AMERICAN HISTORIC INNS

INCORPORATED

Certificate

ɞ *redeemable for* ଓ

One Free Night at a Bed & Breakfast or Country Inn

Advance reservations required.
See "How to Make a Reservation."

ɞ ɞ ɞ ɞ ଓ ଓ ଓ ଓ

Compliments of American Historic Inns, Inc. and participating Bed & Breakfasts and Country Inns.

This certificate entitles the bearer to one free night
at any one of the more than 1,550 Bed & Breakfasts
and Country Inns when the
bearer buys the first night at the regular rate.
See back for requirements.

VOID IF DETACHED FROM BOOK OR ALTERED

VOID IF DETACHED FROM BOOK OR ALTERED

AMERICAN HISTORIC I N N S INCORPORATED

Free night is provided by participating inn.

Please send redeemed certificate to:

American Historic Inns, Inc.

PO Box 669, Dana Point, CA 92629-0669

Inns with most redeemed certificates will be featured on

iLoveinns.com as one of "America's Favorite Inns."

_____

Name of Guest

_____

Guest Home Address

_____

Guest City/State/Zip

_____

Guest Home Phone

_____

Guest Email Address

_____

Name of Bed & Breakfast/Inn

_____

Signature of Innkeeper

Certificate is good for one (1) free consecutive night when you purchase the first night at the regular rate. Offer not valid at all times. Contact inn in advance for availability, rates, reservations, meal plans, cancellation policies and other requirements. If book is purchased at the inn, certificate is valid only for a future visit. Offer valid only at participating inns featured in this Bed & Breakfast Guide. Not valid during holidays. Minimum 2-night stay. Certificate is for no more than two people and no more than one room. Other restrictions may apply. Bed tax, sales tax and gratuities not included. American Historic Inns, Inc. is not responsible for any changes in individual inn operation or policy. By use of this certificate, consumer agrees to release American Historic Inns, Inc. from any liability in connection with their travel to and stay at any participating Inn. This certificate may not be reproduced and cannot be used in conjunction with any other promotional offers. Certificate must be redeemed at participating inn by December 31, 2008. Void where prohibited.

Certificate Expires December 31, 2008

IF BOOK IS PURCHASED AT THE INN, CERTIFICATE IS VALID ONLY FOR FUTURE VISIT

Media Comments

"…lighthouses, schoolhouses, stage coach stops, llama ranches … There's lots to choose from and it should keep B&B fans happy for years." – Cathy Stapells, Toronto Sun

"Anytime you can get superb accommodations AND a free night, well that's got to be great, and it is … I've used this book before, and I must tell you, it's super … The news, information and facts in this book are all fascinating." – On the Road With John Clayton, KKGO, Los Angeles radio

"…helps you find the very best hideaways (many of the book's listings appear in the National Register of Historic Places.)" – Country Living

"I love your book!" – Lydia Moss, Travel Editor, McCall's

"Delightful, succinct, detailed and well-organized. Easy to follow style…"
– Don Wudke, Los Angeles Times

"Deborah Sakach's Bed & Breakfasts and Country Inns *continues to be the premier Bed & Breakfast guide for travelers and tourists throughout the United States."* – Midwest Book Review

"One of the better promotions we've seen." – Baton Rouge Advocate

"…thoughtfully organized and look-ups are hassle-free…well-researched and accurate…put together by people who know the field. There is no other publication available that covers this particular segment of the bed & breakfast industry – a segment that has been gaining popularity among travelers by leaps and bounds. The information included is valuable and well thought out." – Morgan Directory Reviews

"Readers will find this book easy to use and handy to have. An excellent, well-organized and comprehensive reference for inngoers and innkeepers alike."
– Inn Review, Kankakee, Ill.

"This guide has become the favorite choice of travelers and specializes only in professionally operated inns and B&Bs rather than homestays (lodging in spare bedrooms)." – Laguna Magazine

"This is the best bed and breakfast book out. It outshines them all!"
– Maggie Balitas, Rodale Book Clubs

"Most of us military families have lived all over the world, so it takes an unusual book, service or trip to excite us! As I began to look through the book, my heart beat faster as I envisioned what a good time our readers could have visiting some of these very special historic bed and breakfast properties." – Ann Crawford, Military Living

"Absolutely beautiful!" – KQIL talk show radio

"This is a great book. It makes you want to card everything." – KBRT Los Angeles radio talk show

"All our lines were tied up! We received calls from every one of our 40 stations (while discussing your book.)" – Business Radio Network

"For a delightful change of scenery, visit one of these historical inns. (Excerpts from Bed & Breakfasts and Country Inns *follow.) A certificate for one free consecutive night (minimum two nights stay) can be found in the book."* – Shirley Howard, Good Housekeeping

"iLoveInns.com boasts independently written reviews, elegant design, and direct links to inns' URLs." – Yahoo! Internet Magazine referring to iLoveInns.com, winner of their 2002 Best B&B Site.

Comments From Innkeepers

"The guests we receive from the Buy-One-Night-Get-One-Night-Free program are some of the most wonderful people. Most are first time inngoers and after their first taste of the inn experience they vow that this is the only way to travel." – Innkeeper, Mass.

"Guests that were staying here last night swear by your guide. They use it all the time. Please send us information about being in your guide." – Innkeeper, Port Angeles, Wash.

"The people are so nice! Please keep up the great program!"
– K. C, The Avon Manor B&B Inn, Avon-By-the-Sea, N.J.

"I have redeemed several certificates which have led to new loyal customers who, in turn, referred our inn to new guests!" - Manchester Inn Bed & Breakfast, Ocean Grove, N.J.

"We get many good leads from you throughout the year. Anything that we can do to support, we'll be glad to. Thanks for a great publication."
– A Grand Inn-Sunset Hill House, Sugar Hill, N.H.

"We want to tell you how much we love your book. We have it out for guests to use. They love it! Each featured inn stands out so well. Thank you for the privilege of being in your book."
– Fairhaven Inn, Bath, Maine

"We've had guests return two or three times after discovering us through your book. They have turned into wonderful guests and friends." – Port Townsend, Wash.

"I wanted to let you know that I have been getting quite a few bookings from your guide with the certificates."
– Quill Haven Country Inn, Somerset, Pa.

"The response to your book has been terrific and the guests equally terrific! Many are already returning. Thanks for all your hard work." – Rockport, Mass.

"We love your book and we also use it. Just went to New Orleans and had a great trip."
– Gettysburg, Pa.

"I love your directories and your special offers and very much appreciate being a part of American Historic Inns."
– The Hostetler House B&B, St. Glendive, Mt.

"Outstanding! We were offering a variety of inn guide books, but yours was the only one guests bought."
– White Oak Inn, Danville, Ohio

"This has been one of the best B&B programs we have done and the guests have been delightful. Thanks!" – Eastern Shore, Md.

"We have been thrilled with our relationship with American Historic Inns for many years. Many of the travelers you've led to us had never visited our area before. Many of them, likewise, have returned."
– The Thorpe House Country Inn, Metamora, Ind.

"We are grateful that so many of our old friends and new guests have found us through your book. We always recommend your publications to guests who wish to explore other fine country inns of New England."
– Innkeeper, Vt.

Comments About
Bed & Breakfasts and Country Inns

"I purchased 8 of these books in January and have already used them up. I am ordering 8 more. I've had great experiences. This year I've been to California, Philadelphia and San Antonio and by ordering so many books enjoyed getting free night at each place. The inns were fabulous." – D. Valentine, Houston, Texas

"Our office went crazy over this book. The quality of the inns and the quality of the book is phenomenal! Send us 52 books." – M.B., Westport, Conn.

"Every time we look at this book we remember our honeymoon! Every time we make another reservation with the free night certificate we relive our honeymoon! We were married in May and visited three fabulous inns that week, in Cape May, Philadelphia and one near Longwood Gardens. They all served phenomenal food and were beautifully decorated. We went back in the summer we loved it so much. It's like our honeymoon again everytime we use this book. You get such a real feel of America's little towns this way." – S. Piniak, N.J.

"The 300 women who attended my 'Better Cents' seminar went wild for the free-night book. I brought my copy and showed them the value of the free-night program. They all wanted to get involved. Thank you so much for offering such a great value."
– R.R., Making Cents Seminars, Texas

"Thank you for offering this special! It allowed us to get away even on a tight budget."
– D.L., Pittsburgh, Pa.

"I'm ordering three new books. We've never stayed in one we didn't like that was in your book!"
– M.R., Canton, Ohio

"This made our vacation a lot more reasonable. We got the best room in a beautiful top-drawer inn for half the price." – L.A., Irvine, Calif.

"I used your book and free night offer and took my 17-year-old daughter. It was our first B&B visit ever and we loved it. (We acted like friends instead of parent vs. teenager for the first time in a long time.) It was wonderful!" – B.F., Clinton, N.J.

"Thanks! Do we love your B&B offer! You betcha! The luxury of getting a two-day vacation for the cost of one is Christmas in July for sure. Keep up the good work."
– R.R., Grapevine, Texas.

"What a great idea for gifts. I'm ordering five to use as birthday, housewarming and thank-you gifts." – J.R., Laguna Niguel, Calif.

"The best thing since ice cream – and I love ice cream!" – M.C., Cape May, N.J.

"I keep giving your books away as gifts and then don't have any for myself. Please send me three more copies." – D.T., Ridgewood, N.J.

"Out of 25 products we presented to our fund raising committee your book was No. 1 and it generated the most excitement." – H.U., Detroit, Mich.

ഇൗᏟഇൗᏟഇൗᏟഇൗᏟഇൗᏟഇൗᏟ

Dedicated to the memory of Eric G. Stewart, loving father to Josephine and soul mate to Suzanne – a genius with a one-of-a-kind, creative sprit. We will always carry you in our hearts.

ᏟഇᏟഇᏟഇᏟഇᏟഇᏟഇᏟ

American Historic Inns™

Bed & Breakfasts

a n d   C o u n t r y   I n n s

_____

by Deborah Edwards Sakach

Published by

AMERICAN
HISTORIC
INNS
INCORPORATED

PO Box 669
Dana Point
California
92629-0669
www.iLoveInns.com

Bed & Breakfasts and Country Inns

AUTHOR:
Deoborah Sakach

COVER DESIGN:
David Sakach

PRODUCTION MANAGER:
Jamee Danihels, Barbara Naylon

BOOK LAYOUT:
Jamee Danihels and David Sakach

SENIOR EDITOR
Shirley Swagerty

ASSISTANT EDITORS:
Barbara Naylon, Jamee Danihels

DATABASE ASSISTANTS:
Jamee Danihels, Liz Barbosa, Julie Pltz

CARTOGRAPHY:
Maurice Phillips and David Sakach

SCANNING:
Jamee Danihels

PROOFREADING:
Jamee Danihels and Barbara Naylon

For the up-to-the-minute information on participating properties, please visit iloveinns.com.

Publisher's Cataloging in Publication Data
Sakach, Deborah Edwards
American Historic Inns, Inc.
Bed & Breakfasts and Country Inns

1. Bed & Breakfast Accommodations - United States, Directories, Guide Books.
2. Travel - Bed & Breakfast Inns, Directories, Guide Books.
3. Bed & Breakfast Accommodations - Historic Inns, Directories, Guide Books.
4. Hotel Accommodations - Bed & Breakfast Inns, Directories, Guide Books.
5. Hotel Accommodations - United States, Directories, Guide Books.
I. Title. II Author. III Bed & Breakfast, Bed & Breakfasts and Country Inns.

American Historic Inns is a trademark of American Historic Inns, Inc.
ISBN: **1-888050-19-5**
Softcover
Printed in the United States of America.
10 9 8 7 6 5 4 3 2 1

Table Of Contents

How To Make A Reservation

1 Call

The FREE Night offer **requires advance reservations** and is subject to availability.*

To use the Free Night Certificate call the inn of your choice in advance of your stay and identify yourself as holding a Certificate from American Historic Inns, Inc.

Find out what meals, if any, are included in the rates and whether you will have to pay for meals. A few properties participating in this program do not offer a free breakfast.

2 Confirm

Verify your rate and the inn's acceptance of the Free Night Certificate for the dates you are staying. Make a written note of the name of the reservationist and confirmation code, if any.

Confirm availability of the dates you wish to stay. This offer is subject to availability. All holidays are excluded as well as certain local event dates. A consecutive two-night minimum is required.

Ask about cancellation policies as some inns may require at least a two-week notice in order to refund your deposit. (Also, please note some locales require bed tax be collected, even on free nights.)

3 Check-in

Don't forget to take this book with the Free Night Certificate along with you.

---

*The FREE Night is given to you as a gift directly from the innkeeper in the hope that you or your friends will return and share your discovery with others. **The inns are not reimbursed by American Historic Inns, Inc.***

IMPORTANT NOTE

*"Subject to availability" and "anytime based on availability": each innkeeper interprets availability for their own property. Just as airlines may set aside a number of seats for discounted fares, so small inns in our program may use different formulas to manage the number of rooms and the times available for the Buy-One-Night-Get-One-Night-Free program. You must call the innkeeper to see if any of their vacant rooms are available for the free night. While innkeepers have proven to be extremely generous with the program, each reservation must be made by first stating that you wish to use the Free Night Certificate toward your two-night stay. When innkeepers foresee a full house during peak times, they might not be able to accept this certificate. Our innkeepers welcome your reservation and are looking forward to your visit.

How To Use This Book

You hold in your hands a delightful selection of America's best bed & breakfasts and country inns. The innkeeper of each property has generously agreed to participate in our FREE night program. **They are not reimbursed for the second night, but make it available to you in the hope that you will return to their inn or tell others about your stay. This is their gift to you.**

Most knowledgeable innkeepers enjoy sharing regional attractions, local folklore, history, and pointing out favorite restaurants and other special features of their areas. They have invested much of themselves in creating an experience for you to long remember. Many have personally renovated historic buildings. Others have infused their inns with a unique style and personality to enliven your experience with a warm and elegant environment. Your innkeepers are a tremendous resource. Treat them kindly and you will be well rewarded.

Accommodations

You'll find bed & breakfasts and country inns in converted schoolhouses, churches, lighthouses, 18th-century farmhouses, Queen Anne Victorians, adobe lodges, plantations and more.

Many are listed in the National Register of Historic Places and have preserved the stories and memorabilia from their participation in historical events such as the Revolutionary or Civil wars.

The majority of inns included in this book were built in the 18th, 19th and early 20th centuries. We have stated the date each building was constructed at the beginning of each description.

Each inn featured in this guidebook has agreed to honor the certificate for the free night when the first night is purchased at the regular rate. We hope you enjoy the choices we made, and we encourage you to suggest new inns that you discover.

A Variety of Inns

A **Country Inn** generally serves both breakfast and dinner and may have a restaurant associated with it. Many have been in operation for years; some, since the 18th century as you will note in our "Inns of Interest" section. Although primarily found on the East Coast, a few country inns are in other regions of the nation. Always check as to what meals are provided.

A **Bed & Breakfast** facility's primary focus is lodging. It can have from three to 20 rooms or more. The innkeepers usually live on the premises. Breakfast is the only meal served and can be a full-course, gourmet breakfast or a simple buffet. Many B&B owners pride themselves on their culinary skills.

As with country inns, many B&Bs specialize in providing historic, romantic or gracious atmospheres with amenities such as canopied beds, fireplaces, hot tubs, whirlpools, afternoon tea in the library and scenic views.

Some give great attention to recapturing a specific historic period, such as the Victorian or Colonial eras. Many display antiques and other furnishings from family collections.

A **Homestay** is a room available in a private home. It may be an elegant stone mansion in the best part of town or a charming country farm. Homestays have one to three guest rooms. Because homestays are often operated as a hobby-type business and open and close frequently, only a very few unique properties are included in this publication.

Area Codes

Although we have made every effort to update area codes throughout the book, new ones pop up from time to time. For up to the minute phone numbers, please check our Web site at iloveinns.com.

Baths

Most bed & breakfasts and country inns provide a private bath for each guest room. We have included the number of rooms and the number of private baths in each facility.

Beds

K, Q, D, T, indicates King, Queen, Double or Twin beds available at the inn.

Meals

Continental breakfast: Coffee, juice, toast or pastry.
Continental-plus breakfast: A continental breakfast plus

a variety of breads, cheeses and fruit.

Country breakfast: Includes all the traditional fixings of home-cooked country fare.

Full breakfast: Coffee, juice, breads, fruit and an entree.

Full gourmet breakfast: May be an elegant four-course candlelight offering or especially creative cuisine.

Teas: Usually served in the late afternoon with cookies, crackers or other in-between-meal offerings.

Vegetarian breakfast: Vegetarian fare.

Meal Plans

AP: American Plan. All three meals may be included in the price of the room. Check to see if the rate quoted is for two people or per person.

MAP: Modified American Plan. Breakfast and dinner may be included in the price of the room.

EP: European Plan. No meals are included. We have listed only a few historic hotels that operate on an European Plan.

Always find out what meals, if any, are included in the rates. Not every establishment participating in this program provides breakfast, although most do. Inns offering the second night free may or may not include a complimentary lunch or dinner with the second night. Occasionally an innkeeper has indicated MAP and AP when she or he actually means that both programs are available and you must specify which program you are interested in.

Please do not assume meals are included in the rates featured in the book.

Rates

Rates are usually listed in ranges, i.e., $65-175. The LOWEST rate is almost always available during off-peak periods and may apply only to the least expensive room. Rates are subject to change and are not guaranteed. Always confirm the rates when making the reservations. Rates for Canadian listings usually are listed in Canadian dollars. Rates are quoted for double occupancy for two people. Rates for this program are calculated from regular rates and not from seasonal promotional offers.

Breakfast and other meals MAY or MAY NOT be included in the rates and may not be included in the discount.

Smoking

The majority of country inns and B&Bs in historic buildings prohibit smoking; therefore, if you are a smoker we advise you to call and specifically check with each inn to see if and how they accommodate smokers.

Rooms

Under some listings, you will note that suites are available. We typically assume that suites include a private bath and a separate living room. If the inn contains suites that have more than one bedroom, it will indicate as such.

Additionally, under some listings, you will note a reference to cottages. A cottage may be a rustic cabin tucked in the woods, a seaside cottage or a private apartment-style accommodation.

Fireplaces

When fireplaces are mentioned in the listing they may be in guest rooms or in common areas. The fireplace could be either a gas or wood-burning fireplace. If it mentions that the inn contains a fireplace in room, please keep in mind that not every room may have a fireplace. A few inns have fireplaces that are non-working because of city lodging requirements. Please verify this if you are looking forward to an intimate, fireside chat in your room.

State maps

The state maps have been designed to help travelers find an inn's location quickly and easily. Each city shown on the maps contains one or more inns.

As you browse through the guide, you will notice coordinates next to each city name, i.e. C3. The coordinates designate the location of inns on the state map.

Media coverage

Some inns have provided us with copies of magazine or newspaper articles written by travel writers about their establishments, and we have indicated that in the listing. Articles written about the inns may be available either from the source as a reprint, through libraries or from the inn itself. Some inns have also been featured by local radio and TV stations.

Comments from guests

Over the years, we have collected reams of guest comments about thousands of inns. Our files are filled with these documented comments. At the end of some descriptions, we have included a guest comment received about that inn.

Inspections

Each year we travel across the country visiting inns. Since 1981, we have had a happy, informal team of Inn travelers and prospective innkeepers who report to us about new Bed & Breakfast discoveries and repeat visits to favorite inns.

Alabama

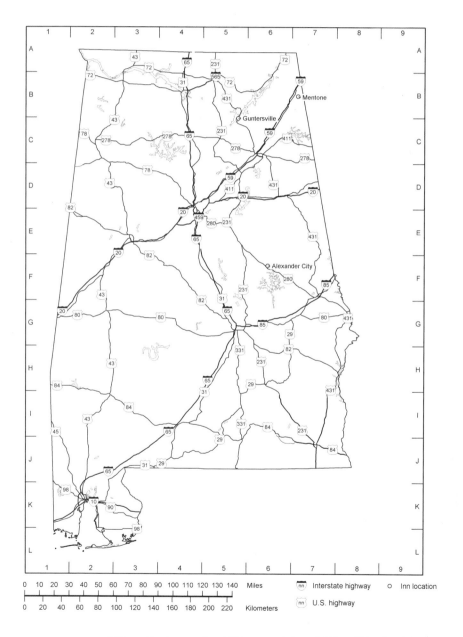

	Miles
0 10 20 30 40 50 60 70 80 90 100 110 120 130 140	Miles
0 20 40 60 80 100 120 140 160 180 200 220	Kilometers

nn Interstate highway   o Inn location

nn U.S. highway

Alexander City

Mistletoe Bough

497 Hillabee St
Alexander City, AL 35010
(256)329-3717 (877)330-3707
Internet: www.mistletoebough.com
E-mail: mistletoebough@charter.net

Circa 1890. When Jean and Carlice Payne purchased this three-story Queen Anne Victorian, it had been in the Reuben Herzfeld family for 103 years. Surrounded by two acres of lawns, tall oak and pecan trees as well as a tulip tree, Victorian Pearl bushes, camellias and brilliant

azaleas, the home has a three-story turret and cupola, balconies, stained-glass windows and a wrap-around porch. The porch ceiling is painted sky blue. A gracious foyer features tongue-and-groove wain-scoting and opens to a ladies' par-lor on one side and a gentlemen's parlor on the other. Fresh flowers, antiques and lace curtains are mixed with traditional and antique Victorian and European furnishings. Upon arrival, guests are pampered with refresh-ments and homemade cookies (frequently with ingredients from Mistletoe's fruit trees and Carlice's herb garden). Other goodies are always on hand. A four-course breakfast is served in the formal dining room with fine china, crystal and silver. The home is in the National Register.

Innkeeper(s): JoAnn & Jesse Frazier. $85-120. 5 rooms with PB. Breakfast and snacks/refreshments included in rates. Types of meals: Full bkfst. Beds: KQD. Cable TV, ceiling fan, telephone and turn-down service in room. Air conditioning. Parlor games, fireplace, badminton and croquet on premises. Antiquing, golf, shopping and water sports nearby.

Location: City.

Certificate may be used: Monday-Thursday, excluding holidays.

Guntersville

Lake Guntersville B&B

2204 Scott St
Guntersville, AL 35976-1120
(256)505-0133 Fax:(256)505-0133
Internet: www.lakeguntersvillebedandbreakfast.com
E-mail: lakeguntersvillebandb@konnekted.com

Circa 1910. The state's largest lake is just a short walk from this turn-of-the-century home that is furnished with many antiques. Boasting more than 900 miles of shoreline, the lake is perfect for fishing and boating. Each of the well-appointed guest bed-rooms have private out-side access; several offer lake views. Weather per-mitting, breakfast is

served on the veranda, surrounded by gorgeous scenery and serenaded by songbirds. The veranda also is appealing for relax-ing on wicker chairs, a swing or hammock.

Innkeeper(s): Carol Dravis. $89-129. 7 rooms, 4 with PB, 4 total suites, including 3 two-bedroom suites, 2 conference rooms. Breakfast and snacks/refreshments included in rates. Types of meals: Full gourmet bkfst, veg bkfst, early coffee/tea, picnic lunch, wine, Afternoon or Evening Tea & Pastries Trays are optional for $10 and Breakfast delivered to room in Basket(our full breakfast optional for $10 delivery fee. Picnic Baskets need advance notice. Beds: KQDT. Cable TV, VCR, DVD, reading lamp, CD player, refrigerator, ceiling fan, clock radio, telephone, coffeemaker, hair dryer, bath amenities, wireless Internet access, iron/ironing board, Writing table, Microwave, Snacks available, Fireplaces non-working, Private entrances most all rooms and Wireless Internet Access in room. Central air. Fax, copier, library, fireplace, gift shop, Wireless Internet access, email, conference areas and Gazebo on premises. Handicap access. Antiquing, art galleries, beach, canoeing/kayaking, fishing, golf, hiking, live theater, museums, parks, shop-ping, sporting events, tennis, water sports, walking trails, Cathedral Caverns, NASA Space Center& Space Camp, St. Bernard Prep School & Ave Maria Grotto/Cullman and Shrine of the Blessed Sacrament/Our Lady of the Angels Monastery/Hanceville nearby.

Location: City, mountains. Peninsula.

Publicity: *Huntsville Times, Sun Herald, Mobile Press, Advertiser Gleam, Birmingham News, Off the Beaten Path, Quimbys 2006, Cruising Guide, Best of the Best from Alabama Cookbooks, Huntsville Times, Decatur Daily, Atlanta Magazine, Arringtons B&B Journal (Best Porches, Best Customer Service, Best B&B Cookbook & Best for Outdoor Sports), Alabama Public TV Bed & Breakfast fund raiser Special, Channel 19, public radio, Huntsville WLRH and Huntsville Public Radio.*

Certificate may be used: Sunday-Thursday, year-round, no holiday weekends.

Alaska

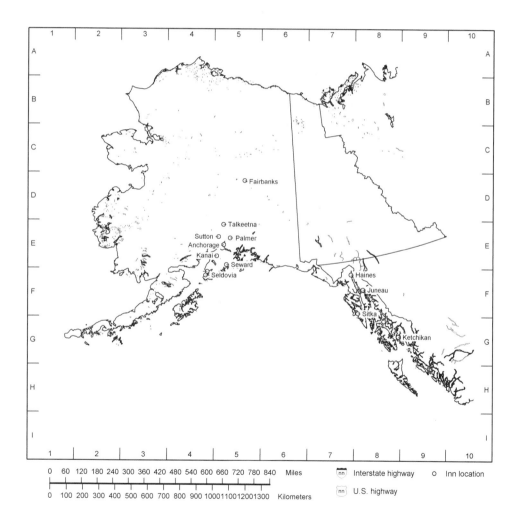

0 60 120 180 240 300 360 420 480 540 600 660 720 780 840   Miles

0 100 200 300 400 500 600 700 800 900 1000 1100 1200 1300   Kilometers

(nn) Interstate highway   O Inn location

(nn) U.S. highway

Anchorage

Alaska Bed and Breakfast and Vacation Rentals

204 East 15th Ave.
Anchorage, AK 99501
(907)278-1111 (888)777-0346 Fax:(907)258-7877
Internet: www.mahoganymanor.com
E-mail: AHI@alaska-bnb-rentals.com

Circa 1947. This elegant inn in the heart of Anchorage stands on a half-acre on the crest of a hill with views of the countryside and mountains. From the rare woods used in construction, to the Alaskan artwork, to the unique floor-to-ceiling indoor waterfall, the beauty of this inn competes with the natural beauty surrounding it. The library is full of books on Alaska for explorers planning their next journey or for guests relaxing at the end of the day. The four guest bedrooms, including a  three-room family suite, come with robes and slippers. A hearty continental breakfast is available to guests whenever they want it in the full-service guest kitchen that is stocked with delights like juice, fruit, rolls, breads, pastries, yogurt and hot and cold cereals. Hot drinks are always available, and hors d'oeuvres or dessert are offered each evening, as well. The inn is a perfect place for releasing creative energies at corporate meetings, and it's excellent for creating lifetime memories at family events. It has a swimming pool and outdoor whirlpool.

Innkeeper(s): Mary Ernst, CTC & Russ Campbell. $129-349. 5 rooms with PB, 1 with FP, 1 with WP, 2 suites, 1 conference room. Breakfast, afternoon tea and snacks/refreshments included in rates. Types of meals: Cont plus, veg bkfst, early coffee/tea and room service. Beds: KQDT. Modem hook-up, data port, cable TV, VCR, DVD, reading lamp, stereo, clock radio, telephone, coffeemaker, turn-down service, desk, voice mail, hair dryer, bathrobes, bath amenities, wireless Internet access, iron/ironing board, hair dryers, iron, ironing board, robes and slippers in room. Fax, copier, spa, swimming, library, parlor games, fireplace, laundry facility, gift shop and gift shop on premises. Limited handicap access. Antiquing, art galleries, bicycling, canoeing/kayaking, cross-country skiing, downhill skiing, fishing, golf, hiking, horseback riding, museums, parks, shopping, sporting events, tennis, water sports, Performing Arts Center, Egan Convention Center and federal buildings and hospitals nearby.

Location: City.

Publicity: *Anchorage Daily News, Alaska Business Monthly and MSNBC documentary.*

Certificate may be used: Sunday-Thursday, Oct. 1-April 30, except holidays and special events, valid on daily rates only.

Alaska House of Jade Bed & Breakfast

3800 Delwood Place
Anchorage, AK 99504
(907)337-3400 (866)337-3410 Fax:(907)333-2329
Internet: www.alaskahouseofjade.com
E-mail: alaskahouseofjade@ak.net

Built specifically with comfort in mind, this custom tri-level home provides gracious hospitality. The innkeepers are fluent in many languages and welcome world travelers. Relax in the living room or on a spacious balcony and sitting area. Spacious suites feature robes, jetted tubs, showers and an intercom system. Bountiful hot gourmet breakfasts and evening desserts are always raved about. The Museum of Natural History and Fine Arts and the Alaska Native Heritage Center are nearby. Visit the Saturday Market for local products to bring home. Ask about day trip activities.

Innkeeper(s): Yves & Dee Memoune. $75-189. 5 rooms, 2 with FP, 4 with WP, 5 total suites, including 1 two-bedroom suite. Breakfast and snacks/refreshments included in rates. Types of meals: Full gourmet bkfst. Beds: KQDT. Cable TV, reading lamp, ceiling fan, clock radio, telephone, desk, hair dryer, wireless Internet access, iron/ironing board, Intercom between rooms and Jetted tubs (three suites) in room. VCR, fax, copier, bicycles, parlor games, fireplace, laundry facility on premises. Limited handicap access. Amusement parks, antiquing, art galleries, bicycling, canoeing/kayaking, cross-country skiing, downhill skiing, fishing, golf, hiking, horseback riding, live theater, museums, parks, shopping, sporting events, tennis, water sports, Native cultural center, Day cruises, Whale watching, Glacier cruises, Botanical gardens, Kenai Fjords and Fishing nearby.

Location: City, mountains. Near Cook Inlet.

Certificate may be used: September, October, April & May. 4 months or last minute, subject to availability.

Alaska's North Country Castle B&B

PO Box 111876, 14600 Joanne Cir
Anchorage, AK 99511
(907)345-7296
Internet: www.castlealaska.com
E-mail: info@castlealaska.com

Circa 1986. Surrounded by woods, this modern, multi-level Victorian cottage-style home offers sparkling treetop views of the Chugach Mountains and Cook Inlet. The B&B is not actually a castle, though guests are treated like royalty. Sit by the fire, play the piano or choose a book from the Alaskana library in the living room. Each guest suite boasts warm floors, vaulted ceilings, bay windows, robes, phone, modem and wireless DSL. The Chugach Suite features two bedrooms, a deck and balconied sitting area. The Turnagain View Suite includes a fireplace, double Jacuzzi/shower with a view and private deck. Innkeepers Wray and Cindy serve a hearty, traditional breakfast in a gazebo-style nook with Alaska blueberry pancakes or baked French toast or specialty egg dishes and fresh fruit, reindeer sausage and juice. Use of a refrigerator, washer, dryer and barbecue grill are available.

Innkeeper(s): Cindy & Wray Kinard. $149-229. 3 rooms with PB, 1 with FP, 1 with WP, 2 total suites, including 1 two-bedroom suite. Breakfast included in rates. Types of meals: Full gourmet bkfst, veg bkfst and Diabetic Breakfast. Beds: QT. Modem hook-up, reading lamp, ceiling fan, clock radio, telephone, turn-down service, desk, some with hot tub/spa, some with fireplace, hair dryer, bathrobes, bath amenities, wireless Internet access, Private treetop decks with sparkling mountain and ocean views in room. TV, VCR, DVD, copier, spa, library, laundry facility, Forest trails, Guest living room w/fireplace, Alaskana library, Piano, Four decks on three levels for wildlife spotting and sunset glowing on premises. Amusement parks, art galleries, bicycling, canoeing/kayaking, cross-country skiing, downhill skiing, fishing, golf, hiking, horseback riding, live theater, museums, parks, shopping, sporting events, bird sanctuary, wilderness mountain trails and coastal trails nearby.

Location: Mountains. Foothills.

Publicity: *Country Magazine (1996), Inn Travelers Magazine (Tops in Alaska 2004), Arrington's B & B Journal (2004), Featured, Inn Traveler Magazine (June 2006) and San Francisco Newspaper.*

Certificate may be used: Sept. 15-Oct. 14, April 15-May 15.

Glacier Bear B&B

4814 Malibu Rd
Anchorage, AK 99517-3274
(907)243-8818 Fax:(907)248-4532
Internet: www.glacierbearbb.com
E-mail: info@glacierbearbb.com

Circa 1986. This cedar-sided contemporary home is located just three blocks from the world's largest float plane lake. The B&B is decorated with Victorian pieces. One bedroom includes a pencil canopy bed, while another offers an antique king bed and a fireplace. The landscaped grounds include an eight-person spa surrounded by ferns, trees and wild berry bushes. The innkeepers offer both a hearty full breakfast or continental fare. Freshly ground coffee, tea, soft drinks and snacks are available throughout the day.

Innkeeper(s): Cleveland & Belinda Zackery. $75-125. 5 rooms, 3 with PB, 1 with FP. Breakfast included in rates. Types of meals: Full bkfst, early coffee/tea and snacks/refreshments. Beds: KQT. Reading lamp, clock radio, telephone and desk in room. VCR, fax, spa, bicycles and parlor games on premises. Cross-country skiing, downhill skiing, fishing, parks, shopping, sporting events, water sports, float plane lake and nature walks nearby.

Location: City.

Certificate may be used: Oct. 1-April 1.

Fairbanks

7 Gables Inn & Suites

4312 Birch Ln
Fairbanks, AK 99709
(907)479-0751 Fax:(907)479-2229
Internet: www.7gablesinn.com
E-mail: gables7@alaska.net

Circa 1982. There are actually 14 gables on this modern Tudor-style inn, which is located a short walk from the University of Alaska and the Chena River. Inside the foyer, a seven-foot waterfall is an amazing welcome. A two-story, flower-filled solarium and a meeting room are wonderful gathering places. Seasonally enjoy the magnificent aurora borealis or a white world of snowflakes and dog mushing, and then relax in a steaming in-room Jacuzzi tub. In summertime the midnight sun allows canoe trips down the river for a progressive dinner from restaurant to deck to dock. The innkeepers received the city's Golden Heart Award for exceptional hospitality.

Innkeeper(s): Paul & Leicha Welton. $60-200. 49 rooms, 31 suites. Breakfast and snacks/refreshments included in rates. Types of meals: Full gourmet bkfst. Beds: KQT. Cable TV, VCR, DVD, reading lamp, clock radio, telephone, desk, hot tub/spa, wireless Internet, most with Jacuzzi tubs, some suites with fireplaces and all suites have full private kitchens in room. Fax, bicycles, library and laundry facility on premises. Antiquing, bicycling, cross-country skiing, downhill skiing, fishing, golf, hiking, museums, parks and shopping nearby.

Location: City.

Certificate may be used: Oct. 1-April 30.

Haines

The Summer Inn Bed & Breakfast

117 Second Avenue
Haines, AK 99827
(907)766-2970 Fax:(906)766-2970
Internet: www.summerinnbnb.com
E-mail: innkeeper@summerinnbnb.com

Circa 1912. This historic farmhouse has an infamous beginning, it was built by a member of a gang of claimjumpers who operated during the Gold Rush. The home affords stunning mountain and water views.

The home is comfortably furnished, and one guest bathroom includes a claw-foot tub original to the home. Breakfasts include fresh fruit and entrees such as sourdough pancakes with ham. The area offers many activities, including museums and a historic walking tour, skiing, snowshoeing, ice fishing, hiking, fishing and much more.

Innkeeper(s): Mary Ellen & Bob Summer. $70-90. 5 rooms. Breakfast and afternoon tea included in rates. Types of meals: Full bkfst, early coffee/tea and snacks/refreshments. Beds: DT. Reading lamp and alarm clocks in room. Fax, library, telephone and BBQ on premises. Art galleries, beach, bicycling, canoeing/kayaking, cross-country skiing, fishing, golf, hiking, live theater, museums, parks, shopping, tennis, water sports and birding nearby.

Location: Ocean community. Coastal town.

Publicity: *American History (April 2000) and Historic Sears Mail Order Houses Roebucks.*

Certificate may be used: Dec. 1-March 31, subject to availability.

Juneau

Pearson's Pond Luxury Inn & Adventure Spa

4541 Sawa Cir
Juneau, AK 99801-8723
(907)789-3772 (888)658-6328 Fax:(907)790-1965
Internet: www.pearsonspond.com
E-mail: book@pearsonspond.com

Circa 1990. View glaciers, visit museums or take a chance at gold-panning streams while staying at this award-winning B&B resort. Landscaped gardens and blueberry bushes border the guests' decks. A full, self-serve breakfast and trail snacks are found in each private kitchenette or in the Breakfast Lounge. The Mendenhall Glacier is within an easy walk and nearby trails offer excellent hiking or mountain biking. River rafting, glacier trekking, or angling for world-class halibut, salmon or freshwater trout may interest the more adventuresome. Soak in a hot tub spa surrounded by a lush forest near a picturesque duck pond. Vacation condos are also available.

Innkeeper(s): Steve & Diane Pearson. $149-449. 7 rooms with PB, 5 with FP, 7 with HT, 2 cottages, 1 conference room. Breakfast, afternoon tea, snacks/refreshments, hors d'oeuvres and wine included in rates. Types of meals: Full bkfst, veg bkfst, early coffee/tea and picnic lunch. Beds: Q. Modem hook-up, data port, cable TV, VCR, DVD, reading lamp, stereo, refrigerator, snack bar, clock radio, telephone, coffeemaker, turn-down service, desk, most with hot tub/spa, voice mail, fireplace, hair dryer, bathrobes, bath amenities, wireless Internet access, iron/ironing board, canopy beds, sitting areas & kitchenettes, most rooms with water view balcony, some rooms with rain shower and some rooms with cathedral ceiling & skylight in room. Fax, copier, spa, bicycles, library, parlor games, laundry facility, gift shop, campfire, BBQs, fishing poles, dock, rowboat, water bike, fitness gym, massage room, yoga area, wedding gazebo, trails and award winning gardens on premises. Limited handicap access. Antiquing, art galleries, beach, bicycling, canoeing/kayaking, cross-country skiing, downhill skiing, fishing, golf, hiking, horseback riding, live theater, museums, parks, shopping, tennis, water sports, wineries, Mendenhall Glacier, Glacier Bay National Park. Mt. Roberts Tramway, Glacier Gardens Rainforest Adventure. Glacier cruises, trekking and dog mushing, rafting and jet skiing nearby.

Location: Waterfront. On lake, in forest, next to mountains & glacier.

Publicity: *MSN.com (#4 in the World Most Romantic Hotel Destination), Arrington's Journal (readers voted it a Most Perfect Stay and Best B&B of Alaska), North American Inns (named a Best Rooms of North America), Frommers and Fodors, Healing Spas and Retreats, Healing Lifestyles, Country Discovery, Pacific Northwest, Atlantic Monthly, Alaska Bride Magazine, Juneau Empire, Capital City Weekly, Sunset Magazine, Country Inns, Good Housekeeping, Discovery network Travel Feature, Big Skies and Glaciers. KING TV in Seattle, WA (featured the inn on Alaska Vacations) and Innkeeper has been interviewed on several local radio stations.*

Certificate may be used: October through April, Sunday through Thursday.

Kenai

Blonde Bear Bed and Breakfast

47004 Emery Street
Kenai, AK 99611
(907)776-8957 (888)776-8956
Internet: www.blondebear.com
E-mail: info@blondebear.com

Circa 2000. Recently built on 21 acres with lawns, rock gardens, perennials and natural forest, this two-story ranch exudes Alaskan Sourdough Hospitality. Blonde Bear Bed and Breakfast is open year round in Kenai, Alaska. Sip homemade wine and locally made treats by the outdoor bonfire. A canoe and a barbecue grill are available to use. Stay in one of the comfortable guest bedrooms with a rustic Alaskan country decor. The Blonde Bear Den features robes, an amenities basket, entertainment center and a private bath with a soaker tub. Wake up to a hearty breakfast before beginning the day's scenic adventures.

Innkeeper(s): George and Tina Showalter. $70-165. 7 rooms, 2 with PB, 1 with HT, 2 total suites, including 1 two-bedroom suite, 1 three-bedroom suite and 1 four-bedroom suite. Breakfast, hors d'oeuvres and wine included in rates. Types of meals: Full gourmet bkfst, early coffee/tea, lunch, picnic lunch and snacks/refreshments. Beds: QDT. Data port, TV, VCR, DVD, reading lamp, stereo, refrigerator, clock radio, telephone, desk, hair dryer, bathrobes, bath amenities, wireless Internet access and iron/ironing board in room. Fax, copier, parlor games and laundry facility on premises. Limited handicap access. Art galleries, beach, bicycling, canoeing/kayaking, cross-country skiing, fishing, golf, hiking, horseback riding, museums, parks, shopping, sporting events, tennis, water sports, flyout fishing, hunting, bear viewing, sightseeing guides, recreation facility includes swimming pool, racketball courts, workout gym and rock wall nearby.

Location: Country, ocean community.

Publicity: *Entrepreneur Magazine (March 2007).*

Certificate may be used: Anytime, November-March, subject to availability.

Ketchikan

Almost Home B&B

412 D-1 Loop Rd N
Ketchikan, AK 99901-9202
(907)225-3273 (800)987-5337 Fax:(907)247-5337
Internet: www.ketchikan-lodging.com/bb15.html
E-mail: wanda@ketchikan-lodging.com

Circa 1981. These rural B&B accommodations, located a few minutes' drive north of Ketchikan, provide guests with a completely outfitted apartment. Guests can choose from two- or three-bedroom units. Each offers linens, phone, cable TV, washer and dryer and a gas barbecue grill. A special welcome is extended to fishing parties. Ketchikan is known for its excellent salmon and halibut fishing and offers several fishing derbies each summer.

Innkeeper(s): Darrell & Wanda Vandergriff. $150. 5 rooms, 4 cottages. Breakfast included in rates. Types of meals: Cont plus. Beds: KDT. Cable TV, reading lamp, refrigerator, clock radio, telephone, gas BBQ, full outfitted kitchen and laundry facility in room. Fishing, live theater, parks, shopping, water sports, totem poles and native culture nearby.

Location: Wooded secluded lot.

Certificate may be used: Oct. 1-June 1.

Palmer

Rose Ridge B&B

8614 E. Highlander Circle
Palmer, AK 99645
(907)745-8604 (877)827-ROSE Fax:(907)745-8608
Internet: www.roseridgebnb.com
E-mail: stay@roseridgebnb.com

Circa 1997. Fifteen secluded acres surround this quiet, modern home in the Matanuska Valley. Watch videos or play games in the family room. A reading area is perfect for curling up with a good book. Guest bedrooms, accented with hand-stitched quilts, also feature VCRs and private entrances. Enjoy a continental breakfast, or a full breakfast from a varied menu, served in the dining room. Walk in the woods or relax on the deck. Pan for gold at nearby Hatcher Pass when visiting Independence Mine and Historical Park.

Innkeeper(s): David & Diane Rose. $75-125. 3 rooms, 2 with PB, 1 guest house. Breakfast included in rates. Types of meals: Country bkfst, veg bkfst and early coffee/tea. Beds: Q. Modem hook-up, data port, TV, VCR, reading lamp, refrigerator, ceiling fan, clock radio, telephone, coffeemaker, desk and hair dryer in room. DVD, fax, library, parlor games and laundry facility on premises. Limited handicap access. Art galleries, bicycling, canoeing/kayaking, cross-country skiing, fishing, golf, hiking, horseback riding, live theater, museums, parks, shopping, tennis, water sports and glacier hikes nearby.

Location: Country, mountains.

Certificate may be used: Anytime, subject to availability.

Sitka

Alaska Ocean View Bed & Breakfast Inn

1101 Edgecumbe Dr
Sitka, AK 99835-7122
(907)747-8310 (888)811-6870 Fax:(907)747-3440
Internet: www.sitka-alaska-lodging.com
E-mail: info@sitka-alaska-lodging.com

Circa 1986. Alaska Ocean View Bed & Breakfast Inn is a red-cedar executive home is located in a quiet neighborhood one block from the seashore and the Tongass National Forest in Sitka. Witness spectacular sunsets over stunning Sitka Sound and on clear days view majestic Mt. Edgecumbe, an extinct volcano located offshore on Kruzoff Island. Binoculars are kept handy for guests who take a special interest in looking for whales and eagles. Guest bedrooms are named after popular local wildflowers. Explore the scenic area after a hearty breakfast.

Innkeeper(s): Carole & Bill Denkinger. $119-219. 3 rooms with PB, 2 with FP, 1 conference room. Breakfast, afternoon tea, snacks/refreshments and hors d'oeuvres included in rates. Types of meals: Full gourmet bkfst, veg bkfst, early coffee/tea and room service. Beds: KQT. Data port, cable TV, VCR, DVD, reading lamp, stereo, refrigerator, ceiling fan, snack bar, clock radio, telephone, coffeemaker, turn-down service, desk, hot tub/spa, most with fireplace, hair dryer, bathrobes, bath amenities, wireless Internet access, iron/ironing board, one room with ocean view balcony, two furnished with table and chairs on patio, HEPA Air cleaners, wine glasses, wine opener, can opener, coffee creamers, cappuccinos, teas, etc. and picnic supplies in room. Fax, copier, spa, library, pet boarding, parlor games, gift shop, water garden fish pond with waterfall area set with table, chairs and stone checkerboard and covered shuttle bus/taxi waiting area on premises. Limited handicap access. Antiquing, art galleries, beach, bicycling, canoeing/kayaking, fishing, golf, hiking, museums, parks, shopping, Whale watching, Wildlife viewing, Underwater discovery tours, Fly fishing, Ocean salmon & halibut fishing, Bird watching, Glaciers, Totem poles, Chamber music concerts, Crab feeds, Russian and Tlingit Indian folk dance, Heli skiing, Hang gliding, Kruzoff Island, Wilderness Hot Springs and Baranof Island nearby.

Location: Mountains, ocean community. One block from Tongass National Forest.

Publicity: *Ladies Home Journal, Washington Post, Sunday New York Times and Alaska Airlines in flight magazine.*

Certificate may be used: Sunday-Wednesday, October-March, Sunday-Wednesday, April-May 7. Space subject to availability. Anytime at the last minute.

Sutton

Matanuska Lodge

34301 West Glenn Hwy
Sutton, AK 99674
(907)746-0378
Internet: www.matanuskalodge.com
E-mail: nuska1@mac.com

Circa 2006. Lavish luxury and traditional comfort are offered at Matanuska Lodge, a newly built log home sitting on two acres in Sutton, Alaska. This romantic getaway, surrounded by wildflowers, is open all year-round and boasts views of the Saddlenotch Mountains and Matanuska Glacier. It is a short walk to enjoy the activities of 100 Mile Lake. The gathering area has games and a big screen TV with DVDs. Appetizers, snacks and beverages are provided. Sit in the English garden, at the picnic table or the fire pit. Stay in a guest bedroom with a whirlpool tub and deck access. One room also features a fireplace. Radiant heated floors and blackout shades are among the pampering amenities. Savor a bountiful breakfast with a continental flair. Dinner is available upon request.

Innkeeper(s): Brenda Goldberg & Rodney Johnson. $200-400. 4 rooms with PB, 1 with FP, 4 with WP. Breakfast, snacks/refreshments and hors d'oeuvres included in rates. Types of meals: Full gourmet bkfst, early coffee/tea and Dinner as well as lunch can be arranged on a one to one basis. There will be an additional fee for this special service. Picnic lunches may also be provided if there is a need. Beds: K. Reading lamp, ceiling fan, clock radio, telephone, turn-down service, hot tub/spa, some with fireplace, hair dryer, bathrobes, bath amenities, wireless Internet access, Beautiful bed covers & Accessories, Arm chairs, Rocking chairs, In-floor heating, Deck access for viewing and sitting in room. Central air. TV, VCR, DVD, fax, copier, spa, library, parlor games and Big screen TV available in gathering area on premises. Bicycling, canoeing/kayaking, cross-country skiing, fishing, hiking, horseback riding, parks, shopping and water sports nearby.

Location: Mountains.

Certificate may be used: Anytime, subject to availability.

Arizona

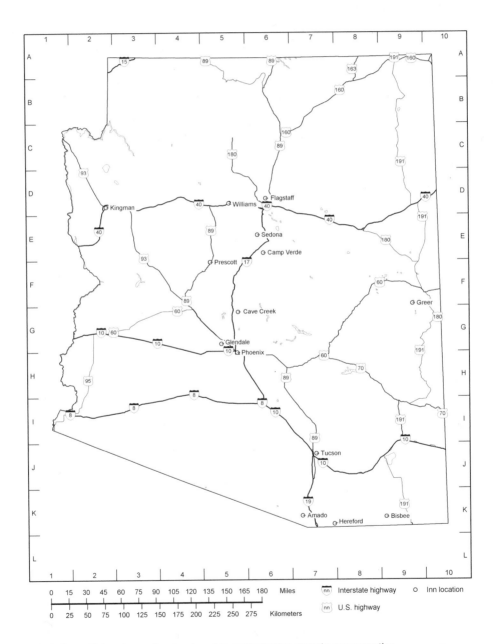

Miles: 0 15 30 45 60 75 90 105 120 135 150 165 180
Kilometers: 0 25 50 75 100 125 150 175 200 225 250 275

Interstate highway   Inn location
U.S. highway

Tell the innkeeper that you have an iLoveInns free-night certificate when you make your reservation.

Camp Verde

Luna Vista Bed and Breakfast

1062 E Reay Rd
Camp Verde, AZ 86322
(928)567-4788 (800)611-4788 Fax:(928) 567-4107
Internet: www.lunavistabandb.com
E-mail: Info@LunaVistaBAndB.com

Circa 2002. Encompassing a total of 16 fenced acres with 5 acres of mesquite and creosote natural forest, 6 acres open field and corrals, 2 acres along Beaver Creek, and three landscaped acres around the modern Santa Fe Pueblo, this upscale B&B ranch resort offers a secluded, equestrian country setting. Luxury guest suites are designed with individual themes featuring numerous works of art, and an incredible assortment of amenities that may include a jetted tub for two, bidet, steam room and private balcony or patio. Hospitality is generous with a hearty breakfast, social hour and snacks and refreshments available any time. Swim in the heated pool with a slide and soak in the spa. Go horseback riding or hike the creekside trails. Ask about spa and beauty packages.

Innkeeper(s): Kala and Frank. $150-235. 5 rooms, 3 with PB, 1 with FP, 2 with WP, 2 two-bedroom suites. Breakfast, Sunday brunch, snacks/refreshments, hors d'oeuvres and wine included in rates. Types of meals: Full gourmet bkfst, veg bkfst, early coffee/tea and Catering and Banquet Services available for weddings and private parties. Beds: KQT. Modem hook-up, data port, cable TV, VCR, DVD, reading lamp, stereo, refrigerator, ceiling fan, snack bar, clock radio, telephone, desk, some with hot tub/spa, some with fireplace, hair dryer, bathrobes, bath amenities and wireless Internet access in room. Central air. Fax, copier, spa, swimming, stable, library, pet boarding, parlor games and gift shop on premises. Handicap access. Antiquing, art galleries, bicycling, canoeing/kayaking, fishing, golf, hiking, horseback riding, live theater, museums, parks, shopping, wineries, Casinos, Sightseeing, Ballooning, Native American Ceremonies, Festivals and Concerts nearby.

Location: Country. Near Sedona Red Rock Country.

Publicity: *Red Rock News, Kudos Magazine, AZ Tourist News, NBC's Arizona Highways TV, ABC's Sonoran Living Live and Las Vegas Talk Radio.*

Certificate may be used: May-August, Sunday-Thursday, subject to availability.

Flagstaff

Starlight Pines Bed & Breakfast

3380 E Lockett Rd
Flagstaff, AZ 86004-4039
(928)527-1912 (800)752-1912
Internet: www.starlightpinesbb.com
E-mail: romance@starlightpinesbb.com

Circa 1996. Tall pine trees and nearby mountains create a peaceful ambiance at this Victorian-styled home. Relax on the wraparound porch with a swing or curl up with a book in front of the fireplace in the parlor. Guest bedrooms include amenities such as a fireplace and/or antique clawfoot tub. Country antiques are placed on oak-plank floors and luxurious spreads top the beds. Bathrobes and bubble baths are found in the private baths. The innkeepers pamper with fresh flowers, gourmet breakfasts, enjoyable conversation and friendly pet Shih Tzus, Mooshu and Taz.

Innkeeper(s): Richard & Michael. $145-169. 4 rooms with PB, 1 with FP, 1 suite. Breakfast included in rates. Types of meals: Full gourmet bkfst, veg bkfst, early coffee/tea and snacks/refreshments. Beds: KQD. Modem hook-

up, data port, reading lamp, refrigerator, some with fireplace, hair dryer, bathrobes and wireless Internet access in room. DVD, fax, parlor games, telephone and 70' x 12' wraparound porch with swing on premises. Antiquing, art galleries, bicycling, cross-country skiing, downhill skiing, fishing, golf, hiking, horseback riding, museums, parks, shopping, sporting events and tennis nearby.

Location: Mountains.

Certificate may be used: December, January and February. Sunday-Thursday only, Anytime, Last Minute-Based on Availability.

Glendale

Glendale Gaslight Inn

5747 W. Glendale
Glendale, AZ 85301
(623)934-9119 Fax:(623)934-0343
Internet: www.GlendaleGaslightInn.com
E-mail: Teresa@GlendaleGaslightInn.com

Circa 1925. Glendale Gaslight Inn is a circa 1925 red brick building that offers a casually elegant setting in historic downtown Glendale, Arizona. Enjoy spacious accommodations with upscale comfort and amenities. Glendale Gaslight Inn is perfect for romantic getaways or business trips. Themed guest bedrooms are an inviting respite. Relax with a fresh pastry at the gourmet coffee bar and later, unwind at the piano wine bar and lounge.

Innkeeper(s): Paul and Teresa Seabrook. $72-245. 9 rooms with PB, 1 suite, 1 conference room. Breakfast included in rates. Types of meals: Cont plus, early coffee/tea, lunch, hors d'oeuvres, wine, Gourmet Specialty Coffees including Mochas, Lattes, Cappuccinos as well as organic herbal teas. Fine assortment of fresh pastries, desserts and ice cream. Fresh sandwiches, fruits and & salads. Beds: KQ. Reading lamp, refrigerator, ceiling fan, snack bar, desk, bathrobes, bath amenities, wireless Internet access, iron/ironing board, Signature white marble-top desk and handwoven Oriental rugs on new beautiful red oak floors in room. Central air. Fax, copier, telephone, Gournmet Coffee House and Live Piano Jazz & Wine Bar on premises. Antiquing, art galleries, bicycling, golf, museums, parks, shopping, sporting events and Many Signature Festivals sponsored by the City of Glendale nearby.

Certificate may be used: June-August, subject to availability.

Hereford

Casa De San Pedro

8933 S Yell Ln
Hereford, AZ 85615-9250
(520)366-1300 (888)257-2050 Fax:(520)366-0701
Internet: www.bedandbirds.com
E-mail: info@bedandbirds.com

Circa 1996. Built around a courtyard and fountain, this Territorial hacienda-style bed & breakfast inn is furnished with hand-carved wood furnishings and accent tiles from Mexico. Its care for the environment as well as its location on ten acres of high prairie grassland adjacent to the San Pedro River and Riparian Reserve create a world-class hideaway for naturalists and ecotourism. Relax by the fire in the Great Room, or research birds on the computer. Romantic guest bedrooms offer quiet privacy and the warm hospitality includes quality concierge services. Experience the made-to-satisfy breakfast that will include old favorites and wonderful new recipes. Special dietary needs are easily accommodated.

Innkeeper(s): Karl Schmitt and Patrick Dome. $149-175. 10 rooms with PB, 6 with FP, 1 conference room. Breakfast, afternoon tea, snacks/refreshments, Full served breakfast each morning featuring fresh seasonal fruit, fresh baked muffins/scones and egg entre' with optional meats. Vegetarian and special diets supported included in rates. Types of meals: Full gourmet bkfst, veg bkfst, early coffee/tea and Picnic lunch for an additional charge. Beds: KD.

Modem hook-up, reading lamp, CD player, ceiling fan, clock radio, telephone, desk, hot tub/spa, most with fireplace, hair dryer, bath amenities, wireless Internet access and iron/ironing board in room. Central air. TV, VCR, DVD, fax, copier, spa, swimming, library, parlor games, laundry facility, gift shop, Ramada for bird watching, Gas grills for your BBQ, Butterfly garden, Xeriscape low water use landscaping and Native habitat for wildlife on premises. Handicap access. Antiquing, art galleries, bicycling, fishing, golf, hiking, live theater, museums, parks, shopping, tennis, wineries, Ramsey Canyon, Miller Canyon, Ash Canyon, Tombstone, Bisbee, Coronado National Monument, Kartchner Caverns, Garden Canyon and Some of the best bird-watching in the nation nearby.

Location: Country, mountains. San Pedro River and Riparian Reserve.

Publicity: *AZ Tourist News, Minneapolis Herald Tribune, Arizona Highways and Rated the Best Breakfasts in the Southwest by Arrington's Inn Traveler magazine.*

Certificate may be used: anytime, based on availability except holidays, Feb.15-May 15, Aug.1-8 or Dec. 24-Jan. 1.

Kingman

Hotel Brunswick

315 E Andy Devine Ave
Kingman, AZ 86401
(928)718-1800 Fax:(928)718-1801
Internet: www.hotel-brunswick.com
E-mail: reservations@Hotel-Brunswick.com

Circa 1909. Built at the turn of the 20th century, the Hotel Brunswick was, for awhile, the tallest building in three counties. The hotel was built to accommodate the many railroad passengers who traveled through Kingman. Later in the century, the hotel fell into disrepair until the current owners purchased the property, restoring the historic charm. Each of the guest rooms has been appointed individually. Rooms range from the spacious honeymoon suite to the cozy, economical Cowboy and Cowgirl rooms. In addition to the accommodations, the hotel includes a European-style café, Mulligan's Bar, and a full-service business center. Your hosts can arrange a massage service or create a honeymoon package with flowers and champagne. Kingman, a stop along the famed Route 66, maintains many historic buildings and sites.

Innkeeper(s): Jason and Jennifer Pfaff. $25-110. 24 rooms, 7 with PB, 8 suites. Breakfast included in rates. Types of meals: Cont plus, early coffee/tea and gourmet dinner. Restaurant on premises. Beds: QDT. Modem hook-up, cable TV, VCR, reading lamp, refrigerator and telephone in room. Air conditioning. Fax, copier and laundry facility on premises. Handicap access. Antiquing, canoeing/kayaking, fishing, golf, hiking, horseback riding, museums, parks, shopping, water sports and ghost towns nearby.

Location: Arid plains.

Publicity: *Kingman Daily Miner, Standard News, Arizona Holidays and TV 77.*

Certificate may be used: June, July, August, subject to availability, holidays excluded. No other discounts apply.

Phoenix

Maricopa Manor

15 W Pasadena Ave
Phoenix, AZ 85013
(602)274-6302 (800)292-6403 Fax:(602)266-3904
Internet: www.maricopamanor.com
E-mail: res@maricopamanor.com

Circa 1928. Secluded amid palm trees on an acre of land, this Spanish-style house features four graceful columns in the entry hall, an elegant living room with a marble mantel and a music room. Completely refurbished suites are very spacious and distinctively furnished with style and good taste. Relax on the private patio or around the pool while enjoying the soothing sound of falling water from the many fountains.

Innkeeper(s): Jeff Vadheim. $99-224. 7 rooms, 4 with FP, 4 with WP, 7 total suites, including 2 two-bedroom suites, 1 conference room. Breakfast and snacks/refreshments included in rates. Types of meals: Cont plus and Breakfast delivered to suite. Beds: KQ. Modem hook-up, data port, cable TV, VCR, DVD, reading lamp, stereo, refrigerator, ceiling fan, clock radio, telephone, coffeemaker, desk, most with hot tub/spa, most with fireplace, hair dryer, bathrobes, bath amenities, wireless Internet access, iron/ironing board and Digital cable with HBO in room. Central air. Fax, copier, spa, swimming, library, parlor games and off-street parking on premises. Handicap access. Amusement parks, antiquing, art galleries, bicycling, golf, hiking, horseback riding, live theater, museums, parks, shopping, sporting events, tennis, water sports and restaurants nearby.

Publicity: *Arizona Business Journal, Country Inns, AAA Westways, San Francisco Chronicle, Focus, Sombrero, NY Times, USA Weekend Magazine, AZ Republic YES Magazine and FOX 15 "Sonoran Living"*

"I've stayed 200+ nights at B&Bs around the world, yet have never before experienced the warmth and sincere friendliness of Maricopa Manor."

Certificate may be used: May 1-Dec. 19.

Sedona

Lodge at Sedona-A Luxury Bed and Breakfast Inn

125 Kallof Place
Sedona, AZ 86336-5566
(928)204-1942 (800)619-4467 Fax:(928)204-2128
Internet: www.lodgeatsedona.com
E-mail: info@lodgeatsedona.com

Circa 1959. Elegantly casual, this newly renovated mission-style B&B sits on three secluded acres with expansive red rock views, mature juniper, sculpture gardens, fountains and a private labyrinth. Enjoy Sunset Snacks in the Fireplace Lounge, Celebration Porch  or outdoor terrace. Artfully decorated king suites feature romantic fireplaces, spa tubs, sitting areas, private decks and entrances. Linger over a five-course breakfast. Massage therapy is available. Exclusive receptions, weddings and executive meetings are accommodated. The lodge offers health club privileges, including access to two swimming pools. The Grand Canyon is a two-hour day trip, and the area includes hiking trails, Jeep tours and hot air balloons.

Innkeeper(s): Innkeeper. $160-339. 15 rooms, 14 with PB, 13 with FP, 2 with HT, 8 with WP, 9 suites, 2 conference rooms. Breakfast, snacks/refreshments and hors d'oeuvres included in rates. Types of meals: Full bkfst, veg bkfst, early coffee/tea, picnic lunch and gourmet dinner. Beds: KQ. Cable TV, VCR, DVD, reading lamp, stereo, refrigerator, ceiling fan, snack bar, clock radio, turn-down service, desk, most with hot tub/spa, fireplace, hair dryer, bathrobes, bath amenities, wireless Internet access and iron/ironing board in room. Central air. Fax, copier, spa, swimming, library, parlor games, telephone, laundry facility, gift shop, Large private decks on all King suites, Celebration Terrace and Free Wireless Internet throughout Lodge on premises. Handicap access. Antiquing, art galleries, bicycling, canoeing/kayaking, cross-country skiing, fishing, golf, hiking, horseback riding, live theater, museums, parks, shopping, tennis, water sports, wineries, jeep tours, cycling, hot air balloon, biplane, casino, camping, adventure tours, wine tours and horseback tours nearby.

Location: Country, mountains. Sedona Red Rock Country.

Publicity: *Real Simple Magazine, Forbes.com, Arizona Republic, Sedona, Red Rock News, San Francisco Examiner, Country Register, New York Post, Bon Appetit, Mountain Living, Sunset Magazine, AZ News, AZ Travel, Arizona Getaways,Road & Travel, Noth American Inns and KPNX Channel 10 Phoenix.*

"What a wonderful hideaway you have! Everything about your inn was and is fantastic! The friendly service made me feel as if I was home. More importantly, the food made me wish that was my home!"
Certificate may be used: Anytime, subject to availability.

Tucson

Cactus Quail Bed & Breakfast

14000 N Dust Devil Dr
Tucson, AZ 85739-9047
(520)825-6767 (888)825-6767 Fax:(520)825-4104
Internet: www.cactusquail.com
E-mail: cactusquail@earthlink.net

Circa 1994. Enjoy spectacular views of the Santa Catalina Mountains from this quiet and peaceful five-acre retreat in Tucson, Arizona. Cactus Quail Bed & Breakfast boasts an outstanding desert landscape with a heated swimming pool and 26-jet spa. Inside this Spanish-tiled hacienda, fresh baked goods, snacks and beverages are accessible at any time. Themed guest bedrooms are decorated with a Southwestern flair. Turndown service includes chocolates on down pillows. A satisfying gourmet breakfast is served in the dining room or on the patio and room service is available. Browse through the gift boutique and Thomas Kinkade viewing gallery. Schedule a relaxing spa service and experience the many activities nearby that include fishing, hiking, horseback riding and adventure tours. The B&B backs up to the National Forest and State Park and is a birder's paradise.

Innkeeper(s): Dan & Linda Cassidy. $99-179. 4 rooms, 3 with PB, 1 with WP. Breakfast and snacks/refreshments included in rates. Types of meals: Full gourmet bkfst and room service. Beds: K. Cable TV, VCR, reading lamp, refrigerator, ceiling fan, clock radio and desk in room. Air conditioning. Fax, copier, spa, library, parlor games, telephone, fireplace, laundry facility, heated pool, gift gallery and Thomas Kinkade viewing gallery on premises. Limited handicap access. Amusement parks, antiquing, art galleries, bicycling, golf, hiking, horseback riding, live theater, museums, parks, shopping, sporting events, Birding, desert trails, Sahuaro National Monuments, Sabino Canyon, Jeep tours, half-day tours and ghost towns nearby.

Location: Country.

Publicity: *Arizona Daily Star, Tucson Explorer and The Phoenix.*

Certificate may be used: Anytime, subject to availability.

Casa Tierra Adobe B&B Inn

11155 W Calle Pima
Tucson, AZ 85743-9462
(520)578-3058 (866)254-0006 Fax:(520)578-8445
Internet: www.casatierratucson.com
E-mail: info@casatierratucson.com

Circa 1988. The Sonoran Desert surrounds this secluded, adobe retreat. The mountain views and brilliant sunsets are spectacular. The interior arched courtyard, vaulted brick ceilings and Mexican furnishings create a wonderful Southwestern atmosphere. Each guest room has a private entrance and patios that overlook the desert landscape. The rooms open up to the courtyard. Freshly ground coffee and specialty teas accompany the full vegetarian breakfast. Old Tucson, the Desert Museum and a Saguaro National Park are nearby. The inn also provides a relaxing hot tub and telescope.

Innkeeper(s): Dave Malmquist. $135-325. 4 rooms with PB, 1 suite. Breakfast and snacks/refreshments included in rates. Types of meals: Full gourmet bkfst, veg bkfst and early coffee/tea. Beds: Q. Data port, refrigerator, ceiling fan, snack bar, clock radio and telephone in room. Air conditioning. TV, VCR, fax, spa, telescope and guest computer with high-speed Internet

connection on premises. Bicycling, golf, hiking and horseback riding nearby.

Location: Country.

Publicity: *Arizona Daily Star, Smart Money Magazine, Washington Post, Phoenix Magazine and Scottsdale Tribune.*

Certificate may be used: April 15-June 15, Aug. 15-Nov. 15.

Williams

Buffalo Pointe Lodge

437 West Route 66
Williams, AZ 86046
(928)635-4341 (800)973-6210 Fax:(928)635-4345
Internet: www.buffalopointe.com
E-mail: info@buffalopointe.com

Circa 1909. Originally built as a mansion, this nostalgic lodge is centrally located in Grand Canyon country. The veranda overlooks historic Route 66. Each guest bedroom is distinctively decorated. Amenities include cable TV, an extensive video library and refrigerators. Breakfast is enjoyed in the intimate on-site restaurant called Special D's. There is much to experience nearby, from pine forests to the scenic red rocks of Sedona.

Innkeeper(s): Kathy and Cary. $68-90. 9 rooms with PB, 1 with FP, 1 two-bedroom suite, 1 conference room. Breakfast, An extended continental breakfast with muffins, bagels, fresh fruit, cereal and a variety of teas and juice and coffee included in rates. Types of meals: Cont plus. Beds: KQD. Cable TV, refrigerator, ceiling fan, clock radio, hair dryer, bath amenities, wireless Internet access and King-size rooms have refrigerators in room. Air conditioning. Fax, copier, parlor games and telephone on premises. Antiquing, art galleries, bicycling, cross-country skiing, downhill skiing, fishing, golf, hiking, horseback riding, parks, shopping, Located at the gateway to the Grand Canyon, 59 miles to the south rim, 7 area fishing lakes, Hiking trails up Bill Williams Mountain into Sycamore Canyon, 18-hole championship golf course, Day trips to Sedona, Jerome, Prescott and Flagstaff nearby.

Location: City, mountains.

Publicity: *Channel 11.*

Certificate may be used: November-March, Sunday-Thursday, subject to availability.

The Sheridan House Inn

460 E Sheridan Ave
Williams, AZ 86046
(928)635-9441 (888)635-9345 Fax:(928)635-1005
Internet: www.grandcanyonbedandbreakfast.com
E-mail: sheridanhouseinn@msn.com

Circa 1988. This two-story house offers porches and decks from which to enjoy its two acres of ponderosa forest. For a queen-size bed and views of pine trees ask for the Willow Room or for sunset views the Cedar Room is the best choice. It also features a bay widow. CD stereo systems and cable TV are in all the rooms. Full breakfasts are served, often on the upstairs deck and a casual buffet dinner is available as well. A fitness room and den with pool table and piano are open to guests, and there is a seasonally available hot tub, as well. The Grand Canyon is 45 minutes away and the Grand Canyon Railroad is within a half mile.

Innkeeper(s): K.C. & Mary Seidner. $135-195. 6 rooms with PB, 1 with FP, 2 two-bedroom suites. Breakfast included in rates. Beds: KQDT. Cable TV, VCR, stereo, ceiling fan, clock radio and telephone in room. TV, spa, library, parlor games, fireplace, Hiking trail, Game room with piano and Pool table on premises. Antiquing, cross-country skiing, downhill skiing, fishing, golf, horseback riding, parks, shopping, tennis and Grand Canyon Railroad nearby.

Location: Mountains.

Publicity: *Williams Grand Canyon News and KPAZ Flagstaff.*

Certificate may be used: Jan. 5-March 31, Sunday-Thursday, excluding holidays

Arkansas

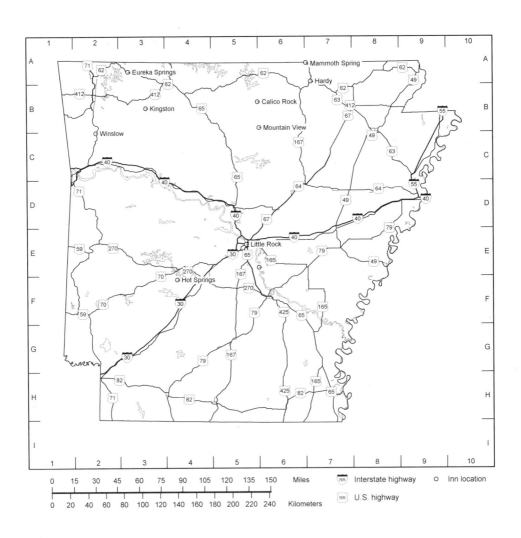

0 15 30 45 60 75 90 105 120 135 150 Miles

0 20 40 60 80 100 120 140 160 180 200 220 240 Kilometers

(nn) Interstate highway   o Inn location

(nn) U.S. highway

Eureka Springs

1884 Bridgeford House B&B

263 Spring St
Eureka Springs, AR 72632-3154
(479)253-7853 (888)567-2422 Fax:(479)253-5497
Internet: www.bridgefordhouse.com
E-mail: innkeeper@bridgefordhouse.com

Circa 1884. Victorian charm abounds at this Queen Anne-Eastlake home, located in the heart of the historic district. Experience generous Southern hospitality upon arrival, when offered homemade treats. Several guest bedrooms feature a double Jacuzzi, fireplace and deck. Savor a gourmet breakfast served on fine china and flatware. The bed & breakfast is just a few blocks from gift boutiques, antique shops, spas, restaurants and much more.

Innkeeper(s): Jeff & Nadara (Sam) Feldman. $109-169. 5 rooms with PB. Breakfast included in rates. Types of meals: Full bkfst, early coffee/tea, snacks/refreshments and room service. Beds: KQ. Cable TV, VCR, reading lamp, refrigerator, clock radio and fans in room. Air conditioning. Telephone on premises. Antiquing, fishing, golf, live theater, shopping and water sports nearby.

Location: City, mountains. Less than one hour from Branson, Mo.

Publicity: *Times Echo Flashlight, Arkansas National Tour Guide and Country Almanac.*

"You have created an enchanting respite for weary people."

Certificate may be used: anytime, subject to availability-except major holidays, major festivals or anytime in October.

5 Ojo Inn B&B

5 Ojo St
Eureka Springs, AR 72632-3220
(479)253-6734 (800)656-6734
Internet: www.5ojo.com
E-mail: bnbinns@5ojo.com

Circa 1890. Guests at 5 Ojo choose between four restored buildings ranging in vintage from an 1891 Victorian to a 1940s cottage. Rooms are decorated with antiques but include modern amenities such as refrigerators and coffeemakers. Most rooms include whirlpool tubs and fireplaces. The Carriage House Cottage and the Anniversary Suite are ideal places for honeymooners or those celebrating a special occasion. Among its romantic amenities, the Anniversary Suite includes a private porch with a swing.

Gourmet breakfasts are served in the Sweet House's dining room, but private dining can be arranged. Eureka Springs with its 63-65 springs, has been a sought after spa town for more than a century.

Innkeeper(s): Richard & Jan Grinnell. $95-160. 10 rooms with PB, 7 with FP, 9 with WP, 3 suites, 2 cottages. Breakfast and snacks/refreshments included in rates. Types of meals: Full gourmet bkfst and picnic lunch. Beds: KQ. Cable TV, VCR, DVD, reading lamp, refrigerator, ceiling fan, snack bar, clock radio, coffeemaker, hair dryer, bath amenities, wireless Internet access, iron/ironing board, Complimentary drinks and snacks, Private entrances, Outdoor hot tub and Cable TV in room. Central air. Fax, spa, library, parlor games, telephone and gift shop on premises. Antiquing, art galleries, bicycling, canoeing/kayaking, fishing, golf, hiking, horseback riding, live theater, museums, parks, shopping, sporting events, water sports, massage therapy, shopping, historic Victorian village, shows and Great Passion Play nearby.

Location: City, mountains. Historic District.

Publicity: *Arkansas Democrat Gazette, Southern Living and Country Inns.*

Certificate may be used: Jan. 2-Dec. 30, Monday-Thursday, except October, holidays and festivals.

Candlestick Cottage Inn

6 Douglas St
Eureka Springs, AR 72632-3416
(479)253-6813 (800)835-5184 Fax:(479)253-2849
Internet: www.candlestickcottageinn.com
E-mail: info@candlestickcottageinn.com

Circa 1882. Woods and foliage surround this scenic country home, nestled just a few blocks from Eureka Springs historic district. Guests are sure to discover a variety of wildlife strolling by the home, including an occasional deer. Breakfasts are served on the tree-top porch, which overlooks a waterfall and fish pond. The morning meal begins with freshly baked muffins and fresh fruit, followed by an entree. Innkeepers Denise and Rita will prepare a basket of sparkling grape juice and wine glasses for those celebrating a special occasion. Guest rooms are decorated in Victorian style, and some include two-person Jacuzzis.

Innkeeper(s): Denise Coleman & Rita Shepler . $89-159. 6 rooms with PB, 4 suites, 1 cottage. Breakfast included in rates. Types of meals: Full bkfst. Beds: KQ. Cable TV, reading lamp, refrigerator, ceiling fan, clock radio, coffeemaker, most with hot tub/spa, hair dryer, bath amenities, wireless Internet access, iron/ironing board, coffee and tea in room. Air conditioning. VCR, fax, copier, parlor games, telephone, laundry facility, soft drinks and bottled water on premises. Antiquing, art galleries, canoeing/kayaking, fishing, golf, hiking, horseback riding, live theater, museums, parks and shopping nearby.

Location: Country, mountains.

Certificate may be used: Sunday-Thursday, excluding holidays.

Cliff Cottage Inn - Luxury B&B Suites & Historic Cottages

Heart of Historic Downtown
Eureka Springs, AR 72632
(479)253-7409 (800)799-7409
Internet: www.cliffcottage.com
E-mail: cliffctg@aol.com

Circa 1880. Comprised of three houses in a row, the Cliff Cottage Inn is just steps to the shops and restaurants of Main Street in Eureka Springs, Arkansas. An 1880 Eastlake Victorian, Sears' first kit home, is a State and National Historic Landmark. It features suites with private front porches and decks tucked into the three-story high rock bluff. The Place Next Door is a Victorian replica boasting two upstairs suites with balconies. The Artist's Cottage is a renovated 1910 Craftsman. Two elegant suites include pure-air

whirlpool tubs, a porch and a deck. A complimentary bottle of champagne or white wine is chilled in the refrigerator; a coffeemaker with imported tea, coffee, hot chocolate and chai are provided. A full gourmet breakfast is delivered each morning.

Innkeeper(s): Sandra CH Smith . $189-230. 8 rooms with PB, 4 with FP, 2 with HT, 6 with WP, 6 suites, 2 cottages, 1 conference room. Breakfast, snacks/refreshments, wine and Gourmet hot breakfast is delivered right to your suite. Optional extra to the cottages as they have fully-equipped kitchens included in rates. Types of meals: Full gourmet bkfst, veg bkfst, early coffee/tea, All suites/cottages have coffeemakers with large selection of imported teas, coffee, hot chocolate, chai, cappucino; also, granola and dry cereals and cookie samplers. Beds: KQ. Modem hook-up, data port, cable TV, VCR, reading lamp, stereo, refrigerator, ceiling fan, snack bar, clock radio, coffeemaker, desk, hot tub/spa, voice mail, most with fireplace, hair dryer, bathrobes, bath amenities, iron/ironing board, In-room massage, Delivered gourmet breakfasts, Suites have two-person Jacuzzi and Cottages have private hot tubs in room. Central air. Spa, library, parlor games, telephone, Complimentary champagne or white wine, In-room beverage bars with complimentary coffee, Imported teas, Hot chocolate, Chai, Cappuccino, Sodas and Concierge service on premises. Amusement parks, antiquing, art galleries, beach, canoeing/kayaking, fishing, golf, hiking, horseback riding, live theater, museums, parks, shopping, tennis, water sports, Great Passion Play (six-minute drive), discount golf, canoe excursions, guided fishing expeditions, horseback trips and carriage rides nearby.

Location: City, mountains. Historic Downtown, 17 steps up from Main St.

Publicity: *Arkansas Democrat Gazette, Country Inns, Modern Bride, Southern Living, Southern Bride, Sandra was guest chef on a CBS-TV cooking show, Romantic Destinations Magazine (One of the Top Six Most Romantic Inns of the South), Southern Bride and American Bed & Breakfast Association (highest rating as well as an Award for Excellence).*

Certificate may be used: January to April, June to August. November-December, Monday, Tuesday, Wednesday, Thursday, no holidays.

The Heartstone Inn & Cottages

35 King's Highway
Eureka Springs, AR 72632-3534
(479)253-8916 (800)494-4921
Internet: www.heartstoneinn.com
E-mail: info@heartstoneinn.com

Circa 1903. A white picket fence leads to this spacious Victorian inn and its pink and cobalt blue wraparound porch filled with potted geraniums and Boston ferns. Located on the Eureka Springs historic loop the inn offers English country antiques, private entrances and pretty linens. Private Jacuzzis, refrigerators and VCRs are available. Pamper yourself in the inn's massage therapy studio. Walk to shops, restaurants and galleries or hop on the trolley to enjoy all the pleasures of the town. Golf privileges at a private club are extended to guests. The New York Times praised the inn's cuisine as the "Best Breakfast in the Ozarks."

Innkeeper(s): Rick & Cheri Rojek. $95-165. 11 rooms with PB, 4 with FP, 6 suites, 2 cottages, 1 conference room. Breakfast and snacks/refreshments included in rates. Types of meals: Full gourmet bkfst. Beds: KQ. Cable TV, VCR, DVD, reading lamp, refrigerator, ceiling fan, clock radio, coffeemaker, desk, some with hot tub/spa, some with fireplace, hair dryer, bathrobes, bath amenities, wireless Internet access, iron/ironing board and whirlpool tub in room. Air conditioning. Fax, copier, spa, library, parlor games, telephone, gift shop, massage therapy and gift shop on premises. Limited handicap access. Amusement parks, antiquing, art galleries, bicycling, canoeing/kayaking, fishing, golf, hiking, horseback riding, live theater, parks, shopping, restaurants and opera nearby.

Location: City, mountains.

Publicity: *Innsider, Arkansas Times, New York Times, Arkansas Gazette, Southern Living, Country Home, Country Inns and USA Today.*

"Extraordinary! Best breakfasts anywhere!"

Certificate may be used: Sunday through Wednesday arrivals during November through April. Other times, last minute only, call for availability.

Hot Springs

Lookout Point Lakeside Inn

104 Lookout Circle
Hot Springs, AR 71913
(501)525-6155 (866)525-6155 Fax:(501)525-5850
Internet: www.lookoutpointinn.com
E-mail: innkeeper@lookoutpointinn.com

Circa 2002. Feel rejuvenated in the tranquil setting of this newly built Arts and Crafts inn sitting on 1 1/2 spectacular acres in the Ouachita Mountains overlooking a serene bay. Nap in a hammock, stroll by a stream and waterfall on garden paths or walk the labyrinth. Gather for afternoon refreshments with dessert, fruit and wine. Luxurious guest bedrooms boast views of Lake Hamilton and include an assortment of amenities to assist business travelers. Stay in a romantic room with a whirlpool tub, fireplace, private terrace or deck. Savor a hearty breakfast with homemade breads and delicious entrees made with fresh herbs grown on-site. Hike the many trails of Lake Catherine State Park or explore Hot Springs National Park. Fish on nearby DeGray Lake.

Innkeeper(s): Ray & Kristie Rosset, Annette Stubbs. $125-300. 10 rooms with PB, 7 with FP, 8 with WP, 1 conference room. Breakfast, snacks/refreshments and wine included in rates. Types of meals: Full gourmet bkfst, veg bkfst, early coffee/tea and picnic lunch. Beds: KQT. Modem hook-up, data port, cable TV, VCR, DVD, reading lamp, stereo, ceiling fan, clock radio, telephone, desk, most with hot tub/spa, voice mail, most with fireplace, hair dryer, bathrobes, bath amenities, wireless Internet access, iron/ironing board, Lake view and Desk in room. Central air. Fax, copier, swimming, library, parlor games, gift shop, snack bar, refrigerator, microwave, coffeemaker, canoe, labyrinth, hammock, waterfalls and gardens on premises. Handicap access. Amusement parks, antiquing, art galleries, bicycling, canoeing/kayaking, fishing, golf, hiking, horseback riding, live theater, museums, parks, shopping, tennis, water sports, Music Festivals, Documentary Film Festival and Garvan Woodland Gardens nearby.

Location: Waterfront.

Publicity: *Southern Living (August 2005), Arrington's Inn Traveler magazine ("Top ten B&B/Inns for Rest & Relaxation in North America" - summer 2004), Active Years magazine ("One of the three top B&B/Inns in Arkansas" - May 2004), Arrington's Bed & Breakfast Journal (May 2004), Past Careers Profile, Good Morning and Arkansas (December 2005).*

Certificate may be used: Dec. 1-Jan. 31, Sunday-Thursday, except Dec. 25-Jan. 2.

Little Rock

The Empress of Little Rock

2120 Louisiana St
Little Rock, AR 72206-1522
(501)374-7966 (877)374-7966 Fax:(501)375-4537
Internet: www.theEmpress.com
E-mail: hostess@theEmpress.com

Day lilies, peonies and iris accent the old-fashioned gardens of this elaborate, three-story Queen Anne Victorian. A grand center hall opens to a double staircase, lit by a stained-glass skylight. The 7,500 square feet include a secret card room at the top of the tower. The Hornibrook Room features a magnificent Renaissance Revival bedroom set with a high canopy. The Tower Room mini-suite has a king-size Austrian bed. The two-course gourmet breakfast is served in the dining room "before the Queen" by candlelight.

Innkeeper(s): Sharon Welch-Blair & Robert Blair. Call for rates. 8 rooms. Breakfast and snacks/refreshments included in rates. Types of meals: Full gourmet bkfst, veg bkfst, early coffee/tea and picnic lunch. Beds: KQT. Modem hook-up, data port, cable TV, VCR, reading lamp, CD player, refrigerator, ceiling fan, snack bar, clock radio, telephone, coffeemaker, turn-down service, desk, hot tub/spa, most with fireplace, hair dryer, bathrobes, bath amenities, wireless Internet access, iron/ironing board, candlelight gourmet breakfast, museum quality antiques, complimentary snacks and homemade "Death by Empress Cookies in room. Central air. Fax, copier, spa, library, parlor games, gift shop, luxury robes, feather beds (removable), champagne picnic lunch,complementary liqueurs, high-speed Internet access, Secret Victorian Moonlight Garden with Gothic Summer House and Quartz Fountain and award winning gardens on premises. Amusement parks, antiquing, art galleries, bicycling, canoeing/kayaking, fishing, golf, hiking, horseback riding, live theater, museums, parks, sporting events, tennis, water sports and wineries nearby.

Location: City. Historic District, Capitol City.

Publicity: *National Geographic Traveler, Nation's Business, Victorian Homes, Victorian Decorating & Lifestyles, Southern Living, Delta SkyMiles Magazine, New York Times, Dallas Morning News, Inn Connections, National Public Television, HGTV programs If Walls Could Talk, Homes Across America and Porches .*

Certificate may be used: Nov. 30-Feb. 28 and June 1-Sept. 15, selected rooms only, any night, no holidays.

California

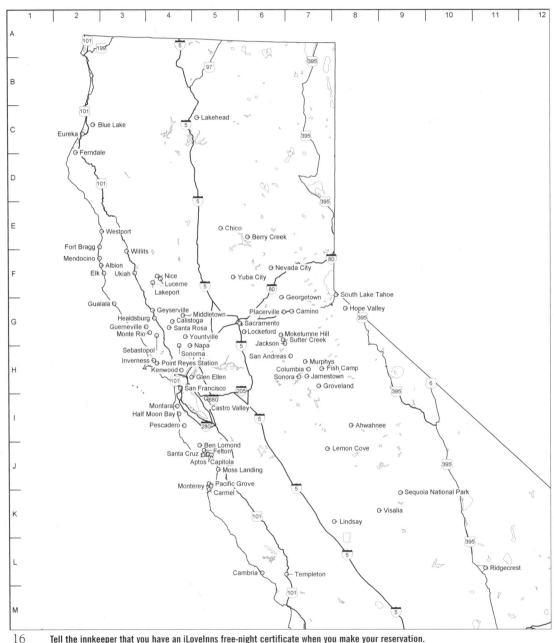

Tell the innkeeper that you have an iLoveInns free-night certificate when you make your reservation.

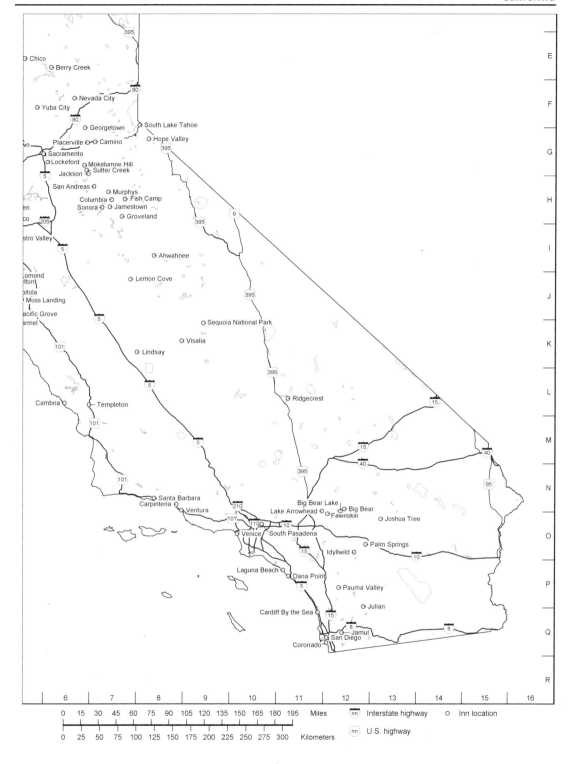

E

F

G

H

I

J

K

L

M

N

O

P

Q

R

Chico
Berry Creek
Nevada City
Yuba City
Georgetown
South Lake Tahoe
Placerville Camino
Hope Valley
Sacramento
Lockeford Mokelumne Hill
Jackson Sutter Creek
San Andreas
Murphys
Columbia Fish Camp
Sonora Jamestown
Groveland

Ahwahnee

Lemon Cove

Sequoia National Park
Visalia
Lindsay

Cambria
Templeton

Ridgecrest

Santa Barbara
Carpinteria
Ventura
Big Bear Lake
Lake Arrowhead Big Bear
Fawnskin
Joshua Tree
Venice South Pasadena
Palm Springs
Idyllwild
Laguna Beach
Dana Point
Pauma Valley
Cardiff By the Sea
Julian
Jamul
San Diego
Coronado

Lomond
ilton
pitola
Moss Landing
acific Grove
armel

stro Valley

80
395
80
395
6
395
395
5
101
5
101
5
101
395
15
15
40
40
95
210
101
110
10
15
10
8
15
8
205
5

6   7   8   9   10   11   12   13   14   15   16

0   15   30   45   60   75   90 105 120 135 150 165 180 195   Miles

0   25   50   75 100 125 150 175 200 225 250 275 300   Kilometers

nn Interstate highway   O Inn location

nn U.S. highway

Ahwahnee

Apple Blossom Inn B&B

44606 Silver Spur Tr
Ahwahnee, CA 93601
(559)642-2001 (888)687-4281
Internet: www.appleblossombb.com
E-mail: appleblossominn@sti.net

Circa 1991. Surrounded by an organic apple farm, this peaceful bed & breakfast is just a stone's throw from Yosemite National Park and offers the ideal location for a stay in Gold Country. Relax by the woodburning stove in the sitting room or on the sundeck. Tastefully furnished guest bedrooms reflect a western decor with natural earth tones or traditional Victorian style. A video library is provided for in-room use. After a hearty breakfast visit the historic Sugar Pine Railroad or ski at nearby Badger Pass Resort. Swim in the inn's pool or soak in the spa overlooking the woods.

Innkeeper(s): Candy Arthur. $99-240. 3 rooms with PB, 1 two-bedroom suite. Breakfast and snacks/refreshments included in rates. Types of meals: Full gourmet bkfst, early coffee/tea and picnic lunch. Beds: KQD. TV, VCR, reading lamp, ceiling fan, clock radio, turn-down service, desk, hair dryer and bathrobes in room. Air conditioning. Fax, copier, spa, parlor games, telephone and fireplace on premises. Limited handicap access. Antiquing, art galleries, bicycling, canoeing/kayaking, cross-country skiing, downhill skiing, fishing, golf, hiking, horseback riding, live theater, museums, parks, shopping, water sports, wineries, Yosemite National Park, Bass Lake, Chukchansi Gold Casino, Sugar Pine Railroad and Historic Highway 49 nearby.

Location: Country, mountains. Yosemite.

Certificate may be used: Nov. 1-March 30, Sunday-Thursday. Holidays excluded.

Sierra Mountain Lodge

45046 Fort Nip Trail
Ahwahnee, CA 93601
(559)683-7673 Fax:(559) 641-2420
Internet: www.sierramountainlodge.com
E-mail: info@sierramountainlodge.com

Circa 1996. Gracing two acres of gardens with gravel paths that lead to sitting areas amid roses and woods, Sierra Mountain Lodge is located in picturesque Ahwahnee, California, near the town of Oakhurst and close to Yosemite National Park. Guest suites boast a simple yet elegant country-style décor with a living room and kitchenette. A private entry connects to a large community deck overlooking Ahwahnee Valley and Sierra Mountains. Enjoy a continental breakfast in the lobby before embarking on the day's scenic adventures. The lodge is open year-round and each season offers a scenic splendor.

Innkeeper(s): John, Brenda & Ken. $85-145. 4 total suites, including 2 two-bedroom suites. Breakfast, snacks/refreshments and Continental breakfast is served daily from 7am-10am in the lobby included in rates. Beds: KQDT. Cable TV, VCR, DVD, reading lamp, CD player, refrigerator, ceiling fan, clock radio, hair dryer, bath amenities and wireless Internet access in room. Air conditioning. Telephone and fireplace on premises. Limited handicap access. Antiquing, art galleries, bicycling, canoeing/kayaking, cross-country skiing, fishing, golf, hiking, horseback riding, live theater, parks, shopping, water sports, wineries, Yosemite National Park, Sequoia National Park, Bass Lake, High Sierra's, Chuchansi Gold Casino and Oakhurst nearby.

Location: Country, mountains. Yosemite National Park, Bass Lake, Oakhurst, High Sierra's.

Certificate may be used: Sunday-Thursday, excluding all holidays.

Albion

Fensalden Inn

33810 Navarro Ridge Rd
Albion, CA 95410-0099
(707)937-4042 (800)959-3850
Internet: www.fensalden.com
E-mail: inn@fensalden.com

Circa 1860. Originally a stagecoach station, Fensalden looks out over the Pacific Ocean as it has for more than 100 years.

The Tavern Room has witnessed many a rowdy scene, and if you look closely you can see bullet holes in the original redwood ceiling. The inn provides 20 acres for walks, whale-watching, viewing deer and bicycling. Relax with wine and hors d'oeuvres in the evening.

Innkeeper(s): Lyn Hamby. $119-239. 8 rooms with PB, 8 with FP, 2 suites, 1 cottage, 2 conference rooms. Breakfast, hors d'oeuvres and wine included in rates. Types of meals: Full bkfst. Beds: KQ. Reading lamp, CD player, refrigerator, ceiling fan, coffeemaker, fireplace and bungalow has Jacuzzi bathtub in room. Fax, copier, parlor games and telephone on premises. Handicap access. Antiquing, art galleries, beach, bicycling, canoeing/kayaking, fishing, golf, hiking, horseback riding, live theater, parks, shopping, tennis and wineries nearby.

Location: Country.

Publicity: *Sunset, Focus, Peninsula, Country Inns, Steppin' Out, LA Times, Vine Times and 1950s B movie The Haunting of Hill House.*

"Closest feeling to heaven on Earth."

Certificate may be used: Anytime, November-April, subject to availability in selected rooms, excluding holidays and special events.

Aptos

Bayview Hotel

8041 Soquel Dr
Aptos, CA 95003-3928
(831)688-8656 (800)422-9843 Fax:(831)688-5128
Internet: www.bayviewhotel.com
E-mail: bay_view_hotel@hotmail.com

Circa 1878. This Victorian hotel is the oldest operating inn on the Monterey Coast. Each of the rooms is decorated with antiques, sitting areas, and some have fireplaces. The inn is just half a mile from beautiful beaches, and a redwood forest is nearby. This inn is an ideal spot for those seeking relaxation or those on a coastal trip. Monterey and San Jose are less than an hour from the hotel, and San Francisco is 90 miles north. Breakfast is served in the inn's dining room. The hotel is close to an abundance of outdoor activities, as well as Nisene Marks State Park.

Innkeeper(s): Christina Locke . $109-269. 12 rooms, 10 with PB, 2 with FP. Breakfast included in rates. Types of meals: Cont plus, early coffee/tea and afternoon tea. Beds: KQD. Cable TV, clock radio and fireplace in room. TV, fax, telephone, fireplace and gift shop on premises. Amusement parks, antiquing, parks, shopping and water sports nearby.

Location: Ocean community.

Publicity: *Mid-County Post and Santa Cruz Sentinel.*

"Thank you so much for all of your tender loving care and great hospitality."

Certificate may be used: Oct. 1-April 1, Sunday-Thursday, subject to availability.

Ben Lomond

Fairview Manor

245 Fairview Ave
Ben Lomond, CA 95005-9347
(831)336-3355
Internet: www.fairviewmanor.com
E-mail: fairviewbandb@aol.com

Circa 1924. The Santa Cruz Mountains serve as a backdrop at this private and restful getaway. The inn is surrounded by nearly three acres of park-like wooded gardens. The Redwood County inn offers comfort and relaxation. The deck off the Great Room overlooks the San Lorenzo River. Built in the early 1920s, the décor reflects that era. Each of the cozy guest bedrooms boasts a private bath and delightful garden view. Enjoy a full country breakfast and afternoon snacks. The inn is an excellent place for family get-togethers as well as small meetings and outdoor weddings. Beaches, thousands of acres of state parks and many wineries are nearby.

Innkeeper(s): Gael Glasson Abayon/Jack Hazelton. $100-159. 5 rooms with PB, 1 conference room. Breakfast, snacks/refreshments, hors d'oeuvres, wine, Raves for our new Breakfast Menu that could include German Apple Pancakes, Eggs Benedict, Citrus Slices in ginger or Blueberry Panckes and just to name a few included in rates. Types of meals: For a nominal charge and we can assist with picnic lunches and such. Beds: KQT. Reading lamp, snack bar, desk, some with fireplace, hair dryer, bath amenities, iron/ironing board and sitting area in room. Parlor games, refrigerator, complimentary drinks, large deck and acreage on premises. Amusement parks, antiquing, art galleries, beach, fishing, golf, hiking, museums, parks, shopping, water sports, wineries, Santa Cruz Beach Boardwalk, Ano Nuevo State Park, Big Basin State Park and Roaring Camp Railroad nearby.

Location: Country, mountains.

Certificate may be used: Sunday through Thursday.

Berry Creek

Lake Oroville Bed and Breakfast

240 Sunday Dr
Berry Creek, CA 95916-9640
(530)589-0700 (800)455-5253 Fax:(530)589-3800
Internet: www.lakeorovillebedandbreakfast.com
E-mail: cheryl@lakeorovillebedandbreakfast.com

Circa 1970. Situated in the quiet foothills above Lake Oroville, this country inn features panoramic views from the private porches that extend from each guest room. Two favorite rooms are the Rose Petal Room  and the Victorian Room, both with lake views and whirlpool tubs. The inn's 40 acres are studded with oak and pine trees. Deer and songbirds abound.

Innkeeper(s): Cheryl & Ron Damberger. $75-165. 6 rooms with PB, 1 conference room. Breakfast included in rates. Types of meals: Full bkfst and early coffee/tea. Beds: KQ. Cable TV, VCR, reading lamp, stereo, refrigerator, ceiling fan, snack bar, clock radio, telephone, turn-down service, desk, hot tub/spa, whirlpool tubs and tape player in room. Air conditioning. TV, fax, copier, spa, library, pet boarding, child care, parlor games and fireplace on premises. Handicap access. Antiquing, fishing, golf, live theater, parks, shopping, tennis and water sports nearby.

Location: Mountains. Lake and valley views.

Publicity: *Oroville Mercury-Register, Chronicle, San Jose Mercury and Most Romantic Weekends.*

Certificate may be used: Anytime, subject to availability.

Big Bear

Gold Mountain Manor Historic B&B

1117 Anita, PO Box 2027
Big Bear, CA 92314
(909)585-6997 (800)509-2604 Fax:(909)585-0327
Internet: www.goldmountainmanor.com
E-mail: info@goldmountainmanor.com

Circa 1928. This spectacular log mansion was once a hideaway for the rich and famous. Ten fireplaces provide a roaring fire in each room in fall and winter. The  Presidential Suite offers a massive rock fireplace embedded with fossils and quartz, facing the two-person Jacuzzi rock tub and four-poster bed. In the Clark Gable room is the fireplace Gable and Carole Lombard enjoyed on their honeymoon. Gourmet country breakfasts and afternoon hors d'oeuvres are served. In addition to the guest rooms, there are home rentals.

Innkeeper(s): Cathy Weil. $129-259. 7 rooms with PB, 7 with FP, 3 suites, 1 conference room. Afternoon tea and snacks/refreshments included in rates. Types of meals: Full gourmet bkfst and early coffee/tea. Beds: Q. Reading lamp, CD player, ceiling fan, clock radio, desk, some with hot tub/spa, fireplace, hair dryer, bathrobes, bath amenities, wireless Internet access, Suites have a Jacuzzi and 2 rooms with DVD Players in room. DVD, fax, spa, library, parlor games, telephone, pool table, kayaks and wireless Internet on premises. Cross-country skiing, downhill skiing, fishing, parks, water sports, hiking/forest and mountain biking nearby.

Location: Mountains. Forest at end of street.

Publicity: *Best Places to Kiss, Fifty Most Romantic Places and Kenny G holiday album cover.*

"A majestic experience! In this magnificent house, history comes alive!"

Certificate may be used: Monday-Thursday, within March 24-Dec.13, no holidays, subject to availability.

Big Bear Lake

Eagle's Nest B&B

41675 Big Bear Blvd, Box 1003
Big Bear Lake, CA 92315
(909)866-6465 (888)866-6465 Fax:(909)866-6025
Internet: www.eaglesnestlodgebigbear.com
E-mail: eaglesnestlodge@earthlink.net

Circa 1983. Named for the American bald eagles that nest in and around Big Bear Lake in California, this lodgepole pine inn features a river rock fireplace in the great room. Antiques, leather furniture and lodge decor provide a warm mountain setting. Surrounded by tall pine trees, the property also includes several cottage suites.

Innkeeper(s): Mark & Vicki Tebo. $110-130. 5 rooms with PB, 3 with FP. Breakfast and snacks/refreshments included in rates. Types of meals: Country bkfst. Beds: Q. Cable TV, reading lamp, ceiling fan, clock radio and fireplace in room. VCR, fax, parlor games, telephone and fireplace on premises. Antiquing, bicycling, canoeing/kayaking, cross-country skiing, downhill skiing, fishing, golf, hiking, horseback riding, live theater, parks, shopping, water sports, mountain biking, rock climbing and movie theatres nearby.

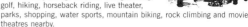

Location: Mountains.

"Each breakfast was delicious and beautiful. A lot of thought and care is obvious in everything you do."

Certificate may be used: Anytime except holidays and weekends from Dec. 15-April 15, subject to availability.

Knickerbocker Mansion Country Inn

869 Knickerbocker Rd
Big Bear Lake, CA 92315
(909)878-9190 (877)423-1180 Fax:(909)878-4248
Internet: www.knickerbockermansion.com
E-mail: knickmail@knickerbockermansion.com

Circa 1920. The inn is one of the few vertically designed log structures in the United States. The inn was built of local lumber by Bill Knickerbocker, the first dam keeper of Big Bear. The inn includes two historic buildings set on two-and-a-half wooded acres, backing to a national forest. Although, the inn offers a secluded setting, the village of Big Bear Lake is within walking distance. The village offers shopping, restaurants, fishing, hiking, mountain biking and excellent downhill skiing.

Innkeeper(s): Stanley Miller & Thomas Bicanic. $110-280. 11 rooms with PB, 2 with FP, 2 total suites, including 1 two-bedroom suite, 1 conference room. Breakfast included in rates. Types of meals: Full gourmet bkfst, early coffee/tea, picnic lunch, snacks/refreshments and gourmet dinner. Restaurant on premises. Beds: KQ. Modem hook-up, data port, cable TV, VCR, DVD, reading lamp, stereo, refrigerator, ceiling fan, clock radio, telephone, coffeemaker, desk, hot tub/spa, voice mail and fireplace in room. Fax, copier, library, parlor games and gift shop on premises. Handicap access. Antiquing, art galleries, bicycling, canoeing/kayaking, cross-country skiing, downhill skiing, fishing, golf, hiking, horseback riding, live theater, museums, parks, shopping, tennis and water sports nearby.

Location: Mountains.

Publicity: *Los Angeles Magazine, Yellow Brick Road, San Bernardino Sun and Daily Press.*

"Best breakfast I ever had in a setting of rustic elegance, a quiet atmosphere and personal attention from the innkeepers. The moment you arrive you will realize the Knickerbocker is a very special place."

Certificate may be used: Sunday-Thursday, non-holiday, subject to availability and prior booking.

Calistoga

Brannan Cottage Inn

109 Wapoo Ave
Calistoga, CA 94515-1136
(707)942-4200 Fax:(707)942-2507
Internet: www.brannancottageinn.com
E-mail: brannancottageinn@sbcglobal.net

Circa 1860. This Greek Revival cottage was built as a guest house for the old Calistoga Hot Springs Resort. Behind a white picket fence towers the original palm tree planted by Sam

Brannan and noted by Robert Louis Stevenson in his "Silverado Squatters." Five graceful arches, an intricate gingerbread gableboard, and unusual scalloped ridge cresting make this a charming holiday house. Six spacious guest rooms feature down comforters; three have four-poster beds. Guests enjoy a full breakfast and evening wine and cheese.

Innkeeper(s): Doug & Judy Cook. $170-225. 6 rooms with PB, 2 suites, 1 conference room. Breakfast included in rates. Types of meals: Full gourmet

bkfst, veg bkfst, early coffee/tea, picnic lunch, hors d'oeuvres and wine. Beds: Q. Cable TV, reading lamp, refrigerator, ceiling fan, clock radio, telephone, hair dryer, bath amenities, wireless Internet access, iron/ironing board, computer hook-up/DSL (by prior arrangement) and mini suites with TV in room. Air conditioning. Fax, copier, library, parlor games, fireplace, free use of pool and mineral water hot tubs at Golden Haven Hot Springs Spa (about 3 blocks away) and office equipment (by prior arrangement) on premises. Limited handicap access. Amusement parks, antiquing, art galleries, bicycling, fishing, golf, hiking, horseback riding, live theater, museums, parks, shopping, tennis, hundreds of wineries, natural attractions like the Petrified Forest and the Old Faithful Geyser of California and access to pool and hot tub at the Golden Haven Hot Sprints (3 blocks away) nearby.

Location: Wine country, Napa Valley.

Publicity: *Food Network ("Tasting Napa").*

Certificate may be used: Nov. 1 to March 31, Sunday through Thursday, subject to availability.

Chelsea Garden Inn

1443 2nd St
Calistoga, CA 94515-1419
(707)942-0948 (800)942-1515 Fax:(707)942-5102
Internet: www.chelseagardeninn.com
E-mail: innkeeper@chelseagardeninn.com

Circa 1940. Located in the heart of Napa Valley, this delightfully different California-style inn features two-room suites with fireplaces and private entrances. The romantic ground-level Palm Suite has a large sitting room with fireplace, day bed and library. The adjoining Lavender Suite is perfect for couples traveling together. Named for its view of the mountains, the second-floor Palisades Suite boasts a four-poster bed and a small balcony overlooking the pool. A full gourmet breakfast is served in the dining room or garden with fresh-brewed coffee from a local roastery. Enjoy evening wine and cheese. Explore the extensive gardens with grapevines, flowers, fruit and nut trees. Swim in the pool or relax by the fire in the social room. Visit local shops, wineries, museums, spas, art galleries and restaurants just two blocks away.

Innkeeper(s): Connie McDonald, Dave and Susan DeVries. $160-275. 5 rooms with PB, 5 with FP, 4 total suites, including 1 two-bedroom suite, 1 cottage, 1 conference room. Breakfast, hors d'oeuvres and wine included in rates. Types of meals: Full gourmet bkfst, early coffee/tea and snacks/refreshments. Beds: KQDT. Modem hook-up, cable TV, VCR, DVD, reading lamp, stereo, refrigerator, ceiling fan, clock radio, coffeemaker, desk, fireplace, hair dryer, bathrobes, bath amenities, wireless Internet access, iron/ironing board, central heating, refrigerator, microwave and video library in room. Central air. Fax, copier, swimming, library, parlor games, telephone, guest computer, free high speed wireless Internet connection, social room with vaulted ceiling, gardens, office telephone with free local calls, complimentary wine and hors d'oeuvres each evening and wine tasting coupons on premises. Limited handicap access. Amusement parks, antiquing, art galleries, bicycling, canoeing/kayaking, fishing, golf, hiking, horseback riding, live theater, museums, parks, shopping, tennis, water sports, wineries, mud baths, massage, ballooning, glider rides and natural wonders and historical sites nearby.

Location: Country. Small town in the Wine Country.

Publicity: *Sunset Magazine, Access Press and The Best Places to Kiss in Northern California.*

Certificate may be used: November through April, Monday-Wednesday.

Fannys

1206 Spring St
Calistoga, CA 94515-1637
(707)942-9491 Fax:(707)942-4810
Internet: www.fannysnapavalley.com
E-mail: fannysnapavalley@comcast.net

Circa 1915. In a shingled Craftsman-cottage style, painted forest green and red, this inn offers an inviting shaded porch with swing, rockers and spots for dining. Inside, comfortable interiors include over-stuffed chairs, a fireplace, library and upstairs guest rooms with plank floors and window seats. The innkeeper, a former restaurateur, provides breakfast and knowledgeable touring suggestions.

Innkeeper(s): Deanna Higgins. $100-180. 2 rooms with PB. Breakfast included in rates. Types of meals: Country bkfst. Beds: Q. Reading lamp, ceiling fan, hair dryer, bath amenities and clock in room. Air conditioning. TV, VCR, fax, library, parlor games, telephone and fireplace on premises. Antiquing, art galleries, canoeing/kayaking, golf, hiking, museums, parks, shopping, tennis, wineries and winery tours & tasting nearby.

Location: Country. Napa Valley.

Certificate may be used: Sunday-Thursday, subject to availability.

Cambria

Olallieberry Inn

2476 Main St
Cambria, CA 93428-3406
(888)927-3222 Fax:(805)927-0202
Internet: www.olallieberry.com
E-mail: info@olallieberry.com

Circa 1873. This restored Greek Revival home features rooms decorated with fabrics and wall coverings and furnished with period antiques. All of the guest rooms feature fireplaces. Butterfly and herb gardens and a 120-year-old redwood grace the front yard. The cheery gathering room boasts a view of the Santa Rosa Creek. Full breakfast with fresh breads, fruits and a special entree start off the day, and wine and hors d'oeuvres are served in the afternoon. The inn is within walking distance to restaurants and shops.

Innkeeper(s): Marjorie Ott. $130-220. 9 rooms with PB, 9 with FP, 1 suite. Breakfast, snacks/refreshments, hors d'oeuvres and wine included in rates. Types of meals: Full gourmet bkfst, veg bkfst and early coffee/tea. Beds: KQ. Reading lamp, refrigerator, fireplace, hair dryer, bathrobes, bath amenities, wireless Internet access and iron/ironing board in room. Fax, library, parlor games, telephone and gift shop on premises. Handicap access. Antiquing, art galleries, beach, bicycling, canoeing/kayaking, fishing, golf, hiking, horseback riding, live theater, museums, parks, shopping, sporting events, tennis, water sports, wineries and Hearst Castle nearby.

Location: Ocean community.

Publicity: *Los Angeles Times, Santa Barbara Independent, Via Magazine, Country Magazine, California Tour and Travel Magazine and Elmer Dills Radio Show.*

"Our retreat turned into relaxation, romance and pure Victorian delight."

Certificate may be used: October through April-Sunday through Thursday nights, excluding holiday periods, subject to availability.

The J. Patrick House

2990 Burton Dr
Cambria, CA 93428-4002
(805)927-3812 (800)341-5258 Fax:(805)927-6759
Internet: www.jpatrickhouse.com
E-mail: jph@jpatrickhouse.com

Circa 1980. This charming log home and carriage house bed & breakfast is nestled in the woods above Cambria's east village. The picturesque grounds include a garden area that separates the main log home from the carriage house, where all but one of the guest rooms are located. Rooms are decorated in a romantic style with country/traditional decor, wood-burning fireplace or stove and private bath. Wine and hors d'oeuvres are served each evening in the main house's fireplaced living room. Fresh fruits, homemade granola and freshly baked breads and muffins are part of the full morning meal. "Killer" chocolate chip cookies and cold milk are served before bedtime.

Innkeeper(s): Ann O'Connor & John Arnott. $175-220. 8 rooms with PB, 7 with FP. Breakfast and wine included in rates. Types of meals: Full bkfst, veg bkfst and early coffee/tea. Beds: KQ. CD player, clock radio, turn-down service, fireplace, massage, champagne, one with wood burning stove, hair dryer and iron/ironing board in room. Fax, library, parlor games, telephone, gift shop, gift shop, wine and hors d'oeuvres, guest refrigerator and sitting room on premises. Antiquing, art galleries, beach, bicycling, canoeing/kayaking, fishing, golf, hiking, horseback riding, parks, shopping, tennis, wineries, Hearst Castle and Paso Robles wine region tasting nearby.

Location: Mountains. Woods.

Publicity: *Karen Brown's, Inn Traveler Magazine Fall 2005, Best Overall for 2006, Elmer Dills, KABC, Channel 7 and Select Registry.*

Certificate may be used: October through March, Monday-Thursday, excluding holiday periods. Based on availability. Limited rooms apply.

The Squibb House

4063 Burton Dr
Cambria, CA 93428-3001
(805)927-9600 Fax:(805)927-9606
Internet: www.squibbhouse.net
E-mail: innkeeper@squibbhouse.net

Circa 1877. A picket fence and large garden surround this Victorian inn with its Italianate and Gothic Revival architecture. Guests may relax in the main parlor, stroll the gardens or sit and rock on the porch. The home was built by a Civil War veteran and young school teacher. The downstairs once was used as a classroom while an addition was being made in the town's school. Each guest room has a fire stove.

Innkeeper(s): Bruce Black. $105-185. 5 rooms with PB, 5 with FP. Breakfast included in rates. Types of meals: Cont plus. Beds: Q. Reading lamp in room. Parlor games, telephone, fireplace and retail shop in historic 1885 carpentry shop on premises. Antiquing, fishing, golf, parks, shopping, Hearst Castle, wine tasting and galleries nearby.

Location: Pine covered hills.

Publicity: *Cambrian.*

Certificate may be used: Sunday-Thursday only, November-March, not valid during holiday weeks.

Carmel

Cobblestone Inn

PO Box 3185
Carmel, CA 93921-3185
(831)625-5222 (800)833-8836 Fax:(831)625-0478
Internet: www.cobblestoneinncarmel.com
E-mail: cobblestoneinn@foursisters.com

Circa 1950. An exterior of wood and cobblestone gathered from the Carmel River provide a friendly facade for visitors to this bed & breakfast located two blocks from the heart of Carmel. Each guest room has its own cobblestone fireplace.

 The inn's English country decor is enhanced with quilts, a colorful antique carousel horse and other early American antiques. In addition to breakfast and afternoon tea, evening wine and hors d'oeuvres are served. Guests can borrow one of the inn's bicycles to explore the area. The beach and shopping are nearby. There is a $20 fee for an additional guest in room, except for children less than 5 years old. Cobblestone is one of the Four Sisters Inns.

Innkeeper(s): Sharon Carey. $125-265. 24 rooms with PB, 24 with FP, 3 suites. Breakfast, afternoon tea, snacks/refreshments, hors d'oeuvres and wine included in rates. Types of meals: Full gourmet bkfst and early coffee/tea. Beds: KQ. Data port, cable TV, VCR, reading lamp, stereo, refrigerator, ceiling fan, snack bar, clock radio, telephone, coffeemaker, turn-down service, desk, some with hot tub/spa, voice mail, fireplace, hair dryer, bathrobes, bath amenities and iron/ironing board in room. Central air. Fax, copier, bicycles, parlor games, afternoon wine and hors d'oeuvres, home-baked cookies, evening turndown service, newspaper delivery, bicycles to borrow and signature breakfast on premises. Handicap access. Antiquing, art galleries, beach, bicycling, canoeing/kayaking, fishing, golf, hiking, horseback riding, live theater, museums, parks, shopping, tennis and wineries nearby.

Location: Ocean community.

Publicity: *Country Inns and Honeymoons.*

Certificate may be used: Sunday – Thursday, December through February, based on promotional discount availability and excludes special event periods, holidays and certain room types. First night must be at full rack rate to receive second night free.

Carpinteria

Prufrock's Garden Inn By The Beach

600 Linden Ave
Carpinteria, CA 93013
(805)566-9696 (877)837-6257
Internet: www.prufrocks.com
E-mail: prufrocksgardeninn@yahoo.com

Circa 1904. Tucked between a mountain wilderness, flower fields and an ocean, this inn is located one block from State Beach Park and 10 minutes from the City Center. Santa Barbara Independent named it a "Most Romantic Getaway," and the L.A. Times voted it a "Readers' Favorite." Other recognitions include being pictured in Land's End catalog and a "Community Beautiful" award. Explore Salt Marsh Park and waterfront bluffs, or visit specialty shops and cafes. The inn is close to an Amtrak station. A quote from The Love Song of J. Alfred Prufrock, by TS Eliot is lived out at this inn: "Time for you and time for me, before the taking of a toast and tea."

Innkeeper(s): Judy & Jim Halvorsen. $99-399. 7 rooms, 8 with PB, 4 with FP, 3 with HT, 3 with WP, 2 two-bedroom suites, 2 cottages. Breakfast, afternoon tea, snacks/refreshments, hors d'oeuvres and 24-hour treats and drinks included in rates. Types of meals: Full gourmet bkfst, early coffee/tea, picnic lunch, Free 24 hour treats and drinks, Home baking twice daily and Fresh squeezed OJ and more. Beds: Q. Cable TV, VCR, DVD, reading lamp, CD player, refrigerator, ceiling fan, clock radio, coffeemaker, desk, some with hot tub/spa, most with fireplace, hair dryer, bathrobes, bath amenities, wireless Internet access, iron/ironing board, Free WiFi, Garden wood-burning fireplaces and Beach amenities in room. Fax, copier, library, parlor games, telephone, Wood-burning fireplaces in garden sitting areas and Beach amenities on premises. Handicap access. Antiquing, art galleries, beach, bicycling, canoeing/kayaking, fishing, golf, hiking, horseback riding, live theater, museums, parks, shopping, sporting events, tennis, water sports, wineries, Tide pooling, Protected seal refuge, Whale and Dolphin watching nearby.

Location: City, mountains, ocean community, waterfront. Santa Barbara/Carpinteria State Beach.

Publicity: *Santa Barbara Independent ("Most Romantic Getaway"), National Geographic Traveler "World's Best Beaches", Local "Community Beautification" award, Land's End catalog, L.A. Times ("Reader's favorite") and Sunset magazine.*

Certificate may be used: Oct. 1-June 30, Sunday-Thursday.

Castro Valley

Deer Crossing Inn

21600 Eden Canyon Rd
Castro Valley, CA 94552
(510)537-4926 Fax:(510)537-6854
Internet: www.deercrossinginn.com
E-mail: info@deercrossinginn.com

Classic and comfortable, Deer Crossing Inn in San Francisco, California spans more than six acres with a faux gold mine to enhance the Old West ambiance offering luxury amenities in a casually elegant setting. Gather by the 16 foot cobblestone fireplace in the Great Room or on the expansive deck that surrounds three sides of the second floor. Play table tennis, air hockey or any number of activities as well as watch movies and eat popcorn in the spacious game room with a beverage bar. The grounds boast a fire pit, wagon wheel waterfall, two ponds and hot tub. Stay in a delightful guest bedroom or The Mayor's Suite that features a Jacuzzi, wood-burning fireplace and private deck. Breakfast is served in the Gold Rush Restaurant, the themed dining room.

Innkeeper(s): Cindi & Rick Hinds. $130-250. 4 rooms with PB, 2 with FP, 1 with WP, 2 suites. Breakfast, afternoon tea, snacks/refreshments and wine included in rates. Types of meals: Country bkfst and early coffee/tea. Beds: QDT. Cable TV, DVD, ceiling fan, telephone, desk, some with fireplace, bath amenities and wireless Internet access in room. Central air. TV, VCR, fax, copier, spa, library, parlor games, gift shop, Air hockey, Table tennis, Fire pit and Ponds on premises. Hiking, horseback riding, parks, shopping, wineries and Rowell Ranch Rodeo Park nearby.

Location: Country, mountains.

Certificate may be used: Sunday-Thursday, subject to availability.

Chico

L'Abri B&B

14350 Hwy 99
Chico, CA 95973
(530)893-0824 (800)489-3319
Internet: www.now2000.com/labri
E-mail: l.janak@att.net

Circa 1972. This ranch-style house is located on more than two acres, with a scenic seasonal creek. All three guest rooms offer a private, outside entrance and each is uniquely decorated. Full breakfasts are offered, often followed by special baked goods and an occasional peach or berry cobbler when in season. Cycle the country roads, go horseback riding or go into town and enjoy light opera and open-air summer concerts.

Innkeeper(s): Lauree Janak. $80-150. 4 rooms with PB, 1 with HT. Breakfast and snacks/refreshments included in rates. Types of meals: Country bkfst, veg bkfst, early coffee/tea and room service. Beds: Q. Modem hook-up, TV, reading lamp, refrigerator, ceiling fan, clock radio, telephone, some with hot tub/spa, hair dryer, bathrobes and morning coffee/juice tray delivered in room. Air conditioning. VCR, DVD, fax, copier, parlor games and fireplace on premises. Antiquing, art galleries, bicycling, canoeing/kayaking, cross-country skiing, downhill skiing, fishing, golf, hiking, horseback riding, live theater, museums, parks, shopping, sporting events, tennis, water sports, Bidwell Park, breweries and world-renowned glass blower studios nearby.

Location: Country.

Certificate may be used: Jan. 2-Dec. 1, Sunday-Thursday, except holidays and special events.

Coronado

Cherokee Lodge

964 D Avenue
Coronado, CA 92118
(619)437-1967 Fax:(619)437-1012
Internet: www.cherokeelodge.com
E-mail: stay@cherokeelodge.com

Experience the delights of Coronado Island while staying at this bed and breakfast located just one block from downtown and four blocks from the beach. Named after the Cherokee roses that framed the property in the late 1800s, it is steeped in history. There are common areas to relax in and one offers a computer to use as well as wireless high-speed Internet. Enjoy comfortable, smoke-free accommodations with a choice of twelve guest bedrooms that feature VCRs and refrigerators. A washer and dryer are available. A continental breakfast is provided daily. Walk to nearby bistros and restaurants.

Innkeeper(s): Karen Johnson. Call for rates. 12 rooms. Beds: KQDT. Modem hook-up, data port, cable TV, VCR, reading lamp, refrigerator, ceiling fan, clock radio, telephone, coffeemaker, desk, hair dryer, bath amenities, wireless Internet access and iron/ironing board in room. Laundry facility and future handicap room on premises. Limited handicap access. Amusement parks, antiquing, art galleries, beach, bicycling, canoeing/kayaking, fishing, golf, live theater, museums, parks, sporting events, tennis, water sports, sailing and kite surfing among locally available water sports nearby.

Location: City, ocean community.

Certificate may be used: October-May, anytime subject to availability, no holidays.

Dana Point

Blue Lantern Inn

34343 Street of the Blue Lantern
Dana Point, CA 92629
(949)661-1304 (800)950-1236 Fax:(949)496-1483
Internet: www.bluelanterninn.com
E-mail: bluelanterninn@foursisters.com

Circa 1990. The four-diamond inn is situated high on a blufftop overlooking a stunning coastline and the blue waters of Dana Point harbor with its pleasure craft, fishing boats and the tall ship, Pilgrim. Each guest room features both a fireplace and a whirlpool tub and many offer private sun decks. Afternoon tea, evening turndown service and bicycles are just a few of the amenities available. In the evening, wine and hors d'oeuvres are served. Shops, restaurants and beaches are nearby, and popular Laguna Beach is just a few miles to the north. There is a $20 fee for an additional guest in room, except for children less than 5 years old. Blue Lantern is one of the Four Sisters Inns.

Innkeeper(s): Lin McMahon. $155-500. 29 rooms with PB, 29 with FP, 2 conference rooms. Breakfast, afternoon tea, snacks/refreshments, hors d'oeuvres and wine included in rates. Types of meals: Full gourmet bkfst. Beds: KQ. Modem hook-up, data port, cable TV, VCR, reading lamp, stereo, refrigerator, ceiling fan, snack bar, clock radio, telephone, coffeemaker, turn-down service, desk, hot tub/spa, voice mail, fireplace, hair dryer, bathrobes, bath

amenities, iron/ironing board, signature breakfast, afternoon wine and hors d'oeuvres, morning newspaper delivery, complimentary sodas and home-baked cookies in room. Central air. Bicycles, library, parlor games, gift shop, complimentary parking and gym on premises. Handicap access. Amusement parks, antiquing, art galleries, beach, bicycling, canoeing/kayaking, fishing, golf, hiking, horseback riding, live theater, museums, parks, shopping, water sports, beach and Dana Point Harbor nearby.

Location: Ocean community, waterfront.

Certificate may be used: Sunday – Thursday, December through February, based on promotional discount availability and excludes special event periods, holidays and certain room types. First night must be at full rack rate to receive second night free.

Elk

Sandpiper House Inn

5520 S Hwy 1
Elk, CA 95432
(707)877-3587 (800)894-9016 Fax:(707)877-1822
Internet: www.sandpiperhouse.com
E-mail: sandpiperhouseinn@yahoo.com

A garden path leads Sandpiper guests to a garden sitting area overlooking the California coast. The path continues onward to a private beach. The historic home was built by a local lumber company. The living room and dining room have virgin redwood paneling. Guest quarters are appointed to look like rooms in an English country home. Canopied beds, Oriental rugs and polished wood floors create a romantic ambiance. Rooms offer either ocean or countryside views, and four have a fireplace. Gourmet breakfasts are served on tables set with lace and fresh flowers. In-house massages also are available.

Innkeeper(s): Gerarda & Barney Stocking. Call for rates. Call inn for details. Breakfast and snacks/refreshments included in rates. Types of meals: Full gourmet bkfst, early coffee/tea, hors d'oeuvres and wine. Beds: KQ. Reading lamp, refrigerator, desk, fireplace, soaking tubs, hair dryers and iron/iron board in room. Library, parlor games, telephone, in-house massage therapy and Internet access on premises. Fishing, live theater, parks, shopping, water sports and wineries nearby.

Location: Ocean community, waterfront.

Certificate may be used: October-March, Monday-Thursday.

Eureka

Carter House Inns

301 L St
Eureka, CA 95501
(707)444-8062 (800)404-1390 Fax:(707)444-8067
Internet: www.carterhouse.com
E-mail: reserve@carterhouse.com

Circa 1884. Superior hospitality is offered in these Victorian inns that grace the historic district. Perched alongside Humboldt Bay, the inn promises appealing views. Proud of their AAA four-diamond rating, luxurious guest bedrooms and suites feature fireplaces, antique furnishings and spas. Begin each morning with a highly acclaimed breakfast. Renowned for regional, seasonal cuisine, for many ingredients are grown in the garden or bought from local purveyors. Restaurant 301 boasts a coveted international Wine Spectator Grand Award, maintaining in its cellars an extensive collection of the world's finest vintages.

Innkeeper(s): Mark & Christi Carter. $155-497. 32 rooms with PB, 15 with FP, 15 suites, 2 cottages, 1 conference room. Breakfast and afternoon tea included in rates. Types of meals: Full gourmet bkfst, early coffee/tea, snacks/refreshments, hors d'oeuvres, wine, gourmet dinner and room service. Restaurant on premises. Beds: KQDT. Cable TV, VCR, reading lamp, stereo, refrigerator, snack bar, clock radio, telephone, turn-down service, desk and hot tub/spa in room. Fax, copier, spa, fireplace, bedtime tea & cookies and wine & hors d'oeuvres before dinner available on premises. Handicap access. Antiquing, fishing, live theater, parks, shopping, sporting events, water sports and beaches nearby.

Location: Ocean community, waterfront.

Publicity: *Sunset, U.S. News & World Report, Country Home, Country Living, Bon Appetit, San Francisco Focus, Northwest Palate, Gourmet, Art Culinare, San Francisco Chronicle, Wine Spectator, New York Times Magazine and Organic Gardening.*

Certificate may be used: Anytime, November-April, subject to availability.

Ships Inn Bed and Breakfast

821 D St
Eureka, CA 95501-1711
(707)443-7583 (877)443-7583 Fax:(707)443-6215
Internet: www.shipsinn.net
E-mail: genie@shipsinn.net

Circa 1887. Built by a master ship builder for a sea captain in 1882, this Victorian bed and breakfast is accented with a nautical décor. It is located just blocks from the quaint Old Town and the new Boardwalk. Relax, read or play games in the Fireside Room with a writing deck and soft music playing in the background. On the first Saturday evening of each month an Arts Alive! reception is held for a local artist or photographer and the artwork hangs in the gallery all month. Each guest bedroom features a private bath, TV, VCR and robes. Stay in the spacious Captain's Quarters, the fantasy Rose Garden Room or the Mission Room with DSL modem. Savor breakfast served in the dining room with general seating or provided in-room.

Innkeeper(s): Genie Wood and Bill Daly. $120-170. 3 rooms with PB, 2 suites. Breakfast included in rates. Types of meals: Full bkfst, veg bkfst, early coffee/tea and room service. Beds: KQ. Modem hook-up, data port, cable TV, VCR, reading lamp, refrigerator, ceiling fan, clock radio, telephone, coffeemaker, turn-down service, desk, fireplace, hair dryer, bathrobes, bath amenities, iron/ironing board, turndown service with ice water and chocolates each evening and down comforters in room. Fax, copier, library, parlor games and featured work by a different artist or photographer each month on premises. Antiquing, art galleries, beach, bicycling, canoeing/kayaking, fishing, golf, hiking, live theater, museums, parks, shopping and wineries nearby.

Location: City, waterfront. The Victorian Seaport.

Certificate may be used: Sept. 15-Dec.15, excluding holidays, Jan. 5-Feb.10, Must mention this promotion up front.

Fawnskin

Inn At Fawnskin

880 Canyon Rd
Fawnskin, CA 92333
(909)866-3200 (888)329-6754 Fax:(909)878-2249
Internet: www.fawnskininn.com
E-mail: innatfawnskin@charter.net

Circa 1976. Listen to the quiet at this contemporary log home on an acre with scores of pine trees. The inn is located across the street from the North Shore of Big Bear Lake. It has four guest bedrooms and is decorated in elegant country style with antiques and reproductions. The large master suite has a rock fireplace, a sitting area and a private balcony that overlooks the lake. Guests are free to use the living room (with its large rock fireplace), TV/VCR/DVD and dining room. A country breakfast

is served on china in the dining room. The meal includes such delicacies as fresh peaches, a brie and ham omelette with maple-smoked bacon, fresh-squeezed orange juice and freshly-ground coffee. The inn is minutes from boating, fishing, biking trails, ski areas, shops and restaurants. Guests enjoy moonlight walks by the lake and skies filled with stars. Guests who listen carefully may be rewarded by hearing innkeeper Nancy, who once sang at the White House, singing as she creates a perfect atmosphere for guests to relax and unwind.

Innkeeper(s): Nancy & Bill Hazewinkel. $135-285. 5 rooms with PB, 4 with FP, 3 suites, 6 cabins. Breakfast included in rates. Types of meals: Full gourmet bkfst, veg bkfst, early coffee/tea, snacks/refreshments, hors d'oeuvres and wine. Beds: KQ. Cable TV, VCR, DVD, reading lamp, CD player, refrigerator, ceiling fan, clock radio, desk, hot tub/spa and fireplace in room. Fax, copier, spa, parlor games and gift shop on premises. Limited handicap access. Antiquing, art galleries, bicycling, canoeing/kayaking, cross-country skiing, downhill skiing, fishing, golf, hiking, horseback riding, live theater, museums, parks, shopping and water sports nearby.

Location: Mountains.

Publicity: *LA Times, Inland Empire magazine and Valley Messenger.*

Certificate may be used: Sunday-Thursday, non-holiday.

Felton

Felton Crest Inn

780 El Solyo Heights Drive
Felton, CA 95018
(831)335-4011 (800)474-4011 Fax:(831)335-4011
Internet: www.feltoncrestinn.com
E-mail: hannapeters@mymailstation.com

Circa 1981. Bright and spacious interiors highlight this New Victorian built in 1981 on one secluded acre that is peacefully bordered by a state park and a private camp in the Santa Cruz Mountains. Colorful stained-glass windows frame the front door that leads to the entry hall. Relax on plush seating in the fireside living room that boasts French doors opening onto the large outdoor deck and surrounding redwoods. Romantic guest bedrooms and suites include sitting areas, fine linens and Jacuzzi baths. Indulge in the Tree Top Penthouse with a private deck, wood stove, and vaulted ceilings with exposed beams. Start the day with a continental breakfast in the dining room before venturing out on one of the scenic hiking trails.

Innkeeper(s): Hannah Peters. $215-295. 4 rooms with PB, 1 with FP. Breakfast included in rates. Types of meals: Cont. Beds: K. Cable TV, VCR, clock radio, telephone, desk, some with fireplace and bath amenities in room. Central air. DVD and fax on premises. Limited handicap access. Amusement parks, antiquing, art galleries, beach, bicycling, canoeing/kayaking, fishing, golf, hiking, horseback riding, live theater, museums, parks, shopping, water sports and wineries nearby.

Location: Mountains.

Certificate may be used: Monday-Thursday.

Ferndale

Collingwood Inn Bed & Breakfast

831 Main Street
Ferndale, CA 95536
(707)786-9219 (800)469-1632 Fax:(707)786-4859
Internet: www.collingwoodinn.com
E-mail: stay@collingwoodinn.com

Circa 1885. Considered a Showboat House, the architecture of this enchanting B&B built in 1885 is non-symmetrical Italianate with Queen Anne flair. Relax in the parlor amid casual elegance and Victorian splendor and enjoy the generous hospitality. Savor afternoon tea, bedtime port and chocolates. Choose a well-appointed guest bedroom or suite that features a private entrance with a deck or balcony, fireplace, feather bed, clawfoot tub, sitting area, garden or village view, robes, fruit basket, fresh flowers, inn-made soap and bubble bath. Designated pet-friendly rooms include treats and necessities. An incredible breakfast is available when desired and made with local, organically grown ingredients. Browse Peter's art gallery and studio. On-site spa services can be arranged.

Innkeeper(s): Chris & Peter. $100-300. 5 rooms with PB, 2 with FP, 1 total suite, including 2 two-bedroom suites, 2 cottages, 2 guest houses. Breakfast, afternoon tea, snacks/refreshments and wine included in rates. Types of meals: Full gourmet bkfst, veg bkfst, Sun. brunch, early coffee/tea, lunch, picnic lunch, hors d'oeuvres, gourmet dinner and room service. Beds: QT. Modem hook-up, data port, cable TV, VCR, DVD, reading lamp, stereo, refrigerator, ceiling fan, clock radio, telephone, coffeemaker, turn-down service, desk, most with hot tub/spa, most with fireplace, hair dryer, bathrobes, bath amenities, wireless Internet access, iron/ironing board, terrycloth robes, complimentary fruit basket, bottled water and bedtime chocolates in room. TV, fax, copier, spa, library, pet boarding, parlor games, laundry facility and gift shop on premises. Handicap access. Antiquing, art galleries, beach, bicycling, canoeing/kayaking, fishing, golf, hiking, horseback riding, live theater, museums, parks, shopping, sporting events, water sports, Humboldt County Fair, Redwood National Forest and Avenue of the Giants nearby.

Location: City, country, mountains. Victorian Village.

Publicity: *San Francisco Chronicle (2003), Fido-friendly Magazine (2003), Times-Standard, The Press Democrat, LA Times (2007), KQED San Francisco (2004), KPLU Seattle (2004), KVIE Sacramento (2004), KPBS San Diego (2004), Travel Channel (2004), GSNetwork (2006), Sony Pictures (2006), HR Radio, Germany/Europe (2004), Outbreak (1995), The Majestic (2001), Blue Skies (1994), A Death in Canaan (1978) and Salem's Lot (1979).*

Certificate may be used: Anytime, November-March, subject to availability.

Fish Camp

Tin Lizzie Inn

7730 Laurel Way
Fish Camp, CA 93623
(559)641-7731 Fax:(559) 641-7731
Internet: www.tinlizzieinn.com
E-mail: modelttours@sti.net

Circa 2006. Recently opened and newly built, Tin Lizzie Inn is a replica of an 1890's Victorian mansion. This B&B offers an elegant and intimate setting just two miles from the south entrance of Yosemite National Park, across from Tenaya Lodge in Fish Camp, California. Tour the town in an original Model T Ford. Relax with a beverage on the front porch; sit by the waterfall or bronze fountain. Enjoy evening treats by the firepit. Stay in the romantic Tin Lizzie Suite that spans the entire second floor and includes a fireplace, clawfoot massage tub and body spray shower. The first-floor Lady Suite features a Jacuzzi tub. Linger over a

gourmet breakfast on the attached private balcony or patio. Bass Lake and the surrounding area is known for its incredible beauty.

Innkeeper(s): David & Sheran Woodworth. $225-450. 2 rooms with PB, 1 with FP, 1 with WP, 1 suite, 1 cottage. Breakfast, afternoon tea and snacks/refreshments included in rates. Types of meals: Full gourmet bkfst, veg bkfst, early coffee/tea, picnic lunch and Evening Treats. Beds: KQ. Cable TV, VCR, DVD, reading lamp, stereo, clock radio, telephone, turn-down service, desk, some with fireplace, hair dryer, bathrobes, bath amenities, wireless Internet access, iron/ironing board, Shower with body sprays, Balcony and Private patio in room. Fax, copier, library, parlor games, Model T and Model A Fords, Firepit, Waterfall, Private patios, Evening treats, Beverages all day, Videos on Henry Ford and the Model T on premises. Antiquing, bicycling, canoeing/kayaking, fishing, golf, hiking, horseback riding, live theater, parks, water sports, Sugar Pine Railroad, Waterfalls, Evening events, Lake and Camping nearby.

Location: Mountains. 2 miles from southern entrance to Yosemite National Park.

Certificate may be used: May-October, Sunday-Thursday, subject to availability.

Fort Bragg

Glass Beach B&B

726 N Main St
Fort Bragg, CA 95437-3017
(707)964-6774
Internet: www.glassbeachinn.com
E-mail: glassbeachinn@hotmail.com

Circa 1920. Each of the guest rooms at this Craftsman-style home is decorated in a different theme and named to reflect the decor. The Malaysian and Oriental Jade rooms reflect Asian artistry, while the Forget-Me-Not and Victorian Rose rooms are bright, feminine rooms with walls decked in floral prints. Antiques are found throughout the home and the back cottage, which includes three of the inn's nine guest rooms. The inn also offers a hot tub for guest use. Breakfasts are served in the inn's dining room, but guests are free to take a tray and enjoy the meal in the privacy of their own room.

Innkeeper(s): Nancy Cardenas/RichardFowler. $60-195. 9 rooms with PB, 4 with FP, 1 suite, 1 cottage. Breakfast and snacks/refreshments included in rates. Types of meals: Country bkfst, afternoon tea and room service. Beds: Q. Cable TV, VCR, reading lamp, refrigerator, clock radio, hot tub/spa and fireplace in room. Spa, parlor games and telephone on premises. Handicap access. Antiquing, art galleries, beach, bicycling, canoeing/kayaking, golf, hiking, horseback riding, live theater, museums, parks, shopping, water sports, wineries and scuba diving nearby.

Location: City, ocean community.

Certificate may be used: Jan. 5-June 4, Oct. 1-Dec. 31, Sunday-Thursday. Most holidays excluded.

Georgetown

American River Inn

Main and Orleans Streets
Georgetown, CA 95634-0043
(530)333-4499 (800)245-6566 Fax:(530)333-9253
Internet: www.americanriverinn.com
E-mail: ariinnkeepers@aol.com

Circa 1853. Just a few miles from where gold was discovered in Coloma stands this completely restored miners' boarding house. Mining cars dating back to the original Woodside Mine Camp are on-site. The lode still runs under the inn. There is a Jacuzzi, croquet field, ping pong and complimentary mountain bikes. In the evenings, guests are treated to complimentary wines and hors d'oeuvres. Georgetown was a designated site for the California gold discovery celebration.

Innkeeper(s): Maria, Will & Betty. $95-130. 12 rooms, 7 with PB, 1 with FP, 1 conference room. Types of meals: Full gourmet bkfst. Beds: KQ. Fax, copier, spa, bicycles and ping pong on premises. Handicap access. Fishing and hiking nearby.

Publicity: *Los Angeles Times, Sunset, Gourmet, Westways and 50 Romantic Getaways.*

"Our home away from home. We fell in love here in all its beauty and will be back for our fourth visit in April, another honeymoon for six days."

Certificate may be used: Anytime, November-April, excluding holidays, Sunday-Thursday May-October, subject to availability.

Geyserville

Hope-Merrill House & Hope Bosworth House

21253 Geyserville Ave.
Geyserville, CA 95441-9637
(707)857-3356 (800)825-4233 Fax:(707)857-4673
Internet: www.hope-inns.com
E-mail: moreinfo@hope-inns.com

Circa 1870. The Hope-Merrill House is a classic example of the Eastlake Stick style that was so popular during Victorian times.

Built entirely from redwood, the house features original wainscoting and silk-screened wallcoverings. A swimming pool, vineyard and gazebo are favorite spots for guests to relax. The Hope-Bosworth House, on the same street, was built in 1904 in the Queen Anne style by an early Geyserville pioneer who lived in the home until the 1960s. The front picket fence is covered with roses. Period details include oak woodwork, sliding doors, polished fir floors and antique light fixtures.

Innkeeper(s): Cosette & Ron Scheiber. $129-250. 12 rooms with PB, 5 with FP, 1 suite. Breakfast included in rates. Types of meals: Full gourmet bkfst, early coffee/tea and picnic lunch. Beds: Q. Reading lamp, ceiling fan and desk in room. Fax, copier, telephone, fireplace, coffee, tea and hot chocolate available 24 hours a day on premises. Antiquing, parks, shopping, water sports, wineries and redwoods nearby.

Location: Wine country.

Publicity: *New York Times, San Francisco Chronicle, San Diego Union, Country Homes, Sunset, Sacramento Union, Los Angeles Times and Bay Area Back Roads.*

Certificate may be used: From Dec. 1-March 31 anyday, Monday-Thursday April 1-Nov. 30.

Glen Ellen

Relais du Soleil

1210 Nuns Canyon Rd.
Glen Ellen, CA 95442
(707)833-6264 Fax:(707)833-6644
Internet: www.relaisdusoleil.com
E-mail: relaisdusoleil@cs.com

Circa 1914. Open year-round, Relais du Soleil means a place to rest in the sun, and this guest ranch on 120 park-like acres in Glen Ellen, California perfectly reflects its French name. Enjoy the casual ambiance and gorgeous scenery in Nuns Canyon at the foot of Mayacamas mountain range. Shade trees accent the deck next to Calabazas Creek. Play horseshoes, darts, croquet or petanque. Sit and stargaze or birdwatch. Stay in an upstairs guest bedroom in the main house or the three-room cottage called the Bunkhouse Suite. Feel welcomed by fresh flowers and a glass of champagne upon arrival. A full ranch breakfast is served on the patio or in the dining room. Take a wine-tasting tour of the nearby Sonoma Valley vineyards.

Innkeeper(s): Tim Korn. $99-250. 5 rooms with PB, 1 cottage. Breakfast, hors d'oeuvres and wine included in rates. Types of meals: World-renowned gourmet breakfast. Beds: QDT. Reading lamp, stereo, refrigerator, clock radio, desk, hair dryer, bathrobes, bath amenities and iron/ironing board in room. TV, VCR, fax, copier, spa, bicycles, library, pet boarding, parlor games, telephone, fireplace, laundry facility, swimming hole, creek, petanque court, small private winery, horseshoes, darts, croquet, great hiking, mushroom hunting, great bird watching, star gazing and Sculpture Garden by Bryan Tedrick on premises. Handicap access. Antiquing, art galleries, bicycling, fishing, golf, hiking, horseback riding, live theater, museums, parks, shopping, tennis, wineries and Jack London State Park nearby.

Location: Country. Sonoma Wine Country.

Publicity: *Travel World International Magazine (Jan. 2006).*

Certificate may be used: Anytime, Sunday-Thursday.

Groveland

Hotel Charlotte

18736 Main Street
Groveland, CA 95321
(209)962-6455 Fax:(209)962-6254
Internet: www.HotelCharlotte.com
E-mail: HotelCharlotte@aol.com

Circa 1921. Gracing one acre in the Sierra Nevada Mountains of California, the Hotel Charlotte is on the way to Yosemite near Stanislaus National Forest. Find entertainment in the game room or relax on the balcony overlooking the gold rush town of Groveland. Beverages are usually available at any time. Listed in the National Register, this bed and breakfast hotel provides comfortable and convenient accommodations. Air-conditioned guest bedrooms feature new, soundproof windows and a variety of sleeping arrangements. Several rooms boast a clawfoot tub, one room with a spa tub. Enjoy a buffet breakfast in the morning. Café Charlotte, the onsite full-service restaurant and bar, offers good food and spirits.

Innkeeper(s): Lynn & Victor. $88-149. 10 rooms with PB, 2 two-bedroom suites, 4 guest houses. Pancake buffet and scrambled eggs with all the fixings included in rates. Types of meals: Country bkfst, veg bkfst, early coffee/tea, picnic lunch, wine, dinner and On-site restaurant is open Thurs.-Sun. from 5:30. A pancake buffet breakfast is included in the room rates and complimentary coffee & tea are available most times. Any other food services are an additional cost and may require a minimum number of participants. Restaurant on premises. Beds: QDT. Modem hook-up, data port, reading lamp, telephone, hair dryer, bath amenities, wireless Internet access, iron/ironing board, Deluxe rooms have televisions with cable and VCRs and most rooms have telephones in room. Central air. TV, fax, copier, library, parlor games, laundry facility, Shared balcony, ice machine for guests, almost anytime beverage service (coffee, tea and iced tea) on premises. Limited handicap access. Antiquing, art galleries, beach, bicycling, canoeing/kayaking, cross-country skiing, fishing, golf, hiking, horseback riding, live theater, museums, parks, shopping, tennis, water sports, wineries, Whitewater river rafting, Yosemite National Park, Stanislaus National Forest and Gold Panning nearby.

Location: Mountains. Yosemite.

Publicity: *Www.tripadvisor.com rates us as number one in Groveland for both our hotel and restaurant.*

Certificate may be used: November 1-March 31, Sunday-Thursday, all holidays excluded.

The Groveland Hotel at Yosemite National Park

18767 Main St.
Groveland, CA 95321-0481
(209)962-4000 (800)273-3314 Fax:(209)962-6674
Internet: www.groveland.com
E-mail: guestservices@groveland.com

Circa 1849. Located 23 miles from Yosemite National Park, the 1992 restoration features both an 1849 adobe building with 18-inch-thick walls constructed during the Gold Rush and a 1914 building erected to house workers for the Hetch Hetchy Dam. Both feature two-story balconies. There is a Victorian parlor, a gourmet restaurant and a Western saloon. Guest rooms feature European antiques, down comforters, some feather beds, in-room coffee, phones with data ports, and hair dryers. The feeling is one of casual elegance.

Innkeeper(s): Peggy A. & Grover C. Mosley. $145-285. 17 rooms with PB, 3 with FP, 3 with WP, 3 suites, 1 conference room. Breakfast and Full Breakfast included in rates. Types of meals: Full bkfst, veg bkfst, early coffee/tea, lunch, picnic lunch, wine, gourmet dinner, room service and The Victorian Room Restaurant is famous for Gourmet California Seasonal Cuisine and the Wine Spectator Magazine "Award of Excellence" wine list. Lunch is available in the restaurant or in the garden courtyard on weekends through the summer months. Restaurant on premises. Beds: KQT. Modem hook-up, data port, TV, reading lamp, CD player, ceiling fan, clock radio, telephone, coffeemaker, desk, some with hot tub/spa, voice mail, some with fireplace, hair dryer, bathrobes, bath amenities, wireless Internet access, iron/ironing board, Our in-room coffee features fresh beans with grinders, all rooms have period antiques, feather beds with down comforters and 600-thread count luxury linens and Our bath robes are plush and comfortable in room. Central air. VCR, fax, copier, library, pet boarding, parlor games, gift shop, Spa services, Special in-room extras for additional fees and Handicap access to some rooms on premises. Limited handicap access. Antiquing, art galleries, bicycling, canoeing/kayaking, cross-country skiing, downhill skiing, fishing, golf, hiking, horseback riding, live theater, museums, parks, shopping, tennis, water sports, wineries, Summer entertainment through the Yosemite Courtyard Theatre (open air theatre), Live entertainment, Jazz & blues, Country music, Big band, Popular music, Tributes to famous stars, Historical dramas (Open weekends from May through September), Yosemite National Park (23 miles), World class White Water Rafting, Caverns to explore, Spelunking, Gold panning, Historic towns to explore, Two art galleries, Mountain Sage Coffee House, The Iron Door, the oldest Saloon in California (right next door) featuring live music and other activities nearby.

Location: Country, mountains. Only 23 miles to Yosemite National Park's Highway 120 gate.

Publicity: *Sonora Union Democrat, Los Angeles Times, Penninsula, Sunset (February 2001-West's Best Inns), Stockton Record, Country Inns Magazine (Top 10 Inns in U.S.), Men's Journal Magazine, 25 Best Hideaways, Associated Press, Huell Howser's California's Gold "Roads Go Through" (Episode #9002) and Wine Spectator Award of Excellence for our wine list.*

Certificate may be used: Oct. 15-April 15, Sunday through Thursday, excluding holidays.

Gualala

North Coast Country Inn

34591 South Hwy One
Gualala, CA 95445
(707)884-4537 (800)959-4537 Fax:(707)884-1833
Internet: www.northcoastcountryinn.com
E-mail: nccinn@gmail.com

Circa 1944. Overlooking the Pacific Ocean, the six guest rooms that comprise North Coast Country Inn are tucked into a pine and redwood forested hillside. Each is furnished with antiques, and include a fireplace, some wet-bar kitchenettes and private deck. There is a very private and secluded hot tub on the hillside or you may relax in the gazebo. Breakfast is served in the breakfast room. Barking sea lions are often heard in the distance.

Innkeeper(s): Phil & Sandy Walker. $156-225. 6 rooms with PB, 6 with FP, 1 conference room. Breakfast and snacks/refreshments included in rates. Types of meals: Full gourmet bkfst, veg bkfst, early coffee/tea and picnic lunch. Beds: KQ. Reading lamp, refrigerator, ceiling fan, clock radio, coffeemaker, turn-down service, hot tub/spa and fireplace in room. TV, VCR, fax, spa, parlor games, telephone and gift shop on premises. Antiquing, art galleries, beach, bicycling, canoeing/kayaking, fishing, golf, hiking, horseback riding, live theater, parks, shopping, tennis and wineries nearby.

Location: Ocean community.

Publicity: *San Francisco Examiner, Wine Spectators, Wine Trader, Motortrend, Los Angeles Times and San Francisco Chronicle.*

"Thank you so much for a very gracious stay in your cozy inn. We have appreciated all the special touches."

Certificate may be used: November-May 31, subject to availability and June-October 31, Sunday-Thursday.

Guerneville

Fern Grove Cottages

16650 Highway 116
Guerneville, CA 95446-9678
(707)869-8105
Internet: www.ferngrove.com
E-mail: innkeepers@ferngrove.com

Clustered in a village-like atmosphere and surrounded by redwoods, these craftsman cottages have romantic fireplaces, private entrances, and are individually decorated. The cottages were built in the 1920s and served as little vacation houses for San Francisco families visiting the Russian River. Some units have a kitchen or wet bar, some have double whirlpool tubs and other cottages are suitable for families. Guests enjoy use of the swimming pool. The cottages are just a few blocks from shops and restaurants, as well as a swimming beach on the river. Visit a nearby redwood state reserve or the Russian River Valley wineries for wine tasting and tours.

Innkeeper(s): Mike & Margaret Kennett. $89-259. 20 cottages with PB, 14 with FP, 1 conference room. Breakfast included in rates. Types of meals: Cont plus and Wines By The Fireside during winter months: on non-event Saturdays. Beds: KQ. Cable TV, VCR, DVD, reading lamp, CD player, refrigerator, clock radio, coffeemaker, some with fireplace, hair dryer and wireless Internet access in room. Swimming, telephone, guest barbeque and picnic/eating area on premises. Limited handicap access. Antiquing, art galleries, beach, bicycling, canoeing/kayaking, fishing, golf, hiking, horseback riding, live theater, museums, parks, shopping, tennis, water sports, wineries, Armstrong Redwood State Reserve, Ocean beaches and Surfing nearby.

Location: River and vineyards.

Certificate may be used: Anytime, November-March, event and holidays excluded, subject to availability.

Half Moon Bay

Landis Shores Oceanfront Inn

211 Mirada Rd
Half Moon Bay, CA 94019
(650)726-6642 Fax:(650)726-6644
Internet: www.landisshores.com
E-mail: luxury@landisshores.com

Circa 1999. Luxuriate in pampered pleasure at this Contemporary Mediterranean bed & breakfast inn overlooking Miramar Beach. Guest bedrooms boast impressive extras that include binoculars, private balconies, fireplaces, robes, radiant heated floors, a generous assortment of personal grooming amenities and mini-refrigerators with bottled water. Marble or granite bathrooms feature whirlpools and separate showers except for the ADA San Francisco Bay room, with a large limestone shower. Enjoy in-room entertainment centers and business services. Choose a movie selection from the library. Savor a gourmet breakfast in the dining room at a table for two or on a tray delivered to the door. The restaurant has a sommelier and an award-winning wine list. Exercise in the fully equipped fitness center or jog along the coastline trail. Guest services can arrange horseback riding or bike rentals.

Innkeeper(s): Ken & Ellen Landis. $295-345. 8 rooms with PB, 8 with FP, 1 conference room. Breakfast, hors d'oeuvres and wine included in rates. Types of meals: Full gourmet bkfst and early coffee/tea. Beds: KQ. Modem hook-up, data port, cable TV, VCR, reading lamp, CD player, refrigerator, clock radio, telephone, coffeemaker, turn-down service, desk, hot tub/spa, voice mail, fireplace, private balconies, wireless Internet access and radiant heated floors in room. Fax, copier, library, parlor games, fitness center, movie library and award-winning wine list on premises. Handicap access. Antiquing, art galleries, beach, bicycling, canoeing/kayaking, fishing, golf, hiking, horseback riding, live theater, parks, shopping, tennis, water sports, wineries, tide pools, redwoods and birdwatching nearby.

Location: Ocean community, waterfront. Beach access.

Publicity: *Half Moon Bay Review, Arrington's Bed & Breakfast Journal, Inn Traveler and KGO Radio (Dining Around with Gene Burns).*

Certificate may be used: All year, Sunday-Thursday.

Old Thyme Inn

779 Main Street
Half Moon Bay, CA 94019-1924
(650)726-1616 (800)720-4277 Fax:(650)726-6394
Internet: www.oldthymeinn.com
E-mail: innkeeper@oldthymeinn.com

Circa 1898. Spend enchanted nights in this "Princess Anne" Victorian inn located on the historic Main Street of Old Town, Half Moon Bay. Its lush, aromatic English flower and herb garden with a bubbling fountain provides a perfect backdrop for casual conversations or romantic tete-a-tetes. Just 28 miles from San Francisco and less than one hour from San Jose and the Silicon  Valley, the inn is within walking distance of a crescent-shaped beach, art galleries, shops and fine dining. Furnished in antiques and adorned with the innkeeper's art collection, it offers seven freshly decorated guest rooms, each with a queen bed and hypoallergenic featherbed and down comforter. Two rooms have both Jacuzzis and fireplaces. Savor the inn's tantalizing full breakfast before a day of relaxing or sightseeing.

Innkeeper(s): Rick & Kathy Ellis. $155-345. 7 rooms with PB, 3 with FP, 3 with WP. Breakfast, hors d'oeuvres and wine included in rates. Types of meals: Full gourmet bkfst, veg bkfst and early coffee/tea. Beds: Q. Cable TV, VCR, reading lamp, clock radio, some with hot tub/spa, some with fireplace, hair dryer, bathrobes, bath amenities, wireless Internet access and iron/ironing board in room. Fax, parlor games, telephone and gift shop on premises. Antiquing, art galleries, beach, bicycling, canoeing/kayaking, fishing, golf, hiking, horseback riding, live theater, parks, shopping, water sports and wineries nearby.

Location: Ocean community.

Publicity: *California Weekends, Los Angeles, San Mateo Times, San Jose Mercury News, Herb Companion and San Francisco Examiner.*

Certificate may be used: Nov. 1 to April 30, Sunday-Thursday (except for Thanksgiving, year-end holidays and Valentine's/President's Day weekends), valid for the Garden or Thyme room only, subject to availability.

Healdsburg

Camellia Inn

211 North St
Healdsburg, CA 95448-4251
(707)433-8182 (800)727-8182 Fax:(707)433-8130
Internet: www.camelliainn.com
E-mail: info@camelliainn.com

Circa 1869. Just two blocks from the tree-shaded town plaza, this Italianate Victorian townhouse elegantly graces a half-acre of award-winning grounds. Architectural details include ceiling medallions, ornate mahogany and Palladian windows. Gather in the double parlor with twin marble fireplaces and antiques. Spacious guest bedrooms feature inlaid hardwood floors with Oriental rugs and chandeliers. Many feature whirlpool tubs for two, gas-log fireplaces, canopy beds, sitting areas and private entrances. The Memento can be used as a family suite with an adjoining room. Savor a hearty breakfast buffet fireside in the main dining room. Relax in the swimming pool, and enjoy the more than 50 varieties of camellias.

Innkeeper(s): Ray, Del and Lucy Lewand. $119-239. 9 rooms with PB, 4 with FP, 1 two-bedroom suite, 2 conference rooms. Breakfast and wine included in rates. Types of meals: Full bkfst. Beds: QD. Modem hook-up, reading lamp, hot tub/spa, fireplace and wireless Internet access in room. Air conditioning. TV, VCR, fax, swimming, parlor games, telephone and gift shop on premises. Limited handicap access. Antiquing, art galleries, beach, bicycling, canoeing/kayaking, fishing, golf, hiking, horseback riding, live theater, museums, parks, shopping, water sports and wineries nearby.

Location: City. Town surrounded by vineyards.

Publicity: *Sunset, Travel & Leisure, New York Times, San Fernando Valley Daily News, San Diego Union, Sacramento Bee, Healdsburg Tribune, Washington Post, Cooking Light and Food & Travel.*

"A bit of paradise for city folks."

Certificate may be used: Anytime, December-April, Sunday-Thursday, subject to availability, excludes holidays & events.

Healdsburg Inn on The Plaza

110 Matheson St, PO Box 1196
Healdsburg, CA 95448-4108
(707)433-6991 (800)431-8663 Fax:(707)433-9513
Internet: www.healdsburginn.com
E-mail: Healdsburginn@foursisters.com

Circa 1900. A former Wells Fargo building, the inn is a renovated brick gingerbread overlooking the plaza in historic downtown Healdsburg. Ornate bay windows, embossed wood paneling and broad, paneled stairs present a welcome smile. There are fireplaces and the halls are filled with sunlight from vaulted, glass skylights. A solarium is the setting for breakfast

and evening wine and hors d'oeuvres. A large covered balcony extends along the entire rear of the building. Shops on the premises sell gifts, toys, quilts and fabric. An antique shop and art gallery can be found there, as well. The surrounding area is full of things to do, including wineries and wine-tasting rooms.

Innkeeper(s): Wanda & Jennifer. $255-295. 10 rooms with PB, 9 with FP, 1 conference room. Breakfast and snacks/refreshments included in rates. Types of meals: Full gourmet bkfst and early coffee/tea. Beds: KQT. Cable TV, VCR, reading lamp, refrigerator, ceiling fan and telephone in room. Air conditioning. TV, fax, copier, parlor games, fireplace and wine tasting on premises. Antiquing, fishing, parks, shopping, water sports, wineries, balloon, canoe and historic walking tour nearby.

Location: Small town.

Publicity: *Healdsburg Tribune, Los Angeles Daily News, New York Times and San Francisco Chronical Travel Section.*

"The first-thing-in-the-morning juice and coffee was much appreciated."

Certificate may be used: Sunday – Thursday, December through February, based on promotional discount availability and excludes special event periods, holidays and certain room types. First night must be at full rack rate to receive second night free.

Madrona Manor, Wine Country Inn & Restaurant

1001 Westside Road
Healdsburg, CA 95448-0818
(707)433-4231 (800)258-4003 Fax:(707)433-0703
Internet: www.madronamanor.com
E-mail: info@madronamanor.com

Circa 1881. This handsome estate consists of five historic structures including the Mansion, Schoolhouse and a Gothic-style Carriage House. Embellished with turrets, bay windows, porches and a mansard roof, the stately inn is surrounded by eight acres of manicured lawns, terraced flower and vegetable gardens and wooded areas. Elegant antique furnishings abound. The inn's noteworthy five-star restaurant offers California cuisine featuring fresh local ingredients served in romantic dining rooms.

Innkeeper(s): Joe & Maria Hadley. $185-445. 17 rooms with PB, 5 suites, 2 conference rooms. Breakfast included in rates. Types of meals: Full gourmet bkfst and dinner. Restaurant on premises. Beds: KQ. Telephone in room. Air conditioning. Fax, fireplace and data port on premises. Handicap access. Antiquing, bicycling, fishing, parks, shopping, sporting events, water sports and wineries nearby.

Location: Country.

Publicity: *Travel & Leisure, Conde Naste, Gourmet, Woman's Day Home Decorating Ideas, US News, Diversions, Money, Good Housekeeping, Wine Spectator, Wine and Spirits and Great Country Inns of America.*

"Our fourth visit and better every time."

Certificate may be used: All year, Sunday through Thursday, excluding holidays.

Hope Valley

Sorensen's Resort

14255 Hwy 88
Hope Valley, CA 96120
(530)694-2203 (800)423-9949
Internet: www.sorensensresort.com
E-mail: info@sorensensresort.com

Circa 1876. Where Danish sheepherders settled in this 7,000-foot-high mountain valley, the Sorensen family built a cluster of fishing cabins. Thus began a century-old tradition of valley hospitality. The focal point of Sorensen's is a "stave" cabin — a reproduction of a 13th-century Nordic house. Now developed as a Nordic ski resort, a portion of the Mormon-Emigrant Trail and Pony Express Route pass near the inn's 165 acres. In the summer, river rafting, fishing, pony express re-rides and llama treks are popular Sierra pastimes. Lake Tahoe lies 20 miles to the north.

Breakfast is included in the rates for bed & breakfast units only. All other cabins are equipped with kitchens.

Innkeeper(s): John & Patty Brissenden. $95-350. 33 rooms, 31 with PB, 23 with FP, 28 cottages, 2 conference rooms. Types of meals: Full bkfst, early coffee/tea, lunch, picnic lunch, snacks/refreshments and gourmet dinner. Restaurant on premises. Beds: QD. Reading lamp and refrigerator in room. Copier, sauna, library, parlor games, telephone, fireplace, e-mail hook-up, complimentary wine, tea and cocoa on premises. Handicap access. Antiquing, cross-country skiing, downhill skiing, fishing, parks and water sports nearby.

Location: Mountains.

Publicity: *Sunset, San Francisco Chronicle, Los Angeles Times, Motorland, Outside, New York Times and Travel & Leisure.*

"In one night's stay, I felt more comfortable, relaxed, and welcome than any vacation my 47 years have allowed. Thank you for the happiness you have given my children."

Certificate may be used: Monday through Thursday, non-holiday, excluding February, July, August and October.

Idyllwild

Cedar Street Inn & Spa

25870 Cedar
Idyllwild, CA 92549
(951)659-4789 Fax:(951)659-1049
Internet: www.cedarstreetinn.com
E-mail: Inn@cedarstreetinn.com

Circa 1988. Relaxation and romance reign at this Victorian country inn which is home to both spa and massage studios. Created from two 1930s homes, this award-winning inn is hidden in the quaint forest village of Idyllwild, California. Themed guest bedrooms and suites feature fireplaces, cable TV and private entrances. Stay in a separate cabin or an adjacent two-bedroom cottage with a fireplace, kitchen and large secluded outdoor deck with a therapeutic hot tub. Thoughtful amenities at the Cedar Creek Inn make each visit a delight. The new spa house is perfect for serious aqua therapy. Hike nearby trails and Strawberry Creek. Ask about weekday specials.

Innkeeper(s): Herb Larson. $90-170. 9 rooms, 12 with PB, 10 with FP, 2 with HT, 1 with WP, 1 suite, 2 cottages, 3 cabins, 1 conference room. Types of meals: Early coffee/tea. Beds: KQDT. Cable TV, VCR, reading lamp, refrigerator, ceiling fan, coffeemaker, desk, some with hot tub/spa, fireplace and wireless Internet access in room. Fax, copier, spa, library, parlor games and WIFI from your laptop on premises. Antiquing, art galleries, bicycling, canoeing/kayaking, cross-country skiing, fishing, golf, hiking, horseback riding, live theater, parks, shopping, wineries, Yoga and Pilates classes and rock climbing nearby.

Location: Mountains.

Publicity: *Destinations of Southern California.*

Certificate may be used: Anytime, November-April, subject to availability.

Inverness

Rosemary Cottages

75 Balboa Avenue
Inverness, CA 94937-0619
(415)663-9338 (800)808-9338
Internet: www.rosemarybb.com
E-mail: innkeeper@rosemarybb.com

Circa 1986. From the windows of this trio of spacious and secluded cottages, enjoy views of a wooded canyon and hillside. The location of Rosemary Cottages near Tomales Bay State Park and Point Reyes National Seashore in Inverness, California is the perfect setting for a scenic vacation or romantic getaway. Select a sunny cottage with a fully equipped kitchen and other pleasing amenities. A satisfying breakfast is made with organic ingredients. Relax in the garden hot tub.

Innkeeper(s): Suzanne Storch. $185-295. 3 cottages with PB, 3 with FP. Breakfast and $225-$295 nightly rate for occupancy of two includes breakfast included in rates. Types of meals: Full bkfst. Beds: QT. DVD, reading lamp, CD player, refrigerator, clock radio, telephone, coffeemaker, desk, hair dryer, bathrobes and iron/ironing board in room. Spa, parlor games, fireplace, Decks, Gas barbeque and Gardens on premises. Antiquing, art galleries, beach, bicycling, canoeing/kayaking, fishing, golf, hiking, horseback riding, parks, shopping, tennis, water sports, wineries, World class birding, Whale watching, Tule elk, Elephant seals, Wildflowers, Redwoods, Marshlands and Excellent restaurants nearby.

Location: Ocean community. Pt. Reyes National Seashore.

Certificate may be used: Nov. 1 through March 31, Sunday through Thursday, excluding holiday weeks.

Ten Inverness Way

10 Inverness Way, PO Box 63
Inverness, CA 94937-0063
(415)669-1648 Fax:(415)669-7403
Internet: www.teninvernessway.com
E-mail: inn@teninvernessway.com

Circa 1904. Shingled in redwood, this handsome bed & breakfast features a stone fireplace, a sunny library with many  good books, and close access to a wonderful hiking area. After an afternoon of hiking, guests can enjoy a soak in the garden hot tub. Inverness is located on Tomales Bay, offering close access to nearby beaches at Point Reyes National Seashore. The Golden Gate Bridge is 45 minutes from the inn.

Innkeeper(s): Teri Mowery. $125-200. 5 rooms, 4 with PB, 1 suite. Breakfast and afternoon tea included in rates. Types of meals: Full gourmet bkfst, veg bkfst, early coffee/tea, picnic lunch and snacks/refreshments. Beds: Q. Reading lamp, ceiling fan, clock radio, hair dryer and iron/ironing board in room. Fax, copier, spa, library, parlor games, telephone, fireplace, gift shop and gift shop on premises. Antiquing, art galleries, beach, bicycling, canoeing/kayaking, fishing, golf, hiking, horseback riding, live theater, museums, parks, shopping, water sports and wineries nearby.

Location: Mountains, ocean community.

Publicity: *Los Angeles Times* ("as snug as a Christmas stocking, as cheery as a roaring fire"), *New York Times, Travel & Leisure, Sunset, Gourmet* and *San Francisco Chronicle.*

"Everything we could have wanted for our comfort was anticipated by our hosts. Great hot tub. Lovely rooms and common areas."

Certificate may be used: Sunday-Thursday, Nov. 1-March 31, holiday periods excluded.

Jackson

Wedgewood Inn

11941 Narcissus Rd
Jackson, CA 95642-9600
(209)296-4300 (800)933-4393 Fax:(209)296-4301
Internet: www.wedgewoodinn.com
E-mail: jeannine@wedgewoodinn.com

Circa 1987. Located in the heart of Sierra gold country on a secluded, five acres, this Victorian replica is crammed full of senti-  mental family heirlooms and antiques. Each room has been designed with careful attention to detail. A baby grand piano rests in the parlor. The carriage house is a separate cottage with its own private entrance. It boasts four generations of family heirlooms, a carved canopy bed, a wood-burning stove and a two-person Jacuzzi tub. The innkeepers' 1921 Model-T, "Henry," is located in its own special showroom. Gourmet breakfasts are served on bone china and include specialties such as cheese-filled blintzes, fruit and baked goods. Breakfast is available in selected guest rooms by request. There is a gift shop on the premises.

Innkeeper(s): Vic & Jeannine Beltz. $155-205. 5 rooms with PB, 1 suite. Breakfast included in rates. Types of meals: Full gourmet bkfst, early coffee/tea and snacks/refreshments. Beds: Q. Refrigerator, ceiling fan, clock radio, turn-down service, desk and Jacuzzi in room. Air conditioning. Fax, copier, parlor games, telephone, croquet, hammocks and horseshoes on premises. Antiquing, cross-country skiing, downhill skiing, fishing, golf, live theater and shopping nearby.

Location: Mountains. Gold Country Foothills.

Publicity: *San Francisco Chronicle, Contra Costa Times, Stockton Record, Country Magazine* and *Victorian Magazine.*

Certificate may be used: Sunday through Thursday inclusive, no holiday weekends.

Jamestown

1859 Historic National Hotel, A Country Inn

18183 Main St,
Jamestown, CA 95327-0502
(209)984-3446 (800)894-3446 Fax:(209)984-5620
Internet: www.national-hotel.com
E-mail: info@national-hotel.com

Circa 1859. Located between Yosemite National Park and Lake Tahoe, in Gold Country, this is one of the 10 oldest continuously operating hotels in the state. The inn maintains its original redwood bar where thousands of dollars in gold dust were once spent. Original furnishings, Gold Rush period antiques, brass beds, lace curtains and regal comforters grace the guest bedrooms. A soaking room is an additional amenity, though all rooms include private baths. Enjoy a daily bountiful buffet breakfast. Arrange for romantic dining at the on-site gourmet restaurant, considered to be one of the finest in the Mother Lode. Order a favorite liquor or espresso from the saloon, or try the area's wine tasting. Favorite diversions include gold panning, live theatre and antiquing, golf and shopping.

Innkeeper(s): Stephen Willey. $150-175. 9 rooms with PB, 1 conference room. Breakfast and Buffet breakfast in dining room for hotel guests included in rates. Types of meals: Country bkfst, Sun. brunch, early coffee/tea, gourmet lunch, picnic lunch, snacks/refreshments, hors d'oeuvres, wine, gourmet dinner, room service, Banquets, meetings, seminars, weddings and receptions. Restaurant on premises. Beds: QT. Modem hook-up, data port, cable TV, VCR, reading lamp, telephone, coffeemaker, desk, hair dryer, bathrobes, bath amenities, wireless Internet access, iron/ironing board, Antique furnishings, Old fashioned claw-footed tub for two soaking room, Pull-chain toilets, Memory foam mattress pads and Alarm clocks in room. Central air. DVD, fax, copier, spa, library, pet boarding, parlor games, highly-acclaimed restaurant with patio dining, original Gold Rush saloon, espresso bar and soaking room for house guests on premises. Antiquing, art galleries, bicycling, canoeing/kayaking, cross-country skiing, downhill skiing, fishing, golf, hiking, horseback riding, live theater, museums, parks, shopping, tennis, water sports, wineries, gold panning, antiquing, shopping, multiple golf courses, Historic Steam Railroad State Park, Columbia Gold Rush State Park, Big Trees State Park, watersports of all types - kayaking, canoeing, rafting, sailing, etc., hiking, fishing and horseback riding nearby.

Location: Country, mountains. Yosemite National Park, Sonora.

Publicity: *Bon Appetit, California Magazine, Focus, San Francisco Magazine, Gourmet, Sunset, San Francisco Chronicle, Modesto Bee, Sacramento Bee, San Jose Mercury, The Union Democrat, Razor Magazine, Fabulous Foods.com, Via Magazine, Stockton Record, San Francisco Downtown Magazine, NBC, Channel 13, PBS, Bound For Glory, Back to the Future-3, Redemption of the Ghost, Little House on the Prairie and Gambler #2.*

Certificate may be used: Last minute availability only.

The Victorian Gold Bed and Breakfast

10382 Willow St
Jamestown, CA 95327-9761
(209)984-3429 (888)551-1852 Fax:(209)984-4929
Internet: www.victoriangoldbb.com
E-mail: innkeeper@victoriangoldbb.com

Circa 1890. Enjoy Gold Country at this Victorian, which was home to Albert and Amelia Hoyt, publishers of the Mother Lode Magnet. In the 1890s, the home served as a boarding house. Today, it offers eight guest rooms with lacy curtains, fresh flowers, clawfoot tubs, marble showers and robes. A full breakfast is served each morning along with The Palm's special blend of coffee. The inn is located two-and-a-half hours from San Francisco and about an hour from Yosemite Valley, and it is within walking distance of Main Street, boutiques, galleries, restaurants and Railtown State Park.

Innkeeper(s): Ken & Anita Spencer. $110-190. 8 rooms with PB. Breakfast included in rates. Types of meals: Full gourmet bkfst and early coffee/tea. Beds: KQD. Cable TV, DVD, reading lamp, refrigerator, clock radio, hair dryer, bathrobes, bath amenities, wireless Internet access and iron/ironing board in room. Central air. Fax and copier on premises. Limited handicap access. Antiquing, cross-country skiing, fishing, golf, hiking, live theater, museums, parks, shopping, water sports, wineries, Railtown State Park and Yosemite and Calaveras Big Trees nearby.

Location: Mountains. California gold country.

Publicity: *Avalon Bay News, San Jose Mercury News, Sacramento Bee, Modesto Bee, San Francisco Chronicle, Sonora Union Democrat, Central Valley Chronicles on KVIE TV and Central Sierra Bank 1999 calendar.*

"The simple elegance of our room and ambiance of the Palm in general was a balm for our souls."

Certificate may be used: Anytime, November-March, subject to availability.

Jamul

Lion's Head Guest House

16001 Skyline Truck Trail
Jamul, CA 91935
(619)669-9061 Fax:(619)669-9062
Internet: www.lionsheadguesthouse.com
E-mail: info@lionsheadguesthouse.com

Circa 1979. Feel refreshed after a pleasurable stay at this stylish bed and breakfast located on eight acres in a quiet, rural setting in the mountains of Jamul. The central location is perfect for experiencing the many sightseeing adventures in the area from horseback riding to beachcombing. Spacious and luxurious guest suites offer upscale amenities. The huge Parisian Suite features two bathrooms, a reading room, dining table and balcony. Sit by the fire and the fountain on the private deck of the Athens Suite. A popular favorite for romantic getaways is the Amethyst Suite with a Jacuzzi tub and entertainment center. Start the day with a satisfying breakfast then relax on the rooftop patio, swim in the pool or soak in the spa.

Innkeeper(s): Tom & Robin Willis. $185-250. 12 rooms, 8 with PB, 1 with FP, 3 with HT, 3 with WP, 1 cottage, 1 guest house. Breakfast and wine included in rates. Types of meals: Country bkfst and early coffee/tea. Beds: KQ. Cable TV, VCR, reading lamp, refrigerator, clock radio, most with hot tub/spa, some with fireplace, hair dryer, bathrobes, bath amenities and iron/ironing board in room. Central air. DVD, spa, swimming, telephone, laundry facility and roof-top patio on premises. Amusement parks, antiquing, art galleries, beach, bicycling, fishing, golf, hiking, horseback riding, live theater, museums, parks, shopping, sporting events, water sports, Tecate Mexico, skydiving, snorkeling and casino nearby.

Location: Country, mountains.

Publicity: *Sunset Magazine (Feb 2005) .*

Certificate may be used: Sunday-Thursday, last minute weekends upon availability.

Joshua Tree

Joshua Tree Inn

61259 29 Palms Hwy.
Joshua Tree, CA 92252-0340
(760)366-1188 Fax:(760)366-3805
Internet: Joshuatreeinn.com
E-mail: joshuatreeinn@gmail.com

Circa 1940. Escape to the peaceful grandeur of the Mojave Desert at this secluded hacienda-style inn on four acres, only

five miles from the national park. Feel enveloped by the awesome mountains while relaxing on the vine-covered veranda. The square horseshoe design allows for privacy with each ground-level guest bedroom and suite facing the large pool and courtyard. Stay in the legendary Gram Parsons Room, named after the songwriter/musician who was one of the many celebrity guests. Hike, climb or simply stargaze from a lounge chair.

$75-145. 10 rooms with PB, 2 suites, 1 conference room. Types of meals: Cont, early coffee/tea and afternoon tea. Beds: KQDT. Cable TV, reading lamp, ceiling fan, clock radio and water cooler in room. VCR, fax, copier, swimming, parlor games, telephone and fireplace on premises. Antiquing, golf, live theater, parks, shopping, tennis and Joshua Tree National Park nearby.

Location: Mountains. Joshua Tree National Park (5 min).

Publicity: *Los Angeles Times and Press Enterprise.*

"Quiet, clean and charming."

Certificate may be used: June-September, excluding holidays and based on availability.

Spin and Margies Desert Hide-A-Way

64491 29 Palms Highway
Joshua Tree, CA 92252
(760)366-9124 Fax:(760)366-2954
Internet: www.deserthideaway.com
E-mail: mindela@earthlink.net

Circa 1950. Escape to this Hacienda-style inn situated on three acres of desert landscape featuring palms, pines, native trees and succulents and a small pond. Four well-designed suites are arranged around an interior courtyard with cactus, yuccas and a soothing fountain. Blending an eclectic mix of Southwest, Mexican and modern furnishings and decor, the private suites include sitting rooms, kitchens and patios.

Innkeeper(s): Drew Reese/Mindy Kaufman. $115-150. 4 rooms with PB. Types of meals: Early coffee/tea. Beds: Q. Cable TV, VCR, reading lamp, stereo, refrigerator, ceiling fan, clock radio, telephone, coffeemaker, desk, fireplace, tape system and full kitchen in room. Air conditioning. Library, parlor games and fireplace on premises. Antiquing, art galleries, bicycling, cross-country skiing, golf, hiking, horseback riding, live theater, museums, parks, shopping, wineries, gifts, Spin & Margies trading post and casino nearby.

Location: Country, mountains. Desert & National Park area.

Publicity: *Malibu Times, LA Times and London Herald.*

Certificate may be used: July 5-Sept. 5, Sunday-Thursday.

Julian

Butterfield B&B

2284 Sunset Dr
Julian, CA 92036
(760)765-2179 (800)379-4262 Fax:(760)765-1229
Internet: butterfieldbandb.com
E-mail: info@butterfieldbandb.com

Circa 1935. On an ivy-covered hillside surrounded by oaks and pines, the Butterfield is a peaceful haven of hospitality and country comfort. Overlooking the countryside, several of the charming guest bedrooms feature fireplaces and fluffy featherbeds. A delicious gourmet breakfast is served in the gazebo during summer or by a warm fire in cooler months. The parlor is a delightful place to enjoy hot beverages and afternoon treats. Whether it is scheduling an in-room massage, or making dinner reservations, the innkeepers are always happy to oblige.

Innkeeper(s): Ed & Dawn Glass. $135-185. 5 rooms with PB, 3 with FP, 1 cottage. Breakfast and snacks/refreshments included in rates. Types of meals: Full gourmet bkfst, veg bkfst and early coffee/tea. Beds: KQD. Cable TV, DVD, reading lamp, stereo, refrigerator, ceiling fan, clock radio, coffeemaker, most with fireplace, hair dryer, bathrobes, bath amenities, wireless Internet access and iron/ironing board in room. Air conditioning. Fax, copier, library, parlor games and telephone on premises. Limited handicap access. Antiquing, art galleries, canoeing/kayaking, fishing, golf, hiking, horseback riding, live theater, museums, parks, shopping and wineries nearby.

Location: Mountains.

Publicity: *South Coast and Travel Agent.*

Certificate may be used: Jan. 7-Aug. 31, Sunday-Thursday.

Orchard Hill Country Inn

2502 Washington Street
Julian, CA 92036-0425
(760)765-1700 (800)716-7242
Internet: www.orchardhill.com
E-mail: information@orchardhill.com

Circa 1992. Reminiscent of America's great national park lodges, this award-winning inn is cradled in the heart of the Julian Historic Mining District. Enjoy the hilltop vistas and warm hospitality. A mountain spring, colorful native gardens and hiking trails lead to abandoned mines. The inn features a guest-only dining room, bar and on-site masseuse. The conference room is available  for weddings and retreats. Air-conditioned cottage rooms with porches offer comfort and abundant amenities that include fireplace, whirlpool tub, wet bar, refrigerator coffee maker and phone with modem. The area is renowned for birding, star gazing, hiking and nearby desert wildflower preserves. Relax and be refreshed in the romantic setting.

Innkeeper(s): Straube Family. $195-425. 22 rooms with PB, 12 with FP, 1 conference room. Breakfast and hors d'oeuvres included in rates. Types of meals: Country bkfst, early coffee/tea, picnic lunch, wine and gourmet dinner. Beds: KQ. Cable TV, VCR, reading lamp, CD player, refrigerator, ceiling fan, clock radio, telephone, coffeemaker, turn-down service, desk, some with hot tub/spa, voice mail, some with fireplace, hair dryer, bathrobes, bath amenities, wireless Internet access and iron/ironing board in room. Air conditioning. Fax, copier, library, parlor games and gift shop on premises. Handicap access. Antiquing, art galleries, bicycling, fishing, hiking, horseback riding, live theater, parks, shopping, wineries, music/art festivals, horse trails and bird watching nearby.

Location: Mountains. Northeast San Diego County.

Publicity: *San Diego Union Tribune, Los Angeles Times, Orange County Register, Orange Coast, San Francisco Chronicle, San Bernardino Sun, Oceanside Blade-Citizen and "Top Six Lodges in the West" Sunset Magazine.*
"The quality of the rooms, service and food were beyond our expectations."

Certificate may be used: Sunday-Thursday, other restrictions may apply.

Villa De Valor - Hildreth House, circa 1898

2020 Third Street
Julian, CA 92036
(760)765-3865 (877)968-4552 Fax:(760)765-3862
Internet: www.villadevalor.com
E-mail: stay@villadevalor.com

Circa 1898. Gracing the heart of the historic district, this formal Victorian bed & breakfast offers a getaway full of elegance and charm. Innkeeper Valorie proudly displays her personal artwork throughout the inn for all to enjoy. A parlor invites conversation. Romantic suites feature private entrances, fireplaces, spacious sitting areas, period furnishings and nostalgic amenities. Intimate table settings accent gourmet candlelight breakfasts. Later, indulge in sweet treats by the fire. Breathe in the mountain air and enjoy the view from the front porch, unwind in an aromatherapy sauna or just relax in the backyard garden gazebo with the sounds of a soothing fountain.

Innkeeper(s): Valorie Ashley. $165-210. 3 rooms with PB, 3 with FP, 2 suites, 1 cottage. Breakfast and snacks/refreshments included in rates. Types of meals: Full gourmet bkfst, veg bkfst and early coffee/tea. Beds: QD. Cable TV, VCR, reading lamp, refrigerator, ceiling fan, clock radio, coffeemaker, desk, wireless Internet access, fireplace, AC, formal parlor sitting area and CD player in room. Library, parlor games, telephone, fireplace, gift shop and evergreen garden with gazebo and water fountain pond on premises. Antiquing, art galleries, bicycling, fishing, hiking, horseback riding, live theater, museums, parks, shopping, wineries, gold mine, star gazing and carriage rides nearby.

Location: Mountains. Lakes nearby.

Publicity: *San Diego Union Tribune, Orange County Register, Arrington's-winner of 2003 "Best Art Collection," 2004 "Best Antiques," 2003 Book of Lists and Best Art Collection, Inn Traveler- feature story in fall issue 2003, LA Times- feature story in December 2003 Travel Section and Feb. 2005 "Best Anniversary & Honeymoon" featured story KPBS* .

Certificate may be used: Jan. 10-Aug. 15, Sunday-Thursday, excludes holidays.

Kenwood

Birmingham Bed and Breakfast

8790 Sonoma Hwy
Kenwood, CA 95452
(707)833-6996 (800)819-1388 Fax:(707)833-6398
Internet: www.birminghambb.com
E-mail: info@birminghambb.com

Circa 1915. Set amongst vineyards, this two-acre Prairie-style country estate with breathtaking views was given historic designation by Sonoma County. A fireplace, library and game table are located in the Victorian breakfast parlor. The sitting parlor offers a reading nook and small visitors center. Romantic guest bedrooms and suites feature four-poster and sleigh beds. The spacious Red Room boasts a soaking tub with shower and a private balcony overlooking the pond and hazelnut trees. Fresh produce from the orchard and garden provides ingredients for seasonal breakfast recipes like artichoke cheese frittata, scones and poached pears. Relax on the wraparound porch facing mountain vistas.

Innkeeper(s): Nancy & Jerry Fischman. $160-295. 5 rooms, 4 with PB, 1 two-bedroom suite, 1 cottage, 1 conference room. Breakfast and afternoon tea included in rates. Types of meals: Full gourmet bkfst, veg bkfst and early coffee/tea. Beds: KQT. Reading lamp, desk, some with fireplace, hair dryer, bath amenities, iron/ironing board, clock and toiletries in room. Central air. Fax, copier, library, parlor games and telephone on premises. Antiquing, art galleries, beach, bicycling, golf, hiking, horseback riding, museums, parks, shopping and wineries nearby.

Location: Country, mountains. Vineyards.

Publicity: *Travel Holiday.*

Certificate may be used: November-April, anytime subject to availability, last minute subject to availability.

Lake Arrowhead

Romantique Lakeview Lodge

28051 Hwy 189
Lake Arrowhead, CA 92352
(909)337-6633 (800)358-5253 Fax:(909)337-5966
Internet: www.lakeviewlodge.com
E-mail: info@lakeviewlodge.com

Circa 1924. Privacy and quiet luxury are found at this elegant Victorian inn boasting fresh mountain air and unobstructed panoramic views of the lake amidst a pine forest. This year-round hideaway has retained an old-fashioned splendor with antique furnishings, lace, crystal, brass and oil paintings. Most of the romantic guest bedrooms and suites feature fireplaces and offer a variety of tasteful decor to choose from. Classic movies are available in the lobby for watching in-room videos. Indulge in Sinful Cinnamon Rolls, fresh fruit and cereal for breakfast.

Explore the scenic beauty, and visit the quaint shopping village.

Innkeeper(s): Megan McElrath, Chris Fischer, Shiela Hall. $79-199. 9 rooms with PB, 7 with FP, 3 suites. Breakfast and snacks/refreshments included in rates. Types of meals: Cont and early coffee/tea. Beds: KQD. Cable TV, VCR, reading lamp, telephone, hair dryer, bath amenities, wireless Internet access, iron/ironing board and fireplace in room. Fax, parlor games, fireplace and classic movies in lobby for VCRs in each guest room on premises. Handicap access. Antiquing, art galleries, bicycling, canoeing/kayaking, cross-country skiing, downhill skiing, fishing, golf, hiking, horseback riding, shopping and water sports nearby.

Location: Mountains.

Certificate may be used: January-June, valid Sunday-Friday. July-December, valid Sunday-Thursday. Holidays excluded.

Lakehead

O'Brien Mountain Inn

18026 O'Brien Inlet Road
Lakehead, CA 96051
(530)238-8026 (888)799-8026 Fax:(530)238-2027
Internet: www.obrienmountaininn.com
E-mail: info@obrienmountaininn.com

Circa 1957. Northern California mountain side retreat located at Shasta Lake. Located on 47 peaceful acres of lush forest, expect a perfect blend of casual comfort and elegant ambiance, with a large dose of style and romance. Careful attention is given to ironed sheets, soft robes, chocolates, candles and fresh flowers. The inn has a musical theme, blending traditional, contemporary and antique furnishings. The decor of the four guest bedrooms incorporate classical, jazz, world beat or folk. The unique Tree House Suite, offers 700 secluded square feet including a fireplace and Jacuzzi tub. CD players, writing paper, bottled water, and private entrances with patios are considered necessary provisions. More treats include refreshments upon arrival, as well as hot beverages and baked goods delivered to each room before a hearty breakfast is served. Activities like billiards, croquet or horseshoes round off a most delightful stay.

Innkeeper(s): Teresa & Greg Ramsey. $140-300. 8 rooms with PB, 4 with FP, 4 total suites, including 1 two-bedroom suite. Breakfast and snacks/refreshments included in rates. Types of meals: Full gourmet bkfst, veg bkfst and early coffee/tea. Beds: KQ. Modem hook-up, data port, VCR, DVD, reading lamp, stereo, refrigerator, ceiling fan, clock radio, telephone, coffeemaker, some with hot tub/spa, some with fireplace, hair dryer, bathrobes, bath amenities, iron/ironing board, fresh flowers, wine, homemade chocolates, private entrances, candles, flowers, bottled water, books, magazines, CD players with various music choices (or you may bring your own) and DVD/VHS players in the suites in room. Central air. Fax, library, parlor games and concierge services on premises. Limited handicap access. Antiquing, art galleries, bicycling, canoeing/kayaking, cross-country skiing, downhill skiing, fishing, golf, hiking, horseback riding, live theater, museums, parks, shopping, sporting events, tennis, water sports, wineries, Lake Shasta, Castle Crags, Mount Shasta, Lassen Peak, Whiskeytown Lake and Burney Falls nearby.

Location: Mountains.

Publicity: *Sunset Magazine, Los Angeles Times, Seattle Post, San Jose Mercury News, Wall Street Journal, California Getaways and Public Access.*

Certificate may be used: October-May.

Lemon Cove

Plantation B&B

33038 Sierra Hwy 198
Lemon Cove, CA 93244-1700
(559)597-2555 (800)240-1466 Fax:(559)597-2551
Internet: www.plantationbnb.com
E-mail: relax@plantationbnb.com

Circa 1908. The history of orange production is deeply
entwined in the roots of California, and this home is located on
what once was an orange plantation.
The original 1908 house burned in
the 1960s, but the current home
was built on its foundation. In keeping with the home's plantation past,
the innkeepers decorated the bed
and breakfast with a "Gone With
the Wind" theme. The comfortable,
country guest rooms sport names
such as the Scarlett O'Hara, the
Belle Watling, and of course, the
Rhett Butler. A hot tub is located in
the orchard, and there also is a heated swimming pool.

Innkeeper(s): Scott & Marie Munger. $139-229. 8 rooms with PB, 2 with FP,
1 with WP, 3 suites. Breakfast and snacks/refreshments included in rates.
Types of meals: Full gourmet bkfst and early coffee/tea. Beds: KQDT. Cable
TV, VCR, reading lamp, ceiling fan and hot tub/spa in room. Air conditioning.
Fax, spa, swimming, parlor games, telephone and fireplace on premises.
Antiquing, cross-country skiing, fishing, golf, parks, shopping, sporting events
and water sports nearby.

Location: Mountains.

Publicity: *Exeter Sun, Kaweah Commonwealth, Los Angeles Times, Fresno
Bee, Visalia Delta Times, Westways Magazine and Sunset Magazine.*

"Scarlett O'Hara would be proud to live on this lovely plantation."
Certificate may be used: Sept. 7-May 15.

Lockeford

Inn At Locke House

19960 N Elliott Rd
Lockeford, CA 95237
(209)727-5715 Fax:(209)727-0873
Internet: www.theinnatlockehouse.com
E-mail: lockehouse@jps.net

Circa 1862. Sitting on a bluff in a quaint landmark town, this
historic rural home is listed in the National Register. Built in
1862, the brick Neo-Georgian farmhouse boasts English country gardens and a wonderful view of the Sierra Foothills. Enjoy
welcome refreshments and beverages. Join the innkeepers for
dessert in one of the parlors by the fire. Listen to the pump
organ or piano, browse the artifacts, books and games. Sleep in
a cherry spool, wrought iron or four-poster pine bed in a guest
bedroom in the Main House; some feature clawfoot tubs and
fireplaces. Indulge in the fabulous three-room Water Tower
Suite with a separate entrance and deck, spiral staircase, clawfoot tub and wrought iron canopy bed. Linger over a gourmet
breakfast with a changing menu in the sunny carriageway.

Innkeeper(s): Richard and Lani Eklund. Call for rates. 5 rooms with PB, 5
with FP, 1 suite. Refreshments and Full Gourmet Breakfast included in rates.
Beds: KQT. Modem hook-up, data port, reading lamp, stereo, ceiling fan, clock
radio, telephone, turn-down service, desk, fireplace, hair dryer, bathrobes,

bath amenities, wireless Internet access and iron/ironing board in room. Air
conditioning. TV, VCR, fax, copier, library, parlor games, DSL & WI-FI, croquet,
badminton, lawn bowling, horseshoes, binoculars for birdwatching, business
services available, guests have access to refrigerator, beverages and snacks in
carriageway on premises. Antiquing, art galleries, bicycling, canoeing/kayaking,
fishing, golf, hiking, horseback riding, live theater, museums, parks, shopping,
sporting events, tennis, wineries, sky diving, farmer's market, craft fairs,
Clements Rodeo, concerts, movie theatre and fine dining nearby.

Location: Country.

Publicity: *Sacramento Magazine, Stockton Record, Lodi News Sentinel,
HGTV "Restore America" and HGTV "If Walls Could Talk"*

Certificate may be used: January-March, July-August, Sunday-Thursday, subject to availability, holidays and special events excluded. Main House only,
peak rates apply.

Mendocino

Brewery Gulch Inn

9401 Coast Hwy One N
Mendocino, CA 95460-9767
(707)937-4752 (800)578-4454 Fax:(707)937-1279
Internet: www.brewerygulchinn.com
E-mail: innkeeper@brewerygulchinn.com

Circa 2000. Ten acres of bliss are found at this distinctive
Craftsman-style inn, built with eco-salvaged, old virgin redwood timbers from Big River. Sitting next to the original historic farmhouse on a scenic hillside, Arts and Crafts furnishings
and ocean views create an eye-pleasing decor. The romantic
guest bedrooms boast fireplaces, private decks, and pampering
touches including terry robes and CD players. Mouth-watering
breakfast al fresco on the common deck or fireside is prepared
with organic ingredients. Relax in the fireplaced Great Room
with afternoon wine and hors d'oeuvres.

Innkeeper(s): Jo Ann Stickle, GM. $170-396. 10 rooms with PB, 10 with FP.
Breakfast, snacks/refreshments, hors d'oeuvres and wine included in rates.
Types of meals: Full gourmet bkfst, veg bkfst, early coffee/tea, gourmet lunch
and picnic lunch. Beds: KQT. Modem hook-up, data port, cable TV, VCR,
DVD, reading lamp, stereo, clock radio, telephone, turn-down service, desk,
hot tub/spa, voice mail, fireplace, hair dryer, bathrobes, bath amenities, wireless Internet access and iron/ironing board in room. Fax, copier, library, parlor
games and gift shop on premises. Handicap access. Antiquing, art galleries,
beach, bicycling, canoeing/kayaking, fishing, golf, hiking, horseback riding,
live theater, museums, parks, shopping, tennis, water sports, wineries, Skunk
steam engine train and historical village nearby.

Location: Ocean community.

Publicity: *Food & Wine, Sunset Magazine, San Francisco Chronicle,
Appellation, NY Times, Gourmet, Wine Enthusiast, Best of California, KGO,
Travel & Leisure, Diablo Magazine 12 Great Gateways and Food & Wine.*

Certificate may be used: November-April, Sunday-Thursday, subject to availability, except during holidays or local special events.

Headlands Inn

10453 Howard Street
Mendocino, CA 95460
(707)937-4431 (800)354-4431 Fax:(707)937-0421
Internet: www.headlandsinn.com
E-mail: innkeeper@headlandsinn.com

Circa 1868. A historic setting by the sea in the village of
Mendocino complements this New England Victorian Salt Box.
The quaintness of the past combines with amenities of the present. Meet new friends sharing afternoon tea and cookies in the
parlor. Almost all of the romantic guest bedrooms feature fireplaces, comfortable feather beds with down comforters, fresh
flowers and bedside chocolates. Some have white-water ocean
views. A cottage provides more spacious privacy. Indulge in a full
breakfast delivered to the room with homemade treats and cre-

ative entrees. The front porch is also an ideal spot for ocean views. Lawn seating gives ample opportunity to enjoy the year-round English garden. Many unique shops and fine restaurants are within walking distance.

Innkeeper(s): Denise & Mitch. $99-229. 7 rooms with PB, 6 with FP, 1 suite, 1 cottage. Breakfast, afternoon tea and snacks/refreshments included in rates. Types of meals: Full gourmet bkfst and veg bkfst. Beds: KQ. Reading lamp, clock radio, desk, fireplace, hair dryer, bathrobes, wireless Internet access, ocean views, feather beds, hair dryers, robes, cottage has cable TV/VCR, refrigerator & microwave and daily morning newspaper delivered in room. DVD, fax, copier, parlor games and telephone on premises. Limited handicap access. Antiquing, art galleries, beach, bicycling, canoeing/kayaking, fishing, golf, hiking, horseback riding, live theater, museums, parks, shopping, tennis and wineries nearby.

Location: Ocean community. Mendocino Village.

Publicity: *"Best Places to Kiss" Romantic Travel Guide and "Best Places to Stay" Travel Guide.*

"If a Nobel Prize were given for breakfasts, you would win hands down. A singularly joyous experience!!"

Certificate may be used: November-March, Sunday-Thursday, excluding holiday periods, subject to availability.

John Dougherty House

571 Ukiah St
Mendocino, CA 95460
(707)937-5266 (800)486-2104
Internet: www.jdhouse.com
E-mail: info@jdhouse.co

Circa 1867. Feel refreshed and rejuvenated by the seaside comfort offered at John Dougherty House in Mendocino, California. Enjoy the spectacular ocean views while relaxing at this delightful bed and breakfast just a short stroll to Mendocino Headlands State Park. Elegantly fresh and immaculate guest

bedrooms and suites welcome sweet dreams. Accommodations feature an assortment of pampering amenities and some boast fireplaces, jetted spa tubs and private decks. Stay in the more secluded Kit's Cabin or the historic Water Tower with an 18-foot ceiling. A bountiful buffet breakfast includes entrees accented with edible flowers from the English garden, homemade scones and locally grown fruit. Special packages are available.

Innkeeper(s): Damien Wood & Andrew Hindman. $140-275. 8 rooms with PB, 7 with FP, 2 two-bedroom suites, 2 cottages. Breakfast included in rates. Types of meals: Cont plus and early coffee/tea. Beds: KQ. Cable TV, DVD, reading lamp, stereo, refrigerator, clock radio, telephone, desk, most with hot tub/spa, most with fireplace, hair dryer, bath amenities and 4 rooms with jetted tubs in room. Copier and parlor games on premises. Limited handicap access. Antiquing, art galleries, beach, bicycling, canoeing/kayaking, fishing, golf, hiking, horseback riding, live theater, parks, shopping, tennis, water sports and wineries nearby.

Location: Country, ocean community. Pacific Coast.

Publicity: *Mendocino Beacon, Country Home, Los Angeles Times (Travel Section August 2001) and San Francisco Times/Tribune.*

"A treasure chest of charm, beauty and views."

Certificate may be used: Sunday-Thursday, January-February, subject to availability.

Packard House B&B

45170 Little Lake Street
Mendocino, CA 95460
(707)937-2677 (888)453-2677 Fax:(707)937-1440
Internet: www.packardhouse.com
E-mail: info@packardhouse.com

Circa 1878. Relax in the casually tranquil setting of modern elegance and style at the Packard House, built in 1878 with Victorian architecture in the heart of the village of Mendocino, California. Each luxurious guest bedroom features a fireplace, jetted spa tub, soft robes and other upscale amenities. After a sweet sleep, select from two breakfast options. Savor a homemade two-course meal in the dining room or indulge in a gourmet breakfast basket in bed. Stroll the local shops and take time to explore the nearby wineries of Anderson Valley. Enjoy the incredible views of the rugged coast.

Innkeeper(s): Damien Wood & Andrew Hindman. $225. 4 rooms with PB, 4 with FP. Breakfast and wine included in rates. Types of meals: Full gourmet bkfst and veg bkfst. Beds: KQ. Cable TV, DVD, reading lamp, CD player, refrigerator, clock radio, telephone, hot tub/spa, fireplace, hair dryer, bathrobes, wireless Internet access and iron/ironing board in room. Central air. Fax, gift shop, gardens and DVD library on premises. Art galleries, beach, bicycling, canoeing/kayaking, fishing, golf, hiking, horseback riding, live theater, parks, shopping, tennis, water sports, wineries, diving, whale watching and bird watching nearby.

Location: Ocean community. Village.

Publicity: *San Francisco Magazine, Via, Sunset Magazine, Marin IS and Pontiac Moon.*

Certificate may be used: Sunday-Thursday: January, subject to availability.

Sea Rock Inn

11101 Lansing St
Mendocino, CA 95460
(707)937-0926 (800)906-0926
Internet: www.searock.com
E-mail: innkeeper@searockinn.com

Circa 1930. Enjoy sea breezes and ocean vistas at this inn, which rests on a bluff looking out to the Pacific. Most of the accommodations include a wood-burning fireplace and feather bed. Four junior suites are available in the Stratton House, and each affords a spectacular ocean view. There are six cottages on the grounds, most offering a sea view. The innkeepers also offer deluxe accommodations in four special suites. Each has an ocean view, wood-burning fireplace, private entrance and a deck, whirlpool or ocean view tub. The grounds, which now feature gardens, were the site of an 1870s brewery. The inn is less than half a mile from Mendocino.

Innkeeper(s): Susie & Andy Plocher. $179-395. 14 rooms with PB, 14 with FP, 8 suites, 6 cottages. Breakfast included in rates. Types of meals: Full bkfst and early coffee/tea. Beds: KQ. Modem hook-up, data port, cable TV, VCR, DVD, reading lamp, clock radio, telephone, coffeemaker, desk, fireplace, hair dryer, bathrobes, bath amenities, wireless Internet access and iron/ironing board in room. Massage facility with infra-red sauna on premises. Antiquing, art galleries, beach, bicycling, canoeing/kayaking, fishing, golf, hiking, horseback riding, live theater, parks, shopping, tennis, water sports and wineries nearby.

Location: Ocean community. Waterfront.

Publicity: *California Visitors Review and Sunset Magazine.*

Certificate may be used: Jan. 3-March 1, Monday-Thursday, excluding holiday periods.

The Inn at Schoolhouse Creek

7051 N Hwy 1
Mendocino, CA 95460
(707)937-5525 (800)731-5525 Fax:(707)937-2012
Internet: www.schoolhousecreek.com
E-mail: innkeeper@schoolhousecreek.com

Circa 1860. The Inn at School House Creek offers private cottages and rooms on its eight acres of rose gardens, forests and meadows. (The inn's gardens have been featured in several magazines.) Many cottages include views of the ocean and all have a fireplace. The inn offers a quiet getaway, while still being close to all of the fun in Mendocino just two miles away. Private beach access to Buckhorn Cove allows guests to enjoy whale watching, sea lions and the crashing waves of the Pacific. Organize your day to include a picnic lunch (available by advance notice) to enjoy at a secluded waterfall in the redwoods. Then take a sunset soak in the inn's ocean view hot tub. The next morning's breakfast may include a hot apple crisp with whipped cream, eggs, fruit and a variety of freshly baked muffins and breads, jams and juices.

Innkeeper(s): Steven Musser & Maureen Gilbert. $149-425. 18 rooms, 19 with PB, 19 with FP, 4 with HT, 6 with WP, 2 two-bedroom suites, 12 cottages, 2 conference rooms. Breakfast, hors d'oeuvres and wine included in rates. Types of meals: Full bkfst, early coffee/tea, picnic lunch and afternoon tea. Beds: KQD. Modem hook-up, cable TV, VCR, DVD, reading lamp, CD player, refrigerator, clock radio, telephone, coffeemaker, desk, hot tub/spa, voice mail and fireplace in room. Fax, spa, sauna, library, pet boarding, child care, parlor games, gift shop, Evening wine and hors d'oeuvres, Ocean view, Hot tub and Sauna on premises. Handicap access. Antiquing, art galleries, beach, bicycling, canoeing/kayaking, fishing, golf, hiking, horseback riding, live theater, parks, shopping, tennis, water sports and wineries nearby.

Location: Ocean community, waterfront.

Certificate may be used: Nov. 1-Feb. 28, Sunday-Thursday, holidays and local festivals excluded.

Whitegate Inn Bed and Breakfast

499 Howard Street
Mendocino, CA 95460
(707)937-4892 (800)531-7282 Fax:(707)937-1131
Internet: www.whitegateinn.com
E-mail: staff@whitegateinn.com

Circa 1883. When it was first built, the local newspaper called Whitegate Inn "one of the most elegant and best appointed residences in town." Its bay windows, steep gabled roof, redwood siding and fish-scale shingles are stunning

examples of Victorian architecture. The house's original wallpaper and candelabras adorn the double parlors. There, an antique 1827 piano, at one time part of Alexander Graham Bell's collection, and inlaid pocket doors take you back to a more gracious time. French and Victorian antique furnishings and fresh flowers add to the inn's elegant hospitality and old world charm. The gourmet breakfasts are artfully presented in the inn's sunlit dining room. The inn is just a block from the ocean, galleries, restaurants and the center of town.

Innkeeper(s): Richard & Susan Strom. $159-319. 6 rooms with PB, 6 with FP, 2 with HT, 2 with WP. Breakfast included in rates. Types of meals: Full gourmet bkfst and snacks/refreshments. Beds: KQ. Cable TV, VCR, DVD, reading lamp, refrigerator, clock radio, telephone, desk and 2 with jet tubs in room. Fax, copier, fireplace, welcome basket, evening sherry, wine,

cheese and wireless Internet on premises. Antiquing, art galleries, beach, bicycling, fishing, golf, wineries and whale watching nearby.

Location: Ocean community.

Publicity: *Insider, Country Inns, Country Home, Glamour, Santa Rosa Press Democrat, San Francisco Chronicle, Bon Appetit, Victoria Magazine, Sunset, San Francisco Examiner, Victorian Decorating, Country Gardener, Cover of Karen Brown's CA Guide and NY Times.*

"We have stayed at over 60 Inns and Whitegate is the best inn we have ever had the pleasure to be a guest at, the service and hospitality are the best."

Certificate may be used: Nov. 1 - May 20, Sunday-Thursday, no holiday periods, selected rooms.

Middletown

Backyard Garden Oasis a B&B

PO Box 1760
Middletown, CA 95461-1760
(707)987-0505
Internet: www.backyardgardenoasis.com
E-mail: greta@backyardgardenoasis.com

Circa 1997. Be renewed by the blend of simple elegance and rustic ambiance in the Collayomi Valley of North Calistoga over Mt. St. Helens. Stay in one of the individual cottages that feature air conditioning, skylight, gas fireplaces, a refrigerator and coffeemaker and access to the video collection. The private redwood decks overlook the Manzanita grove, pond and waterfall. One cottage is wheelchair accessible. Gather in the dining room of the main house for a hearty country breakfast that begins with fresh-squeezed orange juice. Schedule a massage with a certified therapist then soak under the stars in the hot tub. Harbin Hot Springs is ten minutes away and it is a two-hour drive to San Francisco or Sacramento. Take a wine tasting tour of nearby Lake County wineries.

Innkeeper(s): Greta Zeit. $129-149. 4 rooms with PB, 3 with FP, 1 suite, 3 cottages. Breakfast included in rates. Types of meals: Country bkfst, veg bkfst and early coffee/tea. Beds: K. Modem hook-up, data port, cable TV, VCR, reading lamp, stereo, refrigerator, ceiling fan, telephone, coffeemaker, turn-down service, desk, some with hot tub/spa, fireplace, hair dryer, bathrobes, bath amenities, wireless Internet access and iron/ironing board in room. Air conditioning. Fax, spa, creek and pond on property on premises. Limited handicap access. Antiquing, bicycling, canoeing/kayaking, fishing, golf, hiking, horseback riding, museums, parks, tennis, water sports and wineries nearby.

Location: Country, mountains.

Certificate may be used: Available Monday-Thursday, excluding Holidays.

Mokelumne Hill

The Lêger Historic Inn and Restaurant

8304 Main St
Mokelumne Hill, CA 95245
(209)286-1401 Fax:(209)286-2105
Internet: www.hotelleger.com
E-mail: hotelleger@aol.com

Step back in time and experience the nostalgia of the Mother Lode era while still having easy access to modern city life. Guest bedrooms and a suite feature antique furnishings and Victorian beds covered with down-filled duvets. Three rooms boast fireplaces. A restaurant and saloon offer menus for lunch and dinner. Relax in the courtyard after visiting nearby historical sites. The landscaped quarter-acre is a popular wedding spot complete with available horse-drawn carriage.

Innkeeper(s): The Lêger Family. Call for rates. 13 rooms. Types of meals:

Early coffee/tea, lunch and gourmet dinner. Restaurant on premises. Beds: D. Reading lamp, turn-down service, some with fireplace, hair dryer, bath amenities, wireless Internet and iron/ironing board in room. Central air. Fax, copier, swimming, telephone, laundry facility and gift shop on premises. Antiquing, art galleries, bicycling, canoeing/kayaking, cross-country skiing, downhill skiing, fishing, hiking, horseback riding, live theater, museums, parks, shopping, tennis, water sports, wineries and Jackson Rancheria-Casino (7 miles) nearby.

Location: Country, mountains.

Publicity: *Stockton Record, San Jose Sentinel, Newsweek Magazine, Here Comes the Guide Wedding Book, Sunset Magazine, Calaveras Enterprise, Amador Dispatch, Sonora Dispatch, Haunted Hotels and Historical Hotels and Inns.*

Certificate may be used: Sunday-Friday.

Montara

The Goose & Turrets B&B

835 George St.
Montara, CA 94037-0937
(650)728-5451 Fax:(650)728-0141
Internet: goose.montara.com
E-mail: rhmgt@montara.com

Circa 1908. Now a haven focusing on comfort and hospitality, this classic bed & breakfast once served as Montara's first post office, the town hall, and a country club for Spanish-American War veterans. Large living and dining room areas are filled with art and collectibles. Sleep soundly in one of the tranquil guest bedrooms then linger over a leisurely four-course breakfast. Stimulating conversation comes easily during afternoon tea. There are plenty of quiet spots including a swing and a hammock, to enjoy the fountains, orchard, rose, herb and vegetable gardens.

Innkeeper(s): Raymond & Emily Hoche-Mong. $145-190. 5 rooms with PB, 3 with FP. Breakfast and afternoon tea included in rates. Types of meals: Full gourmet bkfst and veg bkfst. Beds: KQDT. Reading lamp, clock radio, desk, some with fireplace, hair dryer, bath amenities, wireless Internet access and iron/ironing board in room. Fax, library, parlor games, telephone, bocce ball court and piano on premises. Antiquing, art galleries, beach, bicycling, canoeing/kayaking, fishing, golf, hiking, horseback riding, live theater, parks, shopping, water sports, wineries, nature reserves, whale watching, aero sightseeing and birding nearby.

Location: Seaside village.

Publicity: *San Diego Union, Tri-Valley, Los Angeles Times, Pilot Getaways, AOPA Magazine, San Jose Mercury News, Half Moon Bay Review, Peninsula Times Tribune, San Mateo Times, Contra Costa Times, The Wall Street Journal, Home & Garden Channel "If Walls Could Talk", Ramblin' with Ramsey and LA Times Travel.*

"You have truly made an art of breakfast and tea-time conversation. We will be back."

Certificate may be used: Anytime, November-March, subject to availability, Christmas and New Years excluded.

Monte Rio

Village Inn & Restaurant

20822 River Blvd
Monte Rio, CA 95462-9758
(707)865-2304 (800)303-2303 Fax:(707)865-2332
Internet: www.villageinn-ca.com
E-mail: village@sonic.net

Circa 1906. A serene setting, year-round attractions, legendary

food and unsurpassed views are easy to appreciate at this all-season resort with handicap access that features an eclectic blend of antiques and contemporary comforts. Soak up the sun on the lawn or on a private balcony. Stylish guest bedrooms are in two buildings and those in the lodge boast separate entrances. All feature upscale amenities, VCRs and a video library, mini refrigerators and microwave ovens. Dine on "Sonoma Fresh" cuisine in the full-service restaurant and bar overlooking the Russian River.

Innkeeper(s): Mark Belhumeur & Philip Hampton. $92-215. 11 rooms with PB, 1 conference room. Breakfast and Basket of apples always available included in rates. Types of meals: Cont plus, picnic lunch, snacks/refreshments, hors d'oeuvres, wine, gourmet dinner and room service. Restaurant on premises. Beds: KQD. Cable TV, VCR, DVD, reading lamp, CD player, refrigerator, ceiling fan, clock radio, coffeemaker, desk, some with fireplace, hair dryer, bathrobes, bath amenities, wireless Internet access, iron/ironing board, microwave, iron, ironing board, Judith Jackson amenities, bathrobes and complimentary videos and popcorn in room. Fax, copier, library, parlor games, telephone, gift shop, full-service restaurant and bar, meeting room and lawn for sunning on premises. Handicap access. Amusement parks, antiquing, art galleries, beach, bicycling, canoeing/kayaking, fishing, golf, hiking, horseback riding, live theater, museums, parks, shopping, tennis, water sports, wineries and Indian casino nearby.

Location: Country, mountains, waterfront.

Publicity: *San Francisco Chronicle (2001), Mobility (2002), AAA/CSAA VIA (2002), Silver Medal Award in Sonoma County Harvest Fair Wine List Competition, Arringtons Bed and Breakfast Journal (Top 15 USA Meeting Facilities), Spirit of Sonoma Award (2003), KRCB San Francisco, Lore says and "Site of 1942 Bing Crosby/Fred Astair movie Holiday Inn best known for introducing the immortalized Irving Berlin song White Christmas." Spectacular views of Russian River & California Redwoods. .*

Certificate may be used: For Sunday-Wednesday arrivals and last minute subject to availability.

Monterey

The Jabberwock

598 Laine St
Monterey, CA 93940-1312
(831)372-4777 (888)428-7253 Fax:(831)655-2946
Internet: www.jabberwockinn.com
E-mail: innkeeper@jabberwockinn.com

Circa 1911. Set in a half-acre of gardens, this Craftsman-style inn provides a fabulous view of Monterey Bay with its famous barking seals. When you're ready to settle in for the evening, you'll find huge Victorian beds complete with lace-edged sheets and goose-down comforters. Three rooms include Jacuzzi tubs. In the late afternoon, hors d'oeuvres and aperitifs are served on an enclosed sun porch. After dinner, guests are tucked into bed with home-

made chocolate chip cookies and milk. To help guests avoid long lines, the innkeepers have tickets available for the popular and nearby Monterey Bay Aquarium.

Innkeeper(s): Dawn Perez & John Hickey. $165-295. 7 rooms with PB, 4 with FP, 3 with HT. Breakfast, afternoon tea, snacks/refreshments, hors d'oeuvres and wine included in rates. Types of meals: Full gourmet bkfst, veg bkfst, early coffee/tea, picnic lunch and Evening Wine. Beds: KQ. Reading lamp, clock radio, some with hot tub/spa, hair dryer, bathrobes, wireless Internet access and three with Jacuzzi for two in room. Fax, copier, spa, library, parlor games, telephone, fireplace and Piano on premises. Antiquing, art galleries, beach, bicycling, canoeing/kayaking, fishing, golf, hiking, horseback riding, live theater, museums, parks, shopping, tennis, water sports, wineries, restaurants, Cannery Row, Carmel shopping and Monterey Bay Aquarium nearby.

Location: City, ocean community, waterfront. 8 blocks to Monterey Bay Aquarium.

Publicity: *Sunset, Travel & Leisure, Sacramento Bee, San Francisco Examiner, Los Angeles Times, Country Inns, San Francisco Chronicle, Diablo* and Elmer Dill's *KABC-Los Angeles TV.*

"Words are not enough to describe the ease and tranquility of the atmosphere of the home, rooms, owners and staff at the Jabberwock."

Certificate may be used: Sunday through Thursday, November through April, excluding holidays.

Napa

Arbor Guest House

1436 G St
Napa, CA 94559-1145
(707)252-8144 (866)627-2262 Fax:(707)252-7385
Internet: www.arborguesthouse.com
E-mail: Susan@arborguesthouse.com

Circa 1906. Innkeepers Jack and Susan Clare have decorated the exterior of their gracious bed & breakfast, which is surrounded by old trees, with lush gardens and three patios. Romantic guest quarters boast beautiful period furnishings. Two of the rooms include spa tubs and three offer fireplaces. Freshly made breakfasts feature homemade breads, scones, fruits and egg dishes and are served in the dining room or at a table in the sunny garden. The many wineries and shops of Napa Valley are nearby.

Innkeeper(s): Beverly and Susan Clare. $119-239. 5 rooms with PB, 3 with FP, 2 with WP. Breakfast and snacks/refreshments included in rates. Types of meals: Full gourmet bkfst, veg bkfst and early coffee/tea. Beds: QD. Reading lamp, ceiling fan, clock radio, coffeemaker, desk, hot tub/spa, fireplace, iron and ironing board in room. Central air. Telephone and high-speed wireless access on premises. Limited handicap access. Amusement parks, antiquing, art galleries, bicycling, canoeing/kayaking, fishing, golf, hiking, horseback riding, live theater, museums, parks, shopping and wineries nearby.

Location: Wine country.

Certificate may be used: January-July, Monday-Thursday, excluding holidays, Anytime, subject to availability.

Blackbird Inn

1755 First St
Napa, CA 94559
(707)226-2450 (888)567-9811
Internet: www.blackbirdinnnapa.com
E-mail: blackbirdinn@foursisters.com

Circa 2001. This meticulously restored hideaway, built with Greene and Greene-type architecture, is within an easy walk to town. The stone pillared porch, leaded glass and blackbird vines are a welcome setting for the wonderful atmosphere found inside. True to the Craftsman-style furnishings and decor, the period lighting accents the subdued colors and warm ambiance. Double-paned windows offer quiet views of the garden fountain. Many of the guest bedrooms feature private decks, spa tubs and fireplaces. Wine and hors d'oeuvres are served in the afternoon. There is a $20 fee for an additional guest in room, except for children less than 5 years old.

Innkeeper(s): Michael Harris. $145-285. 8 rooms with PB, 6 with FP. Breakfast, afternoon tea, snacks/refreshments, hors d'oeuvres and wine included in rates. Types of meals: Full bkfst and early coffee/tea. Beds: KQ. Data port, cable TV, VCR, reading lamp, stereo, clock radio, telephone, turn-down service, hot tub/spa, jetted spa tub and/or private deck and some with fireplace in room. Air conditioning. DVD, fax, parlor games, fireplace, full signature breakfast, afternoon wine and hors d'oeuvres, morning newspaper delivery, evening turndown service, complimentary sodas and home-baked cookies on premises. Handicap access. Antiquing, art galleries, bicycling, golf, hiking,

live theater, museums, parks, shopping, wineries and wine tasting nearby.

Location: City. Downtown Historic Napa.

Certificate may be used: Sunday – Thursday, December through February, based on promotional discount availability and excludes special event periods, holidays and certain room types. First night must be at full rack rate to receive second night free.

Candlelight Inn

1045 Easum Drive
Napa, CA 94558-5524
(707)257-3717 (800)624-0395 Fax:(707)257-3762
Internet: www.candlelightinn.com
E-mail: mail@candlelightinn.com

Circa 1929. Located on a park-like acre with gardens, this elegant English Tudor-style house is situated beneath redwood groves and towering trees that shade the banks of Napa Creek. Six rooms feature a marble fireplace and two-person marble Jacuzzi inside the room. The Candlelight Suite offers cathedral ceilings, stained-glass windows and a private sauna. The inn's breakfast room has French doors and windows overlooking the garden. Breakfast is served by candlelight.

Innkeeper(s): Wendy Tamiso. $209-359. 10 rooms with PB, 6 with FP. Breakfast and snacks/refreshments included in rates. Types of meals: Full gourmet bkfst, early coffee/tea and wine. Beds: KQ. Modem hook-up, cable TV, reading lamp, clock radio, telephone, most with hot tub/spa, voice mail, most with fireplace, hair dryer, bathrobes, bath amenities, wireless Internet access and iron/ironing board in room. Air conditioning. Fax, parlor games, gift shop and Swimming pool on premises. Limited handicap access. Amusement parks, antiquing, art galleries, bicycling, canoeing/kayaking, golf, hiking, horseback riding, live theater, museums, parks, shopping, wineries, hot air ballooning and spas nearby.

Location: Wine country.

Publicity: *Wine Country This Week and CNN.com.*

"We still haven't stopped talking about the great food, wonderful accommodations and gracious hospitality."

Certificate may be used: December-February, Sunday-Thursday, holiday periods excluded, subject to availability.

Hennessey House-Napa's 1889 Queen Anne Victorian B&B

1727 Main St
Napa, CA 94559-1844
(707)226-3774 Fax:(707)226-2975
Internet: www.hennesseyhouse.com
E-mail: inn@hennesseyhouse.com

Circa 1889. Colorful gardens greet you at this gracious Victorian. It was once home to Dr. Edwin Hennessey, a Napa County physician and former mayor. Pristinely renovated, the inn features stained-glass windows and a curving wraparound  porch. A handsome hand-painted, stamped-tin ceiling graces the dining room. The inn's romantic rooms are furnished in antiques. Some offer fireplaces, feather beds and spa tubs. The bathrooms all feature marble floors and antique brass fixtures. There is a sauna and a garden fountain. The innkeepers serve gourmet breakfasts with specialties such as blueberry-stuffed French toast and Eggs Florentine. Tea and cookies are offered at 3 p.m. Later in the evening, wine and cheese is served. Walk to inviting restaurants, shops and theaters. Nearby are the world-famous Napa Valley wineries. The innkeepers will be happy to make recommendations or reservations for wineries, the area's spas and mud baths, hot air balloons, the Wine Train, horseback riding, cycling and hiking.

Innkeeper(s): Kevin Walsh & Lorri Walsh. $135-319. 10 rooms with PB, 6 with FP, 4 with WP. Breakfast included in rates. Types of meals: Full bkfst. Beds: KQT. Modem hook-up, data port, reading lamp, ceiling fan, clock radio, telephone, voice mail, hair dryer, bath amenities, wireless Internet access, iron/ironing board and Some with CD players in room. Air conditioning. TV, fax, sauna, parlor games, fireplace, High Speed Wireless Internet Access and Sauna on premises. Antiquing, shopping, restaurants, shops, Napa Opera House, COPIA-The American Center for Wine, Food and the Arts and Wine Train nearby.

Location: Napa Valley Wine Country.

Publicity: *New York Times, "Journeys – 36 Hours in Napa," (September 2004), "Beautiful Bedrooms – Design Inspirations from the Worlds Leading Inns and Hotels," a book by Tina Skinner, Arrington's Inn "2004 Book of Lists" (Voted one of the 10 best in a wine region nationwide) and NBC11 News.*

"A great place to relax in Napa!"

Certificate may be used: November 25-February 28, Sunday-Thursday, 12/23-12/31 excluded; holidays and weekends excluded.

La Belle Époque

1386 Calistoga Ave
Napa, CA 94559-2552
(707)257-2161 (800)238-8070
Internet: www.napabelle.com
E-mail: roxann@napabelle.com

Circa 1893. This luxurious Victorian inn has won awards for "best in the wine country" and "best breakfast in the nation." Enjoy the experience in the wine cellar and tasting room where guests can casually sip Napa Valley wines. The inn, which is

one of the most unique architectural structures found in the wine country, is located in the heart of Napa's Calistoga Historic District. Beautiful original stained-glass windows include a window from an old church. Six guest rooms offer a whirlpool tub. A selection of fine restaurants and shops are within easy walking distance, as well as the riverfront, art museums and the Wine Train Depot.

Innkeeper(s): Roxann & Derek Archer. $199-419. 9 rooms with PB, 6 with FP, 3 suites, 1 conference room. Breakfast, snacks/refreshments, hors d'oeuvres and wine included in rates. Types of meals: Full gourmet bkfst and early coffee/tea. Beds: KQ. Data port, cable TV, VCR, reading lamp, CD player, ceiling fan, snack bar, clock radio, telephone, desk, hair dryer, bathrobes, bath amenities, wireless Internet access and iron/ironing board in room. Central air. Fireplace and gift shop on premises. Amusement parks, antiquing, art galleries, bicycling, canoeing/kayaking, golf, hiking, horseback riding, live theater, museums, parks, shopping, sporting events, tennis and wineries nearby.

Location: City. Wine country.

"At first I was a bit leery, how can a B&B get consistent rave reviews? After staying here two nights, I am now a believer!"

Certificate may be used: Dec. 3-21, Jan. 2-March 15, Monday-Thursday, holidays excluded and weekends excluded. Cannot be combined with any other promotion.

Stahlecker House B&B Country Inn & Garden

1042 Easum Dr
Napa, CA 94558-5525
(707)257-1588 (800)799-1588 Fax:(707)224-7429
Internet: www.stahleckerhouse.com
E-mail: stahlbnb@aol.com

Circa 1949. This country inn is situated on the banks of tree-lined Napa Creek. The acre and a half of grounds feature rose

and orchard gardens, fountains and manicured lawns. Guests often relax on the sun deck. There is an antique refrigerator stocked with soft drinks and lemonade. Full, gourmet breakfasts are served by candlelight in the glass-wrapped dining room that overlooks the gardens. In the evenings, coffee, tea and freshly made chocolate chip cookies are served. The Napa Wine Train station is five minutes away. Wineries, restaurants, antique shops, bike paths and hiking all are nearby.

Innkeeper(s): Ron & Ethel Stahlecker. $169-299. 4 rooms with PB, 4 with FP, 1 suite. Breakfast and snacks/refreshments included in rates. Types of meals: Full gourmet bkfst and afternoon tea. Beds: QT. TV, reading lamp, clock radio, telephone, turn-down service, desk, hot tub/spa and couple spa/couple shower in room. Air conditioning. Library, parlor games, fireplace and croquet on premises. Antiquing, fishing, golf, hiking, live theater, parks, shopping, tennis, wineries and hot air balloons nearby.

Location: City. Wine country.

Publicity: *Brides Magazine and Napa Valley Traveler.*

"Friendly hosts and beautiful gardens."

Certificate may be used: Monday-Thursday only, Nov. 1 to April 30 (not valid in summer, no holidays).

The McClelland-Priest Bed & Breakfast Inn

569 Randolph Street
Napa, CA 94559
(707)224-6875 (800)290-6881 Fax:(707)224-6782
Internet: www.mcclellandpriest.com

Experience the stately elegance and Victorian splendor of this 1879 historic landmark. Pass through the grand foyer to the formal parlor for an early evening reception with hors d'oeuvres and Napa Valley wines amid European antiques, handcrafted plaster ceilings and authentically ornate chandeliers. Innkeeper/owner Celeste offers concierge services that will assist with local attractions, reservations and travel planning. Take a self-guided, complimentary wine-tasting tour. The onsite Sole Spa and Fitness Center features a variety of treatments and exercise options. Guest suites reflect the luxurious ambiance of a famed writer, composer or artist and boast fireplaces, large soaking tubs or Jacuzzis. The Firenze Suite also includes an outdoor garden terrace. Special packages are available.

Innkeeper(s): Celeste. $189-289. 5 rooms with PB.

Certificate may be used: November 24-February. Block out dates December 24-27, December 29-January 2 and January 7-16.

Nevada City

Emma Nevada House

528 E Broad St
Nevada City, CA 95959-2213
(530)265-4415 (800)916-3662 Fax:(530)265-4416
Internet: www.emmanevadahouse.com
E-mail: mail@emmanevadahouse.com

Circa 1856. The childhood home of 19th-century opera star Emma Nevada now serves as an attractive Queen Anne Victorian inn. English roses line the white picket fence in front, and the

forest-like back garden has a small stream with benches. The Empress' Chamber is the most romantic room with ivory linens atop a French antique bed, a bay window and a massive French armoire. Some rooms have whirlpool baths and TV. Guests

enjoy relaxing in the hexagonal sunroom and on the inn's wrap-around porches. Empire Mine State Historic Park is nearby.

Innkeeper(s): Susan & Andrew Howard. $149-249. 6 rooms with PB, 2 with FP, 2 with WP, 1 two-bedroom suite. Breakfast and afternoon tea included in rates. Types of meals: Full gourmet bkfst, early coffee/tea and snacks/refreshments. Beds: KQ. Modem hook-up, cable TV, VCR, DVD, reading lamp, CD player, ceiling fan, clock radio, desk, some with fireplace, hair dryer, bathrobes, bath amenities, wireless Internet access, iron/ironing board, claw-foot bathtubs and Jacuzzi tubs in room. Central air. Fax, parlor games, telephone and gift shop on premises. Antiquing, art galleries, bicycling, canoeing/kayaking, cross-country skiing, downhill skiing, fishing, golf, hiking, horseback riding, live theater, museums, parks, shopping, tennis, water sports and wineries nearby.

Location: City, country, mountains. Town in foothills.

Publicity: *Country Inns, Gold Rush Scene, Sacramento Focus, The Union, Los Angeles Times, San Jose Mercury News, Sacramento Bee and Karen Browns.*

"A delightful experience: such airiness and hospitality in the midst of so much history. We were fascinated by the detail and the faithfulness of the restoration. This house is a quiet solace for city-weary travelers. There's a grace here."

Certificate may be used: Jan. 2 to April 30, Monday-Thursday, no holidays.

Nice

Featherbed Railroad Company B&B

2870 Lakeshore Blvd, PO Box 4016
Nice, CA 95464
(707)274-4434 (800)966-6322
Internet: featherbedrailroad.com
E-mail: rooms@featherbedrailroad.com

Circa 1940. Located on five acres on Clear Lake, this unusual inn features guest rooms in nine luxuriously renovated, painted and papered cabooses. Each has its own feather bed and private bath, most have Jacuzzi tubs for two. The Southern Pacific cabooses have a bay window alcove, while those from the Santa Fe feature small cupolas.

Innkeeper(s): Lorraine Bassignani. $102-180. 9 rooms with PB. Breakfast included in rates. Types of meals: Full bkfst. Beds: QDT. Cable TV and VCR in room. TV and spa on premises.

Publicity: *Santa Rosa Press Democrat, Fairfield Daily Republic, London Times, Travel & Leisure and Bay Area Back Roads.*

Certificate may be used: Sunday-Thursday, Oct. 15-April 15.

Pacific Grove

Centrella B&B Inn

612 Central Ave
Pacific Grove, CA 93950-2611
(831)372-3372 (800)233-3372 Fax:(831)372-2036
Internet: www.centrellainn.com
E-mail: reserve@centrellainn.com

Circa 1889. Pacific Grove was founded as a Methodist resort in 1875, and this home, built just after the town's incorporation, was billed by a local newspaper as, "the largest, most commodious and pleasantly located boarding house in the Grove." Many a guest is still sure to agree. The rooms are well-appointed in a comfortable, Victorian style. Six guest rooms include fireplaces. The Garden Room has a private entrance, fireplace, wet bar, Jacuzzi tub and a canopy bed topped with designer linens. Freshly baked croissants or pastries and made-to-order waffles are common fare at the inn's continental buffet breakfast. The inn is within walking distance of the Monterey Bay Aquarium, the beach and many Pacific Grove shops.

Innkeeper(s): Marion Taylor. $119-279. 26 rooms with PB, 6 with FP, 2 suites, 5 cottages. Breakfast and snacks/refreshments included in rates. Types of meals: Cont plus. Beds: KQT. Reading lamp and telephone in room. VCR, fax, copier, fireplace and TVs upon request on premises. Antiquing, golf, parks and water sports nearby.

Location: City.

Publicity: *Country Inns, New York Times and San Francisco Examiner.*

"I was ecstatic at the charm that the Centrella has been offering travelers for years and hopefully hundreds of years to come. The bed—perfect! I am forever enthralled by the old beauty and will remember this forever!"

Certificate may be used: Sunday-Thursday, November-February, excluding holidays and special events, subject to availability.

Gosby House Inn

643 Lighthouse Ave
Pacific Grove, CA 93950-2643
(831)375-1287 (800)527-8828 Fax:(831)655-9621
Internet: www.gosbyhouseinn.com
E-mail: gosbyhouseinn@foursisters.com

Circa 1887. Built as an upscale Victorian inn for those visiting the old Methodist retreat, this sunny yellow mansion features an abundance of gables, turrets and bays. During renovation the innkeeper slept in all the rooms to determine just what antiques were needed and how the beds should be situated. Eleven of the romantic rooms include fireplaces and many offer canopy beds. The Carriage House rooms include fireplaces, decks and spa tubs. Gosby House, which has been open to guests for more than a century, is in the National Register. There is a $20 fee for an additional guest in room, except for children less than 5 years old. Gosby House is one of the Four Sisters Inns. The Monterey Bay Aquarium is nearby.

$155-195. 22 rooms with PB, 11 with FP. Breakfast, afternoon tea, snacks/refreshments, hors d'oeuvres and wine included in rates. Types of meals: Full gourmet bkfst and early coffee/tea. Beds: KQD. Stereo, clock radio, telephone, turn-down service, some with hot tub/spa, hair dryer, bath amenities, iron/ironing board, signature breakfast and afternoon wine and hors d'oeuvres, evening turndown service, morning newspaper delivery, bicycles to borrow and home-baked cookies in room. TV, fax, copier, bicycles, parlor games and fireplace on premises. Handicap access. Antiquing, art galleries, beach, bicycling, canoeing/kayaking, golf, hiking, live theater, museums, parks, shopping, tennis, wineries and Monterey Bay Aquarium nearby.

Location: Ocean community.

Publicity: *San Francisco Chronicle, Oregonian, Los Angeles Times and Travel & Leisure.*

Certificate may be used: Sunday – Thursday, December through February, based on promotional discount availability and excludes special event periods, holidays and certain room types. First night must be at full rack rate to receive second night free.

Green Gables Inn

301 Ocean Avenue
Pacific Grove, CA 93950-2903
(831)375-2095 (800)722-1774 Fax:(831)375-5437
Internet: www.greengablesinnpg.com
E-mail: greengablesinn@foursisters.com

Circa 1888. This half-timbered Queen Anne Victorian appears as a fantasy of gables overlooking spectacular Monterey Bay. The parlor has stained-glass panels framing the fireplace and bay windows looking out to the sea. A favorite focal point is an antique carousel horse. Most of the guest rooms have panoramic views of the ocean, fireplaces, gleaming woodwork, soft quilts and teddy bears, and four rooms have spa tubs. Across the street is the Monterey Bay paved oceanfront cycling path. (Mountain bikes may be borrowed from the inn.) There is a $20 fee for an additional guest in room, except for children less than 5 years old. Green Gables is one of the Four Sisters Inns.
Innkeeper(s): Lois DeFord. $120-260. 11 rooms, 7 with PB, 6 with FP, 5 suites. Breakfast, afternoon tea, snacks/refreshments, hors d'oeuvres and wine included in rates. Types of meals: Full gourmet bkfst and early coffee/tea. Beds: KQD. Cable TV, VCR, reading lamp, stereo, ceiling fan, snack bar, clock radio, telephone, turn-down service, desk, some with hot tub/spa, voice mail, hair dryer, bathrobes, bath amenities and iron/ironing board in room. Fax, copier, bicycles, library, parlor games, fireplace, signature breakfast, afternoon wine and hors d'oeuvres, evening turndown service, morning newspaper delivery, home-baked cookies and bicycles to borrow on premises. Handicap access. Antiquing, art galleries, beach, bicycling, canoeing/kayaking, fishing, golf, hiking, horseback riding, live theater, museums, parks, shopping, tennis, water sports, wineries and aquarium nearby.

Location: Ocean community, waterfront.

Publicity: *Travel & Leisure and Country Living.*

Certificate may be used: Sunday – Thursday, December through February, based on promotional discount availability and excludes special event periods, holidays and certain room types. First night must be at full rack rate to receive second night free.

Inn at Seventeen Mile Drive

213 Seventeen Mile Dr
Pacific Grove, CA 93950-2400
(831)642-9514 (800)526-5666 Fax:(831)642-9546
Internet: www.innat17.com
E-mail: innkeeper@innat17.com

Circa 1925. The only challenging part of a visit to this 1920s craftsman-style house is figuring out where the deep blue sea ends and clear skies begin. Located in the heart of the Monterey Peninsula, this two-story, three-building inn offers sea or garden views from the main house, while you will find rustic ambiance,

surrounded by oak and redwood trees, in the cottage and redwood chalet rooms. Relax in the spa beneath the tall trees in the gardens, which are often visited by deer and monarch butterflies, or enjoy a glass of champagne while observing Koi in the fountain ponds. Or, spend time in the wood-paneled dining, sitting and reading rooms while enjoying complimentary hors d'oeuvres and planning a day full of activities.
Innkeeper(s): Dianna and Charlie Wareing. $115-290. 14 rooms with PB, 2 with FP, 1 cottage. Breakfast, snacks/refreshments, hors d'oeuvres and wine included in rates. Types of meals: Full bkfst. Beds: KQ. Data port, cable TV, reading lamp, refrigerator, clock radio, telephone, some with fireplace, hair dryer, bathrobes, bath amenities, wireless Internet access and iron/ironing board in room. Central air. VCR, fax, copier, spa, library and parlor games on premises. Handicap access. Antiquing, art galleries, beach, bicycling, canoeing/kayaking, fishing, golf, hiking, live theater, museums, parks, shopping, sporting events, tennis, water sports, wineries, Monterey Bay Aquarium and The Monarch Butterfly Sanctuary nearby.

Location: Ocean community. Close to golf course.

Certificate may be used: Nov. 1 to March 31, Sunday-Thursday, except holidays, special events. Offer applies to Queen-size rooms only.

Martine Inn

255 Ocean View Blvd
Pacific Grove, CA 93950
(831)373-3388 (800)852-5588 Fax:(831)373-3896
Internet: www.martineinn.com
E-mail: don@martineinn.com

Circa 1899. This turn-of-the-century oceanfront manor sits atop a jagged cliff overlooking the coastline of Monterey Bay, just steps away from the water's edge. Bedrooms are furnished with antiques, and each room contains a fresh rose. Thirteen rooms also boast fireplaces. Some of the museum-quality antiques were exhibited in the 1893 Chicago World's Fair.  Other bedroom sets include furniture that belonged to Edith Head, and there is an 1860 Chippendale Revival four-poster bed with a canopy and side curtains. Innkeeper Don Martine has a collection of vintage MGs, six on display for guests. Twilight wine and hors d'oeuvres are served, and chocolates accompany evening turndown service. The inn is a beautiful spot for romantic getaways and weddings.
Innkeeper(s): Don Martine. $159-425. 24 rooms with PB, 13 with FP, 1 suite, 6 conference rooms. Breakfast, snacks/refreshments, hors d'oeuvres and wine included in rates. Types of meals: Full gourmet bkfst and early coffee/tea. Beds: KQD. Reading lamp, refrigerator, clock radio, telephone, turn-down service, desk, hot tub/spa, most with fireplace, hair dryer, bathrobes, bath amenities and wireless Internet access in room. TV, fax, copier, spa, library, parlor games, evening wine, DSL Internet, billiard table, car display, piano and Wi-fi on premises. Handicap access. Antiquing, art galleries, beach, bicycling, canoeing/kayaking, fishing, golf, hiking, horseback riding, live theater, museums, parks, shopping, sporting events, tennis, water sports, wineries, Monterey Bay Aquarium, Cannery Row, 17-Mile Drive and Fishermans Wharf nearby.

Location: Ocean community, waterfront.

Publicity: *Sunday Oregonian, Bon Appetit, Vacations APAC, Fresno Bee, San Francisco Magazine, Santa Barbara News-Press, Victory Lane and North American Classic MG Magazine.*

"Wonderful, can't wait to return."

Certificate may be used: Anytime, November-February, subject to availability. Not on Valentine's and between Christmas and New Year's.

Palm Springs

Sakura, Japanese B&B Inn

1677 N Via Miraleste at Vista Chino
Palm Springs, CA 92262
(760)327-0705 (800)200-0705 Fax:(760)327-6847
Internet: www.travelbase.com/destinations/palm-springs/sakura
E-mail: pssakurain@yahoo.com

Circa 1945. An authentic Japanese experience awaits guests of this private home, distinctively decorated with Japanese artwork and antique kimonos. Guests are encouraged to leave their shoes at the door, grab kimonos and slippers and discover what real relaxation is all about. Futon beds, and in-room refrigerators and microwaves are provided. Guests may choose either American or Japanese breakfasts, and Japanese or vegetarian dinners also are available. The Palm Springs area is home to more than 100 golf courses and hosts annual world-class golf and tennis charity events. A favorite place for celebrity watching, the area also is the Western polo capital and offers the famous 9,000-foot aerial tram ride that climbs through several temperature zones. There are cycling trails, theater, horseback riding in the canyons and fine dining, skiing and antiquing. During the summer months, the innkeepers conduct tours in Japan.

Innkeeper(s): George & Fumiko Cebra. $45-90. 3 rooms, 2 with PB, 1 suite. Breakfast included in rates. Types of meals: Full bkfst, early coffee/tea, picnic lunch, afternoon tea and dinner. Beds: QDT. TV, VCR, refrigerator and clock radio in room. Central air. Swimming, Jacuzzi, outdoor barbeque and Japanese Gardens on premises. Amusement parks, antiquing, cross-country skiing, fishing, live theater, parks and shopping nearby.

Location: City, mountains. California desert.

Certificate may be used: Anytime, Sunday-Thursday.

Pauma Valley

Cupid's Castle B&B

17622 Hwy 76
Pauma Valley, CA 92061
(760)742-3306 Fax:(760)742-0279
Internet: www.cupidscastlebandb.com
E-mail: cupidscastle@earthlink.net

Circa 1995. Five acres of gardens with fountains, gazebos and a fragrant lemon orchard surround this four-story castle. A fairy grotto garden with willow love seat and arbor is a popular spot for weddings and anniversaries. Inside the B&B, cupids from the innkeeper's collection can be spotted. Romantic guest bedrooms feature two-person Jacuzzi tubs, canopy beds, VCRs and private balconies. A full breakfast is served daily. Arrangements can be made for a special dinner prepared with grilled salmon, New York steak and homemade cheesecake. Palomar Mountain and observatory, wineries and five casinos are nearby. Try hot-air ballooning, cycling or golf.

Innkeeper(s): Ted & Connie Vlasis. $200-275. 4 suites. Breakfast and snacks/refreshments included in rates. Types of meals: Full gourmet bkfst, early coffee/tea and dinner. Beds: K. Modem hook-up, cable TV, VCR, reading lamp, stereo, refrigerator, ceiling fan, clock radio, coffeemaker, desk, hot tub/spa and fireplace in room. Central air. Fax, copier, spa, library, parlor games, fireplace, gift corner and happy hour on premises. Handicap access. Amusement parks, antiquing, art galleries, beach, bicycling, fishing, golf, hiking, horseback riding, live theater, museums, parks, shopping, wineries and casinos nearby.

Location: Country, mountains. Farm.

Publicity: *Featured on San Diego T.V. News, San Diego Hideaways and Arlington's Bed and Breakfast Journal (voted Most Romantic).*

Certificate may be used: Monday through Thursday, Jan. 30 to Dec. 14.

Placerville

Albert Shafsky House Bed & Breakfast

2942 Coloma St
Placerville, CA 95667
(530)642-2776 Fax:(503)642-2109
Internet: www.shafsky.com
E-mail: stay@shafsky.com

Circa 1902. Gold Country hospitality is offered at this Queen Anne Victorian bed and breakfast located just a stroll to the historic district and the shops of Old Hangtown. Enjoy a welcome snack and refreshments in the elegant living room. Pleasantly decorated guest bedrooms are furnished with antiques and offer individually controlled heat and air conditioning as well as feather beds and goosedown comforters during winter. The two-room Lighthouse Suite also boasts a sitting room for a private breakfast. Arrangements can be made for special occasions, or a personalized bouquet of flowers.

Innkeeper(s): Rita Timewell and Stephanie Carlson. $135-185. 3 rooms with PB. Breakfast, snacks/refreshments and wine included in rates. Types of meals: Full gourmet bkfst, veg bkfst, early coffee/tea and hors d'oeuvres. Beds: KQ. Reading lamp, CD player, ceiling fan, clock radio, turn-down service, desk, hair dryer, bathrobes, bath amenities, wireless Internet access and iron/ironing board in room. Air conditioning. TV, VCR, fax, copier, library, parlor games, telephone, fireplace, gift shop, satellite TV, video library, games and guest refrigerator on premises. Limited handicap access. Antiquing, art galleries, canoeing/kayaking, cross-country skiing, downhill skiing, fishing, golf, hiking, horseback riding, live theater, museums, parks, shopping, tennis, water sports, wineries, Apple Hill, Sutter's Mill, Gold Bug Mine, Gold Discovery Park and whitewater rafting nearby.

Location: City, country, mountains. Located a short stroll from historic Placerville, aka Old Hangtown.

Publicity: *Mountain Democrat, San Francisco Chronicle, San Jose Mercury News, The El Dorado Guide, KCRA, Taste of California (Travel Channel), KNCI and KAHI.*

Certificate may be used: Sunday-Thursday, subject to availability.

Point Reyes Station

The Tree House

PO Box 1075
Point Reyes Station, CA 94956-1075
(415)663-8720 (800)977-8720
Internet: www.treehousebnb.com
E-mail: treehousebnb@juno.com

Circa 1970. The Tree House, poised on the tip of Inverness Ridge in West Marin, California, offers an outstanding view of Point Reyes Station. Two of the guest bedrooms feature a fireplace and a private balcony or deck. Start each day with a continental breakfast before exploring the picturesque area. A hot tub is tucked away in a cozy spot of the garden. Hiking and biking on nearby trails and birdwatching are popular activities.

Innkeeper(s): Lisa Patsel. $125-165. 3 rooms with PB, 2 with FP, 1 suite. Breakfast included in rates. Types of meals: Cont plus. VCR, reading lamp, ceiling fan, clock radio and telephone in room. TV, spa, pet boarding and fireplace on premises. Antiquing, parks and shopping nearby.

Location: Mountains. Hiking.

Certificate may be used: Monday-Thursday, January-May, holidays excluded.

Ridgecrest

BevLen Haus Bed & Breakfast

809 N Sanders St
Ridgecrest, CA 93555
(760)375-1988 (800)375-1989 Fax:(760)375-6871
Internet: www.bevlen.com
E-mail: BLH_B&B@iwvisp.com

Circa 1950. Country charm abounds at this bed & breakfast. Two antique cookstoves warm the home, one in the kitchen and another in the sitting room. The garden room includes a Franklin stove. Each of the three guest rooms features country decor with quilt-topped beds. The home is near museums and outdoor attractions. Death Valley National Park is a popular day trip.

Innkeeper(s): Beverly & Leonard de Geus. $55-75. 3 rooms with PB. Breakfast included in rates. Types of meals: Full bkfst. Beds: QDT. Reading lamp, ceiling fan and desk in room. Central air. TV, fax, copier, spa, telephone and fireplace on premises. Antiquing, bicycling, fishing, golf, hiking, museums, parks, shopping and tennis nearby.

Location: Northern Mojave Desert.

Certificate may be used: Anytime, subject to availability.

Sacramento

Amber House

1315 22nd St
Sacramento, CA 95816-5717
(916)444-8085 (800)755-6526 Fax:(916)552-6529
Internet: www.amberhouse.com
E-mail: info@amberhouse.com

Circa 1905. These two historic homes on the city's Historic Preservation Register are in a neighborhood of fine historic homes eight blocks from the capitol. Each guest bedroom is named for a famous poet or composer and features stained glass, antiques from throughout the century, and luxury amenities. All the bathrooms are marble tiled and seven rooms include two-person Jacuzzi tubs. Several rooms boast fireplaces. Start the day with an early morning tray delivered to the door and a two-course gourmet breakfast is served in room or in the dining room at a time you request.

Innkeeper(s): Judith Bommer. $159-279. 10 rooms with PB, 3 with FP, 7 with WP, 1 conference room. Breakfast included in rates. Types of meals: Full gourmet bkfst, early coffee/tea and Cookies and late night beverage delivered to your room. Beds: Q. Modem hook-up, data port, cable TV, VCR, reading lamp, CD player, clock radio, telephone, turn-down service, desk, most with hot tub/spa, voice mail, hair dryer, wireless Internet access and iron/ironing board in room. Air conditioning. Fax, copier, library, parlor games, fireplace and garden on premises.

Location: City.

"Your cordial hospitality, the relaxing atmosphere and delicious breakfast made our brief business/pleasure trip so much more enjoyable."

Certificate may be used: Anytime, subject to availability.

San Diego

A Victorian Heritage Park Inn

2470 Heritage Park Row
San Diego, CA 92110-2803
(619)299-6832 (800)995-2470 Fax:(619)299-9465
Internet: www.heritageparkinn.com
E-mail: innkeeper@heritageparkinn.com

Circa 1889. Situated on a seven-acre Victorian park in the heart of Old Town, this inn is two of seven preserved classic structures. The main house offers a variety of beautifully appointed guest rooms, decked in traditional Victorian furnishings and decor. The opulent Manor Suite includes two bedrooms, a Jacuzzi tub and sitting room. A collection of classic movies is available, and a different movie is shown each night in the inn's parlor. Guests are treated to a light afternoon tea, and breakfast is served on fine china on candlelit tables. The home is within walking distance to the many sites, shops and restaurants in the historic Old Town.

Innkeeper(s): Nancy & Charles Helsper. $140-300. 12 rooms with PB, 3 with WP, 1 two-bedroom suite. Breakfast and afternoon tea included in rates. Types of meals: Full gourmet bkfst and early coffee/tea. Beds: KQT. Reading lamp, clock radio, telephone, turn-down service and desk in room. Air conditioning. VCR, fax, copier, parlor games and gift shop on premises. Antiquing, fishing, live theater, parks, shopping, sporting events, water sports, San Diego Zoo and Tijuana nearby.

Location: City.

Publicity: *Los Angeles Herald Examiner, Innsider, Los Angeles Times, Orange County Register, San Diego Union, In-Flight, Glamour and Country Inns.*

"A beautiful step back in time. Peaceful and gracious."

Certificate may be used: Call innkeeper for dates.

San Francisco

Archbishop's Mansion

1000 Fulton St (at Steiner)
San Francisco, CA 94117-1608
(415)563-7872 (800)543-5820 Fax:(415) 885-3193
Internet: www.thearchbishopsmansion.com
E-mail: jspear@jdvhospitality.com

Circa 1904. This French Empire-style manor was built for the Archbishop of San Francisco. It is designated as a San Francisco historic landmark. The grand stairway features redwood paneling, Corinthian columns and a stained-glass dome. The parlor has a hand-painted ceiling. Each of the guest rooms is named for an opera. Rooms have antiques, Victorian window treatments and embroidered linens. Continental breakfast is served in the dining room, and guests also are treated to a complimentary wine and cheese reception each night.

Innkeeper(s): John Spear . $149-329. 15 rooms with PB, 11 with FP, 5 suites, 2 conference rooms. Breakfast and wine included in rates. Types of meals: Cont plus. Beds: KQ. Modem hook-up, data port, cable TV, VCR, reading lamp, CD player, clock radio, telephone, turn-down service, some with hot tub/spa, most with fireplace, hair dryer, bathrobes, bath amenities, wireless Internet access, iron/ironing board, beautiful canopied beds and other antiques in room. Fax, copier, tennis, library and parlor games on premises. Amusement parks, antiquing, art galleries', beach, bicycling, canoeing/kayaking, fishing, golf, hiking, horseback riding, live theater, museums, parks, shopping, sporting events, tennis, water sports and wineries nearby.

Location: City. On Alamo Square Park.

Publicity: *Travel-Holiday, Travel & Leisure, USA Today, Country Inns and Travel Channel.*

"The ultimate, romantic honeymoon spot."

Certificate may be used: Anytime, Sunday-Thursday, holidays excluded.

Petite Auberge

863 Bush St
San Francisco, CA 94108-3312
(415)928-6000 (800)365-3004 Fax:(415)673-7214
Internet: www.petiteaubergesf.com
E-mail: petiteauberge@jdvhospitality.com

Circa 1917. An ornate baroque design with curved bay windows highlight this five-story hotel that has now been transformed into a French country inn. This Joie de Vivre property boasts antiques, fresh flowers and country accessories. Most guest bedrooms feature working fireplaces. Take a short walk to the Powell Street cable car. In the evenings, wine and cheese, sherry, tea, coffee and cake are served. There is an extra fee for an additional guest in room, except for children less than five years old.

Innkeeper(s): Pamela Flank. $109-269. 26 rooms with PB, 17 with FP, 1 suite. Breakfast included in rates. Types of meals: Full gourmet bkfst, early coffee/tea, afternoon tea and wine. Beds: KQ. Cable TV, reading lamp, clock radio, telephone, fireplace and terry robes in room. Fax, copier and valet parking on premises. Handicap access. Antiquing, art galleries, beach, canoeing/kayaking, fishing, golf, hiking, live theater, parks, shopping, sporting events, tennis, wineries, historic sites, museums and cable nearby.

Location: City. Nob Hill, Union Square.

Publicity: *Travel & Leisure, Oregonian, Los Angeles Times, Brides, Conde Nast Traveler Top 75 in US and 2005 Gold List.*

"Breakfast was great, and even better in bed!"

Certificate may be used: November-February, Sunday-Thursday, excluding holidays and special events.

The Inn San Francisco

943 South Van Ness Ave
San Francisco, CA 94110-2613
(415)641-0188 (800)359-0913 Fax:(415)641-1701
Internet: www.innsf.com
E-mail: innkeeper@innsf.com

Circa 1872. Built on one of San Francisco's earliest "Mansion Rows," this 21-room Italianate Victorian is located near the civic and convention centers, close to Mission Dolores. Antiques, marble fireplaces and Oriental rugs decorate the opulent grand double parlors. Most rooms have featherbeds, Victorian wallcoverings and desks, while deluxe rooms offer private spas, fireplaces or bay windows. There is a rooftop deck with a 360-degree view of San Francisco. Complimentary beverages are always available. The inn is close to the opera, symphony, theaters, Mission Dolores, gift and jewelry centers and antique shopping.

Innkeeper(s): Marty Neely & Connie Wu. $105-295. 21 rooms, 19 with PB, 3 with FP, 3 suites, 1 cottage. Breakfast included in rates. Types of meals:

Full bkfst and afternoon tea. Beds: QD. TV, reading lamp, refrigerator, clock radio, telephone, desk, hot tub/spa, one suite with redwood hot tub, flowers and truffles in room. Fax, fireplace, garden, rooftop view sundeck and parlor on premises.

Location: City.

Publicity: *Innsider, Sunset Magazine, San Francisco Chronicle and American Airlines Magazine.*

"Breakfast; marvelous. The best B&B we've visited. We were made to feel like family."

Certificate may be used: Monday-Thursday, subject to availability, holidays excluded. Check with innkeeper for weekend night availability.

White Swan Inn

845 Bush St
San Francisco, CA 94108-3300
(415)775-1755 (800)999-9570 Fax:(415)775-5717
Internet: www.whiteswaninnsf.com
E-mail: whiteswan@jdvhospitality.com

Circa 1915. This four-story inn is near Union Square and the Powell Street cable car. Beveled-glass doors open to a reception area with granite floors and English artwork. Bay windows and a rear deck contribute to the feeling of an English garden inn. The guest rooms are decorated with bold English wallpapers and prints. All rooms have fireplaces. Turndown service and complimentary newspapers are included, and in the evenings wine, sherry, tea, coffee, cake and hors d'oeuvres are served. There is a $20 fee for an additional guest in room, except for children less than 5 years old.

Innkeeper(s): John Spear GM. $139-309. 26 rooms with PB, 26 with FP, 3 suites, 1 conference room. Breakfast and afternoon tea included in rates. Types of meals: Full gourmet bkfst, early coffee/tea, snacks/refreshments and wine. Beds: KQT. Data port, cable TV, reading lamp, refrigerator, clock radio, telephone, coffeemaker, turn-down service, desk, fireplace, terry robes, newspaper and complimentary beverages in room. Fax, copier, library, parlor games and wireless Internet on premises. Antiquing, art galleries, beach, canoeing/kayaking, fishing, golf, hiking, live theater, museums, parks, shopping, sporting events, tennis and wineries nearby.

Location: City. Nob Hill, Union Square.

Publicity: *Travel & Leisure, Victoria and Wine Spectator.*

"Wonderfully accommodating. Absolutely perfect."

Certificate may be used: December and January, Sunday-Thursday, excluding holidays and special events.

Santa Barbara

Cheshire Cat Inn & Spa

36 W Valerio St
Santa Barbara, CA 93101-2524
(805)569-1610 Fax:(805)682-1876
Internet: www.cheshirecat.com
E-mail: cheshire@cheshirecat.com

Circa 1894. This elegant inn features three Queen Anne Victorians, a Coach House and three cottages surrounded by fountains, gazebos and lush flower gardens. The guest bedrooms and suites are furnished with English antiques, Laura Ashley fabrics and wallpapers or oak floors, pine furniture and down comforters. Some boast fireplaces, Jacuzzi tubs, private balconies, VCRs and refrigerators. Wedgwood china set in the formal dining room or brick patio enhances a delicious break-fast. Local wine and hors d'oeuvres are served in the evening. Spa facilities offer massage and body treatments.

Innkeeper(s): Debbie and Bharti. $189-410. 17 rooms with PB, 3 with FP, 3 with HT, 4 total suites, including 3 two-bedroom suites, 3 cottages, 1 conference room. Breakfast, hors d'oeuvres and wine included in rates. Types of meals: Cont plus, early coffee/tea and room service. Beds: KQT. Cable TV, VCR, reading lamp, refrigerator, ceiling fan, clock radio, telephone, some with hot tub/spa, some with fireplace, hair dryer, bathrobes, wireless Internet access and iron/ironing board in room. Air conditioning. Fax, copier, spa and spa facilities on premises. Antiquing, art galleries, beach, bicycling, canoeing/kayaking, fishing, golf, hiking, horseback riding, live theater, museums, parks, shopping, sporting events, tennis, water sports and wineries nearby.

Location: City.

Publicity: *Two on the Town, KABC, Los Angeles Times, Santa Barbara, American In Flight and Elmer Dills Recommends.*

"Romantic and quaint."

Certificate may be used: Jan. 2-Dec. 23, no holidays/weekends, subject to availability.

The Old Yacht Club Inn

431 Corona Del Mar
Santa Barbara, CA 93103-3601
(805)962-1277 (800)676-1676 Fax:(805)962-3989
E-mail: info@oldyachtclubinn.com

Circa 1912. One block from famous East Beach, this California Craftsman house was the home of the Santa Barbara Yacht Club during the Roaring '20s. It was opened as Santa Barbara's first B&B and has become renowned for its gourmet food and superb hospitality. The Old Yacht Club Inn features an evening social hour. Inviting guest bedrooms boast fresh flowers and a decanter of sherry. Wake up to start the day with a gourmet breakfast.

Innkeeper(s): Eilene Bruce. $99-479. 12 rooms with PB, 1 cottage, 1 conference room. Breakfast included in rates. Types of meals: Full gourmet bkfst, early coffee/tea and gourmet dinner. Beds: KQ. TV, reading lamp, telephone and hot tub/spa in room. Fax, copier, bicycles, fireplace, wine social, beach chairs and beach towels on premises. Antiquing, fishing, live theater, shopping, sporting events and water sports nearby.

Publicity: *Los Angeles, Valley, Bon Appetit and Gourmet.*

"One of Santa Barbara's better-kept culinary secrets."

Certificate may be used: November, December, January, February, Monday-Thursday evenings only. Weekend and holiday periods excluded. Based on availability.

The Upham Hotel & Country House

1404 De La Vina St
Santa Barbara, CA 93101-3027
(805)962-0058 (800)727-0876 Fax:(805)963-2825
Internet: www.uphamhotel.com
E-mail: upham.hotel@verizon.net

Circa 1871. Antiques and period furnishings decorate each of the inn's guest rooms and suites. The inn is the oldest continuously operating hostelry in Southern California. Situated on an acre of gardens in the center of downtown, it's within easy walking distance of restaurants, shops, art galleries and museums. The staff is happy to assist guests in discovering Santa Barbara's varied attractions. Garden cottage units feature porches or secluded patios and several have gas fireplaces.

Innkeeper(s): Jan Martin Winn. $195-550. 50 rooms with PB, 8 with FP, 4 suites, 3 cottages, 3 conference rooms. Breakfast and snacks/refreshments included in rates. Types of meals: Cont plus and early coffee/tea. Beds: KQD.

Cable TV, VCR, DVD, reading lamp, ceiling fan, clock radio, telephone, desk, hair dryer, bathrobes, bath amenities, wireless Internet access, iron/ironing board and master suite has hot tub/spa in room. Fax, copier and fireplace on premises. Antiquing, art galleries, beach, golf, live theater, museums, parks and shopping nearby.

Location: City.

Publicity: *Los Angeles Times, Santa Barbara, Westways, Santa Barbara News-Press and Avenues.*

"Your hotel is truly a charm. Between the cozy gardens and the exquisitely comfortable appointments, The Upham is charm itself."

Certificate may be used: Sunday-Thursday, subject to availability.

White Jasmine Inn Santa Barbara (Glenborough Inn)

1327 Bath St
Santa Barbara, CA 93101-3630
(805)966-0589
Internet: www.whitejasmineinnsantabarbara.com
E-mail: stay@whitejasmineinnsantabarbara.com

Circa 1885. The Victorian and California Craftsman-style homes that comprise the Glenborough are located in the theatre and arts district. Antiques, rich wood trim and elegant fireplace suites with canopy beds are offered. Some rooms also have mini refrigerators or whirlpools tubs. There's always plenty of hospitality and an invitation to try the secluded garden hot tub. Homemade breakfasts, served in the privacy of your room, have been written up in Bon Appetit and Chocolatier. Bedtime cookies and beverages are served, as well. It's a three-block walk to restaurants, shops and the shuttle to the beach.

Innkeeper(s): Marlies Marburg. $98-319. 13 rooms with PB, 13 with FP, 2 with HT, 4 cottages. Breakfast included in rates. Types of meals: Full bkfst. Beds: KQ. TV, reading lamp, ceiling fan, clock radio, telephone, desk, hot tub/spa, fireplace, coffeemaker, robes and some with A/C and mini-fridge in room. Fax, spa and parlor games on premises. Antiquing, fishing, live theater, parks, shopping, sporting events and water sports nearby.

Location: City, mountains, ocean community. Downtown, near wineries.

Publicity: *Houston Post, Los Angeles Times and Pasadena Choice.*

"Only gracious service is offered at the Glenborough Inn."

Certificate may be used: Sunday-Thursday during October-April except holidays based on regularly priced rooms, valid only for Heather room.

Santa Cruz

Cliff Crest Bed & Breakfast Inn

407 Cliff St
Santa Cruz, CA 95060-5009
(831)427-2609 (831)252-1057 Fax:(831)427-2710
Internet: www.cliffcrestinn.com
E-mail: Innkpr@CliffCrestInn.com

Circa 1887. Warmth, friendliness and comfort characterize this elegantly restored Queen Anne Victorian home. An octagonal solarium, tall stained-glass windows, and a belvedere overlook Monterey Bay and the Santa Cruz Mountains. The mood is airy and romantic. The spacious gardens were designed by John McLaren, landscape architect for Golden Gate Park. Antiques and fresh flowers fill the rooms, once home to William Jeter, lieutenant governor of California.

Innkeeper(s): Constantin Gehriger, Adriana Gehriger Gil. $95-245. 6 rooms with PB, 2 with FP, 1 with HT, 1 four-bedroom suite, 1 guest house. Breakfast, Healthy full gourmet breakfast and everything made from scratch included in rates. Types of meals: Full gourmet bkfst, early coffee/tea, Lunches, dinners and and special events are provided to order. Just ask us!. Beds: KQ. Cable TV, DVD, reading lamp, clock radio, telephone, desk, hair dryer, bathrobes, bath amenities, wireless Internet access and iron/ironing board in room. Fax, copier, spa, parlor games, fireplace, Beautiful backyard with ocean view, designed by John MacLaren and the architect of Golden Gate Park in San Francisco on premises. Handicap access. Amusement parks, antiquing, art galleries, beach, bicycling, canoeing/kayaking, fishing, golf, hiking, horseback riding, live theater, museums, parks, shopping, sporting events, tennis, water sports, wineries, Walk to Main Beach, Municipal Wharf and downtown Santa Cruz nearby.

Location: Waterfront.

Publicity: *The New York Times, Sunset Magazine, San Francisco Chronicle Magazine and many guidebooks, Sudden Impact and the 1983 Dirty Harry movie with Clint Eastwood was filmed here.*

"Delightful place, excellent food and comfortable bed."

Certificate may be used: Monday to Thursday, except holidays. Last minute subject to availability.

Pleasure Point Inn

23665 E Cliff Dr
Santa Cruz, CA 95062-5543
(831)475-4657
Internet: www.pleasurepointinn.com
E-mail: inquiries@pleasurepointinn.com

Circa 2001. Located in front of the popular Pleasure Point Surfing Beach, this oceanfront estate was completely remodeled recently. The modern Mediterranean-style architecture and design has an upscale appearance. Guest bedrooms all feature gas fireplaces, custom furniture, private patios and entrances. Some offer heated floor tiles and Jacuzzi tubs. Enjoy the sights and sounds of the sea from the large roof top deck overlooking Monterey Bay. Chaise lounges encourage soaking up the sun by day. A heater gas lamp placed near the outdoor dining tables provides warmth for cool evenings. Gaze at the stars while relaxing in the big hot tub. Capitola Village, only two miles away, offers shopping, dining, a sandy beach and nightly entertainment. Cruises can be arranged at the local yacht harbor.
Innkeeper(s): Jill & Tara. $225-295. 4 rooms with PB, 4 with FP. Breakfast and snacks/refreshments included in rates. Types of meals: Cont plus. Beds: KQ. TV, VCR, DVD, reading lamp, stereo, refrigerator, clock radio, telephone, coffeemaker, desk, most with hot tub/spa, fireplace, hair dryer, wireless Internet access, iron/ironing board, fireplace and some with Jacuzzi tubs in room. Spa on premises. Amusement parks, antiquing, shopping and sporting events nearby.
Location: Waterfront.

Certificate may be used: Sunday-Wednesday from Jan. 10-March 31.

The Darling House A B&B Inn By The Sea

314 W Cliff Dr
Santa Cruz, CA 95060-6145
(831)458-1958 Fax:(831)458-0320
Internet: www.darlinghouse.com
E-mail: ddarling@darlinghouse.com

Circa 1910. It's difficult to pick a room at this oceanside mansion. The Pacific Ocean Room features a fireplace and a wonderful ocean view. The Chinese Room might suit you with its silk-draped, hand-carved rosewood canopy wedding bed.

Elegant oak, ebony, and walnut woodwork is enhanced by the antique decor of Tiffanys and Chippendales. Roses, beveled glass and libraries add to the atmosphere. Beyond the ocean-view veranda are landscaped gardens. Guests often walk to the wharf for dinner.
Innkeeper(s): Karen & Darrell Darling. $95-260. 8 rooms, 1 with PB, 2 with FP, 1 suite, 1 cottage, 1 conference room. Breakfast included in rates. Types of meals: Cont plus. Beds: KQDT. Modem hook-up, VCR, turn-down service, desk, message service, clothes press, reservation service and TV on request in room. Fax, copier, library, parlor games, telephone and fireplace on premises. Limited handicap access. Amusement parks, antiquing, art galleries, beach, bicycling, canoeing/kayaking, fishing, golf, hiking, live theater, museums, parks, shopping, sporting events, tennis, water sports, wineries, Narrow Gauge Railway, aquarium, ocean research, Shakespeare Festival in July and August, Begonia Festival, Cabrillo Music Festival, Jazz Festival, PGA Tournaments and international ocean sport contests nearby.
Location: City, ocean community.

Publicity: *Modern Maturity, Pacific, New York Times, LA Times, Sacramento Bee Fresno, San Francisco Chronicle, Oakland Tribune, Santa Cruz Sentinel, Bay Guardian, San Jose Mercury News and Thrill (ABC made-for-TV movie).*

"So pretty, so sorry to leave."

Certificate may be used: November-April, Sunday-Thursday, holidays excluded.

West Cliff Inn

174 West Cliff Drive
Santa Cruz, CA 95060
(831)649-0908 (800)979-0910 Fax:(831)649-4822
Internet: www.westcliffinn.com
E-mail: westcliffinn@foursisters.com

Boasting seaside serenity in Santa Cruz, California, West Cliff Inn sits on a bluff across from the beach. Originally built in 1877 as a private home, this renovated and stately three-story Victorian Italianate has become a Four Sisters Inn. The coastal décor is inviting with a clean and fresh ambiance. Feel the ocean breeze while relaxing on the wraparound porch. Gather for afternoon wine and appetizers. Stay in a guest bedroom with a marble tile bathroom, fireplace and jetted spa tub. A second-story room boasts a private outdoor hot tub and the two top-floor suites include sitting areas. Breakfast is a satisfying way to begin each day's adventures. Explore the local surfing museum or hit the waves and hang ten. Stroll along the famous beach boardwalk. Seasonal packages are offered.
Innkeeper(s): Four Sisters Inns. Call for rates. Call inn for details.

Certificate may be used: Sunday – Thursday, December through February, based on promotional discount availability and excludes special event periods, holidays and certain room types. First night must be at full rack rate to receive second night free.

Santa Rosa

Melitta Station Inn

5850 Melitta Rd
Santa Rosa, CA 95409-5641
(707)538-7712 (800)504-3099 Fax:(707)538-7565
Internet: www.melittastationinn.com
E-mail: info@melittastationinn.com

Circa 188. Originally built as a stagecoach stop, this inn was the focus for the little town of Melitta. Still located down a country lane with walk-in access to a state park, the station has been charmingly renovated. Oiled-wood floors, a rough-beam cathedral ceiling and French doors opening to a balcony are features of the sitting room. Upon arrival, enjoy English tea and homemade scones. Three inviting guest bedrooms feature antique clawfoot tubs. Linger over a hearty country breakfast in the great room. Wineries and vineyards stretch from the inn to the town of Sonoma. Basalt stone, quarried from nearby hills, was sent by rail to San Francisco where it was used to pave the cobblestone streets.

Innkeeper(s): Jackie & Tim Thresh. $100-230. 6 rooms with PB, 2 total suites, including 1 two-bedroom suite. Breakfast, afternoon tea, snacks/refreshments, Full gourmet 3-course cooked breakfast and complimentary water and sodas included in rates. Types of meals: Full gourmet bkfst, veg bkfst, early coffee/tea and Complimentary water/sodas. Beds: KQ. Cable TV, reading lamp, ceiling fan, some with hot tub/spa, hair dryer, bathrobes, bath amenities and wireless Internet access in room. Central air. Fax, copier, spa, telephone, fireplace, gift shop, Spa/massage services in dedicated area, Relaxation space, 40-jet luxury hot-tub in sun-room, Meeting space for up to 14 (requires overnight room rental), King suite with disabled access & private patio, Public patio with BBQ and Deck area on premises. Limited handicap access. Antiquing, beach, bicycling, canoeing/kayaking, fishing, golf, hiking, horseback riding, live theater, museums, parks, tennis, wineries, Safari West Animal Kingdom, Pacific Coast Air Museum, Luther Burbank Home and Gardens, Charles Schulz Museum and Ice Skating Rink nearby.

Location: Country. Wine country.

Publicity: *Journalist John Clayton (copyright KNX 1070 NEWSRADIO)* .

Certificate may be used: Monday-Thursday, December-February.

Sebastopol

Vine Hill Inn

3949 Vine Hill Rd
Sebastopol, CA 95472
(707)823-8832 Fax:(707)824-1045
Internet: www.vine-hill-inn.com
E-mail: innkeeper@vine-hill-inn.com

Circa 1897. Situated between picturesque apple orchards and vineyards, this Victorian farmhouse is an eclectic country-style bed & breakfast. An intimate ambiance is imparted, with gathering places to play games or converse. Spacious guest bedrooms boast antiques, Egyptian towels and bathrobes. Choose between a clawfoot tub or Jacuzzi. Relax on private decks or porches with gorgeous views. Savor a satisfying breakfast that may include fresh fruit, chicken sausage, frittata and beverages. A swimming pool provides added enjoyment.

Innkeeper(s): Kathy Deichmann. $160-200. 4 rooms with PB. Breakfast included in rates. Types of meals: Full gourmet bkfst. Beds: Q. Reading lamp in room. Central air. Fax, copier, swimming, library, parlor games, telephone and fireplace on premises. Antiquing, art galleries, beach, bicycling, canoeing/kayaking, fishing, golf, hiking, horseback riding, live theater, parks, shopping and wineries nearby.

Location: Country.

Certificate may be used: Anytime, Sunday-Thursday, subject to availability.

Sonoma

Inn at Sonoma

630 Broadway
Sonoma, CA 95476
(707)939-1340 (888)568-9818 Fax:(707)939-8834
Internet: www.innatsonoma.com
E-mail: innatsonoma@foursisters.com

Circa 2002. Located within walking distance to the historic Sonoma Plaza, this delightful new inn is sure to please.

Reflecting a casual California decor, the well-furnished guest bedrooms feature fireplaces and some offer private balconies. Start the day with a sumptuous breakfast, then grab a bicycle to explore the local area. Hors d'oeuvres and afternoon wine are a welcome respite, and the rooftop Jacuzzi is a soothing relaxer. There is a $20 fee for an additional guest in room, except for children less than 5 years old.

Innkeeper(s): Chapman Retterer. $125-240. 19 rooms with PB, 19 with FP. Breakfast, snacks/refreshments and wine included in rates. Types of meals: Full bkfst, veg bkfst, early coffee/tea, afternoon tea and hors d'oeuvres. Beds: KQ. Data port, cable TV, DVD, reading lamp, stereo, ceiling fan, clock radio, telephone, coffeemaker, turn-down service, desk, voice mail, hair dryer, bathrobes, bath amenities, iron/ironing board, DVD player, fireplace, private decks and terry robes in room. Air conditioning. Fax, spa, bicycles, library, parlor games, fireplace, signature breakfast, afternoon wine and hors d'oeuvres, evening turndown, morning newspaper delivery, home-baked cookies and bicycles to borrow on premises. Handicap access. Antiquing, art galleries, bicycling, canoeing/kayaking, golf, hiking, live theater, museums, parks, shopping, tennis and wineries nearby.

Location: City, country. Wine country.

Publicity: *Sunset, Coastal Living and Travel and Leisure.*

Certificate may be used: Sunday – Thursday, December through February, based on promotional discount availability and excludes special event periods, holidays and certain room types. First night must be at full rack rate to receive second night free.

South Pasadena

Bissell House

201 Orange Grove Ave
South Pasadena, CA 91030-1613
(626)441-3535 (800)441-3530 Fax:(626)441-3671
Internet: www.bissellhouse.com
E-mail: info@bissellhouse.com

Circa 1887. Adorning famous Orange Grove Avenue on historic Millionaire's Row, this restored three-story Victorian mansion is a cultural landmark that offers an elegant ambiance and inviting hospitality. Spacious guest bedrooms feature antique furnishings, tasteful décor and modern conveniences that include DSL. Linger over a scrumptious full breakfast in the formal dining room served with crystal glassware, vintage silver and fresh flowers. Apricot bread pudding, egg strata, ginger scones, crème brulee and lemon soufflé French toast are some of the popular specialties. Swim in the pool surrounded by lush foliage or relax in the gorgeous English garden. Visit nearby Old Town Pasadena with a small-town atmosphere and big-city entertainment, boutiques, and upscale restaurants.

Innkeeper(s): Juli Hoyman. $150-350. 5 rooms with PB, 1 with WP. Breakfast, afternoon tea, snacks/refreshments and wine included in rates. Types of meals: Full gourmet bkfst, veg bkfst and early coffee/tea. Beds: KQT. Data port, reading lamp, clock radio, desk, some with hot tub/spa, hair dryer, bath amenities, wireless Internet access, iron/ironing board, Hypoallergenic duvets, Featherbeds, Luxury linens, Comfy robes and DSL in room. Central air. TV, VCR, DVD, fax, copier, swimming, library, parlor games, telephone, fireplace and gift shop on premises. Antiquing, art galleries, golf, hiking, horseback riding, live theater, museums, parks, shopping, sporting events, tennis and wineries nearby.

Location: City.

Publicity: *"9 on the Town" and voted #5 top romantic getaway along with the Ritz Carlton Spa.*

Certificate may be used: Call innkeeper for last minute, subject to availability, holidays excluded.

Sutter Creek

Grey Gables B&B Inn

161 Hanford St
Sutter Creek, CA 95685-1687
(209)267-1039 (800)473-9422 Fax:(209)267-0998
Internet: www.greygables.com
E-mail: reservations@greygables.com

Circa 1897. The innkeepers of this Victorian home offer poetic accommodations both in the delightful decor and by the names of their guest rooms. The Keats, Bronte and Tennyson rooms afford garden views, while the Byron and Browning rooms include clawfoot tubs. The Victorian Suite, which encompasses the top floor, affords views of the garden, as well as a historic churchyard. All of the guest rooms boast fireplaces. Stroll down brick pathways through the terraced garden or relax in the parlor. A proper English tea is served with cakes and scones. Hors d'oeuvres and libations are served in the evenings.

Innkeeper(s): Roger & Susan Garlick. $130-224. 8 rooms with PB, 8 with FP. Breakfast, afternoon tea, hors d'oeuvres and wine included in rates. Types of meals: Full gourmet bkfst, veg bkfst and early coffee/tea. Beds: KQT. Modem hook-up, reading lamp, ceiling fan, clock radio, fireplace, hair dryer, bath amenities and free wireless high speed Internet access in room. Central air. Fax, copier, parlor games and telephone on premises. Handicap access. Antiquing, art galleries, cross-country skiing, downhill skiing, fishing, golf, horseback riding, live theater, museums, parks, shopping, water sports and wineries nearby.

Location: City, mountains. Gold Country.

Certificate may be used: Anytime, Sunday-Thursday, excludes all holidays, some black-out dates.

The Hanford House B&B Inn

61 Hanford St Hwy 49
Sutter Creek, CA 95685
(209)267-0747 (800)871-5839 Fax:(209)267-1825
Internet: www.hanfordhouse.com
E-mail: info@hanfordhouse.com

Circa 1929. Hanford House is located on the quiet main street of Sutter Creek, a Gold Rush town. The ivy-covered brick inn features spacious, romantic guest rooms; eight have a fireplace. The Gold Country Escape includes a Jacuzzi tub, canopy bed, sitting area and a private deck. Guests can enjoy breakfast in their room or in the inn's cheerful breakfast room. Guests can relax in the front of a fire in the Hanford Room, which doubles as facilities for conferences, retreats, weddings and social events. Wineries, antique shops and historic sites are nearby.

Innkeeper(s): Bob & Karen Tierno. $110-249. 10 rooms with PB, 9 with FP, 3 suites, 1 conference room. Breakfast, afternoon tea and snacks/refreshments included in rates. Types of meals: Full gourmet bkfst and early coffee/tea. Beds: KQ. Cable TV, reading lamp, ceiling fan and telephone in room. Air conditioning. VCR, fax and complimentary wireless Internet access on premises. Handicap access. Antiquing, fishing, golf, live theater, water sports, skiing, Gold Rush historic sites and 25 wineries nearby.

Publicity: *Best Places to Kiss and 50 Best Inns in Wine Country.*

Certificate may be used: Jan. 1-Dec. 31; Sunday-Thursday, excluding holidays, first night at peak weekend holiday rates. Second-floor suites are excluded from the program.

Templeton

Carriage Vineyards Bed and Breakfast

4337 S. El Pomar Road
Templeton, CA 93465
(805)227-6807 (800)617-7911 Fax:(805)226-9969
Internet: www.carriagevineyards.com
E-mail: Stay@CarriageVineyards.com

Circa 1995. Named after the owners' horse-drawn carriage collection, this 100-acre ranch is tucked away in the country of the Central Coast. Enjoy vineyards, orchards, pastures, gardens and a creek. Hike the hillsides to be immersed in the peaceful scenery of the area. Tastefully decorated guest bedrooms are furnished with well-placed antiques. The Victoria Room is a second-story master suite featuring an oversize shower and Jacuzzi tub for two. Savor a hot gourmet breakfast served daily. Overnight horse facilities are available.

Innkeeper(s): Kristi & Stan Barefoot. $120-235. 4 rooms with PB. Breakfast included in rates. Types of meals: Full gourmet bkfst. Beds: KQDT. Clock radio, coffeemaker, desk and hot tub/spa in room. Central air. Fax, spa, telephone, fireplace, laundry facility and horse overnight stables on premises. Antiquing, art galleries, beach, live theater, museums, parks, sporting events, water sports and wineries nearby.

Location: Country.

Certificate may be used: Sunday-Thursday excludes holidays and the months of April, May and October.

Country House Inn

91 S Main St
Templeton, CA 93465-8701
(805)434-1598 (800)362-6032
Internet: www.thecountryhouseinn.com
E-mail: countryhouse@tcsn.net

Circa 1886. Built by the founder of Templeton in 1886, this Victorian home and Carriage House is now a designated historic site. Fully restored and furnished in a quaint yet comfortable style, gather in one of the fireside common rooms to relax or chat with new friends. Guest bedrooms and suites boast an assortment of pleasures that includes terry cloth robes. Several rooms have clawfoot tubs, private entrances and a porch with wicker furniture. Enjoy a gourmet breakfast in the dining room. Elegant landscaping and gardens accent the grounds. Croquet is a popular activity on the front lawn. Tour the local vineyards of this rural wine country.

Innkeeper(s): Dianne Garth. $115-130. 5 rooms with PB, 1 with FP, 1 suite. Breakfast included in rates. Types of meals: Full gourmet bkfst, early coffee/tea and afternoon tea. Beds: KQ. Reading lamp, ceiling fan, desk and fireplace in room. Parlor games and telephone on premises. Antiquing, art galleries, beach, canoeing/kayaking, fishing, golf, hiking, horseback riding, live theater, museums, parks, shopping, tennis, water sports, wineries and wine tours nearby.

Location: Wine country.

Publicity: *Los Angeles Times and PM Magazine.*

"A feast for all the senses, an esthetic delight."

Certificate may be used: April-September, Sunday-Thursday; October-March, Sunday-Saturday; last minute based on projected availability.

Ukiah

Vichy Hot Springs Resort & Inn

2605 Vichy Springs Rd
Ukiah, CA 95482-3507
(707)462-9515 Fax:(707)462-9516
Internet: www.vichysprings.com
E-mail: vichy@vichysprings.com

Circa 1854. This famous spa, now a California State Historical Landmark (#980), once attracted guests Jack London, Mark Twain, Robert Louis Stevenson, Ulysses Grant and Teddy Roosevelt. Eighteen rooms and eight cottages comprise the property. Some of the cottages are historic and some are new. The 1860s naturally warm and carbonated mineral baths remain unchanged. A hot soaking pool and historic Olympic-size pool await your arrival. A magical waterfall is a 30-minute walk along a year-round stream.

Innkeeper(s): Gilbert & Marjorie Ashoff. $125-355. 26 rooms with PB, 8 with FP, 1 suite, 8 cottages, 1 conference room. Breakfast and Sunday brunch included in rates. Types of meals: Country bkfst. Beds: QT. Modem hook-up, data port, reading lamp, CD player, refrigerator, clock radio, telephone, coffeemaker, desk, voice mail, some with fireplace, hair dryer, bath amenities, wireless Internet access, iron/ironing board and Wi-Fi high speed in room. Central air. Fax, copier, spa, swimming, naturally sparkling mineral baths, massages, facials, walking, hiking, 700 acres of private park to explore, hot pool and Olympic size pool on premises. Handicap access. Antiquing, beach, bicycling, canoeing/kayaking, fishing, golf, hiking, live theater, museums, parks, shopping, tennis, water sports, wineries, redwood parks, lakes, rivers, Sun House Museum and Montgomery Woods tallest trees in the world nearby.

Location: Country, mountains. 700 acres on property.

Publicity: Sunset, Sacramento Bee, San Jose Mercury News, Gulliver (Japan), Oregonian, Contra Costa Times, New York Times, San Francisco Chronicle, San Francisco Examiner, Adventure West, Gulliver (Italy), Bay Area Back Roads, Huell Hauser California Gold, PBS, California Farm Bureau and Too numerous to mention.

Certificate may be used: Sunday-Thursday; April-September, Sunday-Friday; October-March, excludes holidays.

Venice

Venice Beach House

15 Thirtieth Avenue
Venice, CA 90291
(310)823-1966 Fax:(310)823-1842
Internet: www.venicebeachhouse.com
E-mail: info@venicebeachhouse.com

Circa 1911. Built by Warren and Carla Wilson in 1911 in the Craftsman style of architecture, this faithfully restored home is listed in the National Register. The Wilsons' friends and family included the founder of Venice, Abbot Kinney and a close-knit group of Hollywood stars and local personalities. An ever-growing circle of friends and family are invited to share its casual elegance. Romantic guest bedrooms and spacious suites are tastefully decorated and well-furnished. James Peasgood's Room boasts a double Jacuzzi, cathedral wood ceiling and private balcony. Enjoy the ocean vista in the Pier Suite with a fireplace and sitting room. Tramp's Quarters with a pine beam ceiling and the Olympia Suite with oversized dual shower offer delightful garden views. After breakfast explore the scenic area by bicycle or walk to the beach to rollerblade, surf and people-watch.

Innkeeper(s): Brian Gannon, Mgr.. $145-235. 9 rooms, 5 with PB, 1 with FP, 2 suites. Breakfast, afternoon tea and snacks/refreshments included in rates. Types of meals: Cont plus. Beds: KQDT. Modem hook-up, data port, cable TV, reading lamp, clock radio, telephone, desk and DSL high-speed Internet access in room. Fax, library, fireplace and Venice Beach on premises. Amusement parks, beach, bicycling, canoeing/kayaking, hiking, shopping, water sports, rollerblading and surfing nearby.

Location: Ocean community.

Publicity: Washington Post - "In one of the most popular beach towns in the world, by far the most charming accommodation is the Venice Beach House" and MTV.

"In one of the most popular beach towns in the world, by far the most charming accommodation is the Venice Beach House. — Washington Post"

Certificate may be used: Nov. 30-April 1, subject to availability.

Visalia

Ben Maddox House B&B

601 N Encina St
Visalia, CA 93291-3603
(559)739-0721 (800)401-9800 Fax:(559)739-0729
Internet: www.benmaddoxhouse.com
E-mail: innkeeper@benmaddoxhouse.com

Circa 1876. Sequoia National Park is just 40 minutes away from this late 19th-century home constructed completely of redwood. The parlor, dining room and front guest bedrooms remain in their original pristine state and are tastefully furnished in period antiques. Enjoy a full breakfast served at private tables in the historic dining room or on the deck. The grounds feature a swimming pool, finch aviary, gardens and 100-year-old trees. Ask about small group special events such as weddings, showers, rehearsal dinners, family reunions, corporate retreats and meetings.

Innkeeper(s): Katina & Lucy. $110-130. 6 rooms, 4 with PB. Breakfast included in rates. Types of meals: Full bkfst. Beds: KQ. Cable TV, VCR, reading lamp, refrigerator, ceiling fan, clock radio, hair dryer, bathrobes, bath amenities, wireless Internet access and iron/ironing board in room. Central air. Fax, telephone, complimentary soft beverages, pool open from Memorial Day to Labor Day and holiday tea in the month of December on premises. Handicap access. Antiquing, bicycling, canoeing/kayaking, cross-country skiing, fishing, golf, hiking, horseback riding, live theater, museums, parks, shopping, sporting events, tennis, water sports, Sequoia National park, historic downtown area and restaurants nearby.

Location: City. Historic District.

Publicity: Southland, Fresno Bee, Visalia Times-Delta and has 3-diamond rating for AAA and CABBI.

Certificate may be used: Anytime, subject to availability.

Westport

Howard Creek Ranch

40501 N Hwy One
Westport, CA 95488
(707)964-6725 Fax:(707)964-1603
Internet: www.howardcreekranch.com
E-mail: Please Call 707-964-6725

Circa 1871. First settled as a land grant of thousands of acres, Howard Creek Ranch is now a 60-acre farm with sweeping views  of the Pacific Ocean, sandy beaches and rolling mountains. A 75-foot bridge spans a creek that flows past barns and outbuildings to the beach 200 yards away. The farmhouse is surrounded by green lawns, an award-winning flower garden, and grazing cows, horses and llama. This rustic rural location offers antiques, a hot tub, sauna and heated pool. A traditional ranch breakfast is served each morning.

Innkeeper(s): Charles & Sally Grigg. $75-198. 12 rooms, 11 with PB, 5 with FP, 2 suites, 3 cabins. Breakfast included in rates. Types of meals: Country bkfst and early coffee/tea. Beds: KQD. TV, VCR, reading lamp, refrigerator, ceiling fan, coffeemaker, desk, some with hot tub/spa and some with fireplace in room. Fax, copier, spa, sauna, library, parlor games, telephone, farm animals, hiking trails, beach-combing, whale watching (in season), birdwatching, surfing, exploring tide pools and creek running through ranch on premises. Antiquing, art galleries, beach, bicycling, canoeing/kayaking, golf, hiking, horseback riding, live theater, museums, parks, shopping, water sports, wineries, horseback riding on the beach, state parks, surfing and surf fishing, wildlife observation (fox, bobcat, mountain lion, deer), sealife observation (starfish, sea lions, whales and pelicans) nearby.

Location: Mountains, ocean community.

Publicity: San Francisco Magazine, San Francisco Chronicle, California Country Vacations, Forbes Magazine, Sunset Magazine, Diablo, FYI, Vacations (Americas Best Romantic Inns issue), PBS American Heartland and KETH Channel 54.

"This is one of the most romantic places on the planet."

Certificate may be used: Oct. 15-May 15, Sunday-Thursday, excluding holiday periods.

Willits

Beside Still Waters Farm Luxury Bed & Breakfast Cottages

30901 Sherwood Rd
Willits, CA 95490
(707)984-6130 (877)230-2171
Internet: www.besidestillwatersfarm.com
E-mail: innkeeper@besidestillwatersfarm.com

Circa 2004. Luxury bed & breakfast cottages offer privacy and pampering in a peaceful setting amidst 22 picturesque acres. Indulge in daydreams and rekindle romance while staying at these newly built accommodations in Mendocino County. Each guest suite is a separate cottage situated near the Victorian-style farmhouse for easy access to borrow a game, puzzle or browse for a CD and video. Stroll through the garden flowers. Modern amenities include aromatherapy steam showers, foot spas, heated towel bars, whirlpools for two and cast iron stove fireplaces.

Meadowood Guesthouse, ideal for families, groups and extended stays, boasts a full kitchen and laundry facilities. Breakfast is delivered to each cottage and may feature an egg entrée with fresh-picked herbs, or French toast with lavender maple syrup and homemade sausage.

Innkeeper(s): Earl & Christy Collins. $199-269. 3 cottages with PB, 3 with FP, 3 with HT, 3 with WP, 1 two-bedroom suite, 1 guest house. Breakfast and snacks/refreshments included in rates. Types of meals: Full gourmet bkfst, veg bkfst and early coffee/tea. Beds: KQT. Modem hook-up, data port, cable TV, VCR, DVD, reading lamp, stereo, refrigerator, ceiling fan, snack bar, clock radio, telephone, coffeemaker, turn-down service, desk, hot tub/spa, voice mail, fireplace, hair dryer, bathrobes, bath amenities, wireless Internet access, iron/ironing board, aromatherapy steam-showers and foot spas in room. Air conditioning. Fax, copier, spa, sauna, library, parlor games, laundry facility, gift shop and picnic areas on premises. Antiquing, art galleries, beach, bicycling, canoeing/kayaking, fishing, golf, hiking, horseback riding, live theater, museums, parks, shopping, wineries and whale watching nearby.

Location: Country, mountains.

Publicity: The San Francisco Chronicle, LA Times, Denver Post, Ventura Star, Chicago Tribune and Inn Traveler Magazine.

Certificate may be used: Sunday-Thursday, November-April, excluding holiday periods, subject to availability.

Yountville

Lavender

2020 Webber Ave
Yountville, CA 94599
(707)944-1388 (800)522-4140 Fax:(707)944-1579
Internet: www.lavendernapa.com
E-mail: lavender@foursisters.com

Circa 1999. Stroll through lavender and flower gardens or relax on the veranda of this French farmhouse located in California's Napa Valley wine country. Privacy and elegant country comfort are the order of the day in the inn's eight guest rooms decorated in bold natural colors. The main house has one guest room upstairs and one downstairs. The six cottages, each with its own private entrance and private patio, have King-size beds, spacious bathrooms with two-person bathtubs. The farm breakfast is an all-you-can-eat buffet with a variety of courses sure to please the most discriminating palate. Typical menus include such items as egg entrees, breakfast potatoes, pancakes, muffins, fresh fruit, different breads, oatmeal and cereal. Each afternoon during the complimentary teatime, guests relax with wine, cheese, crackers and baked goods like cookies, pound cake and angel food cake. Guests can walk through the entire small town of Yountville with its Vintage 1870 shopping center, cafes and historic residential homes. Or guests may prefer to check out one of the inn's bicycles and soak up the relaxed atmosphere as they pedal through town. Naturally, many guests spend the day wine tasting and some take the three-hour tour on the Wine Train as it winds its way up the valley at a leisurely five miles per hour. Nearby Calistoga has its own geyser as well as day spas known for a variety of rejuvenating baths. There is a $20 fee for an additional guest in room, except for children less than 5 years old.

Innkeeper(s): Rachel Retterer. $200-250. 8 rooms with PB, 8 with FP. Breakfast and wine included in rates. Types of meals: Full gourmet bkfst. Beds: K. Modem hook-up, data port, cable TV, reading lamp, telephone, turn-down service, desk, hot tub/spa and voice mail in room. Air conditioning. Fax, copier and bicycles on premises. Antiquing, art galleries, bicycling, fishing, golf, hiking, horseback riding, museums, parks, shopping, sporting events, tennis, water sports and wineries nearby.

Location: Wine country.

Certificate may be used: Sunday – Thursday, December through February, based on promotional discount availability and excludes special event periods, holidays and certain room types. First night must be at full rack rate to receive second night free.

Maison Fleurie

6529 Yount St
Yountville, CA 94599-1278
(707)944-2056 (800)788-0369 Fax:(707)944-9342
Internet: www.maisonfleurienapa.com
E-mail: maisonfleurie@foursisters.com

Circa 1894. Vines cover the two-foot thick brick walls of the Bakery, the Carriage House and the Main House of this French country inn. One of the Four Sisters Inns, it is reminiscent of a bucolic setting in Provence. Rooms are decorated in a warm, romantic style, some with vineyard and garden views. Rooms in the Old Bakery have fireplaces. A pool and outdoor hot tub are available and you may borrow bicycles for wandering the countryside. In the evenings, wine and hors d'oeuvres are served. Yountville, just north of Napa, offers close access to the multitude of wineries and vineyards in the valley. There is a $20 fee for an additional guest in room, except for children less than 5 years old.

Innkeeper(s): Rachel Retterer. $130-285. 13 rooms with PB, 7 with FP. Breakfast, afternoon tea and wine included in rates. Types of meals: Full gourmet bkfst. Beds: KQD. Telephone, turn-down service, hot tub/spa, terry robes and newspaper in room. Fax, bicycles, fireplace, outdoor pool and hot tub on premises. Handicap access. Antiquing and wineries nearby.

Location: Country. Napa Valley.

"Peaceful surroundings, friendly staff."

Certificate may be used: Sunday – Thursday, December through February, based on promotional discount availability and excludes special event periods, holidays and certain room types. First night must be at full rack rate to receive second night free.

Yuba City

Harkey House B&B

212 C St
Yuba City, CA 95991-5014
(530)674-1942 Fax:(530)674-1840
Internet: www.harkeyhouse.com
E-mail: lee@harkeyhouse.com

Circa 1875. An essence of romance fills this Victorian Gothic house set in a historic neighborhood. Every inch of the home has been given a special touch, from the knickknacks and photos in the sitting room to the quilts and furnishings in the guest quarters. Camilla's Cottage features a queen bed with a down comforter and extras such as an adjoining kitchen and a gas stove. Full breakfasts of muffins, fresh fruit, juice, waffles and freshly ground coffee are served in a glass-paned dining room or on the poolside patio.

Innkeeper(s): Bob & Lee Jones. $90-195. 4 rooms with PB, 2 with FP, 1 cottage, 1 conference room. Breakfast included in rates. Types of meals: Full bkfst and early coffee/tea. Beds: Q. Cable TV, reading lamp, stereo, ceiling fan, clock radio, telephone, turn-down service, desk and hot tub/spa in room. Air conditioning. TV, VCR, spa, library, parlor games, fireplace and pool on premises. Antiquing, fishing, golf, live theater, parks, shopping, water sports, birding and Sutter Buttes nearby.

Location: Mountains. Rivers.

Publicity: *Country Magazine.*

"This place is simply marvelous...the most comfortable bed in travel."

Certificate may be used: February-November, Sunday-Thursday, excludes holidays.

Colorado

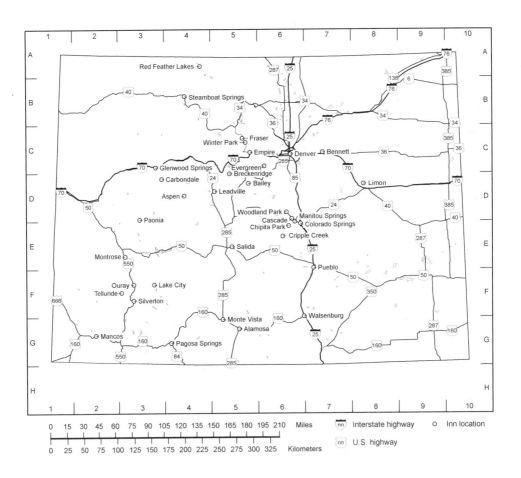

0 15 30 45 60 75 90 105 120 135 150 165 180 195 210   Miles

0 25 50 75 100 125 150 175 200 225 250 275 300 325   Kilometers

Interstate highway   O Inn location

U.S. highway

Aspen

Little Red Ski Haus

118 East Cooper Ave.
Aspen, CO 81612
(970)925-3333 (866)630-6119 Fax:(970)925-7123
Internet: www.littleredskihaus.com
E-mail: info@littleredskihaus.net

Circa 1888. People from all over the world stay at this historic Victorian bed & breakfast that is known to be the area's first. Little Red is in the historic registry and boasts a recent $1 million renovation. An elegant fireplace with an antique mantel graces the parlor and an upright piano is in the music room. Antiques furnish the elegant guest rooms. Enjoy a full gourmet breakfast in the Prospector's Cellar. In the afternoon and evening, guests gather in this charming room that boasts a fireplace and full service bar. Guests can also find time to meet friends and enjoy the hot tub deck. Located close to town, shuttle busses go to the nearby slopes. The gondola is walking distance away.

Innkeeper(s): Beverly Fiore. $159-429. 13 rooms with PB, 2 suites, 1 conference room. Breakfast included in rates. Types of meals: Full gourmet bkfst, picnic lunch and afternoon tea. Beds: KQT. Modem hook-up, data port, cable TV, VCR, reading lamp, ceiling fan, clock radio, telephone, turn-down service, desk, hot tub/spa, voice mail, some with whirlpool tubs and others have instant steam showers in room. Spa, library, parlor games, fireplace, laundry facility, ski lockers and boot room on premises. Handicap access. Antiquing, art galleries, bicycling, canoeing/kayaking, cross-country skiing, downhill skiing, fishing, golf, hiking, horseback riding, live theater, museums, parks, shopping, tennis, water sports, snowmobiling, hot air ballooning, rodeos, white-water rafting, snowshoeing, ice skating, rock climbing, paragliding, Jeep trips and motorcross trips nearby.

Location: Mountains.

Publicity: Aspen Magazine, Boulder Daily Camera, Ski Magazine - voted November 2003 "Inn of the Month," Aspen Times, Aspen Daily News, Du Page County Dairy Herald, Denver Post, ABC Chicago Affiliate, Janet Davies Show and In Gear Cable TV Show.

Certificate may be used: April-May, October-November, Dec. 1-15.

Bennett

Willow Tree Country Inn

49990 E. 64th Ave.
Bennett, CO 80102
(303)644-5551 (800)257-1241 Fax:(303)644-3801
Internet: www.willowtreebb.com
E-mail: willowtreeinn@tds.net

Circa 1920. A peaceful setting permeates this English Tudor inn that sits on 60 acres with magnificent views of the Rocky Mountains. The country décor and antique furnishings are tastefully blended in an uncluttered and inviting way. Enjoy a light supper upon arrival. Watch a glorious sunset from the large covered porch. Read in the sunroom or watch a video by the fire in the parlor. Delightful guest bedrooms boast snow-capped mountain vistas, robes, slippers, a snack basket and a stocked refrigerator. Feel pampered with a complimentary hydrotherapy foot bath and herbal foot massage. Breakfast in the dining room may start with just-baked cinnamon rolls, a fruit plate and green chili strata. Soak in the hot tub after playing croquet, badminton or horseshoes.

Innkeeper(s): Deborah & Gerald Toczek. $69-139. 3 rooms with PB. Breakfast, afternoon tea, snacks/refreshments and dinner included in rates. Types of meals: Full gourmet bkfst, veg bkfst, early coffee/tea and room service. Beds: KD. Refrigerator, ceiling fan, snack bar, clock radio, turn-down service and desk in room. Air conditioning. TV, VCR, spa, parlor games and fireplace on premises. Golf, croquet, horseshoes, badminton and puzzles nearby.

Certificate may be used: Anytime, subject to availability.

Breckenridge

Four Peaks Inn

407 S. Ridge Street
Breckenridge, CO 80424
(970)453-3813
Internet: www.fourpeaksinn.com
E-mail: reservations@fourpeaksinn.com

Circa 1880. Personalized service is the hallmark of this bed and breakfast in Breckenridge, Colorado. Gather for afternoon refreshments, relax in the library by the fire or schedule an on-site reflexology. The outdoor open-loft hot tub and sauna overlook the slopes. A guest kitchenette features a toaster oven, microwave and refrigerator. Boasting a contemporary renovation, the historic section of the home dates back to 1880. Guest bedrooms are located there and reflect the Victorian style with antiques. Banana Streusel French Toast with Amaretto Sauce and a Spinach and Sausage Frittata are popular favorites for a hearty gourmet breakfast at Four Peaks Inn. Dinners can be arranged in advance. Restaurants, shops and the free town shuttle are just outside the door. Ask about specials offered.

Innkeeper(s): Shannon and JJ Bosgraaf. $89-220. 7 rooms, 5 with PB. Types of meals: Full gourmet bkfst, veg bkfst, early coffee/tea, picnic lunch, afternoon tea and wine. Beds: KQDT. Cable TV, VCR, reading lamp, clock radio, hair dryer, bathrobes, bath amenities and iron/ironing board in room. DVD, spa, library, child care and fireplace on premises. Handicap access. Bicycling, canoeing/kayaking, cross-country skiing, downhill skiing, fishing, golf, hiking, horseback riding, live theater, museums, parks and shopping nearby.

Location: Mountains.

Certificate may be used: April-May, September-November.

Carbondale

Ambiance Inn

66 N 2nd St
Carbondale, CO 81623-2102
(970)963-3597 (800)350-1515 Fax:(970)963-1360
Internet: www.ambianceinn.com
E-mail: ambiancein@aol.com

Located in the gorgeous Crystal Valley between Aspen and Glenwood Springs, this contemporary chalet-style home offers all-season accommodations for a wonderful getaway. Relax with one of the books or magazines in the second-floor New Orleans Library, or plan the next day?s activities using the convenient desk. Themed guest bedrooms include sitting areas and soft robes. The Aspen Suite features a ski lodge décor with knotty pine paneling and snowshoes hung on the walls. It is the perfect size for two couples or a large family traveling together. In the morning, savor a lavish breakfast at the oak table in the dining room before exploring the scenic area.

Innkeeper(s): Norma & Robert Morris. Call for rates. 5 rooms. Breakfast included in rates. Types of meals: Full gourmet bkfst, veg bkfst, early coffee/tea and gourmet lunch. Beds: Q. Modem hook-up, reading lamp, refrigerator, ceiling fan, clock radio, telephone, coffeemaker, desk, hot tub/spa, some with fireplace, hair dryer, bathrobes, bath amenities and iron/ironing board in room. Air conditioning. Amusement parks, antiquing, art galleries, bicycling, canoeing/kayaking, cross-country skiing, downhill skiing, fishing, golf, hiking, horseback riding, live theater, museums, parks, shopping, sporting events, tennis, water sports and wineries nearby.

Location: Mountains.

Certificate may be used: Excludes holidays, Christmas week and peak summer weekends.

Cascade

A Rocky Mountain Lodge & Cabins

4680 Hagerman Ave
Cascade, CO 80809-1818
(719)684-2521 (888)298-0348 Fax:(719) 684-8348
Internet: www.rockymountainlodge.com
E-mail: info@rockymountainlodge.com

Circa 1936. Nestled in the Rocky Mountains at Pikes Peak, this rustic log lodge is located in the historic Ute Pass, five miles from Manitou Springs and six miles from Colorado Springs. There are six rooms in the lodge, all with private bathrooms. The Luxury Suite features a fireplace, whirlpool tub for two and oversized two-person body spray shower. Breakfast can be served in-suite. It is perfect for a honeymoon, romantic getaway or anniversary. A signature three-course breakfast is served daily to all guests. The cottage and cabin are within walking distance from the main lodge. The cabin dates to 1909 and includes two bedrooms, a kitchen, bathroom and living room with a fireplace. The two-story cottage, built during the 1930s, has a bedroom and sitting area upstairs and a kitchenette and dining room downstairs.

Innkeeper(s): Brian and Debbie Reynolds. $95-199. 9 rooms, 6 with PB, 4 with FP, 2 with WP, 1 suite, 1 cottage, 1 guest house, 1 cabin. Breakfast, afternoon tea and snacks/refreshments included in rates. Types of meals: Full gourmet bkfst, veg bkfst, early coffee/tea, picnic lunch, 3 course breakfast served for all Bed and Breakfast guests. No meals for Cabin or Cottage guests and but each have a full kitchen. Beds: QDT. Modem hook-up, data port, cable TV, VCR, DVD, reading lamp, stereo, refrigerator, ceiling fan, clock radio, telephone, coffeemaker, desk, some with hot tub/spa, some with fireplace, hair dryer, bathrobes, bath amenities, wireless Internet access, iron/ironing board, Luxury Suite has ceiling fan, clock radio, coffeemaker, DVD player, fireplace, refrigerator, telephone, two-person body spray shower, whirlpool air massage tub for two and private sitting room in room. Air conditioning. Spa, library, parlor games, gift shop, refrigerator, microwave and coffeemaker on premises. Limited handicap access. Amusement parks, antiquing, art galleries, bicycling, cross-country skiing, downhill skiing, fishing, golf, hiking, horseback riding, live theater, museums, parks, shopping, sporting events, tennis, wineries, white water rafting and train trips nearby.

Location: Country, mountains. Colorado Springs.

Publicity: Arrington's Inn Traveler Magazine, Voted "Best to Visit Again & Again", "Best with Nearby Attractions", and "Best for a Honeymoon/Anniversary" for 2004 and 2005 & 2006!.

Certificate may be used: November-April, Sunday-Thursday, subject to availability, holidays excluded.

Chipita Park

Chipita Lodge B&B

9090 Chipita Park Rd
Chipita Park, CO 80809
(719)684-8454 (877)CHI-PITA Fax:(719)684-8234
Internet: www.chipitalodge.com
E-mail: chipitainn@aol.com

Circa 1927. Overlooking Chipita Lake and at the base of Pikes Peak, this native stone and log lodge features a hot tub and gazebo with views of mountains on its two-acre knoll-top location. Formerly the local post office and general store, the lodge boasts rooms with fresh Western decor as well as rooms with Native American influences. A three-course breakfast is served with country-style entrees. Evening and afternoon refreshments are offered before the large stone fireplace in the handsome gathering room or on the deck overlooking the lake. The Garden of the Gods, Manitou Springs and Cripple Creek are nearby.

Innkeeper(s): Kevin & Martha Henry. $100-135. 3 rooms with PB, 1 conference room. Breakfast and snacks/refreshments included in rates. Types of meals: Full gourmet bkfst. Beds: Q. Modem hook-up, reading lamp, CD player, ceiling fan, clock radio and turn-down service in room. Fax, copier, spa, parlor games, telephone and fireplace on premises. Amusement parks, antiquing, art galleries, cross-country skiing, fishing, golf, hiking, horseback riding, live theater, museums, parks, shopping, sporting events and wineries nearby.

Location: Mountains.

Publicity: Denver Post.

Certificate may be used: Nov. 1-March 31, Sunday-Thursday, excluding Thanksgiving, Christmas, New Year's, Valentine's, Easter.

Colorado Springs

Black Forest B&B Lodge & Cabins

11170 Black Forest Rd
Colorado Springs, CO 80908-3986
(719)495-4208 (800)809-9901 Fax:(719)495-0688
Internet: www.blackforestbb.com
E-mail: blackforestbb@msn.com

Circa 1984. Surrounded by the scenic beauty of the Pikes Peak region of Colorado, Black Forest Bed and Breakfast Lodge and Cabins in Colorado Springs sits at the highest point east of the Rocky Mountains. Ponderosa Pines, golden Aspens and fragrant meadows highlight the 20 scenic acres that  boast panoramic views. The rustic mountain setting includes a log pavilion and cabins. Stay in a guest bedroom or suite with a stocked kitchen or kitchenette, fireplace, and whirlpool tub. Select a movie to watch from the video collection. A breakfast tray is delivered to the room each morning. There is an abundance of outdoor activities to enjoy in the area.

Innkeeper(s): Rex and Susan Redden. $75-350. 6 rooms with PB, 5 with FP, 1 with WP, 2 two-bedroom, 2 three-bedroom and 1 four-bedroom suites, 2 cottages, 3 guest houses, 2 cabins, 1 conference room. Breakfast and snacks/refreshments included in rates. Types of meals: Cont plus and early coffee/tea. Beds: KQDT. Modem hook-up, data port, cable TV, VCR, reading lamp, CD player, refrigerator, ceiling fan, snack bar, clock radio, telephone, coffeemaker, desk, most with fireplace, hair dryer, bathrobes, bath amenities, wireless Internet access and iron/ironing board in room. Fax, copier, library, parlor games, laundry facility and gift shop on premises. Limited handicap access. Antiquing, art galleries, bicycling, canoeing/kayaking, cross-country skiing, fishing, golf, hiking, horseback riding, live theater, museums, parks, shopping, sporting events, tennis, water sports, wineries and focus on the family nearby.

Location: Country, mountains.

Certificate may be used: Accepts Weekends, Anytime, subject to availability, Anytime, Last Minute-Based on Availability.

Cheyenne Canon Inn

2030 W Cheyenne Blvd
Colorado Springs, CO 80906
(719)633-0625 (800)633-0625 Fax:(800)633-8826
Internet: cheyennecanoninn.com
E-mail: info@cheyennecanoninn.com

Circa 1921. This massive, 10,000-square foot mansion features Arts and Crafts-style architecture. The manor was built as an upscale casino and bordello. During its heyday, the famous guests included the Marx Brothers and Lon Chaney. The casino room now serves as the location for the inn's nightly wine and cheese hour. The room has more than 100 panes of glass affording views of Cheyenne Canon and Cheyenne Mountain.

The guest rooms and adjacent honeymoon cottage are decorated with treasures and antiques from around the world. There is a greenhouse spa on the second floor and complimentary beverages and fruit always are available. Modem outlets, TVs and in-room phones are among the amenities for business travelers. Downtown Colorado Springs is minutes away, and hiking trails and waterfalls are across the street.

Innkeeper(s): Kevin & Izel Cooke. $105-230. 10 rooms with PB, 4 with FP, 3 suites, 1 cottage, 2 conference rooms. Types of meals: Full bkfst, early coffee/tea, snacks/refreshments and gourmet dinner. Beds: KQ. Cable TV, ceiling fan, telephone, turn-down service and hair dryers in room. Air conditioning. Fax, library and day spa on premises. Antiquing, fishing, golf, hiking, live theater, parks, shopping, sporting events and gambling nearby.

Location: City, mountains.

Publicity: *Denver Post, Colorado Source, Beacon, National Geographic Traveler and Country Inns.*

"It truly was 'home away from home.' You have made it so welcoming and warm. Needless to say our breakfasts at home will never come close to the Cheyenne Canon Inn!!"

Certificate may be used: October through April, Sunday-Thursday.

Holden House-1902 Bed & Breakfast Inn

1102 W Pikes Peak Ave
Colorado Springs, CO 80904-4347
(719)471-3980 (888)565-3980 Fax:(719)471-4740
Internet: www.holdenhouse.com
E-mail: mail@holdenhouse.com

Circa 1902. Built by the widow of a prosperous rancher and businessman, this Victorian inn has rooms named after the

Colorado towns in which the Holden's owned mining interests. The main house, adjacent carriage house and Victorian house next door include the Cripple Creek, Aspen, Silverton, Goldfield and Independence suites. The inn's suites boast fireplaces and oversized tubs for two. Guests can relax in the living room with fireplace, front parlor, veranda with mountain views or garden with gazebo and fountains. There are friendly cats in residence.

Innkeeper(s): Sallie & Welling Clark. $140-160. 5 rooms, 5 with FP, 5 suites. Breakfast, snacks/refreshments, hors d'oeuvres and wine included in rates. Types of meals: Full gourmet bkfst, early coffee/tea and afternoon tea. Beds: Q. Modem hook-up, data port, cable TV, DVD, reading lamp, CD player, refrigerator, ceiling fan, clock radio, telephone, turn-down service, desk, fireplace, hair dryer, bathrobes, bath amenities, iron/ironing board and tubs for two in room. Air conditioning. VCR, fax, copier, library, parlor games and gift shop on premises. Limited handicap access. Antiquing, art galleries, bicycling, fishing, golf, hiking, horseback riding, live theater, museums, parks, shopping, sporting events, tennis, wineries, historic sites, rock climbing and whitewater rafting nearby.

Location: City, mountains. Central to downtown & Historic District.

Publicity: *Denver Post, Victorian Homes, Pikes Peak Journal, Glamour, Country Inns, Vacations, Rocky Mountain News, Cats, Rocky Mountain Motorist, Colorado Springs Business Journal, Colorado Springs Gazette, Colorado Homes and Lifestyles, Home & Away, Country Register, Home Magazine, Rocky Mountain Resorts, KKTV 11, KRDO Radio/TV, KOAA 5/30, FOX News, KVOR Radio, KKLI Radio and 1460 KKCS.*

"Your love of this house and nostalgia makes a very delightful experience."

Certificate may be used: Oct. 15-April 30, Sunday-Thursday, excludes holidays.

Old Town GuestHouse

115 S 26th St
Colorado Springs, CO 80904
(719)632-9194 (888)375-4210 Fax:(719)632-9026
Internet: www.oldtown-guesthouse.com
E-mail: luxury@oldtown-guesthouse.com

Circa 1997. Serving as the gateway to Old Colorado City, this recently built urban inn is surrounded by galleries, boutiques and restaurants. The three-story brick Federal-style design is in keeping with the 1859 period architecture of the historic area. Enjoy the breathtaking views of Pike's Peak and Garden of the Gods. It is entirely handicap accessible, soundproof, has an elevator, sprinklers and a security system, and boasts a four-diamond rating. International videoconferencing is available with WIFI 802.11 wireless fidelity hot spot. Play pool or work out on equipment in the game room and plan to join the innkeepers for a daily social hour. Elegant guest bedrooms are named after flowers and offer luxurious comfort with fireplaces, steam showers or hot tubs on private porches. Linger over breakfast in the indoor/outdoor fireside dining room.

Innkeeper(s): Shirley & Don Wick. $99-215. 8 rooms with PB, 5 with FP, 4 with HT, 1 two-bedroom suite, 1 conference room. Breakfast and snacks/refreshments included in rates. Types of meals: Full bkfst, early coffee/tea, wine, Evening Reception w/Wine, Beer, Sodas and Snacks. Beds: KQT. Cable TV, VCR, DVD, reading lamp, CD player, refrigerator, ceiling fan, clock radio, telephone, coffeemaker, turn-down service, desk, most with hot tub/spa, voice mail, most with fireplace, hair dryer, bathrobes, wireless Internet access, iron/ironing board, steam showers and private outside hot tubs in room. Central air. Fax, copier, spa, library, parlor games, gift shop, Exercise Equipment and Pool table on premises. Handicap access. Antiquing, art galleries, bicycling, cross-country skiing, fishing, golf, hiking, horseback riding, live theater, museums, parks, shopping, sporting events, tennis, gold mine, Cave of the Winds, cliff dwellings, Olympic Training Center and Broadmoor Hotel nearby.

Location: City.

Publicity: *Colorado Springs Gazette, Colorado Springs Business Journal, Sunset Magazine, NBC, CBS and ABC.*

Certificate may be used: Last minute subject to availability.

Room at the Inn A Victorian Bed & Breakfast

618 N Nevada Ave
Colorado Springs, CO 80903-1006
(719)442-1896 (888)442-1896 Fax:(719)442-6802
Internet: www.roomattheinn.com
E-mail: rooms@roomattheinn.com

Circa 1896. A Colorado pioneer built this Queen Anne Victorian, a delightful mix of turret, gables and gingerbread trim. While restoring their century-old Victorian, the innkeepers discovered several hand-painted murals had once decorated the interior. Original fireplace mantels and a collection of antiques add to the nostalgic ambiance. Fresh flowers, turn-down service and a bountiful breakfast are just a few of the amenities. Several rooms include a fireplace or double whirlpool tub.

Innkeeper(s): Dorian & Linda Ciolek. $109-160. 8 rooms with PB, 4 with FP, 2 suites. Breakfast, afternoon tea and snacks/refreshments included in rates. Types of meals: Full bkfst and early coffee/tea. Beds: Q. Reading lamp, telephone, desk, clocks and whirlpool tubs in room. Air conditioning. VCR, fax, copier, parlor games and fireplace on premises. Handicap access. Antiquing, fishing, golf, live theater, parks, shopping, sporting events, museums, fine arts center, Colorado College and downtown nearby.

Location: City.

Publicity: *Denver Post and Colorado Springs Gazette-Telegraph.*

Certificate may be used: Sunday-Thursday, Oct. 15-April 1, subject to availability, not valid on holidays and special events.

Cripple Creek

Whispering Pines Bed and Breakfast

PO Box 1317
Cripple Creek, CO 80813
(719)689-2316
Internet: www.whisperingpinesbandb.net
E-mail: info@whisperingpinesbandb.net

A newly built, Whispering Pines Bed and Breakfast sits on ten acres in the Rocky Mountains, one mile from the historic gold mining town of Cripple Creek, Colorado. Incredible views of several ranges, including the Sangre de Cristo Mountains surround the Victorian-style B&B that boasts natural rock outcroppings, large pine trees and wildflowers. Soak up the sun and the beauty while relaxing on the huge outdoor covered deck with two wicker swings. Game and pool tables are in the recreation room and the community room has a microwave, refrigerator and satellite TV. Beverages are available anytime. Feel pampered in a guest bedroom with a two-person hydrotherapy air tub, some with underwater lights; or stay in a romantic suite with a fireplace. A three-course breakfast welcomes hearty appetites.

Innkeeper(s): Peggy and Ed Schillerberg. Call for rates. Call inn for details. Breakfast and afternoon tea included in rates. Types of meals: Full gourmet bkfst, early coffee/tea and room service. TV, VCR, stereo, refrigerator, ceiling fan, telephone, coffeemaker, desk, hot tub/spa, some with fireplace, hair dryer, bathrobes, bath amenities, iron/ironing board, private baths, hydrotherapy air tubs and satellite TV in all rooms in room. Spa, parlor games and recreation room with pool table and game table on premises.

Certificate may be used: Anytime, subject to availability except for July and August.

Empire

Mad Creek B&B

167 Park Avenue
Empire, CO 80438-0404
(303)569-2003 (888)266-1498
Internet: www.madcreekbnb.com
E-mail: madmadam@aol.com

Circa 1881. There is just the right combination of Victorian décor with lace, flowers, antiques and gingerbread trim on the façade of this mountain town cottage. The home-away-from-home atmosphere is inviting and the Eastlake furnishings are comfortable. Relax in front of the rock fireplace while watching a movie, peruse the library filled with local lore or plan an adventure with local maps and guide books. Empire was once a mining town, conveniently located within 20 to 60 minutes of at least six major ski areas.

Innkeeper(s): Myrna & Tonya Payne. $75-105. 3 rooms with PB. Breakfast, afternoon tea and snacks/refreshments included in rates. Types of meals: Full bkfst and early coffee/tea. Beds: KQD. Reading lamp, ceiling fan, toiletries and down comforters in room. TV, VCR and outdoor hot tub and gazebo where breakfast is served when weather permits among the beautiful wildflower gardens on premises. Antiquing, cross-country skiing, downhill skiing, fishing, horseback riding, parks, shopping, water sports and gambling nearby.

Location: Mountains. Rivers.

Certificate may be used: Oct. 15-Nov. 20, Sunday-Thursday; April 16-May 20, Sunday-Thursday.

The Peck House

83 Sunny Ave.
Empire, CO 80438-0428
(303)569-9870 Fax:(303)569-2743
Internet: www.thepeckhouse.com
E-mail: info@thepeckhouse.com

Circa 1862. Built as a residence for gold mine owner James Peck, this is the oldest hotel still in operation in Colorado. Many pieces of original furniture brought here by ox cart remain in the inn, including a red antique fainting couch and walnut headboards. Rooms such as the Conservatory provide magnificent views of the eastern slope of the Rockies, and a panoramic view of Empire Valley can be seen from the old front porch.

Innkeeper(s): Gary & Sally St. Clair. $65-125. 11 rooms, 9 with PB, 1 suite. Breakfast included in rates. Types of meals: Cont, hors d'oeuvres, wine and gourmet dinner. Restaurant on premises. Beds: QDT. Reading lamp and bath amenities in room. Fax, spa, library, parlor games, telephone, fireplace and gift shop on premises. Antiquing, art galleries, bicycling, cross-country skiing, downhill skiing, fishing, hiking, horseback riding, museums, parks, shopping, Gold Panning and Rafting nearby.

Location: Country, mountains.

Publicity: *American West, Rocky Mountain News, Denver Post and Colorado Homes.*

Certificate may be used: January-May and October-November, Sunday through Thursday, subject to availability.

Evergreen

Bears Inn B&B

27425 Spruce Lane
Evergreen, CO 80439
(303)670-1205 (800)863-1205 Fax:(303)670-8542
Internet: www.bearsinn.com
E-mail: booknow@bearsinn.com

Circa 1924. Guests have been drawn to the stunning mountain views and tradition of hospitality at this historic lodge since the 1920s. Originally a summer resort, this bed and breakfast is now open for year-round enjoyment. The comfortable rustic interior boasts exposed logs and hardwood floors. Gather to read or relax by the inviting, large stone fireplace in the Great Room. Guest bedrooms are decorated and furnished to reflect a theme. Antiques and clawfoot tubs add a nostalgic elegance. Linger over a gourmet candlelight breakfast each morning. Soak up the scenery on the spacious deck with a gas log campfire, or in the outdoor hot tub. Biking, hiking, fishing, ice skating, and cross-country skiing are some of the myriad of local activities available. Wedding parties, as well as corporate, association and religious retreats are always welcome. Visit Denver just 35 miles away.

Innkeeper(s): Vicky Bock. $120-200. 11 rooms with PB, 1 suite, 1 cabin, 1 conference room. Breakfast and snacks/refreshments included in rates. Types of meals: Full gourmet bkfst, veg bkfst and afternoon tea. Beds: KQ. Modem hook-up, data port, cable TV, VCR, reading lamp, clock radio, telephone and wireless Internet access in room. Fax, copier, spa, library, parlor games and fireplace on premises. Amusement parks, antiquing, art galleries, bicycling, canoeing/kayaking, cross-country skiing, downhill skiing, fishing, golf, hiking, horseback riding, live theater, museums, parks, shopping, sporting events, tennis, water sports and wineries nearby.

Location: Mountains.

Certificate may be used: October-April, Sunday-Thursday.

Fraser

Wild Horse Inn Bed and Breakfast

PO Box 609
Fraser, CO 80442
(970)726-0456 Fax:(970)726-9678
Internet: www.wildhorseinn.com
E-mail: info@wildhorseinn.com

Circa 1994. Surrounded by majestic mountains, this inn was built from handhewn 400-year-old Engleman pine logs, moss-covered rock and huge picture windows. Sitting among acres of meadows and trees on a ridge above Fraser Valley, the casual lodge atmosphere exudes a rustic flair with superb hospitality and gracious service. Plan the next day's activities by the massive stone fireplace. Read a book from the library. Munch on a treat from the bottomless cookie jar. Each spacious guest bedroom features a private balcony, cozy robes and a whirlpool bath. Taste buds are teased and tempted with locally roasted coffee, blackberry scones, orange muffins or brioche. Ham crisps with baked eggs and mushrooms, Mexican Frittata or Lemon Souffle Crepes are additional breakfast favorites served in the dining room. Schedule a massage, soak in the hot tub or lounge on a sun deck.

Innkeeper(s): John Cribari and Christine French. $165-245. 10 rooms with PB, 3 cabins. Breakfast, afternoon tea and snacks/refreshments included in rates. Types of meals: Full gourmet bkfst, veg bkfst, early coffee/tea, picnic lunch and room service. Beds: KQT. Modem hook-up, data port, TV, VCR, reading lamp, clock radio, telephone, robes and slippers, private balconies and jetted tubs in room. Fax, spa, sauna, library, parlor games, fireplace, gift shop, massage services, fitness equipment, movie library and winter-season soups on premises. Antiquing, art galleries, bicycling, canoeing/kayaking, cross-country skiing, downhill skiing, fishing, golf, hiking, horseback riding, museums, parks, shopping, water sports, Rocky Mountain National Park, rafting, mountain biking, hot air ballooning, snowmobiling, dog sled rides and ice skating nearby.

Location: Mountains.

Publicity: *Quick Escapes and Travel & Leisure.*

Certificate may be used: April, May, October-Nov. 15.

Glenwood Springs

Sunlight Mountain Inn B&B

10252 County Rd 117
Glenwood Springs, CO 81601
(970)945-5225 (800)733-4757 Fax:(970)947-1900
Internet: sunlightinn.com
E-mail: innkeeper@sunlightinn.com

Circa 1968. Located at the foot of Sunlight Mountain Resort Ski Area, this lodge provides cozy guest rooms decorated in a casual Western style. One room has a fireplace and whirlpool tub. Four Mile Creek runs through the property, which is located at 8,000 feet. The inn originally was known as the Apple Inn and was built by a prominent local citizen, instrumental in the development of the nearby Sunlight Ski Area. A full breakfast, including such items as blueberry pancakes, haystack eggs or perhaps an apple dish is served in the inn's dining room, which overlooks the ski area. During the

winter season, dinner is served. The inn's cuisine is American country — Western style. The inn has an outdoor hot tub. Snowmobiling and horseback riding excursions are available nearby. The inn is 12 miles from a renown hot springs.

Innkeeper(s): Gretchenn DuBois. $65-164. 20 rooms with PB, 1 with FP. Breakfast included in rates. Types of meals: Full gourmet bkfst. Beds: KQDT. Clock radio, telephone and coffeemaker in room. TV, VCR, spa, fireplace and full bar on premises. Art galleries, bicycling, canoeing/kayaking, cross-country skiing, downhill skiing, fishing, golf, hiking, horseback riding, parks, shopping, water sports, snowmobiling and hot springs pool nearby.

Location: Mountains.

Certificate may be used: Anytime, subject to availability.

Leadville

Peri & Ed's Mountain Hide Away

201 W 8th St
Leadville, CO 80461-3529
(719)486-0716 (800)933-3715 Fax:(719)486-2181
Internet: www.mountainhideaway.com
E-mail: solder@mountainhideaway.com

Circa 1879. This former boarding house was built during the boom days of Leadville. Families can picnic on the large lawn sprinkled with wildflowers under soaring pines. Shoppers and history buffs can enjoy exploring historic Main Street, one block away. The surrounding mountains are a natural playground offering a wide variety of activities, and the innkeepers will be happy to let you know their favorite spots and help with directions. The sunny Augusta Tabor room features a sprawling king-size bed with a warm view of the rugged peaks.

Innkeeper(s): Eva Vigil. $49-129. 10 rooms with PB, 2 with FP, 2 cottages. Breakfast included in rates. Types of meals: Full bkfst. Beds: KQDT. Ceiling fan and clock radio in room. VCR, spa, library, parlor games and telephone on premises. Antiquing, cross-country skiing, downhill skiing, fishing, live theater, parks and shopping nearby.

Location: Mountains.

Certificate may be used: October-Dec. 15, April 15-June 30, Monday-Wednesday.

The Ice Palace Inn Bed & Breakfast

813 Spruce St
Leadville, CO 80461-3555
(719)486-8272 (800)754-2840 Fax:(719)486-0345
Internet: icepalaceinn.com
E-mail: stay@icepalaceinn.com

Circa 1899. Innkeeper Kami Kolakowski was born in this historic Colorado town, and it was her dream to one day return and run a bed & breakfast. Now with husband Giles, she has created a restful retreat out of this turn-of-the-century home built with lumber from the famed Leadville Ice Palace. Giles and Kami have filled the home with antiques and pieces of history from the Ice Palace and the town. Guests are treated to a mouth-watering gourmet breakfast with treats such as stuffed French toast or German apple pancakes. Stay in one of our two suites located in the three-story turret and enjoy the incredible view while soaking in a jetted hot tub.

Innkeeper(s): Giles & Kami Kolakowski. $89-169. 5 rooms with PB, 5 with FP, 2 with HT. Breakfast, afternoon tea and snacks/refreshments included in rates. Types of meals: Full gourmet bkfst, veg bkfst, early coffee/tea and room service. Beds: KQDT. Cable TV, VCR, reading lamp, stereo, refrigerator, ceiling fan, clock radio, telephone, coffeemaker, turn-down service, desk, hot tub/spa and fireplace in room. Fax, copier, spa, library, parlor games, gift shop and hot tub on premises. Antiquing, art galleries, bicycling, canoeing/kayaking, cross-country skiing, downhill skiing, fishing, golf, hiking, horseback riding, live theater, museums, parks, shopping, tennis and water sports nearby.

Location: Mountains.

Publicity: *Herald Democrat, The Denver Post, The Great Divide, Good Morning America, CNN, The Fox Report and National Public Radio.*

Certificate may be used: Monday-Thursday year-round; any day in April, May, October and November, excluding holidays, based on availability.

Mancos

Sundance Bear Lodge

38890 Hwy 184, Box 1045
Mancos, CO 81328
(970)533-1504 (866)529-2480
Internet: www.sundancebear.com
E-mail: sue@sundancebear.com

Circa 1985. The Sundance Bear Lodge includes a main lodge, a log cabin, and the guest house, which is a separate three-bedroom home in the trees. It's near Indian digs in the Mesa Verde National Park and Four Corners region. Mancos is a rustic working ranch community. A full breakfast, snack and refreshment are provided. Guests can enjoy hiking, horseback riding, golf, fishing, skiing and bicycling or just stay on site and enjoy the solitude and the beautiful views.

Innkeeper(s): Susan & Bob Scott. $99-185. 5 rooms, 4 with PB, 1 with FP, 1 guest house, 2 cabins. Breakfast and snacks/refreshments included in rates. Types of meals: Full bkfst, veg bkfst, early coffee/tea and Breakfast available between 7:30 and 9:30 AM. Beds: KQDT. TV, VCR, reading lamp, CD player, ceiling fan, clock radio, coffeemaker and hair dryer in room. DVD, fax, copier, spa, sauna, library, telephone, fireplace, laundry facility, horse corral and high-speed Internet on premises. Handicap access. Art galleries, bicycling, cross-country skiing, fishing, golf, hiking, horseback riding, live theater, parks, shopping, wineries, Durango-Silverton narrow gauge train, Mesa Verde National Park and San Juan Skyway nearby.

Location: Country, mountains.

Certificate may be used: November-March, subject to availability; Applies to lodge rooms and guesthouse.

Manitou Springs

Avenue Hotel, A Victorian B&B

711 Manitou Ave
Manitou Springs, CO 80829-1809
(719)685-1277 (800)294-1277
Internet: www.AvenueHotelBandB.com
E-mail: info@avenuehotelbandb.com

Circa 1886. One of Manitou Spring's original hotels, this 1886 Queen Anne shingled Victorian is in the Historic Preservation District, listed in the National Register. Four guest rooms, three

suites and Carriage House are comfortably appointed: from the exotic Oasis Room with its hints of the Far East to the elegance of the Peonies Room, a romantic favorite with King bed and clawfoot tub. Start the day with a hearty breakfast that includes courses like waffles with fresh strawberries and whipped cream, omelets and fresh fruit. Relax on the large front porch or stroll through town shops and restaurants. Within walking or driving distance is the Cog Railroad, Pikes Peak, Cave of the Winds, Cliff Dwellings, the Air Force Academy, the Commonwheel Artist Co-op and a number of museums and art galleries. Hikers will enjoy Mueller State Park, Waldo Canyon, Intemann and Barr Trails and Garden of the Gods.

Innkeeper(s): Kevin Abney . $75-145. 8 rooms, 7 with PB, 3 with FP, 3 total suites, including 2 two-bedroom suites, 1 cottage. Breakfast and snacks/refreshments included in rates. Types of meals: Full bkfst and early coffee/tea. Beds: KQDT. Cable TV, reading lamp, ceiling fan, clock radio, desk, some with hot tub/spa, most with fireplace, hair dryer, wireless Internet access and iron/ironing board in room. VCR, DVD, fax, copier, spa, library, parlor games, telephone and massages on premises. Antiquing, art galleries, bicycling, fishing, golf, hiking, horseback riding, live theater, museums, parks, shopping, sporting events and tennis nearby.

Location: Mountains.

Publicity: *Camille's Magic.*

Certificate may be used: Nov.1 to April 30, Sunday-Thursday, excluding holidays and special events.

Red Crags B&B Inn

302 El Paso Blvd
Manitou Springs, CO 80829-2308
(719)685-1920 (800)721-2248 Fax:(719)685-1073
Internet: www.redcrags.com
E-mail: info@redcrags.com

Circa 1880. Well-known in this part of Colorado, this unique, four-story Victorian mansion sits on a bluff with a combination of views that includes Pikes Peak, Manitou Valley, Garden of the Gods and the city of Colorado Springs. There are antiques throughout the house. The formal dining room features a rare cherrywood Eastlake fireplace. Two of the suites include double whirlpool tubs.  Outside, guests can walk through beautifully landscaped gardens or enjoy a private picnic area with a barbecue pit and a spectacular view. Wine is served in the evenings.

Innkeeper(s): Brett Maddox. $100-200. 8 rooms with PB, 8 with FP, 5 total suites, including 1 two-bedroom suite. Breakfast, afternoon tea, snacks/refreshments and wine included in rates. Types of meals: Full gourmet bkfst, veg bkfst and early coffee/tea. Beds: K. Data port, reading lamp, snack bar, clock radio, telephone, desk, hot tub/spa, fireplace, feather beds, TV available upon request, some with two-person jetted tubs and 3 with air conditioning in room. Fax, copier, spa, parlor games and gift shop on premises. Antiquing, art galleries, bicycling, cross-country skiing, fishing, golf, hiking, horseback riding, live theater, museums, parks, shopping, sporting events, tennis, Pikes Peak, Olympic Training Center, Focus on the Family, Glen Eyrie Castle and Cave of the Winds nearby.

Location: City, mountains.

Publicity: *Rocky Mountain News, Bridal Guide, Denver Post, Los Angeles Times, Springs Woman, Colorado Springs Gazette and Front Range Living.*

"What a beautiful, historical and well-preserved home - exceptional hospitality and comfort. What wonderful people! Highly recommended!"

Certificate may be used: Oct. 15 to April 30, Sunday-Thursday; excluding holidays, subject to availability.

Monte Vista

The Windmill B&B

4340 W Hwy 160
Monte Vista, CO 81144
(719)852-0438 (800)467-3441
Internet: www.thewindmillbandb.com

Circa 1959. This Southwestern-style inn affords panoramic views of the surrounding Sangre De Cristo and San Juan mountain ranges. The 22-acre grounds still include the namesake windmill that once was used to irrigate water in the yard and garden. Now it stands guard over the hot tub. Each of the guest rooms is decorated in a different theme, with a few antiques placed here and there. The plentiful country breakfast is served in a dining room with mountain views.

Innkeeper(s): Sharon & Dennis Kay. $95-125. 4 rooms with PB. Breakfast and snacks/refreshments included in rates. Types of meals: Full gourmet bkfst and early coffee/tea. Beds: KQT. Reading lamp, telephone, turn-down service and desk in room. TV, VCR, spa, parlor games, fireplace and windmill on premises. Handicap access. Antiquing, art galleries, bicycling, cross-country skiing, downhill skiing, fishing, golf, hiking, horseback riding, live theater, museums, parks and shopping nearby.

Location: Mountains.

Certificate may be used: Sunday-Thursday.

Montrose

Uncompahgre Bed and Breakfast

21049 Uncompahgre Rd.
Montrose, CO 81401
(970)240-4000 (800)318-8127 Fax:(970)249-6546
Internet: www.uncbb.com
E-mail: uncompahgre_bnb@yahoo.net

Remodeled both inside and out, this B&B is the perfect base for visiting this year-round scenic locale. The Black Canyon of the Gunnison, America's 55th national park, is only one-half hour away. Go horseback riding or white water rafting. Tour the Ute Museum, take a narrow gauge train trip from Silverton to Durango, or attend a hot air balloon festival. The Montrose Aquatic Center offers an indoor swimming facility. Plan each day's excursions while relaxing in the great room by the fireplace. Stay in the romantic French Country Room with a two-person Jacuzzi, electric fireplace, CD music and candlelight. A complete breakfast can be enjoyed in-room or in the dining room. One of the guest bedrooms is wheelchair accessible and some feature small refrigerators and microwaves.

Innkeeper(s): Richard and Barbara Helm. $70-120. 9 rooms with PB, 1 with FP, 1 with WP. Breakfast, afternoon tea and hors d'oeuvres included in rates. Types of meals: Full gourmet bkfst, veg bkfst and early coffee/tea. Beds: KQT. Data port, cable TV, VCR, DVD, reading lamp, CD player, refrigerator, ceiling fan, clock radio, telephone, coffeemaker, desk, hot tub/spa, some with fireplace, hair dryer, bathrobes and iron/ironing board in room. Fax, copier, library, parlor games and laundry facility on premises. Handicap access. Antiquing, beach, cross-country skiing, downhill skiing, fishing, golf, hiking, horseback riding, live theater, parks, shopping, tennis, wineries and elk and deer hunting in season nearby.

Location: Country. Black Canyon of the Gunnison National Park.

Publicity: *Montrose Daily Press, Denver Post and Public Television.*

Certificate may be used: November-April.

Ouray

Wiesbaden Hot Springs Spa & Lodgings

625 5th St
Ouray, CO 81427
(970)325-4347 Fax:(970)325-4358
Internet: www.wiesbadenhotsprings.com

Circa 1879. Built directly above natural mineral hot springs, this historic lodging establishment has a European flair. Below the main lodge and into the mountain is the natural Vaporcave, where the hot springs flow from thousands of feet below the earth's surface into a 108 degree soaking pool. The remains of an adobe where Chief Ouray resided while using the sacred water

for its medicinal and healing qualities can be seen on the property. The Vaporcave, outdoor swimming pool and Lorelei, a privately rented outdoor soaking spa are all continually flowing hot springs. Therapeutic massage, Raindrop, LaStone and Dry Brushings are also offered as well as Aveda Concept Spa facials, wraps and polishes. The Wiesbaden is considered a place of unequaled ambiance.

Innkeeper(s): Linda Wright-Minter. $94-345. 20 rooms with PB, 2 with FP, 2 total suites, including 1 two-bedroom suite, 2 cottages, 2 guest houses. Types of meals: Early coffee/tea. Beds: KQDT. Cable TV, reading lamp, refrigerator, ceiling fan and telephone in room. Fax, spa, swimming and fireplace on premises. Antiquing, art galleries, bicycling, cross-country skiing, downhill skiing, fishing, golf, hiking, horseback riding, museums, parks, shopping, tennis and water sports nearby.

Location: Mountains.

Publicity: *Travel & Leisure, National Geographic Traveler, Spa, Sunset, Money, Lifestyles, New York Times and many other publications.*

Certificate may be used: Nov. 15-May 15, Sunday through Thursday excluding all holidays. All natural hot springs pools on premises.

Pagosa Springs

Canyon Crest Lodge

201A Yeoman Dr
Pagosa Springs, CO 81147
(970)731-3773 (877)731-1377 Fax:(970)731-5502
Internet: www.canyoncrestlodge.com
E-mail: canyoncrest@pagosa.net

Circa 1998. Sitting on 40 acres of tall pine trees and mountainous rocky terrain with magnificent views of Pagosa Peak, Valley and the Great Divide, this English Country House is a traditional rock structure with 18-inch thick walls. Gather by the large fireplace in the lounge and enjoy the relaxing ambiance. Guest suites are named after famous castles, and can be accessed from the private upper deck. Each suite includes a comfortable sitting area with a TV, and a walk-in closet with robes and slippers. Breakfast is served in the dining room and can be taken to the dining deck or back to the room. Other meals can be arranged in advance. Soak in the hot tub overlooking the gorgeous scenery.

Innkeeper(s): Valerie Green. $100-200. 6 rooms, 1 with FP, 6 suites, 1 conference room. Types of meals: Country bkfst, veg bkfst, early coffee/tea, picnic lunch, afternoon tea, gourmet dinner and room service. Beds: KQ. Modem hook-up, data port, TV, VCR, reading lamp, stereo, refrigerator, snack bar, clock radio, telephone, turn-down service, hot tub/spa and voice mail in room. Fax, copier, spa, sauna, bicycles, library, parlor games, fireplace and laundry facility on premises. Handicap access. Antiquing, art galleries, bicycling, canoeing/kayaking, cross-country skiing, downhill skiing, fishing, golf, hiking, horseback riding, live theater, museums, parks, shopping, sporting events, tennis, water sports and wineries nearby.

Location: Mountains.

Certificate may be used: Anytime, April, May and October, subject to availability.

Paonia

The Bross Hotel B&B

312 Onarga Ave.
Paonia, CO 81428
(970)527-6776 Fax:(970)527-7737
Internet: www.paonia-inn.com
E-mail: brosshotel@paonia.com

Circa 1906. This turn-of-the-century western hotel was restored to its original splendor with a front porch and balcony while being updated with late-century amenities in the mid-1990s. Wood floors and trim, dormer windows and exposed brick walls all add to the Victorian decor. For pleasure, relax in the sitting area or library/TV/game room. A conference room and communications center is perfect for business. Guest bedrooms feature antiques and handmade quilts. Some rooms can be adjoined into suites. Breakfast is an adventure in seasonal culinary delights that cover the antique back bar in the dining room. Visit Black Canyon of the Gunnison National Park, Grand Mesa, West Elk and Ragged Wilderness areas and Fort Uncompaghre-a Living History Museum.

Innkeeper(s): Linda Lentz . $100-115. 10 rooms with PB, 1 conference room. Breakfast and snacks/refreshments included in rates. Types of meals: Full gourmet bkfst, veg bkfst and early coffee/tea. Beds: KQDT. Modem hook-up, data port, ceiling fan and telephone in room. TV, VCR, fax, copier, spa, library and parlor games on premises. Antiquing, art galleries, bicycling, canoeing/kayaking, cross-country skiing, fishing, golf, hiking, horseback riding, museums, parks, shopping, wineries, dinosaur dig and explore the many activities of the Black Canyon of the Gunnison National Park nearby.

Location: Mountains.

Publicity: Denver Post, Grand Junction Sentinel, 52-80 Magazine (the Denver City Magazine, September 2004), Nexus ("brown palace of the town," September-October 2003) and Gourmet (July 2004).

Certificate may be used: Anytime, November-April, subject to availability.

Red Feather Lakes

Red Feather Ranch B&B and Horse Hotel
3105 CR 69
Red Feather Lakes, CO 80545
(970)881-3715 (877)881-5215
Internet: www.redfeatherranch.com
E-mail: info@redfeatherranch.com

Circa 1980. Sitting on 40 scenic acres of wildflowers, meadow, aspen and pine forests, this log-sided mountain lodge is surrounded by numerous hiking trails. Serenity and relaxation come easy here, though activities are endless. A phone and TV/VCR are provided in the common area. Afternoon snacks are offered as well as all-day hot and cold beverages. Guest bedrooms feature rustic pine furniture. The Ponderosa Room is a mini-suite boasting a sleigh bed, panoramic views, couch for watching satellite TV, refrigerator and a coffee maker. Relish a hearty mountain breakfast before embarking on the day's adventures. Borrow a mountain bike, play horseshoes, swing in the hammock, fish in the river or lakes, snowshoe or cross-country ski, ride a horse and then soak in the hot tub or sing along by the campfire.

Innkeeper(s): Carla & David McCandless. $99-149. 5 rooms with PB, 1 suite. Breakfast and snacks/refreshments included in rates. Types of meals: Country bkfst, veg bkfst, early coffee/tea and picnic lunch. Beds: KQD. Reading lamp, clock radio, coffeemaker, turn-down service, desk, hair dryer, bathrobes, bath amenities, wireless Internet access, Towel warmers, Heaters, Electric blankets and Pet friendly in room. TV, VCR, DVD, spa, stable, bicycles, library, pet boarding, parlor games, telephone, fireplace, gift shop and horse boarding accommodations and policies can be found on the web site at www.redfeatherranch.com. Horse Hotel is for guests vacationing with their horses on premises. Antiquing, art galleries, bicycling, canoeing/kayaking, cross-country skiing, fishing, golf, hiking, horseback riding, shopping, sporting events and water sports nearby.

Location: Country, mountains. Located on 40 private acres at 8200 ft. elevation, surrounded by Roosevelt National Forest. One hour Northwest of Ft. Collins.

Publicity: Denver Post, Fort Collins Coloradoan, KFKA 1310AM and Arrington's B&B Journal - voted "Best Horse Lover's B&B"

Certificate may be used: November through February, Excluding Valentine's Day.

Salida

River Run Inn
8495 Co Rd 160
Salida, CO 81201
(719)539-3818 (800)385-6925 Fax:(719)539-9395
Internet: www.riverruninn.com
E-mail: riverrun@amigo.net

Circa 1892. This gracious brick home, a National Register building, is located on the banks of the Arkansas River, three miles from town. It was once the poor farm, a home for the indigent who worked for food and lodging before the welfare system became established. The house has been renovated to reflect a country-eclectic style and has six newly decorated guest rooms, most enhanced by mountain views. The location is ideal for anglers, rafters, hikers, bikers and skiers. A 13-bed, third floor is great for groups. A full country breakfast, afternoon refreshments and evening brandy and sherry complete a memorable visit to the River Run Inn.

Innkeeper(s): Sally Griego & Brad Poulson. $90-125. 6 rooms with PB, 1 with WP. Breakfast and snacks/refreshments included in rates. Types of meals: Full gourmet bkfst, veg bkfst, early coffee/tea, afternoon tea, hors d'oeuvres, wine and Requested picnic lunch and dinners. Beds: KQT. CD player, ceiling fan, clock radio, turn-down service, hair dryer, bathrobes, bath amenities and Reading light over bed in room. TV, DVD, library, parlor games, telephone, gift shop and private fishing in Arkansas River on premises. Antiquing, art galleries, bicycling, canoeing/kayaking, cross-country skiing, downhill skiing, fishing, golf, hiking, horseback riding, live theater, museums, parks, shopping, tennis, water sports, wineries and Snowshoeing nearby.

Location: Country, waterfront. Mountain view.

Publicity: Outside Magazine, Fly Fisherman, Denver Post, Colorado Springs Gazette, CBS Denver, The Travel Channel and MSNBC.com.

"So glad we found a B&B with such character and a great owner as well."

Certificate may be used: March 1-Oct. 31, Sunday-Thursday, excludes holidays, based on availability.

Telluride

San Sophia
330 W Pacific Ave
Telluride, CO 81435-1825
(970)728-3001 (800)537-4781 Fax:(970)728-6226
Internet: www.sansophia.com
E-mail: info@sansophia.com

Circa 1988. An observation tower rises gingerly from the inn's gabled roofline, providing 360-degree views from the valley floor to the 13,000-foot peaks of the Saint Sophia Ridge. Rooms are decorated with brass beds and hand-stitched quilts and feature soaking tubs and bay windows or balconies. The two-story windows of the dining room reveal views of waterfalls plunging from the peaks on one side and ski slopes on the other.

Innkeeper(s): Amy Ullrich. $99-299. 1 room, 16 with PB. Breakfast, afternoon tea, hors d'oeuvres and wine included in rates. Types of meals: Full gourmet bkfst, veg bkfst and early coffee/tea. Cable TV, VCR, reading lamp, CD player, clock radio, telephone, desk, hair dryer, bathrobes, bath amenities, wireless Internet access, iron/ironing board, Aveda bath amenities and Godiva chocolates on your pillow in room. Fax, copier, spa, library, child care, fireplace, Happy Hour every afternoon with microbrewed beers, select wines and tea and hors d'oeuvres on premises. Antiquing, art galleries, bicycling, canoeing/kayaking, cross-country skiing, downhill skiing, fishing, golf, hiking, horseback riding, live theater, museums, parks, shopping, tennis, wineries, mountain climbing, jeeping, old gold mines and glider and balloon rides nearby.

Location: City, mountains. Ski Resort.

Publicity: *Rocky Mountain News, Snow Country, Country Inns, Glamour and New York Times.*

"Telluride is a great town, and your bed and breakfast is part of the charm and beauty of the entire area."

Certificate may be used: Month of October, April, May, July mid-week only, November and December mid-week only.

Walsenburg

La Plaza Inn

118 West Sixth
Walsenburg, CO 81089
(719)738-5700 (800)352-9237 Fax:(719)738-6220

Circa 1907. Stay in the relaxed comfort of this historic stucco inn painted in traditional Southwest colors. Relax in the large well-appointed lobby or second-floor sitting room. Each guest bedroom imparts its own ambiance and is nicely furnished with a mixture of period pieces. Many of the suites feature fully equipped kitchens. Breakfast is individually  served or a buffet is set up in the on-site cafe and bookstore that boasts original 15-foot tin ceilings. Sit in the refreshing shade of the back yard. Enjoy the scenic area by skiing local mountains, hiking nearby trails or engaging in water activities and other outdoor sports.

Innkeeper(s): Martie Henderson. $59-90. 10 rooms with PB, 6 suites, 1 conference room. Breakfast included in rates. Types of meals: Country bkfst, veg bkfst, early coffee/tea and lunch. Restaurant on premises. Beds: KQDT. Modem hook-up, data port, cable TV, VCR, reading lamp, refrigerator, ceiling fan, snack bar, telephone, coffeemaker and desk in room. Air conditioning. Fax, copier, library, parlor games, cafe and bookstore on premises. Antiquing, art galleries, bicycling, canoeing/kayaking, cross-country skiing, fishing, golf, hiking, live theater, museums, parks, shopping, tennis and water sports nearby.

Location: Mountains.

Certificate may be used: Anytime, November-March, subject to availability.

Winter Park

Bear Paw Inn

871 Bear Paw Dr
Winter Park, CO 80482
(970)887-2772 Fax:(970)887-2772
Internet: www.bearpaw-winterpark.com
E-mail: bearpaw@rkymtnhi.com

Circa 1989. Secluded, quiet and romantic, this massive award-winning log lodge is exactly the type of welcoming retreat one might hope to enjoy on a vacation in the Colorado wilderness, and the panoramic views of the Continental Divide and Rocky Mountain National Park are just one reason. The cozy interior is highlighted by log beams, massive log walls and antiques.  There are two guest rooms, both with a Jacuzzi tub. The master has a private deck with a swing. Guests can snuggle up in feather beds topped with down comforters. Winter Park is a Mecca for skiers, and ski areas are just a few miles from the Bear Paw, as is ice skating, snowmobiling, horse-drawn sleigh rides and other winter activities. For summer guests, there is whitewater rafting, golfing, horseback riding and bike trails. There are 600 miles of bike trials, music festivals and much more.

Innkeeper(s): Rick & Sue Callahan. $180-225. 2 rooms with PB. Breakfast and snacks/refreshments included in rates. Types of meals: Full gourmet bkfst and early coffee/tea. Beds: Q. TV, reading lamp, refrigerator, turn-down service, feather beds, finest linens, Jacuzzi tubs and chocolates in room. VCR, fax, copier, telephone, fireplace, 3-course gourmet breakfast and homemade afternoon treats each day on premises. Antiquing, cross-country skiing, downhill skiing, fishing, live theater, shopping, water sports, hot air balloons, mountain bikes and summer rodeos nearby.

Location: Mountains.

Publicity: *Sunset Magazine, Cape Cod Life, Boston Globe, Los Angeles Times, Continental Airlines Quarterly, Denver Post, Rocky Mountain News, Log Homes Illustrated, Colorado Country Life,* voted *"Outstanding Hospitality"* by the Colorado Travel Writers and given 10 stars and chosen *"Best Date Getaway"* by the editors of Denver City Search.

"Outstanding hospitality."

Certificate may be used: October-Nov. 15, April, May, Sunday-Thursday, excluding holiday weeks.

Connecticut

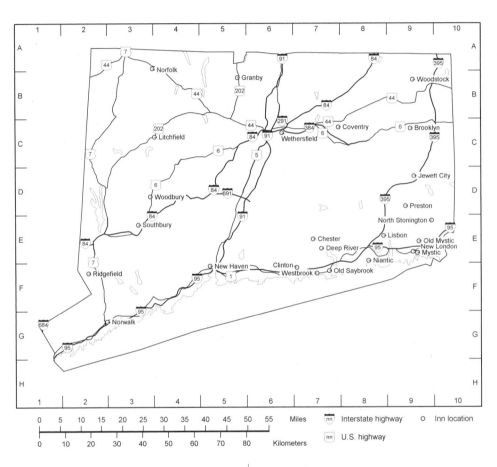

Clinton

3 Liberty Green B&B

3 Liberty St.
Clinton, CT 06413
Fax:860-669-0110
Internet: www.3liberty.com
E-mail: stay@3liberty.com

Circa 1734. Offering a relaxed ambiance, 3 Liberty Green Bed and Breakfast in Connecticut is surrounded by a picturesque setting. Sit on the front porch looking out on the village green while staying at this historic, two-story Center Chimney Colonial listed in the National Register. Tea, treats, bottled water and port wine are available in the parlor. Guest bedrooms and a suite feature two-person Jacuzzi tubs, fireplaces and canopy beds. Ask about spa and massage packages. A delicious home-made breakfast is served in the country kitchen or al fresco. The New England shoreline village of Clinton is a short stroll. Take a waking tour of Liberty Green and Main Street Historic District; tour Chamard Vineyards and shop at the nearby outlet malls. Canoe and kayak rentals are perfect for fishing.

Innkeeper(s): Shelley Nobile. $100-220. 4 rooms with PB, 4 with HT, 4 with WP, 1 two-bedroom suite. Breakfast, afternoon tea, wine, Complimentary tea, Sweets and Port wine cordials included in rates. Types of meals: Full gourmet bkfst, veg bkfst, early coffee/tea, snacks/refreshments, Complimentary tea, sweets and spring water & port wine always available. Beds: QDT. Cable TV, DVD, reading lamp, clock radio, hot tub/spa, bath amenities, wireless

Internet access, All with a King or Queen canopy bed, sitting area, cable/DVD and double Jacuzzi in room. Air conditioning. Fax, copier, spa, telephone, fireplace and Front porch sitting areas overlooking the village green on premises. Antiquing, art galleries, beach, bicycling, canoeing/kayaking, downhill skiing, fishing, golf, hiking, live theater, museums, parks, shopping, wineries, Walk to the beach, antiquing, shops, dining, art galleries & museums, Clinton Crossing Premium Outlets (10 mins), Chamard Vineyards, Essex Steam Train & Riverboat, CT River & Long Island Sound cruises, theater and cinemas nearby.

Location: Ocean community. Picturesque Village Green.

Certificate may be used: Sunday-Thursday, November-May.

Coventry

The Daniel Rust House

2011 Main St
Coventry, CT 06238-2034
(860)742-0032
Internet: www.thebirdinhand.com
E-mail: drhouse1731@sbcglobal.net

Circa 1731. Prepare for a remarkable journey back in time at this former 18th-century tavern. Original wide-board floors, fireplaces and raised paneled walls reflect that era. Romantic canopy beds and Jacuzzi tubs boast added comfort to the guest bedrooms. A secret closet may have harbored runaway slaves during the Underground Railroad. Spacious privacy is offered in the cottage. Conferences and small weddings are accommodated easily. Local universities, Caprilands Herb Farm and Nathan Hale Homestead all are nearby.

Innkeeper(s): Germaine Salvatore & Cathy Mitchell. $120-185. 3 rooms with PB, 2 with FP, 1 with WP, 1 cottage. Breakfast included in rates. Types of meals: Country bkfst and early coffee/tea. Beds: KQDT. Reading lamp, ceiling fan, clock radio, turn-down service, most with fireplace, hair dryer, bathrobes, bath amenities, wireless Internet access and iron/ironing board in room. Air conditioning. Parlor games and telephone on premises. Handicap access. Antiquing, art galleries, beach, bicycling, canoeing/kayaking, cross-country skiing, fishing, golf, hiking, live theater, museums, parks, shopping, sporting events, water sports, wineries and casinos nearby.

Location: Country.

Publicity: *Journal Inquirer, Willimantic Chronicle, The Hartford Courant, WFSB and WRCH.*

"We were delighted then, to find such a jewel in the Bird-In-Hand."

Certificate may be used: Jan. 3-April 1, Sunday-Friday.

Deep River

Riverwind Inn

209 Main St
Deep River, CT 06417-2022
(860)526-2014
Internet: www.riverwindinn.com
E-mail: innkeeper@riverwindinn.com

Circa 1790. Embrace the warmth of this wonderful bed & breakfast built in 1790 with post and beam construction, wood ceilings and a 12-foot stone fireplace. Mingle in one of a variety of common rooms or bask in privacy. Sip a glass of sherry in the keeping room, watch a movie, grab a book from the library, or play a game in one of the upstairs sitting rooms. Air-condi-

tioned guest bedrooms boast a delightful décor accented by stenciling and tasteful furnishings. The Moonlit Suite on the third floor is very popular and offers total privacy. A sitting room with fireplace and a two-person Jacuzzi enhances its romantic ambiance. Sit outside on an Adirondack chair or relax in a rocker on the wraparound porch.

Innkeeper(s): Elaine & Leo Klevens. $120-225. 8 rooms with PB, 2 with FP, 1 with WP, 2 suites. Breakfast, snacks/refreshments and Complimentary Sherry included in rates. Types of meals: Full bkfst. Beds: QDT. Reading lamp, ceiling fan, clock radio, hair dryer, bath amenities, wireless Internet access and iron/ironing board in room. Air conditioning. TV, library and fireplace on premises. Antiquing, art galleries, beach, canoeing/kayaking, golf, live theater, museums, parks, shopping, water sports, wineries, Hiking trails, Great restaurants, Casinos, Connecticut River and Goodspeed Opera House nearby.

Publicity: *Hartford Courant, Country Living, Country Inns, Country Decorating, New York Travel & Leisure, New York Times, Boston Globe and Los Angeles Times.*

"Warm, hospitality, a quiet homey atmosphere, comfortable bed, well thought-out and delightful appointments, delicious light hot biscuits — a great find!"

Certificate may be used: Jan. 2-April 30, Sunday-Thursday, Holidays Excluded, subject to availability.

Granby

The Dutch Iris Inn B&B

239 Salmon Brook Street
Granby, CT 06035
(860)844-0262 (877)280-0743 Fax:(860)844-0248
Internet: www.dutchirisinn.com
E-mail: info@dutchirisinn.com

Circa 1812. For many years this historic Colonial was used as a summer home. Some of the inn's antiques were the original furnishings, including a Louis XIV couch, Chickering grand piano, fainting couch, four-poster bed and marble-top dresser. Relax in the keeping room by a roaring fire, where the previous owners did the cooking. Several guest bedrooms feature working fireplaces. A customized breakfast menu is savored by candlelight and classical music. Half of the three acres feature perennial and bulb gardens, as well as wild blackberries and blueberries. Sip a cold beverage in a rocking chair on the side porch.

Innkeeper(s): Nancy & William Ross. $99-159. 6 rooms with PB, 4 with FP, 2 with WP. Breakfast and snacks/refreshments included in rates. Types of meals: Full bkfst. Beds: KQ. Cable TV, VCR, reading lamp, clock radio, telephone, desk, voice mail, most with fireplace, hair dryer, bath amenities, wireless Internet access, iron/ironing board, wireless Internet access, fireplace and two with whirlpool tubs in room. Air conditioning. Fax and parlor games on premises. Amusement parks, antiquing, art galleries, beach, bicycling, canoeing/kayaking, cross-country skiing, downhill skiing, fishing, golf, hiking, horseback riding, live theater, museums, parks, shopping, tennis, water sports, wineries, private schools: Westminster, Ethel Walker, Avon Olf Farm, Suffield Academy, Loomis Chaffee and Miss Porter's nearby.

Location: Country.

Certificate may be used: Anytime, Sunday-Thursday.

Jewett City

Homespun Farm Bed and Breakfast

306 Preston Rd, Route 164
Jewett City, CT 06351
(860)376-5178 (888)889-6673
Internet: www.homespunfarm.com
E-mail: relax@homespunfarm.com

Circa 1740. The Brewster family, whose great-great grandfather arrived on the Mayflower, owned this Colonial farmhouse for 250 years. Now the Bauers have lovingly renovated the home, which is listed in the National Register. Furnished with antiques and period reproductions, the inn's tasteful decor is accented with an artistic hand-stenciled wood floor and wall border. A sitting room overlooks the golf course and offers gorgeous sunset views. Charming guest bedrooms are well suited for romance, families or business. Luxury abounds with plush robes, candles, aromatherapy personal products, fresh flowers and fine linens on the handmade white oak and pencil post beds. Farm-fresh eggs are part of a scrumptious candlelight breakfast served in the Keeping Room. The extensive grounds, a Certified National Wildlife Federation Backyard Habitat, feature a koi pond, kitchen garden, orchard, grape arbor and flower gardens that welcome birds and butterflies.
Innkeeper(s): Kate & Ron Bauer. $149-189. 2 rooms with PB, 2 with FP. Breakfast and snacks/refreshments included in rates. Types of meals: Full gourmet bkfst, veg bkfst and early coffee/tea. Beds: QT. Cable TV, VCR, DVD, reading lamp, CD player, clock radio, turn-down service, some with hot tub/spa, fireplace, hair dryer, bathrobes, bath amenities, wireless Internet access and iron/ironing board in room. Air conditioning. Fax, library, parlor games, telephone and laundry facility on premises. Limited handicap access. Antiquing, art galleries, beach, bicycling, canoeing/kayaking, fishing, golf, hiking, horseback riding, live theater, museums, parks, shopping, sporting events, wineries, Foxwood Casino and Mohegan Sun Casino nearby.
Location: Country. Just 17 miles from Mystic.
Certificate may be used: Jan. 2 to March 30, Monday-Thursday, Oct. 30 to Dec. 23, Monday through Thursday, no other discounts apply to time frame, subject to availability.

Litchfield

Abel Darling B&B

PO Box 1502
Litchfield, CT 06759
(860)567-0384
Internet: www.abeldarling.com
E-mail: abeldarling@hotmail.com

Circa 1782. The spacious guest rooms in this 1782 colonial home offer a light romantic feel and comfortable beds. Breakfast is served in the sunny dining room and includes home-baked breads and muffins. This bed and breakfast is in the heart of the historic district, and nearby is the village green, hosting many restaurants and boutique shops, and the Litchfield countryside.
Innkeeper(s): Colleen Murphy. $125-150. 3 rooms, 2 with PB. Breakfast included in rates. Types of meals: Cont plus. Beds: QD. Reading lamp, clock radio, desk, hair dryer, bathrobes and iron/ironing board in room. VCR, fax, copier, bicycles, library, parlor games and telephone on premises. Antiquing, art galleries, beach, bicycling, canoeing/kayaking, cross-country skiing, downhill skiing, fishing, golf, hiking, horseback riding, live theater, parks, shopping, tennis and wineries nearby.
Location: Country, mountains.
Publicity: Litchfield County Times and New York Times.
Certificate may be used: Jan. 2-April 30.

Mystic

The Whaler's Inn

20 E Main St
Mystic, CT 06355-2646
(860)536-1506 (800)243-2588 Fax:(860)572-1250
Internet: www.whalersinnmystic.com
E-mail: sales@whalersinnmystic.com

Circa 1901. This classical revival-style inn is built on the historical site of the Hoxie House, the Clinton House and the U.S. Hotel. Just as these famous 19th-century inns offered, the Whaler's Inn has the same charm and convenience for today's visitor to Mystic. Once a booming ship-building center, the town's connection to the sea is ongoing, and the sailing schooners still pass beneath the Bascule Drawbridge in the center of town. More than 75 shops and restaurants are within walking distance.
Innkeeper(s): Richard Prisby. $89-249. 49 rooms with PB, 1 conference room. Types of meals: Cont plus, gourmet lunch and gourmet dinner. Restaurant on premises. Beds: KQD. Reading lamp, desk, cable TV, telephone, voice mail, data port, alarm clock, air conditioning, eight luxury rooms with water views, Jacuzzi tubs and fireplaces in room. TV, telephone and business center on premises. Handicap access. Antiquing, fishing, parks, shopping, water sports, walk to Mystic Seaport and harbor & schooner cruises nearby.
Location: City. Historic downtown Mystic.
Certificate may be used: Nov. 27-April 30, excluding holidays.

New London

Kirkland House Bed & Breakfast

51 Glenwood Ave
New London, CT 06320-4316
(860)437-1500 (877)220-9029
Internet: www.kirklandhouse.com
E-mail: email@kirklandhouse.com

Circa 1896. Listed in the National Register, this historic 1896 Italianate villa with a grand staircase has been lovingly restored. Kirkland House Bed and Breakfast in New London, Connecticut boasts manicured grounds and an inviting wicker-filled porch. Two air-conditioned guest bedrooms boast double mantled fireplaces. One room features a bed with an English-style coronet and a Victorian marble-top dresser. The other room is accented with blue chintz fabric and has a clawfoot tub. Select from a gourmet breakfast menu in the elegant formal dining room. Stroll along a private beach or play tennis nearby. Spa services, a health club and golf are available.
Innkeeper(s): Gail Schwenker. $100-250. 4 rooms, 2 with PB, 2 with FP, 1 two-bedroom suite. Breakfast and afternoon tea included in rates. Types of meals: Full gourmet bkfst and early coffee/tea. Beds: KQT. Reading lamp, clock radio, hair dryer, bathrobes, bath amenities, wireless Internet access and iron/ironing board in room. Air conditioning. TV, DVD, fax, copier, bicycles, library, parlor games, telephone, fireplace, Swimming, Tennis, Gym nearby and In-room Spa services available on premises. Amusement parks, antiquing, art galleries, beach, bicycling, canoeing/kayaking, fishing, golf, hiking, horseback riding, live theater, museums, parks, shopping, sporting events, tennis, water sports, wineries, Historic homes, Mystic Seaport and Mystic Acquarium nearby.
Location: Ocean community.
Certificate may be used: Sunday-Thursday, subject to availability, must identify using coupon when booking room.

Niantic

Inn at Harbor Hill Marina

60 Grand St
Niantic, CT 06357
(860)739-0331 Fax:(860)691-3078
Internet: www.innharborhill.com
E-mail: info@innharborhill.com

Circa 1890. Arise each morning to panoramic views of the Niantic River harbor at this traditional, late-19th-century inn. Travel by boat or car to neighboring cities and enjoy the finest culture New England has to offer. This three-story, harbor-front inn offers rooms filled with antiques and seaside décor. Some have balconies and fireplaces. Experience true adventure at sea on a chartered fishing trip, or spend the day in town shopping or relaxing on the beach, all within walking distance. During the summer, guests can listen to outdoor concerts in the park while overlooking Long Island Sound. Whatever the day has in store, guests can start each morning the right way with a fresh, continental breakfast on the wraparound porch overlooking the marina and gardens.

Innkeeper(s): Sue & Dave Labrie. $135-245. 9 rooms with PB, 5 with FP, 1 suite, 1 conference room. Breakfast, afternoon tea and snacks/refreshments included in rates. Types of meals: Cont plus, early coffee/tea and wine. Beds: QDT. Cable TV, reading lamp, CD player, ceiling fan, clock radio, desk, most with fireplace, hair dryer, wireless Internet access, iron/ironing board, suite and balcony rooms and corner rooms with fireplaces in room. Air conditioning. Fax, copier, parlor games, telephone, gift shop, complimentary boat rides and beach passes on premises. Antiquing, art galleries, beach, bicycling, canoeing/kayaking, fishing, golf, live theater, museums, parks, shopping, sporting events, water sports, wineries, Mohegan Sun Casino, Foxwoods Casino, Mystic Seaport, Mystic Aquarium and outlets nearby.

Location: Waterfront. One to two miles away from beaches.

Publicity: *Mystic Coast & Country and awarded 2005 Golden Pineapple Award in Excellence in Tourism Service and Hospitality.*

Certificate may be used: Nov. 1-March 31, Sunday-Thursday, not valid on holidays.

Norfolk

Blackberry River Inn

538 Greenwoods Road W
Norfolk, CT 06058
(860)542-5100 Fax:(860)542-1763
Internet: www.blackberryriverinn.com
E-mail: blackberry.river.inn@snet.net

Circa 1763. In the National Register, the Colonial buildings that comprise the inn are situated on 27 acres. A library with cherry paneling, three parlors and a breakfast room are offered for guests' relaxation. Guest rooms are elegantly furnished with antiques. Guests can choose from rooms in the main house with a fireplace or suites with a fireplace or Jacuzzi. The Cottage includes a fireplace and Jacuzzi. A full country breakfast is included.

Innkeeper(s): Janette Angel. $85-225. 18 rooms with PB, 1 cottage. Breakfast and afternoon tea included in rates. Types of meals: Full bkfst. Beds: KQT. Cable TV in room. Air conditioning. Swimming, library, fireplace, hiking and fishing on premises. Antiquing, canoeing/kayaking, cross-country skiing, downhill skiing, golf, horseback riding, shopping, tennis, sleigh rides, hay rides, auto racing and music festivals nearby.

Certificate may be used: May to November only, Sunday to Thursday, subject to availability.

Manor House

69 Maple Ave
Norfolk, CT 06058-0447
(860)542-5690 (866)542-5690 Fax:(860)542-5690
Internet: www.manorhouse-norfolk.com
E-mail: innkeeper@manorhouse-norfolk.com

Circa 1898. Charles Spofford, designer of London's subway, built this home with many gables, exquisite cherry paneling and grand staircase. There are Moorish arches and Tiffany windows. Guests can enjoy hot-mulled cider after a sleigh ride, hay ride, or horse and carriage drive along the country lanes nearby. The inn was named by "Discerning Traveler" as Connecticut's most romantic hideaway.

Innkeeper(s): Michael W. Dinsmore. $125-250. 9 rooms with PB, 4 with FP, 1 suite, 1 conference room. Breakfast and afternoon tea included in rates. Types of meals: Full gourmet bkfst, early coffee/tea and room service. Beds: KQDT. Reading lamp, ceiling fan, clock radio, desk and three with double whirlpools in room. Fax, library, parlor games, telephone and fireplace on premises. Antiquing, cross-country skiing, downhill skiing, fishing, live theater, parks, shopping, sporting events and water sports nearby.

Location: Mountains.

Publicity: *Good Housekeeper, Gourmet, Boston Globe, Philadelphia Inquirer, Innsider, Rhode Island Monthly, Gourmet, National Geographic Traveler and New York Times.*

Certificate may be used: Weekdays, excluding holidays and month of October.

North Stonington

Antiques & Accommodations

32 Main St
North Stonington, CT 06359-1709
(860)535-1736 (800)554-7829
Internet: www.antiquesandaccommodations.com
E-mail: call@antiquesandaccommodations.com

Circa 1861. Surrounded by an acre of herb, edible flower, perennial and cutting gardens, this Victorian treasure offers a

romantic setting for a getaway or vacation. Antiques and Accommodations is located in North Stonington, Connecticut. Stay in a pleasant guest bedroom with a canopy bed. Each morning, linger over a delightful breakfast served in the formal dining room. Historic Mystic Seaport, beaches and casinos are just minutes from the inn. Ask about specials and packages available.

Innkeeper(s): Ann & Tom Gray. $110-249. 1 two-bedroom and 1 three-bedroom suites. Breakfast included in rates. Types of meals: Full gourmet bkfst, wine and gourmet dinner. Beds: KQT. Cable TV, VCR, reading lamp, hair dryer, bath amenities and wireless Internet access in room. Air conditioning. TV, fax, copier and fireplace on premises. Antiquing, art galleries, beach, canoeing/kayaking, fishing, golf, hiking, live theater, museums, shopping and wineries nearby.

Publicity: *Country Inns, Woman's Day, New London Day, Connecticut Magazine and Connecticut Public Radio Yankee Travel Guide Editors Choice.*

"I loved the great attention to detail and authenticity. A lovely labor of love."

Certificate may be used: Sunday-Thursday, subject to availability.

Inn at Lower Farm

119 Mystic Rd
North Stonington, CT 06359
(860)535-9075 (866)535-9075
Internet: www.lowerfarm.com
E-mail: info@lowerfarm.com

Circa 1740. Fully restored, this 1740 center-chimney Georgian Colonial boasts six working fireplaces. The bed and breakfast is located on more than four acres of lawns, gardens and cattail marshes. Enjoy the scenic surroundings while relaxing in the hammock or on the comfortable outdoor furniture scattered throughout the property. Swing on the porch swing and breathe in the fresh country air. Well-appointed guest bedrooms feature queen-size beds, en-suite private baths and bright sitting areas with recliner chairs. Three rooms have fireplaces and a fourth includes a whirlpool tub. Wake up to a full country breakfast served by candlelight in front of the original open hearth and beehive oven. In the afternoon gather for tea and homemade cookies.

Innkeeper(s): Mary & Jon Wilska. $100-175. 4 rooms with PB, 3 with FP, 1 with WP, 1 two-bedroom suite, 1 conference room. Breakfast, afternoon tea and snacks/refreshments included in rates. Types of meals: Full gourmet bkfst, veg bkfst and early coffee/tea. Beds: Q. Reading lamp, stereo, clock radio, desk, most with fireplace, hair dryer, bath amenities, Recliner Queen Anne chairs, individual wall-mounted reading lamps, Make-up mirror and Wireless Internet in room. Central air. TV, VCR, fax, copier, library, parlor games, telephone, hammock, porch swing and outdoor sitting areas on premises. Antiquing, art galleries, beach, bicycling, canoeing/kayaking, fishing, golf, hiking, horseback riding, live theater, museums, parks, shopping, sporting events, tennis, water sports, wineries, Foxwood and Mohegan Sun Casinos, birdwatching, foliage tour, cider mill and apple and berry picking nearby.

Location: Country.

Certificate may be used: November through May, Sunday-Thursday.

Norwalk

Silvermine Tavern

194 Perry Ave
Norwalk, CT 06850-1123
(203)847-4558 (888)693-9967 Fax:(203)847-9171
Internet: www.silverminetavern.com
E-mail: innkeeper@silverminetavern.com

Circa 1790. The Silvermine consists of the Old Mill, the Country Store, the Coach House and the Tavern itself. Primitive paintings and furnishings, as well as family heirlooms, decorate the inn. Guest rooms and dining rooms overlook the Old Mill, the waterfall and swans gliding across the millpond. Some guest rooms offer items such as canopy bed or private decks. In the summer, guests can dine al fresco a large deck at the mill pond.

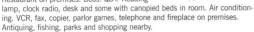

Innkeeper(s): Frank Whitman, Jr. $130-170. 11 rooms, 10 with PB, 1 suite. Breakfast included in rates. Types of meals: Cont, lunch and dinner. Restaurant on premises. Beds: QDT. Reading lamp, clock radio, desk and some with canopied beds in room. Air conditioning. VCR, fax, copier, parlor games, telephone and fireplace on premises. Antiquing, fishing, parks and shopping nearby.

Location: Residential area.

Certificate may be used: No Friday nights, no September or October. No holidays.

Old Saybrook

Deacon Timothy Pratt Bed & Breakfast Inn C.1746

325 Main Street
Old Saybrook, CT 06475
(860)395-1229 (800)640-1195 Fax:(860)395-4748
Internet: www.pratthouse.net
E-mail: stay@pratthouse.net

Circa 1746. Built prior to the Revolutionary War, this slate blue house is an outstanding example of center chimney Colonial-style architecture. Listed in the National Register, the inn's original features include six working fireplaces, hand-hewn beams, wide board floors, a beehive oven and built-in cupboard. Four-poster and canopy beds, Oriental rugs and period furnishings accentuate the New England atmosphere. Fireplaces and Jacuzzi tubs invite romance and relaxation. On weekends a multi-course, candlelight breakfast is served in the elegant dining room. Enjoy homemade muffins or scones, fresh fruit and entrees such as heart-shaped blueberry pancakes or eggs Benedict. Among the variety of local historic house museums to visit, the William Hart house is across the street. The area offers many shopping and dining opportunities as well as galleries to explore. Beaches, a state park and river cruises also are available.

Innkeeper(s): Shelley Nobile. $100-220. 7 rooms with PB, 7 with FP, 7 with HT, 7 with WP, 3 total suites, including 1 two-bedroom suite. Breakfast, afternoon tea and snacks/refreshments included in rates. Types of meals: Full gourmet bkfst, veg bkfst, early coffee/tea, Complimentary tea, coffee, cookies and port wine and spring water is always available to you in our dining room. Beds: QT. Modem hook-up, data port, cable TV, VCR, DVD, reading lamp, stereo, clock radio, telephone, hot tub/spa, fireplace, hair dryer, bath amenities, wireless Internet access, iron/ironing board, massage therapy (fee); each rm w/ fireplace, Jacuzzi, Queen canopy or four-poster bed, comfortable sitting areas, hair dryer, private bath, cable TV, modem line and high speed wireless and stereo/cd player in room. Central air. Fax, copier, spa, bicycles, library, parlor games, gift shop, complimentary tea, hot chocolate, spring water, fresh baked cookies, port wine, guest refrigerator, picturesque grounds, picnic/sitting areas, three-tier fountain, two-person hammock and a swing on a two-century-old maple tree on premises. Antiquing, art galleries, beach, bicycling, canoeing/kayaking, cross-country skiing, downhill skiing, fishing, golf, hiking, horseback riding, live theater, museums, parks, shopping, sporting events, tennis, wineries, lighthouses, waterfront dining, waterfront historic walking park, waterfront golf and mini-golf, spas, playhouses, Essex Steam Train & Riverboat, Goodspeed Opera House, Chamard Vineyards, charming New England village, sightseeing cruises, a short drive to Foxwoods and Mohegan Sun Casinos, Clinton & Westbrook Factory Outlet Malls, Mystic Seaport and Aquarium and Gillette Castle State Park nearby.

Location: Country, ocean community. Historic and shopping district.

Publicity: *Fodor's New England Travel Guide, America's Favorite Inns Book, Elle Magazine, Coastal Living Magazine, Inn Traveller Feature, Entrepreneur's Business Start-Ups Magazine, Inn Spots & Special Places in New England, Waterside Escapes by Woodpond Press, Arrington Publishing Awards: Most Historical Charm (2004), Best Interior Design & Decor (2003) and Best Location For Walking to Shops and Restaurants (2002).*

Certificate may be used: November-May.

Ridgefield

West Lane Inn

22 West Ln
Ridgefield, CT 06877-4914
(203)438-7323 Fax:(203)438-7325
Internet: www.westlaneinn.com
E-mail: west_lane_inn@sbcglobal.net

Circa 1849. Listed in the National Register, this 1849 Victorian mansion combines the ambiance of a country inn with the convenience of a boutique hotel. An enormous front porch is filled with black wrought iron chairs and tables overlooking a manicured lawn on two acres. A polished oak staircase rises to a third-floor landing and lounge. Chandeliers, wall sconces and floral wallpapers accent the intimate atmosphere. Elegant, over-sized guest bedrooms feature individual climate control, four-poster beds and upscale amenities like heated towel racks, voice mail, wireless DSL and refrigerators. Two include fireplaces and a kitchenette. Wake up and enjoy a morning meal in the Breakfast Room before experiencing one of New England's finest towns with a variety of boutiques, museums, antique shops and restaurants.

Innkeeper(s): Maureen Mayer & Deborah Prieger. $145-250. 16 rooms with PB, 2 with FP, 1 suite, 1 conference room. Breakfast included in rates. Types of meals: Full bkfst and room service. Restaurant on premises. Beds: KQ. Cable TV, VCR, reading lamp, refrigerator, ceiling fan, clock radio, telephone, coffeemaker, desk, voice mail, some with fireplace, hair dryer, bath amenities, wireless Internet access, iron/ironing board, free wireless DSL, full private baths and heated towel racks in room. Air conditioning. Fax and copier on premises. Antiquing, cross-country skiing, golf, hiking, live theater, museums, parks, shopping, tennis, wineries, award winning restaurants, boutiquing and movies nearby.

Location: City. New England town.

"Thank you for the hospitality you showed us. The rooms are comfortable and quiet. I haven't slept this soundly in weeks."

Certificate may be used: Anytime, November through April, subject to availability, for standard rooms only and not valid on holidays or Friday and Saturday nights.

Southbury

Cornucopia At Oldfield

782 Main St North
Southbury, CT 06488-1898
(203)267-6707 Fax:(203)267-6773
Internet: cornucopiabnb.com
E-mail: innkeeper@cornucopiabnb.com

Circa 1818. Be surrounded by acres of rolling lawns and gardens that are bordered by huge sugar and Norway maples and the original stone walls. Experience country elegance in a relaxed setting at this stately Georgia Federal home that sits in the historic district. The fireside public rooms include the Keeping Room for watching a DVD or video or playing games. The front parlor offers a more reserved, quiet ambiance. A desk and a library of books, magazines and CDs are on the second floor. Inviting guest bedrooms feature fleece robes and modern amenities. Stay in a room with a clawfoot tub, fireplace or balcony. A full breakfast is served daily in the formal dining room. Sit by the lily pond, relax in the shady gazebo or nap in a hammock. Take a refreshing dip in the swimming pool.

Innkeeper(s): Christine & Ed Edelson. $100-250. 6 rooms, 5 with PB, 4 with FP, 1 with WP, 1 two-bedroom suite, 2 conference rooms. Breakfast, snacks/refreshments and wine included in rates. Types of meals: Full gourmet bkfst, veg bkfst, early coffee/tea, picnic lunch and afternoon tea. Beds: KQT. Reading lamp, CD player, ceiling fan, turn-down service, most with fireplace, hair dryer, bathrobes, bath amenities and wireless Internet access in room. Central air. TV, VCR, DVD, fax, swimming, library, parlor games and telephone on premises. Amusement parks, antiquing, art galleries, canoeing/kayaking, cross-country skiing, downhill skiing, fishing, golf, hiking, horseback riding, live theater, museums, parks, shopping, tennis, water sports and wineries nearby.

Location: Country.

Certificate may be used: Sunday-Thursday, Jan. 1-May 30, subject to availability, no holidays.

Westbrook

Angels' Watch Inn

902 Boston Post Rd
Westbrook, CT 06498-1848
(860)399-8846 Fax:(860)399-2571
Internet: www.angelswatchinn.com
E-mail: info@angelswatchinn.com

Circa 1830. Appreciate the comfortable elegance and tranquil ambiance of this stately 1830 Federal bed and breakfast that is situated on one acre of peaceful grounds in a quaint New England village along the Connecticut River Valley Shoreline. Romantic guest bedrooms are private retreats with canopy beds, fireplaces, stocked refrigerators, strawberries dipped in chocolate, fresh fruit and snack baskets, whirlpools or two-person clawfoot soaking tubs. Maintaining a fine reputation of impeccable standards, the inn caters to the whole person. After breakfast choose from an incredible assortment of spa services that include massage therapy, yoga, intuitive guidance, as well as mind, body and spirit wellness. Go horseback riding then take a sunset cruise. Ask about elopement/small wedding packages and midweek or off-season specials.

Innkeeper(s): Bill , Peggy and Diane. $115-195. 4 rooms, 5 with PB, 5 with FP, 4 with HT. Breakfast, afternoon tea and snacks/refreshments included in rates. Types of meals: Full gourmet bkfst, veg bkfst, early coffee/tea, picnic lunch, wine and dinner. Beds: KQT. Cable TV, DVD, reading lamp, stereo, refrigerator, ceiling fan, snack bar, clock radio, desk, hot tub/spa, fireplace, hair dryer, bathrobes, bath amenities, wireless Internet access, iron/ironing board, complimentary beverages, bottled water, soda and a choice of beer, red wine and white wine or sparkling cider in room. Air conditioning. Fax, copier, spa, parlor games, telephone, laundry facility and Wireless Internet access for laptops on premises. Limited handicap access. Antiquing, art galleries, beach, bicycling, canoeing/kayaking, cross-country skiing, fishing, golf, hiking, live theater, museums, parks, shopping, sporting events, water sports and wineries nearby.

Location: Ocean community.

Publicity: *The Hartford Courant, New Haven Register, Main Street News, Pictorial and ABC affiliate Positively Connecticut.*

Certificate may be used: Sunday-Thursday year-round, holidays and special events excluded. Full season rate apply.

Captain Stannard House

138 South Main Street
Westbrook, CT 06498-1904
(860)399-4634
Internet: www.stannardhouse.com
E-mail: info@stannardhouse.com

Circa 1850. An inn for all seasons, this historic Georgian-style bed & breakfast exudes a casual country elegance that offers comfort and hospitality. Situated in a small shoreline village on Long Island Sound, Pilot's Point marina is within walking distance. Play chess, shoot pool, watch TV or chat by the fire in one of the common areas. Enjoy the peaceful gardens. A guest refrigerator is available for use as needed. Tastefully furnished with antiques, spacious guest bedrooms include in-room temperature control. Linger over a full breakfast in the dining room at a table for two. Just one block from the beach, passes and sand chairs enhance a fun day in the sun. Ask about special events and theme weekends.

Innkeeper(s): Jim & Mary Brewster. $125-195. 8 rooms, 9 with PB. Breakfast and snacks/refreshments included in rates. Types of meals: Full gourmet bkfst and early coffee/tea. Beds: QDT. Reading lamp, hair dryer, bathrobes, bath amenities, wireless Internet access and iron/ironing board in room. Air conditioning. TV, VCR, DVD, fax, copier, bicycles, library, parlor games, telephone, fireplace, billiard room, game rooms for chess, checkers, cards and board games on premises. Limited handicap access. Antiquing, art galleries, beach, bicycling, canoeing/kayaking, fishing, golf, hiking, live theater, museums, parks, water sports, factory outlets, birdwatching and casinos nearby.

Location: Ocean community. Old Saybrook, Clinton, Essex.

Certificate may be used: Anytime November - May, subject to availability.

Westbrook Inn B&B

976 Boston Post Rd
Westbrook, CT 06498-1852
(800)342-3162 Fax:(860)399-8023
Internet: www.westbrookinn.com
E-mail: info@westbrookinn.com

Circa 1876. A wraparound porch and flower gardens offer a gracious welcome to this elegant Victorian inn. The innkeeper, an expert in restoring old houses and antiques, has filled the B&B with fine Victorian period furnishings, handsome paintings and wall coverings. Well-appointed guest bedrooms and a spacious two-bedroom cottage provide comfortable accommodations. Some guest rooms include a fireplace, four-poster canopy bed or balcony. A full breakfast features homemade baked goods that accompany a variety of delicious main entrees. Complimentary beverages are available throughout the day. Enjoy bike rides and walks to the beach. Nearby factory outlets and casinos are other popular activities.

Innkeeper(s): Glenn & Chris . $175-259. 13 rooms with PB, 8 with FP, 3 with WP, 2 suites, 1 cottage, 1 conference room. Breakfast and snacks/refreshments included in rates. Types of meals: Country bkfst and early coffee/tea. Beds: KQT. Data port, cable TV, VCR, reading lamp, refrigerator, clock radio, telephone, desk, most with fireplace, hair dryer, bath amenities, wireless Internet access, iron/ironing board and Period antiques in room. Central air. Fax, copier, bicycles, library, parlor games, gift shop, picturesque gardens, gazebo, bistro-style patio, historic front porch, two-person hammock and cottage with full kitchen on premises. Limited handicap access. Antiquing, art galleries, beach, bicycling, canoeing/kayaking, fishing, golf, hiking, horseback riding, live theater, museums, parks, shopping, sporting events, tennis, wineries, boat cruises, casinos, outlet mall and quaint downtown nearby.

Location: Ocean community.

Publicity: *Harbor News, New Haven Register, Middletown Press, Pictorial Newspaper, Arrington's B&B Journal " Best Inn with Nearby Attraction," voted "the most elegant inn" (2005), NBC (2003) and Comcast Cable.*

Certificate may be used: Nov. 1-May 15, Monday-Thursday, select rooms.

Wethersfield

Chester Bulkley House B&B

184 Main St
Wethersfield, CT 06109-2340
(860)563-4236 Fax:(860)257-8266
Internet: www.chesterbulkleyhouse.com
E-mail: chesterbulkley@aol.com

Circa 1830. Offering the best of both worlds, this renovated Greek Revival structure is ideally located in the historic village of Old Weathersfield with its quaint sites, museums and shops, yet the inn also boasts a 10-minute drive to downtown Hartford with ballet, Broadway shows, opera and the symphony. Hand-carved woodwork, wide pine floors, working fireplaces and period pieces enhance the comfortable ambiance. Cut flowers, pillow chocolates and other thoughtful treats ensure a pleasant and gracious stay for business or leisure.

Innkeeper(s): Tom Aufiero. $95-145. 5 rooms, 3 with PB, 1 suite. Breakfast included in rates. Types of meals: Full gourmet bkfst, veg bkfst, early coffee/tea and afternoon tea. Beds: KQDT. Ceiling fan, clock radio, hair dryer

bath amenities and iron/ironing board in room. Air conditioning. TV, fax, library, telephone and fireplace on premises. Antiquing, downhill skiing, fishing, live theater, parks, shopping and sporting events nearby.

Location: Village.

Certificate may be used: January-August, Sunday to Thursday.

Woodbury

Hummingbird Hill B&B

891 Main St S
Woodbury, CT 06798
(203)263-3733
Internet: hummingbirdbb.com
E-mail: HummingbirdHill@charter.net

Circa 1953. Hummingbird Hill B&B is a traditional, colonial-style in Woodbury, Connecticut. Interiors are in shades of blue and white and flowers from the garden and candles accent the living room. Relax and watch TV or DVDs in the living room in front of a cozy fire. A heated sun porch offers a quiet place to read at any time of the year. An open-air porch and brick patio look out onto the perennial garden, a favorite spot for butterflies, dragonflies, and, of course, the hummingbirds.

Innkeeper(s): Sharon Simmons. $95-125. 2 rooms, 1 with PB. Breakfast and afternoon tea included in rates. Types of meals: Cont plus and early coffee/tea. Beds: KT. Reading lamp, clock radio and telephone in room. Air conditioning. TV, VCR, fireplace and A smoke free property on premises. Amusement parks, antiquing, art galleries, bicycling, cross-country skiing, downhill skiing, golf, hiking, horseback riding, live theater, museums, parks, shopping, wineries, Berry & apple picking, Hot air ballooning and Bird watching nearby.

Location: Country.

Publicity: *Voices, Republican American, Connecticut Vacation Guide and Northwest Connecticut Convention and Visitors Bureau.*

Certificate may be used: Sunday to Thursday, subject to availability.

Longwood Country Inn

1204 Main St S
Woodbury, CT 06798-3804
(203)266-0800
Internet: www.longwoodcountryinn.com
E-mail: inquire@longwoodcountryinn.com

Circa 1789. Amid the backdrop of Litchfield Hills, Longwood Country inn sits on four acres in the historic district of Woodbury, Connecticut. Period furnishings and modern comforts accent this classic Colonial built in 1789 and recently renovated. Overlook the elegant grounds and gardens from the country porch or fireside lounges. Beverages and snacks are always available. Spacious luxury suites boast gas-log fireplaces, whirlpool tubs and French telephone showers. The Restaurant is highly acclaimed for its creative American cuisine. This bed and breakfast is bordered by five acres of ornamental plants and wooded walkways along the Pomperaug River.

Innkeeper(s): Rick Howe. $150-325. 4 rooms, 5 with PB. Breakfast included in rates. Types of meals: Full bkfst. Restaurant on premises. Beds: KQT. Cable TV, reading lamp, clock radio, telephone and desk in room. Air conditioning. Fireplace on premises. Amusement parks, antiquing, art galleries, cross-country skiing, downhill skiing, fishing, golf, horseback riding, shopping, hot air ballooning and jazz nearby.

Location: Country town.

Publicity: *Voices, Yankee Traveler, Hartford Courant, Newtown Bee, Connecticut Magazine and New York Times.*

"Your hospitality will always be remembered."

Certificate may be used: Jan. 7-Feb. 28, Monday-Thursday, excluding weekends, Valentine's and holidays.

Woodstock

B & B at Taylor's Corner

880 Route 171
Woodstock, CT 06281
(860)974-0490 (888)974-0490
Internet: www.taylorsbb.com
E-mail: reservations@taylorsbb.com

Traditional lodging and hearthside cooking is part of the historic yet romantic ambiance of this restored 18th-century central-chimney Colonial and attached Connecticut cottage, listed in the National Register. It boasts two beehive ovens, eight fireplaces, original wide-floor boards, moldings, gunstock beams, mantels and stair rails. Relax by the fireside in the keeping room, parlor or in an Adirondack chair on the patio. Spacious guest bedrooms are furnished with antiques and reproductions. Besides a daily breakfast in the dining room, light snacks and beverages are available. Ask about getaway specials. Popular Old Sturbridge Village is 15 miles away.

Innkeeper(s): Brenda Van Damme. Call for rates. 3 rooms with PB, 3 with FP. Breakfast and snacks/refreshments included in rates. Types of meals: Full bkfst, veg bkfst, early coffee/tea and Gluten-free breakfast available upon request. Beds: QT. Reading lamp, clock radio, fireplace, hair dryer, bath amenities, wireless Internet access and iron/ironing board in room. Air conditioning. TV, DVD, fax, copier, library, parlor games, XBox and movie library on premises. Antiquing, bicycling, cross-country skiing, fishing, hiking, parks, shopping, sporting events and wineries nearby.

Certificate may be used: November-May, anytime subject to availabilty.

Elias Child House B&B

50 Perrin Rd
Woodstock, CT 06281
(860)974-9836 (877)974-9836 Fax:(860)974-1541
Internet: www.eliaschildhouse.com
E-mail: afelice@earthlink.net

Circa 1700. Nine fireplaces warm this heritage three-story colonial home, referred to as "the mansion house" by early settlers. There are two historic cooking hearths, including a beehive oven. Original floors, twelve-over-twelve windows and paneling remain. A bountiful breakfast is served fireside in the dining room and a screened porch and a patio provide nesting spots for reading and relaxing. The inn's grounds are spacious and offer a pool and hammocks. Woodland walks on the 47 acres and antiquing are popular activities.

Innkeeper(s): Anthony Felice, Jr. & MaryBeth Gorke-Felice. $100-135. 3 rooms with PB, 3 with FP, 1 suite. Breakfast included in rates. Types of meals: Country bkfst and early coffee/tea. Beds: QDT. Reading lamp, clock radio, turn-down service, bathrobes, suite has two fireplaces, sitting room and two baths (one with a clawfoot tub) in room. Air conditioning. TV, VCR, DVD, fax, copier, swimming, bicycles, library, parlor games, telephone, fireplace, hearth-cooking demonstrations, cross-country skiing and snowshoeing on premises. Antiquing, bicycling, canoeing/kayaking, fishing, golf, hiking, museums, parks, shopping and wineries nearby.

Location: Country.

Publicity: *Time Out New York, Best Fares Magazine, Distinction, Wine Gazette, Car & Driver Magazine, Worcester Telegram and Gazette.*

"Comfortable rooms and delightful country ambiance."

Certificate may be used: Sunday through Thursday, except holidays, Valentine's Day and certain specialty weekends.

The Inn at Woodstock Hill

94 Plaine Hill Rd
Woodstock, CT 06281-2912
(860)928-0528 Fax:(860)928-3236
Internet: www.woodstockhill.com
E-mail: innwood@gmail.com

Circa 1826. This classic Georgian house with its black shutters and white clapboard exterior reigns over 14 acres of rolling farmland. Inside are several parlors, pegged-wood floors, English country wallpapers and floral chintzes. Four-poster beds and  woodburning fireplaces enhance the special ambience.

Innkeeper(s): Richard Naumann. $100-220. 21 rooms with PB, 8 with FP, 2 two-bedroom suites, 1 cottage, 1 guest house, 4 conference rooms. Breakfast included in rates. Types of meals: Full gourmet bkfst, Sun. brunch, early coffee/tea, gourmet lunch, picnic lunch, snacks/refreshments, hors d'oeuvres, wine, gourmet dinner and room service. Restaurant on premises. Beds: KQDT. Modem hook-up, data port, cable TV, VCR, DVD, reading lamp, clock radio, telephone, coffeemaker, desk, voice mail, most with fireplace, hair dryer, bath amenities, wireless Internet access and iron/ironing board in room. Air conditioning. Fax, copier, library, pet boarding, parlor games, laundry facility, gift shop, phone, TV and broadband Internet at no charge on premises. Handicap access. Antiquing, art galleries, bicycling, cross-country skiing, fishing, golf, hiking, horseback riding, live theater, museums, parks, shopping, sporting events, tennis and wineries nearby.

Location: Country.

Publicity: *Hartford Courant, Worcester Telegram, Connecticut Magazine and Country Inns.*

"You can go to heaven, I'll just stay here!"

Certificate may be used: Accepts Weekends, Anytime subject to availability, Anytime, Last Minute-Based on Availability .

Delaware

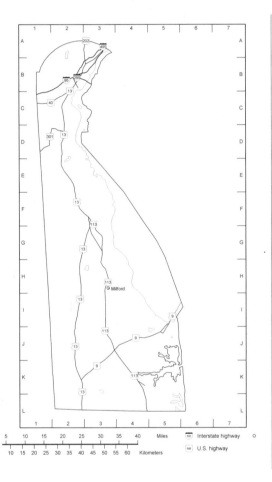

5   10   15   20   25   30   35   40   Miles
10 15 20 25 30 35 40 45 50 55 60   Kilometers

nn Interstate highway
nn U.S. highway

Milford

The Towers B&B

101 NW Front St
Milford, DE 19963-1022
(302)422-3814 (800)366-3814
Internet: www.mispillion.com
E-mail: mispillion@ezol.com

Circa 1783. Once a simple colonial house, this ornate Steamboat Gothic fantasy features every imaginable Victorian architectural detail, all
added in 1891. There are
10 distinct styles of gingerbread as well as towers, turrets, gables, porches and
bays. Inside, chestnut and
cherry woodwork, window

seats and stained-glass windows are complemented with American and French antiques. The back garden boasts a sun-room and swimming pool. Ask for the splendid Tower Room or Rapunzel Suite.

Innkeeper(s): Daniel & Rhonda Bond. $110-160. 4 rooms with PB, 2 suites. Breakfast included in rates. Beds: QD. Reading lamp, ceiling fan and clock radio in room. Air conditioning. Swimming, telephone and fireplace on premises. Antiquing, fishing, live theater, parks, shopping and water sports nearby.

Location: City, ocean community.

Publicity: *Washington Post, Baltimore Sun, Washingtonian and Mid-Atlantic Country.*

"I felt as if I were inside a beautiful Victorian Christmas card, surrounded by all the things Christmas should be."

Certificate may be used: Any night of the week throughout the year, except NASCAR Race weekends and holidays.

Florida

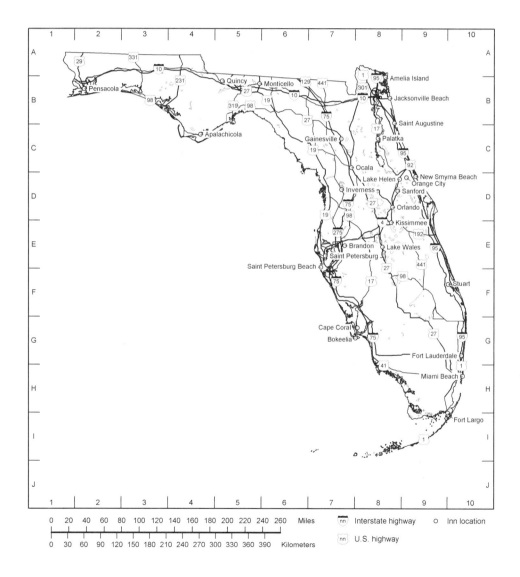

0 20 40 60 80 100 120 140 160 180 200 220 240 260 Miles

0 30 60 90 120 150 180 210 240 270 300 330 360 390 Kilometers

Interstate highway   O Inn location

U.S. highway

Amelia Island

Amelia Island Williams House

103 S 9th St
Amelia Island, FL 32034-3616
(904)277-2328 (800)414-9258
Internet: www.williamshouse.com
E-mail: info@williamshouse.com

Circa 1856. It's not this grand Antebellum mansion's first owner, but its second for whom the house is named. Marcellus Williams and his wife, a great-great-granddaughter of the King of Spain, are its most esteemed residents. Among their many influential guests, the two once hosted Jefferson Davis and, ironically, the first owners used part of the home for the Underground Railroad. It will be hard for guests to believe that the home was anything but opulent. Antiques from nine different countries decorate the home. The guest rooms are romantic; the gourmet breakfast served on the finest china; and the lush, fragrant grounds are shaded by a 500-year-old oak tree. The innkeepers also have restored the historic home next door, which was used as an infirmary during the Civil War. Four of the guest rooms are housed here, complete with clawfoot or Jacuzzi tubs.

Innkeeper(s): Deborah and Byron McCutchen. $219-280. 10 rooms with PB, 5 with FP, 1 with HT, 3 with WP. Breakfast, snacks/refreshments and wine included in rates. Types of meals: Full gourmet bkfst, picnic lunch and gourmet dinner. Beds: KQ. Data port, cable TV, VCR, reading lamp, ceiling fan, clock radio, telephone, coffeemaker, desk, most with hot tub/spa, most with fireplace, hair dryer, bathrobes, Flowers, Bottled water and Cookies upon arrival in room. Air conditioning. Fax, copier, bicycles, library, parlor games, laundry facility, video library, large verandas, balconies, porches, beach towels, bicycles and beach chairs/umbrellas available, daily maid service and concierge service on premises. Handicap access. Antiquing, art galleries, beach, bicycling, canoeing/kayaking, fishing, golf, hiking, horseback riding, live theater, museums, parks, shopping, sporting events, tennis, water sports, sailing, zoo, windsurfing, mo-peds, history tours, ghost tours, carriage rides, Cumberland Island Trips and Fort Clinch Park nearby.

Location: Ocean community. Historic District.

Publicity: *Best 100 in the World Conde Naste Traveler 2004, Waters Edge 2004, Jacksonvillle Magazine 2004, Southern Lady 2004, Country Inns, Southern Living, Southern Accents, Victoria, Veranda, Palm Beach Life, Arrington's Journal, CNN International Travel and Inn Country USA.*

Certificate may be used: May-January mid-week subject to availability. Last minute subject to availability.

Apalachicola

Coombs House Inn

80 6th St
Apalachicola, FL 32320
(850)653-9199 (888)244-8320 Fax:(850)653-2785
Internet: www.coombshouseinn.com
E-mail: info@coombshouseinn.com

Circa 1905. This Victorian manor was built for James N. Coombs, a wealthy lumber baron who served in the Union Army. Despite his Yankee roots, Coombs was an influential figure in Apalachicola. The home has been lovingly restored to reflect its previous grandeur. Co-owner Lynn Wilson is a renown interior designer and her talents accent the inn's high ceilings, tiled fireplaces and period antiques. Bright English fabrics decorate windows and Oriental rugs accentuate the hardwood floors.

Innkeeper(s): Estella Banta, Scott & Ana Wilson. $79-229. 19 rooms, 23 with PB, 1 with WP, 3 suites, 3 guest houses, 1 conference room. Breakfast, afternoon tea, snacks/refreshments, hors d'oeuvres, wine and Weekend wine and cheese receptions 6-7 PM included in rates. Types of meals: Full bkfst, veg

bkfst and early coffee/tea. Beds: KQDT. Modem hook-up, data port, cable TV, reading lamp, refrigerator, ceiling fan, clock radio, telephone, coffeemaker, desk, some with hot tub/spa, hair dryer, bathrobes, bath amenities, wireless Internet access and iron/ironing board in room. Central air. Fax, copier, bicycles, parlor games, fireplace, gift shop, Complimentary beach chairs, Umbrellas and Towels on premises. Handicap access. Antiquing, art galleries, beach, bicycling, canoeing/kayaking, fishing, golf, hiking, horseback riding, live theater, museums, parks, shopping, tennis, water sports and Sailing nearby.

Location: City, ocean community. Historic District.

Publicity: *Southern Living, Florida Design and Country Inns Magazine.*

Certificate may be used: Dec. 1-Jan. 31, weekdays only in specific rooms, pending availability. Please contact innkeeper for availability. No holidays.

Bokeelia

Bokeelia Tarpon Inn

8241 Main St
Bokeelia, FL 33922-1550
(239)283-8961 (866)TARPON2 Fax:(239)283-8215
Internet: www.tarponinn.com
E-mail: Info@tarponinn.com

Circa 1914. Originally known as the 1914 Poe Johnson home, this historic waterfront bed and breakfast is located on the Gulf Coast?s Pine Island. Restored to offer a relaxed pace, it especially caters to fisherfolk. Deepwater fishing is accessible from the private dock and boat ramp. Tackle, rods and equipment can be requested. The Knot Room is filled with fishing resources, memorabilia and a library. Enjoy twilight-time refreshments by the fireplace in the living room. The screened-in second-story porch features sweeping views of Charlotte Harbor and Gasparilla Island. Guest bedrooms are all named for local islands in the Pine Island Sound. An expanded tropical breakfast is sure to please. Golf carts, kayaks, and bikes are available to explore the area. A wine cellar and cigar humidor add to the amenities.

Innkeeper(s): Cynthia Welch. $159-325. 5 rooms with PB. Breakfast, snacks/refreshments, hors d'oeuvres and wine included in rates. Types of meals: Cont plus, picnic lunch and room service. Beds: Q. Modem hook-up, reading lamp, ceiling fan, clock radio, telephone, hair dryer, bathrobes, bath amenities, wireless Internet access and iron/ironing board in room. Air conditioning. VCR, fax, copier, bicycles, parlor games, fireplace, laundry facility and gift shop on premises. Handicap access. Art galleries, beach, bicycling, canoeing/kayaking, fishing, golf, museums, parks, shopping and tennis nearby.

Location: Waterfront.

Certificate may be used: June 30-Dec. 1.

Brandon

Behind The Fence B&B Inn

1400 Viola Dr at Countryside
Brandon, FL 33511-7327
(813)685-8201
Internet: www.floridasecrets.com/fence.htm

Circa 1976. Experience the charm of New England on Florida's west coast at this secluded country inn surrounded by tall pines and oaks. Although the frame of the home was built in the mid-1970s, the innkeepers searched Hillsborough County for 19th-century and turn-of-the-century artifacts, including old stairs, doors, windows, a pantry and the back porch. Guests can stay either in the main house or in a two-bedroom cottage. All rooms are filled with antique Amish-county furniture. The innkeepers serve fresh popcorn on cool nights in front of the fireplace. Breakfast includes fresh fruit, cereals, juices, coffees and delicious Amish sweet rolls.

Innkeeper(s): Larry & Carolyn Yoss. $79-99. 5 rooms, 3 with PB, 1 suite, 1 cottage, 1 conference room. Breakfast and afternoon tea included in rates. Types of meals: Cont plus, early coffee/tea and snacks/refreshments. Beds: DT. Cable TV, reading lamp, refrigerator, clock radio and desk in room. Air conditioning. VCR, swimming, telephone and fireplace on premises. Amusement parks, antiquing, canoeing/kayaking, fishing, horseback riding, parks, shopping, sporting events and water sports nearby.

Location: Subdivision to County Park.

Publicity: *Brandon News, Travel Host, Country Living, Country Home and Florida Secrets.*

"One of the best kept secrets in all of Tampa! Thanks again!"

Certificate may be used: Anytime, subject to availability.

Cape Coral

A-Bayview Bed & Breakfast

12251 Shoreview Drive
Cape Coral, FL 33993-0035
(239)283-7510 Fax:(239)283-7510
Internet: www.webbwiz.com/bayviewbb
E-mail: cbirds@webtv.net

Circa 2000. A magnificent view of Matlacha Bay is seen in a relaxing and tranquil setting from this waterfront bed & breakfast on the Gulf Coast. Newly built in the Old Florida Cracker style of architecture, it features a bright and cheery interior with floral accents. Each spacious, air-conditioned guest suite includes a refrigerator, television and relaxing decks or porches to watch boats, birds, dolphin and manatee. A continental-plus breakfast offers local fruits, cereals, and baked goods. Fish from the pier or canoe the mangroves. Boat dockage is available. Visit the local Caloosa Indian Shell Mounds and Museum. Take a tour of Edison's and Ford's winter estates in Fort Myers.

Innkeeper(s): Diane LeRoy. $99-179. 4 suites. Breakfast included in rates. Types of meals: Cont plus and early coffee/tea. Beds: Q. Cable TV, reading lamp, ceiling fan, telephone and turn-down service in room. Central air. Fax and free use of canoes on premises. Limited handicap access. Amusement parks, antiquing, art galleries, beach, bicycling, canoeing/kayaking, fishing, golf, hiking, horseback riding, live theater, museums, parks, shopping, tennis, water sports and wineries nearby.

Location: Waterfront. In an old Florida fishing village with craft shops.

Certificate may be used: May-November, Sunday-Thursday, excluding holidays, rack rates apply, cannot use in conjunction with any other promotion.

Gainesville

Camellia Rose Inn

205 S. E. 7th Street
Gainesville, FL 32601
(772)528-9562
Internet: www.camelliaroseinn.com
E-mail: info@camelliaroseinn.com

Circa 1903. Recently renovated, Camellia Rose Inn offers modern technology and pleasing amenities wrapped in a warm and cozy ambiance that reflects its Queen Anne-era beginning in historic Gainesville, Florida. Relax on the wraparound porch with a beverage or snack. More than forty different varieties of camellias, azaleas, crape myrtle, oak and red bud trees adorn the grounds. Stay in one of the spacious guest bedrooms with freshly pressed bed linens. Most feature a fireplace and spa shower. The Anticipation master suite boasts a corner bubble tub while Southern Charm has a clawfoot. On the second floor, Stardust includes a private balcony overlooking the gardens. A detached cottage offers even more privacy. Wake up and indulge in a

delicious three-course breakfast in the dining room.

Innkeeper(s): Tom & Patricia McCants. $125-165. 6 rooms with PB. Breakfast, snacks/refreshments, hors d'oeuvres and wine included in rates. Types of meals: Full bkfst, early coffee/tea, Fresh baked cookies and Evening happy hour. Beds: KQT. Cable TV, VCR, DVD, reading lamp, CD player, ceiling fan, snack bar, clock radio, turn-down service, desk, most with fireplace, hair dryer, bathrobes, bath amenities, wireless Internet access, iron/ironing board and Spa showers in all rooms except Master Suite that has a corner bubble tub in room. Central air. Fax, bicycles and library on premises. Handicap access. Antiquing, art galleries, bicycling, canoeing/kayaking, fishing, golf, hiking, horseback riding, live theater, museums, parks, shopping, sporting events, water sports and Shands Teaching Hospital nearby.

Location: City.

Certificate may be used: June-August, anytime subject to availability.

Magnolia Plantation Cottages and Gardens

309 SE 7th Street
Gainesville, FL 32601-6831
(352)375-6653 Fax:(352)338-0303
Internet: www.magnoliabnb.com
E-mail: info@magnoliabnb.com

Circa 1885. This restored French Second Empire Victorian is in the National Register. Magnolia trees surround the house. Five guest rooms are filled with family heirlooms. All bathrooms feature clawfoot tubs and candles. There are also private historic cottages available with Jacuzzis. Guests may enjoy the gardens, reflecting pond with waterfalls and gazebo. Bicycles are also available. Evening wine and snacks are included. The inn is two miles from the University of Florida.

Innkeeper(s): Joe & Cindy Montalto. $90-250. 5 rooms with PB, 5 with FP, 5 with WP, 7 cottages. Breakfast and afternoon tea included in rates. Types of meals: Full bkfst. Beds: Q. TV, reading lamp, ceiling fan, clock radio, turn-down service, desk, hot tub/spa, fireplace, cottages have Jacuzzi, fireplace, full kitchen and private garden in room. Air conditioning. VCR, fax, bicycles, library, telephone and cocktail hour on premises. Antiquing, live theater, parks, shopping and sporting events nearby.

Location: City.

Publicity: *Florida Living Magazine and Inn Country USA.*

"This has been a charming, once-in-a-lifetime experience."

Certificate may be used: Sunday-Thursday, all year or anytime, last minute.

Jacksonville Beach

Fig Tree Inn

185 4th Ave S
Jacksonville Beach, FL 32250
(904)246-8855 (877)217-9830
Internet: www.figtreeinn.com
E-mail: egghouse@comcast.net

Circa 1915. Whether staying here for a romantic getaway or to cheer for a favorite football team, this cedar shake bed & breakfast inn with Victorian accents offers an inviting and relaxing atmosphere. Sip a cool beverage in a rocker or swing on the acclaimed front porch. Games, books and magazines as well as an extensive video library are in the parlor. Wireless high-speed Internet service is available. Stay warm by the fire on cool nights. Themed guest bedrooms feature a handmade willow and canopy bed, Jacuzzi and clawfoot tub. The backyard's namesake produces enough fruit to make fig walnut pancakes, fig jelly and preserves served on scones. A light meal is served weekdays, a full breakfast is enjoyed on weekends. The kitchen can be used at any time. Walk to the beach, only half a block away.

Innkeeper(s): Dawn & Kevin Eggleston. $135-175. 6 rooms with PB, 2 conference rooms. Breakfast, afternoon tea and snacks/refreshments included in rates. Types of meals: Full gourmet breakfast on the weekend; Continental weekdays and special diets upon request. Beds: KQT. Modem hook-up, cable TV, VCR, DVD, reading lamp, stereo, refrigerator, ceiling fan, snack bar, clock radio, telephone, coffeemaker, desk, hot tub/spa, hair dryer, bathrobes, bath amenities, wireless Internet access and iron/ironing board in room. Central air. Fax, copier, spa, bicycles, library, parlor games, fireplace, laundry facility and video library on premises. Limited handicap access. Amusement parks, antiquing, art galleries, beach, bicycling, canoeing/kayaking, fishing, golf, hiking, live theater, museums, parks, shopping, sporting events, tennis, water sports, wineries, cruise ships, NFL and college football nearby.

Location: Ocean community.

Certificate may be used: Special events and holidays excluded.

Key Largo

Tarpon Flats Inn

29 Shoreland Dr
Key Largo, FL 33037-4750
(305)453-1313
Internet: www.tarponflats.com
E-mail: info@tarponflats.com

Circa 1966. Surrounded by a lush tropical setting overlooking Largo Sound, Tarpon Flats Inn and Marina is located on the island of Key Largo just 60 minutes south of Miami, Florida. It has been fully restored and includes the inn, conch house and marina to offer a romantic bed and breakfast experience as well as charter fly fishing and other excursions. Relax on a hammock, enjoy the private sandy beach, swim in the pool or take out a kayak. Delightful guest bedrooms and suites feature a Victorian elegance, Caribbean flair, British Mahogany furnishings, waterfront verandas, entertainment centers and some include kitchenettes. Special packages are available.

Innkeeper(s): Carol Rodgers. $165-220. 6 suites. Breakfast included in rates. Types of meals: Cont. Beds: QT. Modem hook-up, cable TV, VCR, DVD, reading lamp, stereo, refrigerator, ceiling fan, clock radio, coffeemaker and hair dryer in room. Central air. Fax, swimming, bicycles, telephone, laundry facility, Fishing, Scuba diving, Snorkeling, Hammock, Private beach and Pool on premises. Art galleries, beach, canoeing/kayaking, hiking, museums, parks, shopping, water sports, Golf, Fine dining, Eco tours and Dolphin swim nearby.

Location: Ocean community.

Certificate may be used: May 1 to December 15, excluding holidays and weekends. May be used on a 3-night stay including a weekend.

Kissimmee

Wonderland Inn B & B

3601 South Orange Blossom Trail
Kissimmee, FL 34746
(407)847-2477 (877)847-2477 Fax:(407)847-4099
Internet: www.wonderlandinn.com
E-mail: innkeeper@wonderlandinn.com

Circa 1950. Cradled by oaks and orange trees, this brick country inn has been renovated recently to offer gracious Southern hospitality in a relaxed, elegant setting. Artistically-appointed guest bedrooms, suites and a romantic honeymoon cottage feature hand-painted garden scenes and nature murals. Generous amenities include terry cloth robes, refrigerators, coffee makers,

data ports, turndown service and much more. Delve into a delicious breakfast in the Main House, and gather later for a sunset wine and cheese hour. Play croquet, and then indulge in pampering spa services.

Innkeeper(s): Rosemarie O'Shaughnessy, Sonia Bergman - Wedding Planner. $79-159. 11 rooms with PB. Types of meals: Full bkfst and early coffee/tea. Beds: KQD. Modem hook-up, data port, cable TV, VCR, DVD, reading lamp, stereo, refrigerator, ceiling fan, clock radio, telephone and coffeemaker in room. Air conditioning. Fax, library, parlor games, laundry facility and four-course breakfast on premises. Limited handicap access. Amusement parks, antiquing, art galleries, beach, canoeing/kayaking, fishing, golf, hiking, horseback riding, live theater, museums, parks, shopping, water sports, wineries, Disneyworld (15 minutes), Sea World (20 minutes) and Universal (30 minutes) nearby.

Location: City. Minutes from Disneyworld.

Publicity: *Florida Magazine, Florida USA and Tampa Bay.*

Certificate may be used: May-June, subject to availability, no other discounts apply when using this promotion. Excludes holidays and special events.

Lake Helen

The Ann Stevens House

201 E Kicklighter Rd
Lake Helen, FL 32744-3514
(386)228-0310 (800)220-0310 Fax:(386)228-2337
Internet: www.annstevenshouse.com
E-mail: info@annstevenshouse.com

Circa 1895. This three-story, turn-of-the-century vernacular Victorian inn is surrounded by a variety of trees in a quiet, country setting. The inn is listed in the national, state and local historic registers, and offers eight guest rooms, all with private bath. Each room features a different type of country decor, such as Americana, English and country. Guests enjoy hot tubbing in the Victorian gazebo or relaxing on the inn's porches, which feature rockers, a swing and cozy wicker furniture. Borrow  a bike to take a closer look at the historic district. Cassadaga, Stetson University, fine dining and several state parks are nearby.

Innkeeper(s): Ed & Helene Gracy. $130-170. 10 rooms with PB, 1 with FP, 2 with WP. Breakfast and snacks/refreshments included in rates. Types of meals: Country bkfst. Beds: KQ. Cable TV, reading lamp, ceiling fan, clock radio, telephone, desk, some with hot tub/spa, hair dryer, bathrobes, bath amenities, wireless Internet access and private screened porch in room. Central air. VCR, fax, copier, spa, bicycles, library, parlor games, fireplace, gift shop, nature trails through forest and meditation areas on premises. Limited handicap access. Amusement parks, antiquing, beach, bicycling, canoeing/kayaking, fishing, golf, hiking, horseback riding, live theater, parks, sporting events, tennis, water sports and Daytona & New Smyrna beaches nearby.

Location: Country. Small town.

Certificate may be used: April 1-Nov. 30, Sunday-Thursday, excludes holidays.

Lake Wales

Chalet Suzanne Country Inn & Restaurant

3800 Chalet Suzanne Dr
Lake Wales, FL 33859-7763
(863)676-6011 (800)433-6011 Fax:(863)676-1814
Internet: www.chaletsuzanne.com
E-mail: info@chaletsuzanne.com

Circa 1924. Situated on 70 acres adjacent to Lake Suzanne, this country inn's architecture includes gabled roofs, balconies, spires and steeples. The superb restaurant has a glowing reputation and offers a six-course candlelight dinner. Places of interest on the property include the Swiss Room, Wine Dungeon, Gift Boutique, Autograph Garden, Museum, Ceramic Salon, Airstrip and the Soup Cannery. The inn has been transformed into a village of cottages and miniature chateaux, one connected to the other seemingly with no particular order.

Innkeeper(s): Eric & Dee Hinshaw. $169-229. 26 rooms with PB. Breakfast included in rates. Types of meals: Full bkfst, lunch and gourmet dinner. Beds: KDT. Cable TV, reading lamp, clock radio and telephone in room. Air conditioning. TV, VCR, fax, copier, swimming, library, parlor games and spa services on premises. Handicap access. Amusement parks, antiquing, fishing, golf, live theater, parks, shopping, sporting events, tennis and water sports nearby.

Location: Waterfront. Rural-lakefront.

Publicity: *National Geographic Traveler, Southern Living, Country Inns, Uncle Ben's 1992 award and Country Inn Cooking.*

"I now know why everyone always says, 'Wow!' when they come up from dinner. Please don't change a thing."

Certificate may be used: Accepts Weekends, Anytime, Last Minute-Based on Availability; Anytime, subject to availability.

New Smyrna Beach

Night Swan Intracoastal B&B

512 S Riverside Dr
New Smyrna Beach, FL 32168-7345
(386)423-4940 (800)465-4261 Fax:(386)427-2814
Internet: www.nightswan.com
E-mail: info@nightswan.com

Circa 1906. From the 140-foot dock at this waterside bed & breakfast, guests can gaze at stars, watch as ships pass or perhaps catch site of dolphins. The turn-of-the-century home is

decorated with period furnishings, including an antique baby grand piano, which guests are invited to use. Several guest rooms afford views of the Indian River, which is part of the Atlantic Intracoastal Waterway. Seven rooms include a large whirlpool tub. The innkeepers have created several special packages, featuring catered gourmet dinners, boat tours or romantic baskets with chocolate, wine and flowers.

Innkeeper(s): Martha & Chuck Nighswonger. $100-200. 15 rooms with PB, 1 with FP, 3 total suites, including 2 two-bedroom suites, 1 cottage, 1 conference room. Breakfast and snacks/refreshments included in rates. Types of meals: Full bkfst and early coffee/tea. Beds: KQ. Modern hook-up, cable TV, VCR, DVD, reading lamp, refrigerator, ceiling fan, clock radio, telephone, desk, hair dryer, wireless Internet access, iron/ironing board and seven whirlpool tubs in room. Air conditioning. Fax, library, fireplace and laundry facility on premises. Handicap access. Antiquing, art galleries, beach, bicycling, canoeing/kayaking, fishing, golf, horseback riding, live theater, museums, parks, shopping, tennis and water sports nearby.

Location: Waterfront.

Publicity: *Ft. Lauderdale Sun Sentinel and Florida Living.*

Certificate may be used: June 1-Jan. 30, Sunday-Thursday, except holidays.

Ocala

Seven Sisters Inn

820 SE Fort King St
Ocala, FL 34471-2320
(352)867-1170 (800)250-3496 Fax:(352)867-5266
Internet: www.sevensistersinn.com
E-mail: sevensistersinn@msn.com

Circa 1888. Gracing the historic district with its stately elegance, this 1888 Queen Anne Victorian bed & breakfast has been meticulously restored and is listed in the National Register. The furnishings and décor of the themed guest bedrooms reflect the four corners of the world. Sleep in a Sultan's bed in India, explore Egyptian artifacts, lounge in French luxury in Paris or experience the harmony of the Orient in China. A three-room suite instills old-fashioned romance with American accents and a canopy bed. Heated towel bars, whirlpool tubs, fireplaces and stone spa showers are delightful amenities included in most rooms. Award-winning recipes are part of a gourmet breakfast served in Monet's Morning Room with crystal, silver, white china and fine linens. Indulge in afternoon tea after a morning bike ride. Ask about candlelit dinners, special events and packages.

Innkeeper(s): Ken Oden & Bonnie Morehardt. $119-279. 13 rooms, 9 with PB, 7 with FP, 4 with WP. Breakfast, afternoon tea, snacks/refreshments and wine included in rates. Types of meals: Full gourmet bkfst, veg bkfst, early coffee/tea, picnic lunch and Gourmet Candlelight Dinners also available with 2-days notice. Beds: KQ. Modern hook-up, data port, cable TV, VCR, DVD, reading lamp, CD player, ceiling fan, clock radio, telephone, coffeemaker, turn-down service, desk, most with hot tub/spa, most with fireplace, hair dryer, bathrobes, bath amenities, wireless Internet access, Ironing/ironing boards available, All rooms have access to refrigerators and microwaves. in room. Central air. Fax, copier, library, parlor games, gift shop and small pets accommodated in designated guest rooms on premises. Handicap access. Antiquing, art galleries, bicycling, canoeing/kayaking, fishing, golf, hiking, horseback riding, live theater, museums, parks, shopping, water sports, wineries, Day Trips: Ocala National Forest, Silver Springs Park, Rainbow Springs Park, Homosassa Springs Park, Bok Tower Gardens, Disney and Cypress Gardens and much more nearby.

Location: City. Historic District.

Publicity: *Southern Living, Southern Lady, Glamour, Conde Nast Traveler and Country Inns (one of 12 best).*

Certificate may be used: Sunday-Thursday, no holidays or weekends.

Orange City

Alling House Bed and Breakfast

215 E. French Ave.
Orange City, FL 32763
(386)775-7648 Fax:(386)775-7648
Internet: www.allinghousebb.com
E-mail: info@allinghousebb.com

Circa 1908. The Alling House Bed and Breakfast has been well-preserved to reflect its Victorian heritage. Spanning almost three acres in Ocean City, Florida, the landscaped grounds include a goldfish pond. Relax on the front porch accented by shade trees and the surrounding residential neighborhood. Play games, use the guest computer and browse the book and video library in the second-floor common room that has a refrigerator stocked with drinks and snacks. Gather in the family room or parlor and listen to the vintage baby grand piano. Stay in a comfortable guest bedroom furnished with antiques or a cottage with kitchen facilities. Just three miles away, see the manatees at St. John's River and Blue Spring State Park. Daytona and New Smyrna Beach are a 30-minute drive.

Innkeeper(s): Gerald and Nan Hill. $95-135. 6 rooms with PB, 2 with FP, 3 with WP, 3 cottages. Breakfast, snacks/refreshments, Cottages have full kitchens and therefore breakfast is not included in the rate. Breakfast in the main house is available for $5 per person included in rates. Types of meals: Country bkfst, veg bkfst and early coffee/tea. Beds: KQT. Cable TV, VCR, DVD, reading lamp, CD player, refrigerator, ceiling fan, clock radio, coffeemaker, desk, hair dryer, bathrobes, bath amenities, wireless Internet access and iron/ironing board in room. Central air. Bicycles, library, parlor games, telephone and laundry facility on premises. Handicap access. Antiquing, beach, bicycling, canoeing/kayaking, fishing, golf, hiking, horseback riding, live theater, parks, shopping, sporting events, water sports, Hot air balloon rides and Dinner cruises nearby.

Location: City.

Certificate may be used: May-December, excluding NASCAR and Daytona Bike Events.

Orlando

The Courtyard at Lake Lucerne

211 N Lucerne Circle E
Orlando, FL 32801-3721
(407)648-5188 (800)444-5289 Fax:(407)246-1368
Internet: www.orlandohistoricinn.com
E-mail: info@orlandohistoricinn.com

Circa 1885. This award-winning inn, precisely restored with attention to historical detail, consists of four different architectural styles. The Norment-Parry House is Orlando's oldest home. The Wellborn, an Art-Deco Modern Building, offers one-bedroom suites with kitchenettes. The I.W. Phillips is an antebellum-style manor where breakfast is served in a large reception room with a wide veranda overlooking the courtyard fountains  and lush gardens. The Grand Victorian Dr. Phillips House is listed in the National Register of Historic Places. For an enchanting treat, ask for the Turret Room.

Innkeeper(s): David Messina. $89-225. 30 rooms with PB, 1 conference room. Breakfast included in rates. Types of meals: Cont plus. Beds: KQD.

Cable TV, reading lamp, refrigerator, clock radio, telephone, desk and hot tub/spa in room. Air conditioning. TV, copier and fireplace on premises. Amusement parks, antiquing, fishing, live theater, shopping, sporting events and water sports nearby.

Location: City.

Publicity: *Florida Historic Homes, Miami Herald, Southern Living and Country Victorian.*

"Best-kept secret in Orlando."

Certificate may be used: Anytime, subject to availability, on regular rate for standard rooms.

Palatka

Azalea House

220 Madison St
Palatka, FL 32177-3531
(386)325-4547
Internet: www.theazaleahouse.com
E-mail: azaleahouse@gbso.net

Circa 1878. Located within the Palatka Historic District, this beautifully embellished Queen Anne Victorian is painted a cheerful yellow with complementing green shutters. Bay windows, gables and verandas have discrete touches of royal blue, gold, white and aqua on the gingerbread trim, a true "Painted Lady." There are oak, magnolia and palm trees and an 85-year-old, grafted camellia tree with both pink and white blossoms. Double parlors are furnished with period antiques including an arched, floor-to-ceiling mirror. A three-story heart and curly pine staircase leads to the guest rooms. There is a needlework shop on site. Two blocks away is the mile-wide north flowing St. John's River. An unaltered golf course designed by Donald Ross in 1925 is nearby, as well as the Ravine State Botanical Garden. It's 25 minutes to Crescent Beach.

Innkeeper(s): Doug & Jill de Leeuw. $90-150. 6 rooms, 4 with PB. Breakfast and snacks/refreshments included in rates. Types of meals: Full bkfst and early coffee/tea. Beds: Q. Reading lamp, ceiling fan, clock radio, turn-down service and hair dryer in room. Central air. TV, swimming, library, parlor games, telephone, fireplace, gift shop, Needlework shop and Wee Forest Folk Retailer on premises. Antiquing, fishing, golf, live theater, parks, shopping and water sports nearby.

Location: City. Historic district.

Publicity: *American Treasures and 2002 B&B Calendar.*

Certificate may be used: June 1-Aug. 31.

Quincy

Allison House Inn

215 N Madison St
Quincy, FL 32351
(850)875-2511 (888)904-2511 Fax:(850)875-2511
Internet: www.allisonhouseinn.com
E-mail: innkeeper@tds.net

Circa 1843. Crepe myrtle, azaleas, camellias and roses dot the acre of grounds that welcomes guests to the Allison House. A local historic landmark located in the 36-block historic district, the inn is in a Georgian, English-country style with shutters and an entrance portico. It was built for General Allison, who became Governor of Florida. There are two parlors, and all the rooms are appointed with English antiques. Homemade biscotti is always available for snacking and for breakfast, English muffins and freshly baked breads are offered. Walk around the district and spot the 51 historic homes and buildings. Nearby dining opportunities include the historic Nicholson Farmhouse Restaurant.

Innkeeper(s): Stuart & Eileen Johnson. $85-150. 6 rooms with PB. Breakfast and snacks/refreshments included in rates. Types of meals: Full bkfst and wine. Beds: KQD. Modem hook-up, cable TV, reading lamp, ceiling fan, clock radio, telephone, hair dryer, bathrobes, bath amenities, wireless Internet access, iron/ironing board, individual air conditioning controls and hair dryers in room. Air conditioning. Fax and bicycles on premises. Handicap access. Antiquing, art galleries, beach, bicycling, fishing, golf, horseback riding, live theater, sporting events and tennis nearby.

Location: City. Small town.

Certificate may be used: June 15-Sept. 15, Sunday-Thursday.

Saint Augustine

Agustin Inn

29 Cuna St
Saint Augustine, FL 32084-3681
(904)823-9559 (800)248-7846 Fax:(904)824-8685
Internet: www.agustininn.com
E-mail: info@agustininn.com

Circa 1903. Situated in the historic walking district of our nation's oldest city, this Victorian inn captures the ambiance of old downtown St. Augustine. Innkeepers Robert and Sherri Brackett, members of Historic Inns of St. Augustine, FBBI and Superior Small Lodging, have furnished the home in comfortable elegance. The 18 guest bedrooms boast mahogany or canopy beds and oval Jacuzzi-style bath tubs. Some of the bedrooms have private entrances and terraces where early coffee or tea and evening wine and hors d'oeuvres can be enjoyed while overlooking the fragrant courtyards. Sherri's full homemade breakfasts are satisfying and may feature Belgian waffles, quiche, baked French toast, or omelets with homemade biscuits, blueberry muffins or banana bread. Venturing out on the cobblestone streets offers a variety of activities and historical sites.

Innkeeper(s): Laurie-Ann and Stephen Lee. $89-359. 18 rooms with PB, 17 with WP, 1 conference room. Breakfast, snacks/refreshments and Hors d'oeuvres on Friday & Saturday included in rates. Types of meals: Full bkfst, early coffee/tea and Hors d'oeuves on Friday & Saturday. Beds: Q. Cable TV, reading lamp, refrigerator, ceiling fan, clock radio, hair dryer, bath amenities, iron/ironing board and Jacuzzi style bath tubs in room. Central air. Fax, copier and telephone on premises. Handicap access. Antiquing, art galleries, beach, fishing, golf, museums, parks, shopping and wineries nearby.

Location: Historic District.

Certificate may be used: January, June, July, August and September, Sunday-Thursday, excluding holidays, subject to availability.

Casablanca Inn on The Bay

24 Avenida Menedez
Saint Augustine, FL 32084
(904)829-0928 (800)826-2626
Internet: www.casablancainn.com
E-mail: innkeeper@casablancainn.com

Circa 1914. One of Henry Flagler's engineers built this Mediterranean Revival home with its panoramic Matanzas Bay views. Situated in the historic district, Fort Castillo de San Marcos is seen easily from the sprawling veranda. The inn is furnished and decorated with antiques and one-of-a-kind collectibles appropriately placed for comfort and style. Choose from guest bedrooms or suites offering private sun decks and entries, pillow-top mattresses, Jacuzzis and decorative fireplaces. Hospitality is generous with a sumptuous two-course breakfast. Complimentary beverages and fresh-baked cookies are extra enjoyable when gathered on a porch in a rocker over-

looking the ocean. Designated off-street parking is provided, with many attractions, shops, museums and restaurants within an easy walk. Bikes are available for further fresh-air exploration. Voted "Best B&B" by the local residents.

Innkeeper(s): Nancy & Mike Miles. $119-399. 13 rooms, 20 with PB, 10 suites. Breakfast, afternoon tea and snacks/refreshments included in rates. Types of meals: Full gourmet bkfst and early coffee/tea. Beds: Q. Modem hook-up, data port, TV, reading lamp, ceiling fan, clock radio, telephone, desk and hot tub/spa in room. Central air. Fax, bicycles and fireplace on premises. Limited handicap access. Antiquing, art galleries, beach, bicycling, canoeing/kayaking, fishing, golf, hiking, horseback riding, live theater, museums, parks, shopping, sporting events, tennis, water sports, wineries, boating, World Golf Village and Jacksonville Jaguars (NFL) nearby.

Location: City. Historic District of nation's oldest city.

Publicity: *Atlanta Journal* and featured on St. Augustine Ghost tour.

Certificate may be used: June-November, Sunday-Thursday.

Castle Garden B&B

15 Shenandoah St
Saint Augustine, FL 32084-2817
(904)829-3839
Internet: www.castlegarden.com
E-mail: castleg@aug.com

Circa 1860. This newly-restored Moorish Revival-style inn was the carriage house to Warden Castle. Among the seven guest rooms are three bridal rooms with in-room Jacuzzi tubs and sunken bedrooms with cathedral ceilings. The innkeepers offer packages including carriage rides, picnic lunches, gift baskets and other enticing possibilities. Guests enjoy a homemade full, country breakfast each morning.

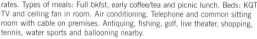

Innkeeper(s): Bruce & Brian Kloeckner. $99-229. 7 rooms with PB, 3 suites. Breakfast included in rates. Types of meals: Full bkfst, early coffee/tea and picnic lunch. Beds: KQT. TV and ceiling fan in room. Air conditioning. Telephone and common sitting room with cable on premises. Antiquing, fishing, golf, live theater, shopping, tennis, water sports and ballooning nearby.

Location: City.

Certificate may be used: Sunday-Thursday. Other times if available.

Centennial House

26 Cordova St
Saint Augustine, FL 32084-3627
(904)810-2218 (800)611-2880 Fax:(904)810-1930
Internet: www.centennialhouse.com
E-mail: innkeeper@centennialhouse.com

Circa 1899. In the heart of the historic district on the horse-drawn carriage route, this meticulously restored home maintains 19th century aesthetics with generous modern amenities. Relax in the garden courtyard and enjoy the landscaped grounds of this premier inn. Impressive suites and guest bedrooms are sound insulated and offer almost every luxury imaginable for leisure or business. The inn is handicap accessible. Savor a complete gourmet breakfast each morning. Special dietary requests are met with gracious hospitality. It is an easy stroll to a wide variety of local sites and attractions.

Innkeeper(s): Geoff & Ellen Fugere. $130-260. 8 rooms with PB, 3 with FP. Breakfast included in rates. Types of meals: Full gourmet bkfst and early coffee/tea. Beds: KQ. Data port, cable TV, VCR, reading lamp, ceiling fan, clock radio, telephone, desk, most with hot tub/spa, some with fireplace, hair dryer, bathrobes, bath amenities, wireless Internet access, iron/ironing board, down pillows, Egyptian cotton towels, video library, complimentary soft drinks, early morning coffee/tea, 19th-century aesthetics and soundproof insulation in room. Central air. Fax, copier, parlor games and video library on premises. Handicap access. Amusement parks, antiquing, art galleries, beach, bicycling, canoeing/kayaking, fishing, golf, hiking, horseback riding, live theater, museums, parks, shopping, sporting events, tennis, water sports and wineries nearby.

Location: City, ocean community.

Certificate may be used: May-October, Sunday-Thursday, excluding holidays, subject to availability.

House Of Sea & Sun Bed & Breakfast

2 B St
Saint Augustine, FL 32080-6905
(904)461-1716 Fax:(904)461-1319
Internet: www.houseofseaandsun.com
E-mail: info@houseofseaandsun.com

Circa 1914. House of Sea and Sun Bed & Breakfast spans more than one acre with oceanfront views. St. Augustine Beach is just 25 feet away with boogie boards, chairs and towels provided. Built in 1914, this Florida B&B offers generous hospitality and comfort. Relax on Victorian antiques by the fireplace in the living room. Stay in a guest suite with a whirlpool, clawfoot or soaking tub. Some rooms lead out onto a brick patio. One-bedroom condo suites boast full kitchens and balconies. Gather in the sunny breakfast room for a morning meal made from original recipes. Bikes are available for exploring the historic area.

Innkeeper(s): Patty Steder. $99-225. 6 rooms with PB, 3 with WP, 4 guest houses. Breakfast, snacks/refreshments and hors d'oeuvres included in rates. Types of meals: Full bkfst and early coffee/tea. Beds: KQ. Cable TV, reading lamp, CD player, refrigerator, ceiling fan, clock radio, coffeemaker, hair dryer, bathrobes, bath amenities, wireless Internet access and iron/ironing board in room. Central air. VCR, DVD, fax, copier, swimming, bicycles, library, parlor games, telephone, fireplace, laundry facility and Pet friendly in some rooms on premises. Limited handicap access. Amusement parks, antiquing, art galleries, beach, bicycling, canoeing/kayaking, fishing, golf, hiking, horseback riding, live theater, museums, parks, shopping, sporting events, tennis, water sports and wineries nearby.

Location: Ocean community, waterfront.

Certificate may be used: Aug. 1-Jan. 31, Monday-Thursday.

Inn on Charlotte Street

52 Charlotte St
Saint Augustine, FL 32084-3647
(904)829-3819 (800)355-5508 Fax:(904)810-2134
Internet: www.innoncharlotte.com
E-mail: innkeeper@innoncharlotte.com

Circa 1918. Majestic palms accentuate the exterior of this brick home, adorned by a sweeping two-story veranda with columns. The inn is located among many gems within the heart of the Old City's historic district for a perfect vacation spot. Furnished with antiques, over-stuffed sofas and wicker, all guest bedrooms include a Jacuzzi tub. Relax on a porch swing and absorb the peaceful sights and sounds. Walk to nearby Castillo de San Marco and the many local shops and restaurants.

Innkeeper(s): Lynne Fairfield. $129-269. 8 rooms with PB, 1 with FP, 7 with WP, 1 suite. Breakfast, snacks/refreshments and wine included in rates. Types of meals: Full gourmet bkfst and early coffee/tea. Beds: KQ. Cable TV, reading lamp, ceiling fan, clock radio, most with hot tub/spa, hair dryer, bath amenities, wireless Internet access and iron/ironing board in room. Central air. Parlor games and telephone on premises. Antiquing, art galleries, beach, bicycling, canoeing/kayaking, fishing, golf, live theater, museums, parks, shopping, sporting events, tennis, water sports, wineries and historical re-enactments nearby.

Location: Nation's oldest city.

Publicity: *Southern Living.*

Certificate may be used: Sunday-Thursday during months of July-September excluding holidays.

Old City House Inn & Restaurant

115 Cordova St
Saint Augustine, FL 32084-4413
(904)826-0113 Fax:Call ahead
Internet: www.oldcityhouse.com
E-mail: relax@oldcityhouse.com

Circa 1873. Strategically located in the center of a city immersed in history, this award-winning inn and restaurant was a former stable. Recently it was locally voted the "best of St. Augustine" and nationally voted one of the "Top 15 inns" for its cuisine. A red-tiled roof, coquina walls, veranda and courtyard add to the Spanish atmosphere. Guest bedrooms boast hand-carved, four-poster beds and high-speed Internet. Some rooms feature Jacuzzi tubs. An expansive daily gourmet breakfast is included. The on-site restaurant is open for lunch and dinner. Unique salads, fresh fish and chicken create the midday menu, while dinner selections boast standards such as Filet Mignon and the more unusual South African Emu or Thai curry entrees. Choose an appetizer of baked brie, low country grits or escargot.

Innkeeper(s): James & Ilse Philcox. $149-239. 7 rooms with PB, 2 with HT, 1 conference room. Breakfast included in rates. Types of meals: Full gourmet bkfst, veg bkfst, Sun. brunch, early coffee/tea, gourmet lunch, afternoon tea, snacks/refreshments, wine and gourmet dinner. Restaurant on premises. Beds: Q. Data port, cable TV, VCR, DVD, reading lamp, CD player, ceiling fan, clock radio, telephone, desk, some with hot tub/spa, voice mail, bath amenities, four-poster hand-carved beds, some with Jacuzzis, telephones and data ports and all private entrances in room. Central air. Fax, copier, bicycles, award-winning and cozy restaurant with full bar and fireside lounge on premises. Handicap access. Antiquing, art galleries, beach, bicycling, canoeing/kayaking, fishing, golf, hiking, horseback riding, live theater, museums, parks, shopping, sporting events, tennis, water sports and wineries nearby.

Location: City, ocean community, waterfront. Historic downtown.

Publicity: *Arrington's B&B Journal: Top 15 Inns Nationally for Cuisine, St. Augustine Record's: Best of St. Augusting; Florida Times Union, Florida Trend, Ft. Lauderdale Sun Sentinel, Florida Secrets, Miami Herald, Daily Mail, Travel Channel, British BBC, Jacksonvile Floria Channel 4 NBC affiliate and Greenboro NC Channel 17 NBC affiliate.*

Certificate may be used: Sunday-Thursday, Non-holidays.

St. Francis Inn

279 Saint George St
Saint Augustine, FL 32084-5031
(904)824-6068 (800)824-6062 Fax:(904)810-5525
Internet: www.stfrancisinn.com
E-mail: info@stfrancisinn.com

Circa 1791. Rich in old-world charm and modern comforts, St. Francis Inn is located in St. Augustine Antigua, Florida, a restored historic district in the nation's oldest city. Walk along the brick-paved streets or ride a complimentary bicycle to tour downtown. Enjoy free admission to the St. Augustine Lighthouse and Museum

and discounts to other popular sites in this seaside city. Swim in the refreshing pool or relax on a private deck or porch. All day long house-blend coffees, hot chocolate, assorted teas and cappuccinos are available. Gather for conversation at the evening social hour. Guest bedrooms and suites boast antiques or reproduction furniture, and several have kitchenettes or refrigerators, electric fireplaces and whirlpool or clawfoot tubs. The Cottage is ideal for a family or for two couples. Start the day's adventures with a delicious buffet breakfast.

Innkeeper(s): Joe Finnegan. $139-269. 17 rooms, 14 with PB, 8 with FP, 4 suites, 1 cottage, 2 conference rooms. Breakfast, snacks/refreshments and hors d'oeuvres included in rates. Types of meals: Full gourmet bkfst, Daily evening social, evening desserts. Bloody Marys and Mimosas with breakfast on weekends and holidays. Inn-baked cookies, apples and coffee and other beverages all day. Complimentary sherry in every room. Picnic Baskets also available . Beds: KQDT. Cable TV, VCR, DVD, reading lamp, CD player, refrigerator, ceiling fan, clock radio, telephone, desk, some with hot tub/spa, most with fireplace, wireless Internet access, Fresh flowers and Sherry greet you in your room in room. Central air. Fax, copier, swimming, bicycles, parlor games, gift shop, Free parking, Fri/Sat/Holiday complimentary local evening transportation, Facilities to spend a day on St. Augustine Beach, Free & discount attractions admissions and Local health club access on premises. Limited handicap access. Antiquing, art galleries, beach, bicycling, canoeing/kayaking, fishing, golf, hiking, horseback riding, live theater, museums, parks, shopping, sporting events, tennis, water sports, wineries, Horse-drawn carriage rides, Trolley tours, Bay cruises, Many superb restaurants, Historic sites, Reenactments, Ghost tours, Festivals, Art fairs and Musical performances nearby.

Location: City. Historic Old City.

Publicity: *Orlando Sentinel.*

"We have stayed at many nice hotels but nothing like this. We are really enjoying it."

Certificate may be used: May 1 to Feb. 10, Sunday-Thursday, excluding holiday periods.

Saint Petersburg

La Veranda Bed & Breakfast

111 5th Ave. N
Saint Petersburg, FL 33701
(727)824-9997 (800)484-8423X8417 Fax:(727)827-1431
Internet: www.laverandabb.com
E-mail: info@laverandabb.com

Circa 1910. Featuring Old World charm in an urban setting, this classic Key West-style mansion is only two blocks from the waterfront. Antiques, Oriental rugs and artwork accent the gracious elegance. Lounge by the fire in the living room or on one of the large wicker-filled wraparound verandas overlooking lush tropical gardens. Romantic one- and two-bedroom suites boast private entrances, as well as indoor and outdoor sitting areas. A gourmet breakfast with Starbucks coffee is served on settings of china, silver and crystal. Corporate services are available with assorted business amenities.

Innkeeper(s): Nancy Mayer. $185-299. 10 rooms, 5 with PB, 5 suites. Breakfast and snacks/refreshments included in rates. Types of meals: Full gourmet bkfst, veg bkfst, early coffee/tea, afternoon tea and room service. Beds: KQT. Cable TV, VCR, reading lamp, CD player, refrigerator, ceiling fan, snack bar, clock radio, telephone, turn-down service, desk and fireplace in room. Air conditioning. Fax, copier, bicycles, library, fireplace and laundry facility on premises. Limited handicap access. Amusement parks, antiquing, art galleries, beach, bicycling, canoeing/kayaking, fishing, golf, hiking, live theater, museums, parks, shopping, sporting events, water sports and wineries nearby.

Location: City.

Publicity: *NY Daily Times and Interstate 75.*

Certificate may be used: Sunday-Thursday, subject to availability.

Larelle House Bed & Breakfast

237 6th Avenue, NE
Saint Petersburg, FL 33701-2603
(727)490-3575 (888)439-8387 Fax:(727)490-5098
Internet: www.larellehouse.com
E-mail: info@larellehouse.com

Circa 1908. Surrounded by a wrought-iron fence, the lushly landscaped grounds of this 1908 three-story Queen Anne Victorian feature a four-tiered, fountain on a brick courtyard. Relax on the spacious wicker-filled front veranda or two back porches with tropical breezes. An in-ground hot tub in the backyard garden sits under a gazebo with Corinthian columns and flowering bougainvillea. Home-made snacks and refreshments and a guest refrigerator are available any time in the dining room. Browse the video and DVD library in the sunroom. Evening wine and cheese are offered in the fireside parlor. Guest bedrooms feature an assortment of pleasing amenities and some boast a bay window, clawfoot tub and pedestal sink. Turndown service includes handmade chocolates and port or sherry. After breakfast take a scenic bike ride.

Innkeeper(s): Ellen & Larry Nist. $119-209. 4 rooms with PB. Breakfast, snacks/refreshments and wine included in rates. Types of meals: Full gourmet bkfst. Beds: KQD. Cable TV, DVD, reading lamp, CD player, ceiling fan, clock radio, turn-down service, desk, hair dryer, bathrobes, bath amenities, and iron/ironing board in room. Central air. VCR, fax, copier, spa, bicycles, library, parlor games, telephone, fireplace, TV/DVD in common area Sun Room, beautiful in-ground hot tub in back yard garden, refreshments and home made snacks available 24/7, guest refrigerator in dining room, wireless Internet access and free phone calls on premises. Amusement parks, antiquing, art galleries, beach, bicycling, fishing, golf, live theater, museums, parks, shopping, sporting events, tennis, water sports, wineries, The Pier, BayWalk, regular weekend events in the numerous waterfront parks, air shows and fireworks from our unique widow's walk for a perfect view nearby.

Publicity: *Superior Small Lodging Association's Highest Honor - The Donal A. Dermody White Glove Award*

Certificate may be used: June-October, Sunday-Thursday, subject to availability when presented at time of reservation, excludes holidays and special events.

Stuart

Inn Shepard's Park Bed and Breakfast

601 SW. Ocean Blvd.
Stuart, FL 34994
(772)781-4244
Internet: www.innshepard.com
E-mail: marilyn@innshepard.com

Circa 1924. Gracing the heart of The River Front Village, this quaint and intimate Key West style home is an easy walk to the shops, restaurants and entertainment of historic downtown. Nap in the hammock surrounded by a garden oasis or relax on the wraparound porch. Socialize in the sunroom or in the main parlor area. Browse the video library. Themed guest bedrooms are air-conditioned and boast an assortment of white or natural wicker accents, an antique mahogany four-poster bed, oak furnishings and an iron bed. Enjoy views of Shepard's Park and Frazier Creek. A breakfast buffet is served on the covered front porch. Take an early-morning bike ride. The waterfront is only 400 feet away. Beach chairs, coolers and a single or double kayak are available.

Innkeeper(s): Marilyn Miller. $85-200. 4 rooms, 2 with PB. Breakfast and snacks/refreshments included in rates. Types of meals: Cont plus and early coffee/tea. Beds: QD. Cable TV and ceiling fan in room. Central air. Bicycles, library and fireplace on premises. Antiquing, art galleries, beach, bicycling, canoeing/kayaking, fishing, golf, horseback riding, live theater, museums, parks and tennis nearby. Location: Ocean community, waterfront.

Certificate may be used: June-September, weekdays excluding holidays.

Georgia

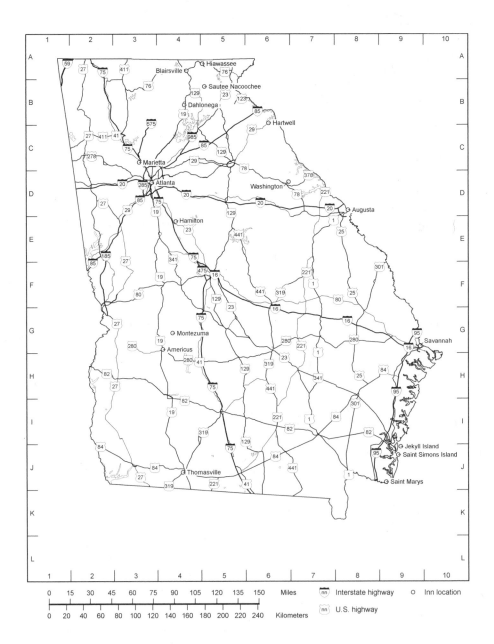

Tell the innkeeper that you have an iLoveInns free-night certificate when you make your reservation.

Atlanta

King-Keith House B&B

889 Edgewood Ave NE
Atlanta, GA 30307
(404)688-7330 (800)728-3879
Internet: www.kingkeith.com
E-mail: kingkeith@mindspring.com

Circa 1890. One of Atlanta's most photographed houses, this Queen Anne Victorian sits among live oaks and prominent homes in the restored neighborhood of Inman Park. Listed in the National Register, it boasts twelve-foot ceilings and carved fireplaces. Play the baby grand piano in one of the elegant public rooms and stroll through the private gardens. Enjoy complimentary snacks and beverages. Romantic guest bedrooms offer a variety of pleasing amenities, gorgeous antiques and some feature clawfoot tubs. The Downstairs Suite includes a Jacuzzi tub, living room and private entrance off the front porch. Originally the servant's quarters, the spacious Cottage is a honeymoon favorite with vaulted ceilings, double Jacuzzi and an elegant garden with a fountain. Linger over a gourmet breakfast served with generous southern hospitality.

Innkeeper(s): Jan & Windell Keith. $90-200. 4 rooms with PB, 1 suite, 1 cottage. Breakfast included in rates. Types of meals: Full bkfst and early coffee/tea. Beds: KQDT. Cable TV, reading lamp, refrigerator, ceiling fan, snack bar, clock radio, telephone, desk, hair dryer and cottage with Jacuzzi and fireplace in room. Air conditioning. Parlor games on premises. Antiquing, golf, live theater, parks, shopping, sporting events, tennis and restaurants nearby.

Location: City. Downtown.

Publicity: *Southern Living, Victorian Homes (cover), Collector Inspector and HGTV.*

Certificate may be used: Good only Sunday, Monday, Tuesday, Wednesday and Thursday.

Blairsville

Misty Mountain Inn & Cottages

4376 Misty Mountain Ln
Blairsville, GA 30512-6648
(706)745-4786 (888)647-8966
Internet: www.jwww.com/misty
E-mail: mistyinn@windstream.net

Circa 1890. This Victorian farmhouse is situated on a four-acre compound and also features six mountainside cottages located in the woods surrounding the inn. Four spacious guest rooms

in the main house have private baths and fireplaces. All are decorated in country antiques with hand-crafted accessories, quilts and green plants. Two cottages boast antique beds and Jacuzzi tubs. The lofted bedroom cottages can comfortably sleep more than two people, offering full baths, living rooms and eat-in kitchens. Flea markets, festivals, antique craft shops,

lakes, waterfalls and hiking trails are located nearby.

Innkeeper(s): Peg Shaw. $70-100. 4 rooms with PB, 10 with FP, 6 cottages. Breakfast included in rates. Types of meals: Full bkfst and early coffee/tea. Beds: QT. Reading lamp, ceiling fan, clock radio, desk, fireplace, private balcony or porch and all cottages have fireplace in room. Air conditioning. Fax and telephone on premises. Limited handicap access. Antiquing, bicycling, canoeing/kayaking, fishing, golf, hiking, horseback riding, live theater, museums, parks, shopping, water sports, wineries and Misty Mountain Model Railroad (open to the public for tours May through December) nearby.

Location: Mountains.

Certificate may be used: December through September except holidays and area festivals and special events.

Dahlonega

Lily Creek Lodge

2608 Auraria Rd
Dahlonega, GA 30533
(706)864-6848 (888)844-2694
Internet: www.lilycreeklodge.com
E-mail: lilycreeklodge@windstream.net

Circa 1984. Seven forested acres surround Lily Creek Lodge, and guests will enjoy grounds that offer gardens, a secluded hot tub, a swimming pool with a waterfall and a treehouse where breakfasts can be served. There is a common area indoors with a large stone fireplace, or guests can relax on the deck or in the pavilion out by the pool. A gazebo and swing also are romantic items guests will discover on the lush grounds. Each room has been decorated with a special theme in mind, from the Montana Suite with its oak log bed to the Geisha Suite with its Asian appointments. On arrival, guests are greeted with a selection of port, wine and homemade cookies or other treat. Dahlonega is rich in history, and it is in this historic town that gold was first discovered in the United States. Guests can look for antiques, pan for gold or enjoy the many outdoor activities.

Innkeeper(s): Don & Sharon Bacek. $109-219. 14 rooms, 13 with PB, 1 with WP, 7 suites, 1 conference room. Breakfast, snacks/refreshments and wine included in rates. Types of meals: Full gourmet bkfst, veg bkfst, picnic lunch and Vegetarian by advance request. Beds: KQ. Cable TV, VCR, DVD, reading lamp, desk, some with hot tub/spa, some with fireplace, bath amenities, wireless Internet access, Some with kitchens, Ceiling fans, Coffeemakers, Bathrobes, Microwave and Clocks available on request in room. Central air. Fax, copier, spa, swimming, library, parlor games, telephone, gift shop, Bocci court, Treehouse, Gazebo, Walking trails, Hammock and Fire pit on premises. Antiquing, art galleries, bicycling, canoeing/kayaking, fishing, golf, hiking, horseback riding, live theater, museums, parks, shopping, water sports, wineries, Arts, Crafts, Waterfalls, Festivals, Apple orchards, Vineyards & Tasting rooms, Zoo and Kangaroo Conservation Center nearby.

Location: Country, mountains. 4 miles from historic town of Dahlonega.

Publicity: *New York Times, Nashville Tennessean, Montgomery Alabama Advertiser, Walking Magazine, Dahlonega Nugget, Atlanta Journal Constitution, Piedmont Review, Blue Ridge Country Magazine, Huntsville Alabama Times and PBS Chattanooga - Southern Accents.*

Certificate may be used: Sunday-Thursday, subject to availability, from Jan. 1 to April 30, excluding holidays and special events.

Hamilton

Magnolia Hall B&B

127 Barnes Mill Rd
Hamilton, GA 31811
(706)628-4566
Internet: www.magnoliahallbb.com
E-mail: kgsmag@juno.com

Circa 1890. Fancy gingerbread trim decorates the wide veranda of this two-story Victorian settled in an acre of magnolias and century-old hollies near the courthouse. Heart-pine floors, tall ceilings, antiques, a grand piano and china, crystal and silver service for breakfast set the mood for a gracious inn stay. One of the house specialties is Baked Georgia Croissant with fresh peaches and toasted almonds. It's five miles to Callaway Gardens and 20 miles to Warm Springs.

Innkeeper(s): Dale & Kendrick Smith. $105-125. 5 rooms with PB, 2 suites. Breakfast and snacks/refreshments included in rates. Types of meals: Full gourmet bkfst and early coffee/tea. Beds: QT. Cable TV, VCR, reading lamp, clock radio, turn-down service, desk and refreshments in room. Air conditioning. Parlor games, telephone, fireplace, rockers and porch swing on premises. Handicap access. Amusement parks, antiquing, fishing, golf, parks, shopping, sporting events, tennis, water sports, Wild Animal Park and FDR Home nearby.

Location: Small town, rural setting.

Publicity: Victorian Homes, Georgia Journal, Georgia Magazine and National Geographic Traveler.

Certificate may be used: Monday-Thursday.

Hartwell

Shuler Manor

714 Early Drive
Hartwell, GA 30643
(706)377-3550 (866)377-3550
Internet: www.shulermanor.com
E-mail: bnb@shulermanor.com

Circa 2000. Retreat to two acres of panoramic lakeside bliss at this newly built Federal-style heirloom quality home. Furnished and decorated with a customized style of traditional and contemporary, the foyer leads to a coffered ceiling game parlor with billiards and two great rooms with stone and granite fireplaces and satellite TV. One suite offers transom windows; one suite has a full wall of windows. Six of seven rooms all have fantastic waterfront views. One suite offers a fireplace and Jacuzzi tub. This sheltered peninsula of Lake Hartwell is a perfect refuge to enjoy wildlife, walk nature paths, explore the gardens, sit on the dock or go fishing. A hot tub is a welcome treat for all.

Innkeeper(s): Gary & Theresa Shuler. $75-165. 7 rooms, 4 with PB, 1 with FP, 3 total suites, including 1 two-bedroom suite and 1 three-bedroom suite, 1 cottage, 1 conference room. Breakfast and snacks/refreshments included in rates. Types of meals: Country bkfst, early coffee/tea and afternoon tea. Beds: KQDT. Modem hook-up, data port, cable TV, VCR, DVD, reading lamp, stereo, refrigerator, ceiling fan, snack bar, clock radio, telephone, coffeemaker, turn-down service, desk, hot tub/spa, some with fireplace, hair dryer, bath amenities, wireless Internet access, iron/ironing board, one suite with fireplace and one suite with Jacuzzi tub in room. Central air. Fax, copier, spa, swimming, library, pet boarding, parlor games, laundry facility, billiards, 2 great rooms with massive fireplaces, TV satellite viewing, outdoor therapeutic hot tub for all guests, panoramic views of lake, dock, horseshoes, swimming, boating and fishing on premises. Handicap access. Antiquing, art galleries, bicycling, canoeing/kayaking, fishing, golf, hiking, horseback riding, live theater, museums, parks, shopping, water sports, wineries, sporting events for Clemson University and/or University of Georgia (45 minute drive), Commerce, GA with 250+ outlet stores, Mall of Georgia, Buford and Greenville/Spartanburg nearby.

Location: Waterfront. On Lake Hartwell with a panoramic view of the lake.

Publicity: Hartwell Sun, Anderson Independent Mail, Simply Southern, Atlanta Woman, Athens Banner Herald and Chic.

Certificate may be used: Sept. 4-April 30, subject to availability.

The Skelton House B&B

97 Benson St
Hartwell, GA 30643
(706)376-7969 (877)556-3790 Fax:(706)856-3139
Internet: www.theskeltonhouse.com
E-mail: info@theskeltonhouse.com

Circa 1896. It is said that history and traditional elegance embrace contemporary comforts and grace at this 1896 Victorian bed and breakfast. Relaxation is easy on one of the two-story covered porches accompanied by refreshments. Take a stroll among the gorgeous gardens that adorn two acres. It is the perfect setting for weddings and other special events. Stay in the romantic Parke's Room suite that features a separate entrance, whirlpool tub with candles and a deck with a rooftop garden. Mama and Papa's Room is handicap accessible. Indulge in a satisfying gourmet breakfast and on Sundays a buffet brunch is too good to miss.

Innkeeper(s): Ruth & John Skelton. $100-135. 7 rooms with PB, 1 conference room. Breakfast, Sunday brunch and snacks/refreshments included in rates. Types of meals: Full gourmet bkfst and early coffee/tea. Beds: QT. Modem hook-up, data port, cable TV, VCR, DVD, reading lamp, ceiling fan, snack bar, telephone, coffeemaker, some with hot tub/spa, hair dryer, bath amenities and iron/ironing board in room. Central air. Fax, copier, library, parlor games and gift shop on premises. Handicap access. Antiquing, canoeing/kayaking, fishing, golf, hiking, horseback riding, live theater, museums, parks, shopping, sporting events, tennis, water sports and wineries nearby.

Location: City.

Certificate may be used: January-March, Sunday-Thursday.

Montezuma

Traveler's Rest B & B

318 N Dooly St
Montezuma, GA 31063-1531
(478)472-0085
Internet: www.travelersrestbb.com
E-mail: travelersrestbb@alltel.net

Circa 1899. Blending the past and the present in the heartland of the South, this 1899 Victorian is romantic and timeless. Relax on a rocking chair with a complimentary soft drink on the wraparound porch. Friendly and attentive service adds to the pleasant ambiance. Movies, books and games are found in the parlor. The Garden Room and guest suites are on the second floor with amenities that include fresh flowers, bottled water, bathrobes and entertainment centers. The Victorian Suite boasts a sitting area and Jacuzzi. A clawfoot tub and shower accent the Civil War Suite with historical pictures in the sitting room. Savor a sumptuous breakfast in the Tea Room. Light or packed lunches, candle-lit dinners and high tea can be arranged when requested in advance. Ask about specials and packages available.

Innkeeper(s): Adele Goodman . $67-97. 4 rooms with PB. Breakfast and snacks/refreshments included in rates. Types of meals: Full gourmet bkfst, veg bkfst, Sun. brunch, early coffee/tea, lunch, picnic lunch, afternoon tea, hors d'oeuvres, wine and gourmet dinner. Cable TV, VCR, DVD, reading lamp, stereo, ceiling fan, clock radio, coffeemaker, turn-down service, desk, some with hot tub/spa, hair dryer, bathrobes, bath amenities, iron/ironing board and day beds/sofa beds in some rooms in room. Central air. Fax, spa, pet boarding, parlor games, gift shop, library (with movies and books), original hard-wood floors, unique staircase, period furnishings and high ceilings on premises. Antiquing, fishing, golf, museums and parks nearby.

Location: Country. Historic South.

Certificate may be used: Anytime, subject to availability.

Saint Simons Island

Village Inn and Pub

500 Mallery St
Saint Simons Island, GA 31522
(912)634-6056
Internet: www.villageinnandpub.com
E-mail: info@villageinnandpub.com

Circa 1930. Between the parks and oceanfront village, this award-winning island B&B inn sits under ancient live oaks. Restored and carefully expanded, the 1930 beach cottage houses the reception, sitting and breakfast areas as well as the Village Pub, a solid mahogany olde English bar and original stone fireplace. Standard and deluxe guest bedrooms are named after historical people with local significance and feature upscale amenities, soothing color palettes, crown molding and custom-built armoires that hold large TVs. Most rooms include a balcony with a view of the pool and flower-filled courtyard or the neighborhood. A generous continental breakfast is available on the sun porch.

Innkeeper(s): Kristy. $140-245. 28 rooms with PB. Breakfast included in rates. Types of meals: Cont plus, wine and Pub on property. Beds: KQD. Modem hook-up, data port, cable TV, reading lamp, ceiling fan, clock radio, telephone, voice mail, hair dryer, bathrobes, bath amenities, wireless Internet access and iron/ironing board in room. Central air. Fax, copier, swimming and fireplace on premises. Antiquing, art galleries, beach, bicycling, canoeing/kayaking, fishing, golf, hiking, horseback riding, live theater, museums, parks, shopping, tennis and water sports nearby.

Location: Ocean community.

Certificate may be used: August through February-based on availability.

Sautee Nacoochee

The Stovall House

1526 Hwy 255 N
Sautee Nacoochee, GA 30571
(706)878-3355
Internet: www.stovallhouse.com
E-mail: info@stovallhouse.com

Circa 1837. This house, built by Moses Harshaw and restored in 1983 by Ham Schwartz, has received two state awards for its restoration. The handsome farmhouse has an

extensive wraparound porch providing vistas of 26 acres of cow pastures and mountains. High ceilings, polished walnut woodwork and decorative stenciling provide a pleasant backdrop for the inn's collection of antiques.

Victorian bathroom fixtures include pull-chain toilets and pedestal sinks. The inn has its own restaurant.

Innkeeper(s): Ham Schwartz. $98. 5 rooms with PB. Breakfast included in rates. Types of meals: Cont and dinner. Restaurant on premises. Beds: KQDT. Ceiling fan and clock radio in room. Air conditioning. Library, parlor games, telephone and fireplace on premises. Amusement parks, antiquing, fishing,

live theater, parks, shopping and water sports nearby.

Location: Mountains.

Publicity: *Atlanta Journal and GPTV - Historic Inns of Georgia.*

"Great to be home again. Very nostalgic and hospitable."

Certificate may be used: Accepts Weekends, Anytime subject to availability, Anytime Last Minute-Based on Availability.

Thomasville

1884 Paxton House Inn

445 Remington Ave
Thomasville, GA 31792-5563
(229)226-5197 Fax:(229)226-9903
Internet: www.1884paxtonhouseinn.com
E-mail: 1884@rose.net

Circa 1884. The picturesque residential neighborhood in the renowned Plantation Region is the perfect setting for this award-winning, historic Gothic Victorian Landmark Home, listed in the National Register. Unique architecture, a grand circular staircase, 12 ornamental fireplaces, 13-foot ceilings, heart-pine floors, a courting window and nine-foot doors reflect remarkable craftsmanship. Museum-quality reproductions, classic antiques, designer fabrics and international collections impart an 18th-century style. Luxurious suites and garden cottages offer upscale amenities that include Egyptian bath towels, terry robes, data ports and sound spas. Breakfast is served with settings of fine china and silver. Indulge in family recipes passed down by generations of Southern chefs. Rock on the wraparound veranda, swim in the indoor lap pool or take a moonlit stroll through the gardens.

Innkeeper(s): Susie M. Sherrod. $165-350. 9 rooms with PB, 3 two-bedroom suites, 2 cottages. Breakfast, afternoon tea and snacks/refreshments included in rates. Types of meals: Full gourmet bkfst, veg bkfst and early coffee/tea. Beds: KQ. Modem hook-up, data port, cable TV, VCR, DVD, reading lamp, refrigerator, ceiling fan, clock radio, telephone, coffeemaker, turn-down service, desk, hot tub/spa, private baths with tub/shower, some with wet bar, iron/ironing board, sound spa, hair dryer, terry robes, goose-down pillows, full-length mirror and high-speed wireless Internet in room. Central air. Fax, copier, spa, swimming, library, parlor games, fireplace, exercise room, computer centers, two with fiber optic high-speed-commercial grade connection, lap pool and lemonade social and teas (by reservation) on premises. Amusement parks, antiquing, art galleries, bicycling, fishing, golf, horseback riding, live theater, museums, parks, shopping, sporting events and tennis nearby.

Location: City.

Publicity: *Fodor's (named the South's and America's "Best" B&B Inn), Frommer's (Four Flags), Southern Living, Travel and Leisure, Georgia Journal ("Best B&B Inn" in the Plantation region of Georgia), American Automobile Association, Times Picayune ("Special Inns of the Southeast"), The Sun ("provides us with a true glimpse of Southern living"), St. Louis Times ("the charm of the 1800s still attracts visitors to Thomasville...[Susie Sherrod's] efforts result in a spectacular variety of blossoms"), WALB TV and WCTV.*

Certificate may be used: July-August, Sunday-Thursday, subject to availability, cannot be combined with any other discount program.

Serendipity Cottage

339 E Jefferson St
Thomasville, GA 31792-5108
(229)226-8111 (800)383-7377 Fax:(229)226-8144
Internet: www.serendipitycottage.com
E-mail: laurag@rose.net

Circa 1906. Serendipity Cottage Bed & Breakfast was built in 1906 as a post Victorian Foursquare. Located by the historic district of Thomasville, Georgia near the border of Florida, it is an easy walk to downtown attractions. Relax on the front porch

with a book from the upstairs library. Peruse the classic menu assortment for afternoon tea and shop in the Cheese Ladies Polish Pottery Shop. Whether staying for business, a vacation or a romantic wedding, the spacious and well-appointed guest bedrooms are peaceful retreats with brass or four-poster beds. Gather each morning for a delightful gourmet breakfast in the enclosed Sun Room before exploring the surrounding scenic area.

Innkeeper(s): Laura & Robert. $125-145. 4 rooms with PB, 2 with FP. Breakfast, snacks/refreshments, Teas and picnic lunches and dinners by special request and advanced reservations included in rates. Types of meals: Full gourmet bkfst, veg bkfst, early coffee/tea, gourmet lunch, picnic lunch, afternoon tea, hors d'oeuvres, gourmet dinner, Teas and picnic lunches and dinners are available by special request and advance notice. Beds: Q. Cable TV, VCR, reading lamp, ceiling fan, clock radio, coffeemaker, hair dryer, bathrobes, bath amenities, wireless Internet access and iron/ironing board in room. Central air. Fax, copier, bicycles, library, parlor games, telephone, fireplace, gift shop and Beautiful koi pond area for relaxing on premises. Amusement parks, antiquing, art galleries, fishing, golf, live theater, museums, parks, shopping, sporting events, Plantation tours and Historical districts nearby.

Location: City.

Publicity: *Tallahassee ABC affiliate channel.*

"Thank you for the wonderful weekend at Serendipity Cottage. The house is absolutely stunning and the food delicious."

Certificate may be used: Call innkeeper, Subject to availability.

Washington

Washington Plantation

15 Lexington Avenue
Washington, GA 30673
(706)678-2006 (877)405-9956 Fax:(706)678-3454
Internet: www.washingtonplantation.com
E-mail: info@washingtonplantation.com

Circa 1828. Period antiques and reproductions furnish this restored 1828 Greek Revival plantation home. Enjoy the seven acres of natural beauty with rose gardens, fountains, a waterfall, stream and koi pond. Scattered seating with tables are shaded by magnolia, oak, dogwood, pecan, hickory, elm and crape myrtle. Relax on a porch rocker or wicker chair. Large, bright guest bedrooms feature lavish draperies, Oriental rugs, brass and crystal chandeliers and fireplaces. Generous upscale amenities pamper and please. Early risers partake of juice and goodies before a full-service Southern breakfast is provided daily. Lunch and dinner can be ordered in advance for an extra charge.

Innkeeper(s): Tom and Barbara Chase. $135-195. 5 rooms with PB, 5 with FP. Breakfast, snacks/refreshments and wine included in rates. Types of meals: Full gourmet bkfst, veg bkfst, early coffee/tea, picnic lunch and gourmet dinner. Beds: KQ. Cable TV, VCR, DVD, reading lamp, stereo, clock radio, telephone, coffeemaker, turn-down service, desk, some with hot tub/spa, fireplace, hair dryer, bathrobes, bath amenities, wireless Internet access and iron/ironing board in room. Central air. Fax, copier, library, parlor games and laundry facility on premises. Antiquing, bicycling, fishing, golf, hiking, horseback riding, live theater, museums, parks, shopping, sporting events, Augusta National Golf Club (one hour) and University of Georgia football stadium (40 miles) nearby.

Location: Country. Historic District.

Publicity: *Washington Tour of Homes, Southern Distinction Magazine, Southern Living Magazine (March and 2006).*

Certificate may be used: June-August anytime, September-May Sunday through Thursday Except April 1-April 10.

Hawaii

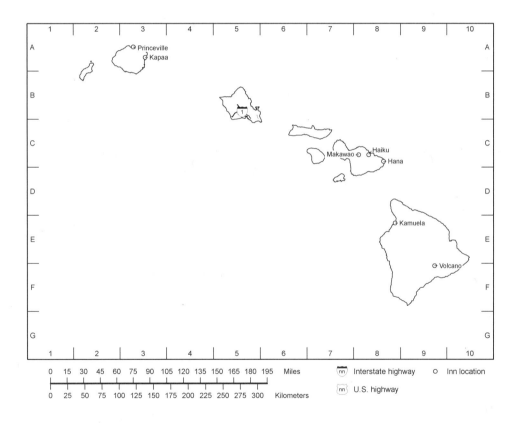

	1	2	3	4	5	6	7	8	9	10	
A			Princeville Kapaa								A
B											B
C							Makawao Haiku Hana				C
D											D
E								Kamuela Volcano			E
F											F
G											G

0 15 30 45 60 75 90 105 120 135 150 165 180 195   Miles

0 25 50 75 100 125 150 175 200 225 250 275 300   Kilometers

(nn) Interstate highway   o Inn location

(nn) U.S. highway

Haiku

Huelo Point Flower Farm

311 Huelo Church Rd
Haiku, HI 96708
(808)572-1850
Internet: www.mauiflowerfarm.com
E-mail: huelopt@maui.net

Experience the Aloha spirit of Hawaii at Huelo Point Flower Farm, a two-acre retreat on sea cliffs overlooking Waipio Bay and the majestic slopes of Mt. Haleakala on the island of Maui. Feel like a local who is surrounded by the paradise of this lush tropical valley on the north shore. Select from spacious Main House, Guest House, glass-walled Gazebo Cottage or Carriage House accommodations that feature private hot tubs, outdoor grills and fully equipped kitchens. Swim in the large pool with a waterfall and relax in the sauna. Pick fresh produce from the organic fruit orchard and enjoy the peaceful oasis.

Innkeeper(s): Ted & Shannon Richardson . Call for rates. 4 rooms, 1 cottage, 3 guest houses. Cable TV, VCR, DVD, reading lamp, stereo, refrigerator, ceiling fan, telephone, coffeemaker, bath amenities, wireless Internet access, Each of our units has a private hot tub, outdoor grill and fully-equipped kitchen in room. Swimming, sauna and laundry facility on premises. Art galleries, beach, bicycling, parks, shopping and water sports nearby.

Location: Country, waterfront. Cliffside rental homes overlook Waipio Bay.

Publicity: *National Geographic Traveler, Travel & Leisure Magazine and San Francisco Examiner Hawaii Magazine (see our web site for reviews).*

Certificate may be used: Last minute (7 days) subject to availability.

Hana

Hana Maui Botanical Gardens B&B

470 Ulaino Road PO 404
Hana, HI 96713
(808)248-7725 Fax:(808)248-7725
Internet: ecoclub.sights/hanamaui
E-mail: JoLoyce@aol.com

Circa 1976. This Hawaiian country farm features a ranch house and duplex with two studio apartments set on 27 acres that include a public botanical garden, fruit trees and flowers. The Flower and Marine studio have a private bath, kitchen, lanai and carport. Also offered is Volcano Heart Chalet near Volcano National Park on the Big Island. The chalet features two keyed rooms, each decorated in an individual theme, private half baths, a shared shower and a shared kitchenette and sitting room with a gas fireplace.

Innkeeper(s): JoLoyce Kaia. $100-125. 2 suites. Types of meals: Cont. Beds: QT. Reading lamp, refrigerator and coffeemaker in room. Parlor games, telephone, no alcohol, no smoking, free access to 10-acre botanical gardens and fruit picking in season on premises. Art galleries, canoeing/kayaking, hiking, horseback riding, museums, parks, shopping and swimming nearby.

Location: Country. Public Botanical garden.

Certificate may be used: Anytime, subject to availability. Reservations may be made only one month in advance to qualify for one night free.

Volcano

A'Alani Volcano Heart Hawaii

11th St
Volcano, HI 96785
(808)248-7725 Fax:(808)248-7725
Internet: ecoclub.com/hanamaui
E-mail: joloyce@aol.com

Circa 1987. This comfortable cedar home can be your base for visiting one of Hawaii's most fascinating landscapes. The entrance to Volcano National Park is just two miles away from this inn, which is nestled in a natural setting of tree ferns and ohia trees. The park features hiking trails around Kilauea volcano crater and through landscape that changes from forest to arid to tropical. The Volcano Art Center, volcano exhibit and observatory are a must for everyone and provide great insight into the Hawaiian culture.

Innkeeper(s): Jo Loyce Kaia. $100-125. 3 rooms. Types of meals: Cont. Beds: QT. Reading lamp, no alcohol and no smoking in room. VCR, telephone, fireplace, laundry facility and sitting room with gas fireplace on premises. Antiquing, art galleries, beach, golf, hiking, horseback riding, museums, parks, shopping, Volcano National Park, Orchid Nursery and Winery nearby.

Location: Mountains. Near Volcano National Park.

Certificate may be used: Reservations may be made only one month in advance to qualify for one free night.

Tara Firma Inn - Volcano

19-4251 Kekoanui Blvd.
Volcano, HI 96785
(808)985-7204 Fax:(808)967-7184
Internet: www.TaraFirmaInn-Volcano.com
E-mail: TaraFirmaInn@Hawaii.rr.com

Circa 1989. Surrounded by the lush tropical rainforest amid giant ferns and gorgeous orchids, this inn is perfectly located to easily exience the many incredible sights and attractions of the island. After a day at the sand and surf relax in the great room with a cool drink. The Fern and Ginger guest bedrooms feature private entrances that lead onto the deck. The second-floor Orchid Suite boasts a sitting area. A continental breakfast buffet is provided daily. Hawaii Volcanoes National Park is just three miles away, a must-see. Tour a nearby macadamia nut farm, visit stunning waterfalls and soak up the natural beauty of a black sand beach.

Innkeeper(s): Kate & Fritz Bell. Call for rates. 3 rooms, 1 with PB, 1 suite. Breakfast, Coffe and tea and water are available anytime included in rates. Types of meals: Cont plus. Beds: QD. Clock radio and hair dryer in room. VCR, DVD, fireplace, coffee makers, refrigerator and a microwave on premises. Art galleries, golf, hiking, museums, parks, shopping, wineries and Hawaii Volcanoes National Park nearby.

Location: Country, mountains. Hawaii Volcanoes National Park.

Certificate may be used: Anytime, subject to availabilty.

Idaho

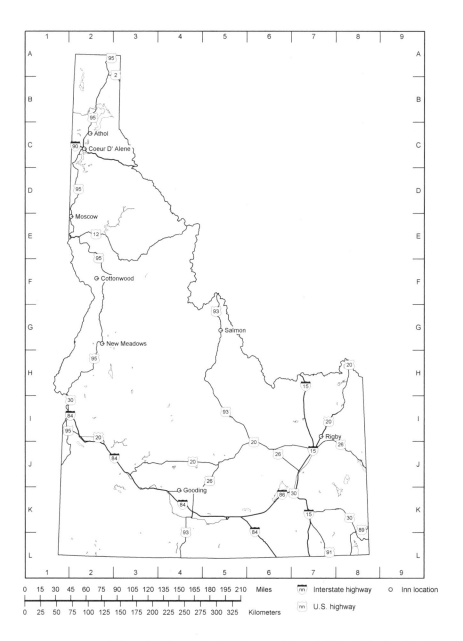

0 15 30 45 60 75 90 105 120 135 150 165 180 195 210 Miles

0 25 50 75 100 125 150 175 200 225 250 275 300 325 Kilometers

nn Interstate highway

nn U.S. highway

○ Inn location

Athol

Cedar Mountain Farm

25249 N Hatch Rd
Athol, ID 83801-8683
(208)683-0572
Internet: www.cedarmountainfarm.com
E-mail: info@cedarmountainfarm.com

Circa 1998. Expect down-home peaceful hospitality at Cedar Mountain Farm in Athol, the heart of Northern Idaho. This working family farm spans 440 acres of field, creek, mountains and forest; perfect for vacations, reunions, retreats, seminars and weddings. Enjoy hiking, biking, sledding, cross-country skiing or snowshoeing. Fish in Sage Creek, watch for birds and wildlife and pet the farm animals. The library invites relaxation and the game closet is well-stocked. Stay in a guest suite or log cabin with kitchen and laundry facilities. The Forest Suite boasts an electric fireplace, and the Bunkhouse offers more space and privacy. Wheelchair-accessible Granny's Woods features a jetted tub, two-headed walk-in shower and can be adjoined with Spring, both located in one wing of the main cabin. Savor a hearty breakfast served family style.

Innkeeper(s): Al and Daryl Kyle. $115-150. 4 rooms with PB, 1 with FP, 1 with WP, 3 two-bedroom suites, 2 cabins, 1 conference room. Breakfast and snacks/refreshments included in rates. Types of meals: Country bkfst, veg bkfst and early coffee/tea. Beds: KQDT. Modem hook-up, reading lamp, ceiling fan, hair dryer and bath amenities in room. TV, VCR, DVD, fax, copier, library, parlor games, laundry facility, desk, refrigerator, kitchen privileges, laundry privileges, snacks, telephone, iron/ironing board and microwave on premises. Limited handicap access. Amusement parks, antiquing, art galleries, beach, bicycling, canoeing/kayaking, cross-country skiing, downhill skiing, fishing, golf, hiking, horseback riding, live theater, museums, parks, shopping, tennis, water sports and wineries nearby.

Location: Country, mountains.

Publicity: *June 2006 issue of Horizon Air Magazine AgraTourism.*

Certificate may be used: Sunday through Thursday during October, November, Early December, January, February, March and April. Not valid with any other special. Good for 2 days only.

Coeur d Alene

The Roosevelt Inn

105 E Wallace Ave
Coeur d Alene, ID 83814-2947
(208)765-5200 (800)290-3358 Fax:(208)664-4142
Internet: www.therooseveltinn.com
E-mail: info@therooseveltinn.com

Circa 1905. This turn-of-the-century, red brick home was named for President Roosevelt and is the oldest schoolhouse in town. Roosevelt translates to Rosefield in Dutch, and the innkeepers have created a rosy theme for the inn. The Bell Tower Suite and the Honeymoon Suite are the favorite room requests, but all rooms offer Victorian antiques and some have lake views. Coeur d' Alene has been recognized by National Geographic Magazine as one of the five most beautiful lakes in the world. The area offers the world's longest floating boardwalk and Tubb's Hill Nature Park. A variety of shops and restaurants are within a five minute stroll from the inn. The natural surroundings offer mountain biking, boating, skiing and hiking.

Innkeeper(s): John & Tina Hough. $89-319. 15 rooms, 12 with PB, 3 with FP, 6 total suites, including 4 two-bedroom suites, 2 conference rooms. Breakfast, afternoon tea and snacks/refreshments included in rates. Types of meals: Full gourmet bkfst, veg bkfst, early coffee/tea, Murder Mystery Dinners and Special party dinners for groups. Beds: KQ. Reading lamp, CD player, clock radio, turn-down service, hair dryer, bath amenities, wireless Internet access and iron/ironing board in room. Central air. TV, VCR, DVD, fax, copier, spa, swimming, sauna, library, pet boarding, parlor games, telephone, fireplace, gift shop and Rose greeting in room on premises. Handicap access. Amusement parks, antiquing, art galleries, beach, bicycling, canoeing/kayaking, cross-country skiing, downhill skiing, fishing, golf, hiking, horseback riding, live theater, museums, parks, shopping, sporting events, tennis, water sports, wineries, Lake Cruises, boating, para sailing, Catamaran Cruises and exercise room & pool at 24 hour fitness center free to all Roosevelt Guests nearby.

Location: City, mountains.

Publicity: *Spokesman Review, Coeur d'Alene Press, KSPS in Spokane, Washington, KETH San Jose and California.*

Certificate may be used: September-May, Sunday-Thursday.

Salmon

Greyhouse Inn B&B

1115 Hwy 93 South
Salmon, ID 83467
(208)756-3968 (800)348-8097
Internet: www.greyhouseinn.com
E-mail: greyhouse@greyhouseinn.com

Circa 1894. The scenery at Greyhouse is nothing short of wondrous. In the winter, when mountains are capped in white and the evergreens are shrouded in snow, this Victorian appears as a safe haven from the chilly weather. In the summer, the rocky peaks are a contrast to the whimsical house, which looks like something out of an Old West town. The historic home is known around town  as the old maternity hospital, but there is nothing medicinal about it now. The rooms are Victorian in style with antique furnishings. The parlor features deep red walls and floral overstuffed sofas and a dressmaker's model garbed in a brown Victorian gown. Outdoor enthusiasts will find no shortage of activities, from facing the rapids in nearby Salmon River to fishing to horseback riding. The town of Salmon is just 12 miles away.

Innkeeper(s): David & Sharon Osgood. $79-115. 9 rooms, 2 with PB, 3 cottages, 2 cabins. Breakfast included in rates. Types of meals: Country bkfst, veg bkfst, early coffee/tea, picnic lunch and dinner. Beds: KQDT. TV, VCR, reading lamp, refrigerator, ceiling fan, clock radio, coffeemaker, desk and bathrobes in room. Bicycles, library, parlor games, telephone, gift shop, carriage house and two log cabin rooms on premises. Antiquing, art galleries, bicycling, canoeing/kayaking, cross-country skiing, downhill skiing, fishing, golf, hiking, horseback riding, live theater, museums, parks, shopping, tennis, water sports, float trips, hot springs and mountain biking nearby.

Location: Mountains.

Publicity: *Idaho Statesman Newspaper, PBS and Travel Channel.*

"To come around the corner and find the Greyhouse, as we did, restores my faith! Such a miracle. We had a magical evening here, and we plan to return to stay for a few days. Thanks so much for your kindness and hospitality. We love Idaho!"

Certificate may be used: Anytime, subject to availability.

Illinois

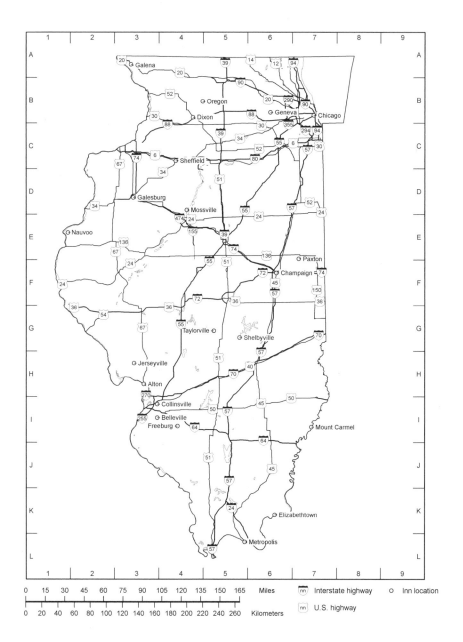

0   15 30 45 60 75 90 105 120 135 150 165   Miles

0 20 40 60 80 100 120 140 160 180 200 220 240 260   Kilometers

[nn] Interstate highway   ○ Inn location

[nn] U.S. highway

Alton

Beall Mansion, An Elegant B&B

407 East 12th Street
Alton, IL 62002-7230
(618)474-9100 (866)843-2325 Fax:(618)474-9090
Internet: www.beallmansion.com
E-mail: bepampered@beallmansion.com

Circa 1903. An eclectic blend of Neoclassic, Georgian and Greek Revival styles, the mansion was designed as a wedding gift by world renown architect, Lucas Pfeiffenberger. Original woodwork, eleven and a half-foot ceilings, leaded-glass windows, pocket doors, crystal chandeliers and imported marble and bronze statuary reflect the era's opulence. Elegantly appointed guest bedrooms are unique in size and decor. Each includes a private bath with shower and clawfoot tub or whirlpool for two, imported marble floor and chandelier. Voted "Illinois Best Bed & Breakfast" by Illinois Magazine's Readers Poll.

Innkeeper(s): Jim & Sandy Belote. $119-328. 5 rooms with PB, 2 with FP, 1 suite, 2 conference rooms. Types of meals: Full gourmet bkfst, veg bkfst, early coffee/tea and room service. Beds: KQD. Modem hook-up, data port, cable TV, VCR, DVD, reading lamp, ceiling fan, clock radio, telephone, turn-down service, desk, most with hot tub/spa, voice mail, some with fireplace, hair dryer, bathrobes, bath amenities, wireless Internet access, iron/ironing board, two-person whirlpool, iron/board, luxury bath amenities, homemade lavender bath salts and high-speed wireless Internet service in room. Central air. Fax, copier, library, parlor games, gift shop, verandah, hammock, badminton, horseshoes and croquet on premises. Amusement parks, antiquing, art galleries, bicycling, canoeing/kayaking, fishing, golf, hiking, horseback riding, live theater, museums, parks, shopping, sporting events, tennis, water sports, wineries, Meeting of the Great Rivers National Scenic Byway, Lewis & Clark Interpretive Center and Trailsite Number 1 and boat rental nearby.

Location: City. On Millionaire's Row in the historic river town of Alton, Ill, 25 min. from the Gateway Arch & downtown St. Louis, Mo., 90 min. from Springfield, Ill.

Publicity: *Illinois Magazine, Illinois Now, AAA Midwest Motorist, AAA Home & Away, BBW Magazine, St. Louis Magazine, The Daily Journal, St. Louis Post Dispatch, Pequot Press, NorthShore Magazine, The Telegraph, Edwardsville Intelligencer, DeForest Times, Show Me St. Louis, News 4 St. Louis, TLC's "While You Were Out", WBGZ, KWMU* and *Silence of the Yams* (a made for TV spoof of *Silence of the Lambs*).

Certificate may be used: December-March, Sunday-Thursday night stays. Reserved at the rack rate. Not available with any other certificate, discount or coupon. Blackout dates apply, subject to availability. Not valid if booked through a third party.

Champaign

Golds B&B

2065 County Road 525 E
Champaign, IL 61822-9521
(217)586-4345
Internet: www.culocalbiz.com/goldsbandb
E-mail: reg@prairienet.org

Circa 1874. Visitors to the University of Illinois area enjoy a restful experience at this bed and breakfast, west of town in a peaceful farmhouse setting on six acres. Antique country furniture collected by the innkeepers over the past 25 years is showcased and is beautifully offset by early American stenciling on the walls. Relax in the parlor or by the fireplace in the living room. A walnut stairway leads to the guest bedrooms with tall windows offering pastoral views. Seasonal produce from the garden are sometimes ingredients in the breakfast fare served in the dining room.

Innkeeper(s): Rita & Bob Gold. $55. 3 rooms, 1 with PB. Breakfast included in rates. Types of meals: Cont plus and early coffee/tea. Beds: QT. Reading lamp and clock radio in room. Air conditioning. TV, VCR, telephone and fireplace on premises. Antiquing, fishing, golf, hiking, live theater, museums, parks, shopping, sporting events and wineries nearby.

Location: Country.

Certificate may be used: Sunday-Thursday.

Chicago

China Doll Guest House

738 West Schubert Avenue
Chicago, IL 60614
(773)525-4967 (866)361-1819 Fax:(773)525-3929
Internet: www.chinadollguesthouse.com
E-mail: chinadollchicago@yahoo.com

Circa 1895. Everything needed is included for a wonderful visit to the Windy City. Stay in a self-contained, one-bedroom garden apartment with exposed brick walls. It is complete with an entertainment system, fireplace, private Jacuzzi, sauna and a fully stocked island kitchen with customized breakfast foods per advance request. A larger accommodation of one to two bedrooms with up to six rooms is available on the second-floor, and features a private deck in addition to all the same amenities. Both apartments have an office with computers, high-speed Internet and other equipment. A laundry room facility is the only shared amenity. Chinese-Mandarin and English are spoken.

Innkeeper(s): Jim & Yanan Haring. $195-295. Call inn for details. Breakfast, afternoon tea and snacks/refreshments included in rates. Types of meals: Cont plus. Beds: QDT. Modem hook-up, data port, cable TV, VCR, reading lamp, stereo, refrigerator, snack bar, clock radio, telephone, coffeemaker, desk, voice mail and fireplace in room. Air conditioning. Fax, copier, spa, library, fireplace, laundry facility, sauna, conference room with projector and air conditioning on premises. Art galleries, beach, bicycling, cross-country skiing, fishing, golf, hiking, live theater, museums, parks, shopping, sporting events and tennis nearby.

Location: City.

Certificate may be used: Anytime, November-April, subject to availability, except holiday periods.

House Of Two Urns

1239 N Greenview Ave
Chicago, IL 60622-3318
(773)235-1408 (800)835-9303 Fax:(773)235-1410
Internet: www.twourns.com
E-mail: info@twourns.com

Circa 1912. This historic townhouse offers guests a unique experience in the Windy City. The house is built in late Victorian style, and innkeeper Kapra Fleming has decorated the B&B in an eclectic style with antiques and family heirlooms. Kapra has included many thoughtful amenities, such as robes, hair dryers, slippers and an alarm clock. Rooms are inviting and tastefully furnished. The spacious loft suite includes a queen and full bed, as well as a private bath. The continental-plus breakfasts include items such as French toast with almonds and bananas or chocolate chip scones. The home is located in the Wicker Park section of Chicago, less than three miles from downtown and six miles from McCormick Center.

Innkeeper(s): Kapra and Miguel. $119-189. 6 rooms, 4 with PB, 3 with FP, 2 with WP, 2 two-bedroom and 1 three-bedroom suites, 3 guest houses. Breakfast and snacks/refreshments included in rates. Types of meals: Full gourmet bkfst, early coffee/tea and Breakfast served between 7 am and 9:30

am daily. Beds: KQDT. Modem hook-up, cable TV, VCR, DVD, reading lamp, CD player, ceiling fan, clock radio, telephone, desk, voice mail, hair dryer, bathrobes, bath amenities, wireless Internet access, iron/ironing board and deck/patios with gas grills available for all units in room. Central air. Fax, copier, spa, library, parlor games, fireplace, laundry facility, gift shop, Free Wi-Fi access and free off-street parking and Local phone calls are also free on premises. Antiquing, art galleries, beach, bicycling, golf, live theater, museums, parks, shopping, sporting events, water sports, excellent boutique shopping and critically acclaimed chefs for dining within walking distance nearby.

Location: City.

Certificate may be used: Jan. 20 to Feb. 10, Monday-Thursday.

Collinsville

Maggie's B&B

2102 N Keebler Ave
Collinsville, IL 62234-4713
(618)344-8283
E-mail: maggiesbnb@mailstation.com

Circa 1900. A rustic two-acre wooded area surrounds this friendly Victorian inn, once a boarding house. Rooms with 11-foot ceilings are furnished with exquisite antiques and art objects collected on worldwide travels. Downtown St. Louis,

the Gateway Arch and the Mississippi riverfront are just 10 minutes away.
Innkeeper(s): Maggie Leyda. $50-100. 4 rooms, 3 with PB, 1 with FP, 1 conference room. Breakfast included in rates. Types of meals: Full bkfst and early coffee/tea. Beds: KQDT. Cable TV, VCR, reading lamp, ceiling fan, clock radio and turn-down service in

room. Air conditioning. TV, spa, library, telephone and fireplace on premises. Handicap access. Amusement parks, antiquing, fishing, live theater, parks, shopping and sporting events nearby.

Location: Country.

Publicity: *USA Today, Cooking Light, Collinsville Herald Journal, Innsider, Belleville News, Democrat, Saint Louis Homes & Gardens, Edwardsville Intelligences, St. Louis Business Journal and St. Louis Post Dispatch.*

"We enjoyed a delightful stay. You've thought of everything. What fun!"

Certificate may be used: Sunday through Thursday, subject to availability.

Dixon

Crawford House Inn

204 E Third St
Dixon, IL 61021
(815)288-3351
Internet: www.crawfordhouseinn.com
E-mail: crawfordinn@grics.net

Circa 1854. In 1854, Joseph Crawford, who counted Abraham Lincoln among his friends, built this Italianate Victorian house that bears his name. Now a B&B, Crawford House offers a glimpse into small-town America. Guest bedrooms feature feather beds. Breakfasts are served with white linens, china and stemware in the dining room. Gourmet breakfasts include juice, coffee, an egg entree, fresh baked goods and seasonal fruits. The streets of Dixon are lined with colorful flower beds. The area is popular for cycling and scenic country trails offer opportunities for walking, horseback riding and cross-country

skiing. Visit the Ronald Reagan boyhood home, John Deere Historical Site or local antique stores. Rock River is two blocks away for boating, fishing and canoeing.

Innkeeper(s): Lyn Miliano. $75-85. 3 rooms, 1 with FP. Breakfast included in rates. Types of meals: Full gourmet bkfst. Beds: KQ. Cable TV, VCR, reading lamp, ceiling fan and clock radio in room. Air conditioning. Library, parlor games and fireplace on premises. Antiquing, bicycling, canoeing/kayaking, fishing, golf, hiking, horseback riding, live theater, museums, parks, shopping, tennis and water sports nearby.

Location: Small town.

Certificate may be used: Anytime, subject to availability.

Elizabethtown

River Rose Inn B&B

1 Main Street
Elizabethtown, IL 62931-0078
(618)287-8811 Fax:(618)287-8853
Internet: www.riveroseinn.com
E-mail: riveroseinn@riveroseinn.com

Circa 1914. Large, shade trees veil the front of this Greek Gothic home, nestled along the banks of the Ohio River. From the grand front entrance, guests look out to polished woodwork and a staircase leading to shelves of books. Rooms are cheerful and nostalgic, decorated with antiques. Each guest room offers something special. One has a four-poster bed, another offers a fireplace. The Scarlet Room has its own balcony and whirlpool tub, and the Rose Room has a private patio with a swing. The Magnolia Cottage is ideal for honeymooners and includes a whirlpool tub for two, fireplace and a deck that overlooks the river. Breakfasts are served in the dining room where guests can enjoy the water views.

Innkeeper(s): Sue Hemphill. $85-125. 5 rooms with PB, 2 with FP, 4 with WP, 1 cottage. Breakfast, snacks/refreshments and Dinner can be arranged for special occasions. Call for menus and pricing included in rates. Types of meals: Full bkfst and early coffee/tea. Beds: Q. Cable TV, VCR, reading lamp, refrigerator, ceiling fan, clock radio, desk, most with hot tub/spa, some with fireplace, bath amenities and iron/ironing board in room. Air conditioning. Spa, swimming, library, parlor games, Library with books and videos, Large inground swimming pool and Hydrotherapy Jacuzzi Spa behind smokehouse overlooking the Ohio River on premises. Limited handicap access. Amusement parks, antiquing, beach, bicycling, canoeing/kayaking, fishing, golf, hiking, horseback riding, museums, parks, shopping, water sports, wineries, Garden of the Gods, Rimrock Forest Trail, Pounds Hollow Recreation, Cave-in-Rock State Park, Metropolis Casino, pirate caves, Shawnee Queen River Taxi boat rides, summer festivals, local antique/craft shops and restaurants nearby.

Location: Country, mountains, waterfront. Quaint rivertown.

Publicity: *Chicago Tribune, Midwest Living, Southern Illinoisan, Triple A Travel Guide, WSIL and CBS Chicago.*

Certificate may be used: November-March, excluding holidays, Sunday-Thursday, some exceptions, subject to availability.

Freeburg

His Rest Bed & Breakfast

8059 Jefferson Road
Freeburg, IL 62243
(618)539-3665
Internet: HisRestBB.com
E-mail: hisrest@sbcglobal.net

Circa 1977. Formerly known as the Westerfield House, this 1977 log home features a rustic luxury and a tranquil serenity.

Relax by the large stone fireplace in the great room. Accommodations include an upper room suite and summer kitchen cottage. Indulge in a bountiful country breakfast daily. Refreshments are also provided throughout the day. Downtown St. Louis is less than half an hour away.

Innkeeper(s): Kevin & Vici Eader . $150-175. 2 rooms with PB, 2 with FP, 1 suite, 1 cabin. Breakfast and snacks/refreshments included in rates. Types of meals: Country bkfst, early coffee/tea, picnic lunch, afternoon tea, hors d'oeuvres, gourmet dinner and room service. Beds: KQT. TV, reading lamp, refrigerator, clock radio, coffeemaker, fireplace, hair dryer, bathrobes and bath amenities in room. Central air. VCR, DVD, library, parlor games, telephone and gift shop on premises. Antiquing, art galleries, golf, horseback riding, live theater, museums, parks, shopping, sporting events, wineries, Ravissant Winery, Orchard's Golf Course, Eckert's Country Farms and Our Lady of the Snows Shrine nearby.

Location: Country.

Certificate may be used: Accepts Weekends, Anytime, subject to availability; Anytime, last minute - based on availability.

Galena

Aldrich Guest House

900 3rd St
Galena, IL 61036-2627
(815)777-3323 Fax:(815)777-3323
Internet: www.aldrichguesthouse.com
E-mail: aldrich@aldrichguesthouse.com

Circa 1845. This elegant Greek Revival home is listed in the National Register of Historic Places. Victorian antiques decorate the interior. Guest rooms include antiques and handmade quilts. Clawfoot tubs and pedestal sinks in the private bathrooms add to the nostalgic charm of the inn. A multi-course, gourmet breakfast is prepared daily served on fine china and linens. The screened porch overlooks the yard where General Grant once drilled Union soldiers. The home is within walking distance of shops and restaurants.

Innkeeper(s): Jim and Marie Nadeau. $90-150. 5 rooms with PB, 3 with FP. Breakfast and snacks/refreshments included in rates. Types of meals: Full bkfst and early coffee/tea. Beds: QT. Reading lamp, stereo, clock radio, most with fireplace, hair dryer, bathrobes, bath amenities and wireless Internet access in room. Central air. TV, VCR, fax, copier, library, parlor games, telephone, gift shop, screened-in porch and gardens on premises. Antiquing, art galleries, bicycling, canoeing/kayaking, downhill skiing, golf, hiking, horseback riding, live theater, museums, parks, shopping, tennis and wineries nearby.

Location: Country.

Publicity: *Chicago Tribune and Telegraph Herald.*

"Thank you for the 'personal touch' you give to your guests."

Certificate may be used: November through August, Monday-Thursday, subject to availability.

Annie Wiggins Guest House

1004 Park Avenue
Galena, IL 61036-2622
(815)777-0336
Internet: www.anniewiggins.com
E-mail: annie@anniewiggins.com

For a nostalgic journey into a bygone era, this Greek Revival mansion is a historical treasure. Built with innovative architecture, Doric and Ionic columns reside with marble fireplaces, brick and woodwork. Several common rooms and a veranda provide places to relax and enjoy panoramic views of the woods and Galena River. The guest bedrooms are resplendently decorated with antiques and touches of yesteryear. Luxurious fine linens, large soaking tubs, candles, private entrances and screened porches are some of the pleasures available.

Innkeeper(s): Bill & Wendy Heiken. $95-235. 7 rooms with PB, 5 with FP. Beds: Q. 400+ thread-count Egyptian cotton sheets, 100% cotton blankets, 6 down pillows, (poly pillows available on request) and pillow-topped Queen-size beds in room.

Certificate may be used: Monday-Thursday, Nov. 5-May 30, except holidays.

Cloran Mansion

1237 Franklin St
Galena, IL 61036-1309
(815)777-0583 (866)234-0583 Fax:(815)777-0580
Internet: www.cloranmansion.com
E-mail: innkeeper@cloranmansion.com

Circa 1880. Historic Galena, Illinois serves as the perfect backdrop for this 1880 red brick Italianate Victorian mansion. The half-acre manicured lawn and gardens feature a romantic gazebo, pond and a firepit. Books, magazines, board games and a movie and CD collection are available in the Library. Spacious guest bedrooms and suites include a fireplace, whirlpool tub, candles, entertainment center, and a mini-refrigerator with complimentary beverages. Antonio's Cottage is pet and child-friendly as well as handicap accessible. Cloran Mansion serves a family-style six-course country breakfast in the dining room on fine china and crystal. For the ultimate pampering, schedule a massage with an onsite therapist.

Innkeeper(s): Carmine and Cheryl Farruggia. $99-225. 6 rooms, 5 with FP, 5 with WP, 6 total suites, including 2 two-bedroom suites, 1 cottage. Breakfast, Early morning coffee and tea and hot chocolate included in rates. Types of meals: Full bkfst, veg bkfst, picnic lunch, snacks/refreshments and gourmet dinner. Beds: KQ. Cable TV, VCR, DVD, reading lamp, stereo, refrigerator, ceiling fan, clock radio, coffeemaker, turn-down service, hot tub/spa, fireplace, hair dryer, bathrobes, bath amenities, wireless Internet access, iron/ironing board and Double Whirlpool/Jacuzzi in room. Central air. Fax, copier, sauna, bicycles, library, parlor games, telephone, pet friendly, gazebo, pond, gardens, fire pit, on-site parking and motorcycle garage parking on premises. Handicap access. Antiquing, art galleries, bicycling, canoeing/kayaking, cross-country skiing, downhill skiing, fishing, golf, hiking, horseback riding, live theater, museums, parks, shopping and wineries nearby.

Location: City.

Certificate may be used: Sunday-Thursday.

Farmers' Guest House

334 Spring St
Galena, IL 61036-2128
(815)777-3456 (888)459-1847 Fax:(815)777-3202
Internet: www.farmersguesthouse.com
E-mail: farmersgh@galenalink.net

Circa 1867. This two-story brick Italianate building was built as a bakery and served as a store and hotel, as well. Rows of arched, multi-paned windows add charm to the exterior. The rooms are decorated with antiques, lace curtains and floral wallpapers. The accommodations include seven rooms with queen-size beds, one room with a double bed, and two, two-room king Master Suites. There's a bar, featured in the movie "Field of Dreams." A hot tub is offered in the backyard. The inn also has a cabin in the woods available for rent.

Innkeeper(s): Kathie, Jess Farlow. $115-225. 9 rooms with PB, 5 with FP, 3 with WP, 3 suites, 1 cottage, 1 cabin. Breakfast, snacks/refreshments and wine included in rates. Types of meals: Full bkfst, veg bkfst and early coffee/tea. Beds: KQD. Cable TV, DVD, reading lamp, stereo, coffeemaker, some with hot tub/spa, hair dryer, bathrobes and wireless Internet access in room. Central air. Fax, copier, spa, library, parlor games, telephone, fireplace, gift shop, hot tub and evening wine and cheese hour on premises. Limited handicap access. Antiquing, art galleries, bicycling, canoeing/kayaking, cross-country skiing, downhill skiing, golf, hiking, horseback riding, live theater, museums, parks, shopping, wineries and hot air ballooning nearby.

Location: City.

Publicity: *Better Homes & Gardens, Country Discoveries, Comforts at Home, Country Extra and Field of Dreams.*

"Neat old place, fantastic breakfasts."

Certificate may be used: All year, must be Sunday-Monday, Monday-Tuesday, Tuesday-Wednesday or Wednesday-Thursday nights. Based on availability.

The Steamboat House Bed and Breakfast

605 S. Prospect
Galena, IL 61036
(815)777-2317 Fax:(815)776-0712
Internet: www.thesteamboathouse.com
E-mail: glenchar@thesteamboathouse.com

Circa 1855. Truly elegant as well as historic, this brick Gothic Revival, pre-Civil War mansion was built for a renowned Mississippi River steamboat captain. The inn exudes luxury while imparting a welcome, friendly ambiance. Main-floor parlors include a library and billiards room. A central parlor on the second floor offers early-morning Gevalia coffee and tea. Enjoy midweek afternoon treats or wine and cheese on the weekends. Each guest bedroom features a fireplace, heirloom furniture, vintage photographs and original artwork. The formal dining room is set with antique china, crystal and silver for a breakfast that is sure to please. Relax on the front porch overlooking roses.

Innkeeper(s): Glen and Char Carlson. $105-145. 5 rooms with PB, 5 with FP. Breakfast, snacks/refreshments and wine included in rates. Types of meals: Full gourmet bkfst and early coffee/tea. Beds: QT. Cable TV, VCR, DVD, reading lamp, CD player, clock radio, fireplace, hair dryer, wireless Internet access, iron/ironing board, heirloom antique furnishings and LCD in room. Central air. Library, parlor games, telephone, gift shop, billiard room, original parlors, large covered front porch and LCD TV on premises. Antiquing, art galleries, bicycling, canoeing/kayaking, cross-country skiing, downhill skiing, fishing, golf, hiking, horseback riding, live theater, museums, parks, shopping, sporting events, tennis, water sports, wineries, historic district and trolley tours nearby.

Location: City. Near downtown Galena.

Publicity: *Country Magazine, Illinois Now Magazine, America's Best Bed & Breakfast Recipes, Chicago Tribune and Daily Herald (northwest Illinois suburbs).*

Certificate may be used: November-February, Monday/Tuesday, Tuesday/Wednesday, Wednesday/Thursday. Bess or Lene Room, subject to availability.

Galesburg

Seacord House

624 N Cherry St
Galesburg, IL 61401-2731
(309)342-4107
E-mail: seacord_housebb@galesburg.net

Circa 1891. A former county sheriff and businessman built this Eastlake-style Victorian, which is located in the town's historic district. The home was named for its builder, Wilkens Seacord, a prominent local man whose family is mentioned in Carl Sandburg's autobiography. In keeping with the house's historical prominence, the innkeepers have tried to maintain its

turn-of-the-century charm. Victorian wallpapers, lacy curtains and a collection of family antiques grace the guest rooms and living areas. The bedrooms, however, feature the modern amenity of waterbeds. For those celebrating romantic occasions, the innkeepers provide heart-shaped muffins along with regular morning fare.

Innkeeper(s): Gwen and Lyle. $47-59. 3 rooms. Breakfast and snacks/refreshments included in rates. Types of meals: Full bkfst, early coffee/tea, Special diets on request, snacks with 2 hour notice and students of Knox parents invited to join them at no charge. Beds: QT. Reading lamp, ceiling fan, clock radio, hair dryer, iron/ironing board, books, games, TV/VCR in library, fireplace and telephone 1st floor, porch swing and patio seating in room. Air conditioning. TV, VCR, fax, library, parlor games, telephone and fireplace on premises. Antiquing, beach, fishing, golf, hiking, parks, sporting events, water sports, on occasion live theater, symphony orchestra and other music nearby.

Location: City.

Certificate may be used: Any day between Nov. 1 and April 1.

Metropolis

Isle of View B&B

205 Metropolis St
Metropolis, IL 62960-2213
(618)524-5838 (800)566-7491
Internet: www.isle-of-view.net
E-mail: kimoff@hcis.net

Circa 1889. Metropolis, billed as the "home of Superman," is not a bustling concrete city, but a quaint, country town tucked along the Ohio River. The Isle of View, a stunning Italianate manor, is just a short walk from shops, restaurants and the Players Riverboat Casino. All the guest rooms are appointed in Victorian design with antiques. The Master Suite was originally the home's library and includes a unique coal-burning fireplace, canopy bed and two-person whirlpool tub.

Innkeeper(s): Kim & Gerald Offenburger. Call for rates. 5 rooms with PB. Breakfast included in rates. Types of meals: Full bkfst. Modem hook-up, cable TV, reading lamp, ceiling fan, telephone, hot tub/spa and some with fireplace in room. Central air. Antiquing, art galleries, bicycling, canoeing/kayaking, fishing, golf, hiking, horseback riding, live theater, museums, parks, shopping, water sports and wineries nearby.

Location: Small Town.

Certificate may be used: Sunday-Friday, subject to availability.

Mossville

Old Church House Inn

1416 E Mossville Rd.
Mossville, IL 61552
(309)579-2300
Internet: www.bedandbreakfast.com/bbc/p210657.asp
E-mail: churchhouse@prodigy.net

Circa 1869. Take sanctuary at this lovingly restored 1869 brick Colonial country church situated on Peoria's north side. The inn offers warm hospitality and comfortable elegance. Relax by a wood-burning fire with afternoon tea or sit on a bench among colorful garden blooms. Each guest bedroom features pampering amenities and distinctive details that may include an antique carved bedstead, handmade quilts and lacy curtains. Chocolates are a pleasant treat with turndown service in the evening.

Innkeeper(s): Dean & Holly Ramseyer. $155. 1 suite. Breakfast included in rates. Types of meals: Cont plus, early coffee/tea, picnic lunch, room service and Gourmet Continental Plus Breakfast. Beds: Q. TV, reading lamp, clock radio, turn-down service and bathrobes in room. Central air. Library, telephone and fireplace on premises. Antiquing, bicycling, cross-country skiing, fishing, golf, hiking, live theater, museums, parks, shopping, sporting events, tennis, water sports, Bike trail and Riverfront nearby.

Location: Country. Village.

Publicity: Chillicothe Bulletin, Journal Star, Country Inns and The Chicago Tribune.

"Your hospitality, thoughtfulness, the cleanliness, beauty, I should just say everything was the best."

Certificate may be used: Monday-Thursday all year or anytime with reservations within 48 hours of requested date.

Nauvoo

Sonora Gardens Farmstead

970 E CR 2100
Nauvoo, IL 62354
(309)221-7286
Internet: www.sonoragardens.com
E-mail: wetfam@frontiernet.net

Circa 1912. Feel welcomed as a guest at this bed and breakfast on a working grain farm in rural Nauvoo, Illinois. Greta and her siblings are fourth-generation farmers whose great-grandparents built this Sears kit home in 1912. Relax in the living room, front porch or kitchen garden sitting area. Stay in a centrally air-conditioned guest bedroom with heirloom furnishings and a whirlpool tub accented by Italian tile. Enjoy a home-cooked breakfast and afternoon refreshments in the dining area. Tractor rides are offered occasionally and bikes are available to explore the area. Sonora Gardens Farmstead is a smoke-free, pet-free environment. Ask for a list of the local attractions and scenic sites.

Innkeeper(s): Greta Wilson Wetzel. $79-140. 2 rooms with PB, 1 with FP, 2 with WP, 1 guest house, 1 cabin. Breakfast and snacks/refreshments included in rates. Types of meals: Full gourmet bkfst, veg bkfst, early coffee/tea, picnic lunch, wine, we pack picnic lunches by request and "Breakfast in Bed" tray is always available. Light breakfast only with our guest house and cabin. . Beds: QDT. Cable TV, VCR, DVD, reading lamp, stereo, refrigerator, ceiling fan, snack bar, clock radio, telephone, coffeemaker, desk, some with fireplace, hair dryer, bathrobes, bath amenities, iron/ironing board in Bed and Breakfast and Guest house, fireplace in the 1880 guest house with a wonderful Americana decor and the cabin has a full kitchen and laundry room in room. Central air. Spa, bicycles, library, laundry facility and we are located on a working grain farm and will offer tractor rides when time allows. on premises. Antiquing, bicycling, fishing, golf, hiking, horseback riding, museums, wineries, many historical sites and shopping nearby.

Location: Country.

Publicity: One local paper and two regional papers.

Certificate may be used: November-March.

Oregon

Pinehill Inn

400 Mix St
Oregon, IL 61061-1113
(815)732-2067 (800)851-0131 Fax:(815)732-1348
Internet: www.pinehillbb.com
E-mail: info@pinehillbb.com

Circa 1874. This Italianate country villa is listed in the National Register. Ornate touches include guest rooms with Italian marble fireplaces and French silk-screened mural wallpaper. Outside, guests may enjoy porches, swings and century-old pine trees. Seasonal events include daily chocolate tea parties featuring the inn's own exotic homemade fudge collection.

Innkeeper(s): Chris & Ken Williams. $80-195. 6 rooms with PB, 4 with FP, 3 with WP, 1 suite. Breakfast and snacks/refreshments included in rates. Types of meals: Full gourmet bkfst, early coffee/tea and wine. Beds: KQDT. Cable TV, VCR, DVD, reading lamp, stereo, refrigerator, ceiling fan, snack bar, clock radio, telephone, desk, most with hot tub/spa, most with fireplace, hair dryer, bathrobes, bath amenities, wireless Internet access and iron/ironing board in room. Central air. Fax, copier, parlor games and laundry facility on premises. Antiquing, art galleries, bicycling, canoeing/kayaking, cross-country skiing, fishing, golf, hiking, horseback riding, live theater, parks, shopping, sporting events, tennis and water sports nearby.

Location: Country.

Publicity: Fox Valley Living, Victorian Sampler, Freeport Journal, Victorian Homes, Chicago Tribune fall foilage route and Passion of the Automobile.

"We enjoyed our stay at Pine Hill, your gracious hospitality and the peacefulness. Our thanks to you for a delightful stay. We may have to come again, if just to get some fudge."

Certificate may be used: Monday-Thursday, November through March.

Paxton

TimberCreek Bed & Breakfast

1559 E. State Route 9
Paxton, IL 60957
(217)379-2589 (877)945-6569 Fax:(217)379-3991
Internet: www.timbercreekbb.com
E-mail: timbercreekbb@illicom.net

Circa 2003. In a secluded meadow on 25 acres with trees and a stream, this newly built country retreat is the perfect place to relax in an upscale setting. The English Cottage décor compliments the hardwood, brick and tile floors, knotty alder beams and white pickled wood ceilings. Play board games or read in the Gathering Room. The Kitchen is stocked with beverages and an evening snack is offered. Stay in a handicap-accessible first-floor suite with a canopy bed and black marble fireplace. The romantic Rose Garden Suite is a honeymoon favorite with a Jacuzzi, two-person shower and 14-foot fireplace. A rustic Americana cabin is also available. Savor a hearty morning meal in the Breakfast Room. Two stone patios feature wrought iron tables and chairs and the porch boasts wood rockers.

Innkeeper(s): Connie Bahler. $99-199. 7 rooms with PB, 3 with FP, 1 with WP, 6 suites, 1 cabin, 1 conference room. Breakfast included in rates. Types of meals: Full bkfst, gourmet lunch, dinner and room service. Beds: KQ. Reading lamp, clock radio, hot tub/spa and fireplace in room. Central air. TV, VCR, DVD, fax, copier and telephone on premises. Antiquing, fishing, golf, hiking, parks, shopping and wineries nearby.

Location: Country.

Certificate may be used: Anytime, subject to availability.

Sheffield

Chestnut Street Inn

301 E Chestnut St
Sheffield, IL 61361
(815)454-2419 (800)537-1304
Internet: www.chestnut-inn.com
E-mail: monikaandjeff@chestnut-inn.com

Circa 1854. Originally built in Italianate style, this mid-19th-century reborn Colonial Revival is the dream-come-true for innkeeper Gail Bruntjen. She spent more than 15 years searching for just the right country home to open a bed & breakfast. With its gracious architectural character and well-organized

interior spaces, the Chestnut Street Inn fit the bill. Classic French doors open to a wide foyer with gleaming chandeliers and a floating spindle staircase.
Sophisticated chintz fabrics and authentic antiques highlight each room. The four guest rooms offer down comforters, four-poster beds and private baths. Guests will be delighted by the gourmet selections offered every morning such as broccoli mushroom quiche, homemade breads and fresh fruit, all exquisitely presented by candlelight on fine China and crystal. Afternoon tea and evening snacks are served in the public rooms. Antiquing, shops ,bicycling, hiking, golf and fishing are located nearby.

Innkeeper(s): Monika & Jeff Sudakov. $95-175. 4 rooms with PB, 1 with FP, 1 suite, 1 conference room. Breakfast and snacks/refreshments included in rates. Types of meals: Full gourmet bkfst, veg bkfst, early coffee/tea, gourmet lunch, wine, gourmet dinner, 4-Course Fixed Price Menu served daily by reservation only and Beer and Wine license on premises. Restaurant on premises. Beds: KQT. Cable TV, VCR, DVD, reading lamp, CD player, clock radio, desk, some with fireplace, hair dryer, bathrobes, bath amenities, wireless Internet access and iron/ironing board in room. Central air. Fax, copier, library, parlor games, telephone, laundry facility and gift shop on premises. Antiquing, bicycling, canoeing/kayaking, fishing, golf, hiking, horseback riding, live theater, museums, parks, shopping, wineries, Bishop Hill, Goods Furniture, Hornbaker Gardens, Tanner's Orchard and Festival 56 nearby.

Location: Country. Village.

Publicity: *The Illinois Review, Illinois Country Living, Inn Traveller Magazine, Star Courier and Bureau County Republican.*

"Without a doubt, the best B&B I've ever been to."

Certificate may be used: Anytime, subject to availability.

Shelbyville

The Shelby Historic House and Inn

816 W Main St
Shelbyville, IL 62565-1354
(217)774-3991 (800)342-9978 Fax:(217)774-2224
Internet: shelbyinn.com
E-mail: kenfry@stewstras.net

Sitting on one acre, The Shelby Historic House and Inn was built as a Queen Anne Victorian and is listed in the National Register of Historic Places. Stay in a gracious guest bedroom or suite. A continental breakfast is a great start to each day. This inn is well known for its conference facilities, and is less than a mile from Lake Shelbyville, a popular boating and fishing spot in Illinois. Guaranteed tee times are available at a neighboring championship golf course. Three state parks are nearby, and the Amish settlement near Arthur is within easy driving distance.

Innkeeper(s): Ken Fry. $65-76. 45 rooms, 6 suites, 1 conference room. Types of meals: Cont. Beds: K. Cable TV, reading lamp, clock radio, telephone and desk in room. Air conditioning. Fax on premises. Handicap access. Antiquing, fishing, live theater, parks, shopping and water sports nearby.

Certificate may be used: Anytime, November-April, subject to availability.

Taylorville

Market Street Inn

220 E Market St
Taylorville, IL 62568-2212
(217)824-7220 (800)500-1466
Internet: www.marketstreetinn.com
E-mail: innkeeper@marketstreetinn.com

Carefully and lovingly renovated, this vintage 1892 Queen Anne Victorian home and Carriage House in Taylorville is perfectly located in central Illinois, in the heart of historic Lincolnland. The common area with a kitchenette is on the third floor. Most of the well-appointed guest bedrooms feature double whirlpool tubs and some have fireplaces. Stay in one of the two romantic suites in the Carriage House with pampering amenities. Wake up each day to enjoy a satisfying fireside breakfast. There are many local attractions and activities to enjoy and plan to take a day trip to St. Louis, Missouri, 93 miles away.

Innkeeper(s): Myrna Hauser. $125-235. 10 rooms with PB, 7 with FP, 8 with WP, 2 suites, 1 cottage. Breakfast included in rates. Types of meals: Country bkfst, veg bkfst, early coffee/tea and wine. Beds: KQ. Cable TV, VCR, DVD, reading lamp, CD player, ceiling fan, clock radio, telephone, desk, most with hot tub/spa, most with fireplace, hair dryer, bathrobes, bath amenities, wireless Internet access, iron/ironing board, fax send and receive and social hour in room. Central air. Fax, copier, bicycles, parlor games, laundry facility, We have a great porch for sitting, sipping and socializing or just being quiet on on premises. Handicap access. Bicycling, fishing, golf, hiking, museums, parks, tennis, Open mike entertainment, Periodic live entertainment, Wine tasting every Saturday, Festivals and Events (see events section on Web site) nearby.

Location: City.

Certificate may be used: May be made 72 hours in advance. Subject to availability. Except holidays and special events.

Indiana

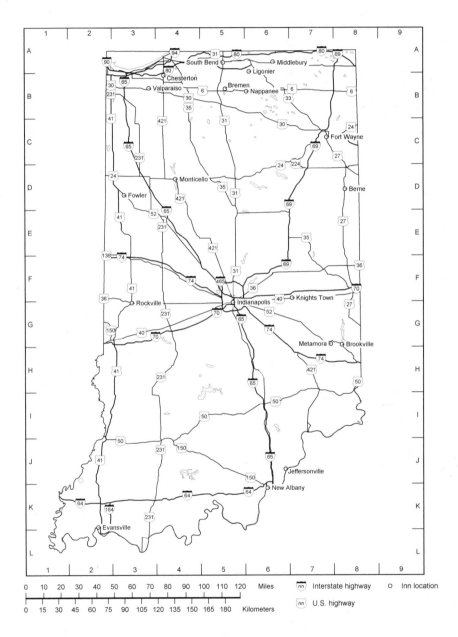

Interstate highway   o Inn location

U.S. highway

0 10 20 30 40 50 60 70 80 90 100 110 120 Miles

0 15 30 45 60 75 90 105 120 135 150 165 180 Kilometers

    Tell the innkeeper that you have an iLoveInns free-night certificate when you make your reservation.

Berne

Historic Schug House Inn

706 W Main St
Berne, IN 46711-1328
(260)589-2303
E-mail: schughousebb@onlyinternet.net

Circa 1907. This Queen Anne home was built in 1907 by Emanuel Wanner. It was constructed for the Schug family, who occupied the home for 25 years, and whom the innkeepers chose the name of their inn. Victorian features decorate the home, including inlaid floors, pocket doors and a wraparound porch. Guest rooms boast walnut, cherry and oak furnishings. Fruit, cheeses and pastries are served on antique china each morning in the dining room. Horse-drawn carriages from the nearby Old Order Amish community often pass on the street outside.

Innkeeper(s): John Minch. $50-60. 9 rooms with PB, 1 conference room. Breakfast included in rates. Types of meals: Cont. Beds: KQDT. TV and telephone on premises.

Certificate may be used: Jan. 2-Dec. 20, except July 20-27 and Aug. 23-30.

Bremen

Scottish Bed and Breakfast

2180 Miami Trail
Bremen, IN 46506
(574)220-6672 Fax:(574)546-5575
Internet: www.scottishbb.com
E-mail: info@scottishbb.com

Close to the Amish region, this year-round bed and breakfast sits on two park-like acres in the country. Practice golf on the putting green. Stay in a comfortable guest bedroom or suite with a Jacuzzi tub, TV and DVD player. The King Suite boasts a private entrance to the indoor swimming pool. Start the day with a hot continental-plus breakfast and enjoy evening refreshments. An assortment of pleasing packages is offered from theater to romance or create a customized getaway.

Innkeeper(s): Homer & Brenda Miller. $99-139. 4 rooms with PB, 1 conference room. Breakfast and snacks/refreshments included in rates. Types of meals: Country bkfst, early coffee/tea and afternoon tea. Data port, TV, DVD, stereo, snack bar, clock radio, telephone, desk, some with hot tub/spa, fireplace, hair dryer, bathrobes, bath amenities, wireless Internet access and iron/ironing board in room. Central air. Fax, swimming, pet boarding, parlor games, laundry facility and gift shop on premises. Antiquing, beach, bicycling, fishing, golf, live theater, parks, shopping, sporting events, Potato Creek State Park, Amish Acres and Blueberry Festival nearby.

Location: Country.

Certificate may be used: Monday-Thursday, October-December, subject to availability. Excluding Holidays and Notre Dame Weekends.

Chesterton

The Gray Goose

350 Indian Boundary Rd
Chesterton, IN 46304-1511
(219)926-5781 (800)521-5127 Fax:(219)926-4845
Internet: www.graygooseinn.com
E-mail: graygoose@verizon.net

Circa 1939. Situated on 100 wooded acres, just under one hour from Chicago, this English country inn overlooks a private lake. Guests can see Canadian geese and ducks on the lake and sur-

rounding area. Rooms are decorated in 18th-century English, Shaker and French-country styles. Some of the rooms feature fireplaces, Jacuzzi and poster beds. Complimentary snacks, soft drinks, coffee and tea are available throughout the day. Strains of Mozart or Handel add to the ambiance.

Innkeeper(s): Tim Wilk . $90-185. 8 rooms with PB, 3 with FP, 3 suites, 1 conference room. Breakfast, afternoon tea and snacks/refreshments included in rates. Types of meals: Full gourmet bkfst, veg bkfst and early coffee/tea. Beds: KQ. Modem hook-up, data port, TV, VCR, reading lamp, ceiling fan, clock radio, telephone, turn-down service, desk, hot tub/spa, fireplace and one room with fireplace and Jacuzzi in room. Central air. Fax, copier, library, parlor games, gift shop, snack/service bar, large screened gazebo and gift shop on premises. Antiquing, art galleries, beach, bicycling, cross-country skiing, downhill skiing, fishing, golf, hiking, horseback riding, live theater, museums, parks, shopping, sporting events, tennis, water sports and wineries nearby.

Location: Waterfront.

Publicity: *Insider, Post-Tribune, Glamour, Country Inns, Midwest Living, Indianapolis Star, Indianapolis Woman and Arrington's Inn Traveler.*

"Extremely gracious! A repeat stay for us because it is such a wonderful place to stay."

Certificate may be used: November to April.

Indianapolis

The Old Northside Bed & Breakfast

1340 North Alabama St.
Indianapolis, IN 46202
(317)635-9123 (800)635-9127 Fax:(317)635-9243
Internet: www.oldnorthsideinn.com
E-mail: garyh@hofmeister.com

Circa 1885. This Romanesque Revival mansion is fashioned out of bricks, and the grounds are enclosed by a wrought-iron fence. Border gardens and an English side garden complete the look. Rooms are decorated with a theme in mind. The Literary Room, which includes a fireplace and Jacuzzi tub, is decorated to honor Indiana authors. Another room honors the Hollywood's golden years. The home has many modern conveniences, yet still retains original maple floors and hand-carved, mahogany woodwork. Full breakfasts are served in the formal dining room or on the patio. Guests can walk to many city attractions.

Innkeeper(s): Gary Hofmeister. $135-215. 7 rooms with PB, 5 with FP, 7 with WP, 1 suite. Breakfast, afternoon tea and snacks/refreshments included in rates. Types of meals: Full bkfst. Beds: KQ. Cable TV, VCR, clock radio, telephone, desk and hot tub/spa in room. Central air. Fireplace on premises. Antiquing, art galleries, bicycling, live theater, museums, parks, shopping and sporting events nearby.

Location: City.

Certificate may be used: August, September, October, November, Sunday-Friday.

Jeffersonville

Market Street Inn

330 West Market Street
Jeffersonville, IN 47130
(812)285-1877 (888)284-1877 Fax:(812)218-0926
Internet: www.innonmarket.com
E-mail: info@innonmarket.com

Circa 1881. One block from the Ohio River, Market Street Inn is a stately, three-story Second Empire mansion built in 1881 and recently restored in downtown Jeffersonville, Indiana. Sit on the front porch or relax on the third-floor deck by the fountain and outdoor fireplace. Guest bedrooms feature fireplaces and each suite also includes a double Jacuzzi tub, separate shower, two sinks, bidet and wet bar. Savor a magnificent breakfast made by a professional chef and served in one of the two dining rooms. Browse through the antique and gift shop for treasures to take home.

Innkeeper(s): Carol & Steve Stenbro. $79-199. 7 rooms with PB, 7 with FP, 6 with WP, 3 suites, 1 conference room. Breakfast and snacks/refreshments included in rates. Types of meals: Full gourmet bkfst, veg bkfst, early coffee/tea, lunch, picnic lunch, afternoon tea and gourmet dinner. Beds: KQT. Modem hook-up, data port, cable TV, VCR, DVD, reading lamp, CD player, ceiling fan, clock radio, telephone, desk, most with hot tub/spa, fireplace, bathrobes, wireless Internet access, Suites have Double Jacuzzis, Separate showers, Two sinks, Bidet and Wet bar in room. Central air. Fax, copier, library and parlor games on premises. Handicap access. Amusement parks, antiquing, art galleries, bicycling, canoeing/kayaking, downhill skiing, fishing, golf, hiking, horseback riding, live theater, museums, parks, shopping, sporting events, tennis, water sports, wineries, Antiques, Candy Museum and Fossil Beds nearby.

Location: City. Near Louisville, KY.

Certificate may be used: Sunday - Thursday, except holidays or Derby, Anytime, subject to availability.

Ligonier

Solomon Mier Manor Bed Breakfast and Antiques

508 South Cavin Street
Ligonier, IN 46767-1802
(260)894-3668
Internet: www.smmanor.com
E-mail: stay@smmanor.com

Circa 1899. This turn-of-the-century Queen Anne-Italianate manor boasts hand-painted ceilings, intricate woodwork and stained-glass windows. The ornate carved staircase is especially appealing with its staircase library. Antiques fill the guest rooms and common areas. The home is eligible to be on the National Register and originally was home to Solomon Mier, one of the area's first Jewish residents who came to the Ligonier area in search of religious tolerance and word of the railroad to come. Guests will find many areas of interest, such as the Shipshewana Flea Market & Auction and the on-site antique shop.

Innkeeper(s): Homer & Brenda Miller. $65-80. 4 rooms with PB. Breakfast, afternoon tea and snacks/refreshments included in rates. Types of meals: Full bkfst and early coffee/tea. Beds: KQDT. Reading lamp, ceiling fan and telephone in room. Air conditioning. TV, VCR, bicycles, library, parlor games, fireplace and gift shop on premises. Fishing, golf, museums, parks, shopping and tennis nearby.

Location: City.

Publicity: *Kendallville News Sun, Ligonier Advanced Leader and Goshen News.*

"Complete and beautiful experience."

Certificate may be used: Anytime, November-March, subject to availability.

Metamora

The Thorpe House Country Inn

19049 Clayborne St.
Metamora, IN 47030
(765)647-5425
Internet: www.metamora.com/thorpehouse
E-mail: thorpe_house@hotmail.com

Circa 1840. The steam engine still brings passenger cars and the gristmill still grinds cornmeal in historic Metamora. The Thorpe House is located one block from the canal. Rooms feature original pine and poplar floors, antiques, stenciling and country accessories. Enjoy a hearty breakfast selected from the inn's restaurant menu. (Popular items include homemade biscuits, egg dishes and sourdough pecan rolls.) Walk through the village to explore more than 100 shops.

Innkeeper(s): Mike & Jean Owens. $70-125. 5 rooms with PB, 1 suite. Breakfast and snacks/refreshments included in rates. Types of meals: Country bkfst, veg bkfst, early coffee/tea, lunch and picnic lunch. Restaurant on premises. Beds: KDT. Central air. TV, VCR, fax, parlor games, telephone, gift shops and pottery studio on premises. Amusement parks, antiquing, art galleries, beach, bicycling, canoeing/kayaking, fishing, golf, hiking, horseback riding, museums, parks, shopping, water sports, flea markets and bird sanctuary nearby.

Location: Restored 1840 canal-town village.

Publicity: *Cincinnati Enquirer, Chicago Sun-Times and Midwest Living.*

"Thanks to all of you for your kindness and hospitality during our stay."

Certificate may be used: Sunday-Thursday or weekends, based on projected availability.

Middlebury

Bee Hive B&B

51129 County Road 35
Middlebury, IN 46540
(574)825-5023
Internet: www.beehivebb.usclargo.com
E-mail: beehivebb@yahoo.com

Circa 1988. This family home is located on 39 acres in the Amish area of Middlebury and was constructed with hand-sawn lumber. Original primitive paintings by Miss Emma Schrock are part of the B&B's collectibles. There is also a collection of antique farm equipment. Guest rooms are in the farmhouse with the exception of Honey Comb Cottage which is a guest house with its own bath. If you'd like to help out with some of the farm chores and are an early riser see if you can coax Herb into letting you help. Afterwards you'll be ready for a full farm breakfast including Treva's home made granola and hearty breakfast casseroles. Ask for advice in discovering the best places to visit in the area.

Innkeeper(s): Herb & Treva Swarm. $70-85. 4 rooms, 1 with PB, 1 cottage. Breakfast included in rates. Types of meals: Country bkfst, early coffee/tea and snacks/refreshments. Beds: QD. TV, VCR, reading lamp, stereo, ceiling fan, clock radio, telephone and coffeemaker in room. Air conditioning. Fax, copier, parlor games and refrigerator on premises. Antiquing, beach, bicycling, canoeing/kayaking, cross-country skiing, downhill skiing, fishing, golf, hiking, live theater, museums, parks, shopping, sporting events, tennis and Amish heartland tours nearby.

Location: Country.

"What a great place to rest the mind, body and soul."

Certificate may be used: Anytime, subject to availability.

Patchwork Quilt Country Inn

11748 County Road 2
Middlebury, IN 46540
(574)825-2417 Fax:(574)825-5172
Internet: www.patchworkquiltinn.com
E-mail: stay@patchworkquiltinn.com

Circa 1875. Located in the heart of Indiana's Amish country, this inn offers comfortable lodging and fine food. Some of the recipes are regionally famous, such as the award-winning Buttermilk Pecan Chicken. All guest rooms feature handsome quilts and country decor, and The Lodge treats visitors to a 5-person hot tub and kitchenette. The smoke-free inn also is host to a gift shop, game room and nature trail.

Innkeeper(s): John & Adrienne Cohoat. $99-199. 15 rooms with PB, 1 with FP, 1 with HT, 3 with WP, 2 total suites, including 1 two-bedroom suite, 6 conference rooms. Breakfast included in rates. Types of meals: Country bkfst, veg bkfst, Sun. brunch, early coffee/tea, gourmet lunch, picnic lunch, snacks/refreshments, hors d'oeuvres and gourmet dinner. Restaurant on premises. Beds: KQDT. Modem hook-up, TV, VCR, reading lamp, refrigerator, clock radio, coffeemaker, some with fireplace, hair dryer, wireless Internet access, iron/ironing board, three whirlpool tubs, one hot tub and some VCRs and DVDs in room. Central air. DVD, fax, copier, library, child care, parlor games, telephone, laundry facility, gift shop, Full service restaurant, game and fitness center, nature trail, meditation cabin, campfire area and movies on premises. Handicap access. Amusement parks, antiquing, art galleries, bicycling, canoeing/kayaking, cross-country skiing, downhill skiing, fishing, golf, hiking, horseback riding, live theater, museums, parks, shopping, sporting events, tennis, water sports, wineries and Amish buggy rides and tours nearby.

Location: Country. Amish Country.

Publicity: *Elkhart Truth, Goshen News, Detroit Free Press* and *CookingVillage.com.*

Certificate may be used: Anytime except Notre Dame football weekends and other special events.

Nappanee

A Victorian Guest House

302 E Market St
Nappanee, IN 46550-2102
(574)773-4383
Internet: www.victorianb-b.com
E-mail: vghouse@bnin.net

Circa 1887. Listed in the National Register, this three-story Queen Anne Victorian inn was built by Frank Coppes, one of America's first noted kitchen cabinet makers. Nappanee's location makes it an ideal stopping point for those exploring the heart of Amish country, or visiting the South Bend or chain of lakes areas. Visitors may

choose from six guest rooms, including the Coppes Suite, with its original golden oak woodwork, antique tub and stained glass. Full breakfast is served at the antique 11-foot dining room table. Amish

Acres is just one mile from the inn.

Innkeeper(s): Christine Lantis. $79-119. 6 rooms with PB. Breakfast and afternoon meal included in rates. Types of meals: Full bkfst, early coffee/tea and snacks/refreshments. Beds: QT. Cable TV, reading lamp, ceiling fan, clock radio, telephone, turn-down service, hair dryer, wireless Internet access and iron/ironing board in room. Air conditioning. Antiquing, golf, live theater, parks, shopping, sporting events, water sports, Amish Acres, Shipshewana and Farmers Market nearby.

Location: City.

Publicity: *Goshen News.*

Certificate may be used: November-March, Monday-Thursday.

Homespun Country Inn

302 N Main St
Nappanee, IN 46550
(574)773-2034 (800)311-2996 Fax:(574)773-3456
Internet: www.homespuninn.com
E-mail: home@hoosierlink.net

Circa 1902. Windows of stained and leaded glass create colorful prisms at this Queen Anne Victorian inn built in 1902. Quarter-sawn oak highlights the entry and first-floor common rooms. Comfortable antiques and family heirlooms accent the inn. Two parlors offer areas to read, do a jigsaw puzzle or watch satellite TV or a movie. Each guest bedroom displays photos of the home's original occupants. Early risers enjoying a cup of coffee or tea might see a passing horse and buggy while sitting on the porch swing. Breakfast is served in the dining room. Ask about the assortment of special packages and how to add a Homespun Memory Gift Bag to a reservation.

Innkeeper(s): Dianne & Dennis Debelak. $89. 5 rooms with PB. Breakfast and snacks/refreshments included in rates. Types of meals: Full bkfst and early coffee/tea. Beds: QDT. Cable TV, VCR, reading lamp, ceiling fan, clock radio and night lights in room. Air conditioning. Fax, copier, parlor games, telephone and fireplace on premises. Antiquing, golf, live theater, parks, shopping, sporting events and tennis nearby.

Location: Amish heritage.

Publicity: *The Elkhart Truth.*

"We have been telling all our friends about how wonderful your establishment is."

Certificate may be used: Any day January-April. Discount based on regular room rates. No other discount applies.

South Bend

Innisfree-A-Celtic-B&B

702 West Colfax
South Bend, IN 46601
(574)283-0740
Internet: www.Innisfree-a-Celtic-BandB.com
E-mail: innisfree.1@juno.com

Circa 1892. Gracing the heart of the West Washington National Historical District, Innisfree- a-Celtic-Bed-and-Breakfast in South Bend, Indiana offers warmth and hospitality. It was built in 1892 in the Queen Anne Victorian style and has been lovingly restored. From the inviting porch to the first-floor parlors to the second-floor balcony there are many places to relax, read or share conversation. Stay in the Michael Collins Room with a fireplace or the Grainne O'Malley Room with a four-poster bed and private sitting area in the turret. Indulge in the spacious Schocklehorne Suite with a whirlpool tub. Wake up to a hearty breakfast before embarking on the day's adventures. Special packages are available.

Innkeeper(s): Cindy and Terry Lewis. $79-155. 6 rooms, 4 with PB, 4 with FP, 1 with WP, 1 suite. Breakfast, snacks/refreshments, Intimate breakfast in room upon request and Complimentary wine/cheese in evening with whole house bookings included in rates. Types of meals: Full gourmet bkfst. Beds: KQDT. Cable TV, reading lamp, stereo, refrigerator, ceiling fan, clock radio, coffeemaker, turn-down service, some with hot tub/spa, most with fireplace, hair dryer, bathrobes, bath amenities, wireless Internet access, iron/ironing board, Chocolate at bedside and Herbal tea/coffee upon arrival in room. Central air. Fax, copier, bicycles, library, parlor games, telephone and laundry facility on premises. Limited handicap access. Antiquing, art galleries, bicycling, canoeing/kayaking, cross-country skiing, fishing, golf, hiking, live theater, museums, parks, shopping, sporting events, water sports, wineries, The Studebaker Mansion and Museum, The College Football Hall of Fame and St. Joseph's River East Race nearby.

Location: City.

Certificate may be used: Anytime, subject to availabilty. Not valid during special events or Notre Dame football games.

Oliver Inn

630 W Washington St
South Bend, IN 46601-1444
(574)232-4545 (888)697-4466 Fax:(574)288-9788
Internet: www.oliverinn.com
E-mail: oliver@michiana.org

Circa 1886. This stately Queen Anne Victorian sits amid 30 towering maples and was once home to Josephine Oliver Ford, daughter of James Oliver, of chilled plow fame. Located in South Bend's historic district, this inn offers a comfortable library and nine inviting guest rooms, some with built-in fireplaces or double Jacuzzis. The inn is within walking distance of downtown and is next door to the Tippecanoe Restaurant in the Studebaker Mansion.

Innkeeper(s): Tom & Alice Erlandson. $95-329. 10 rooms, 8 with PB, 6 with FP, 4 with WP, 4 total suites, including 2 two-bedroom suites, 1 guest house, 1 conference room. Breakfast and snacks/refreshments included in rates. Types of meals: Full gourmet bkfst, early coffee/tea and Adjacent to Tippecanoe Place Restaurant. Beds: KQ. Modem hook-up, data port, cable TV, DVD, reading lamp, CD player, ceiling fan, clock radio, telephone, turn-down service, desk, some with fireplace, hair dryer, bathrobes, bath amenities, wireless Internet access, iron/ironing board and several with double whirlpool tubs in room. Central air. Fax, library, parlor games, gift shop and baby grand with computer disk system on premises. Limited handicap access. Antiquing, art galleries, beach, bicycling, canoeing/kayaking, cross-country skiing, fishing, golf, hiking, live theater, museums, parks, shopping, sporting events, tennis, water sports, wineries, fine dining, Amish country and Notre Dame nearby.

Location: City. Lake Michigan (35 miles), Chicago (90 miles).

Certificate may be used: January through December, Sunday-Thursday.

Valparaiso

Songbird Prairie B & B

174 N 600 W
Valparaiso, IN 46385-9233
(219)759-4274
Internet: www.songbirdprairie.com
E-mail: barbaraandefrain@aol.com

Circa 2000. Recently built in the stately, red-brick Federal style, Songbird Prairie Bed and Breakfast in Valparaiso, Indiana spans six acres with landscaped lawns, woodland areas and lush wetlands. Walk paths through prairie grass and wild rose. Ethan Allen furnishings accent the B&B with a colonial country ambiance. Songbird-themed guest bedrooms and suites feature luxurious European linens, robes and towels, fireplaces and whirlpool tubs. Savor a three-course hot breakfast presented with flowers and creative garnishes in the sunroom overlooking serenading songbirds.Ask about special packages available. Downtown Chicago is just one hour away for a fun trip to the city.

Innkeeper(s): Barbara and Efrain Rivera . $155-185. 4 rooms with PB, 4 with FP, 4 with WP, 1 conference room. Breakfast, snacks/refreshments and Three Course Hot Breakfast served in the sunroom where songbirds serenade and entertain included in rates. Types of meals: Full gourmet bkfst, veg bkfst, early coffee/tea and Non-alcoholic premises. Beds: KQT. Modem hook-up, data port, cable TV, VCR, DVD, reading lamp, CD player, ceiling fan, snack bar, clock radio, turn-down service, fireplace, hair dryer, bathrobes, bath amenities, wireless Internet access and iron/ironing board in room. Central air. Fax, copier, parlor games and gift shop on premises. Amusement parks, antiquing, art galleries, beach, fishing, golf, hiking, horseback riding, live theater, parks, shopping, sporting events, water sports, wineries and National Dunes Lakeshore: Taltree Arboretum nearby.

Location: Country.

Publicity: *2006 nominee for Hotel of the Year, 2003 Sunflower Award from Innsidescoop, 2004 Hotel of the Year PCCVC, 2005 Chosen 1 of 25 Best Undiscovered Inns of America and 2005 Travel Smart one of 24 Best.*

Certificate may be used: Monday-Thursday excluding holiday or special events.

The Inn at Aberdeen

3158 South SR 2
Valparaiso, IN 46385
(219)465-3753 Fax:(219)465-9227
Internet: www.innataberdeen.com
E-mail: innkeeper@innataberdeen.com

Circa 1856. An old stone wall borders this inn, once a dairy farm, horse farm and then hunting lodge. Recently renovated and expanded, this Victorian farmhouse is on more than an acre. An elegant getaway, there's a solarium, library, dining room and parlor for relaxing. The inn offers traditional Queen Anne furnishings in the guest rooms. The Timberlake Suites include fireplaces, two-person Jacuzzi tubs and balconies. The Aberdeen Suite includes a living room and fireplace, while the Alloway Suite offers a living room, kitchenette and a balcony. A conference center on the property is popular for executive meetings and special events, and there is a picturesque gazebo overlooking the inn's beautifully landscaped lawns and English gardens. Golf packages and mystery weekends have received enthusiastic response from guests. There is a golf course, spa and microbrewery adjacent to the inn.

Innkeeper(s): Bill Simon, Val & Chris Urello, Audrey Slingsby, Mandy Johnson, John & Lyn Johnson. $102-195. 11 rooms, 10 with FP, 11 with HT, 11 with WP, 11 suites, 1 conference room. Breakfast, snacks/refreshments, Evening dessert, Flavia Coffee Bar, Hot tea, Cocoa, Snacks and Beverages included in rates. Types of meals: Full gourmet bkfst, early coffee/tea and Our own chef for special functions. Beds: KQ. Modem hook-up, cable TV, VCR, DVD, reading lamp, refrigerator, ceiling fan, snack bar, clock radio, telephone, desk, hot tub/spa, hair dryer, bathrobes, bath amenities, wireless Internet access and iron/ironing board in room. Central air. Fax, copier, swimming, tennis, library, parlor games, fireplace, gift shop, Flavia Coffee Bar, Evening dessert, Unlimited snacks & beverages, Toll-free local calls, Gazebo, Outdoor pool and Golf within Aberdeen on premises. Handicap access. Antiquing, cross-country skiing, downhill skiing, fishing, golf, live theater, parks, shopping, sporting events, tennis and water sports nearby.

Location: Rural.

Publicity: *Midwest Living, Chicago Magazine, Chicago Tribune, Country Inns and Indiana Business Magazine ("Best Retreat Site").*

"Every time we have the good fortune to spend an evening here, it is like a perfect fairy tale, transforming us into King and Queen."

Certificate may be used: Sunday through Thursdays only, excluding holidays.

Iowa

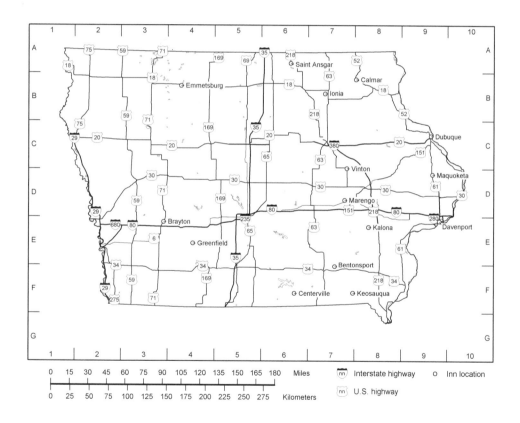

	Miles	
0 15 30 45 60 75 90 105 120 135 150 165 180		Miles
0 25 50 75 100 125 150 175 200 225 250 275		Kilometers

nn Interstate highway   o Inn location

nn U.S. highway

Bentonsport

Mason House Inn of Bentonsport

21982 Hawk Dr
Bentonsport, IA 52565
(319)592-3133 (800)592-3133
Internet: www.masonhouseinn.com
E-mail: stay@masonhouseinn.com

Circa 1846. A Murphy-style copper bathtub folds down out of the wall at this unusual inn built by Mormon craftsmen who stayed in Bentonsport for three years on their trek to Utah. More than half of the furniture is original to the home, including a nine-foot walnut headboard and a nine-foot mirror. The

Caboose Cottage, a self-contained apartment within a real railroad caboose, is the newest lodging addition. It features a kitchen, dining area and Queen bed.

This is the oldest operating pre-Civil War steamboat inn in Iowa. Guests can imagine the days when steamboats made their way up and down the Des Moines River, while taking in the scenery. A full breakfast is served in the main house dining room, but if guests crave a mid-day snack, each room is equipped with its own stocked cookie jar.

Innkeeper(s): Chuck & Joy Hanson. $59-100. 9 rooms with PB, 1 two-bedroom suite, 1 cottage. Breakfast included in rates. Types of meals: Full bkfst and early coffee/tea. Beds: KQDT. Data port, reading lamp, ceiling fan, wireless Internet access and filled cookie jar in room. Air conditioning. TV, VCR, DVD, fax, parlor games, telephone, fireplace and Free wireless Internet access on premises. Handicap access. Antiquing, bicycling, canoeing/kayaking, fishing, golf, hiking, horseback riding, parks, shopping, wineries, Rose Garden, Historic Church and Native American artifact museum nearby.

Location: Country, waterfront. Rural by river.

Publicity: *Des Moines Register, Decatur Herald & Review, AAA Home & Away, Country Magazine, Veteran's View, Iowa Public Television, Today Show and Coast to Coast AM with George Noory.*

"The attention to detail was fantastic, food was wonderful and the setting was fascinating."

Certificate may be used: Anytime, subject to availability.

Calmar

Calmar Guesthouse Bed & Breakfast

103 W North St
Calmar, IA 52132-7605
(563)562-3851
Internet: www.travelassist.com/reg/ia102s.html
E-mail: lbkruse@acegroup.cc

Circa 1890. This beautifully restored Victorian home was built by John B. Kay, a lawyer and poet. Stained-glass windows, carved moldings, an oak and walnut staircase and gleaming woodwork highlight the gracious interior. A grandfather clock ticks in the living room. In the foyer, a friendship yellow rose is incorporated into the stained-glass window pane. Breakfast is served in the formal dining room. The Laura Ingalls Wilder Museum is nearby in Burr Oak. The Bily Brothers Clock Museum, Smallest Church, Luther College, Niagara Cave, Lake Meyer and Norwegian Museum are located nearby.

Innkeeper(s): Lucille Kruse. $59-65. 5 rooms, 1 with PB. Breakfast included in rates. Types of meals: Full bkfst. Beds: Q. Cable TV, VCR, DVD, reading lamp, refrigerator, ceiling fan, clock radio, telephone, coffeemaker, desk, bathrobes, iron/ironing board and clock in room. Air conditioning. Bicycles, library, parlor games and laundry facility on premises. Antiquing, bicycling, canoeing/kayaking, cross-country skiing, fishing, golf, hiking, horseback riding, live theater, museums, parks, shopping, sporting events and water sports nearby.

Location: City.

Publicity: *Iowa Farmer Today, Calmar Courier, Minneapolis Star-Tribune, Home and Away, The Iowan and Alive at five on KWWL.*

"What a delight it was to stay here. No one could have made our stay more welcome or enjoyable."

Certificate may be used: Monday to Thursday, April to October only.

Centerville

One of A Kind

314 W State St
Centerville, IA 52544
(641)437-4540 Fax:(641)437-4540
Internet: www.oneofakindbedandbreakfast.com
E-mail: jjstuff@iowatelecom.net

Circa 1867. This large, three-story brick home with mansard roof and tall bays is the second oldest house in town. The innkeeper has filled the inn with "One of a Kind" craft and decorative items for sale, created on the premises or by local artisans. There is also a tea room, popular for its chicken soup and homemade croissant sandwiches, so of course you can expect a yummy breakfast, as well. Guest quarters are decorated with antiques and reproductions spiced with a variety of collectibles. The largest fish hatchery in the world is a short drive away at Lake Rathbun, but there is plenty to do within walking distance.

Innkeeper(s): Jack & Joyce Stufflebeem. $45-75. 5 rooms, 3 with PB. Breakfast and snacks/refreshments included in rates. Types of meals: Full bkfst, early coffee/tea, lunch, picnic lunch, afternoon tea and gourmet dinner. Beds: QDT. Cable TV, reading lamp, ceiling fan and turn-down service in room. Air conditioning. VCR, fax, copier, parlor games, telephone and tea room on premises. Antiquing, fishing, golf, live theater, parks, shopping, sporting events, tennis and water sports nearby.

Location: Small town.

Certificate may be used: Anytime, subject to availability.

Davenport

The Bishop's House Inn

1527 Brady St
Davenport, IA 52803-4622
(563)322-8303
Internet: www.sau.edu/administration/bishopsinn
E-mail: bishopshouseinn@sau.edu

Circa 1871. Meticulously restored, Bishop's House Inn of St. Ambrose University was built in 1871 and is listed in the National Register of Historic Places. This Italianate mansion in Davenport, Iowa reflects it heritage as a thriving Mississippi River town and boasts an array of Victorian details. Common areas include the Front Parlor, Starburst Parlor, Library and Summer Porch. The Second Floor Parlor is the Biz Hub with a computer, printer and refrigerator with ice maker. Early morning coffee and afternoon refreshments are provided. Stay in a well-appointed guest bedroom or suite with a marble shower stall, clawfoot or whirlpool tub. Linger over a hearty Midwestern breakfast in one of the dining rooms. Laundry facilities are available. Browse for souvenirs at the Gift Boutique.

Innkeeper(s): MaryElise Cervelli. $89-155. 5 rooms with PB, 2 with FP, 1 with WP, 1 suite. Breakfast and snacks/refreshments included in rates. Types of meals: Full bkfst, veg bkfst and early coffee/tea. Beds: Q. Cable TV, reading lamp, refrigerator, ceiling fan, clock radio, telephone, desk, hair dryer, bathrobes, bath amenities, wireless Internet access and iron/ironing board in room. Central air. VCR, DVD, fax, copier, fireplace, gift shop, Complimentary wireless access throughout the Inn, Business center for guests with complimentary use of computer & color printer, Coffee, Tea and Cold drinks on premises. Handicap access. Antiquing, art galleries, bicycling, fishing, golf, live theater, museums, parks, shopping and sporting events nearby.

Location: City.

Certificate may be used: Anytime, subject to availability.

Dubuque

The Hancock House

1105 Grove Ter
Dubuque, IA 52001-4644
(563)557-8989 Fax:(563)583-0813
Internet: www.TheHancockHouse.com
E-mail: chuckdbq@mchsi.com

Circa 1891. Victorian splendor can be found at The Hancock House, one of Dubuque's most striking examples of Queen

Anne architecture. Rooms feature period furnishings and offer views of the Mississippi River states of Iowa, Illinois and Wisconsin. The Hancock House, listed in the National Register, boasts several unique features, including a fireplace judged blue-ribbon best at the 1893 World's Fair in Chicago. Guests can enjoy the porch swings, wicker furniture and spectacular views from the wraparound front porch.

Innkeeper(s): Chuck & Susan Huntley. $80-175. 9 rooms with PB, 3 with FP, 4 with WP, 4 suites. Breakfast and snacks/refreshments included in rates. Types of meals: Full bkfst, veg bkfst and early coffee/tea. Beds: Q. Data port, cable TV, reading lamp, clock radio, desk, bath amenities, wireless Internet access, iron/ironing board and feather mattress in room. Air conditioning. Fax, copier, parlor games, telephone, fireplace, gift shop and gift shop on premises. Antiquing, art galleries, bicycling, canoeing/kayaking, cross-country skiing, downhill skiing, fishing, golf, hiking, horseback riding, live theater, museums, parks, shopping, sporting events, tennis, water sports, wineries and riverboat casino nearby.

Location: City.

Publicity: *Victorian Sampler (Cover).*

Certificate may be used: Sunday-Thursday, excluding holidays.

The Mandolin Inn

199 Loras Blvd
Dubuque, IA 52001-4857
(563)556-0069 (800)524-7996 Fax:(563)556-0587
Internet: www.mandolininn.com
E-mail: innkeeper@mandolininn.com

Circa 1908. This handicapped-accessible three-story brick Edwardian with Queen Anne wraparound veranda boasts a mosaic-tiled porch floor. Inside are inlaid mahogany and rosewood floors, bay windows and a turret that starts in the parlor and ascends to the second-floor Holly Marie Room, decorated in a wedding motif. This room features a seven-piece Rosewood

bedroom suite and a crystal chandelier. A gourmet breakfast is served in the dining room with a fantasy forest mural from the turn of the century. There is an herb garden outside the kitchen. Located just 12 blocks away, is the fabulous National Mississippi River Museum and Aquarium. The inn can equally accommodate both business and pleasure travel.

Innkeeper(s): Amy Boynton. $85-150. 8 rooms, 6 with PB, 1 with FP, 1 two-bedroom suite, 2 conference rooms. Breakfast included in rates. Types of meals: Full gourmet bkfst and early coffee/tea. Beds: KQT. Modem hook-up, cable TV, VCR, reading lamp, clock radio, desk, some with fireplace, bathrobes and wireless Internet access in room. Central air. DVD, fax, parlor games and telephone on premises. Handicap access.

Antiquing, art galleries, bicycling, cross-country skiing, downhill skiing, fishing, golf, hiking, horseback riding, live theater, museums, parks, shopping, sporting events, tennis, water sports and wineries nearby.

Location: City.

Publicity: *USA Today's "10 Best" Places to Stay, Arrington's BNB Journal, 2006 Summer Inn Traveler magazine, Iowan Magazine, Dubuque, Des Moines and Chicago newspapers, Emerging Horizons (Accessible Travel News) Magazine, Lakehom Magazine, Japanese TELPAL F, a Japanese Travel Show, local FOX TV, local television Promo for Cinderella (Cinderella reading her story in the parlour of the Mandolin Inn) and This American Life segment on NPR.*

"From the moment we entered the Mandolin, we felt at home. I know we'll be back."

Certificate may be used: Nov. 1 through Aug. 31, Sunday through Thursday, except for holidays.

Ionia

The Dairy Barn B&B

1436 210th Street
Ionia, IA 50645
(866)394-6302 Fax:(641)394-5376
Internet: www.thedairybarn.com
E-mail: info@thedairybarn.com

The Dairy Barn Bed and Breakfast in Ionia, Iowa is the perfect getaway in the countryside. The stress of city life immediately disappears. Feel welcomed the first night with a farmhand's supper. Ride a bike through the scenic area or stroll along the walking trails. Picnic lunches can be arranged in advance. Guest bedrooms are named after the dairy cows that resided there before renovations took place. The first-floor rooms are handicap accessible. Rooms in the hayloft are accented by a mural. Mabel's and Rosie's Rooms have entrances to a private outside balcony. Linger over Gerrie's hearty breakfast made with farm-fresh ingredients and from recipes collected in the B&B's cookbook available for purchase.

Innkeeper(s): Don & Gerrie Etter. $96. 8 rooms. Breakfast and Supper included in rates.

Certificate may be used: Anytime, subject to availabilty, excluding holidays, weekends and special events.

Maquoketa

Squiers Manor B&B

418 W Pleasant St
Maquoketa, IA 52060-2847
(563)652-6961 Fax:(563)652-5995
Internet: www.squiersmanor.com
E-mail: innkeeper@squiersmanor.com

Circa 1882. Innkeepers Virl and Kathy Banowetz are ace antique dealers, who along with owning one of the Midwest's largest antique shops, have refurbished this elegant, Queen Anne Victorian. The inn is furnished with period antiques that are beyond compare. Guest rooms boast museum-quality pieces such as a Victorian brass bed with lace curtain wings and inlaid mother-of-pearl or an antique mahogany bed with carved birds and flowers. Six guest rooms include whirlpool tubs, and one includes a unique Swiss shower. The innkeepers restored the home's original woodwork, shuttered-windows, fireplaces, gas and electric chandeliers and stained- and engraved-glass windows back to their former glory. They also recently renovated the mansion's attic ballroom into two luxurious suites. The Loft, which is made up of three levels, features pine and wicker furnishings, a sitting room and gas-burning wood stove. On the second level, there is a large Jacuzzi, on the third, an antique queen-size bed. The huge Ballroom Suite boasts 24-foot ceilings, oak and pine antiques, gas-burning wood stove and a Jacuzzi snuggled beside a dormer window. Suite guests enjoy breakfast delivered to their rooms. Other guests feast on an array of mouth-watering treats, such as home-baked breads, seafood quiche and fresh fruits. Evening desserts are served by candlelight.

Innkeeper(s): Virl & Kathy Banowetz. $80-195. 8 rooms with PB, 3 suites. Breakfast included in rates. Types of meals: Full gourmet bkfst. Beds: KQT. Antiquing, cross-country skiing, downhill skiing, fishing, parks, shopping and water sports nearby.

Publicity: Des Moines Register Datebook and Daily Herald.

"We couldn't have asked for a more perfect place to spend our honeymoon. The service was excellent and so was the food! It was an exciting experience that we will never forget!"

Certificate may be used: Sunday-Thursday, except in October, Valentine's week, or on holidays.

Saint Ansgar

Blue Belle Inn B&B

PO Box 205, 513 W 4th St
Saint Ansgar, IA 50472-0205
(641)713-3113 (877)713-3113
Internet: www.bluebelleinn.com
E-mail: innkeeper@bluebelleinn.com

Circa 1896. This home was purchased from a Knoxville, Tenn., mail-order house. It's difficult to believe that stunning features, such as a tin ceiling, stained-glass windows, intricate woodwork and pocket doors could have come via the mail, but these original items are still here for guests to admire. Rooms are named after books special to the innkeeper. Four of the rooms include a whirlpool tub for two, and the Never Neverland room has a clawfoot tub. Other rooms offer a skylight, fireplace or perhaps a white iron bed. During the Christmas season, every room has its own decorated tree. The innkeeper hosts a variety of themed luncheons, dinners and events, such as the April in Paris cooking workshop, Mother's Day brunches, the "Some Enchanted Evening" dinner, Murder Mysteries, Ladies nights, Writer's Retreats, quilting seminars and horse-drawn sleigh rides.

Innkeeper(s): Sherrie Hansen. $45-375. 11 rooms, 8 with PB, 2 with FP, 3 with WP, 5 total suites, including 2 two-bedroom suites and 1 three-bedroom suite, 1 cottage, 1 guest house, 2 conference rooms. Breakfast and snacks/refreshments included in rates. Types of meals: Full gourmet bkfst, veg bkfst, early coffee/tea, gourmet lunch, afternoon tea, gourmet dinner, room service and Visit our main website for a quaterly schedule of events and menus with weekly specials. Restaurant on premises. Beds: KQDT. Cable TV, VCR, reading lamp, stereo, refrigerator, clock radio, coffeemaker, desk, most with hot tub/spa, some with fireplace, bathrobes, bath amenities, wireless Internet access, iron/ironing board, Handicap accessibility and Jacuzzis for two in room. Central air. Fax, copier, library, parlor games, telephone, laundry facility, handicap unit with ramp & roll-in shower, kitchenette with refrigerator and microwave, wireless Internet access, piano, movies, popcorn and complimentary snacks on premises. Handicap access. Antiquing, bicycling, canoeing/kayaking, fishing, golf, hiking, museums, parks, shopping, water sports, wineries, hunting, Music Man Square, Hormel Spam museum and Clear Lake nearby.

Location: Small town.

Publicity: Minneapolis Star Tribune, Post-Bulletin, Midwest Living, Country, AAA Home & Away, Des Moines Register, Country Home, Iowan Magazine, American Patchwork and Quilting, New York Times, HGTV Restore America, KTTC - Rochester and MN.

Certificate may be used: Nov. 1-April 30, Monday-Thursday nights only, holidays excluded, Dec. 26-31 excluded, subject to availability.

Vinton

The Lion & The Lamb B&B

913 2nd Ave
Vinton, IA 52349-1729
(319)472-5086 (888)390-5262
Internet: www.lionlamb.com
E-mail: request@lionlamb.com

Circa 1892. Meticulously restored, this Queen Anne Victorian built in 1892 in Vinton, Iowa is a true Painted Lady with seven colors detailing its stunning exterior that boasts intricate chimneys, gingerbread trim, gables and turrets. Inside, seven fireplaces are accented with ornate wood and tiled mantles. Pocket doors, stained-glass windows, high ceilings and parquet floors highlight the furnishings and décor. Sip lemonade or iced tea on the front porch or in the parlor. Guest bedrooms in the Ellis House are named after the original family members. Stay in the Ellis Suite with a whirlpool tub. Start each day at the Lion & the Lamb Bed & Breakfast with a morning meal served on china. Ask about Murder Mystery Dinners and special packages.

Innkeeper(s): Rachel Waterbury. $75-155. 6 rooms with PB, 1 with WP, 3 conference rooms. Breakfast included in rates. Types of meals: Full bkfst, early coffee/tea, snacks/refreshments and gourmet dinner. Beds: KQ. TV, reading lamp, ceiling fan, clock radio, coffeemaker, bathrobes and wireless Internet access in room. Air conditioning. Parlor games and telephone on premises. Antiquing, cross-country skiing, fishing, golf, hiking, live theater, parks, shopping, tennis and water sports nearby.

Location: City. Small Town.

Publicity: Cedar Valley Times, Waterloo Courier, Cedar Rapids Gazette, Country Discoveries Magazine and KWWL-Channel 7 Neighborhood News.

"It is a magical place!"

Certificate may be used: Sunday to Thursday, September to May, excluding holidays and weekends.

Kansas

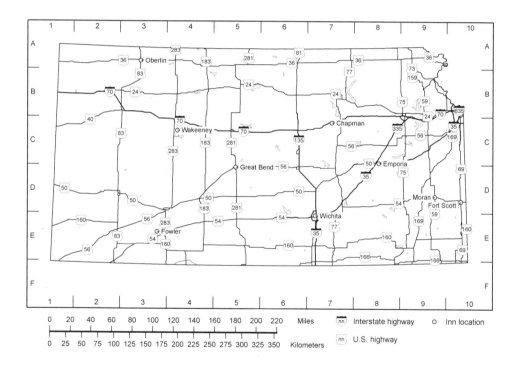

0   20   40   60   80   100   120   140   160   180   200   220   Miles

0   25   50   75   100   125   150   175   200   225   250   275   300   325   350   Kilometers

nn Interstate highway   o Inn location

nn U.S. highway

Fort Scott

Lyons' Twin Mansions Bed & Breakfast and Spa

742 & 750 S National Ave
Fort Scott, KS 66701-1319
(620)223-3644 (800)784-8378 Fax:(620)223-0062
Internet: www.lyonsmansion.com
E-mail: relax@lyonsmansion.com

Circa 1876. For a business trip, vacation or romantic getaway, this landmark Victorian mansion is a luxurious choice. This gracious home has parlors to gather and Paradise, a full service spa. Extreme Media TV, 42" Plasma in one, 50" flat screen in another. All guest rooms have full cable with movie channels. Spacious guest bedrooms offer king-size beds, refined comfort and modern technology with refreshment centers and high-speed Internet. The baths feature oversized jetted whirlpools that are made to look like antique clawfoot tubs. Enjoy a hearty breakfast in the grand dining room, unless a breakfast basket delivered to the door is preferred. The grounds are showcased by a gazebo, fish ponds, picnic areas and an enclosed starlit hot tub. Ask about the creative specialty packages offered such as mystery, private dining and couples and ladies spa packages.

Innkeeper(s): Pat & Larry Lyons and Nate Lyons. $79-175. 8 rooms, 7 with PB, 3 with FP, 4 with WP, 1 two-bedroom suite, 1 cottage, 1 guest house, 3 conference rooms. Breakfast and snacks/refreshments included in rates. Types of meals: Full bkfst, veg bkfst, picnic lunch, gourmet dinner and room service. Beds: K. Modem hook-up, cable TV, VCR, DVD, reading lamp, stereo, refrigerator, ceiling fan, snack bar, clock radio, telephone, coffeemaker, turn-down service, desk, most with hot tub/spa, some with fireplace, hair dryer, bathrobes, bath amenities, wireless Internet access, iron/ironing board, Three with two-person whirlpool and one with two-person therapeutic massage with built in ChromoTherapy in room. Central air. Fax, copier, spa, library, parlor games, laundry facility, High-speed Internet, Outdoor Grill and Picnic area on premises. Antiquing, canoeing/kayaking, fishing, golf, hiking, horseback riding, live theater, museums, parks, shopping, tennis, Olympic-size swimming pool, (open Memorial Day thru Labor Day), city park with playgrounds, community center, tennis, baseball, archery and movie theater nearby.

Publicity: *Midwest Living, Victorian Homes, Kansas Magazine, AAA Midwest Traveler, Travel Kansas Magazine, Fort Scott Tribune and Topeka Capitol Journal.*

Certificate may be used: Accepts weekends, Anytime, subject to availability, Anytime, last minute-based on availability.

Oberlin

The Landmark Inn at The Historic Bank of Oberlin

189 S Penn
Oberlin, KS 67749
(785)475-2340 (888)639-0003
Internet: www.landmarkinn.com
E-mail: info@landmarkinn.com

In 1886, this inn served as the Bank of Oberlin, one of the town's most impressive architectural sites. The bank lasted only a few years, though, and went through a number of uses, from county courthouse to the telephone company. Today, it serves as both inn and a historic landmark, a reminder of the past with rooms decorated Victorian style with antiques. One room includes a fireplace; another has a whirlpool tub. In addition to the inviting rooms, there is a restaurant serving dinner specialties such as buttermilk pecan chicken and roasted beef with simmered mushrooms. The inn is listed in the National Register.

Innkeeper(s): Gary Anderson. Call for rates. 7 suites. Breakfast included in rates. Types of meals: Full gourmet bkfst, early coffee/tea, gourmet lunch, afternoon tea, snacks/refreshments, gourmet dinner and room service. Restaurant on premises. Beds: QD. Cable TV, VCR, reading lamp, ceiling fan, snack bar, clock radio, telephone and desk in room. Air conditioning. Fax, sauna, bicycles, library, parlor games and fireplace on premises. Handicap access. Antiquing, golf, parks, shopping and tennis nearby.

Location: Small town/country.

Publicity: *Kansas Magazine, Dining out in Kansas, Wichita Eagle-Beacon, Salina Journal, Hays Daily News, 2001 Bed & Breakfast Calendar, KSN TV-Wichita, KS, High Plains Public TV and Kansas Public TV Taste of Kansas.*

Certificate may be used: January-April, Sunday-Thursday, subject to availability.

Kentucky

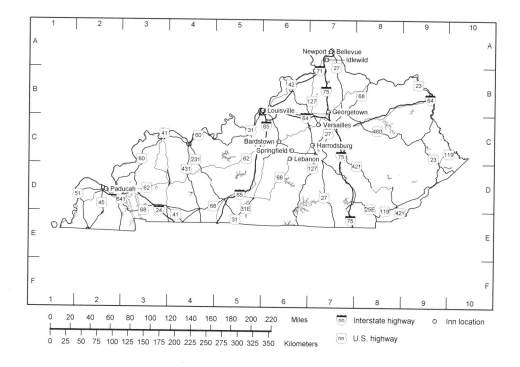

Newport   Bellevue
  Idlewild
71   27

42   75   68   23

127   64

Louisville   Georgetown

41   60   31   65   Versailles   460

27

60   Bardstown   Harrodsburg   23   119

231   62   Springfield   75

431   Lebanon   421

68   127

51   Paducah   62   65   27

45   641   68   24   41   68   31E   25E   119   421

31   75

| 0 | 20 | 40 | 60 | 80 | 100 | 120 | 140 | 160 | 180 | 200 | 220 | Miles |

| 0 | 25 | 50 | 75 | 100 | 125 | 150 | 175 | 200 | 225 | 250 | 275 | 300 | 325 | 350 | Kilometers |

Interstate highway   o   Inn location

U.S. highway

Bellevue

Christopher's B&B

604 Poplar St
Bellevue, KY 41073
(859)491-9354 (888)585-7085
Internet: www.christophersbb.com
E-mail: christophers@insightbb.com

Circa 1889. The former home of Bellevue Christian Church, this unique inn sits in one of the area's three historic districts. The spacious building was transformed into a delightful residence and B&B featuring the original hardwood floors and stained-glass windows. Tastefully decorated and furnished in a Victorian style, the gracious guest bedrooms and suite feature Jacuzzi tubs and VCRs.

Innkeeper(s): Brenda Guidugli. $105-179. 3 rooms with PB, 3 with WP, 1 suite. Breakfast and snacks/refreshments included in rates. Types of meals: Full bkfst, veg bkfst and early coffee/tea. Beds: KQ. Modem hook-up, data port, cable TV, VCR, DVD, reading lamp, stereo, refrigerator, ceiling fan, snack bar, clock radio, telephone, coffeemaker, desk, hair dryer, bathrobes, bath amenities, wireless Internet access, iron/ironing board, Jacuzzi, ironing board, iron, hair dryer and DVD/VHS movies in room. Central air. Fax, copier, parlor games, fireplace, gift shop, continental plus breakfast (weekdays only); full breakfast (weekends) and single/double Jacuzzi tubs on premises. Limited handicap access. Amusement parks, antiquing, art galleries, fishing, golf, hiking, live theater, museums, parks, shopping, sporting events, water sports, Newport Aquarium, Newport on the Levee, Millennium Peace Bell, Riverbend outdoor concerts, Bengals' Paul Brown Stadium, Cincinnati Reds' Great American Ball Park, National Underground Railroad Freedom Center, Cincinnati Zoo, Cincinnati Museum Center, Paramount King's Island, BB Riverboats dinner/lunch cruises and restaurants with a river view nearby.

Location: City. Near Ohio River.

Publicity: *Midwest Living, The Cincinnati Enquirer, The Kentucky Post, Kentucky Monthly, Arts Across Kentucky, AAA Home Away, City Beat, Kentucky Living, Cleveland Magazine, Kentucky Enquirer, Places To Go, Channel 12 Local News and Arrington's Bed and Breakfast Journal 2003 & 2004 Book of Lists (voted "One of the Top 15 B&Bs/Inns for Best Design and Decor").*

Certificate may be used: Sunday-Friday only, subject to availability. During week: Continental plus breakfast, Weekends: full breakfast.

Georgetown

Bryan House Bed & Breakfast

401 West Main Street
Georgetown, KY 40324
(502)863-1060 (877)296-3051
Internet: www.bryanhousebnb.com
E-mail: bryanhouse@bellsouth.net

Circa 1891. Known as "The Jewel of Georgetown," this 1891 Queen Anne with brick, stonework and classic columns has been meticulously restored to maintain its historical integrity yet offer modern conveniences. The Victorian décor is accented with Eastlake and Renaissance Revival furnishings. Overlook the gardens from the covered porch. Romantic guest bedrooms feature antique beds in walnut and oak. The Tasteful Melody Suite and Grapes of Gold Suite boast whirlpool tubs. An award-winning gourmet breakfast may include melon with lime mousse, homemade Danish pastries, almond egg puffs or amaretto stuffed waffles with fresh raspberry maple syrup and beverages.

Innkeeper(s): Jan & Stan Sekula. $75-155. 3 rooms with PB. Breakfast and snacks/refreshments included in rates. Types of meals: Full gourmet bkfst and early coffee/tea. Beds: Q. Cable TV, CD player, ceiling fan, clock radio, turn-down service, hot tub/spa and wireless Internet access in room. Central air. Fax,

copier, library, parlor games, telephone and fireplace on premises. Antiquing, art galleries, bicycling, canoeing/kayaking, fishing, golf, hiking, horseback riding, live theater, museums, parks, shopping, sporting events, tennis, wineries and distilleries nearby.

Location: City.

Certificate may be used: Monday-Thursday, November-March, subject to availability.

Idlewild

First Farm Inn

2510 Stevens Rd
Idlewild, KY 41080
(859)586-0199
Internet: www.firstfarminn.com
E-mail: info@firstfarminn.com

Circa 1870. Elegantly updated, this 1870s farm house and historic wooden barn with tobacco rails are located just outside Cincinnati and surrounded by 21 acres of rolling hills, ponds stocked with bass, centuries-old maple trees, gardens and horses. Situated above the Ohio River, where Kentucky joins Ohio and Indiana, city sites and country pleasures are equally accessible. Spend two hours learning about horses and riding one of the friendly equines. Lessons begin with grooming, working in the arena, then graduating to a trail ride around the farm, along the pond and through the woods. Schedule a massage with a licensed therapist in a spacious guest bedroom furnished with antique oak heirlooms. Indulge in a bountiful homemade breakfast of fresh fruit, assorted breads and an entree served family style around the big dining room table. Sit by the fire or play the grand piano. Relax in the outdoor hot tub; swing or rock on the veranda.

Innkeeper(s): Jen Warner & Dana Kisor. $90-162. 2 rooms with PB. Full healthy balanced all-you-can eat breakfast included in rates. Types of meals: Full gourmet bkfst, veg bkfst, early coffee/tea, Swiss Rosti, Kentucky version of Pasta Carbonara, Multi-grain pancakes with peaches, pumpkin, bananas, blueberries, blackberries and etc. or more conventional breakfasts. Beds: Q. TV, VCR, DVD, reading lamp, CD player, ceiling fan, clock radio, telephone, desk, some with fireplace, hair dryer, bathrobes, bath amenities, iron/ironing board and Massage available (please schedule in advance) in room. Central air. Copier, spa, stable, library, pet boarding, child care, parlor games, Horseback riding lessons, Porch swing, Porch rockers, Tire swing, Hammock, Cats, Dogs, Horses, Grand piano, Fishing pond and Hiking on premises. Amusement parks, antiquing, art galleries, canoeing/kayaking, downhill skiing, fishing, golf, hiking, horseback riding, live theater, museums, parks, shopping, sporting events, tennis, water sports, wineries, Perfect North ski slopes, Big Bone Lick State Park (mammoth and mastodon bones found here in 1740s), 1830s vintage Rabbit Hash General Store, Historic Burlingotn shops and Cabin Arts Quilt Shop nearby.

Location: Country, near downtown Cincinnati.

Publicity: *Kentucky Monthly, Cincinnati Monthly, Chicago Herald, Columbus Parent, Kentucky Post, Cincinnati Enquirer, Louisville Courier-Journal, Indianapolis Monthly, City Beat, The Downtowner, The Community Recorders, Arrington's Inn Traveler named "Best for Rest and Relaxation", Channel 12 One Tank Trip, Channel 6 Travel specials, NPR Brainbrew, WBOB Travel Trips in Cincinnati, N. Kentucky Chamber Small Business Success finalist (2001, 2002, .2003, 2004 and 2005).*

Certificate may be used: Monday-Tuesday, December-March, last minute subject to availability.

Lebanon

Myrtledene B&B

370 N Spalding Ave
Lebanon, KY 40033-1557
(270)692-2223 (800)391-1721
Internet: www.myrtledene.com
E-mail: info@myrtledene.com

Circa 1833. Once a Confederate general's headquarters at one point during the Civil War, this pink brick inn, located at a bend in the road, has greeted visitors entering Lebanon for more than 150 years. When General John Hunt Morgan returned in 1863 to destroy the town, the white flag hoisted to signal a truce was flown at Myrtledene. A country breakfast usually features ham and biscuits as well as the innkeepers' specialty, peaches and cream French toast.

Innkeeper(s): James F. Spragens. $85. 4 rooms, 2 with PB, 1 with FP, 1 conference room. Breakfast included in rates. Types of meals: Full gourmet bkfst, early coffee/tea and afternoon tea. Beds: DT. Reading lamp, clock radio, turn-down service, Makers Mark bourbon and bourbon chocolates in room. Air conditioning. VCR, library, parlor games, telephone and fireplace on premises. Antiquing, fishing, live theater, parks, shopping and water sports nearby.

Location: City.

Publicity: *Lebanon Enterprise, Louisville Courier-Journal, Lebanon/Marion County Kentucky and Sunnyside.*

"Our night in the Cabbage Rose Room was an experience of another time, another culture. Your skill in preparing and presenting breakfast was equally elegant! We'll be back!"

Certificate may be used: Anytime except Sept. 27-28.

Louisville

1853 Inn at Woodhaven

401 S Hubbard Ln
Louisville, KY 40207-4074
(502)895-1011 (888)895-1011 Fax:(502)896-0449
Internet: www.innatwoodhaven.com
E-mail: info@innatwoodhaven.com

Circa 1853. This Gothic Revival, painted in a cheerful shade of yellow, is still much the same as it was in the 1850s, when it served as the home on a prominent local farm. The rooms still feature the outstanding carved woodwork, crisscross window designs, winding staircases, decorative mantels and hardwood floors. Guest quarters are tastefully appointed with antiques, suitable for their 12-foot, nine-inch tall ceilings. Complimentary coffee and tea stations are provided in each room. There are several common areas in the Main House and Carriage House, and guests also take advantage of the inn's porches. Rose Cottage is octagon shaped and features a 25-foot vaulted ceiling, a king bed, fireplace, sitting area, double whirlpool, steam shower and wraparound porch. The National Register home is close to all of Louisville's attractions.

Innkeeper(s): Marsha Burton. $95-225. 8 rooms with PB, 3 with FP, 6 suites, 1 cottage. Breakfast included in rates. Types of meals: Full gourmet bkfst. Beds: KQ. Cable TV, reading lamp, stereo, ceiling fan, clock radio, tele-

phone, desk, coffee, tea, hot chocolate facility, six with double whirlpool and four with steam shower in room. Air conditioning. Fax, copier, library, parlor games, fireplace and wireless Internet on premises. Handicap access. Amusement parks, antiquing, golf, live theater, parks, shopping, sporting events, tennis and water sports nearby.

Location: City.

Publicity: *Courier Journal, New York Times, WAVE and WHAS.*

Certificate may be used: Sunday through Thursday, January through April.

Aleksander House

1213 S First St
Louisville, KY 40203
(502)637-4985 (866)637-4985 Fax:(502)635-1398
Internet: www.aleksanderhouse.com
E-mail: alekhouse@aol.com

Circa 1882. Prints of French impressionists, Toile wall coverings, 13-foot ceilings and original light fixtures, fireplaces and walnut woodwork create a romantic atmosphere at this 1882 Victorian Italianate bed and breakfast. Ask for Katharine's Room and relax in the comfort of an inviting antique four-poster bed. Business travelers appreciate the amenities of Penina's Room which can be combined into a suite with the adjoining Kimberly's Room, making it perfect for families. Belgian waffles with fresh strawberries or Eggs Benedict are favorite breakfast entrees served in the delightful dining room with Queen Anne and Duncan Fyfe furnishings. Aleksander House is a three-story brick inn listed in the National Register and is situated in historic Old Louisville, Kentucky. Get-away specials, spa and sweetheart packages are available.

Innkeeper(s): Nancy R Hinchliff. $115-169. 5 rooms, 4 with PB, 2 with FP, 1 suite. Breakfast and snacks/refreshments included in rates. Types of meals: Full gourmet bkfst, veg bkfst and early coffee/tea. Beds: KQDT. Modem hook-up, data port, TV, VCR, DVD, reading lamp, stereo, refrigerator, ceiling fan, clock radio, telephone, coffeemaker, desk, some with fireplace, hair dryer, bathrobes, bath amenities, wireless Internet access, iron/ironing board, children and pets allowed with some restrictions in room. Central air. Fax, copier, library, parlor games, video library, snacks, beverages, outdoor deck and gardens on premises. Amusement parks, antiquing, art galleries, bicycling, golf, hiking, horseback riding, live theater, museums, parks, shopping, sporting events, tennis, water sports, wineries and river boating nearby.

Location: City.

Publicity: *Country Inns, Louisville Magazine, Today's Woman Magazine, The Courier-Journal, Country Register and Channel 11-WGN.*

Certificate may be used: Monday-Thursday, subject to availability.

Central Park B&B

Old Louisville Historic District
Louisville, KY 40208-2349
(502)638-1505 (877)922-1505 Fax:(502)638-1525
Internet: www.centralparkbandb.com
E-mail: centralpar@win.net

Circa 1884. This three-story Second Empire Victorian is listed in the National Register, and it is located in the heart of "Old Louisville," amid America's largest collection of Victorian homes. Enjoy the fine craftsmanship of the home's many amenities, including the reverse-painted glass ceiling of the front porch and the polished woodwork and stained glass. Among its 18 rooms are seven guest rooms, all with private baths and two with whirlpool tubs. There are 11 fireplaces, some with carved mantels and decorative tile. The Carriage House suite has a full kitchen. Antiques are found throughout. Across the street is Central Park; only 3 minutes from downtown and seven minutes from the airport.

$110-175. 7 rooms with PB, 6 with FP, 2 with WP, 1 suite, 1 guest house,

1 conference room. Breakfast, afternoon tea, snacks/refreshments, hors d'oeuvres and wine included in rates. Types of meals: Full gourmet bkfst, veg bkfst and early coffee/tea. Beds: KQT. Modem hook-up, data port, cable TV, VCR, DVD, reading lamp, stereo, refrigerator, ceiling fan, snack bar, clock radio, telephone, coffeemaker, desk, some with hot tub/spa, fireplace, hair dryer, bathrobes, bath amenities, wireless Internet access, iron/ironing board, coffee/tea and hot chocolate in room. Central air. Fax, copier, tennis, parlor games, laundry facility, gift shop, Massage Therapist available by appointment and BBQ Grill in Garden Patio for guest use on premises. Amusement parks, antiquing, art galleries, bicycling, fishing, golf, hiking, horseback riding, live theater, museums, parks, shopping, sporting events, tennis, wineries and Five dining establishments within walking distance of the inn nearby.

Location: City.

Certificate may be used: January through December, Sunday-Thursday, except holidays and special events.

Newport

Cincinnati's Weller Haus B&B

319 Poplar St
Newport, KY 41073-1108
(859)431-6829 (800)431-4287 Fax:(859)431-4332
Internet: www.wellerhaus.com
E-mail: wellerhaus@insightbb.com

Circa 1880. Set in Taylor Daughter's Historic District and five minutes from downtown Cincinnati, this inn consists of two historic homes. The inn has received awards for preservation, and special features include original woodwork and doors. Secluded gardens are inviting, and there is a wrought iron fence setting off the property. A full breakfast is served by candlelight. Rooms offer antiques and suites feature double Jacuzzi tubs. A sky-lit great room has cathedral ceilings, and an ivy-covered gathering kitchen is open for snacks and drinks. Guests enjoy walking to the Newport Aquarium, Newport on the Levee and the Riverboat Row Restaurants as well as downtown Cincinnati stadiums. Other attractions include live theater and water sports. Business travelers are provided telephones, in room desks, high-speed wireless Internet and a copy machine and fax are on the premises. Private space is available for small meetings. Breakfast can accommodate business schedules.

Innkeeper(s): Leanne Saylor. $125-199. 5 rooms with PB, 3 with FP, 3 with HT, 1 conference room. Breakfast included in rates. Types of meals: Full bkfst, veg bkfst, early coffee/tea and snacks/refreshments. Beds: QDT. Modem hook-up, data port, cable TV, VCR, DVD, reading lamp, stereo, ceiling fan, snack bar, clock radio, telephone, coffeemaker, turn-down service, desk, some with hot tub/spa, some with fireplace, hair dryer, bathrobes, bath amenities, wireless Internet access, iron/ironing board, Suites have Jacuzzi for two, High-speed Internet access, 200+ movie titles, Complimentary snacks and Soft drinks in room. Central air. Fax, copier, library, parlor games, gift shop, Pet friendly in one room, Rendezvous Suite and $25 Pet Fee for pets 20 lbs and under—no cats on premises. Limited handicap access. Amusement parks, antiquing, art galleries, cross-country skiing, downhill skiing, fishing, hiking, horseback riding, live theater, museums, parks, shopping, sporting events, water sports and wineries nearby.

Location: City.

Publicity: *Downtowner, Bellevue Community News, Cincinnati Enquirer, Country Inns, Kentucky Monthly, Arrington's Bed & Breakfast Journal, The Book of Lists and Cincinnati Weekly.*

"You made B&B believers out of us."

Certificate may be used: All year long with a Sunday-Wednesday check-in—NO holidays, special events.

Springfield

1851 Historic Maple Hill Manor B&B

2941 Perryville Rd (US 150 EAST)
Springfield, KY 40069-9611
(859)336-3075 (800)886-7546
Internet: www.maplehillmanor.com
E-mail: stay@maplehillmanor.com

Circa 1851. In a tranquil country setting on 14 acres, this Greek Revival mansion with Italianate detail is considered a Kentucky Landmark home and is listed in the National Register of Historic Places. Numerous architectural features include 14-foot ceilings, nine-foot windows, 10-foot doorways and a grand cherry spiral staircase. Guest bedrooms provide spacious serenity, and some boast fireplaces and or Jacuzzis. Enjoy a full country breakfast, and then take a peaceful stroll through flower gardens and the fruit orchard, or relax on a patio swing or porch rocker. The local area has a rich abundance of attractions including Bardstown, Shaker Village, Bourbon, historic Civil War areas and Lincoln Trails. Lexington and Louisville are within an hour's drive.

Innkeeper(s): Todd Allen & Tyler Horton. $119-179. 7 rooms with PB, 3 with FP, 2 with WP, 4 suites, 1 conference room. Breakfast, afternoon tea and snacks/refreshments included in rates. Types of meals: Full gourmet bkfst, veg bkfst, early coffee/tea, gourmet lunch, picnic lunch, hors d'oeuvres, gourmet dinner and room service. Beds: QDT. TV, VCR, DVD, reading lamp, CD player, ceiling fan, snack bar, clock radio, telephone, coffeemaker, turn-down service, some with hot tub/spa, some with fireplace, hair dryer, bath amenities, wireless Internet access, iron/ironing board, Two with Jacuzzi, three with fireplace, designer linens, antique furnishings, rollaway beds available, some with TV/VCR/DVD/CD player(includes movies/music) and each Guest Room has a private bath in room. Central air. Fax, copier, library, parlor games, laundry facility, gift shop, orchard, grape vineyard, nature walking paths, flower gardens, fountains, patio, Gazebo, snack bar, complimentary homemade evening desserts, 24-hour beverage service, alpaca and llama farm, Fiber Studio & Farm Store and Murder Mystery Events on premises. Limited handicap access. Antiquing, art galleries, bicycling, canoeing/kayaking, fishing, golf, hiking, horseback riding, live theater, museums, parks, shopping, sporting events, tennis, water sports, wineries, My Old Kentucky Home & Golf Course State Park, Stephen Foster Musical, Kentucky Dinner Train, Historic Bardstown, Bernheim Forest, Kentucky Railway Museum, Civil War Museums, Lincoln Homestead State Park & Golf Course, Maywood Golf Course, Abbey of Gethsemani, Lincoln National Museum & Birthplace, Kentucky Bourbon Distilleries, Bourbon Heritage Center, Maker's Mark Bourbon Distillery, Heaven Hill Bourbon Distillery, Jim Beam Bourbon Distillery, Oscar Getz Museum of Whiskey History, Fox Hollow Pottery, Nettie Jarvis Antiques, Kentucky Wine Trail, Antique Shopping, U-Pick Farms, Horse Stables, Shaker Village at Pleasent Hill, Old Fort Harrod State Park, Willisburg Lake, Perryville Civil War Battlefield, Constitution Square, Big Red Stables, Taylorsville Lake, Green River Lake, Herrington Lake, Mt. Zion Covered Bridge, Koenig Farm & Spiinery, St. Catharine Motherhouse, Washington Courthouse, Keeneland, Around the Town Carriage Rides, Basilica of St. Joseph, Old Talbott Tavern, Springhill Winery, Rolling Hills Vineyard, Chateau Du Viex Corbeau Winery, Amish/ Mennonite Shops, Wickland, Wildlife/Natural History Museum, Lincoln Boyhood Home, Abraham Lincoln Museum, Lebanon Civil War Par, Loretto Motherhouse, Pioneer Playhouse Outdoor Dinner Theatre, Ragged Edge Community Theatre and Norton Centre for the Arts nearby.

Location: Country. Rural.

Publicity: *Southern Living, Danville's Advocate-Messenger, Springfield Sun, Cincinnati's Eastside Weekend, Louisville Courier Journal, Lexington Herald-Leader, Arts Across Kentucky, Kentucky Monthly, Arrington's Inn Traveler Magazine,* Voted "Best Breakfast in the Southeast" for 2005 and 2006 by Arrington's B&B Journal, Voted #1 in the US as the B&B with the "most Historical Charm" and voted as "One of Kentucky's Finest B&Bs"

"Thank you again for your friendly and comfortable hospitality."
Certificate may be used: Sunday-Thursday, year-round.

Versailles

Montgomery Inn Bed & Breakfast

270 Montgomery Ave
Versailles, KY 40383
(859)873-4478 (800)526-9801 Fax:(859)873-7099
Internet: www.montgomeryinnbnb.com
E-mail: innkeeper@montgomeryinnbnb.com

Circa 1911. Located in the horse capital of the world, Montgomery Inn Bed & Breakfast is a restored 1911 Victorian in the Kentucky Bluegrass region of Versailles. This family-operated inn offers concierge service and many upscale amenities with Southern hospitality. Munch on fresh-baked cookies in the Library upon check-in, swing on the wraparound porch or nap in the double hammock. Snacks, beverages, and access to a microwave and refrigerator are in the Media Room. Play the antique baby grand piano in the front parlor. Stay in a guest bedroom or spa suite with a two-person whirlpool tub, cotton sateen sheets, oversized Egyptian cotton towels and terry robes. A hearty gourmet breakfast is served in the GardenSide Dining Room. Dinner is available by reservation.

Innkeeper(s): Pam & Michael Matthews. $139-179. 10 rooms, 10 with HT, 10 with WP, 10 total suites, including 1 two-bedroom suite, 1 conference room. Breakfast, snacks/refreshments and wine included in rates. Types of meals: Full gourmet bkfst, early coffee/tea, gourmet lunch, picnic lunch, afternoon tea, hors d'oeuvres and gourmet dinner. Beds: KQ. Cable TV, VCR, DVD, reading lamp, stereo, refrigerator, snack bar, clock radio, telephone, desk, hot tub/spa, hair dryer, bathrobes, bath amenities, wireless Internet access, iron/ironing board, 600-count sheets, Egyptian cotton towels, Wine & beverage set-ups, Periodicals and DVD movies in room. Central air. Fax, copier, library, parlor games, fireplace, laundry facility, gift shop and Complimentary snacks & beverages on premises. Antiquing, art galleries, bicycling, canoeing/kayaking, fishing, hiking, horseback riding, live theater, museums, parks, shopping, sporting events, tennis, wineries, Bourbon Distilleries, Candy factory, Keeneland Horse Racing, Kentucky Horse Park, Red Mile Harness Racing, Shaker Village, Berea Art & Craft Colony, Mammoth National Park, Diamond Caves and Kentucky River nearby.

Location: Country.

Certificate may be used: Not valid during Equestrian Events, subject to availability.

Louisiana

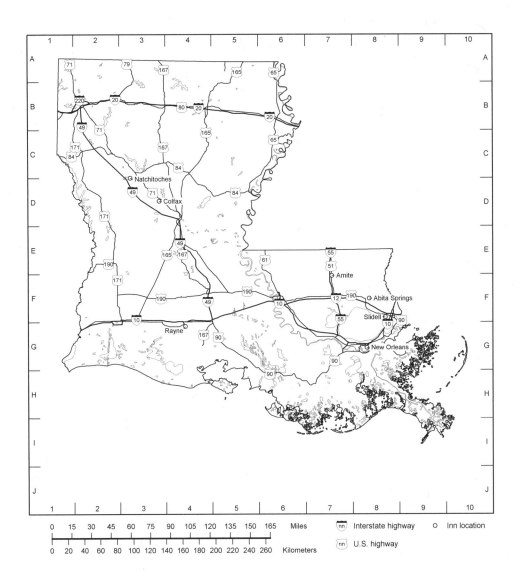

New Orleans

1822 Bougainvillea House

924 Gov. Nicholls St.
New Orleans, LA 70116-3106
(504)522-5000 Fax:(504)522-5000
Internet: www.1822bougainvillea.com
E-mail: patkahn@aol.com

Circa 1822. Built by a plantation owner in 1822, this French Quarter guesthouse boasts the romantic mystique of its historical background. Each luxurious suite includes a bedroom, living/dining room, bath, private entrance and either a patio or balcony. Some feature antique furnishings. Dine on culinary delights at famous restaurants nearby, walk along the levee by the river, shop at the Royal Street boutiques, and plan a visit during Mardi Gras, Creole Christmas or one of the many popular local festivals. Arrange an excursion to the world-class Audubon Zoo, the swamps or take a walking tour of haunted mansions.

Innkeeper(s): Pat Kahn. $125-200. 3 rooms, 5 suites. Types of meals: Early coffee/tea. Beds: KQ. Cable TV, reading lamp, refrigerator, ceiling fan, clock radio, telephone, coffeemaker and desk in room. Central air. Fax, copier, bicycles and laundry facility on premises. Amusement parks, antiquing, art galleries, beach, bicycling, fishing, golf, horseback riding, live theater, museums, parks, shopping, sporting events and tennis nearby.

Location: Heart of the French Quarter.

"We love your home and always enjoy our visits here so much!"

Certificate may be used: June-August, Subject to availability, Paddlewheeler or Riverboat suites only.

1870 Banana Courtyard French Quarter/New Orleans B&B

1422 N. Rampart St.
New Orleans, LA 70116
(504)947-4475 (800)842-4748 Fax:(504)949-5689
Internet: www.bananacourtyard.com
E-mail: bananacour@aol.com

Circa 1870. Everyone feels like an honored guest while staying at this Victorian Creole bed & breakfast extraordinaire. A variety of accommodations are offered, from the main B&B rooms to a romantic 1850s cottage, spacious guest suite, historic townhouse or apartment. Lagniappe means a little something extra, and that is what is offered here. Enjoy a welcome drink, a generous continental breakfast and afternoon beverages. Relaxing is easy in the courtyard on a double hammock. Just outside the gate is the French Quarter, Bourbon Street is only three blocks away.

Innkeeper(s): The Banana Lady. $59-225. 12 rooms with PB, 5 with FP, 1 with WP, 5 total suites, including 4 two-bedroom suites, 3 three-bedroom suites and 2 four-bedroom suites, 4 cottages, 4 guest houses. Breakfast, Generous Continental breakfast served in dining room included in rate for accommodations Cont plus, Available for a fee items such as chocolate covered strawberries, champagne and cakes. Beds: KQDT. Modem hook-up, cable TV, reading lamp, refrigerator, ceiling fan, clock radio, telephone, coffeemaker, turn-down service, some with fireplace, hair dryer, wireless Internet access, iron/ironing board, Balcony, WiFi in all rooms in main B&B and Data port in some in room. Air conditioning. Library, Porch swing, Tropical courtyard, Hammock, Veranda, Add-ons for fee: prepaid tour bookings, Streetcar/transit passes, Add-ons for your room: chocolate covered strawber-

ries, champagne and flowers on premises. Amusement parks, antiquing, art galleries, bicycling, canoeing/kayaking, fishing, golf, horseback riding, live theater, museums, parks, shopping, sporting events, tennis, water sports, bars, music and dance clubs, restaurants, streetcars, riverboats, zoo, aquarium and numerous sightseeing opportunities nearby.

Location: City. French Quarter, Faubourg Marigny.

Certificate may be used: Monday-Thursday, week nights only, June 15-Aug. 15 and Dec. 1-21, excluding some holidays, special events and convention blackout dates.

Andrew Jackson Hotel

919 Royal Street, French Quarter
New Orleans, LA 70116-2792
(504)561-5881 (800)654-0224 Fax:(504)596-6769
Internet: www.FrenchQuarterInns.com
E-mail: gary@FrenchQuarterInns.com

Circa 1860. Encounter the sights and sounds of New Orleans from this historic small hotel situated in the heart of the French Quarter that combines southern style and hospitality. Stay in a balcony suite or a romantic guest bedroom that opens to a tropical gas-lit courtyard that is a classic design of this area. After a late night of music and merriment enjoy a continental breakfast in bed. The staff is trained and available to help make each trip most memorable.

Innkeeper(s): French Quarter Inns. $79-299. 23 rooms with PB, 3 suites, 1 cottage. Breakfast included in rates. Types of meals: Cont and early coffee/tea. Beds: KDT. Cable TV, ceiling fan, telephone and Royal Balcony suites feature views of Royal Street and the Vieux Carre in room. Central air. Tropical courtyard and classic French Quarter fountain on premises. Amusement parks, antiquing, art galleries, bicycling, fishing, horseback riding, live theater, museums, parks, shopping, sporting events, tennis and French Quarter historic district nearby.

Location: City, waterfront. Historic District, French Quarter.

Certificate may be used: Anytime, subject to availability.

Avenue Inn Bed & Breakfast

4125 St. Charles Avenue
New Orleans, LA 70115
(504)269-2640 (800)490-8542 Fax:(504)269-2641
Internet: www.avenueinnbb.com
E-mail: info@avenueinnbb.com

Circa 1891. Set among timeless oaks on famous St. Charles Street is this 1891 Thomas Sully mansion. The inn has high ceilings and hardwood floors, and its 17 guest rooms are furnished with period pieces. Come during Mardi Gras and you can sit on the big front porch and watch the 18 Mardi Gras parades that come down St. Charles Avenue. The French Quarter, Central Business District, Convention Center as well as Tulane and Loyola Universities are all within 1 3/4 miles. Antique shops, restaurants and night spots are within walking distance.

Innkeeper(s): Joe & Bebe Rabhan. $89-299. 17 rooms with PB, 5 with FP. Breakfast included in rates. Types of meals: Cont. Beds: KQD. Modem hook-up, data port, cable TV, reading lamp, ceiling fan, clock radio, telephone, desk and voice mail in room. Central air. VCR, fax, copier, library, parlor games and fireplace on premises. Limited handicap access. Amusement parks, antiquing, art galleries, bicycling, canoeing/kayaking, fishing, golf, live theater, museums, parks, shopping, restaurants, cultural events, sightseeing and day spa nearby.

Location: City.

Certificate may be used: Subject to availability, excludes holidays and special events.

Fairchild House

1518 Prytania St
New Orleans, LA 70130-4416
(504)524-0154 (800)256-8096 Fax:(504)568-0063
Internet: www.fairchildhouse.com
E-mail: info@fairchildhouse.com

Circa 1841. Situated in the oak-lined Lower Garden District of New Orleans, this Greek Revival home was built by architect L.H. Pilie. The house and its guest houses maintain a Victorian ambiance with elegantly appointed guest rooms. Wine and cheese are served upon guests' arrival. Afternoon tea can be served upon request. The bed & breakfast, which is on the Mardi Gras parade route, is 17 blocks from the French Quarter and 12 blocks from the convention center. Streetcars are just one block away, as are many local attractions, including paddle-boat cruises, Canal Place and Riverwalk shopping, an aquarium, zoo, the St. Charles Avenue mansions and Tulane and Loyola universities.

Innkeeper(s): Rita Olmo & Beatriz Aprigliano-Ziegler. $75-165. 9 rooms with PB, 1 suite. Breakfast included in rates. Types of meals: Cont plus. Beds: KQDT. Clock radio, telephone, desk and voice mail in room. Air conditioning. TV, fax and copier on premises. Antiquing, shopping and restaurants nearby.

Location: City.

"Accommodations were great; staff was great ... Hope to see y'all soon!"

Certificate may be used: June 1-Aug. 31. Please call during other seasons.

HH Whitney House on the Historic Esplanade

1923 Esplanade Avenue
New Orleans, LA 70116-1706
(504)948-9448 (877)944-9448 Fax:(504) 949-7939
Internet: www.hhwhitneyhouse.com
E-mail: stay@hhwhitneyhouse.com

Circa 1865. The Civil War had barely ended when builders broke ground on this elegant Italianate mansion. More than a century later, much of its original charm has been maintained. The intricate molding and plasterwork are of the highest quality. Common rooms with Victorian furnishings and appointments complement the architecture. Distinctive antiques include an early 20th-century player piano. A decorative fireplace is featured in each guest bedroom. The Bride's Room, with a lace-draped canopy bed, makes a spacious two- or three-bedroom suite when combined with the Solarium or Groom's rooms. The romantic Honeymoon Suite in the former servants' quarters offers total privacy. Located in the Esplanade Ridge historic district, the French Quarter is just a half-mile walk.

Innkeeper(s): Glen Miller/ Randy Saizan. $75-250. 5 rooms, 3 with PB, 5 with FP. Breakfast and snacks/refreshments included in rates. Types of meals: Full bkfst. Beds: Q. Cable TV, reading lamp, CD player, ceiling fan, clock radio, hair dryer, bathrobes, bath amenities, wireless Internet access, iron/ironing board and safes in room. Central air. VCR, DVD, fax, spa, swimming, parlor games, telephone, fireplace and laundry facility on premises. Amusement parks, antiquing, art galleries, bicycling, canoeing/kayaking, fishing, golf, horseback riding, live theater, museums, parks, shopping, sporting events, tennis, French Quarter and fairgrounds nearby.

Location: City. Near French Quarter, city park and fairgrounds.

Certificate may be used: Last minute bookings, subject to availability.

Hotel Saint Pierre

911 Burgundy Street, French Quarter
New Orleans, LA 70116-3003
(504)524-4401 (800)225-4040 Fax:504-593-9425
Internet: www.FrenchQuarterInns.com
E-mail: gary@FrenchQuarterInns.com

Circa 1780. Experience the atmosphere and architecture of the French Quarter while staying at this historic collection of Creole cottages. The flavors of Bourbon Street are two blocks away. Select a guest bedroom or suite with a balcony overlooking a lush courtyard and swimming pool. After a continental breakfast with southern-style treats, relax and enjoy the hotel's generous blend of comfortable hospitality. There is so much to see and do in New Orleans and this is the perfect home base.

Innkeeper(s): French Quarter Inns. $69-299. 74 rooms with PB, 3 with FP, 7 suites, 14 cottages. Breakfast included in rates. Types of meals: Cont and early coffee/tea. Beds: KDT. Cable TV, ceiling fan, telephone, hot tub/spa, fireplace and wireless Internet access in room. Central air. Fax and two swimming pools on premises. Amusement parks, antiquing, art galleries, bicycling, fishing, golf, live theater, museums, parks, shopping, sporting events, tennis, water sports, historic architecture, national landmarks, fine dining, jazz and live music nearby.

Location: City, waterfront. Historic District, French Quarter.

Certificate may be used: Anytime, subject to availability, restrictions apply, special events excluded.

Lafitte Guest House

1003 Bourbon St
New Orleans, LA 70116-2707
(504)581-2678 (800)331-7971 Fax:(504)581-2677
Internet: www.lafitteguesthouse.com
E-mail: carol@lafitteguesthouse.com

Circa 1849. This elegant French manor house has been meticulously restored. The house is filled with fine antiques and paintings collected from around the world. Located in the heart of the French Quarter, the inn is near world-famous restaurants, museums, antique shops and rows of Creole and Spanish cottages. Between 5:30 p.m. and 7 p.m., there is a wine and cheese social hour on Friday and Saturday.

Innkeeper(s): William Walker. $159-229. 14 rooms with PB, 7 with FP, 2 suites. Breakfast included in rates. Types of meals: Cont plus. Beds: KQ. Modem hook-up, cable TV, refrigerator, ceiling fan, clock radio, telephone, desk and wireless Internet access in room. Air conditioning. Fax, copier, library and fireplace on premises. Amusement parks, antiquing, art galleries, fishing, live theater, parks, shopping, sporting events and water sports nearby.

Location: City.

Publicity: *Glamour, Antique Monthly, McCall's, Dixie and Country Living.*

"This old building offers the finest lodgings we have found in the city — McCall's Magazine."

Certificate may be used: Last two weeks of August and first two weeks of December, Sunday through Thursday, subject to availability.

Magnolia Mansion

2127 Prytania Street
New Orleans, LA 70130
(504)412-9500 (888)222-9235 Fax:(504)412-9502
Internet: www.magnoliamansion.com
E-mail: info@magnoliamansion.com

Circa 1857. Experience a high standard of opulence at this upscale, adults-only, non-smoking bed & breakfast. It is the perfect romantic getaway, quiet and peaceful weekend retreat, or a wonderful place to celebrate an anniversary, birthday, honeymoon or other special occasion. The Mansion is centrally located in what is considered to be "The Gateway To The Garden District." It is just one block from St. Charles Ave. streetcar on the Mardi Gras Parade Route and within minutes of the French Quarter. Relax with friends or read a good book on the wrap-around veranda overlooking the enchanting courtyard surrounded by massive 150-year-old oak trees. Wake each morning from a great night's sleep in a luxurious themed guest bedroom to enjoy a continental breakfast in the formal dining room. Visit the area's major attractions, including the Superdome; enjoy fine dining and ride on a Mississippi River Paddlewheel.

Innkeeper(s): Hollie Vest. $125-750. 9 rooms with PB. Breakfast included in rates. Types of meals: Cont plus and early coffee/tea. Beds: KQT. Modem hook-up, cable TV, VCR, reading lamp, ceiling fan, clock radio, telephone, desk, robes, hair dryers, makeup mirrors, valet, iron and ironing board in room. Central air. Complimentary local calls, video and book library and data ports on premises. Amusement parks, antiquing, art galleries, beach, bicycling, canoeing/kayaking, fishing, golf, hiking, horseback riding, live theater, museums, parks, shopping, sporting events, tennis, water sports and wineries nearby.

Location: City. French Quarter, Superdome, Convention Center, Riverwalk, Antique Shopping, 10 minutes from Mansion.

Publicity: *American Airlines, American Way Inflight Magazine, Times Picayune, Off Beat Publications, Weddings With Style, Chris Rose Times Picayune Columnist, Live on Internet Talk Show and New Orleans Bride on Cox Cable.*

Certificate may be used: Sunday-Thursday, blackout dates and restrictions apply.

Maison Perrier B&B

4117 Perrier St
New Orleans, LA 70115
(504)897-1807 (888)610-1807 Fax:(504)897-1399
Internet: www.maisonperrier.com
E-mail: innkeeper@maisonperrier.com

Circa 1892. Experience Southern hospitality and a casually elegant atmosphere at this bed & breakfast located in the Uptown Garden District. The historic Victorian mansion was built in 1892 with renovations carefully preserving ornamental woodwork, fireplace tiles, chandeliers and antique furnishings while adding modern conveniences. Distinctive guest bedrooms and suites with parlors feature stunning beds, romantic touches that include candles and flowers, whirlpool tubs, terry cloth robes, and private balconies. Praline French toast, apple puff pancakes, creole eggs and potato casserole are among the incredible breakfast favorites that begin and end with New Orleans coffee. Relax in the brick courtyards surrounded by tropical plants.

$79-330. 15 rooms with PB, 8 suites, 4 conference rooms. Breakfast, afternoon tea and snacks/refreshments included in rates. Types of meals: Full gourmet bkfst, veg bkfst, early coffee/tea, picnic lunch, hors d'oeuvres and wine. Beds: KQT. Modem hook-up, data port, cable TV, DVD, reading lamp, stereo, refrigerator, ceiling fan, clock radio, telephone, desk, some with hot tub/spa, voice mail, most with fireplace, hair dryer, bathrobes, bath amenities, wireless Internet access, iron/ironing board, decorative fireplaces, luxury bath amenities and terry cloth robes in room. Central air. Fax, copier, library, parlor games and laundry facility on premises. Limited handicap access. Amusement parks, antiquing, art galleries, beach, bicycling, fishing, golf, horseback riding, live theater, museums, parks, shopping, sporting events, tennis, water sports and wineries nearby.

Location: City. Uptown garden district.

Publicity: *Fodors, Frommers, Travel & Leisure, CNN, HBO (Dane Cook Tour), Fox News, Memphis PBS and WWOZ.*

Certificate may be used: June-Sept. 30, Sunday-Thursday only, subject to availability.

Sully Mansion - Garden District

2631 Prytania St
New Orleans, LA 70130-5944
(504)891-0457 (800)364-2414 Fax:(504)269-0793
Internet: www.sullymansion.com
E-mail: reservations@sullymansion.com

Circa 1890. This handsome Queen Anne Victorian, designed by its namesake, Thomas Sully, maintains many original features common to the period. A wide veranda, stained glass, heart-of-pine floors and a grand staircase are among the notable items. Rooms are decorated in a comfortable mix of antiques and more modern pieces. Sully Mansion is the only inn located in the heart of New Orleans' Garden District.

Innkeeper(s): Nancy & Guy Fournier. $89-200. 8 rooms with PB, 6 with FP. Breakfast and snacks/refreshments included in rates. Types of meals: Cont plus. Beds: KQDT. Cable TV, DVD, reading lamp, stereo, refrigerator, clock radio, telephone, desk, voice mail, bath amenities, wireless Internet access, iron/ironing board, guest refrigerator and "sully's satchel" home away from home medicine chest available to all guests in room. Air conditioning. Fax, copier, library, fireplace and Beautiful wraparound porch allows guests to savor the unique Garden District environment on premises. Amusement parks, antiquing, art galleries, bicycling, fishing, golf, horseback riding, live theater, museums, parks, shopping, sporting events, tennis, wineries, French Quarter, Audobon Zoo, Warehouse district and antique stores of Magazine Street nearby.

Location: City.

Publicity: *Houston Chronicle, Travel & Leisure, New Orleans Times Picayune, Los Angeles Times, Travel & Holiday, San Francisco Chronicle Richmond Times Dispatch and Independent film "Seizure" shot at the inn.*

"I truly enjoyed my stay at Sully Mansion—the room was wonderful, the pastries memorable."

Certificate may be used: Free night Sunday-Wednesday all year except special events (New Years Eve, Sugar Bowl, Mardi Gras, Jazz Fest and Halloween). Not valid during Tulane graduation.

Terrell House

1441 Magazine St.
New Orleans, LA 70130
(504)247-0560 (866)261-9687 Fax:(504)247-0565
Internet: www.terrellhouse.com
E-mail: lobrien@terrellhouse.com

Circa 1858. Gracing the Lower Garden District in an historic area near the French Quarter, Terrell House is a grand three-story Italianate stucco-over-brick antebellum mansion in New Orleans, Louisiana. Relax in elegance and comfort on a porch, in the den or double parlors with period English and American antiques. Air-conditioned guest bedrooms with generous upscale amenities in the main house and the adjacent carriage house look out or open onto the courtyard with lush gardens, fountains and shaded sitting areas. The carriage house is furnished with locally handcrafted cypress furniture. Linger over a satisfying breakfast that reflects warm southern hospitality before exploring the popular sites of the city.

Innkeeper(s): Ed and Linda O'Brien. $125-250. 8 rooms with PB, 1 two-bedroom suite. Breakfast included in rates. Types of meals: Full bkfst, early coffee/tea, snacks/refreshments and hors d'oeuvres. Beds: KQT. Cable TV, reading lamp, ceiling fan, clock radio, coffeemaker, fireplace, hair dryer, bathrobes, bath amenities, wireless Internet access and iron/ironing board in room. Central air. DVD, fax, copier, bicycles, library and telephone on premises. Amusement parks, antiquing, art galleries, bicycling, fishing, golf, live theater, museums, parks, shopping, sporting events, Zoo, St Charles Streetcar, Convention Center and Riverwalk nearby.

Location: City. Near historic French Quarter.

Certificate may be used: July 5-September and December-January, subject to availability.

Rayne

Maison D'Memoire B&B Cottages

8450 Roberts Cove Rd.
Rayne, LA 70578
(337)334-2477
Internet: www.maisondmemoire.com
E-mail: info@maisondmemoire.com

Circa 1850. Tranquil, private and romantic, these cottages exude an irresistible Cajun charm just one mile from Interstate 10, only 15 minutes from Lafayette. Twenty picturesque acres in a country setting include a secluded lake. Each guest house is well-equipped with TV/VCR, full kitchen and individual phone line. Breakfast is delivered to the door each morning. Stay in the Autumn Cottage, listed in the National Register, with a four-poster bed, antique clawfoot tub and veranda. Both the Country Garden Cottage with a back porch and the two-bedroom Prairie Haven Cottage boast a Jacuzzi tub. The Sweet Surrender Cottage is a deluxe suite with a heart-shaped Jacuzzi, electric fireplace and sun porch overlooking the lake. Weddings are popular. The Camellia Cove Retreat Center is perfect for meetings, reunions or other gatherings.

Innkeeper(s): Lyn Guidry. $130-200. 4 cottages, 1 with FP, 3 with HT, 4 total suites, including 1 two-bedroom suite, 1 conference room. Breakfast included in rates. Types of meals: Full bkfst. Beds: KQ. TV, VCR, DVD, reading lamp, CD player, refrigerator, ceiling fan, clock radio, telephone, coffeemaker, most with hot tub/spa, some with fireplace, hair dryer, bathrobes, bath amenities, iron/ironing board, full kitchen, microwave, full breakfast delivered for cabins, iron/ironing board, monogramed robes, hair dryers and Jacuzzi in room. Central air. Antiquing, fishing, golf, hiking, live theater, museums, parks, shopping and tennis nearby.

Location: Country.

Certificate may be used: January, July, August and September; Monday-Thursday; excludes holidays and special events.

Slidell

Woodridge Bed & Breakfast of Louisiana

40149 Crowe's Landing Rd.
Slidell, LA 70461
(985)863-9981 (877)643-7109
Internet: www.woodridgebb.com
E-mail: info@woodridgebb.com

Circa 1979. Generous Southern hospitality and comfort mingled with upscale amenities are offered at this Georgian-style home. Each flower-themed guest suite is furnished with antiques and an adjacent access to the balcony. After a restful night's sleep, linger over a big country breakfast with an abundance of homemade breads, a hot entree, meats and seasonal fruits. Shaded by 100-year-old live oak trees, a swing for two is a pleasant interlude. Enjoy the serene gardens with fountains, a bistro and benches to view the dogwood, magnolia, roses and azalea.

Innkeeper(s): Debbi & Tim Fotsch. $99-169. 5 rooms with PB, 1 with FP, 1 conference room. Breakfast included in rates. Types of meals: Full gourmet bkfst and early coffee/tea. Beds: Q. Cable TV, DVD, ceiling fan, clock radio, telephone, some with fireplace, hair dryer, bath amenities, wireless Internet access and iron/ironing board in room. Central air. Spa, swimming, parlor games, Early morning coffee /tea available, Guest refrigerator, Microwave in common area and Picnic areas on premises. Amusement parks, antiquing, art galleries, beach, bicycling, canoeing/kayaking, fishing, golf, horseback riding, live theater, museums, parks, shopping, sporting events, tennis, water sports, wineries, skydiving, dinner theatre, swamp tours, nature conservatory, space center tours, zoo and aquarium nearby.

Location: Rural, residential, close to city.

Certificate may be used: May 1-Sept. 30 Sunday-Thursday except holiday; subject to availablity.

Maine

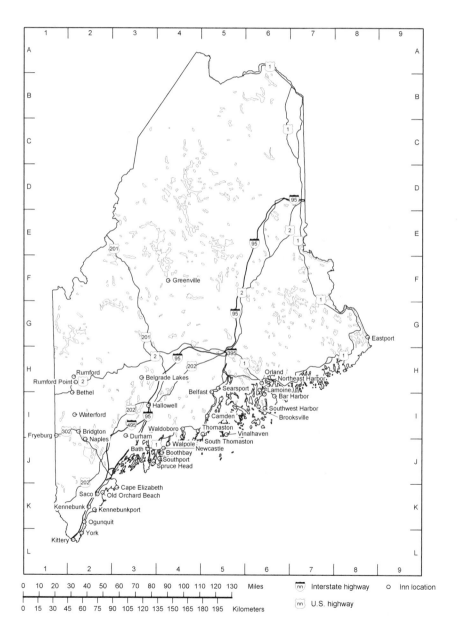

A | B | C | D | E | F | G | H | I | J | K | L

1
1
1
95
2
1
201
Greenville
2
95
1
201
395
Eastport
2
95
202
1
Rumford
Rumford Point 2
Bethel
Belgrade Lakes
Orland
Northeast Harbor
Belfast
Searsport
Lamoine
Bar Harbor
Waterford
202
95
Hallowell
Southwest Harbor
Brooksville
Camden
495
Bridgton
Waldoboro
Thomaston
302
Fryeburg
Naples
Durham
Vinalhaven
South Thomaston
1
Walpole
Bath
Boothbay
Newcastle
Southport
Spruce Head
202
Cape Elizabeth
Saco
Old Orchard Beach
Kennebunk
Kennebunkport
Ogunquit
Kittery
York

0 10 20 30 40 50 60 70 80 90 100 110 120 130 Miles

0 15 30 45 60 75 90 105 120 135 150 165 180 195 Kilometers

[nn] Interstate highway   o Inn location

[nn] U.S. highway

Bar Harbor

Mira Monte Inn & Suites

69 Mount Desert St
Bar Harbor, ME 04609-1327
(207)288-4263 (800)553-5109 Fax:(207)288-3115
Internet: www.miramonte.com
E-mail: mburns@miramonteinn.com

Circa 1864. A gracious 16-room Victorian mansion, the Mira Monte has been renovated in the style of early Bar Harbor. It features period furnishings, pleasant common rooms, a library and wraparound porches. Situated on estate grounds, there are sweeping lawns, paved terraces and many gardens. The inn was one of the earliest of Bar Harbor's famous summer cottages. The two-room suites each feature canopy beds, two-person whirlpools, a parlor with a sleeper sofa, fireplace and kitchenette unit. The two-bedroom suite includes a full kitchen, dining area and parlor. The suites boast private decks with views of the gardens.

Innkeeper(s): Marian Burns. $95-290. 16 rooms with PB, 14 with FP, 3 total suites, including 1 two-bedroom suite. Breakfast and wine included in rates. Types of meals: Full bkfst and early coffee/tea. Beds: KQT. Data port, cable TV, VCR, reading lamp, clock radio, telephone, desk, some with hot tub/spa, voice mail, most with fireplace, hair dryer, bath amenities and iron/ironing board in room. Air conditioning. Library, parlor games, data ports and Internet access on premises. Handicap access. Antiquing, art galleries, bicycling, canoeing/kayaking, cross-country skiing, fishing, golf, hiking, live theater, museums, parks, shopping, water sports, wineries and Acadia National Park nearby.

Location: Mountains, ocean community. Island.

Publicity: *Los Angeles Times.*

"On our third year at your wonderful inn in beautiful Bar Harbor. I think I enjoy it more each year. A perfect place to stay in a perfect environment."

Certificate may be used: May 12-May 20, holidays excluded.

Bath

Fairhaven Inn

118 N Bath Rd
Bath, ME 04530
(207)443-4391 (888)443-4391 Fax:(207)443-6412
Internet: www.mainecoast.com/fairhaveninn
E-mail: fairhvn@gwi.net

Circa 1790. With its view of the Kennebec River, this site was so attractive that Pembleton Edgecomb built his Colonial house where a log cabin had previously stood. His descendants occupied it for the next 125 years. Antiques and country furniture fill the inn. Meadows and lawns, and woods of hemlock, birch and pine cover the inn's 16 acres.

Innkeeper(s): Dawn & Andy Omo. $75-155. 8 rooms, 6 with PB, 1 suite. Breakfast included in rates. Types of meals: Full gourmet bkfst and early coffee/tea. Beds: KQT. Reading lamp and clock radio in room. TV, VCR, fax, library, parlor games, telephone and fireplace on premises. Limited handicap access. Antiquing, art galleries, beach, bicycling, canoeing/kayaking, cross-country skiing, fishing, golf, hiking, live theater, museums, parks, shopping, sporting events, tennis and water sports nearby.

Location: Country. River-country setting.

Publicity: *The State, Coastal Journal and Times Record.*

"The Fairhaven is now marked in our book with a red star, definitely a place to remember and

visit again."

Certificate may be used: Nov. 1-May 20, Sunday-Thursday.

Inn At Bath

969 Washington St
Bath, ME 04530-2650
(207)443-4294 Fax:(207)443-4295
Internet: www.innatbath.com
E-mail: innkeeper@innatbath.com

Circa 1835. Located in the heart of Bath's Historic District, this Greek Revival home is surrounded by fabulous gardens. Well-appointed, spacious guest bedrooms are furnished with antiques. Some feature two-person Jacuzzis, wood-burning fireplaces, sofas, writing desks and private entrances. Breakfast includes buttermilk blueberry pancakes, green chili egg puff, pecan waffles with fresh fruit, homemade granola and organic yogurt. Walk to the Kennebec River, the Chocolate Church Arts Center or local shops, galleries and restaurants. Visit the Maine Maritime Museum. Innkeeper Elizabeth will assist with arranging guided fishing trips; spotting bald eagles, ospreys and seals; taking a lighthouse tour; finding the perfect lobster roll on a dock or booking a sailing excursion.

Innkeeper(s): Elizabeth Knowlton. $140-185. 8 rooms with PB, 4 with FP, 1 suite. Breakfast included in rates. Types of meals: Full bkfst, veg bkfst and early coffee/tea. Beds: KQDT. Cable TV, VCR, reading lamp, clock radio, telephone, some with hot tub/spa, some with fireplace, hair dryer, bath amenities, wireless Internet access, iron/ironing board, Fax and Computer available for guests at no charge in room. Air conditioning. Fax, copier, bicycles and parlor games on premises. Handicap access. Antiquing, art galleries, beach, bicycling, canoeing/kayaking, fishing, golf, hiking, horseback riding, live theater, museums, parks, shopping, sporting events, tennis, water sports, Some winters, great snow for Cross Country Skiing and Downhill Skiing (about 2 hour drive) nearby.

Location: Coastal town.

Publicity: *House Beautiful.*

Certificate may be used: November 1-May 15, Sunday-Thursday, excludes holiday weeks and school weekends and graduations.

Belfast

Belhaven Inn

14 John St
Belfast, ME 04915-6650
(207)338-5435
Internet: www.belhaveninn.com
E-mail: info@belhaveninn.com

Circa 1851. This 16-room 1851 Federal Victorian stands on an acre in the heart of Belfast, a historic harbor community with roots in shipbuilding. Mullioned windows, pumpkin pine floors and carved mantels are some of the many period features of the inn. A circular staircase leads to the four guest bedrooms, each appointed with period pieces. A three-course country breakfast is served daily on the side porch, weather permitting. It includes items such as fruit cup with yogurt or granola, freshly baked muffins, hot breads and a hot entrée of either eggs, pancakes, crepes or sausage. Locally grown berries and produce are used in season. After breakfast relax on the porch or head into Belfast to explore the many art galleries and shops. Take a ride on the vintage Belfast and Moosehead Train or arrange for a boat to explore the islands in the Penobscot Bay or take a drive and explore the nearby lighthouses.

Innkeeper(s): Anne & Paul Bartels. $99-150. 4 rooms with PB, 1 suite. Breakfast included in rates. Types of meals: Country bkfst, early coffee/tea and snacks/refreshments. Beds: QDT. Reading lamp, clock radio and desk in room. TV, VCR, tennis, library, parlor games, telephone, fireplace, badminton and volleyball on premises. Antiquing, art galleries, beach, bicycling, canoeing/kayaking, cross-country skiing, fishing, golf, hiking, horseback riding, live theater, museums, parks, shopping, tennis and wineries nearby.

Location: Country. Coastal community, harbor town.

Certificate may be used: Jan. 1-June 1, Sunday-Thursday, subject to availability.

Londonderry Inn

133 Belmont Ave (Rt 3)
Belfast, ME 04915
(207)338-2763 (877)529-9566 Fax:(207)338-6303
Internet: www.londonderry-inn.com
E-mail: info@londonderry-inn.com

Circa 1803. Built in 1803, this Maine farmhouse provides elegant comfort and spacious common areas to relax and enjoy a wonderful vacation. Choose from five delightful guest bedrooms with modern private baths. Wake up each morning to an old-fashioned farmer's breakfast featuring gourmet foods that may include blueberry pancakes and cranberry muffins served in the large fireplaced country kitchen. Early risers can sip coffee on the screened porch or backyard deck overlooking the garden. Explore six beautiful acres surrounding the inn, pick raspberries in season or catch a glimpse of deer or wild turkeys. Pick a complimentary in-room movie from the extensive video collection of more than 200 films. Visit the area's many historic sites like Fort Knox State Park.

Innkeeper(s): Marsha Oakes. $95-145. 5 rooms with PB. Breakfast and snacks/refreshments included in rates. Types of meals: Country bkfst, early coffee/tea and afternoon tea. Beds: KQD. Cable TV, VCR, reading lamp, CD player, refrigerator, clock radio, telephone, twin sleep sofa, bathrobes and hair dryers in room. Fax, copier, library, fireplace, AC, backyard deck, evening dessert, 200+ video/periodical library and laundry facilities (for a nominal fee) on premises. Antiquing, art galleries, beach, bicycling, canoeing/kayaking, downhill skiing, fishing, golf, hiking, live theater, museums, parks, shopping, water sports, wineries, lighthouses, wild blueberries, strawberries and apples nearby.

Location: Country, ocean community. Two miles from downtown Belfast and harbor.

Certificate may be used: September to June, excluding July and August, any day of the week.

The Alden House Bed & Breakfast

63 Church St
Belfast, ME 04915-6208
(207)338-2151 (877)337-8151 Fax:(207)338-2151
Internet: www.thealdenhouse.com
E-mail: innkeeper@thealdenhouse.com

Circa 1840. Gracefully appointed, this Greek Revival home in Belfast, Maine on gorgeous Penobscot Bay, was built in 1840. Saunter up the hand carved, cherry circular staircase to a sitting area. Relax in front of the fire in the handsome library, enjoy the fireside North Parlor with a grand and player piano. Settle into the South Parlor for games and friendly conversation by the fire. Beautifully restored guest bedrooms boast period antiques, soothing featherbeds, and exciting attributes of days gone by. Delight in sumptuous breakfasts, afternoon tea and baked treats. Sit on the veranda or gazebo and explore the grounds. The Alden House is located in the heart of town, near quaint shops and art boutiques. View magnificent harbor sunrises and sunsets.

Innkeeper(s): Deborah and Ted Hensley. $100-160. 7 rooms, 5 with PB, 1 with FP. Breakfast, afternoon tea and snacks/refreshments included in rates. Types of meals: Full gourmet bkfst, veg bkfst, early coffee/tea and Will meet most dietary requirements or restrictions with 24 hours notice. Beds: QT. Modem hook-up, TV, VCR, reading lamp, turn-down service, some with fireplace, hair dryer, bathrobes, bath amenities, wireless Internet access, Natural body care products, hair dryers, bathrobes, Vermont Sweetwater, gourmet chocolates and fine linens in room. Air conditioning. Fax, library, parlor games, telephone, gazebo and veranda, lovely grounds, early bird refreshments, game table, tea time and scrumptious snacks, 3 working fireplaces in library and parlors, grand and player piano and bagpipe entertainment on premises. Limited handicap access. Antiquing, art galleries, beach, canoeing/kayaking, cross-country skiing, downhill skiing, fishing, golf, hiking, horseback riding, live theater, museums, parks, shopping, tennis, water sports, wineries, Whale watching, lighthouses, Acadia National Park, windjammer sails, Penobscot Marine Museum, The Original Fort Knox, Sear's Island, the largest uninhabited island on the east coast and birding nearby.

Location: Ocean community.

Publicity: *Yankee Magazine (July-August, 2006), DownEast Magazine (November 2005), Travellady.com (December 2005), Bangor Daily News and Waldo Independent.*

Certificate may be used: Nov. 15-May 1, holidays excluded. Last minute projected upon availability.

The Jeweled Turret Inn

40 Pearl St
Belfast, ME 04915-1907
(207)338-2304 (800)696-2304
Internet: www.jeweledturret.com
E-mail: info@jeweledturret.com

Circa 1898. This grand Victorian is named for the staircase that winds up the turret, lighted by stained- and leaded-glass panels and jewel-like embellishments. It was built for attorney James Harriman. Dark pine beams adorn the ceiling of the den, and the fireplace is constructed of bark and rocks from every state in the Union. Elegant antiques furnish the guest rooms. Guests can relax in one of the inn's four parlors, which are furnished with period antiques, wallpapers, lace and boast fireplaces. Some rooms have a ceiling fan and whirlpool tub or fireplace. The verandas feature wicker and iron bistro sets and views of the historic district. The inn is within walking distance of the town and its shops, restaurants and the harbor.

Innkeeper(s): Cathy & Carl Heffentrager. $105-159. 7 rooms with PB, 1 with FP, 1 with WP. Breakfast and afternoon tea included in rates. Types of meals: Full gourmet bkfst, early coffee/tea, Crakers and cheese and sherry served during social hour 5:30-6:30 pm. Beds: QDT. Reading lamp, ceiling fan, clock radio, some with fireplace, bath amenities and one with whirlpool tub in room. TV, parlor games and telephone on premises. Antiquing, art galleries, beach, bicycling, canoeing/kayaking, cross-country skiing, downhill skiing, fishing, golf, hiking, horseback riding, live theater, museums, parks, shopping, tennis, water sports and wineries nearby.

Location: Small historic coastal town.

Publicity: *News Herald, Republican Journal, Waterville Sentinel, Los Angeles Times, Country Living, Victorian Homes and The Saturday Evening Post.*

"The ambiance was so romantic that we felt like we were on our honeymoon."

Certificate may be used: April, May and November, holidays excluded.

Belgrade Lakes

Wings Hill Inn

PO Box 386
Belgrade Lakes, ME 04918-0386
(207)495-2400 (866)495-2400
Internet: wingshillinn.com
E-mail: wingshillinn@earthlink.net

Circa 1800. Enjoy an ideal romantic getaway at this year-round post and beam farmhouse in a picturesque lakefront village. Relaxation comes easy by the fireplace in the Great Room or the extensive screened wraparound porch overlooking the lake. Savor afternoon tea with pastries. The guest bedrooms feature a comfortable elegance. Start each day with a satisfying gourmet breakfast. Intimate candlelit dining is available Thursday through Sunday evenings. Hiking, fishing, boating, golf and cross-country skiing are just outside the front door. Other popular New England sites and activities are an easy drive away.

Innkeeper(s): Christopher & Tracey Anderson. $115-180. 6 rooms with PB, 1 with WP. Breakfast and afternoon tea included in rates. Types of meals: Full bkfst and early coffee/tea. Beds: KQ. TV, VCR, reading lamp, ceiling fan, clock radio, hair dryer and iron/ironing board in room. Air conditioning. Library, parlor games, fireplace and gift shop on premises. Handicap access. Antiquing, cross-country skiing, downhill skiing, fishing, golf, hiking, shopping, sporting events and water sports nearby.

Certificate may be used: November through April, excluding holidays and special events.

Bethel

Chapman Inn

1 Mill Hill Rd.
Bethel, ME 04217-1067
(207)824-2657 (877)359-1498
Internet: www.chapmaninn.com
E-mail: info@chapmaninn.com

Circa 1865. As one of the town's oldest buildings, this Federal-style inn has been a store, a tavern and a boarding house known as "The Howard." It was the home of William Rogers Chapman, composer, conductor and founder of the Rubenstein Club and the Metropolitan Musical Society, in addition to the Maine Music Festival. The inn is a convenient place to begin a walking tour of Bethel's historic district.

Innkeeper(s): Sandra & Fred. $25-129. 10 rooms with PB, 2 suites. Breakfast included in rates. Types of meals: Full bkfst, early coffee/tea and afternoon tea. TV, reading lamp, refrigerator, telephone and desk in room. Air conditioning. VCR, fax, sauna, parlor games and fireplace on premises. Antiquing, cross-country skiing, downhill skiing, fishing, golf, live theater, parks, shopping, tennis and water sports nearby.

Location: Mountains. In village.

Certificate may be used: Oct. 15-June 1, Sunday-Friday except holidays.

L'Auberge Country Inn and Bistro

15 L'Auberge Ln.
Bethel, ME 04217-0021
(207)824-2774 (800)760-2774 Fax:(207)824-3108
Internet: www.laubergecountryinn.com
E-mail: inn@laubergecountryinn.com

Circa 1850. In the foothills of the White Mountains, surrounded by five acres of gardens and woods, this former carriage house was converted to a guest house in the 1920s. Among its seven guest rooms are two spacious suites. The Theater Suite offers a four-poster queen bed and dressing room. The Family Suite can accommodate up to six guests. Mount Abrahms and Sunday River ski areas are just minutes away.

Innkeeper(s): Doron and Sharon Haendel . $69-250. 7 rooms with PB, 1 two-bedroom and 1 three-bedroom suites. Breakfast included in rates. Types of meals: Country bkfst, veg bkfst, early coffee/tea, picnic lunch, hors d'oeuvres, gourmet dinner and room service. Restaurant on premises. Beds: KQDT. Reading lamp, clock radio, turn-down service, desk, some with hot tub/spa, some with fireplace, bath amenities and wireless Internet access in room. Air conditioning. TV, VCR, fax, copier, bicycles, library, pet boarding, child care,

parlor games, telephone, laundry facility, gift shop and gift shop on premises. Limited handicap access. Amusement parks, antiquing, art galleries, beach, bicycling, canoeing/kayaking, cross-country skiing, downhill skiing, fishing, golf, hiking, horseback riding, live theater, museums, parks, shopping, sporting events, tennis, water sports, Gould Academy and National Training Laboratories nearby.

Location: Country, mountains. Resort.

Publicity: *Yankee, Gourmet, Canadian Life, Maine Explorers Guide, Fodors, Frommers, Rough Guides, Tripadvisor.com (4 stars)* and *New York 1 News.*

Certificate may be used: Midweek, Monday through Thursday, non-holiday.

Brooksville

Oakland House Seaside Resort

435 Herrick Rd
Brooksville, ME 04617
(207)359-8521 (800)359-7352 Fax:(207)359-9865
Internet: www.oaklandhouse.com
E-mail: jim@oaklandhouse.com

Circa 1767. It is easy to enjoy this historic inn and its 50 wooded acres with hiking trails, panoramic views and a half-mile of private oceanfront. One of the state's few remaining original coastal resorts, it is still family-owned, now by the fourth generation. Shore Oaks, the private summer home built in Arts and Crafts style, offers seaside accommodations. Relax on vintage furnishings by the weathered stone fireplace in the living room. Guest bedrooms are appointed with period antiques and fine linens. Savor a full breakfast in the dining room. Unwind on porch rockers overlooking the lighthouse and an island. One-to-five bedroom cottages are tucked among the trees or along the shore. Most offer living rooms with woodburning fireplaces and kitchens. The old homestead, the Oakland House, is an acclaimed onsite restaurant.

Innkeeper(s): Jim & Sally Littlefield, Sally & Sean McGuigan. $95-295. 12 rooms, 22 with PB, 14 with FP, 15 cottages, 2 conference rooms. Breakfast, Sunday brunch, dinner, In high season (summer months) these meals are included. Various meal plans are available in the spring and fall. In the fall, the smaller and more intimate oceanfront dining rooms at Shore Oaks Seaside Inn are open and the larger "Rusticator" restaurant in the century-old hotel is closed included in rates. Types of meals: Country bkfst, early coffee/tea, lunch and picnic lunch. Restaurant on premises. Beds: KQDT. Reading lamp, coffeemaker, desk and most with fireplace in room. VCR, DVD, fax, copier, swimming, library, telephone, Row boats, recreation room, dock, moorings, lawn games: tetherball, volleyball, croquet and badminton on premises. Antiquing, art galleries, beach, bicycling, canoeing/kayaking, cross-country skiing, fishing, golf, hiking, museums, parks, shopping, water sports, concerts, musical events, boating, whale watching, lobster boat trips and schooner day trips nearby.

Location: Country, ocean community, waterfront. Lake and ocean.

Publicity: *Victorian Homes Magazine (Oct. 2006), Sunday Eagle-Tribune (September 25, 2005), Coastal Living (September, 2004), Newark Star Ledger (July, 2004), Boston Magazine's Elegant Wedding (Summer 2004), Maine Public Broadcasting's "Home; A Place Apart.", Yankee (April 2002), Yankee's Travel Guide to New England (2005)* and *Metroland (August 2002).*

"We have dreamt of visiting Maine for quite some time. Our visit here at Shore Oaks and the beautiful countryside surpassed our dreams. We will be back to enjoy it again."

Certificate may be used: June - Mid October, any accommodation subject to availablity, day of arrival or day before.

Camden

Blue Harbor House, A Village Inn

67 Elm St, Rt 1
Camden, ME 04843-1904
(207)236-3196 (800)248-3196 Fax:(207)236-6523
Internet: www.blueharborhouse.com
E-mail: info@blueharborhouse.com

Circa 1810. James Richards, Camden's first settler, built this
Cape house on a 1768 homesite. (The King granted him the
land as the first person to fulfill all the conditions of a settler.)
An 1810 carriage house has been refurbished to offer private
suites, some with whirlpool tubs. Breakfast is served on the

sun porch overlooking the
Camden Hills. Dinner, available by reservation, can be a
gourmet affair or an authentic
Maine lobster bake on the
lawn. The bustling harbor is a
five-minute walk away.

Innkeeper(s): Annette and Terry
Hazzard. $95-225. 10 rooms with
PB, 2 suites, 1 conference room. Breakfast and afternoon tea included in
rates. Types of meals: Full gourmet bkfst, early coffee/tea and gourmet dinner.
Beds: KQDT. Cable TV, VCR, reading lamp, refrigerator, clock radio, tele-
phone, turn-down service and desk in room. Air conditioning. TV, fax, bicy-
cles, library and parlor games on premises. Antiquing, cross-country skiing,
downhill skiing, fishing, live theater, parks, shopping and water sports nearby.
Location: Coastal village.
Publicity: *Dallas Morning News, Discerning Traveler and Country Living.*

"I don't know when I've enjoyed my stay in a country inn more."
Certificate may be used: Anytime, November-March, subject to availability.

Camden Windward House B&B

6 High St
Camden, ME 04843-1611
(207)236-9656 (877)492-9656 Fax:(207)230-0433
Internet: www.windwardhouse.com
E-mail: bnb@windwardhouse.com

Circa 1854. Each guest room at this Greek Revival home has
been individually decorated and features names such as the
Carriage Room, Trisha Romance Room, Brass Room, or Silver
Birch Suite. Expansive views of Mt. Battie may be seen from its
namesake room. It offers a pri-
vate balcony, skylights, cathedral
ceilings, sitting area with fireplace, an extra large TV and a
Jacuzzi and separate shower. All
rooms include antiques and
romantic amenities such as candles and fine linens. The

innkeepers further pamper guests with a hearty breakfast featuring a variety of juices, freshly ground coffee and teas and a
choice of items such as featherbed eggs, pancakes, French toast
or Belgian waffles topped with fresh Maine blueberries. After
the morning meal, guests are sure to enjoy a day exploring
Camden, noted as the village where "the mountains meet the
sea." The inn is open year-round.

Innkeeper(s): Jesse & Kristen Bifulco. $110-240. 8 rooms with PB, 5 with
FP, 3 total suites, including 1 two-bedroom suite. Breakfast and afternoon tea
included in rates. Types of meals: Full gourmet bkfst, early coffee/tea and

snacks/refreshments. Beds: KQT. Modem hook-up, cable TV, VCR, reading
lamp, ceiling fan, clock radio, telephone, desk, fireplace, two with Jacuzzi
whirlpool tubs, two with antique clawfoot soaking tubs, phones with data
port, two with private balcony or deck and some with VCRs and/or separate
sitting rooms in room. Air conditioning. Fax, library and parlor games on
premises. Antiquing, art galleries, beach, bicycling, canoeing/kayaking, cross-
country skiing, downhill skiing, fishing, golf, hiking, live theater, museums,
parks, shopping, tennis, water sports and wineries nearby.
Location: Ocean community. Mountains and coastal village.
Certificate may be used: Jan. 2 to May 1, Sunday through Thursday nights.

Captain Swift Inn

72 Elm St
Camden, ME 04843-1907
(207)236-8113 (800)251-0865 Fax:(207)230-0464
Internet: www.swiftinn.com
E-mail: innkeeper@swiftinn.com

Circa 1810. This inviting Federal-style home remains much as
it did in the 19th century, including the original 12-over-12
windows and a beehive oven. The home's historic flavor has
been diligently preserved
and the original five fireplaces, handsome wide pine
floors, restored moldings
and exposed beams add to
the warm and cozy interior.
Air-conditioned guest bedrooms feature warm quilts
on comfortable beds and

private baths. On the first floor a guest bedroom is entirely
handicapped accessible. A full and hearty breakfast is offered
daily and includes specialties such as Blueberry French Toast or
Sausage and Brie Casserole. Situated in Camden, the Captain
Swift Inn is centrally located on the Mid-Coast of Maine to easily explore all that this scenic state has to offer.

Innkeeper(s): Norm & Linda Henthorn. $99-245. 8 rooms with PB, 4 with
FP, 2 with WP, 2 suites. Breakfast and snacks/refreshments included in rates.
Types of meals: Full bkfst, veg bkfst and early coffee/tea. Beds: KQT. Cable
TV, reading lamp, refrigerator, ceiling fan, clock radio, coffeemaker, some with
fireplace, hair dryer, wireless Internet access, 2 new suites featuring loft, fireplaces, whirlpool tubs and King-size beds in room. Air conditioning. Fax and
library on premises. Handicap access. Antiquing, art galleries, beach, bicycling, canoeing/kayaking, cross-country skiing, downhill skiing, fishing, golf,
hiking, horseback riding, live theater, museums, parks, shopping, water
sports, wineries, schooner and windjammer cruises, lighthouses and complimentary gym passes nearby.
Location: Maine Seaport.
Certificate may be used: Anytime, November-April, subject to availability.

Inns at Blackberry Common

82 Elm St
Camden, ME 04843-1907
(207)236-6060 (800)388-6000
Internet: www.innsatblackberrycommon.com
E-mail: innkeepers@blackberryinn.com

Circa 1849. A welcoming inn that was built in 1849, this
Italianate Victorian has been restored to retain and reflect its
original splendor while offering truly modern comfort. Enjoy
afternoon refreshments in one of the spacious parlors, each
with a fireplace, or sitting on the garden patio. Elegant yet
inviting guest bedrooms and spacious suites in the main house
and adjoining carriage house include luxury linens and comfy
robes. Select a room with a gas fireplace and a clawfoot or
whirlpool tub. A multi-course breakfast is served among can-

dles and flowers in the dining room that boasts original tin ceilings with fancy plaster moldings. The seasonal menu features locally grown ingredients as well as herbs and berries picked onsite. Ask about special seaside adventure packages.

Innkeeper(s): Jim & Cynthia Ostrowski. $99-245. 11 rooms with PB, 8 with FP, 3 with HT. Breakfast and snacks/refreshments included in rates. Types of meals: Full gourmet bkfst. Beds: KQT. TV, CD player, refrigerator, ceiling fan, clock radio, coffeemaker, fireplace, some with whirlpools and some with refrigerator in room. Air conditioning. Fax, parlor games and telephone on premises. Antiquing, art galleries, beach, bicycling, canoeing/kayaking, cross-country skiing, downhill skiing, fishing, golf, hiking, live theater, museums, parks, shopping, tennis, water sports, wineries, snowshoeing and lighthouses nearby.

Location: Ocean community.

Publicity: *The Miami Herald, Daughters of Painted Ladies, Yankee Magazine Editor's Pick and NY Times.*

"Charming. An authentic reflection of a grander time."

Certificate may be used: November through May, Sunday through Thursday only, subect to availability. No holidays or special events. Subject to change, must mention at time of reservation, otherwise not valid.

Lord Camden Inn

24 Main Street
Camden, ME 04843
(207)236-4325 (800)336-4325 Fax:(207)236-7141
Internet: www.lordcamdeninn.com
E-mail: info@lordcamdeninn.com

Circa 1893. Lord Camden Inn, a fine luxury boutique inn, has been extensively renovated to offer pampering new amenities while retaining its classic, richly elegant heritage. Adorning the coastal village of Camden, Maine, it boasts award-winning hospitality and comfort. Work out in the Fitness Room and schedule in-room spa services. An assortment of lavish guest bedrooms and suites offer modern-day comfort and a warm and inviting ambiance. Sleep in a Suite Dreams Bed by a gas fireplace and private balcony overlooking the Megunticook River or Camden Harbor and Penobscot Bay. Some rooms are ADA accessible, child and pet friendly. Linger over a breakfast buffet before embarking on the scenic sites and historic attractions of the area. This B&B is a popular choice for intimate weddings and romantic or family getaways.

Innkeeper(s): Matthew Levin. $89-289. 36 rooms with PB, 11 with FP, 7 suites, 1 conference room. Breakfast included in rates. Types of meals: Full bkfst and early coffee/tea. Beds: KQD. Cable TV, DVD, reading lamp, refrigerator, clock radio, telephone, coffeemaker, desk, some with fireplace, hair dryer, bath amenities, wireless Internet access and iron/ironing board in room. Air conditioning. Fax, copier, pet boarding and complimentary full buffet breakfast on premises. Handicap access. Antiquing, art galleries, beach, bicycling, canoeing/kayaking, cross-country skiing, downhill skiing, fishing, golf, hiking, museums, parks, shopping, tennis, water sports, wineries and schooner trips nearby.

Location: Ocean community.

Publicity: *Portland Magazine, Downeast Magazine and New York Times.*

Certificate may be used: Nov.1-June 15.

Cape Elizabeth

Inn By The Sea

40 Bowery Beach Rd
Cape Elizabeth, ME 04107-2599
(207)799-3134 (800)888-4287 Fax:(207)799-4779
Internet: www.innbythesea.com
E-mail: info@innbythesea.com

Circa 1986. This cottage-style resort is like a modern version of the hotels and inns that dotted Maine's coast in its heyday as a

summer spot. The inn has its own private boardwalk leading to Crescent Beach. Guests can enjoy swimming, tennis and shuffleboard without leaving the inn's grounds, which also offer a tea garden and gazebo. The well-appointed rooms are elegant, but not imposing, with Chippendale furnishings, light pine and floral chintz. Guests opting for one of the inn's cozy garden suites can grab a book from the inn's library and enjoy it from a rocker on their own private porch. Cuisine at the inn's gourmet Audubon Room is full of memorable items. In the summer months, the inn opens its outdoor pool patio dining service.

Innkeeper(s): Lori. $169-639. 43 rooms, 6 with FP, 43 suites, 2 conference rooms. Types of meals: Full bkfst, picnic lunch, gourmet dinner and room service. Restaurant on premises. Beds: KQD. Cable TV, VCR, reading lamp, refrigerator, ceiling fan, clock radio, telephone, coffeemaker, turn-down service, microwaves, high-speed Internet access and corporate desk in room. Fax, copier, outdoor pool, volleyball and shuffleboard on premises. Amusement parks, antiquing, cross-country skiing, downhill skiing, fishing, live theater, parks, shopping, sporting events and water sports nearby.

Location: Ocean community.

Certificate may be used: Anytime, November-April, excluding holidays, subject to availability. Guest must mention gift certificate program when making reservations.

Durham

Royalsborough Inn at the Bagley House

1290 Royalsborough Rd
Durham, ME 04222-5225
(207)865-6566 (800)765-1772 Fax:(207)353-5878
Internet: www.royalsboroughinn.com
E-mail: royalsboro@suscom-maine.net

Circa 1772. Six acres of fields and woods surround the Bagley House. Once an inn, a store and a schoolhouse, it is the oldest house in town. Guest rooms are decorated with colonial furnishings and hand-sewn quilts.

Innkeeper(s): Marianne and Jim Roberts. $134-175. 7 rooms with PB, 7 with FP, 1 conference room. Breakfast, afternoon tea and snacks/refreshments included in rates. Types of meals: Full gourmet bkfst, veg bkfst and early coffee/tea. Beds: KQDT. Cable TV, reading lamp, CD player, clock radio, fireplace, hair dryer, bathrobes, bath amenities and wireless Internet access in room. Air conditioning. VCR, fax, library, parlor games, Therapeutic massages & Reiki by appointment and Iron/ironing board on premises. Handicap access. Antiquing, art galleries, beach, canoeing/kayaking, cross-country skiing, downhill skiing, golf, hiking, live theater, museums, parks, shopping, sporting events and 170+ retail shops in Freeport nearby.

Location: Country.

"I had the good fortune to stumble on the Bagley House. The rooms are well-appointed and the innkeepers are charming."

Certificate may be used: November-June, Sunday-Thursday.

Greenville

Greenville Inn

40 Norris Street
Greenville, ME 04441-1194
(207)695-2206 (888)695-6000
Internet: www.greenvilleinn.com
E-mail: innkeeper@greenvilleinn.com

Circa 1885. Lumber baron William Shaw built this inn, which sits on a hill overlooking Moosehead Lake and the Squaw

Mountains. The inn includes many unique features. Ten years were needed to complete the embellishments on the cherry and mahogany paneling, which is found throughout the inn. A spruce tree is painted on one of the leaded-glass windows on the stairway landing. The inn's six fireplaces are adorned with carved mantels, English tiles and mosaics. The inn's

dining room is ideal for a romantic dinner. Fresh, seasonal ingredients fill the ever-changing menu, and the dining room also offers a variety of wine choices.

Innkeeper(s): Terry & Jeff Johannemann. $140-400. 14 rooms with PB, 4 with FP, 1 with WP, 4 two-bedroom suites, 6 cottages, 2 conference rooms. Breakfast included in rates. Types of meals: Country bkfst, veg bkfst, early coffee/tea, picnic lunch, wine and gourmet dinner. Restaurant on premises. Beds: KQD. Cable TV, VCR, DVD, reading lamp, stereo, ceiling fan, desk, some with hot tub/spa, some with fireplace, hair dryer, bathrobes, bath amenities, wireless Internet access, iron/ironing board, exclusive toiletries and in-room amenities specials available in room. Air conditioning. Fax, copier, spa, library, parlor games, telephone, hearty buffet breakfast, fine dining restaurant, full service bar, veranda, private porches and two sitting rooms on premises. Limited handicap access. Antiquing, art galleries, beach, bicycling, canoeing/kayaking, cross-country skiing, downhill skiing, fishing, golf, hiking, horseback riding, live theater, museums, parks, shopping, tennis, water sports, snowmobiling, leaf peeping, whitewater rafting, moose safaris, mountain climbing, sea plane rides, ice fishing, dog sledding and snowshoeing nearby.

Location: Country, mountains. On top of mountain, overlooking lake, town and mountains. Walking distance to town.

Publicity: *Arrington's Book of Lists for 2006, Travel & Leisure, Travel Holiday, Conde Nast-Johansens Recommended Hotels, Inns & Resorts, The Washington Post, Down East Magazine, Portland Press Herald, The Providence Sunday Journal, The Boston Sunday Globe, Morning Sentinel, Aero Zambia Magazine, Gray's Sporting Journal, A Sports Afield Guide, Charleston's Free Time, Yankee Magazine's Travel Guide to New England, National Geographic Guide to America's Hidden Corners, Maine Times, Portland Monthly, Bangor Daily News, Channel 2, NBC/Bangor and Channel 5, ABC/Bangor and voted "New England - Best Places to Stay"*

"The fanciest place in town. It is indeed a splendid place."

Certificate may be used: November 1-May 25, Last minute, subject to availability.

Pleasant Street Inn

26 Pleasant St
Greenville, ME 04441
(207)695-3400 Fax:(207)695-2004
Internet: www.pleasantstreetinn.com
E-mail: innkeeper@pleasantstinn.com

Circa 1889. Situated at the gateway to the Great North Woods, this grand Queen Anne Victorian is a historic gem with rare Tiger Oak woodwork in the foyer, staircase and main parlor. The eclectic décor includes original artwork and antiques. Gather in the entertainment parlor, or in the fourth floor Tower Room with panoramic views of the mountains, village and lake. Romantic and elegant guest bedrooms provide restful retreats. Several rooms may be adjoined as suites. Early risers can visit the Butler's Pantry for a hot beverage before a hearty breakfast served by the fireplace in the dining room or on the huge wraparound porch. Open year-round, it is a short walk to the pubs, shops and restored steamship Katahdin. The East Cove of Moosehead Lake is only half a block away.

Innkeeper(s): Mary Bobletz. $110-175. 6 rooms with PB, 2 suites. Breakfast and snacks/refreshments included in rates. Types of meals: Country bkfst and dinner. Beds: QT. Reading lamp, CD player, ceiling fan and clock radio in room. TV, VCR, fax, parlor games, telephone and fireplace on premises.

Antiquing, art galleries, beach, bicycling, canoeing/kayaking, cross-country skiing, downhill skiing, fishing, golf, hiking, horseback riding, museums, parks, shopping, tennis, water sports, moose safaris, snowmobiling, dogsledding and scenic floatplane rides nearby.

Location: Country, mountains.

Publicity: *Boston Globe and Port City Life Magazine.*

Certificate may be used: November-May 15, excluding holidays.

Hallowell

Maple Hill Farm B&B Inn

11 Inn Road
Hallowell, ME 04347
(207)622-2708 (800)622-2708 Fax:(207)622-0655
Internet: www.MapleBB.com
E-mail: stay@MapleBB.com

Circa 1906. Visitors to Maine's capitol city have the option of staying at this nearby inn, a peaceful farm setting adjacent to an 800-acre state wildlife management area that is available for canoeing, fishing, hiking and hunting. This Victorian Shingle-style inn was once a stagecoach stop and dairy farm. Some rooms include large double whirlpool tubs

and fireplaces. The inn, with its 130-acre grounds and new Gathering Place Hall, easily accommodates conferences, parties and receptions. Guests are welcome to visit the many farm animals. Cobbossee Lake is a five-minute drive from the inn. Nearby downtown Hallowell is listed as a National Historic District and offers antique shops and restaurants.

Innkeeper(s): Scott Cowger & Vince Hannan. $80-200. 8 rooms with PB, 5 with FP, 3 conference rooms. Breakfast and afternoon tea included in rates. Types of meals: Full bkfst, early coffee/tea and snacks/refreshments. Beds: KQD. Cable TV, VCR, reading lamp, telephone, wireless Internet access, three with private decks and four with large whirlpool tubs in room. Fireplace on premises. Handicap access. Antiquing, cross-country skiing, live theater, shopping and water sports nearby.

Location: Country.

Publicity: *Family Fun, An Explorer's Guide to Maine, The Forecaster, Portland Press Herald, Kennebec Journal, Maine Times, Travel and Leisure "Special Hotels" issue as one of 30 Great U.S. Inns and Editor's Pick in the 2002 & 2003 Yankee Magazine Travel Guide to New England.*

"You add many thoughtful touches to your service that set your B&B apart from others, and really make a difference. Best of Maine, hands down!" — Maine Times"

Certificate may be used: May-October, Sunday-Wednesday. November-April, anytime, but not both Friday and Saturday. Discount is off rack rates. Please inquire.

Kennebunk

The Kennebunk Inn

45 Main St
Kennebunk, ME 04043-1888
(207)985-3351 Fax:(207)985-8865
Internet: www.thekennebunkinn.com
E-mail: info@thekennebunkinn.com

Circa 1799. Built in 1799 and serving guests since the 1920s, this historic inn offers full-service hospitality. Feel welcomed in the Phineas Cole Parlour. Guest bedrooms are named after presidents and their first ladies. Two pet-friendly rooms and three family suites are available. For a special treat, make dinner reservations at Academe, the inn's fine dining restaurant. Chef-owners, Brian and Shanna both graduates of the Culinary Institute of America, will tantalize and delight with creativity and execution. Lunch and dinner pub fare is available in The Tavern. The Baitler Board Room is perfect for special events. Free beach passes are provided.

Innkeeper(s): Brian & Shanna O'Hea. $85-120. 22 rooms with PB, 1 with FP, 3 suites, 1 conference room. Breakfast included in rates. Types of meals: Cont plus, early coffee/tea and dinner. Restaurant on premises. Beds: KQDT. Cable TV, VCR, reading lamp, clock radio, telephone and desk in room. Air conditioning. Fax, copier, library, pet boarding, fireplace and online access on premises. Handicap access. Amusement parks, antiquing, cross-country skiing, fishing, golf, live theater, parks, shopping, sporting events, tennis and water sports nearby.

Publicity: *Down East Magazine.*

Certificate may be used: Anytime, subject to availability. Weekends in July, August and first 2 weekends of December are not available.

Kennebunkport

1802 House

15 Locke Street
Kennebunkport, ME 04046-1646
(207)967-5632 (800)932-5632 Fax:(207)967-0780
Internet: www.1802inn.com
E-mail: inquiry@1802inn.com

Circa 1802. The rolling fairways of Cape Arundel Golf Course, old shade trees and secluded gardens create the perfect setting for this historic 19th-century farmhouse. Located along the gentle shores of the Kennebunk River, the inn is accentuated by personal service and attention to detail. Romantic guest bedrooms offer four-poster canopy beds, two-person whirlpool tubs and fireplaces. The luxurious three-room Sebago Suite tucked into a private wing is a favorite choice. Homemade specialties and regional delights are part of a gourmet breakfast served in the sunlit dining room. Popular Dock Square is within walking distance for browsing in boutiques and art galleries. Golf packages are available.

Innkeeper(s): Linda and Jay. $109-389. 6 rooms with PB, 5 with FP, 4 with WP, 1 three-bedroom suite. Breakfast and snacks/refreshments included in rates. Types of meals: Full gourmet bkfst, early coffee/tea and picnic lunch. Beds: Q. Cable TV, VCR, reading lamp, CD player, clock radio, turn-down service, most with hot tub/spa, most with fireplace, hair dryer, bathrobes, wireless Internet access and whirlpool tub in room. Air conditioning. Fax, bicycles, parlor games, telephone, gift shop and gift shop on premises. Antiquing, art galleries, beach, bicycling, canoeing/kayaking, cross-country skiing, fishing, golf, hiking, horseback riding, live theater, museums, parks, shopping, tennis, water sports, wineries and Summer theater nearby.

Location: Ocean community. On the Cape Arundel Golf Course.

Publicity: *Down East Magazine, Golf Digest and Modern Bride.*

Certificate may be used: Sunday through Thursday, November and January-March-April-May.

English Meadows Inn

141 Port Rd
Kennebunkport, ME 04043
(207)967-5766 (800)272-0698
Internet: www.englishmeadowsinn.com
E-mail: innkeeper@englishmeadowsinn.com

Circa 1860. For more than 100 years this Victorian farmhouse has warmly welcomed travelers, and has been lovingly maintained to stay in pristine condition. Peaceful surroundings include at least two acres of manicured lawns, flowers, trees

and antique lilacs. The main house and carriage house offer elegant guest bedrooms furnished with antiques and Oriental rugs. The carriage house boasts a cozy fireplace in the large common room. A guest house has a screened porch amidst the trees. The three-course breakfast may include poached pears, a breakfast souffle and baked blueberry muffins. Dock Square is just a short walk for shopping or restaurants, and there are many historic sites and nearby beaches.

Innkeeper(s): Bruce & Valerie Jackson. $120-285. 10 rooms with PB, 3 with FP, 1 cottage. Breakfast and snacks/refreshments included in rates. Types of meals: Full gourmet bkfst, early coffee/tea and afternoon tea. Beds: KQDT. Reading lamp, CD player, clock radio, some with hot tub/spa, some with fireplace, hair dryer, bath amenities and all rooms with air conditioning in room. Air conditioning. TV, DVD, fax, copier, library, parlor games and telephone on premises. Amusement parks, antiquing, art galleries, beach, bicycling, canoeing/kayaking, cross-country skiing, fishing, golf, hiking, horseback riding, live theater, museums, parks, shopping, tennis and water sports nearby.

Location: Country. Haborside Village.

"An English country house experience in Kennebunkport."

Certificate may be used: Reservation must be made by phone, not booked on-line from website.

Kittery

Enchanted Nights B&B

29 Wentworth St
Kittery, ME 03904-1720
(207)439-1489
Internet: www.enchantednights.org

Circa 1890. The innkeepers bill this unique inn as a "Victorian fantasy for the romantic at heart." Each of the guest rooms is unique, from the spacious rooms with double whirlpool tubs and fireplaces to the cozy turret room. A whimsical combination of country French and Victorian decor permeates the interior. Wrought-iron beds and hand-painted furnishings add to the ambiance. Breakfasts, often with a vegetarian theme, are served with gourmet coffee in the morning room on antique floral china.

Innkeeper(s): Nancy Bogenberger & Peter Lamandia. $52-300. 8 rooms, 6 with PB, 4 with FP, 2 conference rooms. Breakfast included in rates. Types of meals: Full gourmet bkfst, veg bkfst and early coffee/tea. Beds: KQDT. Cable TV, VCR, reading lamp, refrigerator, ceiling fan, clock radio, microwave, five have whirlpools and four have fireplaces in room. Air conditioning. Telephone and refrigerator on premises. Handicap access. Antiquing, art galleries, beach, bicycling, canoeing/kayaking, golf, hiking, horseback riding, live theater, museums, parks, shopping, sporting events, tennis, water sports, wineries, outlet shopping, historic homes, whale watching and harbor cruises nearby.

Location: City, ocean community.

"The atmosphere was great. Your breakfast was elegant. The breakfast room made us feel we had gone back in time. All in all it was a very enjoyable stay."

Certificate may be used: Nov. 1-April 30, Sunday-Thursday. No holidays.

Naples

Augustus Bove House

Corner Rts 302 & 114
Naples, ME 04055
(207)693-6365 (888)806-6249
Internet: www.naplesmaine.com
E-mail: augbovehouse@adelphia.net

Circa 1830. A long front lawn nestles up against the stone foundation and veranda of this house, once known as the Hotel Naples, one of the area's summer hotels in the 1800s. In the 1920s, the inn was host to a number of prominent guests, including Enrico Caruso, Joseph P. Kennedy and Howard Hughes. The guest rooms are decorated in a Colonial style and modestly furnished with antiques. Many rooms provide a view of Long Lake. A fancy country breakfast is provided.

Innkeeper(s): David & Arlene Stetson. $89-250. 10 rooms with PB, 3 suites. Breakfast and afternoon tea included in rates. Types of meals: Full bkfst and early coffee/tea. Beds: KQT. Cable TV and telephone in room. Air conditioning. VCR, fax and spa on premises. Antiquing, cross-country skiing, downhill skiing, fishing, live theater, parks, shopping and water sports nearby.

Location: Waterfront.

Publicity: *Brighton Times, Yankee Magazine and Quality Travel Value Award.*

"Beautiful place, rooms, and people."

Certificate may be used: Sunday-Thursday, must mention certificate before making reservation.

Newcastle

Tipsy Butler B & B

11 High St
Newcastle, ME 04553
(207)563-3394
Internet: www.thetipsybutler.com
E-mail: innkeeper@thetipsybutler.com

Circa 1845. Sprawled on two acres of lawns with gardens bordering the Greek Revival house, this bed and breakfast is open year-round in a delightful coastal village. Sit on one of the two-story covered front porches. Relax with a good book or try your hand at croquet. Spacious, air-conditioned guest bedrooms on all three floors boast views of the twin villages of Damariscotta and Newscastle. Stay in a room with a King-size fourpost bed, floor to ceiling windows or clawfoot tub. Savor the fragrance of hot coffee and a home-cooked breakfast every morning. Begin with a pastry and fresh fruit then linger over a main course of cream cheese-stuffed French toast with wild Maine blueberry sauce, breakfast pizza, cheddar and potato bake, southern pecan pancakes or garden vegetable frittata with a meat entrée and beverages. Special dietary needs are accommodated.

Innkeeper(s): Sarah Davison-Jenkins. $90-190. 4 rooms with PB. Breakfast and afternoon tea included in rates. Types of meals: Full gourmet bkfst, veg bkfst, early coffee/tea and snacks/refreshments. Beds: KQ. TV, VCR, DVD, reading lamp, CD player, clock radio, turn-down service, some with fireplace, hair dryer, bathrobes, bath amenities, wireless Internet access, iron/ironing board, Satellite TV with XM radio stations & HBO, room with a clawfoot tub, room with a four-post Bed and room that can sleep up to 5 people in room. Air conditioning. Fax, copier, library, parlor games, telephone, Croquet and Bocce on premises. Limited handicap access. Antiquing, art galleries, beach, bicycling, canoeing/kayaking, cross-country skiing, downhill skiing, fishing, golf, hiking, horseback riding, live theater, museums, parks, shopping, tennis, water sports and Lighthouse nearby.

Location: Country, ocean community. Coastal Village.

Certificate may be used: November 1 through April 30, last minute, excluding holiday weekends.

Northeast Harbor

The Northeast Harbor Inn (Maison Suisse)

PO Box 1090
Northeast Harbor, ME 04662
(207)276-5223 (800)624-7668
Internet: www.maisonsuisse.com
E-mail: maison@prexar.com

Circa 1892. Stay in the inviting comfort and quiet elegance of the landmark Early Shingle-style main house close to Bar Harbor in a timeless village setting. The recently built harbor-view annex is an adaptation of a century-old design by the same architect. Guest bedrooms and suites are furnished in antiques and boast oversized beds, historic or appropriately coordinated wallpapers. Two rooms include fireplaces. Breakfast is provided at the on-site bakery and restaurant across the street. Choose a hearty New England breakfast or a lighter continental with fresh pastries. The grounds boast a goldfish and iris water garden from the 1950s and a rustic garden with cranberry, blueberry, heather, fern and cedar thyme. Relax in one of the sitting areas and terraces. Visit the many popular attractions of nearby Acadia.

Innkeeper(s): White Family & Friends. $125-395. 16 rooms with PB, 2 with FP, 5 suites. Breakfast and afternoon tea included in rates. Types of meals: Full bkfst and early coffee/tea. Beds: KQT. Cable TV, reading lamp, clock radio, telephone, desk, fireplace, fans and tea/coffee available 24 hours/day in room. Library, parlor games, tennis, laundry, fax, copy, gym, VCR and movie rentals on premises. Handicap access. Amusement parks, antiquing, art galleries, beach, bicycling, canoeing/kayaking, cross-country skiing, fishing, golf, hiking, horseback riding, live theater, museums, parks, shopping, tennis, water sports, tennis, laundry, fax, copy, gym and movie rentals nearby.

Location: Country, ocean community. In the heart of Acadia's best-loved village, near harbor, Acadia Park trails, shops, restaurants, gardens & village services.

Publicity: *Travel and Leisure, USA Weekend, Glamour, Woman's Day and Elle Decor.*

Certificate may be used: During "Pink" and "Orange" price code seasons (visit our rates page on www.maisonsuisse.com) except for anticipated dates of high occupancy (wedding weekends, hiking tour dates etc.).

Ogunquit

Yardarm Village Inn

406 Shore Rd, PO Box 773
Ogunquit, ME 03907-0773
(207)646-7006 (888)927-3276
Internet: www.yardarmvillageinn.com
E-mail: yardarm@maine.rr.com

Circa 1874. In the quiet part of town, just south of the entrance to Perkins Cove, this three-story classic New England inn offers a delightful selection of accommodations. The large veranda is the perfect spot for relaxing on a white wicker rocker. Comfortable guest bedrooms and two-room suites are furnished and decorated in a Colonial-country style. Start the day with homemade blueberry muffins, fruit and beverages. Take an afternoon or evening charter on the Inn's private sailboat past the three-mile beach or along the rocky coast. The on-site wine and cheese shop is well-stocked to satisfy the most discriminating palate.

Innkeeper(s): Scott & Beverlee. $79-135. 10 rooms with PB, 4 suites. Types of meals: Cont, Beer and wine and cheese gift shop on premises. Beds: KQDT. Cable TV, reading lamp, refrigerator, clock radio, hair dryer, bath amenities, wireless Internet access and hair dryers in room. Air conditioning.

Fax, copier, library, parlor games, telephone, fireplace, gift shop, private sailboat charters, wine and cheese shop, hand-painted blueberry dinnerware made in Maine, computer with Internet access, free wireless access and gift shop on premises. Amusement parks, antiquing, art galleries, beach, bicycling, canoeing/kayaking, fishing, golf, hiking, horseback riding, live theater, museums, parks, shopping, tennis, water sports, deep sea fishing, whale watching, boat charters and Marginal way walking trail nearby.

Location: Ocean community.

Certificate may be used: May, June and October, Sunday-Thursday, excluding holidays.

Old Orchard Beach

Atlantic Birches Inn

20 Portland Ave Rt 98
Old Orchard Beach, ME 04064-2212
(207)934-5295 (888)934-5295 Fax:(207)934-3781
Internet: www.atlanticbirches.com
E-mail: info@atlanticbirches.com

Circa 1903. The front porch of this Shingle-style Victorian and 1920s bungalow are shaded by white birch trees. The houses are a place for relaxation and enjoyment, uncluttered, simple havens filled with comfortable furnishings. The guest rooms are decorated with antiques and pastel wallcoverings. Maine's coast offers an endless amount of activities, from boating to whale watching. It is a five-minute walk to the beach and the pier.

Innkeeper(s): Ray & Heidi Deleo. $91-172. 10 rooms with PB, 3 two-bedroom suites. Breakfast included in rates. Types of meals: Cont plus and early coffee/tea. Beds: KQDT. Modem hook-up, data port, cable TV, VCR, DVD, reading lamp, refrigerator, ceiling fan, clock radio, telephone, desk, hair dryer, bath amenities, wireless Internet access and iron/ironing board in room. Air conditioning. Fax, copier, swimming, library, parlor games, badminton, basketball, horseshoes, volleyball, pool towels and pool lounge chairs on premises. Limited handicap access. Amusement parks, antiquing, art galleries, beach, bicycling, canoeing/kayaking, cross-country skiing, downhill skiing, fishing, golf, hiking, horseback riding, live theater, museums, parks, shopping, sporting events, tennis, water sports, wineries, Water parks, Whale-watching tours, Deep sea fishing, Hot air ballooning, Fireworks, Lighthouses, Movie theaters, Outlets, Cemetery tours, Farm stands, Tree farms, Elk farm, Walking trails and Garden tours nearby.

Location: Ocean community.

Publicity: *Down East Magazine - Feb 2004.*

"Your home and family are just delightful! What a treat to stay in such a warm & loving home."

Certificate may be used: Nov.1-June 1, no holidays.

Rumford

Boardwalk

867 Route 120
Rumford, ME 04276
(207)364-2746
Internet: www.boardwalkrumford.com
E-mail: boardwalk@gwi.net

Circa 1924. Sitting along the banks of the Swift River in a country setting in the western mountains of Maine, this is not a typical bed and breakfast. Stay in a three-bedroom condo-style suite with a kitchenette that features a refrigerator, microwave and other assorted amenities. Guest bedrooms are

furnished with Amish-made solid oak furniture and include The Chisholm Room, The Goddard Room and The Giguere Room which can also be used as a den or sitting room. A daily continental breakfast can be enjoyed at the breakfast nook.

Innkeeper(s): Gerry & Joline Boudreau. $65-115. 3 total suites, including 1 two-bedroom suite and 1 three-bedroom suite, 1 conference room. Continental breakfast included in rates. Types of meals: Cont. Beds: QD. Modem hook-up, cable TV, DVD, reading lamp, CD player, refrigerator, ceiling fan, clock radio, telephone, coffeemaker, hair dryer, bath amenities, wireless Internet access and iron/ironing board in room. Air conditioning. Fax, copier and swimming on premises. Limited handicap access. Antiquing, bicycling, canoeing/kayaking, cross-country skiing, downhill skiing, fishing, golf, hiking, tennis and water sports nearby.

Location: Country, mountains. Bethel, Maine.

Certificate may be used: Sept. 1-Nov. 30.

Searsport

Carriage House Inn

120 E. Main Street
Searsport, ME 04974
(207)548-2167 (800)578-2167
Internet: www.carriagehouseinmaine.com
E-mail: info@carriagehouseinmaine.com

Circa 1874. There is a rich history behind this popularly photographed Second Empire Victorian mansion sitting on two acres of landscaped grounds with ocean vistas. It was built in 1874 by a sea captain and later owned by impressionist painter Waldo Peirce, a lifelong friend of Ernest Hemingway who visited the inn. Play the baby grand piano in the elegant parlor showcasing an original marble fireplace or watch a video by firelight in the nautical den. On the second floor a library/sitting area with bay views extends a peaceful spot to read or listen to a book selection on tape. Guest bedrooms with floor-to-ceiling windows are graciously furnished with 19th-century antiques and artifacts. Honeymooners enjoy the spacious Captain's Quarters with a hand-carved cherry canopy bed, marble-top dresser and bay window. A bountiful breakfast is served in the dining room.

Innkeeper(s): Marcia L. Markwardt. $75-125. 3 rooms with PB, 1 guest house. Breakfast, afternoon tea and snacks/refreshments included in rates. Types of meals: Full bkfst, veg bkfst and early coffee/tea. Beds: QD. Reading lamp, CD player, clock radio, desk, hair dryer, bath amenities and wireless Internet access in room. TV, VCR, fax, library, parlor games, telephone and fireplace on premises. Antiquing, art galleries, beach, bicycling, canoeing/kayaking, cross-country skiing, downhill skiing, fishing, golf, hiking, live theater, museums, parks, shopping and water sports nearby.

Location: Ocean community.

Publicity: *Bangor Metro magazine (Dec. 2005 issue) and American Heritage magazine (July 2005 issue) .*

Certificate may be used: Anytime November-May, June-October, Monday-Thursday all subject to availability.

Inn Britannia

132 W. Main Street
Searsport, ME 04974
(207)548-2007 (866)INN-BRIT
Internet: www.innbritannia.com
E-mail: info@innbritannia.com

Circa 1830. Originally a Colonial New England sea captain's home, this five-acre estate is surrounded by English gardens and natural woods. Vibrant Victorian colors accent antiques, stained-glass lamps and memorabilia. Chat by the vintage woodstove in the Drawing Room. The Southampton is a pleasant second-floor common room. A spiral staircase leads to the Pub, a cozy loft with games, television and library. Well-appointed guest bedrooms are stocked with generous amenities. The romantic three-room Windsor Suite features a fireplace, clawfoot soaking tub, oversized tile shower, bay window and a sitting room. Linger over a leisurely multi-course breakfast in the fireside dining room with settings of silver and chintz, fresh flowers and candlelight. Binoculars, bird books, sketch pads, charcoals, water colors, picnic baskets and beach towels are available. Enjoy complimentary sherry and a bottomless cookie jar. Play croquet or take a short walk to Penobscot Bay.

Innkeeper(s): Caren Lorelle & Susan Pluff. $125-205. 7 rooms with PB, 1 with FP, 2 two-bedroom suites. Breakfast included in rates. Types of meals: Full gourmet bkfst, veg bkfst, early coffee/tea, afternoon tea, snacks/refreshments, wine, Dinner is served during the Spring and Winter months, by reservation only. A snack tray is available for room service, as well as wine and for an additional cost and with prior notice. Beds: QDT. Cable TV, reading lamp, clock radio, desk, some with fireplace, hair dryer, bathrobes, bath amenities, wireless Internet access, iron/ironing board, Tea service and Complimentary glass of wine or sherry in room. Air conditioning. VCR, DVD, fax, copier, library, parlor games, telephone, gift shop, Private lane to beach, Computer with Internet access, Complimentary sherry, Fresh home-baked cookies, Afternoon tea or coffee, Refreshments, DVDs, Videos and Games on premises. Limited handicap access. Antiquing, art galleries, beach, bicycling, canoeing/kayaking, cross-country skiing, downhill skiing, fishing, golf, hiking, horseback riding, live theater, museums, parks, shopping, water sports, wineries, Acadia National Park, Lobster Festival, Common Ground Fair, International Folk Festival, The Blue Hill Fair, Belfast New Year's By the Bay Celebration, hunting and snowmobiling nearby.

Location: Ocean community. Penobscot Bay.

Publicity: *Michelin Green Guide for New England, Fodor's Maine Coast, Frommers.com, Boston Herald's Travel Section, Edmond Monthly, Good Times from South Florida, American Eagle, Bangor Daily News, American Eagle Latitudes Magazine, East-West News, Coastal Living, St. Louis Suburban Journal, The New York Daily News and WLIS in CT "Travel with Kal"*

Certificate may be used: Jan. 1-June 30, subject to availability.

South Thomaston

Weskeag at The Water

PO Box 213
South Thomaston, ME 04858-0213
(207)596-6676
Internet: www.weskeag.com
E-mail: weskeag@midcoast.com

Circa 1830. The backyard of this three-story house stretches to the edge of Weskeag River and Ballyhac Cove. Fifty yards from the house, there's reversing white-water rapids, created by the 10-foot tide that narrows into the estuary. Guests often sit by the water's edge to watch the birds and the lobster fishermen. Sea kayakers can launch at the inn and explore the nearby coves and then paddle on to the ocean. The inn's furnishings include a mixture of comfortable antiques. Featherbed eggs are a house specialty.

Innkeeper(s): Gray Smith. $90-150. 9 rooms, 6 with PB. Breakfast included in rates. Types of meals: Full bkfst. Beds: QD. Reading lamp and ceiling fan in room. TV, VCR, library and telephone on premises. Antiquing, art galleries, beach, cross-country skiing, downhill skiing, fishing, live theater, museums and shopping nearby.

Location: Ocean community. Tidal saltwater inlet.

Certificate may be used: Oct. 15 through June 15.

Southport

Lawnmere Inn

65 Hendricks Hill Road
Southport, ME 04576
(207)633-2544 (800)633-7645
Internet: www.lawnmereinn.com
E-mail: innkeepers@lawnmereinn.com

Circa 1898. Sitting at water's edge on Townsend Gut where Boothbay Harbor meets Sheepscot River, the renovated Victorian Lawnmere Inn has operated for more than 100 years in Southport, Maine. Relax on an Adirondack chair on the expansive lawn with delightful views. Bikes and kayaks are available for exploring the scenic area. Gather for conversation in the main lobby, read a book in the second floor sitting area and relax by the fire in the parlor. Stay in a guest bedroom in the Main Inn or adjacent East and West Annex buildings. The one-bedroom Hideaway Cottage boasts a wraparound porch and the Pine View Guest House is perfect for large groups. Savor a country breakfast in the breakfast room. The dining room is open to the public for dinner.

Innkeeper(s): Donna Phelps. $89-189. 36 rooms, 30 with PB, 4 two-bedroom suites, 1 guest house. Breakfast, Sunday brunch and Certain selected items from menu included in rates. Types of meals: Country bkfst, early coffee/tea, lunch, gourmet dinner, Complimentary country breakfast buffet included in room rate available 7:30am-9:30am. Lunch available daily 11:30-2:30, dinner available nightly 5:30pm-9:00pm (some Saturday evenings closed for events). Groggy Lobster pub opens daily at 4pm and full menu & pub menu offered. Childrens menu offered. Complimentary coffee in lobby all day. Restaurant on premises. Beds: KQD. Cable TV, VCR, DVD, reading lamp, clock radio, telephone, voice mail, hair dryer, bath amenities and wireless Internet access in room. Air conditioning. Fax, bicycles, child care, parlor games, fireplace, gift shop, Child care available with advance notice and Pets allowed in certain rooms only (Please call the inn for availability) on premises. Limited handicap access. Antiquing, art galleries, beach, bicycling, canoeing/kayaking, fishing, golf, hiking, horseback riding, live theater, museums, parks, shopping, tennis, water sports, Whale watching, Harbor crusies, Deep sea fishing, Music theater, Opera house theater, Railway antique auto museum, Sunset music cruises and Aquarium nearby.

Location: Waterfront.

Certificate may be used: Sunday-Thursday, May 25 to Columbus Day, when space available.

Southwest Harbor

The Island House

36 Freeman Ridge Road
Southwest Harbor, ME 04679
(207)244-5180
Internet: www.islandhousebb.com
E-mail: islandab@adelphia.net

Circa 2004. Since opening its doors in the mid-1800s, the Island House has offered old-fashioned hospitality and a pleasant retreat. That tradition continues in the newly built bed and breakfast located in a quiet wooded setting nearby. Furnishings from Ann?s and Charlie?s childhood years in Southwest Harbor and Asia blend comfortably with the Maine simplicity of the house.

Innkeeper(s): Ann and Charles Bradford. $75-150. 2 rooms with PB, 1 guest house. Breakfast included in rates. Types of meals: Full bkfst, veg bkfst and early coffee/tea. Beds: KQDT. TV, reading lamp, clock radio, hair dryer, bath amenities and guest house with efficiency kitchen in room. VCR, library, parlor games, telephone, cable TV, CD player, telephone and guest house with private bath on premises. Antiquing, art galleries, beach, bicycling, canoeing/kayaking, cross-country skiing, fishing, golf, hiking, horseback riding, live theater, museums, parks, shopping, sporting events, tennis and water sports nearby.

Location: Ocean community. Mountains, ocean.

"Island House is a delight from the moment one enters the door! We loved the thoughtful extras. You've made our vacation very special!"

Certificate may be used: Sunday-Thursday, November through April.

Spruce Head

Craignair Inn

5 Third Street
Spruce Head, ME 04859
(207)594-7644 (800)320-9997 Fax:(207)596-7124
Internet: www.craignair.com
E-mail: innkeeper@craignair.com

Circa 1930. Craignair originally was built to house stonecutters working in nearby granite quarries. Overlooking the docks of the Clark Island Quarry, where granite schooners once were

loaded, this roomy, three-story inn is tastefully decorated with local antiques. A bountiful continental plus breakfast is served in the inn's dining room which offers scenic ocean and coastline views. Enjoy a candlelit dinner with a bottle of wine from the inn's comprehensive wine list as soft music plays in the background.

Innkeeper(s): Steve & Neva Joseph. $75-240. 20 rooms, 13 with PB. Breakfast included in rates. Types of meals: Cont plus, early coffee/tea, wine, gourmet dinner and Full Bar. Restaurant on premises. Beds: KQT. Cable TV, reading lamp, ceiling fan, telephone, hair dryer and wireless Internet access in room. Air conditioning. Fax, copier, library, parlor games, fireplace and Wireless Internet on premises. Antiquing, art galleries, beach, bicycling, canoeing/kayaking, cross-country skiing, downhill skiing, fishing, golf, hiking, horseback riding, live theater, museums, parks, shopping, tennis and water sports nearby.

Location: Ocean community, waterfront.

Publicity: *Boston Globe, Free Press, Tribune, Country Living Magazine, 2005 Fodor's Choice and selected as "one of twenty five great glorious escapes in the United States".*

"A coastal oasis of fine food and outstanding service with colonial maritime ambiance!"

Certificate may be used: Sunday through Thursday, April, May, September, October, November. Subject to availability. Room in main Inn. Vestry Rooms Excluded.

Vinalhaven

Payne Homestead at the Moses Webster House

14 Atlantic Ave
Vinalhaven, ME 04863
(207)863-9963 (888)863-9963 Fax:(207)863-2295
Internet: www.paynehomestead.com
E-mail: Donna@paynehomestead.com

Circa 1873. Situated on an island, a half-mile from the ferry, this handsome Second Empire French Victorian is at the edge of town. Enjoy a game room, reading nooks and a parlor. The

Coral Room boasts a view of Indian Creek, while shadows of Carver's Pond may be seen through the windows of Mama's Room. A favorite selection is the Moses Webster Room that features a marble mantel, tin ceiling and a bay window looking out at the town. Breakfast usually offers fresh fruit platters and egg dishes with either French toast or pancakes. Restaurants and Lane Island Nature Conservancy are close. Take scenic walks past private fishing boats, ponds and shoreline, all part of the hideaway quality noted by National Geographic in "America's Best Kept Secrets."

Innkeeper(s): Lee & Donna Payne. $90-265. 4 rooms, 1 with PB, 1 two-bedroom suite. Breakfast included in rates. Types of meals: Full bkfst and early coffee/tea. Beds: KQDT. TV, VCR, fax, copier, parlor games and telephone on premises. Limited handicap access. Antiquing, bicycling, canoeing/kayaking and parks nearby.

Location: Ocean community. On an island.

Publicity: *National Geographic's "Best kept secrets" and Boston's New England Travel Magazine.*

"Our first stay in a B&B contributed greatly to the perfection of our honeymoon."

Certificate may be used: Anytime, subject to availability; Anytime last minute based on availability.

Walpole

Brannon-Bunker Inn

349 S St Rt 129
Walpole, ME 04573
(207)563-5941 (800)563-9225
Internet: www.brannonbunkerinn.com
E-mail: brbnkinn@lincoln.midcoast.com

Circa 1820. This Cape-style house has been a home to many generations of Maine residents, one of whom was captain of a ship that sailed to the Arctic. During the '20s, the barn served as a dance hall. Later, it was converted into comfortable guest rooms. Victorian and American antiques are featured, and there are collections of WWI military memorabilia.

Innkeeper(s): Joe & Jeanne Hovance. $90-100. 7 rooms, 5 with PB, 1 suite. Breakfast included in rates. Types of meals: Cont plus. Beds: QDT. TV, reading lamp, clock radio and desk in room. VCR, library, child care, parlor games, telephone and fireplace on premises. Handicap access. Antiquing, art galleries, beach, bicycling, canoeing/kayaking, fishing, golf, hiking, horseback riding, museums, parks, shopping, tennis and water sports nearby.

Location: Country, Damariscotta river.

Publicity: *Times-Beacon Newspaper.*

"Wonderful beds, your gracious hospitality and the very best muffins anywhere made our stay a memorable one."

Certificate may be used: September-June, except holiday weekends, subject to availability.

Waterford

Lake House

686 Waterford Rd.
Waterford, ME 04088
(207)583-4182 (800)223-4182 Fax:(207)583-2831
Internet: www.lakehousemaine.com
E-mail: info@lakehousemaine.com

Circa 1790. Situated on the common, the Lake House was first a hotel and stagecoach stop. In 1817, granite baths were constructed below the first floor. The inn opened as "Dr. Shattuck's Maine Hygienic Institute for Ladies." It continued as a popular health spa until the 1890s. Now noted for excellent country cuisine, there are two dining rooms for non-smokers. The spacious Grand Ballroom Suite features curved ceilings and a sitting area with fireplace, TV and Whirlpool tub.

Innkeeper(s): Allyson & Donald Johnson. $99-265. 8 rooms with PB, 3 with FP, 2 with WP, 2 suites, 1 cottage, 1 conference room. Breakfast, hors d'oeuvres, dinner and Packages available including meals included in rates. Types of meals: Full gourmet bkfst, veg bkfst, snacks/refreshments, wine and Lunch for guests available. Restaurant on premises. Beds: KQ. Data port, cable TV, DVD, reading lamp, refrigerator, ceiling fan, clock radio, telephone, coffeemaker, some with hot tub/spa, some with fireplace, hair dryer, bathrobes, bath amenities, wireless Internet access and iron/ironing board in room. Air conditioning. VCR, fax, copier, library, child care and parlor games on premises. Limited handicap access. Antiquing, beach, bicycling, canoeing/kayaking, cross-country skiing, downhill skiing, fishing, golf, hiking, live theater, parks, shopping, water sports and wineries nearby.

Location: Country, mountains.

Publicity: *Bon Appetit, Downeast, Portland Press Herald and Travel & Leisure.*

"Your hospitality was matched only by the quality of dinner that we were served."

Certificate may be used: Excludes Friday and Saturday nights July 1-Nov. 1, Anytime, subject to availability, Anytime, at the last minute.

Maryland

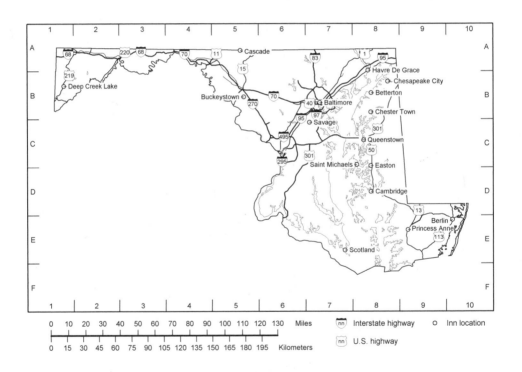

Tell the innkeeper that you have an iLoveInns free-night certificate when you make your reservation.

Annapolis

Georgian House B&B

170 Duke of Gloucester St
Annapolis, MD 21401-2517
(410)263-5618 (800)557-2068
Internet: www.GeorgianHouse.com
E-mail: info@GeorgianHouse.com

Circa 1747. Stay in this 250-year-old home once used by signers of the Declaration of Independence as a clubhouse. Today this pre-Revolutionary home is a landmark in the heart of the historic district, renown for being a comfortable and elegant bed and breakfast. Original yellow pine floors, 16-inch thick brick walls and six fireplaces are accented by fine oil paintings, period window treatments and bed covers. Guest bedrooms with private baths and other modern conveniences pamper and please. Read the paper in the double salon or relax in the garden. Listen to the mini-grand player piano during a satisfying breakfast. Videos, books, a stocked refrigerator and a microwave are found in the second floor library.

Innkeeper(s): Ann & Tom Berger. $170-235. 4 rooms with PB, 1 with FP, 1 suite. Breakfast and snacks/refreshments included in rates. Types of meals: Full gourmet bkfst and early coffee/tea. Beds: Q. Cable TV, VCR, reading lamp, ceiling fan, clock radio, some with fireplace, hair dryer, bathrobes, bath amenities and wireless Internet access in room. Central air. Fax, library, parlor games, telephone, refrigerator and microwave in common area on premises. Antiquing, art galleries, beach, canoeing/kayaking, fishing, golf, live theater, museums, parks, shopping, sporting events, tennis and water sports nearby.

Location: City. Historic Annapolis.

Publicity: *National Geographic Traveler, Chesapeake Life, Washington Post and Washington Times.*

Certificate may be used: weekdays (Sunday-Thursday nights), December-March, subject to availabilty.

Baltimore

Hopkins Inn

3404 St Paul St
Baltimore, MD 21218
(410)235-8600 (800)537-8483 Fax:(410)235-7051
Internet: www.hopkinsinnbaltimore.com
E-mail: info@hopkinsinnbaltimore.com

Circa 1920. Major renovations have turned this inn with Spanish Revival architecture into uptown elegance. Victorian decor and antique furnishings reside with original artwork in tasteful luxury. A meeting room and a conference room are available for business or pleasure. The inviting guest bedrooms have a cozy ambiance. Start the day with a continental breakfast. Centrally located across from Johns Hopkins University on renown Homewood Campus, it is close to all the attractions this area has to offer.

Innkeeper(s): Pat - Mgr.. $89-159. 26 rooms, 15 with PB, 11 suites, 2 conference rooms. Breakfast and afternoon tea included in rates. Types of meals: Cont plus and early coffee/tea. Beds: QDT. Modem hook-up, cable TV, reading lamp, clock radio, telephone and desk in room. Air conditioning. Fax, copier, parlor games, complimentary continental breakfast, afternoon cookies

and tea served daily, garage parking available at $8 per day and front desk open 6 AM-10 PM daily on premises. Antiquing, art galleries, bicycling, golf, hiking, museums, parks, shopping, sporting events, Baltimore Inner Harbor, Union Memorial Hospital, Baltimore Museum of Art, Camden Yards, PSI Net Stadium and Convention Center nearby.

Location: City. Uptown location adjacent to Johns Hopkins University.

Certificate may be used: Monday-Thursday, for further available dates please contact innkeeper.

Berlin

Merry Sherwood Plantation

8909 Worcester Hwy
Berlin, MD 21811-3016
(410)641-2112 (800)660-0358 Fax:(410)641-9528
Internet: www.merrysherwood.com
E-mail: info@merrysherwood.com

Circa 1859. This magnificent pre-Civil War mansion is a tribute to Southern plantation architecture. The inn features antique period furniture, hand-woven, Victorian era rugs and a square grand piano. The ballroom, now a parlor for guests, boasts twin fireplaces and pier mirrors. (Ask to see the hidden cupboards behind the fireside bookcases in the library.) Nineteen acres of grounds are beautifully landscaped and feature azaleas, boxwoods and 125 varieties of trees.

Innkeeper(s): Larry Sadler and Carol Quillen. $150-200. 8 rooms, 6 with PB, 4 with FP, 1 with WP. Breakfast, afternoon tea and snacks/refreshments included in rates. Types of meals: Full gourmet bkfst. Beds: QD. Clock radio, bathrobes and bath amenities in room. Central air. Telephone and fireplace on premises. Antiquing, art galleries, beach, bicycling, fishing, golf, hiking, museums, parks, shopping and water sports nearby.

Publicity: *Washington Post, Baltimore Sun and Southern Living.*

"Pure elegance and privacy at its finest."

Certificate may be used: Anytime, Sunday-Thursday.

Buckeystown

The Inn at Buckeystown

3521 Buckeystown Pike
Buckeystown, MD 21717
(301)874-5755 (800)272-1190 Fax:(301)874-1842
Internet: www.innatbuckeystown.com
E-mail: wellssm714@verizon.net

Circa 1897. Gables, bay windows and a wraparound porch are features of this grand Victorian mansion located on two-and-a-half acres of lawns and gardens (and an ancient cemetery). The inn features a polished staircase, antiques and elegantly decorated guest rooms. Ask for the Victoriana Suite, which boasts a working fireplace and oak decor. A gourmet dinner is served with advance

reservation. High tea and monthly murder mysteries are also offered. The inn also hosts weddings, rehearsals and retreats. The village of Buckeystown is in the National Register.

Innkeeper(s): Janet Wells. $115-250. 7 rooms, 5 with PB. Breakfast included in rates. Types of meals: Full gourmet bkfst, veg bkfst, early coffee/tea and Fine dining restaurant on premises. Beds: QD. Cable TV, reading lamp, refrigerator and desk in room. Air conditioning. TV, VCR, fax, parlor games, telephone, fireplace and tea room on premises. Limited handicap access. Antiquing, art galleries, bicycling, canoeing/kayaking, downhill skiing, fishing, golf, live theater, museums, parks, shopping, sporting events and wineries nearby.

Location: Country.

Publicity: *Mid-Atlantic, Innsider, The Washingtonian, Washington Post, Baltimore Sun,Frederick Magazine (Voted #1 B&B 2003, 2004, 2005), Weekend Wonder, Great Getaway by Baltimore and Washingtonian Magazine, The Afternoon Tea Society and many Red Hat Societies (DC Metro's #1 Tea Room), Channel 9 and Travel Channel.*

"This was one of the best bed and breakfast experiences we have ever had."

Certificate may be used: Sunday-Thursday, subject to availability, except holidays.

Cascade

The Cascade Inn

14700 Eyler Ave
Cascade, MD 21719-1938
(301)241-4161 (800)362-9526
Internet: www.thecascadeinn.com
E-mail: thecascadeinn@comcast.net

Circa 1890. In the mountain village of Cascade, this gracious shuttered Georgian manor is situated on two acres of trees and

wildflowers. Three suites have double whirlpool tubs. The Rose Garden Room and Mt. Magnolia suites have fireplaces and porches overlooking the back garden. The inn is appointed with antiques, lace and white linens, and white wicker. A full breakfast is served every day. Cascade is located in between Frederick, Md., and Gettysburg, Pa.

Innkeeper(s): Jan and Duane Musgrove. $125-150. 5 rooms, 3 with PB, 2 with FP, 3 with WP, 4 total suites, including 1 two-bedroom suite. Breakfast and snacks/refreshments included in rates. Types of meals: Full gourmet bkfst, veg bkfst, early coffee/tea and room service. Beds: KQD. Cable TV, reading lamp, refrigerator, ceiling fan, clock radio, telephone, turn-down service, some with fireplace, hair dryer, bathrobes, bath amenities, wireless Internet access, In-room therapeutic massage available and free local and long distance calls in room. Air conditioning. Library, parlor games and Comcast Digital Cable with FREE HBO and movies On Demand on premises. Handicap access. Antiquing, art galleries, canoeing/kayaking, downhill skiing, fishing, golf, hiking, horseback riding, live theater, museums, parks, shopping, sporting events, water sports, wineries, Near Appalachian Trail, PenMar Park, Catoctin Mountain National Park, Cunningham Falls State Park, Gettysburg, Antietam and Monocacy Battlefields and Boyd's Bear Outlet nearby.

Location: Mountains.

Publicity: *Warm Welcomes, Baltimore Sun, Frederick News and Washington Post.*

"A wonderful balance of luxury and at-home comfort."

Certificate may be used: December-April, Sunday through Thursday.

Chesapeake City

Blue Max

300 Bohemia Ave.
Chesapeake City, MD 21915-1244
(410)885-2781 (877)725-8362 Fax:(410)885-2809
Internet: www.bluemaxinn.com
E-mail: innkeeper@bluemaxinn.com

Circa 1854. Known as "the house with generous porches," this is one of the town's largest residences, built with Georgian architecture by the owner of the sawmill. This elegant inn has working fireplaces and a parlor with a grand player piano. Elaborate upscale amenities in the romantic suites and guest bedrooms include robes, flowers, chocolates and luxurious linens. Whirlpool tubs, a private balcony and second-floor verandas are also featured. Mouth-watering dishes like peaches and kiwi with amaretto cream sauce, apple crisp pancakes and country bacon, and eggs Benedict souffle are enjoyed in the fireside dining room or in the solarium overlooking gardens and a fish pond. A waterfall and gazebo highlight lush landscaping.

Innkeeper(s): Christine Mullen. $100-225. 9 rooms with PB, 2 suites. Breakfast and afternoon tea included in rates. Types of meals: Full gourmet bkfst, early coffee/tea and snacks/refreshments. Beds: KQ. Modem hook-up, data port, cable TV, VCR, reading lamp, CD player, refrigerator, ceiling fan, clock radio, telephone, desk, Jacuzzi for two, fireplace and private balcony in the honeymoon suite in room. Air conditioning. Fax, copier, bicycles, library, parlor games and fireplace on premises. Handicap access. Antiquing, art galleries, bicycling, canoeing/kayaking, fishing, golf, hiking, horseback riding, museums, parks, shopping, tennis and water sports nearby.

Certificate may be used: November -April weekday/weekend. May-September weekdays only (Monday-Thursday). Subject to availability and not valid holidays or special events.

Inn at The Canal

104 Bohemia Ave
Chesapeake City, MD 21915
(410)885-5995 Fax:(410)885-3585
Internet: www.innatthecanal.com
E-mail: mary@innatthecanal.com

Circa 1870. A favorite activity here is watching the parade of boats and ships from the waterfront porch. The Inn at the Canal was built by the Brady family, who owned the tugboats that operated on the canal. Rooms are furnished in antiques and quilts. The dining room and parlor are set off by original hand-painted and elaborately designed ceilings. Guests enjoy European soaking tubs and fine amenities. The historic canal town offers a fine collection of restaurants and shops.

Innkeeper(s): Mary & Al Ioppolo. $95-225. 7 rooms with PB, 1 suite, 1 conference room. Breakfast, afternoon tea and snacks/refreshments included in rates. Types of meals: Full gourmet bkfst, veg bkfst and early coffee/tea. Beds: KQD. Modem hook-up, data port, cable TV, VCR, DVD, reading lamp, CD player, refrigerator, ceiling fan, snack bar, clock radio, telephone, desk, hair dryer, bathrobes, bath amenities, wireless Internet access and iron/ironing board in room. Air conditioning. Fax, library, parlor games and gift shop on premises. Antiquing, art galleries, beach, bicycling, canoeing/kayaking, fishing, golf, hiking, horseback riding, live theater, museums, parks, shopping, sporting events, tennis, water sports and wineries nearby.

Location: Waterfront.

Certificate may be used: Nov. 1-April 15, anytime; April 16-Oct. 31, Monday-Thursday only; All holidays excluded.

Chestertown

Great Oak Manor

10568 Cliff Rd
Chestertown, MD 21620-4115
(410)778-5943 (800)504-3098 Fax:(410)810-2517
Internet: www.greatoak.com
E-mail: innkeeper@greatoak.com

Circa 1938. This elegant Georgian mansion anchors vast lawns at the end of a long driveway. Situated directly on the Chesapeake Bay, it is a serene and picturesque country estate. A

library with fireplace, den and formal parlors are available to guests. With its grand circular stairway, bayside gazebo, private beach and nearby marina, the Manor is a remarkable setting for events such as weddings and reunions. Chestertown is eight miles away.

Innkeeper(s): Cassandra and John Fedas. $155-285. 12 rooms with PB, 5 with FP, 3 total suites, including 2 two-bedroom suites, 2 conference rooms. Breakfast and snacks/refreshments included in rates. Types of meals: Full gourmet bkfst and early coffee/tea. Beds: KQ. Modern hook-up, TV, VCR, DVD, reading lamp, stereo, ceiling fan, clock radio, telephone, turn-down service, desk, most with fireplace, hair dryer, bathrobes, bath amenities and iron/ironing board in room. Central air. Fax, copier, swimming, bicycles, library, parlor games, two computer-ready rooms, private beach, access to next-door Marine, including outdoor pool and 9 hole golf course on premises. Limited handicap access. Antiquing, art galleries, beach, bicycling, canoeing/kayaking, fishing, golf, hiking, horseback riding, live theater, museums, shopping, tennis, water sports and Historic Chestertown nearby.

Location: Country, waterfront.

Publicity: *Philadelphia, Diversions, Road Best Traveled, Washingtonian, Country Inns, Southern Living, New Choices, Chesapeake Life, Time Magazine., Today Show with Peter Greenberg and July 2005.*

"The charming setting, professional service and personal warmth we experienced at Great Oak will long be a pleasant memory. Thanks for everything!"

Certificate may be used: Dec. 3-Dec. 20 and Jan. 2-March. Sunday-Thursday, subject to owner's discretion and availability.

The Inn at Mitchell House

8796 Maryland Pkwy
Chestertown, MD 21620-4209
(410)778-6500
Internet: www.innatmitchellhouse.com
E-mail: innkeeper@innatmitchellhouse.com

Circa 1743. This pristine 18th-century manor house sits as a jewel on 12 acres overlooking Stoneybrook Pond. The guest rooms and the inn's several parlors are preserved and appointed in an authentic Colonial mood, heightened by handsome polished wide-board floors. Eastern Neck Island National Wildlife Refuge, Rock Hall, Chesapeake Farms, St.

Michaels, Annapolis and nearby Chestertown are all delightful to explore. The Inn at Mitchell House is a popular setting for romantic weddings and small corporate meetings.

Innkeeper(s): Tracy & Jim Stone. $100-250. 6 rooms, 5 with PB, 4 with FP. Breakfast, snacks/refreshments and wine included in rates. Types of meals: Full gourmet bkfst, veg bkfst and early coffee/tea. Beds: KQ. Cable TV, VCR, DVD, reading lamp, refrigerator, clock radio, turn-down service, desk, most with fireplace, hair dryer, bath amenities, wireless Internet access and iron/ironing board in room. Air conditioning. Library, parlor games and telephone on premises. Antiquing, art galleries, beach, bicycling, canoeing/kayaking, fishing, golf, hiking, live theater, museums, parks, shopping, sporting events, tennis, water sports and private beach nearby.

Location: Country.

Publicity: *Washingtonian, New York Magazine, Glamour, Philadelphia Inquirer, Baltimore Sun, Kent County News, Ten Best Inns in the Country, New York Times, Washington Post and National Geographic Traveler.*

Certificate may be used: Sunday through Thursday, excluding holidays.

Deep Creek Lake

Haley Farm B&B Spa and Retreat Center

16766 Garrett Hwy
Deep Creek Lake, MD 21550-4036
(301)387-9050 (888)231-3276 Fax:(301)387-7479
Internet: www.haleyfarm.com
E-mail: info@haleyfarm.com

Circa 1920. Surrounded by 65 acres of rolling hills and mountains, this farmhouse has been graciously transformed. Chinese carpets, tapestries and European furnishings are some of the innkeepers' many elegant touches. Three luxury suites include a heart-shaped Jacuzzi, king bed, kitchenette and sitting room with a fireplace. There are also six mini-suites and one deluxe guest bedroom. A three-bedroom lakeside cottage includes a boat dock and gorgeous views. Croquet and badminton are set up on the grounds. Other popular activities are fishing in the trout pond, napping in the hammock or picnicking in the gazebo. Be pampered by the spa and sauna with a facial, massage, reflexology or sunless tanning. Ask about retreats and workshops. Located three hours from Washington, DC it is only minutes from the lake, state parks and a ski and golf resort.

$135-215. 10 rooms with PB, 9 with HT, 9 suites. Breakfast included in rates. Types of meals: Full bkfst. Beds: KQ. Ceiling fan and 9 suites with fireplace and Jacuzzis in room. Air conditioning. VCR, spa, bicycles, library, parlor games, telephone and trout pond on premises. Antiquing, cross-country skiing, downhill skiing, fishing, parks, shopping, water sports and white water rafting nearby.

Location: Country, mountains.

"A beautiful setting for a quiet, romantic escape."

Certificate may be used: Monday-Thursday, November-June excluding holidays. Advance reservation on "Buy-One-Night-Get-One-Night-Free" required for discount.

Havre De Grace

Vandiver Inn, Kent & Murphy Homes

301 S Union Ave
Havre De Grace, MD 21078-3201
(410)939-5200 (800)245-1655 Fax:(410)939-5202
E-mail: vandiverinn@comcast.net

Circa 1886. Three acres surround this three-story historic Victorian mansion. A chandelier lights the entrance. Some of the rooms offer gas fireplaces and clawfoot tubs, and all are furnished with Victorian antiques. For instance, a king-size Victorian bed, original to the house, is one of the features of the Millard E. Tydings Room, also offering a decorative fireplace and sitting area. The innkeeper creates gourmet breakfasts with freshly baked scones or muffins. Spend some time in the garden where a summer gazebo is supported by 12 cedar tree trunks.

Innkeeper(s): Susan Muldoon. $99-149. 17 rooms with PB, 4 with FP. Breakfast included in rates. Types of meals: Full gourmet bkfst, veg bkfst, early coffee/tea, picnic lunch and dinner. Beds: KQDT. Data port, cable TV, reading lamp, clock radio, telephone and desk in room. Central air. Fax, parlor games, fireplace, laundry facility and indoor and outdoor conference rooms on premises. Limited handicap access. Antiquing, beach, canoeing/kayaking, downhill skiing, golf, horseback riding, museums, shopping and wineries nearby.

Certificate may be used: Sunday-Thursday, September-April. Not valid on holidays and other blackout dates.

Princess Anne

The Alexander House Booklovers B & B

30535 Linden Ave
Princess Anne, MD 21853
(410)651-5195
Internet: BookloversBnB.com
E-mail: alexanderbooklover@verizon.net

Circa 1885. Cradled between Chesapeake Bay and the beach, this Queen Anne Victorian graces the historic district with an inviting, wicker-furnished wraparound front porch and a veranda with a flower garden shaded by a large magnolia tree. The bed and breakfast is filled with literary memorabilia and portraits that honor writers and their books. Sit by the fire in the Mark Twain Reading Parlor. Each guest bedroom realistically reflects a famous author. Select the 1920s jazzy Harlem Renaissance of the Langston Hughes Room or the romantic Jane Austen Room with a clawfoot tub and ambiance of Regency England. The Robert Louis Stevenson Room offers 19th-century high-seas adventure. Linger over a gourmet breakfast in the French Café Colette where afternoon tea and evening liqueur are also served. A stocked refrigerator and microwave is available for guest use.

Innkeeper(s): Elizabeth and Peter Alexander. $75-150. 3 rooms with PB. Breakfast, afternoon tea and snacks/refreshments included in rates. Types of meals: Full gourmet bkfst, veg bkfst and early coffee/tea. Beds: QD. Modem hook-up, reading lamp, stereo, desk, some with fireplace, hair dryer and bike rack in room. Central air. Fax, copier, library, parlor games, telephone, gift shop, Internet access, refrigerator and microwave (in cafe) on premises. Antiquing, art galleries, beach, bicycling, canoeing/kayaking, fishing, golf, hiking, live theater, museums, parks, shopping, sporting events, tennis, water sports, wild ponies of Assateague/Chincoteague, Smith and Tangier Islands, boat eco tours, Salisbury Zoo and Ocean City (35 minutes away) nearby.

Location: Country. Historic district.

Publicity: *Salisbury Daily Times, Chesapeake Life Magazine and Today Show NBC (February 2004).*

Certificate may be used: Any day, December and January.

Queenstown

Queenstown Inn Bed & Breakfast

7109 Main St.
Queenstown, MD 21658-2012
(410)827-3396 (888)744-3407 Fax:(866)313-8038
Internet: www.queenstowninn.com
E-mail: qtbb@dmv.com

Circa 1830. Relaxation is easy at this comfortable inn, built with an original cast-iron front. Situated near Chesapeake Bay, take a short walk to a private beach. Boaters are welcome and

can be picked up from a dock a few blocks away. The State Room is a spacious gathering place with wood stove, brick bar, stereo and an organ. It opens to a large screened-in porch overlooking flower gardens. Guest bedrooms and a suite are deliberately without electronics for a calm setting. A satisfying continental-plus breakfast is served in the Historic Room, which features vintage pictures of the Eastern shore and the inn's past. An outlet mall and antique center are nearby.

Innkeeper(s): Josh Barnes, Micheal Lydon. $95-200. 5 rooms, 4 with PB, 1 suite. Breakfast and snacks/refreshments included in rates. Types of meals: Cont plus, veg bkfst and early coffee/tea. Beds: QDT. Reading lamp, ceiling fan and tub with shower in room. Central air. TV, VCR, fax, copier, bicycles, library, parlor games, telephone, fireplace and laundry facility on premises. Handicap access. Antiquing, art galleries, beach, bicycling, canoeing/kayaking, fishing, golf, hiking, live theater, museums, parks, shopping, sporting events, tennis, water sports, outlet shopping, Horsehead Wetlands Center and Wye Island Natural Resources Management area nearby.

Certificate may be used: Monday-Thursday, excluding holidays. Not valid with other specials.

Saint Michaels

Parsonage Inn

210 N Talbot St
Saint Michaels, MD 21663-2102
(410)745-5519 (800)394-5519
Internet: www.parsonage-inn.com
E-mail: parsinn@verizon.net

Circa 1883. A striking Victorian steeple rises next to the wide bay of this brick residence, once the home of Henry Clay Dodson, state senator, pharmacist and brickyard owner. The house features brick detail in a variety of patterns and inlays, perhaps a design statement for brick customers. Porches are decorated with filigree and spindled columns. Waverly linens, late Victorian furnishings, fireplaces and decks add to the creature comforts. Six bikes await guests who wish to ride to Tilghman Island or to the ferry that goes to Oxford. Gourmet breakfast is served in the dining room.

Innkeeper(s): Bonnie & Joe Masslofsky. $100-195. 8 rooms with PB, 3 with FP. Breakfast and afternoon tea included in rates. Types of meals: Full bkfst. Beds: KQD. Reading lamp, ceiling fan, clock radio, bath amenities, two with TV and three with fireplace in room. Central air. TV, bicycles, parlor games, telephone, fireplace, swimming pool and hot tub privileges nearby on premises. Handicap access. Antiquing, art galleries, canoeing/kayaking, fishing, golf, shopping, Chesapeake Bay Maritime Museum and Pickering Creek Audubon Center nearby.

Location: City. Main St of Historic Town.

Publicity: *Philadelphia Inquirer Sunday Travel, Wilmington and Delaware News Journal.*

"Striking, extensively renovated."

Certificate may be used: Sunday through Thursday, Nov.1-May 1.

Scotland

St. Michael's Manor B&B

50200 St Michael's Manor Way
Scotland, MD 20687-3107
(301)872-4025 Fax:(301)872-9330
Internet: stmichaels-manor.com
E-mail: stmichaelsman@olg.com

Circa 1805. Sitting on ten scenic acres with a three-acre vine-yard, lots of wildlife and an incredible natural beauty, this historic country manor house is
located on Long Neck
Creek, just nine miles from
St. Mary's City and 16 miles
from Lexington Park. The
estate offers quiet places to
relax. Guest bedrooms are

furnished with period antiques, beds accented by handmade quilts and gorgeous views of the water. A bountiful country breakfast offers a changing menu with seasonal specialties. Swim in the pool or go canoeing. Take a day trip to Washington, DC, only sixty miles away.

Innkeeper(s): Joe & Nancy Dick. $70-150. 4 rooms, 1 with PB. Breakfast included in rates. Types of meals: Full gourmet bkfst, veg bkfst, early coffee/tea, snacks/refreshments and Wine tasting if desired. Beds: QDT. Reading lamp, clock radio, telephone, desk and voice mail in room. Central air. Fax, copier, swimming, bicycles, library, parlor games, fireplace, laundry facility, rowboat, canoe, paddleboat and bird watching on premises. Antiquing, beach, bicycling, canoeing/kayaking, cross-country skiing, fishing, golf, hiking, live theater, museums, parks, shopping, sporting events, tennis, water sports, wineries, crabbing and boats nearby.

Location: Country, waterfront. Manor House is located on Long Neck Creek, one half mile from the Chesapeake Bay.

Publicity: *Washington Post and St. Mary's Co. Enterprise.*

"Your B&B was so warm, cozy and comfortable."
Certificate may be used: March 1-Oct. 31.

Tilghman

Black Walnut Point Inn

Black Walnut Rd, PO Box 308
Tilghman, MD 21671
(410)886-2452 Fax:(410)886-2053
Internet: www.blackwalnutpoint.com
E-mail: mward@intercom.net

Circa 1843. Located on 57 beautiful acres set aside as a wildlife sanctuary, this handsome Colonial Revival manor commands waterfront views from its private peninsula location. Charter fishing and island river cruises can be arranged by the innkeepers. From its bayside hammock to its nature walk and swimming pool, the inn provides an amazingly private getaway. Accommodations are in the main house as well as the Riverside Cottages. All Cottages have their own living room with fireplace, private bath, kitchen and screened porch facing the river.

Innkeeper(s): Tom & Brenda Ward. $120-225. 7 rooms, 4 with PB, 3 cottages, 1 conference room. Breakfast included in rates. Types of meals: Cont plus and early coffee/tea. Beds: KQDT. TV, VCR, DVD, reading lamp, refrigerator, ceiling fan, clock radio and coffeemaker in room. Central air. Fax, copier, spa, swimming, library, parlor games, telephone and fireplace on premises. Handicap access. Antiquing, art galleries, bicycling, canoeing/kayaking, fishing, golf, parks, shopping, tennis and water sports nearby.

Location: Country, waterfront.

Certificate may be used: November through March, Monday through Thursday Nights.

Massachusetts

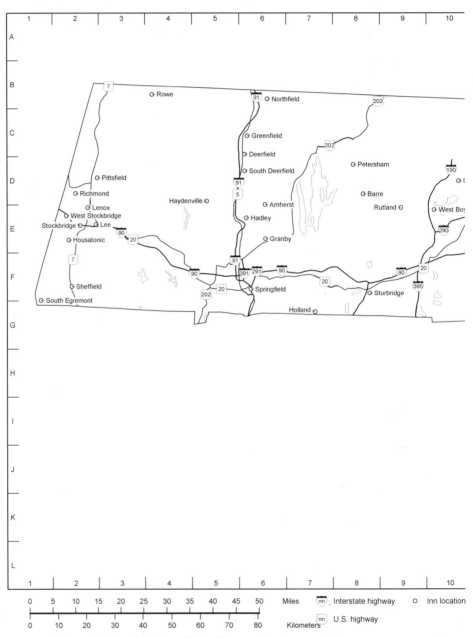

Tell the innkeeper that you have an iLoveInns free-night certificate when you make your reservation.

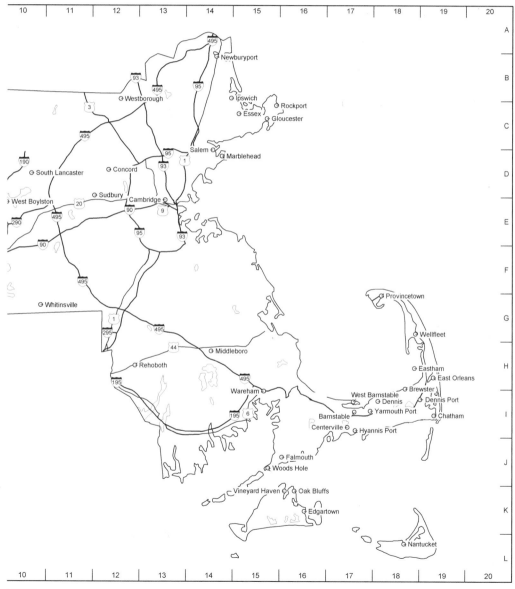

location

Amherst

Allen House Victorian Inn

599 Main St
Amherst, MA 01002-2409
(413)253-5000
Internet: www.allenhouse.com
E-mail: allenhouse@webtv.net

Circa 1886. This stick-style Queen Anne is much like a Victorian museum with guest rooms that feature period repro-

duction wallpapers, pedestal sinks, carved golden oak and brass beds, painted wooden floors and plenty of antiques. Among its many other treasures include Eastlake fireplace mantels. Unforgettable breakfasts include specialties such as eggs Benedict or French toast stuffed with rich cream cheese. Afternoon tea is a treat, and the inn offers plenty of examples of poetry from Emily Dickinson, whose home is just across the street from the inn.

Innkeeper(s): Alan & Ann Zieminski. $75-195. 7 rooms with PB. Breakfast, afternoon tea and snacks/refreshments included in rates. Types of meals: Full bkfst and early coffee/tea. Beds: QDT. Modem hook-up, reading lamp, ceiling fan, clock radio, telephone, desk and down comforters & pillows in room. Air conditioning. Fax, copier, library, parlor games and fireplace on premises. Amusement parks, antiquing, cross-country skiing, downhill skiing, fishing, golf, live theater, parks, shopping, sporting events, tennis and water sports nearby.

Location: Mountains. Small college town.

Publicity: *New York Times, Boston Magazine, Bon Appetit, Yankee Travel and Victorian Homes.*

"Our room and adjoining bath were spotlessly clean, charming, and quiet, with good lighting. Our meals were delicious and appetizing, and the casual, family-like atmosphere encouraged discussions among the guests."

Certificate may be used: Jan. 1-April 1, Sunday-Thursday.

Barnstable

Ashley Manor Inn

3660 Main St, Rt 6A
Barnstable, MA 02630
(508)362-8044 (888)535-2246
Internet: www.ashleymanor.net
E-mail: stay@ashleymanor.net

Circa 1699. This manor house has lived through a succession of expansions, the first addition built in 1750. The final effect is wonderful and mysterious. The inn, thought to be a hiding place for Tories during the Revolutionary War, features a huge open-hearth fireplace with beehive oven and a secret passageway connecting the upstairs and downstairs suites. The inn is reminiscent of a gracious English country house and is filled with Oriental rugs and antiques. All but one of the guest rooms boasts fireplaces, and four have large whirlpool baths. Enjoy complimentary sherry, port and brandy as you relax in the cozy and spacious living room. Two acres of manicured lawns include a regulation-size tennis court. Nature lovers will enjoy the landscape, dotted with cherry and apple trees. The roman-

tic gazebo is the perfect location to view the fountain garden. A full gourmet breakfast is served on the brick terrace or fireside in the formal dining room.

$120-225. 6 rooms with PB, 5 with FP, 4 total suites, including 1 two-bedroom suite. Breakfast included in rates. Types of meals: Full gourmet bkfst and early coffee/tea. Beds: KQT. Modem hook-up, data port, cable TV, VCR, DVD, reading lamp, CD player, refrigerator, clock radio, telephone, coffeemaker, desk, most with hot tub/spa, voice mail, hair dryer, bathrobes, bath amenities, iron/ironing board, fireplace, four with whirlpool baths, flowers, chocolates, beverages and coffee in room. Air conditioning. Fax, copier, bicycles, tennis, library, parlor games, fireplace and gazebo on premises. Antiquing, art galleries, beach, bicycling, canoeing/kayaking, fishing, golf, hiking, live theater, museums, parks, shopping and tennis nearby.

Location: Country.

Publicity: *Chicago Tribune, Boston Globe, Bon Appetit, Tennis, New York Times, Pittsburgh Press, Gourmet, GBH and Newsday.*

"This is absolutely perfect! So many very special, lovely touches."

Certificate may be used: November-May, Sunday-Thursday, subject to availability and excluding holidays.

Beechwood Inn

2839 Main St, Rt 6A
Barnstable, MA 02630-1017
(508)362-6618 (800)609-6618 Fax:(508)362-0298
Internet: www.beechwoodinn.com
E-mail: info@beechwoodinn.com

Circa 1853. Beechwood is a beautifully restored Queen Anne Victorian offering period furnishings, some rooms with fireplaces or seasonal ocean views. Its warmth and elegance make it a favorite hideaway for couples looking for a peaceful and roman-

tic return to the Victorian era. The inn is named for rare old beech trees that shade the veranda.

Innkeeper(s): Debbie & Ken Traugot. $120-200. 6 rooms with PB, 3 with FP. Breakfast and afternoon tea included in rates. Types of meals: Full bkfst and early coffee/tea. Beds: KQD. TV, VCR, reading lamp, refrigerator, wine glasses and corkscrew in room. Air conditioning. Fax, copier, bicycles, parlor games, telephone and fireplace on premises. Antiquing, fishing, live theater, parks, shopping, sporting events, water sports, historic sites, whale watching and bird watching nearby.

Location: Ocean community.

Publicity: *National Trust Calendar, New England Weekends, Rhode Island Monthly, Cape Cod Life, Boston Magazine and Yankee Magazine.*

"Your inn is pristine in every detail. We concluded that the innkeepers, who are most hospitable, are the best part of Beechwood."

Certificate may be used: Nov. 1 through March 31, Sunday through Thursday, except holiday periods.

Lamb and Lion Inn

2504 Main St., Rt. 6A, PO Box 511
Barnstable, MA 02630-0511
(508)362-6823 (800)909-6923 Fax:(508)362-0227
Internet: www.lambandlion.com
E-mail: info@lambandlion.com

Circa 1740. This rambling collection of Cape-style buildings sits on four acres overlooking the Old King's highway. Newly decorated, the inn offers a feeling of casual elegance. The Innkeeper's Pride is a romantic suite with sunken tub, fireplace, kitchenette and a deck overlooking a garden and woods. The Barn-stable is one of the original buildings and now offers three sleeping areas, a living and dining area and French doors to a private patio. A large central courtyard houses a generous sized heated pool and hot tub spa.

Innkeeper(s): Alice & Tom. $145-275. 10 rooms with PB, 8 with FP, 1 with HT, 1 with WP, 6 total suites, including 1 two-bedroom suite and 1 three-bedroom suite, 1 cottage, 1 guest house, 1 cabin, 1 conference room. Breakfast included in rates. Types of meals: Cont plus, early coffee/tea and picnic lunch. Beds: KQ. Cable TV, VCR, DVD, reading lamp, refrigerator, clock radio, telephone, some with hot tub/spa, most with fireplace, hair dryer, bathrobes, bath amenities and wireless Internet access in room. Air conditioning. Fax, copier, spa, swimming, library, parlor games, Heated room in central courtyard and Outdoor hot tub spa on premises. Antiquing, art galleries, beach, bicycling, canoeing/kayaking, cross-country skiing, fishing, golf, hiking, horseback riding, live theater, museums, parks, shopping, sporting events, tennis, water sports, wineries and Whale watching nearby.

Location: Ocean community.

Publicity: *Cape Cod Journal ("EDITOR'S CHOICE ~ 2005") and Arrington's Bed & Breakfast Journal ("One of the Top 15 Best Overall Inns in America").*

Certificate may be used: Oct. 31-May 18, Sunday through Friday, excluding holidays.

Brewster

Old Sea Pines Inn

2553 Main St.
Brewster, MA 02631-1959
(508)896-6114 Fax:(508)632-0084
Internet: www.oldseapinesinn.com
E-mail: info@oldseapinesinn.com

Circa 1900. Formerly the Sea Pines School of Charm and Personality for Young Women, this turn-of-the-century mansion sits on three-and-one-half acres of trees and lawns.

Recently renovated, the inn displays elegant wallpapers and a grand sweeping stairway. On Sunday evenings, mid June through mid September, enjoy a dinner show in conjunction with Cape Cod Repertory Theatre. Beaches and bike paths are nearby, as are village shops and restaurants.

Innkeeper(s): Michele & Stephen Rowan. $80-160. 24 rooms, 19 with PB, 3 with FP, 5 suites, 2 conference rooms. Breakfast included in rates. Types of meals: Full bkfst, early coffee/tea, afternoon tea, snacks/refreshments and room service. Beds: QDT. Cable TV and reading lamp in room. Air conditioning. TV, telephone and fireplace on premises. Handicap access. Antiquing, fishing, live theater, shopping, water sports and dinner theatre in summer nearby.

Publicity: *New York Times, Cape Cod Oracle, For Women First, Home Office, Entrepreneur, Boston Magazine, Redbook, Travel & Leisure and Better Homes & Gardens-British Edition.*

"The loving care applied by Steve, Michele and staff is deeply appreciated."

Certificate may be used: Sunday-Thursday, April 1-June 15 and Sept. 15-Dec. 1.

Cambridge

A Bed & Breakfast In Cambridge

1657 Cambridge St
Cambridge, MA 02138-4316
(617)868-7082 (800)795-7122 Fax:(617)876-8991
Internet: www.cambridgebnb.com
E-mail: doaneperry@yahoo.com

Circa 1897. Located minutes from Harvard Square, this colonial revival house reflects the rich ambiance of the Cambridge historical district. Surround yourself in the finest New England culture, located walking distance from the house. Visit museums, theaters and fine restaurants. Rest under the voluminous trees in the park across the street, or hop on the Red Line for an excursion to Boston. After an active day of sight seeing, return to the warmth of turn-of-the-century antique decor at this three-story home away from home. Enjoy a savory breakfast featuring such delights as home-baked, sesame-orange spice bread and cranberry brody, and spend the afternoon relaxing in an overstuffed chair or Grandmother's cane rockers with some tea or sherry.

Innkeeper(s): Doane Perry. $95-160. 3 rooms. Breakfast and afternoon tea included in rates. Types of meals: Full gourmet bkfst, veg bkfst and early coffee/tea. Beds: KQT. Cable TV, reading lamp, clock radio, telephone, turn-down service, desk and voice mail in room. Air conditioning. Fax, copier and library on premises. Antiquing, art galleries, beach, bicycling, canoeing/kayaking, cross-country skiing, live theater, museums, parks, shopping, sporting events, tennis and water sports nearby.

Location: City.

Certificate may be used: Jan. 7-Feb. 8, Feb. 25-28, Dec. 9-19.

Irving House at Harvard

24 Irving Street
Cambridge, MA 02138-3007
(617)547-4600 (877)547-4600 Fax:(617)576-2814
Internet: www.irvinghouse.com
E-mail: reserve@irvinghouse.com

Circa 1893. Irving House is located in a historic, turn-of-the-century Colonial Revival and has been receiving guests since the 1940s. The simple, comfortable rooms feature a modern hotel decor, and more than half include a private bath. In the mornings, a continental buffet with fruit, pastries and cereals is set up for guests to enjoy. Harvard Square is just minutes away, and guests can walk to the Red Line stop that goes into Boston.

Innkeeper(s): Rachael Solem & Zoia Krastanova. $90-205. 44 rooms, 32 with PB, 1 conference room. Breakfast and afternoon tea included in rates. Types of meals: Cont plus and early coffee/tea. Beds: QDT. TV, reading lamp, clock radio and desk in room. Central air. Fax, laundry facility, off-street parking and DSL on premises. Limited handicap access. Antiquing, art galleries, bicycling, live theater, museums, parks, shopping, sporting events, tennis and downtown Boston nearby.

Location: City. Harvard University, Harvard Square.

Certificate may be used: November-February, subject to availability.

Centerville

Long Dell Inn

436 South Main Street
Centerville, MA 02632-3403
(508)775-2750
Internet: www.longdellinn.com
E-mail: stay@longdellinn.com

Circa 1835. Built by a local sea captain in 1850, this classic Greek Revival home with pumpkin pine floors and detailed moldings is listed in the National Register. Relax in the casually elegant living room with floor-to-ceiling windows or on a hammock in the back yard. Afternoon refreshments are provided and a refrigerator and water cooler are available. Well-appointed guest bedrooms in the main house and carriage house feature generous modern amenities. Read the daily newspaper, then meet new friends over breakfast in the sun parlor. Located in a quiet neighborhood, the delights of Cape Cod are within a short walk.

Innkeeper(s): Kate and Dennis Singletary. $135-175. 7 rooms with PB. Breakfast, snacks/refreshments, hors d'oeuvres and wine included in rates. Types of meals: Full gourmet bkfst, veg bkfst, early coffee/tea and picnic lunch. Beds: KQT. Cable TV, reading lamp, refrigerator, ceiling fan, clock radio, hair dryer, bath amenities, wireless Internet access and iron/ironing board in room. Air conditioning. Library, telephone, fireplace, Beach chairs, Beach towels, Beach umbrellas, Early coffee service at 6 AM, Daily newspaper delivered to room, Afternoon appetizers and Guest refrigerators on premises. Antiquing, art galleries, beach, bicycling, canoeing/kayaking, fishing, golf, hiking, horseback riding, live theater, museums, parks, shopping, tennis, water sports, wineries, Cape Cod Melody Tent concert venue and Ferry boats to islands nearby.

Location: Country.

Certificate may be used: November through April, anytime.

Chatham

Old Harbor Inn

22 Old Harbor Rd
Chatham, MA 02633-2315
(508)945-4434 (800)942-4434 Fax:(508)945-7665
Internet: www.chathamoldharborinn.com
E-mail: info@chathamoldharborinn.com

Circa 1932. This pristine New England bed & breakfast was once the home of "Doc" Keene, a popular physician in the area. A meticulous renovation has created an elegant, beautifully appointed inn offering antique furnishings, designer linens and lavish amenities in an English country decor. A buffet

breakfast, featuring Judy's homemade muffins, is served in the sunroom or on the deck. The beaches, boutiques and galleries are a walk away and there is an old grist mill, the Chatham Lighthouse and a railroad museum. Band concerts are offered Friday nights in the summer at Kate Gould Park.

Innkeeper(s): Judy & Ray Braz. $139-279. 8 rooms with PB, 2 with FP, 1 with WP, 1 suite, 1 conference room. Breakfast, afternoon tea and snacks/refreshments included in rates. Types of meals: Full bkfst, veg bkfst and early coffee/tea. Beds: KQT. Cable TV, VCR, reading lamp, CD player, refrigerator, ceiling fan, clock radio, desk, some with hot tub/spa, some with fireplace, hair dryer, bathrobes, bath amenities, wireless Internet access, iron/ironing board, Jacuzzi in suite, toiletries, welcome package and complementary wireless Internet access in room. Air conditioning. Fax, copier, parlor games, telephone, gift shop, concierge, gift shop, sand chairs, beach umbrel-

las, beach towels, complementary bottled water, soft drinks, coffee and tea service (7:30 p.m.-8:00 p.m.) on premises. Antiquing, art galleries, beach, bicycling, canoeing/kayaking, fishing, golf, hiking, live theater, museums, parks, shopping, sporting events, tennis, water sports, wineries, art festivals, concerts, Cape Cod League Baseball, nature walks and guided Audubon excursions nearby.

Location: Ocean community. Seaside Village/National Seashore.

Publicity: *Honeymoon, Cape Cod Life, Boston, Cape Cod Travel Guide, Country Inns, Cape Cod Dreams and Off Shore.*

Certificate may be used: Nov. 1-April 30, Sunday-Thursday.

Concord

Colonel Roger Brown House

1694 Main St
Concord, MA 01742-2831
(978)369-9119 (800)292-1369 Fax:(978)369-8924
Internet: www.colrogerbrown.com
E-mail: innkeeper@colrogerbrown.com

Circa 1775. This house was the home of Minuteman Roger Brown, who fought the British at the Old North Bridge. The frame for this center-chimney Colonial was being raised on

April 19, 1775, the day the battle took place. Some parts of the house were built as early as 1708. Among the many nearby historic sites are Thoreau's Walden Pond, the Concord Museum, the Alcott House, Old North Bridge, Lexington, the National Heritage Museum, Lowell Mills and much more.

Innkeeper(s): Lauri Berlied. $100-200. 5 suites. Breakfast and afternoon tea included in rates. Types of meals: Cont plus. Beds: QT. Cable TV, reading lamp, refrigerator, snack bar, clock radio, telephone, desk, hot tub/spa, voice mail, color TV, kitchenette and DSL Internet connection in room. Air conditioning. TV, fax, copier, fireplace and data port on premises. Antiquing, cross-country skiing, downhill skiing, fishing, live theater, parks, shopping and water sports nearby.

Location: Town.

Publicity: *Middlesex News, Concord Journal and Washingtonian.*

"The Colonel Roger Brown House makes coming to Concord even more of a treat! Many thanks for your warm hospitality."

Certificate may be used: Nov. 1-April 1, July 1-Aug. 31 on availability.

Hawthorne Inn

462 Lexington Rd
Concord, MA 01742-3729
(978)369-5610 Fax:(978)287-4949
Internet: www.concordmass.com
E-mail: hawthorneinn@concordmass.com

Circa 1870. Share the joy of history, literature, poetry and artwork at this intimate New England bed & breakfast. For 25 years, the inn's ambiance has imparted the spirit of writers and philosophers such as the Alcotts, Emerson, Hawthorne and Thoreau, who once owned and walked the grounds. Antique furnishings, weavings, hardwood floors, a welcoming fireplace and stained-glass windows all exude a wonderful warmth

and gentility. Enjoy afternoon tea on a rustic garden bench in the shade of aged trees and colorful plants. The area offers woods to explore, rivers to canoe, a quaint village with museums, infamous Sleepy Hollow Cemetery, and untold treasures.

Innkeeper(s): Marilyn Mudry & Gregory Burch. $125-315. 7 rooms with PB. Breakfast and afternoon tea included in rates. Types of meals: Cont plus, early coffee/tea, wine and Ask about the Romantic wine package upgrade. Beds: QD. Modem hook-up, data port, reading lamp, clock radio, telephone, desk, voice mail, some with fireplace, hair dryer, bathrobes, bath amenities, wireless Internet access and iron/ironing board in room. Air conditioning. TV, fax, library and parlor games on premises. Antiquing, art galleries, bicycling, canoeing/kayaking, cross-country skiing, fishing, hiking, live theater, museums, parks, shopping, tennis, Homes of Hawthorne, the Alcotts (Little Women), Emerson and Henry Thoreau, Close to Walden Pond, Great Meadows Wildlife refuge, Old North Bridge of the famed "shot heard 'round the world," Public tennis courts, Swimming in historic Walden Pond, Boat rentals on the Concord River, Boston (19 miles) and Cambridge (12 miles) nearby.

Location: Historic Village.

Publicity: *Forbes Magazine, Yankee, New York Times, Los Angeles Times, Boston Globe, Le Monde(France), Early American Life, Evening, National Geographic Traveler, Nono (Japan), guidebook publications such as Select Registry and Karen Brown Guides and Elegant Small Hotels.*

"Surely there couldn't be a better or more valuable location for a comfortable, old-fashioned country inn."

Certificate may be used: January-March, Sunday-Thursday (premium rooms only).

Dennis

Isaiah Hall B&B Inn

152 Whig St.
Dennis, MA 02638
(508)385-9928 (800)736-0160 Fax:(508)385-5879
Internet: www.isaiahhallinn.com
E-mail: info@isaiahhallinn.com

Adjacent to the Cape's oldest cranberry bog is this Greek Revival farmhouse built by Isaiah Hall, a cooper. His grandfather was the first cultivator of cranberries in America and Isaiah designed and patented the original barrel for shipping cranberries. In 1948, Dorothy Gripp, an artist, established the inn. Many examples of her artwork remain. The inn is located in the heart of the Cape and within walking distance to beaches, Dennis village and the Cape Playhouse.

Innkeeper(s): Jerry & Judy Neal. Call for rates. Call inn for details. Breakfast included in rates. Types of meals: Cont plus and early coffee/tea. Beds: KQD. Cable TV, reading lamp, clock radio, telephone, desk, hair dryers, robes and antiques in room. Air conditioning. Fax, parlor games, fireplace, gardens and high-speed Internet access available on premises. Antiquing, fishing, golf, live theater, parks, shopping, water sports, whale watching and bike paths nearby.

Publicity: *Cape Cod Life, New York Times, Golf, National Geographic Traveler, Yankee Travel Guide, Hartford Courant, Best Inn for Relaxing & Unwinding Book of Lists, 2003 Best Hospitality Book of Lists, "Best Mid-Cape B&B" - Silver Award, Cape Cod Life* and voted *"Best Place to Visit Again & Again"*.

"Your place is so lovely and relaxing."

Certificate may be used: Anytime, November-April, subject to availability.

Dennis Port

Joy House Inc., B&B

181 Depot Street
Dennis Port, MA 02639
(508)760-3663 (877)569-4687 Fax:(508)760-6618
Internet: www.joyhousecapecod.com
E-mail: sales@joyhousecapecod.com

Circa 1730. Remodeled for comfort and privacy, this Pre-Revolutionary War, Antique Colonial house is an ideal place to be pampered and served with joy. An old sea captain's home with wide pumpkin pine floors, the foyer gives access to a large common room and fireside sitting area. Listen to classical music or watch cable TV. Attractive guest bedrooms offer a restful stay. Sleep on a four-poster bed under a skylight in the romantic Lighthouse Suite with a decorative fireplace. Wake up to Chef Barbara's breakfast in the dining room. Splendidly landscaped gardens are resplendent with hollies, hydrangeas, roses, rhododendrons and cherry trees.

Innkeeper(s): Barbara and Peter Bach. $110-170. 3 rooms with PB, 2 with FP, 1 two-bedroom suite. Breakfast and snacks/refreshments included in rates. Types of meals: Cont plus and early coffee/tea. Beds: KQD. Modem hook-up, cable TV, VCR, DVD, stereo, refrigerator, snack bar, clock radio, telephone, fireplace, Direct TV and daily newspaper in room. Air conditioning. Fax, copier, spa, library, parlor games and WIFI Internet access on premises. Limited handicap access. Antiquing, art galleries, beach, bicycling, canoeing/kayaking, fishing, golf, hiking, live theater, museums, parks, shopping, tennis, water sports and wineries nearby.

Location: Ocean community.

Certificate may be used: April-June, subject to availability.

East Orleans

The Parsonage Inn

202 Main St.
East Orleans, MA 02643
(508)255-8217 (888)422-8217 Fax:(508)255-8216
Internet: www.parsonageinn.com
E-mail: innkeeper@parsonageinn.com

Circa 1770. Originally a parsonage, this Cape-style home is now a romantic inn nestled in the village of East Orleans and only a mile and a half from Nauset Beach. Rooms are decorated with antiques, quilts, Laura Ashley fabrics and stenciling, and they include the original pine floors and low ceilings. Cooked breakfasts are served either in the dining room or on the brick patio. The innkeepers keep a selection of menus from local restaurants on hand and in the summer season serve appetizers and refreshments each evening while guest peruse their dining choices. The Parsonage is the perfect location to enjoy nature, with the national seashore, Nickerson State Park and whale-watching opportunities available to guests.

Innkeeper(s): Ian & Elizabeth Browne. $90-165. 8 rooms with PB. Breakfast included in rates. Types of meals: Full bkfst. Beds: QT. Cable TV, reading lamp, clock radio, coffeemaker, all with private en-suite bathrooms, one has a kitchen, all rooms have queen bed, two also have a twin bed and some with refrigerator in room. Air conditioning. Fax, parlor games, telephone, fireplace, telephone, refrigerator and grand piano on premises. Antiquing, art galleries, beach, bicycling, canoeing/kayaking, fishing, golf, hiking, horseback riding, live theater, museums, parks, shopping, tennis,

National Sea Shore, Nauset Beach, Skaket Beach and Flax Pond nearby.

Publicity: *Conde Nast Traveler and Bon Appetit.*

"Your hospitality was as wonderful as your home. Your home was as beautiful as Cape Cod. Thank you!"

Certificate may be used: Anytime, November-April, except holidays, subject to availability.

Eastham

Inn at the Oaks

3085 County Road
Eastham, MA 02642
(508)255-1886 (877)255-1886 Fax:(508)240-0345
Internet: www.innattheoaks.com
E-mail: stay@innattheoaks.com

Circa 1870. Originally an 1870 sea captain's home, this Queen Anne Victorian listed in the National Register, graces the Eastham Center Historic District in Massachusetts. Inn at the Oaks offers family-friendly amenities and packages. Children enjoy the outdoor playground and Little Acorns Play Room inside. Play pool, chess, checkers, games, puzzles and use the computer with Internet access in the Billiard Room. Relax on a porch rocker or hammock and read by the fire in the parlor. Select a Suite, Getaway Room or Traditional Room. Some include a fireplace, porch or clawfoot tub. The Carriage House offers two pet-friendly rooms. Savor a country breakfast with specialty entrees in the Gathering Room or on the porch. The signature dish is Abelskivers, Danish pancakes. Spa services feature a two-person hot tub and massage therapy.

Innkeeper(s): Don & Pam Andersen. $120-300. 6 rooms with PB, 2 with FP, 4 total suites, including 2 two-bedroom suites, 1 conference room. Breakfast and afternoon tea included in rates. Types of meals: Full bkfst, veg bkfst, early coffee/tea, Please let us know if you have any special dietary restrictions, gluten free, lactose free, low-carb and vegan etc. Beds: QDT. Cable TV, VCR, DVD, reading lamp, refrigerator, ceiling fan, clock radio, telephone, some with fireplace, bath amenities and wireless Internet access in room. Central air. Fax, copier, spa, library, parlor games, gift shop, game room with pool table, hot tub, playground, play room and DVD lending library on premises. Limited handicap access. Antiquing, art galleries, beach, bicycling, canoeing/kayaking, fishing, golf, hiking, horseback riding, live theater, museums, parks, shopping, sporting events, tennis, water sports, wineries, Whale watching, Cape Cod National Seashore and Summer Childrens' Theatre nearby.

Location: Ocean community.

"A delightful experience—Max Nichols, Oklahoma City Journal Record."

Certificate may be used: June through September, Sunday-Thursday; Oct. 1-May 31, subject to availability.

Falmouth

The Beach Rose Inn

17 Chase Road
Falmouth, MA 02540
(508)540-5706 (800)498-5706 Fax:(508)540-4880
Internet: www.thebeachroseinn.com
E-mail: innkeepers@thebeachroseinn.com

Circa 1863. Gracing the historic district in a peaceful village set-

ting, this meticulously restored inn is listed in the National Register. The Main Inn, Carriage House and a Housekeeping Cottage offer tastefully decorated accommodations. Antique furnishings mingle well with period reproductions, cheery quilts and fine linens. Some guest bedrooms feature a variety of amenities that may include a whirlpool, fireplace, canopy bed, refrigerator, robes and private entrance. A well-presented breakfast is served in the gathering room or on the sun porch. After a day of exploring Cape Cod, sit and chat in the fireside sitting room.

Innkeeper(s): Sheryll & Douglas Reichwein. $110-250. 8 rooms with PB, 2 with FP, 1 with WP, 2 total suites, including 1 two-bedroom suite, 1 cottage. Breakfast, afternoon tea and snacks/refreshments included in rates. Types of meals: Full gourmet bkfst and early coffee/tea. Beds: KQT. Cable TV, VCR, DVD, reading lamp, CD player, refrigerator, ceiling fan, clock radio, some with hot tub/spa, hair dryer, bathrobes, bath amenities, wireless Internet access and iron/ironing board in room. Air conditioning. Fax, copier, spa, telephone and fireplace on premises. Limited handicap access. Antiquing, art galleries, beach, bicycling, canoeing/kayaking, fishing, golf, hiking, horseback riding, live theater, museums, parks, shopping, water sports and Martha's Vineyard nearby.

Location: Country, ocean community. Cape Cod.

Certificate may be used: April 1-May 22 and Oct. 14-Jan. 2. Subject to availability, excluding holidays.

Gloucester

Ancient Thomas Riggs House

27 Vine St.
Gloucester, MA 01930
(978)281-4802
Internet: www.thomasriggshouse.com
E-mail: info@thomasriggshouse.com

Circa 1645. Ancient Thomas Riggs House is an original squared-log house from the late 1640s, the oldest on Cape Ann. A single story was added on in 1704, then a gambrel roof and later a timber-frame wing. Experience a taste of Colonial New England at this romantic bed and breakfast with period furnishings, gardens and a quiet, farm-like setting in Gloucester, Massachusetts. Guest bedrooms feature fireplaces; and the sleeping loft with the Great Room below, boasts a view of Annisquam Harbor. After a restful slumber, savor a hearty breakfast with regional specialties in the dining room, old kitchen, or al fresco. Explore the many nearby historic sites, antique shops and scenic attractions with special itineraries tailored personally by the museum-curator owner.

Innkeeper(s): Barbara Lambert. $100-150. 3 rooms with PB, 1 with FP, 1 two-bedroom suite. Breakfast and afternoon tea included in rates. Types of meals: Country bkfst, veg bkfst and early coffee/tea. Beds: QD. TV, reading lamp, clock radio, desk, some with fireplace, hair dryer, bathrobes, wireless Internet access and iron/ironing board in room. Central air. VCR, library, parlor games and telephone on premises. Antiquing, art galleries, beach, bicycling, canoeing/kayaking, cross-country skiing, fishing, golf, hiking, live theater, museums, parks, shopping, sporting events, tennis and water sports nearby.

Location: City, ocean community.

Publicity: *Gloucester Daily Times (numerous articles), Old House Interior (Dec. 2001), Early Homes (Spring 2004), White Pine Series, Cape Ann Cottages and HGTV's series "If Walls Could Talk" shown numerous times since 2001.*

Certificate may be used: Last minute, December through April based on availability.

Lanes Cove House

6 Andrews Street
Gloucester, MA 01930
(978)282-4647 Fax:(978)283-1022
Internet: www.lanescovehouse.com
E-mail: lanescove@comcast.net

Circa 1860. Overlooking picturesque Lanes Cove, this historic Victorian home is only a ten-minute walk to the village beach. Relax and enjoy the year-round scenery from the large deck. Recently renovated for comfort and privacy, guest bedrooms and a suite with a fully equipped kitchen/sitting room boast ocean views and hardwood floors covered with Oriental rugs. An expanded continental breakfast is served in the dining room including a variety of juices, premium coffees and teas, cereals, fresh fruit, yogurt, local breads, scones and muffins with special spreads and toppings. Cape Ann offers numerous activities and sightseeing adventures. For a taste of city life, Boston is only an hour away.

Innkeeper(s): Anna Andella. $110-125. 3 rooms with PB, 1 suite. Breakfast and afternoon tea included in rates. Types of meals: Cont plus and early coffee/tea. Beds: QT. Cable TV, VCR, reading lamp, refrigerator, ceiling fan, clock radio, telephone, desk, hair dryer, bathrobes, bath amenities, wireless Internet access, iron/ironing board and hand-ironed sheets in room. Air conditioning. Library, parlor games and fireplace on premises. Antiquing, art galleries, beach, bicycling, canoeing/kayaking, cross-country skiing, fishing, golf, hiking, live theater, museums, parks, shopping, water sports, whale watching and great seafood restaurants nearby.

Location: Ocean community.

Certificate may be used: November-April, Sunday-Thursday and anytime at the last minute, based on projected availability.

Greenfield

The Brandt House

29 Highland Ave
Greenfield, MA 01301-3605
(413)774-3329 (800)235-3329 Fax:(413)772-2908
Internet: www.brandthouse.com
E-mail: info@brandthouse.com

Circa 1890. Three-and-a-half-acre lawns surround this impressive three-story Colonial Revival house, situated hilltop. The library and poolroom are popular for lounging, but the favorite gathering areas are the sunroom and the covered north porch.

Ask for the aqua and white room with the fireplace, but all the rooms are pleasing. A full breakfast often includes homemade scones and is sometimes available on the slate patio in view of the expansive lawns and beautiful gardens. A full-time staff provides for guest needs. There is a clay tennis court and nature trails, and in winter, lighted ice skating at a nearby pond. Historic Deerfield and Yankee Candle Company are within five minutes.

Innkeeper(s): Full time staff. $95-295. 9 rooms, 7 with PB, 2 with FP, 1 suite, 1 conference room. Breakfast included in rates. Types of meals: Full bkfst and early coffee/tea. Beds: KQT. Cable TV, reading lamp, refrigerator, ceiling fan, clock radio, telephone, desk, hot tub/spa, two with fireplace and microwave in room. Air conditioning. VCR, fax, copier, tennis, library, parlor games and fireplace on premises. Antiquing, cross-country skiing, downhill skiing, fishing, live theater, parks, shopping, sporting events, water sports,

Old Deerfield and Lunt Silver nearby.

Location: Country, mountains.

Certificate may be used: Nov. 1-April 30.

Hadley

Ivory Creek Bed and Breakfast Inn

31 Chmura Rd
Hadley, MA 01035-9727
(413)587-9747 (866)331-3115 Fax:(413)587-9751
Internet: www.ivorycreek.com
E-mail: pachaderm@aol.com

Circa 1996. Situated waterside on 24 wooded acres of the Mount Holyoke Range, this rambling bed and breakfast boasts a wraparound front porch, decks and balconies for ample opportunities to enjoy the surrounding scenic beauty. Each spacious guest bedroom features a fireplace, Oriental carpets and Continental furnishings. On the first floor a handicapped accessible room has an oversized bath and private deck. A multi-course breakfast served in the fireside dining room or plant-filled sun porch is sure to please. The Metacomet Monadnock Trail crosses the top of the 24-acre grounds for hiking. Mountain bikes and gear are available. Skinner State Park is an easy ride. After the day's adventures enjoy a soak in the hot tub.

Innkeeper(s): Tod & Judith Loebel. $135-250. 6 rooms with PB, 6 with FP, 1 two-bedroom suite, 2 conference rooms. Breakfast, Sunday brunch, snacks/refreshments, Butler's Pantry with complimentary cold beverages, hot tea or coffee, microwave popcorn and granola bars included in rates. Types of meals: Full gourmet bkfst, veg bkfst, early coffee/tea and picnic lunch. Beds: KQT. Modem hook-up, data port, cable TV, reading lamp, ceiling fan, snack bar, clock radio, telephone, turn-down service, desk, fireplace, hair dryer, bath amenities, wireless Internet access, iron/ironing board, all unique, some with decks and balconies in room. Central air. TV, VCR, DVD, fax, copier, spa, library, parlor games, laundry facility, gift shop, hiking trails, mountain bike trails and picnic areas on premises. Handicap access. Amusement parks, antiquing, art galleries, bicycling, canoeing/kayaking, cross-country skiing, fishing, golf, hiking, horseback riding, live theater, museums, parks, shopping, sporting events, water sports, Basketball Hall of Fame, Eric Carle Museum, Yankee Candle Factory, National Yiddish Bookstore and Historic Old Deerfield Village nearby.

Location: Country. Located on the side of the Mount Holyoke Range and bordering Skinner State Park.

Publicity: *Daily Hampshire Gazette (the premier home on the Historic Amherst House Tour 2005).*

Certificate may be used: December-March, Sunday-Thursday excluding holidays (Christmas, New Year's, Valentine's).

Haydenville

Penrose Victorian Inn

133 Main Street
Haydenville, MA 01060
(413)268-3014 (888)268-7711 Fax:(413)268-9232
Internet: www.penroseinn.com
E-mail: zimmer@penroseinn.com

Circa 1820. Experience Victorian elegance at this distinctive Queen Anne that sits on two resplendent acres across from the river. Recently renovated, the inn's antique furnishings and period decor offer a warm hospitality. Common rooms include the music room and parlor. Most of the well-appointed guest bedrooms feature fireplaces. Savor Penrose French toast with fresh seasonal fruit, juice and hot beverages by candlelight. Stroll the perennial and rose gardens with fountain, relax on the porch or go for a swim. Explore Emily Dickens House, Old Deerfield and Calvin Coolidge House, each less than 10 miles away.

Innkeeper(s): Nancy & Dick Zimmer. $95-150. 3 rooms with PB. Breakfast included in rates. Types of meals: Full gourmet bkfst and veg bkfst. Beds: Q. Data port, reading lamp, clock radio, telephone, turn-down service and fireplace in room. Air conditioning. TV, VCR, fax, copier, swimming, library, fireplace and laundry facility on premises. Amusement parks, antiquing, art galleries, bicycling, canoeing/kayaking, cross-country skiing, fishing, golf, hiking, horseback riding, live theater, museums, parks, shopping, sporting events, tennis and water sports nearby.

Location: City. Historic District.

Publicity: *Arrington's Bed and Breakfast Journal (voted "Best in the North" and "Best Near a College or University") and Christmas special with Mark Twain House.*

Certificate may be used: Nov. 30-May 1.

Holland

Restful Paws Bed & Breakfast

70 Allen Hill Rd
Holland, MA 01521-3142
(413)245-7792
Internet: www.restfulpaws.com
E-mail: info@restfulpaws.com

Circa 2003. Known as "the place where pets bring their owners to relax," Restful Paws Bed and Breakfast in Holland, Massachusetts is certainly animal friendly with bean bag pooch beds, an indoor in-ground bone-shaped dog pool, food and water dishes and other desired accessories. There are upscale amenities for humans too. Tastefully decorated and nicely furnished guest bedrooms are handicap accessible and include private entrances. Decide when breakfast is to be served. Breakfast baskets can be delivered to the room or enjoyed in the Gathering Room by a pellet stove and entertainment center. Groomed walking trails, picnic groves, play areas and landscaped gardens accent the 31 wooded acres.

Innkeeper(s): Barbara & Raymond Korny. $164. 4 rooms with PB. Breakfast included in rates. Types of meals: Cont, early coffee/tea and picnic lunch. Beds: Q. Reading lamp, ceiling fan, coffeemaker, hair dryer, bath amenities, Steamer for clothes, Extra blankets, Coffee brewers, Handicap accessible bathrooms, Pet food & water dishes, Pet bean-bag beds and Cleaning supplies in room. Central air. TV, VCR, DVD, fax, copier, library, pet boarding, parlor games, telephone, fireplace, gift shop and "Dogs only" in-ground indoor pool on premises. Handicap access. Antiquing, art galleries, beach, bicycling, canoeing/kayaking, cross-country skiing, fishing, golf, hiking, horseback riding, live theater, museums, parks, shopping, sporting events, water sports, Micro breweries and Fruit orchards nearby.

Location: City, mountains.

Certificate may be used: January and February, Monday-Thursday, subject to availability.

Housatonic

Christine's Bed-Breakfast & Tearoom

325 N Plain Rd
Housatonic, MA 01236-9741
(413)274-6149 (800)536-1186 Fax:(413)274-6296
Internet: www.christinesinn.com
E-mail: innkeepers@christinesinn.com

Circa 1780. Centrally located between Stockbridge and Great Barrington in the middle of the Berkshires, this country cottage farmhouse has sat at the foothill of Tom Ball Mountain for more than 200 years. Large, open beams, slant ceilings and wide-pine floors reflect its original character. Check-in is at the back

parlor, once a small barn. High poster and canopy beds highlight the Colonial-style guest bedrooms. A suite features a fireplace and private terrace. Enjoy breakfast crepes with strawberries or baked French toast with peaches and cream in the garden dining room. Afternoon tea is served on the screened-in porch. Pet friendly. Tea Room open daily 1-4 PM.

Innkeeper(s): Christine Kelsey. $97-217. 4 rooms with PB, 2 with FP, 1 suite. Breakfast and afternoon tea included in rates. Types of meals: Country bkfst, veg bkfst and room service. Beds: QT. Cable TV, VCR, reading lamp, stereo, ceiling fan, clock radio, telephone, turn-down service, desk and fireplace in room. Air conditioning. Fax, copier, library, parlor games and fireplace on premises. Antiquing, art galleries, bicycling, canoeing/kayaking, cross-country skiing, downhill skiing, fishing, golf, hiking, horseback riding, live theater, museums, parks, shopping, sporting events and tennis nearby.

Location: Country, mountains.

Certificate may be used: Mid week only, Nov. 1-May 20.

Hyannis Port

The Simmons Homestead Inn

288 Scudder Ave
Hyannis Port, MA 02647
(508)778-4999 (800)637-1649 Fax:(508)790-1342
Internet: www.simmonshomesteadinn.com
E-mail: simmonshomestead@aol.com

Circa 1805. This former sea captain's home features period decor and includes huge needlepoint displays and lifelike ceramic and papier-mache animals that give the inn a country feel. Some rooms boast canopy beds, and each is individually decorated. Traditional full breakfasts are served in the formal dining room. Evening wine helps guests relax after a day of

touring the Cape. There is a billiard room on the premises and an outdoor hot tub.

Innkeeper(s): Bill Putman. $120-320. 14 rooms with PB, 2 with FP, 2 suites. Breakfast included in rates. Types of meals: Full bkfst and early coffee/tea. Beds: KQT. Reading lamp, ceiling fan, clock radio and desk in room. VCR, fax, copier, bicycles, library, pet boarding, child care, parlor games, telephone, fireplace, billiard room and modem hook-up on premises. Antiquing, fishing, golf, live theater, parks, shopping, tennis and water sports nearby.

Location: Ocean community. Cape Cod.

Publicity: *Bon Appetit, Cape Code Life and Yankee.*

"I want to say that part of what makes Cape Cod special for us is the inn. It embodies much of what is wonderful at the Cape. By Sunday, I was completely rested, relaxed, renewed and restored."

Certificate may be used: Anytime, November-May except holiday weekends, subject to availability. June-October, Sunday-Thursday only, subject to availability.

Ipswich

Ipswich Bed & Breakfast

2 East Street
Ipswich, MA 01938
(978)356-2431 (866)477-9424 Fax:(978)356-5239
Internet: www.ipswichbedbreakfast.com
E-mail: ray.morley@verizon.net

Circa 1864. Stroll on walkways throughout this almost-one-acre estate that is accented by terraced perennial gardens. The Victorian home with Italianate detail was built by a Civil War veteran who became a general merchant. Accommodations include guest bedrooms in the main house and the restored Carriage House, which offers more privacy. The innkeepers will work with food restrictions and preferences. A wholesome breakfast is served in the formal dining room, on the garden deck, in the kitchen with the cook or brought to the room. A tranquil ambiance is imparted during a visit here.

Innkeeper(s): Ray & Margaret Morley. $120-150. 7 rooms, 6 with PB, 1 suite, 1 guest house, 1 conference room. Breakfast, afternoon tea, snacks/refreshments and wine included in rates. Types of meals: Full gourmet bkfst, veg bkfst, Sun. brunch and early coffee/tea. Beds: QT. Modem hook-up, data port, cable TV, VCR, reading lamp, refrigerator, ceiling fan, snack bar, clock radio, telephone, coffeemaker, desk, voice mail, hair dryer, bathrobes, bath amenities, wireless Internet access and iron/ironing board in room. Air conditioning. Fax, copier, library, parlor games, laundry facility and gift shop on premises. Handicap access. Antiquing, art galleries, beach, bicycling, canoeing/kayaking, cross-country skiing, downhill skiing, fishing, golf, hiking, live theater, museums, parks, shopping, tennis and water sports nearby.

Location: Country, ocean community, waterfront.

Publicity: *Arrington's B&B Journal awarded best amenities.*

Certificate may be used: Nov. 1-May 31, subject to availability.

Lee

Devonfield Country Inn

85 Stockbridge Rd
Lee, MA 01238-9308
(413)243-3298 (800)664-0880 Fax:(413)243-1360
Internet: www.devonfield.com
E-mail: innkeeper@devonfield.com

Circa 1800. Devonfield is a gracious English-Style country house built in the late 1800s. Overlooking a pastoral meadow shaded by graceful birch trees with the rolling tapestry of the Berkshire Hills beyond, the B&B sits on 29 acres. In the main house, a fireside living room is complete with grand piano, library and stereo. Relax in the television room and on the porch. A guest pantry is always stocked with coffee, tea, hot chocolate, popcorn and fresh-baked cookies. Browse through the movie library. Many spacious guest bedrooms have wood-

burning fireplaces; some boast Jacuzzis and terry robes. All rooms have complimentary cognac, locally hand-made chocolates and bottled water. A hearty country breakfast proudly features foods locally grown and/or prepared. A tennis court and heated swimming pool offers pleasant onsite activities.

Innkeeper(s): Ronnie & Bruce Singer. $160-350. 10 rooms with PB, 4 with FP, 4 suites, 1 cottage. Beds: KQT. Cable TV, reading lamp and clock radio in room. Air conditioning. Fax, copier, swimming, bicycles, tennis, library, parlor games, telephone and fireplace on premises.

Location: Country, mountains.

Publicity: *Discerning Traveler, New York Magazine and Karen Brown's Guides.*

"A special thank you for your warm and kind hospitality. We feel as though this is our home away from home."

Certificate may be used: November 13-May 24, Room #6, 7 & 8, Sunday through Thursday; Fridays and Saturdays are excluded.

Lenox

Birchwood Inn

7 Hubbard St, Box 2020
Lenox, MA 01240-4604
(413)637-2600 (800)524-1646 Fax:(413)637-4604
Internet: www.birchwood-inn.com
E-mail: innkeeper@birchwood-inn.com

Circa 1767. Experience comfortable country elegance at this Colonial Revival mansion that has welcomed friends since 1767. The inn's antiques, collectibles, quilts, canopy beds and

nine fireplaces create an idyllic getaway. The inn is renowned for sumptuous breakfasts and afternoon tea and was voted "Best Breakfast in New England." Enjoy Berkshire breezes and fireflies on the porch in summer, spring blossoms in stone-fenced gardens, vibrant fall foliage, and the welcome warmth of the firesides in winter. The oldest home in Lenox, it is a short walk from its tranquil hilltop setting to the village's restaurants, galleries and shops.

Innkeeper(s): Ellen Gutman Chenaux. $125-295. 11 rooms with PB, 6 with FP, 4 total suites, including 1 two-bedroom suite, 2 conference rooms. Breakfast and afternoon tea included in rates. Types of meals: Full gourmet bkfst, early coffee/tea, snacks/refreshments and Midnight snack. Beds: KQT. Cable TV, reading lamp, ceiling fan, clock radio, telephone, desk, most with fireplace, hair dryer, bathrobes, bath amenities, wireless Internet access and Free wireless Internet access in room. Air conditioning. VCR, DVD, fax, copier, library, parlor games, gift shop and Free wireless Internet access on premises. Limited handicap access. Antiquing, art galleries, beach, bicycling, canoeing/kayaking, cross-country skiing, downhill skiing, fishing, golf, hiking, horseback riding, live theater, museums, parks, shopping, tennis, water sports, wineries, Tanglewood, music and theater festivals and the Norman Rockwell Museum nearby.

Location: Mountains. Village.

Publicity: *Country Inns, Country Living, New York Magazine, Montreal Gazette, Gourmet Magazine and The Discerning Traveler.*

"Thank you for memories that we will cherish forever."

Certificate may be used: Monday-Thursday, Jan. 5-April 15, holidays excluded.

Walker House

64 Walker St
Lenox, MA 01240-2718
(413)637-1271 (800)235-3098 Fax:(413)637-2387
Internet: www.walkerhouse.com
E-mail: walkerhouse.inn@verizon.net

Circa 1804. This beautiful Federal-style house sits in the center of the village on three acres of graceful woods and restored gardens. Guest rooms have fireplaces and private baths. Each is named for a favorite composer such as Beethoven, Mozart or Handel. The innkeepers' musical backgrounds include associations with the San Francisco Opera, the New York City Opera, and the Los Angeles Philharmonic. Walker House concerts are scheduled from time to time. The innkeepers offer film and opera screenings nightly on a twelve-foot

screen. With prior approval, some pets may be allowed.

Innkeeper(s): Peggy & Richard Houdek. $90-220. 8 rooms with PB, 5 with FP, 1 conference room. Breakfast and afternoon tea included in rates. Types of meals: Cont plus, veg bkfst and early coffee/tea. Beds: QDT. Reading lamp, clock radio and desk in room. Air conditioning. TV, VCR, DVD, fax, copier, library, parlor games, telephone, fireplace, theatre with Internet access and 100-inch screen on premises. Limited handicap access. Antiquing, art galleries, bicycling, cross-country skiing, downhill skiing, fishing, golf, hiking, horseback riding, live theater, museums, parks, shopping, water sports and music nearby.

Location: In small village.

Publicity: *Boston Globe, PBS, Los Angeles Times, New York Times and Dog Fancy.*

"We had a grand time staying with fellow music and opera lovers! Breakfasts were lovely."

Certificate may be used: Nov. 1 to April 30, Sunday through Thursday, excluding holiday periods.

Marblehead

Harborside House B&B

23 Gregory Street
Marblehead, MA 01945
(781)631-1032
Internet: www.harborsidehouse.com
E-mail: stay@harborsidehouse.com

Circa 1850. Enjoy the Colonial charm of this home, which overlooks Marblehead Harbor on Boston's historic North Shore. Rooms are decorated with antiques and period wallpaper. A third-story sundeck offers excellent views. A generous continental breakfast of home-baked breads, muffins and fresh fruit is served each morning in the well-decorated dining room or on the open porch. The village of Marblehead provides many shops and restaurants. Boston and Logan airport are 30 minutes away.

Innkeeper(s): Susan Livingston. $80-100. 2 rooms. Breakfast, afternoon tea and snacks/refreshments included in rates. Types of meals: Cont plus, veg bkfst, early coffee/tea and Homemade cookies. Beds: DT. Modem hook-up, cable TV, VCR, reading lamp, CD player, clock radio, desk, hair dryer, bathrobes, bath amenities, wireless Internet access, iron/ironing board, toiletries, Harbor Sweets candy and fresh flowers in room. Bicycles, library, telephone and fireplace on premises. Antiquing, art galleries, beach, bicycling, canoeing/kayaking, fishing, museums, parks, shopping, water sports, historical house tour and museum nearby.

Location: Waterfront. Historic harbor.

Publicity: *Marblehead Reporter.*

"Harborside Inn is restful, charming, with a beautiful view of the water. I wish we didn't have to leave."

Certificate may be used: January-April, Sunday-Saturday.

The Seagull Inn Bed and Breakfast

106 Harbor Ave
Marblehead, MA 01945-3848
(781)631-1893 Fax:(781)631-3535
Internet: www.seagullinn.com
E-mail: host@seagullinn.com

Circa 1890. Every season is special at this 1890s New England inn that has been completely restored for privacy and comfort. Shaker and hand-crafted furnishings, antiques, original art and woodworking combine to create a pleasant ambiance. Select a video from the library, chat by the fire or listen to music in the casual Harbor Room. Sun-filled guest suites feature four-poster beds. The Lighthouse Suite boasts water views, a roof deck, kitchen and living room. The Seabreeze Suite has an adjoining sitting room with sofa and day bed. Look out on the harbor

from the dining room where a deluxe continental-plus breakfast is served with homemade baked goods, granola, cereals, bagels and cream cheese, ham, smoked salmon, fresh fruit cup and assorted beverages. The extensive gardens invite relaxation.

Innkeeper(s): Ruth & Skip Sigler. $125-225. 3 rooms, 1 with PB, 2 suites. Breakfast and snacks/refreshments included in rates. Types of meals: Cont plus, veg bkfst and early coffee/tea. Beds: QT. Cable TV, VCR, reading lamp, refrigerator, snack bar, clock radio, telephone, coffeemaker, desk, wireless Internet connection, complimentary soft drinks, snacks and bottled water in room. Air conditioning. Fax, copier, bicycles, library, parlor games, fireplace, laundry facility, gift shop, kayaks and croquet on premises. Antiquing, art galleries, beach, bicycling, canoeing/kayaking, cross-country skiing, fishing, golf, live theater, museums, parks, shopping, tennis and water sports nearby.

Location: Ocean community.

Certificate may be used: Anytime, November-March, subject to availability.

Middleboro

On Cranberry Pond B&B

43 Fuller St
Middleboro, MA 02346-1706
(508)946-0768 Fax:(508)947-8221
Internet: www.oncranberrypond.com
E-mail: oncranberrypond@aol.com

Circa 1989. Nestled in the historic "cranberry capital of the world," this 8,000 square-foot modern farmhouse rests on a working cranberry bog. There are two miles of trails to meander, and during berry picking season guests can watch as buckets of the fruit are collected. Rooms are comfortable and well appointed. The Master Suite includes a whirlpool bath for two. A 93-foot deck overlooks the cranberry bog. Innkeeper Jeannine LaBossiere creates gourmet breakfasts and yummy homemade snacks at night. Honeymoons and anniversaries are popular here. There is a spacious conference room with plenty of business amenities. Borrow a fishing rod or one of the innkeeper's mountain bikes for an afternoon's adventure you will long remember. Plymouth, Mass. is nearby and whale watching is a popular activity.

Innkeeper(s): Jeannine LaBossiere- Krushas, Ken Krushas and son Tim. $95-180. 6 rooms, 4 with PB, 2 suites, 2 conference rooms. Breakfast and snacks/refreshments included in rates. Types of meals: Full gourmet bkfst, veg bkfst, early coffee/tea and lunch. Beds: Q. Modem hook-up, data port, cable TV, VCR, reading lamp, CD player, ceiling fan, clock radio, telephone, coffeemaker, turn-down service, desk and hot tub in room. Air conditioning. Fax, copier, bicycles and library on premises. Antiquing, art galleries, beach, bicycling, fishing, golf, live theater, museums, parks, shopping, tennis and wineries nearby.

Location: Oversized Cape.

"Your dedication to making your guests comfortable is above and beyond. You are tops in your field."

Certificate may be used: Accepts weekends, Anytime subject to availability; Anytime, last minute - based on availability.

Nantucket

Brass Lantern

11 N Water St
Nantucket, MA 02554-3521
(508)228-4064 (800)377-6609 Fax:(508)325-0928
Internet: www.brasslanternnantucket.com
E-mail: info@brasslanternnantucket.com

Circa 1838. Ideally located in the residential historic district of town, the Main Inn is a Greek Revival home with a newer

Garden Wing that blends harmoniously. Both sections were renovated recently. The Main Inn offers Old World ambiance enhanced by the traditional elegance of antiques, Oriental rugs, chair rail and wainscoting. The Garden Wing features a more contemporary Nantucket-style decor. Guest bedrooms and suites pamper with Egyptian cotton sheets, fluffy pillows and soft robes. Enjoy a tempting continental breakfast in the sunny dining room or on teak furniture in the garden. Walk down the cobblestone street to the ferry, harbor and other amazing sites and activities in the local area. Rent a bike or take a shuttle bus to explore Sconset and Surfside.

Innkeeper(s): Michelle Langlois. $95-395. 17 rooms, 15 with PB, 3 with FP, 1 two-bedroom suite. Breakfast, afternoon tea and In-season wine and cheese parties on Saturday evenings included in rates. Types of meals: Cont plus and early coffee/tea. Beds: KQDT. Cable TV, reading lamp, refrigerator, clock radio, telephone, voice mail, hair dryer, bathrobes, wireless Internet access and iron/ironing board in room. Air conditioning. Fax, copier, library, child care, parlor games, fireplace and Pet friendly on premises. Antiquing, art galleries, beach, bicycling, canoeing/kayaking, fishing, golf, hiking, live theater, museums, parks, shopping, tennis, water sports and wineries nearby.

Location: Ocean community. The Brass Lantern is ideally located in the residential Historic District in Nantucket Town, an easy walk from Steamship Wharf and the shops and restaurants of Main Street.

Publicity: *Boston Globe.*

Certificate may be used: April-June 15, Sunday-Thursday; Sept.15-Oct. 31, Sunday-Thursday; Last minute subject to availability.

House of The Seven Gables

32 Cliff Rd
Nantucket, MA 02554-3644
(508)228-4706
Internet: www.houseofthesevengables.com
E-mail: walton@nantucket.net

Circa 1880. Originally the annex of the Sea Cliff Inn, one of the island's oldest hotels, this three-story Queen Anne Victorian inn offers 10 guest rooms. Beaches, bike rentals, museums, restaurants, shops and tennis courts are all found nearby. The guest rooms are furnished with king or queen beds and period antiques. Breakfast is served each morning in the guest rooms and often include homemade coffee cake, muffins or Portuguese rolls.

Innkeeper(s): Sue Walton. $100-300. 10 rooms, 8 with PB. Breakfast included in rates. Types of meals: Cont. Beds: KQ. Telephone, fireplace and bird watching on premises. Antiquing, fishing, live theater, shopping and water sports nearby.

Location: The Old Historic District.

"You have a beautiful home and one that makes everyone feel relaxed and at home."

Certificate may be used: Anytime, Sunday-Thursday.

Newburyport

Clark Currier Inn

45 Green St
Newburyport, MA 01950-2646
(978)465-8363
Internet: www.clarkcurrierinn.com
E-mail: ccinn1803@yahoo.com

Circa 1803. Once the home of shipbuilder Thomas March Clark, this three-story Federal-style inn provides gracious accommodations to visitors in the Northeast Massachusetts area. Visitors will enjoy the inn's details added by Samuel McEntire, one of the nation's most celebrated home builders

and woodcarvers. Breakfast is served in the dining room or garden room, with an afternoon tea offered in the garden room. The inn's grounds also boast a picturesque garden and gazebo.

Parker River National Wildlife Refuge and Maudslay State Park are nearby, as well as Plum Island beaches.

Innkeeper(s): Bob Nolan. $95-185. 8 rooms with PB. Breakfast and afternoon tea included in rates. Types of meals: Cont plus. Beds: QDT. Reading lamp, CD player, telephone and desk in room. Air conditioning. Parlor games, sherry and fruit are available in the library on premises. Amusement parks, antiquing, cross-country skiing, fishing, live theater, parks, shopping, water sports and many acclaimed and varied restaurants and shops nearby.

Location: City, waterfront. Historic downtown.

"We had a lovely stay in your B&B! We appreciated your hospitality!"

Certificate may be used: January, February and March.

Northfield

Centennial House

94 Main Street
Northfield, MA 01360
(413)498-5921 (877)977-5950 Fax:(413)498-2525
Internet: www.thecentennialhouse.com
E-mail: info@thecentennialhouse.com

Circa 1811. Celebrate traditional and contemporary New England at this rambling 17-room Federal estate on two acres that was built in 1811 by master craftsmen and recently renovated. Play chess by the huge hearth in the Great Room that resembles an old tavern with hand-hewn beams and a pickled pine ceiling. Look out on rolling lawns and distant hills while meditating in the spacious and airy sunroom with French doors leading onto the terraced lawn and gardens. Savor afternoon tea in the elegant parlor. Guest bedrooms and suites are named and furnished to reflect a local historic area or person. Sleep on a four-poster, brass or sleigh bed. Several rooms boast working fireplaces. A hearty country breakfast is served in the dining room. Retreats, seminars, meetings and special events are welcome.

Innkeeper(s): Joan & Steve Stoia. $104-209. 6 rooms with PB, 3 with FP, 1 with WP, 1 suite. Breakfast included in rates. Types of meals: Country bkfst, veg bkfst, early coffee/tea and 24/7 self-service hot beverages. Beds: KQDT. Cable TV, reading lamp, clock radio, coffeemaker, desk, some with hot tub/spa, most with fireplace, hair dryer and bath amenities in room. Air conditioning. Fax, parlor games, telephone, 24/7 self-service hot beverages and fresh baked afternoon cookies on premises. Amusement parks, antiquing, art galleries, bicycling, canoeing/kayaking, cross-country skiing, downhill skiing, fishing, golf, hiking, horseback riding, live theater, museums, parks, shopping, sporting events, water sports, Crumpin Fox Golf Course, nature center boat cruise in summer, cross country skiing, Magic Wings Butterfly Conservatory and Historic Deerfield nearby.

Location: Country, mountains.

Certificate may be used: November-March, Sunday-Thursday excluding Thanksgiving, Christmas and New Years Eve, subject to availability, Queen rooms Only.

Petersham

Winterwood at Petersham

19 N Main St
Petersham, MA 01366
(978)724-8885
Internet: www.winterwoodinn.net
E-mail: winterwoodatpetersham@verizon.net

Circa 1842. The town of Petersham is often referred to as a museum of Greek Revival architecture. One of the grand houses facing the common is Winterwood. It boasts fireplaces in almost every room. Private dining is available for groups of up to 70 people. The inn is listed in the National Register.

Innkeeper(s): Jean & Robert Day. $149. 6 rooms with PB, 5 with FP. Breakfast included in rates. Types of meals: Cont plus. Beds: QDT. Reading lamp, clock radio and bath amenities in room. Air conditioning. TV, VCR, DVD, fax, copier, library, parlor games, telephone and fireplace on premises. Antiquing, art galleries, bicycling, cross-country skiing, downhill skiing, fishing, golf, hiking and horseback riding nearby.

Location: Country. Town Common.

Publicity: *Boston Globe, Yankee Magazine, Athol Daily News, Greenfield Recorder, The Gardner News and The Fitchburg Sentinel.*

"Between your physical facilities and Jean's cooking, our return to normal has been made even more difficult. Your hospitality was just a fantastic extra to our total experience."

Certificate may be used: Sunday-Thursday, except months of September and October.

Provincetown

Gabriel's at the Ashbrooke Inn

102 Bradford St
Provincetown, MA 02657
(508)487-3232 (800)969-2643
Internet: www.gabriels.com
E-mail: gabrielsma@aol.com

Circa 1830. Experience Gabriel's heavenly setting and cozy hospitality that have been enjoyed by many since 1979. Restored homes are graced with sky-lit common areas to gather in as a group or an individual. Each guest bedroom and suite is distinguished by the name and character of a famous personality. Most feature fireplaces, many boast Jacuzzi tubs and some include kitchenettes, skylights, sleeping lofts and semi-private porches. Modern amenities include high-speed Internet access and computers, voice mail, VCRs and a video library. Savor a full breakfast each morning. Lounge on a sun deck with afternoon wine and cheese. After a work out in the exercise gym, relax in the sauna or steam room. Soak in one of the two soothing outdoor hot tubs. Conveniently located in the heart of quaint Provincetown, the beach is only one block away.

Innkeeper(s): Elizabeth and Elizabeth Brooke. $125-350. 11 rooms with PB, 11 with FP, 10 with WP, 2 suites, 1 conference room. Breakfast, afternoon tea and snacks/refreshments included in rates. Types of meals: Full bkfst, veg bkfst and wine. Beds: QD. Cable TV, VCR, DVD, reading lamp, stereo, refrigerator, ceiling fan, snack bar, clock radio, coffeemaker, desk, hot tub/spa, fireplace, hair dryer, bathrobes, bath amenities, wireless Internet access and iron/ironing board in room. Air conditioning. Fax, copier, sauna, bicycles, library, pet board-

ing, child care, parlor games, telephone and e-mail on premises. Limited handicap access. Antiquing, art galleries, beach, bicycling, canoeing/kayaking, cross-country skiing, fishing, golf, hiking, live theater, museums, parks, shopping, tennis, water sports, wineries and whale watching nearby.

Location: Ocean community.

Certificate may be used: Nov. 1 to April 1 except Saturday Night and Holidays.

Rehoboth

Gilbert's Tree Farm B&B

30 Spring St
Rehoboth, MA 02769-2408
(508)252-6416 Fax:(508)252-6416
Internet: www.gilbertsbb.com
E-mail: jg@gilbertsbb.com

Circa 1835. This country farmhouse sits on 17 acres of woodland that includes an award-winning tree farm. Cross-country skiing and hiking are found right outside the door. If they choose to, guests can even help with the farm chores, caring for horses and gardening. Three antique-filled bedrooms share a second-floor sitting room and bathroom. There are two first-floor rooms with a working fireplace and private bath. The nearby town of Rehoboth is 360 years old.

Innkeeper(s): Jeanne Gilbert. $79-99. 5 rooms, 2 with PB, 1 conference room. Breakfast, afternoon tea and snacks/refreshments included in rates. Types of meals: Full bkfst and early coffee/tea. Beds: KQDT. Reading lamp, desk and two with fireplace in room. VCR, DVD, fax, copier, swimming, stable, library, telephone, fireplace and horse boarding only on premises. Antiquing, cross-country skiing, fishing, live theater, parks, shopping, sporting events and water sports nearby.

Location: Country.

Publicity: *Attleboro Sun Chronicle, Country, Somerset Spectator, Country Gazette and Pawtucket Times.*

"This place has become my second home. Thank you for the family atmosphere of relaxation, fun, spontaneity and natural surroundings."

Certificate may be used: Sunday through Thursday, Dec.1 through April, subject to availability.

Rockport

Emerson Inn By The Sea

One Cathedral Avenue
Rockport, MA 01966
(978)546-6321 (800)964-5550 Fax:(978)546-7043
Internet: www.emersoninnbythesea.com
E-mail: info@emersoninnbythesea.com

Circa 1846. This Greek Revival inn's namesake, Ralph Waldo Emerson, once called the place, "thy proper summer home." As it is the oldest continuously operated inn on Cape Ann, decades of travelers agree with his sentiment. The guest rooms are comfortable, yet tastefully furnished, and some boast ocean views. The grounds

include a heated swimming pool as well as landscaped gardens. Breakfast is included in the rates. Guests also can enjoy dinner at The Grand Cafe, the inn's award winning restaurant.

Innkeeper(s): Bruce & Michele Coates. $99-379. 36 rooms with PB, 2 with FP, 2 two-bedroom suites, 2 cottages, 3 conference rooms. Breakfast and afternoon tea included in rates. Types of meals: Full gourmet bkfst, early coffee/tea, snacks/refreshments, wine and gourmet dinner. Restaurant on premises. Beds: KQDT. Modem hook-up, data port, cable TV, refrigerator, clock radio, telephone, desk, hair dryer, bath amenities, wireless Internet access, iron/ironing board, fireplace, 11 with spa tubs and wireless Internet access in room. Air conditioning. TV, VCR, fax, copier, swimming, sauna, parlor games and gift shop on premises. Limited handicap access. Antiquing, art galleries, beach, bicycling, canoeing/kayaking, fishing, golf, hiking, horseback riding, live theater, museums, shopping and wineries nearby.

Location: Ocean community, waterfront.

Publicity: *Yankee Magazine Travel Guide to New England "Must-See" Destination, Arrington's Inn Traveler, The Discerning Traveler, Karen Brown's Guide to New England and TV 40 Springfield.*

"We were very impressed with every aspect of the Emerson Inn."

Certificate may be used: November-April, May and October, Sunday-Thursday only, subject to availability.

Linden Tree Inn

26 King St
Rockport, MA 01966-1444
(978)546-2494 (800)865-2122 Fax:(978)546-3297
Internet: www.lindentreeinn.com
E-mail: ltree@shore.net

Circa 1870. The breakfasts at this Victorian-style inn keep guests coming back year after year. Guests feast on home-baked treats such as scones, coffee cakes or Sunday favorites, French toast bread pudding, asparagus frittatas and spinach quiche. Each of the bedchambers features individual decor, and the innkeepers offer a formal living room and sun room for relaxation. The cupola affords a view of Mill Pond and Sandy Bay.

Innkeeper(s): Tobey and John Shepherd. $105-148. 16 rooms with PB, 1 two-bedroom suite. Breakfast, afternoon tea and Full breakfast served buffet style included in rates. Types of meals: Full bkfst, early coffee/tea, Breakfast served buffet style and afternoon tea available throught day and evening. Beds: KQT. Reading lamp, clock radio, wireless Internet access, Some with cable TV, Some with CD player and Some with ceiling fans in room. Air conditioning. TV, VCR, DVD, fax, copier, parlor games, telephone, fireplace, Carriage house has semi-efficiency kitchen and DVD player in living room on premises. Amusement parks, antiquing, art galleries, beach, bicycling, canoeing/kayaking, fishing, golf, hiking, live theater, museums, parks, shopping, tennis, water sports and wineries nearby.

Location: Ocean community.

Publicity: *Boston Globe and Boston Magazine.*

"Great coffee! Love that apple walnut bread. Thank you for making this home."

Certificate may be used: Anytime, November-March, subject to availability.

Sally Webster Inn

34 Mount Pleasant St
Rockport, MA 01966-1713
(978)546-9251 (877)546-9251
Internet: www.sallywebster.com
E-mail: sallywebsterinn@hotmail.com

Circa 1832. William Choate left this pre-Civil War home to be divided by his nine children. Sally Choate Webster, the ninth child, was to receive several first-floor rooms and the attic chamber, but ended up owning the entire home. The innkeepers have filled the gracious home with antiques and period reproductions, which complement the original pumpkin pine floors, antique door moldings and six fireplaces. Shops, restaurants, the beach and the rocky coast are all within three blocks of the inn. Whale watching, kayaking, antique shops, music festivals, island tours and museums are among the myriad of nearby attractions. In addition to these, Salem is just 15 miles away, and Boston is a 35-mile drive.

Innkeeper(s): John & Kathy Fitzgerald. $80-135. 7 rooms, 8 with PB, 2 with FP, 1 suite. Breakfast included in rates. Types of meals: Cont plus. Beds:

KQDT. Cable TV, reading lamp, clock radio, some with fireplace, bath amenities, wireless Internet access, iron/ironing board, guest phone and wireless Internet access in room. Air conditioning. DVD, copier, parlor games and telephone on premises. Antiquing, art galleries, beach, bicycling, canoeing/kayaking, fishing, golf, hiking, horseback riding, live theater, museums, parks, shopping, sporting events and water sports nearby.

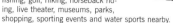

Location: Ocean community.

"All that a bed and breakfast should be."

Certificate may be used: Sunday-Friday, Nov. 15-March, excluding holidays.

Seven South Street Inn

Seven South Street Inn
Rockport, MA 01966-1799
(978)546-6708 (888)284-2730
Internet: www.sevensouthstreetinn.com
E-mail: theinn@sevensouth.net

Circa 1766. Relax in the friendly and gracious atmosphere of this family-owned inn, open year-round. The 1766 Colonial with antiques and reproductions was recently renovated to provide a warm haven of peace and privacy. Gather in the fireside living room, library or sitting room to watch a movie, play games or chat. An outdoor deck is surrounded by colorful, well-kept gardens. Guest bedrooms, a two-room suite and an efficiency suite are inviting accommodations for vacations or extended stays. Enjoy fine linens, towels and robes. Two gourmet breakfast seatings are offered each morning for well-presented, elegant dining that tastes as great as it looks. Swim in the seasonal pool, or ride a bike to explore the scenic area. Make whale watching reservations and visit the local Circles Day Spa.

Innkeeper(s): Debbie & Nick Benn. $79-179. 8 rooms with PB, 1 two-bedroom suite. Breakfast and snacks/refreshments included in rates. Types of meals: Full gourmet bkfst, veg bkfst and early coffee/tea. Beds: QDT. Data port, cable TV, VCR, DVD, reading lamp, stereo, refrigerator, clock radio, telephone, desk, hair dryer, bathrobes, bath amenities, wireless Internet access and iron/ironing board in room. Air conditioning. Swimming, bicycles, library, parlor games and laundry facility on premises. Antiquing, art galleries, beach, bicycling, canoeing/kayaking, cross-country skiing, fishing, golf, hiking, horseback riding, live theater, museums, parks, shopping, tennis, water sports and Whale Watching nearby.

Location: Ocean community.

Certificate may be used: Oct. 1 through May 20, subject to availability.

The Inn on Cove Hill

37 Mount Pleasant St
Rockport, MA 01966-1727
(978)546-2701 (888)546-2701 Fax:(978)546-1095
Internet: www.innoncovehill.com
E-mail: Betsy25@verizon.net

Circa 1771. Pirate gold found at Gully Point paid for this Georgian Federal-style house. A white picket fence and granite walkway welcome guests. Inside, an exquisitely crafted spiral staircase, random-width, pumpkin-pine floors and hand-forged hinges display the original artisan's handiwork. Furnishings include family heirlooms, four-poster canopy beds, and paintings by area artists. Muffin Du Jour is baked fresh each day by Betsy. Take a train to Boston or walk nearby and enjoy whale watching, fishing the local waters, or simply exploring the antique shops and village streets.

Innkeeper(s): Betsy Eck. $110-165. 6 rooms with PB, 1 two-bedroom suite.

Breakfast included in rates. Types of meals: Cont plus and early coffee/tea. Beds: QDT. Cable TV and reading lamp in room. Central air. TV, library, parlor games, telephone and fireplace on premises. Antiquing, art galleries, beach, bicycling, canoeing/kayaking, fishing, golf, hiking, horseback riding, live theater, museums, parks, shopping, tennis, water sports, wineries, state park, castle and train to Boston nearby.

Location: Ocean community.

Certificate may be used: Anytime, November-April, subject to availability.

Rowe

Maple House Bed & Breakfast

51 Middletown Hill Rd
Rowe, MA 01367-9702
(413)339-0107
Internet: www.maplehousebb.com
E-mail: info@maplehousebb.com

Circa 1784. Sitting on a hilltop in the Berkshires, this 200-year-old Colonial homestead farm is also known as The House on the Hill with a View of Yesteryear. Twenty scenic acres provide an assortment of activities. Hike, cross-country ski, nap on a hammock or feed the animals. Relax in the solarium by the brick fireplace. Recently renovated guest bedrooms and a suite feature the original hand-hewn beams and knotty pine flooring with antique furnishings and colorful quilts. Savor a hearty, home-grown and homemade breakfast with choices of baked goods, fruited pancakes, Maple House Granola, fresh egg dishes and much more. Lunch and dinner are available by request for groups of 8 or more. Walk or bike to Rowe Town Forest and play tennis, volleyball or basketball. Swim, fish or canoe at Pelham Lake Park.

Innkeeper(s): Rebecca & Michael Bradley. $70-100. 5 rooms, 3 with PB, 1 suite, 2 conference rooms. Breakfast, afternoon tea and snacks/refreshments included in rates. Types of meals: Country bkfst, veg bkfst, early coffee/tea, gourmet lunch, picnic lunch and gourmet dinner. Beds: KQDT. Modem hookup, reading lamp, clock radio, desk and window fan in room. TV, swimming, bicycles, tennis, library, child care, parlor games, telephone, fireplace, petting farm, snow shoes, hiking and cross-country skiing on premises. Antiquing, art galleries, beach, bicycling, canoeing/kayaking, cross-country skiing, downhill skiing, fishing, hiking, horseback riding, live theater, museums, parks, shopping, tennis and wineries nearby.

Location: Country, mountains.

Publicity: *The Sunday Republican, West County News, Rowe Goal Post and Shelburne Falls Business Association.*

Certificate may be used: Sunday through Thursday anytime.

Salem

Inn on Washington Square

53 Washington Sq
Salem, MA 01970
(978)741-4997
Internet: washingtonsquareinn.com
E-mail: debd731@aol.com

Circa 1850. Overlooking the other historical homes surrounding Salem Common, this Greek Revival house has many original details including wood mouldings and windows. Offering privacy for romance and relaxation, deluxe guest bedrooms feature four-poster or canopy beds, candles, Jacuzzi tubs, a video library for in-room VCRs and one with a fireplace. A breakfast basket of baked goods is delivered to the door. Hot beverages can be made in the personal coffeemakers, or freshly brewed coffee is available in the inn's main sitting area. Perennial gardens and a small koi pond grace the grounds.

Innkeeper(s): Deb D'Alessandro. $100-225. 3 rooms with PB, 1 with FP. Breakfast included in rates. Types of meals: Cont, early coffee/tea and snacks/refreshments. Beds: KQ. Cable TV, VCR, reading lamp, refrigerator, clock radio and coffeemaker in room. Air conditioning. Antiquing, art galleries, beach, fishing, golf, live theater, museums, parks and shopping nearby.

Location: City, ocean community.

Certificate may be used: Monday-Thursday, Nov. 15-May 1.

The Salem Inn

7 Summer St
Salem, MA 01970-3315
(978)741-0680 (800)446-2995 Fax:(978)744-8924
Internet: www.saleminnma.com
E-mail: reservations@saleminnma.com

Circa 1834. Located in the heart of one of America's oldest cities, the inn's 41 individually decorated guest rooms feature an array of amenities such as antiques, Jacuzzi baths, fireplaces and canopy beds. Comfortable and spacious one-bedroom family suites with kitchenettes are available. A complimentary continental breakfast is offered. Nearby are fine restaurants, shops, museums, Pickering Wharf and whale watching boats for cruises.

Innkeeper(s): Melinda Contino. $119-295. 40 rooms with PB, 18 with FP, 11 suites. Breakfast included in rates. Types of meals: Cont plus. Beds: KQT. Cable TV, reading lamp, refrigerator, clock radio, telephone, coffeemaker, desk, hot tub/spa and fireplace in room. Air conditioning. Fax on premises. Antiquing, art galleries, beach, bicycling, canoeing/kayaking, fishing, live theater, museums, parks, shopping, sporting events and water sports nearby.

Location: City.

Publicity: *New York Times, Boston Sunday Globe and Country Living Magazine.*

Certificate may be used: Anytime, at the last minute based on projected availability.

Sheffield

Birch Hill Bed & Breakfast

254 S Undermountain Rd
Sheffield, MA 01257-9639
(413)229-2143 (800)359-3969 Fax:(413)229-3405
Internet: birchhillbb.com
E-mail: info@birchhillbb.com

Circa 1780. A slice of history is felt at this Colonial home that was built during the American Revolution. Graciously situated on 20 scenic acres in the Berkshires, it is adjacent to the Appalachian Trail. The Chestnut Room has a fantastic view and  invites gathering to play the piano or games in front of the fire, listening to a CD or watching TV. Guest bedrooms and suites offer total relaxation. Some feature sitting areas and fireplaces. Creative, mouth-watering breakfasts begin a day of serendipity. Swim in the pool, try croquet and kayak or canoe in the lake across the street. Bicycles are available to explore the local area.

Innkeeper(s): Wendy & Michael Advocate. $125-250. 7 rooms, 5 with PB, 3 with FP, 1 suite, 1 conference room. Breakfast and afternoon tea included in rates. Types of meals: Full gourmet bkfst, veg bkfst and early coffee/tea. Beds: KDT. Reading lamp, CD player, refrigerator, clock radio and fireplace in room. Central air. TV, VCR, fax, copier, swimming, bicycles, library, child care, parlor games, telephone and fireplace on premises. Amusement parks, antiquing, art galleries, beach, bicycling, canoeing/kayaking, cross-country skiing, downhill skiing, fishing, golf, hiking, horseback riding, live theater, museums, parks, shopping, tennis, water sports, skeet shooting and trap shooting nearby.

Location: Country, mountains.

"My experience at your B&B was among the most pleasant I've ever experienced, from the moment I walked in to hear classical music. It was all divine. I can't wait to come back!"

Certificate may be used: Anytime, subject to availability, Sunday-Thursday, excluding July and August.

Staveleigh House

59 Main St
Sheffield, MA 01257-9701
(413)229-2129 Fax:413-528-9888
Internet: www.staveleigh.com
E-mail: innkeeper@staveleigh.com

Circa 1821. The Reverend Bradford, minister of Old Parish Congregational Church, the oldest church in the Berkshires, built this home for his family. Afternoon tea is served and the inn is especially favored for its splendid breakfast and gracious hospitality. Located next to the town green, the house is in a historic district in the midst of several fine antique shops. It is also near Tanglewood, skiing and all Berkshire attractions.

Innkeeper(s): Ali A. Winston. $115-160. 7 rooms, 5 with PB. Breakfast and afternoon tea included in rates. Types of meals: Full bkfst and early coffee/tea. Beds: KQDT. Reading lamp, ceiling fan, clock radio, turn-down service and desk in room. Air conditioning. Telephone, fireplace and terrycloth bath robes on premises. Handicap access. Antiquing, cross-country skiing, downhill skiing, fishing, live theater, parks, shopping, water sports and art galleries nearby.

Location: Village, historic district.

Publicity: *Los Angeles Times, Boston Globe and House and Garden Magazine.*

"The hospitality at Staveleigh House is deeper and more thoughtful than any you will find elsewhere. — House & Gardens Magazine"

Certificate may be used: Sunday-Thursday, November-March, exclude holidays.

South Egremont

Weathervane Inn

17 Main Street
South Egremont, MA 01258
(413)528-9580 (800)528-9580 Fax:(413)528-1713
Internet: www.weathervaneinn.com
E-mail: innkeeper@weathervaneinn.com

Circa 1785. The original post-and-beam New England farmhouse with its beehive oven was added on to throughout its history. It has been restored to combine today's modern amenities with the charm of the inn's historic past. The inn's historic architectural features include broad plank floors, tree trunk supports and granite columns. A full breakfast is offered every morning.

Innkeeper(s): Maxine & Jeffrey Lome. $95-275. 10 rooms, 8 with PB, 2 two-bedroom suites. Breakfast included in rates. Types of meals: Country bkfst, afternoon tea, snacks/refreshments and wine. Beds: KQDT. Modem hook-up, data port, reading lamp, clock radio and telephone in room. Air conditioning. TV, VCR, fax, copier, swimming, library, child care, parlor games and fireplace on premises. Limited handicap access. Antiquing, art galleries, bicycling, cross-country skiing, downhill skiing, fishing, golf, hiking, horseback riding, live theater, museums, parks, shopping, sporting events, water sports and wineries nearby.

Location: Mountains.

Publicity: *New York Times, Berkshire Eagle, Boston Herald, Newsday and Daily News.*

Certificate may be used: Nov.1-March 31, excluding holidays and holiday periods, subject to availability.

Springfield

Lathrop House Bed and Breakfast

188 Sumner Avenue
Springfield, MA 01108
(413)374-2896 Fax:(413)736-6414
Internet: dianamarahenry.com/lathrop
E-mail: dmh@dianamarahenry.com

Circa 1899. Located in the midst of the historic residential district of Forest Park Heights, this 1899 Victorian was known as "The Mansion House." The recently restored Lathrop House Bed and Breakfast features original carved mantels, wood paneling, stained glass and a formal staircase. Swing on a columned porch overlooking the wide lawn. Relax on the veranda, smell the scent of the rose garden or picnic under the shade trees in the back yard. Elegant guest bedrooms with high-ceilings and king beds are accented with contemporary art, in-room libraries, wireless Internet access, designer bathrooms with showers and clawfoot tubs. A generous continental breakfast is provided and available at any time.

Innkeeper(s): Diana Henry. $80-150. 2 rooms, 1 two-bedroom suite. Breakfast and snacks/refreshments included in rates. Types of meals: Cont plus and early coffee/tea. Beds: KQT. Cable TV, VCR, reading lamp, CD player, refrigerator, ceiling fan, snack bar, clock radio, coffeemaker, turn-down service, desk, hair dryer, wireless Internet access and iron/ironing board in room. Air conditioning. Fax, copier, library, parlor games, laundry facility and wireless Internet access on premises. Amusement parks, antiquing, art galleries, beach, bicycling, canoeing/kayaking, fishing, golf, hiking, horseback riding, live theater, museums, parks, shopping, tennis, water sports, wineries, Basketball Hall of Fame, Big E (New England Regional Fair in September), Six Flags New England, Eric Carle Museum of Picture Book Art, National Yiddish Book Center, Yankee Candle Factory and river rides nearby.

Location: City. Historic residential district, Forest Park Heights.

Publicity: *The Springfield Republican, The Jewish Ledger, The Northampton Gazette and Peminder Publications.*

Certificate may be used: Anytime, November-April, subject to availability.

Stockbridge

Historic Merrell Inn

1565 Pleasant St, Rt 102
Stockbridge, MA 01260
(413)243-1794 (800)243-1794 Fax:(413)243-2669
Internet: www.merrell-inn.com
E-mail: info@merrell-inn.com

Circa 1794. This elegant stagecoach inn was carefully preserved under supervision of the Society for the Preservation of New England Antiquities. Architectural drawings of Merrell Inn have been preserved by the Library of Congress. Eight fireplaces in the inn include two with original beehive and warming ovens. An antique circular birdcage bar serves as a check-in desk. Comfortable rooms feature canopy and four-poster beds with Hepplewhite and Sheraton-style antiques. The Riverview Suite is tucked on the back wing of the building and has a private porch which overlooks the Housatonic River.

Innkeeper(s): George Crockett. $99-285. 10 rooms with PB, 4 with FP. Breakfast included in rates. Types of meals: Full bkfst. Beds: KQT. Reading lamp, clock radio, telephone, desk, bathrobes, some with fireplaces and all have wireless web access in room. Air conditioning. Fax, parlor games and fireplace on premises. Antiquing, cross-country skiing, fishing, hiking, live theater, parks, shopping, Tanglewood Music Festival and Norman Rockwell Museum nearby.

Publicity: *Americana, Country Living, New York Times, Boston Globe, Country Accents, Travel Holiday and USA Today.*

"We couldn't have chosen a more delightful place to stay in the Berkshires. Everything was wonderful. We especially loved the grounds and the gazebo by the river."

Certificate may be used: November-April, Except Holiday Weekends.

Sturbridge

Sturbridge Country Inn

530 Main Street
Sturbridge, MA 01566-0060
(508)347-5503 Fax:(508)347-5319
Internet: www.sturbridgecountryinn.com
E-mail: info@sturbridgecountryinn.com

Circa 1840. Shaded by an old silver maple, this classic Greek Revival house boasts a two-story columned entrance. The attached carriage house now serves as the parlor and displays

the original post-and-
beam construction and
exposed rafters. All
guest rooms have indi-
vidual fireplaces and
whirlpool tubs and
include breakfast with

champagne. They are appointed gracefully in colonial style furnishings, including queen-size and four-posters. A patio and
gazebo are favorite summertime retreats. A five-star restaurant
and outdoor heated pool are also on the premesis.

Innkeeper(s): Patricia Affenito. $99-189. 15 rooms with PB, 15 with FP, 15 with WP, 2 suites, 1 conference room. Breakfast included in rates. Types of meals: Cont, early coffee/tea and room service. Restaurant on premises. Beds: KQ. Cable TV, VCR, reading lamp, refrigerator, ceiling fan, clock radio, tele-phone, desk, hot tub/spa, fireplace, hair dryer and iron/ironing board in room. Air conditioning. TV, fax, copier, spa, swimming, restaurant and luxury suites on premises. Antiquing, cross-country skiing, downhill skiing, fishing, live the-ater, parks, shopping, water sports, casinos and old Sturbridge Village nearby.

Location: Rural.

Publicity: *Southbridge Evening News and Worcester Telegram & Gazette.*

"Very cozy and extremely relaxing. The service and attention to detail were outstanding."

Certificate may be used: Anytime, subject to availability in Superior rooms only; Anytime, last minute-based on availability.

Sudbury

Arabian Horse Inn

277 Old Sudbury Rd
Sudbury, MA 01776-1842
(978)443-7400 (800)272-2426 Fax:(978)443-0234
Internet: www.arabianhorseinn.com
E-mail: info@arabianhorseinn.com

Circa 1880. Secluded on nine wooded acres with a horse farm, this 1880 Queen Anne Victorian offers the ultimate in privacy and romance. This inn is the perfect retreat to celebrate birth-days, anniversaries or other special occasions. The three-room Tanah Suite with a canopy bed, two-person Jacuzzi and fire-

place is a honeymoon favorite. A stay in the two-room Orlandra Suite featuring a draped four-poster bed, two-person Jacuzzi and huge balcony is also a popular pleaser. A complete breakfast is made at a flexible time to suit every taste with deli-cious entrees and accompaniments. Enjoy the meal in the Ye Old Worlde Café, on the veranda under the pergola or in-room. Lunch or dinner can be arranged with advance reservation. Tours are gladly given of the original four-story barn with post and beam ceiling and huge cupola.

Innkeeper(s): Joan & Richard Beers. $79-319. 20 rooms, 9 with PB, 1 with FP, 3 with WP, 3 total suites, including 1 two-bedroom suite and 1 three-bed-room suite, 1 cottage, 3 guest houses, 1 conference room. Breakfast, after-noon tea and snacks/refreshments included in rates. Types of meals: Full gourmet bkfst, veg bkfst, Sun. brunch, early coffee/tea, gourmet lunch, picnic lunch, hors d'oeuvres, wine, gourmet dinner, room service and All meals other than Breakfast must be booked during your reservation. Beds: KDT. Modem hook-up, cable TV, VCR, reading lamp, stereo, refrigerator, ceiling fan, clock radio, telephone, coffeemaker, desk, some with fireplace, hair dryer, bathrobes, bath amenities, wireless Internet access, iron/ironing board and Please check with innkeeper for special requirements when making reservation in room. Air conditioning. Fax, copier, spa, stable, library, pet boarding, parlor games and laundry facility on premises. Amusement parks, antiquing, art galleries, beach, bicycling, canoeing/kayaking, cross-country skiing, downhill skiing, fishing, golf, hiking, horseback riding, live theater, museums, parks, shopping, sporting events, tennis, water sports and wineries nearby.

Location: Country. Acton.

Certificate may be used: Anytime, subject to availability.

Hunt House Inn

330 Boston Post Rd.
Sudbury, MA 01776
(978)440-9525 Fax:(978)440-9082
Internet: www.hunthouseinn.com
E-mail: mollyhunthouse@ix.netcom.com

Circa 1850. Well-suited as a bed and breakfast, this early American farmhouse and barn is located in the King Philip Historic District. Fully restored, it is furnished with period antiques and boasts an eclectic decor. The air-conditioned guest bedrooms feature adjoining rooms. The Executive Suite includes a sitting area and separate entrance. Breakfast is a delight every morning, offering combinations of warm muffins, omelettes and egg dishes, fresh fruit, homemade waffles with Vermont maple syrup, sausages and an assortment of vegetarian entrees. Dietary restrictions are accommodated with ease. Visit the historic sites of nearby Boston.

Innkeeper(s): Molly Davidson. $89-99. 3 rooms with PB, 2 two-bedroom suites, 1 conference room. Breakfast, afternoon tea and snacks/refreshments included in rates. Types of meals: Full bkfst, veg bkfst and early coffee/tea. Beds: QT. Modem hook-up, TV, reading lamp, snack bar, clock radio, tele-phone, hair dryer and wireless Internet access in room. Air conditioning. VCR, fax and laundry facility on premises. Antiquing, art galleries, beach, canoeing/kayaking, golf, hiking, live theater, museums, parks, shopping, sporting events, tennis and wineries nearby.

Location: City. In 1638 farming and mill community, near historical Concord, Boston.

Certificate may be used: Monday-Thursday, non holiday.

Vineyard Haven

Hanover House at Twin Oaks

28 Edgartown Rd
Vineyard Haven, MA 02568
(508)693-1066 (800)339-1066 Fax:(508)696-6099
Internet: www.twinoaksinn.net
E-mail: innkeeper@twinoaksinn.net

Circa 1906. When visiting Martha's Vineyard, Twin Oaks offers two pleasurable places to choose from that are within walking distance to the beach, ferry or downtown shops. Stay at the award-winning Clark House, a classic bed & breakfast or the Hanover House, an elegant three-diamond country inn just next door. Gather on one of the porches, the large backyard or private brick patio and gazebo. Complimentary bikes and high-speed Internet access are available on a first come first serve basis. Each of the comfortable guest bedrooms offer Internet access. Join the "breakfast party" for a bountiful continental-plus morning meal.

Innkeeper(s): Steve and Judy Perlman. $99-285. 15 rooms. Breakfast included in rates. Types of meals: Cont plus. Beds: KQD. Cable TV, reading lamp, refrigerator, ceiling fan and two with fireplace in room. Air conditioning. Fax, copier, parlor games and telephone on premises. Antiquing, art galleries, beach, bicycling, canoeing/kayaking, fishing, golf, hiking, horseback riding, live theater, museums, parks, shopping, tennis, water sports and wineries nearby.

Location: Ocean community.

Publicity: *New York Times*.

Certificate may be used: Anytime, subject to availability, except shoulder and summer weekends. Cannot combine with any other discount or program.

Wareham

Mulberry B&B

257 High St
Wareham, MA 02571-1407
(508)295-0684 (866)295-0684
Internet: www.virtualcities.com/ons/ma/z/maza801.htm
E-mail: mulberry257@aol.com

Circa 1847. This former blacksmith's house is in the historic district of town and has been featured on the local garden club house tour. Frances, a former school teacher, has decorated the guest rooms in a country style with antiques. A deck, shaded by a tall mulberry tree, looks out to the back garden. There are two resident cats on the premises.

Innkeeper(s): Frances Murphy. $60-199. 3 rooms. Breakfast included in rates. Types of meals: Full bkfst and afternoon tea. Beds: KDT. TV, reading lamp, clock radio and turn-down service in room. Air conditioning. VCR, parlor games and telephone on premises. Antiquing, cross-country skiing, fishing, live theater, parks, shopping, sporting events, water sports and whale watching nearby.

Location: Atlantic Ocean.

Publicity: *Brockton Enterprise and Wareham Courier*.

"Our room was pleasant and I loved the cranberry satin sheets."

Certificate may be used: Sunday through Thursday, Sept. 15-May 15, Anytime, Last Minute-Based on Availability, no holidays.

Wellfleet

Stone Lion Inn

130 Commercial Street
Wellfleet, MA 02667
(508)349-9565 Fax:(508)349-9697
Internet: www.stonelioncapecod.com
E-mail: info@stonelioncapecod.com

Circa 1871. Built by a sea captain in the 1800s, this French Second Empire Victorian recently has been renovated and redecorated to offer modern indulgences with an old-fashioned charm. Feel right at home in the comfortable living room with games, puzzles, VCR and videotapes. A large selection of books on local history as well as fiction and non-fiction are available to read. Guest bedrooms are named for Brooklyn neighborhoods where the innkeepers once lived or worked. The Clinton Hill boasts a clawfoot tub and shower and a private deck. A hearty breakfast buffet served in the dining room is sure to please. Vegetarian diets are graciously accommodated with advance notice. An apartment and a cottage provide more space and privacy. The grounds feature fish ponds, fountains, a wisteria-covered gazebo and a hammock.

Innkeeper(s): Janet Lowenstein & Adam Levinson. $90-180. 4 rooms with PB, 1 cottage. Breakfast included in rates. Types of meals: Country bkfst. Beds: Q. Reading lamp, refrigerator, ceiling fan, clock radio, hair dryer and wireless Internet access in room. Air conditioning. TV, VCR, DVD, library, parlor games, telephone and gift shop on premises. Antiquing, art galleries, beach, bicycling, canoeing/kayaking, fishing, golf, hiking, live theater, parks, shopping, tennis, water sports, Whale watches, Seal watches, Nature trails, Charter fishing, Sailing, Kite surfing and Live music nearby.

Location: Ocean community.

Publicity: *Conde Nast Traveler (May 2002), Cape Cod Traveler, Boston Globe (July 17, 2005), The Week magazine (August 2005) and Fine Living Network 'Ten Best Vacation Spots in US'.*

Certificate may be used: April and October, Sunday-Thursday, November-March, subject to availability, holidays excluded.

The Inn at Duck Creeke

70 Main St, PO Box 364
Wellfleet, MA 02667-0364
(508)349-9333
Internet: www.innatduckcreeke.com
E-mail: info@innatduckcreeke.com

Circa 1815. The five-acre site of this sea captain's house features both a salt-water marsh and a duck pond. The Saltworks house and the main house are appointed in an old-fashioned style with antiques, and the rooms are comfortable and cozy. Some have views of the nearby salt marsh or the pond. The inn is favored for its two restaurants; Sweet Seasons and the Tavern Room. The latter is popular for its jazz performances.

Innkeeper(s): Bob Morrill & Judy Pihl. $85-135. 25 rooms, 18 with PB. Breakfast included in rates. Types of meals: Cont and dinner. Restaurant on premises. Beds: QDT. Reading lamp, ceiling fan, Eight rooms with air conditioning and the others with ceiling or oscillating fans in room. Fax, parlor games, telephone and fireplace on premises. Antiquing, art galleries, beach, canoeing/kayaking, fishing, golf, hiking, live theater, parks, shopping, tennis, water sports, wineries, National Seashore, Audubon Sanctuary, Bike trails, Marconi site, Whale watching, Wellfleet Historical Museum and Drive-In theater nearby.

Location: Ocean community. Close to harbor, beaches.

Publicity: *Italian Vogue, Travel & Leisure, Cape Cod Life, Providence Journal, New York Times, Provincetown, Conde Nast Traveler, British Vogue and Bon a Parte (Denmark).*

"Duck Creeke will always be our favorite stay!"

Certificate may be used: May 1-June 15, Sunday-Thursday.

West Barnstable

Honeysuckle Hill B&B

591 Main St.
West Barnstable, MA 02668
(508)362-8418 (866)444-5522 Fax:(508)362-8386
Internet: www.honeysucklehill.com
E-mail: stay@honeysucklehill.com

Circa 1810. This Queen Anne Victorian, which is listed in the National Register, is set on a picturesque acre with gardens. The interior is decorated with antiques and white wicker furnishings. The hearty breakfasts include items such as Eggs Benedict, homemade crepes, homemade granola, fresh fruit and cranberry-orange nut muffins. Nearby are the dunes of Sandy Neck Beach. Hyannis is 10 minutes away.

Innkeeper(s): Freddy & Ruth Riley. $134-254. 5 rooms, 4 with PB, 1 two-bedroom suite. Breakfast, snacks/refreshments and wine included in rates. Types of meals: Full gourmet bkfst, Sun. brunch, early coffee/tea and Afternoon tea by request. Beds: KQD. Cable TV, DVD, reading lamp, ceiling fan, clock radio, coffeemaker, desk, hair dryer, bathrobes, bath amenities, wireless Internet access, iron/ironing board, feather beds, fresh flowers, terry cloth robes and hairdryers in room. Air conditioning. Fax, copier, spa, bicycles, library, parlor games, telephone, fireplace, beach towels, chairs and umbrellas, guest refrigerator, fish pond, porch, gardens, barbecue and wireless Internet access on premises. Antiquing, art galleries, beach, bicycling, canoeing/kayaking, fishing, golf, hiking, horseback riding, live theater, museums, parks, shopping, tennis, water sports, wineries, ferries and whale watching nearby.

Location: Ocean community. Cape Cod.

Publicity: *Atlanta Constitution, Saint Louis Journal, Prime Time, Cape Cod Travel Guide, Cape Cod Life, Secondhome, Boston Globe, Triple AAA Travel Guide and Yankee Magazine Travel Guide.*

"The charm, beauty, service and warmth shown to guests are impressive, but the food overwhelms. Breakfasts were divine! — Judy Kaplan, St. Louis Journal"

Certificate may be used: October-May; Monday, Tuesday, Wednesday; subject to availabilty.

Westborough

The Sleigh Maker Inn ~ Bed and Breakfast

87 West Main St
Westborough, MA 01581
(508)836-5546 (877)836-5545 Fax:(508)836-8136
Internet: www.sleighmakerinn.com
E-mail: deborah@sleighmakerinn.com

Circa 1893. Located in the heart of New England in Westborough, Massachusetts this three-story Eastlake Victorian bed and breakfast is in the Boston Metro-West area. It was built as a Christmas gift in 1893 by Forrest W. Forbes, a prominent sleigh maker, for his wife. The company became the largest local

manufacturer and America's oldest. Relax on the wraparound porch with refreshments. Snacks are available any time. The needs of both business and leisure travelers are provided for at this inn. Stay in a themed guest bedroom accented with antiques. One boasts a Jacuzzi tub for two. Gather in the formal dining room for a home-cooked breakfast of classic entrees and accompaniments. Hop on a bicycle to explore the scenic area.

Innkeeper(s): Deborah & James Bergeron. $90-135. 3 rooms with PB, 1 with HT, 1 with WP. Breakfast, snacks/refreshments and wine included in rates. Types of meals: Country bkfst, veg bkfst and early coffee/tea. Beds: Q. TV, reading lamp, clock radio, telephone, desk, hair dryer, bathrobes, bath amenities, wireless Internet access and iron/ironing board in room. Air conditioning. Fax, bicycles and parlor games on premises. Antiquing, art galleries, bicycling, cross-country skiing, fishing, hiking, horseback riding, live theater, museums, parks and wineries nearby.

Location: City, country.

Certificate may be used: June, September, October; certificate may be redeemed at innkeepers discretion or last minute reservations 7 days or less prior to check-in date. Subject to availability. Certificate must be mentioned when calling for availability. For online reservations, please mention in guest notes. Only 1 certificate allowed per participant for any 6-month time period.

Yarmouth Port

Olde Captain's Inn on The Cape

101 Main St Rt 6A
Yarmouth Port, MA 02675-1709
(508)362-4496 (888)407-7161
Internet: www.oldecaptainsinn.com
E-mail: general@oldecaptainsinn.com

Circa 1812. Located in the historic district and on Captain's Mile, this house is in the National Register. It is decorated in a traditional style, with coordinated wallpapers and carpets, and there are two suites that include kitchens and living rooms. Apple trees, blackberries and raspberries grow on the acre of grounds and often contribute to the breakfast menus. There is a summer veranda overlooking the property. Good restaurants are within walking distance.

Innkeeper(s): Sven Tilly. $60-120. 3 rooms, 1 with PB, 2 suites. Breakfast included in rates. Types of meals: Cont plus. Beds: QD. Cable TV, reading lamp and clock radio in room. TV on premises. Antiquing, fishing, live theater, shopping, sporting events and water sports nearby.

Location: Historic district.

Certificate may be used: Anytime, Nov. 1-June 1. Sunday through Thursday, June 1-Nov. 1. Excludes holidays.

One Centre Street Inn

1 Center St
Yarmouth Port, MA 02675-1342
(508)362-9951 (866)362-9951
Internet: www.onecentrestreetinn.com
E-mail: sales@onecentrestreetinn.com

Circa 1824. Originally a church parsonage in the 1800s, this Greek Revival-style inn is listed in the National Register of Historic Places. Just one mile from Cape Cod Bay, the inn has an understated elegance that enhances the comfort and conveniences offered, including Cable TV, VCR, CD clock radio, refrigerators in select rooms, and services and  amenities for business guests. After a restful night's sleep, indulge in a continental breakfast accompanied by locally roasted gourmet coffee from our own Centre Street Coffee House on the screened porch, garden patios or in the sun-filled dining room while listening to bubbling ponds and soft classical music. Take a bike ride into town or a short stroll to the long boardwalk at Gray's Beach.

Innkeeper(s): Mary Singleton. $125-175. 5 rooms, 4 with PB, 1 with FP, 1 suite. Breakfast included in rates. Types of meals: Full gourmet bkfst, early coffee/tea, afternoon tea and snacks/refreshments. Beds: KQDT. Cable TV, VCR, CD player, refrigerator, clock radio, some with fireplace, hair dryer, bath amenities, wireless Internet access, iron/ironing board and CD Clock Radio in room. Air conditioning. Parlor games, telephone and WiFi on premises. Antiquing, art galleries, beach, bicycling, canoeing/kayaking, fishing, golf, hiking, horseback riding, live theater, museums, parks, shopping, tennis, water sports and wineries nearby.

Location: Waterfront. Cape Cod, historic village.

Certificate may be used: Sept. 1-May 31, subject to availability.

Michigan

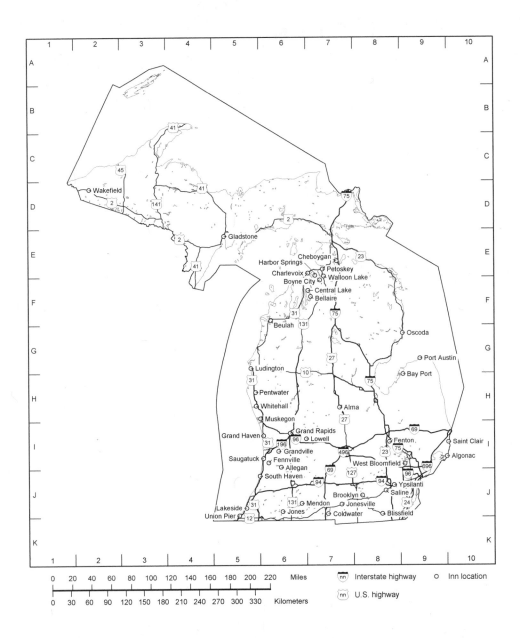

0   20 40 60 80 100 120 140 160 180 200 220   Miles

0   30 60 90 120 150 180 210 240 270 300 330   Kilometers

(nn) Interstate highway   o Inn location

(nn) U.S. highway

Allegan

Castle In The Country Bed and Breakfast

340 M 40 S
Allegan, MI 49010-9609
(269)673-8054 (888)673-8054
Internet: www.castleinthecountry.com
E-mail: info@castleinthecountry.com

Circa 1906. Reflecting its nickname and castle-like appearance, a three-story turret and wide wraparound porch accent this 1906 Queen Anne Victorian adorning five acres of scenic countryside. Gather in one of the several common rooms or sitting areas. A Guest Refreshment Center has a coffee pot and refrigerator. Romantic guest bedrooms and a suite feature fresh flowers, candles, terry robes, handmade bath products, a video library and VCR. Several rooms include whirlpool tubs, fireplaces and CD players. Breakfast is specially prepared and served on fine china and vintage crystal. Innkeepers Herb and Ruth enjoy providing personalized service that ensures a pleasant stay. Ask for an Adventure Map, a helpful tool to enjoy local activities and sites. Many special packages are regularly offered.

Innkeeper(s): Herb & Ruth Boven. $85-205. 10 rooms, 5 with PB, 8 with FP, 7 with WP, 1 two-bedroom suite, 5 conference rooms. Breakfast included in rates. Types of meals: Full gourmet bkfst, veg bkfst, early coffee/tea, picnic lunch, afternoon tea, snacks/refreshments, wine, dinner and room service. Beds: KQT. Modem hook-up, data port, TV, VCR, reading lamp, stereo, refrigerator, ceiling fan, snack bar, clock radio, turn-down service, desk, hot tub/spa, fireplace, antiques, high-quality linens and fabrics, two-person whirlpool tubs plus separate shower, some two-person tiled showers, full gourmet breakfast served daily, with package served in-room, robes, VHS library, CD library, massage by arrangement, handmade soaps and toiletries in room. Central air. DVD, fax, copier, spa, library, parlor games, telephone, gift shop, 65 wooded acres with groomed trails, private lake and ponds, gardens, firepit, wraparound porch, patio, decks, gazebo, screened porch w/dock at private lake and snowshoes bicycles available on premises. Limited handicap access. Antiquing, art galleries, beach, bicycling, canoeing/kayaking, cross-country skiing, downhill skiing, fishing, golf, hiking, horseback riding, live theater, museums, parks, shopping, sporting events, tennis, water sports and wineries nearby.

Location: Country, waterfront.

Publicity: *Arrington's B&B Journal Book of Lists 2002, on the cover of Arrington's B&B Journal 2000, Voted "Most Perfect Stay" 2005 and Voted "Most Romantic Hideaway in North America" 2006.*

Certificate may be used: Sunday-Thursday, Nov. 1-May 31 (excluding holidays).

Alma

Saravilla

633 N State St
Alma, MI 48801-1640
(989)463-4078
Internet: www.saravilla.com
E-mail: Ljdarrow@saravilla.com

Circa 1894. This 11,000-square-foot Dutch Colonial home with its Queen Anne influences was built as a magnificent wedding gift for lumber baron Ammi W. Wright's only surviving child, Sara. Wright spared no expense building this mansion for his daughter, and the innkeepers have spared nothing in restoring the home to its former prominence. The foyer and dining room boast imported English oak woodwork. The foyer's hand-painted canvas wallcoverings and the ballroom's embossed wallpaper come from France. The home still features original leaded-glass windows, built-in bookcases, window seats

and light fixtures. In 1993, the innkeepers added a sunroom with a hot tub that overlooks a formal garden. The full, formal breakfast includes such treats as homemade granola, freshly made coffeecakes, breads, muffins and a mix of entrees.

Innkeeper(s): Linda and Jon Darrow. $90-155. 7 rooms with PB, 3 with FP, 2 with WP, 2 conference rooms. Breakfast and snacks/refreshments included in rates. Types of meals: Full bkfst, early coffee/tea and room service. Beds: KQT. Cable TV, VCR, DVD, reading lamp, ceiling fan, clock radio, telephone, desk, some with hot tub/spa, some with fireplace, bathrobes, bath amenities, wireless Internet access, iron/ironing board and two with whirlpool tub in room. Air conditioning. Fax, spa, library, parlor games and complimentary beverages and snacks available on premises. Antiquing, bicycling, canoeing/kayaking, cross-country skiing, fishing, golf, live theater, sporting events, tennis and Soaring Eagle Casino nearby.

Location: City.

Publicity: *Midwest Living, Michigan Living, Morning Sun, Saginaw News, Sault Sunday., WCMU-TV, WCFX and WCZY.*

"I suggest we stay longer next time. We are looking forward to that visit."

Certificate may be used: Sunday-Thursday from Jan. 2 to Dec. 30, excluding holidays.

Bay Port

Sweet Dreams Inn Victorian B&B

9695 Cedar Street (Off M-25)
Bay Port, MI 48720
(989)656-9952 Fax:(989)656-9952
Internet: hometown.aol.com/sweetdreamsinn/index.html
E-mail: sweetdreamsinn@aol.com

Circa 1890. Enjoy the view of Lake Huron's Wildfowl Bay while staying at this 1890 Victorian mansion. Relax in the sunroom or by the fire in the parlor. Sip refreshments while lounging on the front wraparound porch. A small log cabin called the Doll House boasts videos, games and toys. Four landscaped acres with an outdoor grill and picnic area offer activities that include croquet, horseshoes and volleyball. Choose one of the themed guest bedrooms for a romantic getaway or families may prefer the third-floor two-bedroom Lighthouse Suite with a microwave and small refrigerator in the kitchenette. A home-cooked breakfast is served in the formal dining room. Fishing and hunting are popular and a free public boat launch is only a minute away.

Innkeeper(s): Innkeeper. $85-90. 9 rooms, 5 with PB, 1 two-bedroom suite, 1 conference room. Continental breakfast is included in room rate. Full breakfast is included on special occasions only (most weekends) to be decided by innkeeper included in rates. Beds: QD. Reading lamp, coffeemaker, turn-down service, some with fireplace, hair dryer, bath amenities, wireless Internet access and iron/ironing board in room. TV, VCR, DVD, fax, copier, bicycles, library, parlor games, telephone, gift shop, Wraparound screened-in porch, View of Lake Huron, Volleyball, Croquet, Horseshoes, Gazebo w/grill, Picnic Area, Bonfire pit, Real log cabin for children to play in, Games, Video games, Flower gardens and One minute to boat launch on premises. Antiquing, art galleries, beach, bicycling, canoeing/kayaking, cross-country skiing, fishing, golf, hiking, horseback riding, live theater, museums, parks, shopping, sporting events, tennis, water sports, wineries, A great view of Lake Huron, Sandy beaches, Miniature golf, Go carts, Bumper boats, Bird watching, Hunting on Wildfowl Bay, Jet skis, Lighthouses, Petting zoo, Giant water slide, Farmer's market, Craft & art shows, Town festivals all year long, Historical markers (one right on Cedar St.), Tip of The Thumb Heritage Water Trail, Historical Lake Huron trail (covers over 90 miles of shoreline), great for canoes, kayaks and history buffs nearby.

Location: Country, waterfront.

Publicity: *Huron Daily Tribune, Bad Axe, MI (article on B&B Grand Opening) and Bay City Times Newspaper (destinations).*

Certificate may be used: Sunday-Thursday; subject to availability, no holidays (November-February).

Bellaire

Grand Victorian Bed & Breakfast Inn

402 North Bridge Street
Bellaire, MI 49615-9591
(231)533-6111 (877)438-6111
Internet: www.grandvictorian.com
E-mail: innkeeper@grandvictorian.com

Circa 1895. Featured in Country Inns and Midwest Living magazines, this Queen Anne Victorian mansion boasts three original fireplaces, hand-carved mantels, intricate fretwork and numerous architectural details. Relax with a glass of wine

before the fire in the formal front parlor, or listen to music while playing cards and games in the back parlor. Guest bedrooms offer an eclectic mix of antique furnishings including Victorian Revival, Eastlake and French Provincial. Soak in an 1890s clawfoot tub, or enjoy the park view from a private balcony. Be pampered with an incredible stay in one of the country's most remarkable and unique inns. The gazebo is a perfect spot to while away the day, or take advantage of the area's many nearby activities.

Innkeeper(s): Ken & Linda Fedraw. $95-195. 6 rooms with PB, 4 with FP, 2 with WP. Breakfast and snacks/refreshments included in rates. Types of meals: Full gourmet bkfst. Beds: KQ. Cable TV, VCR, reading lamp, refrigerator, ceiling fan, clock radio, most with fireplace and wireless Internet access in room. Central air. DVD, fax, copier, bicycles, parlor games, telephone and gift shop on premises. Antiquing, art galleries, beach, bicycling, canoeing/kayaking, cross-country skiing, downhill skiing, fishing, golf, hiking, horseback riding, shopping, tennis, water sports, wineries, fine dining, restaurants and touring nearby.

Location: City. Northwest Lower Michigan.

Publicity: *Midwest Living, Country Inns,* featured on Nabisco Cracker/Cookie Boxes Promotion, Traverse Magazine and 2003/5 Arrington's B&B Journal Book of Lists Award—Most Elegant.

"We certainly enjoyed our visit to the Grand Victorian. It has been our pleasure to stay in B&Bs in several countries, but never one more beautiful and almost never with such genial hosts."

Certificate may be used: November 15-May 31.

Beulah

Brookside Inn

115 US Hwy 31
Beulah, MI 49617-9701
(231)882-9688 Fax:(231)882-4600
Internet: www.brooksideinn.com
E-mail: rsvp@brooksideinn.com

Circa 1939. Experience the best of romance at this inn, located near Crystal Lake. Designed for couples, each guest bedroom features a mirrored canopy waterbed or conventional mattress, a three foot deep Polynesian spa and wood-burning stove. Some deluxe rooms boast a loft and offer a larger spa as well as combinations of a sauna, steam bath and French suntanning solarium. Meals include breakfast and dinner, served on the outdoor deck or by the fireplace. Expect fresh flowers, fine wine and great food. The seven-acre grounds showcase a bridge to a flower and herb garden.

Innkeeper(s): Pam & Kirk Lorenz. $235-290. 31 rooms with PB, 31 with FP, 3 conference rooms. Breakfast and dinner included in rates. Types of meals: Full gourmet bkfst, early coffee/tea, gourmet lunch, picnic lunch and snacks/refreshments. Restaurant on premises. Beds: K. Cable TV, VCR, reading lamp, ceiling fan, hot tub/spa, some with sauna steam and tanning bed in room. Air conditioning. Fax, copier, spa, sauna, telephone and fireplace on premises. Handicap access. Downhill skiing, fishing, golf, live theater, parks, sporting events, tennis, water sports, snowmobiling, ice fishing and hot air balloons nearby.

Location: Village.

Publicity: *AAA Travel, Detroit Free Press and Chicago Tribune.*

""Michigan's romantic retreat...works a spell." — Rick Sylvain, Detroit Free Press"

Certificate may be used: Sunday through Thursday, November through June. Not to be combined with any other discounts, Valentines Day 1 day before, 1 day after.

Brooklyn

Dewey Lake Manor

11811 Laird Rd
Brooklyn, MI 49230-9035
(517)467-7122 Fax:517 467 2356
Internet: www.deweylakemanor.com
E-mail: deweylk@frontiernet.net

Circa 1868. This Italianate house overlooks Dewey Lake and is situated on 18 acres in the Irish Hills. The house is furnished in a country Victorian style with antiques. An enclosed porch is a favorite spot to relax and take in the views of the lake while having breakfast. Favorite pastimes include lakeside bonfires in

the summertime and ice skating or cross-country skiing in the winter. Canoe and paddleboats are available to guests.

Innkeeper(s): Barb & Joe Phillips. $79-139. 5 rooms with PB, 5 with FP, 1 with WP, 1 conference room. Breakfast, snacks/refreshments and Certain specials have meals included included in rates. Types of meals: Country bkfst, early coffee/tea, picnic lunch and Can cater lunch & dinner for groups. Beds: Q. Cable TV, VCR, DVD, reading lamp, CD player, refrigerator, ceiling fan, snack bar, clock radio, telephone, coffeemaker, desk, some with hot tub/spa, hair dryer, bathrobes, bath amenities, iron/ironing board, one with Jacuzzi, five with VCR and one with VCR/DVD in room. Central air. Fax, copier, swimming, parlor games, fireplace, gift shop, VCR in sitting room and baby grand piano in parlor on premises. Antiquing, canoeing/kayaking, cross-country skiing, fishing, golf, hiking, horseback riding, live theater, parks, shopping, sporting events, water sports, wineries, Botanical Gardens, car shows at MIS and Civil War Reenactments nearby.

Location: Country, waterfront. Country.

Publicity: *Ann Arbor News, Jackson Citizen Patriot and Toledo Blade.*

"I came back and brought my friends. It was wonderful."

Certificate may be used: November through April, subject to availability, special events excluded.

Central Lake

Bridgewalk B&B

2287 S Main, PO Box 399
Central Lake, MI 49622-0399
(231)544-8122
Internet: www.bridgewalkbandb.com
E-mail: bridgewalkbb@earthlink.net

Circa 1895. Secluded on a wooded acre, this three-story
Victorian is accessible by crossing a foot bridge over a stream.
Guest rooms are simply decorated with Victorian touches, floral
prints and fresh flowers. The Garden Suite includes a clawfoot
tub. Much of the home's Victorian elements have been
restored, including pocket doors and the polished woodwork.
Breakfasts begin with such items as a cold fruit soup, freshly
baked muffins or scones accompanied with homemade jams
and butters. A main dish, perhaps apple-sausage blossoms,
tops off the meal.

Innkeeper(s): Janet & Tom Meteer. $85-115. 5 rooms with PB, 1 suite.
Breakfast included in rates. Types of meals: Full bkfst and early coffee/tea.
Beds: KQT. Reading lamp and ceiling fan in room. Parlor games, telephone
and fireplace on premises. Antiquing, cross-country skiing, downhill skiing,
fishing, parks, shopping, golf and gourmet restaurants nearby.

Location: Village.

Certificate may be used: Sunday-Thursday, can also check Last Minute-
Based on Availability.

Charlevoix

The Inn at Grey Gables

306 Belvedere Avenue
Charlevoix, MI 49720-1413
(231)547-2251 (800)280-4667
Internet: www.innatgreygables.com
E-mail: inn@innatgreygables.com

Circa 1887. Guests at this attractive two-story inn are just a
short walk from a public beach. Visitors have their choice of
seven rooms, including two suites. The Pine Suite features a

kitchen and private
entrance, perfect for honeymooners or for those
enjoying a longer-than-
usual stay. All of the rooms
offer private baths and
most have queen beds.
Guests may opt to relax
and enjoy the beautiful surroundings or take advantage of the
many recreational activities available in the Charlevoix area,
including Fisherman's Island State Park.

Innkeeper(s): Michael Barton & Phillip Anderson. $59-199. 7 rooms with
PB, 1 two-bedroom suite. Breakfast, afternoon tea, snacks/refreshments, hors
d'oeuvres and wine included in rates. Types of meals: Full bkfst. Beds: KQT.
Cable TV, reading lamp, CD player, ceiling fan, snack bar, clock radio, telephone, turn-down service, desk, hair dryer, bathrobes, bath amenities, wireless Internet access and iron/ironing board in room. Air conditioning. DVD,
fax and parlor games on premises. Antiquing, art galleries, beach, bicycling,
canoeing/kayaking, cross-country skiing, downhill skiing, fishing, golf, hiking,
horseback riding, live theater, parks, shopping, tennis, water sports and
wineries nearby.

Location: Country, mountains, waterfront. Public beach 1/2 mile.

Publicity: *USA Today.*

Certificate may be used: Nov. 1-May 24, anytime. Sunday-Thursday, June 1-
30. Sunday-Thursday, September and Oct. 1-30.

Cheboygan

The Gables B&B

314 S Main St
Cheboygan, MI 49721-1953
(231)627-4460
Internet: www.thegablesbnb.com
E-mail: innkeepers@thegablesbnb.com

Circa 1892. The Gables Bed & Breakfast in Cheboygan,
Michigan has proudly welcomed weary travelers since 1892.
Open year-round, this Victorian inn has been restored to its
original grandeur. Hanging baskets line the walkways to the
peaceful English garden in the back. Relax in the outdoor hot
tub. Second-floor guest bedrooms are themed from the Les
Cheneaux with a nautical flair and the Huron's seaside setting,
to the floral Lilac and Trillium rooms. The Wanigan boasts a
north woods décor and features a private balcony. A satisfying
breakfast starts each day right with fresh fruit, hot scones, and
an entrée accompanied by a side of meat. Located near the
Mackinac Bridge, walk to the shops and restaurants. The setting
is perfect for weddings, reunions and other intimate gatherings.

Innkeeper(s): Judy & Jim Churchill. $85-125. 5 rooms, 2 with PB. Breakfast
and snacks/refreshments included in rates. Types of meals: Full bkfst, veg
bkfst and early coffee/tea. Beds: DT. Reading lamp, bathrobes, bath amenities
and wireless Internet access in room. TV, VCR, DVD, fax, spa, parlor games,
telephone and fireplace on premises. Antiquing, beach, bicycling, cross-country skiing, fishing, golf, hiking, live theater, parks, shopping, water sports,
wineries, Mackinaw City, Mackinac Island and Cross in the Woods nearby.

Location: City. Minutes from Mackinaw City and Mackinac Island.

Certificate may be used: Anytime, subject to availability.

Fenton

Wolcott House Bed & Breakfast

610 W Silver Lake Rd
Fenton, MI 48430-2621
(810)714-4317 Fax:(810)714-4318
Internet: www.thewolcotthouse.com
E-mail: wolcotthouse@aol.com

Circa 1900. Once owned by the prominent Wolcott family
who also owned the local mill, this stately red brick Italianate
home has been renovated and provides pleasant lodging.
Wolcott House Bed & Breakfast in Fenton, Michigan is furnished in period décor accented with antiques. Relax in the
parlor by the corner fireplace and vintage Victrola. Stay in the
romantic Honeymoon Suite with a Jacuzzi tub for two and a
fireplace. The President's Room boasts an Americana theme
and the Garden Room is an inviting accommodation. Start each
morning with a gourmet breakfast before embarking on the
day's adventures.

Innkeeper(s): Elaine & Sean Rosekrans. $85-150. 3 rooms, 1 with PB, 1
with FP, 1 with WP, 1 cottage. Breakfast and snacks/refreshments included in
rates. Types of meals: Full gourmet bkfst, early coffee/tea, picnic lunch and
afternoon tea. Beds: QD. Cable TV, VCR, reading lamp, CD player, ceiling fan,
snack bar, clock radio, turn-down service, desk, bathrobes, bath amenities
and iron/ironing board in room. Air conditioning. Fax, copier, bicycles, parlor
games and fireplace on premises. Antiquing, art galleries, beach, bicycling,
canoeing/kayaking, cross-country skiing, downhill skiing, fishing, golf, hiking,
horseback riding, live theater, museums, parks, shopping, sporting events,
tennis and water sports nearby.

Location: City.

Certificate may be used: Anytime, Subject to availability.

Grand Haven

Boyden House Bed & Breakfast

301 South Fifth Street
Grand Haven, MI 49417-1413
(616)846-3538
Internet: www.boydenhouse.com

Circa 1874. A lavish garden surrounds this nineteenth century Victorian/Queen Anne-style home, filled with elegant, cozy, eclectic rooms. Some guest bedrooms feature Jacuzzi tubs and fireplaces. Hardwood floors, massive pocket doors and handcrafted wood details offer a nostalgic journey upon the first step over the threshold of this bed and breakfast in Grand Haven, Michigan. It is an easy walk from Boyden House to shops, restaurants, cafes and the beach. Enjoy a stroll on the boardwalk along the Grand River, ending with a sunset at the lighthouse pier.

Innkeeper(s): Gail Kowalski. $85-175. 7 rooms with PB, 2 with FP. Breakfast included in rates. Types of meals: Full gourmet bkfst and snacks/refreshments. Beds: KQD. Cable TV, VCR, DVD, ceiling fan, some with hot tub/spa, bath amenities, wireless Internet access, individual temperature control and feather beds in room. Central air. Fax, copier, library, telephone, guest lounge with books, CD's, board games, fireplace and cozy seating, expansive porches and abundant landscaping, guest kitchen with snacks and refreshments on premises. Limited handicap access. Amusement parks, antiquing, art galleries, beach, bicycling, canoeing/kayaking, cross-country skiing, downhill skiing, fishing, golf, hiking, horseback riding, live theater, museums, parks, shopping, tennis, water sports and wineries nearby.

Location: Walking distance to downtown, boardwalk and beaches.

Certificate may be used: Anytime, November-April, subject to availability.

Khardomah Lodge

1365 Lake Ave
Grand Haven, MI 49417
(616)842-2990
Internet: www.khardomahlodge.com
E-mail: khardomahlodge@chartermi.net

Circa 1873. A favorite place for family gatherings, the inn's natural wooded surroundings and flower gardens instill an overall sense of well-being. Built in the late 1800s and sitting amongst other historic homes, the lodge's cottage-style decor and antiques create a delightful nostalgia. The great room fireplace is an instant socializer. Choose to stay in the lodge suites or guest bedrooms. A hot tub is the highlight of the hot tub suite. Create memorable meals in the fully-equipped kitchen and gas grill. A catering service also can be arranged. Relax by the fireplace, read a book from the library, watch a video or play a game.

Innkeeper(s): Gayle Gerig, Manager. $60-190. 17 rooms, 3 with PB, 2 with HT, 1 with WP, 2 two-bedroom suites, 1 conference room. Beds: QT. Cable TV, VCR, reading lamp, CD player, refrigerator, ceiling fan, clock radio, telephone, coffeemaker, desk, some with hot tub/spa, fireplace, hair dryer, bath amenities, wireless Internet access, iron/ironing board. The two private suites sleep 2-4 & have whirlpool tubs, kitchens, balcony or deck, fireplaces and cable TV in room. Air conditioning. Spa, library, parlor games, laundry facility, Hot tub outside on private deck for the hot tub suite guests only, Lodge, suites and cottage have their own outdoor grills and decks and a coin laundry is available in-season on premises. Limited handicap access. Amusement parks, antiquing, art galleries, beach, bicycling, canoeing/kayaking, cross-country skiing, fishing, golf, hiking, horseback riding, live theater, museums, parks, shopping, tennis, water sports, wineries, Great boutique shopping and bookstores, great dining options, martini bar and musical fountain plays nightly in-season, outdoor concerts are free weekly, great sailing and fishing nearby.

Location: Lake Michigan.

Publicity: *Hunts Guide, Michigan Meetings and Events, Off the Beaten Bath travel guides, State Historic Travel Guide, Michigan Vacation and Cottage Guide, Grand Rapids Press, Booth Newspapers, 125th birthday feature on Michigan Live TV, WGHN and CMU Public Radio.*

Certificate may be used: November-May, weekdays, suites only, no holidays.

Grand Rapids

Prairieside Suites

3180 Washington Ave SW
Grand Rapids, MI 49418
(616)538-9442 Fax:(616) 538-9440
Internet: www.prairieside.com
E-mail: cheri@prairieside.com

Circa 1920. Stay at this luxury bed and breakfast in Grandville, Michigan. Spacious guest suites feature pampering details that include heated towel bars and tile floors, Jacuzzis, coffee makers, refrigerators, microwaves, CD players and VCRs. Special amenities are offered for business travelers in two suites that boast executive business centers. The European Shower Experience in one of the private baths has three body massage sprays, two shower heads and a seat. Evening snacks are available. A full breakfast is served on the weekends and continental fare is enjoyed during the  week. Swim in the heated outdoor pool with a waterfall, relax in the pergola's double slider, or wander the perennial gardens accented by a fountain. Special arrangements and personal services are gladly taken care of at Prairieside Suites.

Innkeeper(s): Cheri & Paul Antozak. $125-205. 5 rooms with PB, 4 with FP, 5 with WP, 1 conference room. Breakfast, afternoon tea, snacks/refreshments, Cookies, homemade cocoa & Micro Popcorn for a Snack! In-Room Coffee Makers & Tea Service and Soda is waiting in your refrigerator upon arrival! included in rates. Types of meals: Full Breakfast is served in the dining room 30 Sat/Sun. Continental Breakfast: Monday-Friday is packed in your refrigerator for you to eat in the privacy of your room anytime. Beds: K. Modem hook-up, data port, cable TV, VCR, reading lamp, CD player, refrigerator, ceiling fan, clock radio, telephone, coffeemaker, desk, hair dryer, bathrobes, bath amenities, wireless Internet access, iron/ironing board, Jacuzzi tubs, Heated towel bars, Heated toilet seats, TV/VCR/movie library, Refrigerator, Microwave, Coffee pots and Warm cozy robes in room. Central air. Fax, copier, swimming, library, fireplace, gift shop, Video Library of more than 300 titles, music library of 160+ CDs, Make your stay extra special and check out our "Room Service" tab on our website on premises. Antiquing, art galleries, beach, golf, museums, parks, shopping, tennis, wineries, Gourmet/Fine Dining, Lake, Rivertown Crossings Mall & movie theater (2 minutes), Frederick Meijer Gardens, Grand Lady Riverboat, Van Andel Arena & Museum, John Ball Park Zoo, 20+ Restaurants within 5 minutes, pool, Lake Michigan, Kent Trails system, Millenium Park, Bike Trails, Devos Theater, Performing Theater, Picnic area and Downtown Grand Rapids (10 minutes) nearby.

Location: City.

Publicity: *Arrington's Inn Traveler Magazine, (Fall/Winter 2006) and Arrington's 2006 Book of List Voted 3rd "Best Overall Bed & Breakfast" in North America.*

Certificate may be used: November through May, Monday through Thursday excluding holidays, valid for new guests only.

Jones

The Sanctuary at Wildwood

58138 M-40
Jones, MI 49061-9713
(269)244-5910 (800)249-5910 Fax:(269)244-9022
Internet: www.sanctuaryatwildwood.biz
E-mail: info@sanctuaryatwildwood.com

Circa 1973. Travelers in search of relaxation and a little solitude will enjoy the serenity of this estate, surrounded by 95 forested acres. A stroll down the hiking trails introduces guests to a variety of wildlife, but even inside, guests are pampered by the inn's natural setting. One room, named Medicine Hawk, is adorned with a mural depicting a woodland scene. A mural of a pine forest graces the Quiet Solace room. The Keeper of the Wild Room includes a rustic birch headboard. Each of the rooms includes a fireplace, Jacuzzi and service bar. There also are three cottage (6 suites), situated around a pond. >From the  dining and great rooms, guests can watch the abundant wildlife. The innkeeper offers a variety of interesting packages. A heated swimming pool is available during the summer months. Wineries are nearby, and the inn is a half hour from Notre Dame and Shipshewana.

Innkeeper(s): Dick & Dolly Buerkle. $159-219. 11 rooms, 11 with FP, 11 with WP, 11 suites, 3 cottages, 1 conference room. Breakfast included in rates. Types of meals: Full bkfst. Beds: Q. TV, VCR, DVD, reading lamp, stereo, refrigerator, ceiling fan, clock radio, coffeemaker, desk, hot tub/spa, fireplace, bath amenities, Jacuzzi, Fireplace and Cottage suites feature Jenn Air kitchenettes or screened-in porch in room. Air conditioning. Fax, spa, swimming, bicycles, library, parlor games, gift shop, Fishing lake stocked with bluegill/bass & catfish, Walking trails for our guests, Two deer herds, Fox den and Large variety of wild birds on premises. Handicap access. Antiquing, canoeing/kayaking, cross-country skiing, downhill skiing, fishing, golf, horseback riding, shopping, wineries and Amish communities nearby.

Location: Rural, wooded countryside.

Publicity: *The Toledo Blade, Chicago Sun Times, Kalamazoo Gazette, South Bend Tribune, WBCL-Fort Wayne and IN.*

Certificate may be used: Anytime, November-April, subject to availability, excluding holiday periods.

Jonesville

Munro House B&B and Spa

202 Maumee Street
Jonesville, MI 49250-1247
(517)849-9292 (800)320-3792
Internet: www.munrohouse.com
E-mail: info@munrohouse.com

Circa 1834. "The Most Comfortable Lodging in South Central Michigan" is found at this historic Greek Revival mansion in downtown Jonesville. Wake up to a daily, hot and fresh country-style breakfast. Getaway packages including massage and spa services are offered onsite every day. A special event can be planned as desired for any night of the week. Dine at one of the ten restaurants within a mile of Munro House B&B Spa.

Innkeeper(s): Lori & Mike Venturini. $149-219. 7 rooms with PB, 5 with FP, 2 with WP, 2 conference rooms. Breakfast and snacks/refreshments included in rates. Types of meals: Country bkfst. Beds: Q. Cable TV, VCR, DVD, reading lamp, ceiling fan, clock radio, telephone, desk, some with hot tub/spa and wireless Internet access in room. Air conditioning. Fax, copier, library, parlor games, fireplace, massage and day spa services on premises. Antiquing and horseback riding nearby.

Location: City. Village.

"Your home is a wonderful port for the weary traveler. I love it here. The rooms are great and the hospitality unsurpassed."

Certificate may be used: Anytime, subject to availability, Except Valentine's Day, New Years Eve, Hillsdale College & NASCAR Weekends. Any room priced at $159 and up.

Lakeside

Lakeside Inn

15251 Lakeshore Rd
Lakeside, MI 49116-9712
(269)469-0600 Fax:(269)469-1914
Internet: www.lakesideinns.com
E-mail: reservationslk@lakesideinns.com

Circa 1890. Totally renovated in 1995, the Lakeside Inn features original wood pillars and rustic stone fireplaces in the lobby and ballroom. The inn overlooks Lake Michigan located just across the street, and was featured in a USA Today article "Ten Great Places to Sit on the Porch" because of its 100-foot-long veranda. Each individ-  ually decorated room combines the special ambiance of comfortable antique furnishings with modern amenities like TVs, air conditioning and private baths. Many of the rooms are on the lake side, and some offer Jacuzzi tubs. Besides board games or cards for indoor recreation, the inn offers an exercise room and dry sauna. Cycling, horseback riding, swimming, antique shops, art galleries and a state park are nearby.

Innkeeper(s): Connie Williams. $75-175. 31 rooms with PB, 1 suite, 1 conference room. Types of meals: Full bkfst and lunch. Beds: KQDT. TV, reading lamp, clock radio and some with Jacuzzi in room. Air conditioning. Fax, copier, swimming, sauna, bicycles, parlor games, telephone, fireplace and seasonal cafe open for breakfast on premises. Handicap access. Antiquing, art galleries, bicycling, cross-country skiing, fishing, golf, parks, shopping and swimming nearby.

Publicity: *Chicago Tribune, USA Today, Midwest Living, Chicago Magazine, Washington Post and Lake Magazine.*

Certificate may be used: Nov.1 through the Wednesday before Memorial Day Weekend.

Ludington

The Inn at Ludington

701 E Ludington Ave
Ludington, MI 49431-2224
(231)845-7055 (800)845-9170

Internet: www.inn-ludington.com
E-mail: innkeeper@inn-ludington.com

Circa 1890. Experience an informal elegance at this Victorian bed and breakfast in the Great Lakes region near Lake Michigan beach that offers a fine blend of the past and the present. Built in 1890, it has been locally awarded for retaining its  historical integrity during replicate restoration. Lounge by one of the four fireplaces and savor afternoon refreshments. Choose from one of the six ethnically-themed guest bedrooms. Early risers can enjoy fresh coffee, cereal, yogurt and nut bread. A personally tailored meal is offered at an agreed-upon, pre-determined time. Ask about seasonal getaway or family packages, special events and murder mystery weekends.

Innkeeper(s): Kathy & Ola Kvalvaag. $90-225. 7 rooms, 1 with PB, 2 with FP, 1 with HT, 3 suites. Breakfast included in rates. Types of meals: Full bkfst and early coffee/tea. Beds: KQD. Modem hook-up, cable TV, VCR, DVD, reading lamp, ceiling fan, clock radio, desk, some with hot tub/spa, some with fireplace, hair dryer, bath amenities, wireless Internet access and iron/ironing board in room. Air conditioning. Fax, copier, spa, library, parlor games, telephone, laundry facility, gift shop, Free high speed Internet access, One family style apartment (see Web site for details and pictures) and Lovely English Gardens perfect for a wedding on premises. Antiquing, beach, bicycling, canoeing/kayaking, cross-country skiing, fishing, golf, hiking, horseback riding, parks, shopping, tennis and water sports nearby.

Location: Walk in town to beach.

Publicity: *Ludington Daily News, Detroit Free Press, Chicago Tribune, Country Accents and Michigan Living.*

"Loved the room and everything else about the house."

Certificate may be used: November-April, anytime; May, June, September, October, Sunday-Thursday as available at last minute.

Mendon

The Mendon Country Inn

PO Box 98
Mendon, MI 49072
(269)496-8132 (800)304-3366 Fax:(269)496-8403
Internet: www.mendoncountryinn.com
E-mail: innkeeper@mendoncountryinn.com

Circa 1873. This two-story stagecoach inn was constructed with St. Joseph River clay bricks fired on the property. There are eight-foot windows, high ceilings and a walnut staircase. Country antiques are accentuated with woven rugs, collectibles and bright quilts. There are nine antique-filled guest rooms and nine suites which include a fireplace and Jacuzzi tub. Depending on the season, guests may also borrow a tandem bike or arrange for a canoe trip. Special events are featured throughout the year. The inn's Golden Getaway package includes lodging, a dinner for two and special activity, which might be golfing, a river canoe trip, skiing or perhaps a relaxing massage. A rural Amish community and Shipshewana are nearby.

Innkeeper(s): Geff & Cheryl Clarke. $79-149. 16 rooms with PB, 14 with FP, 9 suites, 2 cottages, 1 conference room. Breakfast included in rates. Types of meals: Full bkfst, early coffee/tea and Restaurant dining. Beds: QD. TV, reading lamp, ceiling fan, clock radio, desk, hot tub/spa and most with fireplace in room. Air conditioning. Fax, sauna, bicycles, library, parlor games, telephone and canoeing on premises. Handicap access. Antiquing, cross-country skiing, downhill skiing, fishing, shopping and canoeing nearby.

Location: Waterfront. Rural country.

Publicity: *Innsider, Country Home, Country Magazine and Midwest Living.*

"A great experience. Good food and great hosts. Thank you."

Certificate may be used: Sunday-Thursday throughout the year, plus November-May on weekends, excluding special event weekends.

Muskegon

Hackley-Holt House B & B

523 W Clay Ave
Muskegon, MI 49440-1032
(231)725-7303 (888)271-5609
Internet: www.bbonline.com/mi/hhbb
E-mail: mlarchambault@yahoo.com

Circa 1857. Listed in the National Register, Hackley-Holt House Bed & Breakfast was built in 1857 in the Italianate style of architecture and is located in the Historic Heritage Village of Muskegon, Michigan. Enjoy the Lake Muskegon breeze while sitting on the wraparound porch overlooking colorful perennial gardens. This B&B features a Victorian setting and furnishings. Sit by the fireplace with a carved ornamental mantle in the parlor that boasts original stained glass windows. Beverages and treats are always available. Stay in a centrally air-conditioned guest bedroom with a shower or clawfoot tub. Savor a hearty breakfast in the dining room before taking a trolley or horse-drawn carriage ride. Ask about special packages.

Innkeeper(s): Michelle Archambault. $108-120. 4 rooms with PB. Breakfast and snacks/refreshments included in rates. Types of meals: Full bkfst and early coffee/tea. Beds: KQT. Cable TV, VCR, reading lamp, clock radio, hair dryer and wireless Internet access in room. Central air. Library, telephone and fireplace on premises. Amusement parks, antiquing, art galleries, beach, bicycling, canoeing/kayaking, cross-country skiing, fishing, golf, hiking, horseback riding, live theater, museums, parks, shopping, sporting events, water sports and wineries nearby.

Location: City. Downtown Historic District.

Certificate may be used: October-May.

Port City Victorian Inn, Bed & Breakfast

1259 Lakeshore Dr
Muskegon, MI 49441-1659
(231)759-0205 (800)274-3574 Fax:(231)759-0205
Internet: www.portcityinn.com
E-mail: pcvicinn@comcast.net

Circa 1877. Old world elegance characterizes this Queen Anne Victorian mansion gracing the bluff of Muskegon Lake. The front parlor boasts curved leaded-glass windows with views of the harbor. A paneled grand entryway is accented by the carved posts and spindles of an oak staircase leading up to a TV room and rooftop balcony overlooking the state park. Luxurious honeymoon suites boasts two-person whirlpool baths, and romantic guest bedrooms include desks, modems, refrigerators and ice buckets. Early risers sip morning coffee while reading the local newspaper. A hot breakfast can be delivered to the room, enjoyed in the formal dining room or served in the 14-window sunroom. Ask about special packages available.

Innkeeper(s): Barbara Schossau & Fred Schossau. $125-200. 5 rooms with PB, 2 with FP, 1 with HT, 3 with WP, 3 suites. Breakfast included in rates. Types of meals: Country bkfst, early coffee/tea, snacks/refreshments and room service. Beds: Q. Modem hook-up, data port, cable TV, VCR, DVD, reading lamp, stereo, refrigerator, ceiling fan, snack bar, clock radio, telephone, coffeemaker, turn-down service, desk, some with hot tub/spa, some with fireplace, hair dryer, bathrobes, bath amenities, wireless Internet access, iron/ironing board, double whirlpool tubs, 2-person Jacuzzi, fireplace, hair dryers, robes, lake views and individual remote control air conditioning in room. Central air. Fax, copier, bicycles and parlor games on premises. Amusement parks, antiquing, art galleries, beach, bicycling, canoeing/kayaking, cross-country skiing, fishing, golf, hiking, horseback riding, live theater, museums, parks, shopping, sporting events, tennis, water sports, Lake Michigan, Muskegon Lake and Port City Princess cruise ship nearby.

Location: City, waterfront. Grand Rapids.

Publicity: *Muskegon Chronicle, Detroit Free Press, Arrington's Bed & Breakfast Journal and Arrington's Bed & Breakfast Journal's award "Best In The Midwest."*

"The inn offers only comfort, good food and total peace of mind."

Certificate may be used: Anytime, November-April, subject to availability.

Pentwater

Hexagon House Bed & Breakfast

760 6th St
Pentwater, MI 49449-9504
(231)869-4102 Fax:(231)869-9941
Internet: www.hexagonhouse.com
E-mail: innkeepers@hexagonhouse.com

Circa 1870. Open year round, Hexagon House Bed and Breakfast in the quaint village of Pentwater, is the perfect location for a Lake Michigan vacation. Lake Ludington and Silver Lake sand dunes are also nearby. This hexagonal-designed home surrounded by perennial gardens with sandstone footpaths on three acres, was built in 1870 and boasts Victorian decor. Bikes are available to explore the scenic area or stroll along the adjacent 2.5 wooded trails with a pond and wildlife viewing station. Relax by the fire in the parlor. Stay in the first-floor Cottage Rose Suite with a Jacuzzi and a private porch area. The Cherub room boasts an electric fireplace, clawfoot tub and access to the second-floor wicker-filled wraparound porch. A daily breakfast is made with farm-fresh ingredients.
Innkeeper(s): Amy & Tom Hamel. $100-225. 5 rooms with PB, 2 with FP, 1 suite. Breakfast, snacks/refreshments, hors d'oeuvres and wine included in rates. Types of meals: Full gourmet bkfst, veg bkfst, early coffee/tea, picnic lunch and prior arrangements can be made for dinner at the inn (at an additional charge) or reservations can be made for you at local restaurants. Beds: KQ. TV, VCR, DVD, reading lamp, stereo, refrigerator, ceiling fan, snack bar, clock radio, telephone, hair dryer, bath amenities, wireless Internet access and iron/ironing board in room. Central air. Fax, bicycles, library, parlor games, fireplace, wraparound porches, other meals available upon request, 3 acres, bird watching library and DVD collection on premises. Limited handicap access. Amusement parks, antiquing, art galleries, beach, bicycling, canoeing/kayaking, cross-country skiing, fishing, golf, hiking, horseback riding, museums, parks, shopping, tennis, water sports and wineries nearby.
Location: Country. Near Lake Michigan.
Publicity: *The Ludington Daily News, The Chicago Herald Newspaper, Midwest Living Magazine, Weekend Magazine, Grand Rapids Magazine, Lifestyles Magazine, The Healing Garden Magazine, West Michigan Tourist Guide and The Shoreline Guide Magazine.*
Certificate may be used: Last minute, subject to availabilty.

Petoskey

Terrace Inn

1549 Glendale
Petoskey, MI 49770
(231)347-2410 (800)530-9898
Internet: www.theterraceinn.com
E-mail: info@theterraceinn.com

Circa 1911. Poised in the picturesque Victorian village of Bay View, Petoskey, the 1911 Terrace Inn is located just 45 minutes south of Mackinac Island near sandy Lake Michigan beaches in scenic Northwest Michigan. This year-round bed and breakfast inn is a National Historic Landmark. Feel refreshed by the warm and friendly service perfectly blended with privacy. Sit in a rocker on the wide veranda or relax by the fire in the lobby. Accommodations include themed guest bedrooms, from cottage style to deluxe rooms with fireplaces to whirlpool suites. After a hearty continental breakfast play croquet, then visit the nearby sophisticated downtown area for recreational and cultural activities. The inn's restaurant with owner and chef Mo Rave, offers in-season dinners.
Innkeeper(s): Mo and Patty Rave. $79-179. 38 rooms with PB, 6 with FP, 6

with WP, 6 suites, 2 conference rooms. Breakfast, afternoon tea, dinner and All packages include breakfast and dinner. Special Event may also include lunch. All stays include a continental deluxe breakfast 8 to 10 AM included in rates. Types of meals: Cont plus, early coffee/tea and Complimentary continental deluxe breakfast daily from 8-10 AM. Dinner is available in-season 5-10 and can be charged to your room. Restaurant on premises. Beds: KQT.
Cable TV, DVD, reading lamp, stereo, refrigerator, clock radio, coffeemaker, desk, some with fireplace, hair dryer, bath amenities, wireless Internet access, iron/ironing board, Deluxe Rooms with cable TV & full bath, Whirlpool Suites & Deluxe Whirlpool Suites with kitchenettes, fireplaces & cable, Cottage Rooms are phone and TV-free, all have AC, wireless

Internet and Complimentary breakfast in room. Air conditioning. VCR, copier, bicycles, library, parlor games, telephone, gift shop, Guests have Bay View privileges of the tennis courts, Private beach access (to Lake Michigan), Rec. center, Laundry facilities, Pet boarding, Internet cafes and Day Spas on premises. Limited handicap access. Antiquing, beach, bicycling, canoeing/kayaking, cross-country skiing, downhill skiing, fishing, golf, hiking, live theater, museums, parks, shopping, sporting events, tennis, water sports, Snow shoeing, Boating, Marina, Swimming, Art gallery browsing, Movie theatre, Concerts and Plays nearby.
Location: City. Lake Michigan Resort town-Northwest.
Publicity: *Oakland Press & Observer Eccentric, Midwest Living, Michigan Magazine, Detroit News, the Graphic, Northern Express, Michigan Meetings and Events, Booth News, Traverse Magazine, Hunts Guide, Michigan Vacation Guide, Petoskey News Review, American Historic Inns, Fox News, Michigan Live, Channel 8, Central Michigan University Radio, Interlochen Public Radio and WJML.*
Certificate may be used: Sunday through Thursday, based on availability, not valid holidays or weekends in July or August.

Port Austin

Lake Street Manor

8569 Lake St
Port Austin, MI 48467
(989)738-7720 (888)273-8987
Internet: hometown.aol.com/lakestreetmanor

Circa 1875. As history has shown, the homes of lumber barons are often some of the most luxurious. This Victorian, with its peak roofs and gingerbread trim is no exception. The Culhane family, who made their fortune in the timber business, used this home as their summer retreat. In the 1930s, it was rented out as a summer guest house, and today the innkeeper, Carolyn, has once again opened the doors to visitors. The rooms have charming names: The Garden Basket Room, the Wedding Ring Room and the Raspberry Wine Room, to name a few. The Parlor Room, which includes a bay window, is accessed by double pocket doors, a characteristic feature in Victorian homes. The Bay Room, which is one of the inn's common rooms, includes a hot tub in front of a gas fireplace.
Innkeeper(s): Carolyn and Jack. $75-90. 5 rooms, 3 with PB. Breakfast included in rates. Types of meals: Cont plus and room service. Beds: Q. Cable TV, VCR, reading lamp and ceiling fan in room. Spa, bicycles, parlor games, telephone, gas fireplace, stereo, BBQ, yard games and hot tub on premises. Antiquing, cross-country skiing, fishing, golf, live theater, parks, shopping, tennis, water sports, horseback riding and canoe rental nearby.
Location: City. Lake Huron.
Certificate may be used: May 1-Oct. 31, Sunday-Thursday, no holidays.

Saline

The Homestead B&B

9279 Macon Rd
Saline, MI 48176-9305
(734)429-9625

Circa 1851. The Homestead is a two-story brick farmhouse situated on 50 acres of fields, woods and river. The house has 15-inch-thick walls and is furnished with Victorian antiques and family heirlooms. This was a favorite camping spot for Native Americans while they salted their fish, and many arrowheads have been found on the farm. Activities include long walks through meadows of wildflowers and cross-country skiing in season. It is 40 minutes from Detroit and Toledo and 10 minutes from Ann Arbor.

Innkeeper(s): Shirley Grossman. $75. 5 rooms, 1 conference room. Breakfast and snacks/refreshments included in rates. Types of meals: Full bkfst and early coffee/tea. Beds: DT. TV and reading lamp in room. Air conditioning. VCR, telephone and fireplace on premises. Antiquing, cross-country skiing, parks, shopping and sporting events nearby.

Location: Country.

Publicity: *Ann Arbor News, Country Focus, Saline Reporter* and *Detroit Free Press.*

"We're spoiled now and wouldn't want to stay elsewhere! No motel offers deer at dusk and dawn!"

Certificate may be used: Jan. 2-June 1, Sunday to Friday & Sept. 1-Dec. 30, Sunday to Friday.

Saugatuck

Bayside Inn

618 Water St
Saugatuck, MI 49453
(269)857-4321 Fax:(269) 857-1870
Internet: www.baysideinn.net
E-mail: info@baysideinn.net

Circa 1926. Located on the edge of the Kalamazoo River and across from the nature observation tower, this downtown inn was once a boathouse. The common room now has a fireplace and view of the water. Each guest room has its own deck. The inn is near several restaurants, shops and beaches. Fishing for salmon, perch and trout is popular.

$70-275. 10 rooms with PB, 4 with FP, 2 with WP, 4 total suites, including 1 two-bedroom suite, 1 conference room. Breakfast and snacks/refreshments included in rates. Types of meals: Cont plus and early coffee/tea. Beds: KQ. Modem hook-up, cable TV, DVD, reading lamp, refrigerator, telephone, coffeemaker, desk, some with hot tub/spa, voice mail, some with fireplace, hair dryer, bath amenities, wireless Internet access and iron/ironing board in room. Central air. Fax, copier, spa and parlor games on premises. Limited handicap access. Amusement parks, antiquing, art galleries, beach, bicycling, canoeing/kayaking, cross-country skiing, fishing, golf, hiking, horseback riding, live theater, museums, parks, shopping, sporting events, tennis, water sports and wineries nearby.

Location: City, waterfront.

"Our stay was wonderful, more pleasant than anticipated, we were so pleased. As for breakfast, it gets our A 1 rating."

Certificate may be used: November 1 to March 31, Sunday-Thursday, subject to availability.

Hidden Garden Cottages & Suites

247 Butler St
Saugatuck, MI 49453
(269)857-8109 (888)857-8109 Fax:(269)857-8109
Internet: www.hiddengardencottages.com
E-mail: Indakott@AOL.com

Circa 1879. Perfect for a secluded bed breakfast experience, these elegantly furnished cottages are designed for two. Tucked away in the downtown area, the quiet location is convenient to all of the local shopping, dining and attractions. Each luxurious cottage features a gorgeous canopy or four-poster bed, down comforter and exquisite bed linens. Relax in the romantic seating area by the fireplace with color cable TV, VCR, CD stereo system and a phone. The luxurious bathroom has a whirlpool for two, plush robes and complete bath amenities. A mini-kitchen includes a refrigerator, icemaker and microwave oven. Overlook the intimate courtyard garden and fountains from a private porch that completes the tranquil setting. A continental breakfast is offered each morning. Take a boat cruise on Lake Michigan, play golf or ride the dunes.

Innkeeper(s): Daniel Indurante & Gary Kott. $135-215. 4 rooms with PB, 4 with FP, 4 with WP. Breakfast and snacks/refreshments included in rates. Types of meals: Cont plus. Beds: Q. Cable TV, VCR, reading lamp, stereo, refrigerator, ceiling fan, snack bar, clock radio, telephone, coffeemaker, desk, voice mail, fireplace, hair dryer, bathrobes, bath amenities and iron/ironing board in room. Central air. Limited handicap access. Antiquing, art galleries, beach, bicycling, canoeing/kayaking, cross-country skiing, fishing, golf, hiking, horseback riding, live theater, museums, parks, shopping, sporting events, tennis, water sports and wineries nearby.

Location: City.

Publicity: *Travel Holiday Magazine (September 1998).*

Certificate may be used: September-May.

Twin Oaks Inn

PO Box 818, 227 Griffith St
Saugatuck, MI 49453-0818
(269)857-1600 (800)788-6188 Fax:(269)857-7446
E-mail: twinoaks@sirus.com

Circa 1860. This large Queen Anne Victorian inn was a boarding house for lumbermen at the turn of the century. Now an old-English-style inn, it offers a variety of lodging choices, including a room with its own Jacuzzi. There are many diversions at Twin Oaks, including a collection of videotaped movies numbering more than 700. Guests may borrow bicycles or play horseshoes on the inn's grounds.

Innkeeper(s): Willa Lemken. $110-150. 6 rooms with PB, 1 conference room. Types of meals: Full bkfst, early coffee/tea and snacks/refreshments. Beds: KQ. Cable TV, VCR, reading lamp, stereo, clock radio, desk and hot tub/spa in room. Air conditioning. Parlor games, telephone and fireplace on premises. Antiquing, cross-country skiing, fishing, live theater, parks, shopping and water sports nearby.

Location: Downtown small village.

Certificate may be used: Nov. 1-April 30, Sunday through Thursday.

South Haven

Martha's Vineyard Bed and Breakfast

473 Blue Star Hwy
South Haven, MI 49090
(269)637-9373 Fax:(269)639-8214
Internet: www.marthasvy.com
E-mail: adamson@marthasvy.com

Circa 1852. In a park-like setting of more than four acres with a private beach, this 1852 Federal style estate offers pampered elegance and extravagant hospitality. Gather in the traditionally-decorated parlor. Each spacious guest bedroom boasts a fireplace, antiques, two-person shower, bathrobes and a veranda. A four-course breakfast with silver settings and cloth napkins may include caramel apple pancakes. Indulge in special packages designed as personally requested. Choose golf, massage or an assortment of getaway amenities.

Innkeeper(s): Lou & Ginger Adamson. $99-190. 10 rooms with PB, 10 with FP, 7 with WP. Breakfast included in rates. Types of meals: Full bkfst, veg bkfst and early coffee/tea. Beds: Q. Cable TV, VCR, reading lamp, CD player, ceiling fan, clock radio, most with hot tub/spa, fireplace, hair dryer, bathrobes, bath amenities, wireless Internet access, Bathrobes for guest comfort, Sun porches and Verandah in room. Central air. Fax, copier, swimming, parlor games, telephone and gift shop on premises. Limited handicap access. Antiquing, art galleries, beach, bicycling, canoeing/kayaking, cross-country skiing, downhill skiing, fishing, golf, hiking, horseback riding, live theater, museums, parks, shopping, tennis, water sports and wineries nearby.

Location: Lakeside resort town.

Publicity: *Inn Traveler Magazine - Award for "Most Romantic Hideaway" in North America for four consecutive years.*

Certificate may be used: Valid Sunday through Thursday during months of November through April.

Victoria Resort Bed & Breakfast

241 Oak St
South Haven, MI 49090-2302
(269)637-6414 (800)473-7376
Internet: www.VictoriaResort.com
E-mail: Info@VictoriaResort.com

Circa 1925. Less than two blocks from a sandy beach, this Classical Revival inn offers many recreational opportunities for its guests, who may choose from bicycling, beach and pool swimming, basketball and tennis, among others. The inn's rooms provide visitors several options, including cable TV, fireplaces, whirlpool tubs and ceiling fans. Cottages for families or groups traveling together, also are available. A 10-minute stroll down tree-lined streets leads visitors to South Haven's quaint downtown, with its riverfront restaurants and shops.

Innkeeper(s): Bob & Jan. $70-195. 9 rooms with PB, 4 with FP, 6 with WP, 7 cottages. Breakfast included in rates. Types of meals: Full bkfst. Beds: KQ. Cable TV, VCR, reading lamp, refrigerator, ceiling fan, clock radio, telephone, desk, most with hot tub/spa, most with fireplace, hair dryer, bath amenities and wireless Internet access in room. Central air. Fax, swimming, bicycles, tennis, library, Basketball court, Outdoor pool and Shuffleboard on premises. Antiquing, art galleries, beach, bicycling, canoeing/kayaking, cross-country skiing, downhill skiing, fishing, golf, hiking, horseback riding, museums, parks, shopping, water sports and wineries nearby.

Location: City.

Certificate may be used: September-May, Sunday-Thursday, subject to availability.

Wakefield

Regal Country Inn

1602 E Hwy 2
Wakefield, MI 49968-9581
(906)229-5122 Fax:(906)229-5755
Internet: www.regalcountryinn.com
E-mail: regalinn@charterinternet.com

Circa 1973. Choose from four types of accommodations at this quaint, smoke-free bed & breakfast. Historical rooms feature antique furnishings, scrapbooks and literature documenting nearby towns. Relax on rocker/recliners in a comfortable study bedroom. The Victorians include quilt-topped beds. Country rooms are ideal for families. Savor treats from the 1950s as well as a limited menu and delicious desserts at the inn's Old Tyme Ice Cream Parlour and Soda Fountain. Room service and meals are offered for an added charge. Gather for conversation in the Fireside Room. Hike, fish, ski, golf, snowmobile, visit waterfalls and lighthouses in this scenic Upper Peninsula region. Cultural events and local festivals are held throughout the year.

Innkeeper(s): Richard Swanson. $67-139. 17 rooms with PB. Types of meals: Full gourmet bkfst, early coffee/tea, gourmet lunch, picnic lunch, afternoon tea, snacks/refreshments, gourmet dinner and room service. Restaurant on premises. Beds: KQD. Cable TV, VCR, reading lamp and hair dryer in room. Central air. Fax, copier, sauna, bicycles, parlor games, fireplace, guest office area with dial up, high speed and WiFi Internet access on premises. Antiquing, art galleries, beach, bicycling, canoeing/kayaking, cross-country skiing, downhill skiing, fishing, golf, hiking, horseback riding, live theater, museums, parks, shopping and tennis nearby.

Location: City. On the edge of the old mining and logging community of Wakefield, the western gateway to the Porcupine Mountains Wilderness State Park.

Publicity: *Detroit Free Press.*

"Thanks for all your efforts in making our stay here wonderful. What a delightful inn! This is my first time staying at a B&B and I'm hooked! The town is a real gem, too. You are a great host and truly know how to keep your guests happy."

Certificate may be used: Not available July 1-6. Other times, anytime subject to availability. Cannot be used with any other discounts. Only one discount per stay.

West Bloomfield

The Wren's Nest Bed & Breakfast

7405 West Maple Rd.
West Bloomfield, MI 48322
(248)624-6874
Internet: www.thewrensnestbb.com
E-mail: thewrensnestbb@sbcglobal.net

Circa 1840. Stay at this delightful farmhouse adjacent to a woodland in a country setting. It is surrounded by professionally landscaped grounds that are accented by numerous birdhouses created by the innkeeper, a plethora of perennial and annual flower beds and a heritage vegetable garden with more than 60 varieties of heirloom tomatoes. Watch TV by the fire or play piano in the living room. Relax on one of the two sun porches. Feel at home in one of the comfortable guest bedrooms. Start each morning with a full-course break-

fast made from scratch with fresh ingredients and no preservatives. Personal dietary needs are accommodated with advance notice. This historic bed and breakfast is available for special events, adult or children's tea gatherings and other parties.

Innkeeper(s): Irene Scheel. $95-115. 6 rooms, 3 with PB, 1 guest house, 1 conference room. Breakfast, afternoon tea and snacks/refreshments included in rates. Types of meals: Full gourmet bkfst, veg bkfst and room service. Beds: KQDT. Modem hook-up, data port, cable TV, VCR, reading lamp, stereo, refrigerator, ceiling fan, snack bar, clock radio, telephone, coffeemaker, turn-down service, desk, voice mail and fireplace in room. Central air. Fax, copier, library, laundry facility, heirloom vegetables in the summer and pygmy goats on premises. Limited handicap access. Antiquing, art galleries, beach, bicycling, cross-country skiing, downhill skiing, fishing, golf, hiking, horseback riding, live theater, museums, parks, shopping, sporting events, tennis, water sports, theatres and malls nearby.

Location: City, country.

Publicity: *Detroit News, The West Bloomfield Eccentric, Midwest Living, Japanese Free Press and WDIV 4 Detroit.*

Certificate may be used: Anytime.

Whitehall

White Swan Inn

303 S Mears Ave
Whitehall, MI 49461-1323
(231)894-5169 (888)948-7926
Internet: www.whiteswaninn.com
E-mail: info@whiteswaninn.com

Circa 1884. Maple trees shade this sturdy Queen Anne home, a block from White Lake. A screened porch filled with white wicker and an upstairs coffee room are leisurely retreats. Parquet floors in the dining room, antique furnishings and chandeliers add to the comfortable decor. Chicken and broccoli quiche is a favorite breakfast recipe. Cross the street for summer theater or walk to shops and restaurants nearby.

Innkeeper(s): Cathy & Ron Russell. $85-175. 4 rooms with PB, 2 with FP, 1 with WP. Breakfast and snacks/refreshments included in rates. Types of meals: Full bkfst, veg bkfst, early coffee/tea and Dinner upon request. Beds: KQDT. Cable TV, DVD, reading lamp, ceiling fan, clock radio, desk, some with fireplace, hair dryer, bathrobes, bath amenities, wireless Internet access and one suite with whirlpool tub in room. Air conditioning. Fax, copier, parlor games, telephone, gift shop, beverage center, secure bicycle storage and screened porch on premises. Amusement parks, antiquing, art galleries, beach, bicycling, canoeing/kayaking, cross-country skiing, fishing, golf, hiking, horseback riding, live theater, museums, parks, shopping, sporting events, tennis, water sports, wineries, luge run, dune rides, thoroughbred racing and seasonal festivals nearby.

Location: Small resort town.

Publicity: *White Lake Beacon, Muskegon Chronicle, Michigan Travel Ideas, Bed, Breakfast and Bike Midwest, Book of Lists, Arrington's B&B Journal, Cookbook-Great Lakes, Great Breakfasts, Cookbook-Celebrate Breakfast, WKAR TV ("Best of Bed & Breakfast"), Cookbook-Inn Time for Breakfast and Voted by inngoers-Best in the Midwest 2003.*

"What a great place to gather with old friends and relive past fun times and create new ones."

Certificate may be used: Jan. 5-Dec. 15, Sunday-Thursday.

Ypsilanti

Parish House Inn

103 S Huron St
Ypsilanti, MI 48197-5421
(734)480-4800 (800)480-4866 Fax:(734)480-7472
Internet: www.parishhouseinn.com
E-mail: parishinn@aol.com

This Queen Anne Victorian was named in honor of its service as a parsonage for the First Congregational Church. The home remained a parsonage for more than 50 years after its construction and then served as a church office and Sunday school building. It was moved to its present site in Ypsilanti's historic district in the late 1980s. The rooms are individually decorated with Victorian-style wallpapers and antiques. One guest room includes a two-person Jacuzzi tub. Those in search of a late-night snack need only venture into the kitchen to find drinks and the cookie jar. For special occasions, the innkeepers can arrange trays with flowers, non-alcoholic champagne, chocolates, fruit or cheese. The terrace overlooks the Huron River.

Innkeeper(s): Mrs. Chris Mason. $95-169. 8 rooms with PB, 3 with FP, 1 conference room. Breakfast and snacks/refreshments included in rates. Types of meals: Full gourmet bkfst, veg bkfst and early coffee/tea. Beds: KQD. Modem hook-up, data port, cable TV, VCR, reading lamp, ceiling fan, clock radio, telephone, desk, voice mail, hair dryer, bathrobes, bath amenities and wireless Internet access in room. Central air. DVD, fax, copier, library, parlor games, fireplace and gift shop on premises. Handicap access. Amusement parks, antiquing, art galleries, bicycling, canoeing/kayaking, cross-country skiing, fishing, golf, hiking, live theater, museums, parks, shopping, sporting events, tennis and water sports nearby.

Location: City.

Publicity: *Detroit Free Press, Midwest Living and Ann Arbor News.*

Certificate may be used: December through May, Sunday through

Minnesota

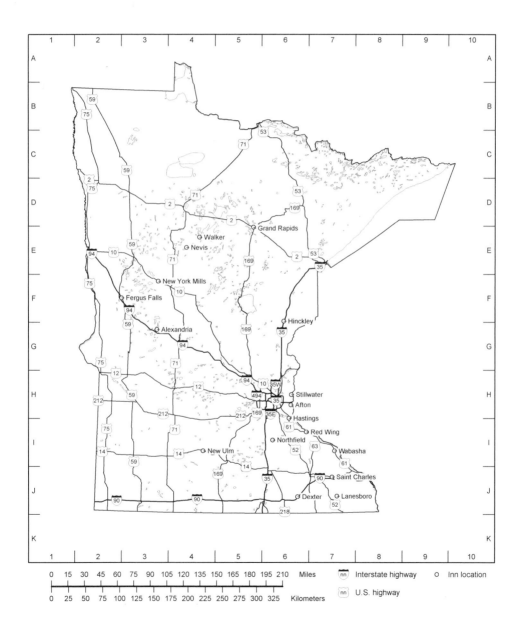

	Miles
0 15 30 45 60 75 90 105 120 135 150 165 180 195 210	Miles
0 25 50 75 100 125 150 175 200 225 250 275 300 325	Kilometers

Interstate highway ○ Inn location

U.S. highway

Afton

The Historic Afton House Inn

3291 S. St. Croix Trail
Afton, MN 55001
(651)436-8883 (877)436-8883 Fax:(651)436-6859
Internet: www.aftonhouseinn.com
E-mail: reservations@aftonhouseinn.com

Circa 1867. Located on two acres of waterfront on the St. Croix River, this historic inn reflects an old New England-style architecture. Guest rooms offer Jacuzzi tubs, fireplaces, waterfront balconies and are decorated with American country

antiques. A restaurant on the premises provides candlelight dining in the Wheel Room. (Ask for Banana Foster, or any flaming dessert—a house specialty.) Or you might prefer to dine in the Catfish Saloon & Cafe, which has a more casual menu. Champagne Brunch cruises are offered on the Grand Duchess May-October. Three charter vessels are available for private cruises for weddings, birthdays, anniversaries, corporate getaways or for groups of 10-350. Visit the inn's web site for online availability.

Innkeeper(s): Gordy & Kathy Jarvis. $79-285. 25 rooms with PB, 19 with FP, 3 total suites, including 2 two-bedroom suites, 2 conference rooms. Breakfast included in rates. Types of meals: Full bkfst, Sun. brunch, lunch, dinner and room service. Restaurant on premises. Beds: KQ. Modem hookup, data port, cable TV, VCR, ceiling fan, clock radio, telephone, desk, hot tub/spa and most with gas fireplace in room. Central air. Fax, copier, spa and gift shop on premises. Handicap access. Antiquing, art galleries, beach, bicycling, cross-country skiing, downhill skiing, fishing, golf, hiking, horseback riding, live theater, museums, parks, shopping, tennis, water sports and wineries nearby.

Location: Country.

Publicity: *St. Paul Pioneer Press, Woodbury Bulletin, Hudson Star Observer and Stillwater Gazette.*

Certificate may be used: Anytime, Sunday-Thursday and available weekends on last minute availability.

Alexandria

Cedar Rose Inn

422 7th Ave W
Alexandria, MN 56308
(320)762-8430 (888)203-5333 Fax:(320)762-8044
Internet: www.cedarroseinn.com
E-mail: florian@cedarroseinn.com

Circa 1903. Diamond-paned windows, gables, a wraparound porch with a swing for two and stained glass enhance the exterior of this handsome three-story Tudor Revival home in the National Register. Located in what was once referred to as the "Silk Stocking District," the home was built by the town's mayor. Arched doorways, Tiffany chandeliers, a glorious open staircase, maple floors and oak woodwork set the atmosphere. There's a library, a formal dining room and a parlor with fireplace and window seat. Request the Noah P. Ward room and enjoy the king-size bed and double whirlpool with mood lights for a special celebration. Wake to the aroma of freshly

baked caramel rolls, scones or cinnamon buns. Entrees of sausage and quiche are favorites. In the evening, enjoy watching the sunset over Lake Winona. Private hiking trails are available for guests or enjoy a day of lake activities, shopping, antiquing or horseback riding.

Innkeeper(s): Aggie & Florian Ledermann. $85-140. 4 rooms with PB, 1 with FP, 2 suites. Breakfast and snacks/refreshments included in rates. Types of meals: Full bkfst, early coffee/tea, picnic lunch, afternoon tea and room service. Beds: KQ. Reading lamp, CD player, refrigerator, clock radio, desk and fireplace in room. Central air. Sauna, library, parlor games and telephone on premises. Antiquing, beach, bicycling, canoeing/kayaking, cross-country skiing, downhill skiing, fishing, golf, hiking, horseback riding, live theater, museums, parks, shopping, tennis, water sports and wineries nearby.

Location: City.

"The Cedar Rose Inn was more than we imagined it would be. We felt like royalty in your beautiful dining room."

Certificate may be used: Anytime, subject to availability.

Fergus Falls

Bakketopp Hus

20517 Hillcrest Rd
Fergus Falls, MN 56537-9649
(218)739-2915 (800)739-2915 Fax:(218)736-1046
Internet: www.bbonline.com/mn/bakketopp/index.html
E-mail: ddn@prtel.com

Circa 1976. From the decks of this wooded home, guests can enjoy the scenery of Long Lake and catch glimpses of wildlife. Antiques, handmade quilts and down comforters decorate the cozy guest rooms. Guest accommodations include one room with a private Jacuzzi and one with a draped canopy bed. Another room is near a fireplace. A bounty of nearby outdoor activities are sure to please nature lovers. Antique shops and restaurants are nearby.

Innkeeper(s): Dennis & Judy Nims. $80-125. 3 rooms with PB. Breakfast, afternoon tea and snacks/refreshments included in rates. Types of meals: Full gourmet bkfst and early coffee/tea. Beds: Q. Reading lamp, clock radio, desk and Jacuzzi in room. Central air. TV, VCR, parlor games, telephone and fireplace on premises. Amusement parks, antiquing, cross-country skiing, fishing, live theater, parks, shopping and water sports nearby.

Location: Waterfront. Lakefront.

Publicity: *Minneapolis Tribune and Minnesota Monthly.*

Certificate may be used: Sunday through Thursday for months of March, November, December, January, February.

Grand Rapids

Morning Glory Bed and Breakfast

726 NW 2nd Ave
Grand Rapids, MN 55744
(218)326-3978 (866)926-3978
Internet: www.morningglorybandb.com
E-mail: karen@morningglorybandb.com

Circa 1960. The many activities of downtown are just a few blocks away from this comfortable two-story brick bed and breakfast. Relax by the wood-burning fireplace in the living room that also has a piano, library, game area and terrace door leading to a private patio with a garden fountain. Cookies and beverages are always available. On the weekends wine and appetizers are also served. Each air-conditioned guest suite features a sitting room. The romantic Champagne and Roses Suite includes a two-person whirlpool and two-sided gas fireplace. In the cheery breakfast room, full breakfast fare is offered week-days and a three-course meal is served on weekends. Play championship golf, bike the Mesabi Trail or take a drive through the Chippewa National Forest on the Edge of the Wilderness Scenic Byway.

Innkeeper(s): Karen and Ron Herbig. $90-125. 4 rooms, 2 with FP, 1 with WP, 4 suites. Breakfast, snacks/refreshments and Wine/cheese on Friday and Saturday from 5-6pm included in rates. Types of meals: Full gourmet bkfst, veg bkfst, early coffee/tea, dinner and Lunch and dinner available for an extra charge. Beds: KQT. Modem hook-up, cable TV, VCR, DVD, reading lamp, CD player, ceiling fan, clock radio, telephone, desk, some with fireplace, hair dryer and wireless Internet access in room. Central air. Copier, library and parlor games on premises. Antiquing, art galleries, beach, bicycling, canoe-ing/kayaking, cross-country skiing, fishing, golf, hiking, live theater, museums, parks, shopping, tennis and water sports nearby.

Location: City.

Certificate may be used: Anytime November-June subject to availability.

Hastings

Classic Rosewood - A Thorwood Property

620 Ramsey Street
Hastings, MN 55033-1137
(651)437-3297 (888)846-7966 Fax:(651)437-4129
Internet: www.classicrosewood.com
E-mail: info@thorwoodinn.com

Circa 1880. This Queen Anne Victorian has several verandas and porches. Grained cherry woodwork and fireplaces add elegance to the inn. All but two of the 15 rooms have fireplaces. In the Mississippi Under the Stars Room, a skylight shines down on the teak whirlpool tub. This 900-square-foot suite features tapestries, paisleys and a copper soaking tub as well as a round shower. The innkeepers serve a formal, five-course afternoon tea on Wednesday and Sundays, which guests can enjoy with a prior reservation.

Innkeeper(s): Dick & Pam Thorsen. $97-277. 8 rooms with PB, 7 with FP, 7 with WP, 3 total suites, including 1 two-bedroom suite, 3 conference rooms. Breakfast and snacks/refreshments included in rates. Types of meals: Full gourmet bkfst, veg bkfst, early coffee/tea, afternoon tea, gourmet dinner and room service. Beds: QDT. Modem hook-up, data port, reading lamp, refrigerator, snack bar, telephone, desk, most with hot tub/spa, most with fireplace, hair dryer, bath amenities, wireless Internet access and iron/ironing board in room. Central air. Fax, copier, spa, library, parlor games, laundry facility and gift shop on premises. Limited handicap access. Antiquing, art galleries, beach, bicycling, canoeing/kayaking, cross-country skiing, downhill skiing, fishing, golf, hiking, horseback riding, live theater, museums, parks, shopping, sporting events, tennis, water sports and wineries nearby.

Location: Small rivertown.

Publicity: *Minneapolis-St. Paul Magazine, Minnesota Monthly, Midwest Living, Glamour, National Geographic Traveler, Jason Davis Show, Channel 5, Channel 11, public television, several local cable shows, KSTP Talk Radio, MPR (Minnesota Public Radio) and Hometown Boy Makes Good (HBO movie).*

Certificate may be used: Nov. 1-Sept. 30, Sunday-Thursday except holidays. Only valid for Whirlpool-fireplace suites.

Hinckley

Dakota Lodge B&B

40497 Hwy 48
Hinckley, MN 55037-9418
(320)384-6052
Internet: www.dakotalodge.com
E-mail: stay@dakotalodge.com

Circa 1975. Designed for comfort and privacy on six scenic acres, the lodge boasts a rustic exterior and a gracious interior. Well-appointed guest bedrooms feature whirlpool tubs and fireplaces. A graciously furnished two-bedroom cottage also is available. Start the day with a satisfying breakfast. A variety of nearby activities include a 32-mile bike trail, casino and antique shops.

Innkeeper(s): Sue & Steve Johnson. $119-149. 4 rooms with PB, 4 with FP, 4 with WP, 1 cottage, 1 guest house, 1 cabin, 1 conference room. Breakfast and snacks/refreshments included in rates. Types of meals: Full bkfst, veg bkfst, early coffee/tea, picnic lunch, wine and room service. Beds: KQT. VCR, DVD, reading lamp, CD player, ceiling fan, clock radio, hair dryer, bath amenities, wireless Internet access and iron/ironing board in room. Central air. TV, fax, copier, library, parlor games, telephone and fireplace on premises. Handicap access. Antiquing, bicycling, canoeing/kayaking, cross-country skiing, fishing, golf, hiking, horseback riding, museums, parks, water sports, Casino, Country music theater and Movie theater nearby.

Location: Country.

Certificate may be used: All year, Monday-Thursday, excluding holidays. Subject to availability.

Lanesboro

Stone Mill Suites

100 Beacon Street East
Lanesboro, MN 55949
(507)467-8663 (866)897-8663 Fax:(507)467-2470
Internet: www.stonemillsuites.com
E-mail: stonemillsuites@hotmail.com

Circa 1885. Combining a historical heritage with modern conveniences, this nineteenth-century stone building was built using limestone quarried from the area's surrounding bluffs. The original clay ceilings and stair railings accent the decor. Themed suites and guest bedrooms reflect local history and its undeniable charm. Relaxing amenities feature a fireplace, whirlpool tub, microwave and refrigerator. Children are welcome, ask about family packages. A generous continental breakfast may include English muffins, bakery items from Lanesboro Pastries, cereal, fruit, beverages and French toast topped with strawberries, blueberries and whipped cream. A variety of museums and the Laura Ingalls Wilder Site are all within a 30-minute drive.

$80-160. 10 rooms with PB, 4 with FP, 7 suites. Breakfast included in rates. Types of meals: Cont plus and early coffee/tea. Beds: KQDT. Modem hook-up, data port, cable TV, VCR, reading lamp, refrigerator, ceiling fan, clock radio, telephone, coffeemaker, desk, hot tub/spa, fireplace and microwave in room. Air conditioning. Fax and parlor games on premises. Handicap access. Antiquing, art galleries, bicycling, canoeing/kayaking, cross-country skiing, fishing, golf, hiking, live theater, museums, parks, shopping and wineries nearby.

Location: Historic Bluff Country.

Publicity: *MN Monthly, Midwest Getaway, Wisconsin State Journal and Minneapolis Star Tribune.*

Certificate may be used: Anytime, Sunday-Thursday, Anytime, subject to availability, Anytime, Last Minute-Based on Availability.

Nevis

The Park Street Inn

106 Park St
Nevis, MN 56467-9704
(218)652-4500 (800)797-1778
Internet: www.parkstreetinn.com
E-mail: psi@unitelc.com

Circa 1912. This late Victorian home was built by one of Minnesota's many Norwegian immigrants, a prominent businessman. He picked an ideal spot for the home, which overlooks Lake Belle Taine and sits across from a town park. The suite includes an all-season porch and a double whirlpool tub. The Grotto Room, a new addition, offers an oversize whirlpool and a waterfall. Oak lamposts light the foyer, and the front parlor is highlighted by a Mission oak fireplace. Homemade fare such as waffles, pancakes, savory meats, egg dishes and French toast are served during the inn's daily country breakfast. Bicyclists will appreciate the close access to the Heartland Bike Trail, just half a block away.

Innkeeper(s): Don & Linda Hayle. $75-125. 4 rooms with PB, 2 with WP, 1 two-bedroom suite. Breakfast included in rates. Types of meals: Full bkfst, early coffee/tea, picnic lunch and snacks/refreshments. Beds: KQD. Reading lamp, stereo, clock radio, some with hot tub/spa, wireless Internet access, TV and DVD in room. Air conditioning. TV, DVD, fax, copier, library, parlor games, telephone, fireplace, VCR available in common area, Movies, Books and Games available on premises. Amusement parks, antiquing, art galleries, beach, bicycling, canoeing/kayaking, cross-country skiing, fishing, golf, hiking, horseback riding, live theater, parks, shopping, water sports, wineries, Itasca State Park, Heartland bike and snowmobile trail, Paul Bunyan State Forest and ATV trails nearby.

Location: Small town.

"Our favorite respite in the Heartland, where the pace is slow, hospitality is great and food is wonderful."

Certificate may be used: Sept. 15 to May 15, anytime, except holidays.

New Ulm

Deutsche Strasse (German Street) B&B

404 South German Street
New Ulm, MN 56073
(507)354-2005 (866)226-9856
Internet: www.deutschestrasse.com
E-mail: info@deutschestrasse.com

Circa 1884. Overlooking the Minnesota River Valley, this stately 1884 home located in the historic district blends Craftsman or Arts and Crafts architecture with a Victorian flair. Common rooms offer a variety of relaxing settings. Play games in the formal dining room, watch the fish in the huge aquarium, sit by the candlelit fireplace in the living room, or play the piano in the Welcome Room. Guest bedrooms exude Old World charm and are furnished with antiques and decorative accents. Breakfast is served on fine crystal and china in the All-Season Sun Porch. Accompanied by the inn's special blend coffee, signature dishes may include homemade granola, German sautéed apples with cinnamon-swirl French toast and Deutsche Strasse Potato Hash.

Innkeeper(s): Gary and Ramona Sonnenberg. $89-179. 5 rooms with PB, 2 with FP. Breakfast and wine included in rates. Types of meals: Full gourmet bkfst and early coffee/tea. Beds: KQD. Reading lamp, some with fireplace, bath amenities, wireless Internet access and filtered drinking water provided to our guests in room. Air conditioning. Library, parlor games, telephone and

gift shop on premises. Limited handicap access. Antiquing, art galleries, beach, bicycling, cross-country skiing, fishing, golf, hiking, museums, parks, shopping, sporting events, tennis, wineries, Morgan Creek Vineyards tours and events, Schell's Brewery tours, Historic home tours: John Lind home and Wanda Gag home, Minnesota Music Hall of Fame, Glockenspiel, putting green, frisbee golf and Minnesota River Valley National Scenic Byway nearby.

Location: City.

Certificate may be used: Last minute based on projected availability.

Red Wing

Moondance Inn

1105 W 4th St
Red Wing, MN 55066-2423
(651)388-8145 (866)388-8145 Fax:(651)388-9655
Internet: www.moondanceinn.com
E-mail: info@moondanceinn.com

Circa 1874. Experience exquisite surroundings at this magnificent Italianate home sitting on two city lots in the historic district. Listed in the National Register, the inn has exterior walls made of thick limestone block, and massive butternut and oak pieces for beams, walls and window sills. A grand staircase, gilded stenciled ceiling, Steuben and Tiffany chandeliers, and a huge living room imparts a European influence. The great room showcases a Red Wing tile and oak fireplace. Each of the spacious guest bedrooms and the Garden Suite features a two-person whirlpool tub and antique furnishings. Luxurious fabrics include gold satin, red silk, brocade, damask and tapestry. A full breakfast buffet is offered on weekends, a hearty meal is served during the week. Appetizers are available mid-afternoon. Retreat to private gardens and a terraced hillside or relax on the front porch.

Innkeeper(s): Mikel Waulk & Chris Brown Mahoney. $125-199. 5 rooms with PB, 1 conference room. Breakfast and snacks/refreshments included in rates. Types of meals: Full gourmet bkfst, veg bkfst, early coffee/tea, gourmet lunch and gourmet dinner. Beds: KQ. Modem hook-up, reading lamp, hot tub and two-person whirlpools in room. Central air. TV, VCR, fax, copier, library, parlor games, telephone, fireplace and porch on premises. Amusement parks, antiquing, art galleries, bicycling, canoeing/kayaking, cross-country skiing, downhill skiing, fishing, golf, hiking, live theater, museums, parks, shopping, sporting events, tennis and water sports nearby.

Location: Small town.

Publicity: *Conde Nast Traveler, Minneapolis Star Tribune, Minneapolis St. Paul Magazine, Minnesota Monthly, Saint Paul, Pioneer Press and Wisconsin Public Radio.*

Certificate may be used: November through March, Sunday through Thursday nights.

Stillwater

Rivertown Inn

306 Olive St W
Stillwater, MN 55082-4932
(651)430-2955 Fax:(651)430-2206
Internet: www.rivertowninn.com
E-mail: rivertown@rivertowninn.com

Circa 1882. This three-story Victorian mansion, built by lumberman John O'Brien, is the town's first bed & breakfast and has recently been renovated and restored by new owners. Framed by a wrought iron fence, the inn boasts a wraparound veranda. Each guest room and suite has been named and decorated after 19th-century poets such as Lord Byron, Browning, Tennyson and Longfellow. Period antiques were chosen to represent the poets' unique styles. Carved or poster beds are featured, and all rooms offer fireplaces and double whirlpool tubs. Among the many amenities are Egyptian cotton bed linens and plush robes. The inn's chef prepares gourmet entrees for breakfast and in the evening light hors d'oeuvres and fine wines are offered. Historic downtown is three blocks away and overlooks the St. Croix River.

Innkeeper(s): Lisa Lothson. $175-325. 9 rooms with PB, 9 with FP, 4 suites. Breakfast included in rates. Types of meals: Full gourmet bkfst, early coffee/tea and snacks/refreshments. Beds: QD. Reading lamp, desk, hot tub/spa, double whirlpool tubs, plush robes, hand milled soaps and Egyptian cotton bed linens in room. Air conditioning. Fax, copier, parlor games, telephone, fireplace, social hour with fine wine and light hors d'oeuvres and in-house chef to prepare gourmet meals (reservations required) on premises. Antiquing, cross-country skiing, downhill skiing, fishing, golf, parks, shopping, sporting events, tennis and water sports nearby.

Location: Three blocks from historic downtown Stillwater.

Publicity: *Country Magazine, Minneapolis Star Tribune, Pioneer Press and Minnesota Monthly.*

Certificate may be used: Valid any season, Sunday-Thursday nights only, holidays excluded.

Wabasha

Historic Anderson House

333 Main St, PO Box 270
Wabasha, MN 55981-0262
(651)565-2500 Fax:(651)565-2600
Internet: www.historicandersonhouse.com
E-mail: info@historicandersonhouse.com

Circa 1856. Said to be Minnesota's oldest continuously operating hotel, the inn has been filled with high-back beds, marble-topped dressers and antiques. A filled cookie jar sits at the front desk, and guests can choose an actual kitty (complete with cat food and litter box) to spend the night in their rooms. Jacuzzi tubs are available, and there's no charge for the warming brick if your feet are cold. Ask about the romantic weekend packages.

Innkeeper(s): Teresa & Mike Smith. $69-189. 22 rooms with PB. Breakfast included in rates. Types of meals: Country bkfst, Sun. brunch, lunch and dinner. Restaurant on premises. Beds: QD. Cable TV, reading lamp and bath amenities in room. Central air. Fax and parlor games on premises. Antiquing, beach, canoeing/kayaking, cross-country skiing, downhill skiing, fishing, golf, hiking, parks, house boat rental, snowmobiling and eagle watching nearby.

Publicity: *The Wall Street Journal, Newsweek., ABC World News Tonight, CBS Evening News, NBC News, People Magazine, Ford Times, Readers Digest, Ladies Home Journal, Insight Magazine, Country Living, Diversion, Omni, Sojurn, The Star, National Enquirer, Continental Air Lines Magazine, Signature Magazine, United Press International, Associated Press and Eye on LA.*

Certificate may be used: November-April, Sunday-Thursday, subject to availability.

Mississippi

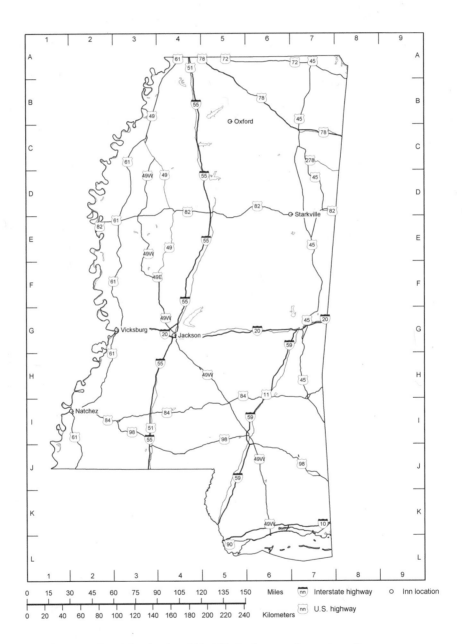

Tell the innkeeper that you have an iLovelnns free-night certificate when you make your reservation.

Jackson

Fairview Inn & Sophia's Restaurant

734 Fairview St
Jackson, MS 39202-1624
(601)948-3429 (888)948-1908 Fax:(601)948-1203
Internet: www.fairviewinn.com
E-mail: fairview@fairviewinn.com

Circa 1908. Surrounded by two acres that include a formal garden with lilies, box hedge and a French sculpture, Fairview Inn & Sophia's Restaurant exudes a romantic ambiance in a

tranquil setting. Bask in the southern hospitality while staying at this 1908 Colonial Revival inn located in the Belhaven historic neighborhood of Jackson, Mississippi. The traditional and elegant décor is

enhanced by antiques and reproductions. A combination study and conference room boasts Tiffany lamps, oil paintings and a Civil War library. Bed & breakfast accommodations are perfect for the business or leisure traveler. Stay in a guest bedroom or suite with fine linens and luxury amenities. Some rooms feature sitting rooms and Jacuzzis. Explore the area shops and museums after breakfast. Complimentary health club facilities are near by.

Innkeeper(s): Peter & Tamar Sharp. $139-289. 18 rooms with PB, 4 conference rooms. Breakfast included in rates. Types of meals: Full bkfst, Sun. brunch, early coffee/tea, snacks/refreshments, wine, gourmet dinner and room service. Restaurant on premises. Beds: KQ. Cable TV, reading lamp, ceiling fan, snack bar, clock radio, telephone, coffeemaker, turn-down service, desk, voice mail, hair dryer, bathrobes, bath amenities, wireless Internet access and iron/ironing board in room. Central air. VCR, fax, copier, library, fireplace, Voice mail, Data ports and Complimentary health club facilities close by on premises. Handicap access. Antiquing, art galleries, golf, live theater, museums, parks, shopping, sporting events, tennis and water sports nearby.

Location: City.

Publicity: *Country Inns, Travel & Leisure, Southern Living* and "Most Outstanding Inn North America 2003" by Conde Nast Johansen.

"Fairview Inn is southern hospitality at its best — Travel and Leisure."

Certificate may be used: Jan. 1 to Dec. 31, except for Thanksgiving and Christmas Day.

Long Beach

Red Creek Inn, Vineyard & Racing Stable

7416 Red Creek Rd
Long Beach, MS 39560-8804
(228)452-3080 (800)729-9670 Fax:(228)452-4450
Internet: redcreekinn.com
E-mail: info@redcreekinn.com

Circa 1899. This inn was built in the raised French cottage-style by a retired Italian sea captain, who wished to entice his bride to move from her parents' home in New Orleans. There are two swings on the 64-foot front porch and one swing that hangs from a 300-year-old oak tree. Magnolias and ancient live oaks, some registered with the Live Oak Society of the Louisiana Garden Club, on four acres. The inn features a par-

lor, six fireplaces, ceiling fans and antiques, including a Victorian organ, wooden radios and a Victrola. The inn's suite includes a Jacuzzi tub.

Innkeeper(s): Karl & Toni Mertz. $49-134. 6 rooms, 5 with PB, 1 with FP, 1 suite, 1 conference room. Breakfast included in rates. Types of meals: Cont plus and early coffee/tea. Beds: QDT. TV and reading lamp in room. Air conditioning. VCR, fax, copier, library, parlor games, telephone and fireplace on premises. Amusement parks, antiquing, fishing, golf, live theater, parks, shopping, water sports and casinos nearby.

Location: Country.

Publicity: *Jackson Daily News, Innviews, Men's Journal, The Bridal Directory, TV Channel 13* and *Mississippi ETV.*

"We loved waking up here on these misty spring mornings. The Old South is here."

Certificate may be used: Sunday-Thursday, May-August and anytime September-April (depending upon availability). Holidays usually excluded.

Natchez

Monmouth Plantation

36 Melrose Ave
Natchez, MS 39120-4005
(601)442-5852 (800)828-4531 Fax:(601)446-7762
Internet: www.monmouthplantation.com
E-mail: luxury@monmouthplantation.com

Circa 1818. Monmouth was the home of General Quitman who became acting Governor of Mexico, Governor of

Mississippi, and a U.S. Congressman. In the National Historic Landmark, the inn features antique four-poster and canopy beds, turndown service and an evening cocktail hour. Guests Jefferson Davis and Henry Clay enjoyed the same acres of gardens, pond and walking paths available today. Elegant, five-course Southern dinners are served in the beautifully appointed dining room and parlors.

Innkeeper(s): Ron & Lani Riches. $195-375. 30 rooms with PB, 18 with FP, 16 suites, 6 cottages, 1 conference room. Breakfast included in rates. Types of meals: Full bkfst, early coffee/tea and dinner. Restaurant on premises. Beds: KQDT. Cable TV, reading lamp, CD player, clock radio, turn-down service and desk in room. Air conditioning. TV, fax, copier, telephone and fireplace on premises. Antiquing and shopping nearby.

Publicity: *Travel & Leisure* top 100 hotels in the world (2006) and *Conde Nast Traveler.*

"The best historical inn we have stayed at anywhere."

Certificate may be used: January-February, June-July, August, November-December, Sunday-Thursday, subject to availability.

Vicksburg

Stained Glass Manor - Oak Hall

2430 Drummond St
Vicksburg, MS 39180-4114
(601)638-8893 (888)VIC-KBNB Fax:(601)636-3055
Internet: www.vickbnb.com
E-mail: vickbnb@magnolia.net

Circa 1902. Billed by the innkeepers as "Vicksburg's historic Vick inn," this restored, Mission-style manor boasts 40 stained-glass windows, original woodwork and light fixtures. Period furnishings create a Victorian flavor. George Washington Maher, who employed a young draftsman named Frank Lloyd Wright, probably designed the home, which was built from 1902 to 1908. Lewis J. Millet did the art for 36 of the stained-glass panels. The home's first owner, Fannie Vick Willis Johnson, was a descendent of the first Vick in Vicksburg. All but one guest room has a fireplace, and all are richly appointed with antiques, reproductions and Oriental rugs. "New Orleans" breakfasts begin with cafe au lait, freshly baked bread, Quiche Lorraine and other treats.

Innkeeper(s): Bill & Shirley Smollen. $99-185. 5 rooms with PB, 3 with FP, 1 cottage, 1 guest house, 1 cabin, 3 conference rooms. Breakfast included in rates. Types of meals: Full gourmet bkfst. Beds: KQDT. Modem hook-up, cable TV, VCR, clock radio, telephone, desk, fireplace and cast iron clawfoot tubs in room. Air conditioning. Fax, sauna, library, parlor games, fireplace and laundry facility on premises. Antiquing, art galleries, bicycling, fishing, golf, hiking, horseback riding, live theater, museums, parks, shopping, tennis, home tours and historic sites nearby.

Location: City. Historic City.

Certificate may be used: Anytime, Sunday-Thursday, subject to availability, excluding holiday weekends, Valentines Day, etc.

Missouri

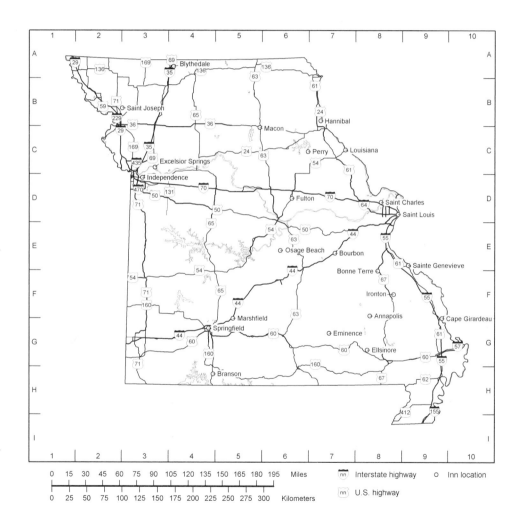

0 15 30 45 60 75 90 105 120 135 150 165 180 195   Miles

0 25 50 75 100 125 150 175 200 225 250 275 300   Kilometers

Interstate highway   o   Inn location

U.S. highway

Annapolis

Rachel's B&B

202 West Second
Annapolis, MO 63620
(573)598-4656 (888)245-7771 Fax:(573)598-3439
Internet: www.rachelsbb.com
E-mail: info@rachelsbb.com

Circa 1921. Formerly the Bolch Mansion, now this renovated Arts and Craft-style B&B is named after the innkeepers' youngest daughter. Annapolis' oldest home, with original glass doorknobs, woodwork, built-in book cases and country elegance, sits on one acre surrounded by mountains and hills. Perfect for a remote romantic getaway, enjoy two-person Jacuzzis, bath salts, robes, fireplace, soft music, romantic in-room videos and private decks. Some rooms are specifically family friendly. In the common room an antique rocking horse is available. There is a large video selection. Enjoy the landscaped grounds with garden pond, goldfish and waterfall, then relax in the outdoor hot tub.

Innkeeper(s): Joe & Sharon Cluck. $90-145. 5 rooms, 5 with FP, 5 with HT, 5 with WP, 5 total suites, including 1 three-bedroom suite, 1 cottage, 1 conference room. Breakfast, snacks/refreshments, Room refrigerators are stocked with drinks, coffee, tea, capuccino, hot cider and hot chocolate and always available at no extra cost included in rates. Types of meals: Full gourmet bkfst, veg bkfst, early coffee/tea, gourmet dinner, Romantic Candlelight dinners by reservations for lodging guest and full restaurant menu. Beds: KQDT. Cable TV, VCR, DVD, reading lamp, stereo, refrigerator, ceiling fan, clock radio, telephone, coffeemaker, turn-down service, desk, hot tub/spa, fireplace, hair dryer, bathrobes, bath amenities, wireless Internet access, iron/ironing board, Satellite TV, refigerators, private entrances, extra fan, clean air filtration system, canopy beds, shower in each room and private decks in room. Central air. Fax, copier, spa, library, parlor games, laundry facility, Beautiful rose gardens with private sitting areas, Fountains, Garden ponds and Massage room on premises on premises. Handicap access. Amusement parks, antiquing, beach, bicycling, canoeing/kayaking, fishing, golf, hiking, horseback riding, live theater, museums, parks, shopping, water sports, fishing, hunting and pottery shops nearby.

Location: Country, mountains. Two hours south of St. Louis.

Publicity: *Missouri Life Magazine 2005 "Fairy Tale Romance", Journal Banner, Mountain Echo, Mustang Club Magazine, One of the Most Handicap accessible B&B's by B&B Journal Book of Lists for 2001, Bed & Breakfast and Bikes Travel Guide Book, Best for Rest and Relaxation 2003, Inn Travelers Magazine (fall 2004), KTJJ, CH. 12 Tour Book 2005, J98 in Farmington, Mo., Dockins Radio Group, Piedmont, Mo, Farmington, Mo. Breakfast on the Radio, Ste. Genevieve, Mo. Radio Station, Breakfast on the Radio (two stations) in Sedalia and Mo.*

Certificate may be used: Anytime, Sunday-Thursday.

Blythedale

Painted Lady

516 Walnut
Blythedale, MO 64426
(660)867-5329
E-mail: jimhitt@grm.net

Circa 1906. It is easy to relax in this quiet setting on four acres in a small-town village. The Queen Anne home is framed by large trees and wrought iron fencing that adjoins the pasture. Sit on the wraparound porch accented with hanging flower baskets. The home's elegant décor features early 1900s antiques and replicas. After a restful night's sleep, wake up to a hearty country breakfast of bacon, eggs, sausage, biscuits and gravy, fresh fruit, homemade cinnamon rolls, pork loin, hash browns, hot coffee and a large pitcher of orange juice. Carriage rides are available, pulled by June, the dapple gray mare. Ask about candlelight dinners.

Innkeeper(s): Tammy and Jim Hitt. $75-125. 4 rooms, 1 with FP. Breakfast included in rates. Types of meals: Full gourmet bkfst, Sun. brunch, picnic lunch and dinner. Beds: KQ. Cable TV, ceiling fan, clock radio, turn-down service, fireplace and bathrobes in room. Central air. Antiquing, fishing and sporting events nearby.

Location: Village.

Certificate may be used: Anytime, subject to availability.

Bonne Terre

Victorian Veranda

207 E School St
Bonne Terre, MO 63628
(573)358-1134 (800)343-1134
Internet: www.victorianveranda.com
E-mail: info@victorianveranda.com

Circa 1868. A veranda encircles this blue and white Queen Anne and there are finely crafted decorative details such as porch columns and dentil work. Furnishings in the dining room are country-style enhanced by light floral wallpaper, fine wood paneling and woodwork around the doors, all painted white. Egg casseroles, potatoes and coffee cakes are served here. There are eight state parks in the area and Cherokee Landing offers canoe trips along the river.

Innkeeper(s): Galen & Karen Forney. $95-135. 4 rooms with PB, 1 two-bedroom suite. Breakfast, afternoon tea, snacks/refreshments and hors d'oeuvres included in rates. Types of meals: Full gourmet bkfst, veg bkfst, early coffee/tea, picnic lunch and room service. Beds: Q. Reading lamp, stereo, refrigerator, ceiling fan, snack bar, clock radio, telephone, desk, hair dryer, bathrobes, bath amenities and iron/ironing board in room. Central air. TV, VCR, parlor games and fireplace on premises. Antiquing, canoeing/kayaking, fishing, golf, hiking, live theater, parks, shopping, sporting events, tennis, water sports, wineries and scuba diving/cave nearby.

Location: Small town.

Certificate may be used: Jan. 2 to Dec. 23, Sunday-Thursday.

Bourbon

Meramec Farm Cabins & Trail Riding Vacations, LLC

208 Thickety Ford Rd
Bourbon, MO 65441
(573)732-4765
Internet: www.meramecfarm.com
E-mail: mfarmbnb@fidnet.com

Circa 1811. This farmhouse inn and cedar guest cabin are found on a working cattle operation, little more than an hour's  drive from St. Louis. Seven generations have lived and worked the farm, which boasts 460 acres. Visitors stay in the 1880s farmhouse or the cabin, built from cedar cut on the farm. The inn's proximity to the Meramec River and Vilander Bluffs provides excellent views and many outdoor activities. Spring visitors are treated to the sight of baby calves. Meramec Caverns and several state parks are nearby.

Innkeeper(s): Carol Springer. $80. 2 cabins. Types of meals: Early coffee/tea and picnic lunch. Beds: QDT. Reading lamp, refrigerator, ceiling fan, clock radio and desk in room. Air conditioning. VCR, DVD, telephone, fireplace, BBQ, Picnic tables, Porches and Kitchens on premises. Antiquing and fishing nearby.

Location: Country.

Publicity: *Midwest Motorist, St. Louis Post-Dispatch and St. Louis.*

Certificate may be used: Anytime, Sunday-Thursday, Nov. 1-April 1, subject to availability.

Branson

Aunt Sadie's Bed & Breakfast & Day Spa

163 Fountain St
Branson, MO 65616-9194
(417)335-4063 (800)944-4250 Fax:(417)336-6772
Internet: www.auntsadies.com
E-mail: info@auntsadies.com

Circa 1964. A tranquil setting surrounds this romantic bed and breakfast on seven acres in Branson, Missouri. Secluded cabins/rooms offer assorted comforts such as private hot tubs. Some also feature whirlpools, refrigerators, microwaves, coffee makers, fireplaces, porch swings, TVs and VCR/DVDs. A breakfast basket is delivered to the cottage, so awake when desired, and leisurely enjoy the morning. Schedule a massage at the day spa and relax with a good book on the private deck. Experience the natural beauty of the Ozark Mountains and explore the Tri-Lake area while staying at Aunt Sadie's Bed & Breakfast & Day Spa.

Innkeeper(s): Dick & Linda Hovell. $120-160. 5 rooms with PB, 4 with FP, 5 with HT, 2 with WP, 1 suite, 4 cottages. Breakfast, snacks/refreshments, A continental breakfast is provided in your room and so you can choose when to awake. included in rates. Types of meals: Cont plus and early coffee/tea. Beds: KQ. Cable TV, VCR, DVD, reading lamp, stereo, refrigerator, ceiling fan, snack bar, clock radio, telephone, coffeemaker, hot tub/spa, hair dryer, bathrobes, bath amenities, wireless Internet access, iron/ironing board and hot tub or whirlpool in room. Air conditioning. Copier, spa, library and parlor games on premises.

Location: Country, mountains.

Certificate may be used: Jan. 30-Sept. 1, Sunday-Thursday.

Cameron's Crag

PO Box 295
Branson, MO 65616
(417)334-4720 (800)933-8529 Fax:(417)335-8134
Internet: www.camerons-crag.com
E-mail: kay@camerons-crag.com

Circa 1993. Sitting high on a bluff, this contemporary bed and breakfast overlooks Lake Taneycomo and the Branson, Missouri skyline. Cameron's Crag offers breathtaking panoramic views of spectacular Ozark scenery, warm hospitality and spacious accommodations. Stay in a guest suite that includes a separate entrance, entertainment center with movie library and private deck area with hot tub. Suites in the detached guest house also offer full kitchens and deluxe whirlpool tubs for two. Innkeeper Kay serves delicious breakfasts using the traditionally southern, local cuisine that blends the influence of early German, French, English and Scandinavian settlers.

Innkeeper(s): Kay and Glen Cameron. $105-155. 4 rooms, 4 with HT, 2 with WP, 4 suites. Breakfast included in rates. Types of meals: Full bkfst and Attempt to accommodate dietary restrictions whenever possible. Beds: K. Cable TV, VCR, DVD, reading lamp, CD player, refrigerator, ceiling fan, clock radio, telephone, coffeemaker, hot tub/spa, hair dryer, bathrobes, bath amenities, iron/ironing board, Microwave, coffee service and refrigerator in room. Central air. Fax, copier and library on premises. Amusement parks, antiquing, beach, bicycling, fishing, golf, hiking, horseback riding, live theater, muse-

ums, parks, shopping, sporting events, tennis, water sports, wineries, Fish hatchery and Lake cruises nearby.

Location: Mountains.

Certificate may be used: Anytime, at the last minute.

Cape Girardeau

Bellevue B&B

312 Bellevue St
Cape Girardeau, MO 63701-7233
(573)335-3302 (800)768-6822 Fax:(573)332-7752
Internet: www.bellevue-bb.com
E-mail: info@bellevue-bb.com

Circa 1891. Within three blocks of Mississippi River front Park, this Queen Anne Victorian with gables and bay windows is in the local historic register. The house is painted deep hunter green with taupe and cranberry trim, emphasizing the historic craftsmanship of its gables, bay windows, balustrades, cornices and stained glass windows. A glider and two wicker rocking chairs sit on the front porch. Inside, the original woodwork remains  as well as several sets of original pocket doors and fireplaces. Ask for the Parkridge Room where a six-foot high antique headboard is the focal point or for the Shea Lorraine or Dearborn rooms, both with large whirlpool tubs. There's a fireplace on the patio for evening get-togethers. SEMO University is nearby.

Innkeeper(s): Marsha Toll. $85-125. 4 rooms with PB, 1 with WP. Breakfast included in rates. Types of meals: Full bkfst. Beds: Q. Cable TV, reading lamp, refrigerator, ceiling fan, clock radio, hair dryer, bath amenities, wireless Internet access, iron/ironing board, whirlpool and some with phone in room. Central air. Antiquing, art galleries, bicycling, fishing, golf, hiking, horseback riding, live theater, parks, shopping and wineries nearby.

Certificate may be used: Sunday-Friday, Jan. 1-April 30, November-December.

Ellsinore

Alcorn Corner B&B

HCR 3 Box 247
Ellsinore, MO 63937
(573)322-5297

Circa 1904. Surrounded by 20 acres, this simple Victorian farmhouse is the kind of bed & breakfast guests will enjoy sharing with their children. There are farm animals, and the innkeeper, a former teacher, is like a grandma to families. Early American furnishings are found in the two guest rooms, and a family-style breakfast with three menu choices is offered.

Innkeeper(s): Virgie Alcorn Evans. $35-50. 2 rooms. Beds: DT. Reading lamp and turn-down service in room. VCR, library, telephone and fireplace on premises. Antiquing, parks, shopping and museums nearby.

Location: Country.

Certificate may be used: May 25 to Nov. 15, Monday-Friday, excluding holidays.

Excelsior Springs

The Inn on Crescent Lake

1261 Saint Louis Ave
Excelsior Springs, MO 64024-2938
(816)630-6745 (866)630-LAKE
Internet: www.crescentlake.com
E-mail: info@crescentlake.com

Circa 1915. Located on 22 acres of lush grounds with woodland and bucolic ponds, this three-story, Georgian-style house is just a half-hour drive from downtown Kansas City and the airport. Spacious suites and guest rooms all have private baths, and guests can choose to have either a whirlpool or clawfoot tub. Enjoy a delicious hot breakfast in the sun-filled solarium. Relax in the outdoor hot tub after a refreshing dip in the pool. Try the paddle boats, or borrow a fishing rod and take out the bass boat.
Innkeeper(s): Ed & Irene Heege. $115-250. 10 rooms with PB, 1 with HT, 6 with WP, 3 suites, 1 cottage. Breakfast included in rates. Types of meals: Country bkfst, veg bkfst and wine. Beds: KQT. Cable TV, DVD, reading lamp, stereo, ceiling fan, clock radio, hair dryer, bath amenities, wireless Internet access and iron/ironing board in room. Central air. Spa, swimming, parlor games, telephone, fireplace, Fishing, Paddle boats and Gas firepit on premises. Handicap access. Amusement parks, antiquing, art galleries, fishing, golf, hiking, live theater, museums, parks and shopping nearby.

Location: Country.

Certificate may be used: Valid from November-April, Sunday-Thursday, higher rates prevail.

Fulton

Romancing The Past Victorian B&B

830 Court St
Fulton, MO 65251
(573)592-1996
Internet: www.romancingthepast.com
E-mail: romancingthepast@sbcglobal.net

Circa 1887. A porch wraps around this pristine Victorian home and offers white wicker furnishings. There's a hammock and hot tub with gazebo in the garden. Finely crafted and restored fretwork, brackets and bay windows decorate the exterior. Polished woodwork, a gracious staircase and parquet floors are highlighted with well-chosen Victorian antiques. The Victorian Rose Room features a private balcony. The Renaissance Suite boasts a fainting couch and carved walnut canopy bed, a sitting room and a large bath decorated in the Neoclassical style. In fact, luxurious baths are the inn's hallmark, as is evidenced by the award-winning spa bathroom in the Miss James Study, and there are both indoor and outdoor spas and aromatherapy.
Innkeeper(s): Jim and Cate Dodson. $105-175. 3 rooms with PB, 3 with FP, 1 with WP, 1 two-bedroom suite. Breakfast included in rates. Types of meals: Full bkfst, veg bkfst, early coffee/tea, picnic lunch, afternoon tea, snacks/refreshments and gourmet dinner. Beds: Q. Cable TV, VCR, DVD, reading lamp, CD player, refrigerator, ceiling fan, clock radio, turn-down service, desk, some with hot tub/spa, most with fireplace, hair dryer, bathrobes, bath amenities, wireless Internet access, iron/ironing board and clock in room. Central air. Fax, copier, spa, library, parlor games, telephone, gift shop, CD player and evening desserts on premises. Limited handicap access. Antiquing, bicycling, fishing, golf, hiking, live theater, parks, shopping, sporting events, tennis, wineries, UMC and bike trails nearby.

Location: City. Small town, beautiful historic neighborhood.

Publicity: *Best Spa Bath, Best Interior Design in Arrington's Bed and Breakfast Journal and Most Historical Charm.*

Certificate may be used: Monday-Thursday, no holidays.

Hannibal

Garth Woodside Mansion

11069 New London Rd
Hannibal, MO 63401-7689
(573)221-2789 (888)427-8409
Internet: www.garthmansion.com
E-mail: innkeeper@garthmansion.com

Circa 1871. Thirty-nine acres of rolling meadows, ponds, woodland and gardens surround this Italian Renaissance Victorian mansion. Upon arrival, enjoy afternoon snacks and a beverage in one of the many antique-filled common rooms. An 1869 Steinway square grand piano offers musical interludes. Relax on the front porch or second-floor balcony. Each guest bedroom includes a feather bed and vintage nightshirts. Ask for the Samuel Clemens Room where Mark Twain slept. Savor a country breakfast. A spacious stone cottage is available with a fireplace in the master bedroom and a two-person whirlpool and shower. The loft boasts a surround sound entertainment center; the private deck overlooks the pond. Two new luxury cottages boast large hot tubs. The onsite fine dining restaurant serves six-course gourmet meals.
Innkeeper(s): Col (Air Force RET) John and Julie Rolsen. $109-395. 8 rooms with PB, 6 with FP, 2 with WP, 3 cottages. Breakfast, afternoon tea and snacks/refreshments included in rates. Types of meals: Full gourmet bkfst and early coffee/tea. Beds: KQD. Data port, reading lamp, CD player, ceiling fan, clock radio, turn-down service, desk, fireplace, hair dryer, bathrobes, bath amenities, wireless Internet access, fireplaces and two-person whirlpool tubs in room. Central air. DVD, parlor games, telephone, gift shop and The Woodside fine dining restaurant on premises. Limited handicap access. Amusement parks, antiquing, fishing, live theater and parks nearby.

Location: Country. Country Estate.

Publicity: *Inn Country USA, Country Inns, Chicago Sun-Times, Glamour, Victorian Homes, Midwest Living, Insider, Country Living, Conde Nast Traveler, Bon Appetit, Missouri Life, Show-Me-Missouri, Saint Louis Post Dispatch, KHMO, KICK-FM, KPCR and WGEM.*

"So beautiful and romantic and relaxing, we forgot we were here to work—Jeannie and Bob Ransom, Insider."

Certificate may be used: November-March; Sunday-Thursday.

Independence

Serendipity B&B

116 S Pleasant St
Independence, MO 64050
(816)833-4719 (800)203-4299
Internet: www.bbhost.com/serendipitybb
E-mail: Please call the inn

Circa 1887. This three-story brick home offers guests the ultimate Victorian experience. Antique furnishings and period appointments create an authentic period ambiance. Victorian children's books and toys, antique pictures, china figurines and a collection of antique colored glassware add to the home's charm. Stereoscopes and music box tunes are other special touches. A full breakfast is served by candlelight in the formal dining room. Outside gardens include arbors, Victorian gazing balls, birdhouses, birdbaths, a hammock, swing and fountain. If time and weather permit, guests may request a ride in an antique car and tour of the house.

Innkeeper(s): Susan & Doug Walter. $95. 6 rooms with PB. Types of meals: Full bkfst. Beds: KQT. Air conditioning. TV, VCR, fax and copier on premises. Amusement parks, antiquing, fishing, golf, live theater, parks, shopping, sporting events, tennis, water sports, historic sites and casinos nearby.

Location: City.

"It was so special to spend time with you and to share your lovely home."

Certificate may be used: Anytime, subject to availability.

Woodstock Inn B&B

1212 W Lexington Ave
Independence, MO 64050-3524
(816)833-2233 (800)276-5202 Fax:(816)461-7226
Internet: www.independence-missouri.com
E-mail: woodstock@independence-missouri.com

Circa 1900. This home, originally built as a doll and quilt factory, is in the perfect location for sightseeing in historic Independence. Visit the home of Harry S Truman or the Truman Library and Museum. The Old Jail Museum is another popular attraction. A large country breakfast is served each morning featuring malted Belgian waffles and an additional entree. Independence is less than 30 minutes from Kansas City, where you may spend the day browsing through the shops at Country Club Plaza or Halls' Crown Center.

Innkeeper(s): Todd & Patricia Justice. $98-219. 11 rooms with PB, 2 suites. Breakfast included in rates. Types of meals: Full bkfst and early coffee/tea. Beds: KQD. Cable TV, VCR, reading lamp, stereo, refrigerator, clock radio, telephone, coffeemaker, turn-down service, desk, hot tub/spa, voice mail and fireplaces in room. Air conditioning. Fax and parlor games on premises. Handicap access. Amusement parks, antiquing, art galleries, fishing, golf, live theater, museums, parks, shopping and sporting events nearby.

Location: City.

Publicity: *Country, San Francisco Chronicle, Independence Examiner, Kansas City Star and New York Times.*

"Pleasant, accommodating people, a facility of good character."

Certificate may be used: Dec. 1-Feb. 28, anytime except during holidays and special events. Subject to availability.

Ironton

Plain & Fancy Bed & Breakfast

HC 69 Box 2554 Hwy 72
Ironton, MO 63650
(573)546-1182 (888)546-1182 Fax:(573)546-4036
Internet: www.plainfancybb.com
E-mail: plainfancybb@hotmail.com

Circa 1908. Plain & Fancy Bed & Breakfast is a peaceful country escape in Eastern Missouri in the heart of Arcadia Valley in Ironton. Sit on Adirondack chairs in the yard; relax on a patio glider by the firepit and take a romantic soak in the hot tub overlooking Stout's Creek. Homemade cookies are a tasty afternoon snack. The upstairs refrigerator is stocked with soda and bottled water. A wedding gazebo and a gift shop are also on the grounds. This post-Victorian farmhouse has been refurbished

with modern amenities. The Red Hat Suite boasts a private porch and an old-fashioned soaking tub. The Amish Room has custom-made, handcrafted Amish furniture and a Jacuzzi. A daily hot breakfast and Sunday brunch is enjoyed in the dining room or breakfast room.

Innkeeper(s): Brenda & Tom Merello. $105-195. 4 rooms with PB, 3 with WP, 1 two-bedroom suite, 1 cottage. Breakfast included in rates. Types of meals: Full bkfst, picnic lunch and dinner. Beds: KQ. Modem hook-up, data port, cable TV, VCR, DVD, reading lamp, stereo, refrigerator, ceiling fan, snack bar, clock radio, desk, most with hot tub/spa, some with fireplace, hair dryer, bathrobes, bath amenities and wireless Internet access in room. Central air. Fax, copier, spa, library and gift shop on premises. Antiquing, bicycling, canoeing/kayaking, fishing, golf, hiking, horseback riding, live theater, parks, shopping, water sports and wineries nearby.

Location: Country.

Certificate may be used: Sunday-Thursday, excluding holidays, not valid for cottage.

Louisiana

Eagle's Nest

221 Georgia
Louisiana, MO 63353-1715
(573)754-9888 Fax:(573)754-5406
Internet: www.theeaglesnest-louisiana.com
E-mail: eaglesnest@big-river.net

Circa 1859. Experience small-town America just a block from the Mississippi River at this inn that was originally an old bank. Four adjacent historic buildings are being restored for expansion to include a cooking school and conference facilities. Lavish guest bedrooms and suites feature Jacuzzi tubs and plush robes. Linger over a scrumptious breakfast in the Bistro. Sip an afternoon beverage and fresh cookies from the bakery on the patio. Soak in the solarium hot tub for a truly stress-free stay.

Innkeeper(s): Karen Stoeckley & Staff. $85-125. 7 rooms with PB, 3 with WP, 1 total suite, including 1 two-bedroom suite and 1 three-bedroom suite, 1 guest house, 2 conference rooms. Breakfast and Sunday brunch included in rates. Types of meals: Full gourmet bkfst, veg bkfst, gourmet lunch, picnic lunch, afternoon tea, snacks/refreshments, wine and gourmet dinner. Restaurant on premises. Beds: Q. Cable TV, reading lamp, ceiling fan, clock radio, telephone, desk, some with hot tub/spa, bathrobes, bath amenities, wireless Internet access and iron/ironing board in room. Central air. Spa, parlor games, fireplace, gift shop, gift shop and winery on premises. Antiquing, art galleries, bicycling, canoeing/kayaking, fishing, golf, hiking, horseback riding, museums, parks, shopping, tennis and wineries nearby.

Location: City. Located in downtown historic Louisiana Mo., just one block from the Mississippi River.

Certificate may be used: Jan. 15 to Nov. 30, any days, subject to availability.

Marshfield

The Dickey House B&B, Ltd.

331 S Clay St
Marshfield, MO 65706-2114
(417)468-3000 (800)450-7444 Fax:(417)859-2775
Internet: www.dickeyhouse.com
E-mail: info@dickeyhouse.com

Circa 1913. This Greek Revival mansion is framed by ancient oak trees and boasts eight massive two-story Ionic columns.

Burled woodwork, beveled glass and polished hardwood floors accentuate the gracious rooms. Interior columns soar in the parlor, creating a suitably elegant setting for the innkeeper's outstanding collection of antiques. A queen-size canopy bed, fireplace and sunporch are featured in the Heritage Room. Some rooms offer amenities such as Jacuzzi tubs and a fireplace. All rooms include cable TV and a VCR. The innkeepers also offer a sun room with a hot tub.

Innkeeper(s): Larry & Michaelene Stevens. $75-165. 3 rooms with PB, 4 suites. Breakfast included in rates. Types of meals: Full gourmet bkfst. Beds: KQD. Cable TV, VCR, reading lamp, ceiling fan, clock radio, telephone and four with double Jacuzzi in room. New sun room with therapeutic hot tub on premises. Handicap access.

Location: Small town.

Certificate may be used: Jan. 10 to April 30, Sunday-Thursday, excluding Valentines Day.

Osage Beach

Inn at Harbour Ridge

6334 Red Barn Road
Osage Beach, MO 65065
(573)302-0411 (877)744-6020
Internet: www.harbourridgeinn.com
E-mail: stay@harbourridgeinn.com

Circa 1999. Romantic and inviting, the Inn at Harbour Ridge Bed and Breakfast boasts a contemporary setting with modern and French décor. Poised on a ridge overlooking Lake of the Ozarks in Central Missouri, there are almost two well-landscaped acres with oak trees, goldfish ponds and an herb garden. A gazebo near the waterfall is the perfect place for a wedding. Osage Beach is conveniently located between Kansas City and St. Louis. Select a delightful guest bedroom that may feature a fireplace, whirlpool, private deck or a patio with a hot tub. An early-morning coffee tray is delivered to each room. Indulge in an incredible breakfast in the solarium dining room. Swim in the cove or sun on the dock. Special requests are granted with pleasure.

Innkeeper(s): Sue Westenhaver. $159-199. 5 rooms, 4 with PB, 4 with FP, 3 with HT, 3 with WP, 1 cottage. Breakfast and snacks/refreshments included in rates. Types of meals: Full gourmet bkfst and early coffee/tea. Beds: KQ. Cable TV, VCR, DVD, reading lamp, stereo, refrigerator, ceiling fan, snack bar, clock radio, telephone, turn-down service, hot tub/spa, fireplace, hair dryer, bathrobes, bath amenities, wireless Internet access, iron/ironing board, Complimentary movie & music library, Private decks or Patios, Goldfish ponds, Gazebo, Swim platform, Dock on Lake and Early morning coffee trays

delivered to your guestroom door in room. Central air. Copier, spa, swimming, library and parlor games on premises. Handicap access. Antiquing, art galleries, beach, fishing, golf, hiking, horseback riding, parks, shopping, tennis, water sports, wineries, Party Cove and Mennonite community nearby.

Location: City. Central Missouri, located halfway between Kansas City and St. Louis, MO.

Publicity: *The Missouri Life Magazine 2006, Named the Lake's Best B & B and 2006 Lake Sun Reader's Choice Award 9/06.*

Certificate may be used: November through March, Sunday through Thursday excluding holidays, Anytime, Last Minute-Based on Availability.

Perry

Kennedy's Red Barn Inn

22748 Joanna Dr
Perry, MO 63462
(573)565-0111 (573)567-4155 Fax:(573)567-4068
Internet: www.redbarninn.com
E-mail: redbarn@redbarninn.com

Circa 1998. Country living is at its best at this old Missouri red barn that has been restored as a delightful home on Mark Twain Lake. Beamed ceilings, an antique staircase, rustic wood floors and lots of room inside and out instill a relaxing ambiance. The main floor includes a gift shop, sitting room, library and dining room where a hearty breakfast is served. Guest bedrooms feature quilt-covered brass beds, lace curtains, antiques and wicker. A red heart whirlpool tub with bath products enhances a romantic setting. After a workout in the exercise room, an outdoor aroma-scented hot tub feels great.

Innkeeper(s): Jack & Rebecca Kennedy. $60-85. 3 rooms, 1 with PB. Breakfast and snacks/refreshments included in rates. Types of meals: Country bkfst, early coffee/tea and afternoon tea. Beds: KQDT. Ceiling fan, clock radio and desk in room. Central air. TV, VCR, fax, copier, spa, bicycles, library, telephone, fireplace, laundry facility and gift shop on premises. Amusement parks, antiquing, art galleries, beach, bicycling, canoeing/kayaking, fishing, golf, hiking, horseback riding, live theater, museums, parks, shopping, tennis and water sports nearby.

Location: Country. Mark Twain Lake.

Publicity: *Courier Post and Lake Gazette.*

Certificate may be used: November-January, anytime.

Saint Joseph

Museum Hill Bed & Breakfast

1102 Felix St
Saint Joseph, MO 64501-2816
(816)387-9663
Internet: www.museumhill.com
E-mail: museumhillbandb@yahoo.com

Circa 1880. Poised on a hill in the historic district overlooking downtown St. Joseph, Missouri, this three-story Italianate red brick mansion was built in 1880 and has been fully restored. Museum Hill Bed & Breakfast features an elegant Great Room with an antique upright piano and inviting sitting areas. Relax with a glass of wine on the wraparound porch with a swing and a grand view of the city. Guest bedrooms boast luxury linens and one room includes a whirlpool tub. Lunch won't be needed after a complete gourmet signature breakfast service. A well-stocked guest kitchen adds to the pampering touches provided. Package deals and getaway specials are offered. The central location is perfect for visiting popular spots in several neighboring states.

Innkeeper(s): John and Beth Courter. $120-160. 4 rooms with PB, 1 with WP, 1 conference room. Breakfast, snacks/refreshments and wine included in rates. Types of meals: Picnic lunch, hors d'oeuvres and gourmet dinner. Beds: QD. Modem hook-up, reading lamp, clock radio, desk, hair dryer, bath amenities, wireless Internet access, Living air purifiers, Soft water, 2" memory foam bed toppers, Extra pillow and 1000 count sheets in room. Central air. TV, VCR, DVD, library, parlor games and telephone on premises. Antiquing, art galleries, beach, bicycling, canoeing/kayaking, cross-country skiing, downhill skiing, fishing, golf, hiking, live theater, museums, parks, shopping, sporting events, tennis, water sports, wineries and Historical walking tours nearby.

Location: Historic Downtown.

Certificate may be used: Good for Empire Rose or Emma's Rose Garden Rooms. Anytime, Monday-Thursday, based on availability. Excludes Trails West and Valentines weekend.

Saint Louis

Lehmann House B&B

10 Benton Place
Saint Louis, MO 63104-2411
(314)422-1483 Fax:(314)621-5449
Internet: www.lehmannhouse.com
E-mail: lehmann.house@sbcglobal.net

Circa 1893. This National Register manor's most prominent resident, former U.S. Solicitor General Frederick Lehmann, hosted Presidents Taft, Theodore Roosevelt and Coolidge at this gracious home. Several key turn-of-the-century literary figures also visited the Lehmann family. The inn's formal dining room, complete with oak paneling and a fireplace, is a stunning place to enjoy the formal breakfasts. Antiques and gracious furnishings dot the well-appointed guest rooms. The home is located in St. Louis' oldest historic district, Lafayette Square.

Innkeeper(s): Marie Davies. $95-110. 5 rooms, 3 with PB, 3 with FP. Breakfast included in rates. Types of meals: Full bkfst, veg bkfst and early coffee/tea. Beds: KQD. Reading lamp, refrigerator, ceiling fan, clock radio, desk, most with fireplace, hair dryer, bathrobes, bath amenities and iron/ironing board in room. Central air. Swimming, tennis, library, parlor games and telephone on premises. Amusement parks, antiquing, art galleries, bicycling, golf, live theater, museums, parks, shopping, sporting events, tennis, museums, zoos and botanical gardens nearby.

Location: City.

Publicity: *St. Louis Post Dispatch and KTVI-St. Louis.*

"Wonderful mansion with great future ahead. Thanks for the wonderful hospitality."

Certificate may be used: Nov. 1-March 30, Sunday-Thursday only, holidays and special events excluded.

Sainte Genevieve

Inn St. Gemme Beauvais

78 N Main St
Sainte Genevieve, MO 63670-1336
(573)883-5744 (800)818-5744 Fax:(573)883-3899
Internet: www.bbhost.com/innstgemme
E-mail: stgemme@brick.net

Circa 1848. This three-story, Federal-style inn is an impressive site on Ste. Genevieve's Main Street. The town is one of the oldest west of the Mississippi River, and the St. Gemme Beauvais is the oldest operating Missouri bed & breakfast. The rooms are nicely appointed in period style, but there are modern amenities here, too. The Jacuzzi tubs in some guest rooms are one relaxing example. There is an outdoor hot tub, as well. The romantic carriage house includes a king-size bed, double

Jacuzzi tub and a fireplace. Guests are pampered with all sorts of cuisine, including full breakfasts served at individual candle-lit tables with a choice of eight entrees. Later, tea, drinks, hors d'oeuvres and refreshments are also served.

Innkeeper(s): Janet Joggerst. $89-179. 9 rooms with PB, 1 with FP, 2 with HT, 1 with WP, 6 suites. Breakfast, afternoon tea, snacks/refreshments and wine included in rates. Types of meals: Full gourmet bkfst and veg bkfst. Restaurant on premises. Beds: KQD. Cable TV, VCR, reading lamp, ceiling fan and clock radio in room. Air conditioning. Fax, library, parlor games, telephone and fireplace on premises. Antiquing, golf, parks, shopping and historic area nearby.

Location: Historic town 60 miles south of St. Louis.

Certificate may be used: Sunday through Thursday, Nov. 1-April 30.

Southern Hotel

146 South Third Street
Sainte Genevieve, MO 63670
(573)883-3493 (800)275-1412 Fax:(573)883-9612
Internet: www.southernhotelbb.com
E-mail: mike@southernhotelbb.com

Circa 1790. Located at the square in historic Sainte Genevieve, the Southern Hotel is a landmark and was known for providing the best accommodations between Natchez and

St. Louis, as well as good food, gambling and pool. Guests now enjoy two parlors, a dining room and a game room on the first floor where a quilt is always underway. Guest rooms offer country Victorian furnishings along with whimsical collectibles. Highlights include a rosewood tester bed, a unique iron bed, several hand-painted headboards and a delicately carved Victorian bed. The clawfoot tubs are hand-painted. Guests also can browse the studio shop as they stroll through the gardens or relax on the long front porch.

Innkeeper(s): Mike & Barbara Hankins. $101-175. 8 rooms with PB, 4 with FP, 2 conference rooms. Breakfast, hors d'oeuvres and wine included in rates. Types of meals: Full gourmet bkfst, veg bkfst, early coffee/tea and snacks/refreshments. Beds: KQD. Reading lamp, ceiling fan, clock radio, most with fireplace, bath amenities, iron/ironing board, Fireplace, Clock radios, Ceiling fan, Ball & clawfoot tub, Bath grains and Antiques in room. Central air. Fax, copier, bicycles, library, parlor games, telephone, gift shop, Art Gallery, Best of Mo Hands, Juried artist and Antique billiard table on premises. Antiquing, art galleries, bicycling, fishing, golf, hiking, museums, parks, shopping, tennis, wineries, 1770 historic tour home and Great River Road Interpretive Center nearby.

Location: City.

Publicity: *Midwest Living, Southern Living, Country Inns, Rural MO #3 in the state, Awarded Best cookbook, Best antiques, PBS, Country Inn Cooking, 25 Most Romantic B&B/Inn 2002 and in the top 15 B&B/Inn Best Cook Book 2003.*

"I can't imagine ever staying in a motel again! It was so nice to be greeted by someone who expected us. We felt right at home."

Certificate may be used: Anytime, Sunday-Thursday.

Springfield

Virginia Rose B&B

317 E Glenwood St
Springfield, MO 65807-3543
(417)883-0693 (800)345-1412

Circa 1906. Three generations of the Botts family lived in this home before it was sold to the current innkeepers, Virginia and Jackie Buck. The grounds still include the rustic red barn.

Comfortable, country rooms are named after Buck family members and feature beds covered with quilts. The innkeepers also offer a two-bedroom suite, the Rambling Rose, which is decorated in a sportsman theme in honor of the nearby Bass Pro. Hearty breakfasts are served in the dining room, and the innkeepers will provide low-fat fare on request.

Innkeeper(s): Jackie & Virginia Buck. $70-120. 4 rooms, 2 with PB, 1 suite. Breakfast included in rates. Types of meals: Full bkfst, early coffee/tea, picnic lunch and snacks/refreshments. Beds: KQT. Reading lamp, clock radio, telephone and turn-down service in room. Air conditioning. VCR, fax and parlor games on premises. Amusement parks, antiquing, fishing, live theater, parks, shopping, sporting events and water sports nearby.

Location: City.

Publicity: *Auctions & Antiques, Springfield Business Journal, Today's Women Journal and Springfield News-leader.*

"The accommodations are wonderful and the hospitality couldn't be warmer."

Certificate may be used: Sunday through Thursday, Jan. 7-Dec. 13, subject to availability and excluding holidays.

Walnut Street Inn

900 E Walnut St
Springfield, MO 65806-2603
(417)864-6346 (800)593-6346 Fax:(417)864-6184
Internet: www.walnutstreetinn.com
E-mail: stay@walnutstreetinn.com

Circa 1894. This three-story Queen Anne gabled house has cast-iron Corinthian columns and a veranda. Polished wood floors and antiques are featured throughout. Upstairs you'll find the gathering room with a fireplace. Ask for the McCann guest room with two bay windows, or one of the five rooms with a double Jacuzzi tub. A full breakfast is served, including items such as strawberry-filled French toast.

Innkeeper(s): Gary & Paula Blankenship. $89-169. 12 rooms with PB, 10 with FP, 5 with WP, 2 suites. Breakfast and Homemade cookies in your room every day! included in rates. Types of meals: Full gourmet bkfst, veg bkfst, early coffee/tea, snacks/refreshments, wine, room service and Special meals for dietary restrictions or special needs. Beds: KQ. Modem hook-up, data port, cable TV, VCR, DVD, reading lamp, stereo, refrigerator, ceiling fan, clock radio, telephone, coffeemaker, turn-down service, desk, hair dryer, bath amenities, wireless Internet access, iron/ironing board, beverage bars, health club access and wake-up calls in room. Central air. Fax, copier, parlor games, fireplace, gift shop and the best porch swing setting in the state! on premises. Handicap access. Amusement parks, antiquing, art galleries, canoeing/kayaking, fishing, golf, hiking, live theater, museums, parks, shopping, sporting events, tennis, Bass Pro Shop, Wonders of Wildlife Museum, 20+ Art Galleries, Springfield Cardinals (St. Louis Cardinals AA team), Springfield Expo Center, restaurants, shopping and entertainment within walking distance nearby.

Location: City.

Publicity: *Southern Living, Women's World, Midwest Living, Victoria, Country Inns, Innsider, Glamour, Midwest Motorist, Missouri, Saint Louis Post, Kansas City Star, USA Today and 417 Magazine.*

"Rest assured your establishment's qualities are unmatched and through your commitment to excellence you have won a life-long client."

Certificate may be used: Sunday-Thursday, excluding holidays and certain dates.

Montana

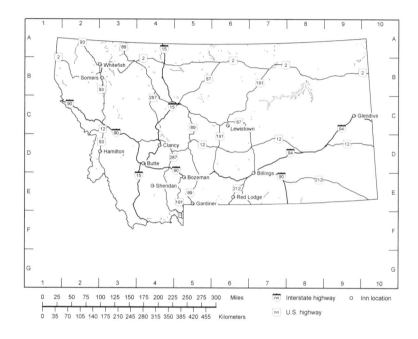

	Miles		
0 25 50 75 100 125 150 175 200 225 250 275 300	Miles		
0 35 70 105 140 175 210 245 280 315 350 385 420 455	Kilometers		

[nn] Interstate highway   O Inn location

[nn] U.S. highway

Bozeman

Olive Branch Inn at the Lindley House

202 Lindley Pl
Bozeman, MT 59715-4833
(406)587-8403 (866)587-8403 Fax:(406)582-8112
Internet: theolivebranchinn.com
E-mail: info@theolivebranchinn.com

The beautiful Montana scenery is a perfect backdrop for this romantic bed & breakfast listed in the National Register. The pampering begins in the guest rooms, which offer plenty of soft, down comforters, feather pillows, fluffy robes and a collection of soaps and oils for a long soak in the tub. Each of the rooms is distinct and memorable. The Marie Antoinette Suite boasts a fireplace, sitting room, clawfoot tub and balcony. The Garden Room offers French Provencal decor with a private garden entrance. Other rooms include items such as wicker furnishings, bay windows, lacy curtains, dramatic wall coverings, a

French bistro table or brass bed. The gourmet breakfasts, which feature special treats such as crepes, souffles and a variety of breads, yogurt and cereals, are a perfect start to the day.

Innkeeper(s): Antoinette Anthony. Call for rates. Call inn for details. Breakfast and afternoon tea included in rates. Types of meals: Full bkfst. Beds: KQT. Antiquing, cross-country skiing, downhill skiing, fishing, live theater, shopping and water sports nearby.

"Elegant, but comfortable. Beautifully restored, wonderful attention to detail."

Certificate may be used: Nov. 1-April 30, Sunday-Wednesday.

Silver Forest Inn

15325 Bridger Canyon Rd
Bozeman, MT 59715-8278
(406)586-1882 (877)394-9357 Fax:775-201-0890
Internet: www.silverforestinn.com
E-mail: info@silverforestinn.com

Circa 1932. This historic log home was originally built as a summer artist colony and school of drama. It later served as a hunting lodge. The unusual turret, stone and massive pine log construction makes for a unique accommodation and the secluded setting adds to the experience. Ask to stay in the Turret Room for an expansive view overlooking Bridger Mountains. It boasts a Queen-size log bed. (The bath is shared.)

Innkeeper(s): Tom Giamanco & Lori Schumacher. $100-150. 5 rooms, 3 with PB, 1 with HT. Breakfast included in rates. Types of meals: Full bkfst and early coffee/tea. Beds: KQ. Reading lamp, clock radio, some with hot tub/spa, hair dryer, bathrobes, bath amenities and wireless Internet access in room. VCR, DVD, spa, library, parlor games, telephone, fireplace, gift shop and hot tub on the outer deck overlooking the Bridger Mountains on premises. Antiquing, art galleries, bicycling, canoeing/kayaking, cross-country skiing, downhill skiing, fishing, golf, hiking, horseback riding, live theater, museums, parks, shopping, sporting events, Yellowstone National Park, Glacier National Park and national forests nearby.

Location: Country, mountains. Ski resorts.

Certificate may be used: October-November, Sunday-Thursday.

Voss Inn

319 S Willson Ave
Bozeman, MT 59715-4632
(406)587-0982 Fax:(406)585-2964
Internet: www.bozeman-vossinn.com
E-mail: vossinn@bridgeband.com

Circa 1883. The Voss Inn is a restored two-story Victorian mansion with a large front porch and a Victorian parlor.

Antique furnishings include an upright piano and chandelier. Two of the inn's six rooms include air conditioning. A full breakfast is served, with freshly baked rolls kept in a unique warmer that's built into an ornate 1880s radiator.

Innkeeper(s): Bruce & Frankee Muller. $120-140. 6 rooms with PB, 3 with FP, 1 suite, 1 conference room. Breakfast and afternoon tea included in rates. Types of meals: Full gourmet bkfst, veg bkfst and Early Coffee. Beds: KQT. Modem hook-up, data port, reading lamp, clock radio, telephone, desk and fireplace in room. Air conditioning. TV, fax, copier, library, parlor games and gift shop on premises. Antiquing, art galleries, bicycling, canoeing/kayaking, cross-country skiing, downhill skiing, fishing, golf, hiking, horseback riding, live theater, museums, parks, shopping, sporting events, tennis, golf, hunting, hiking and biking nearby.

Location: City.

Publicity: *Sunset, Cosmopolitan, Gourmet, Countryside, Country Inns and Victorian Homes.*

"First class all the way."

Certificate may be used: Sunday-Thursday, January-April and October-Dec. 15, subject to availability.

Clancy

Elkhorn View B&B

88 Howard Beer Rd.
Clancy, MT 59634
(406)442-1224 Fax:(406)442-5575
Internet: www.elkviewbb.com
E-mail: elkviewbb@hotmail.com

Circa 2001. Recently custom built from 14-inch diameter logs, this lodge sits on 440 park-like acres with hiking, biking and cross-country ski trails. Exposed trusses, a 32-foot high ceiling, slate floors and massive stone fireplaces create a spacious place to relax. The great room boasts a 61-inch satellite TV. Each guest bedroom is decorated with a theme that reflects the land or culture. Explore the outdoors after a satisfying breakfast or make a reservation for a massage. Enjoy the view from the deck while soaking in the hot tub. A sauna and exercise room is also available.

Innkeeper(s): Ingrid Lietha. $125-180. 4 rooms with PB, 1 conference room. Breakfast, afternoon tea and snacks/refreshments included in rates. Types of meals: Full gourmet bkfst, veg bkfst, early coffee/tea, lunch and dinner. Beds: QD. Modem hook-up, reading lamp, clock radio, telephone, turn-down service, robes, toiletries and reading material in room. Air conditioning. TV, VCR, fax, copier, spa, sauna, bicycles, library, fireplace and laundry facility on premises. Handicap access. Antiquing, art galleries, bicycling, canoeing/kayaking, cross-country skiing, downhill skiing, fishing, golf, hiking, horseback riding, live theater, museums, parks, shopping, sporting events, tennis and water sports nearby.

Location: Country, mountains. Located just 10 miles outside of Helena, convenient yet secluded.

Publicity: *KTVH.*

Certificate may be used: Anytime, Sunday-Thursday.

Glendive

The Hostetler House B&B

113 N Douglas St
Glendive, MT 59330-1619
(406)377-4505 (800)965-8456 Fax:(406)377-8456
E-mail: hostetler@midrivers.com

Circa 1912. Casual country decor mixed with handmade and heirloom furnishings are highlights at this Prairie School home. The inn features many comforting touches, such as a romantic hot tub and gazebo, enclosed sun porch and sitting room filled with books and videos. One room with a private bath and two guest rooms that share a bath are furnished by Dea, an interior decorator. The full breakfasts

may be enjoyed on Grandma's china in the dining room or on the sun porch. The historic Bell Street Bridge and the Yellowstone River are one block from the inn, and downtown shopping is two blocks away. Makoshika State Park, home of numerous fossil finds, is nearby.

Innkeeper(s): Craig & Dea Hostetler. $50-70. 3 rooms. Breakfast included in rates. Types of meals: Full gourmet bkfst and early coffee/tea. Beds: QDT. Reading lamp, ceiling fan and air conditioning in room. VCR, fax, spa, bicycles, library, parlor games, telephone and secretarial service on premises. Antiquing, cross-country skiing, fishing, live theater, parks, shopping, sporting events, water sports and fossil and agate hunting nearby.

Location: City. Small town.

Publicity: *Ranger Review/Circle Banner.*

"Warmth and loving care are evident throughout your exquisite home. Your attention to small details is uplifting. Thank you for a restful sojourn."

Certificate may be used: Accepts Weekends,Anytime, subject to availability.

Hamilton

Deer Crossing B&B

396 Hayes Creek Rd
Hamilton, MT 59840-9744
(406)363-2232 (800)763-2232
Internet: www.deercrossingmontana.com
E-mail: info@deercrossingmontana.com

Circa 1980. This Western-style ranch bed & breakfast is located on 25 acres of woods and pastures. One suite includes a double Jacuzzi tub and another has a private balcony. In addition to the suites and guest rooms, travelers also can opt to stay in the bunkhouse, a historic homestead building with a wood-burning stove. A new creekside log cabin includes a covered porch, fireplace and full kitchen especially appealing to families with small children or long-term guests who want to regroup while enjoying a scenic setting. The area offers many activities, including horseback riding, hiking, fly fishing and historic sites.

Innkeeper(s): Stu & Linda Dobbins. $75-149. 5 rooms, 4 with PB, 2 suites, 2 cabins. Breakfast and snacks/refreshments included in rates. Types of meals: Full bkfst and early coffee/tea. Beds: KQDT. Cable TV, reading lamp, stereo, refrigerator, clock radio, coffeemaker, desk, hair dryer, bathrobes and bath amenities in room. VCR, stable, library, parlor games, telephone, fireplace, satellite dish and fireplace on premises. Antiquing, bicycling, canoeing/kayaking, cross-country skiing, downhill skiing, fishing, golf, hiking, horseback riding, parks, shopping and water sports nearby.

Location: Mountains. Ranch, 50 miles south of Missoula.

Publicity: *Country Magazine and Montana Handbook.*

"It is so nice to be back after three years and from 5,000 miles away!"

Certificate may be used: Oct. 1 to May 1, any day of the week.

Lewistown

Aunt Kissy's Boutique Bed & Breakfast

722 W. Water St.
Lewistown, MT 59457
(406)538-3769 Fax:406-538-5014
Internet: www.auntkissys.com

Circa 1916. Listed in the National Register of Historic Places, this one and a half-story home was built by Croatian stone cutters in 1916. Aunt Kissy's Boutique Bed & Breakfast in Lewistown, Montana has been remodeled for modern comfort but still maintains the fine craftsmanship and unique blend of architectural details. Relax among the ornate gardens or on the covered front porch. Gather in the living room for conversation or a movie near the sandstone fireplace. Snacks, refreshments and afternoon tea are provided. Guest bedrooms and suites boast antique furnishings. Make reservations for any of the onsite spa services available.

Innkeeper(s): Mary Jenni. $120-265. 6 rooms, 3 with PB, 4 suites, 1 guest house, 1 conference room. Breakfast, afternoon tea and snacks/refreshments

included in rates. Types of meals: Full gourmet bkfst, veg bkfst, early coffee/tea, gourmet lunch, picnic lunch, hors d'oeuvres, gourmet dinner, room service, Elegant, gourmet and organic cuisine. Beds: KQD. DVD, reading lamp, ceiling fan, clock radio, turn-down service, hair dryer, bath amenities and wireless Internet access in room. TV, fax, copier, telephone, fireplace and laundry facility on premises. Limited handicap access. Antiquing, art galleries, bicycling, canoeing/kayaking, cross-country skiing, fishing, golf, hiking, parks, shopping, tennis, water sports, Blue Ribbon fishing stream, monthly Art Walk, annual Chokecherry Festival & Hay Bale contest in September and drive-in movie theatre (operates June-September) nearby.

Location: City.

Certificate may be used: Nov. 1-April 30, subject to availability.

Whitefish

Good Medicine Lodge

537 Wisconsin Ave
Whitefish, MT 59937-2127
(406)862-5488 (800)860-5488 Fax:(406)862-5489
Internet: www.goodmedicinelodge.com
E-mail: info@goodmedicinelodge.com

Circa 1974. Fashioned from square cedar logs, this modern Montana-style lodge bed and breakfast boasts a Western décor with comfortable furnishings and textiles reminiscent of Native American themes. Relax by the fire in one of the common areas. Guest bedrooms feature natural cedar walls and ceilings with exposed cedar beams. Two rooms have a fireplace. A European-style breakfast buffet includes homemade baked goods and granola, cereals, yogurt, a specialty entrée, fresh fruit, brewed coffee and juices. The bed and breakfast is located in a mountain setting near Glacier Park, golf courses, cross country and alpine skiing, water sports, fishing and Big Mountain Resort.

Innkeeper(s): Betsy & Woody Cox. $90-220. 9 rooms, 6 with PB, 2 with FP, 2 with WP, 3 total suites, including 2 two-bedroom suites, 1 conference room. Breakfast, hors d'oeuvres and A full breakfast is complimentary to all guests included in rates. Types of meals: Full gourmet bkfst and room service. Beds: KQT. Data port, reading lamp, CD player, refrigerator, ceiling fan, clock radio, telephone, desk, some with hot tub/spa, voice mail, some with fireplace, hair dryer, bathrobes, bath amenities, wireless Internet access and iron/ironing board in room. Central air. TV, VCR, DVD, fax, copier, spa, library, parlor games, laundry facility, gift shop and TV/Library Room with big screen TV on premises. Handicap access. Amusement parks, antiquing, art galleries, beach, bicycling, canoeing/kayaking, cross-country skiing, downhill skiing, fishing, golf, hiking, horseback riding, live theater, museums, parks, shopping, sporting events, tennis and water sports nearby.

Location: City, mountains. Mountains near Glacier National Park and Big Mountain Ski Resort.

Publicity: *USA Today ("Great Places," Sept. 2006), Mountain Sports and Living, Travel America Magazine and Travel Channel ("Wide Open Spaces: Montana & Wyoming").*

Certificate may be used: Oct. 1-April 30.

Nebraska

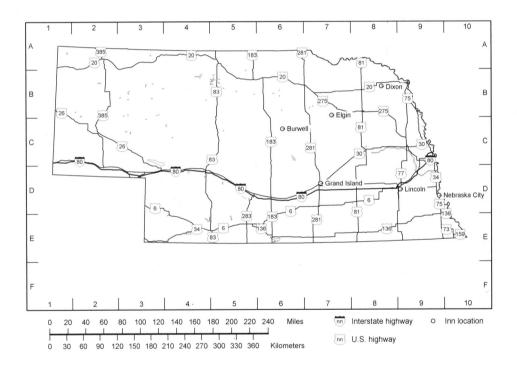

0 20 40 60 80 100 120 140 160 180 200 220 240   Miles

0 30 60 90 120 150 180 210 240 270 300 330 360   Kilometers

(nn) Interstate highway   o   Inn location

(nn) U.S. highway

Lincoln

The Atwood House B&B

740 S 17th St
Lincoln, NE 68508-3799
(402)438-4567 (800)884-6554 Fax:(402)477-8314
Internet: www.atwoodhouse.com
E-mail: larry@atwoodhouse.com

Circa 1894. Located two blocks from the state capitol, this
7,500-square-foot mansion, in the Neoclassical Georgian Revival
style, features four massive columns. Interior columns are
repeated throughout such as
on the dressing room vanity,
on the staircase and on the
parlor fireplace. Classically
appointed, the parlor and
entranceway set an elegant
yet inviting tone. Guest suites
are large and feature spacious
sitting rooms, fireplaces, massive bedsteads and Oriental car-
pets. The 800-square-foot bridal suite consists of three rooms,
and it includes a fireplace, a carved walnut bed and a large
whirlpool tub set off by columns. Breakfast is served on bone
china with Waterford crystal and sterling flatware.

Innkeeper(s): Ruth & Larry Stoll. $85-199. 4 rooms, 2 with FP, 4 suites, 1
cottage, 1 conference room. Breakfast and snacks/refreshments included in
rates. Types of meals: Full gourmet bkfst, veg bkfst and early coffee/tea.
Beds: K. Modem hook-up, cable TV, VCR, DVD, reading lamp, stereo, refrigerator, ceiling fan, clock radio, telephone, coffeemaker, turn-down service,
desk, hot tub/spa, most with fireplace, hair dryer, bathrobes, bath amenities,
wireless Internet access, iron/ironing board and three with two-person
whirlpool in room. Central air. Fax, copier and library on premises. Antiquing,
bicycling, cross-country skiing, fishing, golf, horseback riding, live theater,
parks, shopping, sporting events, tennis and water sports nearby.

Location: City.

Publicity: *Lincoln Journal Star, Midwest Living, Channel 8 local (ABC),
Channel 10/11 local (CBS), KLIN and AM1400.*

"Such a delightful B&B! It is such a nice change in my travels."

Certificate may be used: Jan. 2 to April 30, Monday-Thursday for the Beals,
Atwood or Carriage House suite.

Nebraska City

Whispering Pines

21st Street & 6th Avenue
Nebraska City, NE 68410-9802
(402)873-5850
Internet: www.bbwhisperingpines.com
E-mail: innkeeper@bbwhisperingpines.com

Circa 1878. An easy getaway from Kansas City, Lincoln or
Omaha, Nebraska City's Whispering Pines offers visitors a
relaxing alternative from big-city life. Fresh flowers in each bedroom greet guests at this two-story brick Italianate, furnished
with Victorian and country decor. Situated on more than six
acres of trees, flowers and ponds, the inn is a birdwatcher's
delight. Breakfast is served formally in the dining room, or
guests may opt to eat on the deck with its view of the garden
and pines. The inn is within easy walking distance to Arbor
Lodge, home of the founder of Arbor Day.

Innkeeper(s): Jeanna M. Stavas. $105-115. 5 rooms with PB. Breakfast and
snacks/refreshments included in rates. Types of meals: Full gourmet bkfst,
veg bkfst, afternoon tea and room service. Beds: KQT. Cable TV, reading
lamp, CD player, ceiling fan, clock radio, desk, hair dryer, bathrobes, wireless
Internet access and Bottled water in room. Central air. VCR, DVD, fax, copier,
spa, parlor games, telephone, gift shop, Wraparound porch, Flower and
Water gardens on premises. Antiquing, art galleries, bicycling, fishing, golf,
hiking, horseback riding, live theater, museums, parks, shopping, sporting
events, water sports, wineries and Orchards nearby.

Location: Country.

Certificate may be used: Jan. 2 to Dec. 15, Sunday-Thursday.

Nevada

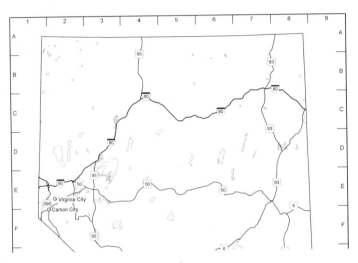

Carson City

Bliss Bungalow
408 West Robinson Street
Carson City, NV 89703-3865
(775)883-6129
Internet: www.blissbungalow.com
E-mail: reservations@blissbungalow.com

Circa 1879. Exquisitely restored, this mansion is one of
Nevada's few historic bed & breakfast inns. Named after its
original owner, the inn was the state's largest residence when
built and it housed the first residential gas lighting and phone
line. The B&B has been updated with modern comforts while
retaining its character. Guest bedrooms feature pillow-top mattresses, Carrera marble and mahogany fireplaces, 10-foot windows, clawfoot tubs, plush towels, fine linens and robes. A spacious family suite is available on the third floor. A hearty breakfast is served on the hand-carved 15-foot Honduras mahogany
dining room table with 19th-century intricate French chairs. An
Arts and Crafts bungalow, circa 1913, is just down the street
with five rooms with private baths and continental breakfast.

Innkeeper(s): Joyce Harrington and Ron Smith. $165-225. 10 rooms with PB.
Breakfast included in rates. Types of meals: Full gourmet bkfst and
Snacks/refreshments at Mansion. Self-serve breakfast at Bungalow. Beds: KQ.
TV, reading lamp, hair dryer and instant hot water in room. Air conditioning.
VCR, fax, copier, library, telephone and fireplace on premises. Antiquing, cross-
country skiing, downhill skiing, fishing, golf, parks, water sports, gambling and
historical tours nearby.

Location: Across from the Governor's Mansion.

*"A Hearst Castle with air conditioning, pillowtop mattresses and
instant hot water."*
Certificate may be used: November-May, Sunday-Thursday, holidays excluded.

Virginia City

Chollar Mansion B & B
P.O. Box 1177
Virginia City, NV 89440
(775)847-9777
E-mail: jeffreywood@peoplepc.com

Circa 1861. The Chollar Mansion, built with Victorian craftsmanship in1861, is listed in the National Register and is the
perfect place to be immersed in the gold and silver mining
mystique as well as the history of Virginia City, Nevada. The
mansion boasts a 164 square foot underground bullion vault.
Relax in the authentic men's parlor with a railroad and mining
library. The paymaster's booth is where the miners got paid
weekly. Accommodations at this bed and breakfast feature spacious guest suites furnished in period Eastlake antiques and an
adjacent cottage decorated in 1930s Art Deco furnishings.
Wake up to the gorgeous easterly sunrise views of Six Mile
Canyon and the surrounding Sierra Nevada Mountain range. A
hearty breakfast is served in the formal dining room.

Innkeeper(s): Jeff & Gena Wood. Call for rates. 4 rooms with PB. Types of
meals: Full bkfst. TV and ceiling fan in room.

Certificate may be used: Jan. 15 to April 15, based upon availability.

New Hampshire

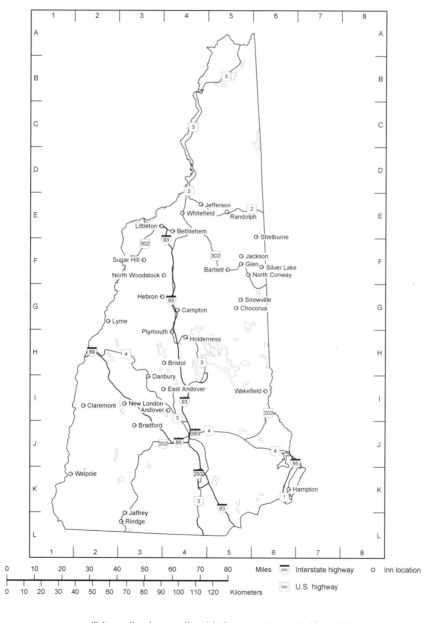

Andover

Highland Lake Inn B&B

32 Maple St
Andover, NH 03216
(603)735-6426
Internet: www.highlandlakeinn.com
E-mail: innkeeper@highlandlakeinn.com

Circa 1767. This early Colonial-Victorian inn overlooks three mountains, and all the rooms have views of either the lake or the mountains. Many guest rooms feature handmade quilts and some have four-poster beds featuring Mascioni linens from Italy.

Guests may relax with a book from the inn's library in front of the sitting room fireplace or walk the seven-acre grounds and enjoy old apple and maple trees, as well as the shoreline of the lake. Adjacent to a 21-acre nature conservancy, there are scenic trails and a stream to explore. Highland Lake is stocked with bass and also has trout. There is beach access to a 200-acre private lake.

Innkeeper(s): Gail and Pecco Beaufays. $135-175. 10 rooms with PB, 2 with FP. Breakfast, snacks/refreshments and Meal plans for groups can be arranged upon request included in rates. Types of meals: Full gourmet bkfst, veg bkfst, Sun. brunch, early coffee/tea, gourmet lunch, picnic lunch, afternoon tea, hors d'oeuvres, gourmet dinner, Sunday Brunch, Lunch and Box Lunch and Dinners can be arranged upon request. Restaurant on premises. Beds: KQT. Cable TV, reading lamp, ceiling fan, clock radio, desk, some with fireplace, hair dryer, bath amenities, wireless Internet access, iron/ironing board, Mascioni linens, Towels from Italy and Molton Brown of London amenities in room. Air conditioning. Fax, swimming, bicycles, library, parlor games, telephone, laundry facility, gift shop and Harney & Sons Fine Teas on premises. Limited handicap access. Antiquing, art galleries, beach, bicycling, canoeing/kayaking, cross-country skiing, downhill skiing, fishing, golf, hiking, live theater, museums, parks, shopping, water sports, NASCAR Track and Greyhound Racing nearby.

Location: Country, mountains, waterfront. Center of 250-year-old historic village.

Publicity: *German Trade, Magazine of the German American Chamber of Commerce, Bedford Record Review, Andover Beacon and WMUR Channel 9.*

"New Hampshire at its most magical."

Certificate may be used: Anytime, subject to availability.

Bethlehem

Adair Country Inn

80 Guider Lane
Bethlehem, NH 03574
(603)444-2600 (888)444-2600 Fax:(603)444-4823
Internet: www.adairinn.com
E-mail: innkeeper@adairinn.com

Circa 1927. Representing all that a New England country inn is hoped to be, enjoy relaxation and tranquility on more than 200 picturesque acres with mountain views and perennial gardens. This four-diamond-rated inn was originally a wedding gift from Frank Hogan to his daughter, Dorothy Adair Hogan. Dorothy hosted many famed guests here, including presidential candidates, Supreme Court justices and actors. Just-baked popovers start the morning fare, followed by fresh fruit, yogurt and specialty dishes such as pumpkin pancakes with Vermont bacon. Homemade cakes and cookies are served during the complimen-

tary afternoon tea service. Make advance reservations for dinner at Tim-Bir Alley restaurant, as it is also open to the public.

$160-375. 9 rooms with PB, 8 with FP, 1 with WP, 1 suite, 1 guest house. Breakfast and afternoon tea included in rates. Types of meals: Full gourmet bkfst, early coffee/tea, picnic lunch and gourmet dinner. Restaurant on premises. Beds: KQT. Reading lamp, stereo, clock radio, turn-down service, desk, hair dryer, bathrobes, bath amenities and wireless Internet access in room. Air conditioning. TV, VCR, DVD, fax, copier, tennis, library, parlor games, telephone, fireplace, gift shop and Pool table on premises. Antiquing, bicycling, canoeing/kayaking, cross-country skiing, downhill skiing, fishing, golf, hiking, horseback riding, live theater, museums, parks, shopping and tennis nearby.

Location: Country, mountains. Franconia, Sugar Hill.

Publicity: *Travel & Leisure, Yankee Connecticut Magazine, New England Travel, Gourmet, Cosmopolitan, New Hampshire Magazine, USA Today, Men's Journal and soon to be featured on HGTV's "If Walls Could Talk."*

"What can we say, we expected a lot — and got much more."

Certificate may be used: November to June, subject to availabilty, not including holidays.

The Mulburn Inn

2370 Main St, Rt 302
Bethlehem, NH 03574
(603)869-3389 (800)457-9440
Internet: www.mulburninn.com
E-mail: info@mulburninn.com

Circa 1908. This English Tudor mansion was once the summer estate of the Woolworth family. The home was built by notable architect Sylvanius D. Morgan, whose inspired design includes many intricate details. The home's romantic ambiance entices a multitude of visitors, and it is within these idyllic walls that

Cary Grant and Barbara Hutton enjoyed their honeymoon. Today, guests also have use of a hot tub.

Innkeeper(s): C. Ferraro and A. Loveless. $85-175. 7 rooms with PB, 1 with FP. Breakfast included in rates. Types of meals: Full gourmet bkfst. Beds: KQ. Reading lamp, clock radio, desk, hair dryer and wireless Internet access in room. Air conditioning. TV, VCR, fax, spa, library, parlor games, telephone and fireplace on premises. Antiquing, bicycling, canoeing/kayaking, downhill skiing, fishing, golf, live theater, parks, shopping, tennis, water sports and romantic getaways nearby.

Location: Mountains.

Publicity: *Cover of Yankee B&B Guide, NECN This is Your Dream House, The Today Show and Home & Garden Channel.*

"You have put a lot of thought, charm, beauty and warmth into the inn. Your breakfasts were oh, so delicious!!"

Certificate may be used: Jan. 1-Sept. 10, Sunday-Thursday; Oct. 25-Dec. 24, Sunday-Thursday.

Bradford

Candlelite Inn

5 Greenhouse Ln
Bradford, NH 03221-3505
(603)938-5571 (888)812-5571
Internet: www.candleliteinn.com
E-mail: candlelite@conknet.com

Circa 1897. Nestled on three acres of countryside in the valley of the Lake Sunapee region, this Victorian inn has all of the grace and charm of an era
gone by. The inn offers a
gazebo porch perfect for
sipping lemonade on a
summer day. On winter
days, keep warm by the parlor's fireplace, while relaxing with a good book.

Enjoy a three-course gourmet breakfast, including dessert, in the sun room overlooking the pond. Country roads invite fall strolls, cross-country skiing and snowshoeing.

Innkeeper(s): Les & Marilyn Gordon. $117-215. 6 rooms with PB, 1 with FP, 2 suites, 1 conference room. Breakfast and snacks/refreshments included in rates. Types of meals: Full gourmet bkfst, early coffee/tea and picnic lunch. Beds: Q. Reading lamp, CD player, ceiling fan, clock radio, some with fireplace, hair dryer, bathrobes, bath amenities, wireless Internet access, some with sitting areas, glass front gas stove, large shower heads and soaking tub in room. Air conditioning. Library, parlor games, telephone, gift shop, piano, afternoon refreshments into the evening, stocked guest refrigerator, porches and pond on premises. Antiquing, art galleries, beach, bicycling, canoeing/kayaking, cross-country skiing, downhill skiing, fishing, golf, hiking, horseback riding, live theater, museums, shopping, sporting events and tennis nearby.

Location: Country, mountains.

Publicity: *Congressional Record, Country Extra Magazine, Inn Traveler Magazine, Accord Publishing B&B calendar, New Hampshire Magazine, Best Recipes from American Country Inns and Bed & Breakfasts—Volume III, Accent Life Style Magazine, NHToDo Magazine, 2006 Yankee Travel Magazine's Editor's Choice and Voted 2001 Inn of the Year.*

Certificate may be used: Sunday through Thursday, excluding holidays, November-May.

Bristol

Pleasant View Bed and Breakfast

22 Hemp Hill Road
Bristol, NH 03222
(603)744-5547 (888)909-2700 Fax:(603)744-9757
Internet: www.pleasantviewbedandbreakfast.com
E-mail: theinnwench@metrocast.net

Circa 1832. Gracing the heart of the state's Lakes Region on a scenic rural road, this bed and breakfast was built as a farm-house prior to 1832 for a local blacksmith with land extending to the shores of Newfound Lake. Relax in country elegance in the great room or on the patio. Play games or read a book from the library by a warm fire. Comfortable guest bedrooms include turndown service. After a satisfying breakfast take a bike ride to enjoy the surrounding beauty.

$95-135. 6 rooms with PB, 1 cottage. Breakfast, afternoon tea and snacks/refreshments included in rates. Types of meals: Full bkfst, early cof-fee/tea and picnic lunch. Beds: KQD. Cable TV, VCR, reading lamp, clock radio, turn-down service, desk, hair dryer, wireless Internet access and iron/ironing board in room. Fax, library, parlor games, fireplace and gift shop on premises. Antiquing, art galleries, beach, bicycling, canoeing/kayaking, cross-country skiing, downhill skiing, fishing, golf, hiking, horseback riding,

live theater, museums, parks, shopping, sporting events, water sports and wineries nearby.

Location: Country.

Certificate may be used: Anytime, Sunday-Thursday, not applicable for cottage.

The Henry Whipple House Bed & Breakfast

75 Summer Street
Bristol, NH 03222
(603)744-6157 Fax:(603)744-6569
Internet: www.thewhipplehouse.com
E-mail: info@thewhipplehouse.com

Circa 1904. Centrally located in scenic New England, this Queen Anne is a grand example of a typical Victorian-era home. Stained-glass windows, oak woodwork, chandeliers and hardwood floors all add to the historic charm. Bedchambers in the main house and two carriage house suites are furnished with antiques, candles, personal spa amenities and plush tow-els. Several rooms feature bronze-engraved fireplaces. Locally grown produce and high-quality meats from Edwards of Surrey, Virginia are used to make a gourmet breakfast of homemade scones or baked goods, eggs Benedict, potato cakes with warm apple sauce, asparagus frittata, crispy bacon and gruyere omelets, tipsy orange French toast and apple pecan pancakes. Enjoy the year-round beauty and activities available nearby.

Innkeeper(s): Sandra Heaney. $100-190. 8 rooms with PB, 2 with FP, 2 suites. Breakfast included in rates. Types of meals: Full gourmet bkfst, veg bkfst and early coffee/tea. Beds: KQDT. Modem hook-up, cable TV, VCR, reading lamp, stereo, refrigerator, ceiling fan, clock radio, telephone, cof-feemaker, desk, some with fireplace, hair dryer, bath amenities and iron/iron-ing board in room. Air conditioning. Fax, copier, library, parlor games and gift shop on premises. Amusement parks, antiquing, art galleries, beach, bicy-cling, canoeing/kayaking, cross-country skiing, downhill skiing, fishing, golf, hiking, horseback riding, live theater, museums, parks, shopping, tennis and water sports nearby.

Location: Country, mountains. Newfound Lake.

Certificate may be used: Accepts Weekends, Anytime, subject to availability; Anytime, last minute - based on availability.

Campton

Mountain-Fare Inn

Mad River Rd, PO Box 553
Campton, NH 03223
(603)726-4283 Fax:(603)726-8188
Internet: www.mountainfareinn.com
E-mail: info@mountainfareinn.com

Circa 1830. Located in the White Mountains between Franconia Notch and Squam Lake, this white farmhouse is sur-rounded by flower gardens in the summer and unparalleled foliage in the fall. Mountain-Fare is an early 19th-century village inn in an ideal spot from which to enjoy New Hampshire's many offerings. Each season brings with it dif-ferent activities, from skiing to biking and hiking or simply taking in the beautiful scenery. Skiers will enjoy the inn's lodge atmosphere during the winter, as well as the close access to ski areas. The inn is appointed in a charming New Hampshire style with country-cottage decor. There's a game room with billiards and a soccer field for playing ball. The hearty breakfast is a favorite of returning guests.

Innkeeper(s): Susan & Nick Preston. $85-145. 10 rooms with PB. Breakfast and afternoon tea included in rates. Types of meals: Full bkfst. Beds: QDT. Reading lamp and clock radio in room. TV, VCR, sauna, telephone, fireplace, game room with billiards and soccer field on premises. Antiquing, cross-country skiing, downhill skiing, fishing, hiking, live theater, parks, sporting events and water sports nearby.

Location: Mountains. New Hampshire White Mountains.

Publicity: *Ski, Skiing and Snow Country.*

"Thank you for your unusually caring attitude toward your guests."

Certificate may be used: Sunday through Thursday nights except Dec. 15-Jan. 2 and Sept. 15-Oct. 20.

Chocorua

Riverbend Inn Bed & Breakfast

273 Chocorua Mountain Highway
Chocorua, NH 03817-0288
(603)323-7440 (800)628-6944 Fax:(603)323-7554
Internet: www.riverbendinn.com
E-mail: info@riverbendinn.com

Circa 1968. Sitting on 15 scenic acres, this secluded country estate is conveniently located between the White Mountains and Lakes Region. Recently renovated, a luxurious decor is accented by antique furnishings. Enjoy afternoon drinks by the fire. Air conditioned guest bedrooms feature cotton linens, mahogany beds, terry robes and cable TV. One room boasts a

private deck and entrance. Breakfast is a multi-course delight that may include favorites like fresh fruit compote and maple yogurt with roasted granola or grapefruit sections with rum-raisin sauce, cinnamon plum cake or cranberry-bran muffins, eggs florentine or Creme Brulee French Toast. Wander through the gorgeous gardens, meadows and be refreshed by the Chocorua River that runs through the grounds. Relax on the deck or in a hammock.

Innkeeper(s): Craig Cox, Jerry Weiss. $95-230. 10 rooms, 6 with PB. Breakfast and snacks/refreshments included in rates. Types of meals: Full gourmet bkfst. Beds: KQD. Cable TV, reading lamp, hair dryer, bathrobes, bath amenities, wireless Internet access, luxurious all-cotton bed linens and massage available in room. Air conditioning. Fax, copier, library, parlor games, telephone, fireplace, gift shop, hammocks, yoga/meditation room and massage available on premises. Antiquing, art galleries, beach, bicycling, canoeing/kayaking, cross-country skiing, downhill skiing, fishing, golf, hiking, horseback riding, live theater, museums, parks, shopping, water sports, sled dog races and scenic train rides nearby.

Location: Country, mountains, waterfront. Babbling brook frontage.

Publicity: *Best Breakfast in New England 2006 Inn Traveler magazine, Best Romantic B&B 2005 New Hampshire Magazine, Best Interior Design and Decor Inn Traveler Magazine, Boston Globe 3-27-05 and New Hampshire Magazine (June 2004 cover).*

"We can't wait to see all four seasons here. Thank you for all the extra touches."

Certificate may be used: November-May, subject to availability, or anytime at the last minute.

Claremont

Goddard Mansion B&B

25 Hillstead Rd
Claremont, NH 03743-3399
(603)543-0603 (800)736-0603 Fax:(603)543-0001
Internet: www.goddardmansion.com
E-mail: info@goddardmansion.com

Circa 1905. This English-style manor house and adjacent garden tea house is surrounded by seven acres of lawns and gardens. Each of the guest rooms is decorated in a different style. One features French Country decor, another sports a Victorian look. The living room with its fireplace, window seats and baby grand piano is a perfect place to relax. Homemade breakfasts, made using natural ingredients and fresh produce, include items such as souffles, pancakes, freshly baked muffins and fruit. The hearty breakfasts are served in the wood paneled dining room highlighted by an antique Wurlitzer jukebox.

Innkeeper(s): Scott Raymond & Keith McAllister. $95-150. 7 rooms, 3 with PB, 1 suite, 2 conference rooms. Breakfast and afternoon tea included in rates. Types of meals: Cont plus, early coffee/tea and snacks/refreshments. Beds: KQDT. Reading lamp, clock radio, hair dryer, bathrobes, bath amenities and wireless Internet access in room. Air conditioning. TV, VCR, fax, copier, library, parlor games, telephone, fireplace and Wireless Internet on premises. Antiquing, art galleries, beach, canoeing/kayaking, cross-country skiing, downhill skiing, fishing, golf, hiking, live theater, museums, parks, shopping, sporting events, tennis and water sports nearby.

Location: Mountains. Rural.

Publicity: *Eagle Times, Yankee (editors pick), Boston Globe and Manchester Union Leader.*

"A perfect romantic getaway spot."

Certificate may be used: Anytime, subject to availability, excluding holidays and foliage season. Only one weekend night, plus one weekday, i.e., not two weekend nights.

Danbury

The Inn at Danbury

67 N.H. Route 104
Danbury, NH 03230
(603)768-3318 (866)DAN-BURY Fax:(603)768-3773
Internet: www.innatdanbury.com
E-mail: info@innatdanbury.com

Circa 1850. Multilingual innkeeper Alexandra imparts a New England hospitality with a European flair at this cozy yet rambling country inn on five wooded acres. The original 1850 roadside farmhouse has evolved into comfortable accommodations with a carriage house and historic wing. Sit by the locally quarried mica stone fireplace in the living room, read a book from the secluded library, converse on the wraparound four-seasons porch, play games in the front game room or relax in the upstairs common room. All the suites and guest bedrooms feature scenic views and either a modern rustic or historically preserved decor. The wait staff in dirndls at the Alphorn Bistro dining room serves authentic Bavarian cuisine and Austrian, Swiss and German family favorites. An adjacent sunroom opens onto a patio and English gardens.

Innkeeper(s): Robert and Alexandra Graf. $99-160. 14 rooms with PB, 2 with FP, 2 two-bedroom suites, 1 guest house, 1 conference room. Breakfast and Any kind of extra meal service can be added included in rates. Types of meals: Country bkfst, veg bkfst, Sun. brunch, early coffee/tea, gourmet lunch, picnic lunch, snacks/refreshments, hors d'oeuvres, wine, gourmet dinner, room service, You may ad on romance and dine package, Chocolate and Cheese or Wine in your room at extra charge. Alphorn Bistro serves Award-winning German Cuisine and has a fantastic Austrian & German Wine List and large European Beer selections. Restaurant on premises. Beds: KQDT. Reading lamp, ceiling fan, clock radio, some with fireplace, bath amenities, wireless Internet access and Some room service available in room. Air conditioning. TV, VCR, DVD, fax, swimming, library, child care, parlor games, telephone, Indoor pool, Award-winning German Restaurant, Full Liquor license, Large German beer List, Fantastic Austrian and German Wine list on premises. Limited handicap access. Antiquing, art galleries, bicycling, canoeing/kayaking, cross-country skiing, downhill skiing, fishing, golf, hiking, horseback riding, live theater, museums, parks, shopping, sporting events, water sports, Cooking classes, Sailing classes, Rock climbing and Massage nearby.

Location: Country, mountains. Rural town.

Publicity: *"Best Wurst" New Hampshire Magazine, Best German Restaurant in NH (2006 & 2007), Best Booth Award and Tasties Chocolate Creation Award from the Care Givers Chocolate festival, American Dream Award, National Restaurant Association - The Restaurant Neighborhood Award, Award-winning German Comfort Food, Best breakfast in New England, Chef Graf cooks on WMUR Channel 9 once a month, New Hampshire Chronicle and THE BIG GUY Show on Sunday Morning.*

Certificate may be used: ANYTIME WEEKDAY'S and Some weekends subject to availability Excluded are: holidays, festivals and Laconia Bike Week in June, some weekends and February.

Glen

Covered Bridge House B&B

Rt 302
Glen, NH 03838
(603)383-9109 (800)232-9109
Internet: www.coveredbridgehouse.com
E-mail: info@coveredbridgehouse.com

Circa 1910. The two-acre grounds at this inn boast the only privately owned covered bridge with a gift shop inside. The bridge, which dates to 1850, houses the inn's gift shop. The grounds also include a private beach area that rests along side a river where guests can go swimming or tubing. Guest rooms are decorated in a country Colonial style with quilts, floral comforters and stenciled walls. Breakfasts include fresh fruit, homemade muffins and made-to-order eggs or perhaps French toast. In warmer weather breakfast is served on the patio.

Innkeeper(s): Dan & Nancy Wanek. $79-124. 6 rooms, 4 with PB, 1 two-bedroom suite. Breakfast included in rates. Types of meals: Full bkfst and early coffee/tea. Beds: KQT. Reading lamp, ceiling fan, clock radio and hair dryer in room. Air conditioning. TV, spa, swimming, telephone and gift shop on premises. Amusement parks, antiquing, bicycling, canoeing/kayaking, cross-country skiing, downhill skiing, fishing, golf, hiking, horseback riding, live theater, parks, shopping and water sports nearby.

Location: Mountains, waterfront.

Certificate may be used: Nov. 1 to May 31, Sunday-Thursday excluding holidays.

Hampton

The Victoria Inn

430 High St
Hampton, NH 03842-2311
(603)929-1437 (800)291-2672
Internet: www.thevictoriainn.com
E-mail: nyhans@thevictoriainn.com

Circa 1875. Elegance and style are featured at this Queen

Anne Victorian inn just a half-mile from the ocean. A romantic gazebo, spacious guest rooms and Victorian furnishings throughout the inn add to its considerable charm. The Honeymoon Suite and Victoria Room are popular with those seeking privacy and luxury. Guests may borrow the inn's bicycles for a relaxing ride or read a book in its deluxe morning room. Common areas include the living room and the sitting room, with its cozy fireplace.

Innkeeper(s): John & Pamela Nyhan. $100-150. 6 rooms with PB, 3 total suites, including 1 two-bedroom suite. Breakfast included in rates. Types of meals: Full bkfst, early coffee/tea and afternoon tea. Beds: KQ. Modem hook-up, cable TV, reading lamp, ceiling fan, clock radio, telephone and turn-down service in room. Air conditioning. VCR, fax, copier, bicycles, library, parlor games and fireplace on premises. Amusement parks, antiquing, beach, bicycling, cross-country skiing, downhill skiing, fishing, golf, hiking, live theater, parks, shopping, sporting events and water sports nearby.

Location: Ocean community.

Certificate may be used: Nov. 1-April 30.

Hebron

CopperToppe Inn & Retreat Center

8 Range Road
Hebron, NH 03241
(603)744-3636 (866)846-3636
Internet: www.coppertoppe.com
E-mail: info@coppertoppe.com

Poised on 15 acres at the top of Tenney Mountain Ridge in the foothills of the White Mountains, Coppertoppe Lodge & Retreat Center overlooks Newfound Lake. The modern setting is in the timeless New England town of Hebron, New Hampshire. Can host up to 150 people for weddings. Feel pampered and appreciated at this intimate and secluded luxury retreat. Beverages and snacks are available all day. Common areas include the living room, library and fitness area. Guest bedrooms and a suite are named after colorful gemstones and boast balconies, large whirlpool tubs and two-person European-style showers. Make a reservation for an in-room spa service. Breakfast is served family-style or as a buffet in the elegant dining room with balcony access.

$135-275. 4 rooms with PB, 1 with FP, 2 with WP, 2 suites, 2 conference rooms. Breakfast, snacks/refreshments and wine included in rates. Types of meals: Full gourmet bkfst, veg bkfst, Sun. brunch, early coffee/tea, lunch, picnic lunch, afternoon tea, gourmet dinner, room service, Gourmet coffee, espresso, cappuccino, tea variety, fresh fruits, fresh baked goods. We customize food service for each guest. Gourmet chefs are available in the area, if you want to plan a dinner party. We use organic or local foods whenever possible. You pick it or catch it and we'll make it. Allergy avoidance is a specialty here. Beds: KQDT. Modem hook-up, data port, cable TV, VCR, DVD, reading lamp, stereo, refrigerator, ceiling fan, snack bar, clock radio, telephone, turn-down service, desk, some with hot tub/spa, some with fireplace, hair dryer, bathrobes, bath amenities, wireless Internet access, iron/ironing board, Towel warmers, slippers, office supplies, flowers or live plants, choice of fiber, feather or memory foam pillows, binoculars, nature guides, restaurant menus, books, magazines, games, puzzles, playing cards and much more in room. Air conditioning. Fax, copier, library, parlor games, laundry facility, gift shop, Yard toys and indoor toys, flip-flops, sunscreen, insect repellent, picnic area, charcoal grill and supplies, Large pond with wildlife, perennial/herb garden, 15 acres of field and woods to explore, dirt road for exercise walks, slopes for sliding, pond for ice skating, room for badminton or croquet, Frisbee or catch, Pet friendly within reason, no surcharge, Cribs, high chair, stools and toddler dish sets available, Kosher, vegetarian and vegan menus are available, Allergy avoidance is a specialty, All stairways are gated and Special requests will be accommodated if possible on premises. Limited handicap access. Amusement parks, antiquing, art galleries, beach, bicycling, canoeing/kayaking, cross-country skiing, downhill skiing, fishing, golf, hiking, horseback riding, live theater, museums, parks, shopping, sporting events, tennis, water sports, wineries, Natural Science Center, mineral and gemstone mines open to the public, glacial caves and features, swimming holes, Audubon centers, guided adventures, dinner cruises, dinner train rides, cooking classes, open mic nights, jazz and folk festivals, marathon, triathlon, motorcycle rally, NASCAR, county fairs, holiday light park in December, brew pubs, D-Acres conservation farm and school, animal farms open to the public with pony rides, pick-your-own farms, cooking classes, quilting retreats, children's camps, family camps and much more nearby.

Certificate may be used: June-September, Sunday-Thursday; October-May; all subject to availability.

Holderness

The Inn on Golden Pond

Rt 3, PO Box 680
Holderness, NH 03245
(603)968-7269 Fax:(603)968-7269
Internet: www.innongoldenpond.com
E-mail: innkeepers@innongoldenpond.com

Circa 1879. Framed by meandering stone walls and split-rail fences more than 100 years old, this inn is situated on 50 acres of woodlands. Most rooms overlook picturesque countryside. Nearby Squam Lake was the setting for the film "On Golden Pond." An inviting, 70-foot screened porch provides a place to relax during the summer.

Innkeeper(s): Bill & Bonnie Webb. $140-195. 8 rooms with PB, 2 suites. Breakfast included in rates. Types of meals: Country bkfst and early coffee/tea. Beds: KQT. Reading lamp, clock radio, turn-down service, desk, hair dryer and wireless Internet access in room. Air conditioning. TV, DVD, fax, library, parlor games, telephone and fireplace on premises. Antiquing, art galleries, beach, bicycling, canoeing/kayaking, cross-country skiing, downhill skiing, fishing, golf, hiking, horseback riding, live theater, museums, parks, shopping, sporting events, tennis and water sports nearby.

Location: Country.

Publicity: *Boston Globe, Baltimore Sun and Los Angeles Times.*

"Another sweet flower added to my bouquet of life."

Certificate may be used: Valid Sunday-Thursday, Not valid in October or on holidays.

Jackson

Inn at Ellis River

17 Harriman Road
Jackson, NH 03846
(603)383-9339 (800)233-8309 Fax:(603)383-4142
Internet: www.InnAtEllisRiver.com
E-mail: stay@InnAtEllisRiver.com

Circa 1893. Imagine a romantic getaway or relaxing vacation at an award-winning New England bed and breakfast, then make that vision a reality by visiting Inn at Ellis River in Jackson, New Hampshire.

Surrounded by the White Mountains, the inn has a trout stream flowing by and nearby hiking trails. Enjoy the intimate ambiance while soaking in the atrium-enclosed hot tub looking out on the river or reading in the sunny sitting room. Gather for afternoon refreshments in the game room and pub, sit in the sauna or swim in the sea-

sonal outdoor heated pool. Period furnishings along with traditional and modern amenities are featured in the guest bedrooms and separate cottage. Many rooms boast two-person Jacuzzis and/or balconies. Most include gas or woodburning fireplaces. Savor a gourmet country breakfast made with local and regional foods.

Innkeeper(s): Frank Baker & Lyn Norris-Baker. $115-299. 21 rooms with PB, 17 with FP, 8 with WP, 2 total suites, including 1 two-bedroom suite, 1 cottage, 1 conference room. Breakfast and snacks/refreshments included in rates. Types of meals: Full gourmet bkfst, veg bkfst, early coffee/tea, gourmet lunch, picnic lunch, wine and gourmet dinner. Beds: KQD. Cable TV, reading lamp, CD player, clock radio, telephone, most with fireplace, hair dryer, bath amenities, wireless Internet access, iron/ironing board, Many rooms with DVD, VCR and Some with balconies or patios in room. Central air. VCR, DVD, fax, copier, spa, swimming, sauna, library, parlor games, gift shop and dinner with advance reservations on premises. Limited handicap access. Amusement parks, antiquing, art galleries, bicycling, canoeing/kayaking, cross-country skiing, downhill skiing, fishing, golf, hiking, horseback riding, live theater, parks, shopping, sporting events, tennis, water sports, Mt. Washington Auto Road, Cog Railway and waterfalls nearby.

Location: Mountains. River frontage.

Publicity: *Yankee Magazine (2007), The Boston Globe (2007), New Hampshire Magazine (2006), The Rutland Herald (2006), Arrington's Inn Traveler (2005) and Inn Traveler's "Best of" Lists (2003 through 2006).*

"We have stayed at many B&Bs all over the world and are in agreement that the beauty and hospitality of Ellis River House is that of a world-class bed & breakfast."

Certificate may be used: Midweek, Sunday-Thursday; January, March, April, May, June and November (non-holiday periods).

Jaffrey

The Benjamin Prescott Inn

Rt 124 E, 433 Turnpike Rd
Jaffrey, NH 03452
(603)532-6637 (888)950-6637 Fax:(603)532-1142
Internet: www.benjaminprescottinn.com
E-mail: innkeeper@benjaminprescottinn.com

Circa 1853. Colonel Prescott arrived on foot in Jaffrey in 1775 with an ax in his hand and a bag of beans on his back. The family built this classic Greek Revival many years later. Now, candles light the windows, seen from the stonewall-lined lane adjacent to the inn. Each room bears the name of a Prescott family member and is furnished with antiques.

Innkeeper(s): Sue & Charlie Lyle. $85-175. 10 rooms with PB, 3 total suites, including 1 two-bedroom suite. Breakfast, afternoon tea, snacks/refreshments, A full British Victorian High Tea (e.g., scones, Devonshire clotted cream and lemon tarts and cucumber sandwiches) may be arranged in advance and is not included in the rate included in rates. Types of meals: Country bkfst and early coffee/tea. Beds: KQDT. Modem hook-up, cable TV, VCR, DVD, reading lamp, refrigerator, ceiling fan, clock radio, telephone, coffeemaker, desk, hair dryer, bath amenities and iron/ironing board in room. Air conditioning. Fax, copier, parlor games, fireplace, We do not board pets and but will help arrange pet boarding for you on premises. Antiquing, art galleries, beach, bicycling, canoeing/kayaking, cross-country skiing, downhill skiing, fishing, golf, hiking, horseback riding, live theater, museums, parks, shopping, water sports, Mount Monadnock/hiking, National Shrine, Lectures, Concerts and Lake beaches nearby.

Location: Country, mountains.

"We have a candle glowing in the window just for you."

Certificate may be used: Nov. 1-May 1, Mid-week May 1-Oct. 31.

The Grand View Inn & Resort

580 Mountain Road
Jaffrey, NH 03452
(603)532-9880 (888)984-7263 Fax:(603)532-6252
Internet: www.thegrandviewinn.com
E-mail: thegrandviewinn@aol.com

Circa 1797. Surrounded by 330 picturesque acres at the base of Mount Monadnock, this resort features a 19th century Colonial mansion, full service spa, world-class restaurant and an equestrian center. It is easy to relax in the warm and inviting country decor and furnishings. Spacious guest suites and bedrooms exude a comfortable, rustic elegance. A satisfying breakfast is served daily. Walk or hike beginner and advanced trails. Swim in an in-ground heated pool and fish or canoe the 30-acre beaver pond. Winter activities include cross country skiing, snowshoeing and snowmobile rentals. Ask about spa and horseback riding packages.

Innkeeper(s): Scott & Kelly Mitchell. $75-250. 9 rooms, 7 with PB, 4 with FP, 2 suites, 1 cottage, 2 conference rooms. Breakfast, afternoon tea and snacks/refreshments included in rates. Types of meals: Cont plus, veg bkfst, early coffee/tea, lunch, picnic lunch, gourmet dinner and room service. Restaurant on premises. Beds: KQT. Telephone, turn-down service and fireplace in room. TV, VCR, fax, copier, spa, swimming, sauna, stable, library, parlor games, fireplace, laundry facility, full service day spa, Restaurant Function Hall and climbing mountain on premises. Limited handicap access. Antiquing, art galleries, bicycling, canoeing/kayaking, cross-country skiing, fishing, golf, hiking, horseback riding, live theater, parks and shopping nearby.

Location: Mountains.

Publicity: *Yankee Magazine 2002—Editor's Choice, named one of the most romantic inns in New Hampshire—2002 and NH Chronicle.*

Certificate may be used: Sunday-Thursday, April-June & September-March, July and August (Monday, Tuesday, Wednesday).

Jefferson

Applebrook B&B

110 Meadows Road / Rt 115A
Jefferson, NH 03583-0178
(603)586-7713 (800)545-6504
Internet: www.applebrook.com
E-mail: info@applebrook.com

Circa 1797. Panoramic views surround this large Victorian farmhouse nestled in the middle of New Hampshire's White Mountains. Guests can awake to the smell of freshly baked muffins made with locally picked berries. A comfortable, fire-lit sitting room boasts stained glass, a goldfish pool and a beautiful view of Mt. Washington.

The romantic Nellie's Nook, includes a king-size bed and a balcony with views of the mountains and a two-person spa. Test your golfing skills at the nearby 18-hole championship course, or spend the day antique hunting. A trout stream and spring-fed rock pool are nearby. Wintertime guests can ice skate or race through the powder at nearby ski resorts or by way of snowmobile, finish off the day with a moonlight toboggan ride. After a full day, guests can enjoy a soak in the hot tub under the stars, where they might see shooting stars or the Northern Lights.

Innkeeper(s): Joy & Tom McCorkhill. $70-175. 12 rooms, 8 with PB, 2 with HT. Breakfast and snacks/refreshments included in rates. Types of meals: Country bkfst, veg bkfst and Dinner available for groups over 10 people. Beds: KQDT. Reading lamp, ceiling fan, clock radio, telephone, desk, some

with hot tub/spa and iron/ironing board in room. TV, VCR, DVD, copier, library, parlor games, fireplace, outdoor kid's play equipment, nature trails and outdoor fire pit on premises. Amusement parks, antiquing, bicycling, canoeing/kayaking, cross-country skiing, downhill skiing, fishing, golf, hiking, live theater, parks, shopping, water sports, Santa's Village, Six Gun City and Story Land nearby.

Location: Mountains.

Publicity: *Coos County Democrat and Berlin Reporter.*

"We came for a night and stayed for a week."

Certificate may be used: January-May and Oct. 15-Dec. 15, Sunday-Thursday.

Littleton

Beal House Inn & Fine Dining Restaurant

2 W Main St
Littleton, NH 03561-3502
(603)444-2661 (866)616-BEAL Fax:(603)444-6224
Internet: www.bealhouseinn.com
E-mail: info@bealhouseinn.com

Circa 1833. This Main Street landmark is centrally located in the White Mountains for year-round enjoyment. Refurbished and elegantly furnished with antiques, the suites feature four-poster beds, fireplaces, Jacuzzis and clawfoot tubs. Relax in luxury with down comforters, bathrobes, coffeemakers, CD players and satellite TV. A feta and fresh spinach frittata with home-baked wheat bread, banana buttermilk pancakes served with local maple syrup, or other delicious recipes may be served for breakfast. Enjoy the pleasant interlude of afternoon tea. The inn's award winning restaurant offers an extensive menu for fine dining and has a popular martini bar. WI-fi and pet friendly.

Innkeeper(s): Brian and Lynn Walker & Blake May. $85-250. 8 rooms with PB, 4 with FP, 2 with WP, 5 total suites, including 1 two-bedroom suite, 1 conference room. Breakfast included in rates. Types of meals: Full gourmet bkfst, veg bkfst, wine, gourmet dinner and room service. Restaurant on premises. Beds: KQD. Modem hook-up, cable TV, VCR, reading lamp, stereo, refrigerator, ceiling fan, clock radio, telephone, coffeemaker, desk, some with hot tub/spa, voice mail, most with fireplace, hair dryer, bathrobes, bath amenities, wireless Internet access, iron/ironing board, Suites have phones and all rooms have complimentary Wi-Fi in room. Central air. Fax, copier, library, pet boarding, parlor games, Pet-friendly suites, One with separate back entrance, Private deck and Enclosed yard on premises. Limited handicap access. Amusement parks, antiquing, art galleries, beach, bicycling, canoeing/kayaking, cross-country skiing, downhill skiing, fishing, golf, hiking, horseback riding, live theater, museums, parks, shopping, tennis, water sports and Snowmobile trails nearby.

Location: Country, mountains. Near Vermont border, west side of White Mountains.

Publicity: *Boston Globe, USA Today, American Historic Country Inns, Glamour, NHToDo, New Hampshire Adventures, Le Soleil, Star Ledger, Miami Herald, Yankee, Courier, Ammonoosuc Times, New Hampshire Magazine, Arrington B&B Journal, WMUR/Channel 9, WSTJ, The Notch and WMTK.*

"These innkeepers know and understand people, their needs and wants. Attention to cleanliness and amenities, from check-in to check-out, is a treasure."

Certificate may be used: Sunday-Thursday, except fall foliage and holidays.

Lyme

The Dowds' Country Inn

PO Box 58
Lyme, NH 03768
(603)795-4712 (800)482-4712 Fax:(603)795-4220
Internet: www.dowdscountryinn.com
E-mail: reservations@dowdscountryinn.com

Circa 1780. This 18th-century inn offers pure New England elegance. The historic home, surrounded by a plentiful six acres, rests on The Common in this charming historic village. The grounds include a duck pond, fountain and gardens- a perfect setting for the many parties and weddings held at the inn. The guest rooms are decorated in a warm, inviting style, many feature stencilled walls or country artwork. The innkeepers serve made-to-order breakfasts and an opulent afternoon tea. The staff will gladly help you plan a day trip to enjoy the charm of the surrounding village and nearby places of interest.

Innkeeper(s): Tami Dowd. $125-230. 22 rooms with PB, 3 suites, 2 conference rooms. Breakfast and afternoon tea included in rates. Types of meals: Country bkfst. Beds: QT. Modem hook-up, reading lamp, clock radio, telephone, turn-down service and desk in room. Air conditioning. VCR, fax, copier, library and gift shop on premises. Handicap access. Antiquing, art galleries, beach, bicycling, canoeing/kayaking, cross-country skiing, downhill skiing, fishing, golf, hiking, horseback riding, live theater, museums, parks, shopping, sporting events, tennis and water sports nearby.

Location: Country, mountains.

Certificate may be used: Nov. 1 through April 1, excluding holidays and group reservations, subject to availability.

North Conway

1785 Inn & Restaurant

3582 White Mountain Hwy
North Conway, NH 03860-1785
(603)356-9025 (800)421-1785 Fax:(603)356-6081
Internet: www.the1785inn.com
E-mail: the1785inn@aol.com

Circa 1785. The main section of this center-chimney house was built by Captain Elijah Dinsmore of the New Hampshire Rangers. He was granted the land for service in the American Revolution. Original hand-hewn beams, corner posts, fireplaces, and a brick oven are still visible and operating. The inn is located at the historical marker popularized by the White Mountain School of Art in the 19th century.

Innkeeper(s): Becky & Charlie Mallar. $69-219. 17 rooms, 12 with PB, 1 suite, 3 conference rooms. Breakfast included in rates. Types of meals: Country bkfst, veg bkfst, early coffee/tea, afternoon tea, snacks/refreshments, hors d'oeuvres, wine, gourmet dinner and room service. Restaurant on premises. Beds: KQDT. Cable TV, VCR, reading lamp, refrigerator, ceiling fan, snack bar, clock radio, coffeemaker, turn-down service and bath amenities in room. Air conditioning. DVD, fax, copier, swimming, bicycles, library, parlor games, telephone, fireplace, cross-country skiing, nature trails and gardens on premises. Limited handicap access. Amusement parks, antiquing, art galleries, beach, bicycling, canoeing/kayaking, cross-country skiing, downhill skiing, fishing, golf, hiking, horseback riding, live theater, museums, parks, shopping, tennis, water sports, walking, gardens, nature trails, rock climbing and ice climbing nearby.

Location: Country, mountains. Famous view of Mt. Washington.

Publicity: Yankee, Country, Bon Appetit, Travel & Leisure, Ski, Travel Holiday, Connecticut Magazine, Better Homes & Gardens, New Hampshire Magazine, Boston Globe, Montreal Gazette, Manchester Union Leader, The Wedding Story and I Dine.

"Occasionally in our lifetime is a moment so unexpectedly perfect that we use it as our measure for our unforgettable moments. We just had such an experience at The 1785 Inn."

Certificate may be used: Anytime, non-holiday, November-June, subject to availability.

Cabernet Inn

Rt 16, Box 489
North Conway, NH 03860
(603)356-4704 (800)866-4704 Fax:(603)356-5399
Internet: www.cabernetinn.com
E-mail: info@cabernetinn.com

Circa 1842. Built prior to the Civil War, this historic home features a deep burgundy exterior highlighted by hunter green shutters and trim. Window boxes filled with flowers add a touch more color. The one-acre grounds are shaded by trees and colored by a variety of flowers. More than half of the guest rooms include a fireplace, and some have double whirlpool tubs. In the afternoons, homemade treats are served, and in the mornings, guests enjoy a full country breakfast with items such as eggs, French toast, pancakes, bacon, sausages and fresh seasonal fruits.

Innkeeper(s): Bruce & Jessica Zarenko. $90-235. 11 rooms with PB, 6 with FP. Breakfast and afternoon tea included in rates. Types of meals: Full Country Breakfast and Afternoon Refreshments. Beds: Q. Reading lamp, ceiling fan, hot tub/spa and antiques in room. Air conditioning. TV, VCR, fax, parlor games, telephone and fireplace on premises. Limited handicap access. Antiquing, art galleries, bicycling, canoeing/kayaking, cross-country skiing, downhill skiing, fishing, golf, hiking, horseback riding, live theater, parks and shopping nearby.

Location: Mountains.

Certificate may be used: November-June, Sunday-Thursday, subject to availability.

Old Red Inn & Cottages

2406 White Mountain Highway
North Conway, NH 03860-0467
(603)356-2642 (800)338-1356 Fax:(603)356-6626
Internet: www.oldredinn.com
E-mail: oldredinn@adelphia.net

Circa 1810. Guests can opt to stay in an early 19th-century home or in one of a collection of cottages at this country inn. The rooms are decorated with handmade quilts and stenciling dots the walls. Several rooms include four-poster or canopy beds. Two-bedroom cottages feature a screened porch. A hearty, country meal accompanied by freshly baked breads, muffins and homemade preserves starts off the day. The inn is near many of the town's shops, restaurants and outlets.

Innkeeper(s): Susan LEFAVE. $79-198. 4 rooms, 15 with PB, 13 with FP, 1 two-bedroom suite, 10 cottages, 10 cabins. Breakfast included in rates. Types of meals: Full bkfst and early coffee/tea. Beds: Q. Cable TV, reading lamp, refrigerator and fireplace in room. Air conditioning. Fax, copier, swimming, parlor games and telephone on premises. Amusement parks, antiquing, bicycling, canoeing/kayaking, cross-country skiing, downhill skiing, fishing, golf, hiking, horseback riding, live theater, parks, shopping, sporting events, tennis and water sports nearby.

Location: Country, mountains.

Certificate may be used: Jan. 2-June 1, Sunday-Thursday, (inn rooms only), non-holiday or vacation weeks.

North Woodstock

Wilderness Inn B&B

50 Courtney Rd. Rts 3 & 112
North Woodstock, NH 03262-9710
(603)745-3890 (888)777-7813
Internet: www.thewildernessinn.com
E-mail: info@thewildernessinn.com

Circa 1912. Surrounded by the White Mountain National
Forest, this charming shingled home offers a picturesque getaway
for every season. Guest rooms, all with private baths, are furnished with antiques and Oriental rugs. The innkeepers also offer
family suites and a private cottage with a fireplace, Jacuzzi and a
view of Lost River. Breakfast is a delightful affair with choices
ranging from fresh muffins to brie cheese omelets, French toast
topped with homemade apple syrup, crepes or specialty pancakes. For the children, the innkeepers create teddy bear pancakes or French toast. If you wish, afternoon tea also is served.
Innkeeper(s): Michael & Rosanna Yarnell. $70-175. 8 rooms, 7 with PB, 1
cottage. Breakfast and See menu on Web site included in rates. Types of
meals: Full gourmet bkfst. Beds: QDT. Cable TV, reading lamp, refrigerator,
coffeemaker, hair dryer, bath amenities, wireless Internet access, iron/ironing
board, cottage has fireplace and two-person Jacuzzi in room. Central air.
Antiquing, bicycling, canoeing/kayaking, cross-country skiing, downhill skiing,
fishing, golf, hiking, horseback riding, live theater, parks, shopping and White
Mountain National Forest nearby.

Location: Country, mountains.

*"The stay at your inn, attempting and completing the 3D jig-saw puz-
zle, combined with those unforgettable breakfasts, and your combined
friendliness, makes the Wilderness Inn a place for special memories."*

Certificate may be used: Anytime, Last Minute-Based on Availability.

Plymouth

Federal House Inn

27 Route 25
Plymouth, NH 03264
(603)536-4644 (866)536-4644
Internet: www.federalhouseinnnh.com
E-mail: stay@federalhouseinnnh.com

Circa 1835. As the name suggests, this bed & breakfast is a historic, brick Federal-style in the foothills of the White Mountains.
In the afternoons, gather by the wood-burning stove in the parlor or on the patio for a wine-and-cheese social with the
innkeepers. Home-baked cookies or other treats also are offered.
Spacious suites boast views of Tenney Mountain. Guest bedrooms feature canopy, sleigh or four-poster beds, luxurious
linens, Caswell-Massey toiletries and turndown service with
handmade gourmet chocolates. A generous New England breakfast buffet is the perfect start to a new day. Spa and beach towels are available for the large Jacuzzi overlooking the gardens.
Innkeeper(s): Andrea and Frank Morese. $109-179. 5 rooms, 3 with PB, 3
with FP. Breakfast, snacks/refreshments and wine included in rates. Types of
meals: Full gourmet bkfst, veg bkfst and early coffee/tea. Beds: Q. Modem
hook-up, cable TV, VCR, DVD, stereo, snack bar, clock radio, desk, hot
tub/spa, some with fireplace, bathrobes, bath amenities, wireless Internet
access, iron/ironing board, 300-thread-count linens, down comforters and pillows and Bose radio in room. Air conditioning. Fax, copier, spa, library, parlor
games and telephone on premises. Antiquing, art galleries, beach, bicycling,
canoeing/kayaking, cross-country skiing, downhill skiing, fishing, golf, hiking,
horseback riding, live theater, parks, shopping, sporting events, water sports,
Holderness School, New Hampton School and Polar Caves nearby.

Location: Country, mountains. Between the Lakes and Mountains.

Publicity: *Editor's Pick Yankee Magazine, "Best Breakfast in New England"
Arrington's B&B Journal, "Best Breakfast in New Hampshire" NH Magazine
and Channel 5 Boston Cronicle.*

Certificate may be used: January-August and November-January (no
September and October). Subject to availability, Sunday-Thursday.

Randolph

Inn At Bowman

1174 US Route 2
Randolph, NH 03593
(603)466-5006 Fax:(603)466-2789
Internet: www.innatbowman.com
E-mail: jerry@ncia.net

Originally a private summer residence, this renovated bed and
breakfast was built in 1948 with the grandeur of a southern-
style plantation. Sit on the front porch amid the tall columns.
Situated in the Presidential Mountains in Randolph, New
Hampshire, the scenic beauty and assortment of activities are
endless. Major hiking trails of the Appalachian Mountains are
nearby. Inn at Bowman offers guest bedrooms and suites that
are welcoming and comfortable. Gather for breakfast and enjoy
the pleasant ambiance. Relax in one of the parlors. Swim in the
outdoor heated pool or soak in the indoor hot tub.
Innkeeper(s): Rich & Jerry & Blanche. $129-249. Call inn for details.
Breakfast and afternoon tea included in rates. Types of meals: Cont plus.
Beds: KQDT. TV, reading lamp, refrigerator, ceiling fan, clock radio, telephone,
coffeemaker, turn-down service, fireplace, bath amenities and iron/ironing
board in room. Air conditioning. Spa, swimming, parlor games and laundry
facility on premises. Handicap access. Amusement parks, antiquing, art galleries, beach, bicycling, canoeing/kayaking, cross-country skiing, downhill skiing, fishing, golf, hiking, horseback riding, live theater, museums, parks,
shopping, tennis and water sports nearby.

Location: Mountains.

Certificate may be used: Sunday-Thursday only. Excluding holidays, ski vacation weeks and foliage weeks, subject to availability, Anytime, subject to
availability, Anytime, at the last minute.

Rindge

Woodbound Inn

247 Woodbound Rd
Rindge, NH 03461
(603)532-8341 (800)688-7770 Fax:(603)532-8341
Internet: www.woodbound.com
E-mail: woodbound@aol.com

Circa 1819. Vacationers have enjoyed the Woodbound Inn
since its opening as a year-round resort in 1892. The main
inn actually was built in 1819, and this portion offers 19
guest rooms, all appointed with classic-style furnishings. The
innkeepers offer more modern accommodations in the
Edgewood Building, and
there are eleven cabins available. The one- and two-bedroom cabins rest along the
shore of Lake Contoocook.
The inn's 162 acres include
a private beach, fishing, hiking, nature trails, tennis
courts, a volleyball court, a
game room and a golf course. There is a full service restau-
rant, a cocktail lounge and banquet facilities on premises. If
for some reason one would want to venture away from the

inn, the region is full of activities, including ski areas, more golf courses and Mount Monadnock.

Innkeeper(s): Rick Kohlmorgen. $99-155. 50 rooms, 45 with PB, 13 cabins, 5 conference rooms. Breakfast included in rates. Types of meals: Full bkfst, lunch and dinner. Restaurant on premises. Beds: QDT. Clock radio, telephone, desk and cabins are lakefront with fireplaces in room. Air conditioning. VCR, copier, swimming, tennis, library, parlor games and fireplace on premises. Handicap access. Amusement parks, antiquing, cross-country skiing, downhill skiing, fishing, live theater, parks, shopping and water sports nearby.

Location: Mountains.

Certificate may be used: Jan. 2-May 15, Oct. 20-Dec. 29 based on availability.

Shelburne

Mt. Washington Bed & Breakfast

421 State Route 2
Shelburne, NH 03581
(603)466-2669 (877)466-2399 Fax:(N/A)
Internet: www.mtwashingtonbb.com
E-mail: mtwashbb@yahoo.com

Circa 1880. Open year-round, antiques and modern country furnishings accent this Federal-style farmhouse built in the 1800s. Sitting on more than five acres at the entrance to the Mount Washington Valley, enjoy looking at the peaks of Mt. Madison, Mt. Adams and the crystal-clear waters of Reflection Pond just outside the door. Relax with afternoon beverages and snacks on the wraparound porch surrounded by colorful flowers. Guest bedrooms are named after local birds and two deluxe suites with whirlpool tubs feature fluffy terrycloth robes, scented bath products and handmade quilts. Savor a hearty breakfast of orange juice, fresh fruit, meat selection and an entrée like the popular Cinnamon French Toast in the Hummingbird Dining Room. Hike, canoe, bike, ski or shop. Packages are available.

Innkeeper(s): Mary Ann Mayer. $90-180. 7 rooms with PB, 2 with WP, 4 suites. Breakfast and snacks/refreshments included in rates. Types of meals: Full bkfst, veg bkfst and Innkeeper will accommodate most dietary requirements if informed in advance. Beds: KQD. TV, VCR, CD player, clock radio, some with hot tub/spa, hair dryer, bathrobes, bath amenities, fluffy robes, scented glycerin soaps, bath/shower scents and two Deluxe Suites have whirlpool tub in room. Air conditioning. Fireplace on premises. Amusement parks, bicycling, canoeing/kayaking, cross-country skiing, downhill skiing, fishing, golf, hiking, horseback riding, live theater, parks, shopping and tennis nearby.

Location: Country, mountains. Mt. Washington Valley.

Publicity: Arrington Inn Journal's Book of Lists, NH ToDo Magazine and Arrington Traveler's Book of Lists Awards.

Certificate may be used: April 1 to May 15, Nov. 1 to Dec. 15. Sunday-Thursday only and subject to availability. Not valid with other specials or offers and daily rates apply.

Wildberry Inn B&B

592 State Rt 2
Shelburne, NH 03581
(603)466-5049
Internet: www.thewildberryinn.com
E-mail: info@thewildberryinn.com

Circa 1877. This colonial salt-box home is located on seven acres in the White Mountains National Forest with the Appalachian Trail passing through part of the property. Rooms are decorated in a fresh country style with quilts and Priscilla curtains. There's a separate suite in the "barn" with fireplace, upstairs bedroom and a downstairs living room with views of the pond, waterfall and garden from its many windows. In winter, snowshoeing, cross-country skiing and snowmobiling are

popular activities. In summer and fall, guests enjoy canoeing and fishing or simply hiking along the property to enjoy the golden oaks, birches, and red and orange maple foliage. Breakfast usually features freshly picked berries in season, homemade breads and dishes to accommodate a lavish pouring of local maple syrup.

Innkeeper(s): Bob & Jackie Corrigan. $85-139. 4 rooms, 3 with PB, 1 with FP, 1 cottage. Breakfast and afternoon tea included in rates. Types of meals: Full gourmet bkfst. Beds: QDT. Data port, TV, VCR, reading lamp, refrigerator, clock radio and coffeemaker in room. Air conditioning. Swimming, telephone, fireplace and laundry facility on premises. Limited handicap access. Antiquing, bicycling, canoeing/kayaking, cross-country skiing, downhill skiing, fishing, golf, hiking, parks, shopping, gourmet dining and snowmobiling nearby.

Location: Country, mountains.

Publicity: The Berlin Daily Sun.

Certificate may be used: Jan.1-July 1 anytime. July 1-Sept. 25 Sunday-Thursday midweek only. Oct. 15-Dec. 23 anytime. Not valid Sept. 26-Oct 14 and Dec. 24-31.

Silver Lake

Lake View Cottage Bed & Breakfast

24 Rosewood Lane
Silver Lake, NH 03875
(603)367-9182 (800)982-0418 Fax:(603)367-9289
Internet: www.lakeviewcottage.com
E-mail: info@lakeviewcottage.com

Circa 1876. In the foothills of the White Mountains between the Lakes Region and Mount Washington Valley, this Victorian bed and breakfast adorns the shore of Silver Lake. Large porches offer expansive water views. Relax in the library or watch TV in a common room. A guest refrigerator is available. Air-conditioned guest bedrooms and suites feature a Victorian Cottage decor, luxury sheets and fresh flowers. Sleep in an antique iron bed in the first-floor Grampa David's Room, with a two-person Jacuzzi, fireplace and sitting room leading to a porch. Each morning enjoy a romantic breakfast with candlelight and crystal. Beach towels are provided for a swim from the dock or beach. Five ski areas are nearby.

Innkeeper(s): Becky Knowles and Jim Coogan. $125-195. 5 rooms with PB, 2 with WP. Breakfast, afternoon tea and snacks/refreshments included in rates. Types of meals: Full gourmet bkfst, veg bkfst, early coffee/tea, room service, Coffee and tea and cocoa are available 24 hours. Beds: KQ. Cable TV, DVD, reading lamp, clock radio, turn-down service, hair dryer, bath amenities, wireless Internet access, High quality Beaudelaire soaps and ammenities in the baths in room. Air conditioning. TV, VCR, fax, copier, swimming, library, parlor games, telephone, fireplace, boating, fishing, hiking and snowmobile trail access on premises. Antiquing, art galleries, beach, bicycling, canoeing/kayaking, cross-country skiing, downhill skiing, fishing, golf, hiking, horseback riding, live theater, parks, shopping, tennis, water sports and snowmobiling nearby.

Location: Mountains, waterfront.

Publicity: Carroll County Independent and Conway Daily Sun.

Certificate may be used: November through March, subject to availability.

Sugar Hill

A Grand Inn-Sunset Hill House

231 Sunset Hill Rd
Sugar Hill, NH 03586
(603)823-5522 (800)786-4455 Fax:(603)823-5523
Internet: www.sunsethillhouse.com
E-mail: innkeeper@sunsethillhouse.com

Circa 1882. This Second Empire luxury inn has views of five

mountain ranges. Three parlors, all with cozy fireplaces, are favorite gathering spots. Afternoon tea is served here. The inn's lush grounds offer many opportunities for recreation or relaxing, and guests often enjoy special events here, such as the Fields of Lupine Festival. The Cannon Mountain Ski Area and Franconia Notch State Park are nearby, and there is 30 kilometers of cross-country ski trails at the inn. Be sure to inquire about golf and ski packages. In the fall, a Thanksgiving package allows guests to help decorate the inn for the holidays as well as enjoy Thanksgiving dinner together. NH Magazine just named Sunset Hill House — A Grand Inn the "Very Best in NH for a Spectacular Meal."

Innkeeper(s): Lon, Nancy, Mary Pearl & Adeline Henderson. $100-499. 27 rooms, 28 with PB, 9 with FP, 9 with WP, 2 two-bedroom suites, 3 conference rooms. Breakfast and afternoon tea included in rates. Types of meals: Full gourmet bkfst, veg bkfst, early coffee/tea, lunch, picnic lunch, snacks/refreshments, hors d'oeuvres, wine, gourmet dinner, room service, Award winning fine dining restaurant, Chaine Des Rotisseurs property, Wine spectator award and casual tavern. Restaurant on premises. Beds: KQDT. Modem hook-up, data port, cable TV, reading lamp, ceiling fan, clock radio, telephone, coffeemaker, desk, some with fireplace, hair dryer, bath amenities, wireless Internet access, iron/ironing board, coffeemaker and wifi access in room. Air conditioning. VCR, fax, copier, swimming, library, parlor games, laundry facility, gift shop, irons available at desk, 24/7 coffee in public areas, golf course with discounted golf privileges for guests of Sunset Hill House, heated mountainside swimming pool, decks with incredible mountain views and full computer center with high speed Internet available for guest use on premises. Handicap access. Amusement parks, antiquing, art galleries, beach, bicycling, canoeing/kayaking, cross-country skiing, downhill skiing, fishing, golf, hiking, horseback riding, live theater, museums, parks, shopping, tennis, water sports, Franconia Notch State Park, Appalachian Trail, rock climbing, day hikes, waterfalls, Flume Gorge, the Basin, Mt. Washington, Cog Railway and Clarks Trading Post nearby.

Location: Country, mountains.

Publicity: *Yankee Travel Guide, Courier, Caledonia Record, Boston Globe, Portsmouth Herald, Manchester Union Leader, Journal Enquirer, Sunday Telegraph, Boston Herald, New Hampshire Magazine, GeoSaison, National Geographic, Traveller, Small Meeting Marketplace, BBW Magazine, Ski Magazine, Peoples Places and Plants Magazine, Korean Times and Deutsche Rundfunk.*

"I have visited numerous inns and innkeepers in my 10 years as a travel writer, but have to admit that few have impressed me as much as yours and you did."

Certificate may be used: Not valid weekends Aug.1-Oct. 15.

Wakefield

Wakefield Inn, LLC

2723 Wakefield Rd
Wakefield, NH 03872-4374
(603)522-8272 (800)245-0841 Fax:(603)218-6714
Internet: www.wakefieldinn.com
E-mail: wakefieldinn@msn.com

Circa 1804. Early travelers pulled up to the front door of the Wakefield Inn by stagecoach, and while they disembarked, their luggage was handed up to the second floor. It was brought in through the door, which is still visible over the porch roof. A spiral staircase, ruffled curtains, wallpapers and a wraparound porch all create the romantic ambiance of days gone by. In the living room, an original three-sided fireplace casts a warm glow on guests as it did more than 190 years ago.

Innkeeper(s): Janel and James Martin. $85-145. 7 rooms with PB, 2 two-

bedroom suites. Breakfast and snacks/refreshments included in rates. Types of meals: Full gourmet bkfst, early coffee/tea and room service. Beds: KQDT. Reading lamp, ceiling fan, clock radio, some with fireplace, hair dryer, bath amenities and wireless Internet access in room. Air conditioning. TV, VCR, DVD, library, parlor games and telephone on premises. Antiquing, art galleries, bicycling, canoeing/kayaking, cross-country skiing, downhill skiing, fishing, golf, hiking, parks, shopping and water sports nearby.

Location: Country.

"Comfortable accommodations, excellent food and exquisite decor highlighted by your quilts."

Certificate may be used: Anytime November-May, May-October Sunday-Thursday, Subject to availability.

Walpole

Inn at Valley Farms B&B and Cottages

633 Wentworth Road
Walpole, NH 03608
(603)756-2855 (877)327-2855 Fax:(603)756-2865
Internet: www.innatvalleyfarms.com
E-mail: info@innatvalleyfarms.com

Circa 1774. Experience New England hospitality at this elegantly restored 1774 Colonial home surrounded by 105 acres of certified organic farmland and bordered by a 500-acre orchard in a picturesque town. Use one of the field guides in the library to identify the many species of the diverse habitats on the farm. Relax by the fire or chat in the plant-filled sunroom. The terraced gardens are seen from the comfortable living room. Award-winning handmade Burdick chocolates and fresh flowers are placed bedside in the large guest bedrooms and Garden Suite with antique furnishings. A multi-course breakfast features recipes using fresh eggs and produce grown onsite. Each cottage includes a private entrance, fully equipped kitchen with stocked refrigerator, two-person shower and mini-library. Each morning a basket of baked goods is delivered to the doorstep. Hike nearby Mt. Monadnock.

Innkeeper(s): Jacqueline Caserta. $150-299. 3 rooms with PB, 2 cottages, 1 guest house, 1 conference room. Breakfast and snacks/refreshments included in rates. Types of meals: Full gourmet bkfst, veg bkfst and early coffee/tea. Beds: KQT. Modem hook-up, cable TV, reading lamp, clock radio, telephone, desk, voice mail, fresh flowers in-season, world-renowned Burdick chocolates at bedside and bathrobes in room. Air conditioning. TV, VCR, fax, copier, library, parlor games, fireplace, picnic table, charcoal grills, pick-your-own organic produce from our gardens and collect your own fresh eggs on premises. Limited handicap access. Antiquing, art galleries, beach, bicycling, canoeing/kayaking, cross-country skiing, fishing, golf, hiking, live theater, museums, parks, shopping, sporting events, tennis and water sports nearby.

Location: Country. 105 acres of rolling farmland and woodland, yet conveniently located to numerous activities.

Publicity: *Yankee Magazine's 2001 Travel Guide to New England.*

Certificate may be used: Sunday-Thursday evenings except holidays or fall-foliage season.

Whitefield

The Lion and The Rose B&B

19 Lancaster Road
Whitefield, NH 03598
(160)383-79200 (186)665-55466
Internet: www.thelionandtherose.com
E-mail: innkeepers@thelionandtherose.com

Circa 1895. Newly restored, this 1895 Queen Anne Victorian in Whitefield is open year-round and offers casual elegance in a smoke-free environment. Relax in the outdoor hot tub overlooking a waterfall and the White Mountains. Gather for afternoon tea and treats in the parlor and enjoy wine and appetizers before going out to dinner. Guest suites and bedrooms are furnished with antiques and reproductions. Stay in the Lion's Den Suite with a two-person Jacuzzi, the Key West Room boasts a clawfoot soaking tub and the White Lilac Room boasts a private deck. Start each day with a candlelight breakfast that may include Stuffed French Toast with Raspberry Sauce, maple sausage, hot muffins, fresh fruit and Key Lime Tartlet. Explore the many local sites and attractions of scenic New Hampshire.

Innkeeper(s): Roger & Chris Croteau. $79-185. 7 rooms with PB, 3 with WP, 1 suite. Breakfast, afternoon tea, snacks/refreshments, hors d'oeuvres and wine included in rates. Types of meals: Full gourmet bkfst, veg bkfst and early coffee/tea. Beds: KQD. Modem hook-up, data port, cable TV, reading lamp, refrigerator, ceiling fan, clock radio, coffeemaker, most with hot tub/spa, hair dryer, bathrobes, bath amenities, wireless Internet access and iron/ironing board in room. Air conditioning. VCR, DVD, spa, parlor games, telephone, fireplace and gift shop on premises. Amusement parks, antiquing, art galleries, bicycling, canoeing/kayaking, cross-country skiing, downhill skiing, fishing, golf, hiking, horseback riding, live theater, parks, shopping, tennis and water sports nearby.

Location: Country, mountains.

Certificate may be used: Anytime, subject to availability.

New Jersey

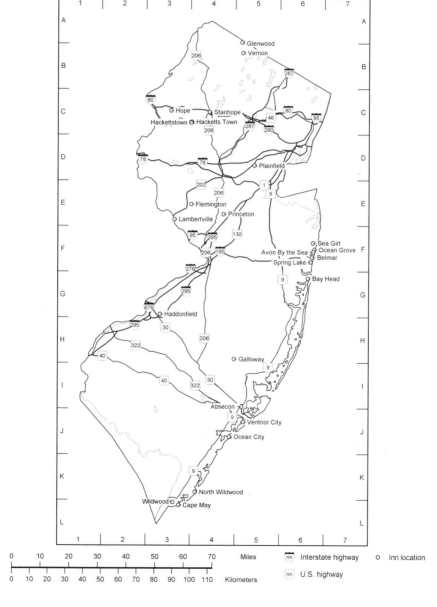

	Miles		
0	10 20 30 40 50 60 70		
0	10 20 30 40 50 60 70 80 90 100 110	Kilometers	

nn Interstate highway   O Inn location

nn U.S. highway

Absecon

Dr. Jonathan Pitney House

57 North Shore Rd
Absecon, NJ 08201
(609)569-1799 (888)774-8639 Fax:(609)569-9224
Internet: www.pitneyhouse.com
E-mail: drpitney@pitneyhouse.com

Circa 1799. A picket fence surrounds this recently renovated Italianate and Colonial inn. It was the home of Dr. Pitney, considered the Father of Atlantic City. Some of the inn's rooms feature Colonial decor, while others are in a Victorian motif. There are clawfoot tubs, whirlpools, ceiling fans and fireplaces. Breakfast is offered gourmet-style and features an entree, freshly baked breads and cakes. Nearby is Atlantic City, Smithville, a winery, beaches, boardwalk, the convention center and a bird sanctuary.

Innkeeper(s): Don Kelly . $100-250. 10 rooms with PB, 10 with FP, 3 with WP, 3 suites. Breakfast and afternoon tea included in rates. Types of meals: Full gourmet bkfst and early coffee/tea. Beds: QD. Cable TV, VCR, ceiling fan and desk in room. Air conditioning. Fax, library, parlor games, telephone and fireplace on premises. Handicap access. Antiquing, fishing, golf, parks, shopping, sporting events, tennis, water sports and casinos nearby.

Certificate may be used: Anytime, November-April, subject to availability.

Avon By The Sea

The Avon Manor B&B & Cottage Rentals

Just North of Spring Lake
Avon By The Sea, NJ 07717-1338
(732)776-7770
Internet: www.avonmanor.com
E-mail: gregmav@aol.com

The Avon Manor was built as a private summer residence in the Colonial Revival style. The handsome facade is graced by a 100-foot wraparound veranda. Light, airy bedrooms are decorated with antiques, wicker and period pieces. Guests breakfast in a sunny dining room or on the veranda.

Innkeeper(s): Greg Dietrich. Call for rates. Call inn for details. Breakfast and afternoon tea included in rates. Types of meals: Full bkfst. Beds: KQT. TV and reading lamp in room. Air conditioning. Child care and fireplace on premises. Amusement parks, antiquing, fishing, live theater, shopping, sporting events and water sports nearby.

Location: Ocean community. Spring Lake.

Certificate may be used: Oct. 1 to May 10, not valid holidays or special events.

Belmar

The Inn at The Shore Bed & Breakfast

301 4th Ave
Belmar, NJ 07719-2104
(732)681-3762 Fax:(732)280-1914
Internet: www.theinnatheshore.com
E-mail: tomvolker@optonline.net

Circa 1880. This child friendly country Victorian actually is near two different shores. Both the ocean and Silver Lake are within easy walking distance of the inn. From the inn's wraparound porch, guests can view swans on the lake. The innkeepers decorated their Victorian home in period style. The inn's patio is set up for barbecues.

Innkeeper(s): Rosemary & Tom Volker. $115-245. 10 rooms, 4 with PB, 4 with FP, 1 conference room. Breakfast, afternoon tea and snacks/refreshments included in rates. Types of meals: Full gourmet bkfst. Beds: KQDT. Modem hook-up, data port, cable TV, VCR, reading lamp, CD player, ceiling fan, clock radio, telephone, voice mail, fireplace, modem, whirlpool tubs, fireplaces and guest pantry in room. Central air. Fax, copier, bicycles, library, parlor games, aquarium, patio with gas grill, guest pantry with refrigerator and microwave on premises. Amusement parks, antiquing, art galleries, beach, bicycling, canoeing/kayaking, fishing, golf, hiking, horseback riding, live theater, museums, parks, shopping, sporting events, tennis and water sports nearby.

Location: Ocean community.

"You both have created a warm, cozy and comfortable refuge for us weary travelers."

Certificate may be used: Anytime, subject to availability, except weekends in June, July and August.

Cape May

Albert Stevens Inn

127 Myrtle Ave
Cape May, NJ 08204-1237
(609)884-4717 (800)890-2287 Fax:(609)884-8320
Internet: www.albertstevensinn.com
E-mail: albertstevensinn@hotmail.com

Circa 1898. Dr. Albert Stevens built this Queen Anne Free Classic house for his home and office. Carved woodwork and Victorian antiques enhance the delightful architectural details. The floating staircase and tower lead to spacious air-conditioned guest bedrooms. Enjoy a complete breakfast as well as afternoon tea and refreshments. Relax in the comfortably heated sunroom, or on the inviting veranda. The outside hot tub offers to soothe and rejuvenate. Free on-site parking is convenient for shopping, restaurants and the beach a short walk away. Beach towels and chairs are gladly provided.

Innkeeper(s): Jim & Lenanne Labrusciano. $100-250. 7 rooms, 10 with PB, 2 with FP, 3 suites. Breakfast, afternoon tea and wine included in rates. Types of meals: Full bkfst and early coffee/tea. Beds: KQD. Cable TV, VCR, DVD, reading lamp, refrigerator, ceiling fan, clock radio, telephone, some with fireplace, hair dryer, bathrobes, bath amenities, wireless Internet access and iron/ironing board in room. Air conditioning. Fax, copier, bicycles, parlor games and Free on-site parking on premises. Amusement parks, antiquing, art galleries, beach, bicycling, canoeing/kayaking, fishing, golf, hiking, live theater, museums, parks, shopping, tennis, water sports, wineries and bird watching nearby.

Location: City, ocean community.

Publicity: *The Jersey Shore, Mid-Atlantic Country, Atlantic City Press, Cape May Star and Wave, The Herald, Washington Post, The New York Times, Philadelphia Inquirer and NBC News.*

Certificate may be used: Oct.30 through April 26, Sunday-Thursday, except weeks that contain a holiday (based on season high rate).

Bedford Inn

805 Stockton Ave
Cape May, NJ 08204-2446
(609)884-4158 (866)215-9507 Fax:(609)884-6320
Internet: www.bedfordinn.com
E-mail: info@bedfordinn.com

Circa 1883. The Bedford, decked in gingerbread trim with verandas on both of its two stories, has welcomed guests since its creation in the 19th century. Electrified gaslights, period wallcoverings and rich, Victorian furnishings create an air of nostalgia. The inn is close to many of Cape May's shops and restaurants, as well as the beach, which is just half a block away. Guests are pampered with breakfasts of quiche, gourmet egg dishes, French toast and freshly baked breads.

Innkeeper(s): Archie & Stephanie Kirk. $100-245. 10 rooms with PB, 2 two-bedroom suites. Breakfast and afternoon tea included in rates. Types of meals: Full bkfst and early coffee/tea. Beds: KQDT. Cable TV, VCR, DVD, reading lamp, ceiling fan, clock radio, some with fireplace, hair dryer, bath amenities and iron/ironing board in room. Air conditioning. Library, parlor games, telephone, refrigerator, free limited driveway parking, hot beverage service 24/7, phone line for computer hook-up and small collection of VHS tapes & DVD's at no charge on premises. Amusement parks, antiquing, art galleries, beach, bicycling, canoeing/kayaking, fishing, golf, hiking, horseback riding, live theater, museums, parks, shopping, tennis, water sports, wineries, house tours, trolley tours, restaurants and beach nearby.

Location: Ocean community.

Certificate may be used: Sunday-Thursday, excluding holidays, based on availability.

Elaine's Victorian Inn

513 Lafayette Street
Cape May, NJ 08204
(609)884-1199 Fax:(609)884-0576
Internet: www.elainescapemay.com
E-mail: info@elainesdinnertheater.com

Circa 1865. Built in 1865 and recently renovated, this all-season B&B inn is just one block from the popular Washington Street Mall in the heart of Cape May, New Jersey. Boasting an enlightened elegance, Elaine's Victorian Inn features panoramic windows in the cheery sun room. Sit on the veranda in relaxing rocking chairs overlooking the one-acre grounds. The New Jersey Shore is only two blocks away and beach chairs are provided. Lavishly furnished guest bedrooms and suites offer upscale amenities. A bountiful breakfast buffet is available daily. Gather for refreshments in the pub and be sure to enjoy the highly acclaimed dinner theater.

Innkeeper(s): Shirley and Ronald Long. $100-265. 12 rooms, 10 with PB, 2 two-bedroom suites, 2 conference rooms. Types of meals: Full gourmet bkfst, veg bkfst, snacks/refreshments, hors d'oeuvres, wine, gourmet dinner, Dinner Theater, Haunted Mansion Restaurant and Victorian Pub. Dining inside or out on our verandah. Restaurant on premises. Beds: Q. Cable TV, reading lamp, hair dryer, bath amenities and iron/ironing board in room. Air conditioning. Fax, copier, telephone, gift shop, Parking, outdoor porches with rockers and beach chairs on premises. Handicap access. Amusement parks, antiquing, art galleries, beach, bicycling, fishing, golf, hiking, horseback riding, live theater, museums, parks, shopping, tennis, water sports, wineries and Haunted Mansion Ghost Tours nearby.

Location: Ocean community, waterfront.

Certificate may be used: Anytime, Sunday-Thursday.

Fairthorne B&B

111 Ocean St
Cape May, NJ 08204-2319
(609)884-8791 (800)438-8742 Fax:(609)898-6129
Internet: www.fairthorne.com
E-mail: fairthornebnb@aol.com

Circa 1892. Antiques abound in this three-story Colonial Revival. Lace curtains and a light color scheme complete the charming decor. There is a new, yet historic addition to the B&B. The innkeepers now offer guest quarters (with fireplaces) in The Fairthorne Cottage, a restored 1880s building adjacent to the inn. The signature breakfasts include special daily entrees along with an assortment of home-baked breads and muffins. A light afternoon tea also is served with refreshments. The proxim-

ity to the beach will be much appreciated by guests, and the innkeepers offer the use of beach towels, bicycles and sand chairs. The nearby historic district is full of fun shops and restaurants.

Innkeeper(s): Diane & Ed Hutchinson. $225-280. 10 rooms, 9 with PB, 7 with FP, 3 with WP, 1 conference room. Breakfast, afternoon tea, snacks/refreshments and hors d'oeuvres included in rates. Types of meals: Full bkfst and early coffee/tea. Beds: KQ. Cable TV, VCR, DVD, reading lamp, CD player, refrigerator, ceiling fan, snack bar, clock radio, most with fireplace, hair dryer, bathrobes, bath amenities, wireless Internet access and iron/ironing board in room. Central air. Fax, bicycles, telephone and gift shop on premises. Amusement parks, antiquing, art galleries, beach, bicycling, canoeing/kayaking, fishing, golf, horseback riding, live theater, museums, parks, shopping, tennis, water sports, wineries and historic lighthouse & Victorian architectural tours nearby.

Location: City. In historic district.

Publicity: *New Jersey Countryside, The Discerning Traveler, Arrington's, NJ Golf, Westchester Magazine and South Jersey Magazine.*

"I feel as if I have come to stay with a dear old friend who has spared no expense to provide me with all that my heart can desire! ... I will savor the memory of your hospitality for years to come. Thanks so much."

Certificate may be used: Nov. 1-May 31, Sunday-Thursday, except holidays.

Gingerbread House

28 Gurney St
Cape May, NJ 08204
(609)884-0211
Internet: gingerbreadinn.com
E-mail: info@gingerbreadinn.com

Circa 1869. The Gingerbread is one of eight original Stockton Row Cottages, summer retreats built for families from Philadelphia and Virginia. It is a half-block from the ocean and breezes waft over the wicker-filled porch. The inn is listed in the National Register. It has been meticulously restored and decorated with period antiques and a fine collection of paintings. The inn's woodwork is especially notable, guests enter through handmade teak double doors.

Innkeeper(s): Fred & Joan Echevarria. $98-295. 6 rooms, 3 with PB, 1 suite. Breakfast and afternoon tea included in rates. Types of meals: Full bkfst. Beds: QD. Cable TV, ceiling fan, bath amenities and wireless Internet access in room. Central air. Fax, parlor games, telephone and fireplace on premises. Antiquing, bicycling, canoeing/kayaking, fishing, golf, hiking, live theater, parks, shopping, tennis, water sports, birding and Victorian homes nearby.

Location: Ocean community.

Publicity: *Philadelphia Inquirer, New Jersey Monthly and Atlantic City Press Newspaper.*

"The elegance, charm and authenticity of historic Cape May, but more than that, it appeals to us as 'home.'"

Certificate may be used: Oct. 14-May 25, Monday-Thursday.

Rhythm of The Sea

1123 W. Beach Ave
Cape May, NJ 08204-2628
(609)884-7788
Internet: www.rhythmofthesea.com
E-mail: rhythm@algorithms.com

Circa 1915. The apt name of this oceanfront inn describes the soothing sounds of the sea that lull many a happy guest into a restful night's sleep. Watching sunsets, strolling the beach, bird watching and whale watching are popular activities. Many of the features of a Craftsman home are incorporated in this seaside inn, such as light-filled spacious rooms, adjoining dining and living areas and gleaming natural wood floors. Mission oak furnishings compliment the inn's architecture. For guests seeking an especially private stay, ask for the three-room suite and arrange for a private dinner prepared by the innkeeper Wolfgang Wendt, a European trained chef. Full breakfasts are provided each morning. Guests are given complimentary beach towels and chairs. There is free parking and complimentary use of bicycles.

Innkeeper(s): Robyn & Wolfgang Wendt. $198-365. 9 rooms, 7 with PB, 2 with FP, 1 suite. Breakfast and snacks/refreshments included in rates. Types of meals: Full bkfst and dinner. Beds: Q. Reading lamp and clock radio in room. Air conditioning. VCR, bicycles, telephone and fireplace on premises. Amusement parks, antiquing, fishing, live theater, shopping and water sports nearby.

Location: Ocean community.

Publicity: *Atlantic City Press, New Jersey Monthly and POV.*

"Your home is lovely, the atmosphere is soothing."

Certificate may be used: November-April, Sunday-Thursday, not valid on holidays or with any other promotional offer. Based on regular rack rate.

The Abbey Bed & Breakfast

34 Gurney St.
Cape May, NJ 08204
(609)884-4506 (866)884-8800 Fax:(609)884-2379
Internet: www.abbeybedandbreakfast.com
E-mail: theabbey@verizon.net

Circa 1869. This historic inn consists of two buildings, one a Gothic Revival villa with a 60-foot tower, Gothic arched windows and shaded verandas. Furnishings include floor-to-ceiling mirrors, ornate gas chandeliers, marble-topped dressers and beds of carved walnut, wrought iron and brass. The cottage adjacent to the villa is a classic Second Empire-style cottage with a mansard roof. A full breakfast is served in the dining room in spring and fall and on the veranda in the summer. Late afternoon refreshments and tea are served each day at 5 p.m. The beautiful inn is featured in the town's Grand Christmas Tour, and public tours and tea are offered three times a week in season.

Innkeeper(s): Colleen. $95-205. 7 rooms with PB. Breakfast and afternoon tea included in rates. Types of meals: Full bkfst and early coffee/tea. Beds: KQD. Reading lamp, refrigerator, ceiling fan, some with air conditioning and antiques in room. Parlor games, beach passes, beach chairs, bicycles, on- and off-site parking and house telephone for local and long distance toll calls on premises. Antiquing, art galleries, beach, bicycling, canoeing/kayaking, fishing, golf,

hiking, horseback riding, live theater, museums, parks, shopping, tennis, wineries, birding, free zoo, nature center, nature walks and Cape May Point State Park nearby.

Location: Ocean community. National Historic District.

Publicity: *Richmond Times-Dispatch, New York Times, Glamour, Philadelphia Inquirer, National Geographic Traveler, Smithsonian and Victorian Homes Magazine.*

"Staying with you folks really makes the difference between a 'nice' vacation and a great one!"

Certificate may be used: Midweek, Sunday or Monday through Thursday. April, May, June, October, except for Victorian Week.

The Carroll Villa B&B

19 Jackson St
Cape May, NJ 08204-1417
(609)884-9619 (877)275-8452 Fax:(609)884-0264
Internet: www.carrollvilla.com
E-mail: manager@carrollvilla.com

Circa 1882. This Victorian hotel is located one-half block from the ocean on the oldest street in the historic district of Cape May. Breakfast at the Villa is a memorable event, featuring dishes acclaimed by the New York Times and Frommer's. Homemade fruit breads, Italian omelets and Crab Eggs Benedict are a few specialties. Meals are served in the Mad Batter Restaurant on a European veranda, a secluded garden terrace or in the sky-lit Victorian dining room. The restaurant serves breakfast, lunch, dinner and cocktails daily. The decor of this inn is decidedly Victorian with period antiques and wallpapers.

Innkeeper(s): Mark Kulkowitz & Pamela Ann Huber. $100-205. 22 rooms with PB, 2 conference rooms. Breakfast included in rates. Types of meals: Full bkfst, lunch and dinner. Beds: QD. Data port, cable TV, VCR, ceiling fan, clock radio, telephone, voice mail, hair dryer, bath amenities, wireless Internet access and iron/ironing board in room. Air conditioning. Fax, copier and fireplace on premises. Amusement parks, antiquing, fishing, live theater, parks and shopping nearby.

Location: City.

Publicity: *Atlantic City Press, Asbury Press, Frommer's, New York Times and Washington Post.*

"Mr. Kulkowitz is a superb host. He strives to accommodate the diverse needs of guests."

Certificate may be used: Sept. 20-May 20, Sunday through Thursday, no holidays, weekends or Christmas week.

The Henry Sawyer Inn

722 Columbia Ave
Cape May, NJ 08204-2332
(609)884-5667 (800)449-5667 Fax:(609)884-9406
Internet: www.henrysawyerinn.com
E-mail: henrysawyerinn@verizon.net

Circa 1877. This fully restored, three-story peach Victorian home boasts a gingerbread embellished veranda, brick-colored shutters and brown trim. Inside, the parlor features Victorian antiques, a marble fireplace, polished wood floors, an Oriental rug, formal wallcoverings, a crystal chandelier and fresh flowers. Guest rooms have been decorated with careful attention to a romantic and fresh Victorian theme, as well. One room includes a whirlpool tub, one includes a private porch, and another a fireplace.

Innkeeper(s): Mary & Barbara Morris. $95-270. 5 rooms with PB, 1 with FP, 2 suites. Breakfast and afternoon tea included in rates. Types of meals: Full bkfst and early coffee/tea. Beds: KQT. Cable TV, reading lamp, ceiling fan, clock radio, small refrigerator and one with whirlpool or private porch in room. Air conditioning. VCR, fax, telephone, fireplace and parking on premises. Antiquing, fishing, golf, live theater, parks, shopping, tennis, water sports, carriage and Victorian trolley nearby.

Certificate may be used: Anytime, November-April, subject to availability.

The Queen Victoria

102 Ocean St
Cape May, NJ 08204-2320
(609)884-8702
Internet: www.queenvictoria.com
E-mail: reservations@queenvictoria.com

Circa 1881. This nationally acclaimed inn, a block from the ocean and shops in the historic district, is comprised of two beautiful Victorian homes, restored and furnished with antiques. "Victorian Homes" magazine featured 23 color photographs of The Queen Victoria, because of its décor and luxurious amenities. Guest rooms offer handmade quilts, antiques, air conditioning, mini-refrigerators and all have private baths. Luxury suites and many rooms have a whirlpool tub and some with handsome fireplace. Afternoon tea is enjoyed while rocking on the porch in summer or before a warm fireplace in winter. Breakfast is hearty buffet style and the inn has its own cookbook. The innkeepers keep a fleet of complimentary bicycles available for guests and there are beach chairs and beach towels as well. The inn is open all year with special Christmas festivities and winter packages.

Innkeeper(s): Doug & Anna Marie McMain. $105-490. 32 rooms with PB, 6 suites. Breakfast and afternoon tea included in rates. Types of meals: Full bkfst and early coffee/tea. Beds: Q. Cable TV, DVD, reading lamp, refrigerator, ceiling fan, clock radio, turn-down service, some with hot tub/spa, some with fireplace, hair dryer, wireless Internet access, iron/ironing board, some with phones and pantry with beverages in room. Air conditioning. Bicycles, parlor games, telephone, gift shop, beach Chairs and beach towels on premises. Amusement parks, antiquing, art galleries, beach, bicycling, canoeing/kayaking, fishing, golf, hiking, live theater, museums, parks, shopping, tennis, water sports, wineries and historic tours nearby.

Location: Waterfront.

Publicity: *Philadelphia Magazine and Baltimore Magazine.*

Certificate may be used: Monday through Thursday, November through March, except holidays and Christmas week.

Flemington

Main Street Manor Bed and Breakfast

194 Main Street
Flemington, NJ 08822
(908)782-4928 Fax:(908)782-7229
Internet: www.mainstreetmanor.com
E-mail: innkeeper@mainstreetmanor.com

Circa 1901. Located in the quaint village of Flemington, this bed and breakfast has been welcoming guests for 13 years. Elegantly restored, the Queen Anne Victorian adorns the historic district. Sip lemonade on the front porch, converse by the fire in the formal front parlor or catch up on reading in the intimate side parlor. Visit local wineries, dine in great restaurants and explore the many shops. All guest bedrooms feature private baths; one room boasts a balcony and another has a clawfoot tub. Each morning a delicious gourmet breakfast is served in the block-paneled dining room. Feel spoiled in the delightful setting so filled with comfort it will be hard to leave.

Innkeeper(s): Donna & Ken Arold. $120-195. 5 rooms with PB, 1 conference room. Breakfast, afternoon tea, snacks/refreshments and wine included in rates. Types of meals: Full gourmet bkfst, veg bkfst, Sun. brunch, early coffee/tea, gourmet lunch, picnic lunch, hors d'oeuvres, room service, All food is prepared on premesis and no preservatives of any kind are used. Fresh-baked goods are always offered for guests to enjoy. Full gourmet breakfasts include fresh and seasonal fruit and ingredients from our local organic farm. The Inn's herb garden helps to supply the fresh herbs which are incorporated into all meals prepared at Main Street Manor. Beds: QT. Modem hook-up, cable TV,

VCR, DVD, reading lamp, stereo, refrigerator, ceiling fan, snack bar, clock radio, coffeemaker, desk, fireplace, hair dryer, bath amenities, wireless Internet access and iron/ironing board in room. Central air. Fax, copier, library, parlor games, gift shop, Afternoon tea with home-baked treats, Fresh seasonal fruit, Complimentary wine & cordials in evening, 24-hour coffee & tea, Bottomless cookie jar, DVD library and Private off-street on-site parking on premises. Antiquing, art galleries, bicycling, canoeing/kayaking, fishing, golf, hiking, horseback riding, live theater, museums, parks, shopping, water sports, wineries, Walking Tour of Historic Downtown, Botanical Gardens - both formal international and informal Wildflower Gardens, Delaware river tubing, Rafting and Personalized itineraries planned by innkeepers for guests at their request nearby.

Location: Country. Historic District.

Certificate may be used: July, August, February and March, Monday through Thursday excluding certain rooms, holidays and special event dates, based on availabilty.

Galloway

White Manor Inn

739 S Second Ave
Galloway, NJ 08205-9542
(609)748-3996 Fax:(609)652-0073
Internet: www.whitemanorinn.com
E-mail: whitemanor@netzero.net

Circa 1932. This quiet country inn was built by the innkeeper's father and includes unique touches throughout, many created by innkeeper Howard

Bensel himself, who became a master craftsman from his father's teachings and renovated the home extensively. Beautiful flowers and plants adorn both the lush grounds and the interior of the home. Everything is comfortable and cozy at this charming B&B, a relaxing contrast to the glitz of nearby Atlantic City.

Innkeeper(s): Anna Mae & Howard R. Bensel Jr. $65-105. 7 rooms, 5 with PB, 1 suite, 1 conference room. Breakfast and snacks/refreshments included in rates. Types of meals: Cont plus and early coffee/tea. Beds: QDT. Ceiling fan in room. Air conditioning. Parlor games and telephone on premises. Amusement parks, antiquing, fishing, live theater, parks, shopping, sporting events, water sports, golf, bird watching and casinos nearby.

Location: Country.

"We felt more like relatives than total strangers. By far the most clean inn that I have seen — spotless!"

Certificate may be used: Nov. 1-April 30, Monday through Thursday.

Lambertville

Chimney Hill Estate Inn

207 Goat Hill Rd
Lambertville, NJ 08530
(609)397-1516 (800)211-4667
Fax:(609)397-9353
Internet: www.chimneyhillinn.com
E-mail: info@chimneyhillinn.com

Circa 1820. Chimney Hill, in the hills above the riverside town of Lambertville, is a grand display of stonework, designed with both Federal and Greek Revival-style architecture. The inn's sunroom is particularly appealing, with its stone walls, fireplaces and French windows looking out to eight acres of gardens and fields. Most of the guest rooms in the estate farmhouse include fireplaces, and some have canopied beds. The Ol' Barn has four suites with fireplaces, Jacuzzis, steam rooms, guest pantries, spiral staircases and loft bedrooms. The

 innkeepers offer adventure, romance and special interest packages for their guests, and the inn is also popular for corporate

retreats. There are plenty of seasonal activities nearby, from kayaking to skiing. New Hope is the neighboring town and offers many charming restaurants and shops, as well.

Innkeeper(s): Terry & Richard Anderson. $135. 10 rooms, 8 with PB, 10 with FP, 4 with WP, 4 suites, 2 conference rooms. Breakfast and snacks/refreshments included in rates. Types of meals: Country bkfst, early coffee/tea, Wine and Cheese - Friday and Saturday evenings and Breakfast in Bed upon request. Beds: KQD. Modem hook-up, data port, cable TV, reading lamp, refrigerator, ceiling fan, snack bar, clock radio, telephone, coffeemaker, desk, most with fireplace, hair dryer, bathrobes, bath amenities, wireless Internet access, iron/ironing board and Jacuzzi in room. Air conditioning. VCR, fax, copier, parlor games, gift shop, Alpaca farm and Garden areas on premises. Limited handicap access. Antiquing, art galleries, bicycling, canoeing/kayaking, fishing, golf, hiking, horseback riding, live theater, museums, parks, shopping, sporting events, tennis, water sports, wineries, Golden Nugget Flea, Market, Peddlers Village, Mitchner Museum, Ivyland Steam Train, New Hope, Frenchtown, Washington Crossing Park, River Country and Doylestown nearby.

Location: Country. Bucks County, PA.

Publicity: *Country Inns (Cover), Colonial Homes Magazine, Country Roads Magazine, NY Times, NJ Magazine, Best Places to Kiss, New Jersey Network, New Jersey Toursim Commercial 2006-2007 and Nassau Broadcasting: 94.5 Hawk Radio-WPST.*

"We would be hard pressed to find a more perfect setting to begin our married life together."

Certificate may be used: Jan. 3-Dec. 20, Monday-Thursday. No holidays, no October dates.

York Street House

42 York St
Lambertville, NJ 08530-2024
(609)397-3007 (888)398-3199 Fax:(609)397-6700
Internet: www.yorkstreethouse.com
E-mail: Innkeeper@YorkStreetHouse.com

Circa 1909. Built by early industrialist George Massey as a 25th wedding anniversary present for his wife, the gracious manor house is situated on almost an acre in the heart of the historic district. Common rooms are warmed by Mercer Tile fireplaces and an original Waterford Crystal chandelier. A winding three-story staircase leads to well-appointed guest bedrooms with period furnishings. Looking out on the lawn and sitting porch, breakfast is served in the dining room, showcasing built-in leaded-glass china and large oak servers. Art galleries, antique shops and restaurants are nearby. Enjoy mule-drawn barges and carriage rides. New Hope, Penn. is a short walk across the Delaware River Bridge, with many quaint shops.

Innkeeper(s): Laurie and Mark Weinstein. $125-275. 6 rooms with PB, 6 with FP, 3 with WP, 1 suite, 1 conference room. Breakfast and snacks/refreshments included in rates. Types of meals: Full gourmet bkfst, veg bkfst, early coffee/tea and picnic lunch. Beds: KQT. Cable TV, reading lamp, ceiling fan, clock radio, desk, fireplace, wireless Internet access and Jacuzzis in room. Air conditioning. VCR, DVD, fax, copier, parlor games and telephone on premises. Antiquing, art galleries, bicycling, canoeing/kayaking, cross-country skiing, fishing, golf, hiking, horseback riding, live theater, museums, parks, shopping, sporting events, water sports and wineries nearby.

Location: Small town.

Certificate may be used: January-April, subject to availability, excludes holidays.

North Wildwood

Candlelight Inn

2310 Central Ave
North Wildwood, NJ 08260
(609)522-6200 (800)992-2632 Fax:(609)522-6125
Internet: www.candlelight-inn.com
E-mail: info@candlelight-inn.com

Circa 1905. Candlelight Inn offers ten guest rooms in a restored Queen Anne Victorian. The home is decorated with an assortment of period pieces. Among its antiques are a Victorian sofa dating to 1855 and an 1890 Eastlake piano. Breakfasts begin with a fresh fruit course, followed by fresh breads and a daily entrée, such as waffles, pancakes or a specialty egg dish. Candlelight Inn is about eight miles from the historic towns of Cape May and Cold Spring Village.

Innkeeper(s): Bill & Nancy Moncrief. $100-270. 10 rooms with PB, 9 with FP, 2 suites. Breakfast, snacks/refreshments and wine included in rates. Types of meals: Full bkfst. Beds: KQ. Cable TV, DVD, reading lamp, stereo, refrigerator, ceiling fan, clock radio, coffeemaker, some with hot tub/spa, fireplace, hair dryer, bathrobes, bath amenities, wireless Internet access and iron/ironing board in room. Central air. VCR, fax, copier, spa, parlor games, telephone, Veranda with rocking chairs, Double hammock, Hot tub and patio deck available to all on premises. Amusement parks, antiquing, beach, bicycling, canoeing/kayaking, fishing, golf, horseback riding, live theater, museums, parks, shopping, tennis, water sports, wineries and the Boardwalk with more rides than Disneyland nearby.

Location: Ocean community.

Publicity: *Atlantic City Press, Camden Courier, the Baltimore Sun and have been on Atlantic City Ch 40 & New York City Ch 4 as desirable places to stay on the "Jersey Shore"*

Certificate may be used: November-April, Monday-Thursday; excluding holidays.

Ocean City

Inn The Gardens Bed & Breakfast

48 Wesley Rd
Ocean City, NJ 08226-4462
(609)399-0800
Internet: www.innthegardens.com
E-mail: innthegardens@aol.com

Circa 1923. Adorning the quiet, residential Gardens neighborhood on the New Jersey Shore, this relaxing bed and breakfast is only eight miles from Atlantic City. Enjoy the ocean breeze while sitting on a porch with a beverage or on the backyard patio surrounded by gardens. Bicycles are provided for scenic rides along the boardwalk. Complimentary beach tags are also provided. Comfortable guest bedrooms feature refrigerators and the Daybreak Room boasts a private balcony. Indulge in an extensive continental breakfast each morning. A computer is available to check e-mail. Ask about specials and packages offered.

Innkeeper(s): Jennifer Torres. $95-169. 7 rooms with PB. Breakfast and afternoon tea included in rates. Types of meals: Cont plus and early coffee/tea. Beds: KQDT. Cable TV, VCR, DVD, reading lamp, refrigerator, ceiling fan, clock radio, hair dryer, wireless Internet access and iron/ironing board in room. Air conditioning. Bicycles, library, parlor games, telephone, laundry facility and beach tags available at no charge on premises. Amusement parks, antiquing, art galleries, beach, bicycling, canoeing/kayaking, fishing, golf, hiking, museums, parks, shopping, water sports, wineries, Atlantic City with concerts, sports events, trade shows and casinos (8 miles) nearby.

Location: Ocean community.

Certificate may be used: October-May, excluding holidays.

Serendipity B&B

712 E 9th St
Ocean City, NJ 08226-3554
(609)399-1554 (800)842-8544 Fax:(609)399-1527
Internet: www.serendipitynj.com
E-mail: info@serendipitynj.com

Circa 1912. The beach and the boardwalk are less than half a block from this renovated Dutch Colonial bed & breakfast for a perfect weekend escape or vacation. Stay in a guest bedroom decorated in pastels and furnished with wicker. Healthy full breakfasts are served in the dining room or, in the summer, on a vine-shaded veranda. Choose from six entrees daily, including vegetarian and high protein selections. Relax on the garden veranda or soak in the spa/hot tub.

Innkeeper(s): Karen Morella. $90-200. 5 rooms with PB. Breakfast and snacks/refreshments included in rates. Types of meals: Full bkfst and veg bkfst. Beds: KQDT. Cable TV, VCR, reading lamp, ceiling fan, clock radio, bathrobes and bottled water in room. Air conditioning. Spa, parlor games, telephone, fireplace, dressing rooms with showers and beach towels, beach chairs, guest refrigerator, microwave, complimentary refreshments and video library on premises. Amusement parks, antiquing, art galleries, beach, bicycling, canoeing/kayaking, fishing, golf, live theater, museums, parks, shopping, water sports, ocean beach and boardwalk nearby.

Location: Ocean community.

Publicity: *Philadelphia Inquirer Magazine, "Best Weekend Escape" Awarded by Arrington's Bed & Breakfast Journal 2004 Book of Lists and "Best Breakfast in the USA" for 2005 awarded by Arrington's Inn Traveler Book of Lists.*

"Serendipity is such a gift. For me it's a little like being adopted during vacation time by a caring sister and brother. Your home is a home away from home. You make it so."

Certificate may be used: November-April, Sunday-Thursday. No holidays. May not be combined with any other offers.

Plainfield

The Pillars of Plainfield Bed and Breakfast Inn

922 Central Ave
Plainfield, NJ 07060
(908)753-0922 (888)PIL-LARS
Internet: www.pillars2.com
E-mail: pillars2@comcast.net

Circa 1870. Victorian and Georgian influences are mingled in the design of this grand historic mansion, which boasts majestic columns and a wraparound porch. An acre of well-manicured grounds and gardens surrounds the home, which is located in Plainfield's Van Wyck Historic District. Guest rooms and suites are appointed with traditional furnishings, and each room has its own special decor. The romantic Van Wyck Brooks Suite includes a fireplace and a canopy bed topped with a down quilt. A wicker table and chairs are tucked into the bay window alcove of the Clementine Yates room. Another spacious room includes a full kitchen. Business travelers will appreciate the private in-room phones with voice mail and wi-fi. Swedish home cooking highlights the morning meal, which is accompanied by freshly ground coffee. Plainfield, the first inland settlement in New Jersey, offers many historic attractions, including the Drake House Museum.

Innkeeper(s): Nancy Fiske and Lamont Blowe. $125-250. 7 rooms with PB, 2 with FP. Snacks/refreshments and Full Gourmet Breakfast included in rates. Types of meals: Full bkfst, veg bkfst and early coffee/tea. Beds: QT. Modem hook-up, data port, cable TV, VCR, reading lamp, ceiling fan, clock radio, telephone, coffeemaker, turn-down service, desk, voice mail and fireplace in room. Air conditioning. Fax, copier, library, parlor games and laundry facility on premises. Amusement parks, antiquing, art galleries, beach, golf, hiking, live theater, museums, parks, shopping, sporting events and tennis nearby.

Location: City.

Certificate may be used: Sunday-Thursday when booked within 2 weeks of arrival date. Does not include Friday or Saturday night booking or Anytime, Last Minute-Based on Availability.

Princeton

Inn at Glencairn

3301 Lawrenceville Road
Princeton, NJ 08540
(609)497-1737 Fax:(609)497-0390
Internet: www.innatglencairn.com
E-mail: innkeeper@innatglencairn.com

Circa 1736. Situated on three park-like acres on a hill in Princeton, New Jersey, this renovated 1736 Georgian manor house is just three miles from downtown. The original smokehouse and stable, both made of stone and a three-story red frame barn are some of the outbuildings at Inn at Glencairn. This bed and breakfast blends the historic setting and traditional décor of antique furnishings with a touch of modern and updated amenities. Relax with refreshments in the parlor or great room by the huge working fireplace under a beamed ceiling with oriental rugs accenting the random-width pine floors. Luxurious guest bedrooms and a two-room suite feature Frette robes and featherbeds with Egyptian cotton linens. Savor a gourmet breakfast that is made with fresh ingredients from local orchards and organic farms.

Innkeeper(s): Bob Riggs. $195-235. 5 rooms with PB, 1 two-bedroom suite. Breakfast, snacks/refreshments and wine included in rates. Types of meals: Full gourmet bkfst, veg bkfst, early coffee/tea and We serve our guests a full gourmet breakfast daily made with fresh ingredients from local farms and orchards. Beverages are available throughout the day and afternoon refreshments are served during the 3:00-5:00 check-in period. Beds: QDT. Modem hook-up, data port, cable TV, reading lamp, hair dryer, bathrobes, bath amenities, wireless Internet access, luxurious beds that include featherbeds, Egyptian cotton linens and down comforters, renovated en-suite baths that feature fluffy cotton towels and Frette bathrobes in room. Central air. Fax, library, parlor games, telephone, fireplace, large gathering spaces include a nearly 500 square foot Great Room with a beamed ceiling and a twelve foot wide original cooking fireplace, fine antiques, a revolving art collection and oriental carpets over original random width pine floors on premises. Limited handicap access. Amusement parks, antiquing, art galleries, bicycling, canoeing/kayaking, cross-country skiing, fishing, golf, hiking, horseback riding, live theater, museums, parks, shopping, sporting events, tennis and wineries nearby.

Location: Country.

Publicity: *New Jersey Monthly, New Jersey Countryside, Princeton Magazine, Trenton Times, Lawrence Ledger, Town Topics and US1.*

Certificate may be used: Anytime, subject to availability, reservation must be made via telephone.

Sea Girt

Beacon House

100 & 104 Beacon Blvd
Sea Girt, NJ 08750-1609
(732)449-5835 Fax:732-282-0974
Internet: www.beaconhouseinn.com
E-mail: beaconhouse@aol.com

Circa 1879. Built in classic Victorian style, this recently renovated inn has been a relaxing getaway for more than a century. Splendidly furnished parlors with fireplaces, crystal chandeliers and oak floors are pleasurable places to while away time. The two main houses, a cottage and a carriage house offer the best in casual elegance. Encounter wicker, brass and chintz in the sunny guest bedrooms. Some boast oceanview balconies, fireplaces and Jacuzzi tubs. Morning is a celebration when a memorable gourmet breakfast is served in the candle-lit dining room. Enjoy the colorful landscape from a rocker on one of the wraparound porches, lounge by the swimming pool, or take a bike ride to the popular boardwalk in this quaint seaside community.
Innkeeper(s): Candace Kadimik. $89-365. 18 rooms with PB, 7 with FP, 2 with WP, 2 two-bedroom suites, 3 cottages, 1 conference room. Breakfast included in rates. Types of meals: Full gourmet bkfst, veg bkfst, early coffee/tea and snacks/refreshments. Beds: KQDT. Cable TV, reading lamp, ceiling fan, clock radio, some with hot tub/spa, most with fireplace, hair dryer, bath amenities and wireless Internet access in room. Central air. VCR, DVD, fax, copier, swimming, bicycles, library, parlor games, telephone, gift shop and Pool on premises. Limited handicap access. Amusement parks, antiquing, art galleries, beach, bicycling, canoeing/kayaking, fishing, golf, hiking, horseback riding, live theater, museums, parks, shopping, tennis and water sports nearby.
Location: Waterfront.
Publicity: *The Coast Star, The Asbury Park Press and Vacations On The Fly.*
Certificate may be used: Anytime, October-April, subject to availability.

Spring Lake

Sea Crest By The Sea

19 Tuttle Ave
Spring Lake, NJ 07762-1533
(732)449-9031 (800)803-9031 Fax:(732)974-0403
Internet: www.seacrestbythesea.com
E-mail: capt@seacrestbythesea.com

Circa 1885. You can hear the surf from most rooms in this Victorian mansion, located an hour from New York city or Philadelphia. Guests will be pampered with Egyptian cotton and  Belgian-lace linens, Queen-size feather beds, fresh flowers and classical music. Eight rooms have Jacuzzis for two and there are eight with fireplaces. Tunes from a player piano announce afternoon tea at 4 p.m.—a good time to make dinner reservations at one of the area's fine restaurants. In the morning family china, crystal and silver add to the ambiance of a full gourmet breakfast. Bicycles are available and the beach is a half block away.
Innkeeper(s): Barbara & Fred Vogel. $320-500. 8 rooms with PB, 8 with FP, 8 with WP, 5 suites, 1 conference room. Breakfast and afternoon tea included in rates. Types of meals: Full gourmet bkfst. Cable TV, VCR, DVD, reading lamp, CD player, refrigerator, ceiling fan, clock radio, telephone, hot tub/spa,

hair dryer, bathrobes, bath amenities, wireless Internet access, iron/ironing board, whirlpools for two, fireplace, complimentary beverage-stocked refrigerators, robes, hair dryers and slippers in room. Central air. Fax, copier, bicycles, parlor games, fireplace, gift shop, evening cordials, passes to premier health fitness club and beach gear on premises. Amusement parks, antiquing, art galleries, beach, bicycling, canoeing/kayaking, fishing, golf, hiking, horseback riding, live theater, museums, parks, shopping, tennis, water sports, wineries and Atlantic Ocean Beach nearby.
Location: Ocean community.
Publicity: *New York Times, New Jersey Monthly Magazine, New York Magazine, Philadelphia Magazine and Washingtonian Magazine.*

"This romantic storybook atmosphere is delightful! A visual feast."
Certificate may be used: Oct. 1-May 15, Sunday-Thursday, subject to availability (excluding holiday periods).

Spring Lake Inn

104 Salem Ave
Spring Lake, NJ 07762-1040
(732)449-2010 Fax:(732)449-4020
Internet: www.springlakeinn.com
E-mail: springlakeinn@aol.com

Circa 1888. Only a block from the beach, this historic Victorian inn boasts an informal seaside atmosphere. Relax on the 80-foot, rocker-lined porch or fireside in the parlor. Well-decorated guest bedrooms and suites offer a variety of peaceful settings including the Turret, surrounded by four windows, and the Tower View suite with sleigh bed and ocean views. Enjoy a leisurely breakfast served in the spacious dining room featuring a 12-foot ceiling. Walk to the town center, with more than 60 shops to explore.
Innkeeper(s): Barbara & Andy Seaman. $99-499. 16 rooms with PB, 8 with FP, 2 suites, 2 conference rooms. Breakfast and snacks/refreshments included in rates. Types of meals: Full gourmet bkfst, Sun. brunch, early coffee/tea and afternoon tea. Beds: QD. Modem hook-up, cable TV, VCR, reading lamp, stereo, refrigerator, ceiling fan, snack bar, clock radio, desk, fireplace, wireless Internet access, beach chairs, beach badges, beach towels and ocean views in room. Air conditioning. Fax, copier, swimming, library, parlor games, telephone and gift shop on premises. Limited handicap access. Amusement parks, antiquing, art galleries, beach, bicycling, canoeing/kayaking, fishing, golf, hiking, horseback riding, live theater, museums, parks, shopping, sporting events, tennis, water sports and wineries nearby.
Location: Ocean community. Two blocks from the lake and one block from the ocean. The town center is within walking distance.
Publicity: *Asbury Press, Westchester Magazine and NJ 12.*
Certificate may be used: Oct. 1 to May 15, subject to availability.

The Normandy Inn

21 Tuttle Ave
Spring Lake, NJ 07762-1533
(732)449-7172 (800)449-1888 Fax:(732)449-1070
Internet: www.normandyinn.com
E-mail: normandy@bellatlantic.net

Circa 1888. In a picturesque seaside town, this historic Italianate Villa with Queen Anne details is just half a block from the ocean. Listed in the National Register, the Colonial Revival and Neoclassicism interior reflect its traditionally elegant Victorian heritage. Relax in spacious double parlours or play the 1886 trumpet-legged grand piano. Fine antiques adorn air-conditioned guest bedrooms. Some rooms feature cozy fireplaces, canopy beds and Jacuzzis. Choose from a selection of hearty country breakfast entrees to savor in the dining room. The inn's exceptional service, romantic ambiance and central location make it the perfect all-season getaway.
Innkeeper(s): The Valori family. $135-396. 18 rooms with PB, 7 with FP, 2 suites, 1 conference room. Breakfast and afternoon tea included in rates.

Types of meals: Full gourmet bkfst and early coffee/tea. Beds: KQDT. Modem hook-up, data port, cable TV, VCR, reading lamp, refrigerator, clock radio, telephone, coffeemaker, desk, fireplace and Jacuzzi tubs in room. Central air. Fax, copier, bicycles, library, parlor games and gift shop on premises. Amusement parks, antiquing, art galleries, beach, bicycling, canoeing/kayaking, fishing, golf, hiking, horseback riding, live theater, museums, parks, shopping, sporting events, tennis and water sports nearby.

Location: Ocean community.

Publicity: *New York Times.*

"The cozy and delicious accommodations of your inn were beyond expectations."

Certificate may be used: Oct. 1 to April 30, Sunday through Thursday, subject to availability.

Stanhope

Whistling Swan Inn

110 Main St
Stanhope, NJ 07874-2632
(973)347-6369 (888)507-2337 Fax:(973)347-6379
Internet: www.whistlingswaninn.com
E-mail: wswan@att.net

Circa 1905. This Queen Anne Victorian has a limestone wraparound veranda and a tall, steep-roofed turret. Family antiques fill the rooms and highlight the polished ornate woodwork, pocket doors and winding staircase. It is a little more than a mile from Waterloo Village and the International Trade Center.

Innkeeper(s): Liz Armstrong. $99-239. 9 rooms with PB, 2 with FP, 3 with WP. Breakfast and snacks/refreshments included in rates. Types of meals: Full bkfst. Beds: Q. Data port, cable TV, VCR, reading lamp, ceiling fan, clock radio, telephone, desk, iron and hair dryer in room. Air conditioning. Fax, copier, bicycles, parlor games, fireplace, tubs for two and Victorian garden on premises. Antiquing, bicycling, canoeing/kayaking, fishing, golf, hiking, horseback riding, live theater, museums, parks, shopping, sporting events, water sports and wineries nearby.

Location: Mountains. Rural village.

Publicity: *Sunday Herald, New York Times, New Jersey Monthly, Mid-Atlantic Country, Star Ledger, Daily Record, Philadelphia, Country and Chicago Sun Times.*

"Thank you for your outstanding hospitality. We had a delightful time while we were with you and will not hesitate to recommend the inn to our listening audience, friends and anyone else who will listen! — Joel H. Klein, Travel Editor, WOAI AM."

Certificate may be used: January-April, Sunday through Thursday nights, excluding holidays.

Ventnor City

Carisbrooke Inn

105 S Little Rock Ave
Ventnor City, NJ 08406-2840
(609)822-6392 Fax:(609)822-9710
Internet: www.carisbrookeinn.com
E-mail: info@carisbrookeinn.com

Circa 1918. Relaxation is easy at this enticing seaside bed & breakfast just a few steps away from the world-famous boardwalk and only one mile from Atlantic City. Delight in the ocean view from the front deck or the tranquility of the back patio. Afternoon refreshments are enjoyed in the sunny Main Parlor,

or by the warmth of a winter fire. Pleasant guest bedrooms feature comfortable amenities and the romantic accents of plants, fresh flowers and lacy curtains. The innkeepers offer a huge breakfast that may include homemade waffles and fresh berries, banana pecan pancakes, Italian frittata with fresh herbs and cheese, Quiche Lorraine and French toast, accompanied by fruit and just-baked muffins and breads. Beach towels and tags are provided for fun in the sun at the shore.

Innkeeper(s): John Battista. $79-315. 8 rooms with PB, 1 with FP. Breakfast, afternoon tea, snacks/refreshments, hors d'oeuvres and wine included in rates. Types of meals: Full gourmet bkfst, veg bkfst and early coffee/tea. Beds: KQ. Cable TV, VCR, DVD, reading lamp, CD player, ceiling fan, clock radio, desk, some with fireplace, hair dryer, bath amenities, wireless Internet access, iron/ironing board and fresh flowers in room. Air conditioning. Fax, copier, library, parlor games, telephone, complimentary tea/coffee/snacks in main parlor, beach tags and towels and chairs (in season) on premises. Amusement parks, antiquing, art galleries, beach, bicycling, canoeing/kayaking, fishing, golf, horseback riding, live theater, museums, parks, shopping, sporting events, tennis, water sports, wineries, Casinos, Shopping, Dining and Clubs nearby.

Location: City, ocean community.

Publicity: *Voted Best on the Shore in Philadelphia Magazine.*

"You have a beautiful, elegant inn. My stay here was absolutely wonderful."

Certificate may be used: Anytime, subject to availability.

Vernon

Alpine Haus B&B

217 State Rt 94
Vernon, NJ 07462
(973)209-7080 Fax:(973)209-7090
Internet: www.alpinehausbb.com
E-mail: alpinehs@warwick.net

Circa 1885. A private hideaway in the mountains, this former farmhouse is more than 100 years old. The renovated Federal-style inn with Victorian accents offers comfortable guest bedrooms named after mountain flowers with a decor reflecting that theme. Antiques also highlight the inn. The adjacent Carriage House has two suites with four-poster beds, stone fireplace and Jacuzzi. A generous country breakfast is enjoyed in the dining room or a continental breakfast on the second-story covered porch with majestic views. The family room and formal sitting room with fireplace are wonderful gathering places for games or conversation. Located next to Mountain Creek Ski and Water Park.

Innkeeper(s): Jack & Allison Smith. $110-225. 10 rooms with PB, 3 with FP, 2 suites, 1 conference room. Breakfast included in rates. Types of meals: Country bkfst, veg bkfst, early coffee/tea and snacks/refreshments. Beds: QDT. Modem hook-up, data port, cable TV, VCR, reading lamp, refrigerator, clock radio, telephone, coffeemaker, desk, some with hot tub/spa, voice mail, hair dryer, wireless Internet access, Internet access and two suites with fireplace and Jacuzzi in room. Central air. Fax, copier, parlor games and fireplace on premises. Handicap access. Antiquing, art galleries, bicycling, canoeing/kayaking, cross-country skiing, downhill skiing, fishing, golf, hiking, horseback riding, live theater, museums, parks, shopping, water sports and wineries nearby.

Location: Country, mountains.

Certificate may be used: Anytime, except Friday-Saturday for the periods Dec. 15 to March 15 and June 15 to Sept. 7 and holiday periods.

Wildwood

Holly Beach Hotel Bed and Breakfast

137 E Spicer Ave
Wildwood, NJ 08260-4724
(609)522-9033 (800)961-7758 Fax:(609)846-0279
Internet: hollybeach.com
E-mail: cynthia@hollybeach.com

Circa 1914. Poised in the heart of town, Holly Beach Hotel Bed and Breakfast is a three-story historic Georgian with an inviting brick front porch with wicker rockers. This non-smoking B&B in Wildwood, New Jersey boasts a Victorian décor with a country flair. Browse through the book and movie library. Stay in one of the air-conditioned guest bedrooms or suites that may feature a whirlpool tub. Gather for a delightful breakfast in the dining room. Beverages are available all the time. Relax in the outdoor hot tub. Picnic tables and a gas grill are provided. Walk to the local museum or look for shells on the beach. Cape May is less than ten minutes away.

Innkeeper(s): Cynthia & Robert Buziak. $89-225. 18 rooms with PB, 3 with FP, 3 with WP, 5 total suites, including 4 two-bedroom suites, 1 cottage, 1 guest house, 1 conference room. Breakfast, afternoon tea, snacks/refreshments, hors d'oeuvres and wine included in rates. Types of meals: Full gourmet bkfst, veg bkfst and early coffee/tea. Beds: KQD. Cable TV, VCR, DVD, reading lamp, refrigerator, ceiling fan, clock radio, some with hot tub/spa, some with fireplace, hair dryer, bathrobes, bath amenities, wireless Internet access and iron/ironing board in room. Air conditioning. Fax, copier, spa, library, parlor games and Wireless Internet on premises. Amusement parks, antiquing, art galleries, beach, bicycling, canoeing/kayaking, fishing, golf, horseback riding, live theater, museums, parks, shopping, tennis, water sports and wineries nearby.

Location: Ocean community.

Certificate may be used: January-April.

New Mexico

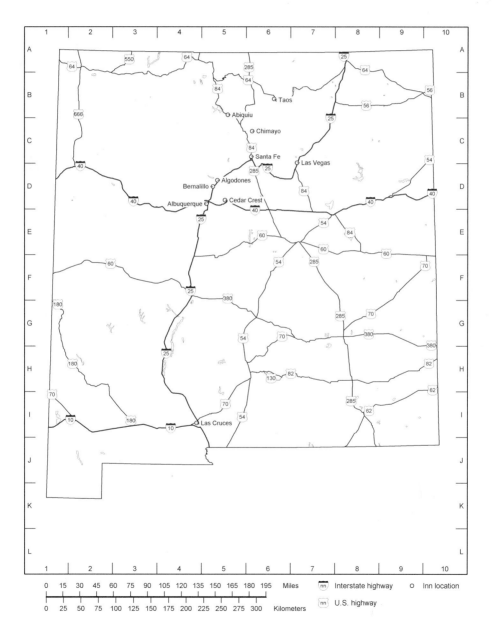

0 15 30 45 60 75 90 105 120 135 150 165 180 195 Miles	nn	Interstate highway	o	Inn location
0 25 50 75 100 125 150 175 200 225 250 275 300 Kilometers	nn	U.S. highway		

Abiquiu

Casa del Rio

PO Box 702
Abiquiu, NM 87510
(505)753-2035 (800)920-1495
Internet: www.casadelrio.net
E-mail: casadelrio@newmexico.com

Circa 1988. These authentic adobe guest houses are filled with local handmade crafts, rugs, bed coverings and furniture. Bathrooms boast handmade Mexican tile, and rooms are decorated in traditional New Mexico style with kiva fireplaces. The patio windows afford a view of cliffs above the Rio Chama, which is just a short walk away. Casa del Rio is near many attractions, including Indian pueblos, the many museums of Ghost Ranch, galleries and an abundance of outdoor activities. The property is halfway between Taos and Santa Fe.

Innkeeper(s): Eileen Sopanen-Vigil. $100-150. 3 rooms with PB, 1 with FP, 1 guest house. Breakfast included in rates. Types of meals: Full bkfst and veg bkfst. Beds: KQT. Reading lamp, refrigerator, clock radio, turn-down service, fireplace and patio in room. Fax, copier, telephone and gift shop on premises. Bicycling, cross-country skiing, downhill skiing, fishing, golf, hiking, museums, parks, shopping, wineries, birding, swimming, rock climbing and rafting nearby.

Location: Country, mountains, waterfront.

Certificate may be used: November-April 15, Sunday-Thursday, excluding major holidays.

Albuquerque

The Mauger

701 Roma Ave NW
Albuquerque, NM 87102-2038
(505)242-8755 (800)719-9189 Fax:(505)842-8835
Internet: www.maugerbb.com
E-mail: maugerbb@aol.com

Circa 1897. Now an elegantly restored Victorian, this former boarding house is listed in the National Register. Guest bedrooms offer amenities that include satellite television, refrigerators, a basket with snacks, voice mail and European down comforters on the beds. The inn

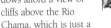

is located four blocks from the convention center/business district and Historic Route 66. Old Town is less than one mile away. There are many interesting museums to visit locally, featuring topics from Native American culture to the atomic age.

Innkeeper(s): Tammy & Mike Ross. $89-209. 8 rooms with PB, 2 guest houses, 1 conference room. Breakfast included in rates. Types of meals: Full bkfst and snacks/refreshments. Beds: KQDT. TV, reading lamp, refrigerator, ceiling fan, snack bar, clock radio, telephone, desk, voice mail, wireless Internet access, coffeemaker, iron and hair dryer in room. Air conditioning. Amusement parks, antiquing, live theater and shopping nearby.

Location: City. Downtown Albuquerque.

Publicity: *Albuquerque Journal, Phoenix Home and Garden, Albuquerque Monthly, National Geographic Traveler, New Mexico Business Week and Golf Digest.*

"Because of your hospitality, kindness and warmth, we will always compare the quality of our experience by the W.E. Mauger Estate."

Certificate may be used: Nov. 15-March 1, except Thanksgiving and Christmas, Sunday-Thursday. Friday and Saturday subject to availability.

Algodones

Hacienda Vargas

PO Box 307
Algodones, NM 87001-0307
(505)867-9115 (800)261-0006 Fax:(505)867-0640
Internet: www.haciendavargas.com
E-mail: stay@haciendavargas.com

Circa 1840. Nestled among the cottonwoods and mesas of the middle Rio Grande Valley, between Albuquerque and Santa Fe, Hacienda Vargas has seen two centuries of Old West history. It once served as a trading post for Native Americans as well as a 19th-century stagecoach stop between Santa Fe and Las Cruces. The grounds contain an adobe chapel, courtyard and gardens. The main house features five kiva fireplaces, Southwest antiques, Spanish tile, a library and suites with private Jacuzzis.

Innkeeper(s): Cynthia & Richard Spence. $79-149. 7 rooms with PB, 6 with FP, 4 suites. Breakfast included in rates. Types of meals: Full bkfst. Beds: QT. Reading lamp, ceiling fan, clock radio, desk and suites have spa in room. Air conditioning. Parlor games, telephone and fireplace on premises. Antiquing, downhill skiing, fishing, live theater, shopping, sporting events, Golf MECCA and car racing nearby.

Location: Valley.

Publicity: *Albuquerque Journal (Country Inns), Vogue and San Francisco Chronicle.*

"This is the best! Breakfast was the best we've ever had!"

Certificate may be used: Sunday-Thursday except holidays or Balloon Fiesta.

Bernalillo

La Hacienda Grande

21 Barros Rd
Bernalillo, NM 87004
(505)867-1887 (800)353-1887 Fax:(505)771-1436
Internet: www.lahaciendagrande.com
E-mail: lhg@swcp.com

Circa 1711. The rooms in this historic adobe inn surround a central courtyard. The first European trekked across the grounds as early as 1540. The land was part of a 1711 land grant from Spain, and owned by descendants of the original family until the innkeepers purchased it. The decor is Southwestern, and each bedchamber is filled with beautiful, handcrafted furnishings. One includes an iron high-poster bed and Jacuzzi tub, and others offer a kiva fireplace. Breakfasts are served in a dining room decorated with wood beams and a brick floor.

Innkeeper(s): Troy & Melody Scott. $109-139. 6 rooms with PB, 5 with FP, 1 conference room. Breakfast included in rates. Types of meals: Full bkfst and early coffee/tea. Beds: KQDT. Reading lamp, clock radio and sitting areas and TV on request in room. Air conditioning. VCR, fax, copier, library, parlor games, telephone, fireplace and phone on premises. Antiquing, cross-country skiing, downhill skiing, fishing, live theater, parks, shopping, sporting events and water sports nearby.

Location: City, country, mountains.

Certificate may be used: All dates except holiday weeks and Albuquerque Balloon Festival (first Saturday in October for 10 days).

Cedar Crest

Elaine's, A B&B

72 Snowline Rd
Cedar Crest, NM 87008-0444
(505)281-2467 (800)821-3092 Fax:(505)281-1384
Internet: www.elainesbnb.com
E-mail: elaine@elainesbnb.com

Circa 1979. Ideally located on the historic Turquoise Trail adjacent to the Cibola National Forest, this three-story log home is situated on four acres of evergreens in the forests of the Sandia Peaks. Over one hundred varieties of birds, including three types of hummingbirds, visit the property. Enchanting mountain views from one of the three balconies are unforgettable. Furnished with European country antiques, several of the guest bedrooms feature private fireplaces and Jacuzzis. Start the day off right with a substantial breakfast of favorite comfort foods. Visit the historic sites, shops and galleries in Albuquerque and Santa Fe, only minutes away from this secluded inn.

Innkeeper(s): Elaine O'Neil. $89-139. 5 rooms, 2 with FP, 5 suites. Breakfast included in rates. Types of meals: Full gourmet bkfst, veg bkfst, early coffee/tea and snacks/refreshments. Beds: KQ. Reading lamp, ceiling fan, most with hot tub/spa, most with fireplace and European country antiques in room. Air conditioning. TV, VCR, DVD, fax, copier, spa, library, parlor games, telephone, over 100 varieties of birds, views of the mountains, three balconies, flagstone patios and garden on premises. Amusement parks, antiquing, art galleries, bicycling, cross-country skiing, downhill skiing, golf, hiking, horseback riding, museums, parks, shopping and wineries nearby.

Location: Mountains. Four acres of evergreens in the forests of the Sandia Peaks.

Publicity: *Fodor's, L.A. Times, Albuquerque Journal, New Mexico Magazine, Fort Worth Star-Telegram, Washington Post, Pittsburgh-Gazette and St. Petersburg Times.*

"Fabulous! Mystical in the spring snow!"

Certificate may be used: Jan. 15-April 15, excluding holidays.

Chimayo

Casa Escondida

64 County Road 0100
Chimayo, NM 87522
(505)351-4805 (800)643-7201 Fax:(505)351-2575
Internet: www.casaescondida.com
E-mail: info@casaescondida.com

Circa 1970. Secluded on six acres in an historic mountain village, this Adobe-style inn features Spanish Colonial architecture. Tongue and groove ceilings, heavy beams known as vigas, French doors, wood, brick and Saltillo tile floors all  add to the warm ambiance. The air is scented with the fragrance of pinon wood from kiva fireplaces. A library offers quiet entertainment. Inviting guest bedrooms include bathrobes to relax in. Some rooms boast gorgeous views, oversized tubs, fireplaces, private access to a deck or patio, and can be made into an adjoining suite. Enjoy a leisurely gourmet breakfast in the sunny dining room, or alfres-

co. Surrounded by trees, an outside hot tub is the perfect spot to relax.

Innkeeper(s): Belinda Bowling. $95-155. 8 rooms with PB, 3 with FP, 1 suite. Breakfast, afternoon tea and snacks/refreshments included in rates. Types of meals: Full bkfst and early coffee/tea. Beds: QT. Reading lamp, ceiling fan, some with fireplace, hair dryer, bathrobes, wireless Internet access, kitchenette, wood-burning stove, oversized tub, private deck, private patio, hair dryer upon request, iron/ironing board upon request and alarm clock upon request in room. Air conditioning. Fax, copier, spa, library, parlor games, telephone, guest phone, laptop hook-up, wireless Internet access, outdoor hot tub, unlimited free local calls and free parking on premises. Limited handicap access. Art galleries, bicycling, canoeing/kayaking, cross-country skiing, downhill skiing, fishing, golf, hiking, horseback riding, live theater, museums, parks, shopping, wineries, hot air ballooning, ancient ruins, Indian pueblos, rafting, bird watching, Southwest cooking classes, casinos, concerts, Cumbre & Toltec Scenic Railroad, Lensic Performing Arts Center, Santa Fe Southern Railway, Santa Fe Horse Park, Santa Fe Farmers Market, Santa Fe Community College Planetarium, laundry facilities and dry cleaning services nearby.

Location: Country, mountains.

Certificate may be used: April-October Sunday-Thursday, November-March Any Day, Excluding holiday periods or special events all year. Discounted rates cannot be combined with any other offers. Discounted rates are not commissionable.

Las Vegas

Plaza Hotel

230 Plaza
Las Vegas, NM 87701
(505)425-3591 (800)328-1882 Fax:(505)425-9659
Internet: www.plazahotel-nm.com
E-mail: lodging@plazahotel-nm.com

Circa 1882. This brick Italianate Victorian hotel, once frequented by the likes of Doc Holliday, Big Nose Kate and members of the James Gang, was renovated in 1982. A stencil pattern found in the dining room inspired the selection of Victorian wallpaper borders in the guest rooms, decorated with period furnishings. Guests also have access to a business center and T-1 internet.

Innkeeper(s): Wid Slick. $71-152. 37 rooms with PB, 4 suites, 1 conference room. Breakfast included in rates. Types of meals: Cont. Restaurant on premises. Beds: KQD. Cable TV, reading lamp, telephone and desk in room. Air conditioning. TV, copier and business center and T-1 Internet on premises. Handicap access. Antiquing, cross-country skiing, fishing, parks, water sports and hot springs nearby.

Location: City.

Certificate may be used: All week, Nov. 1-May 1.

Santa Fe

Alexander's Inn

529 E Palace Ave
Santa Fe, NM 87501-2200
(505)986-1431 (888)321-5123 Fax:(505)982-8572
Internet: www.alexanders-inn.com
E-mail: info@alexanders-inn.com

Circa 1903. Twin gables and a massive front porch are prominent features of this Craftsman-style brick and wood inn. French and American country decor, stained-glass windows and a selection of antiques create a light Victorian touch. The inn also features beautiful gardens of roses and lilacs. The exquisite Southwest adobe casitas are a favorite for families and romantic getaways. Breakfast is often served in the backyard garden. Home-baked treats are offered to guests in the afternoon.

Innkeeper(s): Carolyn Lee. $85-240. 4 cottages, 4 with FP. Welcome basket of fruit, coffee, wine, chips, salsa and etc included in rates. Types of meals: Full gourmet bkfst, early coffee/tea and afternoon tea. Beds: KQT. Cable TV, VCR, reading lamp, refrigerator, clock radio, telephone, desk and hot tub/spa in room. Fax, spa, library, child care, parlor games and fireplace on premises. Antiquing, cross-country skiing, downhill skiing, fishing, live theater, parks, shopping, water sports, museums and Pueblos nearby.

Location: City.

Publicity: *New Mexican, Glamour, Southwest Art and San Diego Union Tribune.*

"Thanks to the kindness and thoughtfulness of the staff, our three days in Santa Fe were magical."

Certificate may be used: Nov. 1-Feb. 28, Sunday-Thursday, no holidays.

Don Gaspar Inn

623 Don Gaspar Avenue
Santa Fe, NM 87505
(505)986-8664 (888)986-8664 Fax:(505)986-0696
Internet: www.dongaspar.com
E-mail: info@dongaspar.com

Circa 1912. This lush, peaceful hideaway is located within one of Santa Fe's first historic districts. Within the Compounds surrounding adobe walls are brick pathways meandering through beautiful gardens, emerald lawns, trees and a courtyard fountain. The elegant Southwestern decor is an idyllic match for the warmth and romance of the grounds. For those seeking privacy, the innkeepers offer the Main House, a historic Mission-style home perfect for a pair of romantics or a group as large as six. The house has three bedrooms, two bathrooms, a fully equipped kitchen and two wood-burning fireplaces. In addition to the main house, there are three suites in a Territorial-style home with thick walls and polished wood floors. There also are two private casitas, each with a gas-burning fireplace. The Fountain Casita includes a fully equipped kitchen, while the Courtyard Casita offers a double whirlpool tub. All accommodations include a TV, telephone, microwave and refrigerators.

Innkeeper(s): Nancy, Michael and Ana. $145-355. 10 rooms with PB, 8 with FP, 3 suites, 3 guest houses. Breakfast included in rates. Types of meals: Full bkfst. Beds: KQ. TV, VCR, reading lamp, refrigerator, ceiling fan, clock radio, telephone, coffeemaker, hot tub/spa, voice mail and fireplace in room. Air conditioning. Fax, copier, fireplace, laundry facility, gardens, courtyard, fountain and two casitas on premises. Handicap access. Antiquing, art galleries, bicycling, cross-country skiing, fishing, golf, hiking, horseback riding, live theater, museums, parks, shopping and tennis nearby.

Location: Mountains.

Publicity: *Sunset, Conde Nast Traveler, Fodors and PBS.*

"Everything was simply perfect."

Certificate may be used: Nov. 1-March 1, Sunday-Thursday, holidays excluded.

Hacienda Nicholas

320 East Marcy Street
Santa Fe, NM 87501
(505)992-8385 (888)284-3170 Fax:(505)982-8572
Internet: www.haciendanicholas.com
E-mail: haciendanicholas@aol.com

Circa 1930. The Southwest meets Provence in this 1930 Adobe Hacienda built around a central garden courtyard full of wisteria, iris, daisies, pansies, geraniums and roses. Heated by an outdoor kiva fireplace on cool days and filled with birdsong on warm days, the courtyard is the perfect place to linger over

a breakfast of homemade muffins and quiche or to return for afternoon tea. The high-ceilinged great room is warmed by a huge fireplace and furnished with overstuffed couches. Just blocks from Santa Fe's historic plaza, the inn's seven guest rooms are elegantly furnished in Mexican décor, each with a wrought iron or carved wood four-poster bed.

Innkeeper(s): Anna Tenaglia. $100-190. 7 rooms with PB, 3 with FP, 3 suites, 1 conference room. Breakfast and afternoon tea included in rates. Types of meals: Full gourmet bkfst and early coffee/tea. Beds: KQ. Cable TV, reading lamp, telephone and fireplace in room. Air conditioning. Fax, fireplace and wine & cheese 5-7 nightly on premises. Handicap access. Antiquing, art galleries, bicycling, canoeing/kayaking, cross-country skiing, downhill skiing, fishing, golf, hiking, horseback riding, live theater, museums, parks, shopping, sporting events, tennis, water sports and wineries nearby.

Location: City.

Publicity: *Travel Holiday.*

Certificate may be used: Nov. 1-Feb. 28, Sunday-Thursday, no holidays.

The Madeleine
(formerly The Preston House)

106 Faithway St
Santa Fe, NM 87501
(505)982-3465 (888)877-7622 Fax:(505)982-8572
Internet: www.madeleineinn.com
E-mail: alexinn@osogrande.com

Circa 1886. Gracing a quiet neighborhood in Santa Fe, New Mexico, this historic and romantic bed and breakfast combines Asian and Victorian décor. Guests are invited for complimentary tea, wine and cheese at Hacienda Nicholas, just across the street. Each delightful guest bedroom is a warm and inviting retreat that features generous upscale amenities to please and pamper both business and leisure travelers. After a satisfying breakfast indulge the senses at the Madeleine's Absolute Nirvana Spa, Tea Room and Gardens. Select a therapeutic massage or treatment from the spa menu. Schedule a facial, bathe in a sea of rose petals  and be sure to visit the blissful gardens and the tea room for delectable treats. Ask about special packages.

Innkeeper(s): Carolyn Lee. $110-210. 7 rooms with PB, 4 with FP, 2 cottages. Breakfast, afternoon tea, snacks/refreshments and wine included in rates. Types of meals: Full gourmet bkfst and early coffee/tea. Beds: KQ. Data port, cable TV, reading lamp, CD player, refrigerator, ceiling fan, clock radio, telephone, coffeemaker, desk, voice mail, some with fireplace, hair dryer, bathrobes, bath amenities, wireless Internet access, iron/ironing board and DSL in room. Air conditioning. Fax, copier, spa, gift shop, NEW: Absolute Nirvana Spa, dedicated to the ancient healing art of using plants, herbs and spices for both inner and outer beauty and we offer traditional Asian spa rituals using only the highest quality organic oils and ingredients on premises. Antiquing, cross-country skiing, downhill skiing, fishing, live theater, parks and shopping nearby.

Location: City, mountains.

Publicity: *Country Inns, Bliss Magazine, New Mexican and Local Flavor .*

"We were extremely pleased — glad we found you. We shall return."

Certificate may be used: Nov. 1-Feb. 28, Sunday-Thursday, no holidays.

Taos

Abbe' de Touchstone - Inn, Spa & Gallery

0110 Mabel Dodge Ln
Taos, NM 87571
(505)758-0192 (800)758-0192 Fax:(505)758-3498
Internet: www.touchstoneinn.com
E-mail: touchstone@taosnet.com

Circa 1800. Touchstone Inn is a quiet, historic adobe estate secluded among tall trees at the edge of Taos Pueblo lands. The grounds have an unobstructed view of Taos Mountain. USA Today calls it "the place to stay in Taos." The inn, connected to a spa and a gallery, features cozy rooms with fireplaces, luxurious textiles, intimate patios and exquisite tiled baths (four of which have Jacuzzi tubs). The inn offers full gourmet vegetarian and continental breakfasts. The spa offers massages, yoga and art classes, facials and therapeutic baths and wraps. Guests enjoy the outdoor hot tub with choice vistas of Taos Mountain. Taos Ski valley is 18 miles to the north.

Innkeeper(s): Bren Price. $145-350. 9 rooms with PB, 6 with FP, 1 total suite, including 2 two-bedroom suites, 1 cottage, 1 guest house, 1 conference room. Breakfast included in rates. Types of meals: Full gourmet bkfst, veg bkfst, For groups and destination Spa packages and we offer lunch and supper along with breakfast. Beds: KQDT. Modem hook-up, cable TV, VCR, reading lamp, stereo, refrigerator, ceiling fan, snack bar, clock radio, telephone, coffeemaker, desk, most with hot tub/spa, most with fireplace, hair dryer, bathrobes, bath amenities, wireless Internet access, iron/ironing board, We are at 7400 feet in elevation so we do not require air conditioning, we do have ceiling fans and four rooms with Jacuzzis in room. DVD, fax, copier, spa, swimming, sauna, tennis, library, parlor games, gift shop, Day spa, Piano, Garden massages, Labyrinth, Beauty spa, Sports spa day pass available and Wireless internet access throughout building on premises. Antiquing, art galleries, bicycling, canoeing/kayaking, cross-country skiing, downhill skiing, fishing, golf, hiking, horseback riding, live theater, museums, parks, shopping, tennis, water sports, wineries, Opera and Labyrinth nearby.

Location: City, mountains. Santa Fe, New Mexico.

Publicity: USA Today, Bride's Magazine, Modern Bride, Mountain Living, Getaways, Mentioned in Winter in Taos by Mabel Dodge Luhan and subject of the book "Taos a Memory" by Miriam Hapgood Dewitt.

Certificate may be used: Monday-Thursday, September through April excluding holidays and fiestas. Last minute subject to availability. Free night does not include breakfast.

Adobe & Pines Inn

4107 State Road 68
Taos, NM 87557
(505)751-0947 (800)723-8267 Fax:(505)758-8423
Internet: www.adobepines.com
E-mail: mail@adobepines.com

Circa 1832. Two country acres create the setting for this classic 1832 Spanish adobe hacienda with its original architectural  details and Southwest eclectic décor and furnishings. Old Taos charm has been transformed into a romantic and luxurious bed and breakfast. Relax on bent apple furniture by the fountain in the back courtyard with an afternoon snack or on secluded patios. Guest bedrooms and suites offer privacy and rejuvenation. Entertainment centers accent the ambiance with music and many rooms feature fireplaces and oversized Jacuzzis. Stay in Puerta Rosa with a dry cedar sauna and

Roman-style soaking tub. Savor the morning with a satisfying gourmet breakfast. Schedule an in-room massage or available spa service. Ask about special packages.

Innkeeper(s): Katherine and Louis Costabel. $98-195. 8 rooms with PB, 8 with FP, 4 with WP, 3 total suites, including 1 two-bedroom suite, 3 cottages. Breakfast included in rates. Types of meals: Full gourmet bkfst, veg bkfst and early coffee/tea. Beds: Q. Cable TV, VCR, DVD, reading lamp, CD player, refrigerator, clock radio, coffeemaker, most with hot tub/spa, hair dryer, bathrobes, bath amenities and iron/ironing board in room. Fax, copier, library, pet boarding, parlor games, telephone, laundry facility, outdoor fire ring, country gardens, hammock and alpacas on premises. Antiquing, art galleries, bicycling, canoeing/kayaking, cross-country skiing, downhill skiing, fishing, golf, hiking, horseback riding, live theater, museums, parks, shopping, tennis, wineries, hot air ballooning and llama trekking nearby.

Location: Country, mountains. High desert.

Publicity: Yellow Brick Road, Denver Post, Los Angeles Times, San Francisco Examiner, New York Times, Weekends for Two in the Southwest, Lonely Planet, New Mexico for Dummies and HGTV.

"The Adobe & Pines Inn warms your soul and your senses with traditional New Mexican decor, hospitality and comfort."

Certificate may be used: Anytime, Sunday-Thursday, not valid Christmas week.

The Historic Taos Inn

125 Paseo Del Pueblo Norte
Taos, NM 87571-5901
(505)758-2233 (800)826-7466 Fax:(505)758-5776
Internet: www.taosinn.com
E-mail: taosinn@newmex.com

Circa 1880. Voted by National Geographic Traveler as one of "America's 54 Great Inns", The Taos Inn is a historic landmark with sections dating back to the 1600s. The inn's authentic adobe pueblo architecture enhances the inviting wood-burning fireplaces (kivas), vigas and wrought iron accents. Handsomely decorated rooms include reflections of the area's exotic tri-cultural heritage of Spanish, Anglo and Indian in the hand-loomed Guatamalan Indian bedspreads, antique armoires and Taos furniture. The Doc Martin's well reviewed restaurant includes the legendary Adobe Bar. Ancient Taos Pueblo and the historic taos Plaza are nearby.

Innkeeper(s): Douglas Smith & Carolyn Haddock. $75-250. 44 rooms with PB, 3 with FP, 3 suites. Types of meals: Full gourmet bkfst, veg bkfst, early coffee/tea, gourmet lunch, snacks/refreshments and gourmet dinner. Restaurant on premises. Beds: KQDT. Cable TV, clock radio, telephone and voice mail in room. Air conditioning. VCR, fax, copier, fireplace, greenhouse, Jacuzzi, full bar (legendary margaritas) with live music seven nights per week and free wireless Internet on premises. Handicap access. Art galleries, bicycling, canoeing/kayaking, cross-country skiing, downhill skiing, fishing, golf, hiking, live theater, museums, parks, shopping and wineries nearby.

Location: City.

Publicity: Travel & Leisure, Gourmet, Bon Appetit, National Geographic Traveler, New York Times, Los Angeles Times, New Mexico Magazine, Inside Oustide Magazine and Wine Spectator Award - 18 years in a row.

"It is charming, warm, friendly and authentic in decor with a real sense of history."

Certificate may be used: All year, Sunday-Thursday, subject to availability. Holiday period exclusions apply. Call for availablity and reservations.

New York

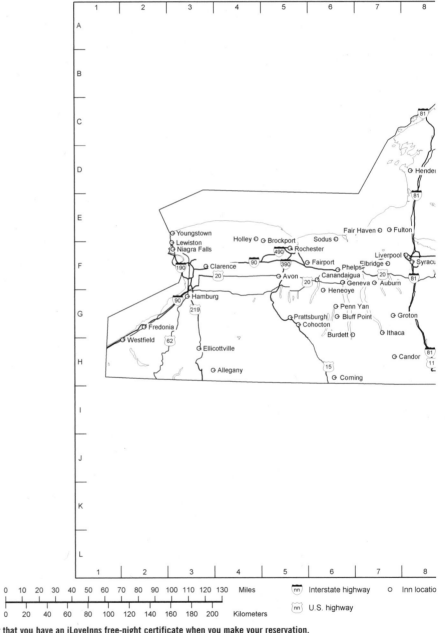

0 10 20 30 40 50 60 70 80 90 100 110 120 130   Miles

0   20   40   60   80   100   120   140   160   180   200   Kilometers

(nn) Interstate highway   o   Inn locatio

(nn) U.S. highway

  Tell the innkeeper that you have an iLoveInns free-night certificate when you make your reservation.

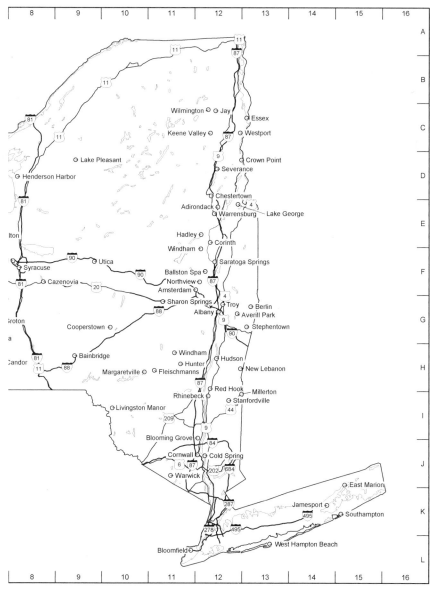

Inn location

Albany

Pine Haven B&B

531 Western Ave
Albany, NY 12203-1721
(518)482-1574
Internet: www.pinehavenbedandbreakfast.com

This turn-of-the-century Victorian is located in Pine Hills, an Albany historic district. In keeping with this history, the

innkeepers have tried to preserve the home's 19th-century charm. The rooms offer old-fashioned comfort with Victorian influences. The Capitol Building and other historic sites are nearby.

Innkeeper(s): Janice Tricarico. Call for rates. Call inn for details. Breakfast included in rates. Types of meals: Cont plus and early coffee/tea. Beds: QDT. Cable TV, reading lamp, clock radio, telephone and desk in room. Air conditioning. Parlor games, fireplace and free off-street parking on premises. Antiquing, cross-country skiing, live theater, parks, shopping and sporting events nearby.

Location: City.

Certificate may be used: Year-round, anytime, subject to availability.

Allegany

Gallets House B&B

1759 Four Mile Rd
Allegany, NY 14706-9724
(716)373-7493 Fax:(716)806-0384
Internet: www.galletshouse.com
E-mail: info@galletshouse.com

Circa 1896. Built by the innkeeper's great uncle Joseph Gallets, who was an oil producer, lumberman and farmer, this historic Victorian home features a third-floor museum with original family photos and heirlooms to browse through. Relax by the fireplaces in the parlor and common room. Enjoy refreshments on the 100-foot porch. Elegant air-conditioned guest bedrooms feature private baths and robes. Two rooms boast whirlpool tubs. Perfect for families and pets, the Carriage House Apartment has three bedrooms, two baths and a full kitchen. Fruits, homemade breads and biscuits are a prelude to sumptuous hot entrees and Joan's memorable French toast or apple cinnamon pancakes for breakfast in the formal dining room. The B&B is near ski resorts, Allegany State Park, St. Bonaventure University, golf courses and a main snowmobile trail. Ask about romance packages and monthly murder mysteries.

Innkeeper(s): Joan & Gary Boser. $85-140. 6 rooms with PB, 2 with FP, 2 with WP, 2 two-bedroom and 1 three-bedroom suites, 1 cottage, 3 guest houses, 1 conference room. Breakfast and snacks/refreshments included in rates. Types of meals: Full gourmet bkfst, veg bkfst, early coffee/tea, afternoon tea and Murder mystery dinner package. Beds: KQDT. Modem hook-up, data port, cable TV, VCR, DVD, reading lamp, CD player, ceiling fan, clock radio, telephone, coffeemaker, desk, some with hot tub/spa, hair dryer, bathrobes, bath amenities, wireless Internet access, iron/ironing board, two with whirlpool tub and wireless Internet connection in room. Air conditioning. Fax, copier, spa, parlor games, fireplace, laundry facility, gift shop and outdoor hot tub on premises. Limited handicap access. Antiquing, art galleries, bicycling, canoeing/kayaking, cross-country skiing, downhill skiing, fishing, golf, hiking, horseback riding, live theater, museums, parks, shopping, sporting events, snowmobile trails, snow tubing and Seneca Allegany Casino nearby.

Location: Country, mountains.

Certificate may be used: March-November, Sunday-Thursday, excluding holidays, subject to availability.

Amsterdam

Halcyon Farm Bed & Breakfast

157 Lang Road
Amsterdam, NY 12010
(518)842-7718 (800)470-2170
E-mail: halcyon@localnet.com

Circa 1800. Situated in historic Mill Point along the Schoharie River, this Federal brick home is surrounded by a peaceful country setting with 300 acres of spacious lawns, blooming perennials, hay fields, woods and the Blue Bank cliff. A living room and adjoining library boasts relaxed seating by the fire. Peach trees shade the private entrance to spacious guest bedrooms that include gas fireplaces. Full gourmet breakfasts may be a selection of the following: basil and vegetable strata, fresh-picked red raspberries and cream, portobello mushrooms with fresh sliced tomatoes and herbed scrambled eggs, homemade sage sausage, crispy parmesan potatoes, buttery currant scones, John's famous cornbread and June's renowned buttermilk blueberry pancakes. Fall is a wonderful time for hiking the cliff and old stagecoach trail behind the farm.

Innkeeper(s): June & John Leonard. $90-150. 5 rooms with PB, 5 with FP, 1 with WP. Breakfast and snacks/refreshments included in rates. Types of meals: Full gourmet bkfst, early coffee/tea and afternoon tea. Beds: KQT. Modem hook-up, data port, reading lamp, clock radio, desk, fireplace, hair dryer, bath amenities, iron/ironing board, TV, DVD and CD player available in the Hidden Room in room. Air conditioning. TV, DVD, fax, copier, library, parlor games, telephone, Guest refrigerator with drinks, Piano, Aerobed for extra person, Free national calling on host phone, Internet access, TV and DVD collection available in the Library on premises. Antiquing, cross-country skiing, fishing, golf, hiking, horseback riding and tennis nearby.

Location: Country. On Schoharie River. Five miles from Mohawk River.

Certificate may be used: Jan. 1 to March 31, Sunday-Thursday.

Averill Park

La Perla at the Gregory House, Country Inn & Restaurant

Rt 43 PO Box 401
Averill Park, NY 12018-0401
(518)674-3774 Fax:(518)674-8916
Internet: www.gregoryhouse.com
E-mail: innkeeper@gregoryhouse.com

Circa 1830. Stockbroker Elias Gregory built what is now the restaurant, as his Colonial home in the 1800s. The newer B&B inn, just twelve years old, blends well with the original house to retain the ambiance of its Victorian heritage. Gather by the dramatic fireplace in the common room which boasts vaulted ceilings, comfy furniture and a big-screen TV. The decor of each well-appointed guest bedroom is inviting. Award-winning La Perla offers Italian continental cuisine and is personally run by innkeeper Alfonso. This rural country town is surrounded by the Adirondacks, Berkshires, Hudson River, Saratoga and Albany with a variety of historic and scenic attractions.

Innkeeper(s): Anna Maria & Alfonso Acampora. $100-125. 12 rooms with PB, 1 conference room. Breakfast included in rates. Types of meals: Cont. Restaurant on premises. Beds: QDT. TV, reading lamp, clock radio, telephone and desk in room. Air conditioning. VCR, fax, copier and fireplace on premises. Amusement parks, antiquing, cross-country skiing, downhill skiing, fishing, live theater, parks, shopping, sporting events and water sports nearby.

Location: Village.

Publicity: *Hudson Valley, Albany Times Union, Schenectady Gazette, Courier and Sunday Record.*

"We experienced privacy and quiet, lovely surroundings indoors and out, excellent service and as much friendliness as we were comfortable with, but no more."

Certificate may be used: November-April, Sunday-Thursday.

Avon

Avon Inn

55 E Main St
Avon, NY 14414-1438
(585)226-8181 Fax:(585)226-8185
Internet: www.avoninn.com

This Greek Revival mansion, in both the state and national historic registers, has been providing lodging for more than a century. After 1866, the residence was turned into a health center that provided water cures from the local sulphur springs. The guest registry included the likes of Henry Ford, Thomas Edison and Eleanor Roosevelt. Though the inn is no longer a health spa, guests can still relax in the garden with its towering trees and fountain or on the Grecian-pillared front porch. A full-service restaurant and conference facilities are on the premises.

Innkeeper(s): Linda Moran. Call for rates. Call inn for details. Breakfast included in rates. Types of meals: Cont. Restaurant on premises. Beds: KQD. Clock radio, telephone and desk in room. Air conditioning. TV, fax and copier on premises. Amusement parks, antiquing, cross-country skiing, downhill skiing, fishing, golf, museums, parks and shopping nearby.

Certificate may be used: All year excluding Saturdays May 1-Nov. 15.

White Oak Bed and Breakfast

277 Genesee Street
Avon, NY 14414
(585)226-6735
Internet: whiteoakbandb.com
E-mail: avon-bnb@frontiernet.net

Circa 1860. Built as a summer home in the 1860s, this distinctive Second Empire Victorian with a mansard roof and wraparound porch has been recently renovated to retain its original charm and traditional decor. A private den/parlor with TV/VCR and board games is a convenient gathering place. Well-placed period furnishings accent the guest bedrooms and spacious Pine Suite. Enjoy the expansive view from the dining room while savoring home-baked breads, fresh fruit, and perhaps a broccoli cheddar omelette with home fries and bacon for breakfast. The one acre of gardens, with flowers for every season, include private sitting areas to chat. Visit nearby Genesee Country Village, a living history village or take day trips to explore the scenic Finger Lakes Region.

Innkeeper(s): Barbara Herman. $105-115. 3 rooms with PB. Breakfast and snacks/refreshments included in rates. Types of meals: Country bkfst, veg bkfst, early coffee/tea and picnic lunch. Beds: QD. Reading lamp, turn-down service and desk in room. Air conditioning. TV, VCR, DVD, library, parlor games, telephone, laundry facility and gift shop on premises. Antiquing, art galleries, bicycling, canoeing/kayaking, fishing, golf, hiking, horseback riding, live theater, museums, parks, shopping and wineries nearby.

Certificate may be used: Anytime, Sunday-Thursday, May 1 through October 31.

Bainbridge

Berry Hill Gardens B&B

242 Ward Loomis Rd.
Bainbridge, NY 13733
(607)967-8745 (800)497-8745 Fax:(607)967-2227
Internet: www.berryhillgardens.com
E-mail: info@berryhillgardens.com

Circa 1820. Located off the beaten path on a secluded lane, this country bed and breakfast graces the heart of Central New York. Two different B&B experiences are offered on 300 acres of gardens, lakes, ponds, woods and meadows. Berry Hill Gardens Inn is situated on a hilltop overlooking miles of rural beauty;

the Buckthorn Lodge is poised in a sunny glen deep in the woods. Find comfortable antiques, fireplaces and all-natural luxury linens. Delicious breakfasts are served in a friendly, healthy informal atmosphere. Conveniently centered between Bainbridge, Afton and Oxford, the scenic Leatherstocking Region features museums, sporting facilities, artisans and fascinating history.

Innkeeper(s): Jean Fowler & Cecilio Rios. $110-165. 8 rooms with PB. Breakfast and snacks/refreshments included in rates. Types of meals: Country bkfst, early coffee/tea and Catered dinners can be provided with advance notice. Beds: KQDT. Reading lamp, ceiling fan, clock radio, desk, hair dryer, bathrobes, bath amenities, wireless Internet access and iron/ironing board in room. TV, VCR, DVD, fax, copier, swimming, library, parlor games, telephone, fireplace, Guest kitchen with refrigerator, microwave, sink and dishes provided in general area, full kitchen and all amenities provided at lodge on premises. Antiquing, art galleries, bicycling, canoeing/kayaking, cross-country skiing, fishing, golf, hiking, horseback riding, live theater, museums, parks, shopping, sporting events, tennis, water sports, wineries and Downhill Skiing is Available at Greek Peak about 45 minutes away nearby.

Location: Country.

Publicity: *Country Living Gardener Magazine (August 2001), Binghamton Press and Sun, People and Places and Plants Magazine (Autumn 2006).*

"The house is just wonderful and our rooms were exceptionally comfortable."

Certificate may be used: Jan. 2-April 30, anytime. May 1-Dec. 20, Sunday through Thursday only. Holidays and special events excluded.

Ballston Spa

Medbery Inn & Spa

48 Front Street
Ballston Spa, NY 12020
(518)-885-SPAS7727
Internet: www.medberyinnandspa.com
E-mail: relax@medberyinnandspa.com

Circa 1878. Indulge in the rejuvenating effects of this feng shui boutique hotel and historic destination spa with relaxing accommodations, natural mineral waters and a full-service spa menu. Luxuriously furnished for the casual and business traveler, choose a candlelit deluxe guest bedroom, or mini-suite with whirlpool tub, body shower and fireplace.

Enjoy the complete line from Stonewall Kitchens and refreshing L?Erbolario fragrances. Savor a dazzling breakfast served daily in the Sans Souci Room. Getaway and spa packages are available. A coordinator will provide assistance in planning and catering special events.

Innkeeper(s): Dolores & Jim Taisey. $125-275. 10 rooms with PB, 3 suites. Breakfast included in rates. Types of meals: Full bkfst and early coffee/tea. Beds: Q. Cable TV, VCR, reading lamp, refrigerator, clock radio and whirlpool in room. Central air. Parlor games, telephone and fireplace on premises. Amusement parks, antiquing, cross-country skiing, downhill skiing, fishing, live theater, parks, shopping, sporting events, water sports and Saratoga Race Course nearby.

Location: Village (historic district).

Publicity: *Country Folk Art Magazine.*

Certificate may be used: Midweek, Sunday-Thursday, January-April.

Blooming Grove

The Dominion House

50 Old Dominion Road
Blooming Grove, NY 10914
(845)496-1826 Fax:(845)496-3492
Internet: www.thedominionhouse.com
E-mail: kathy@thedominionhouse.com

Circa 1880. At the end of a country lane in the scenic Hudson Valley, this Victorian Farmhouse has been adorning four-and-a-half acres since 1880. Original marble mantels, ornate cornice work, wide-plank floors, large pocket doors and eleven-foot ceilings with plaster medallions reflect a well-maintained elegance. The library offers a large book selection or relax by the fire in the oak den. Play a game of pool on the slate-top table and listen to music in the parlor. Large guest bedrooms and a private Honeymoon Cottage are furnished with antiques. A hearty breakfast is served in the dining room with specialty dishes that may include caramel sticky buns, featherlight scones, stuffed croissants, peach French toast and sausage. Swim in the inground pool, play horseshoes or relax on the wraparound porch.

Innkeeper(s): Kathy & Joe Spear. $105-199. 4 rooms, 1 with PB, 1 cottage. Breakfast and snacks/refreshments included in rates. Types of meals: Country bkfst and early coffee/tea. Beds: QDT. Modem hook-up, cable TV, reading lamp, clock radio, telephone and robes in room. Air conditioning. Fax, copier, spa, swimming, library, parlor games, fireplace, slate-top pool table, horseshoes, guest refrigerator and complimentary snacks and drinks on premises. Antiquing, art galleries, canoeing/kayaking, cross-country skiing, downhill skiing, fishing, golf, hiking, live theater, museums, parks, shopping and wineries nearby.

Location: Country.

Certificate may be used: All year, Sunday through Thursday, subject to availability. Excludes holidays.

Bluff Point

Esperanza Mansion

3456 Route 54A
Bluff Point, NY 14478
(315)536-4400 (866)927-4400 Fax:(315)536-4900
Internet: www.esperanzamansion.com
E-mail: info@esperanzamansion.com

Circa 1838. Overlook beautiful Keuka Lake while staying at this classic 1838 Greek Revival mansion that has been meticulously restored. The elegant décor is accented with antique reproductions, period furnishings and colors. Ten scenic acres feature expansive lawns, relaxing porches and patios. The

Mansion Restaurant offers full service and fine food and the Tavern offers more casual fare with an adjoining canopied terrace. There is also a state-of-the-art banquet facility. Guest bedrooms in the Mansion are named for the varieties of grapes grown in the Finger Lakes Region. The Pinot Noir and the Chardonnay rooms can be an adjoining suite. Select a room in the inn with a balcony or patio. Start the day with a deluxe continental breakfast in the fireside dining room.

Innkeeper(s): David and Lisa Wegman. $99-285. 30 rooms with PB, 1 suite, 3 conference rooms. Types of meals: Cont plus, gourmet lunch, picnic lunch, snacks/refreshments, hors d'oeuvres, wine and gourmet dinner. Restaurant on premises. Beds: KQD. Modem hook-up, data port, cable TV, ceiling fan, clock radio, telephone, coffeemaker, desk, voice mail, hair dryer, bath amenities and iron/ironing board in room. Central air. Fax, copier, fireplace and gift shop on premises. Limited handicap access. Antiquing, art galleries, bicycling, canoeing/kayaking, cross-country skiing, downhill skiing, fishing, golf, hiking, museums, parks, shopping, tennis, water sports and wineries nearby.

Location: Country. Overlooking lake.

Certificate may be used: November-March Anytime, April and May, September and October, Sunday-Thursday only.

Brockport

The Victorian B&B

320 S Main St
Brockport, NY 14420-2253
(585)637-7519 Fax:(585)637-7519
Internet: www.victorianbandb.com
E-mail: 5mk320@aol.com

Circa 1889. Within walking distance of the historic Erie Canal, this Queen Anne Victorian inn is located on Brockport's Main Street. Visitors select from five second-floor guest rooms, all with phones, private baths and TVs. Victorian furnishings are found throughout the inn. A favorite spot is the solarium, with its three walls of windows and fireplace, perfect for curling up with a book or magazine. Two first-floor sitting areas with fireplaces also provide relaxing havens for guests. Lake Ontario is just 10 miles away, and visitors will find much to explore in Brockport and Rochester. Brockport is home to the State University of New York and Niagara Falls is an hour away.

Innkeeper(s): Sharon Kehoe. $79-150. 5 rooms with PB. Breakfast and afternoon tea included in rates. Types of meals: Country bkfst, veg bkfst and early coffee/tea. Beds: KQT. Cable TV, reading lamp, clock radio, telephone, desk, hair dryer, bath amenities, wireless Internet access and flower arrangements and/or gift baskets by special arrangement in room. Central air. VCR, fax, library, parlor games, fireplace, iron/ironing board and free off-road parking on premises. Amusement parks, antiquing, art galleries, beach, bicycling, canoeing/kayaking, cross-country skiing, downhill skiing, fishing, golf, hiking, horseback riding, live theater, museums, parks, shopping, sporting events, tennis, water sports, wineries, farmers market and movie theater nearby.

Location: Village, Erie Canal.

Certificate may be used: Oct. 1 to April 30, no holidays and special events.

Canandaigua

1792 Filigree Inn

5406 Bristol Valley Rd.(RT.64S.)
Canandaigua, NY 14424
(585)229-4017 (888)560-7614 Fax:(585)229-4487
Internet: www.filigreeinn.com
E-mail: filigree@filigreeinn.com

Circa 1792. Escape to 1792 Filigree Inn, a four-season country retreat in the Finger Lakes wine country region of New York. Relax on 180 breathtaking acres in Bristol Hills of Canandaigua. Renovated guest suites boast air-conditioned comfort, feather beds, whirlpool tubs, fully equipped kitchens, entertainment centers and a private deck. Each refrigerator is stocked with breakfast foods to enjoy when desired. Ski and snowboard at local Bristol Mountain Resort or try cross-county trails at the nearby Cumming Nature Center. Weddings are popular at this bed and breakfast amid a gorgeous setting and a peaceful ambiance. Ask about special promotions and packages available.

Innkeeper(s): Don & Connie Simmons. $100-180. 8 rooms with PB, 8 with FP, 8 with WP, 4 two-bedroom suites. Breakfast and snacks/refreshments included in rates. Types of meals: Full bkfst. Beds: KQ. Modem hook-up, cable TV, VCR, reading lamp, stereo, refrigerator, snack bar, clock radio, telephone, coffeemaker, fireplace, hair dryer, bath amenities, iron/ironing board, Full kitchens, private decks, dining areas and Jacuzzi tubs in room. Central air. Fax, copier, Hiking trails and snowmobile trails on premises. Limited handicap access. Amusement parks, antiquing, art galleries, beach, bicycling, canoeing/kayaking, cross-country skiing, downhill skiing, fishing, golf, hiking, horseback riding, live theater, museums, parks, shopping, tennis, water sports, wineries, Wine and Culinary Center nearby.

Location: Country, mountains.

Certificate may be used: Sunday-Thursday only, subject to availability.

Bed & Breakfast at Oliver Phelps

252 N Main St
Canandaigua, NY 14424-1220
(585)396-1650 (800)926-1830
Internet: www.oliverphelps.com
E-mail: oliverphelpsbb@aol.com

Circa 1812. Century-old chestnut trees frame this historic Federal-style inn, which has offered elegant accommodations to Finger Lakes visitors since 1986. Gracing Main Street in Canandaigua, New York this B&B features arched entryways, handsome fireplaces and chestnut plank flooring that reflect a time of grace and simplicity. Romantic and spacious guest bedrooms boast poster beds, period antiques and luxurious amenities. Savor a candlelight gourmet breakfast each morning. The surrounding area is filled with attractions for every season and every interest, including winery tours, winter and summer sports, antiquing, shopping, biking and hiking.

Innkeeper(s): Jack & Donna Delehanty. $115-165. 5 rooms with PB, 2 with FP, 1 suite, 1 conference room. Breakfast, afternoon tea and snacks/refreshments included in rates. Types of meals: Full gourmet bkfst, veg bkfst, early coffee/tea and picnic lunch. Beds: KQD. Modem hook-up, cable TV, VCR, reading lamp, clock radio, turn-down service, desk, hair dryer, bathrobes and bath amenities in room. Central air. Copier, spa, bicycles, library, parlor games, telephone and fireplace on premises. Amusement parks, antiquing, art galleries, beach, bicycling, canoeing/kayaking, cross-country skiing, downhill skiing, fishing, golf, hiking, horseback riding, live theater, museums, parks, shopping, tennis, water sports and wineries nearby.

Location: City. Sonnenberg Garden, Granger Homestead.

Certificate may be used: November to May, excluding holidays.

Morgan Samuels B&B Inn

2920 Smith Rd
Canandaigua, NY 14424-9558
(585)394-9232 Fax:(716)394-8044
Internet: www.morgansamuelsinn.com
E-mail: morsambb@aol.com

Circa 1812. A luxurious Victorian estate on 46 acres of peaceful countryside, this inn offers elegance and comfort. Fireplaces, floor to ceiling windows, museum-quality furnishings, stained glass, and wide plank floors are delightful features found in both common and private areas. The guest bedrooms boast French doors leading to balconies that overlook landscaped gardens, fountains and a tennis court, or have a private entrance with an ivy-covered archway. Candlelight and soft music accentuate a lavish gourmet breakfast served in the formal dining room, intimate tea room or glass-enclosed stone porch. Afternoon tea and appetizers are welcome treats.

Innkeeper(s): Brad & Connie Smith. $119-295. 6 rooms with PB, 4 with FP, 3 with WP, 1 suite, 1 conference room. Breakfast, afternoon tea and hors d'oeuvres included in rates. Types of meals: Full gourmet bkfst, early coffee/tea, Gourmet dinner on a pre fixed basis and Afternoon Tea is available upon request. Beds: KQ. Reading lamp, CD player, clock radio, turn-down service, hair dryer, bathrobes, bath amenities, Two rooms have refrigerator and Two rooms have ceiling fans in room. Central air. TV, VCR, DVD, fax, copier, spa, tennis, library, parlor games, telephone, fireplace and gift shop on premises. Antiquing, art galleries, beach, bicycling, canoeing/kayaking, cross-country skiing, downhill skiing, fishing, golf, hiking, horseback riding, live theater, museums, parks, shopping, sporting events, water sports, wineries, Sonnenburg Gardens, Cumming Nature Center, horse racing and Eastman House nearby.

Location: Country.

Certificate may be used: Sunday-Thursday from Nov. 20 to May 20, no holidays.

Candor

The Edge of Thyme, A B&B Inn

6 Main St
Candor, NY 13743-0048
(607)659-5155 (800)722-7365 Fax:(607)659-5155
Internet: www.edgeofthyme.com
E-mail: innthyme@twcny.rr.com

Circa 1840. Originally the summer home of John D. Rockefeller's secretary, this two-story Georgian-style inn offers gracious accommodations a short drive from Ithaca. The inn sports many interesting features, including an impressive stairway, marble fireplaces, parquet floors, pergola (arbor) and windowed porch with leaded glass. Guests may relax in front of the inn's fireplace, catch up with reading in its library or watch television in  the sitting room. An authentic turn-of-the-century full breakfast is served, and guests also may arrange for special high teas.

Innkeeper(s): Prof. Frank & Eva Mae Musgrave. $90-145. 5 rooms, 3 with PB, 2 suites. Breakfast included in rates. Types of meals: Full gourmet bkfst, veg bkfst, early coffee/tea and afternoon tea. Beds: KQDT. Reading lamp, ceiling fan, clock radio and desk in room. Air conditioning. TV, VCR, fax, library, child care, parlor games, telephone, fireplace, gift shop and high tea by appointment on premises. Antiquing, art galleries, cross-country skiing, downhill skiing, fishing, golf, hiking, horseback riding, live theater, museums, parks, shopping, sporting events and wineries nearby.

Location: Village.

Publicity: Historic Inns of the Northeast, 17 newspapers across the US by a freelance writer concentrating on the Finger Lakes, The Ithaca Journal, The Press and Sun Bullitan.

Certificate may be used: Sunday through Thursday. Not valid in May, excluding specific weekends.

Cazenovia

Brae Loch Inn

5 Albany St
Cazenovia, NY 13035-1403
(315)655-3431 Fax:(315)655-4844
Internet: www.braelochinn.com
E-mail: braeloch1@aol.com

Circa 1805. Hunter green awnings accentuate the attractive architecture of the Brae Loch. Since 1946 the
inn has been owned and operated by the
same family. A Scottish theme is
evident throughout, including
in the inn's restaurant. Four of
the oldest rooms have fireplaces
(non-working). Stickley, Harden
and antique furniture add to the
old-world atmosphere, and

many rooms offer canopy beds. Guest rooms are on the second floor above the restaurant.

Innkeeper(s): Jim & Val Barr. $85-155. 12 rooms with PB, 3 with FP, 3 with WP, 1 conference room. Breakfast and You can have a getaway package that includes dinner or brunch included in rates. Types of meals: Cont, Sun. brunch, wine and gourmet dinner. Restaurant on premises. Beds: KQDT. Cable TV, reading lamp, clock radio, telephone, coffeemaker, desk, hair dryer, wireless Internet access, iron/ironing board and All with Tempur-Pedic mattresses in room. Air conditioning. VCR, fax, copier, child care, parlor games, fireplace and gift shop on premises. Antiquing, art galleries, beach, bicycling, cross-country skiing, downhill skiing, fishing, golf, hiking, horseback riding, live theater, museums, parks, shopping, sporting events, tennis, water sports, wineries and swimming just across the street at a public beach nearby.

Location: Small village by lake.

Publicity: The Globe and Mail, Traveler Magazine and CNY.

"Everything was just perfect. The Brae Loch and staff make you feel as if you were at home."

Certificate may be used: Anytime, Sunday-Thursday.

Notleymere Cottage

4641 E Lake Rd
Cazenovia, NY 13035-9357
(315)655-2006 Fax:(315)655-3510
Internet: www.notleymere.com
E-mail: stay@notleymere.com

Circa 1888. Enter Notleymere Cottage Bed & Breakfast to experience an eclectic mix of old and new that is a visual feast. This historic 1888 Victorian shingle-style mansion has been recently restored and painstakingly renovated. Spacious inside with 8,800 square feet, outside it spans two acres on Cazenovia Lake near Syracuse, New York in the Finger Lakes region. Relax in gracious luxury with afternoon tea on the porch or fireside sitting area. Play the baby grand piano in the parlor or listen to a CD while browsing the books in the library. Guest bedrooms feature waterfront or garden views and are exceptionally designed individually with a distinctive décor. Two suites include whirlpool tubs. Gather for a gourmet breakfast in the fireside dining room or lakeside veranda. Boat, fish or swim in the lake.

Innkeeper(s): Bob & Dianna Slodowitz. $140-250. 5 rooms with PB, 2 with

WP, 2 two-bedroom suites. Types of meals: Full bkfst and afternoon tea. Beds: K. Cable TV, DVD, reading lamp, telephone, hair dryer, bath amenities and wireless Internet access in room. Central air. VCR, fax, copier, spa, swimming, bicycles, library, parlor games, fireplace and Boating on Cazenovia Lake on premises. Antiquing, art galleries, bicycling, canoeing/kayaking, cross-country skiing, downhill skiing, fishing, hiking, horseback riding, parks, shopping, sporting events, tennis, water sports, wineries and Local farmers market nearby.

Location: Waterfront.

Certificate may be used: Dec. 1-April anytime; May 1-Nov. 30 Sunday-Thursday; other days subject to availability.

Chestertown

Friends Lake Inn

963 Friends Lake Rd
Chestertown, NY 12817
(518)494-4751 Fax:(518)494-4616
Internet: www.friendslake.com
E-mail: friends@friendslake.com

This Mission-style inn offers its guests elegant accommodations, fine dining in their Four Diamond restaurant and Grand Spectator award-winning wine. Overlooking Friends Lake, the inn provides easy access to the entire Adirondack area. Guests are welcome to borrow a canoe for a lake outing and use the inn's private beach or in-ground swimming pool. Guest rooms are well-appointed and most include four-poster beds. Many have breathtaking lake views or Jacuzzis. Three rooms have a wood-burning fireplace. An outdoor sauna is a favorite spot after a busy day of recreation. The 25km Tubbs Snowshoe Center is on site with wilderness trails and rentals. Trails are available for hiking as well.

Innkeeper(s): John & Trudy Phillips. Call for rates. 17 rooms with PB, 4 with FP, 5 with HT, 1 two-bedroom suite. Breakfast and dinner included in rates. Types of meals: Country bkfst, veg bkfst, picnic lunch, hors d'oeuvres, wine, room service and 4 Diamond Restaurant and Grand Spectator Wine Award. Restaurant on premises. Beds: KQ. Reading lamp, CD player, clock radio, telephone, coffeemaker, turn-down service, some with hot tub/spa, voice mail, some with fireplace, hair dryer, bathrobes, bath amenities, wireless Internet access and iron/ironing board in room. Central air. TV, VCR, fax, copier, spa, swimming, sauna, library, parlor games, gift shop, pool, beach and sauna on premises. Limited handicap access. Amusement parks, antiquing, art galleries, beach, bicycling, canoeing/kayaking, cross-country skiing, downhill skiing, fishing, golf, hiking, horseback riding, live theater, museums, parks, shopping, sporting events, tennis and water sports nearby.

Location: Mountains.

Publicity: Country Inns and New York Times.

"Everyone here is so pleasant, you end up feeling like family!"

Certificate may be used: Sunday-Thursday, November-April, subject to availability, DOES NOT INCLUDE DINNER.

Clarence

Asa Ransom House

10529 Main St
Clarence, NY 14031-1684
(716)759-2315 (800)841-2340 Fax:(716)759-2791
Internet: www.asaransom.com
E-mail: innfo@asaransom.com

Circa 1853. Set on spacious lawns, behind a white picket fence, the Asa Ransom House rests on the site of the first grist mill built in Erie County. Silversmith Asa Ransom constructed an inn and grist mill here in response to the Holland Land Company's offering of free land to anyone who would start and operate a tavern. A specialty of the dining room is "Veal

Perrott" and "Pistachio Banana Muffins."

Innkeeper(s): Robert & Abigail Lenz. $98-175. 9 rooms with PB, 8 with FP, 1 with WP, 2 two-bedroom suites, 1 conference room. Breakfast included in rates. Types of meals: Full gourmet bkfst, early coffee/tea, lunch, afternoon tea, snacks/refreshments, wine and dinner. Restaurant on premises. Beds: KQT. Modem hook-up, cable TV, VCR, DVD, reading lamp, stereo, refrigerator,  clock radio, telephone, turn-down service, desk, hair dryer, bathrobes, wireless Internet access, iron/ironing board, some with porch or balcony and old-time radio tapes in room. Air conditioning. Fax, copier, bicycles, library, parlor games, fireplace, gift shop, Herb and flower gardens on premises. Handicap access. Amusement parks, antiquing, art galleries, bicycling, cross-country skiing, golf, hiking, live theater, museums, parks, shopping, tennis and wineries nearby.

Location: Village.

Publicity: *Toronto Star, Buffalo News, Prevention Magazine, Country Living, Country Inns, Buffalo Spree and Inn Country USA.*

"Popular spot keeps getting better."

Certificate may be used: March-June, September-Dec. 15, Sunday-Thursday.

Cohocton

Ambroselli's Villa Serendip

10849 State Route 371
Cohocton, NY 14826
(585)384-5299 (866)205-6913 Fax:(585)384-5299
Internet: www.villaserendip.com
E-mail: innhost@yahoo.com

Circa 1860. Country Victorian elegance awaits at this Italianate villa surrounded by rolling hills and scenic splendor. Non-smoking guest bedrooms and suites easily accommodate families and honeymooners alike. Cupid's Retreat with a canopy bed and fireplace is perfect for a private romantic getaway. The first-floor Victorian Bride's Dream features a four-poster rice bed and bay window alcove. The Empire Suite offers spaciousness and extra beds as well as a sitting room with a large screen television and VCR. Oven-baked bananas, French toast with glazed pecans, muffins, skillet potatoes with sausage and rosemary, and scrambled eggs with three cheeses are popular breakfast favorites. Visit Canandaigua Lake, Corning Glass Factory and award-winning wineries.

Innkeeper(s): Fran Ambroselli. $95-225. 5 rooms with PB, 2 with FP, 1 with WP, 1 two-bedroom and 1 three-bedroom suites. Breakfast and snacks/refreshments included in rates. Types of meals: Full gourmet bkfst, veg bkfst, early coffee/tea, picnic lunch and afternoon tea. Beds: KQ. Cable TV, VCR, reading lamp, refrigerator, ceiling fan, clock radio, telephone, turn-down service, some with hot tub/spa, some with fireplace, hair dryer, bath amenities, wireless Internet access and iron/ironing board in room. Parlor games and Jacuzzi suite on premises. Handicap access. Antiquing, beach, cross-country skiing, downhill skiing, fishing, golf, hiking, horseback riding, live theater, museums, parks, shopping, Mountain Ski Resort, Swain Ski Resort, Letworth State Park, Stony Brook State Park, Corning Museum of Glass, Keuka Lake and wine tours nearby.

Location: Country, mountains.

Certificate may be used: Anytime, subject to availability, Sunday-Thursday.

Cold Spring

Pig Hill Inn

73 Main St
Cold Spring, NY 10516-3014
(845)265-9247 Fax:(845)265-9154
Internet: www.pighillinn.com
E-mail: pighillinn@aol.com

Circa 1808. The antiques at this stately three-story inn can be purchased, and they range from Chippendale to chinoiserie style. Rooms feature formal English and Adirondack decor with special touches such as four-poster or brass beds, painted rockers and, of course, pigs. The delicious breakfasts can be shared with guests in the Victorian conservatory dining room or a tri-level garden, or it may be served in the privacy of your room. The inn is about an hour out of New York City, and the train station is only two blocks away.

Innkeeper(s): Kyle Gibbs. $150-250. 9 rooms with PB, 6 with FP, 1 conference room. Breakfast and Refreshments or Afternoon Tea included in rates. Types of meals: Full gourmet bkfst and room service. Beds: KQDT. Reading lamp, ceiling fan, clock radio, some with hot tub/spa, most with fireplace, hair dryer, bath amenities, iron/ironing board available and Free high-speed Internet access in room. Central air. TV, fax, copier, spa, library, parlor games, telephone, gift shop and wireless high-speed Internet on premises. Handicap access. Antiquing, beach, bicycling, canoeing/kayaking, cross-country skiing, fishing, golf, hiking, horseback riding, live theater, museums, parks, shopping, sporting events, tennis, water sports, wineries and great restaurants nearby.

Location: Country, mountains. Small Hudson River town.

Publicity: *National Geographic, Woman's Home Journal, Country Inns and Getaways for Gourmets.*

"Some of our fondest memories of New York were at Pig Hill."

Certificate may be used: Monday-Thursday, Nov. 1-April 30, excluding holidays.

Corinth

Agape Farm B&B and Paintball

4839 Rt 9N
Corinth, NY 12822-1704
(518)654-7777 Fax:(518)654-7777
Internet: www.geocities.com/agapefarm
E-mail: agapefarmbnb@adelphia.net

Circa 1870. Amid 33 acres of fields and woods, this Adirondack farmhouse is home to chickens and horses, as well as guests seeking a refreshing getaway. Visitors have their choice of six guest rooms, all with ceiling fans, phones, private baths and views of the tranquil surroundings. The inn's wrap-around porch lures many visitors, who often enjoy a glass of icy lemonade. Homemade  breads, jams, jellies and muffins are part of the full breakfast served here, and guests are welcome to pick berries or gather a ripe tomato from the garden. A trout-filled stream on the grounds flows to the Hudson River, a mile away.

Innkeeper(s): Fred & Sigrid Koch. $120-150. 3 rooms with PB, 1 conference room. Breakfast and snacks/refreshments included in rates. Types of meals: Full gourmet bkfst, veg bkfst and early coffee/tea. Beds: KQDT. Reading lamp, ceiling fan, clock radio, telephone and desk in room. TV, VCR, fax, swimming, child care, parlor games, laundry facility and downstairs HC room and bath on premises. Handicap access. Amusement parks, antiquing, art galleries, beach, bicycling, canoeing/kayaking, cross-country skiing, downhill skiing, fishing, golf, hiking, horseback riding, museums, parks, shopping, sporting events, tennis and water sports nearby.

Location: Country. Saratoga Region.

"Clean and impeccable, we were treated royally."

Certificate may be used: Sept. 15 to June 1, no holidays, premium rooms.

Corning

Rosewood Inn

134 E 1st St
Corning, NY 14830-2711
(607)962-3253
Internet: www.rosewoodinn.com
E-mail: stay@rosewoodinn.com

Circa 1855. Rosewood Inn was originally built as a Greek Revival house. In 1917, the interior and exterior were remodeled in an English Tudor style. Original black walnut and oak woodwork grace the interior, decorated with authentic wallpapers, period draperies and fine antiques. It is within walking distance to historic, restored Market Street and museums.

Innkeeper(s): Stewart & Suzanne Sanders. $95-185. 7 rooms with PB. Breakfast and afternoon tea included in rates. Types of meals: Full bkfst. Beds: QDT. Some with hot tub/spa and some with fireplace in room. Air conditioning. TV, parlor games and telephone on premises. Antiquing, fishing, hiking, museums and wineries nearby.

Location: City.

Publicity: *Syracuse Herald-Journal, New York Times, National Geographic Traveler, Wonderful Hotels and Inns and Innroads.*

"Rosewood Inn is food for the soul! You both made us feel like friends instead of guests. We'll be back!"

Certificate may be used: Anytime, November-March, subject to availability. Not honored on holiday weekends.

Cornwall

Cromwell Manor Inn B&B

174 Angola Rd
Cornwall, NY 12518
(845)534-7136
Internet: www.cromwellmanor.com
E-mail: cmi@hvc.rr.com

Circa 1820. Listed in the National Register of Historic Places, this stunning Greek Revival mansion sits on seven lush acres with scenic Hudson Valley views. It is elegantly furnished with period antiques and fine reproductions. The Chimneys Cottage, built in 1764, features romantic bedrooms with a more rustic

colonial decor. Awaken to the aroma of a gourmet breakfast served in the country dining room or outside veranda. More than 4,000 acres of hiking trails are steps from the front

door. Arrange for a picnic or enjoy a fireside massage. Nap in the hammock, sip wine on the patio next to the classic fountain and watch the sunset from the rear lawn. The farm next door offers unique gifts and treats. Each season has plenty to explore.

Innkeeper(s): Richard. $165-370. 13 rooms, 12 with PB, 7 with FP, 3 total

suites, including 1 two-bedroom suite, 1 conference room. Breakfast and afternoon tea included in rates. Types of meals: Full gourmet bkfst, early coffee/tea, picnic lunch, snacks/refreshments and room service. Beds: KQDT. Reading lamp, CD player, snack bar, clock radio, turn-down service, desk, some with hot tub/spa, most with fireplace, hair dryer, bathrobes, wireless Internet access and iron/ironing board in room. Central air. TV, VCR, fax, copier, parlor games, telephone, refrigerator and coffee maker on premises. Limited handicap access. Antiquing, art galleries, bicycling, canoeing/kayaking, cross-country skiing, downhill skiing, fishing, golf, hiking, horseback riding, live theater, museums, parks, shopping, sporting events, tennis, water sports, wineries, Hudson Valley Mansions, Woodbury Common Premium Outlets, Storm King Art Center, Renaissance Festival, West Point sports and mountain biking nearby.

Location: Country, mountains. Hudson River Valley.

Publicity: *USA Today, New York Times, Wall Street Journal, Fox, CBS Early Show and Top 10 Inns of NY.*

Certificate may be used: Anytime, Sunday-Thursday, subject to availability, holidays excluded.

Dover Plains

Old Drovers Inn

Old Rt 22
Dover Plains, NY 12522
(845)832-9311 Fax:(845)832-6356
Internet: www.olddroversinn.com
E-mail: info@olddroversinn.com

Luxurious accommodations and fine food are featured at this historic Colonial Revival inn, located in the Harlem Valley at the foot of the Berkshires. The inn once served as a resting spot for area

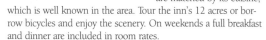

drovers, or cowboys, who were leading cattle to market in New York City. Visitors select from the Cherry, Meeting, Rose or Sleigh rooms. The handsome furnishings and service found at the inn are matched by its cuisine, which is well known in the area. Tour the inn's 12 acres or borrow bicycles and enjoy the scenery. On weekends a full breakfast and dinner are included in room rates.

Innkeeper(s): David Wilson. Call for rates. Call inn for details. Types of meals: Full bkfst, early coffee/tea, lunch, picnic lunch and gourmet dinner. Reading lamp, turn-down service and desk in room. Air conditioning. VCR, telephone and fireplace on premises. Antiquing, cross-country skiing, downhill skiing, golf, live theater and shopping nearby.

Location: Country, mountains.

Publicity: *New York Magazine, Country Inns, New York Times, Town and Country and Relais & Chateaux.*

"This inn is as romantic a treasure as you will ever find."

Certificate may be used: Anytime, subject to availability.

East Marion

Arbor View House B & B

8900 Main Road
East Marion, NY 11939-0226
(631)477-8440 (800)963-8777
Internet: www.Arborviewhouse.com
E-mail: wjoseph@earthlink.net

Circa 1820. Elegant and romantic in Long Island's North Fork Wine Country, this bed and breakfast was originally built with Federal architecture and was later renovated with Victorian design. Relax with afternoon tea and refreshments or sit by the fireplace with a good book. Luxurious guest bedrooms offer an assortment of pleasing amenities that include bottles of spring water, plush robes, entertainment centers and other comforts. Indulge in the spacious Champagne Suite with a whirlpool bath. An optional private deck can be reserved. The Merlot Room boasts a cast iron tub. A four-course brunch-style breakfast is served by candlelight in the formal dining room or al fresco when weather permits. Walk to the beach, tour a local winery or schedule a massage from an extensive spa services menu.

Innkeeper(s): Veda Daley Joseph & Wilfred Joseph. $185-275. 4 rooms with PB, 2 with WP, 1 suite. Breakfast, Sunday brunch, afternoon tea, snacks/refreshments and hors d'oeuvres included in rates. Types of meals: Full gourmet bkfst, early coffee/tea and picnic lunch. Beds: KQ. Modem hook-up, data port, cable TV, VCR, DVD, reading lamp, stereo, ceiling fan, clock radio, turn-down service, desk, some with hot tub/spa, some with fireplace, hair dryer, bathrobes, bath amenities, wireless Internet access, iron/ironing board and Flat Panel TV in room. Air conditioning. Fax, copier, library, parlor games, telephone and Wireless Internet on premises. Limited handicap access. Amusement parks, antiquing, art galleries, beach, bicycling, canoeing/kayaking, cross-country skiing, fishing, golf, hiking, horseback riding, live theater, museums, parks, shopping, sporting events, tennis, water sports, wineries and Birding nearby.

Location: Country. Lake.

Publicity: *Voted "Best of the Best" by Hampton's Dan's Paper in 2005.*

Certificate may be used: Sunday-Thursday December thru March, except holidays and local special events.

Quintessentials B&B and Spa

8985 Main Rd
East Marion, NY 11939-1537
(631)477-9400 (800)444-9112
Internet: www.quintessentialsinc.com
E-mail: innkeeper@quintessentialsinc.com

Feel rejuvenated at this historic 1840's Victorian bed and breakfast in a sea captain's mansion with a Widow's Walk. Situated between the villages of Greenport and Orient on North Fork's East End of Long Island, it is an easy walk to the beach. Complimentary passes and towels are provided. Relax with afternoon tea on the wraparound porch. A second-floor office/sitting area features a computer, high-speed Internet access, fax, desk and refrigerator. Choose to stay in a guest bedroom with a fireplace, private sun deck, clawfoot tub or whirlpool bath and wireless Internet access. Each room boasts upscale amenities, fine linens, fresh flowers, monogrammed robes, mineral water and chocolates on pillows. Savor a lavish brunch-style breakfast and the famous afternoon high tea. Stroll the Japanese meditation garden and schedule a massage or European skin treatment at the on-site, full-service day spa.

Innkeeper(s): Sylvia Daley. $249-299. 5 rooms with PB, 2 suites. Breakfast, afternoon tea and snacks/refreshments included in rates. Beds: KQ. Modem hook-up, cable TV, VCR, DVD, reading lamp, CD player, ceiling fan, clock radio, desk, some with hot tub/spa, some with fireplace, bathrobes, wireless Internet access, hand-made slippers, fluffy towels, deluxe down comforter and pillows, aromatherapy bed and bath products, fresh flowers, bottled water and wrapped sweets and chocolates in room. Air conditioning. Gift shop, Office/Sitting area with computer with high speed Internet, fax, desk, refrigerator, complimentary beach passes, towels, concierge and butler service on premises. Antiquing, art galleries, beach, parks, vineyard tours, Mohegan and Foxwoods casinos and outlet shopping nearby.

Location: East end of Long Island.

Certificate may be used: Anytime, Sunday to Thursday, December through March, except holidays and special events.

Ellicottville

The Jefferson Inn of Ellicottville

3 Jefferson St,
Ellicottville, NY 14731-1566
(716)699-5869 (800)577-8451 Fax:(716)699-5758
Internet: www.thejeffersoninn.com
E-mail: info@thejeffersoninn.com

Circa 1835. The Allegheny Mountains provide a perfect backdrop for this restored Victorian home built by Robert H. Shankland, an influential citizen who owned the local newspaper, along with other enterprises. The home's 100-foot wrap-

around Greek Revival porch was added in the 1920s and patterned after the summer home of President Woodrow Wilson. A full breakfast is served to B&B guests. (There are two separate efficiency units offered to visitors with children or pets.) The only

bed & breakfast within the village, it is located in the center of town where you'll enjoy following the tree-lined streets to restaurants and shops.

Innkeeper(s): Jean Kirsch. $79-209. 7 rooms with PB, 3 with FP, 1 suite. Breakfast included in rates. Types of meals: Full gourmet bkfst, early coffee/tea and picnic lunch. Beds: KQT. Modem hook-up, cable TV, reading lamp, clock radio, telephone, coffeemaker, desk and fireplace in room. Central air. TV, VCR, fax, spa, library and parlor games on premises. Handicap access. Antiquing, art galleries, bicycling, cross-country skiing, downhill skiing, fishing, golf, hiking, horseback riding, museums, parks, shopping, tennis and casino nearby.

Location: Village.

Publicity: *Arrington's Bed and Breakfast Journal, Book of Lists, Genesse Country Magazine, Buffalo Spree Magazine, Olean Chronicle and Ellicottville News.*

"Even though we just met, we are leaving with the feeling we just spent the weekend with good friends."

Certificate may be used: April-June, Sunday to Thursday and November Sunday to Thursday.

Fredonia

The White Inn

52 E Main St
Fredonia, NY 14063-1836
(716)672-2103 (888)FRE-DONI Fax:(716)672-2107
Internet: www.whiteinn.com
E-mail: res@whiteinn.com

Circa 1919. Pleasantly blending the delightful ambiance of yesteryear with the modern elegance of today, this traditional Victorian inn sits in the center of a thriving cultural and historical community. Great attention is given to detail, and the qualities of service and warmth are a

top priority. Meticulously restored, distinctive guest bedrooms provide comfort and style. The Presidential Suite boasts a fireplace and whirlpool tub. Linger over a leisurely breakfast. Known for its

American cuisine, the inn offers fine dining, cocktails and casual fare in the lounge or on the 100-foot-long veranda.

Innkeeper(s): Robert Contiguglia & Kathleen Dennison. $69-179. 23 rooms with PB, 2 with FP, 11 suites, 4 conference rooms. Breakfast included in rates. Types of meals: Full bkfst, lunch and gourmet dinner. Restaurant on premises. Beds: KQD. Cable TV, reading lamp, clock radio, telephone and desk in room. Air conditioning. VCR, fax, copier and fireplace on premises. Antiquing, golf, live theater, parks, shopping and wineries nearby.

Location: City.

Publicity: Upstate New York Magazine, Country Living, US Air Magazine and Buffalo News.

Certificate may be used: Anytime, November-April, excluding holidays and holiday weekends, subject to availability.

Fulton

Battle Island Inn

2167 State Route 48 N
Fulton, NY 13069-4132
(315)593-3699 Fax:(315)598-2635
Internet: www.battle-island-inn.com
E-mail: battleislandinn@usadatanet.net

Circa 1840. Topped with a gothic cupola, this family farmhouse overlooks the Oswego River and a golf course. There are three antique-filled parlors.
Guest accommodations are furnished in a variety of styles including Victorian and Renaissance Revival. There are three wooded acres with lawns and gardens. Guests are often found relaxing on one of the inn's

four porches and enjoying the views. The Honeymoon suite features a canopy bed, full bath and private Jacuzzi.

Innkeeper(s): Diane & Jim Sokolowski. $70-130. 5 rooms, 4 with PB, 1 suite. Breakfast included in rates. Types of meals: Country bkfst, early coffee/tea and snacks/refreshments. Beds: KQD. Cable TV, DVD, reading lamp, refrigerator, ceiling fan, clock radio, telephone, desk and bath amenities in room. Air conditioning. VCR, fax, copier, parlor games, gift shop and refrigerator on premises. Handicap access. Amusement parks, antiquing, cross-country skiing, fishing, golf, live theater, parks, shopping, water sports, wineries and fort nearby.

Location: Country.

Publicity: Lake Effect, Palladium Times, Travel, Journey, Oswego County Business Magazine and Valley News.

"We will certainly never forget our wonderful weeks at Battle Island Inn."

Certificate may be used: November-April, Sunday through Thursday.

Geneva

Geneva On The Lake

1001 Lochland Rd, Rt 14S
Geneva, NY 14456
(315)789-7190 (800)343-6382 Fax:(315)789-0322
Internet: www.genevaonthelake.com
E-mail: info@genevaonthelake.com

Circa 1911. This opulent world-class inn is a replica of the Renaissance-era Lancellotti Villa in Frascati, Italy. It is listed in the National Register. Although originally built as a residence, it became a monastery for Capuchin monks. Now it is one of the finest resorts in the U.S. Renovated under the direction of award-winning designer William Schickel, there are 10 two-

bedroom suites, some with views of the lake. Here, you may have an experience as fine as Europe can offer, without leaving the country. Some compare it to the Grand Hotel du Cap-Ferrat on the French Riviera. The inn has been awarded four diamonds from AAA for more than two decades.

Breakfast is available daily and on Sunday, brunch is served. Dinner is served each evening, and in the summer lunch is offered on the terrace.

Innkeeper(s): William J. Schickel. $138-770. 29 rooms with PB, 3 with FP, 23 suites, 3 conference rooms. Breakfast included in rates. Types of meals: Cont, gourmet dinner and room service. Restaurant on premises. Beds: KQDT. TV, DVD, CD player, refrigerator, clock radio, telephone, turn-down service and desk in room. Air conditioning. VCR, fax, copier, swimming, bicycles, parlor games, fireplace, sailing, fishing, lawn games and boats on premises. Antiquing, cross-country skiing, downhill skiing, live theater, parks, shopping, sporting events, water sports and wineries nearby.

Location: Waterfront.

Publicity: Travel & Leisure, Bon Appetit, Country Inns, The New York Times, Bride's, Catholic Register, Pittsford-Brighton Post, New York, Glamour, Gourmet, Washingtonian, Toronto Star, Globe & Mail, Rochester Democrat & Chronicle and Cooking Light magazine.

"The food was superb and the service impeccable."

Certificate may be used: Sunday through Thursday, Nov. 1 through April 30.

Hadley

Saratoga Rose Inn & Restaurant

4136 Rockwell St
Hadley, NY 12835-0238
(518)696-2861 (800)942-5025 Fax:(518)693-7476
Internet: www.saratogarose.com
E-mail: info@saratogarose.com

Circa 1885. Perched on a hilltop where the Hudson River and Sacanda River meet, this romantic Queen Anne Victorian is conveniently located between nearby Lake George and Saratoga Springs. Guest bedrooms in the Mansion feature High Victorian style decor with original stained-glass windows, hardwood floors and period antiques. The adjacent Carriage House boasts two accommodations. One reflects an Adirondack lodge with log walls and a floor-to-ceiling river-stone fireplace; the other has Southwestern art and fur-

nishings. Hot tubs are in two suites as well as on two private decks overlooking the gardens with a gazebo, waterfall, koi ponds and pristine landscaping. A complete breakfast may include Colorado Eggs Benedict, Toasted Almond French Toast and Italian Frittata. Fine dining is available in candle-lit rooms and on a lantern-lit porch.

Innkeeper(s): Richard Ferrugio, Claude Belanger. $165-205. 6 rooms with PB, 6 with FP, 4 with HT, 1 conference room. Breakfast included in rates. Types of meals: Full gourmet bkfst and gourmet dinner. Restaurant on premises. Beds: KQ. Cable TV, ceiling fan, clock radio, most with hot tub/spa, bathrobes, wireless Internet access and the Colorado Room with refrigerator and coffeemaker in room. Air conditioning. VCR, fax, copier, telephone, fireplace and WiFi access on premises. Limited handicap access. Amusement parks, antiquing, art galleries, beach, bicycling, canoeing/kayaking, cross-country skiing, downhill skiing, fishing, golf, hiking, horseback riding, live theater, museums, parks, shopping, sporting events, tennis and water sports nearby.

Location: Country, mountains.

Publicity: *Getaways for Gourmets*.

"A must for the inn traveler."

Certificate may be used: November-May, Monday-Thursday, may exclude holidays, upon availability.

Henderson Harbor

The Bluff

P.O. Box 429
Henderson Harbor, NY 13651
(315)486-3220
Internet: www.thebluffny.com
E-mail: thebluff@cavtel.net

Circa 1865. The Bluff B&B of the North Country is a three-bedroom cottage with a country motif. It sits on picturesque Lake Ontario in Henderson Harbor, New York. Perfect for a personalized romantic getaway, meals and activities can be selected in advance. Savor a candlelit five-course dinner served home style, after a day of sailing, fishing, golfing, mountain biking or taking a lighthouse tour, with box lunches prepared. Beach towels are provided and it is just 30 steps to a swim in the lake. Gather for afternoon refreshments. After a peaceful sleep wake up and start the day with a complete breakfast menu. Enjoy eating al fresco on the veranda, the grill deck, or in the dining room.

Innkeeper(s): Paul Bryant. $150-240. Call inn for details. Types of meals: Full bkfst, early coffee/tea, picnic lunch, hors d'oeuvres, wine, gourmet dinner and room service. Beds: QD. Clock radio, hair dryer, bath amenities, iron/ironing board and beach towels in room. Air conditioning. Swimming and bicycles on premises. Limited handicap access. Antiquing, beach, bicycling, canoeing/kayaking, fishing, golf, hiking, water sports, wineries and Sailing nearby.

Location: Waterfront.

Certificate may be used: Any Weekday from Aug. 1-Sept. 30.

Honeoye

Greenwoods B&B Inn

8136 Quayle Rd
Honeoye, NY 14471-9736
(716)229-2111
Internet: www.greenwoodsinn.com
E-mail: innkeeper@greenwoodsinn.com

Circa 1990. Exposed beams and rustic wood-paneled walls create a cozy environment in this colossal log home set on seven acres. The innkeepers created wonderful country guest rooms, full of color and individual style. One particularly memorable room includes a red motif with gingham check and lace curtains, a rocking chair, dried flower arrangements hanging from the beams and a bed topped with red and white linens and quilts. Breakfast is a splendid affair with treats such as fresh fruit, huge omelets or stuffed French toast. The area offers plenty of antiquing, historic homes and wineries.

Innkeeper(s): Lisa & Mike Ligon. $99-169. 5 rooms with PB, 3 with FP. Breakfast and snacks/refreshments included in rates. Types of meals: Full gourmet bkfst, veg bkfst, early coffee/tea and picnic lunch. Beds: Q. Modem hook-up, cable TV, VCR, reading lamp, CD player, refrigerator, clock radio, telephone, most with fireplace, hair dryer, bathrobes, bath amenities, wireless Internet access and iron/ironing board in room. Central air. Fax, copier, spa, library, parlor games and sideboard w/complimentary beverages on premises. Antiquing, art galleries, bicycling, canoeing/kayaking, cross-country skiing, downhill skiing, fishing, golf, hiking, horseback riding, live theater, museums,

parks, shopping, tennis, water sports and wineries nearby.

Location: Country. Rural-Hilltop.

Certificate may be used: Monday-Thursday.

Ithaca

A Lake Front Inn-Ithaca's Hotel Alternative

Eastern Shore of Cayuga Lake
Ithaca, NY 14882
(607)533-4804
Internet: www.LakeFrontInn.com
E-mail: info@LakeFrontInn.com

Circa 1930. In the heart of the Finger Lakes region on the scenic shore of Cayuga Lake, experience the timeless accommodations and casual elegance of this Mediterranean country villa B&B inn. Six acres of woodland, meadow gardens and lakefront beach accent the surroundings that inspire and renew. Five terraced hillside levels include private entrances, fireplaces, rich fabrics, cathedral ceilings and period furnishings. Each one is close to the aromatic Swedish sauna and the 30-jet Jacuzzi hot tub. Healthy yet delicious culinary delights are created each morning and served Tuscany style on one of the larger balconies or in-room when requested. Spend a day tasting the fruit of the vine at one of the local wineries on the popular Cayuga Wine Trail.

Innkeeper(s): Diane Rutherford. $165-275. 4 rooms with PB, 2 with FP. Breakfast, snacks/refreshments and wine included in rates. Types of meals: Full gourmet bkfst, veg bkfst, early coffee/tea, picnic lunch, afternoon tea, dinner and room service. Beds: Q. DVD, stereo, refrigerator, telephone, hot tub/spa, fireplace, hair dryer, bathrobes, bath amenities, wireless Internet access and iron/ironing board in room. Spa, sauna and laundry facility on premises. Antiquing, art galleries, beach, bicycling, canoeing/kayaking, cross-country skiing, fishing, golf, hiking, horseback riding, live theater, museums, parks, shopping, tennis, water sports and wineries nearby.

Location: Waterfront.

Certificate may be used: January-March, Monday-Thursday, excluding the Business of Holiday Celebrations.

Log Country Inn - B&B of Ithaca

PO Box 581
Ithaca, NY 14851
(607)589-4771 (800)274-4771 Fax:(607)589-6151
Internet: www.logtv.com/inn
E-mail: wanda@logtv.com

Circa 1969. As the name indicates, this bed & breakfast is indeed fashioned from logs and rests in a picturesque country setting surrounded by 100 wooded acres. The cozy rooms are rustic with exposed beams and country furnishings. There is also a Jacuzzi, fireplace and sauna. The decor is dotted with a European influence, as is the morning meal. Guests enjoy a full breakfast with blintzes or Russian pancakes. The innkeeper welcomes children and pets.

Innkeeper(s): Wanda Grunberg. $85-250. 9 rooms, 3 with PB, 1 suite. Breakfast included in rates. Types of meals: Full bkfst and Wanda's famous cheese blintzes and Russian pancakes and potato pancakes. Beds: QDT. Cable TV, DVD, reading lamp, telephone, desk and hair dryer in room. Air conditioning. TV, VCR, fax, copier, spa, swimming, sauna, library, fireplace, laundry facility and Double Jacuzzi on premises. Antiquing, bicycling, cross-country skiing, downhill skiing, fishing, hiking, live theater, parks, shopping, sporting events, water sports, wineries, Wine vineyards and Ponds nearby.

Location: On the edge of state forest.

Certificate may be used: Jan. 15-May 1, Sunday-Thursday.

Jay

Book and Blanket B&B

Rt 9N, PO Box 164
Jay, NY 12941-0164
(518)946-8323
Internet: www.bookandblanket.com
E-mail: bookinnjay@aol.com

Circa 1860. This Adirondack bed & breakfast served as the town's post office for many years and also as barracks for state troopers. Thankfully, however, it is now a restful bed & breakfast catering to the literary set. Guest rooms are named for authors and there are books in every nook and cranny of the house. Guests may even take a book home with them. Each of the guest rooms is comfortably furnished. The inn is a short walk from the Jay Village Green and the original site of the Historic Jay covered bridge.

Innkeeper(s): Kathy, Fred, Sam & Zoe the Basset Hound. $80-100. 3 rooms, 1 with PB. Breakfast, afternoon tea and snacks/refreshments included in rates. Types of meals: Full bkfst, veg bkfst and early coffee/tea. Beds: QDT. Reading lamp and clock radio in room. TV, VCR, library, parlor games, telephone, fireplace and whirlpool tub on premises. Antiquing, art galleries, beach, bicycling, canoeing/kayaking, cross-country skiing, downhill skiing, fishing, golf, hiking, parks, sporting events, tennis, water sports, Olympic venues i.e. bobsled, luge, ski jump and ice skating nearby.

Location: Country, mountains, waterfront. Small hamlet.

Certificate may be used: Jan. 15 to June 20, Sunday-Thursday.

Keene Valley

Trail's End Inn

62 Trail's End Way
Keene Valley, NY 12943
(518)576-9860 (800)281-9860 Fax:(518)576-9235
Internet: www.trailsendinn.com
E-mail: innkeeper@trailsendinn.com

This charming mountain inn is in the heart of the Adirondack's High Peaks. Surrounded by woods and adjacent to a small pond, the inn offers spacious guest rooms with antique furnishings and

country quilts. All-you-can-eat morning meals in the glassed-in breakfast room not only provide a lovely look at the countryside, but often a close-up view of various bird species. Fresh air and gorgeous views abound, and visitors enjoy invigorating hikes, trout fishing and fine cross-country skiing. Downhill skiers will love the challenge of nearby White Mountain, with the longest vertical drop in the East.

Call for rates. 15 rooms, 8 with PB, 4 with FP, 4 with WP, 2 two-bedroom suites, 3 cottages, 2 conference rooms. Breakfast included in rates. Types of meals: Full bkfst, early coffee/tea, picnic lunch and dinner. Beds: KQDT. Reading lamp, telephone and desk in room. Fax, copier, library, child care, parlor games, fireplace, Guest kitchenette, TV and VCR in living room and Wireless high-speed Internet on premises. Antiquing, cross-country skiing, downhill skiing, fishing, golf, parks, shopping, tennis, water sports, 1980 Olympic headquarters in Lake Placid, rock climbing, ice climbing and major hiking trails nearby.

Location: Mountains.

Publicity: *Outside, Mid-Atlantic and Lake Placid News.*

"Felt like home. What a treasure we found."

Certificate may be used: Jan. 1-June 15 and Oct. 15-Dec. 31; Sunday through Thursday, when available, excluding holiday periods.

Lewiston

Sunny's Roost Bed & Breakfast

421 Plain Street
Lewiston, NY 14092
(716)754-1161
Internet: www.sunnysroost.com
E-mail: sunny@sunnysroost.com

Circa 1900. Formerly a church rectory, Sunny's Roost now nurtures visitors to this area from it's Historic District location. From the inn, guests love to meander the streets and take in the shops, museums and special restaurants. In the summer there are midweek concerts in the park, but often guests just find their way to the back garden and listen amidst the flowers and lawns. Sunny is known for his scones – blueberry, pecan praline and cranberry-orange to name a few.

Innkeeper(s): Sunny and Bob. $90. 4 rooms, 2 with PB. Types of meals: Full bkfst. Beds: KQDT. Reading lamp, ceiling fan, clock radio, turn-down service, hair dryer, bathrobes and wireless Internet access in room. Air conditioning. TV, VCR, DVD, library, parlor games, telephone, laundry facility and gift shop on premises. Antiquing, art galleries, bicycling, fishing, golf, hiking, live theater, museums, parks, shopping, sporting events, water sports, wineries, Old Fort Niagara, Our Lady of Fatima Shrine, Shrine to Saint Jude, Niagara Falls, ArtPark and Seneca Niagara Casino nearby.

Location: Village on Niagara River.

Certificate may be used: Anytime, November-March, subject to availability.

Livingston Manor

Guest House

408 Debruce Rd
Livingston Manor, NY 12758
(845)439-4000 Fax:(845)439-3344
Internet: www.theguesthouse.com
E-mail: andrea@theguesthouse.com

Circa 1980. This 40-acre estate near New York City boasts the best private fly fishing on the Willowemoc River. The inn has five guest bedrooms and three private cottages, one is located on the edge of the woods and across a footbridge that spans the river. This cottage has two bedrooms, a living room, an outdoor Jacuzzi, covered porches and even an enclosed dog run at the back. Guests in the main house and the cottages have views of the pond, woods, river and gardens. Breakfast is a sumptuous beginning to an active, or perhaps, a leisurely day. It includes items such as freshly pressed orange or grapefruit juice, eggs, French toast, pancakes, Belgian waffles and blueberry, corn or oat muffins. Near the inn are golf courses, many tennis courts, hiking, riding and biking trails, cross-country skiing, ice skating and a dozen antique stores.

Innkeeper(s): Shaun & Andrea Plunket. $176-245. 5 cottages. Breakfast included in rates. Types of meals: Room service. Beds: KQT. Cable TV, VCR, reading lamp, refrigerator, ceiling fan, clock radio, telephone, desk and hot tub/spa in room. Air conditioning. Fax, copier, spa, swimming, tennis, pet boarding, parlor games, fireplace, laundry facility and fly fishing on premises. Handicap access. Antiquing, art galleries, bicycling, cross-country skiing, downhill skiing, golf, hiking, horseback riding, live theater, museums, parks, shopping, tennis and water sports nearby.

Location: Country, mountains.

Certificate may be used: Mid-week all months except July, August and Public Holidays. Subject to availability.

Millerton

Simmons' Way Village Inn

53 Main Street
Millerton, NY 12546
(518)789-6235 Fax:(518)789-6236
Internet: www.simmonsway.com
E-mail: info@simmonsway.com

Circa 1854. Enjoy warm American hospitality and charm in this 150-year-old Victorian in the Berkshire foothills. Simmons' Way Village Inn is located in the village of Millerton near Lakeville, Conn., and is the birthplace of famed baseball great Eddie Collins. The inn was chosen by American Express/Hertz as the "Quintessential County Inn 1991." Recently, the inn and restaurant were acclaimed by Gannett papers. Its nine guest bedrooms and one suite, some with fireplaces, are each uniquely decorated with antiques. A full breakfast is included in the tariff. Picnic lunches, dinners, banquets and catering can be arranged through the restaurant on premises. The frequently changing menu includes a variety of fare from seasonal game to pasta to vegetarian and international specialties. Outdoor activities abound, including fishing, hiking, tennis, golf, swimming, boating, cross-country skiing, biking and horseback riding. The inn is near the Lime Rock Race center, summer home of the Boston Symphony Orchestra, historic homes and the Culinary Institute of America.

Innkeeper(s): Jay & Martha Reynolds. $189-225. 9 rooms with PB, 1 suite. Breakfast included in rates. Types of meals: Full bkfst, early coffee/tea, picnic lunch, snacks/refreshments and gourmet dinner. Restaurant on premises. Beds: KQDT. Reading lamp, CD player and clock radio in room. Central air. TV, VCR, fax, copier, library, parlor games, telephone and fireplace on premises. Limited handicap access. Antiquing, art galleries, bicycling, canoeing/kayaking, cross-country skiing, downhill skiing, fishing, golf, hiking, horseback riding, live theater, museums, parks, shopping, tennis and wineries nearby.

Location: Village.

Certificate may be used: November-May anytime subject to availability. Except Thanksgiving and Christmas weeks. June-October; midweek only. Except Holiday weeks and graduation weeks.

New Lebanon

Shaker Meadows

14209 State Route 22
New Lebanon, NY 12125
(518)794-9385 Fax:(518)794-9381
Internet: www.shakermeadows.com
E-mail: shakermeadows@surfbest.net

Circa 1795. Bordering the original Shaker settlement in Lebanon Valley at Mount Lebanon, New York, Shaker Meadows Bed & Breakfast spans fifty acres of meadows and woods in the Berkshire Hills. Built in 1795 and boasting recent renovations, the B&B offers rustic charm and modern conveniences. Relax on a porch, in the library or by the lily pond. Saunter along the peaceful, mile-long walking trail. Enjoy access to a private, sandy beach on Queechy Lake with towels and chairs provided. Delightful guest bedrooms in the farmhouse and spacious suites in the creamery have pastoral and mountain views. Savor a complete breakfast in the dining room. Picnic areas are inviting spots for lunch.

Innkeeper(s): Sean and Jean Cowhig. $85-195. 9 rooms, 6 with PB, 3 total suites, including 1 two-bedroom suite, 1 cottage, 1 guest house, 1 confer-

ence room. Breakfast, Rates include a full breakfast each morning in the Creamery Dining Room (Weekly Farmhouse rates do not include breakfast as most weekly guests prefer to prepare their own; however and breakfast can be requested for any morning at a rate of $10.00 per adult and $6.00 per child) included in rates. Types of meals: Full bkfst, early coffee/tea, picnic lunch, Lunch or dinner in the dining room will be provided for your family or workshop group of up to 50 people with previous arrangement. Rehearsal dinners, BBQs and tented parties on the 100'x24' outdoor tenting site can be arranged. Beds: KQDT. Cable TV, VCR, reading lamp, refrigerator, clock radio, telephone, coffeemaker, hair dryer, bathrobes, bath amenities and iron/ironing board in room. Air conditioning. Fax, library, parlor games and laundry facility on premises. Antiquing, art galleries, beach, bicycling, canoeing/kayaking, cross-country skiing, downhill skiing, hiking, horseback riding, live theater, museums, parks, shopping, sporting events, tennis, water sports, wineries, Tanglewood, Hancock Shaker Village, Old Chatham Shaker Museum, New Lebanon Theatre Barn, Access to private town beach on Queechy Lake, Towels & beach chairs and Norman Rockwell Museum nearby.

Location: Country. Berkshires.

Certificate may be used: Any Sunday-Thursday night and any weekend last minute (one week ahead).

Niagara Falls

Butler House Bed & Breakfast

751 Park Place
Niagara Falls, NY 14301
(716)284-9846 (800)706-5004
Internet: www.butlerhousebb.com
E-mail: butlerhousebb@yahoo.com

Circa 1917. Walk to the majestic Niagara Falls from this three-story 1928 brick home built in the stately Federal style on a quiet, two-way street. Antique and traditional furnishings combine to create a comfortable ambiance. Relax in an easy chair by the fireplace or on the covered veranda. Intimate guest bedrooms with pleasing amenities overlook the tranquil Park Place or the back garden area. Browse through the library of video tapes. A homemade breakfast is served in the dining room. Ask about special packages that are available. Seneca Niagara Casino and Canada are also nearby.

Innkeeper(s): Mike & Marcia Yoder. $89-139. 4 rooms with PB, 1 conference room. Breakfast, afternoon tea and snacks/refreshments included in rates. Types of meals: Full bkfst and early coffee/tea. Beds: QD. Cable TV, VCR, reading lamp, clock radio, desk, hair dryer, bathrobes, bath amenities, wireless Internet access, iron/ironing board and some with ceiling fans in room. Central air. DVD, parlor games and fireplace on premises. Antiquing, art galleries, bicycling, golf, hiking, parks, shopping, sporting events, water sports and wineries nearby.

Location: City. Walking distance to the Falls, other major attractions and Canada.

Certificate may be used: Sunday-Thursday, November-March, Subject to Availability.

North River

Cedarwood B&B

140 Old School House Road
North River, NY 12856
(518)251-5575
Internet: www.cedarwoodbnb.com
E-mail: Cedarwood@Frontiernet.net

Amidst the scenic Adirondack Mountains in North River, New York, Cedarwood Bed & Breakfast sits off a quiet country road. This lovingly restored Victorian farmhouse was built in 1885 and retains its heritage while offering modern conveniences like Wi-Fi service. Groomed cross-country trails are right outside the door and Gore Ski Mountain is just six miles away. Enjoy afternoon refreshments in the fireside sitting room accented with antiques. A pantry features games, a VCR, movies, a refrigerator, microwave and utensils. Two guest bedrooms, Poet's Corner and The Farmer's Wife share a screened porch. Coffee is available for early risers before indulging in a satisfying breakfast. Lake George is a picturesque 30-minute drive and a visit to Lake Placid takes one hour.

Innkeeper(s): Sharalee Falzerano. Call for rates. 3 rooms with PB. Breakfast, afternoon tea and snacks/refreshments included in rates. Types of meals: Full bkfst and Special dietary needs met upon request. Beds: QD. Reading lamp, bath amenities and wireless Internet access in room. Air conditioning. VCR, DVD, fax, copier, library, parlor games, fireplace, Microwave, Refrigerator, Movies and Dishes on premises. Amusement parks, antiquing, bicycling, canoeing/kayaking, cross-country skiing, downhill skiing, fishing, golf, hiking, live theater, museums, shopping and water sports nearby.

Certificate may be used: March 1-June 1 and Aug. 1-Nov. 30.

Penn Yan

Fox Inn

158 Main St
Penn Yan, NY 14527-1201
(800)901-7997
Internet: www.foxinnbandb.com
E-mail: cliforr@aol.com

Circa 1820. Experience the pleasant elegance of a fine, historic home at this Greek Revival Inn. Furnished with Empire antiques, the accommodations include a living room with marble fireplace, sun porch, parlor with billiards table and formal rose gardens. Five guest rooms and one two-bedroom suite each have private baths. The gourmet breakfast provides a selection of nine main entrees. Located near the Windmill Farm Market, the largest farm market in New York, you can spend a casual day shopping or visiting nearby museums or wineries. Or, enjoy more active alternatives such as biking, hiking and picnicking or boating on Keuka Lake.

Innkeeper(s): Cliff & Michele Orr. $109-173. 6 rooms with PB, 1 with FP, 1 suite, 1 conference room. Breakfast included in rates. Types of meals: Full gourmet bkfst and early coffee/tea. Beds: QD. Cable TV, VCR, clock radio, telephone, turn-down service and hot tub/spa in room. Air conditioning. Library, parlor games, fireplace and billiard table on premises. Amusement parks, antiquing, art galleries, beach, bicycling, canoeing/kayaking, cross-country skiing, downhill skiing, fishing, golf, hiking, horseback riding, live theater, museums, parks, shopping, tennis, water sports and wineries nearby.

Publicity: Inn Times "Top 50 Inns in America Award."

Certificate may be used: Anytime, December-April, subject to availability.

Phelps

Yorkshire Inn

1135 State Route # 96
Phelps, NY 14532-9549
(315)548-9675
Internet: www.theyorkshireinn.com
E-mail: innkeeper@theyorkshireinn.com

Circa 1796. Built as a two-story farmhouse in 1796, it was converted to a three-story inn in 1819 to service the stagecoach run. Meticulously restored, this Colonial/Federal inn with a country décor sits on two acres with a stream in the backyard. Located halfway between Rochester and Syracuse, it is the perfect place to stay while visiting the Finger Lakes. Gather for conversation in the living room. Decanters of locally made sherry and port are on the sideboard in the dining room for a nightcap. Guest suites are all on the first floor. The Rose

Room opens out onto the deck. After a hearty breakfast take a driving tour of the lighthouses along Lake Ontario, fish or go wine tasting at nearby vineyards.

Innkeeper(s): Doug and Kathe Latch. $79-119. 2 rooms with PB, 1 two-bedroom suite. Breakfast and wine included in rates. Types of meals: Full bkfst, veg bkfst and early coffee/tea. Beds: Q. Data port, cable TV, reading lamp, coffeemaker, desk, hair dryer, bathrobes, bath amenities, wireless Internet access, iron/ironing board and iPod stereo/alarm clock in room. Air conditioning. Telephone and laundry facility on premises. Limited handicap access. Antiquing, art galleries, beach, bicycling, canoeing/kayaking, cross-country skiing, fishing, golf, hiking, parks, shopping, sporting events, wineries and snowmobiling nearby.

Location: Country.

Publicity: Food Network's All American Festivals.

Certificate may be used: November-March, Sunday-Thursday.

Prattsburgh

Feather Tick 'N Thyme B & B

7661 Tuttle Rd
Prattsburgh, NY 14873-9520
(607)522-4113
Internet: www.bbnyfingerlakes.com
E-mail: info@bbnyfingerlakes.com

Feel revived and refreshed after a stay in the peaceful valley that surrounds this 1890's Victorian Country bed and breakfast inn. Prattsburgh is situated in the New York Finger Lakes wine country between Keuka Lake and Canandaigua Lake. Soak up the scenic view from the wraparound porch. Stroll among the flower gardens by the creek. Enjoy a restful sleep in an ornate iron bed, a four-poster rice bed or a sleigh bed depending upon the room selected. Breakfast is served family style in the dining room with heirloom recipes accented by the collection of depression glass. Feather Tick 'N Thyme B&B offers special weekend packages for a romantic getaway.

Innkeeper(s): Maureen Kunak. $80-100. 4 rooms, 2 with PB. Beds: QD.

Certificate may be used: December through May, Sunday-Thursday, subject to availability.

Rochester

A B&B at Dartmouth House

215 Dartmouth Street
Rochester, NY 14607-3202
(585)271-7872 Fax:on request
Internet: www.DartmouthHouse.com
E-mail: stay@DartmouthHouse.com

Circa 1905. The lavish, four-course breakfasts served daily at this beautiful turn-of-the-century Edwardian home are unforgettable. Innkeeper and award-winning, gourmet cook Ellie Klein starts off the meal with special fresh juice, which is served in the parlor. From this point, guests are seated at the candlelit dining table to enjoy a series of delectable dishes, such as poached pears, a mouth-watering entree, a light, lemon ice and a rich dessert. And each of the courses is served on a separate pattern of Depression Glass. If the breakfast isn't enough, Ellie and husband, Bill, an electrical engineer, have stocked the individually decorated bathrooms with fluffy towels and bathrobes and guests can soak in inviting clawfoot tubs. Each of the bedchambers boasts antique collectibles and fresh flowers. The inn is located in the prestigious turn-of-the-century Park Avenue Historical and Cultural District. The entire area is an architect's dream. Museums, colleges, Eastman School of Music, Highland Park, restaurants and antique shops are

among the many nearby attractions.

Innkeeper(s): Ellie & Bill Klein. $125-150. 4 rooms with PB, 1 two-bedroom suite. Breakfast, afternoon tea and snacks/refreshments included in rates. Types of meals: Full gourmet bkfst, veg bkfst and early coffee/tea. Beds: KQT. Modem hook-up, data port, cable TV, VCR, DVD, reading lamp, refrigerator, ceiling fan, clock radio, telephone, coffeemaker, desk, some with fireplace, hair dryer, bathrobes, bath amenities, wireless Internet access, iron/ironing board, Complimentary wireless/high speed Internet access throughout, fluffy robes, movie library, lighted makeup mirrors, new pillowtop Tempurpedic mattresses, lots of pillows, comfortable recliner rocker chairs and many reading lamps and reading materials in room. Central air. Fax, copier, bicycles, library, parlor games, laundry facility, private, fenced back yard with outdoor furniture and gardens, front porch with comfortable furniture, guest microwave and refrigerator near guest rooms, picnic basket, beverages around the clock, sweet homemade bedtime treat, lots of indoor living plants/greenery, off-street parking and large comfortable covered outdoor open-air porch on premises. Amusement parks, antiquing, art galleries, beach, bicycling, canoeing/kayaking, cross-country skiing, downhill skiing, fishing, golf, hiking, live theater, museums, parks, shopping, sporting events, tennis, water sports, wineries, George Eastman International Museum of Photography, Eastman Theater, GEVA Theater, Auditorium Theater, Little Theater, Park Avenue District, Memorial Art Gallery, Rochester Museum and Science Center, boutiques, cafes, book sellers and antique shops nearby.

Location: City, waterfront. Cultural & historic district.

Publicity: *Democrat & Chronicle, DAKA, Genesee Country Magazine, Seaway Trail Magazine, Oneida News, Travelers News, Country Living, The New York Times Travel Section and innkeeper featured as cooking contest winner on television station WXXI.*

"The food was fabulous, the company fascinating, and the personal attention beyond comparison. You made me feel at home instantly."

Certificate may be used: Jan. 31-April 1, Monday through Thursday, two-night minimum stay.

The Edward Harris House B&B Inn

35 Argyle Street
Rochester, NY 14607
(585)473-9752 (800)419-1213 Fax:(585)473-9752
Internet: www.edwardharrishouse.com
E-mail: innkeeper@edwardharrishouse.com

Circa 1896. Acclaimed as one of the finest early examples of architect Claude Bragdon's work, this Georgian mansion is a restored Landmark home. Its history only enhances the rich warmth, and the immense size reflects a cozy ambiance. Relax in a leather chair in the traditional library. Antiques and collectibles combine well with florals and chintz for a touch of romance. Two guest bedrooms and the Garden Suite boast fireplaces. Four-poster rice beds and hand-painted furniture add to the individual decorating styles. A gourmet candlelight breakfast is served in the formal dining room on crystal and china or on the brick garden patio. Enjoy afternoon tea on the wicker-filled front porch. Walk one block down tree-lined streets to the urban village of Park Avenue. A plethora of historic sites, including The George Eastman House and Strong Museum, are within a one-mile range.

Innkeeper(s): Susan Alvarez. $129-169. 5 rooms with PB, 3 with FP, 2 total suites, including 1 two-bedroom suite, 1 conference room. Breakfast and snacks/refreshments included in rates. Types of meals: Full gourmet bkfst, veg bkfst, early coffee/tea, afternoon tea, hors d'oeuvres, room service and Catering can be arranged easily for lunch or dinner. Please call the Inn. Beds: KQDT. Modem hook-up, data port, cable TV, VCR, DVD, reading lamp,

stereo, refrigerator, ceiling fan, clock radio, telephone, turn-down service, desk, most with fireplace, hair dryer, bathrobes, bath amenities, wireless Internet access, iron/ironing board and Central guest area refrigerator with 24-7 tea service in room. Air conditioning. Fax, copier, library, parlor games, laundry facility, Deaf translation available on staff and Spanish spoken on premises. Limited handicap access. Amusement parks, antiquing, art galleries, beach, bicycling, canoeing/kayaking, cross-country skiing, downhill skiing, fishing, golf, hiking, horseback riding, live theater, museums, parks, shopping, sporting events, tennis, water sports and wineries nearby.

Location: City. Nestled within the Arts/Cultural District of Rochester.

Certificate may be used: Anytime subject to availability, Holiday and Special Events may be excluded. Please call the Inn.

Saratoga Springs

Country Life B&B

67 Tabor Road
Saratoga Springs, NY 12834
(518)692-7203 Fax:(518)692-9203
Internet: www.countrylifebb.com
E-mail: stay@countrylifebb.com

Circa 1829. Near the Battenkill River in the Adirondack foothills, this Flat Front farmhouse sits on 118 acres surrounded by rolling hills. Filled with antiques and traditional furnishings, romantic guest bedrooms feature comfortable terry robes, sherry and candy. A free breakfast is a delicious way to begin the day. Relax on three acres of groomed lawn with flower gardens, a two-person hammock and a porch swing. The bridge across an old mill stream leads to woodland trails. Swim in the ponds with two waterfalls and a rock slide.

Innkeeper(s): Wendy & Richard Duvall. $85-175. 4 rooms with PB. Breakfast and snacks/refreshments included in rates. Types of meals: Country bkfst, veg bkfst and early coffee/tea. Beds: KQ. TV, reading lamp, ceiling fan, clock radio, turn-down service, hair dryer, bathrobes, bath amenities, wireless Internet access, iron/ironing board, sherry, candy, extra blankets, pillows and full-length mirror in room. Air conditioning. Fax, copier, swimming, library, child care, parlor games, telephone, fireplace, coffeemaker and high speed Internet access on premises. Limited handicap access. Antiquing, art galleries, beach, bicycling, canoeing/kayaking, cross-country skiing, downhill skiing, fishing, golf, hiking, horseback riding, live theater, museums, parks, shopping, tennis, water sports, Horse racing and Water sports nearby.

Location: Country, mountains. In the Adirondack foothills, near Saratoga Springs.

Publicity: *Long Island Newsday, Inn Times, NY Times, Country Extra, Long Island Lifestyles Magazine, Washington County Magazine, Glens Falls Business News, ABC TV-Weekend Report and CBS-TV This Morning.*

Certificate may be used: November to May, Sunday-Thursday, holidays excluded, last minute only for weekends, cannot be combined with any other specials or discounts.

Westchester House B&B

102 Lincoln Ave
Saratoga Springs, NY 12866-4536
(518)587-7613 (800)581-7613 Fax:(518)583-9562
Internet: www.westchesterhousebandb.com
E-mail: innkeeper@westchesterhousebandb.com

Circa 1885. This gracious Queen Anne Victorian has been welcoming vacationers for more than 100 years. Antiques from four generations of the Melvin family grace the high-ceilinged rooms. Oriental rugs top gleaming wood floors, while antique clocks and lace curtains set a graceful tone. Guests gather on the wrap-

around porch, in the parlors or gardens for an afternoon refreshment of old-fashioned lemonade. Most attractions are within walking distance.

Innkeeper(s): Bob & Stephanie Melvin. $185-445. 7 rooms with PB, 1 conference room. Breakfast and afternoon tea included in rates. Types of meals: Full bkfst and early coffee/tea. Beds: KQT. Data port, reading lamp, CD player, ceiling fan, clock radio, telephone, desk, voice mail, hair dryer, wireless Internet access and iron/ironing board in room. Air conditioning. TV, fax, copier, library, parlor games, fireplace, baby grand piano, library and free wireless Internet access on premises. Antiquing, art galleries, cross-country skiing, fishing, golf, hiking, horseback riding, live theater, museums, parks, shopping, sporting events, tennis, water sports, opera, ballet, horse racing, race track, Saratoga Performing Arts Center, swimming, spa with mineral baths, Skidmore College and excellent restaurants nearby.

Location: City. Upstate New York small town.

Publicity: *Getaways for Gourmets, Albany Times Union, Saratogian, Capital, Country Inns, New York Daily News, WNYT, Newsday, Hudson Valley and Select Registry Distinguished Inns of America.*

"I adored your B&B and have raved about it to all. One of the most beautiful and welcoming places we've ever visited."

Certificate may be used: Monday, Tuesday, Wednesday, April-June 15, September, November, excluding holiday weekends.

Sharon Springs

Edgefield

153 Washington Street
Sharon Springs, NY 13459
(518)284-3339
Internet: www.edgefieldbb.com
E-mail: dmwood71@hotmail.com

Circa 1865. This home has seen many changes. It began as a farmhouse, a wing was added in the 1880s, and by the turn of the century, sported an elegant Greek Revival facade. Edgefield is one of a collection of nearby homes used as a family compound for summer vacations. The rooms are decorated with traditional furnishings in a formal English-country style. In the

English tradition, afternoon tea is presented with cookies and tea sandwiches. Sharon Springs includes many historic sites, and the town is listed in the National Register.

Innkeeper(s): Daniel Marshall Wood. $135-195. 5 rooms with PB. Breakfast, afternoon tea, hors d'oeuvres and wine included in rates. Types of meals: Full gourmet bkfst and early coffee/tea. Beds: QT. Reading lamp, ceiling fan, clock radio, turn-down service and desk in room. Air conditioning. Library, fireplace, antique furnishings and veranda on premises. Antiquing, cross-country skiing, golf, hiking, live theater, museums, parks, shopping, water sports, wineries and Glimmerglass Opera nearby.

Location: Village.

Publicity: *Conde Nast Traveler (Oct. 2003), Colonial Homes Magazine, Philadelphia Inquirer and Boston Globe.*

"Truly what I always imagined the perfect B&B experience to be!"

Certificate may be used: Sept. 8-30, Oct. 20-June 30, Sunday-Thursday.

Stephentown

Berkshire Mountain House

150 Berkshire Way
Stephentown, NY 12168
(518)733-6923 (800)497-0176 Fax:(518)733-6997
Internet: www.berkshirebb.com
E-mail: info@berkshirebb.com

Circa 1962. This inn is situated on a hill overlooking 50 acres with wooded trails, a spring-fed pond and meadows. Views look out to the Berkshire Mountains. Guest rooms offer a combination of antique and contemporary furnishings, and all have views. The inn's wide deck invites conversation. A private two-bedroom, two-bath cottage overlooks the pond. Tanglewood, Jacobs Pillow and Shaker Village are close by.

Innkeeper(s): Mona & Lee Berg. $85-179. 14 rooms, 9 with PB, 1 with HT, 1 two-bedroom, 1 three-bedroom and 1 four-bedroom suites, 1 cottage, 1 guest house. Breakfast, afternoon tea and wine included in rates. Types of meals: Full gourmet bkfst, veg bkfst and early coffee/tea. Beds: KQDT. Modem hook-up, cable TV, VCR, reading lamp, CD player, refrigerator, ceiling fan, clock radio, telephone, coffeemaker, some with hot tub/spa, hair dryer, bathrobes, iron/ironing board and makeup mirrors in room. Air conditioning. DVD, fax, copier, swimming, library, child care, parlor games, fireplace and laundry facility on premises. Limited handicap access. Antiquing, art galleries, bicycling, canoeing/kayaking, cross-country skiing, downhill skiing, fishing, golf, hiking, horseback riding, live theater, museums, parks, shopping, tennis, water sports, wineries, Hancock Shaker Village, Tanglewood, Shakespeare and Co. Jacobs Pillow, Norman Rockwell Museum, Clark Art Institute, MassMoca and Berkshire Theater Festival nearby.

Location: Country, mountains.

Certificate may be used: Nov. 1-April 15, Sunday-Thursday.

Syracuse

Bed and Breakfast at Giddings Garden

290 West Seneca Tnpke.
Syracuse, NY 13207-2639
(315)492-6389 (800)377-3452
Internet: www.GiddingsGarden.com
E-mail: Stay@GiddingsGarden.com

Circa 1810. Once a prestigious tavern, this two-hundred-year-old Federal-style inn has been restored to include the many original chandeliers and rich douglas fir floors while adding upscale details and amenities. Spacious guest bedrooms feature handpicked antique furnishings and collectibles. Marble baths and floor-to ceiling mirrored showers add to the elegance. Savor a creative gourmet breakfast and enjoy refreshments any time at the complimentary guest station with well-stocked refrigerator and microwave. Sip a glass of wine on the old stone patio or stroll the one-acre grounds that are accented by beautifully landscaped gardens, fish ponds and park benches. Downtown and the university are just five minutes away. Skaneateles Lake and the many wineries of the Finger Lakes are also nearby.

Innkeeper(s): Lorin & Dawn Roder. $130-275. 5 rooms with PB, 2 with FP, 1 with HT, 2 suites, 1 guest house. Breakfast, afternoon tea, snacks/refreshments and hors d'oeuvres included in rates. Types of meals: Full gourmet bkfst, veg bkfst and early coffee/tea. Beds: QD. Cable TV, VCR, DVD, reading lamp, CD player, snack bar, clock radio, telephone, coffeemaker, desk, some with hot tub/spa, some with fireplace, wireless Internet access and iron/ironing board in room. Air conditioning. Fax, copier, Complimentary refreshment center, Concierge services and Off-street parking on premises. Antiquing, cross-country skiing, downhill skiing, fishing, golf, hiking, horseback riding, live theater, museums, parks, shopping, sporting events, tennis, water sports, wineries, Coors Light Balloon Fest, Jazz Fest, Blues Fest, Rosamond Gifford Zoo and Skaneateles Music Festival nearby.

Location: City.

Publicity: *Onondaga Historical Home Tour (featured home)*.

Certificate may be used: Jan. 30 to Dec. 20, Sunday-Friday subject to availability, holidays excluded.

Troy

Olde Judge Mansion B&B

3300 6th Ave
Troy, NY 12180-1206
(518)274-5698 (866)653-5834
Internet: www.oldejudgemansion.com
E-mail: ojm@nycap.rr.com

Circa 1892. Experience the Victorian splendor of oak woodwork, 12-foot ceilings, pocket doors and embossed tin walls at this Gothic Italianate built in 1892. In the oak archway entry, view the photos displayed of historic Troy. Gather in the formal parlor to converse by the glow of kerosene lamps. An inviting Lazy Boy is perfect for video watching in the TV room. A sunny sitting room features reading materials and a chest stocked with forgotten conveniences. Kitchen privileges and laundry facilities are available. A stained-glass Newel Post Lamp on the ornate staircase leads to the comfortable guest bedrooms which are all on the second floor. Enjoy a casual, self-serve expanded continental breakfast buffet in the dining room. Shoot pool, play traditional feather, baseball or electric darts in the recreation/game room.

Innkeeper(s): Christina A. Urzan. $45-65. 5 rooms, 3 with PB. Breakfast, afternoon tea and snacks/refreshments included in rates. Types of meals: Full bkfst and early coffee/tea. Beds: KQDT. Cable TV, VCR, ceiling fan, clock radio, telephone, bathrobes, wireless Internet access, iron/ironing board and broadband hook-up in room. Air conditioning. Fax, parlor games, laundry facility and Jacuzzi in shared bathroom on premises. Antiquing, fishing, golf, museums, parks, shopping, tennis and year-round ice skating nearby.

Location: City.

Certificate may be used: Anytime, subject to availability.

Warrensburg

Country Road Lodge B&B

115 Hickory Hill Rd
Warrensburg, NY 12885-3912
(518)623-2207
Internet: www.countryroadlodge.com
E-mail: mail@countryroadlodge.com

Circa 1929. Originally built for a local businessman as a simple "camp," this bed & breakfast has expanded to offer comfortable accommodations. At the end of a short country road in a secluded setting on the Hudson River, 40 acres of woodlands and fields are surrounded by a state forest preserve. Common rooms boast panoramic views of the river and the Adirondack Mountains. After a restful night's sleep, enjoy homemade bread and muffins in the dining room while selecting from the breakfast menu. Nature walks, bird watching, hiking and cross-country skiing are just out the front door.

Innkeeper(s): Sandi & Steve Parisi. $87-97. 4 rooms with PB. Breakfast included in rates. Types of meals: Country bkfst, veg bkfst and early coffee/tea. Beds: KQT. Reading lamp and ceiling fan in room. Air conditioning. Library, parlor games, telephone, wood burning stove in common room, 24-hour hot and cold beverage counter, screened gazebo, Adirondack lawn chairs, perennial gardens and walking trails on premises. Amusement parks, antiquing, art galleries, beach, bicycling, canoeing/kayaking, cross-country skiing, downhill skiing, fishing, golf, hiking, horseback riding, live theater, museums, parks, shopping, tennis, water sports, whitewater rafting, snowshoeing, scenic drives,

lake cruises, Colonial history sites and garage sales nearby.

Location: Country, mountains, waterfront.

Publicity: *North Jersey Herald & News, New York Times, Adirondack Journal and Christian Science Monitor.*

"Homey, casual atmosphere. We really had a wonderful time. You're both wonderful hosts and the Lodge is definitely our kind of B&B! We will always feel very special about this place and will always be back."

Certificate may be used: Anytime, Sunday-Thursday, excluding July and August, holidays and special events. Not valid with other discount programs.

Glen Lodge B&B

1123 State Route 28
Warrensburg, NY 12885-5606
(518)494-4984 (800)867-2335 Fax:(518)494-7478
Internet: www.TheGlenLodge.com
E-mail: info@TheGlenLodge.com

Feel rejuvenated after a visit to this newly built bed and breakfast that reflects an authentic Adirondack lodge. Relax on one of the large porches or in the quiet sitting room. Furnished entirely with cedar log furniture, watch satellite TV in the Great Room by the stone fireplace. Comfortable guest bedrooms are carpeted and boast private baths. Start each day with classic breakfast favorites such as pancakes, French toast, eggs, bacon, sausage and muffins. Browse through the country store. Situated in the scenic North Country area of upstate New York, activities abound. Ski at nearby Gore and Whiteface Mountains or swim at Lake George. Ask about available packages that include rafting on the Hudson River.

Innkeeper(s): Aimee & Douglas Azaert. Call for rates. Call inn for details. Breakfast included in rates. Types of meals: Country bkfst, veg bkfst and early coffee/tea. Beds: QT. Reading lamp, ceiling fan, clock radio, hair dryer and bath amenities in room. Central air. VCR, sauna, telephone, fireplace and gift shop on premises. Handicap access. Amusement parks, antiquing, art galleries, beach, bicycling, canoeing/kayaking, cross-country skiing, downhill skiing, fishing, golf, hiking, horseback riding, live theater, museums, parks, shopping, tennis, water sports and whitewater rafting nearby.

Location: Mountains.

Publicity: *Arrington's "Best Bed & Breakfast for Sports Enthusiasts" (2004 & 2005)* .

Certificate may be used: October-April, last minute, subject to availability.

The Cornerstone Victorian B&B

3921 Main Street
Warrensburg, NY 12885-1149
(518)623-3308 Fax:(518)623-3979
Internet: www.cornerstonevictorian.com
E-mail: stay@cornerstonevictorian.com

Circa 1904. Replete with gleaming woodwork and polished interior columns, this large wood and stone Victorian home has a wraparound porch overlooking Hackensack Mountain. Inside are stained-glass windows, Victorian furnishings, three terra-cotta fireplaces and a beautiful cherry staircase. Awake each morning to a candlelight breakfast complete with homemade morning cakes, Louise's famous granola and other gourmet entrees. Simply ask the innkeepers, with their 25-year experience in the hospitality field, and they can help you plan your leisure activities in the Lake George/Adirondack and Saratoga Springs area.

Innkeeper(s): Doug & Louise Goettsche. $89-175. 5 rooms with PB, 1 with FP, 1 conference room. Breakfast and snacks/refreshments included in rates. Types of meals: Full gourmet bkfst and early coffee/tea. Beds: KQ. Cable TV, VCR, reading lamp, CD player, ceiling fan, clock radio, some with hot tub/spa, some with fireplace, hair dryer and bath amenities in room. Air conditioning. Fax, copier, library, parlor games, telephone, 24-hour complimentary beverage pantry and daily homemade dessert on premises. Amusement parks, antiquing, art galleries, beach, bicycling, canoeing/kayaking, cross-country skiing, downhill skiing, fishing, golf, hiking, horseback riding, live theater, museums, parks, shopping, tennis, water sports, Lake George and Steamboat Cruises, Gore Mountain Ski Area, Saratoga Springs, Great Escape Amusement Park, Lake Placid Olympic Center, Hyde Collection Art Museum and white-water rafting nearby.

Location: Mountains.

Publicity: *PBS series.*

Certificate may be used: Sunday-Thursday nights, excluding peak season, holiday periods and special rates.

Warwick

Glenwood House B&B and Cottage Suites

49 Glenwood Rd
Warwick, NY 10969
(845)258-5066
Internet: www.glenwoodhouse.com
E-mail: info@glenwoodhouse.com

Circa 1855. Built prior to the Civil War, this restored Victorian farmhouse is secluded on more than two picturesque acres in New York's Pochuck Valley. The spacious front veranda is filled with comfortable wicker furnishings, inviting guests to relax and enjoy the country setting. Guest rooms are decorated with a romantic flair. Three rooms include canopied beds. Deluxe cottage suites include a whirlpool tub for two and a fireplace. Seasonal, farm-fresh fruits start off the breakfast service, which might include an entrée such as Texas-style French toast or buttermilk pancakes accompanied by bacon or sausage. The home is close to ski areas, golf courses, wineries, historic home tours and antique stores. The Appalachian Trail, Hudson River and Greenwood Lake are other nearby attractions.

Innkeeper(s): Andrea & Kevin Colman. $110-295. 7 rooms with PB, 2 with FP, 3 suites, 2 cottages. Breakfast included in rates. Types of meals: Country bkfst. Beds: KQD. Modem hook-up, cable TV, VCR, reading lamp, CD player, refrigerator, ceiling fan, clock radio, desk, hot tub/spa, fireplace and Jacuzzi for two in room. Air conditioning. Copier, spa, library, parlor games and telephone on premises. Antiquing, art galleries, beach, downhill skiing, fishing, golf, hiking, horseback riding, live theater, parks, shopping, tennis, water sports, wineries, Mountain Creek Ski Resort and Water Park, Appalachian Trail, Holly Trail, Artist's Open Studio Tour, Walkill River Wildlife Refuge and Famous Black Dirt Region and 'Onion Capital of The World' nearby.

Location: Country, mountains.

Certificate may be used: Anytime, Sunday-Thursday, non-holiday.

Meadowlark Farm

180 Union Corners Rd
Warwick, NY 10990-2525
(845)651-4286 Fax:(845)651-5286
Internet: www.meadowlarkfarm.com
E-mail: meadow@warwick.net

Circa 1865. Gracing the outskirts of Warwick village in the southern region of the Hudson River Valley, this 1865 English-style farmhouse is a welcoming bed and breakfast. Relax in the living room with low-beamed ceilings or the intimate library. Meadowlark Farm boasts a friendly ambiance, warm hospitality and peaceful grounds. Stay in one of the guest suites then savor a full country breakfast made with fresh vegetables from the garden. Choose to gather in the dining room, on the terrace or share a romantic meal in-suite. The B&B offers customized escorted or self-guided tours of the surrounding area. New York City is just 55 miles away for an easy day trip.

Innkeeper(s): Dorothy Haupt. $85-135. 3 rooms, 2 with PB. Beds: KQ.

Location: Country.

Certificate may be used: Sunday-Thursday, Sept. 4-April 30.

Warwick Valley Bed & Breakfast

24 Maple Ave
Warwick, NY 10990-1025
(845)987-7255 (888)280-1671 Fax:(845)988-5318
Internet: www.wvbedandbreakfast.com
E-mail: loretta@warwick.net

Circa 1900. This turn-of-the-century Colonial Revival is located in Warwick's historic district among many of the town's other historic gems. The B&B includes five guest rooms decorated with antiques and country furnishings. Breakfasts are a treat with entrees such as eggs Benedict, apple pancakes or a savory potato, cheese and egg bake. Wineries, antique shops and many outdoor activities are nearby, and innkeeper Loretta Breedveld is happy to point guests in the right direction.

Innkeeper(s): Loretta Breedveld. $100-145. 5 rooms with PB. Breakfast included in rates. Types of meals: Full gourmet bkfst and early coffee/tea. Beds: KQT. TV, telephone, desk, fireplace, sitting area and high-speed Internet access in room. Central air. VCR, fax, copier and bicycles on premises. Amusement parks, antiquing, cross-country skiing, downhill skiing, fishing, golf, live theater, parks, shopping, sporting events, tennis, water sports and wineries nearby.

Location: Historic village.

Publicity: *Warwick Advertiser.*

Certificate may be used: Anytime, subject to availability, except holidays/holiday weekends.

Westfield

Brick House

7573 East Route 20
Westfield, NY 14787
(716)326-6262 Fax:(716)299-2040
Internet: www.brickhousebnb.com
E-mail: brickhousebnb@adelphia.net

Circa 1840. This brick home was built as a homestead on a large property of farmland and vineyards. The next owner constructed the impressive Greek Revival addition in 1860. The home also served guests as a tea room and later as a family-style eatery. Today, surrounded by the aroma of grapes in the vineyards, guests will enjoy the elegance and charm of the past, which has been wonderfully preserved at Brick House B&B. Full family-style buffet breakfasts are served in the home's formal dining room. Wintertime guests enjoy their morning meal in front of a warm fire. Each of the rooms offers something special. The Heritage Room includes a four-poster bed and high ceilings while the Maple View boasts Gothic crystal windows that look out to the 180+ year old maple trees. The Garden Room is another good choice and features an antique high-post canopy bed. Each evening guests are welcomed with homemade refreshments which change with the seasons.

Innkeeper(s): Randy and Lori DeVaul. $85-150. 5 rooms with PB. Breakfast and snacks/refreshments included in rates. Types of meals: Full bkfst. Beds: KDT. Reading lamp, ceiling fan, clock radio, bath amenities, wireless Internet access and iron/ironing board in room. TV, VCR, DVD, library, parlor games and telephone on premises. Antiquing, art galleries, cross-country skiing, downhill skiing, fishing, golf, horseback riding, live theater, parks, shopping, water sports, wineries, Chautauqua Institute, Fredonia Opera House, Splash Lagoon and Wine Trail nearby.

Location: Country. Vineyards.

Publicity: *Canadian Leisure Ways and Seaway Trail.*

"Your accommodations and hospitality are wonderful! Simply out-standing. The living room changes its character by the hour."

Certificate may be used: November-April, wine weekends exempt.

Westhampton Beach

1900 South Winds Bed & Breakfast

91 Potunk Lane
Westhampton Beach, NY 11978
(631)288-5505 (866)332-3344 Fax:(631)288-5506
Internet: www.southwindsbnb.com
E-mail: info@southwindsbnb.com

In the heart of the village on the South Shore of Long Island, this century-old Country Colonial home is just one mile away from the beach. Fully restored, it is furnished with family antiques and the walls are accented with original watercolor paintings. Offering year-round relaxation, chat by the inviting fireplace, sit on the wicker-filled large front porch or lounge by the swimming pool. The second-floor guest bedrooms have been renovated and feature generous amenities that will make every stay even more pleasant. Indulge in Rosemary's daily breakfasts that start the day right. Experience the area's many delights.

Innkeeper(s): Randy & Rosemary Dean. Call for rates. 4 rooms with PB. Breakfast and snacks/refreshments included in rates. Types of meals: Early coffee/tea and Breakfast. Beds: KQT. Cable TV, VCR, reading lamp, refrigerator, ceiling fan, clock radio, hair dryer, bath amenities, wireless Internet access and iron/ironing board in room. Air conditioning. Swimming and fireplace on premises. Amusement parks, antiquing, art galleries, beach, bicycling, canoeing/kayaking, fishing, golf, hiking, horseback riding, live theater, museums, parks, shopping, tennis and wineries nearby.

Location: City.

Certificate may be used: November-March, except holidays, subject to availability, no other discounts apply.

Westport

The Victorian Lady

6447 Main St
Westport, NY 12993
(877)829-7128
Internet: www.victorianladybb.com
E-mail: victorianlady@westelcom.com

Circa 1856. This Second Empire home features all the delicate elements of a true "Painted Lady," from the vivid color scheme

to the Eastlake porch that graces the exterior. Delicate it's not, however, having stood for more than a century. Its interior is decked in period style with antiques from this more gracious era.

Gourmet breakfast is served by candlelight or on the veranda with views of Lake Champlain, a mere 100 yards from the front door. Lovely gardens surround the home.

Innkeeper(s): Deswert Family. $115-185. 5 rooms, 4 with PB, 1 two-bedroom suite. Breakfast, afternoon tea and snacks/refreshments included in rates. Types of meals: Full gourmet bkfst, early coffee/tea and wine. Beds: KQT. Cable TV, reading lamp, ceiling fan, clock radio, desk and bath amenities in room. Air conditioning. VCR, DVD, fax, copier, library, parlor games, telephone and fireplace on premises. Antiquing, art galleries, beach, bicycling, canoeing/kayaking, cross-country skiing, downhill skiing, fishing, golf,

hiking, horseback riding, live theater, museums, parks, shopping, tennis and water sports nearby.

Location: Mountains, waterfront. Historic village.

Publicity: *Victorian Homes Magazine and local PBS.*

Certificate may be used: Anytime, May 29 to Oct. 15, subject to availability.

Wilmington

Willkommen Hof

5367 NYS Rt 86
Wilmington, NY 12997
(518)946-7669 (800)541-9119 Fax:(518)946-7626
Internet: www.willkommenhof.com
E-mail: willkommenhof@whiteface.net

Circa 1910. This turn-of-the-century farmhouse served as an inn during the 1920s, but little else is known about its past. The innkeepers have created a cozy atmosphere, perfect for relaxation after a day exploring the Adirondack Mountain area. A large selection of books and a roaring fire greet guests who choose to settle down in the reading room. The innkeepers also offer a large selection of movies. Relax in the sauna or outdoor spa or simply enjoy the comfort of your bedchamber.

Innkeeper(s): Heike & Bert Yost. $50-245. 8 rooms, 3 with PB, 1 suite. Breakfast and afternoon tea included in rates. Types of meals: Full bkfst, wine and dinner. Restaurant on premises. Beds: KQDT. TV, VCR, reading lamp, refrigerator, ceiling fan, clock radio, coffeemaker, hot tub/spa and fireplace in room. Fax, copier, spa, sauna, library, parlor games, telephone, fireplace and baby grand piano on premises. Amusement parks, antiquing, art galleries, beach, bicycling, canoeing/kayaking, cross-country skiing, downhill skiing, fishing, golf, hiking, horseback riding, live theater, museums, shopping and water sports nearby.

Location: Mountains.

"Vielen Dank! Alles war sehr schoen and the breakfasts were delicious."

Certificate may be used: Midweek, non-holiday, year-round.

Windham

Albergo Allegria B&B

#43 Route 296, PO Box 267
Windham, NY 12496-0267
(518)734-5560 Fax:(518)734-5570
Internet: www.albergousa.com
E-mail: mail@albergousa.com

Circa 1892. Two former boarding houses were joined to create this luxurious, Victorian bed & breakfast whose name means "the inn of happiness." Guest quarters, laced with a Victorian theme, are decorated with period wallpapers and antique furnishings. One master suite includes an enormous Jacuzzi tub. There are plenty of relaxing options at Albergo Allegria, including an inviting lounge with a large fireplace and overstuffed couches. Guests also can choose from more than 300 videos in the innkeeper's movie collection. Located just a few feet behind the inn are the Carriage House Suites, each of which includes a double whirlpool tub, gas fireplace, king-size bed and cathedral ceilings with skylights. The innkeepers came to the area originally to open a deluxe, gourmet restaurant. Their command of cuisine is evident each morning as guests feast on a variety of home-baked muffins and pastries, gourmet omelettes, waffles and other tempting treats. The inn is a registered historic site.

Innkeeper(s): Lenore Radelich & Gail Giardino. $73-299. 21 rooms with PB, 8 with FP, 9 suites. Breakfast included in rates. Types of meals: Full gourmet bkfst. Beds: KQT. Cable TV, VCR, reading lamp, refrigerator, ceiling fan, clock radio, telephone and desk in room. Air conditioning. Fax, copier, bicycles, parlor games, fireplace, afternoon tea on Saturdays, 24-hour guest pantry with soft drinks and hot beverages and sweets on premises. Handicap access. Amusement parks, antiquing, bicycling, cross-country skiing, downhill skiing, fishing, hiking, parks, shopping, tennis, water sports, bird watching and waterfalls nearby.

Location: Mountains.

Publicity: *Yankee.*

Certificate may be used: Mid-week, Sunday-Thursday, non-holiday.

North Carolina

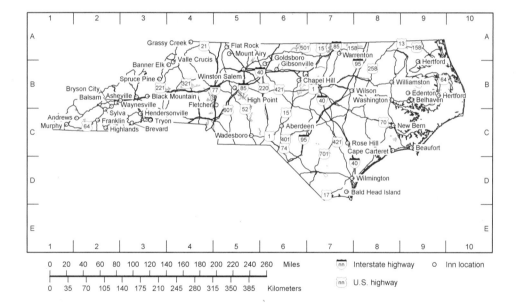

Andrews

Hawkesdene House B&B Inn and Cottages

381 Phillips Creek Road
Andrews, NC 28901
(828)321-6027 (800)447-9549 Fax:(828)321-5007
Internet: www.hawkesdene.com
E-mail: innkeeper@hawkesdene.com

Circa 1994. Want to take a llama trek to a hidden waterfall, pan for gold and sapphires or experience a sunset dinner atop a mountain gazebo? Located in a remote cove of the North Carolina Mountains, this inn offers 20 wooded acres to explore. The bright interiors satisfy the soul and lead the eye to picturesque countryside views, as well. Sample breakfast dishes include stuffed French toast, a fruit smoothie and freshly made muffins all served in the dining room. Bring your own groceries for visits in the pristine cottages. Breakfast is not included for cottage guests. A stream runs through the property. Plan to stay long enough to enjoy fly-fishing, horseback riding, whitewater rafting, canoeing and porch rocking.

Innkeeper(s): Mark & Melissa Harris. $90-145. 5 rooms with PB, 1 suite, 4 cottages. Breakfast included in rates. Types of meals: Full gourmet bkfst and early coffee/tea. Beds: KQDT. Cable TV, VCR, reading lamp, ceiling fan, clock radio, hair dryer, bath amenities and wireless Internet access in room. Central air. Fax, copier, spa, bicycles, library, parlor games, telephone, fireplace, gift shop, gift shop and llama trek suppers on premises. Handicap access. Antiquing, art galleries, bicycling, canoeing/kayaking, fishing, golf, hiking, horseback riding, live theater, museums, parks, shopping, water sports and gem mining nearby.

Location: Mountains.

Publicity: *Atlanta Journal & Constitution.*

Certificate may be used: Anytime, subject to availability.

Asheville

1847 Blake House Inn Bed & Breakfast

150 Royal Pines Drive
Asheville, NC 28704
(828)681-5227 (888)353-5227 Fax:(828)681-0420
Internet: www.blakehouse.com
E-mail: blakehouseinn@charterinternet.com

Circa 1847. Adorning a quiet residential neighborhood in the Historic Royal Pines Area of Asheville, North Carolina, the 1847 Blake House Inn Bed & Breakfast features Italianate architecture with a Gothic Revival influence. The walls are 22-inch thick granite, and the 12-foot ceilings are ornamental plaster. Surrounded by mature pines and sycamores, this B&B has been named a Treasures Tree Preserve of Buncombe County. Enjoy spacious common areas with seating and games. Gather in the Labrador Landing Pub for conversation by a warm fire. The second-floor guest bedrooms each include a sitting area and some feature a clawfoot tub and fireplace. Linger over a two-course breakfast served in one of the two fireside dining rooms or on the porch or patio.

Innkeeper(s): Leslie Kimball. $100-190. 6 rooms with PB, 3 with FP, 1 suite. Breakfast included in rates. Types of meals: Full bkfst, veg bkfst, early coffee/tea and snacks/refreshments. Beds: KQDT. Cable TV, DVD, reading lamp, refrigerator, ceiling fan, snack bar, telephone, coffeemaker, desk, voice mail, some with fireplace, hair dryer, bathrobes, bath amenities, wireless Internet access and iron/ironing board in room. Central air. Child care, parlor games and gift shop on premises. Limited handicap access. Antiquing, art

galleries, bicycling, canoeing/kayaking, cross-country skiing, fishing, golf, hiking, horseback riding, live theater, museums, parks, shopping, sporting events, tennis and wineries nearby.

Location: Mountains.

Certificate may be used: January-April, anytime subject to availability; May-September, Sunday-Thursday subject to availability.

1900 Inn on Montford

296 Montford Ave
Asheville, NC 28801-1660
(828)254-9569 (800)254-9569 Fax:(828)254-9518
Internet: www.innonmontford.com
E-mail: info@innonmontford.com

Circa 1900. This National Register home was one of a few local homes designed by Richard Sharpe Smith, the supervising architect for the nearby Biltmore Estate. The simple exterior and pleasing Arts & Crafts style is flanked by a wide veranda for relaxing and enjoying the neighborhood. English and American antiques fill the elegant inn. Well-appointed guest bedrooms feature King-size beds and fireplaces. Some have whirlpool tubs, and one boasts a clawfoot tub. A secluded, deluxe five-room whirlpool suite also offers a sitting room and private entrance with balcony. Breakfasts include a special fruit dish such as baked banana souffle, a daily entree and dessert. The inn hosts a social hour from 6-7 p.m. daily. Spend the day touring historic homes, or hike and raft in nearby wilderness areas.

Innkeeper(s): Ron and Lynn Carlson. $125-625. 8 rooms with PB, 8 with FP, 3 suites. Breakfast and snacks/refreshments included in rates. Types of meals: Full gourmet bkfst and early coffee/tea. Beds: KQ. Modem hook-up, data port, cable TV, VCR, reading lamp, CD player, refrigerator, ceiling fan, clock radio, telephone, desk, fireplace, high-speed Internet access (wired or wireless), coffee or tea delivered to your door at 8 a.m. and the 1000-square-foot Zelda's Retreat has a 7-body jet shower with steam bath in room. Air conditioning. DVD, fax, copier, library, coffee/tea 24 hours a day, complimentary soda and water on premises. Antiquing, art galleries, bicycling, canoeing/kayaking, downhill skiing, fishing, golf, hiking, horseback riding, live theater, museums, parks, shopping, sporting events, tennis, water sports, wineries, Biltmore Estate and Chimney Rock nearby.

Location: City.

Publicity: *Health Magazine, Jan/Feb 2003, Charlotte Taste Magazine, Asheville Magazine, Knoxville NBC affiliate and Asheville WLOS ABC affiliate.*

Certificate may be used: Jan. 5-Sept. 30, Sunday-Thursday, except holidays.

Albemarle Inn

86 Edgemont Rd
Asheville, NC 28801-1544
(828)255-0027 (800)621-7435 Fax:(828)236-3397
Internet: www.albemarleinn.com
E-mail: info@albemarleinn.com

Circa 1907. In the residential Grove Park area, this AAA four-diamond elegant Greek Revival Mansion graces almost an acre of landscaped grounds. The inn features an exquisite carved-oak staircase and period furnishings. Enjoy late afternoon refreshments on the veranda overlooking award-winning English gardens or fireside in the parlor. Spacious guest bedrooms and suites boast fine linens, antique clawfoot tubs and showers, televisions and phones. Some rooms include a whirlpool tub and a fireplace. A sumptuous candlelight breakfast is served at individual tables in the dining room or on the plant-filled sun porch. Gourmet dishes may include poached cinnamon pears, stuffed French toast with orange sauce and sausages. Inspired by the singing birds, composer Bela Bartok wrote his third piano concerto while

staying here. The inn is a member of Select Registry.

Innkeeper(s): Cathy & Larry Sklar. $100-350. 11 rooms with PB, 1 with FP, 1 with WP, 2 suites. Breakfast, afternoon tea, snacks/refreshments, hors d'oeuvres and wine included in rates. Types of meals: Full gourmet bkfst and early coffee/tea. Beds: KQDT. Modem hook-up, cable TV, reading lamp, ceiling fan, clock radio, telephone, coffeemaker, turn-down service, hair dryer, bathrobes, bath amenities, wireless Internet access, iron/ironing board and Royal Hideaway has 2-person marble whirlpool tub in room. Air conditioning. Fax, copier, parlor games, fireplace and Veranda on premises. Antiquing, art galleries, bicycling, canoeing/kayaking, downhill skiing, fishing, golf, hiking, horseback riding, live theater, museums, parks, shopping, sporting events, tennis, water sports, wineries, golf, Biltmore Estate and Grove Park Resort and Spa nearby.

Location: City, country, mountains. Residential area.

Publicity: National Geographic Traveler, Travel Holiday, Charleston Living & Home Design, Arrington's Inn Traveler, Marquee Magazine and WLOS TV (ABC).

"Most outstanding breakfast I've ever had. We were impressed to say the least!"

Certificate may be used: Sunday-Thursday, Jan. 2-June 30, Aug. 1-Sept. 30, Nov. 1-Dec. 12, except holidays, subject to availability, not to be combined with any other promotions.

Corner Oak Manor

53 Saint Dunstans Rd
Asheville, NC 28803-2620
(828)253-3525 (888)633-3525
Internet: www.corneroakmanor.com
E-mail: info@corneroakmanor.com

Circa 1920. Surrounded by oak, maple and pine trees, this English Tudor inn is decorated with many fine oak antiques and handmade items. Innkeeper Karen Spradley has hand-stitched something special for each room, and the house features handmade items by local artisans. Breakfast delights include entrees such as Blueberry Ricotta Pancakes, Four Cheese and Herb Quiche and Orange French Toast. When you aren't

enjoying local activities, you can sit on the shady deck, relax in the Jacuzzi, play a few songs on the piano or curl up with a good book.

Innkeeper(s): Karen & Andy Spradley. $135-195. 4 rooms with PB, 1 cottage. Breakfast and snacks/refreshments included in rates. Types of meals: Full gourmet bkfst and picnic lunch. Beds: Q. Reading lamp, refrigerator, ceiling fan and one cottage with fireplace in room. Air conditioning. Parlor games, telephone, fireplace and outdoor Jacuzzi on premises. Antiquing, fishing, live theater, parks and shopping nearby.

Location: Quiet neighborhood, 1/2 mile from Biltmore Estate.

"Great food, comfortable bed, quiet, restful atmosphere, you provided it all and we enjoyed it all!"

Certificate may be used: January-March anytime except holidays, April-September & November, Sunday-Thursday only. No holidays, October & December excluded.

Wright Inn & Carriage House

235 Pearson Dr
Asheville, NC 28801-1613
(828)251-0789 (800)552-5724 Fax:(828)251-0929
Internet: www.wrightinn.com
E-mail: info@wrightinn.com

Circa 1899. A true landmark that is timeless in the old-fashioned graciousness and modern conveniences offered, this gabled Queen Anne boasts an award-winning restoration and lavish gardens. Gather in the Coleman Parlor and the Drawing Room with period decor, fireplaces and inviting activities. Romantic suites and guest bedrooms feature distinctive designs; several feature fireplaces and high-speed wireless

Internet. The three-bedroom Carriage House is perfect for larger groups or families. Enjoy a gourmet breakfast and a weekend social hour. Relax on the large wraparound porch and gazebo.

Innkeeper(s): Bob & Barbara Gilmore. $105-325. 11 rooms with PB, 4 with FP, 1 with WP, 1 cottage. Breakfast included in rates. Types of meals: Full gourmet bkfst, early coffee/tea and snacks/refreshments. Beds: KQDT. Cable TV, reading lamp, clock radio, telephone, desk, some with fireplace, hair dryer, bathrobes, bath amenities, wireless Internet access and iron/ironing board in room. Central air. Fax, library, parlor games, weekend social hour included in rates, high-speed wireless Internet and cable TV on premises. Hiking, shopping and water sports nearby.

Location: City. Historic Montford District, Biltmore Estate.

Certificate may be used: January-May, certain rooms eligible-subject to availability, Sunday-Thursday.

Bald Head Island

Theodosia's B&B

2 Keelson Row
Bald Head Island, NC 28461
(910)457-6563 (800)656-1812 Fax:(910)457-6055
Internet: www.theodosias.com
E-mail: stay@theodosias.com

Circa 1817. For a romantic getaway or a quiet retreat, this historic barrier island at the mouth of the Cape Fear River offers a tranquil beauty. Exquisite accommodations are found at this modern Victorian bed & breakfast inn that boasts a southern elegant decor. Stay in the main inn or Carriage House. Delightful guest bedrooms feature splendid views of the harbor, river, marshes and lighthouse from balconies. In the dining room, breakfast entrees may include favorites such as Eggs Benedict, Caramel Soaked French Toast, Egg Souffle and Belgian Waffles. Relax on porch rockers or swings, explore the sites and trips to the beach by bike or electric golf cart. Enjoy use of the golf course, tennis courts and other club facilities. Chat with new friends over afternoon refreshments. Weddings and special events are popular at this idyllic setting.

Innkeeper(s): Pam, Gary and Carson Lawrence. $155-325. 10 rooms with PB. Breakfast and snacks/refreshments included in rates. Types of meals: Full bkfst. Beds: KQ. Cable TV, reading lamp, clock radio, telephone, desk and wireless Internet access in room. Air conditioning. Fax, bicycles, fireplace and Use of golf cart on premises. Handicap access. Fishing, golf, parks, tennis and water sports nearby.

Location: Ocean community, waterfront.

Publicity: The Thomasville Times, Southern Living, Raleigh News and

Observer, Charlotte Observer, Money Magazine and Coastal Living.
Certificate may be used: Sunday-Thursday, Nov. 1-March 31, excludes holidays.

Balsam

Balsam Mountain Inn, Inc.

Seven Springs Drive
Balsam, NC 28707
(828)456-9498 (800)224-9498 Fax:(503)212-9855
Internet: www.balsaminn.com
E-mail: relax@balsammountaininn.com

Circa 1905. This inn, just a quarter mile from the famed Blue Ridge Parkway, is surrounded by the majestic Smoky Mountains. The inn was built in the Neoclassical style and overlooks the scenic hamlet of Balsam. The inn is listed in the National Register of Historic Places and is designated a Jackson County Historic Site. It features a mansard roof and wraparound porches with mountain views. A complimentary full breakfast is served daily, and dinner also is available daily.
Innkeeper(s): Sharon White and Kim Shailer. $125-175. 50 rooms with PB, 8 suites. Breakfast included in rates. Types of meals: Full bkfst, coffee/tea, picnic lunch and dinner. Restaurant on premises. Beds: KD. Reading lamp and desk in room. Fax, copier, parlor games, fireplace, hiking trails and wildflower walks on premises. Handicap access. Antiquing, downhill skiing, fishing, parks, shopping, whitewater rafting, hiking and Blue Ridge Pkwy nearby.

Location: Mountains.

"What wonderful memories we have of this beautiful inn."

Certificate may be used: Sunday through Thursday, November through June & September, excluding holiday periods.

Banner Elk

Beech Alpen Inn

700 Beech Mountain Pkwy
Banner Elk, NC 28604-8015
(828)387-2252 Fax:(828)387-2229
Internet: www.beechalpen.com
E-mail: oceanreal@msn.com

Circa 1968. This rustic inn is a Bavarian delight affording scenic vistas of the Blue Ridge Mountains. The innkeepers offer accommodations at Top of the Beech, a Swiss-style ski chalet with views of nearby slopes. The interiors of both properties are inviting. At the Beech Alpen, several guest rooms have stone fireplaces or French doors that open onto a balcony. Top of the Beech's great room is a wonderful place to relax, with a huge stone fireplace and comfortable furnishings. The Beech Alpen Restaurant serves a variety of dinner fare.
Innkeeper(s): Steve Raymond. $49-149. 25 rooms with PB, 4 with FP. Breakfast included in rates. Types of meals: Cont, early coffee/tea and gourmet dinner. Restaurant on premises. Beds: KQD. Cable TV in room. Fax, copier, parlor games, telephone and fireplace on premises. Antiquing, cross-country skiing, downhill skiing, fishing, live theater, parks, shopping and sporting events nearby.

Location: Mountains.

Certificate may be used: Sunday-Thursday, Jan. 3-Dec. 14.

Black Mountain

Red Rocker Inn

136 N Dougherty St
Black Mountain, NC 28711-3326
(828)669-5991 (888)669-5991
Internet: www.redrockerinn.com
E-mail: info@redrockerinn.com

Circa 1896. Voted as the best B&B in Asheville, Black Mountain and all of Western North Carolina for the past six years, this three-story inn sits on one acre of pristinely landscaped grounds. Located just 14 miles east of Asheville and the famous Biltmore Estate, discover why the Atlanta Journal named this inn one of its "Top 12 Favorites in the Southeast." Elegant, air-conditioned guest bedrooms exude an inviting ambiance. Many feature fireplaces and whirlpool tubs. Each morning sit down to a heaping Southern breakfast that is sure to satisfy. Stroll through gorgeous gardens with a view of the mountains or relax in front of a roaring fire. Red rockers line the expansive wraparound porch, a perfect spot to enjoy tea and hand-dipped macaroons. Special dining packages are available year-round which include homemade specialties and award-winning desserts.
Innkeeper(s): The Lindberg family. $95-190. 17 rooms with PB, 3 with FP. Breakfast, afternoon tea and snacks/refreshments included in rates. Types of meals: Full bkfst, early coffee/tea and dinner. Restaurant on premises. Beds: KQD. Reading lamp, ceiling fan, desk and five with whirlpool tubs in room. Air conditioning. Fax, library, parlor games, telephone and fireplace on premises. Antiquing, downhill skiing, fishing, golf, live theater, parks, shopping, tennis and water sports nearby.

Location: Mountains.

Certificate may be used: Feb. 1 to March 15, Sunday-Thursday; Nov. 15 to Dec. 20, Sunday-Thursday.

Brevard

The Inn at Brevard

315 E Main St
Brevard, NC 28712-3837
(828)884-2105 Fax:(828)885-7996
Internet: www.theinnatbrevard.com
E-mail: brevard@theinnatbrevard.com

Circa 1885. General Stonewall Jackson's troops held reunion dinners at this inn in 1904 and again in 1911. A National and State Historical Landmark, the home's original owner was considered a fine Victorian lady, and her home still reflects the grace of the era. The dining room is open to the public and to guests for Thursday, Friday and Saturday night dinners and Sunday brunch. Full home-cooked country breakfasts are served.
Innkeeper(s): Howard & Faye Yager. $99-225. 15 rooms with PB, 4 with FP, 1 with WP, 2 suites, 3 conference rooms. Breakfast included in rates. Types of meals: Full gourmet bkfst, veg bkfst, Sun. brunch, early coffee/tea, gourmet lunch, picnic lunch, afternoon tea, snacks/refreshments, hors d'oeuvres, wine, gourmet dinner, room service and Special occasion desserts and cakes. Restaurant on premises. Beds: QDT. Cable TV, reading lamp, ceiling fan, snack bar, clock radio, coffeemaker, desk, hair dryer, bath amenities, wireless Internet access, iron/ironing board and All rooms are decorated with antiques in room. Air conditioning. VCR, fax, copier, library, child care, telephone, fireplace, laundry facility, gift shop, Art and Antique gallery on premises. Limited handicap access. Antiquing, art galleries, bicycling, canoeing/kayaking, downhill skiing, fishing, golf, hiking, horseback riding, live theater, museums, parks, shopping, sporting events, tennis and wineries nearby.

Location: Mountains.

Certificate may be used: Jan.1-May 15, Nov. 1-Dec. 30; $165/night Annex, $175/night Main House, does not include breakfast or tax.

Bryson City

Folkestone Inn

101 Folkestone Rd
Bryson City, NC 28713-7891
(828)488-2730 (888)812-3385 Fax:(828)488-0722
Internet: www.folkestone.com
E-mail: innkeeper@folkestone.com

Circa 1926. This farmhouse is constructed of local stone and rock. Pressed-tin ceilings, stained-glass windows and clawfoot tubs remain. The dining room, where breakfast and Saturday

night dinner is served, features floor-to-ceiling windows on all sides with views of the mountains. There is a stream with a rock bridge on the property as well as a garden, and you can walk 10 minutes to waterfall views in the Great Smoky Mountains National Park. All day cookies, snacks, coffee, tea, soft drinks and an optional multi-course dinner available Saturday nights.

Innkeeper(s): Kay Creighton and Peggy Myles. $104-158. 10 rooms with PB. Breakfast included in rates. Types of meals: Full bkfst and snacks/refreshments. Beds: KQ. Reading lamp and central heat in room. Central air. Fax, copier and telephone on premises. Antiquing, fishing, horseback riding, shopping, tubing, rafting, hiking, scenic train and mountain biking nearby.

Location: Mountains.

Publicity: *Asheville Citizen-Times, Atlanta Journal, Lakeland and Palm Beach Post.*

Certificate may be used: Anytime subject to availability excluding July and October.

Cape Carteret

Harborlight Guest House

332 Live Oak Drive
Cape Carteret, NC 28584
(252)393-6868 (800)624-VIEW
Internet: www.harborlightnc.com
E-mail: info@harborlightnc.com

Circa 1963. This three-story home rests on a peninsula just yards from Bogue Sound and the Intracoastal Waterway. In-room amenities might include a massive whirlpool tub, a clawfoot tub or fireplace, and each of the guest suites feature a beautiful water view. The décor is done in a modern, coastal style. Multi-course, gourmet breakfasts begin with fresh juices, coffee, tea and an appetizer, perhaps a stuffed mushroom. From there, guests enjoy a fresh fruit dish followed by a creative entrée. All of which is served in suite or deckside. Museums, an aquarium, historic sites, Hammocks Beach State Park and harbor tours are among the attractions. Fort Macon State Park affords guests an opportunity to view a restored Civil War fort. Popular beaches and horseback riding are just minutes away.

Innkeeper(s): Debbie Mugno & Bob Pickens. $110-300. 7 rooms, 5 with FP, 6 with HT, 7 suites, 1 conference room. Breakfast included in rates. Types of meals: Full gourmet bkfst, early coffee/tea and picnic lunch. Beds: KQ. Modem hook-up, cable TV, VCR, DVD, reading lamp, CD player, refrigerator, ceiling fan, snack bar, clock radio, coffeemaker, turn-down service, most with hot tub/spa, most with fireplace, hair dryer, bathrobes, bath amenities, wireless Internet access, iron/ironing board, complimentary use of robes and slippers for stays of two nights or more, two-person jetted whirlpool tubs and 6

suites with Jacuzzi tub in room. Air conditioning. Fax, copier, library, parlor games, telephone, video library and wireless Internet access on premises. Limited handicap access. Antiquing, art galleries, beach, canoeing/kayaking, fishing, golf, horseback riding, parks, shopping, tennis, water sports and island excursions nearby.

Location: Ocean community, waterfront.

Publicity: *Southern Living, The State Magazine, Carolina Style Magazine, Coastal Living and Cary Magazine.*

Certificate may be used: Nov. 1-Feb. 28, Sunday-Thursday, excluding holidays. Only certain suites available for this special.

Edenton

Trestle House Inn

632 Soundside Rd
Edenton, NC 27932-9668
(252)482-2282 (800)645-8466 Fax:(252)482-7003
Internet: www.trestlehouseinn.com
E-mail: peter@trestlehouseinn.com

Circa 1968. Trestle House is located on a six acres with a lake and a pond filled with large-mouth bass. The interior is unique as it features beams that were actually trestles that once belonged to the Southern Railway Company. Rooms are named for different birds, such as the Osprey and Mallard rooms. Two rooms have a sleigh bed. The morning meal includes home-made breads, breakfast casseroles and fresh orange juice.

Innkeeper(s): Peter L. Bogus. $104-134. 5 rooms with PB, 1 suite. Breakfast included in rates. Types of meals: Full gourmet bkfst. Beds: KQDT. Modem hook-up, data port, cable TV, reading lamp, ceiling fan, clock radio, telephone and desk in room. Central air. VCR, swimming, library, parlor games and fireplace on premises. Amusement parks, antiquing, art galleries, beach, bicycling, canoeing/kayaking, fishing, golf, hiking, live theater, museums, parks, shopping, tennis and water sports nearby.

Location: Waterfront.

Publicity: *North Carolina Traveler and WITN.*

"We have stayed at many B&Bs, but yours is special because it brings us close to nature. Your breakfasts are wonderful and relaxing while eating and watching wildlife in their natural habitat!"

Certificate may be used: Nov. 1-March 31, excluding holidays and holiday weekends.

Flat Rock

Highland Lake Inn

180 Highland Lake Drive
Flat Rock, NC 28731
(828)693-6812 (800)635-5101 Fax:(828)696-8951
Internet: www.hlinn.com/?source=bnbinns
E-mail: lkeeter@hlinn.com

Circa 1900. A great place for families, this farm setting features acres of activities. Besides a visit to the goat barn or watching for the resident peacock, canoe the lake, hike, swim, bike, play volleyball or horseshoes. The inn offers romantic guest bedrooms, some with whirlpool tubs or French doors leading to a porch with rockers. A rustic lodge with cozy rooms and private baths boasts a river rock fireplace in the lobby, billiards and table tennis in the recreation room. There are ten cabin rooms. Cottages with two to four bedrooms have kitchen facilities and some include a washer, dryer and large outside deck. The restaurant boasts an award-winning wine list and meals are made with fresh organic ingredients from the gardens. Explore local Carl Sandburg's home or Flat Rock Playhouse and historic sites in nearby Hendersonville. The Biltmore Estate is 28 miles away.

Innkeeper(s): Jack & Linda Grup. $89-399. 64 rooms, 36 with PB, 17 with FP, 1 suite, 16 cottages, 10 cabins, 3 conference rooms. Breakfast included in rates. Types of meals: Country bkfst, gourmet lunch, picnic lunch and gourmet dinner. Restaurant on premises. Beds: KQT. Modem hook-up, data port, cable TV, reading lamp, refrigerator, ceiling fan, clock radio, telephone, coffeemaker, desk, voice mail, some with fireplace and daily newspaper in room. Air conditioning. VCR, fax, copier, swimming, bicycles, tennis, parlor games, gift shop, variety of conference facilities, yoga studio and in-room massage (by appointment) on premises. Limited handicap access. Antiquing, art galleries, bicycling, canoeing/kayaking, fishing, golf, hiking, horseback riding, live theater, parks, shopping and wineries nearby.

Location: Country, mountains. Western North Carolina.

Publicity: Southern Living, The Southern Gardener, Wine Spectator Magazine (recipient of "Award of Excellence" for having one of the best restaurant wine lists in the world) and PBS.

Certificate may be used: December-March.

Fletcher

Chateau on the Mountain

1048 Sandy Flat Mountain Road
Fletcher, NC 28732
(828)651-9810 (888)591-6281 Fax:(828)651-9811
Internet: www.ChateauOnTheMountain.com
E-mail: innkeepers@ChateauOnTheMountain.com

Circa 1990. Lush landscaping and incredible views of Mt. Pisgah are enjoyed at this ten-acre bed and breakfast built in the style of a French chateau. Poised atop Hoopers Creek Valley in Fletcher, North Carolina, Chateau on the Mountain is surrounded by meadows and mountains. Hiking trails are accented with native plants and wooded areas. Work out in the exercise room, swim in the outdoor pool and schedule spa services. Gather for refreshments or relax by the fire. Stay in a guest bedroom or suite with a sitting area, two-person steam shower, whirlpool, fireplace and adjoining patio or porch with a private hot tub. Accommodations in the Carriage House welcome pets and children. Savor a hearty country breakfast in the formal dining room.
Innkeeper(s): Lee & Jeanne Yudin. $175-325. 6 rooms with PB, 4 with FP, 1 with HT, 5 with WP, 1 conference room. Breakfast, hors d'oeuvres and wine included in rates. Types of meals: Full gourmet bkfst, picnic lunch, snacks/refreshments and Dinner prepared by a personal chef is available with 24-hour notice. Beds: KQ. Cable TV, VCR, DVD, reading lamp, refrigerator, ceiling fan, clock radio, telephone, coffeemaker, turn-down service, desk, some with hot tub/spa, some with fireplace, hair dryer, bathrobes, bath amenities, wireless Internet access and iron/ironing board in room. Central air. Fax, copier, spa, swimming, library, parlor games, laundry facility, gift shop, Pool and Hiking trails on premises. Limited handicap access. Antiquing, art galleries, bicycling, fishing, golf, hiking, horseback riding, live theater, museums, parks, shopping, wineries, Biltmore Estate, Chimney Rock Park, Kayaking, Pisgah Forest, Dupont Forest and Waterfalls nearby.

Location: Country, mountains.

Certificate may be used: Jan. 1-June 30, Aug. 1-31, Nov. 1-Dec 31, subject to availability.

Franklin

Buttonwood Inn

50 Admiral Drive
Franklin, NC 28734-1981
(828)369-8985 (888)368-8985
Internet: www.buttonwoodbb.com
E-mail: info@buttonwoodbb.com

Circa 1920. Trees surround this two-story batten board house located adjacent to the Franklin Golf Course. Local crafts and handmade family quilts accent the country decor. Wonderful breakfasts are served here—often eggs Benedict, baked peaches

and sausage and freshly baked scones with homemade lemon butter. On a sunny morning, enjoy breakfast on the deck and savor the Smoky Mountain vistas. Afterward, you'll be ready for white-water rafting, hiking and fishing.
Innkeeper(s): Liz Oehser. $65-105. 4 rooms with PB. Breakfast and afternoon tea included in rates. Types of meals: Full bkfst and early coffee/tea. Beds: KD. Ceiling fan and clock radio in room. Telephone on premises. Antiquing, bicycling, canoeing/kayaking, fishing, golf, hiking, parks, shopping, sporting events and tennis nearby.

Location: Mountains. County city line.

Certificate may be used: Sunday-Thursday, except October, no weekends or holidays.

Gibsonville

Burke Manor Inn

303 Burke Street
Gibsonville, NC 27249
(336)449-6266 (888)BUR-KE11 Fax:(336)449-9440
Internet: www.burkemanor.com
E-mail: info@burkemanor.com

Circa 1906. Blending the warmth of exceptional hospitality with prestigious service, this historic Victorian bed & breakfast inn features luxurious surroundings, quality reproductions and a comfortable atmosphere. Lavish suites include upscale amenities for the leisure and business traveler alike. Breakfast reflects the quality of food that has given the inn's restaurant a reputation for fine dining. Play tennis, then swim in the heated pool or soak tired muscles in the hot tub. The 3.5 acres provide a peaceful setting for beautiful garden weddings. It is an easy walk from the inn to downtown sites and shops.
Innkeeper(s): Vernon & Lynn Brady. $99-199. 9 rooms with PB, 1 suite, 2 conference rooms. Breakfast and snacks/refreshments included in rates. Types of meals: Full gourmet bkfst, veg bkfst, early coffee/tea and room service. Beds: KQ. Cable TV, reading lamp, stereo, ceiling fan, snack bar, clock radio, telephone, desk, hot tub/spa, voice mail, bathrobes, bath amenities, wireless Internet access, iron/ironing board, high thread count pressed linens, plush robes, candles, heated pool and breakfast in room. Central air. Fax, copier, swimming, tennis, parlor games, 4,800-square-foot wedding reception pavilion and gift shop on premises. Limited handicap access. Amusement parks, antiquing, art galleries, bicycling, canoeing/kayaking, fishing, golf, hiking, live theater, museums, parks, shopping, sporting events, tennis, water sports and wineries nearby.

Location: City.

Publicity: Times News ("Best Bed and Breakfast"), Alamance Chamber of Commerce ("Retailer of the Year"), Greensboro News and Record, Burlington Times News, Crossroads Journal, WFMY TV 2, WBAG and WBAG 1150AM.

Certificate may be used: Anytime, Sunday-Thursday. Some blackout dates and restrictions apply.

Goldsboro

Plum Tree Gardens Bed and Breakfast

109 South George Street
Goldsboro, NC 27530
(919)736-3356
Internet: www.PlumTreeGardens.com
E-mail: plumtreegardens@earthlink.net

Circa 1888. Intimate and gracious, Plum Tree Gardens Bed and Breakfast is located just two blocks from downtown Goldsboro, North Carolina. This historic and meticulously restored Daniels-Stenhouse Victorian home is listed in the National Register and boasts its original copper roof, painted wood siding and antique glass windows. Gather for conversation on the wraparound porch or swing on the screened porch. The grounds are accented with colorful and fragrant flowers, an herb garden and wooded areas. In the afternoon local wine and cheese are served in the formal living room. Inviting guest bedrooms feature fireplaces and eclectic furnishings from vintage to modern. Stay in the Blackberry Room with a private balcony. Early risers can enjoy coffee and muffins before savoring a three-course gourmet breakfast in the dining room.

Innkeeper(s): Shelley Lesak Crabtree. $110-125. 4 rooms, 2 with PB, 4 with FP, 2 conference rooms. Breakfast, hors d'oeuvres, wine and Social hour featuring local wines and Wisconsin cheeses or hors d'oeuvres and three course gourmet breakfast included in price included in rates. Types of meals: Full gourmet bkfst, veg bkfst, early coffee/tea, Social hour featuring local wines and Wisconsin cheeses, Vegetarian breakfast to be ordered ahead with reservation, Special diet requests at time of reservation, Early coffee/tea/juice served with variety basket of muffins and. Beds: D. TV, reading lamp, clock radio, coffeemaker, desk, fireplace, bath amenities, iron/ironing board, Access to phone, Internet, Modem and Voice mail in room. Central air. Library, parlor games, telephone, laundry facility and Gardens on premises. Antiquing, art galleries, beach, bicycling, canoeing/kayaking, fishing, golf, hiking, horseback riding, live theater, museums, parks, shopping, sporting events, tennis, water sports, wineries, Located on Civil War trail and Mountain to Sea bike trail, 90 min. to Beaches, Major colleges, Professional sports and RDU Airport nearby.

Location: City.

Certificate may be used: Anytime, subject to availability.

Grassy Creek

River House

1896 Old Field Creek Rd
Grassy Creek, NC 28631
(336)982-2109 Fax:(336)982-2106
Internet: www.riverhousenc.com
E-mail: riverhouse@skybest.com

Circa 1870. On 180 acres, with a mile of riverfront on the North Fork of the New River in the Blue Ridge Mountains of Ashe County, this year-round country inn and restaurant is ideal for romantic getaways, weddings, honeymoons, reunions, vacations, retreats and seminars. Relax by a warm log fire or on front porch rockers. Choose from guest bedrooms with hot tubs, gas-log fireplaces and porches or stay in one of the secluded cabins by the millpond, river's edge or a log cabin among the trees. A gourmet breakfast is included and served in the renowned restaurant where dinner is offered nightly with libations and an international wine list. Play tennis on one of the full-sized courts, hike or bike. Fishing, tubing and canoeing are also popular available activities.

Innkeeper(s): Gayle Winston. $115-175. 9 rooms with PB, 6 with FP, 4 suites, 1 cottage, 2 cabins, 3 conference rooms. Breakfast included in rates. Types of meals: Full gourmet bkfst, early coffee/tea, gourmet lunch, picnic lunch, afternoon tea, gourmet dinner and room service. Restaurant on premises. Beds: KQT. Reading lamp, refrigerator, ceiling fan, clock radio, desk, hot tub/spa and whirlpool tubs in room. VCR, fax, copier, spa, swimming, tennis, library, parlor games, telephone and fireplace on premises. Antiquing, canoeing/kayaking, cross-country skiing, downhill skiing, fishing, golf, hiking, live theater, parks, shopping, sporting events, tennis and water sports nearby.

Location: Mountains, waterfront.

Certificate may be used: Anytime, Sunday-Thursday, excluding June, July, August and October.

Hertford

1812 on The Perquimans B&B Inn

385 Old Neck Road
Hertford, NC 27944
(252)426-1812

Circa 1812. William and Sarah Fletcher were the first residents of this Federal-style plantation home, and the house is still in the family today. The Fletchers were Quakers and the first North Carolina residents to offer to pay the way for workers who wished to return to Africa. The farm rests along the banks of the Perquimans River, and the grounds retain many original outbuildings, including a brick dairy, smokehouse and a 19th-century frame barn. In the National Register of Historic Places, the inn is appropriately appointed with antiques highlighting the restored mantels and woodwork. The inn is a lovely, pastoral retreat with bikes and canoeing available.

Innkeeper(s): Peter & Nancy Rascoe. $80-85. 4 rooms. Full Plantation Breakfast included in rates. Types of meals: Full bkfst. Beds: KQD. Fireplace in room. Central air. Bicycles, canoeing/kayaking and riverfront on premises.

Location: Riverfront. 12 miles from Historic Edenton.

Certificate may be used: All year, except for weekends in April, May, September, October and major holidays.

Beechtree Inn

948 Pender Rd
Hertford, NC 27944
(252)426-7815
Internet: www.beechtreeinn.net
E-mail: hobbs@beechtreeinn.net

Circa 1760. Experience the 1700s era while enjoying modern amenities during a stay in one of three private small houses at this inn's assembled collection of pre-Civil War buildings on 37 scenic acres of woods, gardens, lawn and farmland. Each restored house is furnished with reproduction furniture made on site, has central air conditioning and heat, a working fireplace, cable TV, VCR, refrigerator, microwave and coffeemaker. Pets are allowed in Flat Branch and Bear Swamp House for an extra fee. Wake up hungry to fully appreciate the hearty country breakfast served each morning. Complimentary refreshments are also provided. A canoe is available to use on Bethel Creek. Beechtree inn restaurant is on site.

Innkeeper(s): Ben and Jackie Hobbs. $90. 4 rooms, 3 with FP, 4 suites, 3 guest houses. Breakfast, afternoon tea and snacks/refreshments included in rates. Types of meals: Full gourmet bkfst. Restaurant on premises. Beds: QT. Modem hook-up, data port, cable TV, VCR, reading lamp, refrigerator, snack bar, clock radio, telephone, coffeemaker, desk and fireplace in room. Central air. DVD, fax, copier, bicycles, pet boarding, parlor games and restaurant on site on premises. Limited handicap access. Antiquing, art galleries, beach, bicycling, canoeing/kayaking, fishing, golf, hiking, museums, parks, shopping, tennis and water sports nearby.

Location: Country. Wooded and farm lands on all sides.

Publicity: *Virginia Pilot, Fine Woodworking, Woodworker's Journal, Southern Living (April 2005) and Coastwatch (July 2005).*

Certificate may be used: This will be honored the weeks we are not having furniture classes. See web site for schedule.

High Point

J.H. Adams Inn

1108 North Main St
High Point, NC 27262
(336)882-3267 (888)256-1289 Fax:(336)882-1920
Internet: www.jhadamsinn.com
E-mail: info@jhadamsinn.com

Circa 1918. A romantic ambiance surrounds this Italian Renaissance inn that was built in 1918 as a private home. It is listed in the National Register and has been completely restored into a 30-room inn with a grand staircase, richly carved moldings, wood floors and a marble fireplace. Gracious hospitality, outstanding comfort, attention to detail and exquisite interiors are central to the inn's heritage. Elegant guest bedrooms and a spacious suite feature Frette linens on premium Sealy mattresses and plush robes. The lavish décor and furnishings reflect the history of the area. Cereals, fruit, muffins, bagels and assorted breads, yogurt and beverages are offered for a continental breakfast. Southern Roots, the inn's restaurant, serves lunch and dinner.

Innkeeper(s): Sue Stanley. $139-239. 31 rooms with PB, 2 with FP, 3 with WP, 2 total suites, including 1 two-bedroom suite, 1 conference room. Breakfast and wine included in rates. Types of meals: Cont and room service. Restaurant on premises. Beds: KQ. Modem hook-up, data port, cable TV, reading lamp, refrigerator, clock radio, telephone, coffeemaker, desk, voice mail, some with fireplace, hair dryer, bathrobes, bath amenities, iron/ironing board, In-room safes and refrigerators stocked with complimentary water in room. Central air. Fax, copier, two handicap-accessible rooms in the South Wing, handicap access to Restaurant and Common Areas on premises. Limited handicap access. Golf, live theater, museums, parks, shopping, wineries and furniture shopping nearby.

Location: City.

Publicity: *Southern Living (July 2004), Our State Magazine "20 Best Inns" and Restore America Fall 2003.*

Certificate may be used: Anytime, subject to availability.

Highlands

Colonial Pines Inn Bed and Breakfast

541 Hickory St
Highlands, NC 28741
(828)526-2060 (866)526-2060
Internet: www.colonialpinesinn.com
E-mail: sleeptight@colonialpinesinn.com

Circa 1937. Secluded on a hillside just half a mile from Highlands' Main Street, this inn offers relaxing porches that boast a mountain view. The parlor is another restful option, offering a TV, fireplace and piano. Rooms, highlighted by knotty pine,

are decorated with an eclectic mix of antiques. The guest pantry is always stocked with refreshments for those who need a little something in the afternoon. For breakfast, freshly baked breads accompany items such as a potato/bacon casserole and baked pears topped with currant sauce. In addition to guest rooms and suites, there are two cottages available, each with a fireplace and kitchen.

Innkeeper(s): Chris & Donna Alley. $85-150. 8 rooms, 5 with PB, 1 with FP, 2 two-bedroom suites, 1 cottage, 1 guest house. Breakfast, afternoon tea and snacks/refreshments included in rates. Types of meals: Full gourmet bkfst,

veg bkfst and early coffee/tea. Beds: KQDT. Data port, cable TV, reading lamp, CD player, refrigerator, ceiling fan, snack bar, telephone, some with fireplace and wireless Internet access in room. DVD, fax and gift shop on premises. Antiquing, art galleries, canoeing/kayaking, downhill skiing, fishing, golf, hiking, horseback riding, live theater, shopping and tennis nearby.

Location: Mountains.

Publicity: *Greenville News, Atlanta Journal, Highlander, Atlanta Constitution and Birmingham News.*

"There was nothing we needed which you did not provide."

Certificate may be used: Valid on Mon, Tues, or Wed during May, June, or Sept, excluding holidays.

Mount Airy

Maxwell House Bed & Breakfast

618 N. Main Street
Mount Airy, NC 27030
(336)786-2174 (877)786-2174
Internet: www.bbonline.com/nc/maxwellhouse
E-mail: maxwellhousebb@hotmail.com

Experience gracious southern hospitality extended at the Historic Merritt House, a 1901 brick and granite Victorian bed and breakfast in the foothills of Blue Ridge Mountains and Wine Country. Oak and pine woodwork, high ceilings, antiques and family heirlooms highlight each room. Relax on willow furniture in the upstairs sitting room and browse the handmade crafts for sale on the hoosier. Gather for afternoon and evening refreshments in the formal dining room or on the wraparound porch. Elegant guest bedrooms are well-appointed and some feature whirlpool tubs. The Maxwell Suite includes a sitting room. Lunch is seldom desired after an indulgently filling breakfast. An assortment of special packages is available.

Innkeeper(s): Roger & Twyla Sickmiller. Call for rates. 4 rooms.

Certificate may be used: Anytime except holiday and festival weekends, subject to availabilty.

Sobotta Manor Bed and Breakfast

347 West Pine Street
Mount Airy, NC 27030
(336)786-2777
Internet: www.bbonline.com/nc/sobotta/index.html
E-mail: sobottamanor@aol.com

Circa 1932. Feel surrounded by a casual elegance at Sobotta Manor Bed and Breakfast in Mount Airy, North Carolina, just ten miles from the Blue Ridge Parkway. Built in 1932 and recently renovated, this stately Tudor-style mansion offers romantic accommodations in the Yadkin Valley, now known for its vineyards. Gather for the social hour and sip a glass of local wine with appetizers. A variety of newspapers are available to read in the parlor and afternoon treats are also provided. The B&B has a complete concierge service. Enjoy a pleasant night's rest in one of the well-appointed guest bedrooms with upscale amenities. Linger over a lavish three-course gourmet breakfast in the European-inspired dining room overlooking the formal English gardens, in the intimate nook or on an open-air porch.

Innkeeper(s): Thurman and Robin Hester. $110-135. 4 rooms with PB. Breakfast and snacks/refreshments included in rates. Types of meals: Full gourmet bkfst, early coffee/tea, wine and Every day starts off with a leisurely but gourmet three-course breakfast served in the European inspired dining room overlooking the formal gardens. Different dining venues such as the cozy breakfast nook or the open-air porches provide for the option for privacy or for conversation with fellow guests. Beds: KQ. Cable TV, DVD, reading lamp, CD player, ceiling fan, clock radio, telephone, turn-down service, hair dryer, bathrobes, bath amenities and wireless Internet access in room. Central air. Fax, copier, bicycles, library, parlor games, fireplace and laundry facility on premises. Antiquing, art galleries, canoeing/kayaking, fishing, golf, hiking, horseback riding, live theater, museums, parks, shopping, sporting events, wineries, mountain biking, road biking, whitewater paddling, campgrounds, winery tours, Andy Griffith Playhouse, Wally Service Station and Squad Car Tour, concerts and jam sessions including Saturday Morning Jam at the Historic downtown cinema, Blue Ridge Jamboree and Thursday Night Jams, Tom Fry's Pickin on the Creek, Bright Leaf Drive In, Blue Ridge Parkway – Known as "America's Favorite Drive" (15 minutes), Mount Rogers National Recreation Area, Appalachian Mountains, Piedmont Regions, Winston-Salem-Greensboro Area, Mount Rogers National Recreation Area Region, Mabry Mill, Horne Creek Farm, Historic Rockford Village, Stone Mountain State Park, Pilot Mountain State Park, Hanging Rock State Park and Outdoor Center, Tanglewood State Park, The Historic Town of Salem, The Museum of Early Southern Decorative Arts (MESDA), The Old Salem Toy Museum and Children's Museum, Reynolda House Museum of Art, Levering Orchard, Yadkin Valley Wines Trail, Panos Old North State Winery and Restaurant, Yadkin Valley Balloon Adventures and Korner's Folly nearby.

Location: City, mountains.

Certificate may be used: Valid Sunday through Thursday, November-August. Holidays and special events excluded.

Murphy

Huntington Hall B&B

272 Valley River Ave
Murphy, NC 28906-2829
(828)837-9567 (800)824-6189 Fax:(828)837-2527
Internet: bed-breakfast-inn.com/
E-mail: info@bed-breakfast-inn.com

Circa 1881. This two-story country Victorian home was built by J.H. Dillard, the town mayor and twice a member of the House of Representatives. Clapboard siding and tall columns

accent the large front porch. An English country theme is highlighted throughout. Afternoon refreshments and evening turndown service are included. Breakfast is served on the sun porch. Murder-mystery, summer-theater, and white-water-rafting packages are available.

Innkeeper(s): Curt & Nancy Harris. $75-125. 5 rooms with PB. Breakfast included in rates. Types of meals: Full gourmet bkfst and early coffee/tea. Beds: KQD. Cable TV, reading lamp, ceiling fan, clock radio, turn-down service and desk in room. Air conditioning. TV, VCR, fax, copier, library, parlor games, telephone and fireplace on premises. Antiquing, fishing, live theater, parks, shopping, tennis and water sports nearby.

Location: Mountains. Small town.

Publicity: *Atlanta Journal, Petersen's 4-Wheel and New York Times.*

"A bed and breakfast well done."

Certificate may be used: Sunday-Thursday any month.

New Bern

Harmony House Inn

215 Pollock St
New Bern, NC 28560-4942
(252)636-3810 (800)636-3113
Internet: www.harmonyhouseinn.com
E-mail: stay@harmonyhouseinn.com

Circa 1850. Long ago, this two-story Greek Revival was sawed in half and the west side moved nine feet to accommodate new hallways, additional rooms and a staircase. A wall was then built to divide the house into two sections. The rooms are dec-

orated with antiques, the innkeeper's collection of handmade crafts and other collectibles. Two of the suites include a heart-shaped Jacuzzi tub. Offshore breezes sway blossoms in the lush garden. Cross the street to an excellent restaurant or take a picnic to the shore.

Innkeeper(s): Ed & Sooki Kirkpatrick. $99-175. 10 rooms with PB, 3 suites, 2 conference rooms. Breakfast included in rates. Types of meals: Full bkfst and early coffee/tea. Beds: KQT. Data port, cable TV, reading lamp, ceiling fan, clock radio, telephone and wireless Internet access in room. Central air. Fax, copier, parlor games and gift shop on premises. Antiquing, art galleries, beach, bicycling, golf, live theater, museums, parks and shopping nearby.

"We feel nourished even now, six months after our visit to Harmony House."

Certificate may be used: Year-round, Sunday through Thursday. Weekends November through February on a space available basis, excluding holidays and special events.

Meadows Inn B&B

212 Pollock St.
New Bern, NC 28560
(252)634-1776 (877)551-1776
Internet: www.meadowsinn-nc.com
E-mail: meadowsinnbnb@earthlink.net

Circa 1847. In the heart of the historic district, this Greek Revival/Federal-style home is considered to be the town's first inn. Boaters enjoy the close proximity to the dock of the Neuse and Trent Rivers with the Intercoastal Waterway only 30 miles away. The Gathering Room is a favorite place to play the baby grand piano or work on a puzzle. Hot and cold beverages always are available. Themed guest bedrooms are spacious and comfortable with non-working fireplaces. Ask about a romantic package in the Victorian Room, or choose the family-friendly two-room suite on the third floor. The morning meal may include quiche, breakfast pizza, scrambled egg enchiladas, or baked French toast to enjoy with fresh fruit, hot breads or muffins and juice.

Innkeeper(s): John & Betty Foy. $96-136. 7 rooms with PB, 1 two-bedroom suite, 1 conference room. Breakfast, snacks/refreshments, wine and Snacks and refreshments included in rates. Types of meals: Full bkfst, early coffee/tea and afternoon tea. Beds: KQDT. Cable TV, reading lamp, refrigerator, ceiling fan, telephone, fireplace, hair dryer and wireless Internet access in room. Air conditioning. VCR, fax, copier, bicycles, parlor games, CD player and refrigerator on premises. Antiquing, art galleries, beach, bicycling, canoeing/kayaking, fishing, golf, hiking, parks and wineries nearby.

Location: City. Confluence of the Neuse and Trent Rivers, 30 miles to Intercoastal Waterway.

Certificate may be used: Anytime, November-April, subject to availability.

New Berne House Inn B&B

709 Broad St
New Bern, NC 28560-4827
(252)636-2250 (866)782-8366
Internet: www.newbernehouse.com
E-mail: nbhinn@esisnet.com

Using bricks salvaged from Tryon Palace, this stately red brick Colonial Revival replica was built by the Taylor family, known for its historic preservation work in North Carolina. Located in the historic district, it is one block to the governor's mansion, Tryon Palace, now a Williamsburg-style living museum. The splendidly refurbished formal parlor is the setting for afternoon tea, and a graceful sweeping staircase leads to guest rooms with canopy beds and antique furnishings.

Innkeeper(s): Barbara Pappas. Call for rates. Call inn for details. Breakfast included in rates. Types of meals: Full gourmet bkfst, early coffee/tea and snacks/refreshments. Beds: KQDT. Ceiling fan, clock radio, telephone and writing table in room. Air conditioning. TV, VCR, fax and copier on premises. Antiquing, live theater and shopping nearby.

Location: City. Historic district.

Publicity: *Charlotte Observer, Raleigh News & Observer and Pinehurst Outlook.*

"In six months of traveling around the country New Berne House was our favorite stop!"

Certificate may be used: Sunday-Thursday, anytime subject to availabilty.

Ocracoke

The Cove B&B

21 Loop Road
Ocracoke, NC 27960-1300
(252)928-4192 Fax:(252)928-4092
Internet: www.thecovebb.com
E-mail: info@thecovebb.com

Circa 1992. For a delightful stay in an historic fishing village on the Cape Hatteras National Seashore, this spacious beach house is the perfect choice. Arrive by ferry and leave all worries on the mainland. Enjoy a complimentary wine reception and pleasant conversation before dining at a nearby restaurant. Watch the sunrise over Pamlico Sound or take in the sunset views of the lighthouse and Historic Portsmouth Island available from the guest bedrooms' private balconies. A complete breakfast could include fruit, eggs, bacon or sausage, biscuits, hash browns or a potato frittata. Take an ecotour, play in the sand, fish in the Gulf stream or grab a bike and explore the village shops.

Innkeeper(s): John and Kati Wharton. $105-205. 6 rooms with PB, 2 with WP. Breakfast and wine included in rates. Types of meals: Full bkfst and early coffee/tea. Beds: QT. Cable TV, reading lamp, ceiling fan, some with hot tub/spa and hair dryer in room. Central air. VCR, DVD, bicycles, parlor games, telephone, Late afternoon wine reception, complimentary bikes and hammock on premises. Beach, bicycling, canoeing/kayaking, fishing, hiking, museums, parks and shopping nearby.

Location: Ocean community. Ocracoke is a historic fishing village on the Cape Hatteras National Seashore.

Certificate may be used: November-March, Weeknights (Sunday-Thursday).

Sylva

Mountain Brook

208 Mountain Brook Rd #19
Sylva, NC 28779-9659
(828)586-4329
Internet: www.mountainbrook.com
E-mail: mcmahon@mountainbrook.com

Circa 1931. Located in the Great Smokies, Mountain Brook in western North Carolina consists of 14 cabins on a hillside amid rhododendron, elm, maple and oak trees. The resort's 200-acre terrain is criss-crossed with brooks and waterfalls, contains a trout-stocked pond and nature trail. Two cabins are constructed with logs from the property, while nine are made from native stone. They feature fireplaces, full kitchens, porch swings and some have Jacuzzi's.

Innkeeper(s): Gus, Michele, Maqelle McMahon. $90-140. 12 cottages with PB, 12 with FP. Types of meals: Early coffee/tea. Beds: KD. Reading lamp,

refrigerator and clock radio in room. Game room and spa/sauna bungalow on premises. Handicap access. Amusement parks, antiquing, downhill skiing, fishing, golf, live theater, shopping, sporting events, tennis, water sports, casino, Great Smokies National Park, railroad and nature trail nearby.

Location: Mountains. Rural.

Publicity: *Brides Magazine, Today and The Hudspeth Report.*

"The cottage was delightfully cozy, and our privacy was not interrupted even once."

Certificate may be used: Feb. 1-Oct. 1, Nov. 1-Dec. 20, holidays excluded.

Tryon

Pine Crest Inn & Restaurant

85 Pine Crest Lane
Tryon, NC 28782-3486
(828)859-9135 (800)633-3001 Fax:(828)859-9136
Internet: www.pinecrestinn.com
E-mail: bnbinns@pinecrestinn.com

Circa 1906. Once a favorite of F. Scott Fitzgerald, this inn is nestled in the foothills of the Blue Ridge Mountains. Opened in 1917 by famed equestrian Carter Brown, the inn offers guests romantic fireplaces, gourmet dining and wide verandas that offer casual elegance. The Blue Ridge Parkway and the famous Biltmore House are a short drive away. Rooms are available in the Main Lodge and cottages. Original buildings include a 200-year-old log cabin, a woodcutter cottage and a stone cottage. Elegant meals are served in a Colonial tavern setting for full breakfasts and gourmet dinners.

Innkeeper(s): Carl Caudle. $89-299. 35 rooms with PB, 29 with FP, 2 with HT, 16 with WP, 8 total suites, including 2 two-bedroom suites and 1 three-bedroom suite, 10 cottages, 2 cabins, 3 conference rooms. Breakfast, snacks/refreshments and Complimentary Port & Sherry in the evenings included in rates. Types of meals: Full gourmet bkfst, veg bkfst, Sun. brunch, early coffee/tea, gourmet lunch, picnic lunch, afternoon tea, hors d'oeuvres, wine, gourmet dinner and room service. Restaurant on premises. Beds: KQDT. Modem hook-up, data port, cable TV, VCR, DVD, reading lamp, CD player, refrigerator, ceiling fan, clock radio, telephone, coffeemaker, turn-down service, desk, most with hot tub/spa, voice mail, most with fireplace, hair dryer, bathrobes, bath amenities, wireless Internet access and iron/ironing board in room. Central air. Fax, copier, swimming, library, parlor games, laundry facility and gift shop on premises. Handicap access. Antiquing, art galleries, bicycling, canoeing/kayaking, fishing, golf, hiking, horseback riding, live theater, museums, parks, shopping, tennis, water sports, wineries, Local Wineries and Numerous area waterfalls nearby.

Location: City, mountains.

Publicity: *Wine Spectator Best of Award of Excellence 9 consecutive years, Select Registry (14 consecutive years), AAA Four-Diamond 13 consecutive years, Southern Living, Our State magazine (August 2006) and Frommer's Budget Travel (2007).*

Certificate may be used: Anytime subject to availability excluding October, holidays and special events.

Tryon Old South B&B

27 Markham Rd
Tryon, NC 28782-3054
(828)859-6965 (800)288-7966 Fax:(828)859-6965
Internet: www.tryonoldsouth.com
E-mail: pat@tryonoldsouth.com

Circa 1910. This Colonial Revival inn is located just two blocks from downtown and Trade Street's antique and gift shops. Located in the Thermal Belt, Tryon is known for its pleasant, mild weather. Guests don't go away hungry from innkeeper Pat Grogan's large Southern-style breakfasts. Unique woodwork abounds in this inn and equally as impressive is a curving staircase. Behind the property is a large wooded area and several waterfalls are just a couple of miles away. The inn is close to Asheville attractions.

Innkeeper(s): Tony & Pat Grogan. $75-105. 4 rooms with PB, 2 guest houses. Breakfast included in rates. Types of meals: Full bkfst, early coffee/tea and wine. Beds: KQD. TV, reading lamp and clock radio in room. Air conditioning. VCR, fax, copier, parlor games, telephone and fireplace on premises. Limited handicap access. Antiquing, art galleries, fishing, golf, hiking, horseback riding, live theater, museums, parks, shopping, wineries and waterfalls nearby.

Location: Mountains. Small town.

Certificate may be used: Anytime except for the months of August, September and October.

Valle Crucis

The Mast Farm Inn

2543 Broadstone Road
Valle Crucis, NC 28691
(828)963-5857 (888)963-5857 Fax:(828) 963-6404
Internet: www.mastfarminn.com
E-mail: stay@mastfarminn.com

Circa 1812. Listed in the National Register of Historic Places, this 18-acre farmstead includes a main house and ten outbuildings, one of them a log cabin built in 1812. The inn features a wraparound porch with rocking chairs, swings and a view of the mountain valley. Fresh flowers gathered from the garden add fragrance throughout the inn. Rooms are furnished with antiques, quilts and mountain crafts. In addition to the inn rooms, there are seven cottages available, some with kitchens.

Before breakfast is served, early morning coffee can be delivered to your room. Organic home-grown vegetables are featured at dinners, included in a contemporary regional cuisine.

Innkeeper(s): Sandra Deschamps Siano & Danielle Deschamps. $125-450. 15 rooms, 8 with PB, 4 with FP, 3 with HT, 7 cottages, 2 guest houses. Breakfast included in rates. Types of meals: Full gourmet bkfst, veg bkfst, early coffee/tea, picnic lunch, snacks/refreshments, wine and gourmet dinner. Restaurant on premises. Beds: KQT. Modem hook-up, data port, reading lamp, CD player, refrigerator, ceiling fan, clock radio, telephone, coffeemaker, hot tub/spa, fireplace, bathrobes and the two cottages have a kitchen in room. Central air. DVD, fax, copier, spa, parlor games and gift shop on premises. Handicap access. Amusement parks, antiquing, art galleries, bicycling, canoeing/kayaking, cross-country skiing, downhill skiing, fishing, golf, hiking, horseback riding, live theater, museums, parks, shopping, water sports, River Sports, Blue Ridge Parkway and Grandfather Mountain nearby.

Location: Country, mountains.

Publicity: *Travel & Leisure, Cooking Light, Blue Ridge Country, Southern Living, New York Times, Our State, Carolina Gardener, Charlotte Taste, Appalachian Voice and The North Carolina Motorsport Association.*

"We want to live here!"

Certificate may be used: May and September only.

Wadesboro

The Forever Inn

214 S Greene St
Wadesboro, NC 28170
(704)695-1304 Fax:(704)695-1369
Internet: theforeverinn.com
E-mail: info@theforeverinn.com

Circa 1910. Gracing a small, southern town, this renovated 1910 Queen Anne Victorian home retains its historical character with original chandeliers, beveled- and leaded-glass windows, detailed woodwork and floors, fireplaces with ceramic tile and octagonal rooms. Read the daily newspaper or watch TV in the library. Gather for conversation in the adjoining living room. Guest bedrooms are named after the colors they reflect and boast upscale amenities. Soak in a clawfoot tub in the Blue Room. The Green Room is a spacious retreat and the Red Room is a suite with a separate sitting room and a bath with a large seated shower. Enjoy a memorable breakfast in the large mahogany dining room before seeing the local sites.

Innkeeper(s): Merrie and Dave. $79-99. 3 rooms with PB. Breakfast included in rates. Types of meals: Full gourmet bkfst. Beds: KQ. Cable TV, reading lamp, ceiling fan, clock radio, hair dryer, bath amenities, wireless Internet access and iron/ironing board in room. Central air. VCR, fax, library, parlor games and telephone on premises. Antiquing, canoeing/kayaking, fishing, golf, hiking, horseback riding, museums, parks, shopping and wineries nearby.

Location: City. Small town.

Publicity: *The Charlotte Observer Travel Section (July 2004)(2), Our State Magazine (February 2006, The Charlotte Observer (April 5, 2006), The Raleigh News & Observer, Food section (Sept. 6 and 2006).*

Certificate may be used: Sunday-Thursday, January, February, March, July, August and September.

Warrenton

Ivy Bed & Breakfast

331 North Main Street
Warrenton, NC 27589
(252)257-9300 (800)919-9886 Fax:(252)257-1802
Internet: www.ivybedandbreakfast.com
E-mail: info@ivybedandbreakfast.com

Circa 1903. Open year-round, this Queen Anne Victorian B&B is located near Lake Gaston and Kerr Lake. It is an easy stroll to quaint downtown shops and an old-fashioned drug store and soda fountain. The one-acre grounds include an English-style box garden with sitting area and fountain. Pat's Porch has inviting rockers and wicker chairs. Evening social hour with appetizers and beverages is hosted in Carter Williams Parlour with a vintage grand piano. Named after the ladies who have lived here, guest bedrooms feature heart pine floors, antiques and Waverly window and bed treatments. Stay in a room with a Jacuzzi and canopy bed or a clawfoot tub and brass bed. The Ivy Suite adjoins two rooms with a connecting bathroom. An incredible three-course candlelit breakfast is served in the Nannie Tarwater Dining Room.

Innkeeper(s): Ellen and Jerry Roth. $100-120. 4 rooms, 3 with PB, 1 with WP, 1 two-bedroom suite, 1 conference room. Breakfast, afternoon tea, snacks/refreshments and A full 3-course candlelit breakfast of your choosing is served at a time that fits your schedule included in rates. Types of meals: Full gourmet bkfst, veg bkfst and early coffee/tea. Beds: Q. Cable TV, reading lamp, clock radio, telephone, hair dryer, bath amenities, wireless Internet access, some rooms with DVD, VCR, Ceiling Fans and Tub with Jacuzzi Jets in room. Central air. Fax, copier, library, parlor games, fireplace, laundry facility, gift shop, Guest refrigerator with soft drinks and bottled water, Coffeemaker, Rocking chairs, Iron/ironing board, Washer/dryer and Wireless high speed Internet on premises. Antiquing, beach, bicycling, canoeing/kayaking, fishing, golf, hiking, horseback riding, live theater, parks, shopping, sporting events, water sports and historic homes nearby.

Location: Country.

Publicity: *Charlotte Magazine, Lake Gaston Gazette, Warren Record and Birmingham News.*

Certificate may be used: Sunday night through Thursday night year round.

Waynesville

Adger House Bed & Breakfast

127 Balsam Drive
Waynesville, NC 28786
(828)452-0861 (866)234-3701 Fax:(828)452-9442
Internet: www.adgerhouse.com
E-mail: info@adgerhouse.com

Circa 1906. Cradled by three wooded acres, this neo-classical revival home has retained much of its original architectural details. High ceilings, hardwood floors and paneled wainscoting complement the period antiques and reproductions. There is ample room to roam, whether enjoying afternoon refreshments in the Eagle's Nest Parlor, reading in a well-stocked library or relaxing in the sunroom. Oversize guest bedrooms are splendidly furnished. Choose a room with a fireplace, loft or double shower. A generous breakfast is served in the Adgerwood Room or al fresco on the patio. Stroll the gardens, or visit the quaint historic village nearby.

Innkeeper(s): Leslie & Bruce Merrell. $95-150. 5 rooms with PB, 2 with FP. Breakfast, afternoon tea and snacks/refreshments included in rates. Types of meals: Full gourmet bkfst and early coffee/tea. Beds: KQT. Reading lamp, ceiling fan, clock radio, some with fireplace, hair dryer, bathrobes and bath amenities in room. TV, library, parlor games, telephone and gift shop on premises. Antiquing, art galleries, bicycling, canoeing/kayaking, downhill skiing, fishing, golf, hiking, horseback riding, live theater, museums, parks, shopping and water sports nearby.

Location: Country, mountains.

Certificate may be used: Sunday-Thursday, November-April, subject to availability.

Yellow House on Plott Creek Road

89 Oakview Dr
Waynesville, NC 28786-7110
(828)452-0991 (800)563-1236 Fax:(704)452-1140
Internet: www.theyellowhouse.com
E-mail: info@theyellowhouse.com

Circa 1885. This manor, which boasts views of the Blue Ridge Mountains, was built as a summer home to a family from Tampa, Fla. The interior of the home is decidedly French country done in romantic colors. Each room is special, from the Batternburg bedding in the Carolina and S'conset rooms to the four-poster bed and mountain view in the Montecito room. Each of the rooms and suites has a fireplace. The Carriage House, S'conset St. Paul de Vence Suite offer whirlpool tubs. Special amenities, such as bathrobes, fresh flowers, a decanter of port, coffee, hair dryers and toiletries thoughtfully have been placed in each room and suite. Each evening, the innkeepers offer wine and cheese, and in the mornings, a gourmet breakfast is served. Guests are free to enjoy their meal on the veranda or in the privacy of their room.

Innkeeper(s): Susan Cerise. $165-265. 10 rooms with PB, 10 with FP, 6 with WP, 7 total suites, including 1 two-bedroom suite, 1 conference room. Breakfast, snacks/refreshments and wine included in rates. Types of meals:

Full gourmet bkfst, veg bkfst, early coffee/tea, picnic lunch and dinner. Beds: KQT. Reading lamp, CD player, refrigerator, ceiling fan, clock radio, telephone, coffeemaker, desk, most with hot tub/spa, hair dryer, bathrobes, bath amenities, wireless Internet access and iron/ironing board in room. Central air. TV, VCR, DVD, fax, copier, library, parlor games, fireplace, gift shop and wireless Internet in main house on premises. Handicap access. Antiquing, art galleries, bicycling, downhill skiing, fishing, golf, hiking, horseback riding, live theater, museums, parks, shopping, tennis, water sports and mountain biking nearby.

Location: Mountains.

Publicity: *Asheville Citizen Times, Mountaineer, WRAL - Raleigh and NC.*

"The scenery and quaintness of this community was only surpassed by the gracious surroundings and hospitality here at the Yellow House."

Certificate may be used: December-May, subject to availability.

Williamston

Big Mill Bed & Breakfast

1607 Big Mill Rd
Williamston, NC 27892-8032
(252)792-8787
Internet: www.bigmill.com
E-mail: info@bigmill.com

Circa 1918. Originally built as a small arts and crafts frame house, the many renovations conceal its true age. The historic farm outbuildings that include the chicken coop, smokehouse, pack house, tobacco barns and potato house, were built from on-site heart pine and cypress trees that were felled and floated down the streams of this 250-acre woodland estate. The Corncrib guest bedroom is in the pack house that originally housed mules. Each of the guest bedrooms feature climate control, stenciled floors, faux-painted walls, hand-decorated tiles on the wet bar and a private entrance. The suite also boasts a stone fireplace and impressive view. The countryside setting includes a three-acre lake with bridges, fruit orchard, vegetable and flower gardens. Eighty-year-old pecan trees planted by Chloe's parents provide nuts for homemade treats as well as shade for the inn.

Innkeeper(s): Chloe Tuttle. $69-135. 4 rooms with PB, 1 with FP, 3 suites, 1 conference room. Breakfast included in rates. Types of meals: Cont plus, veg bkfst, early coffee/tea, gourmet lunch, picnic lunch, gourmet dinner and Catered candlelight meals delivered to your room. Picnic lunches for your outings. Beds: QDT. Modem hook-up, cable TV, VCR, DVD, reading lamp, CD player, refrigerator, ceiling fan, telephone, coffeemaker, desk, some with fireplace, hair dryer, bath amenities, wireless Internet access, iron/ironing board, private entrances, individual climate control, wet bars, kitchenettes with sinks, refrigerators, microwave and coffee pot in room. Central air. Fax, bicycles, parlor games, laundry facility, candlelight dinner in room, lake fishing and off-street parking for any size vehicle on premises. Limited handicap access. Antiquing, bicycling, canoeing/kayaking, fishing, golf, hiking, horseback riding, sporting events, water sports, horse shows, nature trails, nature preserves, boating access, Roanoke River Refuge, Gardner's Creek camping platforms, Bob Martin Agriculture Center, catered meals and Swedish massage upon request nearby.

Location: Country, Carolina countryside.

Publicity: *Down East Magazine, Our State Magazine, Inns, the Perfect Place to Stay, NC Bed & Breakfast Cookbook, Best Recipes from American County Inns and Bed & Breakfasts, WRAL-TV and WITN-TV.*

Certificate may be used: December-February, subject to availability, excluding Valentine's Day, applies to nightly rates only.

Wilmington

C.W. Worth House B&B

412 S 3rd St
Wilmington, NC 28401-5102
(910)762-8562 (800)340-8559 Fax:(910)763-2173
Internet: www.worthhouse.com
E-mail: relax@worthhouse.com

Circa 1893. This beautifully detailed three-story Queen Anne Victorian boasts two turrets and a wide veranda. From the outside, it gives the appearance of a small castle. The inn was renovated in 1995, and it retains many of the architectural details of the original house, including the paneled front hall. Victorian decor is found throughout the inn, including period antiques. The Rose Suite offers a king four-poster bed, sitting room and bath with a clawfoot tub and separate shower. Guests are treated to gourmet breakfasts. Freshly baked muffins and entrees such as eggs Florentine, rosemary and goat cheese strata and stuffed French toast are served. A second-story porch overlooks the garden with dogwood, ponds and pecan trees.

Innkeeper(s): Margi & Doug Erickson. $130-170. 7 rooms with PB, 1 with WP. Breakfast and snacks/refreshments included in rates. Types of meals: Full gourmet bkfst and early coffee/tea. Beds: KQT. Data port, reading lamp, CD player, ceiling fan, clock radio, telephone, desk, some with fireplace, hair dryer, bathrobes, bath amenities, wireless Internet access, iron/ironing board and one guestroom with two-person whirlpool in room. Central air. TV, VCR, DVD, fax, copier, parlor games, gift shop, High-speed wireless Internet access, Porches, Gardens, Ponds and Historic district on premises. Antiquing, art galleries, beach, bicycling, canoeing/kayaking, fishing, golf, horseback riding, live theater, museums, parks, shopping, tennis, water sports, wineries, Fine dining, Carriage and trolley rides, Boat tours, Historic home tours and Historic district walking tours nearby.

Location: City. Near beaches (15-minute drive).

Publicity: *NC Boating Lifestyle Magazine and History Channel Documentary: Isaac's Storm; partially filmed at C. W. Worth House.*

Certificate may be used: Sunday-Thursday; one coupon per reservation, no holidays.

Graystone Inn

100 S 3rd St
Wilmington, NC 28401-4503
(910)763-2000 (888)763-4773 Fax:(910)763-5555
Internet: www.graystoneinn.com
E-mail: contactus@graystoneinn.com

Circa 1906. If you are a connoisseur of inns, you'll be delighted with this stately mansion in the Wilmington Historic District and in the National Register. Recently chosen by American Historic Inns as one of America's Top Ten Romantic Inns, towering columns mark the balconied grand entrance. Its 14,000 square feet of magnificent space includes antique furnishings, art and amenities. A staircase of hand-carved red oak rises three stories. Guests lounge in the music room, drawing room and library. A conference room and sitting area are on the third floor, once a grand ballroom. The elegant guest rooms are often chosen for special occasions, especially the Bellevue, which offers a King bed, sofa and handsome period antiques with a 2-person soaking tub and shower.

Innkeeper(s): Rich & Marcia Moore. $169-359. 9 rooms with PB, 7 with FP, 1 conference room. Breakfast included in rates. Types of meals: Full gourmet bkfst and early coffee/tea. Beds: KQ. Cable TV, reading lamp, ceiling fan, telephone, coffeemaker, turn-down service, desk, some with hot tub/spa, voice mail, hair dryer, bathrobes, bath amenities, wireless Internet access and iron/ironing board in room. Central air. Fax, copier, library, parlor games and fireplace on premises. Antiquing, art galleries, beach, fishing, golf, live theater,

museums, parks, shopping, sporting events, tennis and water sports nearby.
Location: City.

Publicity: *Country Inns, Young Indiana Jones, Matlock, Dawsons Creek, One Tree Hill, Rambling Rose, Mary Jane's Last Dance, Cats Eye, The Locket and The Water is Wide.*

Certificate may be used: Nov. 1-March 31, Sunday-Thursday, holidays excluded.

Rosehill Inn Bed & Breakfast

114 S 3rd St
Wilmington, NC 28401-4556
(910)815-0250 (800)815-0250 Fax:(910)815-0350
Internet: www.rosehill.com
E-mail: rosehill@rosehill.com

Circa 1848. Architect Henry Bacon Jr., most famous for designing the Lincoln Memorial in Washington, D.C., lived

here in the late 19th century. Located in the largest urban historic district in the country, this Neoclassical Victorian was completely renovated in 1995. The guest rooms are spacious and decorated in period furnishings. Breakfast treats include eggs Benedict with Cajun Crab Hollandaise and stuffed French toast with orange syrup.

Innkeeper(s): Patricia & Bob Milton. $119-199. 6 rooms with PB. Breakfast included in rates. Types of meals: Full gourmet bkfst and early coffee/tea. Beds: KQD. Modem hook-up, data port, cable TV, VCR, reading lamp, clock radio, telephone, desk, data port and iron and ironing board in room. Fax on premises. Antiquing, fishing, golf, live theater, parks, shopping, sporting events, tennis, water sports, battleship memorial and beaches nearby.

Location: Historic district.

Publicity: *Southern Living, Wilmington Star News, Wilmington Magazine, Washington Post, Insiders Guide to Wilmington, Atlanta Sun, Philadelphia Inquirer and Oprah Winfrey "The Wedding."*

Certificate may be used: Dec. 1 to Feb. 28 (excluding Feb. 13-15), Sunday-Thursday.

Winston-Salem

Augustus T. Zevely Inn

803 S Main St
Winston-Salem, NC 27101-5332
(336)748-9299 (800)928-9299 Fax:(336)721-2211
Internet: www.winston-salem-inn.com
E-mail: Reservations@winston-salem-inn.com

Circa 1844. The Zevely Inn is the only lodging in Old Salem. Each of the rooms at this charming pre-Civil War inn have a view of historic Old Salem. Moravian furnishings and fixtures permeate the decor of each of the guest quarters, some of which boast working fireplaces. The home's architecture is reminiscent of many structures built in Old Salem during the second quarter of the 19th century. The formal dining room and parlor have wood burning fireplaces. The two-story porch offers visitors  a view of the period gardens and a beautiful magnolia tree. A line of Old Salem furniture has been created by Lexington Furniture Industries, and several pieces were created especially for the Zevely Inn.

Innkeeper(s): Courtney Eagle. $80-205. 12 rooms with PB, 3 with FP, 1 suite. Breakfast and snacks/refreshments included in rates. Beds: KQDT. Cable TV, reading lamp, refrigerator, clock radio, telephone, desk and whirlpool tub in room. Air conditioning. Fax, copier, parlor games and fireplace on premises. Antiquing, live theater, shopping, sporting events and Old Salem Historic District nearby.

Location: City.

Publicity: *Washington Post Travel, Salem Star, Winston-Salem Journal, Tasteful, Country Living, National Trust for Historic Preservation, Homes and Gardens, Homes Across America, Southern Living, Heritage Travel, Top 25 Historic Inns & Hotels and Home & Gardens Network Show.*

"Colonial charm with modern conveniences, great food. Very nice! Everything was superb."

Certificate may be used: November, December, January, February on Sunday, Monday, excluding seasonal events.

Summit Street Inns

420 Summit Street
Winston-Salem, NC 27101
(336)777-1887 (800)301-1887
Internet: www.bbinn.com
E-mail: innkeeper@bbinn.com

Located in a historic urban residential neighborhood, this inn is comprised of two adjacent Victorian homes. Both homes are listed in the National Register and boast such features as wraparound porches, gabled roofs, ornate entrances, beautiful windows and high ceilings. Guest rooms are decorated with Victorian antiques, and each includes a double whirlpool tub. The innkeepers provide many thoughtful amenities, such as stocked mini-refrigerators, microwaves, coffeemakers, stereos, TVs with VCRs

and free movies, irons, bathrobes and hair dryers. There is a Nautilus exercise room and a billiards room. Two gourmet restaurants in historic homes are only two blocks away.

Innkeeper(s): Ken Land, Teri Hail. $99-209. Call inn for details. Breakfast and snacks/refreshments included in rates. Types of meals: Full bkfst and room service. Beds: KQ. Modem hook-up, data port, cable TV, VCR, DVD, reading lamp, stereo, refrigerator, ceiling fan, clock radio, telephone, coffeemaker, desk, hot tub/spa, some with fireplace, hair dryer, bathrobes, bath amenities, wireless Internet access and iron/ironing board in room. Central air. Copier and spa on premises. Antiquing, art galleries, golf, horseback riding, museums, parks, shopping, tennis and wineries nearby.

Location: City.

Publicity: *Southern Living and WXII television.*

Certificate may be used: Sunday-Monday.

North Dakota

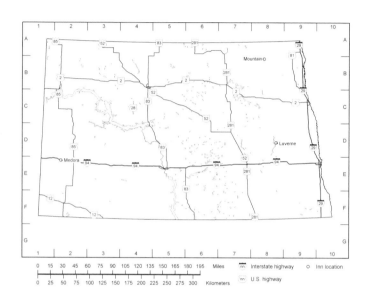

Luverne

Volden Farm

11943 County Rd 26
Luverne, ND 58056
(701)769-2275 Fax:(701)769-2610
Internet: www.voldenfarm.com

Circa 1926. Perennial gardens and a hedge of lilacs surround this redwood house with its newer addition. A favorite room is the North Room with a lace canopy bed, an old pie safe and a Texas Star quilt made by the host's grandmother. Guests enjoy soaking in the clawfoot tub while looking out over the hills. There are two libraries, a music room and game room. The innkeepers also offer lodging in the Law Office, which dates to 1885 and is a separate little prairie house ideal for families. A stream, bordered by old oaks and formed by a natural spring, meanders through the property. The chickens here lay green and blue eggs. Dinner is available by advanced arrangement. Hiking, birdwatching, snowshoeing and skiing are nearby.

Innkeeper(s): JoAnne Wold. $60-95. 4 rooms, 3 with PB, 1 cottage. Breakfast and snacks/refreshments included in rates. Types of meals: Full gourmet bkfst, early coffee/tea, picnic lunch and gourmet dinner. Beds: KDT. Reading lamp, refrigerator, clock radio and desk in room. Bicycles, library, parlor games, telephone, fireplace and meditation garden on premises. Antiquing, cross-country skiing, downhill skiing, fishing, hiking, golf, canoeing, snowshoeing and bird watching nearby.

Location: Country.
Publicity: *Fargo Forum, Horizons, Grand Forks Herald, Mid-West Living and Getaways.*

"Very pleasant indeed! JoAnne makes you feel good. There's so much to do, and the hospitality is amazing!"

Certificate may be used: Anytime, holidays excluded.

Medora

The Rough Riders Hotel B&B

Medora, ND
Medora, ND 58645
(701)623-4444 (800)633-6721 Fax:(701)623-449

Circa 1865. This old hotel has the branding marks of Teddy Roosevelt's cattle ranch as well as other brands stamped into the rough-board facade out front. A wooden sidewalk helps to maintain the turn-of-the-century cow-town feeling. Rustic guest rooms are above the restaurant and are furnished with homesteader antiques original to the area. In the summer, an outdoor pageant is held complete with stagecoach and horses. In October, deer hunters are accommodated. The hotel, along with two motels, is managed by the non-profit Theodore Roosevelt Medora Foundation.

Innkeeper(s): Randy Hatzenbuhler. $45-58. 9 rooms with PB. Breakfast included in rates.

Certificate may be used: Oct. 1-May 1.

Ohio

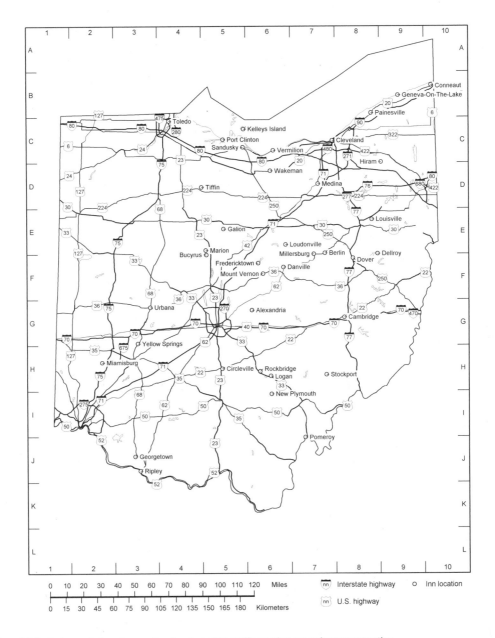

0 10 20 30 40 50 60 70 80 90 100 110 120 Miles

0 15 30 45 60 75 90 105 120 135 150 165 180 Kilometers

(nn) Interstate highway   o Inn location

(nn) U.S. highway

Tell the innkeeper that you have an iLoveInns free-night certificate when you make your reservation.

Alexandria

WillowBrooke Bed 'n Breakfast

4459 Morse Road
Alexandria, OH 43001
(740)924-6161 (800)722-6372
Internet: www.willowbrooke.com
E-mail: wilbrk@aol.com

Circa 1980. There are no worries at this English Tudor Manor House and Guest Cottage located in a secluded 34-acre wooded setting. Furnished in a traditional decor, spacious guest bedrooms and romantic suites offer extensive amenities that pamper and please like feather beds or pillowtop mattresses, candlelight, whirlpool tubs, kitchens and balconies or patios. Families are welcome to stay in the Garden Suite or Guest House. For breakfast, choose from three juices along with French toast and strawberries, scrambled eggs and ham. Enjoy year-round use of the outdoor hot tub, and browse the gift shop for glass oil candles and crystal table accessories.

Innkeeper(s): Sandra Gilson. $115-270. 6 rooms with PB, 3 with FP, 3 suites, 1 cottage, 1 guest house. Breakfast included in rates. Types of meals: Full gourmet bkfst and early coffee/tea. Beds: KQ. Modem hook-up, cable TV, VCR, DVD, reading lamp, stereo, refrigerator, ceiling fan, clock radio, telephone, coffeemaker, turn-down service, desk, most with hot tub/spa, most with fireplace, hair dryer, bathrobes, bath amenities, featherbeds and candlelight in room. Central air. Fax, copier, spa, sauna, parlor games, gift shop, gift shop with Firelight oil candles, crystal table setting accessories and outdoor five-person hydrotherapy hot tub on premises. Limited handicap access. Antiquing, art galleries, beach, bicycling, fishing, golf, hiking, live theater, museums, parks, shopping, sporting events, tennis, wineries, Longaberger Basket Homestead, Heisey Glass Museum and National Trails Raceway nearby.

Location: Country. Located 1/4 mile back into the woods.

Certificate may be used: Monday-Thursday, subject to availability, excludes October.

Ashtabula

Gilded Swan B&B

5024 West Ave
Ashtabula, OH 44004
(440)992-1566 (888)345-7926
Internet: www.thegildedswan.com
E-mail: erswanson@alltel.net

Circa 1902. Romantic interludes and memorable moments are easily experienced at this lavish Queen Anne Victorian in a Lake Erie harbor town. Painstakingly restored, the B&B is furnished with cherished family heirlooms and antiques. Comfortable guest bedrooms and suites boast welcoming decor, canopy beds, whirlpool tubs, a fireplace and pillow chocolates. In the elegant dining room, a sumptuous breakfast may include raspberry-stuffed French toast and grilled sausage links. Afternoon snacks are also offered. Centrally located, the inn is within easy access to wine country, Cleveland's museums, Pennsylvania's attractions and Amish country.

Innkeeper(s): Elaine Swanson. $75-105. 4 rooms, 2 with PB, 1 with FP. Breakfast and snacks/refreshments included in rates. Types of meals: Full gourmet bkfst, early coffee/tea, picnic lunch and afternoon tea. Clock radio, desk, most with hot tub/spa, some with fireplace, bathrobes and bath amenities in room. Central air. TV, parlor games, telephone and gift shop on premises. Amusement parks, antiquing, beach, bicycling, canoeing/kayaking, fishing, golf, hiking, live theater, museums, parks, shopping, water sports and wineries nearby.

Publicity: *Country Extra Magazine.*

Certificate may be used: Anytime, subject to availability.

Berlin

Donna's Premier Lodging B&B

5523 Twp Rd 358
Berlin, OH 44610
(330)893-3068 (800)320-3338
Internet: www.donnasofberlin.com
E-mail: info@donnasb-b.com

Circa 1991. Romantic accommodations on a secluded six-acre wooded hillside include stately Victorian chalets, inviting log cabins, private cottages, villas and bridal suites. The natural setting and luxurious amenities instill a peaceful relaxation. Play pool in a chalet rec room. Snuggle by a fireplace or indulge in the intimacy of a two-person Jacuzzi. Beautifully landscaped grounds offer spots to sit by the 75-foot waterfall, stream and fountain combination. Nature lovers enjoy the serenity of a starlit stroll. Visit nearby Amish Country or go antiquing. Ask about midweek and special sweetheart packages.

Innkeeper(s): Johannes & Donna Marie Schlabach. $99-369. 23 rooms with PB, 23 with FP, 3 suites, 8 cottages, 5 guest houses, 7 cabins. Types of meals: Country bkfst and veg bkfst. Beds: KQ. Cable TV, VCR, DVD, reading lamp, stereo, refrigerator, ceiling fan, clock radio, telephone, coffeemaker, hot tub/spa, fireplace, hair dryer, bath amenities, iron/ironing board, Jacuzzi, mood lighting, 3 with billiards, 9 with kitchenette, 7 with full kitchen and Romancing the Stone cabin has waterfall in room. Central air. Fax, copier, parlor games, gift shop, landscaped grounds with waterfall/stream/pond combination, picnic table and hammock on premises. Limited handicap access. Antiquing, canoeing/kayaking, golf, horseback riding, museums, shopping, tennis, wineries, buggy rides and sleigh rides nearby.

Location: Country.

Publicity: *Country Traveler, Amish Heartland, Country Living Magazine, Canton Repository Newspaper and Neil Zurker's "One Tank Trips"-Channel 8 and TV 27.*

Certificate may be used: November-May, Sunday-Thursday, Honeymoon/Anniversary Villa only.

Bucyrus

Hide Away Country Inn

1601 SR 4
Bucyrus, OH 43302
(419)562-3013 (800)570-8233 Fax:(419)562-3003
Internet: www.hideawayinn.com
E-mail: innkeeper@hideawayinn.com

Circa 1938. Experience a refreshing getaway while staying at this remarkable inn. Because of the inn's outrageous service, even the business traveler will feel rejuvenated after embarking on a rendezvous with nature here. Exquisite guest suites feature private Jacuzzis, fireplaces and amenities that pamper. Savor a leisurely five-course breakfast. Enjoy fine dining in the restaurant, or ask for an intimate picnic to be arranged. A productive conference room instills a personal quiet and inspires the mind.

Innkeeper(s): Debbie Miller. $97-257. 11 rooms with PB, 7 with FP, 10 with WP, 9 suites, 2 guest houses, 2 conference rooms. Breakfast included in rates. Types of meals: Full gourmet bkfst, veg bkfst, early coffee/tea, gourmet lunch, picnic lunch, afternoon tea, snacks/refreshments, hors d'oeuvres, gourmet dinner, room service, 5-Course Breakfast Can be Happily delivered to your suite, as well as Picnic Basket Dinners featuring Cornish Hens, Steak Kabobs, Fried Chicken or Pork Chops. Meals come with appetizer, 2 sides, dessert and sparkling juice, silverware and china and all wrapped up in a huge picnic basket. Restaurant on premises. Beds: KQD. Cable TV, VCR, reading lamp, stereo, refrigerator, ceiling fan, clock radio, telephone, coffeemaker, turn-down service, desk, voice mail, most with fireplace, hair dryer, bathrobes, bath amenities, wireless Internet access and iron/ironing board in room. Air conditioning. Fax, copier, spa, bicycles, library, laundry facility, gift shop, Full kitchen, Restaurant and Patio area, Satellite TV, 5-Course Gourmet

Breakfast, Wireless Internet anywhere on property and 6 acres on premises. Handicap access. Amusement parks, antiquing, bicycling, downhill skiing, fishing, golf, hiking, horseback riding, live theater, museums, parks, shopping, sporting events, water sports, wineries and Baja boats nearby.

Location: Country.

Publicity: *New York Times, Columbus Dispatch, Ohio Country Journal, Akron Beacon Journal, Cleveland Plain Dealer, Travel & Leisure, Neil Zurcker One Tank-Trips-Cleveland, Akron WKBN, Del's Folks and Del's Feasts Cleveland and Cleveland WKYC.*

Certificate may be used: Sunday-Thursday, excluding holidays and special event dates.

Cambridge

Colonel Taylor Inn B&B and Gift Shop

633 Upland Rd
Cambridge, OH 43725
(740)432-7802
Internet: www.coltaylorinnbb.com
E-mail: coltaylor@coltaylorinnbb.com

Circa 1878. Be pampered by warm country hospitality at this 1878 Victorian Painted Lady mansion with a rich historic heritage and modern comforts. The Colonel Taylor Inn B&B in Cambridge, Ohio is open year-round for a perfect vacation, romantic getaway or pleasant business trip. Relax upon arrival with an afternoon snack in one of the two parlors or on one of the three porches. Beverages are always available. Delightful guest bedrooms are on the second floor with working fireplaces and antique furnishings. Most rooms feature four-poster beds and sitting areas by bay windows. The spacious Rose Room also boasts a whirlpool tub. Linger over a five-course breakfast served each morning.

Innkeeper(s): Jim & Patricia Irvin. $135-195. 4 rooms with PB, 4 with FP, 1 two-bedroom suite, 2 conference rooms. Breakfast included in rates. Types of meals: Full gourmet bkfst, veg bkfst, early coffee/tea, picnic lunch, afternoon tea and dinner. Beds: KQD. Cable TV, reading lamp, ceiling fan, clock radio, fireplace, hair dryer, bathrobes, bath amenities, wireless Internet access, iron/ironing board, fireplace, one with bathroom whirlpool tub/fireplace, wireless high speed Internet connection, cable TV in Lilac room and phone available in room. Central air. TV, VCR, library, parlor games, telephone, large-screen TV, two parlors, formal dining room, three porches and wireless Internet on premises. Antiquing, art galleries, beach, bicycling, canoeing/kayaking, cross-country skiing, fishing, golf, hiking, horseback riding, live theater, museums, parks, shopping, tennis, water sports, wineries, glass factories, potteries, festivals and concerts nearby.

Location: Small town historic area.

Publicity: *Mid-West Living Magazine with Trevors tour of the National Rd., RT. 40, Arrington's Bed & Breakfast Journal, Inn Traveler, 4 years of awards, Mid-West Living (Spring 2006) and voted "Best in the USA" & awarded "The Inn with the most Hospitality" 2003 by inngoers.*

Certificate may be used: Monday-Thursday for all months except May and October.

Cedarville

Hearthstone Inn & Suites

10 S Main St
Cedarville, OH 45314-9760
(937)766-3000 (877)644-6466 Fax:(N/A)
Internet: www.hearthstone-inn.com
E-mail: Please call our toll-free number

Circa 2001. Blending regional themes with small-town hospitality, this country inn hotel with an upscale bed and breakfast ambiance is family-owned and non-smoking. Enjoy old-fashioned friendliness, generous service and impeccable cleanliness.

Relax on the wraparound porch or on the leather sofa by the huge Ohio River rock hearth in the Fireplace Lounge with Queen Anne decor. Browse through the historical displays and the cottage gift shop. Pleasant guest bedrooms and Jacuzzi suites feature pampering amenities. Hand-hewn beams beneath the second-floor balcony and mural art accent the Breakfast Commons where a Supreme Selections morning buffet is served. The inn is conveniently located right on the Ohio to Erie Bike Trail.

Innkeeper(s): Stuart & Ruth Zaharek. $94-159. 20 rooms with PB, 2 with HT, 2 suites, 1 conference room. Breakfast included in rates. Types of meals: Cont plus. Beds: KQ. Modem hook-up, data port, cable TV, reading lamp, refrigerator, ceiling fan, clock radio, telephone, coffeemaker, desk, some with hot tub/spa, bath amenities, wireless Internet access and iron/ironing board in room. Air conditioning. VCR, DVD, fax, copier, spa, bicycles, laundry facility and gift shop on premises. Handicap access. Antiquing, bicycling, canoeing/kayaking, fishing, golf, hiking, live theater, museums, shopping and tennis nearby.

Location: Country.

Publicity: *Cincinnati Enquirer, Ohio Magazine and Foder's Travel Guides .*

Certificate may be used: November-January, Sunday-Wednesday; April-May, Sunday-Wednesday. Last minute subject to availability (same day, anytime).

Circleville

Castle Inn Romantic Retreat B&B

610 S Court St
Circleville, OH 43113
(740)477-3986 Fax:(740)477-2342
Internet: www.castleinn.net
E-mail: thecastleinn@aol.com

Circa 1890. Feel like royalty in this romantic castle retreat built by Samuel Ruggles in the late 1800s. The Castle Inn provides accommodations in Circleville, Central Ohio. Authentic documentation of the castle's history adorns the walls of the grand staircase. Gather in the parlor to relax, read or plan the day. Stay in a delightful guest bedroom on the second floor tower or a third-floor honeymoon suite. Select a room with a gas honeycomb fireplace, canopy bed, entertainment center, double Jacuzzi, heart-shaped jetted tub or marble bath with soaking tub.

Innkeeper(s): Jeannie Shaw. $119-279. 6 rooms with PB, 2 with FP, 3 suites. Beds: Q. Cable TV, VCR, CD player, ceiling fan and clock radio in room. Air conditioning.

Certificate may be used: Anytime, subject to availability.

Danville

Red Fox Country Inn

26367 Danville Amity Rd.
Danville, OH 43014-0746
(740)599-7369 (877)600-7310
Internet: www.redfoxcountryinn.com
E-mail: Info@RedFoxCountryInn.com

Circa 1830. This inn, located on 15 scenic central Ohio acres, was built originally to house those traveling on the Danville-Amity Wagon Road and later became a farm home. Amish woven rag rugs and country antiques decorate the guest rooms. Some of the furnishings belonged to early owners, and some date to the 18th century. Four rooms include Amish-made oak beds and

the fifth an 1880s brass and iron double bed. Breakfasts include fresh pastries, fruits, coffee and a variety of delectable entrees. Special dietary needs usually can be accommodated. There are books and games available in the inn's sitting room, and guests also are invited to relax on the front porch. Golfing, canoeing, fishing, horseback riding, hiking, biking, skiing and Mohican State Park are nearby, and the inn is 30 minutes from the largest Amish community in the United States.

Innkeeper(s): Sue & Denny Simpkins. $65-105. 6 rooms, 5 with PB. Breakfast included in rates. Beds: QD. Reading lamp and clock radio in room. Air conditioning. Library, telephone and great place for retreats on premises.

Location: Small town.

Publicity: *Dealers Automotive, Columbus Dispatch, Mount Vernon News and Cincinnati Enquirer.*

"Our dinner and breakfast were '5 star.' Thank you for the gracious hospitality and special kindness you showed us."

Certificate may be used: Weekdays all year-round. Weekends Jan. 1-March 31. Excludes holidays and events at area colleges.

The White Oak Inn

29683 Walhonding Rd, SR 715
Danville, OH 43014
(740)599-6107 (877)908-5923
Internet: www.whiteoakinn.com
E-mail: info@whiteoakinn.com

Circa 1915. Large oaks and ivy surround the wide front porch of this three-story farmhouse situated on 13 green acres. It is located on the former Indian trail and pioneer road that runs along the Kokosing River, and an Indian mound has been discovered on the property. The inn's woodwork is all original white oak, and guest rooms are furnished in antiques. Visitors often shop for maple syrup, cheese and handicrafts at nearby Amish farms. Three cozy fireplace rooms and two cottages provide the perfect setting for romantic evenings.

Innkeeper(s): Yvonne & Ian Martin. $120-205. 12 rooms with PB, 6 with FP, 3 with WP, 2 cottages, 1 conference room. Breakfast and snacks/refreshments included in rates. Types of meals: Country bkfst, veg bkfst, early coffee/tea, gourmet dinner and Romantic dinner baskets delivered to rooms. Beds: KQDT. Reading lamp, CD player, ceiling fan, clock radio, telephone, coffeemaker, some with hot tub/spa, some with fireplace, hair dryer and wireless Internet access in room. Air conditioning. TV, DVD, library, parlor games, gift shop, guest refrigerator and piano on premises. Limited handicap access. Antiquing, bicycling, canoeing/kayaking, fishing, golf, hiking, horseback riding, parks, shopping, water sports, wineries, Amish area, Longaberger Baskets and Roscoe Village nearby.

Location: Country. Rural.

Publicity: *Ladies Home Journal, Columbus Monthly, Cleveland Plain Dealer, Country, Glamour, Columbus Dispatch, Midwest Living, Ohio Magazine and PBS - Country Inn Cooking.*

"The dinner was just fabulous and we enjoyed playing the antique grand piano."

Certificate may be used: Sunday to Thursday nights, year-round.

Dover

Olde World Bed & Breakfast & Tea Room

2982 State Route 516 NW
Dover, OH 44622-7247
(330)343-1333 (800)447-1273
Internet: www.oldeworldbb.com
E-mail: info@oldeworldbb.com

Circa 1881. A quaint atmosphere is imparted at this red brick Victorian farmhouse. The tea parlor features beautifully preserved woodwork found in the pocket doors and fireplace mantel. Themed guest bedrooms and a suite include Parisian, Alpine, Mediterranean and the signature Victorian decor which boasts a carved bed and clawfoot tub. Enjoy an elegant breakfast in the floral-wallpapered dining room with chandelier. The meal may include Swiss eggs, rhubarb muffins, cream scones and grilled local whole hog sausage. Queen's tea is served every Wednesday through Saturday afternoon. The veranda is a favorite retreat while munching on warm, homemade cookies. The Amish countryside and an abundance of antiquing opportunities are nearby.

Innkeeper(s): Jonna Cronebaugh. $85-125. 5 rooms with PB, 1 suite, 1 conference room. Breakfast included in rates. Types of meals: Full gourmet bkfst, lunch, afternoon tea, snacks/refreshments, wine, dinner and room service. Beds: KQ. TV, VCR, reading lamp, CD player, clock radio, fireplace and robes in room. Central air. Fax, spa, parlor games, telephone, gift shop and tea room that serves lunch on premises. Antiquing, canoeing/kayaking, fishing, golf, hiking, horseback riding, live theater, shopping, tennis, water sports, wineries, Amish Country, historical Indian sites, Warther museum, Riverfront Antique Mall, Trumpet in the Land outdoor drama, Zoar Village and Ohio Erie Canal Towpath nearby.

Location: Country.

Publicity: *Ohio Magazine, Columbus Dispatch, Canton Repository, Cleveland Plain Dealer, Ohio Pass Magazine, Home & Away and Country Discovers.*

Certificate may be used: November-April, Sunday-Thursday, subject to availability.

Fredericktown

Heartland Country Resort

3020 Township Rd 190
Fredericktown, OH 43019
(419)768-9300 (800)230-7030 Fax:(419)768-9133
Internet: www.heartlandcountryresort.com
E-mail: heartbb@bright.net

Circa 1996. Peacefully secluded among shady woodlands and rolling hills, this upscale country resort and relaxing retreat is a sprawling haven on more than one hundred acres. The newly constructed log home offers a private setting and luxurious comfort. The refurbished main farmhouse boasts a screened porch and spacious deck. A pool table, games and puzzles are enjoyed in the recreation room. A video library provides a large selection of movies. Stay in a deluxe guest suite with cathedral ceilings, two-person Jacuzzis, full kitchens or kitchenettes, private entrances and porches. Start the day with a scrumptious breakfast. A variety of wrangling and horseback riding activities are available for everyone, from beginners to the experienced. Explore nearby Amish country, Mohican and Malabar State Parks and Kingwood Garden Center.

Innkeeper(s): Dorene Henschen. $120-195. 4 rooms, 3 with PB, 3 with FP, 1 with HT, 3 with WP, 3 suites, 3 cabins, 1 conference room. Breakfast, afternoon tea and snacks/refreshments included in rates. Types of meals: Country bkfst, veg bkfst, early coffee/tea, lunch, picnic lunch, dinner and room service. Beds: QT. TV, VCR, DVD, reading lamp, CD player, refrigerator, ceiling fan, snack bar, clock radio, telephone, coffeemaker, desk, hot tub/spa, fireplace, bathrobes, bath amenities, Suites have Jacuzzis and hot tub on screened porch in room. Central air. Fax, spa, stable, library, pet boarding, parlor games, laundry facility, gift shop, pool table, wrangler activities, chickens, horses, cattle, golden retrievers and cats on premises. Antiquing, bicycling, canoeing/kayaking, cross-country skiing, downhill skiing, fishing, golf, hiking, horseback riding, live theater, museums, parks, shopping, wineries, Amish Country, birding, mid-Ohio raceway, Mohican and Malabar Farm State Parks and Kingwood Garden Center nearby.

Location: Country.

Publicity: *Columbus Dispatch, Country Extra, One Tank Trips, Getaways, Home and Away, Ohio Magazine, Horse and Rider, Cincinnati Enquirer, Arrington's B&B Journal, Columbus Channel 10 and Cleveland Channel 7.*

"Warm hospitality . . . Beautiful surroundings and pure peace & quiet. What more could one want from a B&B in the country? Thank you for an excellent memory!"

Certificate may be used: Monday-Thursday, November-April, subject to availability.

Geneva on the Lake

Eagle Cliff Inn

5254 Lake Road East
Geneva on the Lake, OH 44041
(440)466-1110 Fax:(440)466-0315
Internet: www.eaglecliffinn.com
E-mail: beachclub5@adelphia.net

Circa 1880. Catering to adults, this recently renovated 1880 Victorian inn graces one acre of the Strip in the state's first resort village. It is listed in the National Register, noted as significantly reflecting the dominant recreation history of Geneva On The Lake. Enjoy the relaxed atmosphere while sitting on white wicker cushioned chairs and rockers or a porch swing. Elegantly functional guest bedrooms and a suite offer views of the Strip and lake. The cottages are situated privately in the back. Savor a satisfying daily breakfast. Magnificent sunsets are best viewed from the inn's easy beach access. Sip a local wine from famed Ashtabula County while chatting by the fireplace. Visit the nearby Jenny Munger Museum.

Innkeeper(s): LuAnn & Jerry Busch. $110-139. 7 rooms with PB, 3 cottages. Breakfast, afternoon tea and snacks/refreshments included in rates. Types of meals: Full bkfst, veg bkfst and early coffee/tea. Beds: KQ. Cable TV, reading lamp, stereo, ceiling fan, clock radio, telephone, hair dryer, bath amenities and wireless Internet access in room. Air conditioning. VCR, fax, copier, parlor games, fireplace, laundry facility and parlor & sitting room with fireplace on premises. Amusement parks, antiquing, art galleries, beach, bicycling, canoeing/kayaking, cross-country skiing, fishing, golf, hiking, horseback riding, live theater, museums, parks, shopping, sporting events, tennis, water sports and wineries nearby.

Location: Directly on Geneva-On-the-Lake, Ohio Strip.

Publicity: *"Superior Small Lodging."*

Certificate may be used: Sunday-Thursday, holidays excluded.

The Lakehouse Inn

5653 Lake Road E
Geneva on the Lake, OH 44041
(440)466-8668 Fax:(440)466-2556
Internet: www.thelakehouseinn.com
E-mail: inquiries@thelakehouseinn.com

Circa 1940. In a quaint lakefront location, this inn offers a variety of accommodations that boast a nautical/country décor. Stay "bed and breakfast style" in standard guest bedrooms or Jacuzzi suites with fireplaces, DVD players, microwaves and refrigerators. Renovated cottages include a living room, fully equipped kitchen, bath and one or two bedrooms. Linens, towels, paper goods and cleaning supplies are not provided. The secluded Beach House features a living and dining area, kitchen, Jacuzzi bath, two-person shower, spacious bedroom and outdoor deck. Enjoy the central air and heat as well as panoramic views of Lake Erie and the Geneva Marina.

Innkeeper(s): Andrea Fagnilli. $80-225. 8 cottages, 18 with PB, 4 with FP, 4 with WP, 3 two-bedroom suites, 1 guest house, 1 conference room. Breakfast included in rates. Types of meals: Full bkfst, veg bkfst, early coffee/tea, snacks/refreshments, wine and dinner. Beds: KQDT. Cable TV, DVD, CD player, refrigerator, ceiling fan, clock radio, telephone, fireplace, Jacuzzi tub and high-speed wireless Internet in room. Air conditioning. VCR, fax, copier, swimming, parlor games, gift shop, lakefront winery, lakefront decks, horseshoes, croquet and bocce ball on premises. Amusement parks, antiquing, beach, bicycling, canoeing/kayaking, fishing, golf, hiking, museums, parks, shopping, tennis, water sports, wineries, Geneva-on-the-Lake summer resort, historic Ashtabula Harbor and covered bridges nearby.

Location: Waterfront.

Certificate may be used: October-May, Sunday-Friday, subject to availability.

Georgetown

Bailey House

112 N Water St
Georgetown, OH 45121-1332
(937)378-3087
Internet: www.baileyhousebandb.com
E-mail: baileyho@verizon.net

Circa 1830. The stately columns of this three-story Greek Revival house once greeted Ulysses S. Grant, a frequent visitor during his boyhood when he was sent to buy milk from the Bailey's. A story  is told that Grant accidentally overheard that the Bailey boy was leaving West Point. Grant immediately ran through the woods to the home of Congressman Thomas Hamer and petitioned an appointment in Bailey's place which he received, thus launching his military career. The inn has double parlors, pegged oak floors and Federal-style fireplace mantels. Antique washstands, chests and beds are found in the large guest rooms.

Innkeeper(s): Nancy Purdy. $65-70. 4 rooms, 1 with PB, 2 with FP. Breakfast included in rates. Types of meals: Full bkfst and early coffee/tea. Beds: QD. Cable TV, reading lamp, clock radio, telephone, desk, hair dryer, bath amenities, wireless Internet access, iron/ironing board, fireplace (two rooms) and desk (one room) in room. Air conditioning. VCR, DVD, library, parlor games, fireplace, herb garden, garden shed, screened porch, rustic cabin and unique train display in recreation area on premises. Antiquing, art galleries, fishing, golf, museums, parks, shopping, tennis, water sports, private tours of U.S. Grant Home, historic sites and John Ruthven Art Gallery nearby.

Location: Country. Historic District town.

Publicity: *If Walls Could Talk on HGTV (Feb. 2006).*

"Thank you for your warm hospitality, from the comfortable house to the delicious breakfast."

Certificate may be used: Anytime, subject to availability.

Logan

The Inn At Cedar Falls

21190 SR 374
Logan, OH 43138
(740)385-7489 (800)653-2557 Fax:(740)385-0820
Internet: www.innatcedarfalls.com
E-mail: info@innatcedarfalls.com

Circa 1987. This sophisticated inn, complete with traditional rooms along with separate cottages and cabins, was constructed on 75 acres adjacent to Hocking Hills State Parks and one-half mile from the waterfalls. The kitchen and dining rooms are

in a 19th-century log house. Accommodations in the two-story barn-shaped building are simple and comfortable, each furnished with antiques. There are six fully equipped log cabins and twelve cozy cottages available, each individually decorated. The cabins include a kitchen and living room with a gas-log stove; some have a whirlpool tub. The cottages feature under-the-counter refrigerators, gas-log stoves and whirlpool tubs. There also is a meeting room equipped with a wood-burning stove. Verandas provide sweeping views of woodland and meadow. The grounds include organic gardens for the inn's gourmet dinners, and animals that have been spotted include red fox, wild turkey and white-tail deer.

Innkeeper(s): Ellen Grinsfelder & Terry Lingo. $109-269. 27 rooms, 26 with PB, 17 with FP, 15 with WP, 12 cottages, 5 cabins, 1 conference room. Breakfast, snacks/refreshments and Homemade cookies in the room on arrival included in rates. Types of meals: Full gourmet bkfst, veg bkfst, early coffee/tea, lunch, picnic lunch, wine, gourmet dinner, Picnic lunch, Cheese and fruit trays, Picnic dinner and Brown bag lunch. Restaurant on premises. Beds: KQT. Reading lamp, CD player, refrigerator, clock radio, coffeemaker, desk, hair dryer, bathrobes, wireless Internet access, iron/ironing board, whirlpool tub, cabins and cottages with gas-log stoves and ceiling fans in room. Air conditioning. Fax, copier, parlor games, telephone, fireplace, gift shop and WI-FI on premises. Handicap access. Antiquing, art galleries, bicycling, canoeing/kayaking, cross-country skiing, fishing, golf, hiking, horseback riding, live theater, museums, parks, shopping, mountain bike trails at Lake Hope State Park, 25 miles of hiking trails at surrounding Hocking Hills State Park and year-around park events nearby.

Location: Country. Surrounded on 3 sides by the Hocking Hills State Park.

Publicity: *Country Living, Ohio Magazine, Columbus Dispatch, Country, Post, Channel 4 and Ed Johnson.*

"Very peaceful, relaxing and friendly. Couldn't be nicer."

Certificate may be used: Year-round, Sunday-Thursday only, except holidays.

Mason

Kirkwood Inn

4027 US Route 42
Mason, OH
(513)398-7277 (800)732-4741
Internet: www.kirkwoodinn.com
E-mail: sandraeves@aol.com

Circa 1973. Gracing six acres, this recently renovated Colonial farmhouse and inn features a Williamsburg décor and cherry furnishings. Kirkwood Inn boasts a rich tradition of excellence steeped in history. Surrounded by the sites and major attractions of Cincinnati and Dayton, its location in Mason, Ohio is convenient. Stay in a pleasant guest bedroom or remodeled suite with a Jacuzzi and fireplace. A breakfast buffet is served daily. Experience the best of both worlds; the private intimacy of personal space yet the ambiance of this historic colonial home while dining. Swim in the outdoor pool, relax on the patios and enjoy the bountiful flower gardens and walking paths. Ask about special packages available.

Innkeeper(s): Sandra and David Eves. $59-159. 48 rooms, 1 with FP, 2 suites, 2 conference rooms. Breakfast included in rates. Types of meals: Cont plus, early coffee/tea and snacks/refreshments. Beds: KQ. Modem hook-up, data port, cable TV, DVD, reading lamp, refrigerator, clock radio, telephone, coffeemaker, desk, some with fireplace, hair dryer and bath amenities in room. Air conditioning. Fax, swimming and laundry facility on premises. Limited handicap access. Amusement parks, antiquing, art galleries, bicycling, canoeing/kayaking, fishing, golf, hiking, horseback riding, live theater, museums, parks, shopping, sporting events, tennis and wineries nearby.

Location: Country.

Certificate may be used: Valid November 1-April 1 (Sunday through Thursday), Special Rates and Discounted Rates not applicable. Promotion must be mentioned at time of reservation.

Miamisburg

English Manor B&B

505 E Linden Ave
Miamisburg, OH 45342-2850
(937)866-2288 (800)676-9456
Internet: www.englishmanorohio.com
E-mail: englishmanorohio@yahoo.com

Circa 1924. This is a beautiful English Tudor mansion situated on a tree-lined street of Victorian homes. Well-chosen antiques combined with the innkeepers'

personal heirlooms added to the inn's polished floors, sparkling leaded-and stained-glass windows and shining silver, make this an elegant retreat. Breakfast is served in the formal dining room. Fine restaurants, a water park, baseball, air force museum and theater are close by, as is The River Corridor bikeway on the banks of the Great Miami River.

Innkeeper(s): Julie & Larry Chmiel. $89-125. 5 rooms, 3 with PB, 1 total suite, including 2 two-bedroom suites, 1 conference room. Breakfast included in rates. Types of meals: Full gourmet bkfst, veg bkfst, early coffee/tea, picnic lunch, afternoon tea and dinner. Beds: KQDT. Modem hook-up, data port, reading lamp, clock radio, telephone, turn-down service, bath amenities, wireless Internet access and iron/ironing board in room. Air conditioning. TV, VCR, DVD, bicycles, library, parlor games and fireplace on premises. Amusement parks, antiquing, art galleries, beach, bicycling, canoeing/kayaking, fishing, golf, hiking, horseback riding, live theater, museums, parks, shopping, sporting events, tennis and water sports nearby.

Location: City.

Certificate may be used: Sunday-Thursday all year, upon availability.

Millersburg

Garden Gate Get-A-Way Bed & Breakfast

6041 Township Road 310
Millersburg, OH 44654-9609
(330)674-7608
Internet: www.garden-gate.com
E-mail: info@garden-gate.com

Circa 1996. Well-loved for the perennial gardens and evening campfire, Garden Gate Get-A-Way Bed & Breakfast is a romantic and peaceful retreat in Millersburg, Ohio. Roast marshmallows or enjoy an evening treat while sharing the day's adventures. Each air-conditioned guest bedroom and suite is garden-themed with luxury, five-star amenities and a private entrance along a colorful flower-lined brick path. Some rooms feature a fireplace and one boasts a Jacuzzi. A deluxe, continental breakfast includes homemade baked goods. Breakfast may include Amish Granola Bread, Sausage-Cheddar Puffs, Blueberry Streusel Coffeecake and Lemon-Raspberry Muffins, fruit, cereal, granola, oatmeal, juices, coffee, tea and hot chocolate. Onsite spa services are available.

Innkeeper(s): Herb & Carol Steffey. $105-185. 5 rooms with PB, 2 with FP, 1 suite. Breakfast, snacks/refreshments, Deluxe and continental breakfast and homemade evening snack included in rates. Types of meals: Cont plus. Beds: Q. TV, VCR, DVD, reading lamp, CD player, clock radio, coffeemaker, some with hot tub/spa, some with fireplace, hair dryer, bath amenities, Deluxe and Jacuzzi rooms have a DVD player in room. Central air. Parlor games, telephone, gift shop, evening campfire and perennial gardens on premises. Antiquing, art galleries, bicycling, fishing, golf, hiking, horseback riding, museums, parks, shopping, wineries, Amish community, Rails to Trails and Scenic Byway nearby.

Location: Country.

Certificate may be used: Reservations made 24 hours or less, prior to arrival, based upon availability. Excludes October.

Mount Vernon

Locust Grove Ranch B&B

12480 Dunham Rd.
Mount Vernon, OH 43050
(740)392-6443
Internet: www.locustgroveranch.com
E-mail: cindy@locustgroveranch.com

Circa 2000. Newly built to reflect Federal style, this ranch spans 75 rolling acres with woods and a meandering creek. Black Straight Egyptian Arabian Horses are bred here with new

arrivals each spring. An inviting ambiance is highlighted by country décor, fine antiques and warm hospitality. Read by the fireplace in the great room or play the grand piano. The library is perfect for small gatherings. Spacious guest bedrooms offer pleasant amenities and pampering touches like turndown service or breakfast in bed. Arrange an in-room massage. Breakfast is fuel for the day when served golden wheat waffles with apple pecan syrup, seasoned home fries, fresh berry bowl and cinnamon maple buns. Explore country roads by bike, go horseback riding or swim in the pool. Volleyball, horseshoes and bocce ball are popular activities as well as tractor rides.

Innkeeper(s): Cindy & Marwood Hallett. $109-149. 4 rooms with PB, 1 with FP, 1 conference room. Breakfast and snacks/refreshments included in rates. Types of meals: Full gourmet bkfst, veg bkfst, Sun. brunch, early coffee/tea, picnic lunch, afternoon tea and room service. Beds: Q. Modem hook-up, data port, reading lamp, ceiling fan, clock radio, telephone, turn-down service and fireplace in room. Central air. VCR, DVD, copier, stable, bicycles, library, parlor games, laundry facility, horse boarding, in-room massage and swimming pool on premises. Antiquing, art galleries, bicycling, canoeing/kayaking, downhill skiing, fishing, golf, hiking, horseback riding, parks, shopping, sporting events, tennis and Mid-Ohio Raceway nearby.

Location: Country. Near bike trails & Mid-Ohio Racetrack.

Publicity: *Heart of Ohio Tour.*

Certificate may be used: Anytime, subject to availability.

New Plymouth

Ravenwood Castle

65666 Bethel Rd
New Plymouth, OH 45654-9707
(740)596-2606 (800)477-1541
Internet: www.ravenwoodcastle.com
E-mail: ravenwood@hocking.net

Circa 1995. Although this is a newer construction, the architect modeled the inn after a 12th-century, Norman-style castle, offering a glimpse back at Medieval England. A Great Hall with massive stone fireplace, dramatic rooms and suites with antique stained-glass windows and gas fireplaces make for a unique getaway. The castle, which overlooks Vinton

County's Swan township, is surrounded by 100 acres of forest and large rock formations and is reached by a half-mile private road. There is a seasonal tea room and gift shop on the premises.

Innkeeper(s): Jim & Sue Maxwell. $115-235. 15 rooms with PB, 2 suites, 7 cottages. Breakfast included in rates. Types of meals: Full bkfst, early coffee/tea, picnic lunch, afternoon tea, snacks/refreshments, gourmet dinner and room service. Restaurant on premises. Beds: KQ. Ceiling fan and desk in room. Air conditioning. TV, VCR, fax, copier, parlor games, telephone and pub on premises. Handicap access. Antiquing, fishing, shopping, water sports, caves and waterfalls nearby.

Location: Forested.

Publicity: *US News, World Report, Columbus Dispatch, Cincinnati Enquirer, Midwest Living, USA Today, Honeymoon, Ohio Magazine, Milwaukee Journal Sentinel, Copley News Service, PBS-TV, Country Inn Cooking with Gail Greco and Rand McNally Road Atlas.*

"The atmosphere is romantic, the food excellent, the hospitality super!"

Certificate may be used: Nov. 1-March 31, Sunday-Thursday, except holidays and Christmas week.

Painesville

Fitzgerald's Irish B & B

47 Mentor Ave
Painesville, OH 44077-3201
(440)639-0845
Internet: www.FitzgeraldsBnB.com
E-mail: info@FitzgeraldsBnB.com

Circa 1937. Warm Irish hospitality is extended at this 1937 French Tudor home situated in the historic district. It was recently restored as a landmark of craftsmanship with its castle-like design, unusual turret, slate roof, ornate staircase, hardwood floors and elaborate 11-foot fireplace. Watch satellite TV in the sitting room, play games and relax by the fire in the large gathering room. Lounge on the sun porch overlooking the park-like grounds and frequent birds. Air-conditioned guest bedrooms include pleasing amenities. Sleep on a four-poster or sleigh bed. The third-floor Bushmills Room features a microwave, refrigerator, VCR, CD player, Jacuzzi tub and Roman shower. Savor a full breakfast on weekends and holidays and a generous continental breakfast during the week. Popular trails and beaches of the Great Lakes region are nearby.

Innkeeper(s): Debra & Tom Fitzgerald. $95-150. 5 rooms, 4 with PB. Breakfast included in rates. Types of meals: Full bkfst and early coffee/tea. Beds: Q. TV, VCR, DVD, reading lamp, CD player, ceiling fan, clock radio, telephone, coffeemaker, desk, some with hot tub/spa, hair dryer, bathrobes, bath amenities, wireless Internet access and iron/ironing board in room. Central air. Parlor games and fireplace on premises. Amusement parks, antiquing, art galleries, beach, bicycling, canoeing/kayaking, cross-country skiing, downhill skiing, fishing, golf, hiking, horseback riding, live theater, museums, parks, shopping, sporting events, tennis, water sports and wineries nearby.

Location: City.

Publicity: *New Herald, The Cleveland Plain Dealer, Midwest Irish News, Cleveland Magazine, Arrington's 2003, 2004 & 2005 Book of Lists winner of top 15 B&Bs for interior design and decor and WVIZ the Cleveland PBS station.*

Certificate may be used: Sunday-Thursday, Nov. 1-April 29, holidays excluded, for the Mayo and Dublin rooms only.

Rider's 1812 Inn

792 Mentor Ave
Painesville, OH 44077-2516
(440)354-8200 Fax:(440)350-9385
Internet: www.ridersinn.com
E-mail: ridersinninfo@yahoo.com

Innkeeper(s): Elaine Crane & Gary Herman. $85-105. 10 rooms, 9 with PB, 1 suite, 3 conference rooms. Breakfast included in rates. Types of meals: Full gourmet bkfst, veg bkfst, early coffee/tea, lunch, picnic lunch, afternoon tea, dinner and room service. Beds: KQDT. Cable TV, reading lamp, CD player, refrigerator, ceiling fan, snack bar, clock radio, telephone, turn-down service, desk and voice mail in room. Central air. Fax, copier, library, pet boarding, child care, parlor games, fireplace and laundry facility on premises. Limited handicap access. Antiquing, art galleries, beach, cross-country skiing, fishing, golf, horseback riding, live theater, museums, parks, shopping, sporting events, tennis and wineries nearby.

Location: College town, County Seat.

Publicity: *Business Review, News-Herald, Midwest Living, WEWS, Haunted Ohio V and Channel 5.*

Certificate may be used: Sunday-Friday, year round, not valid on Saturdays.

Sandusky

Wagner's 1844 Inn

230 E Washington St
Sandusky, OH 44870-2611
(419)626-1726 Fax:(419)626-0002
Internet: www.lrbcg.com/wagnersinn
E-mail: wagnersinn@sanduskyohio.com

Circa 1844. This inn originally was constructed as a log cabin. Additions and renovations were made, and the house evolved into Italianate style accented with brackets under the eaves and black shutters on the second-story windows. A wrought-iron fence frames the house, and there are ornate wrought-iron porch rails. A billiard room and screened-in porch are available to guests. The ferry to Cedar Point and Lake Erie Island is within walking distance.

Innkeeper(s): Barb Wagner. $80-100. 3 rooms with PB, 2 with FP. Breakfast included in rates. Types of meals: Cont plus. Beds: Q. Reading lamp, clock radio, desk and fireplace in room. Central air. TV, library, parlor games, tele-

phone and TV on premises. Amusement parks, antiquing, fishing, golf, hiking, museums, parks, shopping, tennis, Lake Erie Islands and golf nearby.

Location: City.

Publicity: *Lorain Journal and Sandusky Register.*

"This B&B rates in our Top 10."

Certificate may be used: Nov. 1 to April 1, Sunday-Thursday.

Stockport

Stockport Mill

1995 Broadway Ave
Stockport, OH 43787
(740)559-2822 Fax:(740)559-2236
Internet: www.stockportmill.com
E-mail: mill@stockportmill.com

Circa 1906. Stay at this century-old restored grain mill on the Muskingum River for a truly authentic historic experience combined with everything desired for a romantic getaway, business retreat or stress-free change of pace. Each of the four floors offers an assortment of common areas and accommodations. Browse the main lobby, an inviting library and the gift gallery showcasing local craftsman and artists. The Massage Therapy Room was the original grain bin. Themed guest bedrooms are named and decorated as a tribute to the local region and its prominent people. Stay in a luxurious suite with a two-person whirlpool spa and private balcony. Riverview Rooms feature clawfoot tubs, southern views of the river and private terraces. Ask about special packages and scheduling events at the Boathouse Banquet Hall.

Innkeeper(s): Dottie Singer. $65-300. 14 rooms with PB, 1 with FP, 1 with HT, 7 total suites, including 1 two-bedroom suite, 1 conference room. Types of meals: Cont, lunch, picnic lunch, snacks/refreshments, hors d'oeuvres, dinner and room service. Restaurant on premises. Beds: KQ. Cable TV, VCR, DVD, reading lamp, ceiling fan, clock radio, telephone, coffeemaker, most with hot tub/spa, some with fireplace, hair dryer, wireless Internet access, iron/ironing board and refrigerator in one suite in room. Air conditioning. Fax, copier, spa, library, parlor games, gift shop, massage therapy by appointment and boat dock on premises. Handicap access. Antiquing, bicycling, canoeing/kayaking, fishing, golf, hiking, live theater, museums, parks, shopping, sporting events, water sports, walk track, boat launching, swimming pool and bowling nearby.

Location: Country, waterfront.

Certificate may be used: Anytime, November-March, subject to availability, suites only (2nd or 3rd floor). Does not include Valentines Day or holidays.

Tiffin

Fort Ball Bed & Breakfast

25 Adams St
Tiffin, OH 44883-2208
(419)447-0776 (888)447-0776 Fax:(419)448-8415
Internet: www.fortball.com
E-mail: ftballbanb@friendlynet.com

Circa 1894. The prominent front turret and wraparound porch are classic details of this Queen Anne Revival house built by John King, builder of the Tiffin Court House and College Hall at Heidelberg College. The innkeepers dedicated more than a year restoring this turn-of-the-century Victorian to its original elegant state. The renovation yielded rich hardwood flooring, wood paneling and many additional architectural details like the elaborate woodwork in the parlor, front entryway and sitting room. Guest rooms are comfortably decorated to accommodate business travelers, families or honeymooners, and offer private and shared baths while some feature whirlpool tubs for two. Breakfast can be enjoyed in the dining room with its elegantly restored woodwork. The inn is within walking distance of the downtown business district, restaurants, antiques, shopping, museums and theater.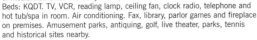

Innkeeper(s): Lenora Livingston. $65-105. 4 rooms, 2 with PB. Breakfast and snacks/refreshments included in rates. Types of meals: Full bkfst and early coffee/tea. Beds: KQDT. TV, VCR, reading lamp, ceiling fan, clock radio, telephone and hot tub/spa in room. Air conditioning. Fax, library, parlor games and fireplace on premises. Amusement parks, antiquing, golf, live theater, parks, tennis and historical sites nearby.

Location: City.

Publicity: *Advertiser-Tribune*.

Certificate may be used: Jan. 10 to Nov. 10, Sunday-Thursday, excluding holidays.

Toronto

Hilltop Haven Bed & Breakfast

228 High Haven Dr
Toronto, OH 43964-2063
(740)537-1250 (877)455-8722
Internet: www.hilltophavenbnb.com

Hilltop Haven Bed & Breakfast in Toronto, Ohio offers accommodations as comfortable as home. Leave this B&B feeling rejuvenated. Relax by the fireplace in the living room. Refreshments are accessible at any time. Stay in one of the centrally air-conditioned guest bedrooms that features antiques, a Victorian or country décor and views of the English Gardens and ponds. Ask about special packages available. The nearby area boasts two marinas with restaurants and the Newburg Landing riverside park and boat launch. Outdoor sports, festivals and historic sites are popular as well as crafts and genealogy research.

Innkeeper(s): Charles and Diana Swearingen. Call for rates. 2 rooms.

Certificate may be used: Based on availability.

Oklahoma

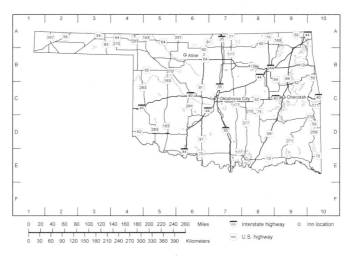

Aline

Heritage Manor

33 Heritage Road
Aline, OK 73716-9118
(580)463-2563 (800)295-2563 Fax:cell 580-541-7087
Internet: www.1aj.org
E-mail: heritage@pldi.net

Circa 1903. This inn provides a way to enjoy and experience the ambiance of the turn of the century. Explore and relax in the inn's peaceful gardens and 80-acre wildlife habitat and watch song birds, butterflies, long-haired cattle, donkeys, llamas and ostriches. The inn invites visitors to enjoy its more than 5,000-volume library and more than a 100 channels on Dish TV. Guests can walk the suspension bridge to two rooftop decks and a widow's walk to view the stars and sunsets. There is also an out-door hot tub for soaking. Dine in the parlor, gazebo, courtyard or tree-top-level deck where the choice of time and menu is entirely up to the guest.

Innkeeper(s): A.J. & Carolyn Rexroat. $55-125. 4 rooms with PB, 1 suite, 2 conference rooms. Breakfast and snacks/refreshments included in rates. Types of meals: Full gourmet bkfst, early coffee/tea, gourmet lunch, picnic lunch, afternoon tea and gourmet dinner. Beds: QD. Cable TV, VCR, DVD, reading lamp, ceiling fan, telephone, desk, wireless Internet access and iron/ironing board in room. Central air. Spa, library, parlor games and fireplace on premises. Handicap access. Antiquing, art galleries, fishing, live theater, museums, parks, shopping, sporting events, water sports and wineries nearby.

Location: Country.

Publicity: *Country, Enid Morning News, Daily Oklahoman, Cherokee Messenger/Republican, Fairview Republican and Discover Oklahoma.*

Certificate may be used: Anytime, subject to availability

Oklahoma City

The Grandison Inn at Maney Park

1200 N Shartel Ave
Oklahoma City, OK 73103-2402
(405)232-8778 (888)799-4667 Fax:(405)232-5039
Internet: www.grandisoninn.com
E-mail: grandison@coxinet.net

Circa 1904. This spacious Victorian has been graciously restored and maintains its original mahogany woodwork, stained glass, brass fixtures and a grand staircase. Several rooms include a Jacuzzi, and all have their own unique decor. The Treehouse Hideaway includes a Queen bed that is meant to look like a hammock and walls are painted with a blue sky and stars. The Jacuzzi tub rests beneath a skylight. The home is located north of downtown Oklahoma City in a historic neighborhood listed in the National Register.

Innkeeper(s): Claudia Wright. $75-200. 8 rooms with PB. Breakfast and snacks/refreshments included in rates. Types of meals: Full bkfst, early coffee/tea, room service, In-room dinners served with wine or champagne, Wine & cheese basket that includes summer sausage, cheese ball, 5-6 individual varieties of cheeses, 4 kinds of crackers, fruits and selection of gourmet cookies. Beds: KQT. Modem hook-up, cable TV, VCR, reading lamp, CD player, ceiling fan, snack bar, clock radio, telephone, desk, hot tub/spa, some with fireplace, hair dryer, bathrobes, wireless Internet access and iron/ironing board in room. Central air. Fax and copier on premises. Handicap access. Antiquing, art galleries, golf, live theater, museums, parks, shopping and sporting events nearby.

Location: City.

Publicity: *Daily Oklahoman, Oklahoma Pride, Oklahoma Gazette, Discover Oklahoma, Tulsa People Magazine, Travel & Leisure, Country Discoveries Magazine, Discover Oklahoma and Oklahoma Living.*

"Like going home to Grandma's!"

Certificate may be used: Anytime, Sunday-Thursday.

Oregon

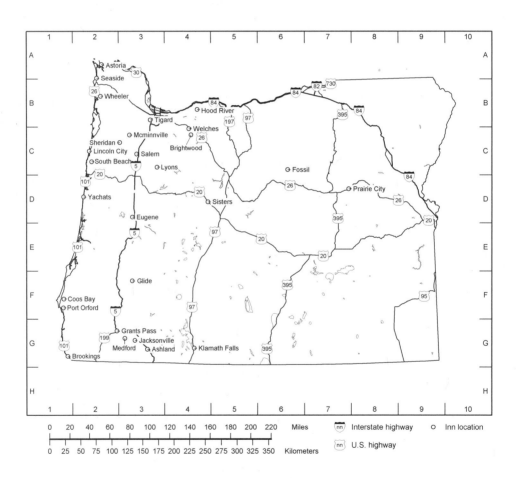

Tell the innkeeper that you have an iLoveInns free-night certificate when you make your reservation.

Astoria

Franklin Street Station Bed & Breakfast

1140 Franklin Ave
Astoria, OR 97103-4132
(503)325-4314 (800)448-1098
Internet: www.astoriaoregonbb.com
E-mail: franklinststationbb@yahoo.com

Circa 1900. Sit out on the balcony and take in views of the Columbia River and beautiful sunsets from this 1900 Victorian-style inn. Ornate craftsmanship and antique furnishings, right down to the clawfoot bathtubs, transport visitors into the past. The six guest rooms are named Starlight Suite, Sweet Tranquility, the Hide-away, the Magestic, Magnolia Retreat and Enchanted Haven. The full breakfast includes dishes like fruit, waffles and sausage. The Flavel House Museum and Heritage Museum within walking distance, and the Astoria Column and Fort Clatsop are a short drive from the inn.

Innkeeper(s): Rebecca Greenway. $80-135. 7 rooms, 5 with PB, 1 with FP, 3 suites. Breakfast included in rates. Types of meals: Full bkfst and Coffee. Beds: Q. Cable TV, VCR, reading lamp, stereo, refrigerator, clock radio, telephone, coffeemaker, fireplace, clawfoot tubs and balconies in room. Copier, library and parlor games on premises. Antiquing, art galleries, beach, fishing, golf, hiking, horseback riding, live theater, museums, parks, shopping, wineries and swimming nearby.

Location: City.

Publicity: *LA Times.*

Certificate may be used: Oct. 15-Jan. 15, Sunday-Friday.

Grandview B&B

1574 Grand Ave
Astoria, OR 97103-3733
(503)325-0000 (800)488-3250
Internet: www.pacifier.com/~grndview/
E-mail: grandviewbedandbreakfast@go.com

Circa 1896. To fully enjoy its views of the Columbia River, this Victorian house has both a tower and a turret. Antiques and white wicker furnishings contribute to the inn's casual, homey feeling. The Bird Meadow Room is particularly appealing to bird-lovers with its birdcage, bird books and bird wallpaper. Breakfast, served in the main-floor turret, frequently includes smoked salmon with bagels and cream cheese.

Innkeeper(s): Charleen Maxwell. $69-130. 10 rooms, 7 with PB, 3 with FP, 2 suites. Breakfast and snacks/refreshments included in rates. Types of meals: Full bkfst. Beds: QT. Parlor games, telephone and fireplace on premises. Antiquing, fishing, live theater, parks, shopping, water sports, historic homes tour, old-fashioned trolley, river walk, aqua center, movie complex and forts nearby.

Location: City.

Publicity: *Pacific Northwest Magazine, Northwest Discoveries, Los Angeles Times, Oregonian and Daily Astorian.*

"I have travelled all over the world and for the first time I found in the country of the computers such a romantic house with such poetic rooms at the Grandview Bed & Breakfast. Thanks, MD from Paris, France."

Certificate may be used: Nov. 1-May 17, holidays okay except two weekends in February may be excluded.

Brookings

South Coast Inn B&B

516 Redwood St
Brookings, OR 97415-9672
(541)469-5557 (800)525-9273 Fax:(541)469-6615
Internet: www.southcoastinn.com
E-mail: innkeeper@southcoastinn.com

Circa 1917. Enjoy panoramic views of the Pacific Ocean at this Craftsman-style inn designed by renowned San Francisco architect Bernard Maybeck. All rooms are furnished with antiques, ceiling fans, CD player, VCRs and TVs. Two guest rooms afford panoramic views of the coastline and there is a separate cottage. A floor-to-ceiling stone fireplace and beamed ceilings make the parlor a great place to gather with friends. There are sun decks and a strolling garden. The Brookings area offers something for everyone. Outdoor activities include hiking, boating, golfing, digging for clams or simply enjoying a stroll along the spectacular coastline. Concerts, galleries, museums, antiques, specialty shops and fine restaurants all can be found within the area.

Innkeeper(s): Michael Clines. $99-159. 6 rooms, 4 with PB, 1 with FP, 2 cottages. Breakfast included in rates. Types of meals: Full gourmet bkfst and early coffee/tea. Beds: KQ. Cable TV, VCR, reading lamp, ceiling fan, clock radio, desk, some with fireplace, hair dryer, bathrobes, hair dryers in baths and 1 with gas fireplace/stove in room. Fax, copier, library, parlor games, telephone, gift shop and continental breakfast in cottage on premises. Antiquing, fishing, live theater, parks, shopping, water sports, Brookings-Harbor area: Flora Pacifica, Harris Beach State Park, Azalea Park, Brandy Peak Distillery, charter fishing, whale watching and Harbor/Chetco Village nearby.

Location: City, ocean community.

"Thank you for your special brand of magic. What a place!"

Certificate may be used: November-April, except holidays.

Coos Bay

Old Tower House Bed & Breakfast

476 Newmark Ave
Coos Bay, OR 97420-3201
(541)888-6058
Internet: www.oldtowerhouse.com
E-mail: oldtowerhouse@yahoo.com

Fully restored and listed in the National Register, Old Tower House Bed & Breakfast offers a delightful setting to relax and enjoy the Oregon coast. Located just a few yards from the ocean in Coos Bay, there are many beaches to explore as well as other activities and attractions. Visit Shore Acres Park and play on one of the top-rated Bandon Dunes golf courses. Browse through the movie collection in the enclosed sun porch. Stay in a guest bedroom in the main house or enjoy the spacious privacy in Ivy Cottage, the original carriage house and tack room. It features a sitting room, microwave and clawfoot tub. A continental breakfast is provided in the formal dining room of the main house or on the sunny veranda.

Innkeeper(s): Stephanie Kramer. Call for rates. Call inn for details. Breakfast and Continental Breakfast included in rate. A gourmet breakfast is offered for an additional $8.50 per person included in rates. Types of meals: Full gourmet bkfst. Cable TV, VCR, reading lamp, refrigerator, clock radio, coffeemaker, hair dryer, bathrobes, bath amenities and wireless Internet access in room. DVD, fax, telephone and fireplace on premises. Antiquing, beach, fishing, golf, hiking, horseback riding, museums, parks and shopping nearby.

Location: Waterfront.

Certificate may be used: December through April, Monday through Thursday, except holidays.

Fossil

Wilson Ranches Retreat Bed and Breakfast

16555 Butte Creek Rd
Fossil, OR 97830
(541)763-2227 (888)968-7698 Fax:(541)763-2719
Internet: www.wilsonranchesretreat.com
E-mail: npwilson@wilsonranchesretreat.com

Circa 1910. Amidst wide open spaces off a quiet country road in North Central Oregon, the Wilson Ranches Retreat Bed and Breakfast in Fossil is a 9,000-acre working cattle and hay ranch. Scenic and secluded, the retreat was designed for comfort and relief from stress. It sits in Butte Creek Valley in the John Day Basin surrounded by the Cascade Mountain Range. Bird watch from the large deck or relax in the living room Called the "best rest in Wheeler County," western-themed guest bedrooms are on the main floor and upstairs as well as two spacious accommodations in the daylight basement that are perfect for families. Hunger disappears after a hearty cowboy breakfast served on the hand-crafted 11-foot knotty pine dining room table. Experience cattle drives, horseback rides, hikes, and four-wheel drive ranch tours.

Innkeeper(s): Phil & Nancy Wilson. $65-85. 7 rooms, 2 with PB, 1 with FP, 1 conference room. Breakfast included in rates. Types of meals: Country bkfst and early coffee/tea. Beds: KQDT. TV, VCR, reading lamp, some with fireplace, hair dryer, bathrobes, bath amenities, iron/ironing board and Microwave in room. Air conditioning. Fax, copier, stable, parlor games and telephone on premises. Limited handicap access. Bicycling, canoeing/kayaking, fishing, golf, hiking, horseback riding, live theater, museums, parks, shopping and tennis nearby.

Location: Country. Ranch.

Certificate may be used: January and February, Monday through Thursday.

Glide

Steelhead Run Bed & Breakfast

23049 N Umpqua Hwy., Scenic Byway 138
Glide, OR 97443-9742
(541)496-0563 (800)348-0563 Fax:(541)496-3200
Internet: www.steelheadrun.com
E-mail: steelhead@steelheadrun.com

Poised on a cliff at the edge of the wild North Umpqua River in Glide, Oregon, Steelhead Run Bed and Breakfast sits on five acres with rolling hills and waterfalls. Play billiards in the game room, watch movies in the theater room or sit by the stone fireplace in the library/parlor. A porch swing and a gazebo invite relaxation. Accommodations include theme-decorated guest bedrooms and three-bedroom family/kitchen apartment suites. Linger over a hearty country buffet breakfast before browsing the fine art gallery, gift store or custom frame shop. Take a refreshing dip in the swimming hole or cast a line in the fishing spot. Enjoy a wide assortment of indoor and outdoor activities.

Innkeeper(s): Nancy & George Acosta. Call for rates. 6 rooms with PB, 3 total suites, including 2 two-bedroom suites, 1 three-bedroom suite and 1 four-bedroom suite, 1 guest house. Breakfast, Early riser large continental breakfast for the fishermen and etc. that want to start their day before the large country buffet breakfast time included in rates. Types of meals: Country bkfst, Can fix special breakfast for vegetarian, diabetics and etc. if they make arrangements in advance. Beds: KQDT. Modem hook-up, TV, VCR, reading lamp, refrigerator, ceiling fan, telephone, coffeemaker, hair dryer, the suites are apartments with private bedroom, family-kitchen-dining rooms, private bathrooms, complete with dishes, stoves, microwaves, toaster and refrigerators in room. Central air. DVD, fax, copier, swimming, library, parlor games,

fireplace, laundry facility, gift shop, Beach and swimming hole on river, fFshing, Gazebo and picnic areas, Fenced playground, Horseshoes, Badminton, Croquet, Foosball, Ping pong, Large game room with billiard table and large screen satellite TV, VHS and DVD, Lots of videos at no charge for guest use, A special apartment with a fenced yard for pet, Barbecues, Access to launch canoes and Rafts in river on premises. Limited handicap access. Antiquing, art galleries, beach, bicycling, canoeing/kayaking, fishing, golf, hiking, live theater, museums, parks, shopping, water sports, wineries, 23 waterfalls in area, fish hatchery, fishing areas, Colliding Rivers, a geographical wonder and historic Native American encampment tourist viewpoint, Tokatee hot springs, County fair grounds, state parks, Little River, Rock Creek River, several other small rivers, Diamond Lake (50 miles) and Crater Lake National Park in Oregon (70 miles) nearby.

Certificate may be used: Jan. 1 through May 15, Oct.15 through Dec. 31 (not available May 16 through Oct.14) No Holidays and not good with any other discounts.

Hood River

Columbia Gorge Hotel

4000 Westcliff Dr
Hood River, OR 97031-9799
(541)386-5566 (800)345-1921 Fax:(541)386-9141
Internet: www.columbiagorgehotel.com
E-mail: cghotel@gorge.net

Circa 1921. This posh hotel is a gem among gems in the National Register of Historic Places. Idyllic guest quarters offer such ornate furnishings as a hand-carved canopy bed that once graced a French castle. The beautifully landscaped grounds, champagne and caviar social hour, turndown service with rose, outdoor river-view dining terrace and a gourmet restaurant are favorite amenities. Last, but not least, are spectacular views of the majestic Columbia River. Guests are treated to the opulent "World Famous Farm Breakfast." The hotel is close to ski areas, golfing and popular windsurfing spots. Pets are welcome!

Innkeeper(s): Boyd & Halla Graves. $189-350. 40 rooms with PB, 2 with FP, 3 conference rooms. Breakfast included in rates. Types of meals: Full bkfst, early coffee/tea, lunch, picnic lunch, afternoon tea, gourmet dinner and room service. Restaurant on premises. Beds: KQD. Cable TV, reading lamp, telephone and turn-down service in room. VCR, fax, copier and fireplace on premises. Antiquing, cross-country skiing, downhill skiing, fishing, live theater, parks, shopping, water sports and windsurfing nearby.

Location: Columbia Gorge, Hood River.

Certificate may be used: Anytime, November-March, excluding holidays, subject to availability.

Jacksonville

Historic Orth House B&B

105 W Main St.
Jacksonville, OR 97530
(541)899-8665 (800)700-7301
Internet: www.orthbnb.com
E-mail: orthbnb@orthbnb.com

Circa 1880. Surrounded by a white picket fence and a half acre of landscaped grounds, this historic, two-story brick Italianate home was built during the Gold Rush and is now listed in the National Register. Large guest bedrooms feature period furnishings and claw-foot tubs. After a satisfying breakfast, stroll among the blooming flower gardens.

Innkeeper(s): Lee & Marilyn Lewis.

$125-250. 4 rooms, 3 with PB, 1 two-bedroom suite. Breakfast included in rates. Types of meals: Cont plus and early coffee/tea. Beds: KQT. Reading lamp, CD player, ceiling fan and clock radio in room. Air conditioning. TV, VCR, fax, copier, telephone and Wireless Internet on premises. Antiquing, art galleries, downhill skiing, fishing, golf, live theater, museums, parks, shopping, wineries, Britt Music Festival and Ashland Shakespeare Festival nearby.

Location: City, mountains. City/Rural.

Publicity: *American Profile, Country Discoveries, Sunset Magazine, AAA Via Magazine and Lippert's Carpet Commercials.*

Certificate may be used: November-April, subject to availability.

TouVelle House

455 N Oregon St
Jacksonville, OR 97530-1891
(541)899-8938 (800)846-8422
Internet: www.touvellehouse.com
E-mail: info@touvellehouse.com

Circa 1916. This Craftsman inn is two blocks away from the main street of this old Gold Rush town. The common areas of this Craftsman inn include The Library, which has a TV and VCR; The Great Room, featuring a large-stoned fireplace; The Sunroom, which consists of many windows; and The Dining Room, featuring an intricate built-in buffet. Guests can relax on either of two spacious covered verandas.

Innkeeper(s): Gary Renninger Balfour/Tim Balfour. $149-170. 6 rooms with PB, 1 suite. Breakfast included in rates. Types of meals: Full gourmet bkfst, veg bkfst, early coffee/tea and snacks/refreshments. Beds: KQT. Reading lamp, CD player, clock radio, hair dryer, bathrobes, bath amenities and wireless Internet access in room. Central air. TV, VCR, DVD, swimming, sauna, library, parlor games, telephone and fireplace on premises. Antiquing, art galleries, bicycling, cross-country skiing, downhill skiing, fishing, golf, hiking, horseback riding, live theater, museums, parks, tennis, water sports, wineries, Britt Festival and Oregon Shakespeare Festival nearby.

"The accommodations are beautiful, the atmosphere superb, the breakfast and other goodies delightful, but it is the warmth and caring of the host that will make the difference in this B&B!! "

Certificate may be used: October-May, subject to availability, except holidays.

Klamath Falls

Thompsons' B&B

1420 Wild Plum Ct
Klamath Falls, OR 97601-1983
(541)882-7938 Fax:541-882-7939
Internet: www.thompsonsbandb.com
E-mail: thompsonbandb@charter.net

Circa 1987. The huge picture windows in this comfortable retreat look out to a spectacular view of Klamath Lake and nearby mountains. Innkeeper Mary Pohll has a collection of dolls and clowns. Popular Moore Park is next door, providing a day of hiking, picnicking or relaxing at the marina. The inn is a perfect site to just relax and enjoy the view. Bird watching is a must, as the inn is home to pelicans, snow geese, bald eagles and many varieties of wild ducks.

Innkeeper(s): Mary & Bill Pohll. $95-105. 4 rooms with PB. Breakfast, snacks/refreshments and wine included in rates. Types of meals: Full bkfst, veg bkfst and early coffee/tea. Beds: K. Cable TV, reading lamp, refrigerator, clock radio, telephone and desk in room. Air conditioning. TV, fax, copier, library, parlor games and laundry facility on premises. Antiquing, bicycling, canoeing/kayaking, fishing, golf, hiking, horseback riding, live theater, museums, parks, shopping, tennis and water sports nearby.

Location: City, mountains.

"Hospitality as glorious as your surroundings."

Certificate may be used: Anytime November-April, subject to availability.

Lincoln City

Brey House

3725 NW Keel Ave
Lincoln City, OR 97367
(541)994-7123
Internet: www.breyhouse.com
E-mail: sbrey@wcn.net

Circa 1941. The innkeepers at this three-story, Cape Cod-style house claim that when you stay with them it's like staying with Aunt Shirley and Uncle Milt. Guest rooms include some with ocean views and private entrances, and the Deluxe Suite offers a living room with fireplace, two baths and a kitchen. The Admiral's Room on the third floor has knotty pine walls, a skylight, fireplace and the best view.

Innkeeper(s): Milt & Shirley Brey. $90-160. 4 rooms with PB, 3 with FP, 2 suites. Breakfast included in rates. Types of meals: Full gourmet bkfst and early coffee/tea. Beds: KQ. Cable TV, VCR, reading lamp, refrigerator, ceiling fan, clock radio, desk and hot tub/spa in room. Parlor games, telephone and fireplace on premises. Antiquing, fishing, golf, live theater, parks, shopping, tennis, water sports and Indian casino nearby.

Location: City, ocean community.

Certificate may be used: September-June, Sunday-Friday. No Saturdays, no holiday weekends.

Coast Inn B&B

4507 SW Coast Ave
Lincoln City, OR 97367
(541)994-7932 (888)994-7932 Fax:(541)994-7935
Internet: www.oregoncoastinn.com
E-mail: coastinn@oregoncoastinn.com

Circa 1939. A short walk from Siletz Bay with its herd of seals, this 4,000-square-foot house is 300 feet from the beach. A serene decor and mission-style furnishings provide a comfortable area to read a good book from the B&Bs library. Enjoy the sights and sounds of the Pacific from a window-wrapped botanical sunroom and deck. Writing journals are placed in the light and airy guest bedrooms and suites featuring luxury beds with down comforters, plush robes and a small refrigerator stocked with bottled water and fruit drinks. One romantic suite's amenities include a gas fireplace, microwave, flat screen TV with DVD and a vintage bathtub. Healthy gourmet breakfasts with fresh Oregon berries and peaches are served in the dining room, accented with vibrant art quilt designs. Small pets are allowed in one room with prior arrangement.

Innkeeper(s): Rosie Huntemann. $100-180. 4 rooms with PB, 1 with FP, 2 suites. Breakfast and snacks/refreshments included in rates. Types of meals: Full gourmet bkfst, early coffee/tea, gourmet dinner and room service. Beds: Q. Cable TV, refrigerator, one bathtub and some with microwaves in room. TV, VCR, fax, copier, library and Internet access on premises. Antiquing, fishing, golf, live theater, parks, tennis, water sports, Oregon Coast Aquarium, factory outlet shopping, beachcombing, whale watching and lighthouses nearby.

Location: Ocean community.

Publicity: *Oregonian & L C Newsguard.*

Certificate may be used: October through April, Sunday-Friday; May through September, Sunday-Thursday, no holidays.

Lyons

Elkhorn Valley Inn B & B

33016 N Fork Rd Se
Lyons, OR 97358-9743
(503)897-3033
Internet: www.elkhornvalleyinnbedandbreakfast.com
E-mail: elkhornvalleyinn@wvi.com

Amid the natural setting of the Opal Creek Wilderness in
Lyons, Oregon, Elkhorn Valley Inn Bed and Breakfast is romantic and relaxing. Porches overlook the lush national forest. A
heated spring-fed spa sits under a blanket of stars by night and
offers breathtaking mountain views during the day. The video
and book library provides indoor entertainment. Lavish guest
bedrooms feature antiques and pampering details. Some rooms
have a fireplace, patio or deck. Rene's Cottage boasts a living
room, kitchenette, two-person spa and clawfoot tub. Enjoy a
bountiful breakfast al fresco in the gazebo or in the warm country kitchen. Three-Pool Park is nearby or hike Trail of Ten Falls
at Silver Falls State Park. Breitenbush River and Hot Springs is
less than one hour away.

Call for rates. 5 rooms with PB, 1 cottage.

Certificate may be used: September to May, all holidays and weekends excluded.

McMinnville

Baker Street B&B

129 SE Baker St
McMinnville, OR 97128-6035
(503)472-5575 (800)870-5575
Internet: www.bakerstreetinn.com
E-mail: cheryl@bakerstreetinn.com

Circa 1914. Restored to its natural beauty, this Craftsman inn
offers three guest bedrooms all year-round. The décor includes
vintage Victorian memorabilia, antiques and a clawfoot or jetted
tub. Le Petite Chateau is a renovated, private two-bedroom cottage with tub/shower bath combination, living room, kitchen
and laundry facilities which is perfect for longer stays or couples traveling together. Situated in the heart of wine country,
gourmet restaurants and wineries are nearby. Visit Salem,
Portland and the coast, just one hour away.

Innkeeper(s): Cheryl Hockaday. $109-159. 4 rooms, 3 with PB, 1 with WP,
1 cottage. Breakfast included in rates. Types of meals: Full bkfst. Beds: KQT.
Cable TV, VCR, reading lamp, refrigerator, ceiling fan, clock radio, coffeemaker, hair dryer, bathrobes, bath amenities, wireless Internet access and
iron/ironing board in room. Central air. Telephone and laundry facility on
premises. Antiquing, art galleries, golf, live theater, museums, parks, shopping, wineries and restaurants nearby.

Location: Small town.

Certificate may be used: February-April, Sunday-Wednesday, excluding
Holidays and regional events.

Medford

Under The Greenwood Tree

3045 Bellinger Ln
Medford, OR 97501-9503
(541)776-0000 Fax:(541)776-0000
Internet: www.greenwoodtree.com
E-mail: utgtree@qwest.net

Circa 1862. Pleasurable luxuries and gracious hospitality are
the hallmarks of this romantic country inn. Ten acres of serene,
idyllic grounds are accented with hand-hewn, hand-pegged
Civil War-era buildings. Professionally decorated guest bedrooms offer amenities such as soft robes, triple sheeting with
fine ironed linens, turndown service with chocolate truffles,
fresh flowers and other pampering treats that surpass expectations. Rely on famous three-course gourmet country breakfasts
made with the freshest ingredients that include herbs, seasonal
fruit and vegetables from the garden. Relax on hammocks and
lounge chairs amongst flower gardens in the shade of 300-year-
old trees before afternoon tea with treats. A furnished porch
and deck provides more enjoyment, or explore the pond and
honeysuckle/rose gazebo.

Innkeeper(s): Joseph & Barbara Lilley. $115-140. 4 rooms with PB.
Breakfast, afternoon tea and snacks/refreshments included in rates. Types of
meals: Full gourmet bkfst, veg bkfst and early coffee/tea. Beds: QD. Reading
lamp, clock radio, telephone, turn-down service, hair dryer, bathrobes and
bath amenities in room. Air conditioning. Fax, copier, bicycles, library and
parlor games on premises. Antiquing, art galleries, bicycling, canoeing/kayak-
ing, cross-country skiing, downhill skiing, fishing, golf, hiking, horseback riding, live theater, museums, parks, shopping, sporting events, tennis, water
sports and wineries nearby.

Location: Country. Farmland.

Publicity: *Sunset Magazine, Romantic Homes and the barn has been seen in
several movies.*

Certificate may be used: October through May based on availability.

Port Orford

WildSpring Guest Habitat

92978 Cemetery Loop
Port Orford, OR 97465
(541)332-0977 (866)333WILD Fax:(775)542-1447
Internet: www.wildspring.com
E-mail: info@wildspring.com

Circa 2004. A peaceful feast for the senses, this intimate boutique resort in Port Orford, on the Oregon coast overlooks the
Pacific Ocean and sits on five acres of Native American grounds
with a second-growth forest, a walking labyrinth and flower gardens. Soak in the open-air slate spa and relax with refreshments
in the Great Hall that has floor-to-ceiling panoramic views.
Natural cedar shingle cottages feature luxury cabin suites with
refrigerators stocked with bottled water. Start each day with a
generous extended continental breakfast buffet. Bikes are available for exploring the scenic area. WildSpring Guest Habitat is
only 60 miles north of California. Ask about the assortment of
themed weekends and special retreats held here.

Innkeeper(s): Dean & Michelle Duarte. $189-259. 5 cottages, 1 conference
room. Breakfast, snacks/refreshments, Help-yourself coffee, teas, hot chocolate, fruit, juices and popcorn and chocolate kisses at any time included in
rates. Types of meals: Cont plus, early coffee/tea and wine. Beds: Q. TV, VCR,
reading lamp, stereo, refrigerator, clock radio, desk, hair dryer, bath amenities,
wireless Internet access, Wine glasses, Corkscrew, Candles, Lighter, Sewing
kit, Hiking guide, Chenille throws, Complimentary bottled water and Spa robes

in room. Fax, copier, spa, bicycles, library, telephone and gift shop on premises. Handicap access. Antiquing, art galleries, beach, bicycling, canoeing/kayaking, fishing, golf, hiking, horseback riding, shopping, tennis, water sports, Wildlife Petting Zoo, Wind surfing and Kite boarding nearby.

Location: Ocean community.

Publicity: *Sunset Magazine, The Week, Portland Monthly, The Oregonian, Oregon Coast Magazine, Natural Awakenings Magazine, The Eugene Register Guard and NPR.*

Certificate may be used: December-April, Monday-Thursday, subject to availability, holiday periods excluded.

Salem

A Creekside Garden Inn

333 Wyatt Ct NE
Salem, OR 97301-4269
(503)391-0837
Internet: www.salembandb.com
E-mail: rickiemh@open.org

Circa 1938. Each room in this Mt. Vernon Colonial replica of George Washington's house has a garden theme. Consider the Picket Fences room. This gracious view room features a fireplace, Queen-size plus daybed, antique toys and a private bath.

The four other upstairs guest rooms offer similar themes. The extensive gardens offer guests an opportunity to stroll along historic Mill Creek or enjoy a round of croquet in the spacious backyard, weather permitting. Hazelnut waffles, confetti hash and oatmeal custard are a few of the breakfast specialties. The inn is just two blocks from the Court-Chemeketa Historic District.

Innkeeper(s): Ms. Rickie Hart. $75-105. 5 rooms, 3 with PB, 1 with FP. Breakfast and snacks/refreshments included in rates. Types of meals: Full gourmet bkfst and early coffee/tea. Beds: QT. Data port, reading lamp and desk in room. VCR, parlor games, telephone and fireplace on premises. Amusement parks, antiquing, golf, live theater, parks, shopping, sporting events, wine country tours and wineries nearby.

Location: City.

Publicity: *Statesman Journal, Sunset, The Oregonian, The Christian Science Monitor and Carlton Food Network (United Kingdom).*

"We all agreed that you were the best hostess yet for one of our weekends!"

Certificate may be used: Nov. 15 to May 1, no holidays.

South Beach

Stone Crest Cellar B&B

9556 South Coast Hwy.
South Beach, OR 97366
(541)867-6621 Fax:(541)867-6622
Internet: www.stonecrestbb.com
E-mail: jjoubert@stonecrestbb.com

Circa 2003. Poised on the edge of the Pacific Ocean, Stone Crest Cellar Bed and Breakfast is just minutes from the town of Newport in South Beach, Oregon. This log and rustic stone B&B features a great room with a 30-foot pine ceiling, an incredible view and a stone fireplace. Relax in the gardens or on waterfront decks. The Joubert family pays close attention to detail and offers a delightful hospitality that is comfortably

informal. Wine and appetizers are served in the late afternoon. Enjoy tea with a sweet treat in the evening. Stay in the first-floor Vineyard Room or the Chardonnay Suite on the second floor. The Shorepine Beach Crest vista from the dining room accents a gourmet breakfast. Spa services can be arranged.

Innkeeper(s): Judy Joubert. $125-165. 2 rooms with PB, 1 suite. Breakfast, hors d'oeuvres and wine included in rates. Types of meals: Full bkfst, veg bkfst, early coffee/tea and afternoon tea. Beds: Q. Cable TV, VCR, reading lamp, clock radio, hair dryer, bathrobes, bath amenities, wireless Internet access and iron/ironing board in room. DVD, fax, library, parlor games, telephone and fireplace on premises. Limited handicap access. Antiquing, art galleries, beach, canoeing/kayaking, fishing, golf, hiking, horseback riding, live theater, museums, parks, shopping, water sports, wineries and Aquarium nearby.

Location: Ocean community.

Certificate may be used: November-April, not valid on holidays and special events, subject to availability.

Wheeler

Old Wheeler Hotel

495 Highway 101 N
Wheeler, OR 97147-0555
(503)368-6000 Fax:(503)368-4590
Internet: www.oldwheelerhotel.com
E-mail: info@oldwheelerhotel.com

Circa 1920. Lovingly restored, this historic downtown refuge boasts stunning views of Nehalem Bay. Feel rejuvenated by the tranquil, non-smoking setting. Relax in the piano lobby or sitting areas. Stay in a guest bedroom or suite with a Jacuzzi or antique tub and fragrant Essential Oils bath amenities, DVD player with an extensive collection, WIFI access and a morning paper delivered to the door. Enjoy a continental breakfast in the common room. Schedule a massage with Janet, the resident licensed therapist. Soak up the incredibly stunning landscape with blue heron, eagles and elk. The local shops, museums and restaurants are within an easy walk.

Innkeeper(s): Winston Laszlo & Maranne Doyle-Laszlo. $60-135. 7 rooms with PB, 3 with WP, 3 two-bedroom and 1 three-bedroom suites. Breakfast and snacks/refreshments included in rates. Types of meals: Cont plus, veg bkfst and early coffee/tea. Beds: KQ. Cable TV, DVD, reading lamp, CD player, ceiling fan, clock radio, some with hot tub/spa, bathrobes, bath amenities, wireless Internet access, Essential oils bath amenities, Daily paper (The Oregonian) and Sound-proof windows in room. Air conditioning. Fax, copier, library, parlor games, telephone, gift shop, Free DVD movies, Iron & ironing board, Hair dryer, Free Wi-FI in common areas, Toaster, Microwave, Fridge and Dishware for guest use on premises. Antiquing, art galleries, beach, bicycling, canoeing/kayaking, fishing, golf, hiking, horseback riding, parks, shopping, water sports, wineries, motor boat rentals and scenic train excursions nearby.

Location: Waterfront. Small town.

Certificate may be used: October through June week nights only. Excludes Fridays, Saturdays, and holiday eves.

Pennsylvania

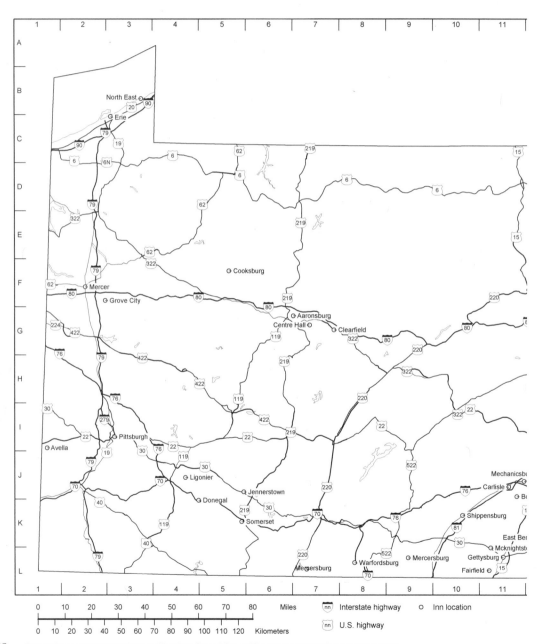

0 10 20 30 40 50 60 70 80   Miles

0 10 20 30 40 50 60 70 80 90 100 110 120   Kilometers

nn Interstate highway   o Inn location

nn U.S. highway

Tell the innkeeper that you have an iLoveInns free-night certificate when you make your reservation.

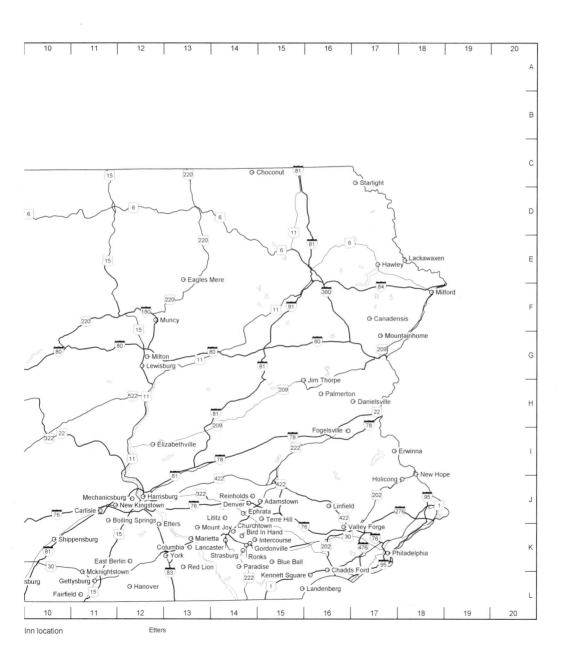

Inn location   Etters

Aaronsburg

Aaronsburg Inn

100 E Aaron Sq
Aaronsburg, PA 16820
(814)349-8626
Internet: www.aaronsburginn.com
E-mail: innkeeper@aaronsburginn.com

Casual and understated with an elegant flair, Aaronsburg Inn and Spa is a boutique country inn with a destination and day spa. Built in 1802 in the Federal style, this inn graces the national historic district in the village of Aaronsburg near State College, Pennsylvania. Experience a restful retreat while receiving excellent service with exquisite detail. Relax by the pool or on a terrace overlooking the gardens. Stay in a luxury guest bedroom with museum-quality antiques, European bedding on cherry canopy beds, period wallpaper and fresh-cut flowers. Several rooms boast fireplaces and two rooms can be adjoined as a spacious suite. Start each day with a bountiful breakfast. Business amenities make work-related activities a pleasure in this environment.

Innkeeper(s): Elizabeth and Ned Irish. Call for rates. Call inn for details.
Certificate may be used: Anytime, subject to availability.

Adamstown

Adamstown Inn

144 W Main St
Adamstown, PA 19501
(717)484-0800 (800)594-4808
Internet: www.adamstown.com
E-mail: stay@adamstown.com

Circa 1830. This restored Victorian with its 1850s pump organ found in the large parlor and other local antiques, fits right into this community known as one of the antique capitals of America (3,000 antique dealers). Other decorations include family heirlooms, Victorian wallpaper, handmade quilts and lace curtains. For outlet mall fans, Adamstown is 10 miles from Reading, which offers a vast assortment of top-quality merchandise.

Innkeeper(s): Kristin Rathman. $79-199. 10 rooms with PB, 8 with FP, 8 with WP, 2 suites, 3 cottages, 1 cabin. Breakfast, afternoon tea and snacks/refreshments included in rates. Types of meals: Cont plus, early coffee/tea and picnic lunch. Beds: KQDT. Cable TV, DVD, reading lamp, CD player, ceiling fan, clock radio, desk, hot tub/spa, hair dryer, bathrobes, bath amenities and wireless Internet access in room. Air conditioning. VCR, copier, spa, library, child care, parlor games, telephone, fireplace and laundry facility on premises. Amusement parks, antiquing, art galleries, bicycling, fishing, golf, hiking, live theater, museums, parks, shopping and wineries nearby.

Location: Lancaster County's Amish Country.

Publicity: *Country Victorian, Lancaster Intelligencer, Reading Eagle, Travel & Leisure, Country Almanac, Lancaster Magazine and Chester County Magazine.*

"Your warm hospitality and lovely home left us with such pleasant memories."

Certificate may be used: Nov. 1-April 15, Sunday through Thursday.

Barnyard Inn B&B and Carriage House

P. O. Box 273
Adamstown, PA 19501
(717)484-1111 (888)738-6624 Fax:(717)484-6100
Internet: www.barnyardinn.com
E-mail: pam@barnyardinn.com

Overlooking the countryside on two-and-a-half wooded acres, this restored German schoolhouse is furnished with family heirlooms and antiques. The huge living room is accented with a corner fireplace and carved wooden mantle. French doors lead to the elegant dining room boasting a crystal chandelier. Well-appointed guest bedrooms and a suite are named after the barnyard of animals found in the mobile petting zoo behind the inn. The Carriage House is a more private and spacious three-room suite with an equipped kitchen.

Innkeeper(s): Pam & Jerry Pozniak. Call for rates. Call inn for details. Breakfast and snacks/refreshments included in rates. Types of meals: Full gourmet bkfst, veg bkfst, early coffee/tea and afternoon tea. Beds: QDT. Cable TV, reading lamp, refrigerator, ceiling fan, clock radio and some with fireplace in room. Central air. TV, fax, copier, parlor games, telephone and gift shop on premises. Amusement parks, antiquing, golf, hiking, live theater, museums, parks, shopping, tennis, wineries, Pennsylvania Dutch attractions and dinner in an Amish home nearby.

Location: Country.

Publicity: *Reading Eagle Newspaper, Lancaster Intelligencer Journal Newspaper, Country Extra Magazine (publishers of Taste of Home magazine) and Arrington's 2004 Book of Lists (Top 15 B&Bs/Inns in North America for "Best Antiques").*

Certificate may be used: Nov. 15 through March 15, Sunday through Thursday, excluding holidays and special events.

Avella

Weatherbury Farm Vacation

1061 Sugar Run Rd
Avella, PA 15312-2434
(724)587-3763 Fax:(724)587-0125
Internet: www.weatherburyfarm.com
E-mail: info@weatherburyfarm.com

Visit Weatherbury Farm Vacation Bed and Breakfast in Avella, Pennsylvania for a kid-friendly family farm stay any time of the year. Built in the 1870s, this working beef and sheep farm with a blacksmith shop is surrounded by country gardens and is just 45 miles southwest of Pittsburgh. Play croquet on the lawn, relax on the porch swing or swim in the pool. Air-conditioned guest bedrooms and suites are located in a cluster of restored historic buildings that include the livery, summer kitchen and farmhouse. After a hearty breakfast everyone interested can assist with morning chores. Help feed rabbits, goats, sheep, chicks and gather eggs from the guinea hens. Kids of all ages can participate in the Official Weatherbury Farm Kids Program and receive a certificate.

Innkeeper(s): Dale, Marcy & Nigel Tudor. $81-169. 2 rooms with PB, 3 suites. Breakfast included in rates. Types of meals: Full bkfst and early coffee/tea. Beds: KQDT. Reading lamp, refrigerator, ceiling fan and bath amenities in room. Air conditioning. VCR, fax, copier, swimming, library, parlor games, telephone, fireplace, Farm Kids Program and Farm Chores on premises. Antiquing, bicycling, fishing, golf, hiking, horseback riding, museums, parks and wineries nearby.

Location: Country.

Publicity: *The New York Times, Pittsburgh Magazine, Arthur Frommer Budget Travel, Parents Magazine, Family Fun, Baltimore Sun, Pittsburgh Post Gazette, Allentown Morning Call, Pittsburgh Business Times, Tribune Review, International Living, Nation's Business. and KDKA.*

"Your home and your hospitality was awesome."
Certificate may be used: January and February excluding holidays, subject to availability.

Bird in Hand

Mill Creek Homestead B&B

2578 Old Philadelphia Pike
Bird in Hand, PA 17505-9796
(717)291-6419 (800)771-2578 Fax:(717)291-2171
Internet: www.millcreekhomestead.com
E-mail: millcreekbnb@hotmail.com

Circa 1793. This 18th-century fieldstone farmhouse is one of the oldest homes in Bird-in-the-Hand. Located in the Pennsylvania Dutch Heartland, the inn is decorated for comfort with Amish influences represented throughout. There are four guest rooms with private baths and fireplaces or stoves. Guests are invited to lounge by the outdoor pool or sit on the porch and watch the horse-drawn buggies go by. A full breakfast is served in the formal dining room, while afternoon refreshments are in the common rooms. The inn is within walking distance of shops, museums, farmers market, antiques and crafts.

Innkeeper(s): Vicki & Frank Alfone. $114-195. 4 rooms with PB, 4 with FP. Breakfast, afternoon tea and snacks/refreshments included in rates. Types of meals: Full bkfst and early coffee/tea. Beds: QT. Reading lamp, stereo, ceiling fan, clock radio, turn-down service, some with hot tub/spa, fireplace, hair dryer, bathrobes, bath amenities, wireless Internet access, robes and hair dryers in room. Central air. TV, VCR, spa, swimming, library, parlor games, telephone and gift shop on premises. Amusement parks, antiquing, art galleries, bicycling, fishing, golf, hiking, live theater, museums, parks, shopping, sporting events, tennis, water sports and wineries nearby.

Location: Country. Country, rural.

Publicity: *Country Inns and Lancaster County Magazine.*

"Thank you for sharing your wonderful home with us. I knew this place would be perfect!"

Certificate may be used: Tuesday-Thursday, Jan. 2-April 30, excluding holidays.

Boiling Springs

Gelinas Manor Victorian B&B

219 Front Street
Boiling Springs, PA 17007
(717)258-6584 (888)789-9411 Fax:(717)245-9328
Internet: www.gelinas-manor.com
E-mail: gelinasmanor@earthlink.net

Circa 1869. One of the first homes in the quiet historic village by the lake, this 1869 Victorian is listed in the National Register. Enjoy comfortable accommodations and a satisfying breakfast before embarking on the day's activities. The well-stocked lake and crystal-clear Yellow Breeches Creek are considered some of the country's best trout fishing areas. The nearby Fly Shop features locally tied flies, fishing gear, clothing and gifts as well as offering experienced tips for any interested fisherman. The famous Allenberry Resort and Playhouse is minutes away for fine dining and entertainment in the evening. Visit the sites of Gettysburg within a 30-minute drive, or savor the fla-

vors of Hershey in an hour. The inn is about 1½ hours away from Pennsylvania Dutch Country in Lancaster County.

Innkeeper(s): Lee & Kitty Gelinas. $65-125. 4 rooms, 3 with PB, 1 two-bedroom suite. Breakfast included in rates. Types of meals: Full gourmet bkfst. Beds: QDT. Cable TV, refrigerator, ceiling fan, clock radio, telephone, turn-down service, bathrobes and bath amenities in room. Air conditioning. Fax, copier, library and fireplace on premises. Amusement parks, antiquing, art galleries, cross-country skiing, downhill skiing, fishing, golf, hiking, live theater, museums, parks, shopping, sporting events and tennis nearby.

Location: Historic Village.

Certificate may be used: Accepts Weekends, Anytime, subject to availability; Anytime, last minute - based on availability.

Canadensis

Brookview Manor Inn

RR 2 Box 2960, Route 447
Canadensis, PA 18325
(570)595-2451 (800)585-7974 Fax:(570)595-7154
Internet: www.brookviewmanor.com
E-mail: innkeepers@thebrookviewmanor.com

Circa 1901. By the side of the road, hanging from a tall evergreen, is the welcoming sign to this forest retreat on six acres

adjoining 250 acres of woodland and hiking trails. The expansive wraparound porch overlooks a small stream. There are brightly decorated common rooms and eight fireplaces. Ten guest rooms include two with Jacuzzis and two deluxe suites. The carriage house has three additional rooms. One of the inn's dining rooms is surrounded by original stained glass, a romantic location for the inn's special six-course dinners prepared by an award-winning New York chef now on staff.

Innkeeper(s): Gaile & Marty Horowitz. $130-250. 10 rooms with PB, 6 with FP, 2 with WP, 2 two-bedroom suites, 1 conference room. Breakfast included in rates. Types of meals: Full gourmet bkfst, veg bkfst and Steakhouse and Italian specialities at MY DAUGHTERS PLACE located at Brookview's Country Cottage. Restaurant on premises. Beds: KQ. Cable TV, VCR, DVD, reading lamp, CD player, ceiling fan, clock radio, turn-down service, most with hot tub/spa, most with fireplace, bath amenities, wireless Internet access, two rooms with Jacuzzis and fireplaces, suites have sitting rooms and private porches, 5 additional rooms at the new Brookview Country Cottage and pool in room. Air conditioning. Fax, copier, swimming, library, parlor games, telephone, swing, wraparound porch overlooking small stream, gourmet dinner available by reservation, scheduled murder mystery weekends, restaurant and Brookview's Country Cottage with 5 additional bedrooms and huge pool on premises. Amusement parks, antiquing, beach, canoeing/kayaking, cross-country skiing, downhill skiing, fishing, golf, hiking, horseback riding, live theater, parks, shopping, water sports, wineries and Pool on premises of sister inn nearby.

Location: Country, mountains.

Publicity: *Mid-Atlantic Country, Bridal Guide, New York Times and Pocono Record.*

"Thanks for a great wedding weekend. Everything was perfect."

Certificate may be used: Sunday to Thursday, subject to availability, not on holiday or special event weeks.

The Merry Inn

Rt 390
Canadensis, PA 18325-0757
(570)595-2011 (800)858-4182 Fax:(570) 595-5088
Internet: www.themerryinn.com
E-mail: merryinnbb@yahoo.com

Circa 1942. Set in the picturesque Pocono Mountains, this bed & breakfast is a 90-minute drive from the metropolitan New York and Philadelphia areas. The turn-of-the-century,

mountainside home was built by two sisters and at one time was used as a boarding house. Current owners and innkeepers Jenepher Weathers & Mary Guy

have decorated their B&B using an eclectic mix of styles. Each guest room is individually appointed, with styles ranging from Victorian to country. Guests enjoy use of an outdoor Jacuzzi set into the mountainside. Bedrooms are set up to accommodate families, and children are welcome here.

Innkeeper(s): Jenepher Weathers & Mary Guy. $105-120. 6 rooms with PB. Breakfast, afternoon tea and snacks/refreshments included in rates. Types of meals: Country bkfst, Sun. brunch, early coffee/tea, lunch and dinner. Beds: KQDT. Cable TV, VCR, reading lamp, snack bar, clock radio, hair dryer and iron/ironing board in room. Central air. Parlor games, telephone, fireplace and outdoor Jacuzzi on premises. Antiquing, art galleries, bicycling, canoeing/kayaking, cross-country skiing, downhill skiing, fishing, golf, hiking, horseback riding, live theater, museums, parks, shopping, sporting events, water sports and golf nearby.

Location: Country, mountains.

Certificate may be used: Anytime midweek, weekends Nov. 15-April 15. No holidays.

Carlisle

Carlisle House

148 South Hanover Street
Carlisle, PA 17013-3420
(717)249-0350 Fax:(717)249-0458
Internet: www.thecarlislehouse.com
E-mail: info@thecarlislehouse.com

Circa 1826. Located in the downtown Historic District, the inn is within easy walking distance of Dickinson College, the Carlisle Fairgrounds, the Historical Museum and some of the best restaurants and shopping in Pennsylvania. Blending a rich history with modern comforts, excellent standards and high-tech amenities for business or leisure, this elegant bed and breakfast offers a memorable stay. Chat with new acquaintances in the sitting room. Relax on the veranda or downstairs patio. Enjoy 24-hour access to the fully equipped kitchen with complimentary fruits and beverages. Guest bedrooms feature period décor and furnishings. Some include a private entrance, fireplace and Jacuzzi bath. The Hydrangea Room becomes a suite when adding loft rooms. The spacious Rose Room boasts an original clawfoot tub. Savor an international-themed quiche breakfast. Conveniently situated in the heart of the state, Gettysburg battlefields, Hershey's Chocolate World, and Lancaster's Amish Country are some of the many day trips available.

Innkeeper(s): Alan & Mary Duxbury. $109-260. 10 rooms with PB, 3 with WP, 2 total suites, including 1 two-bedroom suite. Breakfast and snacks/refreshments included in rates. Types of meals: Full gourmet bkfst,

veg bkfst and early coffee/tea. Beds: KQDT. Modem hook-up, data port, cable TV, DVD, reading lamp, CD player, refrigerator, clock radio, telephone, coffeemaker, turn-down service, desk, voice mail, hair dryer, bathrobes, bath amenities, wireless Internet access, complimentary juices, soda and bottled water, complimentary domestic long-distance and local calls in room. Air conditioning. Fax, copier, library, parlor games, Fresh fruit, ice, coffee, sitting room with Recliners and TV/DVD on premises. Amusement parks, antiquing, art galleries, fishing, golf, hiking, live theater, museums, parks, shopping and sporting events nearby.

Location: City. Downtown Historic District.

Publicity: *Washington Post Travel Escapes, The Dickinsonian, Pittsburgh Mt. Lebanon Magazine, Heart of PA Travel Guide, Central PA Business Journal, Cars & Places, Backroads Magazine, The Sentinel 2004, 2005 and 2006* "Best Bed and Breakfast" in the Carlisle, Shippensburg, Mechanicsburg and Perry County area.

Certificate may be used: Anytime, Sunday-Thursday.

Pheasant Field B&B

150 Hickorytown Rd
Carlisle, PA 17015-9732
(717)258-0717 (877)258-0717
Internet: www.pheasantfield.com
E-mail: stay@pheasantfield.com

Circa 1800. Located on 10 acres of central Pennsylvania farmland, this brick, two-story Federal-style farmhouse features wooden shutters and a

covered front porch. Rooms include a TV and telephone. An early 19th-century stone barn is on the property, and horse boarding is available. The

Appalachian Trail is less than a mile away. Fly-fishing is popular at Yellow Breeches and Letort Spring. Dickinson College and Carlisle Fairgrounds are other points of interest.

Innkeeper(s): Dee Fegan. $95-175. 7 rooms with PB, 1 with FP, 2 with WP, 1 cottage, 1 conference room. Breakfast and snacks/refreshments included in rates. Types of meals: Full bkfst and early coffee/tea. Beds: KQT. Cable TV, VCR, reading lamp, refrigerator, ceiling fan, clock radio, telephone, coffeemaker, desk, some with hot tub/spa, some with fireplace and wireless Internet access in room. Central air. Fax, stable, tennis, library, parlor games, laundry facility, Labyrinth, Piano and Overnight horse boarding on premises. Limited handicap access. Amusement parks, antiquing, art galleries, cross-country skiing, downhill skiing, fishing, golf, hiking, live theater, museums, parks and sporting events nearby.

Location: Country.

Publicity: *Outdoor Traveler, Harrisburg Magazine.* and Voted "Simply The Best" B&B by readers of Harrisburg Magazine for 2005 and 2006.

"You have an outstanding, charming and warm house. I felt for the first time as being home."

Certificate may be used: January and March.

Centre Hall

Keller House B & B

110 W Church St
Centre Hall, PA 16828
(814)364-2225 (888)554-2588
Internet: www.kellerhousebb.com
E-mail: info@kellerhousebb.com

Lovingly restored, this historic 1860 Victorian adorns the lush farm country of Penns Valley in the small village of Centre Hall, Pennsylvania. Antiques and family heirlooms accent the gracious rooms. Relax by the gas fireplace and listen to the Edison Victrola in the sitting room. The porch features wicker furnishings and the covered patio boasts comfortable seating. Hot and cold beverages are available anytime. Guest bedrooms and suites offer upscale amenities and simple pleasures. Select a romantic suite with adjacent sitting room and clawfoot tub and gas fireplace or a double Jacuzzi tub. Keller House B&B serves a delicious breakfast on vintage dinnerware passed down through the generations.

Innkeeper(s): Ernie and Kathy Mowery. Call for rates. 5 rooms with PB, 2 with FP, 1 with WP, 2 suites. Breakfast and snacks/refreshments included in rates. Types of meals: Full bkfst. Beds: QT. Reading lamp, CD player, ceiling fan, clock radio, some with fireplace and bath amenities in room. Air conditioning. TV and telephone on premises. Antiquing, canoeing/kayaking, downhill skiing, fishing, golf, hiking, horseback riding, museums, parks, shopping, sporting events and wineries nearby.

Certificate may be used: December to April, Anytime subject to availability.

Chadds Ford

Pennsbury Inn

883 Baltimore Pike
Chadds Ford, PA 19317-9305
(610)388-1435 Fax:(610)388-1436
Internet: www.pennsburyinn.com
E-mail: info@pennsburyinn.com

Circa 1714. Listed in the National Register, this country farmhouse with hand-molded Flemish Bond brick facade was built originally with Brandywine Blue Granite rubble stone and later enlarged. Retaining its colonial heritage with slanted doorways, winding wood staircases and huge fireplaces, it boasts modern conveniences. There are elegant public sitting areas such as the living room, music room, library with an impressive book collection and breakfast in the dining room. The comfortable guest bedrooms feature antique feather beds and unique architectural details. The eight-acre estate boasts formal gardens that include a fish pond and reflection pool in a serene woodland setting.

Innkeeper(s): Cheryl & Chip Grono. $105-230. 7 rooms, 6 with PB, 5 with FP, 1 suite, 3 conference rooms. Breakfast, afternoon tea and snacks/refreshments included in rates. Types of meals: Full gourmet bkfst, veg bkfst, early coffee/tea, gourmet lunch, picnic lunch and hors d'oeuvres. Beds: KQDT. Modem hook-up, data port, cable TV, VCR, DVD, reading lamp, CD player, refrigerator, ceiling fan, clock radio, telephone, coffeemaker, turn-down service, desk, voice mail, hair dryer, bathrobes, bath amenities, wireless Internet access, iron/ironing board and Three with decorative fireplaces in room. Central air. Fax, copier, library, child care, parlor games, fireplace, laundry facility and gift shop on premises. Limited handicap access. Antiquing, art galleries, bicycling, canoeing/kayaking, fishing, golf, hiking, horseback riding, live theater, museums, parks, shopping, sporting events, tennis, wineries, Longwood Gardens, Winterthur, Brandywine River Museum, Nemours and Hagley nearby.

Location: City, country. Between Philadelphia & Wilmington.

Publicity: *NY Times & LA Times Travel sections, Philadelphia Inquirer Business, LI Press-Away for the Weekend, Main Line Times Travel & Leisure Inn of the Month, Numerous QVC spots and Interviewed on local station WKBW - Ralph Colliers Travel Moment.*

Certificate may be used: Sunday through Thursday, January, February, March, July, August, September and November. Not valid April, May, June, October, December. Anytime, Last Minute-Based on Availability.

Choconut

Addison House B&B

Rural Route 267
Choconut, PA 18818
(570)553-2682
Internet: www.1811addison.com
E-mail: info@1811addison.com

Circa 1811. Addison House was built by one of Choconut's earliest settlers, an Irish immigrant who purchased the vast homestead for just under a dollar an acre. The early 19th-century house is built in Federal style, but its interior includes many Victorian features, from the rich décor to the hand-carved marble fireplaces. A creek rambles through the 260-acre property, and guests will enjoy the secluded, wilderness setting. In the guest rooms, fluffy comforters top antique beds and floral wallcoverings add to the country Victorian ambiance. Breakfasts begin with items such as fresh berries with cream, followed by a rich entrée. The innkeepers are happy to help guests plan their days. The area offers a multitude of outdoor activities, as well as historic sites, antique shops, covered bridges and much more.

Innkeeper(s): Dennis & Gloria McLallen. $65-110. 4 rooms, 1 suite. Breakfast included in rates. Types of meals: Full gourmet bkfst, early coffee/tea and afternoon tea. Beds: D. Turn-down service, ice water and chocolates in room. Central air. TV, VCR, swimming, library, parlor games, telephone, fireplace and afternoon tea and house tour (by appointment) on premises. Antiquing, art galleries, bicycling, canoeing/kayaking, cross-country skiing, fishing, golf, hiking, live theater, museums, parks, shopping, sporting events, wineries and zoo nearby.

Location: Country, mountains. Farm, horses.

Certificate may be used: Jan. 1-Dec. 31.

Churchtown

The Inn at Twin Linden

2092 Main St. RT23
Churchtown, PA 17555-9514
(717)445-7619 Fax:(717) 445-4656
Internet: www.innattwinlinden.com
E-mail: info@innattwinlinden.com

Circa 1849. Experience luxurious elegance at this historic country manor estate. Towering linden trees, the inn's namesake, overlook the brick courtyard. Romantic guest bedrooms and suites feature two-person Jacuzzis or clawfoot tubs, fireplaces and feather beds, some with canopies. Breakfast and afternoon tea are culinary creations by a nationally renowned chef and author of two cookbooks. Relax on wicker-filled porches. The 2.5 acres boast colorful gardens overlooking Mennonite and Amish farm valleys. Play golf at a nearby course, or shop and browse through antiques.

Innkeeper(s): Sue & Norm Kuestner. $125-265. 8 rooms with PB, 7 with FP, 2 with HT, 3 with WP, 2 suites. Snacks/refreshments, Full-course breakfast and early coffee/tea included in rates. Types of meals: Full gourmet bkfst, early coffee/tea, lunch, picnic lunch, hors d'oeuvres, gourmet dinner and room service. Beds: KQDT. Cable TV, VCR, clock radio, turn-down service, desk, most with hot tub/spa, most with fireplace, hair dryer, bathrobes, bath amenities and iron/ironing board in room. Air conditioning. Parlor games, telephone, gift shop, gardens, porches and pergula on premises. Amusement parks, antiquing, art galleries, golf, hiking, live theater, museums, parks, shopping, wineries, buggy rides and hot air ballooning nearby.

Location: Country.

Publicity: *Early American Life, Los Angeles Times, Country Home, Country*

Living, USA Today, National Geographic Traveler, Travel Holiday, Food & Wine and Victoria.

"Your inn exceeds all others."

Certificate may be used: December-August, Sunday-Thursday, anytime at the last minute.

Clearfield

Victorian Loft B&B

216 S Front St
Clearfield, PA 16830-2218
(814)765-4805 (800)798-0456 Fax:(814)765-9596
Internet: www.victorianloft.com
E-mail: pdurant@atlanticbb.net

Circa 1894. Accommodations at this bed & breakfast are available in either a historic Victorian home on the riverfront or in a private, three-bedroom cabin. The white brick home is dressed with colorful, gingerbread trim, and inside, a grand staircase, stained glass and antique furnishings add to the Victorian charm. The suite is ideal for families as it contains two bedrooms, a living room, dining room, kitchen and a bath with a whirlpool tub. The cabin, Cedarwood Lodge, sleeps six and is located on eight, wooded acres near Parker Dam State Park and Elliot State Park. This is a favorite setting for small groups.

Innkeeper(s): Tim & Peggy Durant. $80-145. 5 rooms, 3 with PB, 2 suites, 1 cottage. Breakfast included in rates. Types of meals: Full bkfst, early coffee/tea, Custom blended juices, specialty egg, pancake or French toast main dishes plus homemade bread, coffee cake, cinnamon buns or muffins and fruit salad. Beds: QD. Modem hook-up, cable TV, VCR, reading lamp, stereo, refrigerator, clock radio, telephone, coffeemaker, desk, hair dryer, bathrobes, bath amenities, wireless Internet access, Loft suite has whirlpool bath, kitchette, dining area; Cabin and Second Street Suite have fully equipped eat-in kitchens in room. Central air. DVD, library, parlor games, fireplace, laundry facility, Whirlpool and Grand piano in formal parlor on premises. Antiquing, bicycling, canoeing/kayaking, cross-country skiing, fishing, golf, hiking, horseback riding, live theater, museums, parks, shopping, sporting events, tennis, water sports, wineries, Parker Dam, S.B. Elliot & Curwensville Lake State Parks, Rails to trails and Walking distance to specialty shops nearby.

Location: Mountains. Small town.

Publicity: Clearfield Progress and Tri-County.

"A feeling of old-fashioned beauty. The elegance of roses and lace. All wrapped up into a romantic moment."

Certificate may be used: Monday-Thursday from December-May, subject to availability, Anytime, Last Minute-Based on Availability.

Columbia

The Columbian

360 Chestnut St
Columbia, PA 17512-1156
(717)684-5869 (800)422-5869
Internet: www.columbianinn.com
E-mail: inn@columbianinn.com

Circa 1897. Sip lemonade while relaxing on one of the wraparound porches of this 1897 Colonial Revival mansion. Nap in the hammock, play horseshoes or croquet. Enjoy watching the water fountain bubbling into a trickling stream that flows to the pond with a bridge and garden railroad. Guest bedrooms feature a Victorian or English Country décor. Stay in the two-room Bucher Suite with a gas log fireplace and private balcony. A hearty breakfast includes fresh fruit, homemade granola, sweet breads, pancakes or an egg entrée. Recipes of popular dishes were requested so frequently a cookbook is available for pur-

chase. Walk to historic downtown on the Susquehanna River. Take a driving tour of historic Gettysburg. Specials and packages are offered.

Innkeeper(s): Karen L Umlauf. $100-125. 5 rooms with PB, 3 with FP, 1 suite. Breakfast, afternoon tea, snacks/refreshments and wine included in rates. Types of meals: Full gourmet bkfst, veg bkfst, early coffee/tea, picnic lunch and dinner. Beds: QT. Cable TV, VCR, reading lamp, refrigerator, ceiling fan, snack bar, clock radio, telephone, desk, some with hot tub/spa, most with fireplace, hair dryer, bath amenities, wireless Internet access, iron/ironing board, fruit, candy and flowers in room. Air conditioning. Spa, parlor games and Massage therapy on premises. Amusement parks, antiquing, art galleries, bicycling, canoeing/kayaking, cross-country skiing, downhill skiing, fishing, golf, hiking, horseback riding, live theater, museums, parks, shopping, sporting events, tennis, water sports, wineries, Elizabethtown and Hershey nearby.

Location: City. Town.

Publicity: Philadelphia Inquirer, Lancaster Intelligencer Journal, Columbia News, Washington Post, Potomac and Allentown Morning Call.

"In a word, extraordinary! Truly a home away from home. First B&B experience but will definitely not be my last."

Certificate may be used: December-March, subject to availability; April-November, Sunday-Thursday.

Danielsville

Filbert Bed & Breakfast

3740 Filbert Drive
Danielsville, PA 18038
(610)428-3300
Internet: filbertbnb.com
E-mail: filbertbnb@aol.com

Circa 1800. Feel refreshed in the quiet country setting of this restored 1800 Queen Anne Victorian on six acres in Danielsville, Pennsylvania. Adorning the foothills of Blue Mountains between Lehigh Valley and the Pocono Mountains, The Filbert Bed & Breakfast is a warm and welcoming B&B open all year. Relax on the 60-foot porch, play games or watch movies in the large sitting room or gather for conversation in the greeting parlor. Air-conditioned guest suites boast hardwood floors and antiques. Savor a bountiful breakfast in the dining room before embarking on the day's adventures. Massage and skin care appointments are available from a certified therapist and licensed cosmetologist.

Innkeeper(s): Kathy Silfies. $100-200. 5 total suites, including 1 two-bedroom suite. Breakfast and snacks/refreshments included in rates. Types of meals: Country bkfst and early coffee/tea. Beds: Q. Cable TV, CD player, clock radio, turn-down service, hair dryer, bathrobes, bath amenities and iron/ironing board in room. Air conditioning. VCR, parlor games and telephone on premises. Amusement parks, antiquing, art galleries, bicycling, canoeing/kayaking, cross-country skiing, downhill skiing, fishing, golf, hiking, horseback riding, live theater, museums, parks, shopping, sporting events, water sports and wineries nearby.

Location: Country, mountains.

Certificate may be used: April-November Subject to availability.

Eagles Mere

Crestmont Inn

Crestmont Dr
Eagles Mere, PA 17731
(570)525-3519 (800)522-8767 Fax:570-525-3534
Internet: www.crestmont-inn.com
E-mail: crestmnt@epix.net

Circa 1914. Eagles Mere has been a vacation site since the late 19th century and still abounds with Victorian charm. The Crestmont Inn is no exception. The rooms are tastefully decorated with flowers and elegant furnishings. Suites include two-person whirlpool tubs. A hearty country breakfast is served each morning and guests also are treated to a five-course dinner in the candle-lit dining room. Savor a variety of mouth-watering entrees and finish off the evening with scrumptious desserts. The cocktail lounge is a perfect place to mingle and enjoy hors d'oeuvres, wines and spirits. The inn grounds offer tennis and shuffleboard courts. The Wyoming State Forest borders the property and golfing is just minutes away.

Innkeeper(s): Elna & Fred Mulford. $108-218. 15 rooms with PB, 2 with FP, 5 with WP, 3 two-bedroom suites. Breakfast and snacks/refreshments included in rates. Types of meals: Country bkfst, early coffee/tea, wine and dinner. Restaurant on premises. Beds: KQDT. Cable TV, DVD, reading lamp, refrigerator, clock radio, telephone, some with fireplace, hair dryer, bathrobes and bath amenities in room. Central air. Fax, copier, tennis, parlor games and gift shop on premises. Antiquing, art galleries, beach, canoeing/kayaking, cross-country skiing, fishing, golf, hiking, horseback riding, live theater, museums, parks, shopping, tennis, water sports and wineries nearby.

Location: Mountains. Endless mountain 2,200 feet.

Certificate may be used: Monday through Thursday.

East Berlin

Bechtel Victorian Mansion B&B Inn

400 W King St
East Berlin, PA 17316
(717)259-7760 (800)579-1108
Internet: www.bbonline.com/pa/bechtel/
E-mail: bechtelvictbb@aol.com

Circa 1897. The town of East Berlin, near Lancaster and 18 miles east of Gettysburg, was settled by Pennsylvania Germans prior to the American Revolution. William Leas, a wealthy banker, built this many-gabled romantic Queen Anne mansion, now listed in the National Register. The inn is furnished with an abundance of museum-quality antiques and collections. Rooms are decorated in country Victorian style with beautiful quilts and comforters, lace, dolls and teddy bears.

Innkeeper(s): Richard & Carol Carlson. $105-160. 9 rooms, 7 with PB, 2 suites. Breakfast included in rates. Types of meals: Full bkfst, early coffee/tea and snacks/refreshments. Beds: KQD. Reading lamp and turn-down service in room. Air conditioning. TV, VCR, parlor games, telephone and fireplace on premises. Amusement parks, antiquing, bicycling, downhill skiing, fishing, golf, hiking, live theater, museums, shopping and wineries nearby.

Location: Historic district-German town.

Publicity: *Washington Post and Richmond Times.*

Certificate may be used: Nov. 30-Aug. 31, Sunday through Thursday, excludes holidays and special events.

Ephrata

Doneckers, The Inns

318-324 N State St
Ephrata, PA 17522
(717)738-9502 Fax:(717)738-9554
Internet: www.doneckers.com
E-mail: inns@doneckers.com

Circa 1777. Jacob Gorgas, a devout member of the Ephrata Cloister and a clock maker, noted for crafting 150 eight-day Gorgas grandfather clocks, built this stately Dutch Colonial-style home. Guests can opt to stay in one of three antique-filled homes. The 1777 House, which includes 12 rooms, features hand-stenciled walls, suites with whirlpool baths, fireplaces, original stone masonry and  an antique tiled floor. The home served as a tavern in the 1800s and an elegant inn in the early 1900s. The Homestead includes four rooms, some with fireplaces and amenities such as Jacuzzis, sitting areas and four-poster beds. The Guesthouse features a variety of beautifully decorated rooms each named and themed in honor of local landmarks or significant citizens. All guests enjoy an expansive breakfast with freshly squeezed juice, fruits, breakfast cheeses and other delicacies. The homes are part of the Donecker Community, which features upscale fashion stores, furniture galleries and a restaurant within walking distance of the 1777 House.

Innkeeper(s): Kelly Snyder. $79-250. 31 rooms, 29 with PB, 7 with FP, 12 with HT. Breakfast included in rates. Types of meals: Cont plus, gourmet lunch and gourmet dinner. Restaurant on premises. Beds: KQDT. Cable TV, reading lamp, CD player, clock radio, telephone, some with hot tub/spa, some with fireplace, hair dryer, wireless Internet access, iron/ironing board and some with refrigerator in room. Central air. VCR, fax, bicycles and parlor games on premises. Limited handicap access. Amusement parks, antiquing, art galleries, golf, live theater, museums, parks, shopping, sporting events and wineries nearby.

Location: Small town.

Publicity: *Daily News and Country Inns.*

"A peaceful refuge."

Certificate may be used: Sunday-Thursday, except holidays, year-round.

Historic Smithton Inn

900 W Main St
Ephrata, PA 17522-1328
(717)733-6094
Internet: www.historicsmithtoninn.com
E-mail: smithtoninn@dejazzd.com

Circa 1763. Family run for 236 years, this enchanting inn offers a peaceful and relaxing stay in Lancaster County, just one hour west of Philadelphia. Gather by the fire in the common room. Refreshments on the sideboard include eggnog, hot mulled wine or cider and just-baked apple pie. Inviting guest bedrooms and a luxurious three-room suite are spacious with an intimate ambiance enhanced by well-appointed furnishings, candlelight, chamber music and working fireplaces. Feather beds are gladly provided when requested in advance. Linger leisurely over a satisfying breakfast served daily in the dining room.

Innkeeper(s): Dorothy Graybill. $85-170. 8 rooms with PB, 8 with FP, 1 suite. Breakfast and snacks/refreshments included in rates. Types of meals: Full bkfst. Beds: KQDT. Reading lamp, desk, whirlpools and feather beds in room. Air conditioning. Parlor games, telephone, fireplace, flower gardens and candlelight on premises. Amusement parks, antiquing, art galleries, golf, hiking, live theater, museums, shopping, tennis, wineries, farmland, handcrafts and farmers market nearby.

Location: Village.

Publicity: *New York, Country Living, Early American Life, Washington Post and Philadelphia Inquirer.*

"After visiting over 50 inns in four countries, Smithton has to be one of the most romantic, picturesque inns in America. I have never seen its equal!"

Certificate may be used: January-July, Sunday-Thursday.

Erwinna

Golden Pheasant Inn on the Delaware

763 River Rd
Erwinna, PA 18920-9254
(610)294-9595 (800)830-4474 Fax:(610)294-9882
Internet: www.goldenpheasant.com
E-mail: barbara@goldenpheasant.com

Circa 1857. The Golden Pheasant is well established as the location of a wonderful, gourmet restaurant, but it is also home to six charming guest rooms decorated by Barbara Faure. Four-poster canopy beds and antiques decorate the rooms, which offer views of the canal and river. The fieldstone inn was built as a mule-barge stop for travelers heading down the Delaware Canal. The five-acre grounds resemble a French-country estate, and guests can enjoy the lush surroundings in a plant-filled greenhouse dining room. There are two other dining rooms, including an original fieldstone room with exposed beams and stone walls with decorative copper pots hanging here and there. The restaurant's French cuisine, prepared by chef Michel Faure, is outstanding. One might start off with Michel's special pheasant pate, followed by a savory onion soup baked with three cheeses. A mix of greens dressed in vinaigrette cleanses the palate before one samples roast duck in a luxurious raspberry, ginger and rum sauce or perhaps a sirloin steak flamed in cognac.

Innkeeper(s): Barbara & Michel Faure. $95-225. 6 rooms with PB, 4 with FP, 1 suite, 1 cottage, 3 conference rooms. Breakfast included in rates. Types of meals: Cont plus, early coffee/tea, picnic lunch, snacks/refreshments, gourmet dinner and room service. Restaurant on premises. Beds: Q. Reading lamp, CD player, refrigerator, ceiling fan, clock radio, telephone, coffeemaker, desk, hot tub/spa and fireplace in room. Air conditioning. Fax, copier, swimming, library, parlor games and canal path for walking on premises. Limited handicap access. Antiquing, art galleries, bicycling, canoeing/kayaking, cross-country skiing, fishing, golf, hiking, horseback riding, live theater, museums, parks, shopping, tennis, water sports, wineries, historic Doylestown, New Hope and Washington Crossing nearby.

Location: Country.

Publicity: *The Philadelphia Inquirer, New York Times, Philadelphia Magazine, Food Network and Fox.*

"A more stunningly romantic spot is hard to imagine. A taste of France on the banks of the Delaware."

Certificate may be used: Sunday-Thursday, excluding holidays.

Etters

Canna Country Inn

393 Valley Rd
Etters, PA 17319-8916
(717)938-6077
Internet: www.cannainnbandb.com
E-mail: cannainnbandb@aol.com

Circa 1850. Originally a Pennsylvania Dutch Country barn in the early 1840s, this massive bed and breakfast sits on three acres in the rolling hills. Among the huge wood timbers and exposed stone of the rustic decor are all the upscale modern amenities desired for a relaxing getaway or to maintain job responsibilities. Relax with evening refreshments by the rock fireplace in the living area or on the back deck. Guest bedrooms include Internet access, air conditioning, phone and TV. A two-bedroom suite also features a DVD and CD player. Enjoy a hearty country breakfast served in the formal dining room. Work out in the exercise room and utilize the business center. Explore the park-like setting of the partially wooded grounds with a stream.

Innkeeper(s): June E. Fisher . $45-180. 7 rooms, 6 with PB, 2 with FP, 1 with WP, 2 two-bedroom suites, 1 cottage, 1 conference room. Breakfast, afternoon tea, snacks/refreshments and wine included in rates. Types of meals: Country bkfst, veg bkfst, early coffee/tea, lunch, picnic lunch and Full guest kitchen stocked with snacks and beverages available 24 hours everyday. Beds: KQD. Data port, cable TV, DVD, reading lamp, CD player, refrigerator, ceiling fan, clock radio, telephone, desk, some with hot tub/spa, some with fireplace, hair dryer, bathrobes, bath amenities, wireless Internet access and iron/ironing board in room. Central air. Fax, copier, spa, parlor games, laundry facility, Business center, Meeting room, Banquet facilities, Outdoor 6-person Hot Tub, 3 guest fireplaces and Large common area on premises. Amusement parks, antiquing, art galleries, bicycling, canoeing/kayaking, cross-country skiing, downhill skiing, fishing, golf, hiking, horseback riding, live theater, museums, parks, shopping, sporting events, tennis, water sports and wineries nearby.

Location: Country. Harrisburg.

Publicity: *Harrisburg Magazine and York Dispatch.*

Certificate may be used: Anytime, subject to availability.

Fairfield

The Fairfield Inn 1757

15 West Main Street (Rt. 116 West)
Fairfield, PA 17320
(717)642-5410 Fax:(717)642-5920
Internet: www.thefairfieldinn.com
E-mail: innkeeper@thefairfieldinn.com

Circa 1757. Rich in history, this authentic American treasure has been a continuously operating tavern, restaurant and inn for 180 years and its origins as the Mansion House of the town's founder date back 245 years. Tour the Gettysburg battlefield then retreat to the hospitality and refinement expected from a small luxury hotel yet enjoyed at this inn. Sip a hot beverage by one of the eight fireplaces. Squire Miller's Tavern offers conversation and libations. Renovated guest bedrooms and suites boast air conditioning and cable television. The Mansion House Restaurant serves an imaginative menu of classically prepared and artistically presented dishes. A patio garden is bordered with privacy hedges and filled with flowers. Cooking classes, special dinners and holiday activities are among the many events planned throughout the year.

Innkeeper(s): Joan & Sal Chandon. $120-175. 6 rooms with PB, 2 with FP, 4 with WP, 2 suites, 1 conference room. Breakfast included in rates. Types of meals: Cont, Sun. brunch, lunch, picnic lunch, snacks/refreshments, wine and dinner. Restaurant on premises. Beds: QDT. Cable TV, reading lamp, clock radio, turn-down service, desk, some with fireplace, hair dryer and iron/ironing board in room. Central air. Fax and parlor games on premises. Limited handicap access. Antiquing, bicycling, cross-country skiing, downhill skiing, golf, hiking, horseback riding, live theater, museums, parks, shopping, sporting events, tennis, wineries and Gettysburg National Military Park nearby.

Location: Country. Eight miles west of Gettysburg.

Publicity: *Gettysburg Times, Hanover Evening Sun, York Daily Record, Frederick Magazine, Cleveland Magazine and Travel Channel.*

Certificate may be used: Anytime, November-March, subject to availability, may not be combined with any other discounts, vouchers, coupons or gift certificates.

Fogelsville

Glasbern Country Inn

2141 Pack House Road
Fogelsville, PA 18051
(610)285-4723 Fax:(610)285-2862
Internet: www.glasbern.com
E-mail: innkeeper@glasbern.com

Circa 1985. Gracing more than 200 acres, this renovated, historic Pennsylvania Dutch Post and Beam Barn Structure is now a country inn that specializes in overnight comfort, fine dining and so much more. Accommodations include the Stables, Gate House, Pack House, Farmhouse, Carriage House, Garden Cottage and Barn surrounded by gardens and hillside pastures. Stay in a guest bedroom, spacious bi-level or multi-room suite with a wood-burning or gas fireplace, whirlpool tub, sitting area, cathedral ceilings, Bose Stereo system, wet bar and private deck. Enjoy Contemporary American Cuisine. Browse for treasures in the gift shop. Ask about the popular wedding packages available.

Innkeeper(s): Al Granger. $153-461. 36 rooms with PB, 26 with FP, 31 with WP, 15 suites, 1 cottage, 3 conference rooms. Breakfast included in rates. Types of meals: Country bkfst, early coffee/tea, snacks/refreshments, wine, dinner and room service. Restaurant on premises. Beds: KQ. Modem hookup, data port, cable TV, VCR, DVD, reading lamp, stereo, refrigerator, snack bar, clock radio, telephone, coffeemaker, desk, most with hot tub/spa, voice mail, most with fireplace, hair dryer, bathrobes, bath amenities and iron/ironing board in room. Central air. Fax, copier, spa, swimming, bicycles, pet boarding, laundry facility, gift shop and restaurant on premises. Handicap access. Amusement parks, antiquing, art galleries, bicycling, canoeing/kayaking, cross-country skiing, downhill skiing, fishing, golf, hiking, horseback riding, live theater, museums, parks, shopping, tennis, wineries, Easton's State Theatre, Allentown Art Museum, National Canal Museum, Crayola Factory, Renningers Antiques, Lehigh Valley Mall, Cabelas, Hawk Mountain Sanctuary, Olde Homested Golf Club, Pocono White Water Rafting, Lehigh Valley Disc Golf Club, Lehigh Valley Velodrome, Dorney Park & Wildwater Kingdom and Lehigh Valley Wine Trail nearby.

Location: Country.

"Your place has such charm and warmth."

Certificate may be used: January-August on last minute room reservations only (less than 48 hours prior to arrival), excluding Saturdays.

Gettysburg

Baladerry Inn at Gettysburg

40 Hospital Rd
Gettysburg, PA 17325
(717)337-1342 (800)220-0025
Internet: www.baladerryinn.com
E-mail: baladerry@blazenet.net

Circa 1812. The quiet and private setting on the edge of the Gettysburg Battlefield, this brick country manor was used as a hospital during the Civil War. Additions were added in 1830 and 1977, and the inn has been completely restored. Guests can snuggle up with a book in their comfortable rooms or in the great room, which includes a fireplace. Some guest rooms include a private patio or a fireplace. The spacious grounds offer gardens, a gazebo, a tennis court and terraces. Guided tours of the battlefield can be arranged, and guests also can plan a horseback riding excursion on the battlefield.

Innkeeper(s): Suzanne Lonky. $125-250. 9 rooms with PB, 3 with FP. Breakfast included in rates. Types of meals: Full bkfst, early coffee/tea and snacks/refreshments. Beds: KQT. Reading lamp, clock radio, telephone, desk and private patio overlooking grounds in room. Air conditioning. VCR, tennis and fireplace on premises. Antiquing, cross-country skiing, downhill skiing, fishing, golf, horseback riding, live theater, parks, shopping, sporting events and horseback riding or bicycling on Battlefield nearby.

Location: Country: Edge of battlefield.

Publicity: *Gettysburg Times, Allentown Morning Call, Pennsylvania Magazine and US Air Magazine.*

Certificate may be used: January-March 31 subject to availability. Special program weekends excluded.

James Gettys Hotel

27 Chambersburg St
Gettysburg, PA 17325
(717)337-1334 (888)900-5275 Fax:(717)334-2103
Internet: www.jamesgettyshotel.com
E-mail: info@jamesgettyshotel.com

Circa 1803. Listed in the National Register, this newly renovated four-story hotel once served as a tavern through the Battle of Gettysburg and was used as a hospital for soldiers. Outfitted with cranberry colored awnings and a gold painted entrance, the hotel offers a tea room, nature store and gallery on the street level. From the lobby, a polished chestnut staircase leads to the guest quarters. All accommodations are suites with living rooms appointed with home furnishings, and each has its own kitchenette. Breakfasts of home-baked scones and coffee cake are brought to your room.

Innkeeper(s): Stephanie McSherry. $135-250. 12 suites. Breakfast included in rates. Types of meals: Cont. Beds: QD. Cable TV, reading lamp, refrigerator, clock radio, telephone, coffeemaker and turn-down service in room. Air conditioning. VCR and fax on premises. Handicap access. Amusement parks, antiquing, art galleries, bicycling, cross-country skiing, downhill skiing, fishing, golf, hiking, horseback riding, museums, parks, shopping, tennis and wineries nearby.

Location: Small historic town.

Certificate may be used: Monday through Thursday, excluding holidays and special events, Jan. 1-Dec. 30.

Keystone Inn B&B

231 Hanover St
Gettysburg, PA 17325-1913
(717)337-3888
E-mail: dmartin@superpa.net

Circa 1913. Furniture maker Clayton Reaser constructed this three-story brick Victorian with a wide-columned porch hugging the north and west sides. Cut stone graces every door and window sill, each with a keystone. A chestnut staircase ascends the full three stories, and the interior is decorated with comfortable furnishings, ruffles and lace.

Innkeeper(s): Wilmer & Doris Martin. $95-135. 5 rooms with PB, 1 suite. Breakfast and afternoon tea included in rates. Types of meals: Full bkfst and early coffee/tea. Beds: KQDT. TV, reading lamp and desk in room. Air conditioning. Library, parlor games and telephone on premises. Amusement parks, antiquing, cross-country skiing, downhill skiing, fishing, live theater, parks, shopping, Civil War Battlefield and historic sites nearby.

Location: Small town.

Publicity: *Lancaster Sunday News, York Sunday News, Hanover Sun, Allentown Morning Call, Gettysburg Times, Pennsylvania and Los Angeles Times.*

"We slept like lambs. This home has a warmth that is soothing."

Certificate may be used: November-April, Monday-Thursday.

The Gaslight Inn

33 E Middle St
Gettysburg, PA 17325
(717)337-9100 (800)914-5698 Fax:(717)337-1100
Internet: www.thegaslightinn.com
E-mail: info@thegaslightinn.com

Circa 1872. Gaslights illuminate the brick pathways leading to this 130-year-old Italianate-style, expanded farmhouse. The inn boasts two elegant parlors separated by original pocket doors, a spacious dining room and a first-floor guest room with wheelchair access that opens to a large, brick patio. An open switchback staircase leads to the second- and third-floor guest rooms, all individually decorated in traditional and European furnishings. Some of the rooms feature covered decks,fireplaces, whirlpool tubs and steam showers for two. Guests are invited to enjoy a hearty or heart-healthy breakfast and inn-baked cookies and brownies and refreshments in the afternoon. Winter weekend packages are available and carriage rides, private guides and a variety of activities can be arranged with the help of the innkeepers.

Innkeeper(s): Mike and Becky Hanson. $105-195. 9 rooms with PB, 6 with FP, 2 with HT. Breakfast and snacks/refreshments included in rates. Types of meals: Full gourmet bkfst and early coffee/tea. Beds: KQ. Cable TV, VCR, reading lamp, ceiling fan, clock radio, telephone, some with hot tub/spa, most with fireplace, wireless Internet access and Spa showers for 2 which with the touch of a button provide a 20 minute steam bath in room. Central air. Fax, spa, library, parlor games and Wireless Internet access throughout the inn on premises. Limited handicap access. Antiquing, art galleries, bicycling, cross-country skiing, downhill skiing, fishing, golf, hiking, horseback riding, live theater, museums, parks, shopping, tennis, water sports, wineries and historic educational tours and lectures nearby.

Location: City. Small town, historic site.

Publicity: *Tyler Texas Times, Hanover Sun, Los Angeles Times, Southern Living and Country Inns.*

Certificate may be used: Dec. 1 to March 31, Sunday-Thursday, except New Year's Eve and Valentine's Day.

Gordonville

Osceola Mill House

313 Osceola Mill Rd
Gordonville, PA 17529
(717)768-3758 (800)878-7719
Internet: www.lancaster-inn.com
E-mail: osceolamill@frontiernet.net

Circa 1766. In a quaint historic setting adjacent to a mill and a miller's cottage, this handsome limestone mill house rests on

the banks of Pequea Creek. There are deep-set windows and wide pine floors. Guest bedrooms and the keeping room feature working fireplaces that add to the warmth and charm. Breakfast fare may include tasty regional specialties like locally made Pennsylvania Dutch sausage, and Dutch babies-an oven-puffed pancake

filled with fresh fruit. Amish neighbors farm the adjacent fields, their horse and buggies enhance the picturesque ambiance.

Innkeeper(s): Patricia & Ron Ernst. $99-179. 5 rooms with PB, 4 with FP, 1 cottage. Breakfast included in rates. Types of meals: Full gourmet bkfst. Beds: Q. Cable TV, VCR, DVD, ceiling fan, clock radio, some with fireplace and wireless Internet access in room. Air conditioning. Fax, copier, parlor games and Coffee & Tea is available in Gathering room anytime on premises. Amusement parks, antiquing, art galleries, bicycling, canoeing/kayaking, golf, hiking, live theater, museums, parks, shopping, sporting events and wineries nearby.

Location: Country. Intercourse, Paradise, Strasburg.

Publicity: *The Journal, Country Living, Washington Times, Gourmet and BBC.*

"We had a thoroughly delightful stay at your inn. Probably the most comfortable overnight stay we've ever had."

Certificate may be used: January-March, Sunday-Thursday, subject to availability, excludes holidays and special events, can not be combined with any other offers, discounts or gift certificates.

Grove City

Snow Goose Inn

112 E Main St
Grove City, PA 16127
(724)458-4644 (800)317-4644
Internet: www.bbonline.com/pa/snowgoose
E-mail: msgoose1@earthlink.net

Circa 1895. This home was built as a residence for young women attending Grove City College. It was later used as a family home and offices for a local doctor. Eventually, it was transformed into an intimate bed & breakfast, offering four cozy guest rooms. The interior is comfortable, decorated with antiques and touches country with stenciling, collectibles and a few of the signature geese on display. Museums, shops, Amish farms, colleges and several state parks are in the vicinity, offering many activities.

Innkeeper(s): Orvil & Dorothy McMillen. $75. 4 rooms with PB. Breakfast and snacks/refreshments included in rates. Types of meals: Full gourmet bkfst and early coffee/tea. Beds: QD. Reading lamp, stereo, refrigerator and clock radio in room. Air conditioning. VCR, parlor games, telephone and fireplace on premises. Amusement parks, antiquing, cross-country skiing, downhill skiing, fishing, golf, live theater, parks, shopping, sporting events, tennis and water sports nearby.

Location: City.

Publicity: *Allied News.*

"Your thoughtful touches and homey atmosphere were a balm to our chaotic lives."

Certificate may be used: All year.

Hanover

The Beechmont B&B Inn

315 Broadway
Hanover, PA 17331-2505
(717)632-3013 (800)553-7009 Fax:(717)632-2769
Internet: www.thebeechmont.com
E-mail: innkeeper@thebeechmont.com

Circa 1834. Feel welcomed by centuries of charm at this gracious Georgian inn, a witness to the Battle of Hanover, the Civil War's first major battle on free soil. A 130-year-old magnolia tree shades the flagstone patio and wicker furniture invites a lingering rest on the front porch. The romantic Magnolia Suite features a marble fireplace, whirlpool tub and Queen canopy bed. The inn is noted for its sumptuous breakfasts.

Innkeeper(s): Kathryn & Thomas White. $99-164. 7 rooms with PB, 4 with FP, 1 with WP, 3 suites. Breakfast and snacks/refreshments included in rates. Types of meals: Full gourmet bkfst and early coffee/tea. Beds: QD. Cable TV, ceiling fan, clock radio, telephone, desk, wireless Internet access and fireplace in room. Air conditioning. Fax, copier, parlor games and computer with Internet access on premises. Antiquing, bicycling, cross-country skiing, fishing, golf, hiking, horseback riding, live theater, parks, shopping, sporting events, water sports and wineries nearby.

Location: City.

Publicity: *Evening Sun and York Daily Record.*

"I had a marvelous time at your charming, lovely inn."

Certificate may be used: Sunday-Thursday, Dec. 1-March 31, excluding holidays.

Holicong

Barley Sheaf Farm Estate & Spa

5281 Old York Rd, Rt 202/263
Holicong, PA 18928
(215)794-5104 Fax:(215)794-5332
Internet: www.barleysheaf.com
E-mail: info@barleysheaf.com

Circa 1740. Surrounded by 100 acres of pasture and woodland views in the Bucks County countryside this exclusive destination estate spa boasts luxury accommodations in the historic 1740 Manor House, the Stone Bank Barn and the Guest Cottage. Elegant guest suites offer an assortment of amenities from fireside whirlpool tubs or steam showers to balconies or terraces. Feel indulged by in-suite, all-natural spa treatment rooms. A gourmet buffet brunch is served in the conservatory overlooking the trellis garden and antique French gazebo. Swim in the Olympic-size swimming pool, stroll the scenic walking paths with two ponds and see the miniature horses and sheep. Barley Sheaf Farm Estate & Spa in Holicong, Pennsylvania is centrally located to shopping, entertainment and cultural sites.

Innkeeper(s): Lola Liebert. $250-750. 16 rooms, 14 with FP, 14 with WP, 16 suites, 3 conference rooms. Breakfast, afternoon tea, snacks/refreshments and wine included in rates. Types of meals: Full gourmet bkfst, veg bkfst, early coffee/tea, gourmet lunch and picnic lunch. Beds: KQT. Modem hook-up, cable TV, DVD, reading lamp, stereo, refrigerator, snack bar, clock radio, telephone, coffeemaker, desk, voice mail, most with fireplace, hair dryer, bathrobes, bath amenities, wireless Internet access, iron/ironing board, Steam showers with body sprays and flat screen TV/DVD in room. Central air. VCR, fax, copier, swimming, library and parlor games on premises. Handicap access. Amusement parks, antiquing, art galleries, bicycling, canoeing/kayaking, cross-country skiing, downhill skiing, fishing, golf, hiking, horseback riding, live theater, museums, parks, shopping, tennis, water sports and wineries nearby.

Location: Country.

Publicity: *Country Living, Romantic Inns of America, Philadelphia Magazine,* Philadelphia Enquirer and CNC Business Channel.

Certificate may be used: Monday through Thursday, no holidays.

Intercourse

Carriage Corner

3705 E Newport Rd.
Intercourse, PA 17534-0371
(717)768-3059 (800)209-3059
Internet: www.carriagecornerbandb.com
E-mail: gschuit@comcast.net

Circa 1979. Located in the heart of Amish farmland, this two-story Colonial rests on a pastoral acre. Homemade, country breakfasts are served, often including innkeeper Gordon Schuit's special recipe for oatmeal pancakes. A five-minute walk will take guests into the village where they'll find Amish buggies traveling down the lanes and more than 100 shops displaying local crafts, pottery, quilts  and furniture, as well as art galleries. The innkeepers can arrange for dinners in an Amish home, buggy rides and working Amish farm tours. Longwood Gardens, Hershey's Chocolate World and Gettysburg are also nearby.

Innkeeper(s): Gordon & Gwen Schuit. $68-94. 5 rooms with PB, 1 conference room. Breakfast included in rates. Types of meals: Full bkfst and early coffee/tea. Beds: Q. Cable TV and clock radio in room. Central air. VCR, fax, library, parlor games, telephone and fireplace on premises. Amusement parks, antiquing, art galleries, bicycling, live theater, museums, parks, shopping, wineries, hub of Amish farmland, Amish dinners arranged, buggy rides, working Amish farm tours, Strasburg Steam Railroad, Railroad Museum of PA, "Daniel" at Sight and Sound, festivals and auctions, craft and quilt fairs, farmers' markets and roadside stands, Longwood Gardens, Hershey's Chocolate World and Gettysburg nearby.

Location: Country. Amish farmland.

Certificate may be used: December, January and February, excluding holiday weekends. March-April, November, Sunday through Wednesday, excluding special events.

Jim Thorpe

Harry Packer Mansion

Packer Hill
Jim Thorpe, PA 18229
(570)325-8566
Internet: www.murdermansion.com
E-mail: mystery@murdermansion.com

Circa 1874. This extravagant Second Empire mansion was used as the model for the haunted mansion in Disney World. It was constructed of New England sandstone, and local brick and stone trimmed in cast iron. Past ornately carved columns on the front veranda, guests enter 400-pound, solid walnut doors. The opulent interior includes marble mantels, hand-painted ceilings and elegant antiques. Murder-mystery weekends are a mansion specialty.

Innkeeper(s): Robert & Patricia Handwerk. $150-250. 12 rooms with PB, 4 suites, 3 conference rooms. Breakfast included in rates. Types of meals: Full gourmet bkfst. Beds: Q. Reading lamp, refrigerator, clock radio, turn-down service, desk, hair dryer, bathrobes and bath amenities in room. Air conditioning. TV, parlor games, telephone, fireplace and Murder Mystery Weekends on premises. Antiquing, art galleries, bicycling, canoeing/kayaking, cross-country skiing, downhill skiing, fishing, golf, hiking, museums, parks, shopping, tennis, water sports and wineries nearby.

Location: Mountains.

Publicity: *Philadelphia Inquirer, New York, Victorian Homes, Washington Post, Conde Nast Traveler and winner Best Murder Mystery by Arringtons Book of Lists.*

"What a beautiful place and your hospitality was wonderful. We will see you again soon."

Certificate may be used: Sunday-Thursday year-round except holidays based on availability.

The Inn at Jim Thorpe

24 Broadway
Jim Thorpe, PA 18229
(570)325-2599 (800)329-2599 Fax:(570)325-9145
Internet: www.innjt.com
E-mail: innjt@ptd.net

Circa 1848. This massive New Orleans-style structure, now restored, hosted some colorful 19th-century guests, including Thomas Edison, John D. Rockefeller and Buffalo Bill. All rooms are appointed with Victorian furnishings and have private baths with pedestal sinks and marble floors. The suites include fireplaces and whirlpool tubs. Also on the premises are a Victorian dining Room, Irish pub and a conference center. The inn is situated in the heart of Jim Thorpe, a quaint Victorian town that was known at the turn of the century as the "Switzerland of America." Historic mansion tours, museums and art galleries are nearby, and mountain biking and whitewater rafting are among the outdoor activities.

Innkeeper(s): David Drury. $103-399. 45 rooms, 34 with PB, 5 with FP, 11 with WP, 2 conference rooms. Breakfast included in rates. Types of meals: Cont plus, lunch, dinner and room service. Beds: KQ. Cable TV, DVD, reading lamp, clock radio, telephone, coffeemaker, hair dryer, wireless Internet access, iron/ironing board, 11 suites with whirlpools and some with fireplaces in room. Air conditioning. Fax, copier, fireplace, game room, exercise room and elevator on premises. Handicap access. Antiquing, art galleries, bicycling, canoeing/kayaking, cross-country skiing, downhill skiing, fishing, golf, hiking, horseback riding, museums, parks, shopping and wineries nearby.

Location: Historic Downtown.

Publicity: *Philadelphia Inquirer, Pennsylvania Magazine and Allentown Morning Call.*

"We had the opportunity to spend a weekend at your lovely inn. Your staff is extremely friendly, helpful, and courteous. I can't remember when we felt so relaxed, we hope to come back again soon."

Certificate may be used: Sunday-Thursday excluding holidays and Christmas week and the month of August. All discounts and promotions based on weekend rack rates.

Kennett Square

Kennett House Bed and Breakfast

503 W State St
Kennett Square, PA 19348-3028
(610)444-9592 (800)820-9592 Fax:(610)444-7633
Internet: www.kennetthouse.com
E-mail: innkeeper@kennetthouse.com

Circa 1910. This granite American four-square home features an extensive wraparound porch, a front door surrounded by leaded-

glass windows and magnificent chestnut woodwork. Beyond the foyer are two downstairs parlors with fireplaces, while a second-floor parlor provides a sunny setting for afternoon tea. Rooms are furnished with period antiques and Oriental carpets. An elegant gourmet breakfast is served each morning.

Innkeeper(s): Gilja. $125-175. 4 rooms with PB, 1 suite. Breakfast and snacks/refreshments included in rates. Types of meals: Full gourmet bkfst and early coffee/tea. Beds: Q. Cable TV, reading lamp, ceiling fan, clock radio, hair dryer, bathrobes, bath amenities, wireless Internet access and high-speed Internet access in room. Central air. Fax, copier, library, parlor games, telephone and fireplace on premises. Antiquing, art galleries, bicycling, canoeing/kayaking, fishing, golf, hiking, horseback riding, live theater, museums, parks, shopping, sporting events, wineries, Longwood Gardens, Brandywine Valley attractions and Amish country nearby.

Location: Historic small town.

"Truly an enchanting place."

Certificate may be used: No holidays or holiday weekends. Jan. 1-Feb. 28, all week; March 1-Dec. 31, Sunday-Thursday only.

Lackawaxen

Roebling Inn on the Delaware

155 Scenic Dr
Lackawaxen, PA 18435
(570)685-7900 Fax:(570)685-1718
Internet: www.roeblinginn.com
E-mail: info@roeblinginn.com

Circa 1870. Elegant, country accommodations located just two hours from New York City and two and a half from Philadelphia offer the opportunity to relax and enjoy two pristine rivers, the Delaware and the Lackawaxen. Sit on the front porch or at water's edge amid the mountain beauty and forested landscape. Watch for bald eagles and other birds. Air-conditioned guest bedrooms are comfortably furnished with antiques. Some include a fireplace. Start the day with a bountiful breakfast before exploring the picturesque area. Walk across the Roebling Bridge, America's oldest wire cable suspension bridge, view the picture exhibits and visit the small tollhouse museum. Tour the home of Zane Grey, open seasonally and maintained by the National Park Service. Hike at Minisink Battleground Park, site of a Revolutionary War battle or take in area waterfalls with a self-guided driving/hiking tour.

Innkeeper(s): Don & JoAnn Jahn. $125-165. 6 rooms with PB, 3 with FP, 1 cottage, 1 conference room. Breakfast and snacks/refreshments included in rates. Types of meals: Country bkfst, veg bkfst, early coffee/tea and afternoon tea. Beds: QDT. Cable TV, DVD, reading lamp, CD player, ceiling fan, clock radio, most with fireplace, bath amenities, wireless Internet access, alarm clock, wireless Internet access, some with fireplace and all private bath in room. Air conditioning. Fax, generous cooked-to-order breakfast served at your individual table: eggs, omelettes, oatmeal, pancakes, fruit and more (special diets accommodated), afternoon & evening tea, hot chocolate, cookies, front porch, hammock and sitting room with fireplace on premises. Antiquing, canoeing/kayaking, downhill skiing, fishing, golf, hiking, horseback riding, parks, tennis, water sports, eagle viewing, fishing, drift boat service, white water rafting on the Lackawaxen, tubing/rafting/canoeing on the Delaware and Bethel Woods (30 mins) nearby.

Location: Mountains, waterfront.

Publicity: *New York Times, Pennsylvania Magazine, New York Magazine and New York Daily News.*

Certificate may be used: Monday-Thursday in April and September.

Lancaster

Hollinger House

2336 Hollinger Rd
Lancaster, PA 17602-4728
(717)464-3050 Fax:(717)464-3053
Internet: www.hollingerhousebnb.com
E-mail: majestic@cplx.net

Circa 1870. Become part of the family while staying at this cozy B&B in the heart of Amish Country with hardwood floors, high ceilings and fireplaces. Children of all ages are welcome. Relax on the wraparound veranda. Guest bedroom amenities include bottled water, glycerin soaps and a special blended shampoo. Add romantic touches by requesting an in-room massage by candlelight, soft music, fresh flowers and a welcome basket with an assortment of local goodies, cocktail napkins, glasses, wine, champagne, bottled juices and more. Enjoy a bountiful hot breakfast each morning and the generous hospitality extends to providing evening desserts. Stroll the grounds or go sightseeing. Drive to New York in 2-1/2 hours, two hours to Baltimore, 60 miles to Philadelphia and 35 minutes to Harrisburg.

Innkeeper(s): David & Cindy Mott. $125-295. 9 rooms, 8 with PB, 2 with FP, 1 two-bedroom suite, 3 guest houses, 1 conference room. Breakfast and snacks/refreshments included in rates. Types of meals: Country bkfst. Beds: KQT. Cable TV, reading lamp, clock radio, turn-down service, desk, some with fireplace, hair dryer, bath amenities, wireless Internet access, bottled water, soaps, shampoos and all natural toothpaste in room. Air conditioning. VCR, DVD, fax, copier, library, parlor games, telephone, laundry facility, reading material, cable TV, VCR, High speed Internet access and Wireless Internet access on premises. Amusement parks, antiquing, art galleries, bicycling, canoeing/kayaking, cross-country skiing, downhill skiing, fishing, golf, hiking, horseback riding, live theater, museums, parks, shopping, sporting events, tennis, water sports, wineries, Amish attractions, historic sites, outlet shopping, parks, covered bridges, mini golf, tours and quilt shops nearby.

Location: Country. Rural, private setting.

Publicity: *Victoria Magazine, Hallmark Greeting Cards photo shoot, People's Place photo shoot, Eisenhart Wallpaper photo shoot, Lancaster Magazine, WLAN (one of top B&Bs in Lancaster County), Centennial (Novel, too) and by James Michener.*

Certificate may be used: November-April, Sunday-Thursday; Guest Houses in January, February, March.

O'Flaherty's Dingeldein House B&B

1105 E King St
Lancaster, PA 17602-3233
(717)293-1723 (800)779-7765 Fax:(717)293-1947
Internet: www.dingeldeinhouse.com
E-mail: rooms@dingeldeinhouse.com

Circa 1910. This Dutch Colonial home was once residence to the Armstrong family, who acquired fame and fortune in the tile floor industry. Springtime guests will brighten at the sight of this home's beautiful flowers. During winter months, innkeepers Dave and Gerry Blaich deck the halls with plenty of seasonal decorations. Breakfast by candlelight might include fresh-baked muffins, fruits, the innkeepers' special blend of coffee and mouth-watering omelets, pancakes or French toast. Cozy rooms include comfortable furnishings and cheery wall coverings. With advance notice, the innkeepers can arrange for guests to enjoy dinner at the home of one of their Amish friends.

Innkeeper(s): Dave & Gerry Blaich. $100-165. 6 rooms with PB, 6 with FP, 1 two-bedroom suite. Breakfast and snacks/refreshments included in rates. Types of meals: Full gourmet bkfst and early coffee/tea. Beds: QT. Cable TV, reading lamp, ceiling fan, clock radio, desk, most with fireplace, hair dryer, bathrobes, bath amenities and wireless Internet access in room. Air conditioning. VCR, fax, copier, library, parlor games, telephone and gift shop on premises. Amusement parks, antiquing, art galleries, bicycling, fishing, golf, horseback riding, live theater, museums, parks, shopping, sporting events and wineries nearby.

Location: Residential.

Publicity: *Gourmet.*

Certificate may be used: All year except June, July, August, September and October, Sunday through Thursday. Weekends, January and February.

Landenberg

Cornerstone B&B Inn

300 Buttonwood Rd
Landenberg, PA 19350-9398
(610)274-2143 Fax:(610)274-0734
Internet: www.cornerstoneinn.net
E-mail: info@cornerstoneinn.net

Surrounded by tranquil perennial and water gardens, the historic Cornerstone Bed and Breakfast Inn is an 18th century country estate in picturesque Landenberg, Pennsylvania. Gather by one of the fireplaces in the living room to play games or read. Stay in romantic accommodations that feature canopy beds, antiques and Jacuzzis for two. Wake up and start each day's adventures with a satisfying breakfast. There is much to see and experience in the Brandywine Valley. Tour the Wyeth Museum, visit Longwood Gardens and Winterthur and explore Amish Country. Ask about award-winning getaway packages.

Innkeeper(s): Sue Donato. $90-210. 8 rooms, 5 with FP, 1 suite. Breakfast included in rates. Types of meals: Full bkfst and early coffee/tea. Beds: KQT. Cable TV, reading lamp, clock radio, bath amenities and wireless Internet access in room. Air conditioning. DVD, fax, telephone and fireplace on premises. Amusement parks, antiquing, live theater, parks, shopping and sporting events nearby.

Location: Country.

Certificate may be used: January.

Ligonier

Campbell House B&B

305 E Main St
Ligonier, PA 15658-1417
(724)238-9812 (888)238-9812 Fax:(724)238-9951
Internet: www.campbellhousebnb.com
E-mail: innkeeper@campbellhousebnb.com

Circa 1868. Old-fashioned charm blends with modern confort at this Victorian 1868 city cottage in Ligonier, Pennsylvania. Campbell House Bed and Breakfast is a peaceful retreat with a romantic ambiance. Find complimentary snacks, beverages, videos, wine glasses and ice buckets in the Strawberry Pantry. Relax and let the world go by on the front covered porch. Enjoy the smoke-free environment. Guest bedrooms and suites boast an assortment of pleasing amenities that may include a canopy or sleigh bed and a slipper or clawfoot tub. Start each day with a scrumptious breakfast.

Innkeeper(s): Patti Campbell. $99-190. Call inn for details. Types of meals: Full bkfst, veg bkfst, snacks/refreshments and wine. Cable TV, VCR, DVD, reading lamp, stereo, refrigerator, ceiling fan, snack bar, clock radio, telephone, hair dryer, bathrobes, bath amenities, wireless Internet access and iron/ironing board in room. Central air. Fax, copier, parlor games and gift shop on premises. Amusement parks, antiquing, art galleries, bicycling, canoeing/kayaking, cross-country skiing, downhill skiing, fishing, golf, hiking, live theater, museums, parks, shopping and wineries nearby.

Location: City. Ligonier is an Historical Village.

Certificate may be used: Except June 15 through Oct. 31.

Linfield

Shearer Elegance

1154 Main St
Linfield, PA 19468-1139
(610)495-7429 (800)861-0308 Fax:(610)495-7814
Internet: www.shearerelegance.com
E-mail: contact@shearerelegance.com

Circa 1897. This stone Queen Anne mansion is the height of Victorian opulence and style. Peaked roofs, intricate trim and a stenciled wraparound porch grace the exterior. Guests enter the home via a marble entry,
which boasts a three-story staircase. Stained-glass windows and carved mantels are other notable features. The Victorian furnishings and decor complement the ornate workmanship, and lacy curtains are a romantic touch.

The bedrooms feature hand-carved, built-in wardrobes. The grounds are dotted with gardens. The inn is located in the village of Linfield, about 15 minutes from Valley Forge.

Innkeeper(s): Shirley & Malcolm Shearer. $100-155. 7 rooms with PB, 3 suites, 3 conference rooms. Types of meals: Full bkfst and early coffee/tea. Beds: KQ. Cable TV, VCR, reading lamp, stereo, refrigerator, ceiling fan, clock radio and desk in room. Air conditioning. Fax, copier, library, parlor games and telephone on premises. Amusement parks, antiquing, downhill skiing, fishing, golf, live theater, parks, shopping, sporting events, tennis and outlets nearby.

Location: Country.

Publicity: *Reading, Norristown, Pottstown and Local.*

"Thank you for creating such a beautiful place to escape reality."

Certificate may be used: Jan. 2 to Nov. 10, Sunday through Thursday.

Lititz

Speedwell Forge B&B

465 Speedwell Forge Rd
Lititz, PA 17543
(717)626-1760 (877)EST-1760
Internet: www.speedwellforge.com
E-mail: stay@speedwellforge.com

Circa 1760. Secluded in a valley in Lancaster County, just minutes from Pennsylvania Dutch Country, Speedwell Forge B&B sits on 120 acres along a creek with a cornfield, wolf sanctuary and woodlands in Lititz, Pennsylvania. Built in 1760, this historic Colonial Federal stone house is listed in the National Register of Historic Places. It has been painstakingly restored to maintain the quality craftsmanship it originally reflected. Family heirlooms and antiques accent the interior. Some of the accommodations feature a fireplace and whirlpool tub. The two cottages include a kitchenette. Before exploring the area, start each day with a three-course breakfast. In the evening gather to indulge in a choice of desserts.

Innkeeper(s): Dawn Darlington. $125-225. 5 rooms with PB, 4 with FP, 3 with WP, 1 two-bedroom suite, 2 cottages, 1 conference room. Breakfast included in rates. Types of meals: Full gourmet bkfst, veg bkfst, wine and Evening desserts. Beds: KQDT. Modem hook-up, data port, cable TV, VCR, DVD, reading lamp, CD player, refrigerator, clock radio, telephone, coffeemaker, turn-down service, desk, most with hot tub/spa, voice mail, most with fireplace, hair dryer, bathrobes, bath amenities, wireless Internet access and (Not all rooms have all amenities - please call to ensure we can accommodate your needs) in room. Central air. Library, parlor games, On a beautiful 120-acre farm with creek, Between a lake, Natural park and Wolf sanctuary on premises. Amusement parks, antiquing, art galleries, bicycling, canoeing/kayaking, cross-country skiing, fishing, golf, hiking, horseback riding, live theater, museums, parks, shopping, sporting events, wineries, Hershey (30 minutes), Gettysburg (40 minutes), Philadelphia (one hour),Outlet malls, Small towns, Fine restaurants and Amish nearby.

Location: Country. Between a lake and a natural park.

Publicity: *Gwinnett Daily Post (11/5/06), Lancaster New Era, Lancaster Intelligencer-Journal, Lititz Record-Express, This Old House magazine (October 2005), Harrisburg Patriot-News (10/30/05) and Blue Ridge cable 11 news twice.*

Certificate may be used: November-March, Monday-Thursday, subject to availability.

The Lititz House B&B

301 N Broad St
Lititz, PA 17543
(717)626-5299 (800)464-6764
Internet: www.lititzhouse.com
E-mail: stay@lititzhouse.com

Circa 1904. Experience small-town charm at this 1904 bed and breakfast situated in the heart of downtown in Pennsylvania Dutch Country in Lancaster County. It is mingled with elegant touches for enjoyment and comfort. The first floor has been redecorated with Scandinavian teak, glass and leather furniture on area rugs. Relax in the second-floor sitting room. Air-conditioned guest bedrooms and a two-bedroom suite with private entrances are tasteful and inviting. Let your taste buds rejoice in the elegant gourmet breakfast. Sit on the wraparound front porch rockers, the landscaped decks or the backyard swing amid the flower garden with a fountain.

Innkeeper(s): Pat & Jim Erven. $85-145. 5 rooms, 3 with PB, 1 two-bedroom suite. Breakfast, hors d'oeuvres and wine included in rates. Types of meals: Full gourmet bkfst, veg bkfst, early coffee/tea and snacks/refreshments. Beds: QD. Data port, cable TV, VCR, DVD, reading lamp, ceiling fan, clock radio, hair dryer, bath amenities, wireless Internet access, iron/ironing board, extra fluffy towels, ultra soft sheets and back care mattresses in room. Air conditioning. Amusement parks, antiquing, art galleries, bicycling, fishing, golf, hiking, live theater, museums, parks, shopping, tennis and wineries nearby.

Location: Lancaster County.

Certificate may be used: January-April, subject to availability.

Manheim

Manheim Manor

140 S Charlotte St
Manheim, PA 17545-1804
(717)664-4168 (888)224-4346 Fax:(717)664-0445
Internet: www.manheimmanor.com
E-mail: innkeeper@manheimmanor.com

Adorning a quiet neighborhood in a quaint town, this Victorian home is listed in the National Register. Built from stone and wood, it boasts a pillared front porch with lacy fretwork embellishments. Chestnut wood creates a rich setting for elegant furnishings of double-brocaded love seats and a Louis XV medallion-backed, red-velvet sofa. Offering a variety of decorating styles, well-appointed guest bedrooms feature coordinated wall coverings, window treatments, luxurious fabrics and comfortable furnishings. Indulge in bedside cordials, English toffee, mints and Hershey's chocolates. A bountiful multi-course breakfast is a culinary event, creating a variety of dishes including the all-homemade: granola, yogurt, applesauce and signature Victorian brown bread pudding. Arrangements can be made to join an Amish family for dinner, take a buggy or winter sleigh ride. There is much to explore in Pennsylvania Dutch Country with historical sites and shops within walking distance.

Innkeeper(s): Todd Nath and Laureen Benn. Call for rates. Call inn for details. Breakfast included in rates. Types of meals: Full gourmet bkfst and early coffee/tea. Beds: KQDT. Modem hook-up, cable TV, VCR, reading lamp, stereo, refrigerator, ceiling fan, clock radio, telephone, coffeemaker, desk, hot tub/spa, voice mail and fireplace in room. Central air. Fax, spa, fireplace and laundry facility on premises. Limited handicap access. Amusement parks, antiquing, art galleries, fishing, golf, hiking, horseback riding, live theater, museums, parks, shopping and wineries nearby.

Location: Country.

Certificate may be used: Anytime, November-April, subject to availability.

Rose Manor B&B

124 S Linden St
Manheim, PA 17545-1616
(717)664-4932 (800)666-4932 Fax:(717)664-1611
Internet: www.rosemanor.net
E-mail: inn@rosemanor.net

Circa 1905. A local mill owner built this manor house and it still maintains original light fixtures, woodwork and cabinetry. The grounds are decorated with roses and herb gardens. An herb theme is played out in the guest rooms, which feature names such as the Parsley, Sage, Rosemary and Thyme rooms. The fifth room is named the Basil, and its spacious quarters encompass the third story and feature the roof's angled ceiling. One room offers a whirlpool and another a fireplace. The decor is a comfortable English manor style with some antiques. The inn's location provides close access to many Pennsylvania Dutch country attractions.

Innkeeper(s): Susan Jenal. $99-140. 5 rooms, 3 with PB, 3 with FP, 2 with WP. Breakfast included in rates. Types of meals: Full bkfst and picnic lunch. Beds: QDT. Cable TV, reading lamp, ceiling fan, some with hot tub/spa, some with fireplace and one with whirlpool in room. Air conditioning. Fax, copier, library and telephone on premises. Amusement parks, antiquing, fishing, live theater, parks and shopping nearby.

Location: Small village.

Publicity: *Harrisburg Patriot, Lancaster County Magazine and Central Pennsylvania Life.*

Certificate may be used: January-April; December subject to availability excluding holidays, Anytime, Last Minute-Based on Availability.

Marietta

Olde Fogie Farm

106 Stackstown Rd
Marietta, PA 17547-9502
(717)426-3992 (877)653-3644
Internet: www.oldefogiefarm.com
E-mail: oldefogiefarm@comcast.net

Circa 1841. Enjoy seasonal specials that Tom and Biz offer at this bed & breakfast. Adults are catered to exclusively during November through March. The Chicken Coop and Hayloft suites each feature a fireplace, love seat and breakfast in-room. A hot tub and massage are pampering amenities. From April through October the whole family is welcome. Farm animals

need to be cared for, and after-breakfast chores to be done. An Amish meal can be arranged. The large pond with giant koi is a refreshing place to swim. The picnic pavilion is surrounded by gorgeous landscaping and butterfly gardens.

Innkeeper(s): Tom & Biz Fogie. $95. 2 rooms, 1 with FP, 2 two-bedroom suites. Breakfast included in rates. Types of meals: Country bkfst, veg bkfst and wine. Beds: QDT. Cable TV, VCR, reading lamp, refrigerator, ceiling fan, coffeemaker and some with fireplace in room. Air conditioning. Swimming and sauna on premises. Amusement parks, antiquing, art galleries, beach, bicycling, canoeing/kayaking, cross-country skiing, downhill skiing, fishing, golf, hiking, horseback riding, live theater, museums, parks, shopping, sporting events, tennis, water sports and wineries nearby.

Location: Country. Susquehanna River.

Publicity: *Foders, New York Daily news, New York Times, Washingtonian Magazine, Washington Post, WGAL TV Lancaster, PA, WMBT Harrisburg and PA.*

"You're stuck with us! We'll be here every year. We are already thinking of friends to invite to come here."

Certificate may be used: November through February, subject to availability.

Railroad House Restaurant B&B

280 W Front St
Marietta, PA 17547-1405
(717)426-4141
Internet: www.therailroadhouse.com

Circa 1820. The Railroad House, a sprawling old hotel, conjures up memories of the days when riding the rail was the way to travel. The house was built as a refuge for weary men who were working along the Susquehanna River. When the railroad finally made its way through Marietta, the rail station's waiting  room and ticket office were located in what's now known as the Railroad House. The restored rooms feature antiques, Oriental rugs, Victorian decor and rustic touches such as exposed brick walls. The chefs at the inn's restaurant create a menu of American and continental dishes using spices and produce from the beautifully restored gardens. The innovative recipes have been featured in Bon Appetit. The innkeepers also host a variety of special events and weekends, including murder mysteries and clambakes serenaded by jazz bands. Carriage rides and special walking tours of Marietta can be arranged.

Innkeeper(s): Raphael Aguon. $109-149. 8 rooms with PB, 1 cottage, 1 conference room. Breakfast included in rates. Types of meals: Full gourmet bkfst, early coffee/tea, gourmet lunch, picnic lunch, afternoon tea, snacks/refreshments and gourmet dinner. Restaurant on premises. Beds: QDT. Reading lamp, refrigerator, clock radio and desk in room. Air conditioning. Copier, bicycles, parlor games, telephone, fireplace, gardens and yard games on premises. Amusement parks, antiquing, downhill skiing, fishing, live theater, parks, shopping, sporting events, water sports and music box museum nearby.

Location: Small town.

Certificate may be used: Anytime, subject to availability.

Mechanicsburg

Kanaga House B&B Inn

6940 Carlisle Pike (US Rt 11)
Mechanicsburg, PA 17050
(717)766-8654 (877)9KA-NAGA Fax:(717)697-3908
Internet: www.kanagahouse.com
E-mail: kanagahouse@davtv.com

Circa 1775. Stay in this restored 1775 stone house while visiting the area's many tourist attractions such as Gettysburg Civil War Battlefield, Hershey Chocolate World, Lancaster Dutch Country or Harrisburg (the state capital). The well-appointed guest bedrooms offer canopy beds, and one boasts a fireplace. Tree-studded grounds and a large gazebo are perfect for weddings. The first-floor rooms and catering staff also enhance business meetings and retreats. Walk the nearby Appalachian Trail, or fly fish in the Yellow Breeches and Letort Springs.

Innkeeper(s): Mary Jane & Dave Kretzing. $85-165. 7 rooms with PB, 1 with FP, 1 conference room. Breakfast included in rates. Types of meals: Full bkfst and early coffee/tea. Beds: Q. TV, reading lamp, refrigerator, clock radio, telephone and desk in room. Air conditioning. VCR, copier, fireplace and gazebo with table and chairs on premises. Amusement parks, antiquing, downhill skiing, live theater and shopping nearby.

Location: Rural setting.

Certificate may be used: Oct. 15 to March 31, Sunday-Thursday only, excluding holidays.

Mercersburg

The Mercersburg Inn

405 S Main St
Mercersburg, PA 17236-9517
(717)328-5231 Fax:(717)328-3403
Internet: www.mercersburginn.com
E-mail: innkeeper@mercersburginn.com

Circa 1909. Situated on a hill overlooking the Tuscorora Mountains, the valley and village, this 20,000-square-foot Georgian Revival mansion was built for industrialist Harry Byron. Six massive columns mark the entrance, which opens to a majestic hall featuring chestnut wainscoting and an elegant double stairway and rare scagliola (marbleized) columns. All the rooms are furnished with antiques and reproductions. A local craftsman built the inn's four-poster, canopied king-size beds. Many of the rooms have their own balconies and a few have fireplaces. Thursday through Sunday evening, the inn's chef prepares noteworthy, elegant dinners, which feature an array of seasonal specialties.

Innkeeper(s): Lisa & Jim McCoy. $140-325. 17 rooms with PB, 3 with FP, 2 with WP, 1 cottage, 2 conference rooms. Breakfast included in rates. Types of meals: Full gourmet bkfst, picnic lunch, wine and gourmet dinner. Restaurant on premises. Beds: KQT. Reading lamp, clock radio, telephone, desk, hair dryer, bathrobes, bath amenities, wireless Internet access and iron/ironing board in room. Central air. TV, VCR, fax, copier, parlor games, fireplace and gift shop on premises. Antiquing, beach, bicycling, cross-country skiing, downhill skiing, fishing, golf, hiking, live theater, parks, shopping and water sports nearby.

Location: Mountains. Cumberland Valley.

Publicity: *Mid-Atlantic Country, Washington Post, The Herald-Mail, Richmond News Leader, Washingtonian, Philadelphia Inquirer and Pittsburgh.*

"Elegance personified! Outstanding ambiance and warm hospitality."

Certificate may be used: Sunday-Thursday, excludes holidays.

Milford

Cliff Park Inn & Golf Course

155 Cliff Park Rd
Milford, PA 18337-9708
(570)296-6491 (800)225-6535 Fax:(570)296-5984
Internet: www.cliffparkinn.com
E-mail: escape@cliffparkinn.com

Circa 1850. Located only two miles from the heart of the quaint town, this casually upscale inn offers privacy, seclusion, elegant accommodations, fine dining, and a variety of outdoor activities. It sits on 500 acres within a 70,000-acre national park. Enjoy miles of hiking trails with breathtaking views and play golf on one of the country's oldest 9-hole courses. Choose a newly decorated guest bedroom or suite with a clawfoot tub and separate shower with Bath & Body Works amenities, imported linens, an entertainment center, sunporch  and delightful view. A complimentary continental breakfast with fresh baked breads, granola, bagels & salmon, yogurt, assorted juices and coffee is included in the room rate. A destination in itself, the pub and glass-encased dining room are open for lunch, dinner and Sunday brunch.

Innkeeper(s): Stephanie Brown. $129-249. 12 rooms with PB, 5 suites, 1 conference room. Breakfast and Continental Breakfast included in rates. Types of meals: Full bkfst, lunch, snacks/refreshments and dinner. Restaurant on premises. Beds: KQD. Cable TV, DVD, CD player, clock radio, telephone, voice mail, hair dryer, bath amenities, wireless Internet access and iron/ironing board in room. Air conditioning. Fax, parlor games, fireplace and 9-hole golf course on premises. Limited handicap access. Antiquing, art galleries, bicycling, canoeing/kayaking, cross-country skiing, fishing, golf, hiking, horseback riding, parks and shopping nearby.

Location: Country.

Publicity: *Top 10 Romantic Inn (2005 and iLoveInns.com).*

Certificate may be used: Nov. 1-May 20, Sunday-Thursday.

Milton

Pau-Lyn's Country B&B

1160 Broadway Rd
Milton, PA 17847-9506
(570)742-4110
Internet: www.paulyns.com
E-mail: paulyns@msn.com

Circa 1850. Gracing two acres, this 1857 Victorian brick home provides a year-round environment that is smoke- and alcohol-free. It is considered a restful haven and a walkway to lasting memories. An inviting porch and patio overlook the large lawn. Air-conditioned guest bedrooms are accented with colorful quilts and antiques. The Canal Room features a fireplace and along with the Hideaway Room, are handicap accessible with a ground-level outside entrance. Gather each morning for a hearty country breakfast in the fireside dining room. Special dietary needs will be accommodated with advance notice. Nearby are working farms and dairies, covered bridges, mountains, rivers and valleys.

Innkeeper(s): Paul & Evelyn Landis. $85-100. 7 rooms, 4 with PB. Breakfast included in rates. Types of meals: Country bkfst and early coffee/tea. Beds:

QDT. Modem hook-up, cable TV, reading lamp, refrigerator, clock radio, telephone, some with fireplace, bath amenities and wireless Internet access in room. Central air. VCR, parlor games, large lawn, patio, many trees, birds and porch on premises. Limited handicap access. Amusement parks, antiquing, bicycling, canoeing/kayaking, cross-country skiing, downhill skiing, fishing, golf, hiking, museums, parks, shopping, sporting events, tennis, water sports, wineries, Underground Railroad, Little League museum and field and Knoebels Grove nearby.

Location: Near small town.

Certificate may be used: Year-round, Sunday through Thursday, some weekends. All depends on availability.

Mount Joy

Hillside Farm Bed & Breakfast

607 Eby Chiques Road
Mount Joy, PA 17552-8819
(717)653-6697 (888)249-3406 Fax:(717)653-9775
Internet: www.hillsidefarmbandb.com
E-mail: innkeeper@hillsidefarmbandb.com

Circa 1840. This comfortable farm has a relaxing homey feel to it. Rooms are simply decorated and special extras such as handmade quilts and antiques add an elegant country touch.

Two guest cottages each offer a king bed, whirlpool tub for two, fireplace, wet bar and deck overlooking a bucolic meadow. The home is a true monument to the cow. Dairy antiques, cow knickknacks and antique milk bottles abound. Some of the bottles were found during the renovation of the home and its grounds. Spend the day hunting for bargains in nearby antique shops, malls and factory outlets, or tour local Amish and Pennsylvania Dutch attractions. The farm is a good vacation spot for families with children above the age of 10.

Innkeeper(s): Gary Lintner. $90-250. 5 rooms with PB, 2 with FP, 2 cottages. Breakfast included in rates. Types of meals: Country bkfst, veg bkfst, early coffee/tea and snacks/refreshments. Beds: KQT. TV, VCR, reading lamp, stereo, refrigerator, ceiling fan, snack bar, clock radio and iron/ironing board in room. Central air. Fax, copier, spa, library and telephone on premises. Amusement parks, antiquing, art galleries, bicycling, fishing, golf, hiking, live theater, museums, parks, shopping and wineries nearby.

Location: Country.

Publicity: *Washingtonian Magazine.*

Certificate may be used: January through June, Sunday through Thursday, no holidays or holiday weekends, subject to availability, rooms only.

The Olde Square Inn

127 E Main St
Mount Joy, PA 17552-1513
(717)653-4525 (800)742-3533 Fax:(717)653-0976
Internet: www.oldesquareinn.com
E-mail: oldesquare@dejazzd.com

Situated near the heart of Amish country on the historic town square of friendly Mount Joy, this stately brick house is an inviting and hospitable bed and breakfast. Take a refreshing swim in the seasonal, in-ground pool. Each of the delightful guest bedrooms and the cottage feature a fireplace and some boast whirlpool tubs. Select from a large movie collection. Breakfast can be delivered to the door of the Enchanted Cottage. A homemade breakfast buffet changes daily with a

selection of Dutch Country favorites and signature dishes, such as Baked Oatmeal, Cherry Cobbler, Farmer's Hash and Pineapple Brunch Casserole. Linger in the dining room or take a tray to the porch or brick poolside patio. Relaxation is easy at this comfortable B&B with picturesque surroundings.

Innkeeper(s): Fran & Dave Hand. $109-260. 6 rooms with PB, 6 with FP, 1 with WP, 1 cottage. Breakfast included in rates. Types of meals: Full bkfst and early coffee/tea. Beds: QD. Cable TV, VCR, reading lamp, clock radio and telephone in room. Air conditioning. Fax and fireplace on premises. Amusement parks, antiquing, fishing, live theater, parks, shopping and sporting events nearby.

Location: Small town.

Certificate may be used: November through April, Monday-Thursday. Year-round, last minute-based on availability. Cannot be used on cottage.

The Victorian Rose Bed & Breakfast

214 Marietta Ave
Mount Joy, PA 17552-3106
(717)492-0050 (888)313-7494
Internet: www.thevictorianrosebandb.com
E-mail: victorianrosebb@juno.com

Circa 1897. Central to Hershey and Gettysburg battlefield, The Victorian Rose in Mount Joy is an elegant but comfortable place from which to explore beautiful Lancaster County. Enjoy the stately guest rooms and a number of elegant areas including the library and a formal living room. Guests are treated to innkeeper Doris Tyson's home-baked treats for breakfast, and to her homemade candies at other times. Pennsylvania Dutch Country is just 12 miles from the inn.

Innkeeper(s): Doris L. Tyson. $75-95. 4 rooms, 3 with PB. Breakfast included in rates. Types of meals: Full gourmet bkfst. Beds: Q. TV, VCR, reading lamp, ceiling fan and clock radio in room. Air conditioning. DVD, fax, copier, library, telephone and fireplace on premises. Amusement parks, antiquing, fishing, golf, live theater, museums, parks, shopping and wineries nearby.

Location: Town.

Publicity: *Lancaster Historic Preservation Trust Featured Home 2001 tour and PA Dutch Visitor & Convention Bureau of Authentic B&B Association.*

Certificate may be used: November-May, Sunday-Thursday, subject to availability.

Muncy

The Bodine House B&B

307 S Main St
Muncy, PA 17756-1507
(570)546-8949
Internet: www.bodinehouse.com
E-mail: bodinehouse@alltel.net

Circa 1805. This Federal-style townhouse, framed by a white picket fence, is in the National Register. Antique and reproduction furnishings highlight the inn's four fireplaces, the parlor, study and library. A favorite guest room features a walnut canopy bed, hand-stenciled and bordered walls, and a framed sampler by the innkeeper's great-great-grandmother. Candlelight breakfasts are served beside the fireplace in a gracious Colonial dining room. Also

available is a guest cottage with kitchenette.

Innkeeper(s): David & Marie Louise Smith. $75-135. 3 rooms with PB, 1 with FP, 1 cottage. Breakfast included in rates. Types of meals: Full bkfst and early coffee/tea. Beds: QDT. Cable TV, reading lamp and turn-down service in room. Air conditioning. TV, VCR, fax, bicycles, library, telephone, fireplace and afternoon tea (by request) on premises. Antiquing, canoeing/kayaking, cross-country skiing, fishing, parks, shopping and sporting events nearby.

Location: Village.

Publicity: *Colonial Homes and Philadelphia Inquirer.*

"What an experience, made special by your wonderful hospitality."

Certificate may be used: Sunday through Thursday, year-round, subject to availability.

North East

Grape Arbor Bed and Breakfast

51 East Main St
North East, PA 16428-1340
(814)725-0048 (866)725-0048 Fax:(814)725-5740
Internet: www.grapearborandb.com
E-mail: grapearborandb@aol.com

Circa 1832. Two side-by-side brick Federal mansions with Victorian embellishments have been restored to preserve their antiquity yet provide today's conveniences. Built in the early 1830s as private homes, their history includes having served as a stagecoach tavern, primary school, and possibly a stop on the Underground Railroad. Watch videos, play games or read a book by the fire in the library. Socialize over hors d'oeuvres in the parlor. Elegant guest bedrooms and suites are named for local varieties of grapes and feature antiques, reproductions, data ports, VCRs and fine toiletries. Two main breakfast dishes, pastries and breads, a hot or cold fruit sampler, juice and freshly ground coffee are enjoyed in the formal Dining Room or the light and airy Sun Porch. A guest refrigerator is stocked with beverages and homemade treats are always available.

Innkeeper(s): Dave and Peggy Hauser. $90-160. 8 rooms with PB, 3 with FP, 5 suites. Breakfast and snacks/refreshments included in rates. Types of meals: Full gourmet bkfst and early coffee/tea. Beds: KQD. Data port, cable TV, reading lamp, refrigerator, ceiling fan, clock radio, telephone, coffeemaker, desk, voice mail, fireplace and Jacuzzi in room. Central air. VCR, fax, copier, library, parlor games and fireplace on premises. Limited handicap access. Amusement parks, antiquing, beach, bicycling, cross-country skiing, downhill skiing, fishing, golf, hiking, horseback riding, live theater, parks and wineries nearby.

Location: Lakeside Village.

Certificate may be used: From 1-2 to 4-15, Sunday-Thursday, holidays excluded, subject to availability.

Philadelphia

Rittenhouse 1715, A Boutique Hotel

1715 Rittenhouse Square Street
Philadelphia, PA 19103
(215)546-6500 (877)791-6500 Fax:(215)546-8787
Internet: www.rittenhouse1715.com
E-mail: reservations@rittenhouse1715.com

Circa 1911. Experience elegant luxury at this comfortably renovated carriage house, internationally renown for business or pleasure. Impressive art, impeccable decor, lavish furnishings and extraordinary service are the hallmarks of this inn. The guest bedrooms are spectacular, tranquil retreats. Distinctive amenities include CD players, triple sheeting, turndown service, computer workstations, plush robes and marble bathrooms. Enjoy breakfast in The Cafe and early evening wine and snacks in the gorgeous lobby.

Innkeeper(s): Harriet S. Seltzer. $239-849. 23 rooms with PB, 10 with FP, 4 suites. Breakfast, snacks/refreshments, wine and Wine Reception included in

rates. Types of meals: Cont plus, early coffee/tea, Wine reception every evening in the lobby, coffee and tea available all day and continental breakfast daily. Room service 24 hours per day. Beds: KQD. Modem hook-up, data port, cable TV, reading lamp, CD player, snack bar, clock radio, telephone, turn-down service, desk, some with hot tub/spa, voice mail, some with fireplace, hair dryer, bathrobes, bath amenities, wireless Internet access, iron/ironing board, Large flat screen Plasma TVs, Wireless throughout building & rooms, Data ports in Superior and Deluxe Rooms in room. Central air. Fax, copier, parlor games and Off-premises laundry and dry cleaning services arranged daily on premises. Limited handicap access. Antiquing, art galleries, bicycling, live theater, museums, parks, shopping, sporting events, Fine Dining, Shopping and Museums nearby.

Location: City.

Publicity: *New York Magazine (52 Getaway Weekends, Philadelphia Style), Philadelphia Magazine (Best of Philly® 2002 Winner), Elegant Wedding, Country Living (Inn of the Month) and Washingtonian (Getaway Weekends).*

Certificate may be used: Subject to availability, Sunday-Thursday, January, February, March, July and August. Holidays excluded. No weekends.

Silverstone Bed & Breakfast

8840 Stenton Ave
Philadelphia, PA 19118-2846
(215)242-3333 (800)347-6858 Fax:(215)242-2680
Internet: www.silverstonestay.com
E-mail: yolanta@silverstonestay.com

Italian masons built this Victorian Gothic mansion with silvery stone from the Appalachian Mountains in 1877. Adorning historic Chestnut Hill inside the Philadelphia Metro area of Pennsylvania, this central location in is perfect for walking to local shops and restaurants. Select one of the well-appointed and spacious guest bedrooms or suites. For longer stays, short-term furnished apartments are available. After a satisfying breakfast visit Lancaster's Amish Country or take a day trip to Washington, D.C. or New York City. Laundry facilities and a private guest kitchen are provided. Silverstone Bed & Breakfast offers fresh herbs and vegetables from the garden.

Innkeeper(s): Yolanta. Call for rates. Call inn for details. Cable TV and VCR in room. Laundry facility on premises.

Location: City.

Certificate may be used: July, September, December and January.

Pittsburgh

The Priory

614 Pressley St
Pittsburgh, PA 15212-5616
(412)231-3338 Fax:(412)231-4838
Internet: www.thepriory.com
E-mail: edgpgh@stargate.net

Circa 1888. The Priory, now a European-style hotel, was built to provide lodging for Benedictine priests traveling through Pittsburgh. It is adjacent to Pittsburgh's Grand Hall at the Priory in historic East Allegheny. The inn's design and maze of rooms and corridors give it a distinctly Old World flavor. All rooms are decorated with Victorian furnishings.

Innkeeper(s): John and Suzanne Graf. $134-175. 24 rooms with PB, 3 suites, 1 conference room. Breakfast included in rates. Types of meals: Cont plus. Beds: KQD. Handicap access.

Publicity: *Pittsburgh Press, US Air, Country Inns, Innsider, Youngstown Vindicator, Travel & Leisure, Gourmet, Mid-Atlantic Country and National Geographic Traveler.*

"Although we had been told that the place was elegant, we were hardly prepared for the richness of detail. We felt as though we were guests in a manor."

Certificate may be used: December-March, excludes New Year's Eve and Valentine's Day.

Red Lion

Red Lion Bed & Breakfast

101 S Franklin St
Red Lion, PA 17356
(717)244-4739 Fax:(717)246-3219
Internet: www.redlionbandb.com
E-mail: staywithus@redlionbandb.com

Circa 1920. Explore one of the more popular regions of the state while staying at this unpretentious and quiet three-story brick, Federal-style home. Snuggle up next to the fireplace in the living room with a book from the well-stocked collection of reading material. Sip a cool iced tea on the enclosed sun porch or outside garden patio. Half of the six quaint and comfortable guest bedrooms offer a full bath and queen-size bed. Twin beds and cots are also available for families or groups traveling together. Breakfasts are substantial with quiche, pancakes, stuffed French toast, fresh baked rolls and muffins served alongside fruit or granola. The town has antique and craft shops and is within a 45-minute drive of vineyards, the Amish country of Lancaster, Hershey and the Gettysburg Battlefield.

Innkeeper(s): George & Danielle Sanders. $72-102. 6 rooms, 3 with PB, 1 conference room. Breakfast included in rates. Types of meals: Full bkfst. Beds: QT. TV, VCR, reading lamp, ceiling fan, clock radio, bathrobes and wireless Internet access in room. Air conditioning. Fax, copier, library, parlor games, telephone, fireplace, Off-street parking and Wireless Internet on premises. Limited handicap access. Amusement parks, antiquing, canoeing/kayaking, fishing, golf, hiking, horseback riding, museums, parks, shopping and wineries nearby.

Location: Small town.

Certificate may be used: January and February, subject to availability.

Reinholds

Brownstone Colonial Inn

590 Galen Hall Rd
Reinholds, PA 17569-9420
(717)484-4460 (877)464-9862 Fax:(717)484-4460
Internet: www.brownstonecolonialinn.com
E-mail: info@brownstonecolonialinn.com

Circa 1790. Early German Mennonite settlers built this sandstone farmhouse in 1790. It graces seven scenic acres amidst Amish countryside. Feel relaxed and pampered at this fully restored inn. Guest bedrooms and a suite boast random-width plank floors, locally handcrafted period-authentic furniture, sleigh or pencil post beds and antique Shaker peg boards. Enjoy a hearty country breakfast in the homestead's original smokehouse with brick floor, ceiling beams and open hearth fireplace. Start the day with fresh juices, homemade pastries and jams, a hot entree and fruits grown on-site. Stroll by the fish pond and gardens, or walk the nearby nature trails. An abundance of outlet and antique malls as well as historical and cultural sites are minutes away.

Innkeeper(s): Brenda & Mark Miller. $89-119. 4 rooms with PB, 1 suite. Breakfast and snacks/refreshments included in rates. Types of meals: Full bkfst, early coffee/tea and afternoon tea. Beds: QDT. Modem hook-up, reading lamp, clock radio and desk in room. Central air. VCR, telephone and fireplace on premises. Amusement parks, antiquing, cross-country skiing, fishing, golf, hiking, horseback riding, live theater, museums, parks, shopping, sporting events, water sports and wineries nearby.

Location: Country.

"We can't wait to tell friends and family about your paradise."

Certificate may be used: December-March, Monday-Wednesday.

Ronks

Candlelight Inn B&B

2574 Lincoln Hwy E
Ronks, PA 17572-9771
(717)299-6005 (800)772-2635 Fax:(717)299-6397
Internet: www.candleinn.com
E-mail: candleinn@aol.com

Circa 1920. Located in the Pennsylvania Dutch area, this Federal-style house offers a side porch for enjoying the home's acre and a half of tall trees and surrounding Amish farmland. Guest rooms feature Victorian decor. Three rooms include a Jacuzzi tub and fireplace. The inn's gourmet breakfast, which might include a creme caramel French toast, is served by candlelight. The innkeepers are professional classical musicians. Lancaster is five miles to the east.

Innkeeper(s): Tim & Heidi Soberick. $90-179. 7 rooms with PB, 3 with FP, 3 with HT, 3 with WP. Breakfast and snacks/refreshments included in rates. Types of meals: Full gourmet bkfst. Beds: KQT. Reading lamp, ceiling fan, clock radio, desk, some with hot tub/spa, some with fireplace, bathrobes, bath amenities, amaretto, robes, three with Jacuzzi and fireplaces in room. Central air. TV, fax, parlor games, telephone, badminton, croquet and afternoon refreshments on premises. Amusement parks, antiquing, art galleries, bicycling, fishing, golf, hiking, horseback riding, live theater, museums, parks, shopping, wineries, Sight & Sound theater, Living Waters theater, American Music Theater, Amish farms, Amish crafts and quilts, hot air ballooning, PA Dutch restaurants, farmers' markets, Fulton Opera House, Lancaster Symphony, outlet shopping and arranged dinners with an Amish family nearby.

Location: Country. Suburban-surrounded by farms.

Publicity: *Lancaster Daily News, Pennsylvania Dutch Traveler and Pennsylvania Intelligencer Journal.*

Certificate may be used: December through April, excluding holidays, Sunday through Thursday.

Shippensburg

Field & Pine B&B

2155 Ritner Hwy
Shippensburg, PA 17257-9756
(717)776-7179 Fax:(717)776-0076
E-mail: fieldpine@kuhncom.net

Circa 1790. Local limestone was used to build this stone house, located on the main wagon road to Baltimore and Washington. Originally, it was a tavern and weigh station. The house is surrounded by stately pines, and sheep graze on the inn's 80 acres. The bedrooms are hand-stenciled and furnished with quilts and antiques.

Innkeeper(s): Mary Ellen & Allan Williams. $75-95. 3 rooms, 1 with PB, 1 with FP, 1 suite. Breakfast and snacks/refreshments included in rates. Types of meals: Full gourmet bkfst and early coffee/tea. Beds: QDT. TV, reading lamp, stereo, clock radio, turn-down ser-

vice and desk in room. Air conditioning. VCR, telephone and fireplace on premises. Antiquing, fishing, parks and shopping nearby.

Location: Country.

Publicity: *Central Pennsylvania Magazine.*

"Our visit in this lovely country home has been most delightful. The ambiance of antiques and tasteful decorating exemplifies real country living."

Certificate may be used: Sunday through Thursday, year-round. Plus weekends subject to availability in January, February and March.

Somerset

Quill Haven Country Inn

1519 North Center Ave
Somerset, PA 15501-7001
(814)443-4514 (866)784-5522 Fax:(814)445-1376
Internet: www.quillhaven.com
E-mail: quill@quillhaven.com

Circa 1918. Set on three acres that were once part of a chicken and turkey farm, this historic Arts & Crafts-style home offers guest rooms, each individually appointed. The Bridal Suite includes a four-poster wrought iron bed and sunken tub in the bath. The Country Room includes a decorative pot-bellied stove. Antiques, reproductions and stained-glass lamps decorate the rooms. Guests are treated to a full breakfast with items such as baked grapefruit or apples, homemade breads and entrees such as stuffed French toast or a specialty casserole of ham, cheese and potatoes. Guests can spend the day boating or swimming at nearby Youghiogheny Reservoir, take a whitewater-rafting trip, bike or hike through the scenic countryside, ski at one of three ski resorts in the area or shop at antique stores, outlets and flea markets. Frank Lloyd Wright's Fallingwater is another nearby attraction.

Innkeeper(s): Carol & Rowland Miller. $95-115. 4 rooms with PB. Breakfast and snacks/refreshments included in rates. Types of meals: Full bkfst and early coffee/tea. Beds: KQ. Cable TV, VCR, reading lamp, ceiling fan, clock radio, turn-down service, hair dryer, bathrobes, bath amenities, wireless Internet access and heated mattress pad in room. Air conditioning. Fax, copier, spa, library, parlor games, telephone, fireplace, gift shop, outdoor hot tub, common room with fireplace and mini kitchenette on premises. Amusement parks, antiquing, bicycling, canoeing/kayaking, cross-country skiing, downhill skiing, fishing, golf, hiking, horseback riding, live theater, parks, shopping, tennis, water sports, wineries, Seven Springs, Hidden Valley and Laurel Highlands nearby.

Location: Country, mountains.

Publicity: *Westsylvania Magazine.*

"What a beautiful memory we will have of our first B&B experience! We've never felt quite so pampered in all our 25 years of marriage."

Certificate may be used: Anytime, March-September, subject to availability.

Starlight

The Inn at Starlight Lake

PO Box 27
Starlight, PA 18461-0027
(570)798-2519 (800)248-2519 Fax:(570)798-2672
Internet: www.innatstarlightlake.com
E-mail: info@innatstarlightlake.com

Circa 1909. Acres of woodland and meadow surround the last surviving railroad inn on the New York, Ontario and Western lines. Originally a boarding house, the inn was part of a little village that had its own store, church, blacksmith shop and

creamery. Platforms, first erected to accommodate tents for the summer season, were later replaced by three small cottage buildings that now include a suite with a double whirlpool. A modern three-bedroom house is available for family reunions and conferences. The inn is situated on the 45-acre, spring-fed Starlight Lake, providing summertime canoeing, swimming, fishing and sailing. (No motorboats are allowed on the lake.) Breakfast is served in the lakeside dining area where dinner is also available.

Innkeeper(s): Sari & Jimmy Schwartz. $85-255. 23 rooms, 19 with PB, 1 with FP, 1 suite, 3 cottages. Breakfast included in rates. Types of meals: Full bkfst, Sun. brunch, early coffee/tea, lunch, picnic lunch, snacks/refreshments, wine and dinner. Restaurant on premises. Beds: KQT. Reading lamp, ceiling fan, some with hot tub/spa, some with fireplace and bath amenities in room. TV, VCR, fax, copier, swimming, bicycles, tennis, library, parlor games, telephone, hair dryer and iron/ironing board available at the front desk on premises. Limited handicap access. Antiquing, bicycling, canoeing/kayaking, downhill skiing, fishing, golf, hiking, horseback riding, shopping, tennis, water sports, cross country skiing (right out our front door, bring your own equipment or rent) and try your feet at snow shoeing nearby.

Location: Country, mountains, waterfront.

Publicity: *New York Times, Philadelphia Inquirer, Newsday, Discerning Traveler, Freeman and Travel Network.*

Certificate may be used: Anytime, November-April, subject to availability.

Strasburg

Strasburg Village Inn

1 W Main St, Centre Sq
Strasburg, PA 17579
(717)687-0900 (800)541-1055 Fax:7176873650
Internet: www.strasburg.com
E-mail: angela@greystonemanor.com

Circa 1755. Located on historic Strasburg's Centre Square, this brick inn offers guests a glimpse of early Americana, in the center of the Amish country. Despite the old-fashioned charm, two suites offer the romantic, albeit modern, amenity of Jacuzzi tubs. The inn is adjacent to the Strasburg Country Store and Creamery, the town's oldest operating store. The shop offers a variety of baked goods, a 19th-century soda fountain, a deli with homemade ice cream, penny candy and plenty of collectibles. Guests are treated to a full breakfast at The Creamery. The inn is surrounded by many Pennsylvania Dutch sites, including Amish farms, antique stores and historic villages. Sight and Sound Theater, the Strasburg Railroad and Dutch Wonderland Amusement Park are nearby.

Innkeeper(s): Rich Choromiac. $40-169. 10 rooms with PB, 3 with WP, 1 conference room. Breakfast included in rates. Types of meals: Full bkfst, lunch and picnic lunch. Restaurant on premises. Beds: KQ. TV, clock radio and bath amenities in room. Air conditioning. Amusement parks, antiquing, bicycling, downhill skiing, golf, hiking, horseback riding, live theater, parks, shopping, sporting events and wineries nearby.

Location: Country.

Certificate may be used: Sunday-Thursday, Nov. 1-May 21, excluding holidays.

Terre Hill

The Artist's Inn & Gallery

117 E Main St
Terre Hill, PA 17581
(717)445-0219 (888)999-4479
Internet: www.artistinn.com
E-mail: info@artistinn.com

Circa 1848. Four-course breakfasts and warm and inviting guest rooms are offered at this Federal-style inn. Watch Amish buggies clip clop by from the Victorian veranda and listen to the chimes from the church across the way. Then plan your day with the help of innkeepers Jan and Bruce, avid adventurers who cross-country ski and explore the area's best offerings to share insights with guests. There's an art gallery with works by the resident artist. Guest accommodations are inviting with antiques, gas fireplaces, hardwood floors and decorative painting, wallpapers and borders. The Rose Room offers a Jacuzzi bath. The Garden Suite offers a whirlpool bath for two, massage shower, fireplace, king-size featherbed, private balcony and sitting room. Breakfasts feature breads such as scones or muffins, fruit parfaits, crepes or egg dishes and a luscious dessert—perhaps a pie, cake or tart.

Innkeeper(s): Jan & Bruce Garrabrandt. $115-250. 4 rooms with PB, 3 with FP, 2 suites, 1 cottage. Breakfast and snacks/refreshments included in rates. Types of meals: Full gourmet bkfst, veg bkfst, early coffee/tea and We will happily cater to celiac guests. Beds: KQ. Cable TV, DVD, reading lamp, CD player, ceiling fan, clock radio, turn-down service, some with hot tub/spa, hair dryer, bathrobes, bath amenities, wireless Internet access, iron/ironing board and fresh flowers in room. Central air. Copier, library, parlor games, telephone, fireplace, gift shop and art gallery on premises. Limited handicap access. Amusement parks, antiquing, art galleries, bicycling, cross-country skiing, fishing, golf, hiking, live theater, museums, parks, shopping, tennis, wineries and Amish Attractions nearby.

Location: Country. Small town.

Certificate may be used: Sunday-Thursday, November-April. Holidays excluded.

Valley Forge

The Great Valley House of Valley Forge

1475 Swedesford Road
Valley Forge, PA 19355
(610)644-6759
Internet: www.greatvalleyhouse.com
E-mail: info@greatvalleyhouse.com

Circa 1691. This 300-year-old Colonial stone farmhouse sits on four acres just two miles from Valley Forge Park. Boxwoods line the walkway, and ancient trees surround the house. Each of the  three antique-filled guest rooms is hand-stenciled and features a canopied or brass bed topped with handmade quilts. Guests enjoy a full breakfast before a 14-foot fireplace in the "summer kitchen," the oldest part of the house. On the grounds are a swimming pool, walking and hiking trails and the home's original smokehouse.

Innkeeper(s): Pattye Benson. $99-129. 3 rooms with PB, 1 conference room. Breakfast and Full Gourmet Breakfast included in rates. Types of meals: Full gourmet bkfst, veg bkfst, early coffee/tea, Dietetic, Lunch and Dinner and Weekend brunch available by prior arrangement. Beds: QDT. Modem hook-up, data port, cable TV, DVD, reading lamp, stereo, refrigerator, clock radio, telephone, coffeemaker, turn-down service, desk, hair dryer, bathrobes, bath amenities, wireless Internet access, iron/ironing board and Free Wireless Internet in guest rooms in

room. A/C. Fax, swimming, parlor games, fireplace and grand piano on premises. Antiquing, art galleries, bicycling, canoeing/kayaking, cross-country skiing, fishing, golf, hiking, horseback riding, live theater, museums, parks, shopping, sporting events, water sports, wineries and Antiquing nearby.

Location: Rural/suburban setting.

Publicity: *Valley Forge Convention & Tourism Spring/Summer 2007 Guide, Main Line Philadelphia, Philadelphia Inquirer, Washington Post, New York Times, Suburban Newspaper, Historical Documentary site, Travel cable network and Network TV.*

"As a business traveler, Patty's enthusiasm and warm welcome makes you feel just like you're home."

Certificate may be used: Nov. 1-April 30, both nights must be Sunday-Thursday, excludes holidays.

Warfordsburg

Buck Valley Ranch, LLC

1344 Negro Mountain Rd
Warfordsburg, PA 17267-8168
(717)294-3759 (800)294-3759 Fax:(717)294-6413
Internet: www.buckvalleyranch.com
E-mail: info@buckvalleyranch.com

Circa 1930. Trail riding is a popular activity on the ranch's 64 acres in the Appalachian Mountains of South Central Pennsylvania. State game lands and forests border the ranch. The guest house, decorated in a ranch/cowboy style, is a private farmhouse that can accommodate eight people. Meals are prepared using homegrown vegetables and locally raised meats. Rates also include horseback riding.

Innkeeper(s): Nadine & Leon Fox. $110. 4 rooms. Breakfast included in rates. Types of meals: Full gourmet bkfst. Beds: QDT. Reading lamp, hair dryer, bath amenities and iron/ironing board in room. A/C. Fax, copier, spa, swimming, sauna, stable, parlor games, telephone, gift shop and horseback riding on premises. Amusement parks, antiquing, canoeing/kayaking, skiing, fishing, golf, hiking, parks, shopping, tennis, water sports, C&O Canal, steam train rides and Rails to Trails nearby.

Location: Country, mountains.

Publicity: *Washington Post, Pittsburgh Press, PA bride, Baltimore Sun and Potomac.*

Certificate may be used: Jan. 1-Dec. 31, Sunday-Thursday, excluding weekends and holidays.

York

Friendship House B&B

728 E Philadelphia St
York, PA 17403-1609
(717)843-8299
E-mail: friendshiphouse@yorkinternet.net

Circa 1897. A walk down East Philadelphia Street takes visitors past an unassuming row of 19th-century townhouses. The Friendship House is a welcoming site with its light blue shutters and pink trim. Innkeepers Becky and Karen have added a shot of Victorian influence to their charming townhouse B&B, decorating with wallcoverings and lacy curtains. A country feast is prepared some mornings with choices ranging from quiche to French toast accompanied with items such as baked apples, smoked sausage and homemade breads. Most items are selected carefully from a nearby farmer's market. A cozy gathering place is in the living room with its gas log fireplace.

Innkeeper(s): Becky Detwiler & Karen Maust. $55-70. 3 rooms, 2 with PB, 1 suite. Breakfast and snacks/refreshments included in rates. Types of meals: Full bkfst. Beds: Q. A/C. VCR and telephone on premises. Antiquing, golf, live theater, parks, shopping and museums nearby.

Location: Dutch Country.

Certificate may be used: Jan. 2-March 31.

Rhode Island

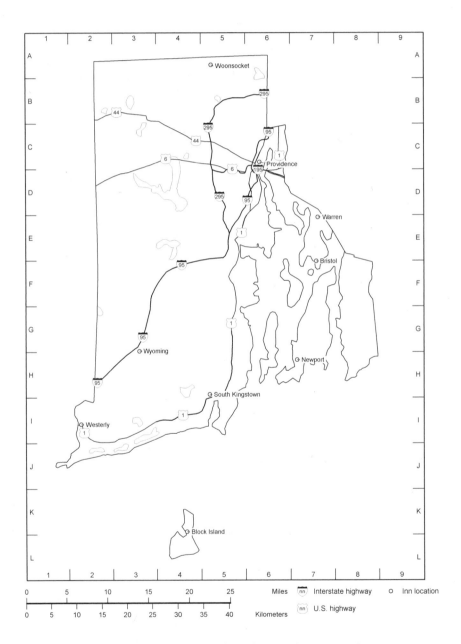

Tell the innkeeper that you have an iLoveInns free-night certificate when you make your reservation.

Block Island

Blue Dory Inn

PO Box 488, 61 Dodge St
Block Island, RI 02807-0488
(401)466-5891 (800)992-7290 Fax:(401)466-9910
Internet: www.blockislandinns.com
E-mail: rundezvous@aol.com

Circa 1887. This Shingle Victorian inn on Crescent Beach offers many guest rooms with ocean views. The Cottage, The Doll House and The Tea House are separate structures for those desiring more room or privacy. Antiques and Victorian touches are featured throughout. Year-round car ferry service, taking approximately one hour, is found at Point Judith, R.I. The island also may be reached by air on New England Airlines or by charter. Mohegan Bluffs Scenic Natural Area is nearby.

Innkeeper(s): Ann Law. $65-495. 12 rooms with PB, 3 suites, 4 cottages, 1 conference room. Breakfast and afternoon tea included in rates. Types of meals: Cont plus and early coffee/tea. Beds: KQDT. Reading lamp, CD player, telephone, desk, most with air conditioning, VCRs and cable TV in room. TV, VCR, fax, copier, swimming, child care and parlor games on premises. Antiquing, beach, fishing, live theater, parks, shopping and water sports nearby.

Location: Ocean community.

"The Blue Dory is a wonderful place to stay. The room was lovely, the view spectacular and the sound of surf was both restful and tranquil."

Certificate may be used: Sept. 15-June 15, Sunday-Thursday.

Bristol

Point Pleasant Inn & Resort

333 Poppasquash Rd
Bristol, RI 02809-1010
(401)253-0627 (800)503-0627 Fax:(401)253-0371
Internet: www.pointpleasantinn.com
E-mail: trishwwi1@aol.com

Circa 1938. Indulge in a slice of paradise at this English country manor house on Poppasquash Point, a peninsula on a hillside overlooking the harbor surrounded by Narragansett Bay. Walk along the teak and granite floors of the 33-room mansion to the music room or the billiard and game room. Select a vintage book to read by the fire in the library or watch the wraparound water vista from the Grand Salon. Savor afternoon tea and treats on the terrace. The Butler's Bar is a complimentary self-service full bar with espresso, wine and cordials. At 5 PM enjoy cocktails and appetizers in the main gallery. Luxurious, air-conditioned guest bedrooms and two romantic suites include generous amenities with Beaudelaire bath products, newspaper delivery, robes, Italian linens, antique accents and oil paintings. Gather for breakfast in the waterfront dining room. Take a sauna after a workout in the exercise room, or soak in the outdoor hot tub and swim in the pool. Ride bikes, kayak, play croquet, tennis or shuffle board.

Innkeeper(s): Trish & Gunter Hafer. $350-675. 6 rooms with PB, 1 with FP, 2 suites, 1 conference room. Breakfast, afternoon tea and snacks/refreshments included in rates. Types of meals: Full gourmet bkfst, veg bkfst, Sun. brunch, early coffee/tea, lunch, picnic lunch, hors d'oeuvres and wine. Beds: KQ. Modem hook-up, data port, cable TV, VCR, reading lamp, stereo, refrigerator, snack bar, clock radio, telephone, coffeemaker, turn-down service, desk, hot tub/spa, fireplace, hair dryers, robes, safes, spa wraps, six different kinds of pillows, customized bottled water, fruit baskets and custom chocolates in room. Central air. Fax, copier, spa, swimming, sauna, stable, bicycles, tennis, library, parlor games, laundry facility, Alcohol is included at no charge, Game room with billiards, Ping pong, Card table, Fitness room, Kayaks, Croquet, Bocce ball, Horseshoes, Volleyball and Water sports on premises. Limited handicap access. Amusement parks, antiquing, art galleries, beach, bicycling, canoeing/kayaking, cross-country skiing, downhill skiing, fishing, golf, hiking, horseback riding, live theater, museums, parks, shopping, sporting events, tennis, water sports, wineries, sailing, harbor tours, Colt State Park, East Bay Bike Path and Newport nearby.

Location: City, ocean community, waterfront.

Publicity: *Southern New England Weddings, Providence Journal, Rhode Island Monthly, East Bay Newspaper, Water Side Escapes, New York Times, Boston Globe, Waterway Getaways and Lanier.*

Certificate may be used: May-October, Monday, Tuesday or Wednesday.

Newport

Agincourt Inn

120 Miantonomi Ave
Newport, RI 02842-5450
(401)847-0902 (800)352-3750
Internet: www.agincourtinn.com
E-mail: info@agincourtinn.com

Circa 1856. This elegant, three-story Stick Victorian inn, listed in the National Register, offers a glimpse of fine living in an earlier age. The innkeepers' attention to detail is evident throughout, with French crystal chandeliers, stained-glass windows and parquet floors in the library as a few of the highlights. Parlors are found on each of the inn's floors. Newport's many attractions, including the Art Museum, sailing and the world famous Newport mansions are just a short drive from the inn.

Innkeeper(s): Randy & Selma Fabricant. $79-250. 8 rooms, 8 with FP, 8 suites. Breakfast included in rates. Types of meals: Cont plus and early coffee/tea. Beds: KQ. Cable TV, VCR, reading lamp, refrigerator, clock radio, fireplace, hair dryer, bath amenities, wireless Internet access, iron/ironing board and refrigerators in room. Air conditioning. Library, parlor games and telephone on premises. Antiquing, art galleries, beach, bicycling, canoeing/kayaking, fishing, golf, hiking, horseback riding, live theater, museums, parks, shopping, sporting events, tennis, water sports, wineries, mansions and sailing nearby.

Location: Ocean community.

Publicity: *Newport Daily News, Providence Journal, West Essex Tribune, Victorian Homes, Victorian, Travel Channel (Haunted Inns), PBS, Local radio station and Mr. Smith.*

"A dream come true! Thanks for everything! We'll be back."

Certificate may be used: Jan. 20-April 30, Monday-Thursday, no holidays, festivals.

America's Cup Inn

6 Mary St
Newport, RI 02840-3028
(401)846-9200 (800)457-7803 Fax:(401)846-1534
Internet: www.americascupinn.com
E-mail: info@americascupinn.com

Circa 1848. This Colonial-style inn is an elegant spot from which to enjoy the seaside town of Newport. Waverly and Laura Ashley prints decorate the individually appointed guest rooms, some of which have four-poster or canopy beds. The innkeeper serves an expanded continental breakfast with items such as fresh fruit, quiche and ham and cheese croissants. Afternoon tea also is served. A day in Newport offers many activities, including touring the Tennis Hall of Fame, taking a cruise through the harbor, shopping for antiques or perhaps taking a trek down Cliff Walk, a one-and-a-half-mile path offering the ocean on one side and historic mansions on the other. Parking is included in the rates.

Innkeeper(s): Marina Stanfield. $89-299. 26 rooms with PB, 1 suite.

Afternoon tea included in rates. Types of meals: Cont plus. Beds: KQDT. Reading lamp and telephone in room. Air conditioning. VCR, fax, copier, parlor games and parking included in rates on premises. Antiquing, parks and shopping nearby.

Location: City, ocean community. Downtown Newport.

"Thank you for your excellent service with a smile."

Certificate may be used: Anytime, November-April, subject to availability.

Cliffside Inn

2 Seaview Ave
Newport, RI 02840-3627
(401)847-1811 (800)845-1811 Fax:(401)848-5850
Internet: www.cliffsideinn.com
E-mail: reservations@legendaryinnsofnewport.com

Circa 1876. The governor of Maryland, Thomas Swann, built this Newport summer house in the style of a Second Empire Victorian. It features a mansard roof and many bay windows. The rooms are decorated in a Victorian motif. Suites have marble baths, and all rooms have fireplaces. Fourteen rooms have a double whirlpool tub. The Cliff Walk is located one block from the inn.

Innkeeper(s): Dixie Kimball. $155-580. 16 rooms with PB, 16 with FP, 14 with WP, 8 suites, 1 cottage, 1 conference room. Breakfast and afternoon tea included in rates. Types of meals: Full gourmet bkfst, early coffee/tea and room service. Beds: KQ. Cable TV, VCR, DVD, reading lamp, stereo, refrigerator, ceiling fan, clock radio, telephone, turn-down service, desk, hot tub/spa, fireplace, hair dryer, bathrobes, bath amenities, wireless Internet access and iron/ironing board in room. Air conditioning. Fax, spa, library, parlor games, gift shop, DVD/video library, fine wine service and Victorian Tea Room on premises. Antiquing, art galleries, beach, bicycling, canoeing/kayaking, fishing, golf, hiking, horseback riding, live theater, museums, parks, shopping, sporting events, tennis, water sports, wineries, Gilded Age Mansions, International Tennis Hall of Fame, Touro Synagogue (oldest in America), Cliff Walk, Museum of Yachting, Fort Adams and historic walking tours nearby.

Location: Ocean community.

Publicity: *New York Times, Boston Globe, Great Tea Rooms of America (Book), Frommer's New England Guidebook, Fodor's Guidebooks, New England Travel&Life, Yankee Magazine, Getaway for Gourmets, National Geographic Travel, Conde Naste Traveler, New York Magazine, Boston Magazine, Connecticut Magazine, Rhode Island Monthly, Bride's Magazine, Discerning Traveler, Robb Report, Inside Philadelphia Magazine, Victorian Homes, BBC's Homes & Antiques, AAA Car&Travel, Good Morning America (ABC-TV), National Geographic, Discovery and Travel Channel.*

"...it captures the grandeur of the Victorian age."

Certificate may be used: January to March, Sunday-Thursday, holidays and school vacation weeks excluded, subject to availability.

Hydrangea House Inn

16 Bellevue Avenue
Newport, RI 02840
(401)846-4435 (800)945-4668 Fax:(401)846-6602
Internet: www.hydrangeahouse.com
E-mail: hydrangeahouse@cox.net

Circa 1876. Well-known for it impeccable service, elegant furnishings, rich warm colors, luxurious fabrics and masterful faux painting, this New England inn is a delightful place to stay. Beach towels are provided for soaking up the sun on the roof deck. After an incredible night's rest, join the first or second seating for a gourmet breakfast in the formal dining room. Start with the special blend Hydrangea House Coffee that complements the signature raspberry pancakes, home-baked breads, granola, seasoned scrambled eggs in puff pastry or other tempting recipes that will provide enough energy for the whole day. Ask about special packages available.

Innkeeper(s): Grant Edmondson / Dennis Blair, Innkeepers. $250-425. 9 rooms with PB, 9 with FP, 7 with HT, 7 with WP, 7 suites. Breakfast and afternoon tea included in rates. Types of meals: Full gourmet bkfst and early

coffee/tea. Beds: KQT. Modem hook-up, data port, cable TV, reading lamp, CD player, clock radio, telephone, turn-down service, desk, fireplace, hair dryer, bathrobes, bath amenities, wireless Internet access and iron/ironing board in room. Central air. Fax and sauna on premises. Antiquing, art galleries, beach, bicycling, canoeing/kayaking, fishing, golf, hiking, horseback riding, live theater, museums, parks, shopping, tennis, water sports and wineries nearby.

Location: City.

Certificate may be used: November-April with Sunday-Wednesday check-ins.

The Burbank Rose B&B

111 Memorial Blvd W
Newport, RI 02840-3469
(401)849-9457 (888)297-5800 Fax:(203)413-4372
Internet: www.burbankrose.com
E-mail: theburbankrose@yahoo.com

Circa 1850. The innkeepers of this cheery, yellow home named their B&B in honor of their ancestor, famed horticultur-

ist Luther Burbank. As a guest, he probably would be taken by the bright, flowery hues that adorn the interior of this Federal-style home. Rooms, some of which afford harbor views, are light and airy with simple decor. The innkeepers serve afternoon refreshments and a substantial breakfast buffet. The home is located in Newport's Historic Hill district and within walking distance of shops, restaurants and many of the seaside village's popular attractions.

Innkeeper(s): Brian Cole. $69-199. 3 rooms with PB, 2 suites. Breakfast included in rates. Types of meals: Cont. Beds: QT. Reading lamp and clock radio in room. Air conditioning. VCR, parlor games and telephone on premises. Antiquing, fishing, live theater, shopping, water sports, sailing, golf and tennis nearby.

Location: City, ocean community, waterfront.

Certificate may be used: Anytime, based on availability. Excluding weekends May-November. Continental breakfast only.

The Melville House

39 Clarke St
Newport, RI 02840-3023
(401)847-0640 (800)711-7184 Fax:(401)847-0956
Internet: www.melvillehouse.com
E-mail: melvillehouse@cox.net

Circa 1750. During the American Revolution this attractive National Register Colonial inn once housed aides to General Rochambeau. Reflecting its historical heritage, the interior decor features early American furnishings. Stay in the spacious Fireplace Suite. A full breakfast is served each morning that may include homemade scones, muffins or coffee cakes and stuffed French toast, pepper frittata or whole wheat pancakes. Take a pleasant walk from this 1750 inn to the waterfront and local sites.

Innkeeper(s): Bob & Priscilla Peretti. $110-209. 6 rooms, 5 with PB, 1 with FP, 1 suite. Breakfast, afternoon tea, snacks/refreshments and Complimentary soft beverages availabile in breakfast room. Bottled water in guestrooms included in rates. Types of meals: Full gourmet bkfst and early coffee/tea. Beds: KQDT. Reading lamp, bath amenities, iron/ironing board and Bottled water in room. Central air. Fax, copier, parlor games, telephone, fireplace,

Refrigerator, Hair dryer, Iron/ironing board, Juice/soda, Tea, Cookies and Complimentary soft beverages available in breakfast room on premises. Limited handicap access. Antiquing, art galleries, beach, bicycling, fishing, golf, hiking, live theater, museums, parks, shopping, tennis, water sports, wineries, the Newport Cliff Walk, Newport Mansions, historic walking tours, Sachuset Point Wildlife Preserve, Newport Harbor tours by sail or motorboat and The International Tennis Hall of Fame nearby.

Location: City, ocean community.

Publicity: *Country Inns, "Lodging Pick" for Newport, Good Housekeeping and New York Post.*

"Comfortable with a quiet elegance."

Certificate may be used: Nov. 1-April 30, Sunday-Thursday, no holidays.

Victorian Ladies Inn

63 Memorial Blvd
Newport, RI 02840-3629
(401)849-9960
Internet: www.victorianladies.com
E-mail: info@victorianladies.com

Circa 1851. Innkeepers Cheryl and Harry have created a comfortable and welcoming atmosphere at this restored three-story Victorian inn and cottage. Intimate and inviting, this traditional New England bed & breakfast features spacious guest bedrooms furnished with period pieces, fine reproductions, rich fabrics and wallcoverings. Linger over a gracious breakfast in the dining room. Stroll through the award-winning gardens, walk over the small bridge and gaze at the koi pond. Relax in the living room while planning activities for the day. Walk to nearby beaches, the Colonial town, famed mansions, cliff walk and harbor front.

Innkeeper(s): Cheryl & Harry Schatmeyer, Jr.. $119-280. 11 rooms with PB, 5 with FP. Breakfast included in rates. Types of meals: Full gourmet bkfst and veg bkfst. Beds: KQ. Cable TV, VCR, reading lamp, CD player, refrigerator, telephone, desk, most with fireplace, hair dryer, wireless Internet access and iron/ironing board in room. Central air. Fax, copier, library, parlor games and gift shop on premises. Antiquing, art galleries, beach, bicycling, canoeing/kayaking, fishing, golf, hiking, horseback riding, live theater, museums, parks, shopping, tennis, water sports and wineries nearby.

Location: Ocean community.

Publicity: *Country Inns, Glamour, Bride Magazine, L.A. Times, Country Victorian, Yankee Magazine, Newport Life Magazine and voted "Best Hotel/B&B" by Newport voters for 6 years.*

"We want to move in!"

Certificate may be used: Feb. 15 to Dec. 15, Sunday-Thursday, (months of July and August excluded).

Providence

Edgewood Manor B&B

232 Norwood Ave
Providence, RI 02905
(401)781-0099 (800)882-3285 Fax:(401)467-6311
Internet: www.providence-lodging.com
E-mail: edgemanor@aol.com

Circa 1905. Built as a private home, this 18-room Greek Revival Colonial mansion has served as a convent, an office, a rooming house and is now restored as an magnificent bed and breakfast. An elegant era is reflected in the coffered, beamed and domed-foyer ceilings, leaded- and stained-glass windows, hand-carved mantels and blend of Victorian and Empire decor. Romantic guest bedrooms feature Jacuzzi tubs and wood-burning fireplaces. Savor a satisfying gourmet breakfast served in the dining room or on the patio. The inn is within walking distance to Narragansett Bay and Roger

Williams Park and Zoo, with 230 acres of magnificent gardens, sculptures and historic buildings.

Innkeeper(s): Joy Generali. $99-329. 15 rooms, 20 with PB, 3 with FP, 8 with WP, 6 total suites, including 2 two-bedroom suites, 3 conference rooms. Breakfast and afternoon tea included in rates. Types of meals: Full gourmet bkfst, wine and Wine and cheese hour on Friday and Saturday Eves. Beds: KQ. Cable TV, VCR, reading lamp, stereo, refrigerator, ceiling fan, clock radio, telephone, most with hot tub/spa, hair dryer, wireless Internet access, iron/ironing board, Two-person Jacuzzi tubs, Wood-burning fireplaces, Gas fireplaces and Afternoon tea in room. Air conditioning. Fax, copier, bicycles, library, fireplace, laundry facility, bicycles for rent and free wireless Internet service on premises. Limited handicap access. Antiquing, art galleries, beach, bicycling, canoeing/kayaking, fishing, golf, hiking, horseback riding, live theater, museums, parks, shopping, sporting events, tennis, wineries, Sailing, Three yacht clubs within walking distance, Roger Williams Park and Botanical gardens within walking distance nearby.

Location: City.

Publicity: *Rated top 25 inns by McMillan travel guides, AAA Inspected three diamond recipient., Featured on National Geographic (2006) and The National Historic Register.*

Certificate may be used: Dec. 1-April 30.

South Kingstown

Admiral Dewey Inn

668 Matunuck Beach Rd
South Kingstown, RI 02879-7053
(401)783-2090 (800)457-2090
Internet: www.admiraldeweyinn.com

Circa 1898. Although the prices have risen a bit since this inn's days as a boarding house (the rate was 50 cents per night), this Stick-style home still offers hospitality and comfort. The National Register inn is within walking distance of Matunuck Beach. Guests can enjoy the sea breeze from the inn's wraparound porch. Period antiques decorate the guest rooms, some of which offer ocean views.

Innkeeper(s): Joan Lebel. $100-150. 10 rooms, 8 with PB. Breakfast included in rates. Types of meals: Cont plus, early coffee/tea and picnic lunch. Beds: QDT. VCR, fax, copier, parlor games, telephone and fireplace on premises. Antiquing, fishing, live theater, parks, shopping and water sports nearby.

Location: Ocean community. Free access to town beach.

Publicity: *Yankee Traveler and Rhode Island Monthly.*

Certificate may be used: Anytime, November-April, subject to availability (holiday weekends excluded). No Weekends.

Warren

Candlewick Inn

755 Main St
Warren, RI 02885-4319
(401)247-2425
Internet: www.candlewickinn.net
E-mail: candlewickinn@msn.com

Circa 1920. Relax with a welcoming cup of tea or glass of wine on the front porch of this intimate yet spacious bungalow. Accented with hardwood floors and high ceilings, the home is furnished with treasured family heirlooms, antiques and handmade quilts. The local newspapers are delivered daily. Wander through the gardens after an incredible breakfast feast with freshbaked breads, specialty butters and other mouth-watering recipes that will satisfy and delight. Ask about seasonal getaway specials.

Innkeeper(s): Joan Wiese. $90-140. 4 rooms, 3 with PB. Breakfast, afternoon tea, These are included for our guests and however your friends and family may be included for a slight charge included in rates. Types of meals: Full bkfst, veg bkfst, early coffee/tea, picnic lunch, snacks/refreshments, wine, dinner and Private dinners or picnic lunches can be arranged with advance notice. Beds: QDT. TV, parlor games, laundry facility, Swimming (2 blocks away), Bicycles & kayaks rentals available, Tennis courts and Bike path behind house on town property on premises. Antiquing, art galleries, beach, bicycling, canoeing/kayaking, fishing, golf, hiking, live theater, museums, parks, shopping, sporting events, tennis, wineries and Roger Williams Park Zoo (25 min drive) nearby.

Location: Ocean community. On the East Bay Bike Path.

Certificate may be used: May 15-Oct. 15, Sunday-Thursday, except holiday weekends. Oct. 16-May 14, all week except holidays, subject to availability.

Westerly

Grandview B&B

212 Shore Rd
Westerly, RI 02891-3623
(401)596-6384 (800)447-6384 Fax:(401)596-3036
Internet: grandviewbandb.com
E-mail: info@grandviewbandb.com

Circa 1910. An impressive wraparound stone porch highlights this majestic Shingle Victorian inn, which also boasts a lovely ocean view from its hilltop site. The inn features 9 guest rooms, a family room with cable TV, a spacious living room with a handsome stone fireplace, and a sun porch where visitors enjoy a hearty breakfast buffet. Antiquing, fishing, golf, swimming and tennis are found nearby as are Watch Hill, Mystic and Newport. The Foxwoods and Mohegan Sun casinos also are nearby.

Innkeeper(s): Patricia Grand. $100-125. 7 rooms, 4 with PB, 1 suite. Breakfast included in rates. Types of meals: Cont plus and early coffee/tea. Beds: KQDT. Reading lamp, refrigerator, ceiling fan, clock radio, 6 with ceiling fans, air conditioning and table fans in room. TV, VCR, fax, copier, library, parlor games, telephone, fireplace and large video library on premises. Antiquing, art galleries, beach, bicycling, canoeing/kayaking, fishing, golf, hiking, live theater, museums, parks, shopping, tennis, water sports, wineries and casinos nearby.

Location: Ocean community.

Certificate may be used: November-April, Sunday-Thursday, subject to availability.

Woonsocket

Pillsbury House Bed & Breakfast

341 Prospect Street
Woonsocket, RI 02895
(401)766-7983 (800)205-4112
Internet: www.pillsburyhouse.com
E-mail: rogerwnri@prodigy.net

Circa 1875. On an historic street in the fashionable North End, this restored Victorian mansion is one of the area's oldest. Boasting original parquet floors, high ceilings and furnished with antiques and period pieces, a grand elegance is

imparted. Sit by the fire in the evenings or on the shaded porch during the day. A guest kitchenette on the second floor includes a microwave, refrigerator stocked with beverages, hair dryer and ironing board. Tastefully decorated guest bedrooms and a suite offer comfort and character. Breakfast in the gracious dining room is a satisfying meal with fresh fruit, homemade baked goods and a hot entree. Located in the heart of the Blackstone River Valley National Heritage Corridor, there is much to see and do.

Innkeeper(s): Susan & Roger Bouchard. $95-135. 4 rooms with PB. Breakfast included in rates. Types of meals: Full bkfst and veg bkfst. Beds: KQT. Clock radio in room. Air conditioning. TV, fax, telephone, complimentary juices, beer and water available in second floor refreshment area on premises. Antiquing, bicycling, canoeing/kayaking, live theater, museums, parks, shopping, wineries, commuter train station to Boston (20 minutes away), South Station (59 minute train ride) and Museum of Work & Culture (1 mile) nearby.

Location: City.

Certificate may be used: Sunday through Thursday, year-round.

Wyoming

Stagecoach House Inn

1136 Main St
Wyoming, RI 02898
(401)539-9600 (888)814-9600
Internet: www.stagecoachhouse.com
E-mail: info@stagecoachhouse.com

Meticulously restored, this historic 1796 Colonial with Victorian décor is an inviting South County country inn. Relax on the front porch overlooking garden shrubs and trees that reflect the original landscaping. Sit by the large fireplace in rocking chairs and listen to the player piano in the lobby. Air-conditioned guest bedrooms and suites feature remote control fireplaces and whirlpool tubs. The honeymoon suite boasts a two-person Jacuzzi and double shower. French doors lead onto the upper deck with a view of the Wood River and horseshoe waterfall. A family suite has two adjoining rooms and a ground-level room is handicapped accessible. A deluxe continental breakfast is served daily.

Innkeeper(s): Deb and Bill Bokon. Call for rates. 12 rooms. Breakfast included in rates. Types of meals: Cont plus. Beds: QT. Data port, cable TV, clock radio, telephone, most with fireplace, hair dryer, iron/ironing board and Jacuzzi tubs in room. Central air. Fax, parlor games, gift shop and one handicap room on premises. Handicap access. Amusement parks, antiquing, beach, bicycling, canoeing/kayaking, cross-country skiing, downhill skiing, fishing, golf, hiking, horseback riding, parks, shopping, sporting events, tennis, water sports, wineries and Casinos nearby.

Location: Country, waterfront.

Certificate may be used: November-March, Sunday-Thursday subject to availability, holidays excluded, standard room only.

South Carolina

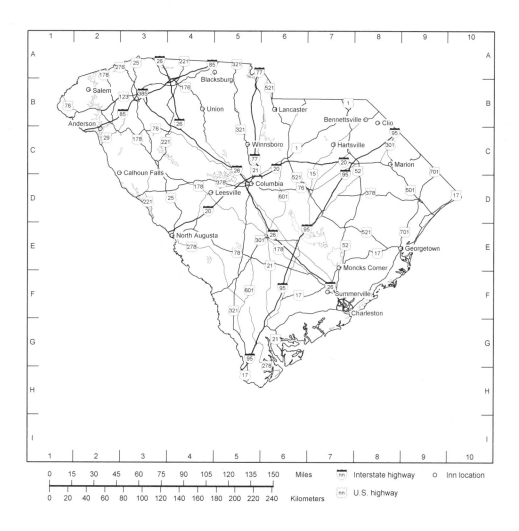

0 15 30 45 60 75 90 105 120 135 150   Miles

0 20 40 60 80 100 120 140 160 180 200 220 240   Kilometers

Interstate highway   ○ Inn location

U.S. highway

Anderson

Evergreen Inn & Spa

1109 S Main St
Anderson, SC 29624-2349
(864)225-1109 Fax:(864)332-1682
Internet: spa-it.com
E-mail: info@spa-it.com

Circa 1834. Surrounded by a garden setting with one of the state's largest crepe myrtle trees, holly trees and huge evergreens planted in the 1800s, these two antebellum mansions sit side by side on three acres. Both of the historical mansions have been fully restored and are listed in the National Register. The inn is the oldest home in the city, and boasts a stately grace and classic Greek Revival architecture. Relax on the wraparound porch accented with columns. Plush themed guest bedrooms offer canopy and four-poster beds, lavish fabrics and rich woods.

Select a complete breakfast made-to-order and served in the upstairs dining area or in-room. Visit the day spa next door for pampering body treatments including skin and hair care. Make reservations for dinner at the on-site 1109 Dining Room, an award-winning restaurant with Swiss chef Peter Ryter.

Innkeeper(s): Myrna Ryter. $125. 5 rooms, 5 with FP, 5 suites, 1 conference room. Breakfast and snacks/refreshments included in rates. Types of meals: Full gourmet bkfst, lunch and gourmet dinner. Restaurant on premises. Beds: KQ. Cable TV, reading lamp, CD player and clock radio in room. Central air. TV, copier, library and gift shop on premises. Handicap access. Antiquing, art galleries, canoeing/kayaking, golf, hiking, museums, parks, shopping, sporting events, tennis, water sports and Spa nearby.

Location: City.

Publicity: *Travel Host Magazine and Greenville News.*

"Fantastic! Very imaginative & fun."

Certificate may be used: Anytime, subject to availability, not valid Clemson Football weekends.

Bennettsville

Breeden Inn, Cottages & Retreat on Main

404 E Main St
Bennettsville, SC 29512
(843)479-3665 (888)335-2996 Fax:(843)479-7998
Internet: www.breedeninn.com
E-mail: info@breedeninn.com

Circa 1886. Four historic buildings in a village-like setting comprise this inn: The 1886 Main House Southern mansion, The Carriage House, The Garden Cottage and two-story Retreat on Main. One especially bountiful cotton crop paid for the construction of the Main House mansion. The inn was named in honor of the A.P. Breeden family who lived in the home for 54 years. The interior of each house features many interesting and varied architectural details. Suites and guest bedrooms delight with exquisite linens, antiques, collectibles, needlework and art. A satisfying morning meal is served in the dining room, breakfast parlor, music parlor, library parlor or on the veranda. Porch swings, rockers and ceiling fans are inviting while overlooking the backyard wildlife habitat with woodland and garden walks.

Innkeeper(s): Wesley & Bonnie Park. $180. 13 rooms with PB, 10 with FP, 3 two-bedroom suites, 2 cottages, 3 guest houses, 1 conference room. Breakfast, snacks/refreshments and Complimentary snack baskets and self-serve around the clock coffee and tea are located in guests hospitality areas within each house included in rates. Types of meals: Full bkfst, veg bkfst, early coffee/tea and The inn offers a full delicious breakfast as well as guests preference of continental or vegetarian/vegan breakfasts. Beds: KQDT. Modem hook-up, data port, cable TV, VCR, DVD, reading lamp, ceiling fan, snack bar, clock radio, telephone, coffeemaker, turn-down service, desk, voice mail, most with fireplace, hair dryer, bathrobes, bath amenities, wireless Internet access, iron/ironing board, Whirlpools for two in four rooms, private phone lines, high speed wireless internet in all rooms, free long distance calls within U.S.A., hair dryer, iron/ironing board, full-length mirror, alarm clock, plush bed linens including down comforter on all beds and some featherbeds in room. Central air. Fax, copier, swimming, bicycles, library, parlor games, laundry facility, gift shop, large in-ground swimming pool, period Koi pond, lovely winding garden walks throughout the grounds with sitting areas, hammocks, fountains, binoculars/field guide books for birding, bicycles, piano, refreshment drink upon arrival, two parlors, gathering room, board games, meeting rooms, five Southern porches with swings,rockers,joggling board, three laundry rooms and three fully equipped period kitchens for guests usage on premises. Antiquing, art galleries, bicycling, fishing, golf, live theater, museums, parks, shopping, tennis, 600-acre Lake Wallace offers two 3.3 mile walking trails, Visitor Center, Local & area antiquing, Museums & self-guided historic walking tours, Dining in two local historic houses, Birding and Kids Funland Park nearby.

Location: Country. Small Southern county seat town. Population 10,000.

Publicity: *Glamour Magazine, Gourmet Magazine, Pee Dee Magazine, Sandlapper Magazine, South Carolina's Official Travel Guide: South Carolina Smiles, pictured on the official map for the state of SC and The National Wildlife Federation.*

"We were absolutely speechless at how lovely and comfortable our room was. Every detail was exquisite, especially the bedding. We had a wonderful romantic weekend. It was just what we were looking for and more. The gardens, your porches, the delicious food and your warm and friendly ways. Staying here was the highlight of our trip."

Certificate may be used: Year-round. Excludes special event dates and holidays.

Charleston

Belvedere B&B

40 Rutledge Ave
Charleston, SC 29401-1702
(843)722-0973 (800)816-1664
Internet: www.belvedereinn.com
E-mail: innkeeper@belvedereinn.com

Circa 1900. This Colonial Revival home with its semicircular portico, Ionic columns and four piazzas boasts a beautiful view of Charleston's Colonial Lake. Bright, airy rooms feature high ceilings with fans, polished wood floors, fireplaces, antique furnishings and Oriental rugs. Relax and enjoy the view on the piazzas or in one of the inn's public rooms. Belvedere B&B is close to many wonderful restaurants and shops.

Innkeeper(s): David S. Spell. $99-195. 3 rooms with PB. Breakfast included in rates. Types of meals: Cont plus. Beds: Q. Cable TV, ceiling fan, clock radio, desk and ornamental fireplaces in room. Air conditioning. VCR, telephone and refrigerator on premises. Antiquing, fishing, live theater, parks, shopping, sporting events and water sports nearby.

Publicity: *Discerning Traveler and Southern Brides.*

Certificate may be used: Last minute subject to availability, Sunday-Thursday.

Columbia

Chesnut Cottage B&B

1718 Hampton St
Columbia, SC 29201-3420
(803)256-1718 (888)308-1718
Internet: www.chestnutcottage.com
E-mail: ggarrett@sc.rr.com

Circa 1850. This inn was originally the home of Confederate General James Chesnut and his wife, writer Mary Boykin Miller Chesnut. She authored "A Diary From Dixie," written during the Civil War but published posthumously in 1905. The white frame one-and-a-half-story house has a central dormer with an arched window above the main entrance. The small porch has four octagonal columns and an ironwork balustrade. Hearty breakfasts are served in the privacy of your room, on the porch or in the main dining room. The innkeepers can provide you with sightseeing information, make advance dinner reservations, as well as cater to any other special interests you might have.

Innkeeper(s): Gale Garrett. $95-225. 5 rooms with PB, 3 with FP, 1 two-bedroom suite. Breakfast and snacks/refreshments included in rates. Types of meals: Country bkfst, veg bkfst, early coffee/tea and room service. Beds: KQ. Modem hook-up, data port, cable TV, VCR, reading lamp, stereo, refrigerator, ceiling fan, snack bar, clock radio, telephone, coffeemaker, turn-down service, desk and fireplace in room. Central air. Fax and copier on premises. Antiquing, art galleries, fishing, hiking, live theater, museums, parks, shopping, sporting events and water sports nearby.

Location: City.

Publicity: *Sandlapper, London Financial Times, State Newspaper and TV show* .

"You really know how to pamper and spoil. Chestnut Cottage is a great place to stay."

Certificate may be used: All year, Sunday through Thursday.

Georgetown

Mansfield Plantation B&B Country Inn

1776 Mansfield Rd
Georgetown, SC 29440-6923
(843)546-6961 (866)717-1776 Fax:(843) 546-1367
Internet: MansfieldPlantation.com
E-mail: mightymansfield@aol.com

Circa 1800. Listed in the National Register, and featured in Mel Gibson's movie, The Patriot, Mansfield Plantation is a perfect respite for those in search of romance and history in a natural, secluded setting. The large dining room and sitting rooms are furnished with the owner's collections of 19th-century American antiques that include paintings, china, silver, furniture and gilt-framed mirrors. Accommodations include three guesthouses, each decorated in a romantic style and boasting fireplaces, hardwood floors, high ceilings, comfortable furnishings and collectibles. The vast grounds (900 private acres), shaded by moss-draped oaks, provide ideal spots for relaxing. Enjoy azalea and camellia gardens, as well as views of the surrounding marshlands. Guests can relax in hammocks or swings, watch for birds or enjoy a bike ride. Boating on the Black River is another possibility. Guests may bring their own boats or rent canoes or kayaks nearby. Among the plantation's notable historic features are a schoolhouse, kitchen, winnowing house, slave village and chapel, all of which predate the Civil War.

Innkeeper(s): Kathryn Green. $135-175. 8 rooms with PB, 8 with FP, 3 guest houses, 1 conference room. Breakfast included in rates. Types of meals: Full gourmet bkfst, veg bkfst, early coffee/tea, picnic lunch and afternoon tea. Beds: KQDT. Cable TV, VCR, DVD, reading lamp, refrigerator, clock radio, coffeemaker, desk, fireplace and iron/ironing board in room. Central air. Fax, bicycles, library, telephone, canoeing, kayaking, water skiing, fishing, hiking and animal/bird watching on premises. Amusement parks, antiquing, art galleries, beach, bicycling, canoeing/kayaking, fishing, golf, horseback riding, live theater, museums, parks, shopping, tennis, water sports, Historic Charleston, Myrtle Beach and Historic Georgetown nearby.

Location: Country, waterfront. On the banks of the Black River, near the ocean.

Publicity: *Georgetown Times, Charleston News & Courier, Sandlapper, Pee Dee Magazine, Charleston Magazine, Carolina Home, South Carolina Homes & Gardens, Grand Strand Magazine, The INNside Scoop, Windshield America (Fine Living Network), Treasure Hunters (NBC) and The Patriot.*

"Handsome furnishings, wildlife walks, sports and hunting opportunities galore, and a sumptuous atmosphere all make for a weekend retreat to remember."

Certificate may be used: Anytime, subject to availability.

The Shaw House B&B

613 Cypress Ct
Georgetown, SC 29440-3349
(843)546-9663
E-mail: shawbandb@sccc.tv

Circa 1972. Near Georgetown's historical district is the Shaw House. It features a beautiful view of the Willowbank marsh, which stretches out for more than 1000 acres. Sometimes giant turtles come up and lay eggs on the lawn. Guests enjoy rocking on the inn's front and back porches and identifying the large variety of birds that live here. A Southern home-cooked breakfast often includes grits, quiche and Mary's heart-shaped biscuits.

Innkeeper(s): Mary & Joe Shaw. $80-95. 3 rooms with PB. Breakfast included in rates. Types of meals: Full bkfst, early coffee/tea and snacks/refreshments. Beds: KQ. Cable TV, reading lamp, stereo, ceiling fan, clock radio, telephone, turn-down service and desk in room. Air conditioning. TV, bicycles, library and fireplace on premises. Amusement parks, antiquing, fishing, live theater, parks, shopping and water sports nearby.

Location: City.

Publicity: *Charlotte Observer and Country.*

"Your home speaks of abundance and comfort and joy."
Certificate may be used: Sunday-Friday, anytime available.

Lancaster

Kilburnie, the Inn at Craig Farm

1824 Craig Farm Road
Lancaster, SC 29720
(803)416-8420 Fax:(803)416-8429
Internet: www.kilburnie.com
E-mail: jtromp@infoave.net

Circa 1828. The area's oldest surviving antebellum home, this Greek Revival was saved from demolition, moved to this 400-acre estate and extensively restored. Listed in the National Register, its historic and architectural significance is seen in the intricate details found in the public rooms. Experience Southern hospitality accented by European charm in a quiet and secluded setting with a classic elegance. Each guest bedroom and suite boasts a fireplace, as do two bathrooms. An unsurpassed two-course breakfast may include fresh-baked bread and muffins, a fruit appetizer of Poached Pears with Blueberries or Southern Pecan Peaches and a main entree of Oven-Shirred Eggs or Herbed Goat Cheese Omelette. Relax on one of the piazza rockers after a stroll on the nature path through the wildlife backyard habitat with bridges spanning the woodlands.

Innkeeper(s): Johannes Tromp. $150-200. 5 rooms with PB, 5 with FP, 1 suite, 1 conference room. Breakfast included in rates. Types of meals: Full gourmet bkfst. Beds: KQ. Modem hook-up, cable TV, VCR, reading lamp, clock radio, telephone, turn-down service, desk, hot tub/spa, fireplace, hair dryer, bath amenities and wireless Internet access in room. Central air. Fax, copier, library and laundry facility on premises. Amusement parks, antiquing, art galleries, canoeing/kayaking, golf, museums, parks, shopping, sporting events and tennis nearby.

Location: Country.

Publicity: Southern Living, Sandlapper Magazine, South Carolina Magazine, Charlotte Observer, Rock Hill Herald, Lancaster News and South Carolina Educational Television (SCETV).

Certificate may be used: Anytime, Sunday-Thursday, except holidays.

Leesville

The Able House Inn

244 E Columbia Ave
Leesville, SC 29070-9284
(803)532-2763 Fax:(803)532-2763
E-mail: ablehouse@pbtcomm.net

Circa 1939. This elegant, white brick home was built by a local druggist. Relax in the tastefully decorated living room or lounge on a comfy wicker chair among the large plants in the sunroom. Guest rooms, named after various relatives, boast beautiful amenities such as a canopied bed or window seats. Jennifer's Room opens into a sitting room with a window seat so large, some guests have snuggled down for a restful night's sleep instead of the large, brass and enamel four-poster bed. Innkeepers offer guests snacks/refreshments in the evening and turn-down service each night. Wake to freshly ground coffee before taking on the day. During the warmer months, innkeepers offer guests the use of their swimming pool.

Innkeeper(s): Jack & Annabelle Wright. $85-100. 5 rooms with PB, 1 suite. Breakfast and snacks/refreshments included in rates. Types of meals: Full bkfst, veg bkfst and early coffee/tea. Beds: QD. Modem hook-up, cable TV, DVD, reading lamp, ceiling fan, clock radio, telephone, turn-down service, desk, hair dryer, bathrobes, bath amenities and iron/ironing board in room. Central air. TV, VCR, fax, copier, spa, swimming, parlor games and fireplace on premises. Antiquing, fishing, golf, live theater, shopping, sporting events, tennis and water sports nearby.

Location: City.

Publicity: Sandlapper and State Newspaper.

"Thank you for the warm Southern welcome. Your place is absolutely beautiful, very inviting. The food was extraordinary!"

Certificate may be used: Sept. 1 to April 1.

Moncks Corner

Rice Hope Plantation Inn Bed & Breakfast

206 Rice Hope Dr
Moncks Corner, SC 29461-9781
(843)849-9000 (800)569-4038
Internet: www.ricehope.com
E-mail: lou@ricehope.com

Circa 1840. Resting on 285 secluded acres of natural beauty, this historic mansion sits among oaks on a bluff overlooking the Cooper River. A stay here is a visit to yesteryear, where it is said to be 45 short minutes and three long centuries from downtown Charleston. Formal gardens boast a 200-year-old camellia and many more varieties of trees and plants, making it a perfect setting for outdoor weddings or other special occasions. Nearby attractions include the Trappist Monastery at Mepkin Plantation, Francis Marion National Forest and Cypress Gardens.

Innkeeper(s): Jamie Edens. $85-165. 5 rooms with PB, 1 conference room. Breakfast included in rates. Types of meals: Full bkfst and early coffee/tea. Beds: KQD. TV, reading lamp, ceiling fan, clock radio and coffeemaker in room. Air conditioning. Copier, tennis, library, parlor games, telephone and fireplace on premises. Antiquing, art galleries, beach, bicycling, canoeing/kayaking, fishing, golf, museums, parks, shopping and tennis nearby.

Location: Country, waterfront. Riverfront.

Publicity: "W" Fasion Magazine photo shoot, Green Power commercial, Japanese TV Documentary, Travel Channel, Haunted Inns and film location for "Consenting Adults" with Kevin Costner.

Certificate may be used: Sunday-Thursday, all year.

Salem

Sunrise Farm B&B

325 Sunrise Dr
Salem, SC 29676-3444
(864)944-0121 (888)991-0121 Fax:(864) 944-7955
Internet: www.bbonline.com/sc/sunrisefarm
E-mail: sfbb@bellsouth.net

Circa 1890. Situated on the remaining part of a 1,000-acre cotton plantation, this country Victorian features large porches with rockers and wicker. Guest rooms are furnished with period antiques, thick comforters, extra pillows and family heirlooms. The "corn crib" cottage is located in the original farm structure used for storing corn. It has a fully equipped kitchen, sitting area and bedroom with tub and shower. The June Rose Garden Cottage includes a river rock fireplace and full kitchen, as well as pastoral and mountain views. The inn offers a full breakfast, snacks and country picnic baskets. Children and pets are welcome.

Innkeeper(s): Julie & Jeff Pierce. $100-140. 6 rooms, 4 with PB, 1 two-bedroom suite, 2 cottages. Breakfast and snacks/refreshments included in rates. Types of meals: Veg bkfst, early coffee/tea, picnic lunch and Breakfast features all-natural and some organic ingredients. Special diets may be accommodated. Beds: KQT. TV, VCR, reading lamp, refrigerator, ceiling fan, snack bar, clock radio, some with fireplace, hair dryer, wireless Internet access, iron/ironing board, free movies and book selection in room. Central air. Parlor games, telephone, llamas, miniature horses, goats, a pot belly pig, cats, dog and sheep on premises. Antiquing, bicycling, canoeing/kayaking, fishing, golf, hiking, horseback riding, live theater, museums, parks, shopping, sporting events, water sports, wineries and boating nearby.

Location: Country, mountains.

Publicity: National Geographic Traveler, Southern Living, Country Extra and Palmetto Places.

Certificate may be used: Nov. 28-May 25, Sunday-Thursday, holidays and special events excluded.

Summerville

King's Inn 2 Bed and Breakfast

207 Central Ave.
Summerville, SC 29483
(843)486-0419 (888)577-5847 Fax:(843)486-0419
Internet: www.kingsinntwo.com
E-mail: info@kingsinntwo.com

Meticulously renovated by the award-winning innkeepers of the original King's Inn, this elegant 1872 Colonial estate offers personalized service and comfort as well as luxury in an elegant setting. Gorgeous landscaping of palmetto palms, mature live oaks, azaleas and camellias highlight the walkways, fountains and statuary. Antiques and an original art collection accent this delightful bed and breakfast in the historic district of Summerville, South Carolina. Watch the large-screen TV in the sun room, adjacent to the yellow parlor with a hand-carved fireplace mantle. Lavish guest bedrooms boast an assortment of upscale amenities from pillow menus and spa robes to bottled water, chocolates and early-morning coffee service. Linger over a multi-course breakfast in the formal dining room or on the veranda overlooking the garden and pool.

Innkeeper(s): Marilyn & Jerry Burkhardt. $139-179. 3 rooms with PB, 1 with WP. Breakfast, afternoon tea, snacks/refreshments and wine included in rates. Types of meals: Full gourmet bkfst, veg bkfst, early coffee/tea, gourmet lunch, picnic lunch, hors d'oeuvres, Small weddings, Private dinners and Parties. Beds: KQ. Cable TV, VCR, DVD, reading lamp, CD player, clock radio, coffeemaker, turn-down service, desk, hair dryer, bathrobes, bath amenities, wireless Internet access, iron/ironing board, Bottled water, Silver ice buckets, Upscale chocolates, Antiques, Original art, Oriental rugs and fresh flowers in room. Central air. Fax, copier, swimming, library, parlor games, telephone, fireplace, Elegant verandas and Breakfast served outside on premises. Antiquing, art galleries, beach, canoeing/kayaking, fishing, golf, hiking, horseback riding, live theater, museums, parks, shopping, tennis, Historic area & shops and Gateway to Charleston nearby.

Certificate may be used: Jan.2-Feb. 12(any day). July and August Sunday-Thursday. Last minute subject to availability.

Union

The Inn at Merridun

100 Merridun Pl
Union, SC 29379-2200
(864)427-7052 (888)892-6020 Fax:(864)429-0373
Internet: www.merridun.com
E-mail: info@merridun.com

Circa 1855. Nestled on nine acres of wooded ground, this Greek Revival inn is in a small Southern college town. During spring, see the South in its colorful splendor with blooming azaleas, magnolias and wisteria. Sip an iced drink on the inn's marble verandas and relive memories of a bygone era. Soft strains of Mozart and Beethoven, as well as the smell of freshly baked cookies and country suppers, fill the air of this antebellum country inn. In addition to a complimentary breakfast, guest will enjoy the inn's dessert selection offered every evening.

Innkeeper(s): Peggy Waller & JD, the inn cat. $99-135. 5 rooms with PB, 3 conference rooms. Breakfast and Evening dessert included in rates. Types of meals: Full gourmet bkfst, gourmet lunch, picnic lunch, afternoon tea, gourmet dinner and Luncheons. Beds: KQT. Reading lamp, ceiling fan, clock radio, telephone, desk, TV/VCR and hair dryers in room. Air conditioning. Fax, copier, library, parlor games, fireplace, refrigerator on each floor for guest use, evening dessert and Miss Fannie's Tea Room on premises. Amusement parks, antiquing, fishing, parks, shopping, sporting events and water sports nearby.

Location: City.

Publicity: *Charlotte Observer, Spartanburg Herald, Southern Living, Atlanta Journal-Constitution, Sandlapper Magazine, SCETV, Prime Time Live, BBC Documentary and Marshall Tucker Band Music Video.*

Certificate may be used: Jan. 15-Nov. 15, Monday-Thursday.

South Dakota

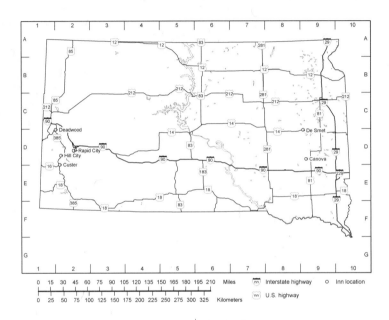

0 15 30 45 60 75 90 105 120 135 150 165 180 195 210 Miles
0 25 50 75 100 125 150 175 200 225 250 275 300 325 Kilometers

⬜ nn Interstate highway   ○ Inn location
⬜ nn U.S. highway

Canova

B&B at Skoglund Farm

24375 438 Avenue
Canova, SD 57321-9726
(605)247-3445
Internet: www.skoglundfarm.com
E-mail: PASkoglund@excite.com

Circa 1917. This is a working farm on the South Dakota prairie. Peacocks stroll around the farm along with cattle, chickens and other fowl. Guests can enjoy an evening meal with the family. The innkeepers offer special rates for families with children. The farm's rates are $30 per adult, $25 per teenager and $20 per child. Children age five and younger stay for free.

Innkeeper(s): Alden & Delores Skoglund.
$60. 4 rooms. Breakfast and dinner included in rates. Types of meals: Full bkfst, early coffee/tea and snacks/refreshments. Beds: QDT. TV, reading lamp and clock radio in room. VCR, library and telephone on premises. Antiquing, fishing, parks, shopping, sporting events and water sports nearby.

Location: Country.

"Thanks for the down-home hospitality and good food."
Certificate may be used: Accepts Weekends, Anytime, subject to availability; Anytime, last minute - based on availability.

Custer

Custer Mansion B&B

35 Centennial Dr
Custer, SD 57730-9642
(605)673-3333 (877)519-4948 Fax:(605)673-6696
Internet: www.custermansionbb.com
E-mail: cusmanbb@gwtc.net

Circa 1891. Situated on one and a half acres of gardens and aspens, this two-story Gothic Victorian was built by one of the original Black Hills homesteaders. Architectural features include Eastlake stick trim, seven gables and stained-glass windows. Antiques fill the guest bedrooms and honeymoon or anniversary suites and family suites. Enjoy a hearty breakfast of fresh fruits, home-baked goods, meats, creative egg dishes, pancakes, waffles and French toast before venturing out for a day of activities in the Black Hills. Conveniently located, all area attractions are close by. After a day of sightseeing, relax in the outdoor hot tub. Pastries and hot and cold beverages are always available.

Innkeeper(s): Bob & Patricia Meakim. $65-130. 6 rooms, 5 with PB, 1 with WP, 1 two-bedroom suite. Breakfast, afternoon tea and snacks/refreshments included in rates. Types of meals: Full gourmet bkfst, veg bkfst and early coffee/tea. Beds: KQT. Cable TV, VCR, reading lamp, ceiling fan, clock radio, hot tub/spa, hair dryer and wireless Internet access in room. Air conditioning. DVD, fax, copier, spa, library, parlor games, telephone and Wireless Internet on premises. Amusement parks, antiquing, art galleries, beach, bicycling, canoeing/kayaking, cross-country skiing, fishing, golf, hiking, horseback riding, live theater, museums, parks, shopping, tennis, water sports and wineries nearby.

Location: Country. Black Hills.

Publicity: *Country Extra Magazine, National Historic Society, Midwest Living Magazine, Classic American Home, Minneapolis Star Tribune and Pilot Getaways.*

Certificate may be used: Oct. 11 to April 30, anytime, subject to availability.

Deadwood

Black Hills Hideaway B&B

11744 Hideaway Rd.
Deadwood, SD 57732
(605)578-3054 Fax:(605)578-2028
Internet: www.enetis.net/~hideaway
E-mail: hideaway@enetis.net

Circa 1976. Guests enjoy the privacy of 67 wooded acres and views of mountain peaks at this bed & breakfast. The eight guest rooms are tucked into a mountain chalet-style home with cathedral ceilings and natural wood interior. The home is located on what was a wagon trail in the late 19th century. The decor is comfortable and there's a huge brick fireplace to enjoy. Each guest room has its own theme, including Western and European themes with antiques. Most rooms have a fireplace, deck and whirlpool or hot tubs. The innkeepers also offer a housekeeping cabin south of Pactola Lake. The home is about 40 miles from Mt. Rushmore and the Crazy Horse Monument. A gold mine, the Passion Play, Spearfish Canyon and other attractions are nearby. Deadwood, a historic national landmark, is 7 miles away.

Innkeeper(s): Ned & Kathy Bode. $109-179. 8 rooms with PB, 7 with FP, 3 with HT, 4 with WP. Breakfast and snacks/refreshments included in rates. Types of meals: Full bkfst, early coffee/tea and dinner. Beds: KQ. VCR, reading lamp, CD player, ceiling fan, clock radio, turn-down service, some with hot tub/spa, most with fireplace and hair dryer in room. TV, fax, copier, bicycles, parlor games, telephone, Robes, Iron and Ironing board on premises. Antiquing, art galleries, bicycling, canoeing/kayaking, cross-country skiing, downhill skiing, fishing, golf, hiking, horseback riding, wineries, gambling, snowmobiling and gold mines nearby.

Location: Mountains.

Certificate may be used: Sept. 16-May 15, Sunday-Thursday, subject to availability.

Hill City

High Country Guest Ranch

12172 Deerfield Rd
Hill City, SD 57745
(605)574-9003 (888)222-4628
Internet: www.highcountryranch.com
E-mail: hcranch@rapidnet.com

Ten cabins set on a grassy meadow offer skylights and private decks. Some have full kitchens, and there are special honeymoon and anniversary accommodations. The inn's special use permit allows guests to enjoy the Black Hills National Forest on horseback with half-day and full-day rides available. The dining room looks like a covered wagon. The ranch is close to Mount Rushmore.

Innkeeper(s): Larry and Bonnie McCaskell. $65-225. 10 cabins, 2 with FP. Beds: Q. Cable TV, VCR, reading lamp, refrigerator, ceiling fan, clock radio and hot tub/spa in room. Air conditioning. Fax, copier, spa, stable, parlor games and telephone on premises. Handicap access. Cross-country skiing, downhill skiing, fishing, golf, live theater, parks, shopping, tennis, water sports, deer and turkey hunting, horseback riding and Mt. Rushmore nearby.

Location: Guest ranch.

Publicity: *Minnesota Monthly.*

Certificate may be used: Sept. 25-May 1.

Rapid City

Coyote Blues Village

23165 Horseman's Ranch Rd, Rapid City, SD 57702
Rapid City, SD 57702
(605)574-4477 (888)253-4477 Fax:(605)574-2101
Internet: www.coyotebluesvillage.com
E-mail: coyotebb@iw.net

Circa 1996. Experience genuine European style with the Streich family from Switzerland in their 9,000-square-foot, two-story European cabin, resting on 30 acres of woodlands in the Black Hills of South Dakota. Four uniquely themed rooms provide style to fit any taste, from "jungle" to "Oriental." Relax in the hot tub just outside the room on the private patio and breathe in the fresh pine scent that fills the crisp air. Rise each morning with the sweet aroma of freshly baked goods from the Swiss Specialty Bakery downstairs. Enjoy breakfast in the dining room or on the deck before an excursion in town.

Innkeeper(s): Christine & Hans-Peter Streich. $50-145. 7 rooms with PB, 4 with HT, 1 two-bedroom suite, 1 conference room. Breakfast and snacks/refreshments included in rates. Types of meals: Full gourmet bkfst, veg bkfst, early coffee/tea, gourmet lunch and gourmet dinner. Beds: KQ. Data port, cable TV, reading lamp, stereo, refrigerator, ceiling fan, clock radio and hot tub/spa in room. VCR, DVD, fax, copier, bicycles, telephone, fireplace, gift shop, weightlifting equipment, sun tanning room and deck with longchairs on premises. Handicap access. Antiquing, art galleries, beach, bicycling, canoeing/kayaking, cross-country skiing, downhill skiing, fishing, golf, hiking, horseback riding, live theater, museums, parks, shopping, tennis, water sports, wineries, 1880 train, caves, pow-wows and rodeos nearby.

Location: Country, mountains.

Certificate may be used: September-May, subject to availabilty, last minute, subject to availabilty.

Tennessee

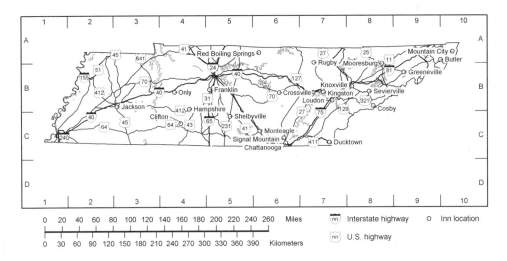

Butler

Iron Mountain Inn B&B & Vacation Cabins

PO Box 30
Butler, TN 37640
(423)768-2446 (888)781-2399
Internet: www.ironmountaininn.com
E-mail: stay@ironmountaininn.com

Circa 1998. Above the clouds on more than 140 acres, this light-filled log home offers breathtaking mountain views. Guest bedrooms feature private balconies and whirlpool tubs. Ask for the Memories or Equestrian with a steam shower. Coffee and sweets are delivered to the door before a full breakfast is served downstairs with tempting dishes such as crepes, Belgian waffles, souffles and omelettes. White-water rafting, horseback riding, fly-fishing or boating on Watauga Lake are favorite activities. This is the perfect location for a romantic wedding or elopement. The innkeeper will help plan a hassle-free, dream-fulfilled day within a budget. Ask about the year-round Sweetheart Special romantic getaway. Pampering includes an in-room massage or a private hideaway in the Creekside Chalet with a hot tub under the stars.

Innkeeper(s): Vikki Woods. $125-350. 4 rooms with PB. Breakfast and Bottomless cookie jar included in rates. Types of meals: Full bkfst, afternoon tea, snacks/refreshments, Bottomless cookie jar and special diets are our specialty. Beds: KQT. Modem hook-up, data port, reading lamp, ceiling fan, clock radio, turn-down service, whirlpools and breakfast in bed with reservation in room. Central air. Fax, copier, library, parlor games, fireplace and laundry facility on premises. Antiquing, art galleries, canoeing/kayaking, cross-country skiing, downhill skiing, fishing, golf, hiking, horseback riding, live theater, water sports, Appalachian Trail, outlet shopping, ghost tours by boat and country auctions nearby.

Location: Mountains. Backs up to National Forest bordered by two creeks.

Publicity: *Awarded #1 Best Place to Stay, Elizabethton Star, USA Today, Johnson City Press, The Tennessee Magazine, Log Home, Country Magazine, Marquee Magazine and PBS.*

Certificate may be used: Mid-week, November-April, in Appalachian Spring or Green rooms, not valid holidays or special events.

Cosby

Creekwalk Inn and Cabins at Whisperwood Farm

166 Middle Creek Road and Highway 321
Cosby, TN 37722
(142)348-74000 (180)096-22246
Internet: www.creekwalkinn.com
E-mail: info@creekwalkinn.com

Circa 1984. Swim or fish in the trout-stocked Cosby Creek while staying at this B&B outside Gatlinburg, Tennessee in the Great Smoky Mountains. Creekwalk Inn and Cabins at Whisperwood Farm in Cosby offers the setting of a log home on a private estate with 3000 feet of water frontage. Firewood is available for outdoor campfires and a guitar is available for strumming and singing along. Beverage service is provided all day. Stay in a guest bedroom with a cathedral ceiling and assorted amenities that may include a creek or meadow view, Jacuzzi, fireplace, robes, balcony or a private outdoor hot tub in a bamboo thicket. Honeymoon and family cabins are also available. Savor a daily gourmet breakfast before exploring the scenic area. The wedding chapel and reception lodge are popular romantic venues.

Innkeeper(s): Janice and Tifton Haynes. $139-310. 7 rooms, 9 with PB, 4 with FP, 2 with HT, 4 with WP, 2 two-bedroom suites, 1 cottage, 14 cabins, 4 conference rooms. Breakfast and Tea and coffee beverage service available 24 hours/day self service. Cabins do not include breakfast included in rates. Types of meals: Full gourmet bkfst, veg bkfst, early coffee/tea, gourmet lunch, picnic lunch, Private chef available with 24 hours notice, private dinners by reservation, fresh fruit and juice served with full gourmet breakfast, vegetarian meals by request, guests may bring own wine and guest refrigerator. Reading lamp, CD player, ceiling fan, some with hot tub/spa, some with fireplace, hair dryer, bathrobes, bath amenities, wireless Internet access, Cathedral ceiling in every bedroom, Creekfront rooms have screen door opening to narrow balcony along the edge of the creek and Hannah Mountain has private hot tub in bamboo thicket down creekside path in room. Central air. DVD, fax, copier, swimming, bicycles, library, telephone, laundry facility, Cosby Creek, stocked with trout & fun for wading & swimming, 3000 feet of creek frontage, Firewood available for outdoor campfires & marshmallow roasts and Guitar available for strumming by the fire. on premises. Handicap access. Amusement parks, antiquing, art galleries, bicycling, canoeing/kayaking, cross-country skiing, downhill skiing, fishing, golf, hiking, horseback riding, live theater, museums, parks, shopping, sporting events, tennis, water sports, wineries, White Water Rafting on the Pigeon River, Dollywood Splash Country, Gatlinburg Aquarium, Biltmore House, Clingman's Dome (eastern continental divide), Appalachian Trail and Mountain music played at local bluegrass restaurant Friday through Sunday night just across the street nearby.

Location: Mountains. Gatlinburg, Knoxville.

Publicity: *Knoxville Sentinel and Cable Wedding Show.*

Certificate may be used: Non-Holiday Weeks. Sunday-Thursday excluding October and Special Events.

Ducktown

The White House B&B

104 Main St, PO Box 668
Ducktown, TN 37326-0668
(423)496-4166 (800)775-4166 Fax:(423)496-9778
Internet: www.ocoee-whitehousebb.com
E-mail: mardan@tds.net

Circa 1898. This Queen Anne Victorian boasts a wraparound porch with a swing. Rooms are decorated in traditional style with family antiques. Innkeepers pamper their guests with Tennessee hospitality, a hearty country breakfast and a mouthwatering sundae bar in the evenings. The innkeepers also help guests plan daily activities, and the area is bursting with possibilities. Hiking, horseback riding, panning for gold and driving tours are only a few choices. The Ocoee River is the perfect place for a river float trip or take on the challenge of roaring rapids. The river was selected as the site of the 1996 Summer Olympic Whitewater Slalom events.

Innkeeper(s): Dan & Mardee Kauffman. $85-94. 3 rooms. Breakfast, afternoon tea and snacks/refreshments included in rates. Types of meals: Full gourmet bkfst and early coffee/tea. Beds: QT. Reading lamp, ceiling fan, clock radio and central heat in room. Central air. VCR, fax, library, parlor games, telephone and fireplace on premises. Antiquing, fishing, golf, parks, shopping, water sports and Ocoee River rafting nearby.

Location: Mountains. Small town in the mountains.

Publicity: *Southern Living.*

"From the moment we walked into your home, we sensed so much hospitality and warmth. You took such good care of us in every way

and lavished so much love on us - and the food!!! Oh, my goodness!!! We'll just have to come back!"

Certificate may be used: Sunday through Thursday, April-November. Everyday, December through March. Holidays and special events excluded.

Greeneville

Nolichuckey Bluffs

295 Kinser Park Lane
Greeneville, TN 37743-4748
(423)787-7947 (800)842-4690 Fax:(423)787-9247
Internet: www.tennessee-cabins.com
E-mail: cabins@usit.net

Circa 1997. Nolichuckey Bluffs is composed of seven cabins located on 16 wooded acres overlooking the river. Redbud Cabin offers two bedrooms, a kitchen, dining area, living room and private Jacuzzi. Six can sleep here, and there are generously sized decks, a fireplace and air conditioning. A full breakfast is served in the country store. Grist Mill and discount golf are found on the property.

Innkeeper(s): Patricia & Brooke Sadler. $90-130. 7 cabins, 5 with FP. Types of meals: Cont and snacks/refreshments. Beds: KQDT. Cable TV, VCR, reading lamp, refrigerator, ceiling fan, clock radio, telephone, coffeemaker, desk, some with hot tub/spa, hair dryer, bath amenities and iron/ironing board in room. Central air. Fax, copier, library, parlor games and laundry facility on premises. Antiquing, fishing, golf, parks, shopping and tennis nearby.

Location: Mountains.

Certificate may be used: Anytime, subject to availability, except holidays and special events.

Jackson

Highland Place B&B Inn

519 N Highland Ave
Jackson, TN 38301-4824
(731)427-1472 (877)614-6305 Fax:(731)427-2430
Internet: www.highlandplace.com
E-mail: relax@highlandplace.com

Circa 1911. Whether traveling for business or pleasure, a stay at this elegant Colonial Revival mansion will relax and inspire. Conveniently located in a quiet downtown historical district, the perfect blend of old and new furnishings provide luxurious comfort and modern convenience. Spacious barely describes the 10-foot-wide hallways, high ceilings, marble fireplace and many exquisite common rooms to gather in and dine together. An audio center enhances the gracious ambiance, and a video library offers further entertainment. The impressive guest bedrooms are well-appointed. Special attention is given to meet personal or corporate needs.

Innkeeper(s): Cindy & Bill Pflaum. $145-175. 4 rooms with PB, 2 with FP, 1 with WP, 2 two-bedroom suites, 2 guest houses, 1 conference room. Breakfast included in rates. Types of meals: Full gourmet bkfst, veg bkfst, early coffee/tea, afternoon tea, snacks/refreshments, wine, gourmet dinner and Inquire about romantic dinner. Beds: Q. Modem hook-up, data port, cable TV, VCR, reading lamp, stereo, ceiling fan, snack bar, clock radio, telephone, turn-down service, desk, some with fireplace, hair dryer, bathrobes, bath amenities, wireless Internet access and iron/ironing board in room. Central air. DVD, fax, copier, library, laundry facility and WiFi Internet access on premises. Antiquing, art galleries, bicycling, fishing, golf, live theater, parks, shopping, sporting events and tennis nearby.

Location: City.

Certificate may be used: Accepts Weekends, Anytime, subject to availability; Anytime, last minute - based on availability.

Kingston

Whitestone Country Inn

1200 Paint Rock Rd
Kingston, TN 37763-5843
(865)376-0113 (888)247-2464 Fax:(865)376-4454
Internet: www.whitestoneinn.com
E-mail: moreinfo@whitestoneinn.com

Circa 1995. This regal farmhouse sits majestically on a hilltop overlooking miles of countryside and Watts Bar Lake. The inn is surrounded by 360 acres, some of which borders a scenic lake where guests can enjoy fishing or simply communing with nature. There are eight miles of hiking trails, and the many

porches and decks are perfect places to relax. The inn's interior is as pleasing as the exterior surroundings. Guest rooms are elegantly appointed, and each includes a fireplace and whirlpool tub. Guests are treated to a hearty, country-style breakfast, and dinners and lunch are available by reservation. The inn is one hour from Chattanooga, Knoxville and the Great Smoky Mountains National Park.

Innkeeper(s): Paul & Jean Cowell. $150-270. 21 rooms with PB, 21 with FP, 2 conference rooms. Breakfast included in rates. Types of meals: Full bkfst, picnic lunch and dinner. Restaurant on premises. Beds: KQ. Cable TV, VCR, reading lamp, stereo, ceiling fan, clock radio, telephone, turn-down service, desk and hot tub/spa in room. Air conditioning. Fax, copier, spa, library, parlor games and fireplace on premises. Handicap access. Antiquing, fishing, golf, shopping and water sports nearby.

Location: Country, mountains, waterfront. Lake.

"Not only have you built a place of beauty, you have established a sanctuary of rest. An escape from the noise and hurry of everyday life."

Certificate may be used: Jan. 1 to March 31, Sunday-Thursday.

Knoxville

Maplehurst Inn

800 W Hill Ave
Knoxville, TN 37902
(865)523-7773 (800)451-1562
Internet: www.maplehurstinn.com
E-mail: sonny@maplehurstinn.com

Circa 1917. This townhouse, located in the downtown neighborhood of Maplehurst, is situated on a hill that overlooks the Tennessee River. A parlor with fireplace and piano invites guests to mingle in the evening or to relax quietly with a book. The inn's favorite room is the Penthouse with king bed, cherry furnishings and a sky lit Jacuzzi. The Anniversary Suite offers a double Jacuzzi and canopy bed. A light informal breakfast is served in the Garden Room overlooking the river, while breakfast casseroles, country potatoes, quiches and breads are offered buffet-style in the dining room. Check there for brownies and cookies if you come back in the middle of the day. The inn is within two blocks of the Convention Center and City Hall as well as several fine restaurants. The University of Tennessee and Neyland Stadium are nearby.

Innkeeper(s): Sonny & Becky Harben. $79-149. 11 rooms with PB, 1 suite. Breakfast and snacks/refreshments included in rates. Types of meals: Full

gourmet bkfst, veg bkfst and early coffee/tea. Beds: KD. Cable TV, VCR, reading lamp, ceiling fan, clock radio, telephone, desk and some with Jacuzzi in room. Air conditioning. Laundry facility on premises. Antiquing, canoeing/kayaking, live theater, museums and parks nearby.

Location: City.

Certificate may be used: Anytime, subject to availability.

Monteagle

Monteagle Inn

204 West Main Street
Monteagle, TN 37356
(931)924-3869 (888)480-3245 Fax:(931) 924-3867
Internet: www.monteagleinn.com
E-mail: suites@monteagleinn.com

Circa 1997. Offering European elegance and comfort, this recently renovated inn is classical in style and design. Adjacent to the courtyard, a large wood-burning fireplace accents the great room that showcases a 1923 baby grand piano family heirloom. Guest bedrooms boast a variety of comfortable furnishings and amenities. Choose a four-poster, iron or sleigh bed with soft linens. Many include balconies. The two-bedroom Cottage boasts a fully equipped kitchen, front porch, dining and living rooms. Enjoy a homemade breakfast in the dining room. The garden gazebo is surrounded by year-round color, designed by a local horticulturist and a prominent landscape architect. Ask about romance and anniversary packages.

Innkeeper(s): Jim Harmon. $160-215. 13 rooms with PB, 1 conference room. Breakfast and snacks/refreshments included in rates. Types of meals: Veg bkfst, early coffee/tea and Full Mountain Gourmet Breakfast. Beds: KQT. Modem hook-up, data port, reading lamp, ceiling fan, clock radio, telephone, desk, voice mail, hair dryer, bathrobes, bath amenities, wireless Internet access, iron/ironing board, down pillows, luxurious European linens, imported bath amenities, antiques and modern reproductions in room. Central air. TV, VCR, DVD, fax, copier, library, parlor games and Handicap Room available on premises. Handicap access. Antiquing, art galleries, bicycling, canoeing/kayaking, fishing, golf, hiking, horseback riding, live theater, parks, shopping, tennis, water sports and wineries nearby.

Location: Country, mountains.

Publicity: *Southern Living, In Tennessee, Sterling Magazine, Chattanooga Times Free Press, Atlanta Journal-Constitution and Charter Cable special on B&B's.*

Certificate may be used: January-March on Sundays, Mondays and Tuesdays.

Mountain City

Prospect Hill B&B Inn

801 W Main St (Hwy 67)
Mountain City, TN 37683
(423)727-0139 (800)339-5084
Internet: www.prospect-hill.com
E-mail: stay@prospect-hill.com

Circa 1889. This three-story shingle-style Victorian manor garners a great deal of attention from passersby with its appealing architecture and commanding hilltop location. Romantic rooms offer tall arched windows, 11-foot ceilings and spectacular views. Fashioned from handmade bricks, it was once home to Major Joseph Wagner, who, like many of his neighbors in far northeastern Tennessee, served on the Union side. The restored home features five guest rooms. A 1910 oak Craftsman dining set complements the oak Stickley furniture (circa 1997) that decorates the living room. Fireplaces, whirlpools and stained glass add luxury to the guest rooms. Prospect Hill boasts views of the Appalachian and Blue Ridge Mountains. From the front window, guests can see three states: Tennessee, Virginia and North Carolina. The inn is within an hour of the Blue Ridge Parkway, Appalachian Trail and Roan and Grandfather mountains, the Virginia Creeper Trail and 25 minutes from Boone, NC.

Innkeeper(s): Judy & Robert Hotchkiss. $89-169. 5 rooms with PB, 4 with FP, 1 cottage, 1 conference room. Breakfast and snacks/refreshments included in rates. Types of meals: Full gourmet bkfst, veg bkfst, early coffee/tea and Snacks in the room. Beds: KQT. Modem hook-up, data port, cable TV, VCR, DVD, reading lamp, CD player, refrigerator, ceiling fan, snack bar, clock radio, telephone, coffeemaker, turn-down service, desk, most with fireplace, hair dryer, bathrobes, bath amenities, iron/ironing board, historic stained glass, balcony or porch, private entrance, bed for one child, scenic views and cottage with LR/DR and fully equipped kitchen in room. Central air. Fax, copier, library, parlor games, laundry facility, gift shop, hiking on 30 acres, access to the Iron Mountain Trail and A Cottage in the Woods has decks and lots of parking on premises. Limited handicap access. Antiquing, art galleries, bicycling, canoeing/kayaking, cross-country skiing, downhill skiing, fishing, golf, hiking, horseback riding, live theater, museums, parks, shopping, water sports, wineries, stables, swimming, fly fishing, outlets, drive-in movies, Appalachian and Virginia Creeper Trails nearby.

Location: Country, mountains. Small town America.

Publicity: *Marquee Magazine, Old-House Journal, Haunted Inns of the Southeast, USA Today (Sleep with a Ghost), Arrington's (named Most Romantic Hideaway), Best Southern Inn, Tennessee Magazine, Four Points Magazine, Blue Ridge Country Magazine, Fresh Outlook Magazine, WCYB-Bristol, VA, Oldies Knoxville, Voted Most Romantic Hideaway (Arrington's-2003) and Best Southern Inn.*

"The most wonderful thing I'll always remember about our stay is, by far, the wonderful home we came back to each night."

Certificate may be used: Sunday to Thursday, except October, July and NASCAR weekends.

Only

Chestnut Hill Ranch and Bed and Breakfast

3001 Browns Bend Road
Only, TN 37140
(931)729-0153 (877)860-9077 Fax:(931)729-0153
Internet: www.chestnuthillranch.com
E-mail: chestnuthillranch@earthlink.net

Just one hour from downtown Nashville, Chestnut Hill Ranch Bed and Breakfast spans 53 lush acres in the Duck River Valley of Only, Tennessee. Built in 1908, the B&B has been renovated and restored to blend a Victorian Country ambiance with modern conveniences. Walk through the woods or explore the countryside on a bike. At the end of the day, soak in the hot tub in the large gazebo. Relax on the big attached decks or look out at the pond and farm animals from the picture window in the Great Room. Themed guest bedrooms are comfortable and inviting; some feature gas log fireplaces. A hearty breakfast and evening refreshments are provided. Arrange for special gatherings to be held in the spacious Event Center.

Innkeeper(s): Dr. Sharon J. Boisvert-Tanley and George Tanley. Call for rates. Call inn for details. Types of meals: Full gourmet bkfst, veg bkfst, early coffee/tea, lunch, picnic lunch, afternoon tea, snacks/refreshments, gourmet dinner, room service, 3 course Dinners, Group luncheons, picnic lunches and dinners and catering available. Advanced reservations required for meals. Beds: QDT. Reading lamp, ceiling fan, bathrobes and bath amenities in room. Central air. TV, VCR, DVD, fax, spa, library, telephone, fireplace, gift shop, New Event Center with 1200 square feet of entertainment area, stained glass windows and fireplace for Wedding and Anniversary celebrations on premises. Limited handicap access. Antiquing, bicycling, canoeing/kayaking, hiking, horseback riding, live theater, shopping, Mennonite community and Loretta Lynn's Hurricane Mills Resort nearby.

Location: Country.

Certificate may be used: Monday-Thursday only, No weekends.

Texas

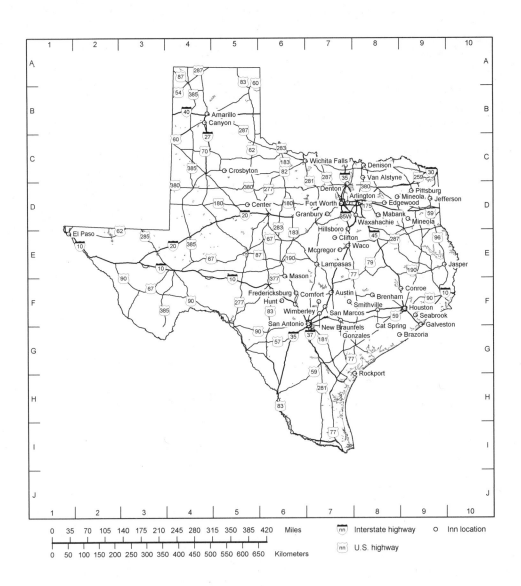

Tell the innkeeper that you have an iLoveInns free-night certificate when you make your reservation.

Amarillo

Parkview House B&B

1311 S. Jefferson St.
Amarillo, TX 79101-4029
(806)373-9464 Fax:(806)373-3166
Internet: ParkviewHousebb.com
E-mail: Parkviewbb@suddenlink.net

Circa 1908. Experience generous Texas hospitality at this lovingly restored, historic Victorian inn. Relax on the wraparound
porch or in a hammock. The Music Room invites listening to a
varied selection of old and new recordings and DVDs. An old-

world charm and treasures collected from around the world create
the ambiance of The Global Room,
perfect for chatting over a glass of
wine with other guests. Intimate
guest bedrooms and suites feature
personal robes and VCRs. Several
include clawfoot tubs. The Garden
Cottage boasts a living room and kitchen with beverage-stocked
refrigerator. Enjoy a gourmet continental breakfast in the formal
dining room or newly remodeled country kitchen with fireplace.
Stroll among the rose and herb gardens with a Koi pond, fountains and statuary. Soak in the hot tub under the stars.

Innkeeper(s): Carol & Nabil Dia. $85-135. 5 rooms, 3 with PB, 1 suite, 1
cottage. Breakfast included in rates. Types of meals: Full gourmet bkfst, early
coffee/tea and snacks/refreshments. Beds: QD. Cable TV, VCR, reading lamp,
clock radio, hot tub/spa, bathrobes, wireless Internet access, some ceiling
fans, desks and telephones in room. Air conditioning. Fax, copier, spa, bicycles, parlor games, telephone, fireplace and Computer on premises.
Amusement parks, antiquing, bicycling, hiking, horseback riding, live theater,
museums, parks, shopping, tennis, water sports and bird watching nearby.

Publicity: *Lubbock Avalanche, Amarillo Globe News, Accent West, Sunday
Telegraph Review, Channel 7 and Ranked #1 in Amarillo by Tripadvisor.com.*

*"You are what give B&Bs such a wonderful reputation. Thanks very
much for the wonderful stay! The hospitality was warm and the
ambiance incredible."*

Certificate may be used: Anytime, Monday to Thursday, excluding some
holidays and weekends, based on availability. American Historic Inns must
be mentioned.

Austin

Carrington's Bluff

1900 David St
Austin, TX 78705-5312
(512)479-0638 (888)290-6090 Fax:(512)478-2009
Internet: www.carringtonsbluff.com
E-mail: phoebe@carringtonsbluff.com

Circa 1877. Relax in the peacefulness of this country inn on a
tree-lined bluff in the city. Carrington's Bluff Bed and Breakfast
sits on an acre in the heart of Austin. The spacious porch is
perfect for lingering while gentle breezes rustle through a 500-
year-old native oak tree. Inside, the rooms are furnished with
English and American antiques and are accented with country
fabrics and décor. Stay in a guest bedroom in the historic main
house, or in the Writer's Cottage across the street. Each accommodation is tastefully furnished and boasts an inviting
ambiance. As the aroma of just-brewed gourmet coffee beckons, a full breakfast of fresh fruit, yogurts, homemade granola,
baked goods, and a hot specialty entrée is served on fine china.

Innkeeper(s): Phoebe Williams. $105-225. 8 rooms with PB. Breakfast,
afternoon tea and snacks/refreshments included in rates. Types of meals: Full
gourmet bkfst, veg bkfst, early coffee/tea and room service. Beds: KQ. Cable
TV, VCR, reading lamp, ceiling fan, clock radio, telephone, coffeemaker, desk,
hair dryer, bathrobes, bath amenities, wireless Internet access and iron/iron-
ing board in room. Central air. DVD, fax, copier, library, parlor games and
fireplace on premises. Limited handicap access. Antiquing, art galleries, bicycling, canoeing/kayaking, fishing, golf, live theater, museums, parks, shopping, sporting events, tennis and water sports nearby.

Publicity: *InStyle Magazine, Inn Traveler, USA Today, Dallas Morning News,
Houston Chronicle, Texas Monthly, Austin American Statesman, Austin
Home and Gardens, Houston Home and Gardens, Women's Sport and
Fitness, American Airlines Destinations, Country Inns Magazine, Elle Decor,
Travel Weekly. and PBS Special.*

"Victorian writer's dream place."

Certificate may be used: Sunday-Thursday, subject to availability, excluding
special events.

Brazoria

Roses & The River

2434 County Road 506
Brazoria, TX 77422
(979)798-1070 (800)610-1070 Fax:(979)798-1070
Internet: www.rosesandtheriver.com
E-mail: rosesandtheriver@yahoo.com

Circa 1980. This Texas farmhouse rests beside the banks of the
San Bernard River. There is a sweeping veranda lined with rockers, and the two-acre grounds are well landscaped with an
impressive rose garden. Each of the three guest rooms has been
decorated with a rose theme. Rooms are named New Dawn,
Rainbow's End and Rise 'n Shine. Two rooms view the river
and one views the rose gardens. Breakfasts include unique
treats such as a "blushing orange cooler," baked Alaska grapefruit, homemade sweet rolls and savory egg dishes. The area
offers many attractions, including two wildlife refuges, Sea
Center Texas, where guests can learn about marine life, the
Center for the Arts and Sciences and several historical sites.

Innkeeper(s): Mary Jo & Dick Hosack. $150. 3 rooms with PB. Breakfast
included in rates. Types of meals: Full gourmet bkfst, veg bkfst, early
coffee/tea and hors d'oeuvres. Beds: Q. Cable TV, VCR, DVD, reading lamp,
ceiling fan, clock radio, coffeemaker and desk in room. Central air. Fax, copier, library, telephone, fireplace and laundry facility on premises. Amusement
parks, antiquing, beach, fishing, golf, live theater, museums, parks, shopping,
water sports and wineries nearby.

Location: Country, waterfront.

Publicity: *Brazosport Facts, Texas Monthly and Great Stays of Texas.*

Certificate may be used: Anytime, subject to availability.

Brenham

Mariposa Ranch B&B

8904 Mariposa Ln
Brenham, TX 77833-8906
(979)836-4737 (877)647-4774
Internet: www.mariposaranch.com
E-mail: info@mariposaranch.com

Circa 1865. Several buildings comprise the inn: a Victorian, an
1820 log cabin, a quaint cottage, a farmhouse and a 1836
Greek Revival home. Guests relax on the veranda, stroll through
the Live Oaks or explore the ranch's 100 acres of fields and
meadows. The inn is furnished with fine antiques. Ask for the
Texas Ranger Cabin and enjoy a massive stone fireplace, sofa,
clawfoot tub and loft with queen bed. Jennifer's Suite boasts a

king canopy bed and two fireplaces. The "Enchanted Evening" package offers champagne, fruit, flowers, candlelight, candy and an optional massage. Guests can select a room with a Jacuzzi for two or a clawfoot tub for additional luxury.

Innkeeper(s): Johnna & Charles Chamberlain. $79-250. 11 rooms with PB, 7 with FP, 2 two-bedroom and 1 three-bedroom suites, 2 cottages, 2 guest houses, 3 cabins, 4 conference rooms. Breakfast included in rates. Types of meals: Full gourmet bkfst, gourmet lunch, picnic lunch, snacks/refreshments, gourmet dinner and room service. Restaurant on premises. Beds: KQT. Modem hook-up, cable TV, VCR, reading lamp, CD player, refrigerator, ceiling fan, clock radio, coffeemaker, most with hot tub/spa, most with fireplace, bathrobes, bath amenities and iron/ironing board in room. Central air. Fax, copier, parlor games, telephone, gift shop, porches to enjoy the evenings, live oak trees, the countryside and animals on premises. Limited handicap access. Antiquing, bicycling, fishing, golf, hiking, horseback riding, live theater, museums, parks, shopping, sporting events, tennis, water sports, wineries, George Bush Library, Washington-On-The-Brazos State Park and Museum, Blue Bell Creamery, The Antique Rose Emporium, Unity Theatre and Festival Hill nearby.

Location: Country. Texas hill country.

Publicity: *Southern Living, Texas Monthly, Public Television and NBC station in Houston.*

Certificate may be used: January-December, Sunday-Thursday, subject to availablilty. Not on holidays or special events.

Cat Spring

BlissWood Bed & Breakfast

13300 Lehmann Legacy Ln
Cat Spring, TX 78933
(713)301-3235 Fax:(979)865-5594
Internet: www.blisswood.net
E-mail: carol@blisswood.net

Surrounded by a tranquil country setting, this working ranch graces more than 650 acres, located just one hour west of Houston. Exotic animals abound from American bison and Corriente cattle to llamas and camels. Picnic at the gazebo looking out on Enchanted Lake, ride a horse across the meadows and creeks, try catch and release bass fishing or sit by a pond watching ducks, swans and geese glide by. A seven-circuit labyrinth is in the Mystical Forest. A variety of accommodations include the two-story Texas Farmhouse, Log Cabin or Lehmann House with a clawfoot, antique tin or Jacuzzi tub. The Dog Trot House includes a pool, deck, patio and fireplace. Stay in the secluded Writer's Cabin secluded among the live oaks. Enjoy the smoke-free environment and a deluxe continental breakfast.

Innkeeper(s): Carol Davis. Call for rates. 9 cottages.

Publicity: *Southern Living Magazine.*

Certificate may be used: Sunday–Thursday or anytime at last minute based on availability. NO holidays or antique week.

Denison

Inn of Many Faces Victorian B&B

412 W Morton St
Denison, TX 75020-2422
(903)465-4639 Fax:(903)465-3328
Internet: www.innofmanyfaces.com
E-mail: theinn@sbcglobal.net

Circa 1897. Resplendently sitting in the middle of towering pecan trees on two wooded acres, this restored Queen Anne Victorian provides rest and relaxation. A collection of whimsical faces are displayed throughout the house and gardens reflecting its name, Inn of Many Faces. Themed guest bedrooms offer spacious accommodations. The Katy Room is a romantic retreat dressed in toile that boasts a fireplace, Jacuzzi tub and shower. The Texoma room features a plush king-size bed, fireplace and sitting area with two-person Jacuzzi and shower. All the rooms include a large gourmet breakfast with fresh fruit, baked entree, breakfast meats and breads. The B&B is located four short blocks from antique shops and art galleries on Main Street and near Lake Texoma for boating, fishing and golfing.

Innkeeper(s): Charlie & Gloria Morton. $99-149. 4 rooms with PB, 2 with FP, 1 conference room. Breakfast and snacks/refreshments included in rates. Types of meals: Full gourmet bkfst, veg bkfst and early coffee/tea. Beds: KQD. Cable TV, VCR, DVD, reading lamp, CD player, ceiling fan, clock radio, hot tub/spa, wireless Internet access and fireplace in room. Central air. Fax, copier, parlor games, telephone, fireplace and massages available on premises. Antiquing, art galleries, fishing, golf, hiking, horseback riding, live theater, museums, parks, shopping, sporting events, tennis, water sports and wineries nearby.

Location: City.

Publicity: *Dallas Morning News, Texas Highways, Herald Democrat, McKinney Courier-Gazette and Frisco Style.*

Certificate may be used: Anytime, Sunday-Thursday.

Denton

Heritage Inn Bed and Breakfast Cluster

815 N Locust St
Denton, TX 76201-2952
(940)565-6414 (888)565-6414 Fax:(940)565-6515
Internet: www.theheritageinns.com
E-mail: innkeeper@theheritageinns.com

Circa 1902. Three separate historic homes make up this bed and breakfast cluster and have been restored with a distinct style and flair. The Redbud House was the first of the inns and honors the pioneer spirit of local founders. The Magnolia House, a two-story farmhouse, boasts secluded upstairs suites and a balcony. Giuseppe's Italian Restaurant on the first floor features four dining rooms with Victorian décor and a patio. The most recent addition is the newly opened Pecan House, part of the original Hoard Farm. Relax by the fire in the parlor or on the back porch swing. Generous amenities offer comfort and pleasure. Enjoy a complete breakfast in the dining room or while lounging in a queen-size bed. Soak in the hot tub that is enclosed in a redwood gazebo.

Innkeeper(s): Donna and John Morris. $90-160. 12 rooms with PB, 2 two-bedroom suites, 3 guest houses, 2 conference rooms. Breakfast, Sunday brunch and snacks/refreshments included in rates. Types of meals: Full gourmet bkfst, veg bkfst, early coffee/tea and room service. Restaurant on premises. Beds: QDT. Cable TV, VCR, reading lamp, refrigerator, ceiling fan, clock radio, telephone, desk, hot tub/spa, voice mail, fireplace and DVD player upon request in room. Central air. Copier, spa, library and parlor games on premises. Limited handicap access. Antiquing, art galleries, canoeing/kayaking, fishing, golf, hiking, horseback riding, live theater, museums, parks, shopping, sporting events, water sports, wineries, Storytelling festival and Art & Jazz Festival nearby.

Location: City.

Publicity: *Dallas Morning News, Fort Worth Star Telegram and Texas Monthly.*

Certificate may be used: January, June, July and August. Not honored during NASCAR weeks (week days only). Not valid with any other discount.

Fort Worth

MD Resort Bed & Breakfast

601 Old Base Road
Fort Worth, TX 76078
(817)489-5150 (866)489-5150 Fax:(817)489-5036
Internet: www.mdresort.com
E-mail: innkeeper@mdresort.com

Circa 1999. Stay at a home away from home at this antique-filled country lodge and working ranch on 37 T-shaped acres. Enjoy a large meeting room, living room with big screen TV, game room and limited access to the full kitchen. Each of the guest bedrooms is decorated in a theme, such as German, Western, Victorian or safari, to name just a few. A full home-cooked breakfast will satisfy the heartiest of appetites. A completely furnished barn apartment also is available. The large spa and swimming pool are especially refreshing interludes after a nature walk. Lunch and dinner are served by reservation. A laundry room is accessible when needed.

Innkeeper(s): Donna Davis. $99-499. 15 rooms, 12 with PB, 6 with WP, 4 total suites, including 1 two-bedroom suite, 1 guest house, 1 cabin, 1 conference room. Breakfast and Breakfast served in main lodge dining area at 9 AM each day included in rates. Types of meals: Country bkfst, lunch, picnic lunch, snacks/refreshments, dinner, room service, Romantic In-Room Ribeye Steak Dinner for two = $100, includes salad, baked potato and bread and specialty dessert. Restaurant on premises. Beds: KQDT. Modem hook-up, cable TV, VCR, refrigerator, ceiling fan, snack bar, clock radio, coffeemaker, hair dryer, wireless Internet access, iron/ironing board and wireless high-speed Internet access in room. Central air. DVD, fax, copier, spa, swimming, stable, pet boarding, parlor games, telephone, fireplace, laundry facility, gift shop, Recreation room with pool table, Games, TV/Cable, Darts, Microwave, Mini-fridge, Table and Chairs on premises. Handicap access. Amusement parks, antiquing, art galleries, bicycling, fishing, golf, hiking, horseback riding, live theater, museums, parks, shopping, sporting events, water sports, Texas Motor Speedway and Exotic Feline Sanctuary nearby.

Location: City, country. 37-acre ranch, in the country and close to the city.

Publicity: *Wise County Messenger and Times Record.*

Certificate may be used: Sunday-Thursday, except on holidays or TMS (Texas Motor Speedway) weekends. Cannot be combined with any other offers.

Texas White House B&B

1417 8th Ave
Fort Worth, TX 76104-4111
(817)923-3597 (800)279-6491 Fax:(817)923-0410
Internet: www.texaswhitehouse.com
E-mail: txwhitehou@aol.com

Circa 1910. A spacious encircling veranda shaded by an old elm tree, graces the front of this two-story home located within five minutes of downtown, TCU, the zoo and many other area attractions. The inn's parlor and living room with fireplace and gleaming hardwood floors are the most popular spots for relaxing when not lingering on the porch. Guest rooms are equipped with phones and television, and early morning coffee is provided before the inn's full breakfast at a time convenient to your personal schedule. Suites include hot tub, sauna and fireplace. Baked egg casseroles and freshly made breads are served to your room or in the dining room. The owners are Fort Worth experts and keep abreast of cultural attractions and are happy to help with reservations and planning. The inn is popular with business travelers — secretarial services are available, etc. — during the week and appealing to couples on weekends.

Innkeeper(s): Grover & Jamie McMains. $105-235. 5 rooms with PB, 1 with FP, 2 suites, 1 conference room. Breakfast and snacks/refreshments included in rates. Types of meals: Full gourmet bkfst, early coffee/tea and room ser-

vice. Beds: KQ. Cable TV, VCR, reading lamp, CD player, refrigerator, ceiling fan, clock radio, telephone, coffeemaker, turn-down service, desk, some with hot tub/spa, some with fireplace, hair dryer, bathrobes, wireless Internet access, iron/ironing board and one suite with dry heat sauna in room. Central air. Fax, copier, laundry facility and gift shop on premises. Limited handicap access. Antiquing, art galleries, golf, live theater, museums and parks nearby.

Location: City.

Certificate may be used: Sunday-Thursday, no holidays. Nights must be consecutive; May 1-Sept. 30.

The Castle Cottage

3513 Williams Rd
Fort Worth, TX 76116
(817)366-2675
Internet: www.thecastlecottage.net
E-mail: dee@thecastlecottage.net

Circa 1945. The Castle Cottage Romantic Bed and Breakfast graces a quiet neighborhood near the cultural district just eight miles from downtown Fort Worth, Texas. Whether traveling for business or pleasure, be pampered by the non-hosted privacy while any needs are considered and met. The cottage was built in 1945 and recently renovated. It features a fully equipped kitchen and dining area. Relax in the living room or sit at the table in the back yard. The surrounding Dallas/Fort Worth area offers much to do and many sights to see.

Innkeeper(s): Dee Micheletti. $150-165. 1 suite. Types of meals: Cont. Beds: K. Data port, cable TV, VCR, DVD, reading lamp, stereo, refrigerator, ceiling fan, clock radio, telephone, coffeemaker, turn-down service, fireplace, hair dryer, bathrobes, bath amenities, wireless Internet access and iron/ironing board in room. Central air. Amusement parks, antiquing, art galleries, beach, bicycling, canoeing/kayaking, cross-country skiing, fishing, golf, hiking, horseback riding, live theater, museums, parks, shopping, sporting events, tennis and water sports nearby.

Location: City.

Certificate may be used: Anytime subject to availablity.

Fredericksburg

Alte Welt Gasthof (Old World Inn)

142 East Main Street
Fredericksburg, TX 78624
(830)997-0443 (888)991-6749 Fax:(830)997-0040
Internet: www.texas-bed-n-breakfast.com
E-mail: stay@texas-bed-n-breakfast.com

Circa 1915. Located on the second floor above a Main Street shop, Alte Welt is in a Basse Block building in the historic district. The entryway opens to an antique-filled foyer. A three-room suite offers a white sofa, silver accents including a silver, tin ceiling, wood floors and an antique iron four-poster bed draped in soft gauze. An armoire with TV and a small refrigerator and microwave add convenience. The innkeeper collects antique, crocheted and embroidered linens for the guest rooms. There is a spacious deck with hot tub adjoining one of the suites. Together, the two suites can accommodate as many as 4 people, who enjoy the freedom of simply going downstairs to Main Street and all its boutiques, shops and restaurants.

Innkeeper(s): Ron & Donna Maddux. $150-165. 2 suites. Breakfast included in rates. Types of meals: Cont and early coffee/tea. Beds: Q. Cable TV, reading lamp, refrigerator, ceiling fan, clock radio, telephone, desk, hot tub/spa, microwave and coffee bar in room. Air conditioning. Antiquing, fishing, golf, parks, shopping, tennis, museums and hunting nearby.

Certificate may be used: Jan. 2 to Feb. 5 and Sept. 3-23, Sunday-Thursday, suite No. 1 only.

Galveston

Coastal Dreams Bed & Breakfast

3602 Ave P
Galveston, TX 77550
(409)770-0270 (866)770-0270
Internet: www.coastaldreamsbnb.com
E-mail: lana@coastaldreamsbnb.com

Circa 1887. Built in 1887 and recently renovated, Coastal Dreams Bed and Breakfast is a relaxing and romantic getaway on the island of Galveston, Texas. Swim in the pool, soak in the spa or lounge on the large, shaded deck. Books, movies, cards and games are available in the hospitality area. Afternoon refreshments are served in the formal dining room. Comfortably pleasant guest bedrooms and a suite are located on the second floor and are named after coastal places. Start each day with a home-cooked breakfast accented by soft music and good conversation. Walk along the beach, shop the famous Strand or visit Moody Gardens. Ask about specials and packages offered.

Innkeeper(s): Lana Lander. $105-165. 4 rooms with PB, 1 with WP, 1 suite. Breakfast, afternoon tea and snacks/refreshments included in rates. Types of meals: Full gourmet bkfst, early coffee/tea, picnic lunch, wine, Picnic lunches, wine and champagne available at additional cost. Beds: KQ. Cable TV, VCR, DVD, reading lamp, CD player, refrigerator, ceiling fan, snack bar, clock radio, coffeemaker, hair dryer, bath amenities, wireless Internet access and iron/ironing board in room. Central air. Fax, copier, spa, swimming, library, telephone and fireplace on premises. Antiquing, art galleries, beach, bicycling, fishing, golf, horseback riding, live theater, museums, parks, shopping, tennis, water sports, wineries, Moody Gardens and Schlitterbahn Waterpark nearby.

Location: City, ocean community, waterfront. .

Certificate may be used: September-February, Sunday through Thursday, Not valid holidays or local special events.

Houston

Palms on West Main

807 W Main St #1
Houston, TX 77006
(713)522-7987 Fax:(713)522-3150
Internet: www.palmsonwestmain.com
E-mail: meadeandsmith@pdq.net

Circa 1914. Centrally located in Houston's historic museum district, this early 20th-century Dutch Colonial home can be found in the same neighborhood where Howard Hughes grew up, possessing unique architecture and mature trees. The inn's host, Tom Meade, a member of the Greater Houston Preservation Alliance, has restored many original designs of the house and enjoys providing ample information on Houston's history and attractions. Private access to each suite is located off the "Key West" deck, filled with tropical plants and fountains. Fireplaces and individual design distinguish each room. With many activities in the Houston area, guests get prepared each morning with a hearty breakfast.

Innkeeper(s): Tom Meade, Rick Smith. $89-109. 3 rooms, 2 with FP, 3 suites. Breakfast included in rates. Types of meals: Full bkfst. Beds: KQ. Cable TV, VCR, reading lamp, ceiling fan, telephone and desk in room. Air conditioning. Fax, bicycles and fireplace on premises. Amusement parks, antiquing, art galleries, bicycling, golf, live theater, museums, parks, shopping and sporting events nearby.

Location: City.

Certificate may be used: Anytime, subject to availability.

Robin's Nest

4104 Greeley St
Houston, TX 77006-5609
(713)528-5821 (800)622-8343 Fax:(713)528-6727
Internet: www.therobin.com
E-mail: robin@therobin.com

Circa 1898. Robin's Nest adorns the museum and arts district, known as The Montrose, in Houston, Texas. This circa 1898 two-story Queen Anne Victorian is much like an intimate European hotel but with a touch of funky American flair. Relax on the wraparound porch or in the parlor. Upstairs there is a tea/coffee station. Inviting guest bedrooms offer a sweet respite from the day's adventures. Whirlpool suites boast private entrances and porches. Murder mystery parties and weddings are popular events at this bed and breakfast inn. Situated near downtown theaters and gourmet restaurants, Galveston and Johnson Space Center are about an hour away.

Innkeeper(s): Robin Smith, Jessica Whatley. $95-175. 7 rooms, 6 with PB, 2 with WP, 1 conference room. Breakfast included in rates. Types of meals: Full gourmet bkfst, veg bkfst and early coffee/tea. Beds: QDT. Modem hook-up, cable TV, reading lamp, refrigerator, ceiling fan, clock radio, telephone, coffeemaker, desk, some with hot tub/spa, hair dryer and wireless Internet access in room. Central air. Fax, copier and library on premises. Amusement parks, antiquing, fishing, live theater, museums, parks, shopping, sporting events, water sports and Downtown nearby.

Location: City. Inside 610 Loop very near downtown, George R. Brown Convention Center and Texas Medical Center.

Publicity: *Houston Home and Garden, Houston Business Journal, Woman's Day, Houston Metropolitan, Houston Post, Southern Living, Texas Monthly, Houston Chronicle, Inside Houston and Houston Press ("Best Houston B&B" 2002).*

"Fanciful and beautiful, comfortable and happy. We saw a whole new side of Houston, thanks to you."

Certificate may be used: Sunday-Thursday, all year, Anytime, Last Minute-Based on Availability, Anytime, based on availability.

Jefferson

1st Bed & Breakfast in Texas Pride House

409 E.Broadway
Jefferson, TX 75657
(800)894-3526 Fax:(903)665-3901
Internet: www.jeffersontexas.com
E-mail: sreisenauer@msn.com

Circa 1888. Mr. Brown, a sawmill owner, built this Victorian house using fine hardwoods, sometimes three layers deep. The windows are nine-feet tall on both the lower level and upstairs. The rooms include amenities such as fireplaces, balconies, canopy beds and private entrances. Most boast original stained-glass windows, and each room is named after a steamboat that once docked in Jefferson. One room is decorated in crimson reds and features a gigantic clawfoot tub that has received an award from Houston Style Magazine for "best bathtub in Texas." A wide veranda stretches around two sides of the house.

Innkeeper(s): Sandra and David Reisenauer. $89-149. 10 rooms with PB, 3 with FP, 2 suites, 1 conference room. Breakfast and snacks/refreshments includ-

ed in rates. Types of meals: Full gourmet bkfst, early coffee/tea, picnic lunch, wine, Dessert buffet on weekends and also from scratch beignets and pumpkin rolls. Beds: KQT. Cable TV, DVD, reading lamp, ceiling fan, snack bar, clock radio, telephone, desk, some with fireplace, hair dryer, wireless Internet access, iron/ironing board and Most rooms have featherbed toppers in room. Central air. Fax, parlor games, complimentary refreshments and weekend dessert buffet on premises. Handicap access. Antiquing, canoeing/kayaking, fishing, golf, hiking, horseback riding, live theater, museums, parks, shopping, water sports, Steamboat tours, Home tours, Water skiing, Antebellum home tours, Steam train, 35 antique stores, Ghost walk and Ghost train nearby.

Location: City. Piney Woods.

Publicity: *Woman's Day, Country Home, Texas Highways and Texas Homes.*

"No five star hotel can compare to the hospitality of Pride House."

Certificate may be used: Sunday-Thursday, holidays and Jefferson special events excluded.

McKay House

306 E Delta St
Jefferson, TX 75657-2026
(903)665-7322 (800)468-2627 Fax:903 665-8551
Internet: www.mckayhouse.com
E-mail: innkeeper@mckayhouse.com

Circa 1851. For more than 15 years, the McKay House has been widely acclaimed for its high standards, personal service and satisfied guests. Both Lady Bird Johnson and Alex Haley have enjoyed the gracious Southern hospitality offered at the McKay House. The Greek Revival cottage features a front porch with pillars. Heart-of-pine floors, 14-foot ceilings and documented wallpapers complement antique furnishings. A full "gentleman's" breakfast is served in the garden conservatory by the gable fireplace. Orange French toast, home-baked muffins and shirred eggs are a few of the house specialties. In each of the seven bedchambers you find a Victorian nightgown and old-fashioned nightshirt laid out for you. History abounds in Jefferson, considered the "Williamsburg of the Southwest."

Innkeeper(s): Hugh Lewis. $66-149. 7 rooms with PB, 5 with FP, 1 two-bedroom suite, 1 cottage, 1 conference room. Breakfast, snacks/refreshments and wine included in rates. Types of meals: Full gourmet bkfst, veg bkfst, early coffee/tea, lunch, picnic lunch, dinner and room service. Beds: KQ. Modem hook-up, data port, cable TV, VCR, DVD, reading lamp, stereo, ceiling fan, snack bar, clock radio, telephone, desk, voice mail, most with fireplace, hair dryer, bath amenities, wireless Internet access and iron/ironing board in room. Central air. Fax, library and parlor games on premises. Handicap access. Antiquing, art galleries, canoeing/kayaking, fishing, golf, hiking, horseback riding, live theater, museums, parks, shopping, water sports and wineries nearby.

Location: City, country.

Publicity: *Southern Accents, Dallas Morning News, Country Home and Bride.*

"The facilities of the McKay House are exceeded only by the service and dedication of the owners."

Certificate may be used: Sunday through Thursday, not including spring break or festivals/holidays; space available, reserved one week in advance please.

Old Mulberry Inn

209 E Jefferson St
Jefferson, TX 75657-2017
(903)665-1945 (800)263-5319
Internet: www.jeffersontexasinn.com
E-mail: mulberry3@charter.net

Circa 1996. Nineteenth-century charm meets modern-day comfort in this plantation-style home. The property sits atop Quality Hill in the town which once was a busy river port in the 1800s.

The wide-plank heart-pine flooring, from a cotton gin near Dallas, provides a soft backdrop to the inn's antiques. Relax on the sofa in the library to gaze at clouds painted on the ceiling 30 feet overhead. In the morning, enjoy coffee and biscotti on one of three porches. Then move to the dining room and partake of a three-course breakfast, featuring such delicacies as yogurt parfait, artichoke quiche and mulberry almond coffee cake.

Innkeeper(s): Donald & Gloria Degn. $89-189. 9 rooms with PB, 1 with FP, 1 with WP, 1 suite. Breakfast included in rates. Types of meals: Full gourmet bkfst, veg bkfst, early coffee/tea and snacks/refreshments. Beds: KQ. Cable TV, VCR, reading lamp, CD player, ceiling fan, clock radio, some with hot tub/spa, some with fireplace, hair dryer, bath amenities, wireless Internet access, New cottage suite/rooms have cable with VCR/DVD players, individual thermostats, refrigerators, coffeemakers, hair dryers, private entrances off porches, three have 2-person soaking tubs and two have 2-person showers in room. Central air. Fax, copier, library, parlor games, telephone and video library on premises. Antiquing, canoeing/kayaking, fishing, golf, live theater, museums, parks, water sports, casinos and potteries nearby.

Publicity: *Southern Living, Dallas Morning News, Texas Highways, Houston Chronicle, LA Times, Named one of the "Top 10 Texas Retreats" by SouthernLiving.com (May 2007)., Shreveport News, AAA 3 diamond award since 1999, Best Recipes from American Country Inns and Bed and Breakfasts and Texas Bed & Breakfast Cookbook.*

Certificate may be used: Anytime, Sunday-Friday, except holiday/special event weekends. Anytime, January and August.

McGregor

Lighthouse Bed & Breakfast

421 S Harrison St
McGregor, TX 76657-1562
(254)840-2589 (800)616-0603 Fax:(254)840-3988
Internet: www.thelighthousebandb.com
E-mail: stay@thelighthousebandb.com

Circa 1894. The romantic charm of the past is highlighted at this recently restored Queen Anne Victorian. The inn's gingerbread trim and wraparound porch with swing and rockers are welcoming first impressions. Grace and elegance are reflected in the six generations of family heirloom antiques and furnishings. The appealing guest bedrooms feature a variety of comforts that may include clawfoot tubs, fireplaces, VCRs, canopy and brass beds. A candle-lit breakfast is served family-style on fine china with silver settings and vintage linens. The stained-glass garden gazebo is showcased on a landscaped lawn.

Innkeeper(s): Jerry & Jan Walters. $80-150. 13 rooms with PB, 2 with FP, 1 suite. Breakfast and snacks/refreshments included in rates. Types of meals: Full bkfst and early coffee/tea. Beds: KQD. Modem hook-up, cable TV, VCR, reading lamp, ceiling fan, clock radio, telephone, desk and fireplace in room. Central air. TV, spa, library, parlor games, fireplace and laundry facility on premises. Antiquing, art galleries, fishing, golf, hiking, horseback riding, live theater, museums, parks, shopping, sporting events and tennis nearby.

Location: Suburban.

Certificate may be used: Jan. 2-Dec. 30, Sunday-Thursday.

Mineola

Munzesheimer Manor

202 N Newsom St
Mineola, TX 75773-2134
(903)569-6634 (888)569-6634 Fax:(903)569-9940
Internet: www.munzesheimer.com
E-mail: innkeeper@munzesheimer.com

Circa 1898. Let time stand still while staying at this historic 1898 Victorian home that was built entirely with pine and cedar. Its classic features include many bay windows, large rooms with high ceilings and original fireplaces with mantles. Sip lemonade on the spacious wraparound porch with wicker furniture and rockers. Relax in one of the two inviting parlors. Choose an upstairs guest bedroom in the main house or an adjacent ground-floor cottage room with a private entrance. The pleasing accommodations feature central heat and air conditioning and American and English antiques. Soak in a claw-foot tub with bath salts before sleeping in a vintage nightgown or nightshirt. A gourmet breakfast is served on china and silver in the formal dining room.

Innkeeper(s): Bob & Sherry Murray. $90-120. 7 rooms with PB, 3 with FP, 3 cottages. Breakfast included in rates. Types of meals: Full bkfst and early coffee/tea. Beds: KQDT. Reading lamp, refrigerator and ceiling fan in room. Air conditioning. VCR, fax, telephone and fireplace on premises. Antiquing, golf, live theater, parks, shopping and tennis nearby.

Publicity: *Country, Dallas Morning News, Southern Bride, Houston Chronicle, San Antonion News and Southern Living.*

Certificate may be used: January-December, Monday-Thursday.

New Braunfels

Acorn Hill Bed & Breakfast

250 School House
New Braunfels, TX 78132-2458
(830)907-2597 (800)525-4618 Fax:(830)964-5486
Internet: www.acornhillbb.com
E-mail: acornhill@acornhillbb.com

Circa 1910. Enjoy wandering the five scenic acres of gardens and fields while staying at this year-round bed & breakfast with a log house that was originally a school and themed cottages conveniently located only five minutes from the Guadalupe River and downtown Gruene. Overlook the hills from a porch rocker. Play the converted pump organ and make calls from an antique phone booth. Suites and cottages feature fireplaces and some boast Jacuzzi tubs. Indulge in an all-you-can-eat multi-course breakfast buffet in the log house dining room. Swim in the in-ground pool or soak in the relaxing hot tub. Browse through the antique and gift shop for treasures to take home. Barbecue pits and picnic tables are provided throughout the grounds. The Victorian Garden is an ideal setting for weddings.

Innkeeper(s): Richard & Pam Thomas. $100-175. 6 rooms with PB, 6 with FP, 3 suites, 3 cottages, 1 conference room. Breakfast included in rates. Types of meals: Country bkfst, veg bkfst, early coffee/tea and picnic lunch. Beds: KQ. TV, VCR, reading lamp, refrigerator, ceiling fan, clock radio, coffeemaker, desk, hot tub/spa and fireplace in room. Central air. Fax, spa, swimming, parlor games, telephone and gift shop on premises. Limited handicap access. Amusement parks, antiquing, art galleries, bicycling, canoeing/kayaking, fishing, golf, hiking, horseback riding, live theater, museums, parks, shopping, sporting events, tennis, water sports and wineries nearby.

Location: Country.

Certificate may be used: November 1 to March 1, Sunday-Thursday only.

Firefly Inn

120 Naked Indian Trail
New Braunfels, TX 78132-1865
(830)905-3989 (800)687-2887
Internet: www.fireflyinn.com
E-mail: info@fireflyinn.com

Circa 1983. Romance the Texas Hill Country in New Braunfels, Canyon Lake, Gruene near the Guadalupe River. The Country Victorian decor and quality handcrafted furniture provide comfort and style. Each guest suite offers several spacious rooms, including a kitchen. To add to the pampering, an excel-

lent breakfast is delivered to the door each morning, ready to satisfy. Spectacular views can be seen from the private deck or porch overlooking the meadows. Picnic tables in the courtyard, small ponds with waterfalls and a hot tub surrounded by mountain hills and fresh air are pleasurable treats to enjoy. A small intimate wedding in the gazebo is complete with a pastor available to perform the ceremony.

Innkeeper(s): Jack & Kathy Tipton. $125-175. 4 cottages, 4 suites. Breakfast included in rates. Types of meals: Full bkfst. Beds: QT. TV, reading lamp, refrigerator, ceiling fan, coffeemaker, hot tub/spa and iron/ironing board in room. Air conditioning. VCR, spa, telephone and laundry facility on premises. Amusement parks, antiquing, beach, canoeing/kayaking, fishing, golf, live theater, museums, parks, shopping, tennis, water sports, wineries, Schlitterbahn, Natural Bridge Caverns, Sea World and Fiesta Texas nearby.

Location: Country. Texas hill country.

Publicity: *San Antonio Wedding Pages 2002 & 2003, Dallas Morning News, San Antonio Express and "Show Me Texas."*

Certificate may be used: Sept. 15 through February, Sunday through Thursday, excluding holidays and special events.

Gruene Mansion Inn

1275 Gruene Rd
New Braunfels, TX 78130-3003
(830)629-2641 Fax:(830)629-7375
Internet: www.gruenemansioninn.com
E-mail: frontdesk@gruenemansioninn.com

Circa 1872. Overlook the Guadalupe River from the porches of this Victorian mansion located on three acres in Hill Country, adjacent to the state's oldest dance hall. The inn has been designated a Historic Landmark and is listed in the National Register. The Mansion, barns, corn crib, carriage house and other outbuildings have all been refurbished to offer quiet and private guest bedrooms, cottages and guest houses. A rustic Victorian elegance is the ambiance and style of decor that blends antiques, fine fabrics and wall coverings. Savor breakfast entrees that boast a Mexican flair and flavor. For a day trip, visit the Alamo, 30 miles away.

Innkeeper(s): Judi & Cecil Eager/Jackie Skinner. $165-299. 31 rooms, 30 with PB, 2 two-bedroom suites, 1 cottage, 1 conference room. Breakfast included in rates. Types of meals: Full bkfst and snacks/refreshments. Beds: KQDT. Cable TV, reading lamp, refrigerator, ceiling fan, clock radio, coffeemaker, some with fireplace, hair dryer, bath amenities, wireless Internet access and iron/ironing board in room. Central air. VCR, fax, copier, telephone, gift shop, porch with rocking chairs looking at Guadalupe River and gift shop on premises. Handicap access. Amusement parks, antiquing, art galleries, bicycling, canoeing/kayaking, fishing, golf, hiking, horseback riding, live theater, museums, parks, shopping, sporting events, tennis, water sports, wineries and oldest dance hall in Texas nearby.

Location: City, country, waterfront. Hill country of Texas.

Publicity: *San Antonio Express News, Austin American Statesmen and New Braunfels Herald Zietung.*

Certificate may be used: January-February, Sunday-Thursday, Sunday Hauses only; September, Sunday-Thursday, Sunday Hauses only.

Pittsburg

Carson House Inn & Grille

302 Mount Pleasant St
Pittsburg, TX 75686-1335
(903)856-2468 (888)302-1878 Fax:(903)856-0709
Internet: www.carsonhouse.com
E-mail: mailus@carsonhouse.com

Circa 1878. The city's oldest occupied home, this bed & breakfast with manicured lawns, a Koi pond and patio, also features a highly acclaimed restaurant. The interior was built using more than one mile of curly pine. The milled lumber, known for its interesting grain pattern, came from diseased trees, now thought to be extinct. The Carson Room boasts a sleigh bed, sitting area and private entrance. It adjoins the Abernathy Room with a brass bed. The Camp Room offers a relaxing two-person whirlpool tub. The private Carson and Barnes Railroad Car, decorated with artifacts, is a fitting tribute to local history. A refrigerator, two-person shower and a Jacuzzi just outside make this a perfect retreat. A cooked-to-order breakfast is made when desired.

Innkeeper(s): Eileen & Clark Jesmore. $79-99. 8 rooms with PB, 1 suite, 1 cottage. Breakfast included in rates. Types of meals: Full gourmet bkfst, veg bkfst, gourmet lunch, snacks/refreshments, gourmet dinner and room service. Restaurant on premises. Beds: KQD. Modem hook-up, data port, cable TV, VCR, reading lamp, refrigerator, ceiling fan, clock radio, telephone, coffeemaker, turn-down service, desk, hot tub/spa and voice mail in room. Central air. Fax, fireplace and laundry facility on premises. Antiquing, bicycling, fishing, golf, hiking, horseback riding, live theater, museums, parks, shopping and water sports nearby.

Location: City.

Publicity: *Dallas Morning News, Gourmet Magazine, Texas Parks & Wildlife and Romantic America.*

Certificate may be used:

Rockport

Anthony's By Sea Bed & Breakfast

732 S Pearl St
Rockport, TX 78382-2420
(361)729-6100 (800)460-2557 Fax:(361)729-2450
Internet: www.anthonysbythesea.com
E-mail: anthonysbythesea@sbcglobal.net

Circa 1997. This quiet, casual retreat is hidden away beneath huge oak trees, near the ocean in an area known as the Texas Riviera. Choose from comfortably furnished single rooms or suites with private baths and sitting areas. Separate guest house has a fully equipped kitchen, spacious living area and sleeps up to six, making it ideal for families and small groups. A sparkling pool and covered lanai provide the most popular areas for relaxing or enjoying the gourmet breakfasts. Located within walking distance of Rockport Beach, a variety of water activities are available, as well as local shopping, restaurants and museums.

Innkeeper(s): Smitty & Beth. $105. 6 rooms, 4 with PB, 1 suite, 1 guest house, 1 conference room. Breakfast included in rates. Types of meals: Full gourmet bkfst and early coffee/tea. Beds: KQD. Cable TV, VCR, reading lamp, refrigerator, ceiling fan and clock radio in room. Central air. Fax, swimming, pet boarding, parlor games, laundry facility and pets allowed on premises. Limited handicap access.

Location: City, ocean community.

Publicity: *New York Times.*

Certificate may be used: Anytime, November-March, subject to availability.

San Antonio

Brackenridge House

230 Madison
San Antonio, TX 78204-1320
(210)271-3442 (800)221-1412 Fax:(210)226-3139
Internet: www.brackenridgehouse.com
E-mail: brackenridgebb@aol.com

Circa 1901. Each of the guest rooms at Brackenridge House is individually decorated. Clawfoot tubs, iron beds and a private veranda are a few of the items that guests might discover. Several rooms include kitchenettes. Blansett Barn, often rented by families or those on an extended stay, includes two bedrooms, a bathroom, a full kitchen and living and dining areas. Many of San Antonio's interesting sites are nearby. The San Antonio Mission Trail begins just a block away, and trolleys will take you to the Alamo, the River Walk, convention center and more. Coffeehouses, restaurants and antique stores all are within walking distance. Small pets are welcome in Blansett Barn.

Innkeeper(s): Bennie & Sue Blansett. $110-250. 6 rooms with PB, 3 suites, 1 cottage. Breakfast included in rates. Types of meals: Full gourmet bkfst and early coffee/tea. Beds: KQD. Modem hook-up, data port, cable TV, VCR, reading lamp, refrigerator, ceiling fan, clock radio, telephone, coffeemaker, desk, microwave, iron, ironing board, hair dryer and wireless Internet connection in room. Air conditioning. Fax, copier, spa and parlor games on premises. Amusement parks, antiquing, fishing, golf, live theater, parks, shopping, sporting events and tennis nearby.

Location: City. 1/2 mile to Alamo & Riverwalk.

Publicity: *San Antonio Express News, Huntington Beach Herald, New York Times and Seattle Times.*

"Innkeeper was very nice, very helpful."

Certificate may be used: Monday through Thursday, June through September; January and February no holidays.

Christmas House B&B

2307 McCullough
San Antonio, TX 78212
(210)737-2786 (800)268-4187 Fax:(210)734-5712
Internet: www.christmashousebnb.com
E-mail: christmashsb@earthlink.net

Circa 1908. Located in Monte Vista historic district, this two-story white inn has a natural wood balcony built over the front porch. The window trim is in red and green, starting the Christmas theme of the inn. (There's a Christmas tree decorated all year long.) Guest rooms open out to pecan-shaded balconies. The Victorian Bedroom offers pink and mauve touches mixed with the room's gold and black decor. The Blue & Silver Room is handicap accessible and is on the first floor. Antique furnishings in the inn are available for sale.

Innkeeper(s): Penny & Grant Estes. $85-125. 4 rooms with PB, 1 suite. Breakfast and snacks/refreshments included in rates. Types of meals: Full bkfst, veg bkfst and early coffee/tea. Beds: KQ. Reading lamp, ceiling fan, clock radio and desk in room. Central air. TV, fax, library, parlor games, fireplace, laundry facility and ADA room on premises. Handicap access. Amusement parks, antiquing, art galleries, bicycling, golf, live theater, museums, parks and shopping nearby.

Publicity: *Fort Worth Star Telegram.*

"What a treat to rise to the sweet smell of candied pecans and a tasty breakfast."

Certificate may be used: Sunday-Thursday, not on holidays or during Fiesta.

Inn on the Riverwalk

129 Woodward Pl
San Antonio, TX 78204-1120
(210)225-6333 (877)866-3946 Fax:(210)271-3992
Internet: www.innonriver.com
E-mail: innontheriverwalk@yahoo.com

Circa 1916. Located in a restored river home, the inn is encircled by an iron fence and shaded by a tall pecan tree. There are gables and a wraparound porch. Inside are polished pine floors and tall ceilings. Antiques, Jacuzzi tubs, fireplaces and private porches are among the guest room offerings. A third-floor penthouse offers French doors opening to a private balcony. There is a large Jacuzzi and King-size bed. Stroll to the Riverwalk for scenic shopping, restaurants and entertainment. The Convention Center is four blocks away.

Innkeeper(s): Johanna & Scott Kiltoff. $119-225. 15 rooms with PB, 2 with FP, 5 with HT, 2 with WP, 3 two-bedroom suites. Breakfast included in rates. Types of meals: Full bkfst. Beds: KQT. Cable TV, reading lamp, stereo, refrigerator, ceiling fan, snack bar, clock radio, telephone, desk, voice mail, hair dryer, bath amenities, wireless Internet access, iron/ironing board, All with refrigerators and 7 with spa in room. Air conditioning. Fax, copier, fireplace, Internet access and outdoor patio overlooking river on premises. Amusement parks, antiquing, art galleries, bicycling, fishing, golf, hiking, horseback riding, live theater, museums, parks, shopping, tennis, water sports, wineries, river and museums nearby.

Certificate may be used: Anytime, subject to availability.

San Marcos

Crystal River Inn and Day Spa

326 W Hopkins St
San Marcos, TX 78666-4404
(512)396-3739 (888)396-3739 Fax:(512)396-6311
Internet: www.crystalriverinn.com
E-mail: info@crystalriverinn.com

Circa 1883. Tall white columns accent this Greek Revival inn that features a fireside dining room with a piano and wet bar. Innkeepers encourage a varied itinerary, including sleeping until noon and having breakfast in bed to participating in a hilarious murder mystery. Rock the afternoon away on the veranda or curl up by the fireplace in a guest bedroom by the headwaters of crystal-clear San Marcos River. Clawfoot tubs, four-poster and canopied beds add to the pleasing ambiance. Shop at the state's largest outlet mall that features more than 200 designer stores.

Innkeeper(s): Mike & Cathy. $110-175. 12 rooms with PB, 4 with FP, 4 two-bedroom suites, 1 cabin, 1 conference room. Breakfast included in rates. Types of meals: Full gourmet bkfst, early coffee/tea, lunch, picnic lunch and dinner. Beds: KQDT. Cable TV, VCR, reading lamp, stereo, refrigerator, ceiling fan, clock radio, telephone, coffeemaker, desk, some with fireplace, hair dryer, bathrobes, bath amenities, wireless Internet access, iron/ironing board, fresh flowers, fruit, amenity baskets with many toiletries, vintage magazines and sound machines in room. Central air. Fax, copier, library, child care, laundry facility, gift shop, gardens, fish pond, veranda and 2 long-term stay apartments on premises. Handicap access. Amusement parks, antiquing, bicycling, canoeing/kayaking, fishing, golf, hiking, live theater, museums, parks, shopping, sporting events, tennis, wineries, pools and river for water sports nearby.

Location: City. Small town.

Publicity: *Texas Monthly, USA Today, Country Inns, Southern Living, Dallas Morning News, Houston Chronicle, Boston Globe, Texas Highways and Continental Airlines flight magazine.*

"Thanks for a smashing good time! We really can't remember having more fun anywhere, ever!"

Certificate may be used: Sunday-Thursday, year-round, except for holiday weeks (Thanksgiving, Memorial Day, July 4th, etc.).

Smithville

Katy House Bed & Breakfast

201 Ramona St.
Smithville, TX 78957-0803
(512)237-4262 (800)843-5289 Fax:(512)237-2239
Internet: www.katyhouse.com
E-mail: bblalock@austin.rr.com

Circa 1909. Shaded by tall trees, the Katy House's Italianate exterior is graced by an arched portico over the bay-windowed living room. Long leaf pine floors, pocket doors and a graceful

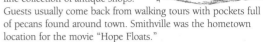

stairway accent the completely refurbished interior. The inn is decorated almost exclusively in American antique oak and railroad memorabilia. A 1909 caboose is being restored to be used as a guest room. Historic Main Street is one block away with a fine collection of antique shops. Guests usually come back from walking tours with pockets full of pecans found around town. Smithville was the hometown location for the movie "Hope Floats."

Innkeeper(s): Bruce & Sallie Blalock. $95-125. 5 rooms with PB, 1 suite, 2 cottages. Breakfast and snacks/refreshments included in rates. Types of meals: Full bkfst, early coffee/tea and picnic lunch. Beds: Q. Cable TV, VCR, reading lamp, ceiling fan, clock radio, telephone, hair dryer, bath amenities, wireless Internet access and iron/ironing board in room. Air conditioning. Fax, bicycles, library, fireplace and gift shop on premises. Antiquing, art galleries, bicycling, canoeing/kayaking, fishing, golf, hiking, horseback riding, museums, parks and shopping nearby.

Location: Small town.

Publicity: *Dallas Morning News, San Antonio Express, Houston Chronicle, Austin Business Journal Magazine "A", Heart of the Pines Magazine and Texas Country Reporter.*

Certificate may be used: Sunday through Thursday, except holidays.

Waxahachie

The BonnyNook

414 W Main St
Waxahachie, TX 75165-3234
(972)938-7207 Fax:(972)937-7700
Internet: www.bonnynook.com
E-mail: vaughn@hyperusa.com

Circa 1887. Each of the five guest rooms at this Queen Anne "Painted Lady" is filled with plants and antiques from around the world. The Sterling Room, a large octagon-shaped chamber, features a hand-carved mahogany canopy bed. The Morrow

Room boasts a 100-year-old sleigh bed and an antique clawfoot tub with a shower. Three of the guest baths offer whirlpool tubs. Bon Appetit featured BonnyNook as part of an article on bed & breakfasts. The hearty breakfasts feature such notable items as blueberry pudding coffeecake or Southern crepes filled with vegetables and eggs. Innkeeper Bonnie Franks keeps a special Coffee Nook filled with teas, coffee, hot cocoa and a refrigerator for her guests. Don't forget to ask about the inn's special cookies. BonnyNook is only two blocks from antique shops, boutiques and restaurants. Gourmet, six-course meals are available by reservation. Massage also is available by reservation.

Innkeeper(s): Vaughn & Bonnie Franks. $125-160. 5 rooms with PB. Breakfast and snacks/refreshments included in rates. Types of meals: Full bkfst, early coffee/tea and gourmet dinner. Beds: KQD. Reading lamp, ceiling fan, clock radio, telephone, desk, hot tub/spa and some with Jacuzzis in room. Air conditioning. Fax, copier, parlor games, coffee nook with refrigerator and ice buckets/ice on premises. Antiquing, parks and shopping nearby.

Location: Small town.

Publicity: *Texas Highways, Dallas Morning News, Forbes, Texas People & Places and Bon Appetit.*

"This was a wonderful retreat from the everyday hustle and bustle and we didn't hear a phone ring once!"

Certificate may be used: Anytime, subject to availability, Sunday-Thursday.

Utah

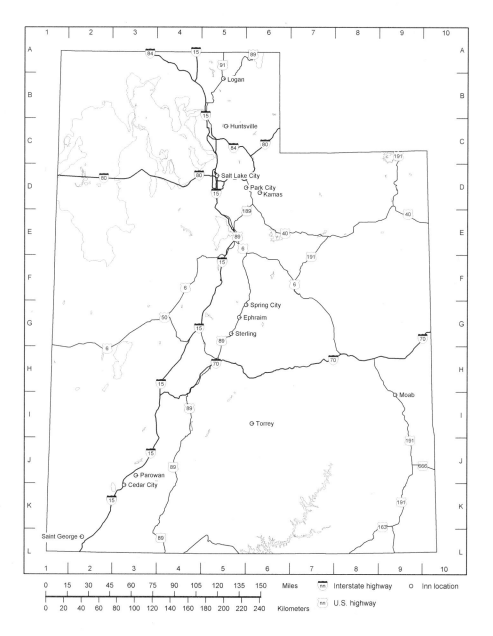

Legend:
- Interstate highway
- U.S. highway
- Inn location

Cedar City

Amid Summer's Inn Bed & Breakfast

140 South 100 West
Cedar City, UT 84720
(435)586-2600
Internet: www.amidsummersinn.com
E-mail: amidsummersinn@yahoo.com

Circa 1935. It is just a block and a half to the Utah Shakespearean Festival and a short walk to downtown Cedar City from this 1930's three-story cottage. The bed and breakfast boasts a formal front parlor with an inviting sitting area. Stay in one of the themed guest bedrooms or spacious suites like the elegant Enchanted Memories, on the upper level. The two-bedroom Garden Suite on the lower level features a kitchenette. Gather in the gorgeous dining room for a lavish breakfast each morning. Explore Bryce Canyon and Zion National Parks while enjoying Amid Summer's Inn.

Innkeeper(s): Gary and Charlene Elsasser. $75-129. 8 rooms with PB, 2 with WP, 2 two-bedroom suites, 1 conference room. Breakfast, afternoon tea and snacks/refreshments included in rates. Types of meals: Full gourmet bkfst, early coffee/tea and room service. Beds: KQT. Cable TV, VCR, DVD, reading lamp, refrigerator, ceiling fan, clock radio, telephone, turn-down service, desk, hair dryer, bath amenities, wireless Internet access and iron/ironing board in room. Central air. Fax, copier, library, fireplace and Expanded cable on premises. Handicap access. Antiquing, art galleries, bicycling, canoeing/kayaking, cross-country skiing, downhill skiing, fishing, golf, hiking, horseback riding, live theater, museums, parks, shopping, sporting events, tennis, water sports, hiking, walking trails, canyons, parowan gap petroglyphs, dinosaur tracks, fort, lakes, Zion National Park, Bryce Canyon National Park, Cedar Breaks National Monument and scenic byway loop nearby.

Location: City, mountains.

Publicity: *Arrington's Inn Traveler rated Charlene and Gary Elsasser as "Best Innkeeper", #8 B&B/Country Inn throughout all North America and also featured in Desert Saint's Magazine and Cedar City newspaper.*

Certificate may be used: Nov. 1-May 31.

Stratford Bed & Breakfast

161 South 200 West
Cedar City, UT 84720
(435)867-5280 (877)530-5280
Internet: www.stratfordbb.com
E-mail: marybeth@stratfordbb.com

Just two blocks from Main Street, this whimsical bed & breakfast adorns a quiet, tree-lined neighborhood in the historic downtown area. Sit on the inviting front porch with a glass of lemonade overlooking the hummingbirds in the garden. Watch cable TV or a video in the parlor. After sleeping under a quilt in a comfortable bed, read the morning paper before breakfast. Enjoy a family-style meal in front of the bay window of the breakfast room that includes fruit, an entree and just-baked breads with homemade jams and jellies. Take a shady one-block stroll to the Utah Shakespeare Festival.

Innkeeper(s): Mary Beth Cook. Call for rates. Call inn for details. Breakfast and snacks/refreshments included in rates. Types of meals: Full bkfst and early coffee/tea. Beds: KQT. Modem hook-up, data port, ceiling fan, feather beds and iron/ironing board in room. Central air. TV, VCR, telephone, fireplace and backyard picnic area on premises. Limited handicap access. Antiquing, art galleries, bicycling, cross-country skiing, downhill skiing, fishing, golf, hiking, live theater, museums, parks, Utah Shakespearean Festival, Neil Simon Festival, Zion National Park, Cedar Breaks National Park and Brian Head Ski Resort nearby.

Location: City.

Certificate may be used: Anytime, subject to availability.

The Garden Cottage Bed & Breakfast

16 North 200 West
Cedar City, UT 84720
(435)586-4919 (866)586-4919 Fax:435-586-9105
Internet: www.thegardencottagebnb.com
E-mail: romance@thegardencottagebnb.com

Circa 1920. Taste the gracious ambiance of Merrie Olde England at this quaint English cottage across from the Utah Shakespearean Festival. At the top of a winding staircase, antique-filled guest bedrooms feature Victorian furnishings and handmade vintage linens with embroidery and lace. A pleasing breakfast usually includes home-baked breads, fresh fruit, quiche, juice smoothies, hot chocolate, tea, cider and coffee. The B&B is surrounded by an award-winning, old-fashioned garden to enjoy. Arrington's Bed and Breakfast Journal recently named the inn as one of the Top 15 B&B/Country Inns.

Innkeeper(s): Gary & Diana Simkins. $109-139. 5 rooms with PB. Breakfast and snacks/refreshments included in rates. Types of meals: Full gourmet bkfst and early coffee/tea. Beds: QT. Reading lamp, hair dryer, bath amenities, wireless Internet access, iron/ironing board and Snacks available all day in room. Central air. TV, VCR, fax, copier, library, parlor games, telephone, fireplace, Satellite TV, Snacks available all day and Shady lush gardens with seating and swing to relax in on premises. Antiquing, art galleries, bicycling, cross-country skiing, downhill skiing, fishing, golf, hiking, horseback riding, live theater, museums, parks, shopping, sporting events, tennis, water sports, Utah Shakespearean Festival, Zion National Park, Bryce Canyon National Park, Cedar Breaks National Monument, Utah Summer Games, Brian Head Ski Resort, Neil Simon Festival, Canyon Country Western Arts Festival and Cedar City Skyfest (a balloon festival) nearby.

Location: Mountains. Small rural town in the mountains.

Publicity: *St. George Magazine (June 2007), Voted Best Bed and Breakfast in Mountain Living Magazine, The Spectrum Newspaper, the Cedar City Magazine, The Daily News and The Review.*

Certificate may be used: Anytime, Nov. 1-May 31.

Moab

Cali Cochitta Bed & Breakfast Inn

110 S 200 East
Moab, UT 84532
(435)259-4961 (888)429-8112 Fax:(435)259-4964
Internet: www.moabdreaminn.com
E-mail: calicochitta@moabdreaminn.com

Circa 1870. This two-story sandstone brick Victorian is in Red Rock Country, which is known for its beautiful panoramas. Innkeeper Kim's beautiful garden has a fountain and is lit by torches at night. She grows both flowers and herbs. The inn is decorated with period Victorian pieces and is full of music and candlelight at night. It has five guest bedrooms including one suite and one cottage. Innkeeper David Boger has 20 years in food management at country clubs and fine restaurants and has catered for international organizations and dignitaries including President George Bush. He cooks with fresh herbs from Kim's garden. Breakfasts include such gourmet fare as crab quiche, homemade blueberry muffins, banana bread, coffee cakes and fresh seasonal berries with the inn's secret Grand Marnier sauce. Other culinary requests, from picnic lunches to candlelight dinners, can be accommodated upon request. The inn is near Arches and Canyonlands National Park and not far from the town of Moab. Guests may enjoy antiquing, shopping touring museums and visiting wineries. Or they may go bicycling, canoeing, fishing, golfing, hiking or horseback riding. David and Kim suggest that guests get up early at least one morning during their stay, and sit on the front porch with a cup of coffee, tea or juice and soak in the magnificent Southern Utah sunrise.

Innkeeper(s): David & Kim Boger. $75-145. 6 rooms with PB, 1 suite, 2 cottages. Breakfast, afternoon tea and snacks/refreshments included in rates. Types of meals: Full gourmet bkfst, early coffee/tea, lunch, picnic lunch and gourmet dinner. Beds: QD. Cable TV, VCR, reading lamp, refrigerator, ceiling fan, clock radio, telephone, turn-down service, desk, hair dryer, bathrobes, bath amenities, wireless Internet access and iron/ironing board in room. Central air. Library, child care, parlor games and hot tub outside in gardens for guest use on premises. Handicap access. Antiquing, art galleries, bicycling, canoeing/kayaking, cross-country skiing, fishing, golf, hiking, horseback riding, live theater, museums, parks, shopping, tennis, water sports, wineries, rock climbing, river rafting and 4x4 nearby.

Location: Country. Remote location by two national parks and Colorado River.

Publicity: *Sunset Magazine and PBS.*

Certificate may be used: January, February excluding holidays and special events. Sunday through Wednesday, subject to availability.

Park City

Old Town Guest House

1011 Empire Ave
Park City, UT 84060
(435)649-2642 (800)290-6423#3710 Fax:(435)649-3320
Internet: www.oldtownguesthouse.com
E-mail: Dlovci@cs.com

Circa 1900. Centrally located, this historic inn is perfect for hikers, skiers and bikers to enjoy all that the mountains offer. Experience convenience and affordability accented with adventure and inspiration. Some of the comfortable guest bedrooms and suites feature lodge-pole pine furnishings and a jetted tub or fireplace. A Park City Breakfast is included and sure to please hungry appetites. The innkeepers' motto of "play hard, rest easy" is pleasantly fulfilled. Assistance is offered in making the most of any stay. Refuel with afternoon snacks and relax in the hot tub.

Innkeeper(s): Deb Lovci Engel. $89-250. 4 rooms with PB, 1 with FP, 1 suite. Breakfast, afternoon tea and snacks/refreshments included in rates. Types of meals: Country bkfst, veg bkfst, early coffee/tea and Hearth mountain breakfast served each morning. Beds: QT. Modem hook-up, data port, cable TV, VCR, DVD, reading lamp, stereo, refrigerator, ceiling fan, snack bar, clock radio, telephone, desk, some with hot tub/spa, voice mail, some with fireplace, hair dryer, bathrobes, bath amenities, wireless Internet access, iron/ironing board, Internet access, ski storage, boot dryers and guest refrigerator in room. Fax, spa, parlor games, laundry facility, ski boot dryers, video library, afternoon snacks, bike storage, ski storage, computer and day packs on premises. Antiquing, art galleries, bicycling, canoeing/kayaking, cross-country skiing, downhill skiing, fishing, golf, hiking, horseback riding, live theater, museums, parks, shopping, tennis, Park City Mountain Resort (walking distance), Deer Valley (free shuttle), The Canyons (free shuttle), snowshoeing and for Summer there are hiking/biking trails from the Inn nearby.

Location: Mountains. Ski areas and mountain biking trails.

Publicity: *Utah Outdoor Magazine, Utah Outdoors July 2002, Voted, "Best Inn for Outdoor Enthusiasts" in 01,02,03,04 & 05 and voted inn "with best outdoor activities."*

Certificate may be used: Anytime, subject to availability.

Salt Lake City

Ellerbeck Mansion B&B

140 North B St
Salt Lake City, UT 84103-2482
(801)355-2500 (800)966-8364 Fax:(801)530-0938
Internet: www.ellerbeckbedandbreakfast.com
E-mail: ellerbeckmansion@qwest.net

Circa 1892. Pleasantly located in the city's downtown historic district, this Victorian inn has been renovated for modern comfort and lovingly restored with original moldings, hardwood floors and stained glass. Impressive fireplaces can be found in the splendid main floor and upstairs galleries as well as in several of the six guest bedrooms. Different seasonal motifs adorn the bedrooms, so every day is a holiday in Christmas Wishes, complete with a sleigh bed. Autumn Winds and Spring Breeze can serve as an ideal suite for families. Enjoy a continental breakfast that is delivered to each room at an agreed-upon time. After exploring the local sites and nearby attractions, the turndown service, evening chocolates and complimentary soft drinks are welcome additions.

Innkeeper(s): Debbie Spencer. $115-135. 6 rooms with PB, 3 with FP. Breakfast and snacks/refreshments included in rates. Types of meals: Full bkfst. Beds: KQ. Modem hook-up, cable TV, reading lamp, clock radio, telephone, turn-down service and fireplace in room. Central air. Fax and fireplace on premises. Antiquing, art galleries, bicycling, downhill skiing, hiking, horseback riding, live theater, museums, parks, shopping, sporting events and Historic Temple Square nearby.

Certificate may be used: Sunday-Wednesday nights except for black out periods and holidays. Cannot be used with any other discount or coupons.

Parrish Place B&B

720 Ashton Ave
Salt Lake City, UT 84106-1802
(801)832-0970 (888)832-0869 Fax:(801)832-0643
Internet: www.parrishplace.com
E-mail: info@parrishplace.com

Circa 1890. Listed in the National Register, this historic, late Victorian mansion was built in 1890 and has been graciously restored. Located in picturesque Salt Lake City, Utah, Parrish Place Bed & Breakfast features original antique art prints by Maxfield Parrish. Gather in the parlor accented by a stained-glass window or feel surrounded by tropical plants and a soothing fountain in the conservatory. Innkeepers Karin and Jeff are both massage therapists. Soak in the hot tub after scheduling a massage for total relaxation. Vibrant and rich guest bedrooms boast fresh flowers, a video library, robes and some have fireplaces, jetted tubs or a two-headed shower. Breakfast is served in the dining room with an original carved fireplace.

Innkeeper(s): Jeff & Karin Gauvin. $89-129. 5 rooms with PB, 2 with WP, 1 conference room. Breakfast and snacks/refreshments included in rates. Beds: Q. Cable TV, VCR, DVD, reading lamp, clock radio, turn-down service, some with hot tub/spa, hair dryer, bathrobes, bath amenities, wireless Internet access and iron/ironing board in room. Air conditioning. Fax, spa, parlor games, telephone, fireplace, gift shop and Massage Therapy on premises. Limited handicap access. Amusement parks, antiquing, art galleries, bicycling, canoeing/kayaking, cross-country skiing, downhill skiing, fishing, golf, hiking, horseback riding, live theater, museums, parks, shopping, sporting events, tennis and 7 National Parks within a half-day drive nearby.

Location: City, mountains.

Publicity: *NY Times (November 13, 2005), Going to: Salt Lake City By Melissa Sanford and HGTV House Hunters.*

Certificate may be used: Sunday-Thursday Nights.

The Anton Boxrud B&B

57 S 600 E
Salt Lake City, UT 84102-1006
(801)363-8035 (800)524-5511 Fax:(801)596-1316
Internet: www.antonboxrud.com
E-mail: antonboxrud@comcast.net

Circa 1901. One of Salt Lake City's grand old homes, this Victorian home with eclectic style is on the register of the Salt Lake City Historical Society. The interior is furnished with antiques from around the country and Old World details. In the sitting and dining rooms, guests will find chairs with intricate carvings, a table with carved swans for support, embossed brass door knobs and stained and beveled glass. There is an out-door hot tub available to guests. The inn is located just a half-block south of the Utah Governor's Mansion in the historic district. A full homemade breakfast and evening snack are provided.

Innkeeper(s): Jane Johnson. $69-140. 7 rooms, 5 with PB, 1 suite. Breakfast included in rates. Types of meals: Full bkfst, early coffee/tea, snacks/refreshments and gourmet dinner. Beds: KQT. Reading lamp, clock radio, desk and wireless Internet access in room. Telephone and fireplace on premises. Amusement parks, antiquing, cross-country skiing, downhill skiing, fishing, live theater, shopping, sporting events and water sports nearby.

Location: City.

Publicity: *Salt Lake Tribune*.

"Made us feel at home and well-fed. Can you adopt us?"
Certificate may be used: Anytime, subject to availability.

Vermont

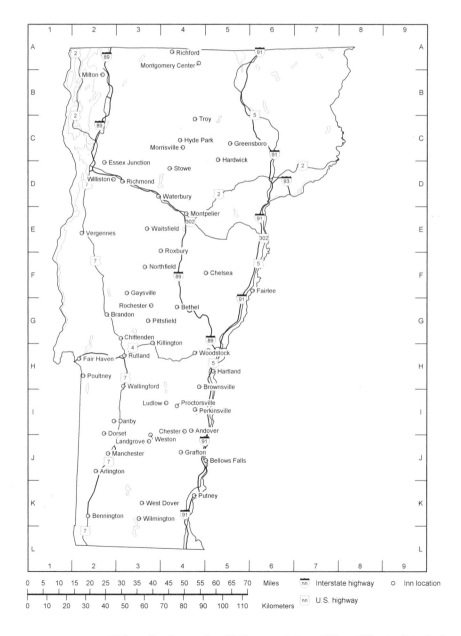

	1	2	3	4	5	6	7	8	9

A
Richford
Montgomery Center
Milton

B
Troy

C
Hyde Park
Morrisville
Greensboro
Hardwick
Essex Junction
Stowe

D
Williston
Richmond
Waterbury
Montpelier

E
Vergennes
Waitsfield

F
Roxbury
Northfield
Chelsea

G
Gaysville
Fairlee
Rochester
Bethel
Brandon
Pittsfield

H
Chittenden
Killington
Woodstock
Fair Haven
Rutland
Hartland
Poultney
Brownsville
Wallingford
Ludlow
Proctorsville
Perkinsville

I
Danby
Dorset
Chester
Andover
Landgrove
Weston

J
Manchester
Grafton
Bellows Falls
Arlington

K
Putney
West Dover
Bennington
Wilmington

Arlington

Hill Farm Inn

458 Hill Farm Rd
Arlington, VT 05250-9311
(802)375-2269 (800)882-2545 Fax:(802)375-9918
Internet: www.hillfarminn.com
E-mail: stay@hillfarminn.com

Circa 1790. One of Vermont's original land grant farmsteads, Hill Farm Inn has welcomed guests since 1905 when the widow Mettie Hill opened her home to summer vacationers. The farm is surrounded by 50 peaceful acres that border the Battenkill River. Guests can relax and enjoy the simple life and visit the inn's sheep, goats and chickens or soak in the 360-degree views of the mountains. Accommodations are charming and cozy, and summer guests have the option of staying in one of four cabins. A large, country breakfast of homemade fare starts off each day.

Innkeeper(s): Al & Lisa Gray. $100-220. 15 rooms with PB, 3 with FP, 6 total suites, including 2 two-bedroom suites, 4 cabins. Breakfast and afternoon tea included in rates. Types of meals: Full gourmet bkfst and snacks/refreshments. Beds: KQDT. Cable TV, VCR, reading lamp, CD player, refrigerator, ceiling fan, clock radio, some with fireplace, hair dryer, bath amenities, wireless Internet access and two kitchenettes in room. Air conditioning. Fax, copier, library, parlor games, telephone, gift shop, farm animals, nature trails, volleyball and children's play equipment on premises. Amusement parks, antiquing, art galleries, bicycling, canoeing/kayaking, cross-country skiing, downhill skiing, fishing, golf, hiking, horseback riding, live theater, museums, parks, shopping, tennis, water sports and families welcome nearby.

Location: Country, mountains. One mile of river frontage.

Publicity: *Providence Journal, Boston Globe, Innsider, Country and New York Times.*

"I have already taken the liberty of changing the meaning of relaxation in the dictionary to 'Hill Farm Inn.' Thank you. . . It was great."

Certificate may be used: Nov. 1-Sept. 1, Sunday-Thursday; excluding holiday periods.

Bennington

Alexandra B&B Inn

916 Orchard Road
Bennington, VT 05201
(802)442-5619 (888)207-9386
Internet: www.alexandrainn.com
E-mail: alexandr@sover.net

Circa 1859. Located on two acres at the edge of town, Alexandra is a Colonial-style inn. There are king or queen beds in all the rooms, as well as fireplaces and views of Bennington Monument and the Green Mountains. Each bath offers water jets and showers. A full gourmet breakfast is served. Bennington College and the business district are five minutes from the inn.

Innkeeper(s): Daniel & Amanda Tarquino. $105-165. 13 rooms, 12 with PB, 12 with FP, 9 with WP. Breakfast and afternoon tea included in rates. Types of meals: Full gourmet bkfst, veg bkfst, early coffee/tea, wine, gourmet dinner and room service. Restaurant on premises. Beds: KQT. Modem hook-up, data port, cable TV, DVD, CD player, clock radio, telephone, desk, most with hot tub/spa, fireplace, hair dryer, bath amenities, wireless Internet access, iron/ironing board, Some with sitting Area and Panoramic windows in room. Air conditioning. Fax, copier, parlor games and Full Bar and Gourmet

Restaurant open only to the guests on premises. Limited handicap access. Antiquing, art galleries, bicycling, canoeing/kayaking, cross-country skiing, downhill skiing, fishing, golf, hiking, horseback riding, live theater, museums, parks, shopping, sporting events, tennis and wineries nearby.

Location: Country, mountains. Outskirts of small town.

Certificate may be used: Nov. 1-May 22, excludes holidays.

South Shire Inn

124 Elm St
Bennington, VT 05201-2232
(802)447-3839 Fax:(802)442-3547
Internet: www.southshire.com
E-mail: relax@southshire.com

Circa 1887. Built in the late 1800s, this inn boasts a mahogany-paneled library, soaring 10-foot ceilings, and three of the guest rooms include one of the home's original fireplaces. Guest rooms feature antiques and Victorian décor. Rooms in the restored carriage house include both a fireplace and a whirlpool tub. Guests are pampered with both a full breakfast, as well as afternoon tea. Local attractions include the Bennington Museum, antique shops, craft stores, covered bridges and skiing.

Innkeeper(s): George & Joyce Goeke. $110-225. 9 rooms with PB, 7 with FP, 1 suite. Breakfast and afternoon tea included in rates. Types of meals: Full bkfst, veg bkfst and early coffee/tea. Beds: KQD. Cable TV, VCR, reading lamp, ceiling fan, clock radio, telephone and whirlpool tubs in room. Central air. Fax, copier, library, parlor games, fireplace and guest refrigerator on premises. Antiquing, art galleries, bicycling, canoeing/kayaking, cross-country skiing, downhill skiing, fishing, golf, hiking, horseback riding, live theater, museums, parks, shopping, Rutland Railroad, Boston & Maine Railroad, Vermont Railway, Bennington train station and Southern Western Vermont Medical Center (SWVMC) nearby.

Location: Country, mountains.

Certificate may be used: Sunday-Thursday, Nov. 1-May 31, excluding holidays and special events.

Brandon

Churchill House Inn

3128 Forest Dale Road
Brandon, VT 05733
(802)247-3078 (800)320-5828
Internet: www.churchillhouseinn.com
E-mail: stay@churchillhouseinn.com

Circa 1872. Caleb Churchill and his son, Nathan, first built a three-story lumber mill, a grist mill and a distillery here, all water powered. Later, with their milled lumber, they constructed this 20-room house. Because of its location, it became a stagecoach stop and has served generations of travelers with comfortable accommodations. The inn is adjacent to Green Mountain National Forest, and excellent hiking, biking, skiing and fishing are just steps away. The inn serves a four-course dinner and a full breakfast.

Innkeeper(s): Seth & Olya Hopkins. $100-180. 8 rooms with PB, 4 with WP. Breakfast, afternoon tea, snacks/refreshments, 4-course dinner $30pp and picnic-lunch $6pp included in rates. Types of meals: Full gourmet bkfst, veg bkfst, early coffee/tea, picnic lunch, hors d'oeuvres, wine and dinner. Beds: KQDT. Reading lamp, stereo, ceiling fan, clock radio, hair dryer, bath amenities, wireless Internet access, iron/ironing board and antique furnishings in room. Fax, copier, swimming, library, parlor games, telephone, fireplace, gift shop and Complimentary beverage bar on premises. Limited handicap access. Antiquing, art galleries, beach, bicycling, canoeing/kayaking, cross-country skiing, downhill skiing, fishing, golf, hiking, horseback riding, museums, parks, shopping, sporting events, tennis, water sports, historic sites and covered bridges nearby.

Location: Country, mountains. Middlebury College.

Publicity: *Gourmet, Yankee and Country.*

"We felt the warm, welcoming, down-home appeal as we entered the front hall. The food was uncommonly good — home cooking with a gourmet flair!"

Certificate may be used: Anytime, November-April, subject to availability, Anytime, Last Minute-Based on Availability.

Lilac Inn

53 Park St
Brandon, VT 05733-1121
(802)247-5463 (800)221-0720 Fax:(802)247-5499
Internet: www.lilacinn.com
E-mail: innkeeper@lilacinn.com

Circa 1909. For some, the scenery is enough of a reason to visit Vermont. For those who need more, try the Lilac Inn. The restored inn's beautiful furnishings, polished woodwork and fireplaces add to the ambiance. Canopy beds dressed with fine linens, flowers, whirlpool tubs and sitting areas grace the guest rooms. A full, gourmet breakfast is included in the rates. The inn is a popular site for unforgettable romantic weddings. The landscaped, two-acre grounds include ponds, a gazebo and hundreds of perennials and annuals. Flowers decorate the ground's stone walls.

Innkeeper(s): Shelly & Doug Sawyer. $115-295. 9 rooms with PB, 3 with FP, 4 conference rooms. Breakfast included in rates. Types of meals: Full gourmet bkfst, early coffee/tea, snacks/refreshments, hors d'oeuvres, wine, gourmet dinner and room service. Restaurant on premises. Beds: KQT. Cable TV, DVD, reading lamp, CD player, ceiling fan, clock radio, desk, some with fireplace, hair dryer, bathrobes, bath amenities, wireless Internet access and iron/ironing board in room. Central air. Fax, copier, library, parlor games and telephone on premises. Handicap access. Antiquing, art galleries, beach, bicycling, canoeing/kayaking, cross-country skiing, downhill skiing, fishing, golf, hiking, horseback riding, live theater, museums, parks, shopping, sporting events, water sports, Shelburne Museum, Ben & Jerry's, Vermont Teddy Bear Factory, Maple Museum, Marble Museum, Robert Frost Trail, Lake Champlain, Warren Kimble, Fran Bull, Killington and Pico nearby.

Location: Country. Small town.

Publicity: *Yankee and Vermont & Country Inns.*

"Tasteful, charming and personable."

Certificate may be used: Anytime, subject to availability.

Bristol

Inn at Baldwin Creek & Mary's Restaurant

1868 North Rte 116
Bristol, VT 05443
(802)453-2432 (888)424-2432 Fax:(802)453-4825
Internet: www.innatbaldwincreek.com
E-mail: info@innatbaldwincreek.com

Circa 1797. Gracing 25 scenic acres at the base of the Green Mountains, this classic New England farmhouse with white clapboard and black shutters is a warm and welcoming B&B inn. Wade and fish in Baldwin Creek, hike on scenic trails and play croquet, volleyball or badminton on the extensive grounds. Swim seasonally in the in-ground heated pool. Adirondack chairs accent the lawns. Gather for afternoon tea. Families appreciate the children's playground area, kid's menu

in the restaurant, toy box and age-appropriate videos. Second-floor guest bedrooms and a two-room suite feature pampering amenities to enhance every stay. A hearty, farm-fresh breakfast is provided daily. Ask about special packages available.

Innkeeper(s): Linda Harmon and Douglas Mack. $75-185. 5 rooms with PB, 2 with FP. Breakfast and afternoon tea included in rates. Types of meals: Full gourmet bkfst, veg bkfst, early coffee/tea, picnic lunch, snacks/refreshments and gourmet dinner. Restaurant on premises. Beds: KQT. VCR, reading lamp, CD player, ceiling fan, clock radio, coffeemaker, turn-down service, some with fireplace, hair dryer, bathrobes, bath amenities, wireless Internet access and iron/ironing board in room. Air conditioning. Fax, copier, swimming, parlor games, telephone and gift shop on premises. Limited handicap access. Antiquing, art galleries, beach, bicycling, canoeing/kayaking, cross-country skiing, downhill skiing, fishing, golf, hiking, horseback riding, live theater, museums, parks, shopping, sporting events, tennis and water sports nearby.

Location: Country, mountains.

Certificate may be used: Sunday-Thursday, April-August.

Chester

Hugging Bear Inn & Shoppe

244 Main St
Chester, VT 05143
(802)875-2412 (800)325-0519
Internet: www.huggingbear.com
E-mail: inn@huggingbear.com

Circa 1850. Among the 10,000 teddy bear inhabitants of this white Victorian inn, several peek out from the third-story windows of the octagonal tower. There is a teddy bear shop on the premises and children and adults can borrow a bear to take to bed with them. Rooms are decorated with antiques and comfortable furniture. A bear puppet show is often staged during breakfast.

Innkeeper(s): Georgette Thomas. $65-165. 6 rooms with PB. Breakfast included in rates. Types of meals: Country bkfst and early coffee/tea. Beds: KQDT. Reading lamp and teddy bear in room. Air conditioning. TV, VCR, parlor games, telephone, fireplace, 10,000 teddy bears and library on premises. Antiquing, cross-country skiing, downhill skiing, fishing, golf, parks, shopping and swimming nearby.

Location: Mountains.

Publicity: *Rutland Daily Herald, Exxon Travel, Teddy Bear Review, Teddy Bear Scene and Boston Globe.*

Certificate may be used: November, March-June 15, except holidays.

Park Light Inn

232 Depot Street
Chester, VT 05143
(802)875-4417 (888)875-4417 Fax:(802)875-5227
Internet: www.parklightinn.com
E-mail: innkeepers@parklightinn.com

Circa 1906. Victorian charm adds to the architectural interest at this rare two-story Queen Anne Colonial that was built in 1906 and reflects quaint, scenic New England. It is furnished with antiques and is accented by lace curtains, period photos and oil paintings on canvas. Stroll the rock gardens and flower beds with a fieldstone wall and mountain views from the side and back yards. Family friendly, play billiards in the great room or relax by the fire in the sitting room. Soak in the hot tub or walk to the town green. Themed guest bedrooms and a spacious suite are named after national parks. The Central Park Room boasts a clawfoot soaking tub. Linger over a hearty three-course country breakfast in the dining room.

Innkeeper(s): Jo-Ann and Jack . $95-265. 5 rooms with PB, 1 with FP, 5 with HT, 2 total suites, including 1 two-bedroom suite, 1 conference room. Breakfast included in rates. Types of meals: Full gourmet bkfst, Sun. brunch, early coffee/tea, gourmet lunch, afternoon tea, snacks/refreshments and gourmet dinner. Restaurant on premises. Beds: KQT. Modem hook-up, data port, cable TV, VCR, DVD, reading lamp, stereo, refrigerator, ceiling fan, clock radio, telephone, coffeemaker, turn-down service, desk, hot tub/spa, some with fireplace, bathrobes, bath amenities, wireless Internet access and iron/ironing board in room. Air conditioning. Fax, copier, parlor games and gift shop on premises. Antiquing, art galleries, beach, bicycling, canoeing/kayaking, cross-country skiing, downhill skiing, fishing, golf, hiking, horseback riding, live theater, museums, parks, shopping, sporting events, tennis, water sports, wineries and fine dining nearby.

Location: Country, mountains.

Publicity: *NY Daily News (January 2005 Travel) and Boston Globe (September 2006 Travel).*

Certificate may be used: April 1-June 30, Sunday-Thursday, last minute, subject to availabilty.

Quail Hollow Inn

225 Pleasant St
Chester, VT 05143
(802)875-2794 (888)829-9874 Fax:(802)875-2794
Internet: www.quailhollowinn.com
E-mail: quailinn@vermontel.net

Circa 1860. Enjoy the one and a half scenic acres of quiet, country setting that surround this Victorian bed and breakfast. Watch television, play the piano or play chess in the Great Room, originally the old hay loft. Gather for refreshments and a game of darts in the popular Behind The Barn Pub, situated off a covered porch with a view of the woods behind the inn. Comfortable and inviting guest bedrooms are wonderful retreats. A newly renovated suite offers two bedrooms and a spacious bath with an antique clawfoot tub and a shower. A generous breakfast is served on Polish pottery in the dining room that is decorated with family heirlooms from Germany and Austria. Stroll the grounds and relax on spacious green areas.

Innkeeper(s): Peter Stearns & Bob Elkinson. $99-179. 7 rooms with PB, 2 suites. Breakfast included in rates. Types of meals: Full gourmet bkfst and veg bkfst. Beds: KQDT. Ceiling fan, clock radio, turn-down service, desk, hair dryer, bath amenities and wireless Internet access in room. Air conditioning. TV, VCR, DVD, fax, copier, spa, parlor games, telephone, fireplace, gift shop and Wireless Internet Access on premises. Antiquing, art galleries, bicycling, canoeing/kayaking, cross-country skiing, downhill skiing, fishing, golf, hiking, horseback riding, live theater, museums, parks, shopping, tennis, water sports and wineries nearby.

Location: Country.

Certificate may be used: April 1 to May 31, August 15 to September 15, November 1 to December 15 (Mid-Week, Sunday-Thursday only with specified dates).

Chittenden

Mountain Top Inn & Resort

195 Mountain Top Rd
Chittenden, VT 05737
(802)483-2311 (800)445-2100 Fax:(802)483-6373
Internet: www.mountaintopinn.com
E-mail: stay@mountaintopinn.com

Circa 1870. Breathtaking views are among the endless pleasures enjoyed at this four-season post and beam traditional mountain lodge that sits on a high meadow hilltop in the Green Mountains National Forest. On-site cross-country ski and equestrian centers as well as beachfront access to a pristine lake are some of the recreational activities available at this 345-acre

resort. The owners have renovated for comfort and style. Stay in a luxury lodge room with fine linens and two-person whirlpool tub; or a rustic cabin or private chalet with a fireplace. The Resort offers various types of massage therapy. Linger over a candlelit meal of exceptional New American cuisine made with fresh

local ingredients while surrounded by a refined mountain lodge ambiance. Enjoy a horse-drawn sleigh ride, snowshoeing, ice skating, sledding, a guided trail ride, mountain biking, fly-fishing, clay bird shooting or playing tennis.

$150-545. 26 rooms with PB, 3 suites, 10 guest houses, 5 cabins, 1 conference room. Breakfast and snacks/refreshments included in rates. Types of meals: Country bkfst, veg bkfst, early coffee/tea, gourmet lunch, picnic lunch, hors d'oeuvres, wine, gourmet dinner and Afternoon snacks. Restaurant on premises. Beds: KQ. Modem hook-up, data port, cable TV, reading lamp, CD player, clock radio, telephone, coffeemaker, desk, voice mail, hair dryer, bath amenities and wireless Internet access in room. Air conditioning. VCR, DVD, fax, copier, swimming, stable, bicycles, tennis, pet boarding, child care, parlor games, fireplace, laundry facility, gift shop, Horseback riding, kayaks & canoes, private beach, lawn games, fly-fishing, clay bird shooting, xc skiing and snowshoeing, horse drawn sleigh rides, snowmobiling and dog sledding, massage therapist and stalls available for boarding guest horses on premises. Handicap access. Antiquing, art galleries, bicycling, downhill skiing, fishing, golf, hiking, live theater, museums, parks, shopping, water sports and wineries nearby.

Location: Mountains. Lakefront.

Publicity: *Boston Globe, Ski Magazine, New York Times, Vermont Magazine, Washington Post, National Geographic, Traveler.com, Newsday, Select Registry, Conde Nast Johansens, Country Living, Rutland Business Journal and Channel 5 WCVB Boston.*

"Twenty years ago we spent a very enjoyable week here with our daughter. The inn, the service and atmosphere were superior at that time and we are glad to report that it hasn't changed."

Certificate may be used: March 1-May 31, Sunday-Thursday and Oct. 21-Dec. 20, Sunday-Thursday, subject to availability.

Danby

Silas Griffith Inn

178 South Main Street
Danby, VT 05739
(802)293-5567 (888)569-4660 Fax:(802) 293-5559
Internet: www.silasgriffith.com
E-mail: stay@silasgriffith.com

Circa 1891. Originally on 55,000 acres, this stately Queen Anne Victorian mansion features solid cherry, oak and bird's-eye maple woodwork. Considered an architectural marvel, an eight-foot, round, solid-cherry pocket door separates the original music room from the front parlor.

Innkeeper(s): Brian & Catherine Preble. $149-275. 10 rooms with PB, 10 with FP, 1 two-bedroom suite, 2 conference rooms. Breakfast included in rates. Types of meals: Full gourmet bkfst, early coffee/tea, lunch, picnic lunch, wine and dinner. Restaurant on premises. Beds: KQT. Data port, cable TV, reading lamp, clock radio, telephone, voice mail, fireplace, bath amenities and wireless Internet access in room. Air conditioning. VCR, DVD, fax, copier, spa, swimming, library, parlor games and gift shop on premises. Limited handicap access. Antiquing, art galleries, beach, bicycling, canoeing/kayaking, cross-country skiing, downhill skiing, fishing, golf, hiking, horseback riding, live theater, museums, parks, shopping, tennis and water sports nearby.

Location: Mountains. Country Village.

"Never have I stayed at a B&B where the innkeepers were so friendly, sociable and helpful. They truly enjoyed their job."
Certificate may be used: Anytime, subject to availability.

Essex Junction

The Inn at Essex

70 Essex Way
Essex Junction, VT 05452-3383
(802)878-1100 (800)727-4295 Fax:(802)878-0063
Internet: www.vtculinaryresort.com
E-mail: innfo@vtculinaryresort.com

Circa 1989. The area's only full-service resort hotel, this inn has been recently renovated by artist Susan Sargent using vibrant colors, plush fabrics and country eclectic design with a Scandinavian flair. The relaxing environment features standard accommodations to fireplace, whirlpool and kitchen suites. In-room spa services are available. The two restaurants are operated by New England Culinary Institute, offering casual American fare to cutting-edge dining. The new four-season glass-enclosed atrium and additional meeting rooms serve as the ideal setting for special events and conferences. Enjoy the tennis courts, an outdoor swimming pool and culinary-theme gardens. Play golf next door at Links at Lang Farm. Skiing and area attractions are nearby.

Innkeeper(s): Jim Glanville. $99-499. 120 rooms with PB, 50 with FP, 30 total suites, including 2 two-bedroom suites, 8 conference rooms. Breakfast included in rates. Types of meals: Full gourmet bkfst, veg bkfst, Sun. brunch, early coffee/tea, gourmet lunch, picnic lunch, snacks/refreshments, hors d'oeuvres, wine, gourmet dinner and room service. Restaurant on premises. Beds: KQD. Data port, cable TV, DVD, clock radio, telephone, coffeemaker, turn-down service, desk, some with hot tub/spa, voice mail, some with fireplace, hair dryer, bathrobes, bath amenities, iron/ironing board, pay-per-view movies and complimentary high speed Internet access in room. Central air. Fax, tennis, child care, parlor games, laundry facility, gift shop, golf course, hiking, antiques, skiing and outdoor pool on premises. Handicap access. Antiquing, art galleries, beach, bicycling, canoeing/kayaking, cross-country skiing, downhill skiing, fishing, golf, hiking, horseback riding, live theater, museums, parks, shopping, sporting events, tennis, water sports, wineries and hands on cooking classes by the New England Culinary Institute nearby.
Location: Country.
Certificate may be used: November-July, Sunday-Thursday.

Fair Haven

Haven Guest House Bed & Breakfast

1 Fourth Street
Fair Haven, VT 05743
(802)265-8882
Internet: havenguesthousevt.com
E-mail: baumannvt@adelphia.net

Circa 1900. Gracious and inviting, the huge wraparound porch with pillars and hanging plants beckons and welcomes relaxation at Haven Guest House Bed & Breakfast. Located near Lake Bomoseen in the picturesque hills of central Vermont in Fair Haven, it was built in 1900 and renovated to reflect its glorious heritage. The B&B is furnished with antiques that are accented by lace floor-length curtains. Gather for conversation in one of the three common rooms. Complimentary beverages are provided. Air-conditioned guest bedrooms are cheerful and pleasant with quilt-covered beds and delightful furnishings. After a good night's sleep, select a gourmet breakfast from a menu each morning in the dining room.

Innkeeper(s): Werner & Gisela Baumann. $99-129. 4 rooms with PB. Breakfast, Full Breakfast and your choice from our gourmet menu included in rates. Types of meals: Full gourmet bkfst, early coffee/tea, Tea, coffee, soda and and more will be served at arrival. Beds: KQT. Cable TV, reading lamp, ceiling fan, clock radio, desk, hair dryer, bath amenities and wireless Internet access in room. Air conditioning. Library, parlor games and fireplace on premises. Antiquing, art galleries, bicycling, canoeing/kayaking, cross-country skiing, downhill skiing, fishing, golf, hiking, horseback riding, museums, sporting events and water sports nearby.
Location: City.
Certificate may be used: Nov. 1-April 30, Sunday-Thursday.

Fairlee

Silver Maple Lodge & Cottages

520 US Rt 5 South
Fairlee, VT 05045
(802)333-4326 (800)666-1946
Internet: www.silvermaplelodge.com
E-mail: scott@silvermaplelodge.com

Circa 1790. This old Cape farmhouse was expanded in the 1850s and became an inn in the '20s when Elmer & Della Batchelder opened their home to guests. It became so successful that several cottages, built from lumber on the property, were added. For 60 years, the Batchelder family continued the operation. They misnamed the lodge, however, mistaking silver poplar trees on the property for what they thought were silver maples. Guest rooms are decorated with many of the inn's original furnishings, and the new innkeepers have carefully restored the rooms and added several bathrooms. A screened-in porch surrounds two sides of the house. Three of the cottages include working fireplaces and one is handicap accessible.

Innkeeper(s): Scott & Sharon Wright. $69-104. 16 rooms, 14 with PB, 3 with FP, 8 cottages. Breakfast included in rates. Types of meals: Cont. Beds: KQDT. TV, reading lamp, refrigerator, clock radio and desk in room. VCR, copier, bicycles, parlor games, telephone and fireplace on premises. Handicap access. Antiquing, cross-country skiing, downhill skiing, fishing, live theater, parks, shopping and water sports nearby.
Location: Country.
Publicity: *Boston Globe, Vermont Country Sampler, Travel Holiday, Travel America* and *New York Times.*

"Your gracious hospitality and attractive home all add up to a pleasant experience."
Certificate may be used: Sunday-Thursday, Oct. 20-Sept. 20.

Hyde Park

Fitch Hill Inn

258 Fitch Hill Rd
Hyde Park, VT 05655-9363
(802)888-3834 (800)639-2903 Fax:(802)888-7789
Internet: www.fitchhillinn.com
E-mail: innkeeper@fitchhillinn.com

Circa 1797. Sitting on three and a half acres of hilltop land, this quiet 1797 Federalist-style home overlooks the picturesque Green Mountains. Surrounding the inn are numerous flower-filled gardens and woods to enjoy strolling through. Guest bedrooms share a period-furnished living room with a wood stove, a TV room and a movie library. The second-floor honeymoon

New Hampshire Suite features a sleigh bed, gas fireplace, two-person jetted tub and a wet bar with sink, refrigerator and microwave. A ground–floor suite includes a butler's kitchen, whirlpool tub and private entrance with deck. All the rooms boast wonderful garden and mountain views. A full hot breakfast is served in the dining room. It is easy to enjoy the tranquility of this 18th-century home  with a three-level deck and year-round hot tub. Relax on one of the two covered porches with a spectacular vista.

Innkeeper(s): Julie & John Rohleder. $100-210. 6 rooms with PB, 2 with FP, 2 with WP, 2 suites. Breakfast and snacks/refreshments included in rates. Types of meals: Full bkfst, veg bkfst and early coffee/tea. Beds: KQDT. Cable TV, VCR, reading lamp, CD player, refrigerator, ceiling fan, clock radio, telephone, coffeemaker, desk, some with fireplace, hair dryer, bathrobes, bath amenities, wireless Internet access, iron/ironing board and Window air conditioning in room. Air conditioning. Library, parlor games, gift shop, Guest computer with high-speed Internet, Covered porches & large deck, Gardens and woods on 3+ acres on premises. Amusement parks, antiquing, art galleries, bicycling, canoeing/kayaking, cross-country skiing, downhill skiing, fishing, golf, hiking, horseback riding, live theater, museums, parks, shopping, tennis, water sports, wineries, sleigh & carriage rides, snowmobiling and snowshoeing nearby.

Location: Country, mountains.

Publicity: *Stowe Reporter, Morrisville News Dispatch, Out & About, Eco-Traveller, Country Living, Bon Appetit and Yankee Magazine.*

Certificate may be used: March, April, May, except Memorial Day weekend, and November, except Thanksgiving weekend.

Killington

Cortina Inn & Resort

103 US Route 4
Killington, VT 05751
(802)773-3333 (800)451-6108 Fax:(802)775-6948
Internet: www.cortinainn.com
E-mail: cortina1@aol.com

Circa 1966. This property combines the amenities of a resort hotel with the ambiance of a country inn. Guests can reserve room packages that include breakfast; the cuisine is highly recommended. The brunches include carved meats and homemade breads along with traditional breakfast fare. Dinner is a special occasion with delicious appetizers and unique main dishes. Each of the rooms is individually decorated and includes original artwork. Some suites feature Jacuzzis and wet bars. The inn boasts an indoor swimming pool, exercise room and a masseur to soothe worn muscles.

Innkeeper(s): Ted Bridges. $89-199. 96 rooms with PB, 14 with FP, 1 with HT, 5 with WP, 7 total suites, including 2 two-bedroom suites, 5 conference rooms. Afternoon tea included in rates. Types of meals: Full gourmet bkfst, veg bkfst, Sun. brunch, early coffee/tea, picnic lunch, snacks/refreshments, wine, gourmet dinner and room service. Restaurant on premises. Beds: KQD. Modem hook-up, data port, cable TV, reading lamp, clock radio, telephone, coffeemaker, desk, some with hot tub/spa, voice mail, some with fireplace, hair dryer, bath amenities, wireless Internet access, iron/ironing board, some with fireplace, hot tub/spa, refrigerator and VCR in room. Air conditioning. VCR, fax, copier, spa, swimming, sauna, bicycles, tennis, library, child care, parlor games, laundry facility, gift shop and art gallery on premises. Handicap access. Amusement parks, antiquing, art galleries, bicycling, canoeing/kayaking, cross-country skiing, downhill skiing, fishing, golf, hiking, horseback riding, live theater, museums, parks, shopping, sporting events, tennis, water sports, wineries, Ice skating, Sleigh rides, Snowshoe tours, Walking tours and Guided sightseeing tours nearby.

Location: Country, mountains.

Publicity: *Travel Agent East Magazine, New York Post, Ski Magazine and Travel Channel.*

Certificate may be used: Anytime, Black October, Dec. 25-Jan. 3, Feb. 13-26.

The Cascades Lodge & Restaurant

Killington Village, 58 Old Mill Rd
Killington, VT 05751-9710
(802)422-3731 (800)345-0113 Fax:(802)422-3351
Internet: www.cascadeslodge.com
E-mail: info@cascadeslodge.com

Circa 1980. Breathtaking views and modern amenities are found at this contemporary three-story country lodge in the heart of the Green Mountains. Guests enjoy an exercise area, indoor pool with sundeck, sauna and whirlpool. A bar and award-winning restaurant are on the premises, and the inn's amenities make it an ideal spot for meetings, reunions or weddings. Within walking distance is an 18-hole golf course and the Killington Summer Theater.

Innkeeper(s): Amy Jones. $82-349. 45 rooms with PB, 5 suites. Continental Breakfast included in rates. Types of meals: Early coffee/tea, dinner and Restaurant on Premises Seasonal. Beds: QD. Cable TV, clock radio, telephone and desk in room. VCR, fax, copier, spa, sauna, parlor games and fireplace on premises. Handicap access. Antiquing, cross-country skiing, downhill skiing, fishing, live theater, parks and shopping nearby.

Location: Mountains. Walk to slopes and golf.

Certificate may be used: Anyday, May 1 to Nov. 1, space available.

The Vermont Inn

H.C. 34 Box 37J
Killington, VT 05751
(802)775-0708 (800)541-7795 Fax:(802)773-5810
Internet: www.vermontinn.com
E-mail: relax@vermontinn.com

Circa 1840. Surrounded by mountain views, this rambling red and white farmhouse has provided lodging and superb cuisine for many years. Exposed beams add to the atmosphere in the living and game rooms.  The award-winning dining room provides candlelight tables beside a huge fieldstone fireplace.

Innkeeper(s): Jennifer & Mitchell Duffy. $100-245. 16 rooms with PB, 6 with FP, 3 with HT. Breakfast and afternoon tea included in rates. Types of meals: Full bkfst, early coffee/tea and gourmet dinner. Beds: QT. Ceiling fan, clock radio, two with Jacuzzi tub and 5 with fireplace in room. Air conditioning. VCR, fax, copier, spa, swimming, sauna, tennis, library, parlor games, telephone, fireplace and screened porch on premises. Handicap access. Antiquing, cross-country skiing, downhill skiing, fishing, live theater, parks, shopping and water sports nearby.

Location: Mountains.

Publicity: *New York Daily News, New Jersey Star Leader, Rutland Business Journal, Bridgeport Post Telegram, New York Times, Boston, Vermont and Asbury Park Press.*

"We had a wonderful time. The inn is breathtaking. Hope to be back."

Certificate may be used: May-September, November-March (Non-Holiday).

Ludlow

Echo Lake Inn

PO Box 154
Ludlow, VT 05149-0154
(802)228-8602 (800)356-6844 Fax:(802)228-3075
Internet: echolakeinn.com
E-mail: echolkinn@aol.com

Circa 1840. An abundance of year-round activities at an ideal location in the state's central mountain lakes region make this authentic Victorian inn a popular choice. Built as a summer hotel in 1840, its rich heritage includes visits from many historic figures. Relax in the quiet comfort of the living room with its shelves of books and a fireplace or gather for refreshments in The Pub. The assortment of guest bedrooms, suites and condos ensure perfect accommodations for varied needs. Some boast two-person Jacuzzi tubs and fireplaces. Dining is a treat, with the fine country restaurant

highly acclaimed for its excellent food, attentive service and casual ambiance. Tennis, badminton and volleyball courts are adjacent to the large swimming pool. Take out a canoe or rowboat from the dock on crystal-clear Echo Lake or fly fish the Black River.

Innkeeper(s): Laurence V. Jeffery. $89-380. 23 rooms with PB, 2 two-bedroom and 1 three-bedroom suites. Breakfast included in rates. Types of meals: Full bkfst, veg bkfst, early coffee/tea, wine, gourmet dinner and room service. Restaurant on premises. Beds: KQDT. Cable TV, VCR, reading lamp, CD player, ceiling fan, clock radio, desk, hair dryer, bathrobes, bath amenities, wireless Internet access and iron/ironing board in room. Air conditioning. DVD, fax, copier, spa, swimming, tennis, library, child care, parlor games, telephone, fireplace, fine dining, children's paddling pool, all-weather surface, back board and night lighting, house racquets and balls, volleyball and badminton on premises. Antiquing, beach, canoeing/kayaking, cross-country skiing, downhill skiing, fishing, golf, hiking, horseback riding, live theater, shopping, water sports, wineries, Okemo Skiing, one of Vermont's best trout fishing rivers, fly fishing and rowing nearby.

Location: Mountains.

Publicity: *Vermont, Bon Appetit, Gourmet, Vermont Magazine ("turn-of-the-century charm with modern luxury") and Restaurants of New England.*

"Very special! We've decided to make the Echo Lake Inn a yearly tradition for our family."

Certificate may be used: April 1-Sept. 20, Oct. 20-Dec. 12, Jan. 1-March 31, Sunday-Thursday, non-holiday.

Golden Stage Inn

399 Depot St
Ludlow, VT 05153
(802)226-7744 (800)253-8226 Fax:(802)226-7882
Internet: www.goldenstageinn.com
E-mail: goldenstageinn@tds.net

Circa 1788. The Golden Stage Inn was a stagecoach stop built shortly before Vermont became a state. It served as a link in the Underground Railroad and was the home of Cornelia Otis Skinner. Cornelia's Room still offers its original polished wide-pine floors and view of Okemo Mountain, and now there's a four-poster cherry bed, farm animal border, wainscoting and a comforter filled with wool from the inn's sheep. Outside are gardens of wildflowers, a little pen with two sheep, a swimming

pool and blueberries and raspberries for the picking. Breakfast offerings include an often-requested recipe, Golden Stage Granola. Home-baked breakfast dishes are garnished with Johnny-jump-ups and nasturtiums from the garden. Guests can indulge anytime by reaching into the inn's bottomless cookie jar. The inn offers stay & ski packages at Okemo Mountain with 24 hours advance notice, and it's a 20 minute drive to Killington access.

Innkeeper(s): Sandy & Peter Gregg. $79-300. 10 rooms, 8 with PB, 1 with FP, 1 with WP, 1 two-bedroom suite. Breakfast, afternoon tea, snacks/refreshments and Our famous "Bottom-Less Cookie Jar! included in rates. Types of meals: Country bkfst, veg bkfst, early coffee/tea, dinner and Famous for our "Bottom-Less Cookie Jar!" Beds: KQDT. Cable TV, reading lamp, clock radio, some with fireplace and hair dryer in room. Central air. TV, VCR, fax, copier, swimming, library, pet boarding, parlor games, telephone, gift shop, gardens and sheep on premises. Handicap access. Antiquing, art galleries, bicycling, canoeing/kayaking, cross-country skiing, downhill skiing, fishing, golf, hiking, horseback riding, live theater, museums, parks, shopping, Covered bridges, Weston Priory and President Calvin Coolidge State Historic Site nearby.

Location: Country, mountains.

Publicity: *Journal Inquirer, Gourmet and Los Angeles Times.*

"The essence of a country inn!"

Certificate may be used: Sunday-Thursday, year-round; excludes fall foliage and premium times. Cannot be combined with other offers.

The Governor's Inn

86 Main St
Ludlow, VT 05149-1113
(802)228-8830 (800)GOVERNOR
Internet: www.thegovernorsinn.com
E-mail: info@thegovernorsinn.com

Circa 1890. Enter this Victorian country house and feel surrounded by the warm hospitality and gracious elegance befitting Governor Stickney's home. Afternoon tea, sweets and savory sandwiches are served in the parlor with extraordinary slate fireplaces, polished woodwork and oriental rugs. Retire to an inviting bed chamber warmed by a gas fireplace to read, watch cable TV or relax in the whirlpool. Awake to a bountiful breakfast that may feature apple cinnamon pancakes or Cuckoo's Nest Souffle served with antique cups, saucers and chocolate pots. Explore Vermont from this delightful location.

Innkeeper(s): Cathy & Jim Kubec. $159-319. 8 rooms with PB, 6 with FP, 1 suite. Breakfast and afternoon tea included in rates. Types of meals: Full gourmet bkfst, early coffee/tea, picnic lunch and gourmet dinner. Beds: KQDT. Cable TV, VCR, DVD, clock radio, turn-down service, some with hot tub/spa, most with fireplace, hair dryer, bathrobes, iron/ironing board, afternoon tea, suite with two-person aqua-massage tub and video/DVD library in room. Air conditioning. Fax, copier, parlor games, telephone and Culinary Magic Cooking Seminars on premises. Antiquing, art galleries, bicycling, canoeing/kayaking, cross-country skiing, downhill skiing, fishing, golf, hiking, horseback riding, live theater, museums, parks, shopping, historical sites, priory, sleigh rides and snowmobiling nearby.

Location: Mountains.

Publicity: *Select Registry and Yankee Travel Guide (Editor's Pick).*

Certificate may be used: May through September (no Fridays or Saturdays) subject to availability.

Manchester

Wilburton Inn

River Road (off Historic Route 7A)
Manchester, VT 05254
(802)362-2500 (800)648-4944 Fax:(802)362-1107
Internet: www.wilburton.com
E-mail: wilbuinn@sover.net

Circa 1902. Shaded by tall maples, this grand Victorian estate sits high on a hill overlooking the Battenkill Valley, set against a majestic mountain backdrop. In addition to the three-story brick mansion, there are four villas and a five-bedroom house. Carved mahogany paneling, Oriental carpets and leaded-glass

windows are complemented by carefully chosen antiques. Besides accommodations, the Teleion Holon Holistic Retreat offers yoga, workshops, vegetarian meals

and healing treatments. Spanning 20 acres in Manchester, Vermont enjoy the three tennis courts, a pool, green lawns, sculptured gardens and panoramic views. Country weddings are a Wilburton Inn specialty. Enjoy dining on New American cuisine in a setting of classic elegance.

Innkeeper(s): Georgette Levis. $135-315. 35 rooms with PB, 8 with FP, 2 with WP, 3 guest houses, 5 conference rooms. Breakfast included in rates. Types of meals: Full gourmet bkfst, afternoon tea, snacks/refreshments, wine, gourmet dinner and room service. Restaurant on premises. Beds: KQD. Cable TV, VCR, DVD, reading lamp, refrigerator, clock radio, telephone, some with hot tub/spa, some with fireplace, hair dryer, bath amenities, wireless Internet access and iron/ironing board in room. Air conditioning. Fax, copier, swimming, tennis, parlor games and gift shop on premises. Handicap access. Antiquing, art galleries, beach, bicycling, canoeing/kayaking, cross-country skiing, downhill skiing, fishing, golf, hiking, horseback riding, live theater, museums, parks, shopping and water sports nearby.

Location: Country, mountains.

Publicity: *Great Escapes TV, Travelhost, Getaways For Gourmets, Country Inns, Bed & Breakfast, Gourmet, Best Places to Stay In New England and New York Times.*

"Simply splendid! Peaceful, beautiful, elegant. Ambiance & ambiance!"

Certificate may be used: Only all April, any day, all month.

Milton

The Sampler House Bed & Breakfast

22 Main St
Milton, VT 05468
(802)893-2724
Internet: www.samplerhouse.com
E-mail: deborah@samplerhouse.com

Circa 1830. Warm and inviting, the Sampler House Bed & Breakfast in historic Milton Village was built in the Cape style in 1830 and has been delightfully restored to offer four-season comfort. Relax on outdoor seating on the front porch, back patio or on Adirondack chairs on the lawn. Stay in a comfortable guest bedroom on the first or second floor. The Cabbage Rose features a faux wood stove and garden-style tub. The Iris Suite encompasses two floors and includes a fully equipped kitchen, entertainment center and private entrance. Savor a hearty Vermont breakfast in the Gathering Room each morning. Year-round activities abound from outdoor water sports at nearby lakes to snow play or gondola rides at an area ski resort.

Innkeeper(s): Deborah Dolby & Peter Martin. $75-125. 3 rooms with PB, 1 with FP, 1 with WP. Breakfast included in rates. Types of meals: Full bkfst and Additional services upon special request. Beds: QT. TV, VCR, DVD, reading lamp, CD player, desk, some with fireplace, hair dryer, bath amenities, wireless Internet access and iron/ironing board in room. Air conditioning. Copier, library, pet boarding and laundry facility on premises. Antiquing, art galleries, beach, bicycling, canoeing/kayaking, cross-country skiing, downhill skiing, fishing, golf, hiking, horseback riding, live theater, museums, parks, shopping, sporting events, tennis, water sports and wineries nearby.

Location: Small town.

Certificate may be used: November-April, except holidays, subject to availability.

Montgomery Center

Phineas Swann B&B Inn

195 Main St
Montgomery Center, VT 05471
(802)326-4306 Fax:(802)326-4310
Internet: www.phineasswann.com
E-mail: info@phineasswann.com

Circa 1880. Newly remodeled and restored, Phineas Swann Bed & Breakfast Inn is an elegant New England treasure located in the hills of Vermont in Montgomery Center, just north of Stowe near Jay Peak Resort. Common areas are plentiful at this very pet-friendly inn, beginning with the Reception Hall and Front Room accented with Victorian furnishings. The Living Room features a masonry

fireplace and provides beverages and fresh-baked treats all day. The Music Room has a player piano and the Den is a sitting room/library with a large

plasma TV. Stay in a lavish guest bedroom in the main house or upscale suite in the Carriage House with a fireplace and Jacuzzi. River House Suites also include a full kitchen and decks overlooking the Trout River. Linger over a gourmet breakfast in the expanded dining room with sun room.

Innkeeper(s): John Perkins & Jay Kerch. $89-256. 7 rooms with PB, 4 with FP, 5 with WP, 4 total suites, including 3 two-bedroom suites, 2 cottages, 1 conference room. Breakfast, afternoon tea and snacks/refreshments included in rates. Types of meals: Full gourmet bkfst, veg bkfst, early coffee/tea, picnic lunch, wine and Early and all day coffee/tea/spring water & snacks. Beds: QDT. Modem hook-up, data port, cable TV, VCR, DVD, reading lamp, stereo, refrigerator, ceiling fan, snack bar, clock radio, telephone, coffeemaker, turndown service, desk, hot tub/spa, most with fireplace, hair dryer, bathrobes, bath amenities, wireless Internet access and iron/ironing board in room. Central air. Fax, copier, spa, bicycles, tennis, library, parlor games and gift shop on premises. Limited handicap access. Antiquing, art galleries, bicycling, canoeing/kayaking, cross-country skiing, downhill skiing, fishing, golf, hiking, horseback riding, live theater, museums, parks, shopping, sporting events and tennis nearby.

Location: Country, mountains, waterfront. On River.

Publicity: *Country Living Magazine, The Boston Phoenix, Out Magazine, Yankee Magazine, Off The Beaten Path Press, Boston Magazine (one of top five romantic inns in New England) , Travel-Travel, Channel 3 news, Channel 5 news and Nominated for Innkeepers of the year 2006.*

Certificate may be used: Anytime during October 20 through November 18 and anytime during April 13 and May 24.

Montpelier

Betsy's B&B

74 E State St
Montpelier, VT 05602-3112
(802)229-0466 Fax:(802)229-5412
Internet: www.BetsysBnB.com
E-mail: BetsysBnB@comcast.net

Circa 1895. Within walking distance of downtown and located in the state's largest historic preservation district, this Queen Anne Victorian with romantic turret and carriage house features lavish Victorian antiques throughout its interior. Bay windows, carved woodwork, high ceilings, lace curtains and wood floors add to the authenticity. The full breakfast varies in content but not quality, and guest favorites include orange pancakes.

Innkeeper(s): Jon & Betsy Anderson. $70-120. 12 rooms with PB, 5 two-bedroom suites. Breakfast included in rates. Types of meals: Full bkfst. Beds: QDT. Data port, cable TV, reading lamp, clock radio, telephone, desk, voice mail, hair dryer, bath amenities, wireless Internet access and iron/ironing board in room. Air conditioning. VCR, DVD, fax, copier, parlor games, fireplace, laundry facility and refrigerator on premises. Antiquing, art galleries, beach, bicycling, canoeing/kayaking, cross-country skiing, downhill skiing, fishing, hiking, live theater, museums, parks, shopping and water sports nearby.

Location: City. Residential in small city.

Certificate may be used: Nov. 1-April 30, holiday weekends excluded.

Morrisville

Village Victorian B & B

107 Union St
Morrisville, VT 05661-6061
(802)888-8850 (866)266-4672
Internet: www.villagevictorian.com
E-mail: philip@villagevictorian.com

Circa 1890. In a typical New England setting, this 1890s Victorian imparts warmth and peace to all who stay here. Sitting in a quiet village in the Lamoille Valley, it is located just seven miles from Stowe. Relax on the porches and patios, or walk through the gardens. Play games by the fire in the living room, read a book or practice the piano. Elegant air-conditioned guest bedrooms offer a variety of pleasant amenities from robes to a video library. Stay in the third-floor Aster Suite with vaulted ceilings, sitting room and Jacuzzi tub. Breakfast in the dining room always includes a taste of Vermont with seasonal fruit, Cabot cheese and yogurt, Sugarwoods Farm Pure Maple Syrup and Green Mountain Coffee Roasters fresh-ground coffee. A laundry facility, microwave, refrigerator, iron and board are available.

Innkeeper(s): Philip and Ellen Wolff. $90-160. 5 rooms with PB, 1 suite. Breakfast included in rates. Types of meals: Full bkfst, afternoon tea, dinner, Dinner or Tea by advance reservation and not included in room rate. Beds: Q. Cable TV, VCR, hair dryer, wireless Internet access and iron/ironing board in room. Air conditioning. TV, fax, library, parlor games, telephone, laundry facility, gift shop, refrigerator, complimentary soda, microwave and video library on premises. Antiquing, art galleries, beach, bicycling, canoeing/kayaking, cross-country skiing, downhill skiing, fishing, golf, hiking, horseback riding, live theater, museums, parks, shopping, sporting events, tennis, water sports and wineries nearby.

Location: City, mountains. Village in the Lamoille Valley.

Certificate may be used: Nov.1-Dec. 13, April 1-June 11.

Northfield

The Northfield Inn

228 Highland Ave
Northfield, VT 05663-5663
(802)485-8558
Internet: www.TheNorthfieldInn.com
E-mail: TheNorthfieldInn@aol.com

Circa 1901. A view of the Green Mountains can be seen from this Victorian inn, which is set on a mountainside surrounded by gardens and overlooking an apple orchard and pond. The picturesque inn also affords a view of the village of Northfield and historic Norwich University. Rooms are decorated with antiques and Oriental rugs, and bedrooms feature European feather bedding and brass and carved-wood beds.

Many outdoor activities are available on the three-acre property, including croquet, horseshoes, ice skating and sledding. Visitors may want to take a climb uphill to visit the Old Slate Quarry or just relax on one of the porches overlooking the garden with bird songs, wind chimes and gentle breezes.

Innkeeper(s): Aglaia Stalb. $95-179. 12 rooms with PB, 2 suites. Breakfast and snacks/refreshments included in rates. Types of meals: Full bkfst. Beds: QDT. Cable TV, reading lamp, ceiling fan, clock radio, telephone and central cooling system available in room. TV, VCR, bicycles, library, parlor games, fireplace, lounge and fitness center on premises. Antiquing, cross-country skiing, downhill skiing, fishing, golf, hiking, live theater, parks, shopping, sporting events, water sports, sledding, flying, fairs, auctions. Veteran's and Labor Day Festivals and Parade, Vermont Quilt Festival and 5 covered bridges in Northfield nearby.

Location: Mountains.

Publicity: *Conde Nast Traveler and Gentlemen's Quarterly.*

"There's no place like here."

Certificate may be used: November through April, Monday-Thursday as available, Holiday and special events excluded.

Perkinsville

The Inn at Weathersfield

1342 Route 106
Perkinsville, VT 05151
(802)263-9217 Fax:(802)263-9219
Internet: www.weathersfieldinn.com
E-mail: stay@weathersfieldinn.com

Circa 1792. Perfectly suited for a quiet getaway, this stately Georgian-style inn with post and beam interior was built in 1792 and thought to have been a stop on the Underground Railroad. Decorated in a rustic elegance, each guest bedroom and suite includes cozy robes and slippers. Many feature fireplaces, four-poster beds, CD stereos, whirlpool or clawfoot tubs and private rooftop decks. Choose a hot, made-to-order breakfast from a menu. Roam the 21 wooded acres with a pond, walking trails, gardens, back roads and an outdoor starlit amphitheater. The candlelit dining room offers New Vermont cuisine, and lighter fare is available in the Pub on select nights.

Relax by the fire in the study after a full day of skiing. A computer provides high-speed Internet access for guest use.

Innkeeper(s): Jane and David Sandelman. $150-285. 12 rooms with PB, 6 with FP, 3 suites, 1 conference room. Breakfast, afternoon tea and snacks/refreshments included in rates. Types of meals: Full gourmet bkfst, veg bkfst, early coffee/tea, picnic lunch and gourmet dinner. Restaurant on premises. Beds: KQDT. Modem hook-up, cable TV, reading lamp, stereo, clock radio, desk, fireplace, robes and slippers in room. VCR, fax, copier, sauna, stable, library, pet boarding, parlor games, fireplace, high-speed Internet, gift shop and full service restaurant on premises. Antiquing, art galleries, bicycling, canoeing/kayaking, cross-country skiing, downhill skiing, fishing, golf, hiking, horseback riding, live theater, museums, parks and shopping nearby.

Location: Country, mountains. Set on 21 wooded acres.

Certificate may be used: Sunday-Thursday excluding Sept. 15- Nov. 1, Christmas week, New Years, Presidents week.

Pittsfield

Casa Bella Inn

3911 Main St, Rt 100
Pittsfield, VT 05762-0685
(802)746-8943 (877)746-8943 Fax:(802)746-8395
Internet: www.casabellainn.com
E-mail: info@casabellainn.com

Circa 1835. Originally built as a stagecoach stop, this full-service country inn sits in a scenic mountain valley and exudes a New England ambiance with accents of Tuscany. It has been recently renovated to provide modern comfort and a relaxed, casual atmosphere. Sit on one of the two-story porches overlooking the village green. In-room massage services are available. Savor a full breakfast after a restful sleep in a well-appointed guest bedroom. The warm hospitality continues with afternoon refreshments. Northern Italian cuisine is featured in the on-site restaurant that seats 30. Visit the Green Mountain National Forest and go tubing in the White River. Experience the many winter activities available at nearby Killington Ski Resort. The fall colors are a must-see annual event.

Innkeeper(s): Franco & Susan Cacozza. $95-145. 8 rooms with PB. Breakfast and afternoon tea included in rates. Types of meals: Full gourmet bkfst, snacks/refreshments and gourmet dinner. Restaurant on premises. Beds: QDT. Reading lamp and clock radio in room. Library, parlor games and telephone on premises. Antiquing, art galleries, bicycling, canoeing/kayaking, cross-country skiing, downhill skiing, fishing, golf, hiking, horseback riding, parks, shopping, tennis, water sports, fly fishing and snowmobiling nearby.

Location: Country, mountains.

Certificate may be used: May-August, Sunday-Thursday, subject to availability, excludes holidays, anytime, subject to availability.

Poultney

Bentley House B&B

399 Bentley Ave
Poultney, VT 05764
(802)287-4004 (866)570-9827
Internet: www.thebentleyhouse.com
E-mail: bentleyhousebb@comcast.net

Circa 1890. This three-story peaked turret Queen Anne inn is located next to Green Mountain College. Stained glass, polished woodwork and original fireplace mantels add to the Victorian atmosphere, and the guest rooms are furnished with antiques of the period. A sitting room adjacent to the guest rooms has its own fireplace.

Innkeeper(s): Pam Mikkelesen. $99-145. 4 rooms with PB. Breakfast included in rates. Types of meals: Full bkfst. Beds: Q. Ceiling fan, clock radio, turn-

down service, hair dryer, bathrobes and iron/ironing board in room. TV, VCR, telephone and fireplace on premises. Limited handicap access. Antiquing, beach, cross-country skiing, fishing, parks, shopping and water sports nearby.

Location: Mountains. Small rural college town.

Publicity: *Rutland Herald and Rutland Business Journal.*

"Your beautiful home was delightful and just the best place to stay!"

Certificate may be used: January-May, Sunday-Thursday.

Richmond

The Richmond Victorian Inn

191 East Main Street
Richmond, VT 05477-0652
(802)434-4410 (888)242-3362 Fax:(802)434-4411
Internet: www.richmondvictorianinn.com
E-mail: innkeeper@richmondvictorianinn.com

Circa 1850. This Queen Anne Victorian, with a three-story tower, is accented with green shutters, a sunburst design, fish scale shingles and a gingerbread front porch. The Tower Room is filled with white wicker, delicate flowered wallpaper and an antique brass bed. The Gold Room features a Queen-size bed and a Jacuzzi, while the Pansy Room features an antique bed, white walls and a stenciled pansy border. There are hardwood floors and leaded-glass windows throughout. From the tree-shaded porch, enjoy the inn's lawns and flower gardens after a full breakfast.

Innkeeper(s): Frank & Joyce Stewart. $95-160. 6 rooms with PB. Breakfast and snacks/refreshments included in rates. Types of meals: Full gourmet bkfst, veg bkfst, early coffee/tea and afternoon tea. Beds: QDT. Reading lamp, clock radio, antique furnishings, cozy quilts, down comforters and plush robes in room. TV, VCR, DVD, fax, library, parlor games, telephone and British-style afternoon tea (Sundays from 2-5 p.m. September-Mother's Day) on premises. Antiquing, art galleries, beach, bicycling, canoeing/kayaking, cross-country skiing, downhill skiing, fishing, golf, hiking, live theater, museums, parks, shopping, sporting events, water sports, wineries, artists' studios, Audubon Center, Huntington Gorge and Little River State Park nearby.

Location: Country, mountains. Small Vermont town, 12 miles east of Burlington.

Publicity: *Hartford Courant (2003), Out and About in Vermont 5th Ed., Rogers (2004), Best Recipes of American Country Inns and Bed and Breakfasts - Maynard (2004).*

"I have stayed at many B&Bs, but by far this is the most wonderful experience. The hospitality was #1, the food was A+. Rooms very comfortable. I felt like family. Hope our paths cross again."

Certificate may be used: November-April, non-holidays, subject to availability and prior booking. May not be combined with other promotions.

Rochester

Liberty Hill Farm

511 Liberty Hill Rd
Rochester, VT 05767-9501
(802)767-3926 Fax:(802)767-6056
Internet: www.libertyhillfarm.com
E-mail: beth@libertyhillfarm.com

Circa 1825. A working dairy farm with a herd of registered Holsteins, this farmhouse offers a country setting and easy access to recreational activities. The inn's location, between the White River and the Green Mountains, is ideal for outdoor enthusiasts and animal lovers. Stroll to the barn, feed the calves or climb up to the hayloft and read or play with the kittens. Fishing, hiking, skiing and swimming are popular pastimes of guests, who are treated to a family-style dinner and full breakfast, both featuring many delicious home-made specialties.

Innkeeper(s): Robert & Beth Kennett. $170. 7 rooms. Breakfast and Dinner at 6PM included in rates. Types of meals: Full bkfst, early coffee/tea and dinner. Beds: QDT. Reading lamp, clock radio and desk in room. VCR, swimming, library, child care, parlor games, telephone, working dairy farm and private beach for swimming and fishing on premises. Antiquing, art galleries, beach, bicycling, canoeing/kayaking, cross-country skiing, downhill skiing, fishing, golf, hiking, live theater, museums, parks, shopping, sporting events, water sports and wineries nearby.

Location: Riverfront in the country and mountains.

Publicity: *New York Times, Boston Globe, Vermont Life, Family Circle, Family Fun, Woman's Day, Country Home, Boston Chronicle, Yankee and Good Morning America.*

"We had a wonderful time exploring your farm and the countryside. The food was great."

Certificate may be used: Jan. 1 to May 20, Sunday-Thursday nights, Anytime, Last Minute-Based on Availability.

Stowe

Brass Lantern Inn B&B

717 Maple St
Stowe, VT 05672-4250
(802)253-2229 (800)729-2980 Fax:(802)253-9384
Internet: www.brasslanterninn.com
E-mail: info@brasslanterninn.com

Circa 1810. This rambling farmhouse and carriage barn rests at the foot of Mt. Mansfield. A recent award-winning renovation has brought a new shine to the inn, from the gleaming plank floors to the polished woodwork and crackling fireplaces and soothing whirlpool tubs. Quilts and antiques fill the guest rooms, and many, like the Honeymoon Room, have their own fireplace, whirlpool tub and mountain view. A complimentary afternoon and evening tea is provided along with a full Vermont-style breakfast. The inn is a multi-time winner of the Golden Fork Award from the Gourmet Dinners Society of North America.

Innkeeper(s): Joe and Nancy Beres. $89-199. 9 rooms with PB, 6 with FP, 6 with WP. Breakfast and afternoon tea included in rates. Types of meals: Country bkfst, veg bkfst and early coffee/tea. Beds: Q. Modem hook-up, TV, reading lamp, stereo, clock radio, most with hot tub/spa, most with fireplace, hair dryer, wireless Internet access, six with whirlpool tubs, fireplace and mountain views in room. Air conditioning. VCR, DVD, fax, copier, spa, library, parlor games, telephone, gardens, patio and green hotel on premises. Antiquing, art galleries, beach, bicycling, canoeing/kayaking, cross-country skiing, downhill skiing, fishing, golf, hiking, horseback riding, live theater, museums, parks, shopping, sporting events, tennis, water sports, wineries, tours, historic district, sleigh/surrey rides, dog sled, snowshoe, Ben & Jerry's, cider mill, glass blowing and covered bridges nearby.

Location: Mountains. Village/country.

Publicity: *Vermont, Vermont Life, Innsider, Discerning Traveler, Ski, Arrington's B&B Journal, Yankee and Ski Year.*

"The little things made us glad we stopped."

Certificate may be used: Midweek and limited weekends during April, May and to mid-June; late October, November and to mid-December excluding holidays.

Honeywood Inn

4583 Mountain Rd
Stowe, VT 05672
(802)253-4846 (800)821-7891 Fax:(802)253-7050
Internet: www.honeywoodinn.com
E-mail: honeywd@aol.com

Circa 1980. Stowe needs no introduction to its famous outdoor resort facilities. The Honeywood Inn is perfectly situated to take advantage of these activities in every season of the year. Cross-country ski trails leave right from the front door, and during the warm months, a 5.3-mile bike and walking path winds through some of Vermont's most splendid scenery, crossing wooden bridges and working farms. The inn resembles a Swiss chalet, while the interior decor has a homey, country feel. Some guest rooms feature canopy, brass or sleigh beds; others boast a spa. If the night is star filled, an outdoor hot tub makes a fun nightcap. In the morning, a light breakfast of fresh fruit, homemade muffins and cereal is followed by a more substantial one of waffles with homemade raspberry sauce, apple-cinnamon pancakes, or eggs Benedict. During the summer you'll enjoy this in the patio garden. The center of Stowe is only a stroll away along the recreation path. Here you can browse through the numerous antique and craft shops.

Innkeeper(s): Carolyn & Bill Cook. $109-259. 10 rooms, 8 with PB, 2 with FP, 2 suites. Breakfast included in rates. Types of meals: Full gourmet bkfst and veg bkfst. Beds: KQD. Reading lamp, ceiling fan, clock radio and some with hot tubs in room. Air conditioning. TV, VCR, fax, copier, spa, swimming, bicycles, parlor games, telephone and fireplace on premises. Antiquing, art galleries, beach, bicycling, canoeing/kayaking, cross-country skiing, downhill skiing, fishing, golf, hiking, horseback riding, live theater, museums, parks, shopping, tennis, water sports and wineries nearby.

Location: Mountains, with babbling brook on property.

Certificate may be used: Jan. 3-Sept. 14, Oct. 15-Dec. 20 Sunday-Thursday.

Troy

Victorian Manor

1430 Vermont Route 101
Troy, VT 05868
(908)928-9061 (802)988-9880 Fax:(908)928-9062
Internet: www.inglenookvermont.com
E-mail: kkjohnsen@verizon.net

Circa 1837. Sitting on 22 acres, this 1837 Victorian farmhouse overlooks the Missisquoi River Valley, as well as Vermont and Canadian mountains. Common rooms include a formal living and dining room, family room and fully equipped kitchen. Enjoy use of the sauna, VCR, washer and dryer. Six guest bedrooms can comfortably accommodate 15. Ride the aerial tramway at nearby Jay Peak Ski and Summer Resort. Play golf at one of the many nearby courses. It is only three miles to the Canadian border. Stowe and Burlington, Vermont are only one hour away. Inglenook Lodge, North Troy Village Restaurant & Pub and The Craving are nearby restaurants to try.

Innkeeper(s): Karen & Henry Johnsen/Inglenook Lodge Staff. $495-725. 6 rooms with PB, 1 suite, 3 conference rooms. Beds: KQDT. Cable TV, VCR, DVD, reading lamp, CD player, refrigerator, ceiling fan, snack bar, clock radio, telephone, coffeemaker, voice mail, hair dryer, bath amenities, iron/ironing board, amenities are available to all occupants and as this facility is rented as a whole house in room. Sauna, stable, parlor games, laundry facility and currently unoccupied nine stall horse barn on premises. Limited handicap access. Antiquing, beach, cross-country skiing, downhill skiing, fishing, golf, horseback riding, live theater, museums, parks, shopping, sporting events, wineries, Jay Peak Ski/Summer Resort, six golf courses, Lake Memphremagog, boating, swimming, Canadian border and Missisquoi River valley nearby.

Location: Country, mountains. One hour north of Stowe & Burlington, VT.

Publicity: *Yankee Magazine (1992).*

Certificate may be used: April 1-Oct. 31 limited to one night per period of occupancy based on standard non-discounted rates.

Vergennes

Strong House Inn

94 W Main St
Vergennes, VT 05491-9531
(802)877-3337 Fax:(802)877-2599
Internet: www.stronghouseinn.com
E-mail: innkeeper@stronghouseinn.com

Circa 1834. This Federal-style home boasts views of the Green Mountains and the Adirondack range. Several rooms offer working fireplaces and all are richly appointed. Country breakfasts and afternoon refreshments are served. Nearby Lake Champlain offers boating and fishing. Golf, hiking, skiing and

some of the finest cycling in Vermont are all part of the area's myriad of outdoor activities. Innkeeper Mary Bargiel is an avid gardener and decorates the grounds with flowers and herb gardens. The innkeepers offer a selection of special weekends including Valentine's Day, quilting, gardening and murder mystery.

Innkeeper(s): Hugh & Mary Bargiel. $95-310. 14 rooms with PB, 4 with FP, 1 suite, 1 conference room. Breakfast and snacks/refreshments included in rates. Types of meals: Country bkfst and early coffee/tea. Beds: KQDT. Cable TV, VCR, reading lamp, stereo, refrigerator, clock radio, telephone, coffeemaker, desk, hot tub/spa, voice mail and wireless Internet access in room. Central air. Fax, copier, library, parlor games, fireplace and gift shop on premises. Handicap access. Antiquing, art galleries, bicycling, canoeing/kayaking, cross-country skiing, downhill skiing, fishing, golf, hiking, horseback riding, museums, parks, shopping and tennis nearby.

Location: Country.

Publicity: *New York Times, Vermont Magazine, Addison County Independent and RETN.*

"Blissful stay...Glorious breakfast!"

Certificate may be used: Nov. 1-May 15, Sunday-Thursday, subject to availability.

Waitsfield

Mad River Inn

Tremblay Rd, PO Box 75
Waitsfield, VT 05673
(802)496-7900 (800)832-8278 Fax:(802)496-5390
Internet: www.madriverinn.com
E-mail: madriverinn@madriver.com

Circa 1860. Surrounded by the Green Mountains, this Queen Anne Victorian sits on seven scenic acres along the Mad River. The charming inn boasts attractive woodwork throughout, highlighted by ash, bird's-eye maple and cherry. Guest rooms feature European feather beds and include the Hayden Breeze Room, with a King brass bed, large windows TV and A/C,

and the Angelina Mercedes Room with a four-poster bed and picturesque views. The inn sports a billiard table, gazebo, organic gardens and a hot tub overlooking the mountains. Guests can walk to a recreation path along the river.

Innkeeper(s): Luc & Karen Maranda. $115-165. 8 rooms with PB. Breakfast and afternoon tea included in rates. Types of meals: Full gourmet bkfst. Beds: KQ. Reading lamp, ceiling fan, turn-down service and desk in room. VCR, fax, spa, parlor games, telephone and fireplace on premises. Antiquing, cross-country skiing, downhill skiing, fishing, live theater, shopping, sporting events, water sports and Vermont Icelandic Horse Farm nearby.

Location: Mountains.

Publicity: *Innsider, Victorian Homes, Let's Live, Skiing, AAA Home & Away, Tea Time at the Inn, Travel & Leisure, Ski Magazine and NY Times.*

"Your hospitality was appreciated, beautiful house and accommodations, great food & friendly people, just to name a few things. We plan to return and we recommend the Mad River Inn to friends & family."

Certificate may be used: Midweek only, non-holiday or foliage season. Jan. 5 to Sept. 20, Oct. 25-Dec.15.

Waitsfield Inn

5267 Main St.
Waitsfield, VT 05673
(802)496-3979 (800)758-3801 Fax:(802)496-3970
Internet: www.waitsfieldinn.com
E-mail: lodging@waitsfieldinn.com

Circa 1825. This Federal-style inn once served as a parsonage and was home to several state senators of the Richardson family. The 1839 barn offers a Great Room with fireplace and wood-plank floors, or in winter you may enjoy sipping spiced Vermont apple cider and munching on fresh cookies in the sitting room. Guest quarters are furnished with period antiques, quilts or comforters and some rooms have exposed beams or hand stenciling. A full breakfast is served in the dining room, with a choice of 14 delicious items as prepared by the inns chef. As the inn is in the village of Waitsfield, the entire town's sites are nearby including a beautiful covered bridge. Visit Glen Moss Waterfall, fly fish, canoe, try a glider, golf or watch a polo match. Snowshoeing, skiing and visits to the New England Culinary Institute and Ben & Jerry's Ice Cream Factory are popular activities.

Innkeeper(s): Mike & Ronda Kelley. $79-174. 14 rooms with PB. Breakfast included in rates. Types of meals: Country bkfst and Dinners for groups or families. Beds: QDT. Hair dryer, bath amenities, wireless Internet access and iron/ironing board in room. Air conditioning. TV, VCR, fax, copier, library, parlor games, telephone, fireplace, gift shop and Complimentary WiFi on premises. Antiquing, art galleries, beach, bicycling, canoeing/kayaking, cross-country skiing, downhill skiing, fishing, golf, hiking, horseback riding, live theater, parks, shopping, tennis, water sports, Quilters, Glassblowers, Pottery, Artists, Coffee shops, Restaurants, Farmers Market, Cheese makers and Bread makers nearby.

Location: Mountains. Village.

Certificate may be used: Sunday-Thursday, January-March and July 1-Sept. 12. Anytime April-June and November-December, all holiday weeks and foliage season excluded.

Waterbury

Thatcher Brook Inn

1017 Waterbury Stowe Road
Waterbury, VT 05676-0490
(802)244-5911 (800)292-5911 Fax:(802)244-1294
Internet: www.thatcherbrook.com
E-mail: info@thatcherbrook.com

Circa 1899. Listed in the Vermont Register of Historic Buildings, this restored Victorian mansion features a rambling porch with twin gazebos and a covered walkway leading to the historic Wheeler House. Guest rooms are decorated in classic country style. Five rooms have fireplaces, and seven have whirlpool tubs.

Innkeeper(s): Lisa & John Fischer. $80-350. 22 rooms with PB, 5 with FP, 5 with WP, 1 suite. Breakfast included in rates. Types of meals: Full bkfst. Beds: KQD. Cable TV, reading lamp, ceiling fan, clock radio, telephone, some with hot tub/spa, bath amenities, wireless Internet access, most have air conditioning, seven have whirlpools and most have TV in room. Air conditioning. Fax, parlor games, fireplace and Wireless Internet access on premises. Handicap access. Antiquing, bicycling, canoeing/kayaking, cross-country skiing, downhill skiing, fishing, golf, hiking, horseback riding, live theater, museums, parks, shopping, water sports, wineries, Ben and Jerry's Tours, Cold Hollow Cider Mill, sleigh rides, horseback riding, kayaking, golf and skiing nearby.

Location: Mountains. Village.

"The room was most comfortable and charming. I also enjoyed your pleasant veranda watching the world pass by. Most relaxing. We entered your inn as strangers and left feeling like family."

Certificate may be used: November through June, Sunday through Thursday, Holiday periods excluded.

West Dover

Deerfield Valley Inn

PO Box 1834
West Dover, VT 05356
(802)464-6333 (800)639-3588 Fax:(802)464-6336
Internet: www.deerfieldvalleyinn.com
E-mail: deerinn@vermontel.com

Circa 1885. Built as a country house in 1885 at the foothills of the Green Mountains, the inn is listed in the National Register and features the original wax-rubbed ash encasements and millwork. It was converted into one of the first inns in Mount Snow and new wings have been added. Sit by the fire in the living room. Enjoy a light afternoon tea. Intimate yet spacious guest bedrooms boast pleasant furnishings and décor. Sleep in the canopy bed in Room 5 with a sitting area and wood-burning fireplace. A bountiful, hearty breakfast is served in the pleasant dining room. The picturesque area offers many year-round activities. Golf packages are available.

Innkeeper(s): Doreen Cooney. $94-169. 9 rooms with PB, 5 with FP. Breakfast and snacks/refreshments included in rates. Types of meals: Country bkfst and veg bkfst. Beds: KQDT. Cable TV, VCR, DVD, reading lamp, CD player, ceiling fan, clock radio, most with fireplace and bath amenities in room. A/C. Fax, copier, parlor games and telephone on premises. Antiquing, art galleries, bicycling, canoeing/kayaking, cross-country skiing, downhill skiing, fishing, golf, hiking, horseback riding, live theater, museums, parks, shopping, tennis, water sports and wineries nearby.

Certificate may be used: Mid March-mid September, anytime subject to availabilty, mid October-mid December anytime subject to availabilty, Mid December-mid March Sunday to Thursday only, non-holidays.

Snow Goose Inn

259 Rte. 100
West Dover, VT 05356
(802)464-3984 (888)604-7964 Fax:(802)464-5322
Internet: www.snowgooseinn.com
E-mail: stay@snowgooseinn.com

Circa 1959. Three acres of Vermont countryside create a secluded setting for the Snow Goose Inn. Renovations in 1998 include the addition of Southern pine floors and private decks. Hand-hewn beams from an old country barn were fashioned into a new grand entry and a duplex honeymoon suite was created. (The new suite offers two decks with mountain and valley views, a Jacuzzi tub, fireplace and sitting area.) Most of the other antique-filled rooms also include a fireplace, VCR, stereo and double Jacuzzi tub. Hypo-allergenic feather mattresses and comforters are additional features. Hearty breakfasts include cereals, fresh fruit, juices, breads and entrees such as wild mushrooms and herb scrambled eggs, French toast stuffed with bananas. Evening wine and cheese is offered on one of the porches with views to the pond and flower gardens or by fireside in winter.

Innkeeper(s): Cyndee & Ron Frere. $115-395. 13 rooms with PB, 9 with FP, 8 with HT, 2 suites. Breakfast, snacks/refreshments, hors d'oeuvres and wine included in rates. Types of meals: Full gourmet bkfst, veg bkfst and early coffee/tea. Beds: KQDT. Cable TV, VCR, reading lamp, stereo, refrigerator, ceiling fan, clock radio, turn-down service, desk, wireless Internet access, wood-burning fireplace and two-person Jacuzzi tub in room. A/C. Fax, copier, parlor games, telephone, fireplace and three acres of informal gardens on premises. Handicap access. Antiquing, art galleries, bicycling, canoeing/kayaking, cross-country skiing, downhill skiing, fishing, golf, horseback riding, live theater, museums, parks, shopping, tennis, water sports and wineries nearby.

Location: Country, mountains.

Certificate may be used: Anytime, Sunday-Thursday, subject to availability.

West Glover

Rodgers Country Inn

582 Rodgers Rd
West Glover, VT 05875
(802)525-6677 (800)729-1704 Fax:(802)525-1103
Internet: www.virtualvermont.com/rodgers
E-mail: jnrodger@together.net

Passed down through generations of the same family since the early 1800s, Rodgers Country Inn is open year round offering friendly hospitality. This B&B is surrounded by fields, woods and mountains in West Glover, Vermont. Relax on the enclosed porch, browse through a magazine on the deck or play table tennis in the Game Room. Stay in a guest bedroom or spacious secluded cabin by the pond that sleeps seven. Home-cooked meals are served family-style in the farmhouse kitchen and dining area. Fish, swim or go boating at nearby Shadow Lake or Lake Parker. Ski, snowshoe and snowmobile on the grounds locally. Leaf Peepers love the fall and maple sugaring to make syrup can be experienced in the spring.

Innkeeper(s): Nancy H. Rodgers . Call for rates. Call inn for details. Breakfast, dinner, Breakfast with Double Occupancy charge of $70 and Breakfast and Dinner with Double Occupancy charge of $90 included in rates. Types of meals: Country bkfst and early coffee/tea. TV, VCR, DVD, spa, Televison, DVD and VCR in main room on premises.

Certificate may be used: April, May, June.

Wilmington

The Inn at Quail Run

106 Smith Rd
Wilmington, VT 05363
(802)464-3362 (800)343-7227 Fax:(802)464-7784
Internet: www.theinnatquailrun.com
E-mail: quailrunvt@aol.com

Circa 1970. Enjoy the serenity of the Vermont countryside at this inn surrounded by 12 private acres and mountain views. Brass and antique beds are covered with comforters perfect for snuggling. A hearty country breakfast is served each morning. Murder-mystery and Christmas Inn Vermont packages add an extra flair to vacations. Relax in the sauna after working out in the exercise room or solar-heated pool. Skiing and sleigh rides make good use of the Vermont winter. Country Theatre, flea markets and the Marlboro Music Festival are nearby attractions.

Innkeeper(s): Victoria & Ray Lawhorne. $100-210. 13 rooms with PB, 4 with FP, 1 suite, 1 cottage. Breakfast and snacks/refreshments included in rates. Types of meals: Country bkfst, early coffee/tea, picnic lunch, afternoon tea and dinner. Beds: KQT. Cable TV, clock radio, some with fireplace, bath amenities and iron/ironing board in room. Air conditioning. VCR, spa, swimming, library, pet boarding, child care, parlor games, telephone and gift shop on premises. Amusement parks, antiquing, art galleries, beach, bicycling, canoeing/kayaking, cross-country skiing, downhill skiing, fishing, golf, hiking, horseback riding, museums, parks, shopping, tennis, water sports and wineries nearby.

Location: Mountains.

Certificate may be used: Anytime, subject to availability.

The Red Shutter Inn & Restaurant

41 West Main Street
Wilmington, VT 05363
(802)464-3768 (800)845-7548 Fax:(802)464-3141
Internet: www.redshutterinn.com
E-mail: innkeeper@redshutterinn.com

Circa 1894. This colonial inn sits on a five-acre hillside amid maples, pine oaks and evergreens. Tucked behind the inn is the renovated carriage house; among its charms is a cozy fireplace suite. In the summer, guests can enjoy gourmet dining by candlelight on an awning-covered porch. The Red Shutter Inn, with its fireplaces in the sitting room and dining room, antique furnishings and view of a rushing river, provide a congenial atmosphere. Antique shops, galleries and craft shops are within walking distance.

Innkeeper(s): Amie & Hannah. $100-300. 9 rooms with PB, 3 with FP, 4 with WP, 2 suites, 1 conference room. Breakfast included in rates. Types of meals: Full gourmet bkfst, veg bkfst, hors d'oeuvres, wine, gourmet dinner, Fine Dining Restaurant and fully licensed cocktail bar. Restaurant on premises. Beds: QD. Cable TV, VCR, DVD, reading lamp, ceiling fan, clock radio, hair dryer, bath amenities, wireless Internet access, iron/ironing board, Whirlpool tubs and Air conditioning in room. Air conditioning. Fax, copier, library, telephone, fireplace, In-house Massage Service, Fine dining restaurant and Fully licensed cocktail bar on premises. Antiquing, art galleries, beach, bicycling, canoeing/kayaking, cross-country skiing, downhill skiing, fishing, golf, hiking, horseback riding, live theater, museums, parks, shopping, tennis and water sports nearby.

Location: Country, mountains. Lake nearby.

Publicity: *USA Weekend.*

"You've made The Red Shutter Inn a cozy and relaxing hideaway."

Certificate may be used: March-June anytime, July-October, Sunday-Thursday, November-Dec. 18, anytime, Dec. 19-February, Sunday-Thursday. Not available holiday weekends, subject to availability, anytime at the last minute.

Trail's End, A Country Inn

5 Trail's End Ln
Wilmington, VT 05363-7925
(802)464-2055 (800)859-2585 Fax:(802)464-5532
Internet: www.trailsendvt.com
E-mail: reservations@trailsendvt.com

Circa 1955. Situated among the pines in a secluded setting on ten picturesque acres, Trail's End – A Country Inn, offers romantic accommodations and traditional New England hospitality. Relax with an assortment of onsite activities. Swim in the outdoor heated pool or play billiards on the 8-foot Olthausen table in the game room. The clay tennis court and stocked trout pond provide more enjoyment. Stay in a guest bedroom furnished with family heirlooms and antiques accented by a sophisticated country decor. Each fireplace suite boasts a canopy bed, whirlpool tub, refrigerator, microwave and wet bar. A daily breakfast menu offers classic selections. Recipes of inn specialties can be found in the cookbook available for purchase. Located in Wilmington, Vermont, this B&B is within five minutes of skiing at Mount Snow or Haystack.

Innkeeper(s): Lois Smith. $110-250. 16 rooms with PB, 6 with FP, 2 with WP, 2 two-bedroom suites, 1 conference room. Breakfast and snacks/refreshments included in rates. Types of meals: Full gourmet bkfst, early coffee/tea, picnic lunch, afternoon tea, dinner and Dinners available at busy times. Beds: QT. Cable TV, VCR, DVD, reading lamp, stereo, refrigerator, ceiling fan, clock radio, turn-down service, desk, most with hot tub/spa, most with fireplace, hair dryer, wireless Internet access, Serta Posture Pedic pillow top beds, Full private bath with Oxygenator shower heads, Curved shower poles, TV/VCR/DVD, HoMedics iSOUNDSPA Sound Machine clock radio with I-Pod docking station and Hair dryer in room. Fax, copier, spa, swimming, sauna, bicycles, library, child care, parlor games, telephone, gift shop and Vermont's Ultimate Spa the Phoenician Rejuvenation Center included at no extra charge on premises. Antiquing, cross-country skiing, downhill skiing, fishing, live theater, parks, shopping, water sports and Marlboro Music Festival nearby.

Location: Country, mountains.

Publicity: *Yankee Magazine, Boston Globe, Inn Times, Snow Country, Sun Country, Changing Times, PM Magazine* and Mt. Snow's 40th Anniversary.

"Thank you again for an absolutely wonderful weekend."

Certificate may be used: March 15-June 15, Sunday-Friday.

Woodstock

Applebutter Inn

Happy Valley Rd
Woodstock, VT 05091
(802)457-4158 (800)486-1734 Fax:(802)457-4158
Internet: www.applebutterinn.com
E-mail: aplbtrn@comcast.net

Circa 1854. Gracious hospitality and comfort are equally enjoyed at this elegant 1854 country home. Authentically restored, this Federal gabled inn listed in the National Register boasts original wide pine floors, Oriental rugs and rare antiques. Relax by the fire in the Yellow Room or browse through the extensive book collection. Play the Mason & Hamlin grand piano in the Music Room. Several of the spacious and romantic guest bedrooms feature fireplaces. The Cameo Room also has a separate entrance. Sleep well on an 18th century pencil-post bed in the King David Room with a private porch. Sit in the morning sun of the breakfast room and savor a gourmet meal highlighted by Barbara's own applebutter. Play croquet on the expansive lawn, or sit on the porch with afternoon tea and fresh-baked cookies. Located in the tranquil hamlet of Taftsville, seasonal activities and fine dining are close by.

Innkeeper(s): Barbara & Michael. $95-195. 6 rooms with PB, 4 with FP, 1 conference room. Breakfast, afternoon tea and Pastries included in rates. Types of meals: Full gourmet bkfst, veg bkfst, early coffee/tea and snacks/refreshments. Beds: KQD. Cable TV, VCR, reading lamp, hair dryer, bath amenities and wireless Internet access in room. Air conditioning. DVD, fax, copier, library, parlor games, telephone, fireplace, Baby Grand Piano and Free Wi-Fi throughout the Inn on premises. Limited handicap access. Antiquing, art galleries, bicycling, canoeing/kayaking, cross-country skiing, downhill skiing, fishing, golf, hiking, horseback riding, live theater, museums, parks, shopping, sporting events and Spa services nearby.

Location: Country, mountains.

Publicity: *Los Angeles Times, Yankee and Food & Wine.*

Certificate may be used: November-April, Sunday-Thursday excluding holiday weeks, subject to availability.

Ardmore Inn

23 Pleasant St, PO Box 466
Woodstock, VT 05091
(802)457-3887 (800)497-9652
Internet: www.ardmoreinn.com
E-mail: ardmoreinn@aol.com

Circa 1867. Stroll to the village green or the covered bridge from this restored 1850 Victorian-Greek Revival home sitting on one acre in the historic district. Arrive as a guest but leave as a friend after staying here. Gracious accommodations include spacious guest bedrooms with an elegant ambiance, antiques, oriental rugs and Vermont marble bathrooms. The Sheridan also features a Jacuzzi tub. Satisfying breakfasts and afternoon refreshments are included. Walk to the nearby shops and restaurants.

Innkeeper(s): Charlotte & Cary Hollingsworth. $115-215. 5 rooms with PB, 2 with FP, 1 with WP. Breakfast and snacks/refreshments included in rates. Types of meals: Country bkfst, veg bkfst and early coffee/tea. Beds: KQ. Reading lamp, clock radio, telephone, desk, some with fireplace, hair dryer, bath amenities, wireless Internet access and iron/ironing board in room. Air conditioning. Fax, copier, library and parlor games on premises. Antiquing, art galleries, bicycling, canoeing/kayaking, cross-country skiing, downhill skiing, fishing, golf, hiking, horseback riding, live theater, museums, parks, shopping, tennis, water sports, mountain biking, fly fishing and snowshoeing nearby.

Location: Mountains. Village.

Certificate may be used: Anytime, subject to availability, except Sept. 15-Oct. 15.

Charleston House

21 Pleasant St
Woodstock, VT 05091-1131
(802)457-3843
Internet: charlestonhouse.com
E-mail: charlestonhousevermont@comcast.net

Circa 1835. This authentically restored brick Greek Revival town house, in the National Register, welcomes guests with shuttered many-paned windows and window boxes filled with pink blooms. Guest rooms are appointed with period antiques and reproductions, an art collection and Oriental rugs. Some of the rooms boast four-poster beds,  and some feature fireplaces and Jacuzzis. A hearty full breakfast starts off the day in the candlelit dining room, and the innkeepers serve afternoon refreshments, as well. Area offerings include winter sleigh rides, snow skiing, auctions, fly fishing, golfing and summer stock theater, to name a few.

Innkeeper(s): Dieter & Willa Nohl. $135-240. 9 rooms with PB. Breakfast included in rates. Types of meals: Full bkfst. Beds: QT. TV in room. Jacuzzis and fireplaces on premises. Antiquing, cross-country skiing, downhill skiing, fishing and golf nearby.

Location: City.

Publicity: *Harbor News, Boston Business Journal, Weekend Getaway, Inn Spots and Special Places.*

Certificate may be used: Nov. 1 to May 31, except holidays.

Virginia

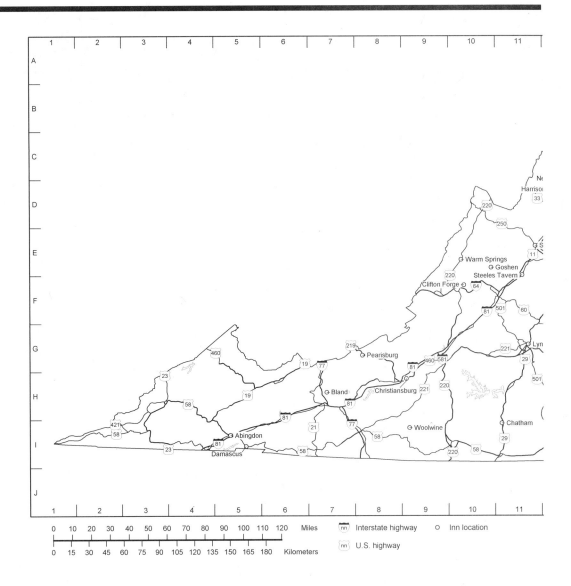

0   10   20   30   40   50   60   70   80   90   100   110   120   Miles

0   15   30   45   60   75   90   105   120   135   150   165   180   Kilometers

nn   Interstate highway   ○   Inn location

nn   U.S. highway

Tell the innkeeper that you have an iLoveInns free-night certificate when you make your reservation.

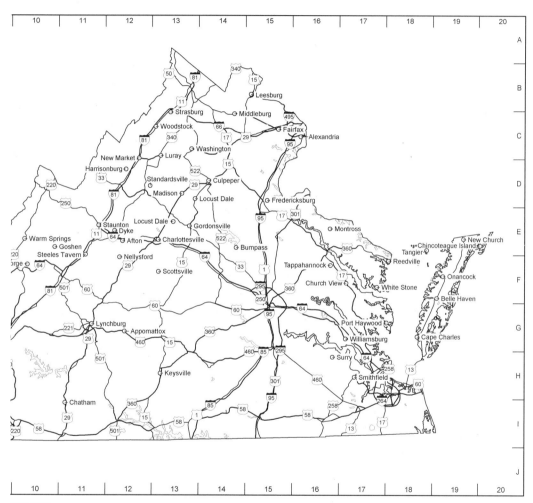

Inn location

Afton

Afton Mountain Bed & Breakfast

10273 Rockfish Valley Hwy
Afton, VA 22920-2771
(540)456-6844 (800)769-6844 Fax:(540)456-7255
Internet: www.aftonmountain.com
E-mail: stay@aftonmountain.com

Circa 1848. Surrounded by 140-year-old silver maples adorning 10 acres in the foothills of the Blue Ridge Mountains, this Victorian farmhouse features original heart pine floors and staircase, a stained-glass entryway and a variety of antiques. Air-conditioned guest bedrooms boast luxurious beds for the ultimate in comfort and include unique furnishings. A sumptuous breakfast begins with fresh fruit, homemade baked goods and an entree specialty. Stroll in the formal rose garden or swim in the pool. Relax on one of the spacious porches with just-baked cookies and a beverage. Tour scenic Skyline Drive, sample wines at local award-winning vineyards, golf or ski. Ask about special packages. Gift certificates are available for the perfect anniversary, birthday, or romantic getaway. Charlottesville and Monticello are nearby.

Innkeeper(s): Orquida and Dan Ingraham. $85-165. 5 rooms with PB, 1 with WP. Breakfast, afternoon tea and snacks/refreshments included in rates. Types of meals: Full gourmet bkfst and early coffee/tea. Beds: KQDT. Reading lamp, stereo, ceiling fan, clock radio, turn-down service, desk, hair dryer, iron/ironing board, XM Satellite Radio available in Jefferson, Goodwin and Shenandoah Rooms in room. Air conditioning. TV, VCR, DVD, fax, copier, swimming, library, parlor games and telephone on premises. Antiquing, art galleries, bicycling, canoeing/kayaking, cross-country skiing, downhill skiing, fishing, golf, hiking, horseback riding, live theater, museums, parks, shopping, sporting events, tennis and wineries nearby.

Location: Country, mountains.

Certificate may be used: Jan. 1-Sept. 15, Nov. 15-Dec. 31, Sunday-Thursday, no holidays.

Alexandria

Alexandria & Arlington Almost Heaven Bed and Breakfast

6339 Brocketts Crossing
Alexandria, VA 22315-3552
(703)921-9043
Internet: www.bedandbreakfastinnvirginia.com
E-mail: cthorneclark@yahoo.com

Circa 1982. Take advantage of the many historic and picturesque attractions in the surrounding area while staying at this stately red brick four-story home. Alexandria Arlington Almost Heaven Bed and Breakfast Inn provides the perfect home-away-from-home experience. Beverages and snacks are always available. Play billiards, darts, air hockey or electronic basketball. After sitting in the indoor sauna, swim in the in-ground pool and soak in the spa. It is an easy walk to the metro for visits to Washington, DC or Mount Vernon, just two of the many places to tour. Guest bedrooms and suites are quiet retreats to enjoy. A daily self-serve continental-plus breakfast is provided during the week and a made-to-order breakfast menu is offered on the weekends and holidays.

Innkeeper(s): Carolyn Clark . $100-159. Call inn for details. Breakfast, afternoon tea, Daily serve yourself breakfast, Hot made-to-order breakfast by menu served Saturday and Sunday and Holidays included in rates. Types of meals: Full bkfst, early coffee/tea and snacks/refreshments. Data port, TV,

VCR, DVD, stereo, refrigerator, ceiling fan, clock radio, telephone, coffeemaker, desk, hot tub/spa, some with fireplace, hair dryer, bathrobes, bath amenities, wireless Internet access, iron/ironing board and Sauna in room. Central air. Fax, copier, spa, swimming, sauna, bicycles, library, laundry facility and On-site free parking on premises. Amusement parks, antiquing, art galleries, bicycling, canoeing/kayaking, fishing, golf, hiking, horseback riding, live theater, museums, parks, shopping, sporting events, tennis and wineries nearby.

Location: City. Washington, DC.

Certificate may be used: Last minute, subject to availability, Dec. 1-Feb. 28.

Bland

Valley View Retreat & Antiques

350 Valley View Lane
Bland, VA 24315
(276)688-4332 (N/A) Fax:(N/A)
Internet: www.valleyviewretreat.com
E-mail: knanken@earthlink.net

Embrace the serenity found in the small-town atmosphere of Bland, Virginia, while staying at this Colonial-style home that graces more than four acres. Valley View Retreat and Antiques opens its doors to one set of guests at a time. A couple or single may stay in the air-conditioned master bedroom suite. For families there is also an extra room for the children. Enjoy the fireside living room and a sun room in complete privacy. Relax on the front porch and rear patio. Breakfast, lunch and dinner are included, but a barbecue grill and a kitchen are also available. Browse through the B&B's gift shop for a treasured memento to take home. A tandem bicycle is provided for the perfect way to ride along and explore the country roads.

Innkeeper(s): Kenneth & Nancy Prosch. $120-140. 2 rooms, 1 with PB. Breakfast, lunch, dinner and Breakfast and Dinner are included in the room rates. Guests that are staying multiple days can use barbeque and kitchen to make lunches. We provide lunches for guests that reserve for one week included in rates. Types of meals: Full bkfst, early coffee/tea, picnic lunch, afternoon tea, snacks/refreshments and We offer a full Breakfast and full Dinner on a fairly Flexible schedule. Lunch provided for guests staying a full week. Beds: QT. Cable TV, VCR, reading lamp, stereo, clock radio, hair dryer and bath amenities in room. DVD, fax, copier, bicycles, parlor games, telephone, fireplace, laundry facility, gift shop, 14 free HBO movie channels, a bicycle built for two for our guests to take out and enjoy the country roads, bocce ball, badminton, lots of games like scrabble and puzzles on premises. Antiquing, art galleries, bicycling, canoeing/kayaking, cross-country skiing, downhill skiing, fishing, hiking, live theater, museums, parks, Lots of biking trails, the Appalachian Trail runs through nearby and Scenery to die for nearby.

Location: Country, mountains.

Certificate may be used: Monday-Thursdays, November-March.

Cape Charles

Cape Charles House

645 Tazewell Ave
Cape Charles, VA 23310-3313
(757)331-4920 Fax:(757)331-4960
Internet: capecharleshouse.com
E-mail: stay@capecharleshouse.com

Circa 1912. A local attorney built this 1912 Colonial Revival home on the site of the town's first schoolhouse. The Cape Charles House is the recipient of the Governor's Award for Virginia Bed and Breakfast Hospitality. Oriental rugs cover lovingly restored hardwood floors. The owners have skillfully combined antiques, heirlooms, artwork, fabrics and collections. Spacious guest bedrooms are named after historically significant townspeople. The premier Julia Wilkins Room features a whirlpool tub/shower and balcony. Gourmet breakfasts served in the formal dining room may include favorites like fresh mango-stuffed croissants in an egg custard with grated nutmeg and orange liqueur. Enjoy late afternoon wine and cheese as well as tea and sweets. Visit the historic Victorian village and swim the quiet bay beach. Bikes, beach towels, chairs and umbrellas are available.

Innkeeper(s): Bruce & Carol Evans. $120-200. 5 rooms with PB. Breakfast, afternoon tea and snacks/refreshments included in rates. Types of meals: Full gourmet bkfst, veg bkfst, early coffee/tea and wine. Beds: KQ. Cable TV, DVD, reading lamp, CD player, ceiling fan, clock radio, desk, hair dryer, bath amenities, wireless Internet access, iron/ironing board and Jacuzzi (two rooms) in room. Air conditioning. TV, VCR, fax, copier, bicycles, parlor games, telephone and fireplace on premises. Antiquing, art galleries, beach, bicycling, canoeing/kayaking, fishing, golf, hiking, museums, parks, shopping, tennis, water sports and wineries nearby.

Location: Small town.

Publicity: *Coastal Living, Chesapeake Magazine, Chesapeake Life and HGTV "If Walls Could Talk"*

"We'll rave, recommend, and we'll return. The culinary magic of your enchanting breakfasts are beyond comparison, unless you consider the charming effects of your warm and generous spirits."

Certificate may be used: November through March, Sunday-Thursday.

Charlottesville

The Foxfield Inn

2280 Garth Rd
Charlottesville, VA 22901
(434)923-8892 (866)369-3536 Fax:(434)923-0963
Internet: www.foxfield-inn.com
E-mail: stay@foxfield-inn.com

Circa 1951. Experience luxury and peacefulness in this single-story, completely restored colonial home situated on three acres just seven miles from Charlottesville. Guest rooms are tastefully decorated with various luxuries, from four-poster cherry canopy beds to an in-room Jacuzzi, to fireplaces and bay windows. Centrally located near Virginia's historic areas, wineries and Jefferson's Monticello, there are plenty of activities to satisfy every taste for travel. Take a day trip to Washington, D.C., only two hours away, or perhaps a 10-minute drive into Charlottesville to enjoy the amenities of the city. Within walking distance are hiking and biking trails, golf and fishing, as well. Get each day started with gourmet coffee from the coffee bar and a full country breakfast featuring eggs Benedict, scones and fresh fruit.

Innkeeper(s): Mary Pat & John Hulburt. $135-260. 5 rooms with PB, 4 with FP. Breakfast and snacks/refreshments included in rates. Types of meals: Country bkfst and early coffee/tea. Beds: Q. Reading lamp, stereo, ceiling fan, clock radio, turn-down service, fireplace, canopy bed and Bose CD/radio in room. Central air. TV, VCR, spa, parlor games, telephone and heated outside spa on premises. Limited handicap access. Antiquing, bicycling, canoeing/kayaking, downhill skiing, fishing, golf, hiking, horseback riding, live theater, parks, shopping, sporting events, tennis, wineries, Jefferson's Monticello, Madison's Montpelier and Monroe's Ash Lawn Highland nearby.

Location: Country.

Certificate may be used: December to March, Monday-Thursday, excluding holidays.

The Inn at Monticello

Rt 20 S, 1188 Scottsville Rd
Charlottesville, VA 22902
(434)979-3593 (877)-RELAX-VA
Internet: www.innatmonticello.com
E-mail: stay@innatmonticello.com

Circa 1850. Thomas Jefferson built his own home, Monticello, just two miles from this gracious country home. The innkeepers have preserved the historic ambiance of the area. Rooms boast such pieces as four-poster beds covered with fluffy, down comforters. Some of the guest quarters have private porches or fireplaces. Breakfast at the inn is a memorable gourmet-appointed affair. Aside from the usual home-made rolls, coffee cakes and muffins, guests enjoy such entrees as pancakes or French toast with seasonal fruit, egg dishes and a variety of quiche. The front porch is lined with chairs for those who wish to relax, and the grounds feature several gardens to enjoy.

Innkeeper(s): Bob Goss & Carolyn Patterson. $195. 5 rooms with PB, 2 with FP. Breakfast and afternoon tea included in rates. Types of meals: Full gourmet bkfst and early coffee/tea. Beds: KQT. Reading lamp and desk in room. Air conditioning. Fax, parlor games, fireplace and afternoon tea with Virginia wine on premises. Antiquing, downhill skiing, live theater, parks, shopping, sporting events, Blue Ridge Parkway Sky Line Drive and wineries nearby.

Location: Historic, 1 mile to city.

Publicity: *Washington Post, Country Inns, Atlantic Country Magazine, Gourmet and Bon Appetit.*

"What a magnificent room at an extraordinary place. I can't wait to tell all my friends."

Certificate may be used: Sunday-Thursday, January-February, no holidays.

Chincoteague Island

Inn at Poplar Corner

4248 Main St
Chincoteague Island, VA 23336-2802
(757)336-6115 Fax:(757)336-5776
Internet: www.innatpoplarcorner.com
E-mail: admin@innatpoplarcorner.com

Circa 1998. Experience the charm of island life while staying at this award-winning three-story Victorian with a romantic 1800s ambiance. Visit the wildlife preserve or the pristine beaches of Assateague Island. Inn at Poplar Corner offers generous Eastern Shore hospitality in Chincoteague Island, Virginia. Relax with afternoon treats and a beverage on the wraparound veranda accented by refreshing breezes. Beach towels, chairs, bikes and binoculars are available for outdoor excursions. Meander through the downtown waterfront shops and restaurants. Guest bedrooms feature oversize whirlpool tubs, robes, luxury organic bath products and some boast a bay view. Select the Main View room on the second floor with a private balcony. Gourmet breakfasts served in the dining room feature fresh local specialties.

Innkeeper(s): Linda Snyder. $139-229. 4 rooms with PB, 4 with WP, 1 conference room. Breakfast, afternoon tea, snacks/refreshments, hors d'oeuvres and wine included in rates. Types of meals: Full gourmet bkfst and early coffee/tea. Beds: Q. Refrigerator, clock radio, hot tub/spa, bathrobes, bath amenities and wireless Internet access in room. Air conditioning. DVD, fax, copier, spa, bicycles, library, parlor games, telephone, fireplace, laundry facility and gift shop on premises. Antiquing, art galleries, beach, bicycling, fishing, hiking, museums, parks, shopping and water sports nearby.

Location: Ocean community.

Certificate may be used: Any week night.

Christiansburg

The Oaks Victorian Inn

311 E Main Street
Christiansburg, VA 24073
(540)381-1500 (800)336-6257 Fax:(540)381-3036
Internet: www.theoaksvictorianinn.com
E-mail: stay@theoaksvictorianinn.com

Circa 1889. Poised on the highest hill in the small town of Christiansburg in the mountain highlands of Southwest Virginia, The Oaks Victorian Inn is an award-winning Queen Anne Victorian. Listed in the National Register, its historic heritage of 1889 has been preserved while lovingly restored. Manicured lawns, 300-year-old white oak trees, perennial gardens, a gazebo, fish pond, brick terrace and fountain accent the pleasant two-acre setting. Relax on a rocker on the wraparound porch. Stay in a guest bedroom or suite with a fireplace, stocked mini-refrigerator, whirlpool or clawfoot tub. The Garden Cottage offers a romantic hideaway. Savor a three-course breakfast by the fire with candlelight and soft music. Regional dishes and original recipes are served on fine china, silver and lace tablecloths.

Innkeeper(s): Lois and John Ioviero. $120-200. 7 rooms with PB, 4 with FP, 1 with HT, 2 with WP, 1 cottage, 1 conference room. Breakfast and snacks/refreshments included in rates. Types of meals: Full gourmet bkfst and early coffee/tea. Beds: KQ. Data port, cable TV, VCR, DVD, reading lamp, stereo, refrigerator, ceiling fan, clock radio, telephone, turn-down service, desk, some with hot tub/spa, some with fireplace, hair dryer, bathrobes, bath amenities, wireless Internet access, Snacks & mini refrigerators in each room stocked with complimentary water, juice and soda in room. Central air. Fax, copier, spa, sauna, bicycles, library, parlor games, valet, laundry and pressing, Library of books, magazines, movies, parlor games, refreshments and snacks on premises. Antiquing, bicycling, canoeing/kayaking, cross-country skiing, downhill skiing, fishing, golf, hiking, horseback riding, live theater, museums, parks, shopping, sporting events, tennis, water sports and wineries nearby.

Location: Mountains. Small town historic district, mountains.

Certificate may be used: Anytime December-March, except holidays. Sunday-Thursday, April-November, except holidays, all subject to availability.

Church View

Dragon Run Inn

35 Wares Bridge Rd
Church View, VA 23032
(804)758-5719
Internet: www.dragon-run-inn.com
E-mail: runninn@oasisonline.com

Circa 1913. Built with cypress from Dragon Run Swamp in 1913, this country farm house offers the ambiance of yesterday and the amenities of today. Relax on the large front porch, or play a game on the picnic table under a big shady tree. Planned arrivals with reservations are greeted with fresh flowers, fruit basket, homemade treats and beverages. Keeping in character with the surroundings, guest bedrooms are named after farm animals. Each room boasts antique furnishings, a cheery decor and a romantic Jacuzzi tub. Enjoy a hearty country breakfast before exploring the scenic area. Tour Lighthouse Island, with one of the oldest lighthouses on Chesapeake Bay.

Innkeeper(s): Ivan & Sue Hertzler. $110. 3 rooms with PB, 3 with WP. Breakfast and snacks/refreshments included in rates. Types of meals: Country bkfst, veg bkfst, early coffee/tea and Meals other than breakfast available if arrangements are made at the time of reservation. Beds: QD. Reading lamp, CD player, clock radio, desk, hair dryer, bath amenities, iron/ironing board, Whirlpool, Fruit basket and Flowers in room. Air conditioning. TV, VCR, copier, library, parlor games, telephone and laundry facility on premises. Limited handicap access. Amusement parks, antiquing, art galleries, bicycling, canoeing/kayaking, fishing, golf, hiking, live theater, museums, parks, shopping, tennis and wineries nearby.

Location: Country.

Certificate may be used: Sunday-Thursday, subject to availability.

Clifton Forge

Firmstone Manor

6209 Longdale Furnace Rd
Clifton Forge, VA 24422-3618
(540)862-0892 (800)474-9882 Fax:(540)862-0158
Internet: www.firmstonemanor.com
E-mail: stay@firmstonemanor.com

Circa 1873. Built by the ironmaster of the Longdale Furnace Company, this Victorian is located in the historic district named for the firm. The home boasts many unusual original features, including a wraparound porch with a built-in gazebo and a view onto a walking wedding maze.

There are more than 12 acres and a budding orchard to enjoy as well as views of the surrounding Shenandoah Valley and the Allegheny Mountains from all the rooms. Large guest bedrooms are elegantly appointed with ceiling fans and most have fireplaces. Civil War sites, museums, children's activities, shopping, lakes and state parks are in the area. Stay on-site and relax in a hammock under a 150-year-old tree with a good book and the sounds of a stream in the background.

Innkeeper(s): Barbara Jarocka. $90-130. 6 rooms with PB, 1 suite, 2 cottages. Breakfast, snacks/refreshments and wine included in rates. Types of meals: Full gourmet bkfst, veg bkfst, early coffee/tea, lunch, picnic lunch, afternoon tea, gourmet dinner, Breakfast in bed, bonfire cook outs and outside grill for guest use. Beds: KQT. Cable TV, VCR, DVD, reading lamp, ceiling fan, telephone, fireplace, hair dryer, bathrobes and iron/ironing board in room. Air conditioning. Fax, library, child care, parlor games, laundry facility, croquet, badminton and fishing pond on premises. Antiquing, art galleries, bicycling, canoeing/kayaking, cross-country skiing, downhill skiing, fishing, golf, hiking, horseback riding, live theater, museums, parks, shopping, sporting events, water sports, wineries and drive-in movie nearby.

Location: Country, mountains. National Forest, property surrounded by pristine streams.

"We'll catch your dreams."

Certificate may be used: Anytime, Subject to availability.

Culpeper

Fountain Hall B&B

609 S East St
Culpeper, VA 22701-3222
(540)825-8200 (800)298-4748
Internet: www.fountainhall.com
E-mail: visit@fountainhall.com

Circa 1859. The well-appointed, oversized guest bedrooms and suites offer comforts galore. Some feature a private porch, whirlpool tub, plush robes and sweeping views of neighboring farms. Enjoy a leisurely breakfast of just-baked flaky croissants with butter and jam, fresh fruits, yogurt, hot and cold cereals and beverages. The surrounding area is steeped in rich American history, and the meticulously landscaped grounds feature seasonal gardens and a lawn groomed for croquet and bocce ball.

Innkeeper(s): Steve & Kathi Walker. $95-150. 6 rooms with PB, 2 suites. Breakfast and snacks/refreshments included in rates. Types of meals: Cont plus and early coffee/tea. Beds: QDT. Modem hook-up, data port, cable TV, VCR, reading lamp, CD player, refrigerator, ceiling fan, clock radio, telephone and desk in room. Air conditioning. Fax, parlor games and fireplace on premises. Handicap access. Antiquing, art galleries, bicycling, canoeing/kayaking, fishing, golf, hiking, horseback riding, museums, parks, shopping and wineries nearby.

Location: Small town.

Publicity: *Culpeper Star Exponent, New York Times, Washington Post, Richmond Channel 8 and Local TV.*

"A great inn you run. We still look back on our stay at Fountain Hall as a standout."

Certificate may be used: Nov. 15-March 31, Sunday to Thursday, Rooms are limited, please mention certificate in advance of placing reservation.

Damascus

Mountain Laurel Inn

22750 Jeb Stuart Hwy
Damascus, VA 24236
(276)475-5956 (888)684-6698 Fax:(276)475-3399
Internet: www.mountainlaurelinn.com
E-mail: info@mountainlaurelinn.com

Circa 1901. A Swedish lumber baron built Mountain Laurel. The home served as post office and the owner as postmaster. The Victorian farmhouse's exterior features a wraparound veranda, and the home is surrounded by three acres of peaceful grounds. Each room has been decorated individually with American and European antiques. Florence's Room, named for the original owner's daughter, includes a fireplace. The Rambo Suite, named to honor the home's first family, includes a Jacuzzi tub and a living room. The home borders the Appalachian Trail, and the area offers plenty of activities, including South Holston Lake, two state parks, the Virginia Creeper Trail, Barter Theatre and the annual Virginia Highlands Festival.

Innkeeper(s): Nathalie & Jim Graham. $69-109. 6 rooms, 2 with PB, 2 with FP, 2 suites. Breakfast included in rates. Types of meals: Country bkfst, early coffee/tea, picnic lunch and dinner. Beds: QDT. Cable TV, reading lamp, ceiling fan and desk in room. Central air. Fax, copier, telephone, fireplace, croquet and volleyball on premises. Antiquing, art galleries, beach, bicycling, fishing, golf, hiking, horseback riding, live theater, museums, parks, shopping, sporting events and wineries nearby.

Location: Country.

Certificate may be used: April to November, anytime subject to availability.

Dyke

Cottages at Chesley Creek Farm

2390 Brokenback Mtn. Road
Dyke, VA 22935
(434)985-7129 (866)709-9292 Fax:(434)985-3594
Internet: www.chesleycreekfarm.com
E-mail: info@chesleycreekfarm.com

Be immersed in the tranquil beauty surrounding these newly built cottages in the Blue Ridge Mountains near Charlottesville,

Virginia. Sitting on 200 acres in the midst of wooded properties, there are miles of hiking trails and a road that leads up to Brokenback Mountain. Stay in the Creek House, Pines, LaurelWood or Ridge Cottage that feature fully equipped kitchens, two-person Jacuzzi tubs, a gas grill on the deck and a seasonal in-ground swimming pool. Contemporary and romantic, the setting invites relaxation and a stress-free getaway.

Innkeeper(s): Chuck Swinney and Stu White. $175-200. 4 cottages with PB, 2 with FP, 4 with WP. Types of meals: No meals provided. Beds: Q. Reading lamp, stereo, refrigerator, ceiling fan, clock radio, coffeemaker, hot tub/spa, fireplace, hair dryer, bathrobes, bath amenities, Fully equipped kitchen, everything provided except food - gas BBQ grill on deck, 2-person Jacuzzi tubs and covered porches/open decks in room. Central air. Seasonal swimming pool and 2 hiking trails on premises.

Location: Country, mountains.

Certificate may be used: Anytime, subject to availability.

Gordonsville

Sleepy Hollow Farm B&B

16280 Blue Ridge Tpke
Gordonsville, VA 22942-8214
(540)832-5555 (800)215-4804 Fax:(540)832-2515
Internet: www.sleepyhollowfarmbnb.com
E-mail: shfbnb@ns.gemlink.com

Circa 1785. Many generations have added to this brick farmhouse creating somewhat of an optical illusion, as the historic home appears much smaller from a distance. The pink and white room often was visited by a friendly ghost, believed to be a Red Cross nurse during the Civil War, according to local stories. She hasn't been seen since the house was blessed in 1959. Accommodations also are available in Chestnut Cottage, which offers two suites with downstairs sitting areas and bedrooms and baths upstairs. One suite has a fireplace. The other suite includes a deck, full kitchen, whirlpool room and Franklin wood stove. The grounds include abundant wildlife, flower gardens, an herb garden, a gazebo and pond for swimming and fishing.

Innkeeper(s): Beverley Allison . $75-175. 6 rooms with PB, 2 with FP, 3 suites. Breakfast included in rates. Types of meals: Full bkfst, early coffee/tea and snacks/refreshments. Beds: QDT. Cable TV, VCR, reading lamp, refrigerator, clock radio, telephone and some with desks in room. Air conditioning. Fax, library, two rooms with whirlpools. In the main house cake and cookies available on sideboard on premises. Antiquing, art galleries, downhill skiing, fishing, golf, hiking, live theater, museums, parks, shopping, sporting events, tennis, wineries, steeplechase race, historic homes and fine dining nearby.

Location: Country.

Publicity: *Orange County Review, City Magazine, Town & County, Washington Post, New York Times and Country Inn Magazine.*

"This house is truly blessed."

Certificate may be used: Anytime, Sunday-Thursday.

Goshen

The Hummingbird Inn

PO Box 147, 30 Wood Lane
Goshen, VA 24439-0147
(540)997-9065 (800)397-3214
Internet: www.hummingbirdinn.com
E-mail: stay@hummingbirdinn.com

Circa 1853. This early Victorian villa is located in the
Shenandoah Valley against the backdrop of the Allegheny
Mountains. Both the first and second floors offer wraparound verandas. The rustic den and one
guest room comprise the oldest portions
of the inn, built around 1780. Dinners
are available by advance reservation
(Friday and Saturday). An
old barn and babbling creek
are on the grounds.
Lexington, the Virginia
Horse Center, Natural
Bridge, the Blue Ridge Parkway and antiquing are all nearby.

Innkeeper(s): Pam & Dick Matthews. $130-175. 5 rooms with PB, 5 with
FP, 2 with WP. Breakfast and snacks/refreshments included in rates. Types of
meals: Country bkfst, veg bkfst, early coffee/tea, picnic lunch, wine and dinner. Beds: KQ. Reading lamp, ceiling fan, snack bar, fireplace, hair dryer,
bathrobes, bath amenities and wireless Internet access in room. Air conditioning. TV, VCR, fax, library, parlor games, telephone, gift shop and Trout
stream on premises. Limited handicap access. Antiquing, canoeing/kayaking,
cross-country skiing, downhill skiing, fishing, golf, hiking, horseback riding,
live theater, museums, parks, shopping, wineries, herb farm, working grist
mill and mineral baths nearby.

Location: Mountains.

Publicity: *New York Times Escapes section, USA Today, Time magazine, Out
Here (Tractor Supply magazine), Rockbridge Discovery, the Country Register,
Purple Roofs e-news, Blue Ridge Country, Inn Spots and Special Places,
WRIR, public radio Richmond and VA.*

*"We enjoyed our stay so much that we returned two weeks later on our
way back for a delicious home-cooked dinner, comfortable attractive
atmosphere, and familiar faces to welcome us after a long journey."*

Certificate may be used: Dec. 1-May 1, Sunday-Thursday, excluding holidays.

Harrisonburg

By The Side Of The Road

491 Garbers Church Rd
Harrisonburg, VA 22801
(540)801-0430 Fax:n/a
Internet: www.bythesideoftheroad.com
E-mail: stay@bythesideoftheroad.com

Circa 1789. Built in 1790, this Flemish Bond brick home sits in
the heart of historic Shenandoah Valley in Harrisonburg, Virginia.
By the Side of the Road is a peaceful country retreat just minutes
from the excitement of city life with Blue Ridge Parkway and
Skyline Drive close by. The bed and breakfast boasts extensive
gardens with perennials bordering the walkway and edible flower
and herb gardens. Luxurious accommodations include oversized
whirlpool or clawfoot tubs, fireplaces, feather beds and other
upscale amenities. The spacious yet intimate cottages are perfect
for feeling pampered. Breakfast is delivered to the door. The
delightful Main House suites feature 15-inch brick walls that
ensure privacy. Gather in the Common Room for the morning
meal served on vintage china and sterling flatware.

Innkeeper(s): Janice & Dennis Fitzgerald. $149-289. 7 rooms, 7 with FP, 4
with WP, 7 total suites, including 2 two-bedroom suites, 3 cottages.
Breakfast and snacks/refreshments included in rates. Types of meals: Full
gourmet bkfst, veg bkfst, early coffee/tea, picnic lunch and Breakfast baskets
delivered to your cottage door. Beds: KQT. Modem hook-up, data port, cable
TV, VCR, DVD, reading lamp, CD player, refrigerator, ceiling fan, clock radio,
telephone, coffeemaker, turn-down service, desk, most with hot tub/spa, hair
dryer, bath amenities, wireless Internet access, iron/ironing board and
Featherbeds in room. Central air. Library, parlor games and fireplace on
premises. Limited handicap access. Amusement parks, antiquing, art galleries, bicycling, canoeing/kayaking, downhill skiing, fishing, golf, hiking,
horseback riding, live theater, museums, parks, shopping, sporting events,
tennis, water sports and wineries nearby.

Location: City, country, mountains.

Certificate may be used: December-January, Monday-Thursday, subject to
availability.

Locust Dale

The Inn at Meander Plantation

2333 North James Madison Hwy.
Locust Dale, VA 22948-9701
(540)672-4912 (800)385-4936 Fax:(540)672-0405
Internet: www.meander.net
E-mail: inn@meander.net

Circa 1766. This historic country estate was built by Henry Fry,
close friend of Thomas Jefferson who often stopped here on his
way to Monticello. The mansion is serenely decorated with elegant
antiques and period reproductions, including four-poster beds.
Healthy gourmet breakfasts are prepared by Chef Suzie. Enjoy
views of the Blue Ridge Mountains from the rockers on
the back porches. Ancient for-
mal boxwood gardens, sur-
rounding natural woodlands,
meadows, pastures and
Robinson River frontage are
part of Meander Conservancy,
offering educational programs
and back-to-nature packages.

Innkeeper(s): Suzie Blanchard, Suzanne Thomas. $120-200. 8 rooms with
PB, 5 with FP, 4 suites, 1 conference room. Breakfast included in rates.
Types of meals: Full bkfst, early coffee/tea, lunch, picnic lunch,
snacks/refreshments and gourmet dinner. Beds: KQ. Reading lamp, clock
radio and desk in room. Air conditioning. VCR, fax, stable, library, pet boarding, child care, parlor games, telephone, fireplace, restaurant service
Thursday and Friday and Saturday on premises. Antiquing, cross-country skiing, downhill skiing, fishing, live theater, parks, shopping, sporting events and
wineries nearby.

Location: Country.

*"Staying at the Inn at Meander Plantation feels like being immersed
in another century while having the luxuries and amenities available
today."*

Certificate may be used: Year-round, Sunday through Thursday, excluding
holidays and October.

Luray

The Woodruff Collection of Victorian Inns

138 E Main St
Luray, VA 22835
(540)743-1494 Fax:(540)743-1722
Internet: www.woodruffinns.com
E-mail: woodruffinns@woodruffinns.com

Circa 1882. Prepare to be pampered. The Woodruffs entered the B&B business after years of experience in hotel management and restaurant businesses. They have not missed a detail, ensuring a perfect, relaxing visit. The Rooftop Skylight Fireside Jacuzzi Suite is often the room of choice because of its interesting shape and architecture, located where the attic was before restoration. The suite boasts skylights, Jacuzzi tub for two and antique stained glass. Tasteful antiques and fresh bouquets of flowers framed by candlelight add a special ambiance. Besides the extra attention and comfortable accommodations, the Woodruffs include coffee and afternoon dessert tea, in-room coffee or tea and a full fireside breakfast in the rates. Candlelight sets the mood for the gourmet dinner, and none of the spectacular meals are to be missed. A romantic finish to each evening is a private dip in one of the garden hot tubs.

Innkeeper(s): Lucas & Deborah Woodruff. $119-289. 5 rooms with PB, 9 with FP, 4 suites, 1 conference room. Breakfast included in rates. Types of meals: Full bkfst, afternoon tea and gourmet dinner. Beds: KQ. Reading lamp, clock radio, coffeemaker, desk and coffeemaker in room. Air conditioning. Fax, spa, parlor games, telephone, fireplace, two outdoor gardens, Jacuzzi tubs for two, afternoon dessert, tea and coffee on premises. Antiquing, downhill skiing, fishing, parks, shopping, water sports, caverns, Shenandoah River and Skyline Drive nearby.

Location: Mountains.

Publicity: *Potomac Living, Cascapades Magazine, Blue Ridge Country Magazine, Cooperative Living, Virginia Wine Gazette, Food and Wine Magazine, Gourmet Magazine, Washington Times* and recipient of Virginia's gold three cluster wine award.

Certificate may be used: Jan. 5 to March 15, Monday-Thursday, lodging only.

Lynchburg

Federal Crest Inn

1101 Federal St
Lynchburg, VA 24504-3018
(434)845-6155 (800)818-6155 Fax:(434)845-1445
Internet: www.federalcrest.com
E-mail: inn@federalcrest.com

Circa 1909. The guest rooms at Federal Crest are named for the many varieties of trees and flowers native to Virginia. This handsome red brick home, a fine example of Georgian Revival architecture, features a commanding front entrance flanked by columns that hold up the second-story veranda. A grand staircase, carved woodwork, polished floors topped with fine rugs and more columns create an aura of elegance. Each guest room offers something special and romantic, from a mountain view to a Jacuzzi tub. Breakfasts are served on fine china, and the first course is always a freshly baked muffin with a secret message inside.

Innkeeper(s): Ann & Phil Ripley. $135-200. 5 rooms, 4 with PB, 4 with FP, 2 suites, 1 conference room. Breakfast, afternoon tea and snacks/refreshments included in rates. Types of meals: Full bkfst and early coffee/tea. Beds: Q. Cable TV, VCR, reading lamp, clock radio, turn-down service, desk, wireless Internet access and telephone in room. Air conditioning. Fax, copier, parlor games, telephone, fireplace, gift shop, conference theater with 60-inch TV (Ballroom) with stage, '50s cafe with antique jukebox and video library on premises. Antiquing, fishing, golf, live theater, parks, shopping, sporting events and tennis nearby.

Location: City, mountains. Central Virginia.

Publicity: *Washington Post, News & Advance, Scene and Local ABC.*

"What a wonderful place to celebrate our birthdays and enjoy our last romantic getaway before the birth of our first child."

Certificate may be used: Jan. 2-July 30, Sunday-Thursday.

Residence Bed & Breakfast

2460 Rivermont Avenue
Lynchburg, VA 24503-1546
(434)845-6565 (888)835-0387
Internet: www.theresidencebb.com
E-mail: stay@theresidencebb.com

Circa 1915. Situated on one acre in the Rivermont Historic District, many celebrities have been entertained at this Colonial Revival estate that was built in 1915 for the presidents of Randolph-Macon Women's College. Gather for conversation and refreshments by the fire. Recently renovated with an eclectic décor and modern conveniences, guest bedrooms and a suite offer a generous assortment of pleasing amenities. A full gourmet breakfast is served daily. Bikes are available for exploring the scenic area. Visit the many historic sites nearby. Appomattox is 20 miles away, and Jefferson's Monticello is 65 miles away. It is only 30 minutes to the Blue Ridge Parkway.

Innkeeper(s): George & JoAnne Caylor. $125-195. 4 rooms, 3 with PB, 1 two-bedroom suite. Breakfast and snacks/refreshments included in rates. Types of meals: Full gourmet bkfst and veg bkfst. Beds: KQT. Modem hook-up, cable TV, VCR, reading lamp, ceiling fan, snack bar, clock radio, telephone, turn-down service, desk, hair dryer, bathrobes, bath amenities and wireless Internet access in room. Central air. DVD, fax, copier, bicycles and fireplace on premises. Antiquing, art galleries, bicycling, canoeing/kayaking, fishing, golf, hiking, live theater, museums, parks, shopping, sporting events, tennis, water sports and wineries nearby.

Location: City. In Rivermont Historic District and 30 minutes to Blue Ridge Parkway.

Certificate may be used: November-February, Monday-Thursday, limit one free night.

Madison

Dulaney Hollow at Old Rag Mountain B&B Inn

3932 South F.T. Valley Rd - Scenic VA Byway, Rt 231
Madison, VA 22727
(540)923-4470 Fax:(540)923-4841
E-mail: oldragmtninn@nexet.net

Circa 1903. Period furnishings decorate this Victorian manor house on 15 acres of the Blue Ridge Mountains. There is also a cabin, cottage and hayloft suite available amid the shaded lawns and old farm buildings. Enjoy a delicious country breakfast. Take a bicycle jaunt or hike the hills around the Shenandoah River and National Park. Monticello, Charlottesville and Montpelier are within an hour's drive.

Innkeeper(s): Susan & Louis Cable. $130-155. 6 rooms, 3 with PB, 2 with FP, 3 cottages, 1 conference room. Breakfast included in rates. Types of meals: Country bkfst, veg bkfst and early coffee/tea. Beds: QDT. Refrigerator, ceiling fan, coffeemaker and desk in room. Air conditioning. VCR, fax, copier, swimming, pet boarding, telephone, fireplace and Internet access on premises. Antiquing, canoeing/kayaking, cross-country skiing, downhill skiing, fishing, golf, hiking, horseback riding, live theater, museums, parks, shopping, sporting events, tennis, water sports, wineries, Civil War sites, historic sites and battlefields, Shenandoah National Park and wildlife preserve nearby.

Location: Mountains. Blue Ridge Mountains.

Publicity: *Madison Eagle and Charlottesville Daily Progress.*

Certificate may be used: Jan. 1 through Dec. 31 (only on weekday nights, Monday through Thursday; not weekends, not any holidays).

Middleburg

Briar Patch Bed & Breakfast

23130 Briar Patch Lane
Middleburg, VA 20117
(703)327-5911 (866)327-5911 Fax:(703)327-5933
Internet: www.briarpatchbandb.com
E-mail: info@briarpatchbandb.com

Circa 1805. Leave stress behind when staying at this historic farm that sits on 47 rolling acres of land that once was where the Civil War's Battle of the Haystacks was fought in 1863. Located in the heart of horse, antique and wine country, it is just 20 minutes from Dulles Airport and 45 minutes from Washington, DC. Overlook the Bull Run Mountains while sitting on the front porch. Antique-filled guest bedrooms in the main house are named after the flowers and feature canopy or four-poster beds. Two rooms can adjoin to become a suite. A separate one-bedroom cottage includes a fully equipped kitchen, dining area and living room. Breakfast is provided in the large kitchen or outside patio. Swim in the pool or soak in the year-round hot tub.

Innkeeper(s): Becky Croft - Manager, Owners - Ellen Goldberg & Dan Haendel. $95-270. 9 rooms, 3 with PB, 3 with FP, 3 two-bedroom suites, 1 cottage. Breakfast included in rates. Types of meals: Full breakfast on weekends and Continental on weekdays. Beds: KQ. Reading lamp, CD player, ceiling fan, some with fireplace, hair dryer, bathrobes, wireless Internet access and iron/ironing board in room. Air conditioning. TV, VCR, DVD, fax, copier, spa, swimming, library, parlor games and telephone on premises. Limited handicap access. Antiquing, art galleries, bicycling, canoeing/kayaking, fishing, golf, hiking, horseback riding, museums, parks, shopping, tennis and wineries nearby.

Location: Country.

Certificate may be used: Valid Monday through Thursday.

New Church

The Garden and The Sea Inn

4188 Nelson Rd.
New Church, VA 23415-0275
(757)824-0672 (800)824-0672
Internet: www.gardenandseainn.com
E-mail: innkeeper@gardenandseainn.com

Circa 1802. Gingerbread trim, a pair of brightly colored gables and two, adjacent verandas adorn the exterior of this Victorian. A warm, rich Victorian decor permeates the antique-filled guest rooms, an ideal setting for romance. Most rooms include whirlpool tubs. The inn's dining room serves gourmet dinners by reservation. Pets are very welcome.

Innkeeper(s): Tom & Sara Baker. $75-205. 8 rooms with PB, 1 conference room. Breakfast included in rates. Types of meals: Full bkfst, snacks/refreshments and gourmet dinner. Restaurant on premises. Beds: KQ. TV, reading lamp, ceiling fan, clock radio and some with fireplace in room. Air conditioning. VCR, fax, copier, library, parlor games, telephone and outdoor heated pool on premises. Handicap access. Antiquing, beach, fishing, parks, shopping and water sports nearby.

Publicity: *Washington Post, Modern Bride and Southern Living.*

Certificate may be used: Sunday through Thursday in April, May, June, October and November.

New Market

Cross Roads Inn B&B

9222 John Sevier Rd
New Market, VA 22844-9649
(540)740-4157 (888)740-4157
Internet: www.crossroadsinnva.com
E-mail: lsmith18@juno.com

Circa 1925. This Victorian is full of Southern hospitality. Bountiful breakfasts and homemade treats are served as an afternoon refreshment. The home is decorated with English floral wallpapers, antiques and old family furnishings. Four-poster and canopy beds are topped with fluffy, down comforters. The historic downtown area is within walking distance.

Innkeeper(s): Sharon & Larry Smith. $95-135. 6 rooms with PB. Breakfast, snacks/refreshments and wine included in rates. Types of meals: Full gourmet bkfst, veg bkfst and picnic lunch. Beds: KQDT. Cable TV, reading lamp, ceiling fan, clock radio, hair dryer, bath amenities, wireless Internet access, iron/ironing board and several with Jacuzzi or fireplace in room. Air conditioning. VCR, fax, parlor games, telephone and fireplace on premises. Handicap access. Antiquing, bicycling, canoeing/kayaking, downhill skiing, fishing, golf, hiking, horseback riding, live theater, parks, shopping, sporting events, water sports, wineries and musical summer festivals nearby.

Location: Mountains. Small town.

Certificate may be used: November to September, Sunday-Thursday.

Pearisburg

Inn at Riverbend

125 River Ridge Dr.
Pearisburg, VA 24134
(540)921-5211 Fax:(540)921-2720
Internet: www.innatriverbend.com
E-mail: stay@innatriverbend.com

Circa 2003. Expansive views of the New River and the surrounding valley are incredibly breathtaking while staying at this contemporary bed and breakfast. Enjoy refreshments in front of the stone fireplace in a great room with a wall of French doors and windows. Two levels of huge wraparound decks offer an abundance of space to appreciate the scenic beauty and assortment of birds. Watch a movie or gather as a group in the TV/meeting room. Luxury guest bedrooms are delightful retreats that have access to decks or terraces and feature pressed linens, specialty personal products, stocked refrigerators, and other generous amenities. Several rooms boast whirlpool tubs. After a three-course breakfast, sample some of the area's many outdoor activities. The Appalachian Trail is only two miles away.

Innkeeper(s): Linda & Lynn Hayes. $130-250. 7 rooms with PB, 1 conference room. Breakfast and snacks/refreshments included in rates. Types of meals: Full bkfst, veg bkfst, early coffee/tea, lunch, picnic lunch and gourmet dinner. Beds: KQT. Cable TV, reading lamp, ceiling fan, clock radio, turndown service, desk and wireless Internet access in room. Central air. VCR, DVD, fax, library, parlor games, telephone, fireplace and gift shop on premises. Limited handicap access. Antiquing, bicycling, canoeing/kayaking, cross-country skiing, downhill skiing, fishing, golf, hiking, live theater, museums, parks, shopping, sporting events, tennis and wineries nearby.

Location: Country, mountains. Overlooking the New River.

Certificate may be used: Anytime, December-March except holidays; Sunday-Thursday, April-November except holidays, all subject to availability.

Reedville

Fleeton Fields B & B

2783 Fleeton Road
Reedville, VA 22539
(804)453-5014 (800)497-8215 Fax:(804)453-5014
Internet: www.fleetonfields.com
E-mail: info@fleetonfields.com

Circa 1945. For a romantic getaway on the Chesapeake Bay, this brick Colonial-style bed and breakfast sits in a park-like setting on 15 tranquil acres at the edge of Fleeton's historic hamlet. Victorian and period furnishings reside amiably with modern amenities. Well-appointed guest suites are spacious and inviting with fresh flowers, soft bathrobes, mini-refrigerators and scenic views. The Garden Suite also features a private entrance, sitting room and fireplace. A multi-course gourmet breakfast is served on fine china, silver and crystal. Explore the area on a bicycle or on a two-car cable ferry over Little Wicomico River. Launch the inn's canoe or kayak on the pond. Visit the Reedville Fisherman's Museum. The enjoyable activities are endless.

Innkeeper(s): Marguerite Slaughter. $135-195. 3 suites. Breakfast included in rates. Types of meals: Full gourmet bkfst and afternoon tea. Beds: Q. Cable TV, VCR, reading lamp, refrigerator, telephone, some with fireplace, hair dryer, bathrobes, bath amenities, iron/ironing board, clocks and soft drinks provided in room. Central air. TV, fax, copier, bicycles and library on premises. Antiquing, art galleries, beach, bicycling, canoeing/kayaking, fishing, golf, hiking, museums, shopping, wineries and Tangier and Smith Island Cruise nearby.

Location: Country, waterfront.

Certificate may be used: November-March.

Smithfield

Church Street Inn

1607 S Church St
Smithfield, VA 23430-1831
(757)357-3176
Internet: www.smithfieldchurchstreetinn.com
E-mail: reservations@smithfieldchurchstreetinn.com

Circa 1980. This Colonial inn is located in a historic seaside town, boasting more than 60 homes that date back to the mid-18th century. St. Luke's Church, the oldest in the United States, dating back to 1632, is located near the inn. Antiques and reproductions fill the rooms, and the suites offer the added amenities of fireplaces and whirlpool tubs. The inn also houses a gift boutique and one of the area's finest antique shops, featuring old clocks and period furniture.

Innkeeper(s): Peter & Angie Lowry. $99-149. 11 rooms with PB, 2 with FP, 2 suites, 1 conference room. Breakfast included in rates. Types of meals: Cont and early coffee/tea. Beds: QDT. Cable TV, reading lamp, clock radio, telephone, desk, fireplace (three rooms) and Jacuzzis in room. Air condition-

ing. VCR, library and parlor games on premises. Handicap access. Amusement parks, antiquing, fishing, live theater, parks, shopping, water sports, Air & Space Museum and Norticus nearby.

Location: Historic small town.

Certificate may be used: Sunday through Thursday, all year, based on availability, excluding holidays.

Four Square Plantation

13357 Foursquare Rd
Smithfield, VA 23430-8643
(757)365-0749 Fax:(757)365-0749
Internet: www.innvirginia.com
E-mail: foursquareplantation@att.net

Circa 1807. Located in the historic James River area, the original land grant, "Four Square" was established in 1664 and consisted of 640 acres. Now in the National Register and a Virginia Historic Landmark, the Federal style home is called Plantation Plain by Virginia preservationists. The inn is furnished with family period pieces and antiques. The Vaughan Room offers a fireplace, Empire furnishings and access by private staircase. Breakfast is served in the dining room. The inn's four acres provide a setting for weddings and special events. Tour Williamsburg, Jamestown, the James River Plantations and Yorktown nearby.

Innkeeper(s): Roger & Donna. $75-85. 3 rooms with PB, 3 with FP. Breakfast included in rates. Types of meals: Full gourmet bkfst and early coffee/tea. Beds: KQT. Cable TV, reading lamp, ceiling fan, telephone and turn-down service in room. Air conditioning. VCR, fax, copier and parlor games on premises. Antiquing, golf and shopping nearby.

Location: Country. Three miles from Smithfield.

Publicity: *Daily Press and Virginia Pilot.*

Certificate may be used: Sunday-Thursday, Jan.1-March 31, Nov.1-Dec.23, no holidays.

Stanardsville

Blue Ridge Mountain Inn

9 Golden Horseshoe Rd
Stanardsville, VA 22973
(434)566-2555
Internet: www.blueridgemountaininn.com
E-mail: pots4u2@aol.com

Circa 2000. Bordering Shenandoah National Park in a secluded setting, this newly built inn is perfect for a peaceful escape or romantic hideaway. Encompassing five acres with lush gardens, lily ponds with koi and goldfish, the views of the Blue Ridge Mountains are breathtaking. Stay in inviting guest bedrooms or cottages with generous amenities. The incredible first-floor Mountain Spring Room features a whirlpool bath for two. Start the day with a European-style continental breakfast. Special packages are available. Intimate weddings, showers and other gatherings are popular in these gorgeous surroundings. Browse the gallery and shop of Blue Ridge Pottery.

Innkeeper(s): Heather Tusing. $119-199. 5 rooms, 7 with PB, 1 with WP, 2 cottages. Breakfast included in rates. Types of meals: Cont. Beds: K. TV, reading lamp, CD player, refrigerator, ceiling fan, clock radio, telephone, coffeemaker, voice mail, hair dryer, bath amenities, wireless Internet access and iron/ironing board in room. Central air. Spa, fireplace and Wireless Internet access on premises. Antiquing, bicycling, canoeing/kayaking, cross-country skiing, downhill skiing, fishing, golf, hiking, horseback riding, live theater, parks, shopping, sporting events, water sports and wineries nearby.

Location: Mountains.

Certificate may be used: Dec. 1-March 1 and the month of June, excludes event weekends.

South River Country Inn

3003 South River Rd
Stanardsville, VA 22973
(434)985-2901 (877)874-4473 Fax:(434)985-3833
Internet: www.southrivercountryinn.com
E-mail: jabraun@earthlink.net

In the heart of South River Valley, this original Virginia-style farmhouse has been restored to provide modern comforts while retaining its authentic charm. The spectacular Blue Ridge Mountains are seen from each of the guest bedrooms, some of which feature Jacuzzi tubs for two. A wholesome country breakfast starts the day on this working farm. Hike, fish in one of the ponds or relax in a front porch swing, rocker or hammock. Shenandoah River activities are just a short drive away.

Innkeeper(s): Judy & Cliff Braun. Call for rates. 4 rooms. Breakfast included in rates. Types of meals: Country bkfst, veg bkfst, early coffee/tea, lunch, picnic lunch and dinner. Beds: QDT. Reading lamp, stereo, refrigerator, clock radio, telephone, coffeemaker and satellite TV in room. Central air. TV, DVD, fax, swimming, parlor games, laundry facility and fishing on premises. Antiquing, art galleries, bicycling, canoeing/kayaking, downhill skiing, fishing, golf, hiking, horseback riding, live theater, museums, parks, shopping, sporting events and wineries nearby.

Location: Country, mountains.

Certificate may be used: December 15-March 15, Sunday-Thursday.

The Lafayette Inn

146 E. Main St
Stanardsville, VA 22973
(434)985-6345
Internet: www.thelafayette.com
E-mail: info@thelafayette.com

Circa 1840. Rich with a local legacy, this historic landmark was built in 1840 and stands as a stately three-story Federalist red brick building in downtown Stanardsville, Virginia. Huge porches are accented with white colonnades. Surrounded by scenic beauty, Shenandoah National Park is just 10 minutes away. The Lafayette Inn features romantic, well-appointed guest bedrooms and suites with generous amenities to make each stay most comfortable. Dicey's Cottage, the original two-story slave quarters, provides spacious privacy, Jacuzzi tubs, gas fireplaces, a kitchenette and a deck. A country-style breakfast is served in the coffee and tea house, transformed daily from being the Tavern where lunch and dinner are available. There is much to see and experience in the area. Take a tour of local vineyards, shop for pottery or visit nearby Monticello. Ask about special packages offered.

Innkeeper(s): Alan & Kaye Pyles. $105-195. 7 rooms, 2 with PB, 4 suites, 1 cottage. Breakfast and Sunday Brunch is optional included in rates. Types of meals: Country bkfst, Inn guests can reserve a "Taste of the Lafayette Inn" dinner for Monday through Wednesday evenings — 7:00pm seating (advanced reservations required), $50 per person. Enjoy amuse, seafood gumbo, shrimp and grits, tournedos of beef and jumbo crab cake and dessert. Or choose the "Vegetarian Taste" of amuse, tomato bisque, "shrimpless" and grits and vegetable wellington and dessert. Beds: KQ. Central air. Antiquing, hiking, shopping and wineries nearby.

Location: Country, mountains.

Certificate may be used: Any Monday-Thursday.

Staunton

Staunton Choral Gardens

216 W. Frederick St.
Staunton, VA 24401
(540)885-6556
Internet: www.stauntonbedandbreakfast.com
E-mail: Stay@StauntonBedandBreakfast.com

Circa 1915. Stay in the heart of the Shenandoah Valley at this wonderfully restored, gracious Sam Collins brick inn and 150-year-old award-winning Carriage House, a large, luxurious two-story private suite, in historic downtown Staunton, Virginia. Guest bedrooms feature upscale amenities that include wireless high-speed Internet service, lush featherbed-topped mattresses and central air conditioning. A fireplace, refrigerator and microwave are also available in some rooms. Enjoy thoughtful touches of fresh flowers, candies, and personal products. Savor multi-course breakfasts and afternoon refreshments. Relax in one of the three gardens. A large goldfish pond and fountain accent the courtyard garden; there is ample seating in the shade garden and a roof-covered swing welcomes rainy-day pleasures at Staunton Choral Gardens. A kennel area is available.

Innkeeper(s): Carolyn Avalos. $60-200. 3 rooms with PB, 1 with FP, 2 two-bedroom suites, 1 cottage. Breakfast, afternoon tea and snacks/refreshments included in rates. Types of meals: Full gourmet bkfst and room service. Beds: KQD. Cable TV, VCR, reading lamp, CD player, refrigerator, ceiling fan, clock radio, coffeemaker, desk, fireplace and wireless Internet access in room. Central air. Pet boarding, parlor games, telephone and kennel area on premises. Antiquing, art galleries, bicycling, fishing, golf, hiking, live theater, museums, parks, shopping, tennis and wineries nearby.

Location: City.

Certificate may be used: Last minute, subject to availabilty.

Steeles Tavern

Sugar Tree Inn

P.O. Box 10
Steeles Tavern, VA 24476
(540)377-2197 (800)377-2197
Internet: www.sugartreeinn.com
E-mail: innkeeper@sugartreeinn.com

Circa 1983. A haven of natural beauty sitting on 28 wooded acres high in the Blue Ridge Mountains, this elegantly rustic log inn imparts peace and solitude. Relax on a porch rocker, perfect for bird watching. Stargaze from the hot tub on the mountainside deck. Choose a book or game from the upstairs library. Spacious accommodations include guest bedrooms in the main lodge and log house as well as two suites in the Grey House. Stone fireplaces, whirlpool tubs, separate sitting rooms, outside decks and other pleasing amenities are welcome indulgences. Look out on the wildflowers and chipmunks during a hearty breakfast in the glass-walled dining room. Make reservations for a candlelight dinner with quiet music and Virginia wine, served Wednesday through Saturday at the inn's restaurant. Walk the nature trail by a rushing creek or explore the Appalachian Trail.

Innkeeper(s): Jeff & Becky Chanter. $145-265. 13 rooms with PB, 13 with FP, 2 suites, 1 cottage, 1 cabin. Breakfast and snacks/refreshments included in rates. Types of meals: Country bkfst, veg bkfst, early coffee/tea, picnic lunch and gourmet dinner. Restaurant on premises. Beds: KQDT. VCR, reading lamp, CD player, ceiling fan, clock radio, coffeemaker, some with hot tub/spa, fireplace, hair dryer, bathrobes and bath amenities in room. Air conditioning. TV, spa, telephone and gift shop on premises. Limited handicap access. Antiquing, art galleries, bicycling, canoeing/kayaking, cross-country skiing, downhill skiing, fishing, golf, hiking, horseback riding, live theater, museums, parks and shopping nearby.

Location: Mountains.

Publicity: *Washingtonian Magazine ("Top 10 Country Inns") and Hampton Roads Magazine ("Mountain Magic").*

Certificate may be used: Anytime, at the last minute.

Tangier

The Bay View Inn

16408 W Ridge Rd
Tangier, VA 23440
(757)891-2396
Internet: www.tangierisland.net
E-mail: ptopus@yahoo.com

Circa 1907. Whether arriving on the island by boat or plane, a visit to this remote fishing village is sure to erase city stress. Accommodations at this year-round, waterfront bed and breakfast include two guest bedrooms in the main house and nine cottages. Gather for a country breakfast in the dining room. Relax on the front porch or the deck. Explore the island on a bike or walk along the beach. There is also Duck hunting every December and January; hunting guides are available. Ask about boat docking fees.

Innkeeper(s): Kathy Crockett. $100-125. Call inn for details. Types of meals: Country bkfst and Dinner available in the off season for an additional charge. Beds: QDT. Cable TV, reading lamp, refrigerator and bath amenities in room. Air conditioning. Bicycles and Internet access on premises. Limited handicap access. Art galleries, beach, bicycling, canoeing/kayaking, fishing and shopping nearby.

Location: Waterfront.

Publicity: *National Geographic, Southern Living, Chesapeake Life and Travel & Leisure.*

Certificate may be used: Nov. 15-March 15.

Tappahannock

Essex Inn

203 Duke St
Tappahannock, VA 22560
(804)443-9900 (866)ESSEXVA
Internet: www.EssexInnVa.com
E-mail: info@EssexInnVA.com

Circa 1850. Authentically restored to its original splendor, this 1850 Greek Revival mansion is furnished with period antiques, reproductions and family heirlooms that reflect an old-world elegance. The Essex Inn is located one block from the Rappahannock River in the heart of the Tappahannock downtown historic district. Relax in the private brick courtyard, screened-in porch or the sunroom. The Music Room, with a baby grand piano, and the library have an inviting fireplace. A butler's pantry includes a microwave, refrigerator, coffee and ice maker as well as wine, beer and snacks. Spacious guest bedrooms in the main house boast fireplaces. The servants' quarters are now indulgent suites with custom amenities. Savor the specialty recipes Melody creates for incredible three-course breakfasts before exploring scenic Virginia.

Innkeeper(s): Reeves and Melodie Pogue. $140-180. 8 rooms with PB, 6 with FP, 4 suites. Breakfast, snacks/refreshments and wine included in rates. Types of meals: Full gourmet bkfst and Afternoon snacks. Beds: KQ. Modem hook-up, data port, cable TV, VCR, DVD, reading lamp, ceiling fan, clock radio, desk, most with fireplace, hair dryer, bathrobes, bath amenities, wireless Internet access, iron/ironing board, Irons, Bubble bath and Suites include

full kitchens in room. Central air. Fax, copier, library, pet boarding, parlor games, telephone, Guest Butler's Pantry with microwave, refrigerator, coffee maker, ice machine, beer, wine and snacks on premises. Amusement parks, antiquing, art galleries, beach, bicycling, canoeing/kayaking, fishing, golf, horseback riding, live theater, museums, parks, shopping, sporting events, water sports and wineries nearby.

Location: Waterfront. Small Town.

Publicity: *The Rappahannock Times and Virginia Living Magazine.*

Certificate may be used: Accepts Weekends, Anytime, subject to availability; Anytime, last minute - based on availability.

Washington

Caledonia Farm - 1812 B&B

47 Dearing Rd (Flint Hill)
Washington, VA 22627
(540)675-3693 (800)262-1812
Internet: www.bnb1812.com

Circa 1812. This gracious Federal-style stone house on the National Register is beautifully situated on 115 forever protected acres adjacent to Shenandoah National Park. It was built by a Revolutionary War officer, and his musket is displayed over a mantel. The house, a Virginia Historic Landmark, has been restored with the original Colonial color scheme retained. All rooms have working fireplaces, air  conditioning and provide views of stone-fenced pastures and the Blue Ridge Mountains. The innkeeper is a retired international broadcaster.

Innkeeper(s): Phil Irwin. $140. 2 rooms, 2 with FP, 2 suites, 1 conference room. Breakfast and snacks/refreshments included in rates. Types of meals: Full gourmet bkfst. Beds: D. VCR, reading lamp, refrigerator, snack bar, clock radio, telephone, turn-down service, desk, hot tub/spa and Skyline Drive view in room. TV, fax, copier, spa, bicycles, library, parlor games, fireplace, hay ride and lawn games on premises. Antiquing, fishing, hiking, live theater, parks, shopping, water sports, wineries, caves, stables and battlefields nearby.

Location: Country, mountains.

Publicity: *Country, Country Almanac, Country Living, Blue Ridge Country, Discovery, Washington Post, Baltimore Sun and Pen TV/Cable 15/PBS X3.*

"We've stayed at many, many B&Bs. This is by far the best!"

Certificate may be used: Anytime, subject to availability, except 3-day holiday weekends and all of October.

Fairlea Farm Bed & Breakfast

636 Mt Salem Ave., PO Box 124
Washington, VA 22747-0124
(540)675-3679 Fax:(540)675-1064
Internet: www.fairleafarm.com
E-mail: longyear@shentel.net

Circa 1960. View acres of rolling hills, farmland and the Blue Ridge Mountains from this fieldstone manor house. Rooms are decorated with crocheted canopies and four-poster beds. Potted plants and floral bedcovers add a homey feel. The stone terrace is set up for relaxing with chairs lined along the edge. As a young surveyor, George Washington laid out the boundaries of the historic village of Little Washington, which is just a 5-minute walk from Fairlea Farm, a working sheep and cattle farm.

Innkeeper(s): Susan & Walt Longyear. $195-220. 4 rooms with PB, 1 suite. Breakfast and afternoon tea included in rates. Types of meals: Full gourmet bkfst and early coffee/tea. Beds: QT. Reading lamp, refrigerator, turn-down service and desk in room. Air conditioning. VCR, fax, copier, parlor games, telephone and fireplace on premises. Antiquing, fishing, horseback riding, live theater, vineyards, Shenandoah National Park and Civil War battlefields nearby.

Location: Country, mountains. Village/working farm, 70 miles west of Washington, DC.

Certificate may be used: December-February, Suite only, No Holidays or Saturdays.

White Stone

Flowering Fields B&B

232 Flowering Field
White Stone, VA 22578-9722
(804)435-6238 Fax:(804)435-6238
E-mail: holisticlaw@verizon.net

Circa 1790. Flowering Fields Bed & Breakfast·sits in White Stone near the mouth of the Rappahannock River before it flows into the Chesapeake Bay. This tranquil B&B is hidden away in the waterfront area known as the Northern Neck of Virginia and claims to be "where southern hospitality begins." Families will enjoy the game room with a pool table or watching movies by the fire in the gathering room. Refreshing lemonade is on the welcome table in the large foyer in the summertime. Browse through the library's extensive collection of health, diet and cookbooks as well as paperbacks to read. Formal but inviting and comfortable guest bedrooms include sitting areas. Linger over a relaxing and delicious breakfast accented with Lloyd's famous blue crab crabcakes. Activities are endless in this scenic and central location.

Innkeeper(s): Lloyd Niziol & Susan Moenssens. $95-125. 6 rooms, 2 with PB, 1 suite, 1 conference room. Breakfast, afternoon tea and snacks/refreshments included in rates. Types of meals: Full gourmet bkfst, veg bkfst and early coffee/tea. Beds: KQDT. Reading lamp, ceiling fan, clock radio, some cable, some desks and sitting area in room. Air conditioning. VCR, fax, copier, bicycles, library, parlor games, telephone, fireplace, advance notification for handicap access and first-floor room with private bath on premises. Antiquing, fishing, golf, parks, shopping, water sports, Williamsburg and Excellent bird watching nearby.

Certificate may be used: January, February, March and April, Monday-Sunday. (7 days a week).

Williamsburg

A Williamsburg White House

718 Jamestown Rd
Williamsburg, VA 23185
(757)229-8580 (866)229-8580
Internet: www.awilliamsburgwhitehouse.com
E-mail: info@awilliamsburgwhitehouse.com

Circa 1904. Just four blocks from historic downtown, this spacious century-old Colonial estate graces a picturesque neighborhood. Decorated around an elegant and traditional presidential theme, the common rooms include the JFK library, where a fireside game of chess can be played while sipping sherry in a leather chair, and the Diplomatic Reception Room where afternoon wine and delicious treats are served. Guest bedrooms are considered Presidential Suites with four-poster and canopy feather beds, robes, sitting areas and motif-matching memorabilia. Enjoy a sumptuous full breakfast in the Reagan Dining Room.

Innkeeper(s): Debbie & John Keane. $115-199. 4 rooms with PB, 3 suites. Breakfast, snacks/refreshments and wine included in rates. Types of meals: Full gourmet bkfst and early coffee/tea. Beds: KQ. Cable TV, clock radio, telephone, turn-down service and bathrobes in room. Central air. Fax, library,

parlor games and fireplace on premises. Amusement parks, antiquing, art galleries, bicycling, canoeing/kayaking, fishing, golf, hiking, horseback riding, live theater, museums, parks, shopping, sporting events and wineries nearby.

Location: Historic Williamsburg.

Certificate may be used: Jan. 3-Feb. 28, Sunday-Thursday, excluding holidays, subject to availability.

An American Inn - Williamsburg Manor B&B

600 Richmond Rd
Williamsburg, VA 23185
(757)220-8011 (800)422-8011 Fax:(757)220-0245
Internet: www.williamsburg-manor.com
E-mail: Williamsburg@occassions.hrcoxmail.com

Circa 1927. Built during the reconstruction of Colonial Williamsburg, this Georgian brick Colonial is just three blocks from the historic village. A grand staircase, culinary library, Waverly fabrics, Oriental rugs and antiques are featured. Breakfasts begin with fresh fruits and home-baked breads, followed by a special daily entree. Gourmet regional Virginia dinners also are available.

Innkeeper(s): Laura & Craig Reeves. $159-225. 5 rooms with PB, 1 two-bedroom suite. Breakfast, snacks/refreshments and Full Regional Breakfast prepared by Chef/Caterer owner included in rates. Types of meals: Full gourmet bkfst, veg bkfst, early coffee/tea, gourmet lunch, picnic lunch, afternoon tea and gourmet dinner. Beds: QT. Modem hook-up, data port, cable TV, DVD, reading lamp, CD player, ceiling fan, clock radio, telephone, voice mail, hair dryer, bath amenities, wireless Internet access and iron/ironing board in room. Central air. VCR, fax, copier, spa, child care, parlor games, fireplace, freshly baked cookies and lemonade on premises. Limited handicap access. Amusement parks, antiquing, art galleries, beach, bicycling, canoeing/kayaking, fishing, golf, hiking, horseback riding, live theater, museums, parks, shopping, sporting events, tennis, water sports and wineries nearby.

Location: City. Colonial Williamsburg.

Publicity: *Virginia Gazette, Williamsburg Magazine, Gourmet Magazine, San Francisco Reader and Daily Press.*

"Lovely accommodations - scrumptious breakfast."

Certificate may be used: Midweek Monday-Thursday, subject to availability.

Colonial Gardens

1109 Jamestown Rd
Williamsburg, VA 23185
(757)220-8087 (800)886-9715 Fax:(757)253-1495
Internet: www.colonialgardensbandb.com
E-mail: colonialgardensbandb@verizon.net

Circa 1965. Gracing three landscaped acres in Williamsburg, Virginia, Colonial Gardens Bed & Breakfast offers an Old World European-style opulence and elegance. Escape to the romantic enchantment of this brick Colonial B&B just one mile from Colonial Williamsburg and less than ten minutes from Busch Gardens and Water Country USA. Gather for wine and appetizers in the library where a guest computer is available to use. Browse for a movie from the DVD or video collection. Spacious guest bedrooms and two suites with fireplaces are comfortable and inviting. Savor a gourmet breakfast served on china, crystal and silver with creative and delicious signature entrees. The surrounding area is steeped in historic sites and attractions.

Innkeeper(s): Karen & Ron Watkins. $135-185. 4 rooms with PB, 2 with FP, 2 total suites, including 1 two-bedroom suite. Breakfast, snacks/refreshments, wine and Picnic lunch extra charge included in rates. Types of meals:

Full gourmet bkfst, veg bkfst, early coffee/tea, picnic lunch, hors d'oeuvres, Early evening wine and cheese and fruit. Beds: KQT. Modem hook-up, data port, cable TV, VCR, DVD, reading lamp, stereo, ceiling fan, snack bar, clock radio, telephone, turn-down service, desk, most with fireplace, hair dryer, bathrobes, bath amenities, wireless Internet access, iron/ironing board and 2 suites with fireplace in room. Central air. Fax, bicycles, library, parlor games, gift shop, VCR/DVD library, Guest computer in Library and High speed Internet Wi Fi throughout house on premises. Amusement parks, antiquing, art galleries, bicycling, golf, live theater, museums, parks, shopping, wineries and plantations nearby.

Location: Small town.

Publicity: *Mid Atlantic Country Magazine, Unique Inns & Bed & Breakfasts of Virginia and Travel & Leisure.*

Certificate may be used: Monday-Thursday, exclusive of all holidays, October and December.

Legacy Of Williamsburg Bed & Breakfast

930 Jamestown Rd
Williamsburg, VA 23185-3917
(757)220-0524 (800)962-4722
Internet: www.legacyofwilliamsburgbb.com
E-mail: legacy@tni.net

Circa 1976. Designed to reflect the ambiance of an 18th century tavern inn, the hardwood pine floors, crown molding, brick fireplaces and candlelight are just the first steps in crossing the threshold of time. Play a game of chance in the Tavern Room. Cards, darts or billiards are popular. Read a book by the fire in the library. Three spacious suites feature comfy terry robes, welcome snacks, personal products, fireplaces and soft comforters on queen beds. Some rooms boast feather beds. A hearty, hot breakfast is served by the host, authentically dressed in period attire in the fireside Keeping Room with music from that era playing in the background. Convenient off-street parking is provided and complimentary beverages are always available. Feel more immersed in history by visiting Colonial Williamsburg just five blocks away. Arrive at William and Mary within five minutes.

Innkeeper(s): Joan & Art Ricker. $145-185. 4 rooms with PB, 3 with FP, 3 suites. Breakfast and afternoon tea included in rates. Types of meals: Full gourmet bkfst, veg bkfst and early coffee/tea. Beds: Q. Modem hook-up, cable TV, reading lamp, refrigerator, telephone, fireplace, bathrobes, iron/ironing board and clock in room. Central air. VCR, library and parlor games on premises. Amusement parks, antiquing, art galleries, beach, bicycling, fishing, golf, horseback riding, live theater, museums, parks, shopping, tennis, water sports and wineries nearby.

Location: City.

Publicity: *Pam Lanier Inn of the year 1997.*

Certificate may be used: Sunday-Thursday, January-March, excludes holidays.

Woolwine

Old Spring Farm Bed & Breakfast, Ltd.

7629 Charity Hwy (Hwy 40)
Woolwine, VA 24185
(276)930-3404
Internet: www.oldspringfarm.com

Circa 1883. Distinct traditions linger at this 1883 authentic French Country farm-stay on 25 acres in Blue Ridge Mountains Wine Country just 50 miles south of Roanoke in Woolwine, Virginia. Old Spring Farm Bed & Breakfast is accented with antiques and collectibles. Calamity Jane features a feather bed, balcony with pastoral view and a Jacuzzi. Stay in the rustic and charming Mountaineer or the sophisticated Le Chat with a reading nook and gas-log stove. Le Chanticleer is the honey-

moon suite with a Jacuzzi, gas-log stove, Tempurpedic bed and private deck. For extended stays the Country House Retreat is a full efficiency. Savor a wholesome "full-tummy nice breakfast" served with an artistic, gourmet flair. Afterwards, take a guided walking tour of the farm and visit with the Bengal-Manx kittens, foals, llamas and lambs.

Innkeeper(s): Suzanne V. Pabst. $125-150. 5 rooms with PB, 1 conference room. Types of meals: Full gourmet bkfst, early coffee/tea, picnic lunch and snacks/refreshments. Beds: KQDT. TV, reading lamp, ceiling fan, clock radio, Refrigerator, Coffeemaker, Microwave, Gas log stove in all except Calamity Jane, Second bed for additional fee and Private deck or balcony off all but Mountaineer Room in room. Air conditioning. VCR, telephone, laundry facility and Decks on premises. Limited handicap access. Antiquing, art galleries, canoeing/kayaking, fishing, golf, hiking, museums, shopping, sporting events, wineries, Swimming and Nextel stock car race nearby.

Location: Mountains.

Publicity: *4-Star Best Bed & Breakfast-City Magazine, Washington Post and Gourmet Magazine.*

Certificate may be used: Anytime, subject to availability.

The Mountain Rose B&B Inn

1787 Charity Hwy
Woolwine, VA 24185
(276)930-1057 Fax:(276)930-2165
Internet: www.mountainrose-inn.com
E-mail: info@mountainrose-inn.com

Circa 1901. This historic Victorian inn, once the home of the Mountain Rose Distillery, sits on 100 acres of forested hills with plenty of hiking trails. A trout-stocked stream goes through the property and a swimming pool provides recreation.  Each room has an antique mantled fireplace, which has been converted to gas logs. Guests can relax by the pool or in rocking chairs on one of the six porches. The innkeepers look forward to providing guests with casually elegant hospitality in the Blue Ridge Mountains. The Blue Ridge Parkway, Chateau Morrisette Winery, Mabry Mill, The Reynolds Homestead, Laurel Hill Jeb Stuart Birthplace, Patrick County Courthouse and the Patrick County Historical Museum are located nearby. A three-course breakfast is offered every morning.

Innkeeper(s): Mike & Dora Jane Barwick. $120-150. 5 rooms with PB, 5 with FP. Breakfast, afternoon tea and snacks/refreshments included in rates. Types of meals: Full bkfst and early coffee/tea. Beds: KQT. TV, DVD, reading lamp, clock radio, desk, fireplace, hair dryer, bathrobes, wireless Internet access, iron/ironing board, satellite TV and porch access in room. Central air. VCR, fax, copier, swimming, parlor games, telephone, Trout-stocked creek, Hiking trails and Tennis courts are a mile away on premises. Antiquing, art galleries, fishing, golf, hiking, horseback riding, live theater, parks, shopping, sporting events, tennis, water sports, wineries and Nascar racing nearby.

Location: Mountains.

Publicity: *Enterprise, Bill Mountain Bugle, New York Times, The Parkway Edition, "Best Romantic Getaway" City Magazine and The Martinsville Bulletin.*

Certificate may be used: Year-round, Sunday-Thursday; Weekends, December-March, subject to availability.

Washington

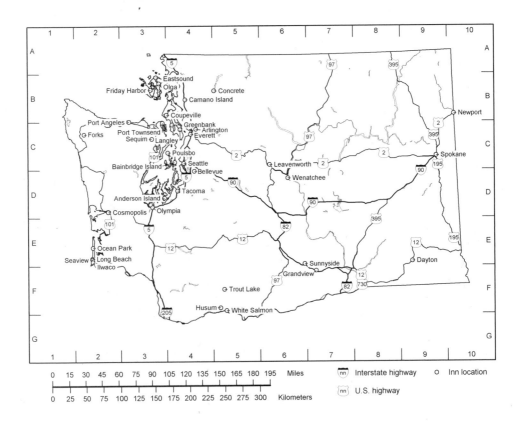

Tell the innkeeper that you have an iLoveInns free-night certificate when you make your reservation.

Anderson Island

The Inn at Burg's Landing

8808 Villa Beach Rd
Anderson Island, WA 98303-9785
(253)884-9185
Internet: www.burgslandingbb.com
E-mail: innatburgslanding@excite.com

Circa 1987. A short ferry trip from Steilacoom and Tacoma, this log homestead boasts beautiful views of Mt. Rainier, Puget Sound and the Cascade Mountains. The master bedroom features a skylight and a private whirlpool bath. After a full breakfast, guests can spend the day at the inn's private beach. Golf, hiking and freshwater lakes are nearby, and the area has many seasonal activities, including Fourth of July fireworks, the Anderson Island fair and parade in September.

Innkeeper(s): Ken & Annie Burg. $90-140. 4 rooms, 2 with PB, 1 with WP. Breakfast included in rates. Types of meals: Full bkfst, veg bkfst and early coffee/tea. Beds: QT. Cable TV, VCR, DVD, reading lamp, clock radio and hair dryer in room. Parlor games, telephone and fireplace on premises. Amusement parks, antiquing, art galleries, beach, bicycling, downhill skiing, fishing, golf, hiking, live theater, museums, parks, shopping, sporting events, tennis, Romantic dining, Bike/walking trail along the waterfront, Catch a Rainiers game at Cheney Stadium, Point Defiance Zoo & Aquarium and Gig Harbor nearby.

Location: Waterfront. Puget Sound.

Publicity: *Sunset, Tacoma News Tribune, Portland Oregonian and Seattle Times.*

Certificate may be used: Anytime, subject to availability.

Bainbridge Island

Holly Lane Gardens

9432 Holly Farm Ln NE
Bainbridge Island, WA 98110-1637
(206)842-8959
Internet: www.hollylanegardens.com
E-mail: dusb2@aol.com

Holly Lane Gardens on Bainbridge Island in Washington offers quiet solitude and natural beauty amid a flower farm with walking paths and gardens. Relax in the libraries, gather by the big stone fireplace or play the grand piano. Soak in the hot tub after an evening telling stories around a fire pit. Stay in the first-floor suite, second-floor guest bedroom or private cottage in a woodland setting. All boast garden and Olympic Mountain views. Appetites are quickly aroused and easily satisfied with a bountiful breakfast that features delicious homemade foods. There is much to see and experience in the scenic Northwest. Take the ferry to Seattle to experience the city sites and attractions.

Innkeeper(s): Ms. Dusabek. Call for rates. Call inn for details.

Certificate may be used: October-April, last minute, subject to availabilty.

Bellevue

Columns on the Park

1844 140th Avenue Southeast
Bellevue, WA 98005
(206)622-6565 Fax:(425)644-6969
Internet: www.columnsonthepark.com
E-mail: ColumnsOnThePark@aol.com

Circa 1955. Embellished with an Italian sensibility, this deluxe bed and breakfast is romantic for an intimate wedding and wonderfully suited for business travel. Situated in a quiet neighborhood near the college, Sea-Tac International Airport is just 20 minutes away. Inviting guest bedrooms boast original artwork, handcrafted and antique furnishings, fresh flowers, luxury and vintage linens, down comforters and pillows, Turkish terry spa robes and entertainment centers. Stay in The May 1845 Suite named for the date that Elizabeth Barrett met Robert Browning. It opens up onto a back terrace with checked marble and limestone. The April 1847 Suite reflects when the Brownings moved to Florence and features access to the lower garden and patio. A vegetarian breakfast is made daily with local organic ingredients and products when possible. Soak in the spa under the stars.

Innkeeper(s): Heidi Behrens-Benedict. $115-125. 2 rooms, 1 conference room. Breakfast included in rates. Types of meals: Full gourmet bkfst, veg bkfst and early coffee/tea. Beds: QD. DVD, reading lamp, CD player, refrigerator, hot tub/spa, hair dryer, bathrobes and alarm clock in room. TV, VCR, fax, copier, spa, library, parlor games, telephone, fireplace, laundry facility and garden seating on premises. Limited handicap access. Antiquing, art galleries, beach, bicycling, canoeing/kayaking, fishing, golf, hiking, live theater, museums, parks, shopping, sporting events, tennis, water sports, wineries, 45 minutes to cross country and downhill skiing, Bellevue Golf Club, The Golf Club at Newcastle, Glendale Country Club, Tam O'Shanter Golf Club, kayaking at Enatai Beach, rowing at Sammamish Rowing, Redmond Velodrome, St. Michele Winery, Columbia Winery and Washington Dinner Train nearby.

Location: City.

Certificate may be used: November-March, Tuesday, Wednesday, Thursday.

Camano Island

The Inn at Barnum Point

464 S Barnum Rd
Camano Island, WA 98282-8578
(360)387-2256 (800)910-2256
Internet: www.innatbarnumpoint.com
E-mail: barnum@camano.net

Circa 1991. The Inn at Barnum Point is a Cape Cod-style B&B located on the bay on Camano Island, Washington. Enjoy listening to the water lap at the shoreline, watching deer in the orchard and sneaking a kiss under an heirloom apple tree. The newest accommodation is the 900-square-foot Shorebird Room with deck, fireplace and soaking tub overlooking Port Susan Bay and the Cascade Mountains.

Innkeeper(s): Carolin Barnum Dilorenzo. $125-225. 3 rooms with PB, 3 with FP. Breakfast included in rates. Types of meals: Full gourmet bkfst and early coffee/tea. Beds: Q. TV, VCR, reading lamp, refrigerator, clock radio and telephone in room. Fax, copier, parlor games and fireplace on premises. Antiquing, golf, live theater, parks, shopping and water sports nearby.

Location: Waterfront.

Certificate may be used: Anytime, Subject to availability.

Eastsound

Turtleback Farm Inn

1981 Crow Valley Rd
Eastsound, WA 98245
(360)376-4914 (800)376-4914 Fax:(360)376-5329
Internet: www.turtlebackinn.com
E-mail: info@turtlebackinn.com

Circa 1895. Guests will delight in the beautiful views afforded from this farmhouse and the newly constructed Orchard House, which overlooks 80 acres of forest and farmland, duck ponds and Mt. Constitution to the east. Rooms feature antique furnishings and many boast views of the farm, orchard or sheep pasture.

Beds are covered with wool comforters made from sheep raised on the property. Bon Appetit highlighted some of the breakfast recipes served at Turtleback; a breakfast here is a memorable affair. Tables set with bone china, silver and fresh linens make way for a delightful mix of fruits, juice, award-winning granola, homemade breads and specialty entrees. Evening guests can settle down with a game or a book in the fire-lit parlor as they enjoy sherry, tea or hot chocolate.

Innkeeper(s): William & Susan C. Fletcher. $100-245. 11 rooms with PB, 4 with FP. Breakfast included in rates. Types of meals: Full bkfst, early coffee/tea and picnic lunch. Beds: KQD. Reading lamp and clock radio in room. Library, parlor games, telephone, fireplace and refrigerator with self-serve beverage bar in dining room on premises. Handicap access. Fishing, live theater, parks, shopping and water sports nearby.

Location: Country.

Publicity: *Los Angeles Times, USA Today, Travel & Leisure, Contra Costa Sun, Seattle Times, Northwest Living, Sunset, Food & Wine, Gourmet, Northwest Travel, New York Times and Alaska Air.*

"A peaceful haven for soothing the soul."

Certificate may be used: November-April, Sunday through Thursday, subject to availability. Holidays and special event dates are excluded.

Friday Harbor

Friday's Historical Inn

PO Box 2023, 35 First St
Friday Harbor, WA 98250
(360)378-5848 (800)352-2632 Fax:(360)378-2881
Internet: www.friday-harbor.com
E-mail: stay@friday-harbor.com

Circa 1891. A visit to San Juan Island should include a stay at this restored turn-of-the-century inn that was originally the San Juan Island Hotel. Gracious service and knowledgeable advice are abundantly shared to ensure a wonderful experience. Choose a romantic guest bedroom or suite featuring a two-person Jacuzzi tub, luxuriously appointed bed and fireplace. A homemade continental breakfast is served daily. Bicycles are available for exploring the island. Lime Kiln Whale Watch Park is perfect for spotting orcas, or ask about taking a charter. Kayaking is just one more of the area's many outdoor adventures.

Innkeeper(s): Laura & Adam Saccio. $55-265. 15 rooms. Breakfast and afternoon tea included in rates. Types of meals: Cont plus and snacks/refreshments. Beds: KQDT. Data port, cable TV, VCR, reading lamp, refrigerator, ceiling fan, snack bar, clock radio, coffeemaker, desk, hot tub/spa and fireplace in room. Fax, spa, bicycles, parlor games and fireplace on premises. Handicap access. Antiquing, art galleries, beach, bicycling, canoeing/kayak-

ing, fishing, golf, hiking, horseback riding, live theater, museums, parks, shopping, tennis and wineries nearby.

Location: Ocean community.

Certificate may be used: October-March, Sunday-Thursday, subject to availability.

States Inn

2687 West Valley Rd
Friday Harbor, WA 98250-8164
(360)378-6240 (866)602-2737 Fax:(360)378-6241
Internet: www.statesinn.com
E-mail: ranch@statesinn.com

Circa 1910. This sprawling ranch home has ten guest rooms, each named and themed for a particular state. The Arizona and New Mexico rooms, often booked by families or couples traveling together, can be combined to create a private suite with two bedrooms, a bathroom and a sitting area. The oldest part of the house was built as a country school and later used as a dance hall, before it was relocated to its current 60-acre spread. Baked French toast, accompanied by fresh fruit topped with yogurt sauce and homemade muffins are typical breakfast fare.

Innkeeper(s): Richard Foote & Angel Michaels. $75-225. 10 rooms, 8 with PB, 1 with FP, 1 two-bedroom suite, 1 conference room. Breakfast included in rates. Types of meals: Full gourmet bkfst, veg bkfst, early coffee/tea, snacks/refreshments and dinner. Beds: KQDT. Reading lamp, clock radio, some with fireplace and wireless Internet access in room. Fax, stable, library, parlor games, telephone, working ranch with livestock and trailriding on premises. Handicap access. Antiquing, art galleries, beach, bicycling, canoeing/kayaking, fishing, golf, hiking, horseback riding, live theater, museums, parks, shopping, tennis, water sports, wineries, sea kayaking, whale watching and birding nearby.

Location: Country, ocean community. Pastoral valley with stream running through property.

Publicity: *Glamour, Conde Naste, USA Today and CITI TV Vancouver.*

Certificate may be used: Oct. 1-April 15, anytime based on availability.

Wharfside Bed & Breakfast

204 Front Street/Port of Friday Harbor
Friday Harbor, WA 98250
(360)378-5661
Internet:
www.fridayharborlodging.com/slowseason/index.html
E-mail: wharfside@rockisland.com

Circa 1973. Stay aboard the West Coast's original cruising B&B at the Port of Friday Harbor in Washington. Wharfside Bed & Breakfast on the Slow Season is an elegantly restored, 60-foot traditional sailing vessel that has been nationally recognized. Experience overnight cruising accommodations in the San Juan Islands with two spacious and private staterooms. Enjoy the fresh air while savoring breakfast on deck or inside the sky-lit salon. It is an easy walk to shops and the ferry. German, Italian or seafood dinners are available. Ask about seasonal rates and special packages.

Innkeeper(s): Ilse Konnen. $159-289. 1 room with PB. Breakfast included in rates. Types of meals: Full gourmet bkfst, snacks/refreshments, dinner and German and Italian cuisine. Beds: QT. TV, DVD, reading lamp, stereo, refrigerator, clock radio, hair dryer, wireless Internet access and iron/ironing board in room. Telephone on premises. Antiquing, art galleries, beach, bicycling, canoeing/kayaking, fishing, hiking, museums, shopping, water sports, wineries and Whale watching nearby.

Location: Waterfront.

Certificate may be used: October-March, Monday-Friday.

Grandview

Cozy Rose Inn

1220 Forsell Rd
Grandview, WA 98930
(509)882-4669 (800)575-8381 Fax:(509)882-4234
Internet: www.cozyroseinn.com
E-mail: stay@cozyroseinn.com

Circa 1908. Enjoying Washington's wine country from the privacy of your own luxurious suite is only part of the unforgettable experience that awaits at this delightful country inn, which combines a Cape Cod and farmhouse-style design with French Country decor. Walk through family vineyards and orchards to be renewed in a relaxing six-acre setting. Each romantic, villa-style suite includes a private bath, fireplace, stereo, refrigerator, microwave and a separate entrance with a private deck overlooking vineyards and orchards. Some also include a Jacuzzi. The Suite Surrender boasts an incredible view and includes Italian furniture, Jacuzzi tub, walk-in tiled shower and flat screen satellite TV/DVD/VCR. Feel truly pampered by a full candlelight breakfast that may include huckleberry pancakes, delivered to each suite. After a day of sightseeing, biking or golfing, soak in the Under The Stars hot tub. Make friends with the two pet llamas, Chocolate and Stubborn.

Innkeeper(s): Mark & Jennie Jackson. $99-229. 5 rooms, 5 with FP, 5 suites. Breakfast included in rates. Types of meals: Country bkfst, veg bkfst and gourmet dinner. Beds: K. Cable TV, reading lamp, stereo, refrigerator, ceiling fan, clock radio, telephone, coffeemaker, desk, hot tub/spa, wireless Internet access, VCR/DVD only in Suite Surrender, individual entrance with private deck, high speed wireless Internet access, music, microwave, coffee and teas in room. Central air. Fax, bicycles, laundry facility, satellite TV, Under the Stars hot tub and dinners by prior arrangement on premises. Antiquing, golf, hiking, museums, parks, jogging, walking, 18-hole golf course, microbreweries, 40 wineries and vineyards nearby.

Location: Country.

Publicity: *Northwest's Best Places to Kiss and Romantic America.*

Certificate may be used: November-February, Sunday-Thursday nights. No holidays or special event weekends. Rack rate only and consecutive nights only. Upgrage upon check in only if available.

Greenbank

Guest House Log Cottages

24371-SR 525, Whidbey Island
Greenbank, WA 98253
(360)678-3115 (800)997-3115
Internet: www.guesthouselogcottages.com
E-mail: stay@guesthouselogcottages.com

Circa 1925. These storybook cottages and log home are nestled within a peaceful forest on 25 acres. The log cabin features stained-glass and criss-cross paned windows that give it the feel of a gingerbread house. Four of the cottages are log construction. Ask for the Lodge and enjoy a private setting with a pond just beyond the deck. Inside are two Jacuzzi tubs, a stone fireplace, king bed, antiques and a luxurious atmosphere.

Innkeeper(s): Don & Mary Jane Creger. $130-325. 6 cottages with PB, 6 with HT. Breakfast included in rates. Types of meals: Full bkfst and early coffee/tea. Beds: KQ. TV, VCR, DVD, reading lamp, stereo, refrigerator, ceiling

fan, clock radio, telephone, turn-down service, desk, hot tub/spa, fireplace, hair dryer, bath amenities, iron/ironing board, kitchen and Jacuzzi in room. Air conditioning. Fax, copier, spa, swimming, swimming pool, hot tub and 25 beautiful forested acres on premises. Limited handicap access. Antiquing, art galleries, beach, bicycling, canoeing/kayaking, fishing, golf, hiking, horseback riding, live theater, museums, parks, shopping, tennis, water sports and wineries nearby.

Location: Mountains, ocean community. Island - wooded.

Publicity: *Los Angeles Times, Woman's Day, Sunset, Country Inns and Bride's.*

"The wonderful thing is to be by yourselves and rediscover what's important."

Certificate may be used: Nov. 1-March 15, Monday-Thursday only, either Farm Guest or Carriage House Cottages.

Langley

Saratoga Inn

201 Cascade Ave
Langley, WA 98260
(360)221-5801 (800)698-2910 Fax:(360)221-5804
Internet: www.saratogainnwhidbeyisland.com
E-mail: saratogainn@foursisters.com

Circa 1994. This romantic, island inn is located away from the hustle and bustle of Seattle. To reach the inn, guests hop aboard a ferry and take a 20-minute journey from the city to quiet Whidbey Island. The inn offers 15 elegantly appointed guest rooms, each with a fireplace. Each room also boasts a water view. Guests enjoy a full breakfast and afternoon with a variety of goodies. Guests can spend the day exploring the island, or hop aboard the ferry to visit the sites of Seattle. There is a $20 fee for an additional guest in room, except for children less than 5 years old. Saratoga Inn is a Four Sisters Inn.

Innkeeper(s): Tomoko Speaks. $115-275. 16 rooms, 15 with PB, 15 with FP. Breakfast, afternoon tea, snacks/refreshments and hors d'oeuvres included in rates. Types of meals: Full gourmet bkfst and early coffee/tea. Beds: KQD. Modem hook-up, data port, cable TV, VCR, reading lamp, CD player, clock radio, telephone, turn-down service, desk, voice mail, fireplace, hair dryer, bathrobes, bath amenities, iron/ironing board, signature breakfast, afternoon tea and hors d'oeuvres, morning newspaper delivery, complimentary sodas and home-baked cookies in room. Central air. Fax, bicycles and parlor games on premises. Handicap access. Antiquing, art galleries, beach, bicycling, canoeing/kayaking, fishing, golf, hiking, horseback riding, live theater, museums, parks, shopping, water sports and wineries nearby.

Location: Waterfront.

Certificate may be used: Sunday – Thursday, December through February, based on promotional discount availability and excludes special event periods, holidays and certain room types. First night must be at full rack rate to receive second night free.

Leavenworth

Autumn Pond Bed & Breakfast

10388 Titus Rd
Leavenworth, WA 98826-9509
(509)548-4482 (800)222-9661
Internet: www.autumnpond.com
E-mail: info@autumnpond.com

Circa 1992. This modern ranch-style inn is set at the base of the Cascade Mountains and offers stunning views, which one can enjoy from the outdoor hot tub. The interior is welcoming, with bright, country prints on the beds and country furnishings. Exposed beams add a rustic touch to the dining area and living room. Guests can feed the ducks at the pond or fish for trout. After a homemade breakfast, head into Leavenworth and explore the shops and sites of this historic Bavarian town.

Innkeeper(s): John & Jennifer Lorenz. $99-119. 6 rooms with PB. Breakfast included in rates. Types of meals: Full bkfst and early coffee/tea. Beds: Q. Reading lamp and clock radio in room. Air conditioning. Telephone, fireplace and pond on premises. Antiquing, cross-country skiing, downhill skiing, fishing, golf, live theater, parks, shopping, water sports, whitewater rafting, cross country skiing, hiking and mountain biking nearby.

Location: Mountains.

Certificate may be used: March 1 to May 31, Sunday-Thursday only.

Ocean Park

Charles Nelson Guest House

26205 Sandridge Road
Ocean Park, WA 98640
(360)665-3016 (888)862-9756 Fax:(360)665-5962
Internet: www.charlesnelsonbandb.com
E-mail: cnbandb@charlesnelsonbandb.com

Circa 1928. Originally purchased from a Sears & Roebuck catalog, this Dutch Colonial home that overlooks Willapa Bay and Long Island's wildlife refuge has been impressively restored. Relax by firelight in the living room on the lambskin rug, or enjoy the view from the sunroom. Guest bedrooms are furnished with a blend of antiques and period furnishings. Homemade muffins, scones or sweet rolls with honey butter and jam accompany sausage and a double-cheese-and-bacon quiche for a typical breakfast in the dining room. Bird watch from the back deck, or gaze at the goldfish and koi in the pond. A nap on a nearby hammock is an inviting respite.

Innkeeper(s): Curt and Ginger Bish. $160-180. 3 rooms with PB. Breakfast and snacks/refreshments included in rates. Types of meals: Full gourmet bkfst, veg bkfst and early coffee/tea. Beds: KQT. Cable TV, DVD, reading lamp, CD player, clock radio, turn-down service, hair dryer, bathrobes and bath amenities in room. VCR, fax, copier, library, parlor games, telephone, fireplace and laundry facility on premises. Antiquing, art galleries, beach, bicycling, canoeing/kayaking, fishing, golf, hiking, horseback riding, museums, parks and shopping nearby.

Location: Ocean community.

Publicity: *Seattle Home and Lifestyles.*

Certificate may be used: Anytime, November-March, subject to availability.

Olympia

Swantown Inn Bed & Breakfast

1431 11th Ave SE
Olympia, WA 98501-2411
(360)753-9123 (877)753-9123 Fax:(360)252-6423
Internet: www.swantowninn.com
E-mail: yourhosts@swantowninn.com

Circa 1887. Explore the Puget Sound area from this historical Queen Anne/Eastlake Victorian mansion situated in a peaceful neighborhood. Listed in the state and city registers, this local landmark features distinctive woodwork inside and out. Common rooms offer pleasurable pursuits that include gameboards, piano or television by a warm fire. A writing desk, fax and phone line provides a workspace for computer use. Relax in elegantly appointed guest bedrooms. The spacious Astoria Room boasts a four-poster bed, sitting area with Capitol view and a two-person Jacuzzi tub. Ask about an accompanying Relaxation Package. A continental breakfast can be brought to the door, or linger over a splendid multi-course meal in the grand dining room. Organic vegetable and flower gardens span a half acre with an orchard and gazebo.

Innkeeper(s): Nathan and Casey Allan. $99-179. 4 rooms with PB, 1 with WP. Breakfast included in rates. Types of meals: Full gourmet bkfst, veg bkfst and early coffee/tea. Beds: KQT. Reading lamp, CD player, clock radio, desk, some with hot tub/spa, hair dryer, bathrobes, bath amenities and wireless Internet access in room. TV, VCR, fax, copier, parlor games, telephone, fireplace, gift shop, sumptuous gourmet breakfast, organic gardens and orchard, gazebo and piano on premises. Antiquing, art galleries, beach, bicycling, canoeing/kayaking, fishing, golf, hiking, live theater, museums, parks, shopping, tennis, wineries, Washington State Capitol Campus, Olympia Farmer's Market and Wolf Haven International nearby.

Location: City, ocean community. Swantown Inn is located in Washington's capital city, Olympia, a waterfront community tucked into a valley at the foot of South Puget Sound.

Publicity: *The Olympian, Lonely Planet, Off the Beaten Path - Washington, The Rough Guide and Absolutely Every Bed & Breakfast in Washington.*

Certificate may be used: Sunday through Thursday nights, excludes June through September and holiday weekends.

Port Angeles

Five SeaSuns Bed & Breakfast

1006 S Lincoln St
Port Angeles, WA 98362-7826
(360)452-8248 (800)708-0777 Fax:(360)417-0465
Internet: www.seasuns.com
E-mail: info@seasuns.com

Circa 1926. Take a respite from the rush of today at this restored, historic home that reflects the 1920s era of sophistication with a sense of romance and refinement. Guest bedrooms depict the seasons of the year and are furnished with period antiques. Pleasing amenities include whirlpool or soaking tubs, balconies and water or mountain views. Artfully presented gourmet breakfasts are served by candlelight with fine china and silver. Relax on the porch or wander the picturesque gardens that highlight the estate-like grounds. Explore nearby Olympic National Park and the Ediz Hook Coast Guard Station. The Underground History Walk is ten blocks. Visit the Makah Indian Museum 75 miles away.

Innkeeper(s): Jan & Bob Harbick. $95-150. 5 rooms with PB, 1 suite, 1 cottage. Breakfast, afternoon tea and snacks/refreshments included in rates. Types of meals: Full bkfst, veg bkfst and early coffee/tea. Beds: QD. Reading lamp and turn-down service in room. TV, VCR, fax, parlor games, telephone and fireplace on premises. Antiquing, art galleries, beach, bicycling, canoeing/kayaking, cross-country skiing, fishing, hiking, live theater, museums, parks, shopping and wineries nearby.

Location: City, ocean community.

Publicity: *Arrington B&B Journal "Best Breakfast" award for 2003 and "Best Garden" for 2004.*

Certificate may be used: Anytime, November-April, subject to availability except holiday weekends.

Inn at Rooster Hill

112 Reservoir Road
Port Angeles, WA 98383
(360)452-4933 (877)221-0837 Fax:(360)457-1839
Internet: www.innatroosterhill.com
E-mail: info@innatroosterhill.com

Circa 1993. Inn at Rooster Hill was built as a bed and breakfast on more thsn two wooded acres with a pond in Port Angeles, Washington. The four-story French Country B&B offers a relaxing and inviting place to stay in the Pacific

Northwest. Soak in the outdoor Jacuzzi after a workout in the exercise room. Quiet guest bedrooms and suites meet a variety of needs with amenities that include high-quality bedding, DVD/CD players, beverages and gourmet popcorn. The romantic Elizabeth Suite also features a whirlpool tub. Breakfast can be savored in the dining room, delivered in-room or a tray taken onto the porch. Ask about customized murder mysteries. Ride the ferry to Victoria, British Columbia, hike Olympic National Park and tour local lavender farms.

Innkeeper(s): Layne and Peggy Frehner. $95-175. 5 rooms with PB, 2 with WP. Breakfast, snacks/refreshments and In-room coffee/tea and bottled water along with gourmet popcorn included in rates. Types of meals: Country bkfst, early coffee/tea, room service and Will accommodate diabetic and vegetarian needs. Inn-style seating open from 8:30-9:00 a.m. Breakfast available to go by request. Beds: KQD. Cable TV, DVD, reading lamp, CD player, refrigerator, ceiling fan, snack bar, clock radio, coffeemaker, desk, hair dryer, bath amenities, wireless Internet access and Elizabeth suite has a whirlpool tub in room. VCR, fax, copier, spa, library, parlor games, telephone, fireplace, workout room with bow flex/treadmill/healthrider, office facilities fax/email/copies available and great place to take a nice long walk on premises. Antiquing, art galleries, beach, bicycling, canoeing/kayaking, cross-country skiing, fishing, golf, hiking, horseback riding, live theater, museums, parks, shopping, water sports, wineries, ferry to Victoria, B.C., Hoh National Rain Forest and Lavender Festival in July nearby.

Location: Country, mountains, ocean community, waterfront. Sequim, 15 miles.

Certificate may be used: Anytime, November-March, subject to availability. September-April Sunday-Thursday, Anytime, subject to availability.

Tudor Inn

1108 S Oak St
Port Angeles, WA 98362-7745
(360)452-3138
Internet: www.tudorinn.com
E-mail: info@tudorinn.com

This English Tudor inn has been tastefully restored to display its original woodwork and fir stairway. Guests enjoy stone fireplaces in the living room and study. A terraced flower garden with 100-foot oak trees graces the property.

Innkeeper(s): Betsy Schultz. $115-145. 5 rooms with PB, 1 with FP. Breakfast and afternoon tea included in rates. Types of meals: Full bkfst. Beds: KQT. TV, VCR, library, parlor games, telephone, fireplace and English gardens on premises. Antiquing, cross-country skiing, downhill skiing, fishing, live theater, parks, shopping, water sports and scenic flights nearby.

Location: City, mountains.

Publicity: *Seattle Times, Oregonian, Los Angeles Times and Olympic Magazine.*

"Delicious company and delicious food. Best in hospitality and warmth. Beautiful gardens!"

Certificate may be used: Sunday through Thursday nights from October 16 to May 15. Friday-Saturday nights 24-hour last minute. Subject to availability.

Port Townsend

Ann Starrett Mansion

744 Clay St
Port Townsend, WA 98368-5808
(888)385-3205
Internet: www.starrettmansion.com
E-mail: edel@starrettmansion.com

Circa 1889. George Starrett came from Maine to Port Townsend and became the major residential builder. By 1889, he had con-

structed one house a week, totaling more than 350 houses. The Smithsonian believes the Ann Starrett's elaborate free-hung spiral staircase is the only one of its type in the United States. A frescoed dome atop the octagonal tower depicts four seasons and four virtues. On the first day of each season, the sun causes a ruby red light to point toward the appropriate painting. The mansion won a "Great American Home Award" from the National Trust for Historic Preservation.

Innkeeper(s): Edel Sokol. $110-185. 11 rooms with PB, 2 with FP, 2 suites, 2 cottages, 2 conference rooms. Breakfast included in rates. Types of meals: Cont. Beds: KQDT. Cable TV, reading lamp, refrigerator, clock radio, telephone and desk in room. Fax and fireplace on premises. Antiquing, cross-country skiing, fishing, live theater, parks, shopping and whale watching nearby.

Location: Seaport Village.

Publicity: *Peninsula, New York Times, Vancouver Sun, San Francisco Examiner, London Times, Colonial Homes, Elle, Leader, Japanese Travel, National Geographic Traveler, Victorian, Historic American Trails, Sunset Magazine, PBS and Day Boy Night Girl.*

"Staying here was like a dream come true."

Certificate may be used: Nov. 1-March 30, Sunday through Thursday, must mention certificate at time of reservation.

Commanders Beach House

400 Hudson St
Port Townsend, WA 98368-5632
(360)385-1778 (888)385-1778
Internet: www.commandersbeachhouse.com
E-mail: stay@commandersbeachhouse.com

Circa 1934. Commander's Beach House is the only bed and breakfast in Victorian Port Townsend, Washington boasting 2,000 feet of unspoiled Admiralty Inlet beach. This historic Colonial Revival is located on 200 acres at Point Hudson Marina. Its rich maritime heritage and relaxed nautical flair create a pleasant ambiance. Sit by the fire in the living room or on the sunny, covered veranda. Select one of the spacious and cheery guest bedrooms or suites at this seaside retreat and be lulled asleep by the waves. A gourmet breakfast with seasonal cuisine is served in the setting desired. A sample menu may include fresh peaches and blackberries with spearmint sauce, seafood soufflé with rosemary potatoes, blackberry tart and peach/ mango juice, coffee and tea. Individual tables offer scenic views overlooking Point Wilson Lighthouse, Mount Baker, the ferries and Whidbey Island.

Innkeeper(s): Gail & Jim Oldroyd. $99-200. 4 rooms, 3 with PB, 1 with FP. Breakfast, afternoon tea and wine included in rates. Types of meals: Full gourmet bkfst and veg bkfst. Beds: Q. Reading lamp, clock radio, some with fireplace, hair dryer, bathrobes, bath amenities, iron/ironing board and feather beds in room. Swimming, library, parlor games, telephone, beach chairs and blankets on premises. Antiquing, art galleries, beach, bicycling, canoeing/kayaking, fishing, golf, hiking, live theater, museums, parks, shopping, tennis, water sports, wineries, whale watching and sailboat charters nearby.

Location: Ocean community, waterfront.

Publicity: *We have received high praise in the Vancouver, B.C. Sun's travel section and as well as the Olympian in Olympia Wa. and the Kitsap Penninsula Sun in Kitsap Co. Wa.*

Certificate may be used: Nov. 1-April 30, Sunday-Thursday, subject to availabilty.

The English Inn

718 F St
Port Townsend, WA 98368-5211
(360)385-5302 (800)254-5302
Internet: www.English-Inn.com
E-mail: stay@english-inn.com

Circa 1885. Have a fabulous time while enjoying the feel of this truly unique yet traditional English bed and breakfast. The stunning 1885 Italianate Victorian home is filled with gorgeous antiques and historic British memorabilia. Be greeted by a warm

and welcoming ambiance. Relax by the fire in the cozy parlor or watch the sunset from the garden gazebo. Delightful guest bedrooms provide comfortable beds, sitting areas, private baths and views of the Olympic Mountains or the colorful gardens. The inn's gracious hosts offer wonderful food and an unforgettable experience. The central location is convenient to all the local sites and activities.

Innkeeper(s): Martin & Jennifer MacGillonie. $120-135. 4 rooms with PB. Breakfast included in rates. Types of meals: Full gourmet bkfst, veg bkfst, early coffee/tea and afternoon tea. Beds: Q. Reading lamp and desk in room. Parlor games and fireplace on premises. Antiquing, art galleries, beach, bicycling, canoeing/kayaking, fishing, golf, hiking, live theater, museums, parks, shopping, water sports and wineries nearby.

Location: Victorian seaport.

Certificate may be used: Jan. 1-May 31 and Nov. 1-Dec. 31, Sunday-Thursday.

Seattle

Inn at Harbor Steps

1221 First Ave
Seattle, WA 98101
(206)748-0973 (888)728-8910 Fax:(206)748-0533
Internet: www.innatharborsteps.com
E-mail: innatharborsteps@foursisters.com

Circa 1997. This inn is located in the heart of downtown Seattle, within walking distance of antique shops, restaurants, Pike Place Market, boutiques and the Seattle Art Museum. The romantic guest rooms include king-size beds, sitting areas and fireplaces. In-room amenities include refrigerators, data ports and voice mail. The inn has a media room, business center and fitness room. Guest can borrow bicycles. In addition to all these modern amenities, guests are pampered with a gourmet breakfast and afternoon tea. There is a $20 fee for an additional guest in room, except for children less than 5 years old. The inn, one of the Four Sisters Inns, is located at the base of a luxury residential high-rise.

Innkeeper(s): Gregory Crick. $165-235. 28 rooms with PB, 20 with FP, 3 conference rooms. Breakfast, afternoon tea and snacks/refreshments included in rates. Types of meals: Full gourmet bkfst and hors d'oeuvres. Beds: KQ. Modem hook-up, data port, cable TV, VCR, DVD, reading lamp, stereo, refrigerator, ceiling fan, snack bar, clock radio, telephone, coffeemaker, turn-down service, desk, some with hot tub/spa, voice mail, hair dryer, bathrobes, bath amenities, iron/ironing board, European balcony and sitting area in room. Central air. Fax, spa, swimming, sauna, bicycles, library, parlor games, fireplace, gym, lap pool, sauna, state of the art media room and private parking on premises. Handicap access. Amusement parks, antiquing, art galleries, bicycling, canoeing/kayaking, fishing, golf, hiking, live theater, museums, parks, shopping and sporting events nearby.

Location: City.

Publicity: *Coastal Living, Travel and Leisure, NY Times and Sunset.*

Certificate may be used: Sunday – Thursday, December through February, based on promotional discount availability and excludes special event periods, holidays and certain room types. First night must be at full rack rate to receive second night free.

Seaview

Shelburne Inn

4415 Pacific Way, PO Box 250
Seaview, WA 98644
(360)642-2442 (800)INN-1896 Fax:(360)642-8904
Internet: www.theshelburneinn.com
E-mail: innkeeper@theshelburneinn.com

Circa 1896. The Shelburne is known as the oldest continuously operating hotel in the state of Washington, and it is listed in the National Register. The front desk at the hotel is a former church altar. Art nouveau stained-glass windows rescued from a church torn down in Morecambe, England, now shed light and color on the dining room.

The guest rooms are appointed in antiques. Just a 10-minute walk from the ocean, the inn is situated on the Long Beach Peninsula, a 28-mile stretch of seacoast that includes bird sanctuaries and lighthouses. The inn offers a full gourmet breakfast.

Innkeeper(s): David Campiche & Laurie Anderson. $135-279. 15 rooms with PB, 2 suites, 1 conference room. Breakfast included in rates. Types of meals: Full gourmet bkfst, lunch, gourmet dinner and room service. Restaurant on premises. Beds: QD. Fax and copier on premises. Handicap access. Antiquing and fishing nearby.

Publicity: *Better Homes & Gardens, Bon Appetit, Conde Nast Traveler, Esquire, Gourmet, Food & Wine and Travel & Leisure.*

"Fabulous food. Homey but elegant atmosphere. Hospitable service, like being a guest in an elegant home."

Certificate may be used: Midweek, October through May, excluding holidays.

Sequim

Lost Mountain Lodge

303 Sunny View Drive
Sequim, WA 98382-7283
(360)683-2431 (888)683-2431 Fax:(360)683-2996
Internet: www.lostmountainlodge.com
E-mail: getaway@lostmountainlodge.com

Circa 1993. Indulge in an idyllic escape or romantic interlude at this award-winning getaway on six secluded acres surrounded by the Olympic Peninsula and snow-capped mountains. Enjoy the classic Northwest-style lodge or the Craftsman Bungalow farm house and private cottages. Soak in the Sundance hydrotherapy spa on the expansive deck overlooking three huge ponds and a rock waterfall. Relax on a covered porch, garden patio, gazebo, swing or hammock. A 24-hour beverage center offers refreshments whenever desired. Watch a film from the extensive library. Huge guest suites are tasteful and refined with line-dried and hand-pressed high-thread-count linens on King-size beds topped with down comforters covered by European duvets. All accommodations feature fireplaces and hydro spas. Explore the scenic area after a full breakfast. Ask about distinctively designed packages.

Innkeeper(s): Dwight & Lisa Hostvedt. $175-350. 5 rooms with PB, 5 with FP, 5 with WP, 4 suites, 2 cottages, 1 guest house, 1 conference room. Breakfast, afternoon tea, snacks/refreshments, hors d'oeuvres and wine included in rates. Types of meals: Full bkfst, veg bkfst and early coffee/tea. Beds: K. Cable TV, VCR, DVD, reading lamp, stereo, snack bar, clock radio, turn-down service, desk, fireplace, hair dryer, bathrobes, bath amenities, iron/ironing board, King beds in every suite, hydrotherapy spas, down comforters with European duvets and 400+ thread count linens in room. Air conditioning. Fax, copier, spa, library, parlor games, telephone, gift shop, complimentary beverage refreshment center including lattes, cappuccino & espresso (24-hours), 32-inch widescreen flat-panel HDTV-DVD in all lodge suites, multiple hydrospas at the lodge and cottages on premises. Limited handicap access. Antiquing, art galleries, beach, bicycling, canoeing/kayaking, cross-country skiing, downhill skiing, fishing, golf, hiking, horseback riding, live theater, museums, parks, shopping, water sports, wineries, Olympic National Park, Dungeness Spit, National Wildlife Refuge and over 50 lavendar farms in Sequim nearby.

Location: Country, mountains, ocean community. Olympic National Park nearby.

Publicity: *Coastal Living (March 2006), Seattle Magazine, Mountain Living Magazine, Best Weekend Escape in North America 2005 (Arrington's), Best Places Northwest 2005, Best Places to Kiss in the Northwest, Karen Brown's Guide to the Pacific Northwest 2004 & 2005 and Best of Taste (PBS program).*

Certificate may be used: Nov. 1 to March 31, Monday-Thursday, except Valentine's Day and Holidays, subject to availability.

Sunnyside

Sunnyside Inn B&B

800 E Edison Ave
Sunnyside, WA 98944-2206
(509)839-5557 (800)221-4195
Internet: www.sunnysideinn.com
E-mail: sunnyside@sunnysideinn.com

Circa 1919. This wine country inn offers spacious rooms, decorated in a comfortable, country style. Most of the rooms include baths with double Jacuzzi tubs. The one bedroom without a Jacuzzi, includes the home's original early 20th-century fixtures. Two rooms offer fireplaces. A full breakfast is served, as well as evening snacks.

Innkeeper(s): Karen & Don Vlieger. $79-119. 13 rooms with PB, 2 with FP. Breakfast and snacks/refreshments included in rates. Types of meals: Full Country Breakfast. Beds: KQ. Cable TV, VCR, reading lamp, ceiling fan, clock radio, telephone, most with hot tub/spa, some with fireplace, hair dryer, bath amenities, wireless Internet access and iron/ironing board in room. Air conditioning. Library, parlor games and Video library on premises. Antiquing, art galleries, bicycling, cross-country skiing, fishing, golf, museums, parks, shopping, tennis, wineries and 40 wineries within 15 mile radius of inn nearby.

Location: City. Wine Country.

Publicity: *Country Magazine and Northwest Best Places.*

Certificate may be used: Nov. 1-June 30, Sunday-Thursday, excluding holidays and special events.

Tacoma

Branch Colonial House

2420 North 21st St
Tacoma, WA 98406
(253)752-3565 (877)752-3565
Internet: www.branchcolonialhouse.com
E-mail: stay@branchcolonialhouse.com

Circa 1904. Built in the early 20th century, this historic bed & breakfast looks out to the Puget Sound. The home, part of Tacoma's annual historic home tour, features Colonial Revival architecture. Several guest rooms afford a view of the Puget Sound, and the suites include a whirlpool tub. The Branch Quarters also has a fireplace. Tacoma is within easy driving distance of Seattle, and the town offers shops, museums, a zoo and an aquarium.

Innkeeper(s): Robin Korobkin. $129-199. 6 rooms with PB, 1 with FP, 3 suites, 3 conference rooms. Breakfast included in rates. Types of meals: Full gourmet bkfst, veg bkfst, early coffee/tea and snacks/refreshments. Beds: KQ. Modem hook-up, data port, cable TV, DVD, reading lamp, stereo, refrigerator, ceiling fan, snack bar, clock radio, telephone, coffeemaker, desk, some with hot tub/spa, some with fireplace, hair dryer, bathrobes and bath amenities in room. VCR, fax, copier, library, parlor games and laundry facility on premises. Amusement parks, antiquing, art galleries, beach, bicycling, canoeing/kayaking, fishing, golf, hiking, horseback riding, live theater, museums, parks, shopping, sporting events and water sports nearby.

Location: City.

Publicity: *Tacoma's New Tribune.*

Certificate may be used: Sunday-Thursday, subject to availability. Blackout dates do apply, call ahead to confirm. Rooms available: Branch, Prospect and Sunroom.

Chinaberry Hill - An 1889 Grand Victorian Inn

302 Tacoma Ave N
Tacoma, WA 98403
(253)272-1282 Fax:(253)272-1335
Internet: www.chinaberryhill.com
E-mail: chinaberry@wa.net

Circa 1889. In the 19th century, this Queen Anne was known as far away as China for its wondrous gardens, one of the earliest examples of landscape gardening in the Pacific Northwest. The home, a wedding present from a husband to his bride, is listed in the National Register. The innkeepers have selected a unique assortment of antiques and collectibles to decorate the manor. The house offers two Jacuzzi suites and a guest room, all eclectically decorated with items such as a four-poster rice bed or a canopy bed. There are two lodging options in the Catchpenny Cottage, a restored carriage house steps away from the manor. Guests can stay either in the romantic carriage suite or the Hay Loft, which includes a bedroom, sitting room, clawfoot tub and a unique hay chute. In the mornings, as the innkeepers say, guests enjoy "hearty breakfasts and serious coffee." Not a bad start to a day exploring Antique Row or Pt. Defiance, a 698-acre protected rain forest park with an aquarium, gardens, beaches and a zoo. Seattle is 30 minutes away.

Innkeeper(s): Cecil & Yarrow Wayman. $135-225. 6 rooms with PB, 1 with FP, 3 with HT, 2 two-bedroom suites, 1 cottage, 1 guest house. Breakfast and snacks/refreshments included in rates. Types of meals: Full gourmet bkfst and early coffee/tea. Beds: QT. Modem hook-up, cable TV, VCR, reading lamp, clock radio, telephone, desk, some with fireplace, hair dryer, bathrobes, bath amenities, iron/ironing board and some bay views in room. Air conditioning. Fax, library, parlor games, wraparound porch, historic estate gardens w/100+ yr. old trees and rock walls that give the property a tucked away feeling on premises. Amusement parks, antiquing, artgalleries, beach, bicycling, canoeing/kayaking, cross-country skiing, downhill skiing, fishing, golf, hiking, horseback riding, live theater, museums, parks, shopping, sporting events, tennis, water sports, wineries, zoo & aquarium, gardens, 14 miles of old growth forested trails, Point Defiance Park, International Glass Museum, Glass Bridge, New Tacoma Art Museum, Washington State History Museum, hot shops for watching blown glass artisans at work, Farmer's Market and parasailing nearby.

Location: City, ocean community.

Publicity: *Sunset Magazine, Travel and Leisure Magazine, Best Places Northwest, Best Places to Kiss Northwest, Recommended Country Inns of the Pacific Northwest, Amazing Getaways, Seattle P-I, Romantic Days & Nights in Seattle, The Oregonian, The Tacoma News Tribune and Tacoma Weekly.*

Certificate may be used: November, January-March, Monday-Wednesday. Seven days prior to reservation. Excludes holidays and special events.

Plum Duff House

619 North K Street
Tacoma, WA 98403
(253)627-6916 (188)862-71920 Fax:(253)272-9116
Internet: www.plumduff.com
E-mail: plumduffhouse@gmail.com

Circa 1901. Friendly and casual with a relaxing ambiance and genuine hospitality, Plum Duff House in the North Tacoma district in Washington was built in 1901 in the Victorian style. Antiques, country and modern furnishings mix in an appealing and inviting way. Relax by the fire in the living room or gather in the enclosed sun porch for a game of chess or browse for a book off the shelf. Snacks and beverages are available at any time. Stay in a comfortable guest bedroom or a suite that boasts a fireplace and Jacuzzi tub. After a satisfying breakfast explore the Great Pacific Northwest. Take day trips to Seattle, Puget Sound, Mt. Rainier and the Olympic Peninsula.

Innkeeper(s): Peter & Robin Stevens. $90-150. 4 rooms with PB, 1 with FP, 1 with WP, 1 two-bedroom suite. Breakfast included in rates. Types of meals: Full bkfst. Beds: KQDT. Cable TV, VCR, refrigerator, ceiling fan, clock radio, telephone, desk, hair dryer, bathrobes, bath amenities, wireless Internet access and iron/ironing board in room. Air conditioning. Fax, copier, spa, bicycles, library, parlor games and fireplace on premises. Amusement parks, antiquing, art galleries, beach, downhill skiing, fishing, golf, hiking, live theater, museums, parks, shopping and sporting events nearby.

Location: City.

Certificate may be used: November-March, Sunday-Thursday, last minute, subject to availabilty.

Trout Lake

The Farm Bed & Breakfast

490 Sunnyside Rd
Trout Lake, WA 98650-9715
(509)395-2488
Internet: www.thefarmbnb.com
E-mail: farmbnb@gorge.net

Circa 1890. Extraordinary views of Mt. Adams and Mt. Hood instill a quiet serenity at this 1890 wooden farmhouse on six acres. Relax on a deck shaded by aspen and weeping willow trees or sit inside by the fire. Two comfortably furnished guest bedrooms feature antique quilts and furniture, fresh flowers and terry robes. Wake up hungry to fully enjoy the generous country breakfast served in the dining room on family heirloom silver, vintage pewter and crystal. Favorites include Dean's homemade huckleberry pancakes, French toast, 400 Mile

Oatmeal and Dutch Babies served with fresh bacon and sausage from Otto's. The gorgeous grounds with barn and arbor are perfect for dream weddings. Trout Lake Festival of the Arts is hosted here each summer, with juried local artists, live music and regional food and drink. Windsurf at Columbia River Gorge Scenic Area or kayak the White Salmon River.

Innkeeper(s): Rosie & Dean Hostetter. $90-100. 2 rooms. Breakfast, afternoon tea and snacks/refreshments included in rates. Types of meals: Full bkfst and early coffee/tea. Beds: QDT. Desk and clocks in room. VCR, bicycles, telephone and perennial flower gardens on premises. Antiquing, canoeing/kayaking, cross-country skiing, downhill skiing, fishing, shopping, water sports, wineries, Festival of the Arts in July, white water rafting, mountain climbing at Mt. Adams, Mt. St. Helens and Mt. Rainier nearby.

Location: Country.

Certificate may be used: Oct. 15-May 31, excluding holidays.

Wenatchee

Apple Country Bed & Breakfast

524 Okanogan Ave
Wenatchee, WA 98801
(509)664-0400 Fax:(509)664-6448
Internet: www.applecountryinn.com
E-mail: innkeepers@applecountryinn.com

Circa 1920. One of the first houses built in the Okanogan Heights area, this Craftsman home with an inviting front porch has been recently renovated. Stay in a spacious guest bedroom in the main house or in the carriage house that offers a one-bedroom apartment. More than just a morning meal, breakfast is highlighted with delicious entrees and fresh-baked breads. Gourmet candlelight dinners are available for an extra charge. After a day of local skiing, soak in the large hot tub.

Innkeeper(s): Jerry & Sandi Anderson. $75-110. 6 rooms, 4 with PB, 1 cottage, 1 guest house. Breakfast included in rates. Types of meals: Full gourmet bkfst, veg bkfst, early coffee/tea and gourmet dinner. Beds: QD. Cable TV, reading lamp, stereo, clock radio, telephone, hot tub/spa, hair dryer, bathrobes, wireless Internet access and iron/ironing board in room. Air conditioning. Spa, parlor games, large front porch, outside hot tub available, full breakfast daily and private dinner at request with extra cost on premises. Antiquing, beach, bicycling, canoeing/kayaking, cross-country skiing, downhill skiing, fishing, golf, hiking, live theater, museums, parks, shopping, sporting events, water sports, wineries, Many local wineries and Mission Ridge ski resort (12 miles) nearby.

Location: City, mountains.

Publicity: *Arlington's Bed and Breakfast Journal voted most comfortable B&B in 2003, Cooking Channel (Food 911 - Tyler's Ultimate) and Wendi Myster Travels in the Northwest.*

Certificate may be used: Anytime, Sunday-Thursday.

Washington, D.C.

Aaron Shipman House

13th and Q Streets
Washington, DC 20009
(202)328-3510 (877)893-3233 Fax:(413)582-9669
Internet: www.aaronshipmanhouse.com
E-mail: reservations@bedandbreakfastdc.com

Circa 1887. This three-story Victorian townhouse was built by Aaron Shipman, who owned one of the first construction companies in the city. The turn-of-the-century revitalization of Washington began in Logan Circle, considered to be the city's first truly residential area. During the house's restoration, flower gardens, terraces and fountains were added. Victorian antiques, original wood paneling, stained glass, chandeliers, as well as practical amenities such as air conditioning and laundry facilities, make this a comfortable stay. There is a furnished apartment available, as well.

Innkeeper(s): For Reservations Kathy, Alan or Steve. $100-275. 7 rooms, 6 with PB, 1 with FP, 1 with WP. Breakfast included in rates. Types of meals: Full bkfst. Breakfast is served family style and 8AM weekdays and 9AM weekends and holidays. Beds: QDT. Data port, TV, clock radio, telephone, desk, hair dryer, wireless Internet access, Most rooms have a fireplace, one is a working wood-burning, the remaining are decorative and One room with Jacuzzi tub in room. Central air. Library, fireplace and laundry facility on premises. Antiquing, art galleries, bicycling, golf, horseback riding, live theater, museums, parks, shopping, sporting events, tennis, Mational Monuments, Smithsonian, Washington Convention Center, White House and Library of Congress nearby.

Location: City. Logan Circle, Downtown Washington DC.

"This home was the highlight of our stay in Washington! This was a superb home and location. The Reeds treated us better than family."

Certificate may be used: Sunday-Thursday, Jan. 1-March 15, not valid holiday weekends or special events.

Adams Inn

1744 Lanier Pl NW
Washington, DC 20009-2118
(202)745-3600 (800)578-6807 Fax:(202)319-7958
Internet: www.adamsinn.com
E-mail: adamsinn@adamsinn.com

Circa 1908. These restored town houses have fireplaces, a library and parlor, all furnished urban country-style, as are the guest rooms. Former residents of this neighborhood include Tallulah Bankhead, Woodrow Wilson and Al Jolson. The Adams-Morgan area is home to diplomats, radio and television personalities and government workers. A notable firehouse across the street holds the record for the fastest response of a horse-drawn fire apparatus. Located in the restaurant area, over 100 restaurants and shops are within walking distance.

Innkeeper(s): Anne Owens. $99-139. 26 rooms, 16 with PB. Breakfast included in rates. Types of meals: Cont plus and early coffee/tea. Beds: QDT. Reading lamp,

clock radio and high speed Internet in room. Air conditioning. Parlor games, telephone, fireplace, guest kitchen and coin-op laundry facilities on premises. Antiquing, parks and walking distance to Metro and buses nearby.

Publicity: *Travel Host.*

"We enjoyed your friendly hospitality and the home-like atmosphere. Your suggestions on restaurants and help in planning our visit were appreciated."

Certificate may be used: Dec. 1-March 1, Sunday-Thursday.

The Embassy Inn

1627 16th St NW
Washington, DC 20009-3063
(202)234-7800 (800)423-9111 Fax:(202)234-3309
Internet: www.embassy-inn.com
E-mail: susandcinns@aol.com

Circa 1910. This restored inn is furnished in a Federalist style. The comfortable lobby offers books and evening sherry. Conveniently located, the inn is seven blocks from the Adams Morgan area of ethnic restaurants. The Embassy's philosophy of innkeeping includes providing personal attention and cheerful hospitality. Concierge services are available. The inn does not have an elevator or parking on site.

Innkeeper(s): Delores Bunch. $119-169. 38 rooms with PB. Breakfast included in rates. Beds: DT. Cable TV, reading lamp, clock radio, telephone and free HBO in room. Air conditioning. Fax, copier and Washington Post daily on premises. Antiquing, live theater, museums, parks and White House nearby.

Publicity: *Los Angeles Times, Inn Times, Business Review and N.Y. Times.*

"When I return to D.C., I'll be back at the Embassy."

Certificate may be used: Anytime, subject to availability.

The Windsor Inn

1842 16th St NW
Washington, DC 20009-3316
(202)667-0300 (800)423-9111 Fax:(202)667-4503
Internet: www.windsor-inn-dc.com
E-mail: susandcinns@aol.com

Circa 1910. Recently renovated and situated in a neighborhood of renovated townhouses, the Windsor Inn is the sister property to the Embassy Inn. It is larger and offers suites as well as a small meeting room. The refurbished lobby is in an Art Deco style and a private club atmosphere prevails. It is six blocks to the Metro station at Dupont Circle. There are no elevators or parking on site.

Innkeeper(s): Kristen Hackett. $119-225. 45 rooms with PB, 2 suites, 1 conference room. Breakfast included in rates. Beds: QDT. TV, reading lamp, clock radio, telephone and some with refrigerators in room. Air conditioning. Fax, copier and daily Washington Post on premises. Antiquing, live theater and parks nearby.

Publicity: *Los Angeles Times, Inn Times, Sunday Telegram, WCUA Press Release and New York Times.*

"Being here was like being home. Excellent service, would recommend."

Certificate may be used: Anytime, subject to availability.

West Virginia

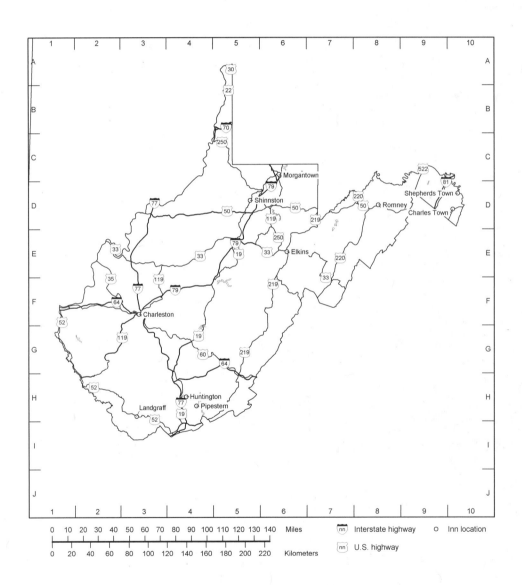

1	2	3	4	5	6	7	8	9	10

0 10 20 30 40 50 60 70 80 90 100 110 120 130 140   Miles

0   20   40   60   80   100   120   140   160   180   200   220   Kilometers

(nn) Interstate highway   ○ Inn location

(nn) U.S. highway

Charles Town

The Washington House Inn

216 S George St
Charles Town, WV 25414-1632
(304)725-7923 (800)297-6957 Fax:(304)728-5150
Internet: www.washingtonhouseinnwv.com
E-mail: emailus@washingtonhouseinnwv.com

Circa 1899. This three-story brick Victorian was built by the descendants of President Washington's brothers, John Augustine and Samuel. Carved oak mantels, spacious guest rooms, antique furnishings and refreshments served on the wraparound veranda or gazebo make the inn memorable. For business travelers, data ports are available. Harpers Ferry National Historic Park, Antietam, and the Shenandoah and Potomac rivers are all within a 15-minute drive. Thoroughbred racing, slot machines and car racing are some of the popular area attractions.

Innkeeper(s): Mel & Nina Vogel. $125-250. 7 rooms with PB, 1 suite, 1 conference room. Breakfast and snacks/refreshments included in rates. Types of meals: Full bkfst and early coffee/tea. Beds: QT. Cable TV, reading lamp, ceiling fan, clock radio, telephone and desk in room. A/C. VCR, fax, copier, parlor games, Internet and antiques and collectibles for sale on premises. Antiquing, fishing, golf, live theater, parks, shopping, water sports, history, museums, horse racing, car racing and slots nearby.

Location: City.

Publicity: *Washington Post - Feb 03, Good Housekeeping - April 03, Travel Holiday - May 03, Recreation News - May 03, Woman's Day and The Today Show.*

Certificate may be used: Sunday-Thursday, Nov. 1-July 31.

Elkins

Tunnel Mountain B&B

Rt 1, Box 59-1
Elkins, WV 26241-9711
(304)636-1684 (888)211-9123
E-mail: beardslee@meer.net

Circa 1939. Nestled on five acres of wooded land, this three-story Fieldstone home offers privacy in a peaceful setting. Rooms are tastefully decorated with antiques, collectibles and crafts. Each bedroom boasts a view of the surrounding mountains. The chestnut and knotty pine woodwork accentuate the decor. The fireplace in the large common room is a great place for warming up after a day of touring or skiing. Guests can also enjoy the Riverside Retreat, a cottage on the river. The area is home to a number of interesting events, including a Dulcimer festival and the state's largest festival, the Mountain State Forest Festival.

Innkeeper(s): Anne & Paul Beardslee. $80-90. 3 rooms with PB, 1 cottage. Breakfast included in rates. Types of meals: Country bkfst. Beds: QD. Cable TV, reading lamp and clock in room. A/C. Parlor games, telephone, fireplace and one great room on premises. Antiquing, art galleries, beach, bicycling, canoeing/kayaking, cross-country skiing, downhill skiing, fishing, golf, hiking, horseback riding, live theater, museums, parks, shopping, sporting events, tennis, water sports, rock climbing and mountain biking nearby.

Location: Mountains.

Publicity: *Blue Ridge Country, Washington Post and WBOY.*

Certificate may be used: November to May, Sunday-Thursday. Not valid for cottage.

Huntington

Heritage Farm Museum & Village

3350 Harvey Rd
Huntington, WV 25704-9112
(304)522-1244
Internet: www.heritagefarmmuseum.com
E-mail: hfmv@comcast.net

Award-winning Heritage Farm Museum & Village spans 500 acres in Huntington, West Virginia, just five miles from Ohio River and Beech Fork Lake. Created expressly to preserve their Appalachian heritage, newly built accommodations include a farmhouse and four log houses made with 100-year-old logs. Each home includes a full kitchen, laundry facilities, covered porches, a wood-burning fireplace and central heat and air conditioning. Swim in the outdoor swimming pool and experience the many activities offered all year round. Visit the Farm Zoo, take the Nature Walk and tour the three museums. Three meeting and reception halls are perfect for various size events and the Log Church is popular for country weddings.

Innkeeper(s): Mike Perry. Call for rates. 14 rooms, 2 with FP, 5 guest houses. Beds: KQDT. Refrigerator, coffeemaker, some with fireplace and iron/ironing board in room. A/C. Swimming, laundry facility and 20'x40' swimming pool for use in summer season on premises.

Location: Country.

Publicity: *Huntington Quarterly and Herald Dispatch.*

"My son and wife were married in the little log church and a dinner was enjoyed by all at the main inn. A year later, we returned to celebrate their anniversary, now the entire family will spend Thanksgiving at the Strawberry Inn! A quiet, beautiful place to enjoy. Thanks for giving our family such wonderful memories!!"

Certificate may be used: January-March, Monday-Wednesday, based on availability.

Landgraff

Elkhorn Inn & Theatre

On Route 52
Landgraff, WV 24829
(304)862-2031 (800)708-2040 Fax:(304)862-2031
Internet: www.elkhorninnwv.com
E-mail: elisse@elkhorninnwv.com

Circa 1922. Named for the trout-filled Elkhorn Creek that runs behind the inn, this historic Italianate brick building with archways and a balcony on the Coal Heritage Trail has been lovingly restored by Dan and Elisse. Period antiques and 1930s furnishings complement an international art collection. Paintings, prints, ceramics, stained glass, sculpture and textiles are for sale. Stay in a guest bedroom or suite with handmade vintage quilts, clawfoot tubs and bubble baths. A family suite with two adjoining rooms is available. Alto Grande Coffee, offered exclusively at the inn, accompanies a continental breakfast. Located near Pinnacle Rock State Park and Panther State Forest, there are ATV and bike trails on Burke Mountain. McDowell County is also a popular hunting and fishing area.

Innkeeper(s): Elisse & Dan Clark. $75-145. 13 rooms, 3 with PB, 1 two-bedroom suite. Breakfast included in rates. Types of meals: Cont, veg bkfst, Sun. brunch, early coffee/tea, lunch, afternoon tea, snacks/refreshments, hors d'oeuvres, wine, gourmet dinner, Weddings, dinner parties, buffet dinner parties and other special events. Beds: QDT. Reading lamp, ceiling fan, clock radio, desk, bathrobes, wireless Internet access, down and vintage quilts, down/feather pillows, individual fans and heaters in room. A/C. TV, VCR, DVD, fax, library, parlor games, telephone, fireplace, laundry facility, gift shop, Wireless Internet access, Gift Shop with an international collection of for-sale artwork, Jewelry, Books, Vintage quilts and locally-made hand-crafted coal gifts, Balcony with umbrella tables and chairs, Fireplace lounge, Outdoor Patio Cafe under the arches, Theatre available for summer events such as weddings, concerts and meetings on premises. Antiquing, fishing, golf, hiking, live theater, museums, parks, shopping, Trout fishing on Elkhorn Creek at the Inn, Pinnacle Rock State Park, Panther State Forest, Blackwolf Golf Course, Hatfield-McCoy ATV trails (Pinnacle Creek trails, Pineville trailhead), McDowell County ATV trails, 3 area stocked trout streams, Anawalt Lake, Berwind Lake, Kimball WWI African-American Memorial, Coal Heritage Trail and "railfan" sites, "History in our Mountains" Musuem in Welch, Skygusty ATV Racetrack, Pocahontas Va. Coal Mine Museum, Antiquing, Day spas & Mercer Mall in Bluefield, "October Sky" Rocketboys Festival in Coalwood, Oktoberfest in Welch & Bramwell and October Italian Festival in Bluefield nearby.

Location: Country, mountains, waterfront. On Elkhorn Creek, near Bluefield.

Publicity: *NY Daily News, Preservation Magazine, ConventionSouth, Charleston Gazette, Charleston Daily Mail, The WV State Journal, Bluefield Daily Telegraph, Welch News, West Virginia Wild & Wonderful Magazine, Trains Magazine, Railfan & Railroad Magazine, Blue Ridge Country, The Artists Magazine, ATV Illustrated Magazine, All-Terrain-Vehicle Magazine, Appalachian Journal; diynetwork.com "Best Built Homes in America", HGTV "Building Character" and 'ReZoned"; Speed Channel "Two Wheel Tuesday", "Traveling the Mountain State", WVNS News 59 (CBS), WVVA News Channel 6 (NBC), WELC Radio AM/FM; 100.9 The Mix, www.atv.com, www.retreatsonline.com, www.hawk.com, www.trailsheaven.com (Hatfield & McCoy ATV trails) and www.byways.org (Coal Heritage Trail).*

Certificate may be used: Year-round, Sunday-Thursday, subject to availability.

Shepherdstown

Thomas Shepherd Inn

300 W German St.
Shepherdstown, WV 25443
(304)876-3715 (888)889-8952
Internet: www.thomasshepherdinn.com
E-mail: info@thomasshepherdinn.com

Built as a Lutheran parsonage using Federal architecture, this inn has been renovated to offer gracious hospitality in a traditional style. Spacious common rooms like the large living room with a fireplace or the book-filled library offer several seating areas with comfortable antique furnishings. The porch invites quiet relaxation. Appealing guest bedrooms provide a retreat from distractions of phone or television. Savor a hearty breakfast served family style that may include favorites like apple cranberry crisp, tomato mushroom and cheese omelet, local bacon, and poppyseed muffins with homemade asian pear marmalade.

Innkeeper(s): Jim Ford & Jeanne Muir. $115-175. 6 rooms with PB, 1 with FP. Breakfast included in rates. Types of meals: Full bkfst, veg bkfst and early coffee/tea. Beds: QD. Reading lamp, clock radio, wireless Internet access, bottled water, soap, shampoo and bath gel in room. Central air. TV, VCR, DVD, fax, copier, library, parlor games, telephone, fireplace and Wireless Internet access on premises. Antiquing, art galleries, bicycling, canoeing/kayaking, fishing, golf, hiking, horseback riding, live theater, museums, parks, shopping, water sports and wineries nearby.

Location: Small town.

Certificate may be used: Monday-Thursday, subject to availability.

Shinnston

Gillum House Bed & Breakfast

35 Walnut St
Shinnston, WV 26431
(304)592-0177 (888)592-0177 Fax:(304)592-1882
Internet: www.gillumhouse.com
E-mail: relax@gillumhouse.com

Circa 1912. The architectural style of a 1912 house is reflected in this comfortable inn. Original works of art, painted by the

one of the innkeepers, grace the walls. The second-floor library offers books to savor and finish reading at home. Antique-filled guest bedrooms pamper with fresh flowers, candles, Egyptian cotton or flannel linens, down comforters and fluffy robes. Breakfast is a healthy, low-fat culinary delight, accented with locally made maple syrup. The nearby West Fork River Trail entertains hikers, bicyclists and equestrians.

Innkeeper(s): Kathleen A. Panek. $89-115. 3 rooms, 1 with PB. Breakfast included in rates. Types of meals: Full bkfst, veg bkfst, early coffee/tea, picnic lunch, A full breakfast is served family-style and special diet needs are our specialty, We offer packages that include a packed lunch and/or dinners and We have over 75 varieties of tea for our tea drinking guests. Beds: QD. Cable TV, VCR, DVD, reading lamp, CD player, clock radio, bathrobes, bath amenities, decorative fireplaces, hair dryer & curling iron in both bathrooms, massage can be arranged, private bath with clawfoot tub and a shower and The Harris and Rosi's Room share a bathroom that has a 60 inch shower in room. Air conditioning. Fax, copier, bicycles, library, parlor games, telephone, laundry facility, gift shop, concierge service, phone in common room, Internet access in common room, art gallery in library and escort service provided from I-79 exit on premises. Antiquing, art galleries, bicycling, fishing, golf, hiking, horseback riding, live theater, museums, parks, shopping, sporting events, wineries, 9 covered bridges, 7 state parks, Chapel of Perpetual Adoration, 2 drive-in theaters, several hand-blown glass factories with tours, historic sites, Mother's Day shrine, rail-trails, birding and overnight stabling (2.5 miles) nearby.

Location: City. Six miles west of I-79, small city (pop. 2,300).

Publicity: *Pittsburgh Post-Gazette, Clarksburg Exponent-Telegram, Shinnston News, Akron Beacon Journal, Blue Ridge Outdoors, West Virginia State Journal, Charleston Gazette-Mail, Long Weekends, New York Times, WBOY, Speed Channel, WCHS, C-FAX, "Inn to Inn Hiking Guide to the Virginias," Off the Beaten Path- West Virginia, Fourth Edition (vignette), Good Morning West Virginia and Vol. II.*

Certificate may be used: Anytime except holidays, WVU home games or October per availability.

Weirton

Rosemont Manor

P. O. Box 99
Weirton, WV 26062
(304)794-4100
Internet: www.rosemontmanor.com
E-mail: rose@rosemontmanor.com

Circa 1929. Secluded on a bluff with a breathtaking view of the Ohio Valley and River, this 10,000 square foot classic stone mansion has two wraparound porches, manicured lawns, a wedding gazebo and wooded areas. Flagstone walkways lead to the huge outdoor swimming pool. The Great Room features wall murals, an entertainment area, a wood-burning fireplace with Italian marble and panoramic vistas from the adjoining second-floor deck. The Conference Room also boasts a stone fireplace and opens to the first-floor porch. A tanning bed, treadmill and free weihts are available in the Fitness Room. Gorgeous guest suites offer lavish amenities for business or leisure. An American cooked breakfast is served daily.

Innkeeper(s): Rosemary Susko. $100-200. 7 rooms, 4 with PB, 3 with FP, 4 suites, 1 conference room. Breakfast included in rates. Types of meals: Full bkfst and early coffee/tea. Beds: KDT. TV, VCR, DVD, reading lamp, CD player, ceiling fan, clock radio, desk, hair dryer, bathrobes, bath amenities and wireless Internet access in room. Air conditioning. Copier, parlor games, telephone, fireplace and laundry facility on premises. Antiquing, bicycling, fishing, golf, hiking, museums, parks, shopping, sporting events and water sports nearby.

Location: City, mountains. Overlooking Ohio Valley & River.

Publicity: *"Reckless" (1984) starring Darryl Hannah and Aiden Quinn.*

Certificate may be used: October-March, Anytime, subject to availability, Last minute, subject to availability.

Wisconsin

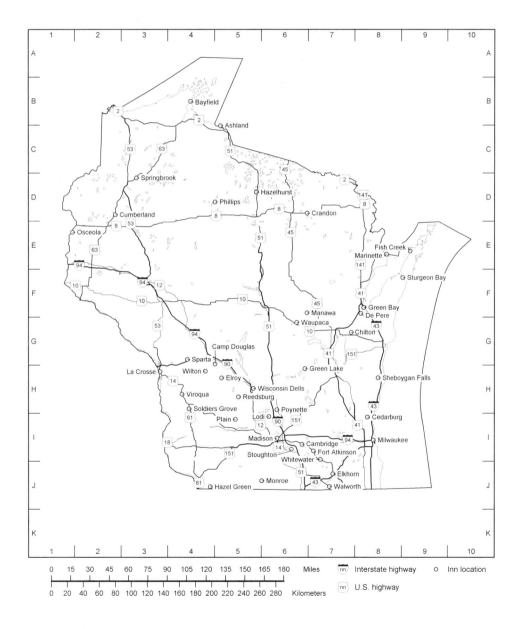

	1	2	3	4	5	6	7	8	9	10	

0 15 30 45 60 75 90 105 120 135 150 165 180   Miles

0 20 40 60 80 100 120 140 160 180 200 220 240 260 280   Kilometers

Interstate highway	o Inn location
U.S. highway	

Appleton

Franklin Street Inn B & B

318 E Franklin St
Appleton, WI 54911-5437
(920)993-1711 (888)993-1711
Internet: www.franklinstreetinn.com
E-mail: info@franklinstreetinn.com

Romance is in the air at this Queen Anne Victorian bed and breakfast inn. The award-winning Franklin Street Inn B&B offers premier accommodations with period décor and antiques in an historic neighborhood of Appleton, Wisconsin. Relax on the wraparound porch overlooking the fountain and garden landscaping or gather in the pleasant fireside parlor. A guest refrigerator is stocked with beverages. Delicious treats include home-baked snacks. Stay in one of the delightful guest bedrooms or suites. The third-floor castle-themed Turret Suite Royale and the Franklin Suite feature two-person whirlpool tubs and gas fireplaces. Onsite massage therapy is available. Savor a four-course breakfast with signature entrees served in-room or in the formal dining room.

Innkeeper(s): Judy and Ron Halma. $99-299. 4 rooms with PB, 2 with FP, 2 with WP, 2 total suites, including 1 three-bedroom suite, 1 conference room. Breakfast and snacks/refreshments included in rates. Types of meals: Full gourmet bkfst, veg bkfst, early coffee/tea and room service. Beds: KQDT. Cable TV, VCR, DVD, reading lamp, stereo, refrigerator, ceiling fan, snack bar, clock radio, telephone, coffeemaker, turn-down service, desk, some with hot tub/spa, some with fireplace, hair dryer, bathrobes, bath amenities, wireless Internet access and iron/ironing board in room. Central air. Antiquing, art galleries, bicycling, canoeing/kayaking, cross-country skiing, fishing, golf, hiking, live theater, museums, parks, shopping, sporting events, tennis, water sports, wineries, Green Bay Packer games, Oshkosh Experimental Aircraft Association (EAA), Fox River Mall and Big Picture Theater nearby.

Certificate may be used: Monday-Thursday, November and January, any day March-May.

Ashland

Second Wind Country Inn

30475 Carlson Road
Ashland, WI 54806
(715)682-1000
Internet: www.secondwindcountryinn.com
E-mail: catchyourbreath@secondwindcountryinn.com

Circa 2004. Encompassing 35 magnificent acres, this non-smoking log and timber lodge offers an incredible view of Lake Superior's Chequamegon Bay area. Relax in the gathering room with a Northwoods lodge décor or on one of the outdoor decks. Three guest suites feature a luxurious ambiance and whirlpool tubs. The Bear Den is handicap accessible. The Northern Lights Loft includes a kitchenette with refrigerator and microwave. Wake up after a restful sleep and enjoy a home-cooked breakfast. Gather for a late-night bonfire and evening treats. Browse the Second Wind Mercantile for gifts to bring home.

Innkeeper(s): Mark and Kelly Illick. $89-159. 3 rooms, 3 with WP, 3 total suites, including 1 three-bedroom suite, 1 conference room. Breakfast and Sunday brunch included in rates. Types of meals: Country bkfst, early coffee/tea and snacks/refreshments. Beds: Q. Reading lamp, CD player, refrigerator, ceiling fan, clock radio, coffeemaker, hot tub/spa, hair dryer, bath amenities and wireless Internet access in room. Central air. VCR, copier, spa, library, parlor games, telephone, gift shop, Free wireless Internet, Fire ring, Outside decks, Cross country skiing, Hiking trails, ATV and Snowmobile trail on premises. Handicap access. Antiquing, art galleries, beach, bicycling, canoeing/kayaking, cross-country skiing, downhill skiing, fishing, golf, hiking,

horseback riding, live theater, museums, shopping and water sports nearby.

Location: Country.

Publicity: *The Sounder.*

Certificate may be used: November-June, Sunday-Thursday.

The Residenz

723 Chapple Avenue
Ashland, WI 54806
(715)682-2425 Fax:(715)685-9953
Internet: www.residenzbb.com
E-mail: therez@ncis.net

Circa 1889. The Residenz is a restored 1891 Queen Anne Victorian mansion that offers gracious hospitality in Ashland, near Chequamegon Bay. Be pampered and immersed in the beauty of Lake Superior's South Shore and Wisconsin's North Woods while staying at this elegant B&B inn. Enjoy evening dessert in the foyer before turning in to sleep in a guest bedroom with an antique sleigh bed covered with a colorful quilt that accents the décor or in the spacious two-room Spruce Suite. Early risers can sip coffee before a gourmet two-course breakfast served in the formal dining room. Walk to the City Museum or browse the shops of Historic Main Street. The Sea Caves at Apostle Islands National Lakeshore are a must-see adventure.

Innkeeper(s): Bob & Reba Rice. $55-110. 5 rooms, 3 with PB, 1 two-bedroom suite. Breakfast and Evening dessert and tea included in rates. Types of meals: Full gourmet bkfst, early coffee/tea and Evening dessert and tea. Beds: KQDT. Cable TV, VCR, DVD, reading lamp, CD player, ceiling fan, clock radio, desk, bathrobes, bath amenities and wireless Internet access in room. Air conditioning. Fax, copier, library, telephone and fireplace on premises. Antiquing, beach, bicycling, canoeing/kayaking, cross-country skiing, downhill skiing, fishing, golf, hiking, horseback riding, live theater, museums, parks, shopping, tennis, water sports, wineries, hiking, bird watching, boating, canoeing and snowmobiling nearby.

Location: Waterfront. Lake Superior's Chequamegon Bay.

Certificate may be used: November-April.

Bayfield

Old Rittenhouse Inn

301 Rittenhouse Ave
Bayfield, WI 54814-0584
(715)779-5111 (800)779-2129 Fax:(715)779-5887
Internet: www.rittenhouseinn.com
E-mail: gourmet@rittenhouseinn.com

Circa 1892. Two historic Queen Anne mansions, a guest house and a private cottage comprise this elegant Victorian inn and gourmet restaurant just a few blocks from downtown. Under massive gables, a wraparound veranda is filled with white wicker furniture, geraniums and petunias. The inn boasts 22 working fireplaces amidst antique furnishings. Well-appointed guest bedrooms and luxury suites offer a variety of romantic amenities that may include whirlpools as well as views of Madeline Island and Lake Superior. The two-story Fountain Cottage is just uphill. For breakfast indulge in baked muffins served with Rittenhouse Jams, Jellies and a cup of coffee accompanied by dishes such as Wild Bayfield Blueberry Crisp or Moonglow Pears Poached in White Zinfandel.

Innkeeper(s): Jerry, Mary, Mark, Wendy, and Julie Phillips. $99-349. 26

rooms with PB, 19 with FP, 17 with WP, 7 total suites, including 2 two-bed-room suites, 2 cottages, 2 guest houses. Breakfast, Continental Breakfast included in room rate and Full Breakfast available for $8.50/houseguest and $11.50/person for walk ins included in rates. Types of meals: Full gourmet bkfst, gourmet lunch, snacks/refreshments, wine, gourmet dinner, room service, Weddings, Reunions and catered special events. Restaurant on premises. Beds: KQD. Reading lamp, CD player, clock radio, coffeemaker, desk, most with hot tub/spa, most with fireplace, hair dryer, bath amenities, wireless Internet access, Whirlpool and Antiques in room. Air conditioning. Fax, copier, telephone and gift shop on premises. Handicap access. Antiquing, art galleries, beach, bicycling, canoeing/kayaking, cross-country skiing, downhill skiing, fishing, golf, hiking, horseback riding, live theater, museums, parks, shopping, tennis, water sports, Apple orchards, Apostle Islands National Lakeshore, Gaylord Nelson Wilderness Preserve, Big Top Chautauqua, Sailing, Charters and Microbrewery nearby.

Location: Country, waterfront.

Publicity: *Wisconsin Trails, Midwest Living, National Geographic Traveler, Country Inns, Minnesota Monthly, Bon Appetit, Gourmet, Better Homes and Gardens, Lake Superior Magazine, Victoria, Minneapolis/St.Paul Magazine, St. Paul Pioneer Press, Milwaukee Journal, Wisconsin State Journal and Chicago Tribune.*

"The whole decor, the room, the staff and the food were superb! Your personalities and talents give a great warmth to the inn."

Certificate may be used: Nov. 1 to May 14, Wednesday and Thursday.

Thimbleberry Inn B&B

38085 Pagent Rd.
Bayfield, WI 54814-1007
(715)779-5757 (800)881-5903 Fax:(715)779-5690
Internet: www.thimbleberryinn.com
E-mail: locey@thimbleberryinn.com

Circa 1992. The waters of Lake Superior sparkle beside the 400-foot shoreline adjacent to this natural wood home. The

peaceful forest setting adds to the romance of the rooms, which include fireplaces. Innkeeper Sharon Locey writes a food column and has written her first cookbook. Her culinary expertise makes breakfast a gourmet treat. A Longaberger basket with coffee and muffins is delivered to your room prior to the full breakfast. While enjoying your morning meal, watch for wildlife and bald eagles as they soar over the Locey's 40 acres.

Innkeeper(s): Craig & Sharon Locey. $99-169. 3 rooms with PB, 3 with FP, 1 suite. Breakfast included in rates. Types of meals: Full bkfst and early coffee/tea. Beds: KQ. Reading lamp and clock radio in room. Antiquing, cross-country skiing, downhill skiing, fishing, shopping and sailboat nearby.

Location: Waterfront. On Lake Superior.

Certificate may be used: Jan. 2-May 15, Nov. 1-Dec. 15, Sunday-Thursday.

Camp Douglas

Sunnyfield Farm B&B

N6692 Batko Rd
Camp Douglas, WI 54618
(608)427-3686 (888)839-0232
Internet: www.sunnyfield.net
E-mail: soltvedt@mwt.net

Circa 1899. Scenic bluffs and rich land surround this 100-year-old, three-story farmhouse boasting 10-foot ceilings. Lovingly restored, the original hardwood floors and hand-carved oak woodwork reside easily with brass ceiling tiles and family heirlooms. Guest bedrooms feature a country decor with

handmade quilts and stenciling. The Rose Room has an adjoining room that is perfect for families or groups. A private studio apartment on the third floor offers a cozy yet spacious suite with living room, kitchen and sky windows for stargazing. Wake up to a complete country breakfast served in the spacious dining room. Three of the 160 acres are manicured lawns to enjoy. Wisconsin Dells is just 30 minutes away.

Innkeeper(s): Susanne & John Soltvedt. $80-120. 4 rooms, 2 with PB. Breakfast included in rates. Types of meals: Country bkfst and early coffee/tea. Beds: QT. Reading lamp, ceiling fan and desk in room. TV, VCR, DVD, library, parlor games, telephone and laundry facility on premises. Antiquing, art galleries, bicycling, canoeing/kayaking, cross-country skiing, fishing, golf, hiking, parks, shopping and water sports nearby.

Location: Country.

Certificate may be used: November through April, anytime, subject to availability.

Cedarburg

Stagecoach Inn B&B

W 61 N 520 Washington Ave
Cedarburg, WI 53012
(262)375-0208 (888)375-0208 Fax:(262)375-6170
Internet: www.stagecoach-inn-wi.com
E-mail: info@stagecoach-inn-wi.com

Circa 1853. This historic Greek Revival inn has been welcoming travelers since its earliest days, when it served as a stagecoach stop between Milwaukee and Green Bay. The innkeepers used 19th-century photographs to help authenticate the inn's meticulous restoration. In addition to the nine guest rooms, the inn houses a pub where the continental-plus breakfasts are served in the mornings and complimentary wine in the afternoon. The innkeepers have owned Stagecoach Inn since the early 1980s. In 1991, they restored Weber Haus, an 1847 house across the street from the inn. Weber Haus offers three suites with whirlpool tubs. Two of the suites include a fireplace, and there is a secret garden to explore and enjoy. Many attractions are within walking distance, including a historic district, antique shops, cultural center, galleries, a winery and restaurants.

Innkeeper(s): Brook & Liz Brown. $85-150. 12 rooms with PB, 2 with FP, 6 with WP, 6 suites, 1 conference room. Breakfast included in rates. Types of meals: Cont plus and room service. Beds: QDT. Cable TV, reading lamp, CD player, telephone and suite has whirlpool tub in room. Air conditioning. VCR, fax, Wireless Internet and Wine Social on premises. Antiquing, art galleries, bicycling, golf, hiking, live theater, museums, parks, shopping, wineries, Cedar Creek Settlement, Pioneer village, Silver Creek Brewery, General Store Museum, Inter-Urban Bike Trail and Cultural Center nearby.

Location: City, country.

Publicity: *Milwaukee, Visions, Midwest Living, Travel Host, Innsider, Wisconsin Trails, Country Life, Business Journal, Country Living, Chicago Tribune, Country Crafts and Better Homes/Crafts.*

"Cedarburg is a lovely town and this is a great place from which to explore it. We hope to return."

Certificate may be used: January-April, Sunday-Thursday, No Holidays.

The Washington House Inn

W 62 N 573 Washington Ave
Cedarburg, WI 53012-1941
(262)375-3550 (800)554-4717 Fax:(262)375-9422
Internet: www.washingtonhouseinn.com
E-mail: whinn@execpc.com

Circa 1886. This three-story cream city brick building is in the National Register. Rooms are appointed in a country Victorian style and feature antiques, whirlpool baths and fireplaces. The original guest registry, more than 100 years old, is displayed proudly in the lobby, and a marble trimmed fireplace is often lit for the afternoon wine and cheese hour. Breakfast is continental and is available in the gathering room, often including recipes from a historic Cedarburg cookbook for items such as home-made muffins, cakes and breads.

Innkeeper(s): Wendy Porterfield. $95-245. 34 rooms with PB, 3 suites, 1 conference room. Breakfast included in rates. Types of meals: Cont plus and snacks/refreshments. Beds: KQD. Cable TV, VCR, reading lamp, ceiling fan, clock radio, telephone and wireless Internet access in room. Air conditioning. TV, fax, copier and sauna on premises. Antiquing, cross-country skiing, fishing, live theater, parks, shopping and sporting events nearby.

Location: City. Historic district.

Publicity: *Country Home and Chicago Sun-Times.*

Certificate may be used: Sunday-Thursday only on $145-$245 rooms, no holidays or festival dates.

De Pere

James St. Inn
201 James St
De Pere, WI 54115-2562
(920)337-0111 (800)897-8483 Fax:(920)337-6135
Internet: www.jamesstreetinn.com
E-mail: jamesst@netnet.net

Circa 1995. An old flour mill on the Fox River is the foundation for this wonderful inn. The comfortable great room is a relaxing place to enjoy a glass of wine with the region's legendary cheese. Spacious waterfront suites

feature excellent views and lavish amenities for leisure or business needs; plus, six penthouse suites were added recently. A generous continental-plus breakfast is served daily.

Innkeeper(s): Kevin Flatley & Joan Hentges. $74-224. 36 rooms with PB, 10 with FP, 16 with WP, 32 suites, 1 conference room. Breakfast, snacks/refreshments and wine included in rates. Types of meals: Cont plus, early coffee/tea, lunch, dinner and room service. Restaurant on premises. Beds: KQD. Data port, cable TV, reading lamp, refrigerator, snack bar, clock radio, telephone, coffeemaker, desk, some with hot tub/spa, some with fireplace, hair dryer, bath amenities, wireless Internet access, iron/ironing board, decks over the river and evening wine & cheese in room. Air conditioning. VCR, fax, copier, library, parlor games and Andrew's Mediterranean Bistro on premises. Handicap access. Amusement parks, antiquing, bicycling, cross-country skiing, fishing, golf, live theater, museums, parks, shopping, sporting events and water sports nearby.

Location: Waterfront. Riverfront, historic downtown.

Publicity: *Midwest Living, Newmonth, Green Bay Press-Gazette and WLUK-Gastank Getaway.*

Certificate may be used: Jan. 1-April 30 and Nov. 1-Dec. 31, Sunday-Friday.

Elroy

East View B&B
33620 County P Rd
Elroy, WI 53929
(608)463-7564
Internet: www.eastviewbedandbreakfast.com
E-mail: eastview@centurytel.net

Circa 1994. This comfortable ranch house offers splendid views of the countryside, with its rolling hills covered with woods. Autumn is a particularly scenic time for a visit, when the trees explode in color. The three guest rooms are simply furnished in a homey, country style with quilts topping the beds. Each room offers a pleasing view. Breakfast comes in several courses, with fresh fruit, homemade breads, a daily entree and finally a dessert. The area provides opportunities for hiking, biking, canoeing or browsing at local craft stores.

Innkeeper(s): Dom & Bev Puechner. $80. 3 rooms with PB. Breakfast included in rates. Types of meals: Full bkfst and early coffee/tea. Beds: QD. Reading lamp, ceiling fan, clock radio, telephone and turn-down service in room. Air conditioning. Walking trails on premises. Amusement parks, antiquing, cross-country skiing, golf and shopping nearby.

Location: Country.

Publicity: *Country Inns and Midwest Living Magazine.*

"What a wonderful treat it was to stay at East View. The view was magnificent and the breakfasts superb."

Certificate may be used: Anytime, subject to availability.

Fish Creek

Thorp House Inn & Cottages
4135 Bluff Ln, PO Box 490
Fish Creek, WI 54212
(920)868-2444
Internet: www.thorphouseinn.com
E-mail: innkeeper@thorphouseinn.com

Circa 1902. Every season surrounds this bed & breakfast inn and its cottages with a natural beauty. Listed in the National Register, an extensive restoration has preserved details like authentic lighting and documentary wallcoverings. Fine antique furnishings and accessories accented with European lace enhance the gracious ambiance. Relax in the library or by the fire in the double parlor. Warm hospitality is enjoyed on the summer sitting porch with

refreshments from the stocked pantry. Choose a well-appointed guest bedroom or stay in one of the quaint country cottages. A beach house is also available.

Innkeeper(s): Christine & Sverre Falck-Pedersen. $95-195. 5 rooms with PB, 6 cottages. Types of meals: Cont plus and early coffee/tea. Beds: KQDT. Reading lamp, refrigerator, three with whirlpool and two with fireplace in room. Central air. Parlor games, telephone and fireplace on premises. Antiquing, cross-country skiing, fishing, live theater, parks, shopping, water sports, summer art school and music festival nearby.

Location: Small village.

Publicity: *Green Bay Press-Gazette, Milwaukee Journal/Sentinel, McCall's, Minnesota Monthly and Madison PM.*

"Amazing attention to detail from restoration to the furnishings. A very first-class experience."

Certificate may be used: Sunday-Thursday, Nov. 1-April 30, Not valid on Friday and/or Saturdays. Holidays excluded. Available only on rack rates and cannot be combined with any other discounts.

Green Bay

The Astor House B&B

637 S Monroe Ave
Green Bay, WI 54301-3614
(920)432-3585 (888)303-6370
Internet: www.astorhouse.com
E-mail: astor@execpc.com

Circa 1888. Located in the Astor Historic District, the Astor House is completely surrounded by Victorian homes. Guests have their choice of five rooms, each uniquely decorated for a range of ambiance, from the Vienna Balconies to the Marseilles Garden to the Hong Kong Retreat. The parlor, veranda and many suites feature a grand view of City Centre's lighted church towers. This home is also the first and only B&B in Green Bay and received the Mayor's Award for Remodeling and Restoration. Business travelers should take notice of the private phone lines in each room, as well as our wireless high-speed Internet access.

Innkeeper(s): Greg & Barbara Robinson. $120-159. 5 rooms with PB, 4 with FP, 3 suites. Breakfast included in rates. Types of meals: Cont plus. Beds: KQDT. Cable TV, VCR, reading lamp, stereo, refrigerator, clock radio, telephone, gas fireplaces and double whirlpool tub (4 of 5 rooms) in room. Air conditioning. Amusement parks, antiquing, cross-country skiing, fishing, live theater, parks, shopping, sporting events and water sports nearby.

Location: City.

Publicity: *Chicago Sun-Times and Corporate Reports.*

Certificate may be used: Anytime, Sunday-Thursday, subject to availability. Excludes special events like holidays and Packer Football Games. May be used only for rooms with whirlpool and fireplace.

Green Lake

McConnell Inn

497 S Lawson Dr
Green Lake, WI 54941-8700
(920)294-6430 (888)238-8625
Internet: www.mcconnellinn.com
E-mail: info@mcconnellinn.com

Circa 1901. This stately home features many of its original features, including leaded windows, woodwork, leather wainscoting and parquet floors. Each of the guest rooms includes beds covered with handmade quilts and clawfoot tubs. The grand, master suite comprises the entire third floor and boasts 14-foot vaulted beam ceilings, Victorian walnut furnishings, a Jacuzzi and six-foot oak buffet now converted into a unique bathroom vanity. Innkeeper Mary Jo Johnson, a pastry chef, creates the wonderful pastries that accompany an expansive breakfast with fresh fruit, granola and delectable entrees.

Innkeeper(s): Mary Jo Johnson and Scott Johnson. $85-175. 5 rooms with PB, 2 with FP, 2 with WP, 1 suite. Breakfast included in rates. Types of meals: Full gourmet bkfst and early coffee/tea. Beds: KQ. Cable TV, VCR, reading lamp, refrigerator, ceiling fan, clock radio, hot tub/spa, some with fireplace, hair dryer, bathrobes and iron/ironing board in room. Central air. Library, parlor games and telephone on premises. Antiquing, art galleries, beach, bicycling, canoeing/kayaking, cross-country skiing, fishing, golf, hiking, horseback riding, live theater, museums, parks, shopping, sporting events, tennis and water sports nearby.

Certificate may be used: November-April, excluding holidays, subject to availability.

Hazel Green

Wisconsin House Stagecoach Inn

Main & Fairplay Streets
Hazel Green, WI 53811-0071
(887)854-2233 (877)854-2233
Internet: www.wisconsinhouse.com
E-mail: wishouse@mhtc.net

Circa 1846. Located in southwest Wisconsin's historic lead mining region, this one-time stagecoach stop will delight antique-lovers. The spacious two-story inn once hosted Ulysses S. Grant, whose home is just across the border in Illinois. One of the inn's guest rooms bears his name and features a walnut four-poster bed. Don't miss the chance to join the Dischs on a Saturday evening for their gourmet dinner, served by reservation only.

Innkeeper(s): Ken & Pat Disch. $75-125. 8 rooms, 6 with PB, 2 two-bedroom suites. Breakfast included in rates. Types of meals: Full gourmet bkfst, early coffee/tea, snacks/refreshments and gourmet dinner. Beds: KQDT. Reading lamp and bath amenities in room. Air conditioning. TV, VCR, DVD, fax, copier, library, parlor games and telephone on premises. Antiquing, art galleries, bicycling, canoeing/kayaking, cross-country skiing, downhill skiing, fishing, golf, hiking, horseback riding, live theater, museums, parks and wineries nearby.

Location: City.

Publicity: *Travel & Leisure, Milwaukee Magazine, Chicago Magazine, Milwaukee Journal and Wisconsin Trails.*

Certificate may be used: May through October anytime, rooms with shared baths only. Other months all rooms available.

Hazelhurst

Hazelhurst Inn

6941 Hwy 51
Hazelhurst, WI 54531
(715)356-6571
Internet: www.hazelhurstinn.com
E-mail: hzhrstbb@newnorth.net

Circa 1969. Situated in the scenic Northwoods, this country inn graces 18 wooded acres that are adjacent to the Bearskin State Trail. Outdoor enthusiasts appreciate the hiking, swimming, fishing, golfing, hunting, snowmobiling, cross-country skiing, horseback riding, boating and the many other activities the area offers. Enjoy a hearty breakfast each morning after a peaceful night's rest in a comfortable guest bedroom. Families are welcome here. Soak up the view from the sitting room or just relax by the fire.

Innkeeper(s): Sharon Goetsch. $75-90. 4 rooms, 3 with PB. Breakfast included in rates. Types of meals: Country bkfst. Beds: Q. Reading lamp, ceiling fan and clock radio in room. VCR, pet boarding, telephone and fireplace on premises. Antiquing, beach, bicycling, canoeing/kayaking, cross-country skiing, fishing, golf, hiking, horseback riding, live theater, museums, shopping, tennis and water sports nearby.

Location: Northwoods.

Certificate may be used: Anytime, subject to availability.

Lodi

Victorian Treasure Inn

115 Prairie St
Lodi, WI 53555-1240
(608)592-5199 (800)859-5199 Fax:(608)592-7147
Internet: www.victoriantreasure.com
E-mail: innkeeper@victoriantreasure.com

Circa 1897. Victorian Treasure features seven individually decorated guest rooms spread among two 19th-century Queen Anne Victorians. The interiors boast stained- and leaded-glass windows, pocket doors, rich restored woods and expansive porches. Five suites include a whirlpool tub, fireplace, wet bar, TV/VCR and stereo. Guests are greeted with a wine and cheese reception. Full, gourmet breakfasts may include specialties such as eggs Florentine, herb vegetable quiche, or stuffed French toast topped with a seasonal fruit sauce. Guests enjoy hiking along the National Scenic Ice Age Trail which passes beside the inn.

Innkeeper(s): Renee & Eric Degelau. $119-289. 9 rooms, 8 with PB, 5 with FP, 7 total suites, including 2 two-bedroom suites and 1 three-bedroom suite, 1 guest house, 1 conference room. Breakfast, afternoon tea, snacks/refreshments and wine included in rates. Types of meals: Full gourmet bkfst, veg bkfst, early coffee/tea and room service. Beds: KQ. Modem hook-up, data port, cable TV, VCR, DVD, reading lamp, stereo, refrigerator, ceiling fan, snack bar, clock radio, telephone, coffeemaker, turn-down service, desk, most with hot tub/spa, most with fireplace, hair dryer, bathrobes, bath amenities, wireless Internet access and iron/ironing board in room. Central air. Fax, copier, library, parlor games, gift shop and gift shop on premises. Antiquing, art galleries, beach, bicycling, canoeing/kayaking, cross-country skiing, downhill skiing, fishing, golf, hiking, horseback riding, live theater, museums, parks, shopping, sporting events, tennis, water sports, wineries, eagle watching, Taliesin, House on the Rock, Frank Lloyd Wright, Ice Age Trail, Wollersheim winery and Devil's Lake State Park nearby.

Location: Small Victorian town.

Publicity: *Recommended Romantic Inns, Wisconsin State Journal, Chicago Sun-Times, Milwaukee Magazine, Wisconsin Trails, Victorian Homes and Country Inn Cooking with Gail Greco.*

"An elegant, romantic getaway that everyone wants to return to again and again."

Certificate may be used: Sunday-Thursday, November-March, excluding holidays, subject to availability.

Madison

Arbor House, An Environmental Inn

3402 Monroe St
Madison, WI 53711-1702
(608)238-2981
Internet: www.arbor-house.com
E-mail: arborhouse@tds.net

Circa 1853. Nature-lovers not only will enjoy the inn's close access to a 1,280-acre nature preserve, they will appreciate the innkeepers' ecological theme. Organic sheets and towels are offered for guests as well as environmentally safe bath products. Arbor House is one of Madison's oldest existing homes and features plenty of historic features, such as romantic reading chairs and antiques, mixed with modern amenities and unique touches. Five guest rooms include a whirlpool tub and three have fire-

places. The Annex guest rooms include private balconies. The innkeepers offer many amenities for business travelers, including value-added corporate rates. The award-winning inn has been recognized as a model of urban ecology. Lake Wingra is within walking distance as are biking and nature trails, bird watching and a host of other outdoor activities. Guests enjoy complimentary canoeing and use of mountain bikes.

Innkeeper(s): John & Cathie Imes. $125-230. 8 rooms with PB, 3 with FP, 1 suite, 1 conference room. Breakfast included in rates. Types of meals: Full bkfst. Beds: KQ. Cable TV, VCR, reading lamp, stereo, ceiling fan, clock radio, telephone and desk in room. Air conditioning. Fax, copier, sauna and fireplace on premises. Handicap access. Antiquing, cross-country skiing, fishing, parks, shopping, sporting events and water sports nearby.

Location: City.

Publicity: *Money Magazine, New York Times, Natural Home, Travel & Leisure, Midwest Living and Insider's List Cable TV-Top 10 Eco-Hotels.*

"What a delightful treat in the middle of Madison. Absolutely, unquestionably, the best time I've spent in a hotel or otherwise. B&Bs are the only way to go! Thank you!"

Certificate may be used: November-April, Sunday-Thursday, excluding holidays (John Nolen and Cozy Rose guest rooms only).

Milwaukee

The Brumder Mansion

3046 W Wisconsin Ave
Milwaukee, WI 53208
(414)342-9767 (866)793-3676 Fax:(414)342-4772
Internet: www.brumdermansion.com
E-mail: brumdermansion@sbcglobal.net

Circa 1910. Built in the English Arts & Crafts style, this majestic brick home with Victorian and Gothic elements is furnished with elegant antiques. Common rooms feature huge oak fireplaces and exquisite woodwork, like the foyer's massive Gothic oak stairway. The lavish parlor's comfortable chairs invite relaxation, and the library has a large selection of games, magazines and books. A friendly atmosphere is enhanced with complimentary wine or beverages and homemade snacks or chocolates. Spacious guest bedrooms offer romantic settings with decorative painting and fine linens. Three suites include a double whirlpool, exquisite marble showers, CD player and TV/VCR. Enjoy the many flowers and view of the boulevard from the front porch.

Innkeeper(s): Carol Hirschi. $79-215. 5 rooms with PB, 5 with FP, 4 with WP, 4 suites, 1 conference room. Breakfast and snacks/refreshments included in rates. Types of meals: Full bkfst, veg bkfst and early coffee/tea. Beds: KQT. Cable TV, VCR, reading lamp, CD player, ceiling fan, clock radio, hot tub/spa, fireplace and 3 with whirlpools in room. Central air. Fax, copier, spa, library, parlor games, telephone and fireplace on premises. Antiquing, art galleries, beach, live theater, museums, parks, shopping, sporting events, water sports and wineries nearby.

Location: City.

Publicity: *Milwaukee Magazine and HBO.*

Certificate may be used: Sunday-Thursday, Jan. 2-May 15, except Valentine's.

Monroe

Victorian Garden B&B

1720 16th St
Monroe, WI 53566-2643
(608)328-1720 (888)814-7909

Circa 1890. The original charm of this blue and white three-story Victorian home still remains today. Antiques and collectibles are found throughout the house, along with a vintage doll and teddy bear collection. Wraparound porches and flower gardens are great for relaxing. Accommodations include the

White Lace and Roses Suite featuring a clawfoot tub and shower for two. The Rosebud Room overlooks the hand-carved Italian fountain, and the Ivy Room is a quiet corner setting. A full breakfast is served in the formal dining room. Local attractions include the Monroe Depot and historic square. Come stay and visit with us, the pleasure is all ours.

Innkeeper(s): Judy & Ron Marsh. $89-109. 3 rooms with PB. Breakfast included in rates. Types of meals: Full bkfst. Beds: QD. Air conditioning. Antiquing, bicycling, cross-country skiing, fishing, golf, hiking, parks and sporting events nearby.

Location: City.

Certificate may be used: Dec. 1-March 31, excluding Dec. 24-Jan. 2, subject to availability, no holidays.

Osceola

St. Croix River Inn

305 River St, PO Box 356
Osceola, WI 54020-0356
(715)294-4248 (800)645-8820
Internet: www.stcroixriverinn.com
E-mail: innkeeper@stcroixriverinn.com

Circa 1908. Timeless elegance is imparted at this meticulously restored stone house that blends old world charm with new world luxuries. Indulge in dramatic vistas from this gorgeous setting on the bluffs of the

river. A comfortable ambiance embraces this inn where complimentary coffee is always found in the sitting room. There is also a wine and beverage bar. Select a book or game from the

entertainment closet. Videos and CDs are also available for use in the private suites that all feature a fireplace and a hydromassage tub. A sumptuous breakfast served to each room is highlighted with spectacular views of the water.

Innkeeper(s): Ben & Jennifer Bruno. $125-250. 7 rooms, 7 with FP, 7 with WP, 7 suites. Breakfast and snacks/refreshments included in rates. Types of meals: Full gourmet bkfst, veg bkfst, early coffee/tea, picnic lunch and wine. Beds: Q. Cable TV, VCR, DVD, reading lamp, stereo, refrigerator, snack bar, clock radio, telephone, coffeemaker, turn-down service, hot tub/spa, voice mail, fireplace, hair dryer, bathrobes, bath amenities, wireless Internet access, Fireplace, Hydromassage tub and Spa-quality amenities in room. Central air. Parlor games, Perched on the bluffs of the river and most rooms offer a private patio or balcony with spectacular river views on premises. Handicap access. Antiquing, beach, bicycling, canoeing/kayaking, cross-country skiing, downhill skiing, fishing, golf, hiking, live theater, parks, shopping, water sports, wineries, Snowmobile trails, Scenic train ride, Dinner cruises, Spa services, Casino and Fine dining nearby.

Location: Country, waterfront.

Publicity: *Chicago Sun-Times, Skyway News and St. Paul Pioneer Press.*

Certificate may be used: Nov. 30 to April 30, Sunday-Thursday, excluding holidays.

Poynette

Jamieson House

407 N Franklin St
Poynette, WI 53955-9490
(608)635-4100 Fax:(608)635-2292
Internet: www.Jamiesonhouse.com
E-mail: jamiesonhouse@charter.net

Circa 1878. Bask in the tranquil peace that is found at this Victorian bed and breakfast and event center in the small town of Poynette, Wisconsin just north of Madison. Surrounded by an acre of garden land, Jamieson House has a yellow brick façade and is tastefully furnished with antiques, reproductions and modern accents. Watch a movie in the living room, play a game or do crafts in the Bank, named after the room's previous purpose. The Sun Room boasts three walls of windows. Spacious guest bedrooms and suites feature whirlpool tubs. Several include fireplaces. Linger over a homemade breakfast served each morning in the formal dining room. Lake Wisconsin is nearby and it is an easy drive to two ski areas and Wisconsin Dells.

Innkeeper(s): Ned & Kathleen O'Reilly. $85-165. 6 rooms with PB, 3 with FP, 6 with WP. A full breakfast is served and all dietary restrictions are accommodated included in rates. Types of meals: Country bkfst, veg bkfst and Gluten-free or sugar-free breakfast. Beds: KQ. Cable TV, VCR, reading lamp, CD player, refrigerator, clock radio, coffeemaker, hot tub/spa, some with fireplace, bathrobes, bath amenities and wireless Internet access in room. Central air. DVD, fax, copier, spa, bicycles, parlor games, telephone and Wireless Internet access on premises. Antiquing, beach, bicycling, canoeing/kayaking, cross-country skiing, downhill skiing, fishing, golf, hiking, horseback riding, museums, parks, shopping, sporting events, water sports and wineries nearby.

Location: Country. Small village.

Certificate may be used: Sunday-Thursday, anytime, excluding holidays, weekends and holidays at the last minute.

Reedsburg

Parkview B&B

211 N Park St
Reedsburg, WI 53959-1652
(608)524-4333 Fax:(608)524-1172
Internet: www.parkviewbb.com
E-mail: info@parkviewbb.com

Circa 1895. Tantalizingly close to Baraboo and Spring Green, this central Wisconsin inn overlooks a city park in the historic district. The gracious innkeepers delight in tending to their guests' desires and offer wake-up coffee and a morning paper. The home's first owners were in the hardware business, so there are many original, unique fixtures, in addition to hardwood floors, intri-

cate woodwork, leaded and etched windows and a suitors' window. The downtown business district is just a block away.

Innkeeper(s): Tom & Donna Hofmann. $80-98. 4 rooms, 2 with PB, 1 with FP. Breakfast and snacks/refreshments included in rates. Types of meals: Full gourmet bkfst, veg bkfst and early coffee/tea. Beds: QT. Reading lamp, CD player, refrigerator, ceiling fan, clock radio and 1 with fireplace in room. Central air. TV, fax and parlor games on premises. Antiquing, art galleries, bicycling, canoeing/kayaking, cross-country skiing, downhill skiing, fishing, golf, hiking, horseback riding, live theater, parks, shopping, wineries and state parks nearby.

Location: City. Population of 8,500 people.

Publicity: *Reedsburg Report and Reedsburg Times-Press.*

"Your hospitality was great! You all made us feel right at home."
Certificate may be used: Sunday-Thursday, May 1-Oct. 31, holidays not included anytime remainder of year.

Sheboygan Falls

The Rochester Inn

504 Water St
Sheboygan Falls, WI 53085-1455
(920)467-3123 (866)467-3122
Internet: www.rochesterinn.com
E-mail: info@rochesterinn.com

Circa 1848. This Greek Revival inn is furnished with Queen Anne Victorian antiques, wet bars and four-poster beds. The most romantic offerings are the 600-square-foot suites. They include living rooms with camel back couches and wing back chairs on the first floor and bedrooms with double whirlpool tubs on the second floor. Sheboygan Falls is one mile from the village of Kohler.

Innkeeper(s): Sean & Jacquelyn O'Dwanny. $109-170. 6 rooms, 5 with HT, 6 total suites, including 5 two-bedroom suites. Breakfast and snacks/refreshments included in rates. Types of meals: Full gourmet bkfst, early coffee/tea and afternoon tea. Beds: Q. Data port, cable TV, VCR, reading lamp, refrigerator, clock radio, telephone, coffeemaker, desk, hot tub/spa and whirlpool in room. Central air. Laundry facility on premises. Antiquing, art galleries, beach, bicycling, canoeing/kayaking, cross-country skiing, fishing, golf, hiking, horseback riding, parks, shopping, tennis, water sports, black Wolf Run, Kohler and Whistling Straits nearby.

Location: Small town.

Certificate may be used: Sunday-Thursday, Nov. 1-May 1, some restrictions apply.

Sparta

The Franklin Victorian Bed & Breakfast

220 E Franklin St
Sparta, WI 54656-1804
(608)366-1427 (888)594-3822 Fax:(608)366-1226
Internet: www.franklinvictorianbb.com
E-mail: innkeeper@franklinvictorianbb.com

Circa 1900. Escape to this Victorian treasure located in the Hidden Valleys of Southwestern Wisconsin. This area is considered to be the Bicycling Capital of America and the famous Elroy-Sparta state biking trail is nearby. Relax with a book and a homemade treat from the bottomless cookie jar. In the early evening, enjoy a wine and cheese reception. Guest bedrooms are elegant and spacious retreats. After a scrumptious full breakfast, adventures await. Explore Amish country, go hiking, experience Warren Cranfest, cranberry harvesting and an abundance of water and snow sports. This all-season inn offers year-round activities. Ask about Murder Mystery Weekends. Bike storage and shuttles are provided.

Innkeeper(s): Jennifer & Steve Dunn. $98-129. 4 rooms with PB, 1 with FP, 1 with WP, 1 suite. Breakfast, snacks/refreshments and wine included in rates. Types of meals: Full bkfst, veg bkfst, early coffee/tea and room service. Beds: KQ. Reading lamp, CD player, refrigerator, ceiling fan, clock radio, coffeemaker, turn-down service, some with hot tub/spa, some with fireplace, hair dryer, bathrobes, bath amenities, wireless Internet access, iron/ironing board and Business Travelers Free High Speed Wireless Internet is available in room. Central air. TV, VCR, DVD, library, parlor games, telephone and High Speed Wireless Internet Available on premises. Antiquing, art galleries, beach, bicycling, canoeing/kayaking, cross-country skiing, downhill skiing, fishing, golf, hiking, horseback riding, museums, parks, shopping, sporting events, tennis and water sports nearby.

Location: City.

Publicity: *La Crosse Tribune, Sparta Newspaper and "Voted by inngoers in Arrington's 2006 Book of Lists as one of the Top 12 B&Bs/Inns in North America for "Most Historical Charm"*

Certificate may be used: Anytime, November-March, subject to availability.

Stoughton

Naeset-Roe Inn

126 E Washington St
Stoughton, WI 53589
(608)877-4150
Internet: www.naesetroe.com
E-mail: naesetroe@naesetroe.com

Circa 1878. A prominent local architect built this historic Italianate home, which is listed in the National Register. The brick exterior is decked with goldenrod trim with scarlet accents. Guest rooms are decorated with antiques. Two rooms include a whirlpool tub, one has a clawfoot tub and the other offers a large soaking tub. Beds are dressed with fine, hand-ironed linens. The Victorian décor is accentuated by the soft glow of candlelight. Massage service is available, as are honeymoon packages. The library offers a large selection of books and magazines, as well as some antique books .Bountiful buffet breakfasts are served by candlelight and might begin with a baked grapefruit with a chocolate cherry liqueur sauce. From there, guests partake of an asparagus quiche with a side of fresh salsa, potatoes and homemade bread. Lastly, guests are treated to pecan rolls and a plate featuring a selection of the state's famous cheeses. The town of Stoughton offers close access to Madison, Cambridge and Janesville.

Innkeeper(s): Carl Povlick. $90-150. 4 rooms with PB, 2 with FP, 2 with WP, 1 conference room. Breakfast included in rates. Types of meals: Full gourmet bkfst, veg bkfst, early coffee/tea, snacks/refreshments and If you have dietary needs let the innkeeper know. No one ever goes away hungry. Beds: Q. TV, VCR, reading lamp, CD player, clock radio, most with hot tub/spa, some with fireplace, hair dryer, bath amenities, wireless Internet access and iron/ironing board in room. Central air. DVD, library, parlor games, telephone and Private garden for your relaxation on premises. Antiquing, art galleries, beach, bicycling, canoeing/kayaking, cross-country skiing, fishing, golf, hiking, horseback riding, live theater, museums, parks, shopping, sporting events, tennis, water sports and wineries nearby.

Location: City.

Publicity: *Women in Business, Wisconsin State Journal, The Stoughton Courier Hub and a New Magazine.*

"You have not missed an item to make your B&B welcoming!"
Certificate may be used: November-May 10, anytime subject to availability.

Sturgeon Bay

Garden Gate Bed & Breakfast

434 N 3rd Ave
Sturgeon Bay, WI 54235
(920)743-9618 (877)743-9618
Internet: doorcountybb.com
E-mail: stay@doorcountybb.com

Circa 1890. Open year-round, historic 1890 Garden Gate Bed & Breakfast exudes a romantic Victorian elegance. The oak-paneled foyer features a stairwell with hand-turned spindles. The parlor boasts an antique oak fireplace mantle with Doric columns and a beveled oval mirror. Verandas beckon relaxation. Sleep in a guest bedroom with a quilt-covered bed and an entertainment center. Nine-panel pocket doors accent the dining room where a delightful daily breakfast is served with soft music by candlelight. Early risers can enjoy coffee and tea first. Ask about specials available. Located in Sturgeon Bay, Wisconsin in Door County, this area is home to a wide variety of outdoor activities and amusements.

Innkeeper(s): Robin Vallow. $100-145. 4 rooms with PB, 3 with FP, 1 with WP, 1 suite. Breakfast included in rates. Types of meals: Full gourmet bkfst, early coffee/tea, snacks/refreshments and wine. Cable TV, DVD, reading lamp, stereo, refrigerator, ceiling fan, snack bar, clock radio, fireplace, bath amenities and Whirlpool suite in room. Central air. VCR on premises. Antiquing, art galleries, beach, bicycling, canoeing/kayaking, fishing, golf, hiking, horseback riding, live theater, museums, parks, shopping, water sports and wineries nearby.

Location: City.

Certificate may be used: Sunday-Thursday, except holidays.

Scofield House B&B

908 Michigan St
Sturgeon Bay, WI 54235-1849
(920)743-7727 (888)463-0204 Fax:(920)743-7727
Internet: www.scofieldhouse.com
E-mail: stay@charterinternet.com

Circa 1902. Mayor Herbert Scofield, prominent locally in the lumber and hardware business, built this late-Victorian house with a sturdy square tower and inlaid floors that feature intricate borders patterned in cherry, birch, maple, walnut, and red and white oak. Oak moldings throughout the house boast raised designs of bows, ribbons, swags and flowers. Equally lavish decor is featured in the guest rooms with fluffy flowered

comforters and cabbage rose wallpapers highlighting romantic antique bedsteads. Baked apple-cinnamon French toast is a house specialty. Modern amenities include many suites with fireplaces and double whirlpools. "Room at the Top" is a sky-lit 900-square-foot suite occupying the whole third floor and furnished with Victorian antiques.

Innkeeper(s): Dan & Vicki Klein. $80-220. 6 rooms with PB, 5 with FP, 5 with WP. Breakfast and afternoon tea included in rates. Types of meals: Full bkfst. Beds: Q. Cable TV, VCR, DVD, reading lamp, stereo, refrigerator, ceiling fan, clock radio, most with hot tub/spa, most with fireplace, hair dryer, bath amenities and double whirlpools in room. Air conditioning. Fax, parlor games, telephone and Free video library on premises. Antiquing, art galleries, bicycling, canoeing/kayaking, cross-country skiing, downhill skiing, fishing, golf, hiking, horseback riding, live theater, museums, parks, shopping, water sports and wineries nearby.

Location: City. Surrounded by 250 miles of shoreline.

Publicity: *Innsider, Glamour, Country, Wisconsin Trails, Green Bay Press Gazette, Chicago Tribune, Milwaukee Sentinel-Journal, Midwest Living, Victorian Decorating & Lifestyle, Country Inns and National Geographic Traveler.*

"You've introduced us to the fabulous world of B&Bs. I loved the porch swing and would have been content on it for the entire weekend."

Certificate may be used: Monday-Thursday, Nov. 15-April 30.

The Reynolds House B&B

111 So 7th Ave
Sturgeon Bay, WI 54235
(920)746-9771 (877)269-7401 Fax:(920)746-9441
Internet: www.reynoldshousebandb.com
E-mail: hahull@reynoldshousebandb.com

Circa 1900. A three-story, red-roofed Queen Anne Victorian

house, the Reynolds House is painted in two shades of teal and yellow with white trim on its balustrades and brackets. Leaded-glass windows and a stone veranda that wraps around the front of the house are features. Rooms are cheerfully decorated and offer antique beds, attractive bed coverings and wallpapers. Tucked under the gable, the Winesap Suite includes a whirlpool, sitting room and fireplace. The innkeeper's kitchen garden furnishes fresh herbs to accent breakfast dishes, as well as flowers for the table.

Innkeeper(s): Heather Hull. $70-195. 4 rooms with PB, 3 with FP, 1 suite. Breakfast and snacks/refreshments included in rates. Types of meals: Full gourmet bkfst and early coffee/tea. Beds: Q. Cable TV, ceiling fan, clock radio and some with whirlpool in room. Central air. TV, VCR, fax, copier, library, parlor games, telephone and fireplace on premises. Antiquing, art galleries, beach,  bicycling, cross-country skiing, fishing, golf, hiking, horseback riding, live theater, museums, parks, shopping, tennis and wineries nearby.

Publicity: *Door County Magazine, Midwest Living Magazine (Voted Best in the Midwest June 2001 & 2003) and Arrington Inn Traveler's (Best Breakfast 2004).*

Certificate may be used: November-April, subject to availability.

White Lace Inn

16 N 5th Ave
Sturgeon Bay, WI 54235-1795
(920)743-1105 (877)948-5223 Fax:(920)743-8180
Internet: www.WhiteLaceInn.com
E-mail: Romance@WhiteLaceInn.com

Circa 1903. The romantic White Lace Inn is composed of four beautifully restored Victorian houses connected by meandering garden paths. Inviting rooms and suites offer fine antiques and ornate Victorian or canopy beds. The inn's suites include oversized whirlpool baths, fireplaces, white linens, down comforters and many other amenities. Often the site for romantic anniversary celebrations, a favorite suite has a two-sided fireplace, magnificent walnut Eastlake bed, English country fabrics and a whirlpool. Lemonade or hot chocolate and cookies are offered upon arrival. In the morning, the delectable offerings include items such as cherry apple crisp and creamy rice pudding. Year-round activities invite frequent visits — the Festival of Blossoms, the Lighthouse Walk, Cherry Festival and the Classic Wooden Boat event, for instance. Take museums and gallery strolls, and enjoy the area's great restaurants.

Innkeeper(s): Dennis & Bonnie Statz. $70-235. 18 rooms with PB, 15 with FP, 12 with HT, 5 suites, 4 guest houses. Breakfast and snacks/refreshments included in rates. Types of meals: Full bkfst and Special dietary needs can be accommodated with advance notice. Beds: KQD. TV, VCR, stereo, most with hot tub/spa, most with fireplace, hair dryer, bath amenities, iron/ironing board, 12 with whirlpool tubs and 9 with fireplace and whirlpool in room. Air conditioning. DVD, fax, parlor games, telephone, gift shop and Wedding Ceremonies on premises. Handicap access. Antiquing, art galleries, beach, bicycling, canoeing/kayaking, cross-country skiing, fishing, golf, hiking, horseback riding, live theater, museums, parks, shopping, sporting events, tennis, water sports and wineries nearby.

Publicity: *Milwaukee Sentinel, Brides, National Geographic Traveler, Wisconsin Trails, Milwaukee, Country Home and Midwest Living.*

""Each guest room is an overwhelming visual feast, a dazzling fusion of colors, textures and beautiful objects. It is one of these rare gems that established a tradition the day it opened." — Wisconsin Trails"

Certificate may be used: Sunday through Thursday, Nov. 1-April 30 with some restrictions, at "high season" rate.

Viroqua

Viroqua Heritage Inn B&B's

217 & 220 E Jefferson St
Viroqua, WI 54665
(608)637-3306 (888)443-7466
Internet: www.herinn.com
E-mail: rhodsent@mwt.net

Circa 1890. It is easy to relax at this handsome 1897 three-story English Tudor Revival inn with gables and leaded windows in Viroqua, Wisconsin. Find a quiet hideaway on the sunporch, or wander in the garden by the pond. The trellis bench is an inviting spot for meditation. A favorite accommodation is the two-room suite with its own enclosed porch and pocket doors. Ask for a guest bedroom with a whirlpool tub or fireplace. The inn sometimes features murder mystery weekends. A full breakfast is served on weekends, and an expanded continental breakfast is offered during the week.

Innkeeper(s): Nancy Rhodes. $60-120. 8 rooms, 6 with PB, 2 with FP, 1 with WP. Breakfast included in rates. Types of meals: Full bkfst and early coffee/tea. Beds: KQD. TV, reading lamp, clock radio, telephone, coffee pots and one with whirlpool bath in room. Air conditioning. VCR, DVD, bicycles, library, child care, parlor games, fireplace, refrigerator, exercise club, whirlpool tub, organic cooking, coffee pub and spa services on premises. Antiquing, cross-country skiing, downhill skiing, fishing, live theater, parks, shopping, water sports, Amish shopping and community built city park nearby.

Location: Wisconsin "Main Street" Town.

Publicity: *Smithsonian Magazine, Readers' Digest and Milwaukee Magazine.*

"Wonderful house, great hosts."

Certificate may be used: Anytime, November-April, subject to availability.

Waupaca

Cleghorn Bed & Breakfast

E1268 Cleghorn Rd
Waupaca, WI 54981
(715)258-5235 (800)870-0737 Fax:(715)258-5235
Internet: www.cleghornbnb.com
E-mail: info@cleghornbnb.com

Circa 1985. Three acres surround this country house with a log facade. The inn boasts interiors of barn-board walls and Amish furnishings and quilts. For instance, there are some hand-crafted bedsteads including a four-poster. A large stone fireplace in the living room and woodland views from the dining room enhance the country setting. Dutch pancakes with apple topping and maple butter is a favorite breakfast item. Nearby are antique shops, art galleries, streams for canoeing and back roads for cycling.

Innkeeper(s): Bob & Linda Yerkes. $89-125. 3 rooms with PB, 2 with FP. Breakfast included in rates. Types of meals: Full bkfst and early coffee/tea. Beds: QT. Reading lamp, ceiling fan, clock radio and turn-down service in room. Air conditioning. VCR, telephone and fireplace on premises. Antiquing, cross-country skiing, fishing, golf, parks, shopping and water sports nearby.

Certificate may be used: Sept. 1 to June 15, Sunday-Thursday and Nov. 1 to May 1, subject to availability, last minute based on projected availability.

Crystal River Inn B&B

E1369 Rural Rd
Waupaca, WI 54981-8246
(715)258-5333 (800)236-5789 Fax:(715)258-5310
Internet: www.crystalriver-inn.com
E-mail: crystalriverinn@charter.net

Circa 1853. The stately beauty of this historic Greek Revival farmhouse is rivaled only by its riverside setting. Each room features a view of the water, garden, woods or all three. A Victorian gazebo, down comforters and delicious breakfasts, with pecan sticky buns, a special favorite, add to guests' enjoyment. A recent addition to the inn's offerings include a newly restored historic cottage. With luxurious decor it includes two bedrooms, a living room with fireplace and private porches. It may be reserved singly or together. Exploring the village of Rural, which is in the National Register, will delight those interested in bygone days. Recreational activities abound, with the Chain O'Lakes and a state park nearby.

Innkeeper(s): Deb and Robert Benada. $68-138. 7 rooms, 5 with PB, 4 with FP, 2 cottages, 1 conference room. Breakfast and snacks/refreshments included in rates. Types of meals: Full bkfst and early coffee/tea. Beds: KQ. TV, reading lamp, ceiling fan, clock radio, telephone, desk, hot tub/spa and fireplace in room. Central air. VCR, DVD, fax and copier on premises. Limited handicap access. Antiquing, art galleries, beach, canoeing/kayaking, cross-country skiing, downhill skiing, golf, hiking, parks, shopping, sporting events, tennis and water sports nearby.

Location: Waterfront. 23 Lakes.

Publicity: *Resorter, Stevens Point Journal, Wisconsin Trails Magazine, Fox Cities Magazine and Appleton Post Crescent.*

"It was like being king for a day."

Certificate may be used: Sunday through Thursday (June-October), other times November-May anytime.

Whitewater

Victoria-On-Main B&B

622 W Main St
Whitewater, WI 53190-1855
(262)473-8400
E-mail: viconmain@sbcglobal.net

Circa 1895. This graceful Queen Anne Victorian, shaded by a tall birch tree, is in the heart of Whitewater National Historic District, adjacent to the University of Wisconsin. It was built for Edward Engebretson, mayor of Whitewater. Yellow tulip and sunny daffodils fill the spring flower beds, while fuchsias and geraniums bloom in summertime behind a picket fence. The inn's gables, flower-filled veranda and three-story turret feature a handsome green tin roof. Each guest room is named for a Wisconsin hardwood. The Red Oak Room, Cherry Room and Bird's Eye Maple Room all offer handsome antiques in their corresponding wood, Laura Ashley prints, antique sheets, pristine heirloom-laced pillowcases and down comforters. A hearty breakfast is sometimes served on the wraparound veranda, and there are kitchen facilities available for light meal preparation. Whitewater Lake and Kettle Moraine State Forest are five minutes away.

Innkeeper(s): Nancy Wendt. $85-95. 3 rooms, 1 with PB, 1 with FP. Breakfast included in rates. Types of meals: Full bkfst and early coffee/tea. Beds: D. Reading lamp and ceiling fan in room. Air conditioning. Telephone on premises. Antiquing, cross-country skiing, fishing, live theater, parks, shopping and water sports nearby.

"We loved it. Wonderful hospitality."

Certificate may be used: June - September and January, Sunday - Thursday.

Wisconsin Dells

Bowman's Oak Hill Bed and Breakfast

4169 State Hwy 13
Wisconsin Dells, WI 53965
(608)253-5638 (888)253-5631
Internet: bowmansoakhillbedandbreakfast.com
E-mail: bowmansoakhillbb@aol.com

Circa 1969. Thirteen acres of country peacefulness surround this estate with lawns, gardens, fields and a cottage ranch home built in the 1960s. This smoke-free, adult retreat is "where comfort comes with your key." Relaxation is easy on the front porch wicker furniture or three-season sun porch. Sit in wing-backed chairs and watch a movie from the video library in the living room. Afternoon and evening snacks and refreshments are offered. Air-conditioned guest bedrooms boast family heirloom furniture, sitting areas and cozy robes. Fresh fruit smoothies are a house specialty for breakfast that includes a hot egg dish and warm baked goods or pancakes. An outdoor covered swing and sitting areas provide romantic settings. Walk in the woods, play croquet or a game of horseshoes.

Innkeeper(s): David and Nancy Bowman. $75-165. 4 rooms with PB. Breakfast and snacks/refreshments included in rates. Types of meals: Full gourmet bkfst, veg bkfst and early coffee/tea. Beds: QD. Reading lamp, ceiling fan, clock radio, turn-down service, desk, some with hot tub/spa, hair dryer, bathrobes, bath amenities, iron/ironing board, antiques, two comfortable chairs and quilts in room. Air conditioning. TV, VCR, library, parlor games and telephone on premises. Amusement parks, antiquing, art galleries, bicycling, canoeing/kayaking, cross-country skiing, downhill skiing, fishing, golf, hiking, horseback riding, live theater, museums, parks, shopping, water sports, wineries and water parks nearby.

Location: Country. Near Downtown River District.

Publicity: Ad-lit publications.

Certificate may be used: November-May excluding Memorial Day Weekend, Sunday-Thursday, subject to availability, Anytime, Last Minute-Based on Availability.

Thunder Valley Inn-Bed & Breakfast, Farm Restaurant and Scandinavian Gift Hus

W15344 Waubeek Road
Wisconsin Dells, WI 53965-9005
(608)254-4145 (877)254-4145
Internet: www.thundervalleyinn.com
E-mail: info@thundervalleyinn.com

Circa 1880. The Wisconsin Dells area is full of both Scandinavian and Native American heritage, and the innkeepers of this country inn have tried to honor the traditions. The inn even features a Scandinavian gift shop. Chief Yellow Thunder, for whom this inn is named, often camped out on the grounds and surrounding area. The inn's restaurant is highly acclaimed. Everything is homemade, including the wheat the innkeepers grind for the morning pancakes and rolls. There is a good selection of Wisconsin beer and wine, as well. Guests can stay in the Farmhouse, Swedish Guest Hus, or Wee Hus, all of which offer microwaves and refrigerators.

Innkeeper(s): Anita, Kari, and Sigrid Nelson. $69-139. 10 rooms with PB, 1 with WP, 4 total suites, including 3 two-bedroom suites, 1 cottage, 2 guest houses, 3 conference rooms. Breakfast, Sunday brunch, snacks/refreshments and A full farm breafkast is included with all room rates included in rates.

Types of meals: Country bkfst, veg bkfst, early coffee/tea, picnic lunch and dinner. Restaurant on premises. Beds: KQDT. Modem hook-up, TV, VCR, DVD, reading lamp, CD player, refrigerator, ceiling fan, clock radio, coffeemaker, desk, bath amenities, iron/ironing board, Most rooms have TV/VCRs, Access to extensive video library & mini-fridges, Many have microwaves, Individual A/C units in the Wee Hus and the Swedish Hus in room. Central air. Library, parlor games, telephone, gift shop, Old one-room schoolhouse, Pet farm animals including kittens, goat & bunny, Visit working dairy farm by arrangement, On-site farm restaurant, Dinner shows May thru mid-October with a 25% discount for B&B guests, Guest entertainers Saturday evenings throughout the summer season, Picnic areas, Evening campfires with marshmallow roasting and Scandinavian Gift Hus on premises. Handicap access. Amusement parks, antiquing, art galleries, beach, bicycling, canoeing/kayaking, cross-country skiing, downhill skiing, fishing, golf, hiking, horseback riding, live theater, museums, parks, shopping, water sports, wineries, Wisconsin Dells Boat Tours, original Wisconsin Ducks, Wollersheim Winery, Circus World Museum, Rick Wilcox Magic Theatre, Noah's Ark Waterpark, Sundara Spa, Tommy Bartlett's Ski, Sky, and Stage Show and Devil's Lake State Park nearby.

Location: Country. One mile from the fabulous Wisconsin Dells.

Publicity: *Wisconsin Trails Magazine, Country Inns, Midwest Living Magazine, Chicago Sun-Times, Milwaukee Journal-Sentinel, National Geographic Travel Magazine, St. Paul Pioneer Press, Eau Claire Leader-Telegram, AAA Home & Away Magazine.* and *WMTV-Madison.*

"Thunder Valley is a favorite of Firstar Club members — delicious food served in a charming atmosphere with warm Scandinavian hospitality."

Certificate may be used: Sunday through Thursday, November through May, except holidays and upon availability. Does not apply to $65 rooms.

White Rose Inns

910 River Road
Wisconsin Dells, WI 53965
(608)254-4724 (800)482-4724 Fax:(608)254-4585
Internet: www.thewhiterose.com
E-mail: info@thewhiterose.com

Circa 1904. Overlooking the Wisconsin River and one block from downtown, these historic Victorian mansions are ornately decorated and boast original woodwork, stairways and architectural details. White Rose Inns offers a tranquil, smoke-free environment. Well-appointed guest bedrooms with gorgeous colors and fabrics feature soft lighting and whirlpool baths. World-famous omelets, quiche du jour, home-fried potatoes, croissants, fresh fruit with yogurt, and Belgian waffles with strawberries and cream are some of the menu items served for breakfast in the Mediterranean dining room. Walk the lavish gardens, swim in the outdoor heated pool, and schedule a massage. Nearby Wisconsin Dells, created by the Northern Glacier, reflects ice-age history and provides great hiking and biking trails. Devil's Lake State Park is just 10 miles away.

Innkeeper(s): Mariah & Roger Boss. $80-225. 21 rooms with PB, 5 with FP, 15 with WP, 3 two-bedroom suites, 3 conference rooms. Breakfast included in rates. Types of meals: Full gourmet bkfst, veg bkfst, early coffee/tea, wine, 10% discount at Cheese Factory Restaurant, B&B and dinner packages at local restaurants and several restaurants within 3 blocks. Beds: KQDT. Cable TV, VCR, reading lamp, desk and wireless Internet access in room. Central air. Fax, copier, swimming, telephone, fireplace, Murder Mystery dinner parties and meeting rooms on premises. Limited handicap access. Amusement parks, antiquing, art galleries, beach, bicycling, canoeing/kayaking, cross-country skiing, downhill skiing, fishing, golf, hiking, horseback riding, live theater, museums, parks, shopping, tennis, water sports, wineries, outlet mall, America's largest indoor and outdoor waterparks and boat tours of spectacular natural scenery nearby.

Location: City, waterfront. One block from downtown beside the Wisconsin River.

Publicity: *Best Wisconsin Romantic Weekends, Isthmus newspaper, Wisconsin State Journal, Milwaukee State Journal, Arringtons Inn Traveler magazine and Fun In Wisconsin magazine.*

Certificate may be used: Anytime, October-April, subject to availability.

Wyoming

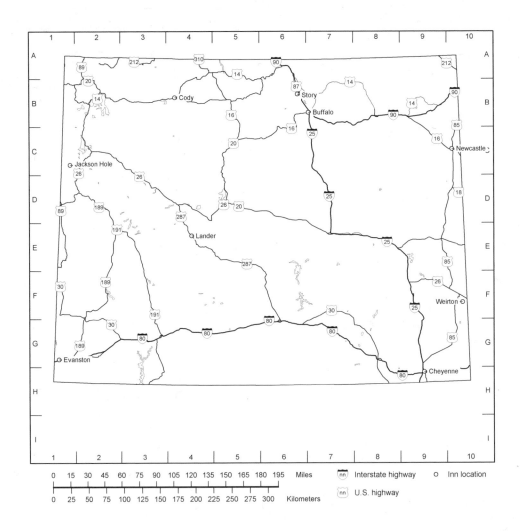

Tell the innkeeper that you have an iLoveInns free-night certificate when you make your reservation.

Cody

Mayor's Inn Bed & Breakfast

1413 Rumsey Ave
Cody, WY 82414
(307)587-0887 (888)217-3001
Internet: www.mayorsinn.com
E-mail: reserve@MayorsInn.com

Circa 1909. Considered the town's first mansion, this stylish two-story, turn-of-the-century home was built for Cody's first elected mayor. A romantic Victorian ambiance is achieved with warm hospitality, antiques, soft lighting, chandeliers and splendid wall and ceiling papers. The parlor inspires nostalgia. The guest bedrooms feature either a brass bed and clawfoot tub, a lodge pole pine bed, jetted tub and western art, or an open, sunny room with double shower. The suite boasts a fresh water hot tub and CD player. Offering private seating, breakfast is served in both of the dining rooms. The Carriage House is a cottage with a fully equipped kitchen.

Innkeeper(s): Bill & DaLeLee Delph. $80-210. 5 rooms, 4 with PB, 1 with HT, 1 with WP, 1 cottage, 1 conference room. Breakfast included in rates. Types of meals: Full bkfst and early coffee/tea. Beds: KQD. Cable TV, DVD, reading lamp, stereo, clock radio, some with hot tub/spa, hair dryer, bathrobes, bath amenities, wireless Internet access, iron/ironing board, telephone in common area and individual climate controls in room. Central air. Fax, parlor games and telephone on premises. Antiquing, art galleries, bicycling, canoeing/kayaking, cross-country skiing, downhill skiing, fishing, golf, hiking, horseback riding, live theater, museums, parks, shopping, tennis, water sports, Nightly rodeo from June to September and Seasonal trolley tours nearby.

Location: Historic downtown Cody, one block off the main street.

Publicity: *Cody Enterprise, The Telegraph Travel, Country Extra Magazine and Bed & Breakfast American Magazine.*

Certificate may be used: Anytime, November-April, subject to availability.

Jackson Hole

Sassy Moose Inn

3895 Miles Rd
Jackson Hole, WY 83014
(307)733-1277 (800)356-1277 Fax:(307)733-5927
Internet: www.sassymoose.com
E-mail: craigerwy@aol.com

Circa 1992. All of the rooms at this log-house-style inn have spectacular Teton views. The Mountain Room has a rock fireplace, queen bed and mountain cabin decor. The River Room's decor is dominated by the colors of the Snake River and accented with antiques. The inn is five minutes from Teton Village and the Jackson Hole Ski Resort. Teton Pines Golf Course and Nordic Trails are just across the road. After a day of activities, enjoy sharing your experiences over tea, wine or relaxing in the large hot tub.

Innkeeper(s): Polly Kelley. $139-215. 5 rooms with PB, 5 with FP, 1 suite. Breakfast included in rates. Types of meals: Full bkfst, early coffee/tea and afternoon tea. Beds: KQ. TV, VCR, DVD, reading lamp, clock radio and desk in room. Air conditioning. Fax, copier, spa, library, child care, parlor games, telephone, fireplace and limited laundry on premises. Cross-country skiing, downhill skiing, fishing, live theater, parks, shopping and water sports nearby.

Location: Mountains. Snake River.

Certificate may be used: Anytime except June through September and December Holiday Season.

Newcastle

EVA-Great Spirit Ranch B&B

1262 Beaver Creek Rd
Newcastle, WY 82701
(307)746-2537
Internet: www.wyomingbnb-ranchrec.com/evagreatspirit

Circa 1984. Amidst spectacular scenery of mountains and woods, guests will find this modern log home. Although the home is new, it rests on what was an old stagecoach route. A century-old barn is located on the property, as well as ruins of a 19th-century bunkhouse. The interior features hardwood floors and high ceilings, and the guest rooms are comfortably furnished in a modern style. There are two rooms with private baths and two adjoining rooms with a shared bath. Irene offers spring and fall hunting packages, where guests can search for deer, elk and wild turkey on the 525-acre property and adjacent Bureau of Land Management and state lands. The vast acreage borders Black Hills National Forest in South Dakota.

Innkeeper(s): Irene Ward. $55-80. 4 rooms, 2 with PB. Breakfast included in rates. Types of meals: Full bkfst. Beds: KQT. Reading lamp, clock radio and fans in room. VCR, library, parlor games, telephone, fireplace, cross-country skiing, games and fireplace on premises. Handicap access. Antiquing, downhill skiing, fishing, golf, parks, snowmobile trails and sightseeing nearby.

Location: Mountains.

Publicity: *News Letter Journal.*

"We enjoyed a very homely introduction to the wild west!"

Certificate may be used: Sept. 15 to May 15, Sunday-Saturday. Bed & breakfast stay only. Hunting packages and Romantic Getaways excluded.

Puerto Rico

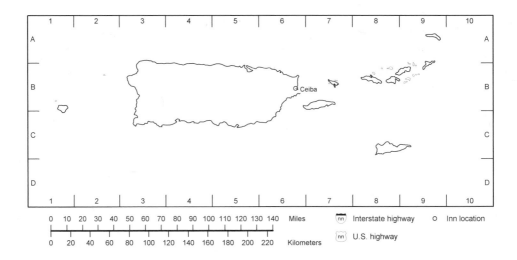

0 10 20 30 40 50 60 70 80 90 100 110 120 130 140   Miles
0 20 40 60 80 100 120 140 160 180 200 220   Kilometers

⬡ Interstate highway   ○ Inn location
⬡ U.S. highway

Maricao

Parador La Hacienda Juanita

Road 105, PO Box 777
Maricao, PR 00606-0777
(787)838-2550 (800)981-7575 Fax:(809)838-2551
Internet: www.haciendajuanita.com
E-mail: reservations@haciendajuanita.com

Circa 1976. This hacienda-style building once served as the main lodge for a coffee plantation. There are 24 acres situated 1600 feet above sea level in the mountains. Antique coffee-making implements decorate the lobby and bunches of bananas usually hang from the ceiling of the veranda. Breakfast usually includes grapefruit, oranges and guavas grown on the farm. The Rain Forest Reserve and Maricao Fish Hatchery are five miles away.

Innkeeper(s): Victoria E. Martinez Rivera. $72. 22 rooms, 21 with PB, 1 conference room. Types of meals: Full bkfst, lunch and dinner. Restaurant on premises. Beds: KDT. Reading lamp and ceiling fan in room. Fax, copier and telephone on premises. Handicap access.

Location: Mountains.

". . .This is the most beautiful place I've ever seen. We fell in love with your hacienda and Maricao and want to live there."

Certificate may be used: March-May except holidays and long weekends. August-November, except holidays and long weekends. Subject to availability.

Canada

British Columbia

Courtenay

Belle Vue Bed & Breakfast

5782 Coral Road
Courtenay, BC V9J 1W9
(250)898-8702 (866)898-8702 Fax:(250)898-8703
Internet: www.bellevuebb.ca
E-mail: belvues@yahoo.com

Circa 1994. A pleasurable fusion of East and West blend amiably at this beachfront California Colonial-style home overlooking the Strait of Georgia to the coastal mountains beyond. Become acquainted with American, Chinese, Middle Eastern and European art. Relax on French and Chinese furniture accented by Turkish lamps that highlight Persian carpets. Guest bedrooms boast balcony access and stocked refrigerators. Elderdowns grace the beds, though hypoallergenic alternatives are available. International flavors enhance a delicious breakfast served on English china with Russian silver, Belgian crystal and Thai brass.

Innkeeper(s): Walter & Haideh Jordan. $105-140. 3 rooms with PB, 2 with FP, 1 with WP, 2 cottages, 2 guest houses. Breakfast included in rates. Types of meals: Full gourmet bkfst, veg bkfst, snacks/refreshments, wine and In room coffee and tea. Beds: Q. Cable TV, VCR, reading lamp, refrigerator, telephone, coffeemaker, some with hot tub/spa, hair dryer, bathrobes, bath amenities, iron/ironing board, whirlpool bath and shower Gabi's room, Pascha's room double-size shower with shower stick, Seth's room tub/shower combo and two self-catering vacation rentals each with whirlpool bath in room. Fax, copier, spa, swimming, library, parlor games, fireplace, Two kayaks available for guest rental, boat, canoe and fishing gear rentals one block away on premises. Antiquing, art galleries, beach, bicycling, canoeing/kayaking, cross-country skiing, downhill skiing, fishing, golf, hiking, horseback riding, live theater, museums, parks, shopping, tennis, water sports, wineries, caving, fossil hunting and bird watching nearby.

Location: Country, ocean community, waterfront. On the Strait of Georgia, minutes north of Courtenay and Comox.

Certificate may be used: Oct. 15 to April 30, subject to availability.

Sooke

Ocean Wilderness Inn & Spa Retreat

9171 West Coast Road
Sooke, BC V0S 1N0
(250)646-2116 (800)323-2116 Fax:(250)646-2317
Internet: www.oceanwildernessinn.com
E-mail: info@oceanwildernessinn.com

Circa 1940. The hot tub spa of this log house inn is in a Japanese gazebo overlooking the ocean. Reserve your time for a private soak, terry bathrobes are supplied. Experience massage and mud treatments, ocean treatments and herbal wraps while meditation enhances your creative expression. The inn will arrange fishing charters, nature walks, wilderness treks and beachcombing. Coffee is delivered to your room each morning

on a silver service. Guests are invited to enjoy breakfast in their room or in the dining lounge. Rooms include antiques, sitting areas and canopy beds. Two of the rooms have hot tubs for two with spectacular ocean and Olympic Mountain views. Rates are in Canadian funds.

Innkeeper(s): Lori LeCount. $115-190. 7 rooms with PB. Breakfast included in rates. Types of meals: Full bkfst, veg bkfst and early coffee/tea. Beds: KQT. Reading lamp, refrigerator, clock radio, hair dryer, bathrobes and wireless Internet access in room. Fax, spa, telephone, fireplace, laundry facility and gift shop on premises. Limited handicap access. Antiquing, beach, canoeing/kayaking, fishing, golf, hiking, live theater, museums, parks, shopping, whale watching and Galloping Goose biking trail nearby.

Location: Waterfront.

Publicity: *Puget Sound Business Journal, Getaways from Vancouver, Travel Holiday Magazine and Seattle Times.*

"Thank you for the most wonderful hospitality and accommodations of our entire vacation."

Certificate may be used: Nov.1-March 30.

Valemount

Rainbow Retreat B&B

PO Box 138
Valemount, BC V0E 2Z0
(250)566-9747
Internet: www.spiralmountain.com

This authentically fashioned log cabin home rests beside an old fur-trader's route nestled in the Canadian Rockies and surrounded by woods. Guests are sure to see plenty of birds and wildlife, including the occasional deer that march across the grounds. The innkeepers have kept the rustic touch, but added Victorian flair such as stained glass and a grand piano. Hearty breakfasts start off the day and gourmet dinners are made-to-order. The secluded retreat is just a few minutes from Mount Robson Provincial Park, and it's just a short walk to Fraser River, especially popular during the annual salmon spawning run.

Innkeeper(s): Keith Burchnall. $50-70. 2 rooms. Breakfast included in rates. Types of meals: Full bkfst.

Certificate may be used: Anytime, except July and August.

Vernon

Richmond House 1894

4008 Pleasant Valley Rd
Vernon, BC V1T 4M2
(250)549-1767 (866)267-4419
Internet: www.richmondhousebandb.com
E-mail: richmondhouse@home.com

Because of its central location, this Victorian inn is an ideal spot for outdoor enthusiasts to base their daily activities. The ski area of Silverstar Mountain is a 30-minute drive and two major lakes (Okanagan and Kalamalka) are 10 minutes from the inn. Internationally renowned Predator Ridge golf course is 20 minutes away. A fireplace in the living room brings warmth in the winter months, and an outdoor deck and hot tub are enjoyed year-round. The innkeeper can direct you to adventure travel packages and local wineries. Breakfasts include a variety of quiche or stuffed French toast with peach sauce.

Innkeeper(s): Keith Brookes & Colleen Couves. $75. 3 rooms. Breakfast included in rates. Types of meals: Full bkfst. Reading lamp, ceiling fan and clock radio in room. Library, telephone, fireplace and lounge on premises. Antiquing, cross-country skiing, downhill skiing, golf and shopping nearby.

Location: Mountains.

Certificate may be used: Oct. 1-Dec. 22 and Jan. 3-April 30.

Victoria

Claddagh House B&B

1761 Lee Ave
Victoria, BC V8R 4W7
(250)370-2816 (877)377-2816 Fax:(250)592-0228
Internet: www.claddaghhouse.com
E-mail: info@claddaghhouse.com

Circa 1913. In a tranquil neighborhood, hospitality abounds at this romantic Victorian inn, fully modernized. Garden views are found in the sunny guest bedrooms. Ask for the spacious top-floor Tara Suite, an ideal indulgence for two or a perfect family setting. Fresh flowers, Belgian chocolates, a double Jacuzzi and down duvets are lavish rejuvenating touches. Select a satisfying breakfast from a substantial menu, to be made when desired. Relax on the front porch, stroll by the pond and fountain, or experience the diversity of Victoria.

Innkeeper(s): Elaine & Ken Brown. $149-249. 3 rooms, 2 with PB, 1 suite. Breakfast, afternoon tea and snacks/refreshments included in rates. Types of meals: Full gourmet bkfst, early coffee/tea and picnic lunch. Beds: KQDT. Ceiling fan and desk in room. VCR, fax, copier, bicycles, library, parlor games, telephone and fireplace on premises. Antiquing, bicycling, fishing, golf, hiking, live theater, parks, shopping, water sports, whale watching, castle tours, gardens and boating nearby.

Location: Residential.

Certificate may be used: Oct. 1 to May 1, Sunday-Thursday, excluding holidays.

Prancing Horse Retreat

573 Ebadora Lane
Victoria, BC V0R 2L0
(250)743-9378 (877)877-8834 Fax:(250)743-9372
Internet: www.prancinghorse.com
E-mail: stay@prancinghorse.com

Circa 1998. Breathtaking scenery and a spectacular setting surround this premier mountain-top retreat with fantastic views of the Olympic Mountains. This red-roofed Victorian villa boasts a turret with stained-glass windows and luxury accommodations. Indulge in a deluxe suite that features fresh flowers, Aveda bath products and Bernard Callebaut Chocolate. Luxury suites also include double soaker tubs, fireplaces and private decks. Savor a gourmet breakfast that is accented by just-squeezed orange juice and champagne in the dining room or on the spacious patio overlooking the valley. Colorful gardens with terraced rocks lead to a multi-tiered deck with a gazebo and hot tub.

$175-375. 7 total suites, including 1 two-bedroom suite. Breakfast included in rates. Types of meals: Full gourmet bkfst and early coffee/tea. Beds: Q. Data port, cable TV, VCR, CD player, refrigerator, clock radio, telephone, coffeemaker, hot tub/spa, most with fireplace, hair dryer, bathrobes, bath amenities, wireless Internet access and iron/ironing board in room. Fax and spa on premises. Antiquing, beach, fishing, golf, hiking, horseback riding, live theater, museums, parks, shopping, tennis, water sports and wineries nearby.

Location: Mountains, waterfront.

Certificate may be used: Anytime, November-March, subject to availability.

Scholefield House B&B

731 Vancouver St
Victoria, BC V8V 3V4
(250)385-2025 (800)661-1623 Fax:(250)383-3036
Internet: www.scholefieldhouse.com
E-mail: mail@scholefieldhouse.com

Circa 1892. Located on a quiet street downtown and three blocks from the Empress Hotel, this authentically restored Victorian B&B is shaded by tall trees that line the wide boulevards. A picket fence and gabled front entrance provide an inviting welcome to guests. Rooms are furnished with antiques and period decor, and each has a private bath. The five-course champagne breakfast is served fireside in the Parlor and edible flowers decorate the abundant servings of eggs Florentine, French toast with Brie, smoked salmon and other entrees. Two favorite spots are the private library where guests may enjoy a glass of sherry or tea and coffee and outside, an English herb and rose garden. The innkeeper is an author, who enjoys the historic register home's connection to the original owner, who founded the library in the Legislature Building. Stroll to the Inner Harbour, restaurants, antique shops, and theater in Victoria's flower-filled environment sometimes called "more English than England."

Innkeeper(s): Tana Dineen. $79-249. 3 rooms with PB, 1 with FP, 2 with WP. Breakfast included in rates. Types of meals: Full gourmet bkfst. Beds: KQ. Cable TV, reading lamp, CD player, ceiling fan, clock radio, turn-down service, most with hot tub/spa, some with fireplace, hair dryer, bathrobes, bath amenities, wireless Internet access, iron/ironing board, 2 with Jacuzzi-for-two and 1 with fireplace in room. VCR, fax, library, parlor games, telephone and Wireless Internet access on premises. Antiquing, art galleries, beach, bicycling, canoeing/kayaking, fishing, golf, hiking, horseback riding, live theater, museums, parks, shopping, tennis, water sports, wineries, whale watching, salmon fishing, Butchart Gardens and English high tea nearby.

Location: City.

Publicity: New York Times, Travel Section June 2003 - "In Victoria and it would be difficult to find more comfortable or elegant accommodations than the Scholefield House." .

Certificate may be used: Nov. 1-April 30.

Whistler

Belle Neige Bed & Breakfast

8597 Drifter Way
Whistler, BC V0N 1B8
(604)938-9225 Fax:(604)938-9762
Internet: www.whistlersuites.net
E-mail: fun@look.ca

Circa 1993. Peacefully set amongst Whistler and Blackcomb Mountains, this new West Coast-style home offers year-round pleasure. The inn's extraordinary panoramic scenery is a breath-taking experience. Each kitchen suite features a private entrance, ensuite bath/shower and the extra comforts of cozy housecoats and goose-down duvets. Italian prosciuto frittata, apple cinnamon pancakes and Quebec-style French toast with pure Canadian maple syrup are some of the items served for breakfast. A variety of breakfast service options suit each guests' budget or style, including self-catered, in-suite continental or fully served. After a day of skiing, soak under the stars and the snowflakes in the apres-ski outdoor hot tub Jacuzzi.

Innkeeper(s): Myrna & Todd. $69-199. 1 room, 2 with PB, 2 suites. Types of meals: Full gourmet bkfst. Beds: KQT. TV, VCR, DVD, reading lamp, CD player, refrigerator, clock radio, coffeemaker, hair dryer, bathrobes and iron/ironing board in room. Fax, spa, bicycles, child care, telephone and laundry facility on premises. Amusement parks, art galleries, beach, bicycling, canoeing/kayaking, cross-country skiing, downhill skiing, fishing, golf, hiking, horseback riding, museums, parks, shopping, sporting events, tennis and water sports nearby.

Location: Mountains.

Publicity: History Channel and The Origins of Christmas.

Certificate may be used: April 10-June 30, Oct. 4-Nov. 25.

Golden Dreams B&B

6412 Easy St
Whistler, BC V0N 1B6
(604)932-2667 (800)668-7055 Fax:(604)932-7055
Internet: www.goldendreamswhistler.com
E-mail: Ann@goldendreamswhistler.com

Circa 1986. Experience the many secrets of great B&B stays at this established inn. Surrounded by mountain views and the beauty of nature, this West Coast home features a private guest living room with wood fireplace where the innkeepers share their knowledge of the locale. Velour robes, duvets and sherry decanters are provided in the guest bed rooms, which have Victorian, Wild West and Aztec themes. After a wholesome breakfast, valley trail and bus stop are just outside. Whistler village and skiing are only one mile away. Relax in the hot tub and enjoy house wine and snacks. A large BBQ sundeck and guest kitchen are convenient amenities. Town Plaza village condos are also available for families. Discount skiing, sight-seeing passes and airport transport booking services are available.

Innkeeper(s): Ann & Terry Spence. $85-175. 3 rooms. Breakfast and afternoon tea included in rates. Types of meals: Full gourmet bkfst, veg bkfst, early coffee/tea, hors d'oeuvres and wine. Beds: QDT. Reading lamp, clock radio, hair dryer, bathrobes, wireless Internet access, iron/ironing board, Hot Tub sandals, decanter of sherry, complimentary house wine, snacks, use of guest refrigerator, microwave, coffee/tea making, local information, maps and ski atlas in room. TV, VCR, fax, spa, bicycles, library, telephone, fireplace, Stainless Steel BBQ, guest kitchen, private guest living room with wood fireplace, stereo, CD player, heated slate entrance and bathroom floors, outdoor ski storage racks and free off-street parking on premises. Art galleries, beach, bicycling, canoeing/kayaking, cross-country skiing, downhill skiing, fishing, golf, hiking, horseback riding, parks, shopping, sporting events, tennis, water sports, World Class alpine village with outstanding downhill skiing on 2

HUGE mountains! Also, Zip Trekking, white water rafting and canoeing, heli-skiing and bungy jumping! nearby.

Location: Mountains. Trailside location just one mile to village ski lifts.

"Great house, great food, terrific people."

Certificate may be used: April 15-June 15 and Sept. 30-Nov. 15, except holidays. Three condos in village December-April only.

New Brunswick

Hillsborough

Ship's Lantern Inn

17 Pleasant Street
Hillsborough, NB E4H 3A6
(506)734-3221 (186)673-47997
Internet: www.shipslantern.com
E-mail: info@shipslantern.com

Circa 1786. Be captivated by the casual elegance of this 18th century Georgian inn with gingerbread trim and large verandas. An included Welcome Package features a variety of treats to choose from. The first floor sitting room is highlighted by an Italian marble fireplace and distinctive antiques. For avid readers or history buffs there are magazines and books to peak interest and provide background of the inn and local area. Generous amenities ensure the feeling of being pleasantly pampered. Several of the guest suites offer whirlpool baths. Select from a breakfast menu in the Lewis or Duffy dining rooms.

Innkeeper(s): Brenda & Cole Belliveau. $135-150. 9 rooms, 5 with PB, 1 with FP, 4 with WP, 4 suites. Types of meals: Full gourmet bkfst, picnic lunch and snacks/refreshments. Beds: KQT. Cable TV, reading lamp, ceiling fan, snack bar, clock radio, telephone, desk, some with fireplace, hair dryer, bath amenities and iron/ironing board in room. Air conditioning. Antiquing, art galleries, beach, bicycling, canoeing/kayaking, cross-country skiing, golf, hiking, horseback riding, museums, parks, shopping, sporting events, tennis, water sports, wineries, Public Library, Arena and Hopewell Rocks (15 minutes) nearby.

Location: Country.

Certificate may be used: Anytime, subject to availability.

Rexton

Jardine's Inn

104 Main Street
Rexton, NB E4W 2B3
(506)523-7070 (866)523-7070 Fax:(866)523-7072
E-mail: hudsonj@nb.sympatico.ca

Circa 1850. Nominated as a Provincial Historic Site, this inn was built with deal construction, using three-inch wood that is pegged together upright. Guest bedrooms are named after Jardine ships. Sleep on a sleigh bed with down duvet, and soak in an antique clawfoot tub. Breakfast delights include grapefruit marinated in Grand Marnier, apple blossom tart with maple sauce, citrus French toast and orange juice with a dollop of mango sorbet. Savor afternoon tea and scones in the tea room. A variety of on-site activities are offered. Make reservations for a lobster supper, learn of the area's rich folklore on an Evening Lantern Guided Walking Tour down Water Street and be sure to view the display of artwork and crafts made by local artists.

Innkeeper(s): Jean & Jack Hudson. $89-125. 5 rooms with PB. Breakfast and afternoon tea included in rates. Types of meals: Breakfast. Beds: QT. Cable TV, reading lamp, ceiling fan and clock radio in room. TV, VCR, fax, bicycles, parlor games, telephone and gift shop on premises. Antiquing, beach, bicycling, canoeing/kayaking, fishing, golf, hiking, horseback riding, live theater, museums, parks and water sports nearby.

Location: Country.

Certificate may be used: During the month of May and the month of October.

Saint Andrews

Kingsbrae Arms Relais & Chateaux

219 King St
Saint Andrews, NB E5B 1Y1
(506)529-1897 Fax:(506)529-1197
Internet: www.kingsbrae.com
E-mail: reservations@kingsbrae.com

Circa 1897. With its splendid ocean views and ridgeline location, this shingle-style was built at the turn of the century on a choice piece of land. Today a trip to the manor house is a bit like traveling to a welcoming English country estate. The five guest rooms and three suites have been decorated with the utmost of elegance. Each room has a fireplace, and beds are dressed with fine linens and puffy comforters. Guests might find a room with a canopy bed draped with velvet or perhaps a bath with a clawfoot tub, marble walls and a wood floor. For those who wish to relax, the library is a masculine retreat with a fireplace and dark, exposed wood beams. Guests also can take a swim in the outdoor, heated swimming pool. The innkeepers pamper you with a gourmet morning feast and tea in the afternoon. One also can arrange to enjoy a five-course dinner, as rates are MAP. The inn has a Canada Select five-star rating and holds a four-star rating from Mobile. It has been selected as a Grand Award Winner of Andrew Harper's "Hideaways of the Year."

Innkeeper(s): Harry Chancey & David Oxford. $585-985. 8 rooms with PB, 8 with FP, 3 suites, 1 conference room. Breakfast, snacks/refreshments and dinner included in rates. Types of meals: Full gourmet bkfst, early coffee/tea, lunch and afternoon tea. Restaurant on premises. Beds: KQ. Cable TV, VCR, reading lamp, CD player, ceiling fan, clock radio, telephone, coffeemaker, turn-down service, desk, whirlpools and Jacuzzi in room. Air conditioning. Fax, copier, swimming, bicycles, library, parlor games, fireplace, patio and piano on premises. Antiquing, cross-country skiing, fishing, golf, parks, shopping, tennis, water sports and whale watching nearby.

Publicity: *Boston Globe, Atlantic Monthly, Canadian House & Home and CBC TV & Radio.*

Certificate may be used: Anytime, at the last minute.

Nova Scotia

Bridgewater

Fairview Inn Bridgewater

25 Queen Street
Bridgewater, NS B4V 1P1
(902)543-2233 (800)725-8732 Fax:(902)530-3323
Internet: www.nsinns.com
E-mail: info@nsinns.com

Circa 1863. Recently restored, this plantation-style inn is the area's oldest continually operating, and boasts a quiet, relaxed setting for business or leisure. Memorable suites feature historical themes and are enhanced with hardwood floors, antique furnishings, local original artwork and data ports. Stay in a suite with a canopy bed and Jacuzzi tub. A satisfying breakfast starts the day. Dine on the covered veranda, poolside or in the dining

room. Room service is available. Swim in the heated outdoor pool and hot tub.

Innkeeper(s): Mr. Stephen O'Leary. $48-108. 26 rooms with PB, 4 suites. Types of meals: Full bkfst, lunch and dinner. Restaurant on premises. Beds: QDT. Modem hook-up, data port, cable TV, VCR, reading lamp, ceiling fan, clock radio, telephone, turn-down service, desk, hot tub/spa and voice mail in room. Fax, copier, spa, swimming, fireplace, laundry facility and pool on premises. Antiquing, art galleries, beach, bicycling, canoeing/kayaking, cross-country skiing, fishing, golf, hiking, horseback riding, live theater, museums, parks, shopping, water sports and wineries nearby.

Location: Small town.

Certificate may be used: Anytime, November-April, subject to availability.

Halifax

West Dover Seaside Cottages

7029 Peggy's Cove Road
Halifax, NS B3H 4E1
(902)423-1102 (800)725-8732 Fax:(902)423-8329
Internet: www.nsinns.com
E-mail: info@nsinns.com

Peggy's Cove Parkland, a small fishing village is the bordering setting for these seaside accommodations. Stay in modern Hillside Cottages boasting harbor views, one or two bedrooms, full kitchens, balconies, gas grills and picnic tables. Some include fireplaces, as does the Deluxe Boathouse. Built on stilts over the water, the wharf is its deck. Full housekeeping service is provided. Ask about vacation packages and day adventures.

$75-205. 9 cottages. Beds: Q. Cable TV, reading lamp, refrigerator, clock radio and coffeemaker in room. Telephone on premises. Canoeing/kayaking, fishing, golf, hiking and shopping nearby.

Certificate may be used: Anytime, subject to availability.

Liverpool

Lane's Privateer Inn & B&B

27-33 Bristol Ave, PO Box 509
Liverpool, NS B0T 1K0
(902)354-3456 (800)794-3332 Fax:(902)354-7220
Internet: www3.nssympatico.ca/ron.lane
E-mail: ron.lane@ns.sympatico.ca

Circa 1798. For more than 30 years, three generations of the Lane family have run this historic lodge nestled among Nova Scotia's scenic coast and forests. The inn is a participant in "A Taste of Nova Scotia," which features a group of fine eateries that meet strict government standards. Lane's hosts a "Sip and Savour" series throughout the year, featuring wine tastings and gourmet meals. Breakfast at the inn is a treat with specialty menus featuring such items as haddock cakes and eggs Benedict. Nearby Kejimkujik National Park offers plenty of outdoor activities, and beaches are only a few miles away. Liverpool offers many fine shops and restaurants to enjoy.

Innkeeper(s): The Lane Family, Ron, Carol, Susan & Terry. $50-85. 30 rooms, 27 with PB. Breakfast included in rates. Types of meals: Lunch, picnic lunch, afternoon tea, gourmet dinner and room service. Restaurant on premises. Beds: QDT. Antiquing, cross-country skiing, fishing, live theater and water sports nearby.

Publicity: *Encore Travel, Providence and Rhode Island News.*

"Warm and relaxed atmosphere!"

Certificate may be used: Oct. 31-June 1, based on availability.

Queensland

Surfside Inn

9609 Hwy #3
Queensland, NS
(902)857-2417 (800)373-2417 Fax:(902)857-2107
Internet: www.thesurfsideinn.com
E-mail: info@thesurfsideinn.com

Circa 1880. Befitting its name, this Victorian inn overlooks Queensland Beach and all of St. Margaret's Bay. Originally a sea captain's home, restoration has maintained the elegant ambiance of that era while offering present-day amenities. Luxurious guest bedrooms and suites boast whirlpool tubs and lake or ocean views. Breakfast on the deck includes yogurt, secret-recipe granola, maritime brown bread and blueberry preserves. Relax over a delicious dinner by candlelight in the dining room. The bay area offers a variety of land activities and water sports.

Innkeeper(s): Michelle & Bill Batcules. $89-199. 8 rooms with PB. Breakfast included in rates. Types of meals: Cont plus, veg bkfst, snacks/refreshments, gourmet dinner and room service. Restaurant on premises. Beds: QD. Cable TV, VCR, reading lamp, ceiling fan, clock radio and hot tub/spa in room. Fax, copier, spa, swimming, telephone, fireplace and laundry facility on premises. Limited handicap access. Amusement parks, antiquing, art galleries, beach, bicycling, canoeing/kayaking, cross-country skiing, fishing, golf, hiking, horseback riding, live theater, museums, parks, shopping, sporting events, tennis, water sports and wineries nearby.

Location: Waterfront.

Certificate may be used: Oct. 1-May 15, Sunday-Thursday.

Smith's Cove

Harbourview Inn

25 Harborview Rd
Smith's Cove, NS B0S 1S0
(902)245-5686 (877)449-0705 Fax:(902)484-6520
E-mail: innkeeper@theharbourviewinn.com

The Winchester House at Harbourview Inn is romantic in a historic Nova Scotia setting among dense woods at Smith's Cove. The inn offers more than two miles of water frontage with a great view of Annapolis Basin and sweeping Fundy tides. Play shuffleboard then take a refreshing swim in the pool. Each of the tastefully decorated guest bedrooms and spacious suites feature air conditioning and a sitting area. Start each day with a complimentary breakfast before exploring the surrounding Digby County area with its wide variety of activities and attractions.

Call for rates. 9 rooms.

Certificate may be used: May 15-June 25 and Sept. 15-Oct. 15.

Ontario

Cayuga

River Inn

1459 Haldimand Rd 17
Cayuga, ON N0A 1E0
(905)774-8057 (866)824-7878
Internet: www.bbcanada.com/riverinn
E-mail: riverinn@linetap.com

Circa 1972. River Inn B&B boasts a 14-acre park-like setting on the Heritage Grand River. Located off the Grand River Scenic Parkway between the small towns of Cayuga and Dunnville in Ontario, this bed and breakfast is only one hour from Niagara Falls and 90 minutes from Toronto. Soak up the sun on the redwood deck before taking a refreshing swim in the pool. Gather in the TV room to play games or watch a movie. Accommodations include guest bedrooms in the main house with kitchen privileges or stay in the guest house that features a living room, kitchenette, and private deck. Breakfast and afternoon tea are provided.

Innkeeper(s): Frank and Helen Belbeck. $65-115. 4 rooms with PB, 1 guest house. Breakfast and afternoon tea included in rates. Types of meals: Full gourmet bkfst, veg bkfst, early coffee/tea and snacks/refreshments. Beds: KQDT. Cable TV, reading lamp, ceiling fan, clock radio, telephone, desk, hair dryer, bath amenities and iron/ironing board in room. Central air. TV, swimming, parlor games and fireplace on premises. Antiquing, art galleries, beach, bicycling, canoeing/kayaking, fishing, golf, hiking, horseback riding, live theater, museums, parks, shopping, water sports and wineries nearby.

Location: Waterfront.

Certificate may be used: November-April, subject to availability.

Chatham

Jordan House

RR #6
Chatham, ON N7M 5J6
(519)436-0839
Internet: www.jordan-house.com
E-mail: reservations@jordan-house.com

Circa 1900. Since 1838 the Jordan family has owned this fifty-acre estate, and hosts John and Barbara act the part of the historic original owners of this Victorian Queen Anne house, in period 1900s attire. Luxury and comfort combine in this large home boasting tastefully decorated rooms furnished with antiques, accented with fresh flowers and featuring an Edwardian decor. Air-conditioned guest bedrooms are named after local and British counties, as well as reflecting the direction they face. Some of the pleasurable amenities include feather bed mattress tops, down duvets and blackout blinds behind draperies. Savor a morning meal full of classic favorites.

Innkeeper(s): John & Barbara Jordan. $98-123. 4 rooms with PB. Breakfast included in rates. Types of meals: Full gourmet bkfst, veg bkfst and early coffee/tea. Beds: KQDT. Modem hook-up, data port, TV, reading lamp, ceiling fan, clock radio, telephone, turn-down service, desk, some with fireplace, hair dryer, bathrobes, bath amenities and iron/ironing board in room. Air conditioning. VCR, DVD, library, pet boarding, parlor games and complimentary high speed wireless Internet on site on premises. Limited handicap access. Antiquing, art galleries, beach, bicycling, fishing, golf, horseback riding, museums and shopping nearby.

Location: Country.

Certificate may be used: Anytime, subject to availability.

Collingwood

Pretty River Valley Country Inn

RR 1
Collingwood, ON L0M 1P0
(705)445-7598
Internet: www.prettyriverinn.com
E-mail: inn@prettyriver.infosathse.com

Circa 1980. Each of the guest rooms at this log inn includes a fireplace, and suites have the added amenity of a double whirlpool tub. The secluded, 120-acre estate offers views of the Pretty River Valley as well as the Blue Mountains. The innkeepers provide an ample breakfast, highlighted by items such as eggs Benedict. A collection of menus from local restaurants is kept on hand. Each season brings outdoor fun. Downhill and cross-country skiing, water sports on the bay and golfing are nearby, and there are plenty of antique shops to explore.

Innkeeper(s): Linda Proudfoot & Paul Bilewicz. $145-270. 11 rooms with PB, 11 with FP, 2 suites, 1 conference room. Breakfast included in rates. Types of meals: Full bkfst. Beds: QT. Refrigerator, clock radio and two with whirlpool in room. Air conditioning. Fax, spa, pet boarding, telephone and fireplace on premises. Antiquing, bicycling, cross-country skiing, downhill skiing, fishing, golf, hiking, parks, shopping, tennis, water sports and kennel across street nearby.

Location: Country, mountains. In valley surrounded by hills.

Publicity: *Toronto Sun and Century Homes.*

Certificate may be used: All year, Sunday to Thursday.

Gananoque

Manse Lane B&B

465 Stone St S
Gananoque, ON K7G 2A7
(613)382-8642 (888)565-6379
Internet: www.bbcanada.com/942.html

Circa 1860. Four comfortable guest rooms, two with a private bath, are available at this bed & breakfast. Breakfasts include items such as cereal, fruit, yogurt, cheeses, breads, bacon and eggs. Guests are within walking distance of local attractions.

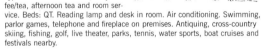

Innkeeper(s): Jocelyn & George Bounds. $100-160. 4 rooms, 2 with PB. Breakfast included in rates. Types of meals: Full bkfst, early coffee/tea, afternoon tea and room service. Beds: QT. Reading lamp and desk in room. Air conditioning. Swimming, parlor games, telephone and fireplace on premises. Antiquing, cross-country skiing, fishing, golf, live theater, parks, tennis, water sports, boat cruises and festivals nearby.

"Thoroughly enjoyed the stay. It was great to see you again."

Certificate may be used: Nov. 1 through April 15, seven days a week.

Kingston

Hotel Belvedere

141 King St E
Kingston, ON K7L 2Z9
(613)548-1565 (800)559-0584 Fax:(613)546-4692
Internet: www.hotelbelvedere.com
E-mail: reserve@hotelbelvedere.com

Circa 1880. Hotel Belvedere began its life as a private mansion, built in the Georgian style of architecture. Eventually, it was transformed into a hotel and then into a boarding house. Thankfully, it has been restored and refurbished back to its original state. The interior boasts the fine woodwork, carved mantels and marble floors one expects in a grand mansion. Elegant guest rooms are decorated in period style with antiques, and beds are dressed with fine white linens. In warm weather, the innkeepers serve a continental breakfast on the private terrace. Guests can enjoy the morning fare in their room or in front of a warm fire in the living room. Secluded three hours from Toronto along the shores of Lake Ontario, Kingston is a charming site for a getaway. Historic homes, museums and dinner cruises are among the offerings in town. The town once served as the capital of Canada.

Innkeeper(s): Donna Mallory & Ian Walsh. $110-250. 20 rooms with PB, 2 suites, 1 conference room. Breakfast included in rates. Types of meals: Cont plus and early coffee/tea. Beds: KQDT. Modem hook-up, data port, TV, reading lamp, telephone, desk and hot tub/spa in room. Air conditioning. Fax, copier, library, fireplace and laundry facility on premises. Limited handicap access. Antiquing, art galleries, beach, bicycling, canoeing/kayaking, cross-country skiing, fishing, golf, hiking, live theater, museums, parks, shopping, sporting events, tennis and water sports nearby.

Publicity: *New York Times, Globe & Mail, National Geographic Traveler, Toronto Star, A Taste of Life and Canadian Travel Show.*

Certificate may be used: Nov. 1 through March 31 on Friday, Saturday, Sunday.

Kitchener

Mornington Crescent Bed & Breakfast

11 Sunbridge Crescent
Kitchener, ON N2K 1T6
(519)763-6557 (877)763-6557
Internet: www.morningtoncres.ca
E-mail: bandb@morningtoncres.ca

Circa 1970. Just minutes from the city, yet this modern bungalow style bed & breakfast sits peacefully secluded in historic and scenic Menn County. Stay here at any time of the year while traveling for business or leisure. Deluxe guest bedrooms and a suite feature pampering amenities as well as high speed and wireless Internet access. Relax in a double whirlpool tub by candlelight before sleeping in a handcrafted Mennonite bed by a fireplace. A well-stocked library offers videos and reading materials to borrow. After a complete breakfast, made as requested, take one of the walking trails from the back yard. Swim in the heated pool or soak in the hot tub.

Innkeeper(s): Carolyn Steele. $75-120. 4 rooms, 2 with PB, 1 with FP, 1 conference room. Breakfast included in rates. Types of meals: Full bkfst, veg bkfst, early coffee/tea and afternoon tea. Beds: KQT. Cable TV, VCR, reading lamp, refrigerator, clock radio, coffeemaker, desk, fireplace and suite has microwave in room. Central air. Fax, copier, spa, swimming, bicycles, library, pet boarding, parlor games, telephone, high-speed wireless Internet and heated in-ground pool on premises. Antiquing, bicycling, canoeing/kayaking, cross-country skiing, fishing, golf, hiking, horseback riding, live theater, parks and shopping nearby.

Certificate may be used: Anytime, November-April, subject to availability.

New Hamburg

The Waterlot

17 Huron St
New Hamburg, ON N3A 1K1
(519)662-2020 Fax:(519)662-2114
Internet: www.waterlot.com
E-mail: waterlot@waterlot.com

Circa 1844. Located beside a mill pond, this Victorian home boasts an imaginative architecture with gothic gables frosted with gingerbread trim and an unusual cupola. It houses the inn's most important asset, a French-country restaurant, Le Bistro, which seats 125 people. Overlooking the Nith River as it flows through the backyard, the restaurant has been well-known for three decades. Guest rooms are simple and housed beneath each of the inn's twin gables.

Innkeeper(s): Gord & Leslie Elkeer. $80-120. 3 rooms, 1 suite. Breakfast included in rates. Types of meals: Cont plus, lunch, picnic lunch and gourmet dinner. Restaurant on premises. Beds: KQD. Clock radio in room. Fax, copier, parlor games, telephone and fireplace on premises. Amusement parks, antiquing, cross-country skiing, downhill skiing, fishing, golf, live theater, parks, shopping and tennis nearby.

Location: Waterfront.
Certificate may be used: April 1-Feb. 28, (closed March).

Niagara Falls

Bampfield Hall

4761 Zimmerman Ave.
Niagara Falls, ON L2E 3M8
(905)353-8522 (877)353-8522
Internet: www.niagaraniagara.com
E-mail: niagbnb@mergetel.com

Circa 1872. Designed with Neo-Gothic architecture, this historic home boasts etched glass, a turret, gracefully curved staircase and patterned wood floors. Family heirlooms and collections are found throughout. Relaxing conversations are popular in the living room, which reflects a 1930s Hollywood decor. Guest bedrooms and a suite are comfortably furnished. The private Jesters Suite is a top-floor room at the back of the house and boasts a Jacuzzi tub. Enjoy a satisfying breakfast in the large dining room.

Innkeeper(s): David & Doddy. $50-115. 3 rooms with PB. Breakfast included in rates. Types of meals: Full gourmet bkfst and veg bkfst. Beds: KQ. Amusement parks, antiquing, art galleries, beach, bicycling, fishing, golf, hiking, horseback riding, live theater, museums, parks, shopping, tennis and wineries nearby.

Location: City.
Certificate may be used: Nov. 1-April 30, Sunday-Thursday, except Christmas, New Year's and Valentine's Day.

Niagara Inn

4300 Simcoe Street
Niagara Falls, ON L2E 1T6
(905)353-8522 (877)353-8522
Internet: www.niagaraniagara.com
E-mail: niagbnb@mergetel.com

Circa 1887. Victorian in design and decor with eclectic accents, this bed & breakfast exudes a feeling of nostalgia. Original detailed woodwork and stained glass reflect the quality craftsmanship of the era. Comfortable guest bedrooms feature

antique furnishings. Savor a leisurely breakfast that includes delicious entrees and homemade baked goods. Explore the scenic locale on available bicycles.

Innkeeper(s): David Tetrault. $50-105. 3 rooms with PB. Breakfast included in rates. Types of meals: Full gourmet bkfst and veg bkfst. Beds: Q. Cable TV, reading lamp, refrigerator, ceiling fan and clock radio in room. Air conditioning. TV, bicycles, library and telephone on premises. Limited handicap access. Amusement parks, antiquing, art galleries, beach, bicycling, fishing, golf, hiking, horseback riding, live theater, museums, parks, shopping, tennis, water sports and wineries nearby.

Location: City.
Certificate may be used: Nov. 1-April 30, Sunday-Thursday, excluding Christmas, New Year's and Valentine's Day.

Niagara On The Lake

Post House Country Inn / Burke House Inn

95 Johnson Street
Niagara On The Lake, ON L0S 1J0
(905)468-9991 (877)349-7678 Fax:(905)468-9989
Internet: www.posthouseinn.com
E-mail: post@posthouseinn.com

Circa 1835. Originally the town's post office, and also used for educating the local children, this circa 1835 building is now an elegant country inn. Decorated and furnished in a luxurious old world style, relaxation comes easy while sitting by the fire in the living room. Guest bedrooms are glorious retreats with pampering amenities. Lavish suites feature a two-person Jacuzzi and most boast a marble bath and fireplace. Stay in Mrs. Connell's Boudoir, a two-room suite with a four-poster bed. The second floor Coach Suite has original pine plank flooring. The renovated Carriage Room with poolside access once housed the horses. A resplendent breakfast is served in the sun-filled conservatory overlooking the heated pool and gardens.

Innkeeper(s): Barbara Ganim. $109-359. 8 rooms with PB, 8 with FP, 4 with WP, 1 cottage, 2 conference rooms. Breakfast and Full epicurean breakfast with attention to healthy start. Diets may be accommodated included in rates. Types of meals: Full gourmet bkfst, veg bkfst, early coffee/tea and room service. Beds: KQT. Modem hook-up, cable TV, VCR, reading lamp, clock radio, turn-down service, desk, most with hot tub/spa, fireplace, hair dryer, bathrobes, bath amenities, wireless Internet access, iron/ironing board and central piped-in Spa music in room. Central air. Fax, copier, spa, swimming, library, parlor games, telephone, breakfast in room can be requested, full concierge service and special assistance for arranging details of engagements on premises. Limited handicap access. Amusement parks, antiquing, art galleries, bicycling, canoeing/kayaking, cross-country skiing, fishing, golf, hiking, live theater, museums, parks, shopping, sporting events, tennis, water sports, wineries, Niagara Falls (12 minutes away with 2 Casinos), Toronto (1 1/2 hours), Butterfly Conservatory and Aviary nearby.

Location: Waterfront. Historic Canadian Town.
Certificate may be used: November-April, Sunday-Thursday.

Ottawa

Auberge McGee's Inn

185 Daly Ave
Ottawa, ON K1N 6E8
(613)237-6089 (800)262-4337 Fax:(613)237-6201
Internet: www.mcgeesinn.com
E-mail: contact@mcgeesinn.com

Circa 1886. Gracing historic Sandy Hill, this restored Victorian mansion offers luxurious and peaceful getaways. It was built for John McGee, Canada's Fourth Clerk of the Privy Council. The

portico is reminiscent of his Irish roots featuring pillars that were common in Dublin architecture. Well-appointed guest bedrooms and suites are comfortable and include generous amenities as well as modern conveniences. Some boast fireplaces and Jacuzzis. Sitting in the heart of the city, walk to nearby Byward Market and Parliament Hill. Visit the many museums or the popular Rideau Center.

Innkeeper(s): Jason, Judy, Sarah & Ken Armstrong. $118-184. 14 rooms with PB, 3 with FP, 3 with WP, 3 suites. Breakfast included in rates. Types of meals: Full bkfst, veg bkfst, early coffee/tea and afternoon tea. Beds: KQT. Data port, cable TV, reading lamp, CD player, refrigerator, clock radio, telephone, coffeemaker, desk, some with hot tub/spa, voice mail, some with fireplace, hair dryer, bathrobes, bath amenities and wireless Internet access in room. Air conditioning. VCR, DVD, fax and free parking on premises. Limited handicap access. Antiquing, art galleries, bicycling, canoeing/kayaking, cross-country skiing, downhill skiing, fishing, golf, hiking, horseback riding, live theater, museums, parks, shopping, sporting events and water sports nearby.

Location: City.

Publicity: *Country Inns, Ottawa Citizen, LaPresse, Ottawa. and CBC.*

Certificate may be used: November-April, excluding Feb. 2 to 28 (Winterlude) and holiday weekends.

Inn on Somerset

282 Somerset St W
Ottawa, ON K2P 0J6
(613)236-9309 (800)658-3564 Fax:(613)237-6842
Internet: www.innonsomerset.com
E-mail: info@innonsomerset.com

Circa 1895. Enjoy a delightful stay at this grand Victorian home built in 1895. Relax in front of the fireplace in the living room or take a leisurely stroll beside the Rideau Canal. Well-appointed guest bedrooms are furnished with period antiques and feature Internet access. Two rooms boast a fireplace and one has a sun porch. A hearty breakfast is served in the gracious dining room from 7:30 to 9 a.m. Work out in the exercise room, use the sauna or be entertained by the home theatre. A washer and dryer are available. The inn is located in the heart of Ottawa, an easy walk to Parliament Hill, shopping and fine restaurants.

Innkeeper(s): George & Richard. $95-130. 11 rooms, 5 with PB, 1 with FP. Breakfast included in rates. Types of meals: Full bkfst. Beds: QDT. Reading lamp, clock radio, telephone and desk in room. Air conditioning. VCR, fax, copier, fireplace and sauna on premises. Antiquing, cross-country skiing, downhill skiing, live theater, parks, shopping, sporting events and tourist attractions nearby.

Location: City.

Publicity: *Ottawa Citizen.*

Certificate may be used: November through January.

Peterborough

King Bethune House, Guest House & Spa

270 King St
Peterborough, ON K9J 2S2
(705)743-4101 (800)574-3664
Internet: www.kingbethunehouse.com
E-mail: marlis@sympatico.ca

Circa 1893. This brick Victorian is downtown on a quiet tree-shaded street. Restored hardwood floors, original trim

throughout, tall ceilings and handsome windows grace the interiors. Guest rooms are large with ensuite baths and offer antiques, as well as desks, data ports, TVs and VCRs. The Spa Suite has a king bed and private entrance as well as a private hot tub, sauna, steam bath and massage therapy room. There's a restful walled garden with fireplace and patio, a favorite spot for breakfast. All guests can arrange spa services by appointment.

Innkeeper(s): Marlis Lindsay. $149-299. 3 rooms, 2 with PB, 1 with HT, 1 suite, 1 conference room. Breakfast included in rates. Types of meals: Full gourmet bkfst, veg bkfst, early coffee/tea, picnic lunch, hors d'oeuvres, room service, There is a wine cellar on the premises and catering is arranged for events and celebrations such as weddings, parties, business meetings and etc. Beds: KQ. Data port, cable TV, VCR, reading lamp, stereo, refrigerator, ceiling fan, clock radio, telephone, coffeemaker, turn-down service, desk, some with hot tub/spa, hair dryer, bathrobes, bath amenities and wireless Internet access in room. Central air. DVD, spa, sauna, bicycles, library, parlor games, laundry facility, spa with steambath, massage therapy room and private outdoor garden hot tub on premises. Limited handicap access. Amusement parks, antiquing, bicycling, cross-country skiing, downhill skiing, fishing, golf, live theater, parks, shopping, sporting events, tennis and water sports nearby.

Location: City, country.

Publicity: *Canadian Country Inns, Peterborough Examiner, CHEX TV, CKPT and Country 105.*

"We still have not found better accommodations anywhere."

Certificate may be used: Jan. 30-Nov. 30, Sunday-Monday.

Waterloo

Hillcrest House

73 George Street
Waterloo, ON N2J 1K8
(519)744-3534 Fax:(519)744-9523
Internet: www.hillcresthouse.ca
E-mail: info@hillcresthouse.ca

Circa 1882. Gracing a quiet residential street, this historic bed and breakfast was built with Italianate architecture in 1882 and is listed as a City of Waterloo Heritage Landmark. The intimate size and first-class service create the perfect atmosphere for a business or leisure stay. The library is stocked with books and magazines. Be entertained in the Games Room. The large parlor with a fireplace is an inviting spot to gather. Schedule an in-house spa service. Spacious guest suites feature upscale amenities, high-speed Internet access, and two suites boast separate sitting rooms with TVs and VCRs. A gourmet breakfast is a satisfying event with delicious main dishes, home-baked tarts or pastries and fresh fruit. Picnic lunches can be arranged and corporate meals planned. Theater tickets and dinner reservations can be secured before arrival.

Innkeeper(s): Stefan and Wendy Schuster. $120-135. 3 rooms with PB, 1 conference room. Breakfast and snacks/refreshments included in rates. Types of meals: Full gourmet bkfst, veg bkfst, Sun. brunch, early coffee/tea, gourmet lunch, picnic lunch, afternoon tea, hors d'oeuvres and gourmet dinner. Beds: QT. Modem hook-up, data port, cable TV, DVD, reading lamp, CD player, ceiling fan, clock radio, telephone, desk, hair dryer, bathrobes, bath amenities and iron/ironing board in room. Fax, spa, bicycles, library, parlor games, fireplace and laundry facility on premises. Antiquing, art galleries, bicycling, canoeing/kayaking, downhill skiing, golf, hiking, live theater, museums, parks, shopping, sporting events, tennis and water sports nearby.

Location: City.

Certificate may be used: Anytime, subject to availability.

Westport

Stepping Stone Inn

328 Centreville Rd, RR 2
Westport, ON K0G 1X0
(613)273-3806 Fax:(613)273-3331
Internet: www.steppingstoneinn.com
E-mail: stepping@rideau.net

Circa 1840. Multi-colored limestone warms in the afternoon sun on this historic house located on more than 150 acres. Flower beds surround the wraparound veranda decorated in white gingerbread and fretwork. Rooms are furnished with antiques, and there is a solarium and dining room that overlook flower gardens, a picturesque swimming pond and waterfall. Guest rooms include luxury suites with Jacuzzis, fireplaces and private entrances. Plan ahead and the inn's chef will create a custom menu for you. Stepping Stone is popular for garden weddings and corporate meetings. The grounds offer a beaver pond, pastures and nature trails. The Rideau Canal System and many lakes are nearby.

Innkeeper(s): Madeleine Saunders. $75-150. 10 rooms with PB, 3 with FP, 3 suites, 1 cabin, 1 conference room. Breakfast included in rates. Types of meals: Full gourmet bkfst, early coffee/tea, picnic lunch, afternoon tea and gourmet dinner. Restaurant on premises. Beds: QT. Reading lamp and 5 with Jacuzzis in room. Air conditioning. Fax, swimming, telephone and fireplace on premises. Handicap access. Antiquing, cross-country skiing, fishing, golf, hiking, live theater, parks, shopping, tennis, water sports and skating nearby.

Certificate may be used: Feb. 1 to Dec. 15, Sunday to Thursday, subject to availability.

Wiarton

Gadd-About Bed & Breakfast

501 Frank
Wiarton, ON N0H 2T0
(519)534-5282 (800)354-9078
Internet: www.gadd-about.ca
E-mail: info@gadd-about.ca

Circa 1892. Be immersed in the elegant, old-world charm of Gadd-About Bed & Breakfast in the village of Wiarton at the Gateway to the Bruce Peninsula and Colpoy's Bay in Ontario. This Victorian B&B boasts original details that include stained-glass window transoms, mahogany paneling with plate racks and an oak and tile fireplace in the parlour. Use the Polaris (Meade) telescope to star gaze, relax on the veranda or in the living room that looks out onto the large porch. Ride the tandem bike or play the antique Heinzman upright grand piano in the Discovery Room. Stay in a guest bedroom with a fireplace and a bathroom with a Jacuzzi tub. Coffee and muffins are available in the second-floor foyer before enjoying a complete breakfast in the formal dining room.

Innkeeper(s): Danielle Paterson. $110. Call inn for details. Breakfast and snacks/refreshments included in rates. Types of meals: Full gourmet bkfst, early coffee/tea, Dinners can be arranged for groups, Packed lunches for hikers etc. and Specialty diets are accommodated. Modem hook-up, reading lamp, CD player, clock radio, most with fireplace, hair dryer, bathrobes, bath amenities, wireless Internet access and iron/ironing board in room. Air conditioning. TV, VCR, fax, copier, spa, bicycles, parlor games, telephone and laundry facili-

ty on premises. Amusement parks, antiquing, art galleries, beach, bicycling, canoeing/kayaking, cross-country skiing, fishing, golf, hiking, horseback riding, live theater, museums, parks, shopping, tennis, 2 Motor Speedways, mountain biking and BMX tracts and trails, Dog sledding in winter, birding, lighthouse tours, rural garden tours, motorcycle and historic walking tours nearby.

Location: Small village on Colpoy's Bay (Georgian Bay).

Publicity: *Toronto Star, Toronto Sun, Destinations and Descovery, Chatham Daily News Travel and Wiarton Echo.*

Certificate may be used: Anytime, November-March, subject to availability.

Windsor

Ye Olde Walkerville B & B

1104 Monmouth Rd
Windsor, ON N8Y 3L8
(519)254-1507 Fax:(519)252-5542
Internet: www.wescanada.com
E-mail: walkervillebb@wescanada.com

Circa 1903. Exuding an upscale romantic ambiance and informal friendliness, this Victorian manor provides an adult-oriented tranquility and relaxation. Excellent service resulting in complete satisfaction is the accomplished desire of this award-winning bed & breakfast. Stay in Samantha's Suite or one of the impressive guest bedrooms, each named after the hosts' grandchildren. Enjoy cable TV and free local phone calls in a smoke-free environment. Choose a chef-prepared breakfast from a varied menu selection that is sure to please. Quantities are made-to-order.

Innkeeper(s): Wayne Strong. $189-289. 5 rooms with PB, 1 with FP, 1 suite. Breakfast included in rates. Types of meals: Full gourmet bkfst, veg bkfst, early coffee/tea and picnic lunch. Beds: KQ. Cable TV, VCR, reading lamp, clock radio, telephone, desk, hot tub/spa and fireplace in room. Central air. Fax, copier, spa, parlor games and fireplace on premises. Art galleries, bicycling, golf, horseback riding, live theater, museums, parks, shopping, sporting events and wineries nearby.

Publicity: *Windsor Star and CBC.*

Certificate may be used: September-November, January-May, Sunday-Thursday, excludes all holidays.

Prince Edward Island

Cardigan

Cardigan River Inn

57 Owens Wharf Rd.
Cardigan, PE C0A 1G0
(902)583-2331 (800)425-9577 Fax:(902)583-2331
Internet: www.cardiganriverinn.com
E-mail: cardiganriverinn@hotmail.com

Known locally as the Road's End Mansion, this renovated five-star waterfront estate graces a 26-acre knoll with a generous amount of salt-river frontage. Listen to music in the living room by firelight, gaze at the library's waterview and enjoy afternoon tea in the sunroom. Splendid guest bedrooms feature period antiques, whirlpool baths with showers, fireplaces, thoughtful personal amenities and use of an extensive video library. Each morning choose from a multi-selection menu for breakfast in the dining room. Manicured grounds boast the area's oldest and largest linden trees. A gazebo is perfect for watching boats sail by. Call the inn for additional travel packages.

$145-240. 4 rooms with PB, 3 with FP, 4 with WP, 2 suites. Whirlpool tub in room.

Certificate may be used: Sept. 9-Oct. 31, Sunday-Friday.

Roseneath B&B

RR #6
Cardigan, PE C0A 1G0
(902)838-4590 (800)823-8933 Fax:(902)838-4590
Internet: www.resebb.ca
E-mail: sleep@rosebb.ca

Circa 1868. Located on 90 acres, this Victorian farm house has scroll-decorated gables and a wraparound porch. It has been in the present family since 1920, and the innkeeper's father once ran the old saw mill. The inn has antiques and quilts, and artwork collected during many years of living overseas. Guests are welcome to play the pump organ or gramophone or borrow binoculars for bird watching (bald eagles, blue jays and herons). Nearby attractions include seal-watching cruises, the Wood Islands Ferry, Orwell Historic Village and Charlottetown. Rates are quoted in Canadian dollars.

Innkeeper(s): Edgar & Brenda Dewar. $95-160. 4 rooms with PB. Breakfast and afternoon tea included in rates. Types of meals: Full bkfst and early coffee/tea. Beds: QDT. Reading lamp, desk and washbasin in room. VCR, fax, copier, bicycles, library, parlor games and telephone on premises. Cross-country skiing, fishing, golf, live theater, parks, shopping and water sports nearby.

Location: Country.

Certificate may be used: Oct. 30 to May 1, subject to availability. Rates are in Canadian dollars.

Summerside

Willowgreen Farm B&B

117 Bishop Dr
Summerside, PE C1N 5Z8
(902)436-4420 (888)436-4420
Internet: www.willowgreenfarm.com
E-mail: email@willowgreenfarm.com

Circa 1920. Recently renovated, this 1920 farmhouse offers simple country elegance in the city. Willowgreen Farm Bed and Breakfast adorns about 120 acres with sheep and goats in the orchard. The relaxed and tranquil setting in Summerside, Prince Edward Island is inviting with the porch and other outdoor sitting areas as well as walking paths. Inside, gather by the fire for casual conversation. Guest bedrooms feature antiques and some suites boast double whirlpool tubs. Savor a varied breakfast menu that is created with fresh seasonal produce and homemade recipes. Special dietary needs are accommodated. The on-site Craft Nook has hand-knit sweaters, blankets, quilted items and yarn for sale.

Innkeeper(s): Steven & Laura Read . $40-100. 8 rooms with PB, 2 with WP. Breakfast included in rates. Types of meals: Full bkfst, picnic lunch, Picnic lunches by previous arrangement (included in some packages) and Dinner off-season by arrangement. Beds: KQD. Some rooms have some of the following - fireplace with Victorian cover (not a working fireplace), one has AC, 2 have TVs, most have ceiling fans, there is on premises a guest fridge, iron/ironing board, telephone, reading lamps and hair dryer in room. TV, VCR, parlor games, telephone, laundry facility and gift shop on premises. Antiquing, art galleries, beach, bicycling, canoeing/kayaking, cross-country skiing, fishing, golf, live theater, museums, parks, shopping, tennis, water sports, College of Piping and Celtic Arts, Dinner Theatre and Anne of Green Gables Museums nearby.

Location: City.

Certificate may be used: Sept. 15-June 15 (not June 16-Sept. 14. Based on availability. Based on rooms over $70. Not to be used with other specials.

Inns of Interest

African-American History

Deacon Timothy Pratt Bed & Breakfast Inn C.1746
.... Old Saybrook, Conn.
The Alexander House Booklovers B & B
.... Princess Anne, Md.
Munro House B&B and Spa ..... Jonesville, Mich.
Hexagon House Bed & Breakfast
.... Pentwater, Mich.
The Signal House .... Ripley, Ohio
Post House Country Inn / Burke House Inn
.... Niagara On The Lake,
The Great Valley House of Valley Forge
.... Valley Forge, Pa.
Rockland Farm Retreat............ Bumpass, Va.
Firmstone Manor............ Clifton Forge, Va.
Sleepy Hollow Farm B&B....... Gordonsville, Va.
Golden Stage Inn .... Ludlow, Vt.
The Inn at Weathersfield......... Perkinsville, Vt.
Elkhorn Inn & Theatre .... Landgraff, W.Va.

Animals

Alaska's North Country Castle B&B
.... Anchorage, Alaska
Casa De San Pedro............ Hereford, Ariz.
Lodge at Sedona-A Luxury Bed and Breakfast Inn
.... Sedona, Ariz.
Collingwood Inn Bed & Breakfast
.... Ferndale, Calif.
The Inn at Schoolhouse Creek
.... Mendocino, Calif.
Cedar Mountain Farm............ Athol, Idaho
Greyhouse Inn B&B............ Salmon, Idaho
Canaan Land Farm B&B....... Harrodsburg, Ky.
First Farm Inn .... Idlewild, Ky.
1851 Historic Maple Hill Manor B&B
.... Springfield, Ky.
Restful Paws Bed & Breakfast
.... Holland, Mass.
Royalsborough Inn at the Bagley House
.... Durham, Maine
Greenville Inn .... Greenville, Maine
The Wren's Nest Bed & Breakfast
.... West Bloomfield, Mich.
Meramec Farm Cabins & Trail Riding Vacations, LLC
.... Bourbon, Mo.
Chimney Hill Estate Inn .... Lambertville, N.J.
Stone Crest Cellar B&B .... South Beach, Ore.
Barley Sheaf Farm Estate & Spa
.... Holicong, Pa.
Willowgreen Farm B&B .... Summerside,
The Shaw House B&B......... Georgetown, S.C.
Sunrise Farm B&B .... Salem, S.C.
MD Resort Bed & Breakfast.... Fort Worth, Texas
Southwind.................... Wimberley, Texas
The Garden, Bed & Breakfast Inn
.... Spring City, Utah
Hill Farm Inn.................. Arlington, Vt.
Arlington's River Rock Inn
.... Arlington, Wash.

Barns

Thunder Valley Inn-Bed & Breakfast, Farm Restaurant, and Scandinavian Gift Hus
.... Wisconsin Dells, Wis.
Heritage Farm Museum & Village
.... Huntington, W.Va.

Fensalden Inn .... Albion, Calif.
Deer Crossing Inn........... Castro Valley, Calif.
The Hancock House............ Dubuque, Iowa
Greyhouse Inn B&B............ Salmon, Idaho
Sonora Gardens Farmstead .... Nauvoo, Ill.
Pinehill Inn.................... Oregon, Ill.
1851 Historic Maple Hill Manor B&B
.... Springfield, Ky.
Oakland House Seaside Resort
.... Brooksville, Maine
Inn Britannia................ Searsport, Maine
Brannon-Bunker Inn........... Walpole, Maine
The Mast Farm Inn........... Valle Crucis, N.C.
Big Mill Bed & Breakfast ...... Williamston, N.C.
Highland Lake Inn B&B.......... Andover, N.H.
Candlelite Inn .... Bradford, N.H.
Mt. Washington Bed & Breakfast
.... Shelburne, N.H.
Inn at Glencairn .... Princeton, N.J.
Hide Away Country Inn .... Bucyrus, Ohio
The Inn At Cedar Falls .... Logan, Ohio
Weatherbury Farm Vacation .... Avella, Pa.
Pheasant Field B&B .... Carlisle, Pa.
Pennsbury Inn .... Chadds Ford, Pa.
Canna Country Inn................ Etters, Pa.
Barley Sheaf Farm Estate & Spa
.... Holicong, Pa.
Cornerstone B&B Inn .... Landenberg, Pa.
Willowgreen Farm B&B .... Summerside,
MD Resort Bed & Breakfast..... Fort Worth, Texas
Jackson Fork Inn LLC.......... Huntsville, Utah
The Hummingbird Inn............ Goshen, Va.
Dulaney Hollow at Old Rag Mountain B&B Inn
.... Madison, Va.
Hill Farm Inn.................. Arlington, Vt.
Churchill House Inn............. Brandon, Vt.
Silas Griffith Inn............... Danby, Vt.
Phineas Swann B&B Inn .. Montgomery Center, Vt.
Waitsfield Inn .... Waitsfield, Vt.
Arlington's River Rock Inn
.... Arlington, Wash.
Thunder Valley Inn-Bed & Breakfast, Farm Restaurant, and Scandinavian Gift Hus
.... Wisconsin Dells, Wis.
Heritage Farm Museum & Village
.... Huntington, W.Va.

Boats

First Farm Inn .... Idlewild, Ky.
1851 Historic Maple Hill Manor B&B
.... Springfield, Ky.
Oakland House Seaside Resort
.... Brooksville, Maine

Greenville Inn .... Greenville, Maine
Lake View Cottage Bed & Breakfast
.... Silver Lake, N.H.
Notleymere Cottage .... Cazenovia, N.Y.
The Bluff .... Henderson Harbor, N.Y.
The Bay View Inn .... Tangier, Va.

Bordellos

Hotel Charlotte............... Groveland, Calif.
The Groveland Hotel at Yosemite National Park
.... Groveland, Calif.
1859 Historic National Hotel, A Country Inn
.... Jamestown, Calif.
Cheyenne Canon Inn..... Colorado Springs, Colo.
Inn at Villalon .... Newport, R.I.

Castles

Ravenwood Castle........ New Plymouth, Ohio

Churches & Parsonages

Casa De San Pedro............. Hereford, Ariz.
Collingwood Inn Bed & Breakfast
.... Ferndale, Calif.
Washington Plantation .... Washington, Ga.
The Hancock House........... Dubuque, Iowa
Old Church House Inn .... Mossville, Ill.
Christopher's B&B............ Bellevue, Ky.
The Parsonage Inn .... East Orleans, Mass.
The Parsonage on The Green B&B
.... Lee, Mass.
Parsonage Inn .... Saint Michaels, Md.
Parish House Inn .... Ypsilanti, Mich.
Deutsche Strasse (German Street) B&B
.... New Ulm, Minn.
The Abbey Bed & Breakfast....... Cape May, N.J.
Post House Country Inn / Burke House Inn
.... Niagara On The Lake,
Inn at Villalon .... Newport, R.I.
Phineas Swann B&B Inn .. Montgomery Center, Vt.
Waitsfield Inn .... Waitsfield, Vt.

Civil War

Washington Plantation .... Washington, Ga.
Mason House Inn of Bentonsport
.... Bentonsport, Iowa
Aldrich Guest House .... Galena, Ill.
The Steamboat House Bed and Breakfast
.... Galena, Ill.
Myrtledene B&B................. Lebanon, Ky.
1851 Historic Maple Hill Manor B&B
.... Springfield, Ky.
The General Rufus Putnam House
.... Rutland, Mass.
Munro House B&B and Spa ..... Jonesville, Mich.
Southern Hotel............ Sainte Genevieve, Mo.
Fairview Inn & Sophia's Restaurant
.... Jackson, Miss.
1847 Blake House Inn Bed & Breakfast
.... Asheville, N.C.
The Inn at Brevard............. Brevard, N.C.

Chateau on the Mountain . . . . Fletcher, N.C.
Plum Tree Gardens Bed and Breakfast
. . . . Goldsboro, N.C.
Pheasant Field B&B . . . . Carlisle, Pa.
Pennsbury Inn . . . . Chadds Ford, Pa.
The Inn at Twin Linden . . . . Churchtown, Pa.
Baladerry Inn at Gettysburg
. . . . Gettysburg, Pa.
James Gettys Hotel . . . . Gettysburg, Pa.
The Beechmont B&B Inn . . . . Hanover, Pa.
Red Lion Bed & Breakfast . . . . Red Lion, Pa.
Inn at Villalon . . . . Newport, R.I.
Chesnut Cottage B&B. . . . . Columbia, S.C.
McKay House . . . . Jefferson, Texas
Firmstone Manor . . . . Clifton Forge, Va.
The Hummingbird Inn. . . . . Goshen, Va.
By The Side Of The Road. . . . . . . Harrisonburg, Va.
Essex Inn. . . . . Tappahannock, Va.
The Inn at Weathersfield. . . . . Perkinsville, Vt.
Gillum House Bed & Breakfast
. . . . Shinnston, W.Va.

Cookbooks Written by Innkeepers

"Heartstone Inn Breakfast Cookbook"
The Heartstone Inn & Cottages
. . . . Eureka Springs, Ark.

"The Old Yacht Club Inn Cookbook"
The Old Yacht Club Inn . . . . . . Santa Barbara, Calif.

"Breakfast Inn Bed"
Garth Woodside Mansion. . . . . Hannibal, Mo.

"By Request, The White Oak Cookbook"
The White Oak Inn . . . . Danville, Ohio

"Favorite Recipes of Whitestone Country Inn"
Whitestone Country Inn . . . . Kingston, Tenn.

"Trail's End Cookbook"
Trail's End, A Country Inn
. . . . Wilmington, Vt.

Farms and Orchards

Fool's Cove Ranch B&B . . . . Kingston, Ark.
Lodge at Sedona-A Luxury Bed and Breakfast Inn
. . . . Sedona, Ariz.
Apple Blossom Inn B&B. . . . . Ahwahnee, Calif.
Collingwood Inn Bed & Breakfast
. . . . Ferndale, Calif.
The Inn at Schoolhouse Creek
. . . . Mendocino, Calif.
Albert Shafsky House Bed & Breakfast
. . . . Placerville, Calif.
Howard Creek Ranch . . . . Westport, Calif.
Black Forest B&B Lodge & Cabins
. . . . Colorado Springs, Colo.
Homespun Farm Bed and Breakfast
. . . . Jewett City, Conn.
The Inn at Woodstock Hill . . . . Woodstock, Conn.
Washington Plantation . . . . Washington, Ga.
Sonora Gardens Farmstead. . . . . Nauvoo, Ill.
Canaan Land Farm B&B. . . . . . . Harrodsburg, Ky.
First Farm Inn . . . . Idlewild, Ky.
1851 Historic Maple Hill Manor B&B
. . . . Springfield, Ky.
Gilbert's Tree Farm B&B. . . . . . . Rehoboth, Mass.
The Alexander House Booklovers B & B
. . . . Princess Anne, Md.
Royalsborough Inn at the Bagley House
. . . . Durham, Maine

Greenville Inn . . . . Greenville, Maine
Maple Hill Farm B&B Inn. . . . . . Hallowell, Maine
Grand Victorian Bed & Breakfast Inn
. . . . Bellaire, Mich.
Plain & Fancy Bed & Breakfast
. . . . Ironton, Mo.
The Mast Farm Inn . . . . Valle Crucis, N.C.
Big Mill Bed & Breakfast . . . . . . Williamston, N.C.
Volden Farm. . . . . Luverne, N.D.
Highland Lake Inn B&B. . . . . Andover, N.H.
Brass Heart Inn . . . . Chocorua, N.H.
Inn at Ellis River . . . . Jackson, N.H.
Chimney Hill Estate Inn . . . . . . Lambertville, N.J.
Halcyon Farm Bed & Breakfast
. . . . Amsterdam, N.Y.
Berry Hill Gardens B&B. . . . . Bainbridge, N.Y.
Agape Farm B&B and Paintball
. . . . Corinth, N.Y.
Hide Away Country Inn . . . . Bucyrus, Ohio
Weatherbury Farm Vacation . . . . Avella, Pa.
Pennsbury Inn . . . . Chadds Ford, Pa.
The Inn at Twin Linden . . . . Churchtown, Pa.
Barley Sheaf Farm Estate & Spa
. . . . Holicong, Pa.
Speedwell Forge B&B. . . . . Lititz, Pa.
Red Lion Bed & Breakfast . . . . Red Lion, Pa.
Field & Pine B&B. . . . . Shippensburg, Pa.
Willowgreen Farm B&B . . . . Summerside,
Inn at Villalon . . . . Newport, R.I.
B&B at Skoglund Farm. . . . . Canova, S.D.
Rockland Farm Retreat. . . . . Bumpass, Va.
Firmstone Manor . . . . Clifton Forge, Va.
The Hummingbird Inn. . . . . Goshen, Va.
Old Spring Farm Bed & Breakfast, Ltd.
. . . . Woolwine, Va.
Hill Farm Inn. . . . . Arlington, Vt.
Alexandra B&B Inn . . . . Bennington, Vt.
Churchill House Inn . . . . Brandon, Vt.
Phineas Swann B&B Inn . . Montgomery Center, Vt.
Liberty Hill Farm. . . . . Rochester, Vt.
Turtleback Farm Inn . . . . Eastsound, Wash.
Justin Trails Resort . . . . Sparta, Wis.
Thunder Valley Inn-Bed & Breakfast, Farm
Restaurant, and Scandinavian Gift Hus
. . . . Wisconsin Dells, Wis.
Heritage Farm Museum & Village
. . . . Huntington, W.Va.

French & Indian War

Ancient Thomas Riggs House
. . . . Gloucester, Mass.

Gardens

Alaska's North Country Castle B&B
. . . . Anchorage, Alaska
Lookout Point Lakeside Inn
. . . . Hot Springs, Ark.
Luna Vista Bed and Breakfast
. . . . Camp Verde, Ariz.
Casa De San Pedro. . . . . Hereford, Ariz.
Lodge at Sedona-A Luxury Bed and Breakfast Inn
. . . . Sedona, Ariz.
The Inn at Schoolhouse Creek
. . . . Mendocino, Calif.
Deacon Timothy Pratt Bed & Breakfast Inn C.1746
. . . . Old Saybrook, Conn.
The Inn at Woodstock Hill . . . . Woodstock, Conn.

Azalea Inn & Gardens . . . . Savannah, Ga.
Serendipity Cottage. . . . . Thomasville, Ga.
Washington Plantation . . . . Washington, Ga.
The Hancock House . . . . Dubuque, Iowa
Blue Belle Inn B&B . . . . Saint Ansgar, Iowa
Beall Mansion, An Elegant B&B
. . . . Alton, Ill.
Aldrich Guest House . . . . Galena, Ill.
Sonora Gardens Farmstead. . . . . Nauvoo, Ill.
First Farm Inn . . . . Idlewild, Ky.
Cincinnati's Weller Haus B&B
. . . . Newport, Ky.
1851 Historic Maple Hill Manor B&B
. . . . Springfield, Ky.
Woodridge Bed & Breakfast of Louisiana
. . . . Slidell, La.
Ancient Thomas Riggs House
. . . . Gloucester, Mass.
Gabriel's at the Ashbrooke Inn
. . . . Provincetown, Mass.
Honeysuckle Hill B&B . . . . West Barnstable, Mass.
The Inn at Mitchell House . . . . Chestertown, Md.
Greenville Inn . . . . Greenville, Maine
Inn Britannia. . . . . Searsport, Maine
Fairview Inn & Sophia's Restaurant
. . . . Jackson, Miss.
Plum Tree Gardens Bed and Breakfast
. . . . Goldsboro, N.C.
Pine Crest Inn & Restaurant
. . . . Tryon, N.C.
The Mast Farm Inn . . . . Valle Crucis, N.C.
Yellow House on Plott Creek Road
. . . . Waynesville, N.C.
Whispering Pines. . . . . Nebraska City, Neb.
Adair Country Inn . . . . Bethlehem, N.H.
A Grand Inn-Sunset Hill House
. . . . Sugar Hill, N.H.
Abbe' de Touchstone - Inn, Spa & Gallery
. . . . Taos, N.M.
Notleymere Cottage . . . . Cazenovia, N.Y.
The Edward Harris House B&B Inn
. . . . Rochester, N.Y.
Garden Gate Get-A-Way Bed & Breakfast
. . . . Millersburg, Ohio
Post House Country Inn / Burke House Inn
. . . . Niagara On The Lake,
Pheasant Field B&B . . . . Carlisle, Pa.
Kennett House Bed and Breakfast
. . . . Kennett Square, Pa.
The Artist's Inn & Gallery
. . . . Terre Hill, Pa.
Inn at Villalon . . . . Newport, R.I.
Breeden Inn, Cottages & Retreat on Main
. . . . Bennettsville, S.C.
The Garden Cottage Bed & Breakfast
. . . . Cedar City, Utah
The Hummingbird Inn. . . . . Goshen, Va.
By The Side Of The Road. . . . . . . Harrisonburg, Va.
Colonial Gardens. . . . . Williamsburg, Va.
Alexandra B&B Inn . . . . Bennington, Vt.
Phineas Swann B&B Inn . . Montgomery Center, Vt.
Trail's End, A Country Inn
. . . . Wilmington, Vt.
Plum Duff House . . . . Tacoma, Wash.
Naeset-Roe Inn . . . . Stoughton, Wis.

Glacier Viewing

Alaska's North Country Castle B&B
. . . . Anchorage, Alaska
Matanuska Lodge. . . . . Sutton, Alaska

Gold Mines & Gold Panning

Alaska's North Country Castle B&B
. . . . Anchorage, Alaska
Casa De San Pedro. . . . . Hereford, Ariz.
Lodge at Sedona-A Luxury Bed and Breakfast Inn
. . . . Sedona, Ariz.
Deer Crossing Inn. . . . . Castro Valley, Calif.
Hotel Charlotte. . . . . Groveland, Calif.
The Groveland Hotel at Yosemite National Park
. . . . Groveland, Calif.
1859 Historic National Hotel, A Country Inn
. . . . Jamestown, Calif.
Albert Shafsky House Bed & Breakfast
. . . . Placerville, Calif.
Lily Creek Lodge. . . . . Dahlonega, Ga.
Greyhouse Inn B&B. . . . . Salmon, Idaho
Echo Lake Inn . . . . Ludlow, Vt.

Hot Springs

Lookout Point Lakeside Inn
. . . . Hot Springs, Ark.
Vichy Hot Springs Resort & Inn
. . . . Ukiah, Calif.
Wiesbaden Hot Springs Spa & Lodgings
. . . . Ouray, Colo.
Greyhouse Inn B&B. . . . . Salmon, Idaho
The Inn on Crescent Lake . . Excelsior Springs, Mo.
Firmstone Manor. . . . . Clifton Forge, Va.
The Hummingbird Inn. . . . . Goshen, Va.

Inns Built Prior to 1800

188 Melitta Station Inn. . . . . . Santa Rosa, Calif.
1645 Ancient Thomas Riggs House
. . . . Gloucester, Mass.
1691 The Great Valley House of Valley Forge
. . . . Valley Forge, Pa.
1699 Ashley Manor Inn . . . . Barnstable, Mass.
1700 Elias Child House B&B
. . . . Woodstock, Conn.
1711 La Hacienda Grande . . . . . . Bernalillo, N.M.
1714 Pennsbury Inn. . . . . Chadds Ford, Pa.
1720 Bed & Breakfast at Roseledge Herb Farm
. . . . Preston, Conn.
1727 Apple Blossom B&B. . . . . York, Maine
1730 Joy House Inc., B&B. . . . Dennis Port, Mass.
1731 The Daniel Rust House
. . . . Coventry, Conn.
1734 3 Liberty Green B&B . . . . . . Clinton, Conn.
1736 Inn at Glencairn . . . . Princeton, N.J.
1739 The Ruffner House . . . . Luray, Va.
1740 Homespun Farm Bed and Breakfast
. . . . Jewett City, Conn.
1740 Inn at Lower Farm. North Stonington, Conn.
1740 Red Brook Inn. . . . . Old Mystic, Conn.
1740 Lamb and Lion Inn . . . . . . Barnstable, Mass.
1740 Barley Sheaf Farm Estate & Spa
. . . . Holicong, Pa.
1743 The Inn at Mitchell House
. . . . Chestertown, Md.
1746 Deacon Timothy Pratt Bed & Breakfast Inn
C.1746
. . . . Old Saybrook, Conn.

1747 Georgian House B&B. . . . . . Annapolis, Md.
1750 The General Rufus Putnam House
. . . . Rutland, Mass.
1750 The Melville House . . . . Newport, R.I.
1752 The Olde Stage Coach B&B
. . . . Jennerstown, Pa.
1755 Strasburg Village Inn
. . . . Strasburg, Pa.
1757 The Fairfield Inn 1757
. . . . Fairfield, Pa.
1760 Glasgow B&B Inn . . . . Cambridge, Md.
1760 Beechtree Inn . . . . Hertford, N.C.
1760 Speedwell Forge B&B . . . . Lititz, Pa.
1763 Blackberry River Inn . . . . . . Norfolk, Conn.
1763 Historic Smithton Inn
. . . . Ephrata, Pa.
1766 Seven South Street Inn
. . . . Rockport, Mass.
1766 Osceola Mill House . . . . . . Gordonville, Pa.
1766 The Inn at Meander Plantation
. . . . Locust Dale, Va.
1767 Birchwood Inn. . . . . Lenox, Mass.
1767 Oakland House Seaside Resort
. . . . Brooksville, Maine
1767 Highland Lake Inn B&B
. . . . Andover, N.H.
1770 The Parsonage Inn . . . . . East Orleans, Mass.
1771 The Inn on Cove Hill. . . . . Rockport, Mass.
1772 Royalsborough Inn at the Bagley House
. . . . Durham, Maine
1774 Inn at Valley Farms B&B and Cottages
. . . . Walpole, N.H.
1775 Colonel Roger Brown House
. . . . Concord, Mass.
1775 Kanaga House B&B Inn . Mechanicsburg, Pa.
1777 Doneckers, The Inns . . . . Ephrata, Pa.
1779 Ira Allen House . . . . Manchester, Vt.
1780 Hotel Saint Pierre . . . . . . New Orleans, La.
1780 Christine's Bed-Breakfast & Tearoom
. . . . Housatonic, Mass.
1780 Birch Hill Bed & Breakfast
. . . . Sheffield, Mass.
1780 The Dowds' Country Inn
. . . . Lyme, N.H.
1782 Abel Darling B&B . . . . . . Litchfield, Conn.
1783 The Towers B&B. . . . . Milford, Del.
1784 Maple House Bed & Breakfast
. . . . Rowe, Mass.
1785 Weathervane Inn . . . South Egremont, Mass.
1785 1785 Inn & Restaurant
. . . . North Conway, N.H.
1785 Sleepy Hollow Farm B&B
. . . . Gordonsville, Va.
1786 Kenniston Hill Inn . . . . . . Boothbay, Maine
1786 Ship's Lantern Inn . . . . Hillsborough, N.H.
1787 Brass Heart Inn . . . . Chocorua, N.H.
1788 Golden Stage Inn . . . . Ludlow, Vt.
1789 Longwood Country Inn . . Woodbury, Conn.
1789 By The Side Of The Road
. . . . Harrisonburg, Va.
1790 Riverwind Inn . . . . Deep River, Conn.
1790 Silvermine Tavern . . . . Norwalk, Conn.
1790 Ivy Lodge . . . . Nantucket, Mass.
1790 Fairhaven Inn . . . . Bath, Maine
1790 Lake House. . . . . Waterford, Maine
1790 Southern Hotel. . . . . . Sainte Genevieve, Mo.
1790 Hacienda Antigua Inn . . Albuquerque, N.M.

1790 Brownstone Colonial Inn
. . . . Reinholds, Pa.
1790 Field & Pine B&B . . . . . . Shippensburg, Pa.
1790 Flowering Fields B&B. . . . . White Stone, Va.
1790 Hill Farm Inn . . . . Arlington, Vt.
1790 Silver Maple Lodge & Cottages
. . . . Fairlee, Vt.
1791 St. Francis Inn . . . . . . Saint Augustine, Fla.
1791 Sedgwick Inn . . . . Berlin, N.Y.
1792 Bridges Inn at Whitcomb House
. . . . West Swanzey, N.H.
1792 1792 Filigree Inn . . . . Canandaigua, N.Y.
1792 The Inn at Weathersfield
. . . . Perkinsville, Vt.
1793 Cove House . . . . Kennebunkport, Maine
1793 Mill Creek Homestead B&B
. . . . Bird in Hand, Pa.
1793 Echo Ledge Farm InnEast Saint Johnsbury, Vt.
1794 Historic Merrell Inn. . . . . Stockbridge, Mass.
1794 The Whitehall Inn. . . . . . . New Hope, Pa.
1794 Inn at the Laveau Farm
. . . . Waitsfield, Vt.
1795 Canaan Land Farm B&B . . Harrodsburg, Ky.
1795 Shaker Meadows . . . . . . New Lebanon, N.Y.
1795 Living Spring Farm B&B
. . . . Adamstown, Pa.
1796 Yorkshire Inn . . . . Phelps, N.Y.
1796 Catamount B&B . . . . Williston, Vt.
1797 The Grand View Inn & Resort
. . . . Jaffrey, N.H.
1797 Applebrook B&B. . . . . Jefferson, N.H.
1797 Inn at Baldwin Creek & Mary's Restaurant
. . . . Bristol, Vt.
1797 Fitch Hill Inn. . . . . Hyde Park, Vt.
1798 Edgartown Inn . . . . Edgartown, Mass.
1798 Lane's Privateer Inn & B&B
. . . . Liverpool,
1799 The Kennebunk Inn . . . . Kennebunk, Maine
1799 Dr. Jonathan Pitney House
. . . . Absecon, N.J.

Jailhouses

Lodge at Sedona-A Luxury Bed and Breakfast Inn
. . . . Sedona, Ariz.
Hotel Charlotte. . . . . Groveland, Calif.
Washington Plantation . . . . Washington, Ga.
1851 Historic Maple Hill Manor B&B
. . . . Springfield, Ky.
Inn at Villalon . . . . Newport, R.I.

Lighthouses

Deacon Timothy Pratt Bed & Breakfast Inn C.1746
. . . . Old Saybrook, Conn.
Ancient Thomas Riggs House
. . . . Gloucester, Mass.
Harborside House B&B . . . . . . Marblehead, Mass.
Oakland House Seaside Resort
. . . . Brooksville, Maine
Inn Britannia. . . . . Searsport, Maine
Grand Victorian Bed & Breakfast Inn
. . . . Bellaire, Mich.
The Bluff . . . . Henderson Harbor, N.Y.
Stone Crest Cellar B&B . . . . . . South Beach, Ore.
Inn at Villalon . . . . Newport, R.I.
Second Wind Country Inn . . . . . . Ashland, Wis.

Literary Figures Asscociated

Inns of Interest

With Inns

Jack London
Vichy Hot Springs Resort & Inn
.... Ukiah, Calif.

D.H. Lawrence
Vichy Hot Springs Resort & Inn
.... Ukiah, Calif.

Mark Twain/Samuel Clemens
Vichy Hot Springs Resort & Inn
.... Ukiah, Calif.

Louisa May Alcott
Hawthorne Inn .... Concord, Mass.

Ralph Waldo Emerson
Hawthorne Inn .... Concord, Mass.

Nathaniel Hawthorne
Hawthorne Inn .... Concord, Mass.

Henry Beston
Inn at the Oaks .... Eastham, Mass.

Ralph Waldo Emerson
Emerson Inn By The Sea .... Rockport, Mass.

Nathaniel Hawthorne
Emerson Inn By The Sea .... Rockport, Mass.

Ralph Waldo Emerson
The Island House ...... Southwest Harbor, Maine

Nathaniel Hawthorne
The Island House ...... Southwest Harbor, Maine

Mark Twain/Samuel Clemens
Garth Woodside Mansion........ Hannibal, Mo.

Llama Ranches

Collingwood Inn Bed & Breakfast
.... Ferndale, Calif.

Washington Plantation .... Washington, Ga.
1851 Historic Maple Hill Manor B&B
.... Springfield, Ky.

Royalsborough Inn at the Bagley House
.... Durham, Maine

Chimney Hill Estate Inn .... Lambertville, N.J.

Adobe & Pines Inn .... Taos, N.M.

Phineas Swann B&B Inn .. Montgomery Center, Vt.

Log Cabins/Houses

Matanuska Lodge.............. Sutton, Alaska
Ocean Wilderness Inn & Spa Retreat
.... Sooke,

Knickerbocker Mansion Country Inn
.... Big Bear Lake, Calif.

Collingwood Inn Bed & Breakfast
.... Ferndale, Calif.

Wild Horse Inn Bed and Breakfast
.... Fraser, Colo.

Washington Plantation .... Washington, Ga.
Cedar Mountain Farm............. Athol, Idaho
Canaan Land Farm B&B......... Harrodsburg, Ky.
1851 Historic Maple Hill Manor B&B
.... Springfield, Ky.

Ancient Thomas Riggs House
.... Gloucester, Mass.

Oakland House Seaside Resort
.... Brooksville, Maine

Sweet Dreams Inn Victorian B&B
.... Bay Port, Mich.

Pine Crest Inn & Restaurant
.... Tryon, N.C.

The Mast Farm Inn .... Valle Crucis, N.C.
Elaine's, A B&B .... Cedar Crest, N.M.

Greenwoods B&B Inn .... Honeoye, N.Y.
Log Country Inn - B&B of Ithaca
.... Ithaca, N.Y.

Heartland Country Resort.... Fredericktown, Ohio
The Inn At Cedar Falls .... Logan, Ohio
Pennsbury Inn .... Chadds Ford, Pa.
Roddy Tree Ranch .... Hunt, Texas
The Inn at Burg's Landing . Anderson Island, Wash.
Arlington's River Rock Inn
.... Arlington, Wash.

Guest House Log Cottages ..... Greenbank, Wash.
Thunder Valley Inn-Bed & Breakfast, Farm
Restaurant, and Scandinavian Gift Hus
.... Wisconsin Dells, Wis.

Heritage Farm Museum & Village
.... Huntington, W.Va.

Movie Locations

Outbreak
Collingwood Inn Bed & Breakfast
.... Ferndale, Calif.

Holiday Inn
Village Inn & Restaurant .... Monte Rio, Calif.

Isaac's Storm
C.W. Worth House B&B....... Wilmington, N.C.

Consenting Adults
Rice Hope Plantation Inn Bed & Breakfast
.... Moncks Corner, S.C.

National Historic Register

The Heartstone Inn & Cottages
.... Eureka Springs, Ark.

Lodge at Sedona-A Luxury Bed and Breakfast Inn
.... Sedona, Ariz.

Collingwood Inn Bed & Breakfast
.... Ferndale, Calif.

Hotel Charlotte.............. Groveland, Calif.
The Groveland Hotel at Yosemite National Park
.... Groveland, Calif.

Vichy Hot Springs Resort & Inn
.... Ukiah, Calif.

Kirkland House Bed & Breakfast
.... New London, Conn.

Deacon Timothy Pratt Bed & Breakfast Inn C.1746
.... Old Saybrook, Conn.

The Inn at Woodstock Hill .... Woodstock, Conn.
Washington Plantation .... Washington, Ga.
Mason House Inn of Bentonsport
.... Bentonsport, Iowa

The Hancock House........... Dubuque, Iowa
Beall Mansion, An Elegant B&B
.... Alton, Ill.

Aldrich Guest House .... Galena, Ill.
Cincinnati's Weller Haus B&B
.... Newport, Ky.

1851 Historic Maple Hill Manor B&B
.... Springfield, Ky.

The Beach Rose Inn .... Falmouth, Mass.
Ancient Thomas Riggs House
.... Gloucester, Mass.

Winterwood at Petersham .... Petersham, Mass.
Merry Sherwood Plantation.......... Berlin, Md.
Carriage House Inn........... Searsport, Maine
Lake House .... Waterford, Maine
Hackley-Holt House B & B .. Muskegon, Mich.
Terrace Inn .... Petoskey, Mich.
Classic Rosewood - A Thorwood Property

.... Hastings, Minn.
Museum Hill Bed & Breakfast
.... Saint Joseph, Mo.

Fairview Inn & Sophia's Restaurant
.... Jackson, Miss.

Aunt Kissy's Boutique Bed & Breakfast
.... Lewistown, Mont.

The Inn at Brevard.............. Brevard, N.C.
Plum Tree Gardens Bed and Breakfast
.... Goldsboro, N.C.

Pine Crest Inn & Restaurant
.... Tryon, N.C.

The Mast Farm Inn .... Valle Crucis, N.C.
Wakefield Inn, LLC .... Wakefield, N.H.
Notleymere Cottage .... Cazenovia, N.Y.
The Edward Harris House B&B Inn
.... Rochester, N.Y.

Eagle Cliff Inn .... Geneva on the Lake, Ohio
Speedwell Forge B&B.............. Lititz, Pa.
Inn at Villalon .... Newport, R.I.
Edgewood Manor B&B .... Providence, R.I.
Breeden Inn, Cottages & Retreat on Main
.... Bennettsville, S.C.

1st Bed & Breakfast in Texas Pride House
.... Jefferson, Texas

Katy House Bed & Breakfast
.... Smithville, Texas

Parrish Place B&B .... Salt Lake City, Utah
Park Light Inn .... Chester, Vt.
Silas Griffith Inn.............. Danby, Vt.
Apple Country Bed & Breakfast
.... Wenatchee, Wash.

The Franklin Victorian Bed & Breakfast
.... Sparta, Wis.

Naeset-Roe Inn .... Stoughton, Wis.

Old Mills

Silvermine Tavern.............. Norwalk, Conn.
Big Mill Bed & Breakfast ...... Williamston, N.C.
Asa Ransom House.............. Clarence, N.Y.
Pennsbury Inn .... Chadds Ford, Pa.
The Hummingbird Inn............. Goshen, Va.
The Mountain Rose B&B Inn ...... Woolwine, Va.

Oldest Continuously Operated Inns

Lodge at Sedona-A Luxury Bed and Breakfast Inn
.... Sedona, Ariz.

Hotel Charlotte.............. Groveland, Calif.
1859 Historic National Hotel, A Country Inn
.... Jamestown, Calif.

The Inn at Schoolhouse Creek
.... Mendocino, Calif.

Vichy Hot Springs Resort & Inn
.... Ukiah, Calif.

1857 Florida House Inn .... Amelia Island, Fla.
St. Francis Inn .... Saint Augustine, Fla.
Mason House Inn of Bentonsport
.... Bentonsport, Iowa

House Of Two Urns.............. Chicago, Ill.
Gabriel's at the Ashbrooke Inn
.... Provincetown, Mass.

Emerson Inn By The Sea .... Rockport, Mass.
Oakland House Seaside Resort
.... Brooksville, Maine

Royalsborough Inn at the Bagley House
.... Durham, Maine

Greenville Inn . . . . Greenville, Maine
Lawnmere Inn . . . . Southport, Maine
Classic Rosewood - A Thorwood Property
. . . . Hastings, Minn.
Southern Hotel . . . . Sainte Genevieve, Mo.
Pine Crest Inn & Restaurant
. . . . Tryon, N.C.
The Mast Farm Inn . . . . Valle Crucis, N.C.
Highland Lake Inn B&B . . . . Andover, N.H.
Candlelite Inn . . . . Bradford, N.H.
Lake View Cottage Bed & Breakfast
. . . . Silver Lake, N.H.
A Grand Inn-Sunset Hill House
. . . . Sugar Hill, N.H.
Wakefield Inn, LLC . . . . Wakefield, N.H.
The Fairfield Inn 1757 . . . . Fairfield, Pa.
Strasburg Village Inn . . . . Strasburg, Pa.
The Bellevue House . . . . Block Island, R.I.
Breeden Inn, Cottages & Retreat on Main
. . . . Bennettsville, S.C.
Smith House Inn . . . . Crosbyton, Texas
McKay House . . . . Jefferson, Texas
Hill Farm Inn . . . . Arlington, Vt.
Churchill House Inn . . . . Brandon, Vt.
Casa Bella Inn . . . . Pittsfield, Vt.

Plantations

Historic Coalson Plantation & Inn
. . . . Thomasville, Ga.
Washington Plantation . . . . Washington, Ga.
1851 Historic Maple Hill Manor B&B
. . . . Springfield, Ky.
Merry Sherwood Plantation . . . . Berlin, Md.
Monmouth Plantation . . . . Natchez, Miss.
Plum Tree Gardens Bed and Breakfast
. . . . Goldsboro, N.C.
Mansfield Plantation B&B Country Inn
. . . . Georgetown, S.C.
Rice Hope Plantation Inn Bed & Breakfast
. . . . Moncks Corner, S.C.
The Inn at Meander Plantation
. . . . Locust Dale, Va.
Four Square Plantation . . . . Smithfield, Va.

Ranches

Casa De San Pedro . . . . Hereford, Ariz.
Lodge at Sedona-A Luxury Bed and Breakfast Inn
. . . . Sedona, Ariz.
The Inn at Schoolhouse Creek
. . . . Mendocino, Calif.
Howard Creek Ranch . . . . Westport, Calif.
Cedar Mountain Farm . . . . Athol, Idaho
Wilson Ranches Retreat Bed and Breakfast
. . . . Fossil, Ore.
MD Resort Bed & Breakfast . . . . . Fort Worth, Texas
Hasse House and Ranch . . . . Mason, Texas

Revolutionary War

Washington Plantation . . . . Washington, Ga.
Ashley Manor Inn . . . . Barnstable, Mass.
Colonel Roger Brown House . . . . . . Concord, Mass.
Hawthorne Inn . . . . Concord, Mass.
Ancient Thomas Riggs House
. . . . Gloucester, Mass.
Inn at Glencairn . . . . Princeton, N.J.
Pennsbury Inn . . . . Chadds Ford, Pa.
Kennett House Bed and Breakfast

. . . . Kennett Square, Pa.
Speedwell Forge B&B . . . . Lititz, Pa.
The Great Valley House of Valley Forge
. . . . Valley Forge, Pa.
Inn at Villalon . . . . Newport, R.I.
The Melville House . . . . Newport, R.I.
Phineas Swann B&B Inn . . Montgomery Center, Vt.
Gillum House Bed & Breakfast
. . . . Shinnston, W.Va.

Schoolhouses

Casa De San Pedro . . . . Hereford, Ariz.
The Inn at Schoolhouse Creek
. . . . Mendocino, Calif.
Vichy Hot Springs Resort & Inn
. . . . Ukiah, Calif.
Washington Plantation . . . . Washington, Ga.
The Roosevelt Inn . . . . Coeur d' Alene, Idaho
Woodridge Bed & Breakfast of Louisiana
. . . . Slidell, La.
Old Sea Pines Inn . . . . Brewster, Mass.
Royalsborough Inn at the Bagley House
. . . . Durham, Maine
Barnyard Inn B&B and Carriage House
. . . . Adamstown, Pa.
Trail's End, A Country Inn
. . . . Wilmington, Vt.
States Inn . . . . Friday Harbor, Wash.
East Highland School House B&B
. . . . Phillips, Wis.
Thunder Valley Inn-Bed & Breakfast, Farm
Restaurant, and Scandinavian Gift Hus
. . . . Wisconsin Dells, Wis.
Heritage Farm Museum & Village
. . . . Huntington, W.Va.

Space Shuttle Launches

The Higgins House . . . . Sanford, Fla.
Pennsbury Inn . . . . Chadds Ford, Pa.

Stagecoach Stops

Luna Vista Bed and Breakfast
. . . . Camp Verde, Ariz.
Fensalden Inn . . . . Albion, Calif.
Hotel Charlotte . . . . Groveland, Calif.
1859 Historic National Hotel, A Country Inn
. . . . Jamestown, Calif.
Albert Shafsky House Bed & Breakfast
. . . . Placerville, Calif.
Melitta Station Inn . . . . Santa Rosa, Calif.
Mason House Inn of Bentonsport
. . . . Bentonsport, Iowa
Maple House Bed & Breakfast
. . . . Rowe, Mass.
Historic Merrell Inn . . . . Stockbridge, Mass.
Maple Hill Farm B&B Inn . . . . Hallowell, Maine
Lake House . . . . Waterford, Maine
Sweet Dreams Inn Victorian B&B
. . . . Bay Port, Mich.
The Mendon Country Inn . . . . Mendon, Mich.
Southern Hotel . . . . Sainte Genevieve, Mo.
Mt. Washington Bed & Breakfast
. . . . Shelburne, N.H.
Wakefield Inn, LLC . . . . Wakefield, N.H.
Hacienda Antigua Inn . . . . Albuquerque, N.M.
Hacienda Vargas . . . . Algodones, N.M.
Penguin Crossing B&B . . . . Circleville, Ohio

The Olde Stage Coach B&B . . . . . Jennerstown, Pa.
The Great Valley House of Valley Forge
. . . . Valley Forge, Pa.
Churchill House Inn . . . . Brandon, Vt.
Golden Stage Inn . . . . Ludlow, Vt.
Phineas Swann B&B Inn . . Montgomery Center, Vt.
Casa Bella Inn . . . . Pittsfield, Vt.
Wisconsin House Stagecoach Inn
. . . . Hazel Green, Wis.

Still in the Family

Vichy Hot Springs Resort & Inn
. . . . Ukiah, Calif.
Cedar Mountain Farm . . . . Athol, Idaho
Sonora Gardens Farmstead . . . . Nauvoo, Ill.
Ancient Thomas Riggs House
. . . . Gloucester, Mass.
Oakland House Seaside Resort
. . . . Brooksville, Maine
Meramec Farm Cabins & Trail Riding Vacations, LLC
. . . . Bourbon, Mo.
Aunt Kissy's Boutique Bed & Breakfast
. . . . Lewistown, Mont.
The Mast Farm Inn . . . . Valle Crucis, N.C.
Big Mill Bed & Breakfast . . . . . . Williamston, N.C.
Lake View Cottage Bed & Breakfast
. . . . Silver Lake, N.H.
Brae Loch Inn . . . . Cazenovia, N.Y.
A B&B at Dartmouth House . . . . . . Rochester, N.Y.
Northern Plantation B&B . . . . Urbana, Ohio
Speedwell Forge B&B . . . . Lititz, Pa.
Willowgreen Farm B&B . . . . Summerside,
Wise Manor . . . . Jefferson, Texas
Hasse House and Ranch . . . . Mason, Texas
Catamount B&B . . . . Williston, Vt.

Taverns

Lodge at Sedona-A Luxury Bed and Breakfast Inn
. . . . Sedona, Ariz.
Fensalden Inn . . . . Albion, Calif.
Hotel Charlotte . . . . Groveland, Calif.
1859 Historic National Hotel, A Country Inn
. . . . Jamestown, Calif.
The Daniel Rust House . . . . Coventry, Conn.
Silvermine Tavern . . . . Norwalk, Conn.
Red Brook Inn . . . . Old Mystic, Conn.
The Ann Stevens House . . . . Lake Helen, Fla.
Birchwood Inn . . . . Lenox, Mass.
Chapman Inn . . . . Bethel, Maine
Southern Hotel . . . . Sainte Genevieve, Mo.
Halcyon Farm Bed & Breakfast
. . . . Amsterdam, N.Y.
Bed and Breakfast at Giddings Garden
. . . . Syracuse, N.Y.
Rider's 1812 Inn . . . . Painesville, Ohio
Pennsbury Inn . . . . Chadds Ford, Pa.
Historic Smithton Inn . . . . Ephrata, Pa.
James Gettys Hotel . . . . Gettysburg, Pa.
Inn at Villalon . . . . Newport, R.I.

Train Stations & Renovated Rail Cars

Featherbed Railroad Company B&B
. . . . Nice, Calif.
Melitta Station Inn . . . . Santa Rosa, Calif.
Deacon Timothy Pratt Bed & Breakfast Inn C.1746
. . . . Old Saybrook, Conn.

Mason House Inn of Bentonsport
. . . . Bentonsport, Iowa
Pine Crest Inn & Restaurant
. . . . Tryon, N.C.
The Inn at Twin Linden . . . . Churchtown, Pa.
Red Lion Bed & Breakfast . . . . Red Lion, Pa.
Katy House Bed & Breakfast
. . . . Smithville, Texas
Cape Charles House . . . . Cape Charles, Va.
Firmstone Manor . . . . Clifton Forge, Va.
Elkhorn Inn & Theatre . . . . Landgraff, W.Va.

Tunnels, Caves, Secret Passageways

Luna Vista Bed and Breakfast
. . . . Camp Verde, Ariz.
Casa De San Pedro . . . . Hereford, Ariz.
Lodge at Sedona-A Luxury Bed and Breakfast Inn
. . . . Sedona, Ariz.
Albert Shafsky House Bed & Breakfast
. . . . Placerville, Calif.
The Steamboat House Bed and Breakfast
. . . . Galena, Ill.
Ashley Manor Inn . . . . Barnstable, Mass.
Merry Sherwood Plantation . . . . Berlin, Md.
Sweet Dreams Inn Victorian B&B
. . . . Bay Port, Mich.
Munro House B&B and Spa . . . . . Jonesville, Mich.
Pine Crest Inn & Restaurant
. . . . Tryon, N.C.
The Great Valley House of Valley Forge
. . . . Valley Forge, Pa.
Inn at Villalon . . . . Newport, R.I.
Firmstone Manor . . . . Clifton Forge, Va.

Underground Railroad

Amelia Island Williams House
. . . . Amelia Island, Fla.
Mason House Inn of Bentonsport
. . . . Bentonsport, Iowa
The Steamboat House Bed and Breakfast
. . . . Galena, Ill.
The Alexander House Booklovers B & B
. . . . Princess Anne, Md.
Highland Lake Inn B&B . . . . Andover, N.H.
Halcyon Farm Bed & Breakfast
. . . . Amsterdam, N.Y.
Post House Country Inn / Burke House Inn
. . . . Niagara On The Lake,
Pheasant Field B&B . . . . Carlisle, Pa.
Pennsbury Inn . . . . Chadds Ford, Pa.
Kennett House Bed and Breakfast
. . . . Kennett Square, Pa.
The Great Valley House of Valley Forge
. . . . Valley Forge, Pa.
Inn at Villalon . . . . Newport, R.I.
Lilac Inn . . . . Brandon, Vt.
Rosebelle's Victorian Inn . . . . Brandon, Vt.
Golden Stage Inn . . . . Ludlow, Vt.
Thunder Valley Inn-Bed & Breakfast, Farm
Restaurant, and Scandinavian Gift Hus
. . . . Wisconsin Dells, Wis.

Unusual Architecture

Alaska's North Country Castle B&B
. . . . Anchorage, Alaska
Cliff Cottage Inn - Luxury B&B Suites & Historic

Cottages
. . . . Eureka Springs, Ark.
Lodge at Sedona-A Luxury Bed and Breakfast Inn
. . . . Sedona, Ariz.
Deer Crossing Inn . . . . Castro Valley, Calif.
Bissell House . . . . South Pasadena, Calif.
Kirkland House Bed & Breakfast
. . . . New London, Conn.
Serendipity Cottage . . . . Thomasville, Ga.
Washington Plantation . . . . Washington, Ga.
Blue Belle Inn B&B . . . . Saint Ansgar, Iowa
Dog Bark Park Inn B&B . . . . . . Cottonwood, Idaho
Hansen House Mansion . . . . Chicago, Ill.
The Steamboat House Bed and Breakfast
. . . . Galena, Ill.
1851 Historic Maple Hill Manor B&B
. . . . Springfield, Ky.
HH Whitney House on the Historic Esplanade
. . . . New Orleans, La.
Ancient Thomas Riggs House
. . . . Gloucester, Mass.
Restful Paws Bed & Breakfast
. . . . Holland, Mass.
Greenville Inn . . . . Greenville, Maine
Grand Victorian Bed & Breakfast Inn
. . . . Bellaire, Mich.
Khardomah Lodge . . . . Grand Haven, Mich.
Hexagon House Bed & Breakfast
. . . . Pentwater, Mich.
Terrace Inn . . . . Petoskey, Mich.
Museum Hill Bed & Breakfast
. . . . Saint Joseph, Mo.
Fairview Inn & Sophia's Restaurant
. . . . Jackson, Miss.
Albemarle Inn . . . . Asheville, N.C.
Yellow House on Plott Creek Road
. . . . Waynesville, N.C.
A Grand Inn-Sunset Hill House
. . . . Sugar Hill, N.H.
Abbe' de Touchstone - Inn, Spa & Gallery
. . . . Taos, N.M.
Adobe & Pines Inn . . . . Taos, N.M.
Notleymere Cottage . . . . Cazenovia, N.Y.
The Edward Harris House B&B Inn
. . . . Rochester, N.Y.
Brick House . . . . Westfield, N.Y.
Pennsbury Inn . . . . Chadds Ford, Pa.
Kennett House Bed and Breakfast
. . . . Kennett Square, Pa.
Speedwell Forge B&B . . . . Lititz, Pa.
The Great Valley House of Valley Forge
. . . . Valley Forge, Pa.
Inn at Villalon . . . . Newport, R.I.
Edgewood Manor B&B . . . . Providence, R.I.
Cape Charles House . . . . Cape Charles, Va.
Firmstone Manor . . . . Clifton Forge, Va.
Essex Inn . . . . Tappahannock, Va.
Silas Griffith Inn . . . . Danby, Vt.
White Rose Inns . . . . Wisconsin Dells, Wis.
Heritage Farm Museum & Village
. . . . Huntington, W.Va.
Elkhorn Inn & Theatre . . . . Landgraff, W.Va.
Rosemont Manor . . . . Weirton, W.Va.

Unusual Sleeping Places

In a water tower
John Dougherty House . . . . Mendocino, Calif.

In a caboose
Featherbed Railroad Company B&B
. . . . Nice, Calif.
In a bank
The Landmark Inn at The Historic Bank of Oberlin
. . . . Oberlin, Kan.
In a trading post
Hacienda Vargas . . . . Algodones, N.M.
On or next to an archaeological dig site
The White Oak Inn . . . . Danville, Ohio
Baby birthing rooms
Bettinger House Bed & Breakfast
. . . . Plain, Wis.

War of 1812

The Inn at Mitchell House . . . . . Chestertown, Md.
The Bluff . . . . Henderson Harbor, N.Y.
Post House Country Inn / Burke House Inn
. . . . Niagara On The Lake,

Waterfalls

Alaska's North Country Castle B&B
. . . . Anchorage, Alaska
Lookout Point Lakeside Inn
. . . . Hot Springs, Ark.
Casa De San Pedro . . . . Hereford, Ariz.
Deer Crossing Inn . . . . Castro Valley, Calif.
Vichy Hot Springs Resort & Inn
. . . . Ukiah, Calif.
Serendipity Cottage . . . . Thomasville, Ga.
Ancient Thomas Riggs House
. . . . Gloucester, Mass.
Greenville Inn . . . . Greenville, Maine
Chateau on the Mountain . . . . Fletcher, N.C.
Pine Crest Inn & Restaurant
. . . . Tryon, N.C.
The Mast Farm Inn . . . . Valle Crucis, N.C.
Yellow House on Plott Creek Road
. . . . Waynesville, N.C.
Whispering Pines . . . . Nebraska City, Neb.
Hannah's House Bed & Breakfast
. . . . Berlin, Ohio
The Inn At Cedar Falls . . . . Logan, Ohio
Post House Country Inn / Burke House Inn
. . . . Niagara On The Lake,
Phineas Swann B&B Inn . . Montgomery Center, Vt.
Arlington's River Rock Inn
. . . . Arlington, Wash.
Second Wind Country Inn . . . . Ashland, Wis.

Who Slept/Visited Here

Lillian Russell
Bayview Hotel . . . . Aptos, Calif.
Clark Gable
Gold Mountain Manor Historic B&B
. . . . Big Bear, Calif.
Carole Lombard
Gold Mountain Manor Historic B&B
. . . . Big Bear, Calif.
Gram Parsons
Joshua Tree Inn . . . . Joshua Tree, Calif.
President William McKinley
Cheshire Cat Inn & Spa . . . . . Santa Barbara, Calif.
Mark Twain (Samuel Clemens)
Vichy Hot Springs Resort & Inn
. . . . Ukiah, Calif.

Jack London
Vichy Hot Springs Resort & Inn
. . . . Ukiah, Calif.

Theodore Roosevelt
Vichy Hot Springs Resort & Inn
. . . . Ukiah, Calif.

Ulysses Grant
Vichy Hot Springs Resort & Inn
. . . . Ukiah, Calif.

Robert Louis Stevenson
Vichy Hot Springs Resort & Inn
. . . . Ukiah, Calif.

The Carnegies
1857 Florida House Inn. . . . . . Amelia Island, Fla.

John D. Rockefeller
1857 Florida House Inn. . . . . . Amelia Island, Fla.

Ulysses S. Grant
1857 Florida House Inn. . . . . . Amelia Island, Fla.

Jefferson Davis
Amelia Island Williams House
. . . . Amelia Island, Fla.

Abraham Lincoln
Aldrich Guest House . . . . Galena, Ill.

Ulysses S. Grant
Aldrich Guest House . . . . Galena, Ill.

Abraham Lincoln
Patchwork Inn . . . . Oregon, Ill.

Martin Van Buren
Old Hoosier House. . . . . Knightstown, Ind.

Louis Armstrong
Hotel Saint Pierre. . . . . New Orleans, La.

Tennessee Williams
Hotel Saint Pierre. . . . . New Orleans, La.

Anthony Edwards
Classic Rosewood - A Thorwood Property
. . . . Hastings, Minn.

Samuel Clemens (Mark Twain)
Garth Woodside Mansion. . . . . Hannibal, Mo.

Calvin Coolidge
Lehmann House B&B . . . . Saint Louis, Mo.

Theodore Roosevelt
Lehmann House B&B . . . . Saint Louis, Mo.

William H. Taft
Lehmann House B&B . . . . Saint Louis, Mo.

Henry Clay
Monmouth Plantation . . . . Natchez, Miss.

Jefferson Davis
Monmouth Plantation . . . . Natchez, Miss.

General Quitman
Monmouth Plantation . . . . Natchez, Miss.

F. Scott Fitzgerald
Pine Crest Inn & Restaurant
. . . . Tryon, N.C.

Ernest Hemmingway
Pine Crest Inn & Restaurant
. . . . Tryon, N.C.

Cary Grant
The Mulburn Inn . . . . Bethlehem, N.H.

Barbara Hutton
The Mulburn Inn . . . . Bethlehem, N.H.

Woolworth Family
The Mulburn Inn . . . . Bethlehem, N.H.

Big Nose Kay
Plaza Hotel . . . . Las Vegas, N.M.

Billy the Kid
Plaza Hotel . . . . Las Vegas, N.M.

Teddy Roosevelt
Notleymere Cottage . . . . Cazenovia, N.Y.

President McKinley
Colonel Taylor Inn B&B and Gift Shop
. . . . Cambridge, Ohio

Lillian Hellman
Barley Sheaf Farm Estate & Spa
. . . . Holicong, Pa.

Marx Brothers
Barley Sheaf Farm Estate & Spa
. . . . Holicong, Pa.

S.J. Perlman
Barley Sheaf Farm Estate & Spa
. . . . Holicong, Pa.

Buffalo Bill Cody
The Inn at Jim Thorpe . . . . Jim Thorpe, Pa.

Thomas Edison
The Inn at Jim Thorpe . . . . Jim Thorpe, Pa.

John D. Rockefeller
The Inn at Jim Thorpe . . . . Jim Thorpe, Pa.

Dwight D. Eisenhower
Swann Hotel . . . . Jasper, Texas

General George Patton
Swann Hotel . . . . Jasper, Texas

Alex Haley
McKay House . . . . Jefferson, Texas

Lady Bird Johnson
McKay House . . . . Jefferson, Texas

Thomas Jefferson
The Inn at Meander Plantation
. . . . Locust Dale, Va.

Elizabeth Taylor
Residence Bed & Breakfast . . . . Lynchburg, Va.

Gerald Ford
Residence Bed & Breakfast . . . . Lynchburg, Va.

Georgia O'Keeffe
Residence Bed & Breakfast . . . . Lynchburg, Va.

President Calvin Coolidge
Echo Lake Inn . . . . Ludlow, Vt.

Henry Ford
Echo Lake Inn . . . . Ludlow, Vt.

Thomas Edison
Echo Lake Inn . . . . Ludlow, Vt.

Martin Sheen
Justin Trails Resort . . . . Sparta, Wis.

World War II

The Goose & Turrets B&B . . . . Montara, Calif.
Carriage House Inn. . . . . Searsport, Maine
Adair Country Inn . . . . Bethlehem, N.H.
Inn at Villalon . . . . Newport, R.I.

INN EVALUATION FORM

Please copy and complete for each stay and mail to the address shown. Since 1981 we have provided this evaluation form to millions of travelers. This information helps us follow the changes in the inns listed in this guide.

Name of Inn: _____

City and State: _____

Date of Stay: _____

Your Name: _____

Address: _____

City/State/Zip: _____

Phone: (__ __ __) __ __ __ – __ __ __ __

E-mail: _____

Please use the following rating scale for the next items.
1: Outstanding.   2: Good.   3: Average.   4: Fair.   5: Poor.

Location	1	2	3	4	5
Cleanliness	1	2	3	4	5
Food Service	1	2	3	4	5
Privacy	1	2	3	4	5
Beds	1	2	3	4	5
Bathrooms	1	2	3	4	5
Parking	1	2	3	4	5
Handling of reservations	1	2	3	4	5
Attitude of staff	1	2	3	4	5
Overall rating	1	2	3	4	5

Comments on Above: _____

_____

_____

_____

_____

MAIL THE COMPLETED FORM TO:
American Historic Inns, Inc.
PO Box 669
Dana Point, CA 92629-0669
(949) 497-2232
www.iLoveInns.com

INN EVALUATION FORM

Please copy and complete for each stay and mail to the address shown. Since 1981 we have provided this evaluation form to millions of travelers. This information helps us follow the changes in the inns listed in this guide.

Name of Inn: _____

City and State: _____

Date of Stay: _____

Your Name: _____

Address: _____

City/State/Zip: _____

Phone: (__ __ __) __ __ __ – __ __ __ __

E-mail: _____

Please use the following rating scale for the next items.
1: Outstanding.   2: Good.   3: Average.   4: Fair.   5: Poor.

	1	2	3	4	5
Location	1	2	3	4	5
Cleanliness	1	2	3	4	5
Food Service	1	2	3	4	5
Privacy	1	2	3	4	5
Beds	1	2	3	4	5
Bathrooms	1	2	3	4	5
Parking	1	2	3	4	5
Handling of reservations	1	2	3	4	5
Attitude of staff	1	2	3	4	5
Overall rating	1	2	3	4	5

Comments on Above: _____

_____

_____

_____

_____

MAIL THE COMPLETED FORM TO:
American Historic Inns, Inc.
PO Box 669
Dana Point, CA 92629-0669
(949) 497-2232
www.iLoveInns.com

AMERICAN HISTORIC INNS
INCORPORATED

iLoveInns.com

PO Box 669
Dana Point
California
92629-0669
(949) 497-2232
Fax (949) 497-9228
www.iLoveInns.com

Order Form

Date: __ __ / __ __ / __ __   Shipped: __ __ / __ __ / __ __

Name: _____

Street: _____

City/State/Zip: _____

Phone: (__ __ __) __ __ __ – __ __ __ __   E-mail: _____

QTY.	Prod. No.	Description	Amount	Total
_____	AHI19	Bed & Breakfasts and Country Inns	$24.95	_____
_____	AHIC2	Classic Country Inns and Bed & Breakfasts Travel Club (reg. $59.95)$49.95		_____
		Subtotal		_____
		California buyers add 7.75% sales tax		_____

Shipping and Handling on Other Books and Travel Club Orders
STANDARD (10-20 days): $4 for first book. Add $2.00 for each additional copy.
PRIORITY (3-5 days): $6.00. Add $4.00 each add'l copy. 2ND-DAY AIR: $15.00. Add $6.00 each add'l copy.   _____

TOTAL   _____

❏ Check/Money Order   ❏ Discover   ❏ Mastercard   ❏ Visa   ❏ American Express

Account Number __ __ __ __ __ __ __ __ __ __ __ __ __ __ __ __   Exp. Date __ __ / __ __

Name on card _____

Signature _____

Publications From American Historic Inns

Bed & Breakfast and Country Inns, 19th Edition

By Deborah Edwards Sakach

Imagine the thrill of receiving this unique book with its FREE night certificate as a gift. Now you can let someone else experience the magic of America's country inns with this unmatched offer. *Bed & Breakfasts and Country Inns* is the most talked about guide among guests.

This fabulous guide features approximately 1,550 inns from across the United States and Canada. Best of all, no other bookstore guide offers a FREE night certificate.* This certificate can be used at any one of the inns featured in the guide.

American Historic Inns, Inc. has been publishing books about bed & breakfasts since 1981. Its books and the FREE night offer have been recommended by many travel writers and editors, and featured in: *The New York Times, Washington Post, Los Angeles Times, Boston Globe, Chicago Sun Times, USA Today, Orange County Register, Baltimore Sun, McCalls, Good Housekeeping, Cosmopolitan, Consumer Reports* and more.

*With purchase of one night at the regular rate required. Subject to limitations.

472 pages, paperback, 500 illustrations   **Price $24.95**

Classic Country Inns and Bed & Breakfast Travel Club

Membership From American Historic Inns, Inc.

SAVE! SAVE! SAVE! We offer an exclusive discount club that lets you enjoy the excitement of bed & breakfast and country inn travel again and again. As a member of this special club, you'll receive benefits that include savings of 25% to 50% off every night's stay!

Your membership card will entitle you to tremendous savings at some of the finest inns in America. Members receive a guide with nearly 1,000 participating bed & breakfasts and country inns to choose from. Plan affordable getaways to inns nearby or visit an area of the country you've always wanted to experience.

The best part of being an American Historic Inns Travel Club Member is that the card can be used as many times as you like.

In addition to your card, you will get a FREE night's stay certificate—truly a club membership that's hard to pass up!

All travel club members receive:
- Travel club card entitling holder to 25% to 50% off lodging.
- FREE night's stay certificate.
- Guide to nearly 1,000 participating inns across America.

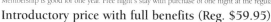

Membership is good for one year. Free night's stay with purchase of one night at the regular rate. Travel Club card is transferable. Discount and certificate cannot be combined.

Introductory price with full benefits (Reg. $59.95)   **$49.95**

www.iLoveInns.com

- More than 19,000 bed & breakfasts and country inns.

- Color photos and room descriptions.

- Use our easy Innfinder Search to quickly access inns near your destination.

- Online room availability, booking and guest reviews.

- Or use our Advanced Search to look for inns that meet your specific needs.

- Search for inns in our Free Night program.

- Send reservation requests via e-mail.

- See our specially selected Featured Inns.

- Learn about bed & breakfast hot spots across the country.

- Find out where the top inns are, including our famous picks for the Top 10 Most Romantic Inns.

- Trip and event planning tools.